Federal Revenues, Expenditures, and Budget Balances, 1967 - 1989
(percentage of GDP, national accounts basis)

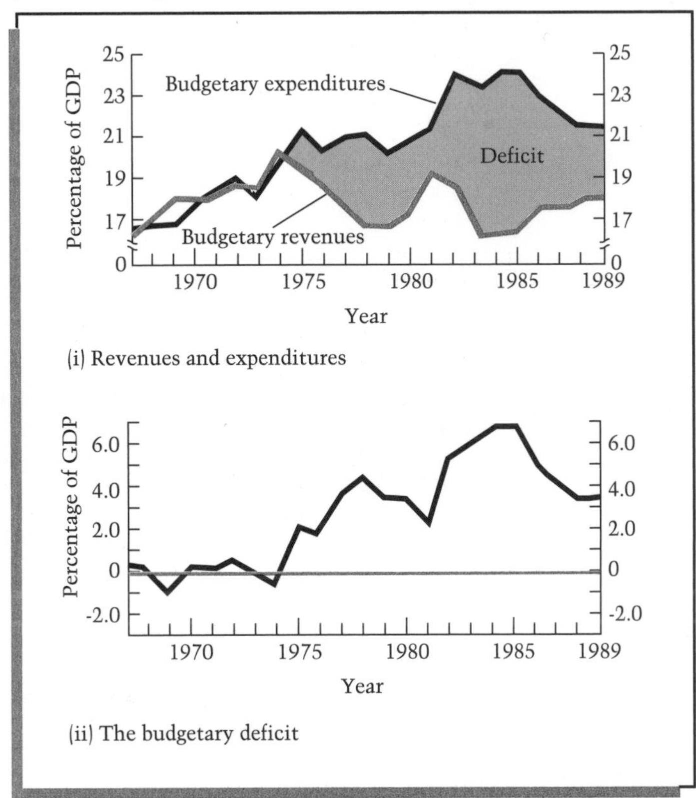

ECONOMICS

Seventh Canadian Edition

ECONOMICS

Richard G. Lipsey
Simon Fraser University

Douglas D. Purvis
Queen's University

Peter O. Steiner
The University of Michigan

HarperCollins*Publishers*

Senior Editor: John Greenman
Project Editor: Nora Helfgott
Design Supervisor: Jaye Zimet
Text Design: Graphics, Etcetera
Cover Design: Kay Cannizzaro
Cover Photos: *Clockwise on the front cover from top left position:* Grain elevator, Thunder Bay, Thomas Kitchin/First Light; Oil upgrader, Regina, Saskatchewan, Thomas Kitchin/First Light; Bay & King Streets, Toronto, Alan Sirulnikoff/First Light; Ford plant, Lorraine C. Parow/First Light; Farming, Quebec, Joe Viesti/Viesti Associates. *Center photo:* Parliament Building, Ontario, Joe Viesti/Viesti Associates.
Production Manager: Kewal K. Sharma
Production Assistant: Jeffrey Taub
Compositor: Ruttle, Shaw, & Wetherill, Inc.
Printer and Binder: Arcata Graphics/Hawkins
Cover Printer: New England Book Components, Inc.

Economics, Seventh Canadian Edition

Library of Congress Cataloging-in-Publication Data

Lipsey, Richard G., 1928-
Economics / Richard G. Lipsey, Douglas D. Purvis, Peter O. Steiner. — 7th Canadian ed.
p. cm.
Includes index.
ISBN 0-06-044125-9
1. Economics. I. Purvis, Douglas D. II. Steiner, Peter Otto, 1922- . III. Title.
[HB171.5.L733 1991] 90-29877
330—dc20 CIP

91 92 93 94 9 8 7 6 5 4 3 2 1

Dedicated to Dennis and Dorothy Purvis,
who will celebrate their fiftieth wedding anniversary
during the life of this edition.

Brief CONTENTS

Detailed CONTENTS

PREFACE

Economics is a living discipline. Through seven editions of *Economics,* our basic motivation has been to provide a text that reflects the tremendous changes in that discipline over the decades.

The first major theme of this book is to reflect the key characteristic that marks any science: the systematic confrontation of theory with observation. Today most economists agree that their subject is more than a stage for parading pet theories and is not just a container for collecting masses of unrelated institutional and statistical material. Economists are expanding the frontiers of knowledge about the economic environment and are learning to understand and sometimes to control it, but new problems and new events are always challenging existing knowledge. Economists are therefore continually concerned with how theory, institutions, and facts relate to each other. Every theory is subject to empirical challenge.

A second major theme of this book concerns the relationship between economic theory and economic policy. Decades of systematic observations have provided an ever-growing understanding of how things relate quantitatively. This knowledge has increased economists' ability to make sensible and relevant statements about public policy. True, there remain many areas where economists' knowledge is painfully sparse, as current debates about our international competitiveness and about the nature of an appropriate monetary policy remind us.

The third major feature of the book has to do with the way we view students. We have tried to be as honest with them as possible within the limits of an introductory textbook. No subject worth studying is always easy, and we do not approve of slipping particularly hard bits of analysis past students without letting them see what is happening and what has been assumed, nor do we approve of teaching them things that they will have to unlearn if they continue their study of economics (a practice sometimes justified on the grounds that it is important to get to the big issues quickly). In short, we have tried to follow Albert Einstein's advice: *Make things as simple as possible, but not simpler.*

Effective criticism of existing ideas is the springboard to progress in science. We believe that introductory economics should introduce students to methods for testing, criticizing, and evaluating the present state of the subject. We do not believe that it is wrong to suggest to students the possiblity of criticizing current economic theory. Students will always criticize and evaluate their course content, and their criticisms are more likely to be informed and relevant if they are given practice and instruction in how to challenge what they have been taught in an effective, constructive manner.

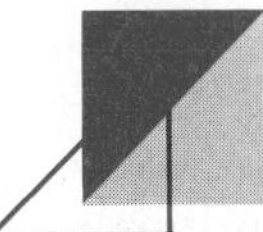

Major Revisions in This Edition

The revisions introduced in this seventh edition are the result of an extensive series of reviews and feedback from our users. There are many major additions to the coverage of the book, including several completely new chapters, but we have also worked to improve the "teachability" and readability of the book. Every part of the book has been thoroughly reviewed with these goals in mind.

Some of the most important changes are as follows.

Changes in Microeconomics

1. Chapter 1 now reports on the remarkable shift toward markets that has occurred worldwide, especially in the major socialist countries. A new box, "Will *Perestroika* Succeed?" highlights some of the problems that a rapid shift toward reliance on markets might encounter even if the shift is beneficial in the long run.

2. In Chapter 5, following the development in the sixth edition, the distinction between long-run

and short-run elasticity is stressed, for both demand and supply elasticities. In this edition we have extended that discussion to incorporate the distinction (made by the famous nineteenth-century British economist Alfred Marshall) between short-run and long-run responses of markets to supply and demand shocks, stressing that prices can "overshoot" (i.e., adjust by more than is required for long-run equilibrium) in the short run.

3. Chapter 6 has been rewritten to emphasize *applying* the tools developed in Chapters 4 and 5 rather than attempting complete coverage of the topics chosen for illustrative purposes. Although students will learn quite a bit about Canadian rent control and agricultural policies, the main purpose of the chapter is to use the discussion of these policies as a vehicle for giving students practice in applying price theory.

4. The basic theory of demand was completely restructured in the sixth edition in order to give instructors maximum flexibility in covering the material. This was achieved by putting the two most important theories—indifference curves and marginal utility—in separate appendixes to Chapter 7. The text of Chapter 7 does as much with demand theory as can be done by stressing the budget constraint and rational choice without developing either marginal utility or indifference curves. Surprisingly much can be done, but few users will bypass both appendixes. Not everyone likes this structure, but overall, user response has been positive, so we have maintained it in this edition.

5. Chapter 8 is almost entirely new. It starts off with some material on *using* demand theory that was included in the sixth edition, but it then turns to an extended treatment of a new and currently fashionable topic: the economics of uncertainty. Boxes on the economics of gambling and the market for used cars will appeal to students and can be read separately from the text itself.

6. The basic material on production and costs is relatively unchanged from the sixth edition, but two new boxes—on transnational corporations and flexible production techniques—highlight important recent developments. The nature of mass production techniques, which remained basically unchanged from Adam Smith's pin factory to Henry Ford's Model T factory, has undergone profound changes in the past two decades. Much of the shift in competitive advantage toward Japan is based on that nation's early superiority in the revolutionary new production techniques.

7. The structure of Part 4 has been altered so that all of the positive analysis is done before introducing efficiency considerations. Chapter 14, on imperfect competition, has been completely rewritten to improve its teachability and to increase its coverage of modern industrial organization theory. Chapter 15 has been updated to cover current Canadian competition policy. Chapter 16 now contains a new section on foreign investment in Canada, a topic of great interest to most students.

8. There is a completely new section on exhaustible resources in Chapter 17, the first chapter in our discussion of income distribution.

9. Chapter 21 contains an updated discussion of Canadian trade policy, a life-and-death matter to Canada, where 50 percent of private-sector income is generated through exports.

10. We have included a new chapter (23) on environmental and social regulation. The two "core" micro policy chapters, 22 and 24, have been extensively reworked; this includes a new box on social choice theory in the former, and expanded coverage of tax reform and fiscal federalism in the latter.

Changes in Macroeconomics

1. This is now the fourth edition in which the macroeconomics material has relied mainly on the tools of aggregate demand and aggregate supply. We have maintained the simplified structure introduced in the sixth edition: The first seven macroeconomics chapters develop the basic model and some simple applications before "elaboration" begins, in Chapter 33. From a teaching standpoint, this is a major improvement; it not only simplifies the introduction to macroeconomics, but it also means that the whole macro development follows an even flow, with concepts introduced only as they are needed. Aggregate demand is encountered only after the aggregate expenditure function has been developed, and aggregate supply is introduced at the end of the first comparative statics analysis in Chapter 29.

2. The detailed treatment of index numbers has been combined with national income accounting in one chapter, 29. The treatment of both topics is simpler yet more comprehensive than in previous editions. Because the basic concepts are covered in Chapter 26, Chapter 27 may be omitted without loss of continuity.

3. Chapter 29, on aggregate supply, continues to

distinguish the factors influencing the slope of the *SRAS* curve and the forces that cause it to shift. The distinction between the short-run aggregate supply (*SRAS*) curves and the long-run aggregate supply (*LRAS*) curves, important for most of the remaining chapters, is carefully examined. We feel that it is worth making the effort required to establish this distinction because as economists, we are concerned about the many textbooks that carry out the bulk of their analysis with a single, stable *AS* curve. This simplifies teaching, but it risks serious confusion. The alert student facing a fixed *AS* curve and an *AD* curve that can be shifted by policy will wonder why anyone would hesitate to pay the price of a once-and-for-all increase in the price level in order to obtain a permanent increase in output and employment. To avoid such serious confusion, we stress the distinction between the shifting short-run *AS* curve and the vertical long-run *AS* curve.

4. Chapter 31 has been rewritten to integrate it more fully into the surrounding chapters and to redirect it toward its initial purpose, elucidating the role of fluctuations and cycles as motivation for studying economic policy. Chapter 32, "An Introduction to Fiscal Policy," has also been thoroughly rewritten and condensed. Chapters 31 and 32 now appear essentially as applications of the aggregate demand and aggregate supply apparatus that the student has just studied. All extraneous material has been eliminated or moved. For example, the accelerator theory of investment is now discussed in the Appendix to Chapter 31, and detailed discussion of the debate on government budget deficits, which requires understanding of the monetary issues covered in Chapters 33–35, now appears in the all-new Chapter 39.

5. Part 9, on money, banking, and monetary policy, has been thoroughly revised. The discussion in Chapter 33 is written to accommodate the likelihood of reserve requirements being eliminated in Canada during the life of this edition; we show that the basic principles of deposit expansion still apply when actual reserves are in excess of *target* reserves, where the latter incorporate reserve requirements and prudent financial management of the financial institution. Chapter 35 focuses more on the external value of the Canadian dollar in the formulation and appraisal of monetary policy. Another related change is increased attention to the globalization of financial markets.

6. The chapter on inflation, 36, has been reworked and greatly simplified. The emphasis is now more on long-term inflation control and less on the issue of breaking entrenched inflation, which had been important at the time of the previous edition.

7. Chapter 38, "Economic Growth," has also received some attention, especially regarding the new endogenous growth models that are currently attracting attention. It also develops the modern theme that growth and cycles are really part of the same phenomenon and hence should be studied in a common model.

8. To emphasize the continuing importance of the issue and to provide maximum flexibility for the instructor, the material on budget deficits and the related political economic issues now appears in a self-contained chapter, Chapter 39. (The Ricardian neutrality proposition is discussed in the appendix to that chapter.) Macroeconomic controversies are now confronted in Chapter 40, to which a lot of new material has been added, including treatment of real business cycle theory and several aspects of the so-called neo-Keynesion economics. (This chapter may be omitted if the instructor feels that its content should be left for a more advanced course.)

9. Finally, the material on the international monetary situation has been updated and revised to reflect current issues. Of most interest here is the inclusion of a new chapter on the policy issues created by the openness of the economy—the role of exchange rates and external balances and their impact on policy choices and on the consequences of those choices.

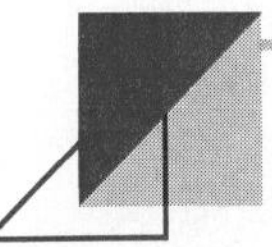

Teaching Aids

Key ideas in economics. New to this edition are four full-color insert sections that repeat important conceptual diagrams from the text with abbreviated captions as a review device for students. Each of these diagrams is intended to be a memory-jogger that says to the student, "Do you remember and understand this concept? If not, return to the proper chapter and reread it in detail."

Tag lines and captions for figures and tables. The boldface tag line below or next to a figure or table states briefly the central conclusion to be drawn from the illustration; the lightface caption gives information needed to reach that conclusion. Each title, tag line, and caption, along with the figure or table, form a self-contained unit, useful for reviewing.

Boxes. The "boxes" contain examples or materials that are relevant extensions of the main text but need not be read as part of the text sequence. They are all optional. Some present additional theoretical material. Others contain expansions and applications of points already covered in the text. The boxes give flexibility in expanding or contracting the coverage of specific chapters.

End-of-chapter material. Each chapter has a Summary, a list of Topics for Review, and Discussion Questions. The questions are designed for class discussion or for "quiz sections." Answers appear in the Instructor's Manual.

Appendixes. The appendixes provide more detailed discussion of certain topics. They directly follow the chapters to which they are related.

Mathematical notes. Mathematical notes are collected in a separate section at the end of the book. Since mathematical notation and derivation are not necessary to understand the principles of economics but are helpful in more advanced work, this segregation seems to be a sensible arrangement. Mathematical notes provide clues to the uses of mathematics for the increasing number of students who have some background in math, without loading the text with notes that are useless and offputting to other readers. Students with a mathematical background have often told us that they find the notes helpful.

Glossary. The glossary covers widely used definitions of economic terms. Because some users treat micro- and macroeconomics in that order, and others in the reverse order, words in the glossary are printed in boldface type when they are first mentioned in *either half* of the text.

Endpapers. Inside the front cover on the left is a list of the most commonly used abbreviations in the text; on the right appears a figure representing the evolution of the federal budget deficit. Inside the back cover on the left is an illustration showing the labor force, employment, and unemployment. On the right is a table of selected time series, showing useful data on the Canadian economy for selected years beginning with 1926.

Supplements

Our book is accompanied by a workbook, *Study Guide and Problems,* prepared by Professors Kenneth Grant, William Furlong, and the text authors. This workbook is designed to be used either in the classroom or by students working on their own.

An *Instructor's Manual,* prepared by us, and a *Test Bank,* prepared by Geoffrey Barnard, are available to instructors adopting the book. The test bank is also available in computerized form; contact HarperCollins Canada Ltd., 1995 Markham Road, Scarborough, Ontario, M1B 5M8.

Two new software programs for students accompany the seventh edition: *Macroview,* a simulation of the Canadian economy, and *Micro Tutorial,* a review of microeconomic concepts. The *Lipsey Disc,* previously available, has been updated for the seventh edition.

For this edition, all illustrations in 15 key theory chapters are reproduced as two- or four-color transparency acetates. In addition, the remaining figures in the text are reproduced in the form of transparency masters. All of these are available free to adopters.

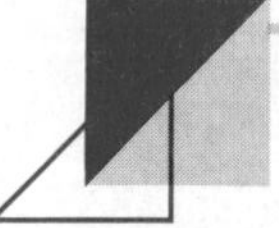

Using the Book

Needs of students differ; some want material that goes beyond the average class level, but others have gaps in their backgrounds. To accommodate the former, we have included more material than we would assign to every student. Also, because there are many different kinds of first-year economics courses in colleges and universities, we have included more material than normally would be included in any single course.

Although teachers can best design their own courses, it may help if we indicate certain views of our own as to how this book *might* be adapted to difference courses.

Sequence

The choice of macro first or micro first is partly a personal one that cannot be decided solely by objective criteria. We believe, however, that there are good reasons for preferring the micro-macro order. The thrust over the past 20 years has been to examine the micro underpinnings of macro functions and to erect macroeconomics on a firmer base of micro behavioral relationships. Virtually every current macro controversy turns on some micro underpinning. For "micro firsters" this poses no problem. For "macro firsters" it is often hard to explain what is at issue.

Changes occur not only in economic theory but also in the topics that excite students. Many of today's problems that students find most challenging—discrimination, social policy, equal-pay legislation, poverty, pollution, and free trade with the United States—are microeconomic in character. The micro-macro order, moreover, reflects the historical evolution of the subject. A century of Classical and neo-Classical development of microeconomics preceded the Keynesian development of macroeconomics.

For those who prefer the macro-micro order, we have attempted to make reversibility easy. The overview chapter that ends Part 1 provides a base on which to build either the microeconomics of Part 2 or the macroeconomics of Part 8. Chapter 4 should be assigned after Chapter 3, even in macro-first courses. Where further microeconomics concepts are required—as in the macro investment chapter—we have added brief sections to make the treatment self-contained while providing review material for those who have covered the microeconomic section.

One-Term Courses

Thorough coverage of most of the book supposes a two-term course in economics. A number of first courses in economics are only one term (or equivalent) in length, and our book can be easily adapted to such courses. Suggestions for use of this book for such courses are given on page xxvii.

ACKNOWLEDGMENTS

The starting point for this book was *Economics,* Ninth Edition, by Richard G. Lipsey, Peter O. Steiner, Douglas D. Purvis, and Paul N. Courant. It would be impossible to acknowledge here all the teachers, colleagues, and students who contributed to that book. Hundreds of users have written to us with specific suggested improvements, and much of the credit for the fact that the book does become more and more teachable belongs to them. We can no longer list them individually but we thank them all most sincerely.

David Scoones and Gillian Hamilton provided excellent research assistance. A number of individuals provided reviews of the sixth edition that were most helpful in preparing the present edition. These are Torben Andersen, Red Deer College; Ronald G. Bodkin, University of Ottawa; Chris Clark, British Columbia Institute of Technology; Barry Cozier, Concordia University; M. H. I. Dore, Brock University; C. M. Fellows, Mount Royal College; S. W. Kardasz, University of Waterloo; George Kondor, Lakehead University; Victor Olshevski, University of Winnipeg; and P. L. Siklos, Wilfred Laurier University. In addition, the key micro chapters of this revision were read by Trudy Ann Cameron, UCLA; Vernon Dow, Cambrian College; and A. Gyasi Nimarko, Vanier College. The core macro chapters were seen by Sohrab Abizadeh, University of Winnipeg; G. C. Church, University of Regina; Geoffrey B. Hainsworth, University of British Columbia; Peter Howitt, University of Western Ontario; and Nicholas Rowe, Carleton University. William Furlong and Kenneth Grant, two of our study guide authors, have contributed to this edition as well.

Special thanks are due to Elaine Fitzpatrick, Patricia Casey-Purvis, Ellen McKay, and Dana Miltchen for careful and efficient handling of the manuscript at all stages.

Note that Peter O. Steiner is no longer actively involved in the writing of this book. His name remains on the list of coauthors in recognition of the many contributions that he made in the past that remain integral to the book. We express our appreciation for his contributions and for those of Paul N. Courant, who participated in the writing of the ninth U.S. edition of *Economics*.

Richard G. Lipsey
Douglas D. Purvis

Suggested Outlines for a ONE-TERM COURSE

Note: A one-term course can cover about 20 to 22 full chapters. The core consists of about 18 chapters. Selections from other chapters, as listed below or according to the instructor's own preferences, can produce courses with various emphases.

Basic core chapters for courses covering both micro and macro

INTRODUCTION

1 The Economic Problem
2 Economics As a Social Science
3 An Overview of the Market Economy

MICROECONOMICS

4 Demand, Supply, and Price
5 Elasticity and Market Adjustment
9 The Role of the Firm
10 Production and Cost in the Short Run
11 Production and Cost in the Long and the Very Long Run
12 Competitive Markets
13 Monopoly
17 Factor Mobility and Factor Pricing
20 The Gains from Trade
22 Benefits and Costs of Government Intervention

MACROECONOMICS

26 An Introduction to Macroeconomics
27 Measuring Macroeconomic Variables
28 National Income and Aggregate Expenditure
29 National Income and the Price Level in the Short Run
30 National Income and the Price Level in the Long Run
32 An Introduction to Fiscal Policy
33 The Nature of Money and Monetary Institutions
34 The Role of Money in Macroeconomics

Chapters that can be added to give different emphases to different courses[1]

MICROECONOMICS

* 6 Supply and Demand in Action: Price Controls and Agriculture
14 Patterns of Imperfect Competition
*15 Public Policy Toward Monopoly and Competition
18 More on Factor Markets
*19 Labor Markets and Discrimination
*21 Barriers to Free Trade
*24 Taxation and Public Expenditure
*25 Social Policy

MACROECONOMICS

*35 Monetary Policy
36 Inflation
37 Employment and Unemployment
38 Economic Growth
*39 Government Budget Deficits
*40 Macroeconomic Controversies
41 Exchange Rates and the Balance of Payments
*42 Alternative Exchange Rate Systems

[1] Chapters marked with an asterisk are particularly appropriate for courses with a heavy policy orientation. Chapters not listed here or in the core seem to us to be lower priority in a one-term course, but they are not necessarily too difficult.

TO THE STUDENT

A good course in economics will give you insight into how an economy functions and into some currently debated policy issues. Like all rewarding subjects, economics will not be mastered without effort. A book on economics must be worked at. It cannot be read like a novel.

Each of you must develop an individual technique for studying, but the following suggestions may prove helpful. It is usually a good idea to read a chapter quickly in order to get the general run of the argument. At this first reading you may want to skip the "boxes" of text material and any footnoes. Then, after reading the Topics for Review and the Discussion Questions, reread the chapter more slowly, making sure that you understand each step of the argument. With respect to the figures and tables, be sure you understand how the conclusions stated in the brief tag lines with each table or figure have been reached. You should be prepared to spend time on difficult sections; occasionally, you may spend an hour on only a few pages. Paper and a pencil are indispensable equipment in your reading. It is best to follow a difficult argument by building your own diagram while the argument unfolds rather than by relying on the finished diagram as it appears in the book. It is often helpful to invent numerical examples to illustrate general propositions. The end-of-chapter questions require you to apply what you have studied. We advise you to outline answers to some of the questions. In short, you should seek to understand economics, not merely to memorize it.

After you have read each part in detail, reread it quickly from beginning to end. It is often difficult to understand why certain things are done when they are viewed as isolated points, but when you reread a whole part, much that did not seem relevant or entirely comprehensible will fall into place in the analysis.

We call your attention to the glossary at the end of the book. Any time you run into a concept that seems vaguely familiar but is not clear to you, check the glossary. The chances are that the term will be there, and its definition will remind you of what you once understood. If you are still in doubt, check the index entry to find where the concept is discussed more fully. Incidentally, the glossary, along with the captions that accompany figures and tables and the end-of-chapter summaries, may prove very helpful when reviewing for examinations.

The bracketed colored numbers in the text itself refer to a series of 46 mathematical notes that are found starting on page M-1. For those of you who like mathematics or prefer mathematical argument to verbal or geometric exposition, these may prove useful. Others may ignore them.

We hope that you will find the book rewarding and stimulating. Students who used earlier editions made some of the most helpful suggestions for revision, and we hope you will carry on the tradition. If you are moved to write to us, please do.

ECONOMICS

PART 1

THE NATURE OF ECONOMICS

Chapter 1

The Economic Problem

Turn on the TV news, read your local newspaper, glance at *MacLean's, Saturday Night,* or *Time* magazine, and you will see for yourself that many of the world's most pressing problems are economic.

How can Mexico, Brazil, and many other less developed countries escape from the crushing burden of international debt under which they are now struggling? Are the developed nations right in making the adoption of more market-oriented economic policies a precondition of increased foreign aid to these LDCs? Why did communism fail to deliver acceptable living standards to the citizens of the socialist countries of Eastern Europe and the republics of the USSR? Will these countries be able to make the transition from centrally controlled to market-based economies without too many setbacks and too much transitional suffering? Is the growth of vast transnational corporations that conduct business across the entire globe making the nation-state obsolete, at least as a vehicle for controlling one country's economic destiny? Does the population explosion mean that the growth of mouths to feed will outrun the growth of food to feed those mouths? Will rising manufacturing output, particularly in the developing nations, cause such an increase in pollution and resource exhaustion as to threaten future living standards or even our survival? Are economists right in urging that environmental protection is often best accomplished using free market incentives rather than direct government intervention?

Your media survey of press, radio, and TV will also show the importance of economic issues in the problems facing Canada today.

Does the size of the federal government's budget deficit affect the average person's living standards? Is the Bank of Canada right to be pursuing a goal of zero inflation? Who benefits from supply management schemes that cause Canadian consumers to pay more for many farm products than American consumers do? Is Ontario right in controlling the prices charged for rented accommodations, or are most other provinces right in letting rents be determined by free markets? Is the Canada–U.S. Free Trade Agreement on balance a good or a bad thing for the average Canadian? What would be the effect on our living standards if Canada broke up into two or more independent nations? Canadians are justly proud of their country's elaborate social welfare schemes, but can the country afford them?

Of course, not all the world's problems are primarily economic. Political, biological, social, cultural, and philosophical issues often predominate. However, as the following examples suggest, no matter how "noneconomic" a particular problem may seem, it will almost always have a significant economic dimension.

1. The crises that lead to wars often have economic roots. Nations often fight for oil and rice and land to live on, although the rhetoric of their leaders evokes God, Glory, and the Fatherland.
2. The current rate of world population growth is 2.2 persons a second, or about 70 million a year; the economic consequences are steady pressures on the environment and the food supply. Unless the human race can find ways to deal with these pressures, increasing millions face starvation and increasing billions face rising levels of environmental degradation.
3. The *greenhouse effect* describes the possibility of a gradual warming of the earth's climate due to a cumulative buildup of CO_2 in the atmosphere. If the possibility proves a reality, such things as the melting of the polar ice cap and further warming of desert regions will alter the earth's physical geography dramatically. Perhaps even more dramatic will be the economic consequences of resulting changes in consumption patterns and production possibilities.

What Is Economics?

So far we have identified a handful of the important current issues on which economics can shed some light. One way to define *economics* is to say that it is the social science that deals with such problems. Another definition, perhaps better known, is Alfred Marshall's: "Economics is a study of mankind in the ordinary business of life." A more penetrating definition might be the following:

Economics is the study of the use of scarce resources to satisfy unlimited human wants.

Scarcity is inevitable and is central to economic problems. What are society's resources? Why is scarcity inevitable? What are the consequences of scarcity?

Resources and Commodities

A society's resources consist of natural gifts such as land, forests, and minerals; human resources, both mental and physical; and manufactured aids to production such as tools, machinery, and buildings. Economists call such resources **factors of production**[1] because they are used to produce those things that people desire. The things produced are called **commodities**, which may be divided into goods and services. **Goods** are tangible (e.g., cars or shoes), and **services** are intangible (e.g., haircuts or education). Notice the implication of positive value contained in the terms *goods* and *services*. (Compare the terms *bads* and *disservices*.)

People use goods and services to satisfy many of their wants. The act of making them is called **production**, and the act of using them to satisfy wants is called **consumption**. Goods are valued for the services they provide. An automobile, for example, helps to satisfy its owner's desires for transportation, mobility, and possibly status.

Scarcity

For most of the world's 5 billion human beings, scarcity is real and ever present. In relation to desires (for more and better food, clothing, housing, schooling, entertainment, and so forth), existing resources are woefully inadequate; there are enough to produce only a small fraction of the goods and services that are wanted.

Are not the advanced industrialized nations rich enough that scarcity is nearly banished? After all, they have been characterized as affluent societies. Whatever affluence may mean, it does not mean the end of the problem of scarcity. Most households that earn $80,000 a year (a princely amount by world standards) have no trouble spending it on things that seem useful to them. Yet it would take twice the present output of the Canadian economy to produce enough to allow all Canadian households to earn that amount.

[1] Definitions of the terms in boldfaced type can be found in the glossary at the back of the book.

Choice

Because resources are scarce, all societies face the problem of deciding what to produce and how to divide the products among their members. Societies differ in who makes the choices and how they are made, but the need to choose is common to all. Just as scarcity implies the need for choice, so choice implies the existence of cost.

Opportunity Cost

A decision to have more of one thing requires a decision to have less of something else. It is this that makes the first decision costly. We look first at a trivial example and then at one that vitally affects all of us; both examples involve precisely the same fundamental principles.

Consider the choice that must be made by a small boy who has 10 cents to spend and who is determined to spend it all on candy. For him there are only two kinds of candy in the world: gumdrops, which sell for 1 cent each, and chocolates, which sell for 2 cents. The boy would like to buy 10 gumdrops and 10 chocolates, but he knows (or will soon discover) that this is not possible: It is not an *attainable combination* given his scarce resources. There are, however, several attainable combinations: 8 gumdrops and 1 chocolate, 4 gumdrops and 3 chocolates, 2 gumdrops and 4 chocolates, and so on. Some of these combinations leave him with money unspent, and he is not interested in them. Only six combinations, as shown in Figure 1-1, are both attainable and use all his money.

FIGURE 1-1 A Choice Between Gumdrops and Chocolates

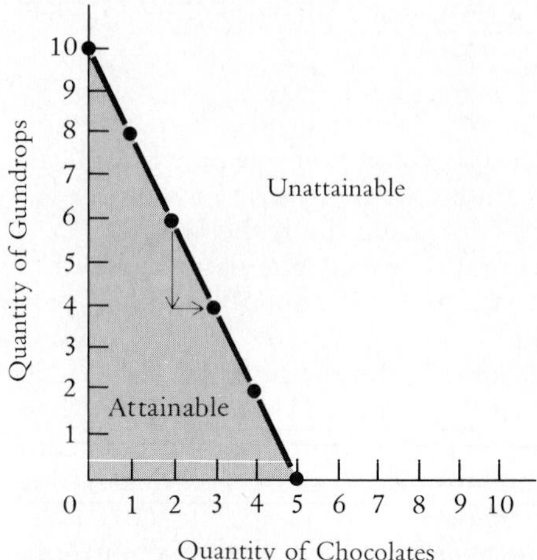

A limited amount of money forces a choice among alternatives. Six combinations of gumdrops and chocolates are attainable and use all of the boy's money. The negatively sloped line provides a boundary between attainable and unattainable combinations. The arrows show that the opportunity cost of 1 more chocolate is 2 gumdrops. In this example the opportunity cost is constant and therefore the boundary is a straight line.

After careful thought, the boy has almost decided to buy 6 gumdrops and 2 chocolates, but at the last moment he decides that he simply must have 3 chocolates. What will it cost him to get this extra chocolate? One answer is 2 gumdrops. As seen in the figure, this is the number of gumdrops he must forgo to get the extra chocolate. Economists describe the 2 gumdrops as the *opportunity cost* of the third chocolate.

Another answer is that the cost of the third chocolate is 2 cents. However, given the boy's budget and his intentions, this answer is less revealing than the first one. Where the real choice is between more of this and more of that, the cost of "this" is usefully looked at as what you cannot have of "that." The idea of opportunity cost is one of the central insights of economics.

Opportunity cost is the cost of using resources for a certain purpose, where the cost is measured by value of the best alternative use of those resources. If, for example, resources that could have produced 20 miles of road are used instead to produce two small hospitals, the opportunity cost of a hospital is 10 miles of road; looked at the other way round, the opportunity cost of a mile of road is one-tenth of a hospital.

Every time a choice must be made, opportunity costs are incurred.

Production Possibilities

Although the choice between gumdrops and chocolates is a minor consumption decision, the essential nature of the decision is the same whatever the choice being made. Consider, for example, the important choice between military and civilian goods. It is not possible to produce an unlimited quantity of both military and civilian goods. If resources are fully employed and the government wishes to produce more arms, less civilian goods can be produced. The opportunity cost of increased arms production is forgone production of civilian goods.

The choice is illustrated in Figure 1-2. Because resources are limited, some combinations—those that would require more than the total available supply of resources for their production—cannot be attained. The negatively sloped curve on the graph divides the combinations that can be attained from those that cannot. Points above and to the right of this curve cannot be attained because there are not enough resources; points below and to the left of the curve can be attained without using all of the available resources; and points on the curve can just be attained if all the available resources are used. The curve is called the **production possibility boundary** or **production possibility curve**. It has a negative slope because, when all resources are being used, having more of one kind of goods requires having less of the other kind.

FIGURE 1-2 A Production Possibility Boundary

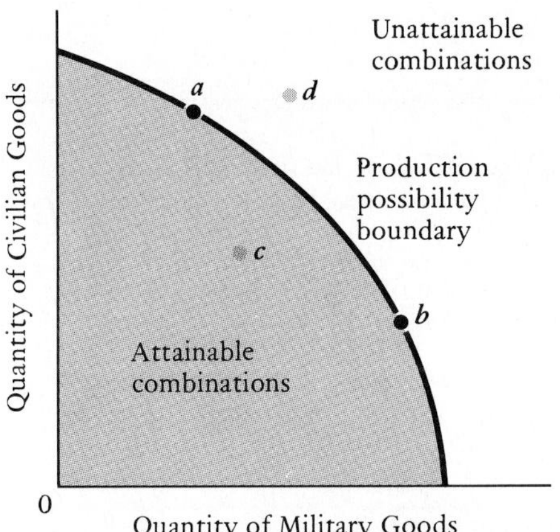

The negatively sloped boundary shows the combinations that are just attainable when all of the society's resources are efficiently employed. The quantity of military goods produced is measured along the horizontal axis, the quantity of civilian goods along the vertical axis. Thus any point on the diagram indicates some amount of each kind of good produced. The production possibility boundary separates the attainable combinations of goods such as *a*, *b*, and *c* from unattainable combinations such as *d*. It is negatively sloped because resources are scarce: When resources are fully employed, more of one good can be produced only if resources are freed by producing less of the other goods. Points *a* and *b* represent full and efficient use of society's resources. Point *c* represents either inefficient use of resources or failure to use all the available resources.

A production possibility boundary illustrates three concepts: scarcity, choice, and opportunity cost. Scarcity is indicated by the unattainable combinations above the boundary, choice by the need to choose among the alternative attainable points along the boundary, and opportunity cost by the negative slope of the boundary.

The shape of the production possibility boundary in Figure 1-2 implies that more and more civilian goods must be given up to achieve equal successive increases in military goods. This shape, referred to as *concave* to the origin, indicates that the opportunity cost of either good grows larger and larger as we increase the amount of it that is produced. A straight-line boundary, as in Figure 1-1, indicates that the opportunity cost of one good in terms of the other stays constant, no matter how much of it is produced. As we shall see, there are reasons to believe that the case of rising opportunity cost applies to many important choices.[2]

Four Key Economic Problems

Although modern economies are complex, many basic decisions that must be made by consumers and producers are not very different from those made in a primitive economy in which people work with few tools and barter with their neighbors. Nor do capitalist, socialist, and communist economies differ in

[2] The importance of scarcity, choice, and opportunity cost has led some people to define economics as the study of the allocation of scarce resources among competing ends. The issues emphasized by this definition are important, but, as will be seen in the next section, other important issues are also involved.

their need to solve the same basic problems, although they do differ, of course, in how they solve them. Most problems studied by economists can be grouped under four main headings.

1. What Is Produced and How?

The allocation of scarce resources among alternative uses, called **resource allocation**, determines the quantities of various goods that are produced. Choosing to produce a particular combination of goods means choosing a particular allocation of resources among the industries or regions producing the goods because, for example, producing much of one good requires that many resources be allocated to its production.

Further, because resources are scarce, it is desirable that they be used efficiently. Hence it matters which of the available methods of production is used to produce each of the goods that is to be produced.

2. What Is Consumed and by Whom?

What is the relationship between the economy's production of commodities and the consumption enjoyed by its citizens? Economists want to understand what determines the distribution of a nation's total output among its people. Who gets a lot, who gets a little, and why? What role does international trade play in this?

Questions 1 and 2 fall within **microeconomics**, the study of the allocation of resources and the distribution of income as they are affected by the free working of the price system and government policies that seek to influence it.

3. How Much Unemployment and Inflation Exist?

When an economy is in a recession, unemployed workers would like to have jobs, the factories in which they could work are available, the managers and owners would like to be able to operate their factories, raw materials are available in abundance, and the goods that could be produced by these resources are wanted by individuals in the community, but for some reason resources remain unemployed. This forces the economy within its production possibility boundary, at a point such as *c* in Figure 1-2.

The world's economies have often experienced bouts of prolonged and substantial changes in price levels. In recent decades the course of prices has almost always been upward. The 1970s and early 1980s saw accelerating inflation, not only in Canada but also in most other parts of the world. Then inflation slowed while unemployment soared. Were these two events related?

Why do governments worry that reductions in either unemployment or inflation will be at the cost of temporarily increasing the other?

4. Is Productive Capacity Growing?

The capacity to produce commodities to satisfy human wants grows rapidly in some countries, expands slowly in others, and actually declines in still others. Growth in productive capacity can be represented by a pushing outward of the production possibility boundary, as shown in Figure 1-3. If an economy's capacity to produce goods and services is growing, combinations that are unattainable today will become attainable tomorrow. Growth makes it possible to have more of all goods.

FIGURE 1-3 The Effect of Economic Growth on the Production Possibility Boundary

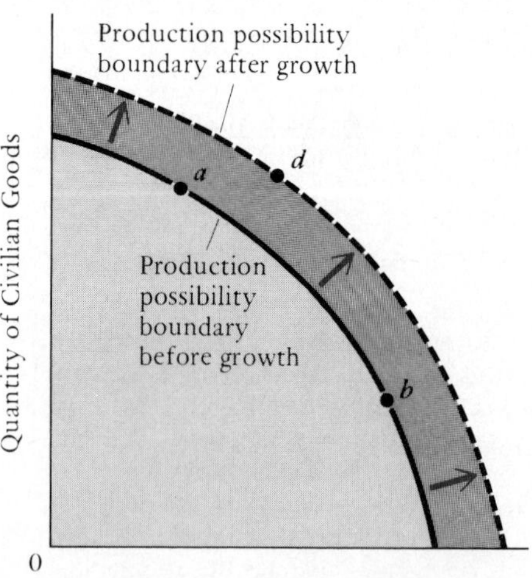

Economic growth shifts the boundary outward and makes it possible to produce more of all commodities. Before growth in productive capacity, points *a* and *b* were on the production possibility boundary and point *d* was an unattainable combination. After growth, as shown by the dark-shaded band, point *d* and many other previously unattainable combinations are attainable.

Questions 3 and 4 fall within **macroeconomics**, the study of the determination of economic aggregates such as total output, total employment, the price level, and the rate of economic growth.

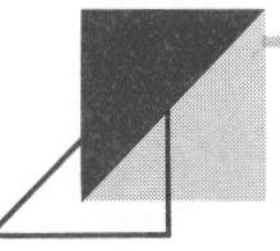

Alternative Economic Systems

An economic system is a distinctive method of providing answers to the basic economic questions just discussed. All such systems are complex. They include producers of every sort, whether publicly or privately owned, domestically owned or foreign-controlled. They include consumers of every sort, young and old, rich and poor, working and nonworking. They include laws—such as those relating to property rights—rules, regulations, taxes, subsidies, and everything else that governments use to influence what is produced, how it is produced, and who gets it. They also include customs of every conceivable kind, and the entire range of contemporary mores and values.

Social organization is a particulary important part of any economic system because it can influence the use of resources. Three of its aspects need to be distinguished: *ownership, control,* and *objectives.*

Consider land, which is one of any country's important productive resources. Its *ownership* may be in the hands of the state or of private individuals. In the latter case, there may be a few large landowners, numerous small peasant farmers, or any mixture of both. *Control* of the current uses of the land may lie with the owners, may be devolved onto tenant farmers, or may be exercised through directives issued by the state. *Objectives* (often called *goals*) of those who have control over the land may vary from time to time and from place to place. Some people may be very money-conscious and cultivate crops that yield the largest return; others may go for immediate return at the expense of the long-term fertility of the land; still others may be primarily concerned to preserve its productivity. (These distinctions will be considered in more detail shortly.)

Types of Economic Systems

We have seen that the concept of an economic system encompasses many different institutional arrangements and behavior patterns. It is helpful, however, to suppress many of the details of particular systems in order to distinguish three major types, called *traditional, command,* and *market.*

Traditional Systems

A **traditional economic system** is one in which behavior is based primarily on tradition, custom, and habit. Young men follow their fathers' occupations—hunting, fishing, and so on. Women do what their mothers did—typically cooking and field work. There is little change in the pattern of goods produced from year to year, other than those imposed by the vagaries of nature. The techniques of production also follow traditional patterns, except when the effects of an occasional new invention are felt. Finally, production is allocated among the members according to long-established traditions. In short, the answers to the economic questions of what to produce, how to produce, and how to distribute are determined by traditions.

Such a system works best in an unchanging environment. Prehistoric studies show that systems did change, but only very gradually, or very occasionally when large external shocks made some form of adaptation unavoidable. A climatic change, the discovery of a new crop, and the invention of a new tool are obvious examples. Under static conditions, a system that does not continually raise problems of choice can prove effective in meeting people's economic and social needs.

Traditional systems were common in earlier times. Today only a few small, isolated, self-sufficient communities still retain wholly traditional systems. In many less developed countries, however, many aspects of economic behavior are still governed by traditional patterns.

Command Systems

In command systems, economic behavior is determined by some central authority, which makes the bulk of the necessary decisions on what to produce, how to produce it, and who gets it. Such economies are characterized by the *centralization* of decision making. Because centralized decision makers usually lay down elaborate and complex plans for the behavior that they wish to impose, the terms **command economy** and **centrally planned economy** are usually used synonymously to refer to this type of economic system.

Central planning of all economic decisions in a large, modern industrial nation is an extremely complex business. Planners need to know the entire range of technological possibilities for production and to have full details of the supplies of all factors of production with their characteristics. On the basis of this information, the planners must settle on their choice of goods and services to be produced and how to produce them. Although planners may allocate commodities by such direct means as rationing, they often use prices. In this case, they set the prices of consumer goods and leave individuals to buy what they wish at the state-controlled prices. Even then, however, the planners must predict the pattern of consumers' demands in order to issue the correct production orders. Whenever they get the quantities wrong, there are queues for some scarce goods and unsold surpluses of others.

The sheer quantity of data required for central planning of an entire economy is enormous, and the task of analyzing it to produce a fully integrated plan can hardly be exaggerated. Moreover, the plan is not once-and-for-all. It must be a rolling process, continually changing to take account not only of current data but also of future trends in labor supplies, technological developments, and people's tastes for various goods and services. Doing so involves the planners in *forecasting*. This is a notoriously difficult business, not least because of the unavailability of all essential, accurate, and up-to-date information.

Today one-third of the world's population lives in the Soviet Union and China, countries that have for decades relied heavily on central planning to deal with the basic economic questions.

Market Systems

In the third type of economic system, the decisions about resource allocation are made without any central direction. Instead, they result from innumerable independent decisions made by individual producers and consumers; such a system is known as a **free market economy** or, more simply, a **market economy**.

In such an economy, decisions relating to the basic economic issues are decentralized. They are nonetheless coordinated. The main coordinating device is the set of market-determined prices—which is why free market systems are often called *price systems*. Since much of this book is devoted to studying how market systems work, little more needs to be said about them at this point.

Mixed Systems

It is useful for studying basic principles to deal with only two pure types of modern economic systems, centrally controlled and market economies. When we look in detail at *any* real economy, however, we discover that its economic behavior is the result of some mixture of central control and market determination. In practice, every economy is a **mixed economy** in the sense that it combines significant elements of both the command principle and the market principle in determining economic behavior. Furthermore, within any economy, the degree of the mix will vary from sector to sector. For example, in many planned economies the command principle is used much more to determine behavior in heavy goods industries, such as steel, than in the agriculture. Farmers are often given substantial freedom to produce and sell what they wish in response to varying market prices.

When we speak of a particular real economy as being a centrally planned economy, we mean only that the degree of the mix is weighted heavily toward the command principle. When we speak of an economy as being a market economy, we mean only that the degree of the mix is weighted heavily toward decentralized decision making in response to market signals. It is important to realize that such distinctions are always matters of degree and that almost every conceivable mix of command and market principles can be found in one real economy or another.

At the outset of our discussion of economic systems we noted two basic ways in which economies can differ: who owns the productive resources and who controls their use. Let us examine these questions more closely.

Ownership of Resources

Who owns a nation's farms and factories, its coal mines and forests? Who owns its railways, streams, and golf courses? Who owns its houses and hotels?

One characteristic of market economies is that the basic raw materials, the productive assets of the society, and the goods produced in the economy are predominantly privately owned. By this standard Canada is predominantly a market economy. However, even in Canada, public ownership extends beyond the usual basic services such as schools and local transport systems to include other activities such as electric power utilities and housing projects.

In contrast, in a planned economy the productive assets are predominantly publicly owned. Although the Soviets officially designate their economy as socialist, for several years some private ownership has existed in three sectors—agriculture, retail trade, and housing—and the government is moving to extend it to several other sectors. However, even though the USSR is not a pure socialist economy, public ownership is sufficiently widespread to place the USSR near one end of a spectrum while Canada lies near the other. Other countries fall between them on the spectrum.

The Decision Process (Coordinating Principles)

We have seen that in a market system, decisions are made in a decentralized way by the interaction of individuals in markets, while in a centrally planned economy, centralized decision makers decide what is to be done and issue appropriate commands to achieve the desired results.

Again, no country offers an example of either system working alone. But it is true that some economies, such as those of Canada, the United States, France, and Singapore, rely much more heavily on market decisions than others, such as the economies of China, the Soviet Union, and Cuba. Yet even in Canada the command principle has some sway. Minimum wages and quotas on some agricultural outputs and on textile imports are obvious examples. More subtle examples are public expenditures and taxes that in effect transfer command of some resources from private individuals to public officials.

In planned economies, where targets, quotas, and directives are important aspects of the decision-making system, the command principle predominates, but the market principle has always operated to some extent. For example, at the retail level, people have always had considerable discretion in how to spend their income on a wide variety of goods.

A key plank in Marxian economic proposals was public ownership of the means of production. Yet modern experience suggests that economic behavior usually depends more on the decision pattern than on the ownership pattern. Thus in the United Kingdom, when many key industries were publicly owned, their control was vested in semiautonomous boards over which Parliament exerted little control. By and large, the boards tried to make their enterprises profitable, and to the extent that they succeeded, their behavior was similar to that of profit-seeking, privately owned firms. In contrast, firms in Hitler's Germany were under a high degree of state control, even though they were privately owned. The behavior of these firms was very different from that of privately owned firms that are managed in order to earn profits for their owners.

Command Versus Market Determination

For over a century a great debate raged on the relative merits of the command principle versus the market principle for organizing economic affairs. The so-called socialist economies of the USSR, Eastern Europe, and China have been command economies for much of this century. The United States and most of the countries of Western Europe were primarily market economies—although some Western European nations incorporated major portions of the command principle. The successes of the USSR and China in the early stages of industrialization suggested to many observers earlier in this century that the command principle was at least as good, if not a better, way of organizing economic behavior than the market principle.

Ends and Means

To understand debates about relative desirability of different systems—as well as countless other debates about economic matters—we need first to distinguish between the goals of our actions and the means that we use to achieve those goals.

Our goals are called **ends**; they are the things that we strive for. The things that we use to achieve our ends are our **means**; they are the methods of achieving our goals.

In the economic aspects of our life, most people's ends include (1) achieving a satisfactory and, ideally, a rising living standard, (2) maintaining a reasonable quality of the environment in which they live, and (3) as far as possible, protecting themselves and others from the consequences of such serious disas-

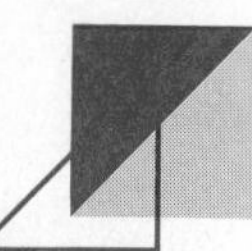

BOX 1-1

Will *Perestroika* Succeed?

At the start of 1989, Mikhail Gorbachev was in the midst of attempting a major restructuring of the Soviet economy. Fast on the heels of *glasnost* ("openness"), his dramatic initiative to reform and open up Russian society and politics, Gorbachev unveiled *perestroika* ("restructuring"), an equally dramatic shift in the Soviet economy away from state planning toward increased reliance on markets.

Perestroika generated enormous interest in Western countries. Many observers expressed doubt as to whether the reforms could succeed, since the long period of centrally planned mismanagement had wreaked such havoc with the economy. As *The Economist* put it:

> Much of the country's industry has yet to reach the technological and competitive standards achieved by capitalist economies in the 1950s. . . . After decades of being told that the state will provide, many ordinary Russians . . . expect it to go on doing just that. . . . When Mr. Gorbachev rattles on about the need for competition and a market, even a "socialist" one, he meets blank incomprehension. . . . The entrepreneurial sparks that glowed briefly at the start of the century have long since been snuffed out.

A key step in the reform, and one that is necessary if the reform is to succeed, is to let prices adjust freely in response to market pressures. However, when market forces and prices have been suppressed for so long, and when enormous amounts of purchasing power have been accumulated by citizens who have few goods available on which to spend their incomes, the *initial* reaction to freeing prices can be devastating. As *The Economist* said:

> In a country where the price of a basic loaf has not changed in 30 years, putting up prices is dangerous. . . . Free prices tomorrow would bring the sort of inflation that would make perestroika go pop. Yet, without freer prices pretty soon, both as a guide to what people want to buy and as an incentive to cut costs, perestroika will simply go phut.

Dramatic reactions to economic reform have caused governments to fall or to reverse course many times throughout history. Early in the 1980s reforms in Poland were halted when people rioted over rising food prices, and the world was shocked when riots over the same issue occurred in Venezuela in late 1988. In both cases the reforms were modest compared to what Gorbachev was attempting. The changes involved in *perestroika* are enormous, and the Russian people, like most other people, can be expected to react negatively and defensively when their everyday lives are affected by such far-reaching changes.

Indeed, by mid 1990 Gorbachev had backed down on some of his proposed economic reforms. Cooperatives had been set up to produce and sell many lines of goods, and they did succeed in putting an array of formerly unattainable goods onto

---

ters as the loss of one's job, the onset of a major disability, or the bankruptcy of one's employer.

All three examples represent a broad group of ends. The first relates to our material living standards. The second relates to the quality of the environment in which we live and work. The third relates to our social welfare system—the system that is intended to shield citizens from the worst consequences of disasters and to provide a "living standard safety net" below which no one should be forced to sink for any reason. Although many others exist, these three are our major economic ends.

Debates over means. Many political and economic debates relate to the alleged potency of alternative means to achieve agreed ends. Consider some examples.

The two great systems of command and free market economies were both seen as means to higher living standards and better control over our environ-

store shelves. Not surprisingly, the workers in these co-ops began to make large profits because they were providing what consumers desperately wanted. Jealousy over the profits, however, led to social unrest, and most co-ops were shut down. Production and distribution of these goods was returned to the planned sector of the economy, thus removing both the profits from the co-op owners and the plentiful supplies of goods that were the source of the profits. More fundamentally, after much debate, the government decided to follow through with its next comprehensive five-year plan—the big planning exercise that sets targets for all forms of production over the following half decade. By relying on the command signals of the planned economy, Gorbachev was accepting what had already gone on for decades. Western observers had no reason to doubt that it would continue to produce what it had produced for decades: low output of shoddy goods delivered only sporadically to shops. They doubted that reforming the planning apparatus would result in much change in economic performance. Nothing less than sweeping away the apparatus itself, as was being done in the former Soviet satellite countries of Eastern Europe, would, they felt, do the job.

Often gradual reform has a better chance of success, but governments do not always have the time to pursue gradual policies; their leaders may get thrown out of office before the reforms have had their effect. Certainly, many observers think that a major issue governing the chances of success for *perestroika* are whether Gorbachev's political skills are powerful enough to allow him to remain in office long enough to see the reforms through to a point where the benefits become apparent to the Russian people.

At the beginning of the 1990s, similar problems beset the governments of the Eastern European countries as they attempted to introduce market systems into economies that had been devastated by decades of central planning. Before these countries could be restructured as modern industrial societies, many inefficient firms had to go bankrupt, many jobs had to be lost, many workers had to learn new attitudes and work habits, and a financial infrastructure had to be created—modern commercial banks, insurance companies, stock exchanges, and a host of other sophisticated financial institutions that service modern industry. Could the transition be made quickly enough to prevent the rise to power of populist political parties? These parties would be dedicated to abandoning the policies of integration into Western European free market economies in order to avoid the short-run pain of adjustment, but would thereby eliminate the possibility of long-term gain. The issue currently hangs in the balance.

ment. Starting in 1989, the countries of Eastern Europe made the choice to move toward a free market system because their citizens thought that it was, among other things, a superior means to the end of higher living standards.

Arguments about nationalizing industries usually relate to the efficiency of industries functioning under this type of system of ownership and control. Few advocates of nationalizing industries see it as an end in itself but rather as a means to higher living standards. The current move to privatize production is the consequence of considerable evidence that state-owned industries function, at best, as well as privately owned firms and, at worst, substantially less efficiently.

Few people want government intervention into the markets for privately rented accommodations or farm production for its own sake. Instead, they hope that such intervention will be a means toward higher incomes for producers or lower prices to consumers,

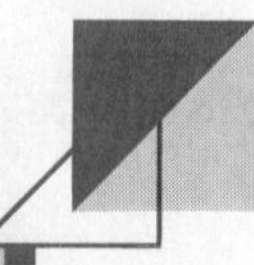

BOX 1-2

The Failure of Central Planning

The year 1989 signaled to the world what many economists had long argued: the superiority of a market-oriented price system over central planning as a method of organizing economic activity. The failure of central planning had many causes, but four were particularly significant.

The failure of coordination. In centrally planned economies, a body of planners tries to coordinate all the economic decisions about production, investment, trade, and consumption that are likely to be made by the producers and consumers throughout the country. This has proved impossible to do with any reasonable degree of efficiency. Bottlenecks in production, shortages of some goods, and gluts of others have plagued the Soviet economy for decades. For example, in 1989 much of a bumper harvest rotted on the farm because of shortages of storage and transportation facilities, and for years there has been an ample supply of black-and-white television sets and severe shortages of toilet paper and soap.

Failure of quality control. Central planners can monitor the number of units produced by any factory and reward those who overfulfill their production targets and punish those who fall short. It is much harder, however, for them to monitor quality. A constant Soviet problem, therefore, has been the production of poor-quality products. Factory managers are concerned to meet their quota by whatever means are available, and once the goods pass out of their factory, what happens to them is someone else's headache. The quality problem is so serious that very few Eastern European manufactured products seem able to stand up to the newly permitted competition from superior goods produced in the advanced market societies.

In market economies, poor quality is punished by low sales, and retailers soon give a signal to factory managers by shifting their purchases to other suppliers. The incentives that obviously flow from such private-sector purchasing discretion are generally absent from command economies, where purchases and sales are planned centrally.

Incentives. In market economies, relative wages and salaries provide incentives for labor to move from place to place, and the possibility of losing one's job provides an incentive to work diligently. This is a harsh mechanism that punishes losers with loss of income (although the social safety net provides floors to the amount of economic punishment that can be suffered). In planned economies, workers usually have complete job security. Industrial unemployment is rare, and even when it does occur, new jobs are usually found for those who lose theirs. Although the high level of security is attractive to many, it has proved impossible to provide sufficient incentives for reasonably hard and effi-

which in turn means a rise in the living standards of those concerned. Opponents argue that these means are inappropriate to the ends. They say, for example, that the long-term result of provincial marketing boards is that consumers will be worse off and only a few farmers better off than if the market had been left unregulated.

Debates over ends. The interests of various groups who are pursuing different ends can conflict. Everyone may agree, for example, that a particular agricultural policy makes farmers better off, but at the expense of consumers who must pay higher prices for their products. In this case, there is a real conflict between groups. The issue then becomes to decide between competing ends—improving the lot of farmers or that of consumers—rather than judging between alternative means to agreed ends.

Conflicts can also emerge over ends in that different groups put different values on alternative ends.

cient work under such conditions. In the words of Oxford historian Timothy Garton Ash, who wrote eyewitness chronicles of the developments in Eastern Europe from 1980 to 1990, the social contract between the workers and the government in the Eastern countries was "We pretend to work, and you pretend to pay us."

Because of the absence of a work-oriented incentive system, income inequalities do not provide the normal free market incentives. Income inequalities have been used instead to provide incentives for party members to toe the line. The major gap in income standards is between party members on the one hand and non–party members on the other. The former have access to such privileges as special stores where imported goods are available, special hospitals providing sanitary and efficient medical care, and special resorts where good vacations are available. In contrast, nonmembers have none of these things.

Environmental degradation. Fulfilling production plans becomes the all-embracing incentive in planned economies, to the exclusion of most other considerations, including the environment. As a result, environmental degradation has occurred in all the countries of Eastern Europe on a scale unknown in advanced Western nations. A particularly disturbing example occurred in central Asia, where high quotas for cotton output led to indiscriminate use of pesticides and irrigation. Birth defects are now found in nearly one child in three, and the vast Aral Sea has been half drained, causing incalculable environmental effects.

The failure to protect the environment stems from a combination of the pressure to fulfill plans and the lack of a political marketplace where citizens can express their preferences for the environment over economic gain. Imperfect though the system may be in democratic market economies, the record of environmental protection has been vastly better than that of command economies.

The price system. In contrast to the failures of command economies, the performance of the free market price system is excellent. One theme of this book is *market success*: how the price system works to coordinate with relative efficiency the decentralized decisions made by private consumers and producers, providing the right quantities of relatively high-quality outputs and incentives for efficient work. It is important, however, not to conclude that doing things better means doing things perfectly. Another theme of this book is *market failure*: how and why the unaided price system sometimes fails to produce efficient results and fails to take account of social values that cannot be expressed through the marketplace.

When environmental groups oppose the establishment of a local pulp mill while potential employees support it, the two groups are applying different values to two competing ends: more local job creation and more environmental protection.

The Shift Toward Free Market Systems

The 1980s witnessed a worldwide shift toward the use of markets. Margaret Thatcher in the United Kingdom and Ronald Reagan in the United States were modern politicians with the highest profiles who pushed policies that reduced the role of government in the economy and increased the role played by markets. Other Western countries, however, also deregulated key industries, privatized large government enterprises, and initiated other promarket reforms. Even in Canada, privatization has been extensive, covering numerous small firms that had in earlier decades come under government control for a variety of reasons, as well as such large, well-known enterprises as Air Canada and PetroCan.

The trend was also evident among planned economies. Major economic reforms in China introduced substantial reliance on market signals and market rewards. This trend was interrupted, however, after the 1989 suppression of the student democracy movement in the Tienanmen Square massacre. In the USSR, General Secretary (later President) Gorbachev's commitment to *perestroika* introduced what may turn out to be revolutionary promarket changes in the Russian economy. As Box 1-1 notes, however, the verdict of history is not yet in on the success of these Russian experiments.

Eastern Europe, 1989

The most dramatic changes were reserved for Eastern Europe. In the year 1989, an amazed world watched as Poland, East Germany, Czechoslovakia, Hungary, Bulgaria, and Romania rejected their centrally planned economies. In all of those countries, the system of single-party government to manage political affairs, combined with central planning to manage economic affairs, was rejected in favor of a system of multiparty democracies to manage political affairs and free markets to manage economic affairs.[3]

There is now no doubt among the majority of citizens and government officials in those countries that decentralized decisions, coordinated by such market signals as prices, wages, and profits, provide a more efficient way of managing economic affairs than a system that tries to coordinate them fully and consciously by bureaucrats employing the apparatus of central planning. The countries of Eastern Europe are now racing to embrace multiparty political systems and market economies.

The demise of these centrally planned, dictatorial economies can be traced to twin failures: They could not deliver living standards that ordinary citizens knew were available in market economies, and they could not falsify the famous dictum of the British historian Lord Acton: "Power tends to corrupt, and absolute power corrupts absolutely."[4]

Great social issues are difficult to settle and often just fade away to be replaced by other issues without being resolved. Rarely in human history has such a decisive verdict been delivered on two competing systems. The verdict has been rendered by ordinary people voting with their feet, their presence at the barricades, and sometimes their lives, for the democratic political and free market economic systems over the reality of dictatorial, centrally planned systems.

Box 1-2 gives some of the reasons why central planning has been a failure in Eastern Europe and the USSR.

The Lessons of Eastern Europe

Already people are debating the lessons to be learned from the failure of the planned economies of the countries of Eastern Europe. These economies featured highly centralized planning, and their failure suggests the superiority of decentralized markets over centrally planned ones as coordinating and signaling devices. Put another way, it demonstrates the superiority of mixed economies with substantial elements of market determination over fully planned command economies. However, it does *not* demonstrate, as some have asserted, the superiority of pure free market economies over mixed economies.

There is no guarantee that free markets will handle, on their own, such problems as controlling pollution and producing sustainable growth. (Indeed, as we shall see in later chapters, much economic theory is devoted to explaining why free markets often fail to do these things.) Mixed economies, with significant degrees of government intervention, are needed to do these jobs.

Furthermore, acceptance of the free market over

[3] In the Marxian theory of the socialist state, a planned economy was combined with a dictatorial government (the "dictatorship of the proletariat"). Although planned economies must necessarily be accompanied by a high degree of state coercion, there is nothing in principle to prevent the combination of a planned economy with democratically elected governments. In practice, however, planned economies have almost invariably been combined with one-party governments. It remains to be seen if Gorbachev's reforms will produce the combination of a planned economy with a stable, multiparty democracy. In contrast, because market economies feature decentralized decision making, market economies can be, and in practice have been, combined with all types of political systems, from full democracy to rigid dictatorship.

[4] Of course, the decline of economic performance and the social disintegration resulting from the increasing need for bribery and corruption to cope with the growing scarcity of ordinary goods and services stretched over decades. What came with such sudden speed was the public acceptance that the planned economies had been falling steadily behind the Western economies. When the economies finally reached a state of near collapse, the need for reform could be ignored no longer. Once begun, the speed of reform became hard to control.

central planning as a background organizing device of economic decisions provides no one with an excuse to ignore the country's many pressing social issues. It still leaves people free to debate the kinds, amounts, and directions of government interventions into the workings of our market-based economy that will help to achieve social goals.

It follows that there is still plenty of room for disagreement about the degree of the mix in any modern mixed economy—room enough to accommodate such divergent views as could be expressed by the Progressive Conservative, Liberal, and NDP parties in Canada. People can accept the free market as an efficient way of organizing economic affairs and still disagree about many things such as the optimal amount and types of government regulation of and assistance to the functioning of the economy, the types of measures needed to protect the environment, and the optimal amount and design of social services and other policies intended to redistribute income from more fortunate to less fortunate citizens.

Alternative Systems: A Final Word

Judging from their behavior, the citizens of most advanced economies have reached two conclusions. First, it is more efficient to have the majority of a country's production and consumption decisions made by independent producers and consumers and coordinated through the price system than to have them made by government officials and coordinated through central plans. Second, the unaided price system (often called a *laissez faire system*) is unable to cope with many of society's problems, and these need to be handled through substantial government intervention. Taken together, these two conclusions provide a presumption for mixed economies over either extreme of laissez faire or complete central planning. Judging further from their behavior, the degree of the mix between market determination and government intervention that best suits the needs of any particular society varies substantially from country to country and from time to time.

1. **All countries have mixed economies.**
2. **Among countries, the mixture differs in ways that are appreciable and significant.**
3. **Over time, the mixture changes.**

No particular mix seems to do everything better than any other particular mix; indeed, each has its strengths and weaknesses, and each may be better suited to the needs and values of some particular society. Thus to talk of "better" and "worse" in this context may be misleading. Although almost all economies today are moving toward more reliance on decentralized market forces, the differences among the mixes to be found in various economies are still enormous and will remain so in the foreseeable future.

SUMMARY

1. Most of the world's pressing problems have an economic aspect, and many are primarily economic. A common feature of such problems is that they concern the use of limited resources to satisfy virtually unlimited human wants.
2. Scarcity is a fundamental problem faced by all economies. Not enough resources are available to produce all the goods and services that people would like to consume. Scarcity makes it necessary to choose. All societies must have a mechanism for choosing what commodities will be produced and in what quantities.
3. The concept of opportunity cost emphasizes the problem of scarcity and choice by measuring the cost of obtaining a unit of one commodity in terms of the number of units of other commodities that could have been obtained instead.
4. Four basic questions must be answered in all economies: What commodities are being produced and how? What commodities are being consumed and by whom? What are the unemployment and inflation rates, and are they related? Is productive capacity changing?

5. Not all economies resolve these questions in the same ways or equally satisfactorily. Economists study how these problems are addressed in various societies and the consequences of using one method rather than another to provide solutions.
6. We can distinguish three pure types of economies: traditional, command, and free market. In practice, all economies are mixed economies in that their economic behavior responds to mixes of tradition, government command, and price incentives.
7. Arguments about which economic system to adopt in general and about such specific economic issues as privatization usually look at these arrangements as means toward the ends of achieving high and rising living standards and other major economic goals.
8. Among the important dimensions in which economies can differ from one another are the pattern of ownership of goods and resources and the decision process used, with a particularly important distinction between command and market coordinating principles.
9. In the late 1980s, events in Eastern Europe and the USSR led to the general acceptance that the system of fully centrally planned economies had failed to produce minimally acceptable living standards for its citizens. All of these countries are now moving toward greater market determination and less state command in their economies. At the beginning of the 1990s, several Eastern European countries were rapidly becoming predominantly market economies, and the USSR was moving more cautiously in that direction.

TOPICS FOR REVIEW

Scarcity and the need for choice
Choice and opportunity cost
Production possibility boundary
Resource allocation
Unemployed resources
Growth in productive capacity
Alternative economic systems
Public versus private ownership
Market versus command systems

DISCUSSION QUESTIONS

1. What does each of the following questions tell you about the policy conflicts perceived by the person making the statement and about how that person has resolved them?
   a. "It is an industry worth several hundred jobs to our province; we cannot afford to forgo it." British Columbia Premier William Vander Zalm explaining the decision to organize a killing of wolves in northern British Columbia so that more game animals could grow up to be shot by hunters.
   b. "The annual seal hunt must be stopped even if it destroys the livelihood of the seal hunters." An animal rights advocate opposing the seal hunt in the Gulf of St. Lawrence.
   c. "Considering our limited energy resources and the growing demand for electricity, Canada really has no choice but to use all of its possible domestic energy sources, including nuclear energy. Despite possible environmental and safety hazards, nuclear

power is a necessity," A representative of the electricity industry replying to criticisms from *Energy Probe*.

d. "The proposed pulp mills in northern Alberta must be opposed because of the pollution they cause, even though they bring new, diversified jobs to Alberta and even though they are based on the most advanced, pollution-minimizing technologies." An opponent of the proposal to construct new pulp and paper mills in the Peace River District of northern Alberta during the 1990s.

e. "Damn the pollution—we want the jobs." A labor leader in Brazil advocating permission to build new pulp mills in his country.

2. What is the difference between scarcity and poverty? If everyone in the world had enough to eat, could we say that food was no longer scarce?

3. Evidence accumulates that the use of chemical fertilizers, which increases agricultural production greatly, damages water quality. Show the choice between more food and cleaner water involved in using such fertilizers. Use a production possibility curve with agricultural output on the vertical axis and water quality on the horizontal axis. In what ways does this production possibility curve reflect scarcity, choice, and opportunity cost? How would an improved fertilizer that increased agricultural output without further worsening water quality affect the curve? Suppose that a pollution-free fertilizer were developed; would this mean that there would no longer be any opportunity cost in using it?

4. Identify the coordinating principle and the incentive system suggested by each of the following:

a. Taxes on tobacco and alcohol

b. Production targets assigned to a Russian factory manager by the state planning agency

c. Legislation establishing minimum wages to be paid

d. A provincial government directing its agencies to use local suppliers of goods rather than buying from other provinces

e. Legislation prohibiting the sale and use of cocaine

f. Rent controls combined with government subsidizing of the building of rental accommodations in Ontario

5. Pick one of the major socialist countries that have recently introduced market-oriented reforms and discuss the start-up problems that the reforms encounter. Explain why you think these problems will or will not persist over the next few years.

6. Discuss the following statement by Professor Paul McCracken, a former chairman of the U.S. President's Council of Economic Advisers:

> One of the mysteries of semantics is why the government-managed economies ever came to be called *planned,* and the market economies *unplanned.* It is the former that are in chronic chaos, in which buyers stand in line hoping to buy some toilet paper or soap. It is the latter that are in reasonable equilibrium—where if you want a cake of soap or a steak or a shirt or a car, you can go to the store and find that the item is magically there for you to buy. It is the liberal economies that reflect a highly sophisticated planning system, and the government-managed economies that are primitive and unplanned.

Chapter 2

Economics As a Social Science

Economics is generally regarded as a social science. What exactly does it mean to be scientific? Can economics ever hope to be in any way "scientific" in its study of the aspects of human behavior with which it is concerned?

The Distinction Between Positive and Normative

The success of modern science rests partly on the ability of scientists to separate their views on what *does* happen from their views on what they *would like* to happen. For example, until the nineteenth century, most people in the Western world believed that the earth was only a few thousand years old. About 200 years ago evidence that some existing rocks were millions or even billions of years old began to accumulate. Most people found this hard to accept: It forced them to rethink their religious beliefs. Many people wanted the evidence to be wrong; they wanted rocks to be only a few thousand years old. Nevertheless, the evidence accumulated until today most people accept that the earth is neither thousands, nor millions, but 4 or 5 billion years old.

This advance in our knowledge came because the question "How old are observable rocks?" could be separated from the feelings of scientists (many of them devoutly religious) about the age they would have liked the rocks to be. Distinguishing what is true from what we would like to be true depends on recognizing the difference between positive and normative statements.

Positive statements concern what is, was, or will be. **Normative statements** concern what one believes ought to be. Positive statements, assertions, or theories may be simple or complex, but they are basically about matters of fact.

Disagreements over positive statements are appropriately handled by an appeal to the facts.

Normative statements, because they concern what ought to be, are inextricably bound up with philosophical, cultural, and religious systems. A normative statement is one that makes, or is based on, a *value judment*—a judgment about what is good and what is bad.

Disagreements over normative statements cannot be handled merely by an appeal to facts.

Some related issues about disagreements among economists are discussed in Box 2-1.

The Distinction Illustrated

The statement "It is impossible to break up atoms" is a positive statement that can quite definitely be (and of course has been) refuted by empirical observations, while the statement "Scientists ought not to break up atoms" is a normative statement that involves ethical judgments. The questions "What government policies will reduce unemployment?" and "What policies will prevent inflation?" are positive ones, while the question "Ought we to be more concerned about unemployment than about inflation?" is a normative one.

The Importance of the Distinction

If we think that something ought to be done, we can deduce other things that, if we wish to be consistent, ought to be done, but we can deduce nothing about what is done (i.e., about what is true). Similarly, if we know that two things are true, we can deduce other things that must be true, but we can deduce nothing about what is desirable (i.e., about what *ought* to be).

It is logically impossible to deduce normative statements from only positive statements or positive statements from only normative ones.

Positive statements assert things about the world. If it is possible for a statement to be proved wrong by empirical evidence, we call it a *testable statement*. Many positive statements are testable, and disagreements over them are appropriately handled by an appeal to the facts.

In contrast, normative statements are never testable. Disagreements over such normative statements as "It is wrong to steal" or "It is immoral to have sexual relations out of wedlock" cannot be settled by an appeal to empirical observations. Thus for a rational consideration of normative questions, different techniques are needed from those used for a rational consideration of positive questions. Because of this, it is convenient to separate normative and positive inquiries. We do this not because we think the former are less important than the latter but merely because they must be handled in different ways.

As an example of the importance of this distinction, consider the question "Has the payment of generous unemployment benefits increased the amount of unemployment?" This positive question can be turned into a testable hypothesis such as "The higher the benefits paid to the unemployed, the higher will be the total amount of unemployment." If we are not careful, however, our attitudes and value judgments may get in the way of our study of this hypothesis. Some people are opposed to all welfare measures and believe in an individualistic self-help ethic. They may hope that the hypothesis is correct because its truth then could be used as an argument against welfare measures in general. Others feel that welfare measures are desirable, reducing misery and contributing to human dignity. They may hope that the hypothesis is wrong because they do not want any welfare measures to come under attack. In spite of different value judgments and social attitudes, however, evidence is accumulating on this particular hypothesis. As a result, we have more knowledge than we had 10 years ago of why and by how much unemployment benefits increase unemployment. This evidence could never have been accumulated or accepted if investigators had not been able to distinguish their feelings about how they wanted the answer to turn out from their assessment of evidence on how people actually behaved.

The distinction between positive and normative statements allows us to keep our views on how we would like the world to work separate from our views on how the world actually does work. We may be interested in both. It can only obscure the truth, however, if we let our views on what we would like to be bias our investigations of what actually is. It is for this reason that the separation of positive from normative statements is one of the foundation stones of science and that scientific inquiry, as it is normally understood, is usually confined to positive questions. Some important limitations on the distinction between positive an normative are discussed in Box 2-2.

Positive and Normative Statements in Economics

Economics, like other sciences, is concerned with questions, statements, and hypotheses that could conceivably be shown to be false by actual observations of the world. It is not necessary to show them to be either consistent or inconsistent with the facts tomorrow or the next day; it is only necessary to be

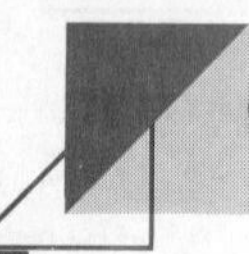

BOX 2-1

Why Economists Disagree

If you listen to a discussion among economists on "The National," "Sunday Morning," or "As It Happens," or if you read about their debates in the daily press or weekly magazines, you will find economists constantly disagreeing among themselves. Why do economists disagree, and what should we make of this fact?

In a recent column in *Newsweek,* Charles Wolf, Jr., suggests four reasons for the disagreement among economists: (1) Different economists use different benchmarks (inflation is *down* compared with last year but *up* compared with the 1950s). (2) Economists fail to make it clear to their listeners whether they are talking about short-term or long-term consequences (tax cuts will stimulate consumption in the short run and investment in the long run). (3) Economists often fail to acknowledge the full extent of their ignorance. (4) Different economists have different values, and these normative views play a large part in their public discussions.

There is surely some truth in each of these assessments, but there is also a fifth reason: the public's *demand for disagreement.* For example, suppose that all economists were in fact agreed on the proposition that unions are not a major cause of inflation. This view would be unpalatable to some individuals. Those who are hostile to unions, for instance, would like to blame inflation on them and would be looking for an intellectual champion. Fame and fortune would await the economist who espoused their cause, and a champion would soon be found.

Disagreement will always exist. It is also true that any disagreement that does exist will likely get exaggerated by the media. This is not necessarily intentional; it happens because of the nature of reporting. When the media cover an issue, they naturally wish to give both sides of it. Normally, the public will hear one or two economists on each side of a debate, regardless of whether the profession is divided right down the middle or is nearly unanimous in its support of one side. Thus the public will not know that in one case a reporter could have chosen from dozens of economists to present each side, while in another case the reporter had to spend three days trying to find someone willing to take a particular side because nearly all the economists contacted thought it was wrong. On many issues, the profession overwhelmingly supports one side. In their desire to show both sides of the case, however, the media present the public with the appearance of a profession equally split over all matters.

Thus anyone seeking to discredit some particular economist's advice by showing that there is disagreement among economists will have no trouble finding evidence to support his or her case. But those who wish to know if there is a majority view or even a strong consensus will find one on a surprisingly large number of issues, such as the housing shortages caused by rent control laws and the unemployment caused by minimum wage laws. Of course, economists disagree on many issues, especially those that involve recent and incompletely understood events, and there will always be controversies at the frontiers of current research.

able to imagine evidence that could show them to be false.

Normative questions cannot be settled by a mere appeal to facts. In democracies, such normative questions as "Should we subsidize higher education?" and "Should we send food to Ethiopia?" are often settled by voting.

Economists need not confine their discussions to positive, testable statements. Economists can usefully hold and discuss value judgments as long as they do not confuse such judments with evaluations of testable statements.

Indeed, the pursuit of what appears to be a normative statement will often turn up positive hy-

BOX 2-2

Limits on the Positive-Normative Distinction

Although the distinction between positive and normative statements is useful, it has a number of limitations.

The classification is not exhaustive. The classifications *positive* and *normative* do not cover all statements that can be made. For example, there is an important class, called *analytic statements,* whose validity depends only on the rules of logic. Thus the sentence "If all humans are immortal and if you are a human, then you are immortal" is a valid analytic statment. It tells us that *if* two things are true, *then* a third thing must be true. The validity of this statement is not dependent on whether or not its individual parts are in fact true. Indeed, the sentence "All humans are immortal" is a positive statement that has been decisively refuted. Yet no amount of empirical evidence on the mortality of humans can upset the truth of the *if-then* sentence quoted. Analytic statements—which proceed by logical analysis—play an important role in scientific work and form the basis of much of our ability to theorize.

Not all positive statements are testable. A positive statement asserts something about the universe. It may be empirically true or false in the sense that what it asserts may or may not be true of the universe. If it is true, it adds to our knowledge of what can and cannot happen. Many positive statements are refutable: If they are wrong, this can be ascertained (within a margin for error of observation) by checking them against data. For example, the positive statement that the earth is less than 5,000 years old was tested and refuted by a mass of evidence accumulated in the nineteenth century.

The statement "Extraterrestrials exist and frequently visit the earth in visible form" is also a positive statement. It asserts something about the universe, but we could never refute this statement with evidence because, no matter how hard we searched, believers could argue that we did not look in the right places or in the right way, that extraterrestrials do not reveal themselves to nonbelievers, or any one of a host of other alibis. Thus some positive statements are irrefutable.

The distinction is not unerringly applied. Because the positive-normative distinction helps the advancement of knowledge, it does not follow that all scientists automatically and unerringly apply it. Scientists are human beings. Many have strongly held values, and they may let their value judgments get in the way of their assessment of evidence. Nonetheless, the desire to separate what is from what we would like to be is a guiding light, an ideal, of science. The ability to do so, albeit imperfectly, is attested to by the acceptance, first by scientists and then by the general public, of many ideas that were initially extremely unpalatable—ideas such as the age of the earth and the theory of evolution.

potheses on which the *ought* conclusion depends. For example, there are probably relatively few people who believe that government control of industry is in itself good or bad. Their advocacy or opposition will be based on beliefs that can be stated as positive rather than normative hypotheses; for example, "Government control reduces efficiency, changes the distribution of income, and leads to an increase of state control in other spheres." A careful study of this subject would reveal enough positive economic questions to keep a research team of economists occupied for many years.

The Scientific Approach

An important aspect of the scientific approach consists of relating questions to evidence. When presented with a controversial issue, scientists will look for all relevant evidence. If they find that the issue is framed in terms that make it impossible to gather evidence for or against it, they will then usually try to recast the question so that it can be answered by an appeal to evidence.

In some fields scientists are able to generate observations that will provide evidence against which to test their hypotheses. Experimental sciences such as chemistry and some branches of psychology have an advantage because it is possible for them to produce relevant evidence through controlled laboratory experiments.

Other sciences such as astronomy and economics cannot do this. They must wait for natural events to produce observations that can be used as evidence in testing their theories. The evidence that then arises does not come from laboratory conditions under which everything is held constant except the forces being studied. Instead, it arises from situations in which many things are changing at the same time, and great care is therefore needed in drawing conclusions from what is observed.

The ease or difficulty with which one can collect evidence does not determine whether a subject is scientific or nonscientific.

Later in this chapter we shall consider some of the problems that arise when analyzing evidence that is not generated under controlled laboratory conditions. For the moment, however, we shall consider some general problems that are more or less common to all sciences and are particularly important in the social sciences.

Is Human Behavior Predictable?

Social scientists seek to understand and to predict human behavior. A scientific prediction is based on discovering stable response patterns, but are such patterns possible with anything so complex as human beings? Sometimes this question is answered "no" on the basis of the following argument. Whereas the natural sciences deal with inanimate matter that is subject to natural laws, the social sciences deal with human beings who have free will and hence cannot be subject to such laws.

This view implies that inanimate matter will show stable response patterns but human beings will not. For example—so goes this argument—if you put a match to a piece of dry paper, the paper will burn, whereas if you subject human beings to torture, some will break down and do what you want them to do and others will not. Even more confusing, the same individual may react differently to torture at different times.

Does human behavior show sufficiently stable responses to factors influencing it to be predictable within an acceptable margin of error? This positive question can be settled only by an appeal to evidence and not by a priori speculation. (**A priori** may be defined as that which is prior to actual experience.) The question itself might concern either the behavior of groups or that of isolated individuals.

Group Behavior Versus Individual Behavior

There are many situations in which group behavior can be predicted accurately without certain knowledge of individual behavior. The warmer the weather, for example, the more people visit the beach and the higher the sales of ice cream. It may be hard to say if or when one individual will buy an ice cream cone, but a stable response pattern can be seen among a large group of individuals. Although social scientists cannot predict which particular individuals will be killed in auto accidents during the next holiday weekend, they can come very close to knowing the total number who will die. The more objectively measurable data they have (e.g., the state of the weather on the days in question and the trend in gasoline prices), the more closely they will be able to predict total deaths.

The well-known fact that pollsters usually do a good job of predicting elections on the basis of surveys provides evidence that human attitudes do not change capriciously. If group behavior were truly capricious, there would be no point in trying to predict anything on the basis of such surveys. The fact that 80 percent of the voters who were surveyed said they intended to vote for a certain candidate would give no information about the probable outcome of the election. Today's information would commonly be reversed tomorrow.

The difference between predicting individual and group behavior is illustrated by the fact that economists can predict with fair accuracy what households as a group will do when their take-home pay is increased. Some indivuals may do surprising and unpredictable things, but the overall response of all households to a permanent change in tax rates that will leave more money in their hands is predictable within quite a narrow margin of error. This stability in the response of households' spending to a change in their available income is the basis of economists' ability to predict successfully the outcome of major revisions in the tax laws.

This does not mean that people never change their minds or that future events can be foretold by a casual study of the past. The stability discussed here is a stable response to causal factors (e.g., next time it gets warm, ice cream sales will rise) and not merely inertia (e.g., ice cream sales will go on rising in the future because they have risen in the past).

The "Law" of Large Numbers

Successfully predicting the behavior of large groups of people is made possible by the statistical "law" of large numbers. Broadly speaking, this law asserts that random movements of many individual items tend to offset one another. The law is based on one of the most beautiful constants of behavior in the whole of science, natural and social, and yet it can be derived from the fact that human beings make errors! The law is based on the statistical relationship called the *normal curve of error.*

What is implied by this law? Ask any one person to measure the length of a room, and it will be almost impossible to predict in advance what sort of error of measurement will be made. Dozens of things will affect the accuracy of the measurement; furthermore, the person may make one error today and a quite different one tomorrow. But ask 1,000 people to measure the length of the same room, and we can predict within a small margin just how this *group* will make its errors. We can assert with confidence that more people will make small errors than will make large errors; that the larger the error, the fewer will be the number making it; that roughly the same number of people will overstate as will understate the distance; and that the larger the number of people making the measurement, the smaller the average of their errors will tend to be.

If a common cause should act on each member of the group, the average behavior of the group can be predicted even though any one member may act in a surprising fashion. If, for example, each of the 1,000 individuals is given a tape measure that understates "actual" distances, it can be predicted that, on the average, the group will understate the length of the room, It is, of course, quite possible that one member who had in the past been consistently undermeasuring distance because of psychological depression will now overmeasure the distance because the state of his health has changed, but some other event may happen to another individual that will turn her from an overmeasurer into an undermeasurer. Individuals may act strangely for inexplicable reasons, but the group's behavior, when the inaccurate tape is substituted for the accurate one, will be predictable precisely because the odd things that one individual does will tend to cancel out the odd things that some other individual does.

Irregularities in individual behavior tend to cancel one another out, and the regularities tend to show up in repeated observations.

The Nature of Scientific Theories

When some regularity between two or more things is observed, we may ask why this should be so. A *theory* is an attempt to answer this question, and by providing an explanation for the regularity, it enables us to predict as yet unobserved events. For example, national income theory predicts that under certain specified circumstances, a reduction in tax rates will reduce the unemployment rate. The simple theory of market behavior predicts that under specified conditions, a partial failure of the potato crop will cause an increase in the incomes of potato farmers.

Theories are used in explaining observed phenomena. A successful theory enables us to predict behavior.

Any explanation whatsoever of how given observations are linked together is a theoretical construction. Theories are used to impose order on our observations, to explain how what we see is linked together. Without theories, there would be only a shapeless mass of meaningless observations.

The choice is not between theory and observation but between better or worse theories to explain observations.

Misunderstandings about the place of theories in scientific explanation give rise to many misconceptions. One of these is illustrated by the phrase "True in theory but not in practice." The next time you hear someone say this (or, indeed, the next time you say it yourself), you should immediately reply, "All right, then, tell me what does happen in practice." Usually you will not be told mere facts, but you will be given an alternative theory—a different explanation of the facts. The speaker should have said, "The theory in question provides a poor explanation of the facts—that is, it is contradicted by some factual observations. I have a different theory that does a much better job."

A theory consists of (1) a set of definitions that clearly define the *variables* to be used, (2) a set of *assumptions* that outline the conditions under which the theory is to apply, (3) one or more *hypotheses* about the relationships among the variables, and (4) *predictions* that are deduced from the assumptions of the theory and can be tested against actual empirical observations. We shall consider these constituents one by one.

Variables

A **variable** is a magnitude that can take on different possible values. Variables are the basic elements of theories, and each one needs to be carefully defined.

Price is an example of an important economic variable. The price of a commodity is the amount of money that must be given up to purchase one unit of that commodity. To define a price, we must first define the commodity to which it is attached. Such a commodity might be one dozen grade A large eggs. The price of such eggs sold in, say, supermarkets in Weyburn, Saskatchewan, defines a variable. The particular values taken on by that variable might be $1.22 on July 1, 1990, $1.29 on July 8, 1991, and $1.25 on July 15, 1992.

There are many distinctions between kinds of variables; we shall discuss two of the most important.

Endogenous and exogenous variables. An **endogenous variable** is a variable that is explained within a theory. An **exogenous variable** influences endogenous variables but is itself determined by factors outside the theory.

Consider the theory that the price of apples in Vancouver on a particular day is a function of several things, one of which is the weather in the Okanagan Valley during the previous apple-growing season. We can safely assume that the state of the weather is not determined by economic conditions. The price of apples in this case is an endogenous variable—something determined within the framework of the theory. The state of the weather in the Okanagan Valley is an exogenous variable; changes in it influence prices because the changes affect the output of apples, but the state of the weather is not influenced by the prices.

Other words are sometimes used for the same distinction. One frequently used pair is *induced* for endogenous and *autonomous* for exogenous; another is *dependent* for endogenous and *independent* for exogenous.

Stock and flow variables. A *flow variable* has a time dimension; it is so much per unit of time. The quantity of grade A large eggs purchased in Weybridge is a flow variable. No useful information is conveyed if we are told that the number purchased was 2,000 dozen eggs unless we are also told the period of time over which these purchases occurred. Sales of 2,000 dozen per hour would indicate an active market in eggs, while sales of 2,000 dozen per month would indicate a sluggish market.

A *stock variable* has no time dimension; it is just so much. Thus the number of eggs in the egg producer's co-op warehouse—for example, 20,000 dozen eggs—is a stock variable. All those eggs are there at one time, and they remain there until something happens to change the stock held by the co-op. The stock variable is just a number, not a rate of flow of so much per day or per month.

Economic theories use both flow variables and stock variables, and it takes a little practice to keep them straight. The amount of income earned is a flow; there is so much per year, per month, or per hour. The amount of a household's expenditure is also a flow—so much spent per week or per month. The amount of money in a bank account or a miser's hoard (earned, perhaps, in the past but unspent) is a stock—just so many thousands of dollars. The key test is always whether a time dimension is required to give the variable meaning.

Assumptions

Assumptions are essential to theorizing. Students are often greatly concerned about the justification of assumptions, particularly if they seem unrealistic.

An example will illustrate some of the issues involved in this question of realism. Much of the theory that we are going to study in this book uses the assumption that the sole motive of all people who run firms is to make as much money as they possibly can, or, as economists put it, firms are assumed to be run so as to *maximize their profits*. The assumption of profit maximization allows economists to make predictions about the behavior of firms. They study the effects that alternatives open to firms would have on profits, and then predict that the alternative selected will be the one that produces most profits.

Profit maximization may seem like a rather crude assumption. Surely the managers of firms sometimes have philanthropic or political motives. Does this not discredit the assumption of profit maximization by showing it to be unrealistic?

To make successful predictions, however, the theory does not require that managers be solely and unwaveringly motivated by the desire to maximize profits. All that is required is that profits be a sufficiently important consideration that a theory based on the assumption of profit maximization will produce predictions that are substantially correct.

This illustration shows that it is not always appropriate to criticize a theory because its assumptions seem unrealistic. All theory is an abstraction from reality. If it were not, it would merely duplicate the world and would add nothing to our understanding of it. A good theory abstracts in a useful way; a poor theory does not. If a theory has ignored some really important factors, its predictions will be contradicted by the evidence—at least where an ignored factor exerts an important influence on the outcome.

Put this way, the statement becomes an empirical assertion. The only way to test it is to see if the predictions that follow from the theory do or do not fit the facts that the theory is trying to explain. If they do, the theorist was correct in the assumption that profit maximization could be assumed for the particular purposes at hand. In this case the criticism that the theory is unrealistic because firms are not always solely concerned to maximize their profits is completely beside the point.

Models

Economists often speak of using *economic models* when they are developing and testing theories. The term *model* conveys the idea that we are abstracting from reality, but the term can also cause some confusion, since it is used in several ways. Typically, a model refers to an explicit statement of the definitions, assumptions, and behavioral hypotheses being used. Sometimes it refers to a rather general statement of the theory under consideration; for example, one model of consumption is that household consumption expenditure is positively related to the household's disposable income. However, sometimes the term *model* refers to a more specific case of the general theory that arises when specific values are attached to the relationships; for example, one specific model of consumption is that when the typical household's disposable income rises by $1,000, its consumption expenditures will rise by $900.

Hypotheses

Relations among variables. The critical step in theorizing is formulating hypotheses. A hypothesis is a statement about how two or more variables are related. For example, it is a basic hypothesis of economics that the quantity produced of any commodity depends on its own price in such a way that the higher the price, the larger the quantity produced. To illustrate, the higher the price of eggs, the larger the quantity of eggs that farmers will produce. Stated in more formal terms, the hypothesis is that the two variables, price of eggs and quantity of eggs, are positively related.[1]

Functional relations. A **function**, also known as a *functional relation,* is a formal expression of a relationship between two or more variables.

The particular hypothesis that the quantity of eggs produced is negatively related to the price of eggs is an example of a functional relation in economics. In its most general form, it merely says that quantity produced is related to price. The more specific hypothesis is that as the price of eggs rises, the quantity produced also rises.

In the case of many hypotheses of this kind, economists can be even more specific about the nature of the functional relation. On the basis of detailed factual studies, economists often have a pretty good idea of by how much the quantity produced will change as a result of specified changes in price; that is, they can predict magnitude as well as direction.

Predictions

A theory's predictions are the propositions that can be deduced from that theory. An example of a prediction would be a deduction that *if* firms maximize

[1] When two variables are related in such a way that an increase in one is associated with an increase in the other, they are said to be *positively related*. When two variables are related in such a way that an increase in one is associated with a decrease in the other, they are said to be *negatively related*.

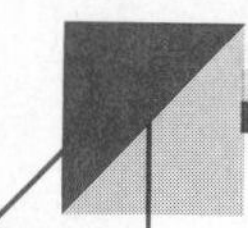

BOX 2-3

Can Hypotheses Be Proved or Refuted?

Most hypotheses in economics are universal. They say that whenever certain specified conditions are fulfilled, cause X will always produce effect Y. Such universal hypotheses cannot be proved correct with certainty. No matter how many observations are collected that agree with the hypothesis, there is always some chance that a long series of atypical observations has been made or that there have been systematic errors of observation. After all, the mass of well-documented evidence accumulated several centuries ago on the existence of the power of witches is no longer accepted, even though it fully satisfied most contemporary observers. The existence of observational errors, even on a vast scale, has been shown to be possible, although (one fervently hopes) it is not very frequent. Observations that disagree with the theory may begin to accumulate, and after some time a theory that looked nearly certain may begin to look rather shaky.

By the same token, a universal hypothesis can never be proved false with certainty. Even when current observations consistently conflict with the theory, it is still possible that a large number of atypical cases has been selected or systematic errors of observation have been made. For instance, evidence was once gathered "disproving" the theory that high income taxes tend to discourage work. More recent research suggests that economists may have been wrong to reject this theory. As a result of measurement errors and bad experimental design, the conflicting evidence may not have been as decisive as was once thought.

There is no absolute certainty in any knowledge. No doubt some of the things we now think are true will eventually turn out to be false, and some of the things we currently think are false will eventually turn out to be true. Yet even though we can never be certain, we can assess the balance of evidence. Some hypotheses are so unlikely to be true, given current evidence, that for all practical purposes we may regard them as false. Other hypotheses are so unlikely to be false, given current evidence, that for all practical purposes we may regard them as true. This kind of practical decision must always be regarded as tentative. Every once in a while we will find that we have to change our mind: Something that looked right will begin to look doubtful, or something that looked wrong will begin to look possible.

their profits and *if* certain other assumptions and hypotheses of the theory hold true, *then* a rise in the rate of corporate tax will cause a reduction in the amount of investment that firms make in new plant and equipment. The prediction is that the rise in the tax rate will be accompanied by a fall in investment. The reasons that lie behind the prediction are contained in the assumptions and hypotheses that constitute the theory in question.

It should be apparent from this discussion that a scientific prediction is not the same thing as a prophecy.

A scientific prediction is a conditional statement that takes the form: *If* this occurs, *then* such and such will follow.

If hydrogen and oxygen are combined under specified conditions, *then* water will be the result. *If* the government cuts taxes, *then* the rate of unemployment will decrease. It is important to realize that this second prediction is very different from the statement: "I prophesy that in two years' time there will be a large reduction in unemployment because I believe the government will decide to cut tax rates." The government's decision to cut tax rates in two years' time will be the outcome of many influences, both economic and political. If the economist's prophecy about unemployment turns out to be wrong because in two years' time the government does not cut tax rates, then all that has been learned is that the economist is not a good guesser about the behavior of the government. However, *if* the government does cut tax rates (in two years' time or at any other time) and *then* the rate of unemployment does not decrease, a conditional scientific prediction in economic theory has been contradicted.

Testing Theories

A theory is tested by confronting its predictions with evidence. It is necessary to discover if certain events are followed by the consequences predicted by the theory. For example, is an increase in the corporate tax rate followed by a decline in business investment? (Box 2-3 provides further discussion of what can be learned from testing theories.)

Generally, theories tend to be abandoned when they are no longer useful, and theories cease to be useful when they cannot predict the consequences of actions in which one is interested better than the next best alternative. When a theory consistently fails to predict better than the available alternatives, it is either modified or replaced. Figure 2-1 summarizes the discussion of theories and their testing.

Refutation or confirmation. The scientific approach to any issue consists of setting up a theory that will explain it and seeing if that theory can be refuted by evidence.

The alternative to this approach is to set up a theory and then look for confirming evidence. Such an approach is hazardous because the world is sufficiently complex that *some* confirming evidence can be found for any theory, no matter how unlikely the theory may be. For example, the advocates of conspiracy theories, such as the theory that U.S. President John F. Kennedy's assassination was a plot involving many persons and at least two gunmen, can always find some confirming evidence. The scientific way to deal with such questions is to set up the simplest theory—in this case, that the president was assassinated by Lee Harvey Oswald acting alone—and then see if the evidence can refute it.

An example of the unfruitful approach of seeking confirmation is frequently seen when a leader—be it a Canadian prime minister or a foreign dictator—is surrounded by sycophants who provide only evidence that confirms the leader's existing views. This approach is usually a road to disaster, because the leader's decisions become more and more out of touch with reality.

A wise leader adopts a scientific approach instinctively, constantly checking the realism of accepted views by encouraging subordinates to criticize them. This tests how far the leader's existing views correspond to all available evidence and encourages amendment in the light of evidence that conflicts with the current views.

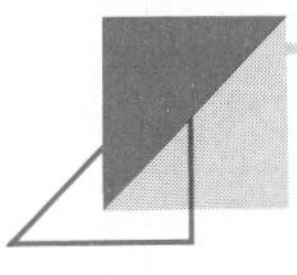

The Measurement and Testing of Economic Relations[2]

It is one thing for economists to theorize that two or more variables are related; it is quite another for them to be able to say how these variables are related. Economists might generalize on the basis of a casual observation that when households receive more income, they are likely to buy more of most commodities. But precisely how much will the consumption of a particular commodity rise as household incomes rise? Are there exceptions to the rule that the purchase of a commodity rises as income rises? For estimating precise magnitudes and for testing general rules or hypotheses, common sense, intuition, and casual observation do not take us very far. More systemtic statistical analysis is required.

Statistical analysis is used to test the hypothesis that two or more things are related and to estimate the numerical values of the function that describes the relation.

In practice, the same data can be used simultaneously to test whether a relationship exists and, if it does exist, to provide a measure of it.

We have seen that economics is a nonlaboratory science. It is rarely possible to conduct controlled experiments with the economy. However, millions of uncontrolled experiments are going on every day. Households are deciding what to purchase given changing prices and incomes; firms are deciding what to produce and how to produce it; and the government is involved in the economy through its various taxes, subsidies, and controls. Because all these ac-

[2] The appendix to this chapter gives a more detailed discussion of the use of graphs in economics.

FIGURE 2-1 The Interaction of Deduction and Measurement in Theorizing

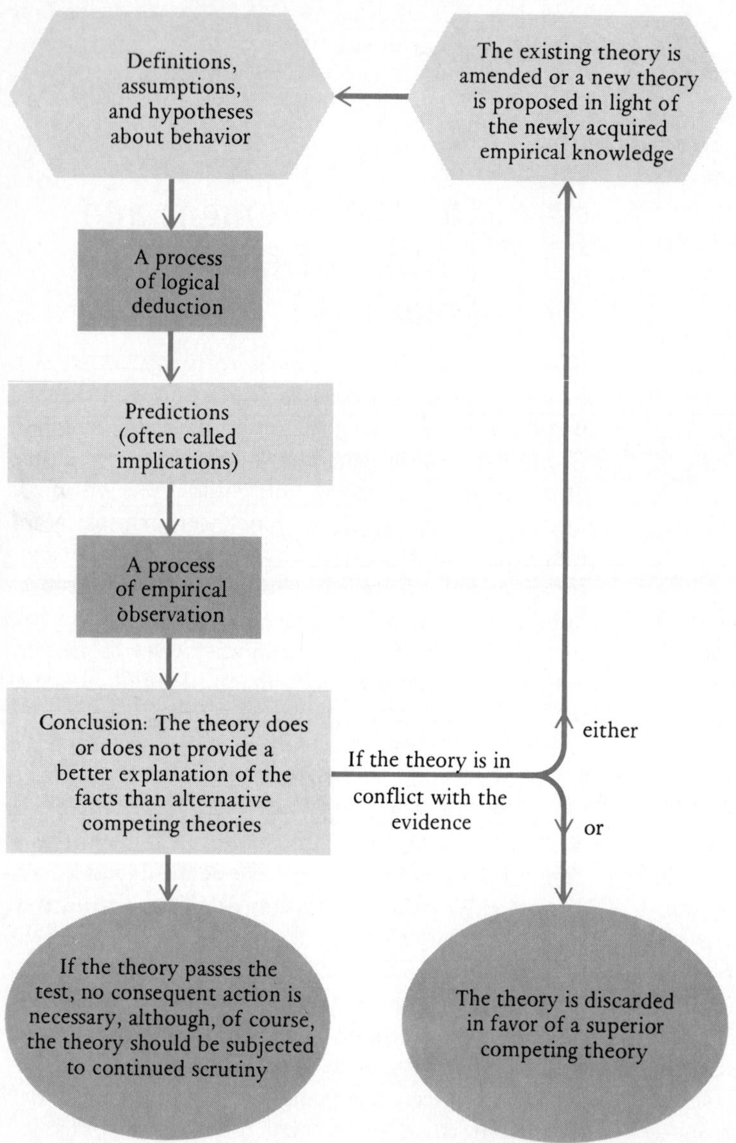

Theory and observation are in continuous interaction. Starting (at the top left) with the assumptions of a theory and the definitions of relevant terms, the theorist deduces by logical analysis everything that is implied by the assumptions. These implications are the predictions of the theory. The theory is then tested by confronting its predictions with evidence. If the theory is in conflict with facts, it will usually be amended to make it consistent with those facts (thereby making it a better theory); in extreme cases it will be discarded, to be replaced by a superior alternative. The process then begins again: The new or amended theory is subjected first to logical analysis and then to empirical testing.

tivities can be observed and recorded, a mass of data is continually produced by the economy.

The variables that interest economists, such as the volume of unemployment, the price of wheat, and the share of income going to wage earners, are generally influenced by many factors, all of which vary simultaneously. If economists are to test their theories about relations among variables in the economy, they must use statistical techniques designed for situations in which other things cannot be held constant.

Fortunately, such techniques exist, although their application is often neither simple nor straightforward. The appendix to this chapter provides a discussion of some tabular and graphical techniques for describing the data and displaying some of the more obvious relationships. Further examination of the data involves using techniques studied in elementary statistics courses. More advanced courses in econometrics study the array of techniques designed to test economic hypotheses and to measure economic relations in the messy circumstances in which economic evidence is often generated.

The Decision to Reject or Accept

Yet even though we can never be *certain* that a hypothesis is true or false, we do have to make decisions. To do so it is necessary to accept some hypotheses (to act as if they were proved) and reject some hypotheses (to act as if they were refuted). Just as a jury can make two kinds of errors (finding an innocent person guilty or letting a guilty person go free), so can statistical decision makers make two kinds of errors. They can reject hypotheses that are true, and they can accept hypotheses that are false. Luckily, like a jury, they can also make correct decisions—and indeed, they expect to do so most of the time.

Although the possibility of error cannot be eliminated in statistics, it can be controlled.

The method of control is to decide in advance how large a risk to take of accepting a hypothesis that is in fact false.[3] Conventionally in statistics, this risk is often set at 5 percent or 1 percent. When the 5 percent cutoff point is used, we will accept the hypothesis if the results that appear to establish it could have happened by chance no more than 1 time in 20. Using the 1 percent decision rule gives the hypothesis a more difficult test. A hypothesis is accepted only if the results that appear to establish it could have happened by chance no more than 1 time in 100.

Consider the hypothesis that a certain coin is "loaded," favoring heads over tails. The coin is flipped 100 times and comes up heads 53 times. This result is not strong evidence in favor of the hypothesis because such an unbalanced result could happen by chance more than 22 percent of the time. Thus the hypothesis of a head-biased coin would not be accepted on the basis of this evidence using either a 1 percent or a 5 percent cutoff. Had the experiment produced 65 heads and 35 tails, a result that would occur by chance less than 1 percent of the time, we would (given a 1 percent or a 5 percent cutoff) accept the hypothesis of a loaded coin.[4]

When action must be taken, some rule of thumb is necessary, but it is important to understand, first, that no one can ever be certain about being right in rejecting any hypothesis and, second, that there is nothing magical about arbitrary cutoff points. Some cutoff point must be used whenever decisions have to be made.

Finally, recall that the rejection of a hypothesis is seldom the end of inquiry. Decisions can be reversed should new evidence come to light. Often the result of a statistical test of a theory is to suggest a new hypothesis that "fits the facts" better than the old one. Indeed, in some cases just looking at a scatter diagram or making a standard statistical analysis uncovers apparent relationships that no one anticipated and leads economists to formulate a new hypothesis.

[3] Return to the jury analogy: Our notion of a person's being innocent unless the jury is persuaded of guilt "beyond a reasonable doubt" rests on our wishing to take only a small risk of accepting the hypothesis of guilt if the person tried is in fact innocent.

[4] The actual statistical testing process is more complex than this example suggests but must be left to a course in statistics.

SUMMARY

1. It is possible, and fruitful, to distinguish between positive and normative statements. Positive statements concern what is, was, or will be, whereas normative statements concern what ought to be. Disagreements over positive, testable statements are appropriately settled by an appeal to the facts. Disagreements over normative statements can never be settled in this way.

2. The success of scientific inquiry depends on separating positive questions about the way the world works from normative questions about how one would like the world to work, formulating positive questions precisely enough so that they can be settled by an appeal to evidence, and then finding means of gathering the necessary evidence.
3. Some people feel that although natural phenomena can be subject to scientific inquiry and "laws" of behavior, human phenomena cannot. The evidence, however, is otherwise. Social scientists have observed many stable human behavior patterns. These form the basis for successful predictions of how people will behave under certain conditions.
4. The fact that people sometimes act strangely, even capriciously, does not destroy the possibility of scientific study of group behavior. The odd and inexplicable things that one person does will tend to cancel out the odd and inexplicable things that another person does.
5. Theories are designed to give meaning and coherence to observed sequences of events. A theory consists of a set of definitions of the variables to be employed, a set of assumptions under which the theory is meant to apply, and a set of hypotheses about how things behave. Any theory has certain logical implications that must be true if the theory is true. These are the theory's predictions.
6. A theory provides predictions of the type "*if* one event occurs, *then* another event will also occur." An important method of testing theories is to confront their predictions with evidence. The progress of any science lies in finding better explanations of events than are now available. Thus in any developing science, one must expect to discard present theories and replace them with demonstrably superior alternatives.
7. Theories are tested by checking their predictions against evidence. In some sciences these tests can be conducted under laboratory conditions where only one thing changes at a time. In other sciences testing must be done using the data produced by the world of ordinary events. (The appendix to this chapter provides a brief discussion of some of the elementary statistical techniques used to test hypotheses when many variables are changing at once.)

TOPICS FOR REVIEW

Positive and normative statements
Testable statements
The law of large numbers and the predictability of human behavior
Variables, assumptions, and predictions in theorizing
Functional relations
Prediction versus prophecy
Measurement and testing

DISCUSSION QUESTIONS

1. A baby doesn't "know" of the theory of gravity, yet in walking and eating the child soon begins to use its principles. Distinguish between behavior and the explanation of behavior. Does a business executive or a farmer have to understand economic theory to behave in a pattern consistent with economic theory?
2. "If human behavior were completely capricious and unpredictable, life insurance could not be a profitable business." Explain. Can you think of any businesses that do *not* depend on predictable human behavior?

3. Write five statements about inflation. (It does not matter whether the statements are correct, but you should confine yourself to ones that you think might be correct.) Classify each statement as positive or normative. If your list contains only one type of statement, try to add a sixth statement of the other type.
4. Each of the following unrealistic assumptions is sometimes made. See if you can visualize situations in which each of them might be useful.
   a. The earth is flat.
   b. There are no differences between men and women.
   c. There is no tomorrow.
   d. People are wholly selfish.
5. "The following theory of wage determination proceeds on the assumption that labor unions do not exist." Of what use can such a theory be in Canada today?
6. What may at first appear to be untestable statements can often be reworded so that they can be tested by an appeal to evidence. How might you do that with respect to each of the following assertions?
   a. The Canadian economic system is the best in the world.
   b. Unemployment insurance is eroding the work ethic and encouraging people to become wards of the state rather than productive workers.
   c. Robotics ought to be outlawed, because it will destroy the future of working people.
   d. Laws requiring equal pay for work of equal value will spell disaster for women.
7. There are hundreds of eyewitnesses to the existence of flying saucers and other UFOs. There are films and eyewitness accounts of Nessie, the Loch Ness monster. Are you persuaded of their existence? If not, what would it take to persuade you? If so, what would it take to make you change your mind?
8. "The simplest way to see that capital punishment is a strong deterrent to murder is to ask yourself whether you might be more inclined to commit murder if you knew in advance that you ran no risk of ending in the electric chair, in the gas chamber, or on the gallows." Comment on the methodology of social investigation implied by this statement. What alternative approach would you suggest?

Appendix to Chapter 2

Graphing Relations Among Variables

The popular saying "The facts speak for themselves" is almost always wrong when there are many facts. Theories are needed to explain how facts are linked together, and summary measures are needed to assist in sorting out what facts show in relation to theories. The simpest means of providing compact summaries of a large number of observations is the use of tables and graphs. Graphs play an important role in economics by representing geometrically both observed data and the correspondence among variables that are the subject of economic theory.

Because the surface of a piece of paper is two-dimensional, a graph may readily be used to represent pictorially any correspondence between two variables. Flip through this book and you will see dozens of examples. Figure 2A-1 shows generally how a coordinate graph can permit the representation of any two measurable variables.[1]

FIGURE 2A-1 A Coordinate Graph

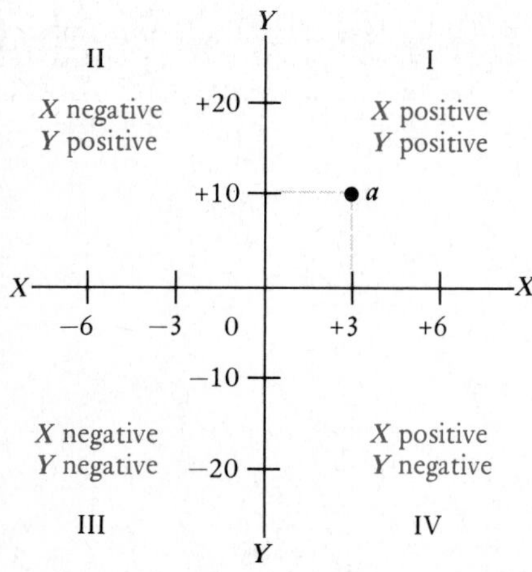

The axes divide the total space into four quadrants according to the signs of the variables. In the upper right-hand quadrant, both X and Y are greater than zero; this is usually called the *positive quadrant*. Point a has *coordinates* $Y = 10$ and $X = 3$ in the coordinate graph. These coordinates *define* point a.

FIGURE 2A-2 The Relationship Between the Price of Carrots and the Quantity of Carrots That Purchasers Wish to Buy: A Numerical Illustration

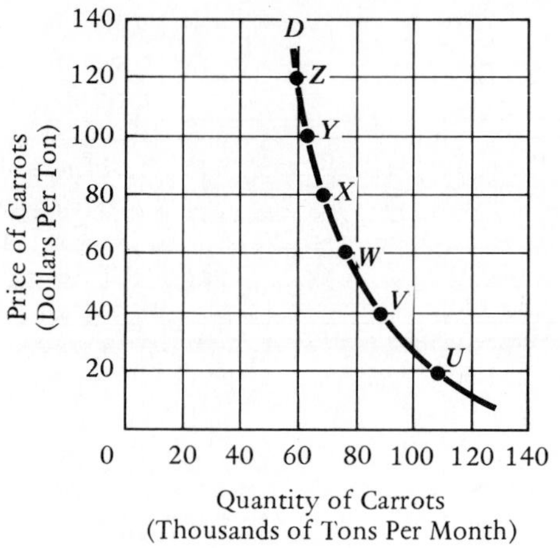

A two-dimensional graph can show how two variables are related. The two variables, the price of carrots and the quantity that people wish to purchase, are shown by the downward-sloping curve labeled D. Particular points on the curve are labeled U through Z. For example, point Z shows that at a price of \$120, the demand to purchase carrots is 60,000 tons per month.

Representing Theories on Graphs

Figure 2A-2 shows a simple two-variable graph, which will be analyzed in detail in Chapter 4. For now it is sufficient to notice that the graph permits

[1] Economics is often concerned only with the positive values of variables, and the graph is confined to the upper right-hand (or "positive") quadrant. Whenever a variable has a negative value, one or more of the other quadrants must be included.

FIGURE 2A-3 **The Relationship Between the Price of a Commodity and the Quantity of the Commodity That Purchasers Wish to Buy**

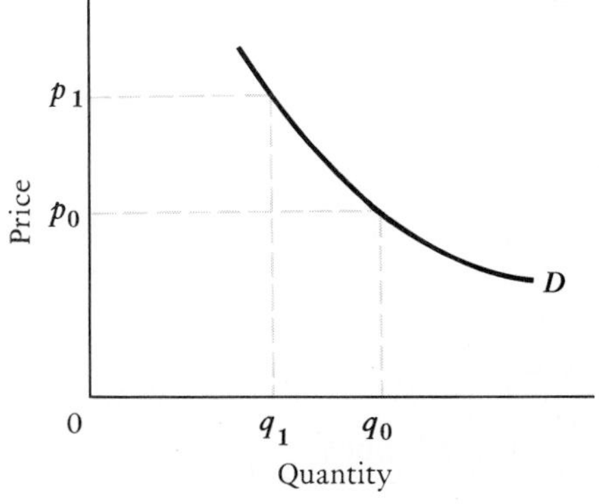

Graphs can illustrate general relationships between variables as well as between specific quantities. Here, in contrast to Figure 2A-2, price and quantity are shown as general variables. The demand curve illustrates a quantitatively unspecified *negative* relationship between price and quantity. For example, at the price p_0 the quantity that purchasers demand is q_0, while at the higher price of p_1 purchasers demand the lower quantity of q_1.

us to show the relationship between two variables, the *price* of carrots on the vertical axis and the *quantity* of carrots per month on the horizontal axis.[2] The downward-sloping curve, labeled D for a *demand curve,* shows the relationship between the price of carrots and the quantity of carrots buyers wish to purchase.

Figure 2A-3 is very much like Figure 2A-2, with one difference. It generalizes from the specific example of carrots to an unspecified commodity and focuses on the slope of the demand curve rather than on specific numerical values. Note that the quantity labeled q_0 is associated with the price p_0, and the quantity q_1 is associated with the price p_1.

Straight Lines and Their Slopes

Figure 2A-4 illustrates a variety of straight lines. They differ according to their slopes. **Slope** is defined as the ratio of the vertical change to the corresponding horizontal change as one moves along a curve.

The symbol Δ is used to indicate a change in any

[2] The choice of which variable to put on which axis is discussed in footnote 4 on page 90 and in math note [8] (regarding math notes, see footnote 3 on page 34).

FIGURE 2A-4 **Four Straight Lines with Different Slopes**

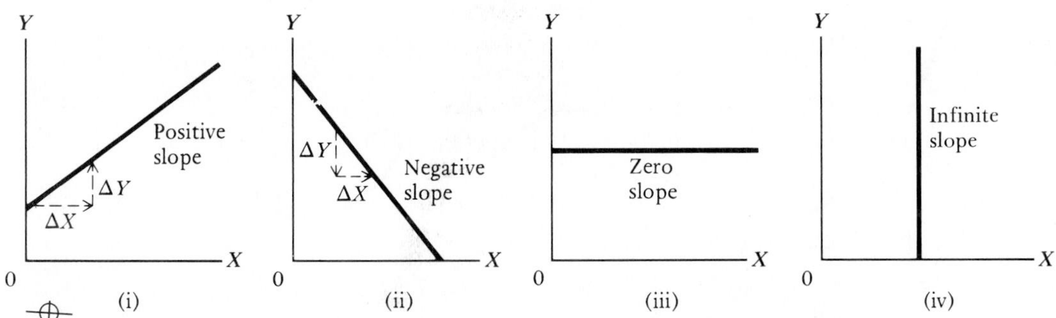

The slope of a straight line is constant but can vary from one line to another. The direction of slope of a straight line is characterized by the signs of the ratio $\Delta Y/\Delta X$. In (i) that ratio is positive because X and Y vary in the same direction; in (ii) the ratio is negative because X and Y vary in opposite directions; in (iii) it is zero because Y does not change as X changes; in (iv) it is infinite.

FIGURE 2A-5 Two Straight Lines with Different Slopes

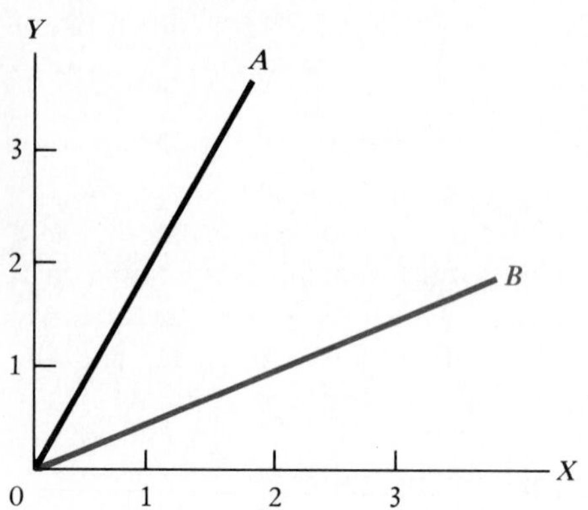

Slope is a quantitative measure. Both lines have positive slopes and thus are similar to Figure 2A-4(i). However, curve *A* is steeper (i.e., has a greater slope) than curve *B*. For each 1-unit increase in *X*, the value of *Y* increases by 2 units along curve *A* but by only ½ unit along curve *B*. The ratio $\Delta Y/\Delta X$ is 2 for curve *A* and ½ for curve *B*.

variable. Thus ΔX means "the change in *X*," and ΔY means "the change in *Y*." The ratio $\Delta Y/\Delta X$ is the slope of a straight line. When both increase or decrease together, the ratio is positive and the line is positively sloped, as in part (i) of Figure 2A-4. When ΔY and ΔX have opposite signs, that is, when one increases while the other decreases, the ratio is negative and the line is negatively sloped, as in part (ii). When ΔY does not change, the line is horizontal, as in part (iii), and the slope is zero. When ΔX is zero, the line is vertical, as in part (iv), and the slope is often said to be infinite, although the ratio $\Delta Y/\Delta X$ is indeterminate. **[1]**[3]

Slope is a quantitative measure, not merely a qualitative one. For example, in Figure 2A-5 two upward-sloping straight lines have different slopes. Line *A* has a slope of 2 ($\Delta Y/\Delta X = 2.0$); line *B* has a slope of 1/2 ($\Delta Y/\Delta X = 0.5$).

Curved Lines and Their Slopes

Figure 2A-6 shows four curved lines. The line in part (i) is plainly upward-sloping and in part (ii) downward-sloping. The other two change from one to the other, as the labels indicate. Unlike straight lines, whose slope is the same at every point on the line, the slope of a curve changes. The slope of a curve must be measured at a particular point and is defined

[3] Notes giving mathematical demonstrations of the concepts presented in the text are designated by colored reference numbers. These notes can be found beginning on page M-1.

FIGURE 2A-6 Four Curved Lines

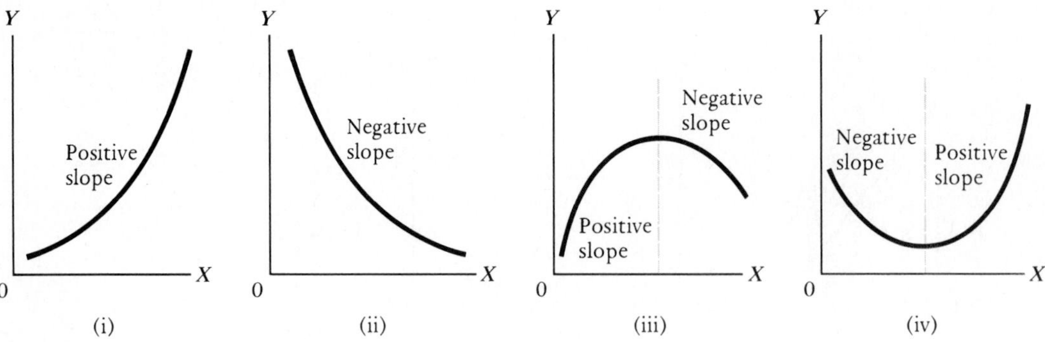

The slope of a curved line is not constant and may change direction. The slopes of the curves in (i) and (ii) change in size but not direction, whereas those in (iii) and (iv) change in both size and direction. Unlike that of a straight line, the slope of a curved line cannot be defined by a single number because it changes as the value of *X* changes.

as the slope of a straight line that just touches (is tangent to) the straight line at that point. This is illustrated in Figure 2A-7. The slope at point A is measured by the slope of the tangent line a. The slope at point B is measured by the slope of the tangent line b.

FIGURE 2A-7 Defining the Slope of a Curve

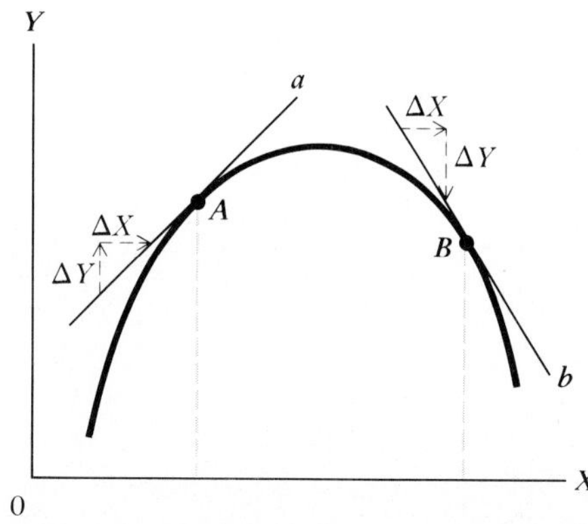

The slope of a curve at any point on the curve is defined by the slope of the straight line that is tangent to the curve at that point. The slope of the curve at point A is defined by the slope of the line a, which is tangent to the curve at point A. The slope of the curve at point B is defined by the slope of the tangent line b.

Graphing Observations

A coordinate graph such as that shown in Figure 2A-1 can be used to diagram the observed values of two variables as well as the theoretical relationships between them. For example, curve D in Figure 2A-2 might have arisen as a freehand line drawn to generalize actual observations of the points labeled U, V, W, X, Y, Z. Although that graph was not constructed from actual observations, many graphs are. To illustrate, we take the very simple hypothesis that the income taxes paid by families increase as their incomes increase.

A Sample

To begin with, observations must be made of family income and tax payments. It is not practical to do so for all families, so a small number (called a *sample*) is studied on the assumption that these households are typical of the entire group.

It is important that the sample be what is called a random sample. A **random sample** is chosen according to a rigidly defined set of conditions guaranteeing, among other things, that every member of the group from which we are selecting the sample has an equal chance of being selected. Choosing the sample in a random fashion has two important consequences.

First, it reduces the chance that the sample will be unrepresentative of the population from which it is selected. Second, and more important, it allows us to calculate just how likely it is that the sample will be unrepresentative by any specified amount. For example, if the average amount of income tax paid by the households in our sample is \$2,000, then it is most likely that the average tax paid by all households is in the vicinity of \$2,000. But that is not necessarily so. The sample might be so unrepresentative that the actual figure for average tax paid is only \$1,500, or it might be \$2,750. If the sample is random, we are able to calculate the probability that the actual data for the whole population differs from the data in our sample by any stated amount.

The reason for the predictability of random samples is that such samples are chosen by chance, and chance events are predictable.

That chance events are predictable may sound surprising, but consider these questions. If you pick a card from a deck of ordinary playing cards, how likely is it that you will pick a heart? An ace? An ace of hearts? You play a game in which you pick a card and win if it is a heart and lose if it is anything else; a friend offers you \$5 if you win against \$1 if you lose. Who will make money if the game is played a large number of times? The same game is played again, but now you get \$3 if you win and pay \$1 if you lose. Who will make money over a large number of draws? If you can answer these questions (we will bet that most of you can), you must believe that chance events are in some sense predictable.

To test the hypothesis about taxes, we have chosen a random sample of 212 families from data collected by the Survey Research Center of the Univer-

FIGURE 2A-8 A Scatter Diagram Relating Taxes Paid to Family Income

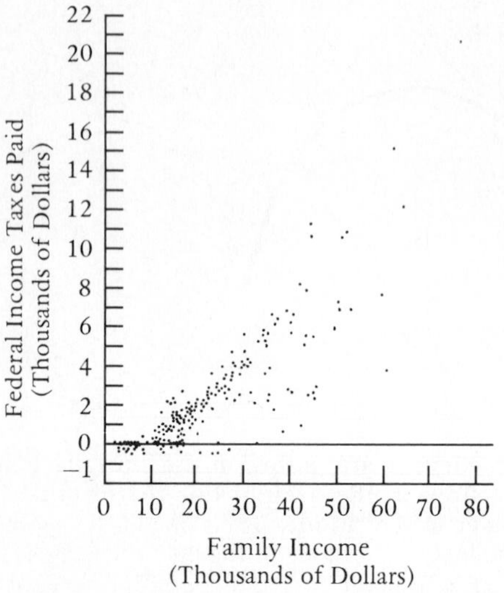

The scatter pattern shows a clear tendency for taxes paid to rise with family income. Family income is measured along the horizontal axis, and federal income taxes paid are measured along the vertical axis. Each dot represents a single family in the sample and is located on the graph according to the family's income and taxes paid. The dots fall mainly within a narrow, rising band, suggesting the existence of a systematic relationship between income and taxes paid, but they do not fall along a single line, which suggests that things other than family income affect taxes paid. The data are for 1979. (Negative amounts of tax liability arise because of such things as capital losses that may be carried forward.)

sity of Michigan. For each family we record its income and the federal income tax it pays as well as some other data that will be useful to us later.[4]

There are several ways in which the data may be used to evaluate the hypothesis.

Scatter diagram. One is the **scatter diagram**, which plots paired values of two variables. Figure 2A-8 is a scatter diagram that relates family income to federal income tax payments. Income is measured on the horizontal axis and taxes paid on the vertical axis. Any point in the diagram represents a particular family's income combined with the tax payment of that family. Thus each family for which there are observations can be represented on the diagram by a dot, the coordinates of which indicate the family's income and the amount of taxes it paid in 1979.

The scatter diagram is useful because if there is a simple relationship between the two variables, it will be apparent to the eye once the data are plotted. For example, Figure 2A-8 makes it apparent that more taxes tend to be paid as income rises. It also makes it apparent that the relationship between taxes and income is approximately linear. A rising straight line fits the data reasonably well between about $10,000 and $40,000 of income. Above $40,000 and below $10,000 the line does not fit the data as well, but since more than two-thirds of the families sampled have incomes in the $10,000 to $40,000 range, the straight line provides a fairly good description of the basic relationship for middle-income families.

The graph also gives some idea of the strength of the relationship. If income were the only determinant of taxes paid, all the dots would cluster closely around a line or a smooth curve; as it is, the points are somewhat scattered, and particular incomes are often represented by several households, each with a different amount of taxes paid.

TABLE 2A-1 Federal Tax Payments Cross-classified by Family Income

Annual family income	Average income tax payment	Number of families
$ 0–9,999	$ 70	38
10,000–19,999	893	76
20,000–29,999	2,470	42
30,000–39,999	4,205	28
40,000–99,000	7,755	28
100,000 or more	—	0

Tax payments tend to increase as family income increases. The data on 212 families are grouped into the income classes shown in the first column. The average tax payment for families in each income group is calculated and listed in the second column. When we read down this second column, we find an unbroken rise in tax payments. This cross-classification reduces 212 individual observations to a mere 5. More (or less) detail could have been preserved by varying the size of the income classes used in the first column.

[4] Since at this stage we are interested in methods rather than results, there is no problem in using data for American rather than Canadian households.

There is some scattering of the dots because the relationship is not "perfect"; in other words, there is some variation in tax payments that cannot be associated with variations in family income. These variations in tax payments occur mainly for two reasons. First, factors other than income influence tax payments, and some of these other factors will undoubtedly have varied among the families in the sample. Second, inevitably there will be some errors in measurement. For example, a family might have incorrectly reported its tax payments to the person who collected our data.

Cross-classification table. A cross-classification table provides another way to examine the hypothesis that tax payments vary directly with income. Table 2A-1 cross-classifies families by their incomes and their average tax payments. At the loss of considerable detail, the table makes clear the general tendency for tax payments to rise as income rises.

Extending the Analysis to Three Variables

The scatter diagram shows that not all variation in income tax payments can be accounted for by observed variations in family income. If it could, all the dots would lie on a line. Since they do not, some other factors must influence tax payments. Why might one family with an income of $25,000 pay 20 percent more in income taxes than another family with the same income?

One reason is difference in family size, for the tax laws provide exemptions based on the number of family members. (There will be other reasons too, such as differences in itemized deductions for medical expenses or charitable donations.) We anticipate that family size will be an important second reason. The survey also collected data on family size, which we now use.

There are now *three* observations for each of the 212 families: annual income, federal income tax payments, and family size. How should these data be handled? The scatter diagram technique is not available because the relationship among three sets of data cannot conveniently be shown on a two-dimensional graph.

The data may, however, be classified into groups once again. This time we are studying two variables that are thought to influence tax payments, and the data have to be cross-classified in a more complicated manner, as shown in Table 2A-2.

TABLE 2A-2 Federal Tax Payments Cross-classified by Family Income and Family Size

Annual family income	Number of family members: 3 or less	4 or 5	6 or more
$ 0–9,999	$ 175	$ 142	$ 26
10,000–19,999	1,028	995	507
20,000–29,999	2,950	2,491	935
30,000–39,999	5,349	3,802	2,372
40,000–49,999	9,459	8,624	4,193
100,000 or more	—	—	—

Tax payments tend to vary positively with family income and negatively with family size. Each row in the table shows the effect of family size on tax payments for a given level of income. For example, reading across the second row, we see that families with incomes between $10,000 and $19,999 paid an average of $1,028 if the family had less than 4 members, $995 if the family had 4 or 5 members, and $507 if the family had 6 or more members. The declining numbers across each row show that for each income group, tax payments tend to decline as family size increases. Each column in the table shows the effect of income on tax payments for a given family size. The increase in taxes paid as we move down each column shows that tax payments increase with family income.

The table can be used to hold one variable roughly constant while allowing another to vary. Reading across each row, we see that income is held constant within a specified range and family size is varied; reading down each column, we see that size of family is held constant within a specified range and income is varied.

Time-Series Data

The data used in the example of Figure 2A-8 are **cross-sectional data** (several measurements or observations made at the same point in time) because the incomes of and taxes paid by different households are compared over a single period of time—the year 1979. Scatter diagrams may also be drawn for a number of observations taken on two variables at successive periods of time.

For example, if one wanted to know whether there was any simple relationship between personal income and personal consumption in Canada be-

TABLE 2A-3 Personal Income and Consumption in Canada, 1965–1989 (*in 1981 dollars*)

Year	Disposable personal income per capita	Personal consumption expenditures per capita
1965	$ 5,592	$5,200
1966	5,840	5,392
1967	5,976	5,524
1968	6,124	5,704
1969	6,292	5,904
1970	6,372	5,940
1971	6,960	6,184
1972	7,252	6,523
1973	7,792	6,895
1974	8,167	7,135
1975	8,538	7,351
1976	8,870	7,712
1977	8,951	7,823
1978	9,227	7,952
1979	9,389	8,007
1980	9,533	8,071
1981	9,771	8,065
1982	9,920	7,732
1983	9,505	7,970
1984	9,835	8,240
1985	10,041	8,578
1986	10,046	8,844
1987	10,302	9,150
1988	10,533	9,213
1989	10,970	9,629

Source: CANSIM series D1, D490000, D10111, D10012.

Real disposable income per capita and real personal consumption expenditures have both grown since 1965. The former has increased from $5,592 to nearly $11,000 over the period, while the latter grew from $5,200 to nearly $10,000.

FIGURE 2A-9 A Scatter Diagram Relating Consumption and Disposable Income

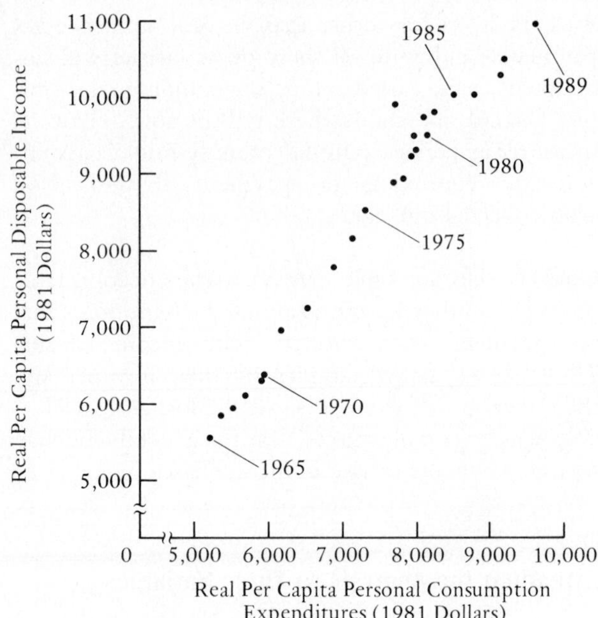

This scatter diagram shows paired values of two variables. The data of Table 2A-3 are plotted here. Each dot shows the values of per capita personal consumption expenditures and per capita disposable personal income for a given year. A close, positive, linear relationship between the two variables is obvious. Note that in this diagram the axes are shown with a break in them to indicate that not all the values of the variables between $5,000 and zero are given. Since no *observations* occurred in those ranges, it was unnecessary to provide space for them.

tween 1965 and 1989, data would be collected for the levels of personal income and expenditure per capita in each year from 1965 to 1989, as is done in Table 2A-3. This information could be plotted on a scatter diagram, with income on the X axis and consumption on the Y axis. The data are plotted in Figure 2A-9, and they do indeed suggest a systematic, almost linear relationship.

Figure 2A-9 is a scatter diagram of observations taken repeatedly over successive periods of time. Such data are called **time-series data**, and plotting them on a scatter diagram involves no new techniques. When cross-sectional data are plotted, each point gives the values of two variables for a particular unit (say, a family); when time-series data are plotted, each point tells the values of two variables for a particular year.

Instead of studying the relationship between income and consumption suggested in the preceding paragraph, a study of the pattern of the changes in either one of these variables over time could be made. Figure 2A-10 shows this information for consumption. Time is one variable, and consumption expenditure is the other. However, time is a special variable; the order in which successive events happen is important. The year 1985 followed 1984; they were not two independent and unrelated years. In contrast,

FIGURE 2A-10 A Time Series of Consumption Expenditures, 1965–1989

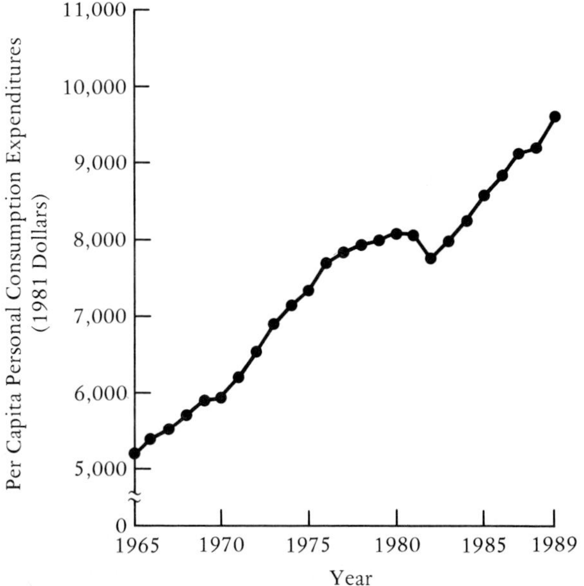

A time series plots values of a single variable in chronological order. This graph shows that with only minor interruptions, consumption measured in 1981 dollars rose from 1965 to 1989. The data are given in the last column of Table 2A-3.

two randomly selected households are independent and unrelated. For this reason it is customary to draw in the line segments connecting the successive points, as has been done in Figure 2A-10.

Such a figure is called a *time-series graph* or a *time series*. This kind of graph makes it easy to see if the variable being considered has varied in a systematic way over the years or if its behavior has been more or less erratic.

Ratio (Logarithmic) Scales

All the foregoing graphs use axes that plot numbers on a natural arithmetic scale, with distances between two values shown by the size of the numerical difference. If *proportionate* rather than *absolute* changes in variables are important, it is more revealing to use a ratio scale rather than a natural scale. On a **natural scale** the distance between numbers is proportionate to the absolute difference between those numbers.

FIGURE 2A-11 The Difference Between Natural and Ratio Scales

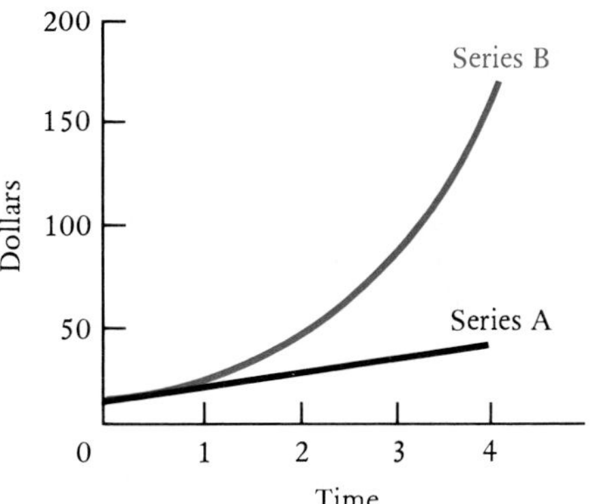

(i) A natural scale

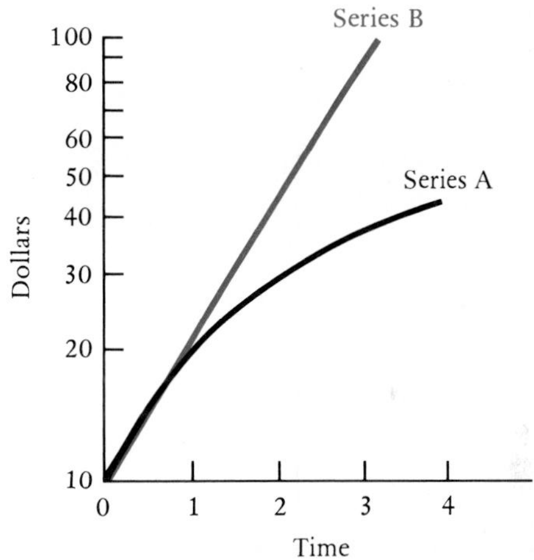

(ii) A ratio scale

On a natural scale, equal distances represent equal amounts; on a ratio scale, equal distances represent equal percentage changes. The two series in Table 2A-4 are plotted in each chart. Series A, which grows at a constant absolute amount, is shown by a straight line on a natural scale but by a curve of diminishing slope on a ratio scale because the same absolute growth represents a decreasing percentage growth. Series B, which grows at a rising absolute rate but a constant percentage rate, is shown by a curve of increasing slope on a natural scale but by a straight line on a ratio scale.

TABLE 2A-4 Two Series

Time period	Series A	Series B
0	$10	$ 10
1	18	20
2	26	40
3	34	80
4	42	160

Series A shows constant absolute growth ($8 per period) but declining percentage growth. Series B shows constant percentage growth (100 percent per period) but rising absolute growth.

Thus 200 is placed halfway between 100 and 300. On a **ratio scale** the distance between numbers is proportionate to the percentage difference between the two numbers (which can also be measured as the absolute difference between their logarithms). Equal distances anywhere on a ratio scale represent equal percentage changes rather than equal absolute changes. On a ratio scale the distance between 100 and 200 is the same as the distance between 200 and 400, between 1,000 and 2,000, and between any two numbers that stand in the ratio 1:2 to each other. For obvious reasons a ratio scale is also called a **logarithmic scale**.

Table 2A-4 shows two series, one growing at a constant absolute amount of 8 units per period and the other growing at a constant rate 100 percent per period. In Figure 2A-11 the series are plotted first on a natural scale and then on a ratio scale. The natural scale makes it easy for the eye to judge absolute variations, and the logarithmic scale makes it easy for the eye to judge proportionate variations.[5]

FIGURE 2A-12 A Contour Map of a Small Mountain

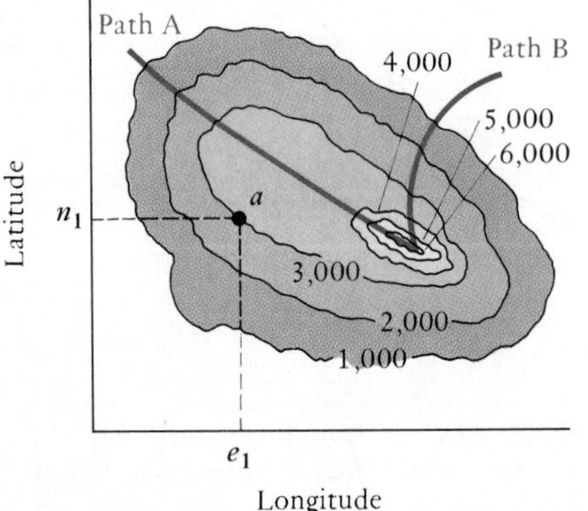

A contour map shows three variables in two-dimensional space. This familiar kind of three-variable graph shows latitude and longitude on the axes and altitude on the contour lines. The contour line labeled 1,000 connects all locations with an altitude of 1,000 feet, the contour line labeled 2,000 connects those with an altitude of 2,000 feet, and so forth. Point a, for example, has latitude n_1, longitude e_1, and an altitude of 3,000 feet. Where the lines are closely bunched, they represent a steep ascent; where they are far apart, a gradual one. Clearly, path A is a gentler climb from 3,000 to 4,000 feet on this mountain than path B.

FIGURE 2A-13 Three Variables Shown in Two Dimensions

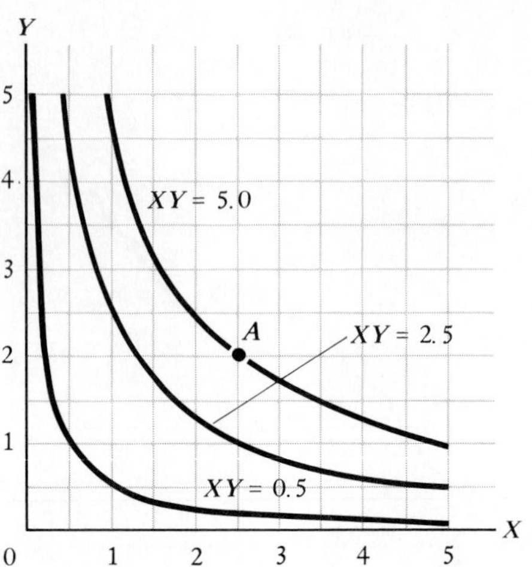

This graph illustrates examples of the three-variable function $XY = a$. The function $XY = a$ is called a *rectangular hyperbola*. The figure shows three members of the family. For example, point A represents $Y = 2.0$, $X = 2.5$, and $a = 5.0$.

[5] Graphs with a ratio scale on one axis and a natural scale on the other are frequently encountered in economics. In the cases just illustrated there is a ratio scale on the vertical axis and a natural scale on the horizontal (or time) axis. Such graphs are often called *semi-log graphs*. In scientific work, graphs with ratio scales on both axes are frequently encountered. Such graphs are often referred to as *double-log graphs*.

Graphing Three Variables in Two Dimensions

Often we want to show graphically more than two dimensions. For example, a topographic map seeks to show latitude, longitude, and altitude on a two-dimensional page. This is done by using contour lines, as in Figure 2A-12. Now consider the function $XY = a$, where X, Y, and a are variables. Figure 2A-13 plots this function for three different values of a. The variables X and Y are represented on the two axes. The variable a is represented by the labels on the curves. Several examples of this procedure occur throughout the book (see, for example, the discussion of indifference curves in Appendix A to Chapter 7 and isoquants in the appendix to Chapter 11).

Chapter 3

An Overview of the Market Economy

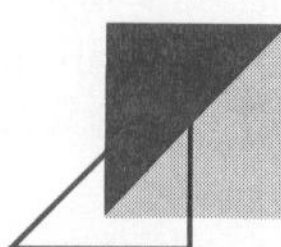

The Evolution of Market Economies

Until about 10,000 years ago, all human beings were hunter-gatherers, providing for their wants and needs by using foods that were freely provided by nature. The Neolithic agricultural revolution changed all that. People gradually abandoned their nomadic life of hunting and food gathering and settled down to tend crops and domesticated animals. Since that time all societies have faced the problem of choice under conditions of scarcity.

Surplus, Specialization, and Trade

Along with permanent settlement, the agricultural revolution brought surplus production. Farmers could produce substantially more than they needed for survival. The agricultural surplus allowed the creation of new occupations. Freed from having to grow their own food, new classes (such as artisans, soldiers, priests, and government officials) turned their talents to performing specialized services and producing goods other than food. They also produced more than they themselves needed, so they traded the excess to obtain whatever other goods they required.

The allocation of different jobs to different people is called **specialization of labor**. Specialization has proved to be extraordinarily efficient compared with self-sufficiency, for at least two reasons. First, individual talents and abilities differ, and specialization allows each person to do the job he or she can do relatively best, while leaving everything else to be done by others. Second, a person who concentrates on one activity becomes better at it than could a jack-of-all-trades.

The exchange of goods and services in early societies commonly took place by simple mutual agreement among neighbors. In the course of time, however, trading became centered in particular gathering places called **markets**. Today we use the term *market economy* to refer to a society in which people specialize in productive activities and meet most of their material wants through exchanges voluntarily agreed on by the contracting parties.

Specialization must be accompanied by trade. People who produce only one thing must trade much of their production in order to obtain all the other things they require.

The earliest market economies depended on **barter**, the trading of goods directly for other goods. However, barter can be a costly process in terms of time spent searching out satisfactory exchanges. The evolution of money made trading easier. Money eliminates the inconvenience of barter by allowing the two sides of the barter transaction to be separated. If a farmer has wheat and wants a hammer, he does not have to search for an individual who has a hammer and wants wheat. He merely has to find someone who wants wheat. The farmer takes money in exchange, then finds another person who wishes to trade a hammer and swaps the money for the hammer.

By eliminating the need for barter, money greatly facilitates trade and specialization.

The Division of Labor

Market transactions in early economies mainly involved consumption goods. Producers specialized in making a commodity and then traded it for the other products they needed. Over the past several hundred years, many technical advances in methods of production have made it efficient to organize agriculture and industry on a large scale. These technical developments have made use of what is called the **division of labor**, a further step in the specialization of labor involving specialization within the production process of a particular commodity. The labor involved is divided into a series of repetitive tasks, and each individual performs a single task that may be just one of hundreds of tasks necessary to produce the commodity. Today it is possible for an individual to work on a production line without knowing what commodity emerges at the end of that line!

To gain the advantages of the division of labor, it became necessary to organize production in large factories. With this development, urban workers lost their status as artisans and became members of the working class, wholly dependent on their ability to sell their labor to factory owners. The day of artisans who made and sold their own goods was over. Today's typical workers do not earn their incomes by selling commodites they personally have produced; rather, they sell their labor services to firms and receive money wages in return. They have increasingly become cogs in a machine they do not fully understand or control. Adam Smith, the eighteenth century Scottish political economist, was the first to develop the idea of the division of labor, as discussed in Box 3-1.

Markets and Resource Allocation

As explained in Chapter 1, *resource allocation* refers to the distribution of the available factors of production among the various uses to which they might be put. There are not enough resources to produce all the goods and services that could be consumed. It is therefore necessary to allocate the available resources among their various possible uses and in so doing to choose what to produce and what not to produce. In a market economy, millions of consumers decide what commodities to buy and in what quantities; a vast number of firms produce these commodities and buy the factor services that are needed to make them; and millions of factor owners decide to whom they will sell these services. These individual decisions collectively determine the economy's allocation of resources.

In a market economy, the allocation of resources is the outcome of countless independent decisions made by consumers and producers, all acting through the medium of markets.

Our main objective in this chapter is to provide an overview of this market mechanism.

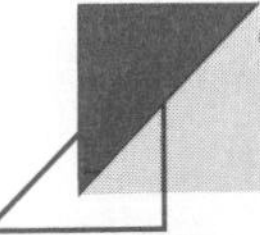

The Decision Makers

Economics is about the behavior of people. Much that we observe in the world and that economists assume in their theories can be traced back to decisions made by individuals. There are millions of individuals in most economies. To make a systematic study of their behavior more manageable, we categorize them into three important groups: households, firms, and the government, collectively known as **agents**.[1] These groups are economic the-

[1] Although in basic economic theory we can get away with three sets of decision makers, it is worth noting that there are others. Probably the most important are such nonprofit organizations as private universities and hospitals, charities such as the Canadian Cancer Society, and funding organizations such as the Donner Foundation. These bodies have an important influence on the allocation of the economy's resources.

BOX 3-1

The Division of Labor

Adam Smith begins his classic *The Wealth of Nations* (1776) with a long study of the division of labor.

The greatest improvements in the productive powers of labour . . . have been the effects of the division of labour.

To take an example . . . the trade of the pinmaker; a workman not educated to this business (which the division of labour has rendered a distinct trade), nor acquainted with the use of the machinery employed in it could scarce, perhaps, with his utmost industry, make one pin in a day, and certainly could not make twenty. But in the way in which this business is now carried on . . . it is divided into a number of branches. . . . One man draws out the wire, another straightens it, a third cuts it, a fourth points it, a fifth grinds it at the top for receiving the head; to make the head requires two or three distinct operations; to put it on is a peculiar business, to whiten the pins is another; it is even a trade by itself to put them into the paper; and the important business of making a pin is, in this manner, divided into about eighteen distinct operations, which, in some manufactories, are all performed by distinct hands, though in others the same man will sometimes peform two or three of them.

Smith observes that even in smallish factories, where the division of labor is exploited only in part, output is as high as 4,800 pins per person per day!

Later Smith discusses the general importance of the division of labor and the forces that limit its application.

Each animal is still obliged to support and defend itself, separately and independently, and derives no sort of advantage from that variety of talents with which nature has distinguished its fellows. Among men, on the contrary, the most dissimilar geniuses are of use to one another; the different produces of their respective talents, by the general disposition of truck, barter, and exchange, being brought, as it were, into a common stock, where every man may purchase whatever part of the produce of other men's talents he has occasion for.

As it is the power of exchanging that gives occasion to the division of labour, so the extent of this division must always be limited by the extent of that power, or, in other words, by the extent of the market. When the market is very small, no person can have any encouragement to dedicate himself entirely to one employment for want [i.e., lack] of the power to exchange all that surplus part of the produce of his own labour, which is over and above his own consumption, for such parts of the produce of other men's labour as he has occasion for.

Smith notes that there is no point in specializing to produce a large quantity of pins, or anything else, unless there are enough persons making other commodities to provide a market for all the pins that are produced. Thus the larger the market, the greater the scope for the divsion of labor and the higher the resulting opportunities for efficient production.

ory's cast of characters, and the market is the stage on which their play is enacted.

Households

A **household** is defined as all the people who live under one roof and who make joint financial decisions or are subject to others making such decisions for them. The members of households are often referred to as *consumers* because they buy and consume most of the consumption goods and services produced by the economy. Economic theory gives households a number of attributes.

First, economists assume that each household makes consistent decisions, as though it were composed of a single individual. Thus economists ignore many interesting problems of how the household reaches its decisions. Family conflicts and the moral and legal problems concerning parental control over minors are dealt with by other social sciences. These problems are avoided in economics by the assumption that the household is the basic decision-making unit of consumption behavior.

Second, economists assume that when buying commodities and selling factor services, households are the principal owners of factors of production. They sell the services of these factors to firms and receive their incomes in return.

Third, economists assume that each household seeks maximum *satisfaction* or *well-being* or *utility,* as the concept is variously called. The household tries to do this within the limitations of its available resources.

Firms

A **firm** is defined as the unit that employs factors of production to produce commodities that it sells to other firms, to households, or to government. For obvious reasons a firm is often called a *producer.* Elementary economic theory gives firms several attributes.

First, economists assume that each firm makes consistent decisions, as though it were composed of a single individual. Thus economics ignores the internal problems of how particular decisions are reached. In doing this, economists assume that the firm's internal organization is irrelevant to its decisions. This allows them to treat the firm as the unit of behavior on the production or supply side of commodity markets, just as the household is treated as the atom of behavior on the consumption or demand side.

Second, economists assume that most firms make their decisions with a single goal in mind: to make as much profit as possible. This goal of *profit maximization* is analogous to the household's goal of utility maximization.

Third, economists assume that in their role as producers, firms are the principal users of the services of factors of production. In markets where factor services are bought and sold, the roles of firms and households are thus reversed from what they are in commodity markets: In factor markets, firms do the buying and households do the selling.

Government

The term **government** is used in economics in a broad sense to include all public officials, agencies, government bodies, and other organizations belonging to or under the direct control of federal, state, and local governments. For example, in Canada the term *government* includes the prime minister and his cabinet, the Bank of Canada, provincial premiers and legislators, mayors and city councils, commissions and regulatory bodies, income tax inspectors, judges, the military, and the police force. It is not important to draw up a comprehensive list, but one should have in mind a general idea of the organizations that have legal and political power to exert control over individual decision makers and over markets.

It is *not* a basic assumption of economics that the government always acts in a consistent fashion. Two important reasons for this may be mentioned here. First, the mayor of Montreal, an Alberta MLA, and the minister of finance in Ottawa represent different constituencies, and therefore they may express different and conflicting views and objectives.

Second, individual public servants, whether elected or appointed, have personal objectives (such as staying in office, achieving higher office, power, prestige, and personal aggrandizement) as well as public service objectives. Although the balance of importance given to the two types of objectives will vary among persons and among types of office, both will almost always have some importance. It would be a rare MP, for example, who would vote against a measure that slightly reduced the "public good" if this vote almost guaranteed his defeat at the next election. ("After all," the MP could reason, "if I am defeated, I won't be around to vote against *really* bad measures.")

Decisions on interrelated issues of policy are made by many different bodies. Federal and provincial legislatures pass laws, the courts interpret laws, the governments decide which laws to enforce with vigor and which not to enforce, the Department of Finance and the Bank of Canada influence monetary conditions, and a host of other agencies and semiautonomous bodies determine actions in respect to different aspects of policy goals. Because of the multiplicity of decision makers, it would be truly amazing if fully consistent behavior resulted.

Another problem arises from the fact that in a democracy, an important goal of legislators and political officials is their own and their leader's reelection. This means, for example, that any measure that imposes large costs and few obvious benefits over the short run is unlikely to find favor, no matter how large the long-term benefits are. There is a strong bias toward shortsightedness in an elective system. Although much of this bias stems from an inability to grasp long-run consequences or a selfish unwillingness to look beyond the present, some of it reflects genuine uncertainty about the future.

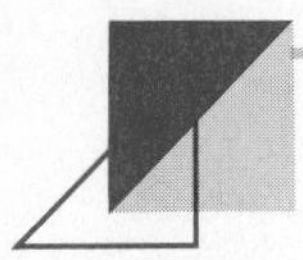

Markets and Economies

We have seen that households, firms, and the government are the main actors in the economic drama. Their action takes place in individual markets.

Markets

The word *market* originally designated a place where goods were traded. The famous Petticoat Lane in London is a modern example of a market in the everyday sense, and most cities have fruit and vegetable markets. Much early economic theory attempted to explain price behavior in just such markets. Why, for example, can you sometimes obtain great bargains at the end of the day and at other times get what you want only at prices that appear exorbitant in relation to prices quoted only a few hours earlier?

As theories of market behavior were developed, they were extended to cover commodities such as wheat. Wheat produced anywhere in the world can be purchased almost anywhere else in the world, and the price of a given grade of wheat tends to be nearly uniform the world over. When we talk about the wheat market, the concept of a market has been extended well beyond the idea of a single place to which the producer, the storekeeper, and the householder go to sell and buy.

We also speak of the "foreign exchange market," which has no more specific location than the international telephone network and computer hookups whereby dealers buy and sell dollars, sterling, francs, yen, and other currencies. Markets may indeed use all conceivable means of communication including the press, as in the case of the markets for many secondhand goods such as automobiles. If you have a car to sell or want to buy one, you will discover that "the market" comprises the local press, specialized magazines, and used-car dealers' sales lots.

Economists distinguish two broad types of markets: **product markets** (sometimes called *goods markets*), in which outputs of goods and services are sold, and **factor markets**, in which the services of factors of production are sold.

Economies

An **economy** is rather loosely defined as a set of interrelated production and consumption activities. It may refer to this activity in a region of one country (for example, the economy of the Maritimes), in a country (the Canadian economy), or in a group of countries (the economy of Western Europe). In any economy the allocation of resources is determined by the production, sales, and purchase decisions made by firms, households, and the government.

In Chapter 1 we learned three important things about economies. First, a *free market economy* is one in which the decisions of individual households and firms (as distinct from the government) exert the major influence over the allocation of resources. Second, the opposite of a free market economy is a *command economy,* in which the major decisions about the allocation of resources are made by the government and in which firms produce and households consume only as directed. Third, in practice, all economies are *mixed economies* in that some decisions are made by firms, households, and the government acting through markets and some are made by the government using the command principle.

Sectors of an Economy

Parts of an economy are usually referred to as **sectors** of that economy. For example, the agricultural sector is the part of the economy that produces agricultural commodities.

Market and Nonmarket Sectors

Producers make commodities. Consumers use them. Commodities may pass from one group to the other in two ways: They may be sold by producers and bought by consumers through markets, or they may be given away.

When commodities are bought and sold, producers expect to cover their costs with the revenue they obtain from selling the product. We call this *marketed production,* and we refer to this part of the economy's activity as belonging to the **market sector**.

When the product is given away, the costs of

production must be covered from some source other than sales revenue. We call this *nonmarketed production,* and we refer to this part of the economy's activity as belonging to the **nonmarket sector**. In the case of private charities, the money required to pay for factor services may be raised from the public by voluntary contributions. In the case of production by the government—which accounts for the bulk of nonmarketed production—the money is provided from government revenue, which in turn comes mainly from taxes.

Whenever a government enterprise *sells* its output, its production is in the market sector. Most of the government's output, however, is in the nonmarket sector, often by the very nature of the product provided. For example, one could hardly expect the criminal to pay the judge for providing the service of criminal justice. Other products are in the nonmarket sector because governments have decided that there are advantages to removing them from the market sector. This is the case, for example, with much of Canadian education. Public policy places it in the nonmarket sector even though much of it could be provided by the market sector.

Private and Public Sectors

An alternative division of an economy's productive activity is between private and public sectors. The **private sector** refers to all production that is in private hands, and the **public sector** refers to all production that is in public hands. The distinction between the two sectors depends on the legal distinction of ownership. In the private sector, the organization that does the producing is owned by households or other firms; in the public sector, it is owned and controlled by the government. The public sector includes all production of goods and services by the government plus all production of crown corporations and other government-operated industries that is sold to consumers through markets.

The distinction between market and nonmarket sectors is economic; it depends on whether or not the producer earns revenue by selling output to users. The distinction between the private and the public sectors is legal; it depends on whether the producing organizations are privately or publicly owned.

Microeconomics and Macroeconomics

As we saw in Chapter 1, there are two different but complementary ways of viewing the economy. The first, *microeconomics,* studies the detailed workings of individual markets and interrelationships between markets. The second, *macroeconomics,* suppresses much of the detail and concentrates on the behavior of broad aggregates.[2]

An Overview of Microeconomics

Early eonomists observed the market economy with wonder. They saw that most commodities were made by a large number of independent producers, yet in approximately the quantities that people wanted to purchase them. Natural disasters aside, there were neither vast surpluses nor severe shortages of products. They also saw that in spite of the ever-changing geographical, industrial, and occupational patterns of demand for labor services, most laborers were able to sell their services to employers most of the time. Visitors from planned economies often have a similar reaction. How, they ask, can there be such an abundance of the right things, produced at the right time and delivered to the right place?

How indeed does the market produce this order in the absence of conscious coordination? It is one thing to have the same good produced year in and year out when people's wants and incomes do not change; it is quite another thing to have production adjusting continually to changing wants, incomes, and techniques of production. Yet this adjustment is accomplished relatively smoothly by markets—albeit with occasional, and sometimes serious, interruptions.

Markets work without conscious central control because individual agents make their private decisions in response to publicly known signals, such as prices, wages, and profits, while these signals, in turn, respond to the collective actions entailed by the sum of all individual decisions. In short:

The great discovery of eighteenth century economists was that the price system is a social con-

[2] The prefixes *micro-* and *macro-* derive from the Greek words *mikros,* "small," and *makro,* "large."

trol mechanism that coordinates decentralized decision making.

In *The Wealth of Nations,* Adam Smith spoke of the price system as "the invisible hand." It allows decision making to be decentralized under the control of millions of individual producers and consumers but nonetheless to be coordinated. Two examples may help to illustrate how this coordination occurs.

A Change in Demand

For the first example, assume that housholds wish to purchase more of some commodity than previously. To see the market's reaction to such a change, imagine a situation in which farmers find it equally profitable to produce either of two crops, carrots or brussels sprouts, and so are willing to produce some of both commodities, thereby satisfying the demands of households that wish to consume both. Now imagine that consumers develop a greatly increased desire for brussels sprouts and a diminished desire for carrots. This change might have occurred because of the discovery of hitherto unsuspected nutritive or curative powers of brussels sprouts.

When consumers buy more brussels sprouts and fewer carrots, a shortage of brussels sprouts and a glut of carrots develop. To unload their surplus stocks of carrots, merchants reduce the price of carrots because it is better to sell them at a reduced price than not to sell them at all. Sellers of brussels sprouts, however, find that they are unable to satisfy all their customers' demands for that product. Brussels sprouts have become more scarce, so merchants charge more for them. As the price rises, fewer people are willing and able to purchase brussels sprouts. Thus the rise in their price limits the quantity demanded to the available supply.

Farmers see the rise in the price of brussels sprouts and the fall in the price of carrots. Brussels sprout production has become more profitable than in the past because the costs of producing brussels sprouts remain unchanged while their market price has risen. Similarly, carrot production is less profitable than in the past because costs are unchanged while the price has fallen. Attracted by high profits in brussels sprouts and deterred by low profits or potential losses in carrots, farmers expand the production of brussels sprouts and curtail the production of carrots. Thus the change in consumers' tastes, working through the price system, causes a reallocation of resources—land and labor—out of carrot production and into brussels sprout production.

As the production of carrots declines, the glut of carrots on the market diminishes and their price begins to rise. At the same time, the expansion in brussels sprout production reduces the shortage, and the price begins to fall. These price movements will continue until it no longer pays farmers to contract carrot production and to expand brussels sprout production. When all of the adjustments have occurred, the price of brussels sprouts is higher than it was originally but lower than it was when the shortage sent the price soaring before output could be adjusted; and the price of carrots is lower than it was originally but higher than when the initial glut sent the price tumbling before output could be adjusted.

The reaction of the market to a change in demand leads to a transfer of resources. Carrot producers reduce their production; they will therefore be laying off workers and generally demanding fewer factors of production. Brussels sprout producers expand production; they will therefore be hiring workers and generally increasing their demand for factors of production.

Labor can probably switch from carrot to brussels sprout production without much difficulty. Certain types of land, however, may be better suited for growing one crop than the other. When farmers increase their brussels sprout production, their demands for the factors especially suited to growing brussels sprouts also increase—and this creates a shortage of these resources and a consequent rise in their prices. Meanwhile, with carrot production falling, the demand for land and other factors of production especially suited to carrot growing is reduced. A surplus results, and the prices of these factors are forced down.

Thus factors particularly suited to brussels sprout production will earn more and will obtain a higher share of total national income than before. Factors particularly suited to carrot production, however, will earn less and will obtain a smaller share of the total national income than before.

Changes of this kind will be studied more fully later; the important thing to notice now is how changes in demand cause reallocations of resources in the directions required to cater to the new levels of demand.

A Change in Supply

As a second example, consider a change originating with producers. Begin as before with a situation in which farmers find it equally profitable to produce either brussels sprouts or carrots and in which consumers are willing to buy, at prevailing prices, the quantities of these two commodities that are being produced. Now imagine that, at existing prices, farmers become more willing to produce brussels sprouts than in the past and less willing to produce carrots. This shift might be caused, for example, by a change in the costs of producing the two goods—a rise in carrot costs and a fall in brussels sprouts costs that would raise the profitability of brussels sprout production and lower that of carrot production.

What will happen now? For a short time, nothing at all will happen; the existing supply of brussels sprouts and carrots on the market is the result of decisions made by farmers at some time in the past. Farmers, however, now begin to plant fewer carrots and more brussels sprouts, and soon the quantities on the market begin to change. The quantity of brussels sprouts available for sale rises, and the quantity of carrots falls. A shortage of carrots and a glut of brussels sprouts result. The price of carrots consequently rises, and the price of brussels sprouts falls. This provides the incentive for two types of adjustments. First, households will buy fewer carrots and more brussels sprouts. Second, farmers will move back into carrot production and out of brussels sprouts.

This example began with a situation in which a shortage of carrots caused the price of carrots to rise. The rise in the price of carrots removed the shortage in two ways: It reduced the quantity of carrots demanded, and it increased the quantity offered for sale (in response to the rise in the profitability of carrot production). Remember that there was also a surplus of brussels sprouts that caused the price to fall. The fall in price removed the surplus in two ways: It encouraged consumers to buy more of this commodity, and it reduced the quantity of brussels sprouts produced and offered for sale (in response to a fall in the profitability of brussels sprout production).

These examples illustrate a general point:

The price system is a mechanism that coordinates individual, decentralized decisions.

The existence of such a control mechanism is beyond dispute. How well it works in comparison with alternative coordinating systems has been in serious dispute for over a century, although, as we noted at the end of Chapter 1, the world has recently experienced a dramatic shift toward increased reliance on market forces.

Microeconomics and Macroeconomics Compared

Microeconomics and macroeconomics differ in the questions each asks and in the level of aggregation each uses. Microeconomics deals with the determination of prices and quantities in individual markets and with the relationships among these markets. Thus it looks at the details of the market economy. It asks, for example, how much labor is employed in the fast food industry and why the amount is increasing. It asks about the determinants of the output of brussels sprouts, pocket calculators, automobiles, and McDonald's hamburgers. It asks, too, about the prices of these goods—why some prices go up and others down. For example, economists interested in microeconomics analyze how prices and outputs respond to exogenous shocks caused by events in other markets or by government policy. They ask how a technical innovation, a government subsidy, or a drought will affect the price and output of beet sugar and the employment of farm workers.

In contrast, macroeconomics focuses on much broader aggregates. It looks at such things as the total number of people employed and unemployed, the average level of all prices, national output, and aggregate consumption. Macroeconomics asks what determines these aggregates and how they respond to changing conditions. Whereas microeconomics looks at demand and supply with regard to particular commodities, macroeconomics looks at aggregate demand and aggregate supply.

An Overview of Macroeconomics

We can group together all the buyers of the nation's output and call their total desired purchases *aggregate desired expenditure*. We can also group together all the producers of the nation's output and call their total desired sales *aggregate supply*. Determining the magnitude of these and explaining why they change are among the major problems of macroeconomics.

Major changes in aggregate desired expenditure are called *demand shocks,* and major changes in aggregate supply are called *supply shocks.* Such shocks will cause important changes in the broad averages and aggregates that are the concern of macroeconomics, including total output, total employment, and average levels of prices and wages. Government actions sometimes cause demand or supply shocks; at other times, they are reactions to such shocks, used in an attempt to cushion or to change the effects of such shocks.

The Circular Flow of Income

One way to gain insight into aggregate demand and aggregate supply is to view the economy as a giant set of flows. A major part of aggregate demand arises from the purchases of consumption commodities by the nation's households. These purchases generate income for the firms that produce and sell commodities for consumption. A major part of aggregate supply arises from the production and sale of consumption goods by the nation's firms. This production generates income for all the factors that are employed in making these goods.

The large colored arrows in Figure 3-1 show the interaction between firms and households in two sets of markets—factor markets and product markets—through which their decisions are coordinated. Consider households first. The members of households want commodities to keep themselves fed, clothed, housed, entertained, healthy, and secure. They also want commodities to educate, edify, beautify, stupefy, and otherwise amuse themselves. Households have resources with which to attempt to satisfy these wants, but not all their wants can be satisfied with the resources available. Households are forced, therefore, to make choices as to which goods and services to buy in product markets that offer them myriad ways to spend their incomes.

Now consider firms. They must choose among the products they might produce and sell, among the ways of producing them, and among the various quantities (and qualities) they can supply. Firms must also buy factors of production. Payments by firms to factor owners provide the factor owners with incomes. The recipients of these incomes are households whose members want commodities to keep themselves fed, clothed, housed, and entertained.

We have now come full circle! The action of this drama involves firms and households interacting with one another.

Payments flow from households to firms through product markets and back to households again through factor markets.

If the economy consisted only of households and firms, if households spent all the income they received on buying goods and services produced by firms, and if firms distributed all their receipts to households either by purchasing factor services or by distributing profits to owners, the circular flow would be simple indeed. Everything received by households would be passed on to firms, and everything received by firms would be passed back to households. The circular flow would be a completely closed system, aggregate demand and aggregate supply would consist only of consumption goods, and macroeconomics would involve little more than measuring the flows of production of and expenditure on consumption goods.

The circular flow is not, however, a completely closed system. First, households do not spend all their income. Some of their income is saved, and some goes to governments as taxes. Further, some household expenditures go to purchases of imports from foreign firms. These three *leakages* from the circular flow are shown by the black arrows flowing out of the households in Figure 3-1. (Of course, firms may also save and pay taxes, but these leakages are omitted from the figure for simplicity.)

A second reason why the circular flow is not a closed system is that there are elements of aggregate demand that do not arise from household spending. One important component of aggregate demand stems from firms that borrow in order to purchase such investment goods as plant and equipment. A further major component of aggregate demand comes from governments—federal, provincial, and local. They add to total expenditure on the nation's output by spending on a whole range of goods and services, from national defense through the provision of justice to the building of roads and schools. A third component of aggregate demand arises from sales of exports to foreign purchasers. These three major additions to the circular flow of income are shown by the black arrows flowing into the firms' sales receipts in Figure 3-1. (Of course, households may also receive payments from government and

FIGURE 3-1 The Circular Flow of Expenditures and Income

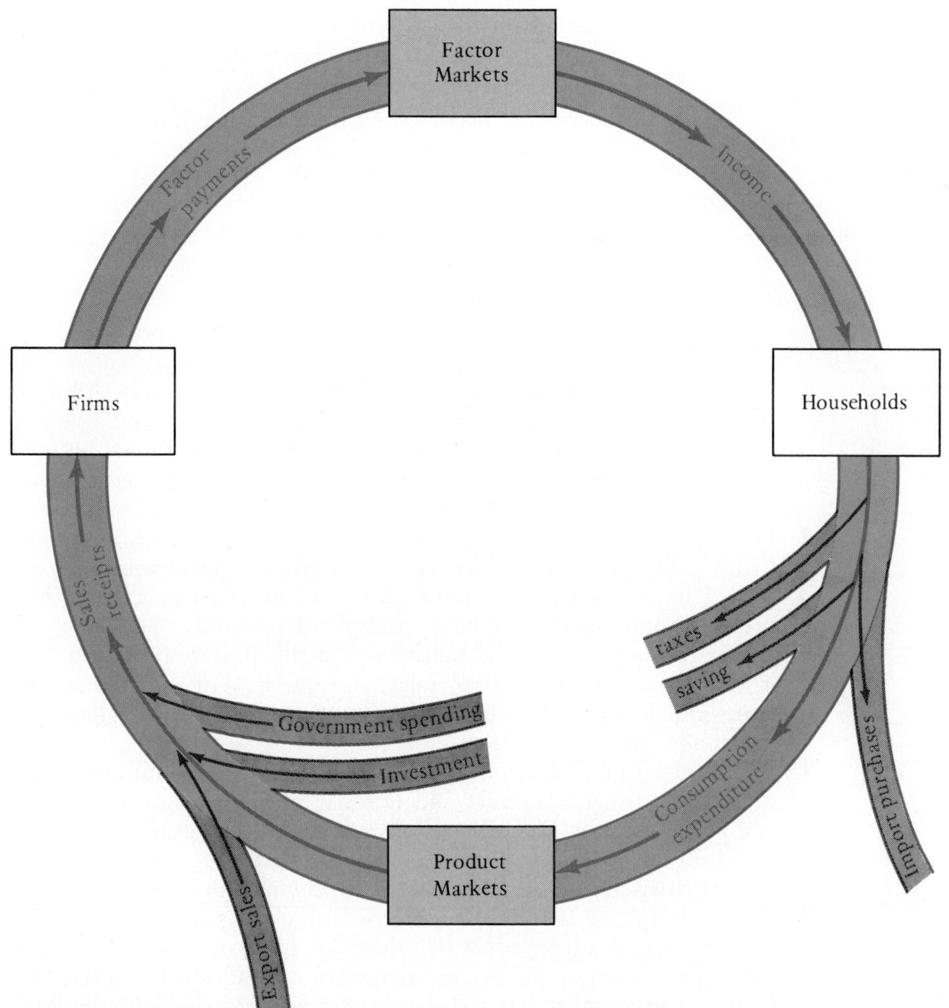

The interaction of firms and households in product and factor markets generates a circular flow of expenditure and income. Factor services are sold by households through factor markets to firms; this leads to a flow of income from firms to households, as shown in the top half of the figure. Commodities are sold by firms through product markets to households; this leads to a flow of receipts from households to firms, as shown in the bottom half of the figure. If these primary flows, shown by the colored arrows, were the only flow, the circular flow would be a closed system.

However, the circular flow is not a closed system because there exist other flows that give rise to leakages and additions to the primary flows. Three leakages—household savings, household tax payments, and household expenditures on imports—are shown by the smaller, black arrows flowing out of the households. Three additions—investment expenditures, government expenditures, and sales of exports—are shown by the smaller, black arrows flowing into the firms' sales receipts.

may borrow from financial institutions to finance current consumption expenditures, but for simplicity these additions are omitted from the figure.)

When any one of these elements of aggregate demand changes, aggregate output and total income earned by households are likely to change as a result. Thus studying the determinants of total consumption, investment, and government spending is crucial to understanding the causes of changes both in the nation's total output and in the employment generated by the production of that output.

The Next Step

Soon you will be going on to study microeconomics or macroeconomics. Whichever branch of the subject you study first, it is important to remember that microeconomics and macroeconomics are complementary, not competing, views of the economy. Both are needed for a full understanding of the functioning of a modern economy.

SUMMARY

1. Modern market economies are based on the specialization and division of labor, which necessitate the exchange of goods and services. Exchange takes place in markets and is facilitated by the use of money. Much of economics is devoted to the study of how markets work to coordinate millions of individual, decentralized decisions.
2. In economic theory, three kinds of decision makers—households, firms, and government—interact in markets. Households are assumed to maximize their satisfaction and firms to maximize their profits. Government may have multiple objectives.
3. A free market economy is one in which the allocation of resources is determined by production, sales, and purchase decisions made by firms and households acting in response to such market signals as prices and profits.
4. Subdivisions of an economy are called sectors. Economies are commonly divided into market and nonmarket sectors and into public and private sectors. These divisions cut across each other; the first is based on the economic distinction of how costs are covered, and the second is based on a legal distinction of ownership.
5. A key difference between microeconomics and macroeconomics is in the level of aggregation to which attention is directed. Microeconomics looks at prices and quantities in individual markets and how they respond to various shocks that impinge on those markets. Macroeconomics looks at broader aggregates such as aggregate consumption, employment and unemployment, and rate of change of the price level.
6. The questions asked in microeconomics and macroeconomics differ, but they are complementary parts of economic theory. They study different aspects of a single economic system, and both are needed for an understanding of the whole.
7. Microeconomics deals with the determination of prices and quantities in individual markets and the relationships among those markets. It shows how the price system provides signals that reflect changes in demand and supply and to which producers and consumers react in an individual but nonetheless coordinated manner.
8. The macroeconomic interactions between households and firms through markets may be illustrated in a circular flow diagram that traces money flows between households and firms. These flows are the starting point for studying the circular flows of aggregate income that are key elements of macroeconomics.

9. Household purchases of consumption goods generate income for firms whose payments to factors then flow back to the households as income. This circular flow is not a simple closed system, because not all income received by households is spent for the output of firms, and some receipts of firms are not paid out to households. Also, some payments to firms do not result from the spending of households, and some payments to households do not result from the spending of firms. The flows of expenditure in the economy help to determine total output, total income, and total employment.

TOPICS FOR REVIEW

Specialization and division of labor
Economic decision makers
Markets and market economies
Market and nonmarket sectors
Private and public sectors
The price system as a social control mechanism
Relationship between microeconomics and macroeconomics

DISCUSSION QUESTIONS

1. Suggest some examples of specialization and division of labor among people you know.
2. There is a greater variety of specialists and specialty stores in large cities than in small towns having populations with the same average income. Explain this in economic terms.
3. Define the household of which you are a member. Consider your household's income last year. What proportion of it came from the sale of factor services? Identify other sources of income. Approximately what proportion of the expenditures by your household became income for firms?
4. "It is not from the benevolence of the butcher, the brewer, or the baker that we expect our dinner, but from their regard to their self-interest. We address ourselves, not to their humanity, but to their self-love, and never talk to them of our necessities, but of their advantages." Do you agree with this quotation from *The Wealth of Nations*? How are "their self-love" and "our dinner" related to the price system? What are assumed to be the motives of firms and of households?
5. Trace the effect of a sharp change in consumer demand away from red meat and toward poultry as a result of continuing reports that too much red meat in a diet is unhealthy.
6. Make a list of other decision makers in the economy today that do not fit into the categories of firm, household, and government. Are you sure that the concept of a firm will not stretch sufficiently to cover some of the items on your list?
7. Trace out some significant microeconomic and macroeconomic effects of an aging population, such as is predicted for many advanced industrialized countries in the twenty-first century.
8. Which, if any, of the arrows in Figure 3-1 does each of the following affect in the first instance?
   a. Households increase their consumption expenditures by reducing saving.
   b. The government lowers income tax rates.
   c. In view of a recession, firms decide to postpone production of some new products.
   d. Consumers like the new model cars and borrow money from the banking system to buy them in record numbers.

PART 2

A GENERAL VIEW OF THE PRICE SYSTEM

Chapter 4

Demand, Supply, and Price

Some people believe that economics begins and ends with the "laws" of supply and demand. It is, of course, too much to hope for "economics in one lesson." (An unkind critic of a book with that title remarked that the author needed a second lesson.) Still, the so-called laws of supply and demand are an important part of our understanding of the market system.

As a first step, we need to understand what determines the demand for commodities and the supply of them. Then we can see how demand and supply together determine the prices of goods and services and the quantities that are bought and sold. Finally, we examine how the price system allows the economy to respond to the many changes that impinge on it. Demand and supply help us in understanding the price system's successes and its failures, as well as the consequences of such government intervention as price controls, minimum wage laws, and sales taxes.

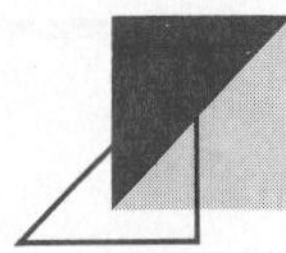

Demand

Table 4-1 shows Canadian consumer expenditure for selected years. What determines its composition? Why does it change? Why did the fraction of total consumer expenditure for food decline from more than one-third in 1910 to less than one-fifth by 1988? Why has the proportion of income spent on services increased by much less in Canada (from 40 percent to 47.3 percent) than in the United States (from 32 percent to 52 percent)? Why do some Canadians heat their homes with electricity, others with oil, and still others with natural gas? How have Canadians reacted to the large changes in fuel prices that occurred in the 1970s and 1980s? Why have the maid and the washerwoman been replaced by the vacuum cleaner and the washing machine?

Quantity Demanded

The total amount of a commodity that all households wish to purchase in some time period is called the **quantity demanded** of that commodity.[1] It is important to notice three things about

[1] In this chapter we concentrate on the demand of *all* households for commodities. Of course, what all households do is only the sum of what each individual household does, and in Chapters 7 and 8 we shall study the behavior of individual households in greater detail.

TABLE 4-1 Composition of Personal Consumption Expenditures, 1951 and 1989 *(percentages)*

	1951		1989	
Durable goods		9.2		15.5
Automobiles and parts	5.4		7.8	
Furniture and household equipment	2.8		5.8	
Other	1.0		1.9	
Semidurable goods		16.0		10.1
Clothing and footwear	9.1		5.8	
Other	6.9		4.3	
Nondurable goods		34.7		27.1
Food	27.1		11.3	
Electricity, gas, and other fuels	3.0		3.0	
Gasoline, oil, and grease	2.0		3.0	
Other	2.6		9.8	
Services		40.1		47.3
Housing and household services	13.6		18.1	
Health services	2.6		4.2	
Other	23.9		25.0	

Sources: Statistics Canada, 13–001, 13–20; Department of Finance, *Economic Review*.

Nondurables and semidurables have declined in relative importance, while durables and services have increased.

this concept. First, quantity demanded is a *desired* quantity. It is the amount households wish to purchase, given the price of the commodity,[2] other prices, their incomes, tastes, and so on. This may be different from the amount that households actually succeed in purchasing. If sufficient quantities are not available, the amount that households wish to purchase may exceed the amount they actually do purchase. To distinguish these two concepts, the term *quantity demanded* is used to refer to desired purchases, and a phrase such as *quantity actually bought* or *quantity exchanged* is used to refer to actual purchases.

Second, *desired* does not refer to idle dreams but to effective demands, that is, to the amounts people are willing to buy given the price they must pay for the commodity.

Third, quantity demanded refers to a continuous *flow* of purchases. It must therefore be expressed as so much per period of time: 1 million units per day, 7 million per week, or 365 million per year. For example, being told that the quantity of new television sets demanded (at current prices) in Canada is 50,000 means nothing unless you are also told the period of time involved. Fifty thousand television sets demanded per day would be an enormous rate of demand; 50,000 per year would be a very small rate. (The important distinction between stocks and flows was discussed on page 24.)

What Determines Quantity Demanded?

The amount of some commodity that all households wish to buy in a given time period is influenced by the following important variables: **[2]** [3]

Commodity's own price
Average household income
Prices of related commodities
Tastes

[2] When economists say that something is "given," they do not mean that it is provided free! Instead they mean that the quantity is held constant. So "given the price of the commodity" means that the price of that commodity is assumed not to change during the period under discussion.

[3] Notes giving mathematical demonstrations of the concepts presented in the text are designated by colored reference numbers. These notes can be found beginning on page M-1.

Distribution of income among households
Population size

We cannot understand the separate influence of each of these variables if we try to consider what happens when everything changes at once. Instead, we consider the influence of the variables one at a time. To do this, we hold all but one of them constant. Then we let that one selected variable vary and study how it affects quantity demanded. We can do the same for each of the other variables in turn, and in this way we can come to understand the importance of each.[4] Once this is done, we can aggregate the separate influences of the variables to discover what would happen if several things changed at the same time—as they often do in practice.

Holding all other influencing variables constant is often described by the words "other things being equal" or "other things given" or by the equivalent Latin phrase, ***ceteris paribus***. When economists speak of the influence of the price of wheat on the quantity of wheat demanded, *ceteris paribus,* they refer to what a change in the price of wheat would do to the quantity demanded if all other forces that influence the demand for wheat did not change.

Demand and Price

We are interested in developing a theory of how commodities get priced. To do this we need to study the relationship between the quantity demanded of each commodity and that commodity's own price. This requires that we hold all other influences constant and ask: How will the quantity of a commodity demanded vary as its own price varies?

A basic hypothesis of economics is that the price of a commodity and the quantity that will be demanded are related *negatively,* other things being equal.[5] That is to say, the lower the price, the higher the quantity demanded, and the higher the price, the lower the quantity demanded.

Why might this be so? Commodities are used to satisfy desires and needs, and there is almost always more than one commodity that will satisfy any given desire or need. Such commodities compete for the purchasers' attention. Hunger may be satisfied by meat or vegetables, a desire for green vegetables by broccoli or spinach. The need to keep warm at night may be satisfied by several woolen blankets or one electric blanket, or a sheet and a lot of oil burned in the furnace. The desire for a vacation many be satisfied by a trip to the seashore or to the mountains, the need to get there by different airlines, a bus, a car, a train. And so it goes. Name any general desire or need, and there will be at least two and often dozens of different commodities that will satisfy it.

Now consider what happens if we hold income, tastes, population, and the prices of all other commodities constant and vary only the price of one commodity. As that price goes up, the commodity becomes an increasingly expensive way to satisfy a want. Some households will stop buying it altogether; others will buy smaller amounts; still others may continue to buy the same quantity. Because many households will switch wholly or partly to other commodities to satisfy the same want, less will be bought of the commodity whose price has risen. As meat becomes more expensive, for example, households may switch to some extent to meat substitutes; they may also forgo meat at some meals and eat less meat at others.

Alternatively, as the prices goes down, the commodity becomes a cheaper method of satisfying a want. Households will buy more of it. Consequently, they will buy less of similar commodities the prices of which have not fallen and which as a result have become expensive *relative to* the commodity in question. When a bumper tomato harvest drives prices down, shoppers switch to tomatoes and cut their purchases of many other vegetables that now look relatively more expensive.

The Demand Schedule and the Demand Curve

A **demand schedule** is one way of showing the relationship between quantity demanded and the price of that commodity, other things being equal.

[4] A relationship in which many variables (in this case average income, population, tastes, and many prices) influence a single variable (in this case quantity demanded) is called a *multivariate* relationship. The technique of studying the effect of each of the influencing variables one at a time, while holding the others constant, is common in mathematics, and there is a specific concept, the *partial derivative,* designed to do so.

[5] In this chapter we introduce this fundamental relation as a hypothesis. In a later chapter we will derive it as a prediction that follows from more basic assumptions about consumers' tastes.

It is a numerical tabulation showing the quantity that is demanded at selected prices.

Table 4-2 is a hypothetical demand schedule for carrots. It lists the quantity of carrots that would be demanded at various prices on the assumption that all other influences on quantity demanded are held constant. We note in particular that average household income is fixed at $20,000 because later we will wish to see what happens when income changes. The table gives the quantities demanded for six selected prices, but actually a separate quantity would be demanded at each possible price from one cent to several hundreds of dollars.

A second method of showing the relationship between quantity demanded and price is to draw a graph. The six price-quantity combinations shown in Table 4-2 are plotted on the graph shown in Figure 4-1. Price is plotted on the vertical axis, and quantity is plotted on the horizontal axis. The smooth curve drawn through these points is called a **demand curve**. It shows the quantity that purchasers would like to buy at each price. The negative slope of the curve indicates that the quantity demanded increases as the price falls.

Each point on the demand curve indicates a single price-quantity combination. The demand curve as a whole shows more.

The demand curve represents the relationship between quantity demanded and price, other things being equal.

TABLE 4-2 A Demand Schedule for Carrots

	Price per ton	Quantity demanded when average income is $20,000 per year (thousands of tons per month)
U	$ 20	110.0
V	40	90.0
W	60	77.5
X	80	67.5
Y	100	62.5
Z	120	60.0

The table shows the quantity of carrots that would be demanded at various prices, *ceteris paribus*. For example, row *W* indicates that if the price of carrots were $60 per ton, consumers would desire to purchase 77,500 tons of carrots per month, given the values of the other variables that affect quantity demanded, including average household income.

FIGURE 4-1 A Demand Curve for Carrots

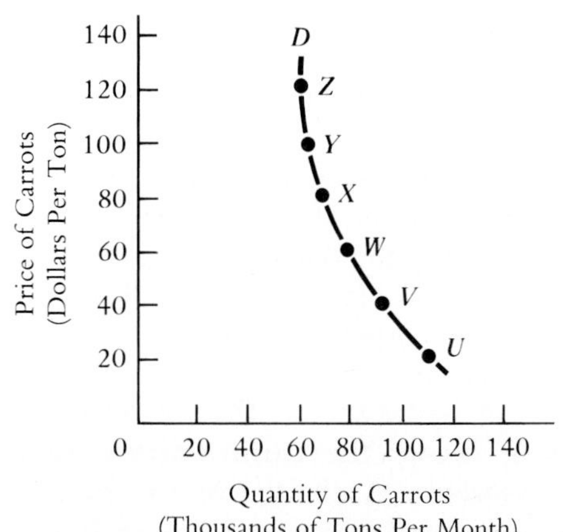

This demand curve relates quantity of carrots demanded to the price of carrots; its downward slope indicates that quantity demanded increases as price falls. The six points correspond to the price-quantity combinations shown in Table 4-2. Each row in the table defines a point on the demand curve. The smooth curve drawn through all of the points and labeled *D* is the demand curve.

When economists speak of the demand in a particular market as being given or known, they are referring not just to the particular quantity being demanded at the moment (i.e., not just to one point on the demand curve) but, instead, to the entire demand curve—to the relationship between desired purchases and all the possible alternative prices of the commodity.

Thus the term **demand** refers to the entire relationship between the quantity of a commodity and the price of that commodity (as shown, for example, by the demand schedule in Table 4-2 or the demand curve in Figure 4-1). In contrast, a single point on a demand schedule or curve is the *quantity demanded* at that point (for example, at point *W* in Figure 4-1, 77,500 tons of carrots a month are demanded at a price of $60 per ton).

Shifts in the Demand Curve

The demand schedule is constructed and the demand curve is plotted on the assumption of *ceteris paribus*, but what if other things change, as surely they must?

What if, for example, households find themselves with more income? If they spend their extra inome, they will buy additional quantities of many commodities *even though their prices are unchanged.*

If households increase their purchases of any one commodity whose price has not changed, the purchases cannot be represented on the original demand curve. They must be represented on a new demand curve, which is to the right of the old curve. Thus the rise in household income shifts the demand curve to the right, as shown in Figure 4-2. This illustrates the operation of an important general rule.

A demand curve is drawn on the assumption that everything except the commodity's own price is held constant. A change in any of the variables previously held constant will shift the demand curve to a new position.

A demand curve can shift in many ways; two of them are particularly important. In the first case, more is bought at *each* price, and the demand curve shifts rightward so that each price corresponds to a higher quantity than it did before. In the second case, less is bought at *each* price, and the demand curve shifts leftward so that each price corresponds to a lower quantity than it did before.

FIGURE 4-2 Two Demand Curves for Carrots

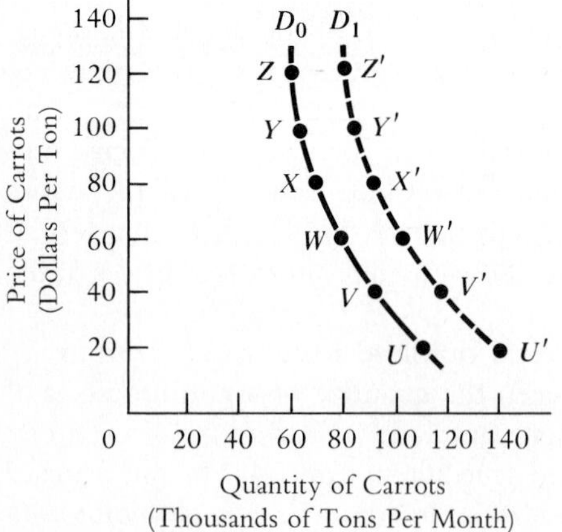

The rightward shift in the demand curve from D_0 to D_1 indicates an increase in the quantity demanded at each price. The lettered points correspond to those in Table 4-3. A rightward shift in the demand curve indicates an increase in demand in the sense that more is demanded at each price and that a higher price would be paid for each quantity.

The influence of changes in variables other than price may be studied by determining how changes in each variable shift the demand curve. Any change will shift the demand curve to the right if it increases the amount that households wish to buy, other things remaining equal, and to the left if it decreases the amount that households wish to buy, other things remaining equal. Note that changes in people's *expectations* about *future* values of variables such as income and prices can influence demand; however, for simplicity we cast the discussion in terms of actual changes in the current values of these variables.

Average household income. If households receive more income on average, they can be expected to purchase more of most commodities even though commodity prices remain the same.[6] Considering all households, we expect that no matter what price we pick, more of any commodity will be demanded than was previously demanded at that price. This shift is illustrated in Table 4-3 and Figure 4-2.

A rise in average household income shifts the demand curve for most commodities to the right. This indicates that more will be demanded at each price.

Other prices. We saw that the negative slope of a commodity's demand curve occurs because the lower its price, the cheaper the commodity becomes relative to other commodities that can satisfy the same needs or desires. These other commodities are called **substitutes.** Another way for the same change to come about is for the price of the substitute commodity to rise. For example, carrots can become cheap relative to cabbage either because the price of carrots falls or because the price of cabbage rises. Either change will increase the amount of carrots that households are prepared to buy.

A rise in the price of a substitute for a commodity shifts the demand curve for the com-

[6] Such commodities are called *normal goods*. Commodities for which the amount purchased falls as income rises are called *inferior goods*. These concepts are defined and discussed in Chapter 5.

TABLE 4-3 Two Alternative Demand Schedules for Carrots

Price per ton p	Quantity demanded when average household income is \$20,000 per year (thousands of tons per month) D_0		Quantity demanded when average household income is \$24,000 per year (thousands of tons per month) D_1	
\$ 20	110.0	U	140.0	U'
40	90.0	V	116.0	V'
60	77.5	W	100.8	W'
80	67.5	X	87.5	X'
100	62.5	Y	81.3	Y'
120	60.0	Z	78.0	Z'

An increase in average household income increases the quantity demanded at each price. When average income rises from \$20,000 to \$24,000 per year, quantity demanded at a price of \$60 per ton rises from 77,500 tons per month to 100,800 tons per month. A similar rise occurs at every other price. Thus the demand schedule relating columns p and D_0 is replaced by one relating columns p and D_1. The graphical representations of these two functions are labeled D_0 and D_1 in Figure 4-2.

modity to the right. More will be purchased at each price.

For example, a rise in the price of cabbage could cause the demand curve for carrots to shift to the right as in Figure 4-2.

Complements are commodities that tend to be used jointly. Cars and gasoline are complements; so are golf clubs and golf balls, electric stoves and electricity, and an airplane trip to Calgary and lift tickets at Banff. Since complements tend to be consumed together, a fall in the price of either one will increase the demand for both.

A fall in the price of a complementary commodity will shift a commodity's demand curve to the right. More will be purchased at each price.

For example, a fall in the price of airplane trips to Calgary will lead to a rise in the demand for lift tickets at Banff even though their price is unchanged.

Tastes. Tastes have a large effect on people's desired purchases. A change in tastes may be long-lasting, such as the shift from fountain pens to ball-point pens or from slide rules to pocket calculators; or it may be a short-lived fad such as hula hoops or pet rocks. In either case, a change in tastes in favor of a commodity shifts the demand curve to the right. More will be bought at each price.

Distribution of income. If a constant total of income is redistributed among the population, demands may change. If, for example, the government increases the deductions that may be taken for children on income tax returns and compensates by raising basic tax rates, income will be transferred from childless person to households with large families. Demands for commodities more heavily bought by childless persons will decline, while demands for commodities more heavily bought by households with large families will increase.

A change in the distribution of income will cause a rightward shift in the demand curves for commodities bought most by households whose incomes increase, and it will cause a leftward shift in the demand curves for commodities bought most by households whose incomes decrease.

Population. Population growth does not by itself create new demand. The additional people must have purchasing power before demand is changed. Extra people of working age who are employed, however, will earn new income. When this happens, the demands for all the commodities purchased by the new income earners will rise. Thus the following statement is usually true:

A rise in population will shift the demand curves for commodities to the right, indicating that more will be bought at each price.

The reasons that demand curves shift are summarized in Figure 4-3.

Movements Along the Demand Curve Versus Shifts of the Whole Curve

Suppose that you read in today's newspaper that the soaring price of carrots has been caused by a greatly increased demand for that commodity. Tomorrow you read that the rising price of carrots is greatly

FIGURE 4-3 Shifts in the Demand Curve

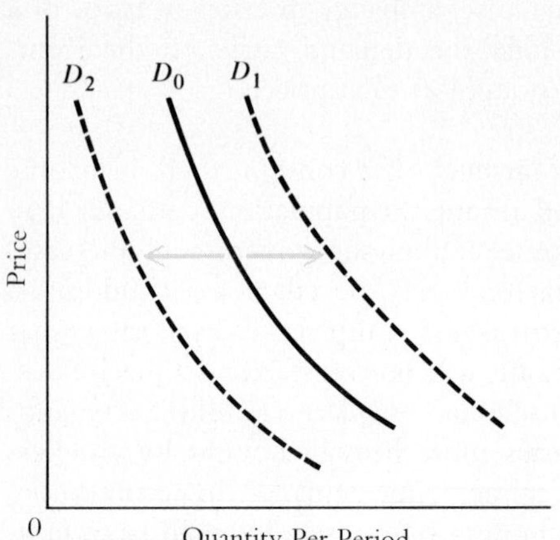

The rightward shift in the demand curve from D_0 to D_1 indicates an increase in demand; a leftward shift from D_0 to D_2 indicates a decrease in demand. An increase in demand means that more is demanded at each price. Such a rightward shift can be caused by a rise in income, a rise in the price of a substitute, a fall in the price of a complement, a change in tastes that favors that commodity, an increase in population, or a redistribution of income toward groups that favor the commodity.

A decrease in demand means that less is demanded at each price. Such a leftward shift can be caused by a fall in income, a fall in the price of a substitute, a rise in the price of a complement, a change in tastes that disfavors the commodity, a decrease in population, or a redistribution of income away from groups that favor the commodity.

reducing the typical household's purchases of carrots as shoppers switch to potatoes, yams, and peas. The two statements appear to contradict each other. The first associates a rising price with rising demand; the second associates a rising price with declining demand. Can both statements be true? The answer is yes because they refer to different things. The first describes a shift in the demand curve; the second describes a movement along a demand curve in response to a change in price.

Consider first the statement that the increase in the price of carrots has been caused by an increased demand for carrots. This statement refers to a shift in the demand curve for carrots. In this case the demand curve must have shifted to the right, indicating more carrots demanded *at each price*. This shift will, as we shall see later in this chapter, increase the price of carrots.

Now consider the statement that fewer carrots are being bought because carrots have become more expensive. This refers to a movement along a given demand curve and reflects a change between two specific quantities being bought—one before the price rose and one afterward.

So what lay behind the two stories might have been something like the following explanations.

1. A rise in the population is shifting the demand curve for carrots to the right as more carrots are demanded at each price. This in turn is raising the price of carrots (for reasons we will soon study in detail). This was the first newspaper story.
2. The rising price of carrots is causing each individual household to cut back on its purchase of carrots. This causes a movement upward to the left along any particular demand curve for carrots. This was the second newspaper story.

To prevent the type of confusion caused by our two newspaper stories, economists have developed a specialized vocabulary to distinguish shifts of curves from movements along curves.

We have seen that *demand* refers to the *whole* demand curve. Economists reserve the term **change in demand** to describe a shift in the whole demand curve, that is, a change in the amount that will be bought at *every* price.

An increase in demand means that the whole demand curve will shift to the right; a decrease in demand means that the whole demand curve will shift to the left.

Any point on a demand curve represents a specific amount being bought at a specified price. It represents, therefore, a particular quantity demanded. A movement along a demand curve is referred to as a **change in quantity demanded.** [3]

A movement down a demand curve is called an increase (or a rise) in the quantity demanded; a movement up a demand curve is called a decrease (or a fall) in the quantity demanded.

FIGURE 4-4 **Shifts of and Movements Along the Demand Curve**

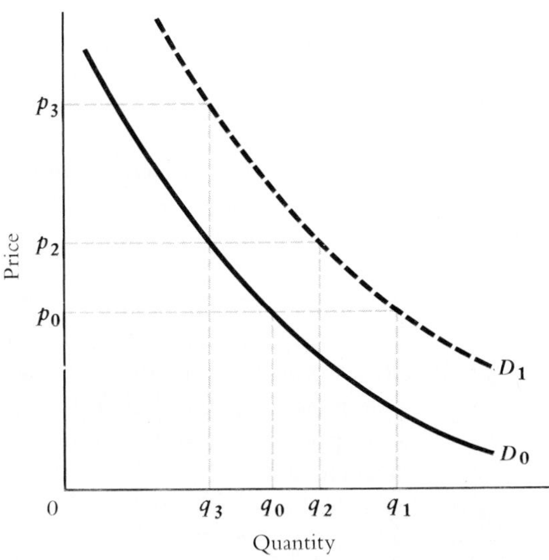

A rise in demand means that more will be bought at each price, but it does not mean that more will be bought under all circumstances. The demand curve is originally D_0 and price is p_0 at which q_0 is bought. Demand then increases to D_1, which implies that at the old price of p_0 there is a larger quantity demanded, q_1. Now assume that the price rises above p_0. This causes quantity demanded to fall below q_1. *The shift in the demand curve means that more is bought at each price. A movement upward along the demand curve means that less will be bought in response to a rise in price.* The net effect of these two changes can be either an increase or a decrease in the quantity demanded. In this figure a rise in price to p_2 means that the quantity demanded, q_2, is still in excess of the original quantity q_0, while a rise in price to p_3 means that the final quantity, q_3, is below the original quantity q_0.

To illustrate this terminology, look again at Table 4-3. When average income is $20,000, an increase in price from $60 to $80 decreases the *quantity demanded* from 77,500 to 67,500 tons per month. An increase in average income from $20,000 to $24,000 increases *demand* from D_0 to D_1.

Figure 4-4 shows the combined effect of a rise in demand, shown by a rightward shift in the whole demand curve, and a fall in the quantity demanded, shown by a movement upward to the left along a given demand curve in response to a change in price.

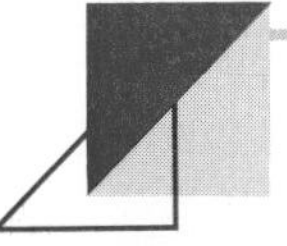

Supply

Canada's private sector produced goods and services worth more than $513 billion in 1989. A broad classification of what was produced is given in Table 4-4. The percentages shown in Table 4-4 reflect some of the changes that have taken place over 38 years.

Economists have as many questions to ask about production and its changing composition as they do about consumption. For example, why have the country's manufacturing industries declined in relative importance? What is the significance of the rising importance of service industries?

Dramatic changes have also occurred within each of the categories shown in the table. Why, for example, did the aluminum industry grow much faster than the steel industry? Even within any single industry, some firms prosper and grow while others

TABLE 4-4 **Domestic Product by Industry of Origin, 1951 and 1989 *(percentage distribution)***

Industry group[a]	1951	1989
Agriculture, forestry, fishing, and trapping	15.5	5.0
Mining, quarrying, and oil wells	4.4	7.0
Manufacturing	31.2	23.0
Construction	5.4	10.0
Transportation, storage, and communication	10.0	6.0
Utilities	2.2	3.0
Wholesale and retail trade	11.5	15.0
Finance, insurance, and real estate	9.5	18.0
Other services	10.3	13.0
	100.0	100.0

Source: Statistics Canada, 11–003, 13–201.
[a] Excluding government and government enterprises.

Since 1951 agriculture, mining, and manufacturing have all declined in relative importance, while utilities, finance, and services have gained. Construction, transportation, and trade show considerable fluctuation with no evident trend.

decline. Indeed, about one-third of the firms in a typical industry at the beginning of any decade are no longer present at the end. Furthermore, a similar proportion of the jobs that exist at the beginning of any decade have gone by the end of the decade, to be replaced by new and often quite different jobs. Why and how do new jobs, new firms, and new industries come into being while other types of jobs, firms, and industries shrink or disappear altogether?

All of these questions and many others are aspects of a single question: *What determines the quantities of commodities that will be produced and offered for sale?*

Full discussion of these questions of supply will come later (in Part 4). For now it suffices to develop the basic relationship between the price of a commodity and the quantity that will be produced and offered for sale by firms, and to understand what forces lead to shifts in this relationship.

Quantity Supplied

The amount of a commodity that firms wish to sell in some time period is called the **quantity supplied** of that commodity. Quantity supplied is a flow; it is so much per unit of time. Note also that quantity supplied is the amount that firms are willing to offer for sale; it is not necessarily the amount they succeed in selling. That is expressed by the term *quantity actually sold* or *quantity exchanged.* Although households may desire to purchase an amount that differs from what firms desire to sell, they cannot succeed in buying what someone else does not sell. A purchase and a sale are merely two sides of the same transaction. Looked at from the buyer's side, there is a purchase; looked at from the seller's side, there is a sale.

Since desired purchases do not have to equal desired sales, quantity demanded does not have to equal quantity supplied, but because no one can buy what someone else does not sell, the quantity actually purchased must equal the quantity actually sold.

What Determines Quantity Supplied?

The amount of a commodity that firms will be willing to produce and offer for sale is influenced by the following important variables:[4]

Commodity's own price
Prices of inputs
Goals of firms
State of technology

The situation is the same here as it is on the demand side. There are several influencing variables, and we will not get far if we try to discover what happens when they all change at the same time. So, again, we use the convenient *ceteris paribus* technique to study the influence of the variables one at a time.

Supply and Price

Since we want to develop a theory of how commodities get priced, we study the relationship between the quantity supplied of each commodity and that commodity's own price. We start by holding all other influences constant and asking: How do we expect the quantity of a commodity supplied to vary with its own price?

A basic hypothesis of economics is that for many commodities, the price of the commodity and the quantity that will be supplied are related *positively,* other things being equal.[7] That is to say, the higher the commodity's own price, the more its producers will supply, and the lower the price, the less producers will supply.

[7] In this chapter we introduce this key relation as a hypothesis. In a later chapter we will derive it as a prediction from more fundamental hypotheses about the conditions that firms face.

TABLE 4-5 A Supply Schedule for Carrots

	Price per ton	Quantity supplied (thousands of tons per month)
u	$ 20	5.0
v	40	46.0
w	60	77.5
x	80	100.0
y	100	115.0
z	120	122.5

The table shows the quantities that producers wish to sell at various prices, *ceteris paribus*. For example, row *y* indicates that if the price were $100 per ton, producers would wish to sell 115,000 tons of carrots per month.

Why might this be so? It is because the profits that can be earned from producing a commodity are almost certain to increase if the price of that commodity rises while the costs of inputs used to produce it remain unchanged. This will make firms, which are in business to earn profits, wish to produce more of the commodity whose price has risen and less of other commodities.[8]

The Supply Schedule and the Supply Curve

The general relationship just discussed can be illustrated by a **supply schedule**, which shows the relationship between quantity supplied of a commodity and the price of the commodity, other things being equal. A supply schedule is analogous to a demand schedule; the former shows what producers would be willing to sell, while the latter shows what households would be willing to buy, at alternative prices of the commodity. Table 4-5 presents a hypothetical supply schedule for carrots.

[8] Notice, however, the qualifying word *many* in the hypothesis printed in color. It is used because, as we shall see in Part 4, there are exceptions to this rule. Although the rule states the usual case, a rise in price (*ceteris paribus*) is not always necessary to call forth an increase in quantity supplied.

FIGURE 4-5 A Supply Curve for Carrots

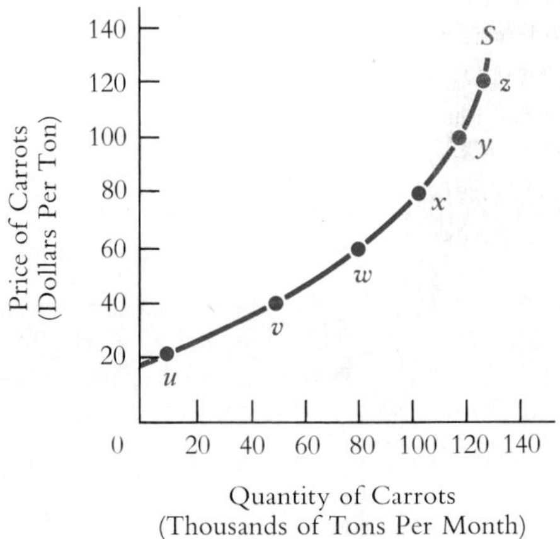

This supply curve relates quantity of carrots supplied to the price of carrots; its upward slope indicates that quantity supplied increases as price increases. The six points correspond to the price-quantity combinations shown in Table 4-5. Each row in the table defines a point on the supply curve. The smooth curve drawn through all of the points and labeled *S* is the supply curve.

A **supply curve**, the graphical representation of the supply schedule, is illustrated in Figure 4-5. While each point on the supply curve represents a specific price-quantity combination, the whole curve shows more.

The supply curve represents the relationship between quantity supplied and price, other things being equal; its positive slope indicates that quantity supplied varies in the same direction as does price.

When economists speak of the conditions of supply as being given or known, they refer not just to the particular quantity being supplied at the moment, that is, not to just one point on the supply curve. Instead, they are referring to the entire supply curve, to the complete relationship between desired sales and all possible alternative prices of the commodity.

Supply refers to the entire relationship between the quantity supplied of a commodity and the price of that commodity, other things being equal. A single point on the supply curve refers to the *quantity supplied* at that price.

TABLE 4-6 Two Alternative Supply Schedules for Carrots

Price per ton p	Quantity supplied before cost-saving innovation (thousands of tons per month) S_0		Quantity supplied after innovation (thousands of tons per month) S_1	
$ 20	5.0	*u*	28.0	*u'*
40	46.0	*v*	76.0	*v'*
60	77.5	*w*	102.0	*w'*
80	100.0	*x*	120.0	*x'*
100	115.0	*y*	132.0	*y'*
120	122.5	*z*	140.0	*z'*

A cost-saving innovation increases the quantity supplied at each price. As a result of a cost-saving innovation, the quantity that is supplied at $100 per ton rises from 115,000 to 132,000 tons per month. A similar rise occurs at every price. Thus the supply schedule relating p and S_0 is replaced by one relating p and S_1.

Shifts in the Supply Curve

A shift in the supply curve means that at each price a different quantity will be supplied than previously. An increase in the quantity supplied at each price is shown in Table 4-6 and is graphed in Figure 4-6. This change appears as a rightward shift in the supply curve. In contrast, a decrease in the quantity supplied at each price would appear as a leftward shift. A shift in the supply curve must be the result of a change in one of the factors that influence the quantity supplied other than the commodity's own price. The major possible causes of such shifts are summarized in the caption of Figure 4-7 and will be considered briefly in the text.

For supply, as for demand, there is an important general rule:

A change in any of the variables (other than the commodity's own price) that affects the amount of a commodity that firms are willing to produce and sell will shift the supply curve for that commodity.

FIGURE 4-6 Two Supply Curves for Carrots

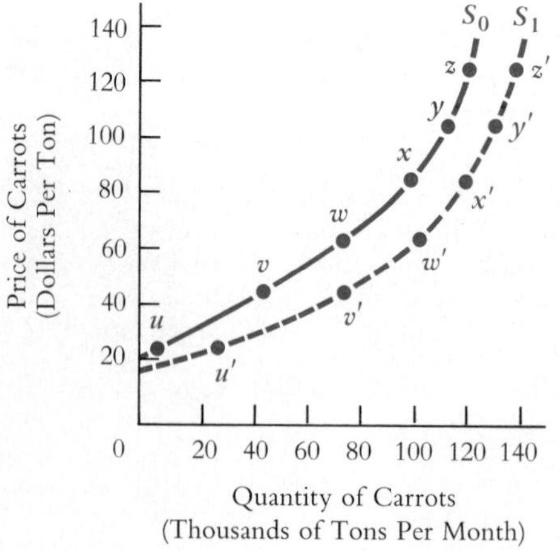

The rightward shift in the supply curve from S_0 to S_1 indicates an increase in the quantity supplied at each price. The lettered points correspond to those in Table 4-6. A rightward shift in the supply curve indicates an increase in supply such that more carrots are supplied at each price.

FIGURE 4-7 Shifts in the Supply Curve

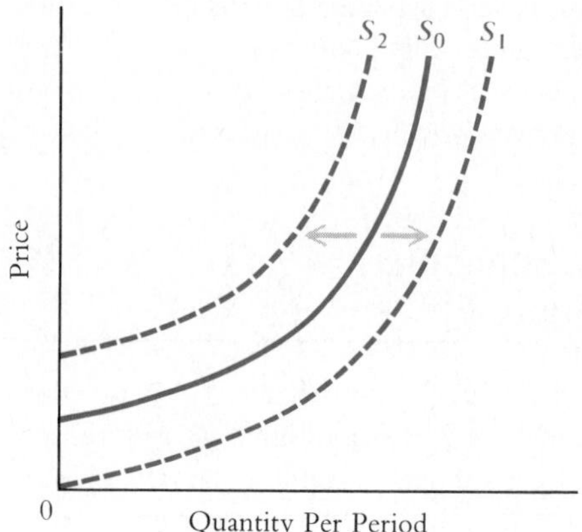

A shift in the supply curve from S_0 to S_1 indicates an increase in supply; a shift from S_0 to S_2 indicates a decrease in supply. An increase in supply means that more is supplied at each price. Such a rightward shift can be caused by certain changes in producers' goals, improvements in technology, or decreases in the costs of inputs that are important in producing the commodity.

A decrease in supply means that less is supplied at each price. Such a leftward shift can be caused by certain changes in producers' goals or increases in the costs of inputs that are important in producing the commodity.

Prices of inputs. All things that a firm uses to produce its outputs, such as materials, labor, and machines, are called the firm's *inputs*. Other things being equal, the higher the price of any input used to make a commodity, the less will be the profit from making that commodity. We expect, therefore, that the higher the price of any input used by a firm, the lower will be the amount that the firm will produce and offer for sale at any given price of the commodity.

A rise in the price of inputs shifts the supply curve to the left, indicating that less will be supplied at any given price; a fall in the cost of inputs shifts the supply curve to the right.

Goals of the firm. In elementary economic theory, the firm is assumed to have a single goal: profit maximization. A firm might, however, have other goals either in addition to or as substitutes for profit maximization; we discuss this possibility in detail in Chapter 16. However, as long as the firm prefers more profits to less, it will respond to changes in the profitabilities of alternative courses of action, and supply curves will have a positive slope.

A change in the importance that a firm gives to other goals may shift the supply curve one way or the other, indicating a changed willingness to supply the quantity at any given price and hence a changed level of profitability.

Technology. At any time, what is produced and how it is produced depend on what is known. Over time, knowledge changes; so do the quantities of individual commodities supplied. The enormous increase in production per worker that has been going on in industrial societies for about 200 years is largely due to improved methods of production. Yet the Industrial Revolution is more than a historical event; it is a present reality. Discoveries in chemistry have led to lower costs of production for well-established products, such as paints, and to a large variety of new products made of plastics and synthetic fibers. Such inventions as transistors and silicon chips have radically changed products such as computers, audiovisual equipment, and guidance control systems, and the consequent development of compact computers is revolutionizing the production of countless other nonelectronic products.

Any technological change that decreases production costs will increase the profits that can be earned at any given price of the commodity. Since increased profitability leads to increased production, this change shifts the supply curve to the right, indicating an increased willingness to produce the commodity and offer it for sale at each possible price.

Movements Along the Supply Curve Versus Shifts of the Whole Curve

As with demand, it is important to distinguish movements along supply curves from shifts of the whole curve. Economists reserve the term **change in supply** to describe a shift of the whole supply curve. This means a change in the quantity supplied at each price of the commodity. A movement along the supply curve indicates a *change in the quantity supplied* in response to a change in the price of the commodity. Thus an increase in supply means that the whole supply curve has shifted to the right; an increase in the quantity supplied means a movement upward to the right along a given supply curve.

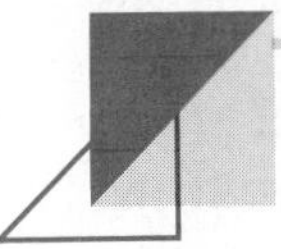

Determination of Price by Demand and Supply

So far demand and supply have been considered separately. Now what we really want to know is this: How do the two forces interact to determine price in a competitive market? Table 4-7 brings together

TABLE 4-7 Demand and Supply Schedules for Carrots and Equilibrium Price

(1) Price per ton p	(2) Quantity demanded (thousands of tons per month) D	(3) Quantity supplied (thousands of tons per month) S	(4) Excess demand (+) or excess supply (−) (thousands of tons per month) $D - S$
$ 20	110.0	5.0	+105.0
40	90.0	46.0	+ 44.0
60	77.5	77.5	0.0
80	67.5	100.0	− 32.5
100	62.5	115.0	− 52.5
120	60.0	122.5	− 62.5

Equilibrium occurs where quantity demanded equals quantity supplied—where there is neither excess demand nor excess supply. These schedules are those of Tables 4-2 and 4-5. The equilibrium price is $60. For lower prices there is excess demand; for higher prices there is excess supply.

the demand and supply schedules from Tables 4-2 and 4-5. The quantities of carrots demanded and supplied at each price may now be compared.

There is only one price, $60 per ton, at which the quantity of carrots demanded equals the quantity supplied. At prices less than $60 per ton there is a shortage of carrots because the quantity demanded exceeds the quantity supplied. This is often called a situation of **excess demand**. At prices greater than $60 per ton there is a surplus of carrots because the quantity supplied exceeds the quantity demanded. This is called a situation of **excess supply**.

To discuss the determination of market price, suppose first that the price is $100 per ton. At this price 115,000 tons would be offered for sale, but only 62,500 tons would be demanded. There would be an excess supply of 52,500 tons per month. We assume that sellers will then cut their prices to get rid of this surplus and that purchasers, observing the stock of unsold carrots, will offer less for what they are prepared to buy.

Excess supply causes downward pressure on price.

Next consider the price of $20 per ton. At this price there is excess demand. The 5,000 tons produced each month are snapped up quickly, and 105,000 tons of desired purchases cannot be made. Rivalry between would-be purchasers may lead them to offer more than the prevailing price in order to outbid other purchasers. Also, perceiving that they could have sold their available supplies many times over, sellers may begin to ask a higher price for the quantities that they do have to sell.

Excess demand causes upward pressure on price.

Finally, consider a price of $60. At this price producers wish to sell 77,500 tons per month, and purchasers wish to buy that quantity. There is neither a shortage nor a surplus of carrots. There are no unsatisfied buyers to bid the price up, nor are there unsatisfied sellers to force the price down. Once the price of $60 has been reached, therefore, there will be no tendency for it to change.

An equilibrium implies a state of rest, or balance, between opposing forces. The **equilibrium price** is the one toward which the actual market price will tend. It will persist once established, unless it is disturbed by some change in market conditions.

The price at which the quantity demanded equals the quantity supplied is called the equilibrium price.

Any other price is called a **disequilibrium price**: a price at which quantity demanded does not equal quantity supplied. The price will be changing. A market that exhibits either excess demand or excess supply is said to be in a state of **disequilibrium**.

A condition that must be fulfilled if equilibrium is to be obtained in some market is called an **equilibrium condition**. In a competitive market, the equality of quantity demanded and quantity supplied is an equilibrium condition. **[5]**

This same story is told in graphical terms in Figure 4-8. The quantities demanded and supplied at any price can be read off the two curves; the excess supply or excess demand is shown by the horizontal distance between the curves at each price. The figure makes it clear that the equilibrium price occurs where

FIGURE 4-8 Determination of the Equilibrium Price of Carrots

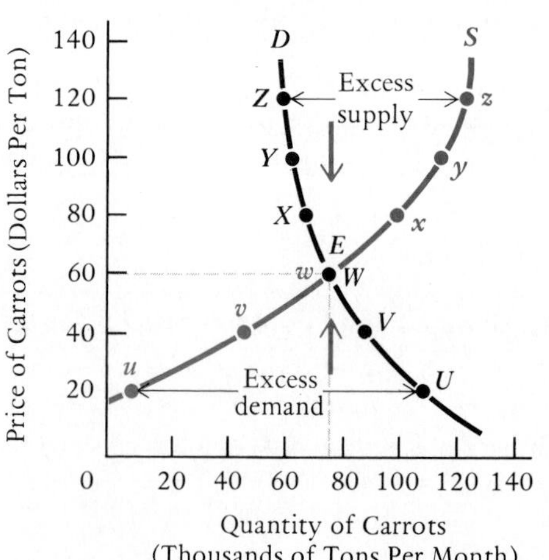

The equilibrium price corresponds to the intersection of the demand and supply curves. Equilibrium is indicated by *E*, which is point *W* on the demand curve and point *w* on the supply curve. At a price of $60 quantity demanded equals quantity supplied. At prices above equilibrium there is excess supply and downward pressure on price. At prices below equilibrium there is excess demand and upward pressure on price. The pressures on price are represented by the vertical arrows.

the demand and supply curves intersect. Below that price there will be excess demand and hence upward pressure on the existing price. Above that price there will be an excess supply and hence downward pressure on the existing price. These pressures are represented by the vertical arrows in the figure.

The Laws of Demand and Supply

Changes in any of the variables other than price that influence quantity demanded or supplied will cause a shift in the supply curve or the demand curve, or both. There are four possible shifts: (1) a rise in demand (a rightward shift in the demand curve), (2) a fall in demand (a leftward shift in the demand curve), (3) a rise in supply (a rightward shift in the supply curve), and (4) a fall in supply (a leftward shift in the supply curve).

Each of these shifts causes changes that are described by one of the four "laws" of demand and supply. Each of the laws summarizes what happens when an initial position of equilibrium is upset by some shift in either the demand curve or the supply curve and a new equilibrium position is then established. The sense in which it is correct to call these propositions "laws" is discussed in Box 4-1.

To discover the effects of each of the curve shifts that we wish to study, we use the method known as **comparative statics**, short for *comparative static equilibrium analysis*.[9] In this method we derive predictions by analyzing the effect on the equilibrium position of some change in which we are interested. We start from a position of equilibrium and then introduce the change to be studied. The new equilibrium position is determined and compared with the original one. The differences between the two positions of equilibrium must result from the change that was introduced, because everything else has been held constant.

The four laws of demand and supply are derived in Figure 4-9, which generalizes our specific discussion about carrots. Study the figure carefully. Previously, we had given the axes specific labels, but from here on we will simplify. Because it is intended to apply to any commodity, the horizontal axis is simply labeled *Quantity*. This should be understood to mean quantity per period in whatever units output is measured. *Price*, the vertical axis, should be understood to mean the price measured as dollars per unit of quantity for the same commodity. The four laws of demand and supply are as follows:

1. **A rise in demand causes an increase in both the equilibrium price and the equilibrium quantity exchanged.**
2. **A fall in demand causes a decrease in both the equilibrium price and the equilibrium quantity exchanged.**
3. **A rise in supply causes a decrease in the equilibrium price and an increase in the equilibrium quantity exchanged.**
4. **A fall in supply causes an increase in the equilibrium price and a decrease in the equilibrium quantity exchanged.**

Formal demonstrations of these "laws" are given in the caption to Figure 4-9. The intuitive reasoning behind each is as follows. (1) A rise in demand creates a shortage, and the unsatisfied buyers bid up the price. This causes a larger quantity to be produced, with the result that at the new equilibrium, more is bought and sold at a higher price. (2) A fall in demand creates a glut, and the unsuccessful sellers bid the price downward. As a result, less of the commodity will be produced and offered for sale. At the new equilibrium, both price and quantity bought and sold are lower than they were originally. (3) An increase in supply creates a glut, and the unsuccessful suppliers force the price down. This increases the quantity demanded, and the new equilibrium is at a lower price and a higher quantity bought and sold. (4) A reduction in supply creates a shortage that causes the price to be bid up. This reduces the quantity demanded, and the new equilibrium is at a higher price and a lower quantity bought and sold.

In this chapter we have studied many forces that can cause demand or supply curves to shift. These were summarized in Figures 4-3 and 4-7. By combining this analysis with the four laws of demand and supply, we can link many real-world events that cause demand or supply curves to shift with changes in market prices and quantities. For example, a rise in the price of a commodity's substitute will shift the commodity's demand curve to the right, as in Figure 4-3, thus leading to a rise in both the commodity's price and the quantity that is bought and sold, as in part (i) of Figure 4-9.

[9] The term *statics* is used because we are not concerned about the actual path by which the market goes from the first equilibrium position to the second. Analysis of that path would be described as dynamic analysis.

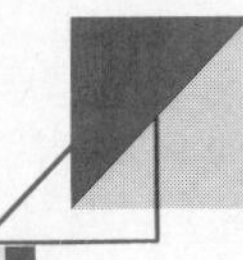

BOX 4-1

Laws, Predictions, Hypotheses

In what sense can the four propositions developed for supply and demand be called "laws"? They are not like bills passed by Parliament, interpreted by courts, and enforced by the police; they cannot be repealed if people do not like their effects. Nor are they like the laws of Moses, revealed to humanity by the voice of God. Are they natural laws similar to Newton's law of gravity? In labeling them *laws,* classical economists clearly had in mind Newton's laws as analogies.

The term *law* is used in science to describe a theory that has stood up to substantial testing. A law of this kind is not something that has been proved to be true for all times and all circumstances, nor is it regarded as immutable. As observations accumulate, laws may be modified or the range of phenomena to which they apply may be restricted or redefined. Einstein's theory of relativity, as one example, forced such amendments and restrictions on Newton's laws.

The laws of supply and demand have stood up well to many empirical tests, but no one believes that they explain all market behavior. They are thus laws in the sense that they predict certain kinds of behavior in certain situations and the predicted behavior occurs sufficiently often to lead people to continue to have confidence in the predictions of the theory. They are not laws—any more than are the laws of natural science—that are beyond being challenged by present or future observations that may cast doubt on some of their predictions. Nor is it a heresy to question their applicability to any particular situation.

Laws, then, are hypotheses that have led to predictions that account for observed behavior. They are theories that, in some circumstances at least, have survived attempts to refute them and have proved useful. It is possible, in economics as in the natural sciences, to be impressed both with the "laws" we do have and with their limitations: to be impressed, that is, both with the power of what we know and with the magnitude of what we have yet to understand.

The theory of the determination of price by demand and supply is beautiful in its simplicity. Yet, as we shall see, it is powerful in its wide range of applications. The usefulness of this theory in interpreting what we see in the world around us is further discussed in Box 4-2.

Prices and Inflation

The theory we have developed explains how individual prices are determined by the forces of demand and supply. To facilitate matters, we have made *ceteris paribus* assumptions. Specifically, we have assumed the constancy of all prices except the one we are studying (and occasionally one other price when we wish to see how change in that price affects the market being studied). Does this mean that our theory is inapplicable to an inflationary world in which all prices are rising at the same time? Fortunately the answer is no.

The price of a commodity states the amount of money that must be spent to acquire one unit of that commodity. This is called the **absolute price**, or *money price.* A **relative price** is the ratio of two absolute prices; it expresses the price of one good in terms of (i.e., *relative to*) another.

We have mentioned several times that what matters for demand and supply is the price of the commodity in question relative to the prices of other commodities; that is, what matters is the *relative price.*

In an inflationary world we are often interested in the price of a given commodity as it relates to the average price of all other commodities. If, during a period when the general price level rose by 40 per-

FIGURE 4-9 The Four "Laws" of Demand and Supply

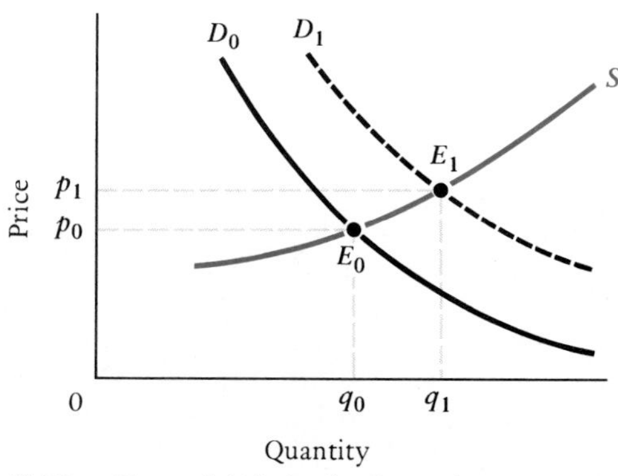

(i) The effects of shifts in the demand curve

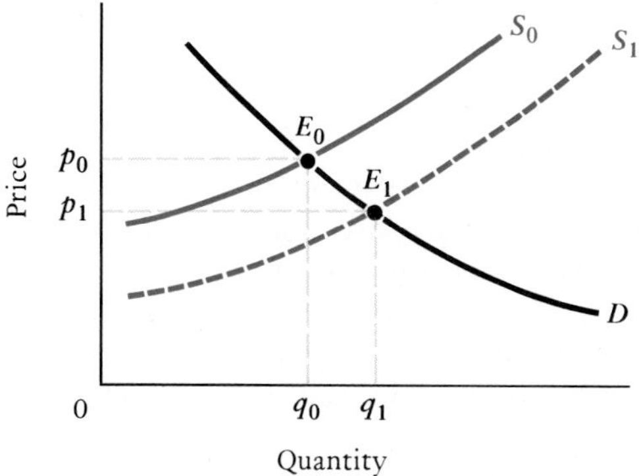

(ii) The effects of shifts in the supply curve

The effects on equilibrium price and quantity of shifts in either demand or supply are called the laws of demand and supply. *A rise in demand.* In (i) assume that the original demand and supply curves are D_0 and S, which intersect to produce equilibrium at E_0, with a price of p_0 and a quantity of q_0. An increase in demand shifts the demand curve to D_1, taking the new equilibrium to E_1. Price rises to p_1 and quantity to q_1.

A fall in demand. In (i) assume that the original demand and supply curves are D_1 and S, which intersect to produce equilibrium at E_1, with a price of p_1 and a quantity of q_1. A decrease in demand shifts the demand curve to D_0, taking the new equilibrium to E_0. Price falls to p_0 and quantity falls to q_0.

A rise in supply. In (ii) assume that the original demand and supply curves are D and S_0, which intersect to produce equilibrium at E_0, with a price of p_0 and a quantity of q_0. An increase in supply shifts the supply curve to S_1, taking the new equilibrium to E_1. Price falls to p_1 and quantity rises to q_1.

A fall in supply. In (ii) assume that the original demand and supply curves are D and S_1, which intersect to produce equilibrium at E_1, with a price of p_1 and a quantity of q_1. A decrease in supply shifts the supply curve to S_0, taking the new equilibrium to E_0. Price rises to p_0 and quantity falls to q_0.

cent, the price of oranges rose by 60 percent, then the price of oranges rose relative to the price level as a whole. Oranges became *relatively* expensive. However, if oranges had risen in price by only 30 percent when the general price level rose by 40 percent, then the relative price of oranges would have fallen. Although the money price of oranges rose substantially, oranges became *relatively* cheap.

In Lewis Carroll's famous story *Through the Looking-Glass,* Alice finds a country where you have to run in order to stay still. So it is with inflation. A commodity's price must rise as fast as the general level of prices rises just to keep its relative price constant.

It has been convenient in this chapter to analyze changes in particular prices in the context of a constant price level. The analysis is easily extended to an inflationary period by remembering that any force that raises the price of one commodity when other prices remain constant will, given general inflation, raise the price of that commodity faster than the price level is rising. For example, a change in tastes in favor of carrots that would raise their price by 20 percent when other prices were constant, would raise their price by 32 percent if at the same time the general price level rises by 10 percent.[10] In each case

[10] Let the price level be 100 in the first case and 110 in the second. Let the price of carrots be 120 in the first case and x in the second. To preserve the same relative price we need x such that $120/100 = x/110$, which makes $x = 132$.

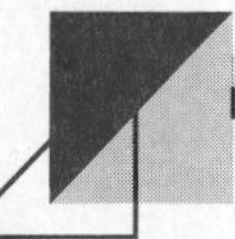

BOX 4-2

Demand and Supply: What Really Happens

"The theory of supply and demand is neat enough," said the skeptic, "but tell me what really happens."

"What really happens," said the economist, "is that first, demand curves have a negative slope; second, supply curves have a positive slope; third, prices rise in response to excess demand; and fourth, prices fall in response to excess supply."

"But that's theory," insisted the skeptic. "What about reality?"

"That is reality as well," said the economist.

"Show me," said the skeptic.

The economist produced the following passages from articles in the *New York Times*.

Increased demand for macadamia nuts causes price to rise above competing nuts. Major producer now plans to double the size of its orchards during the next five years.

* * *

OPEC countries once again fail to agree on output quotas. Output soars and prices plummet.

* * *

Last summer, Rhode Island officials reopened the northern third of Narragansett Bay, a 9,500-acre fishing ground that had been closed since 1978 because of pollution. Suddenly clam prices dropped, thanks to an underwater population explosion that had transformed the Narragansett area into a clam harvester's dream.

* * *

Increasing third-world agricultural production threatens the stability of North American agriculture. In the 1970s North American farm prosperity was built on rising demand due to world prosperity and on falling output in Eastern Europe. Farm experts now worry that the propensity will prove fragile in the face of major increases in world output.

* * *

The effects of [the first year of] deregulation of the nation's airlines were spectacular: cuts in air fares of up to 70 percent in some cases, record passenger jam-ups at the airports, and a spectacular increase in the average load factor [the proportion of occupied seats on the average commercial flight].

The skeptic's response is not recorded, but you should be able to tell which clippings illustrate each of the economist's four statements about "what really happens."

the price of carrots rises 20 percent *relative to the average of all prices.*

In price theory, whenever we talk of a change in the price of one commodity, we mean a change relative to other prices.

If the price level is constant, this change requires only that the money price of the commodity in question rise. If the price level is itself rising, this change requires that the money price of the commodity in question rise faster than the price level.

SUMMARY

1. The amount of a commodity that households wish to purchase is called the *quantity demanded.* It is a flow expressed as so much per period of time. It is determined by the commodity's own price, average household income, the prices of related commodities, tastes, the distribution of income among households, and the size of the population.

2. Quantity demanded is assumed to increase as the price of the commodity falls, *ceteris paribus*. The relationship between quantity demanded and price is represented graphically by a demand curve that shows how much will be demanded at each market price. A movement along a demand curve indicates a change in the quantity demanded in response to a change in the price of the commodity.
3. A shift in a demand curve represents a change in the quantity demanded at each price and is referred to as a *change in demand*. The demand curve shifts to the right (an increase in demand) if average income rises, if the price of a substitute rises, if the price of a complement falls, if population rises, or if there is a change in tastes in favor of the product. The opposite changes shift the demand curve to the left (a decrease in demand).
4. The amount of a commodity that firms wish to sell is called the *quantity supplied*. It is a flow expressed as so much per period of time. It depends on the commodity's own price, the costs of inputs, the goals of the firm, and the state of technology.
5. Quantity supplied is assumed to increase as the price of the commodity increases, *ceteris paribus*. The relationship between quantity supplied and price is represented graphically by a supply curve that shows how much will be supplied at each market price. A movement along a supply curve indicates a change in the quantity supplied in response to a change in price.
6. A shift in the supply curve indicates a change in the quantity supplied at each price and is referred to as a *change in supply*. The supply curve shifts to the right (an increase in supply) if the costs of producing the commodity fall or if, for any reason, producers become more willing to produce the commodity. The opposite changes shift the supply curve to the left (a decrease in supply).
7. The *equilibrium price* is the one at which the quantity demanded equals the quantity supplied. At any price below equilibrium there will be excess demand; at any price above equilibrium there will be excess supply. Graphically, equilibrium occurs where the demand and supply curves intersect.
8. Price is assumed to rise when there is excess demand and to fall when there is excess supply. Thus the actual market price will be pushed toward the equilibrium price, and when it is reached, there will be neither excess demand nor excess supply, and the price will not change until either the supply curve or the demand curve shifts.
9. Using the method of *comparative statics,* the effects of a shift in either demand or supply can be determined. A rise in demand raises both equilibrium price and equilibrium quantity; a fall in demand lowers both. A rise in supply raises equilibrium quantity but lowers equilibrium price; a fall in supply lowers equilibrium quantity but raises equilibrium price. These are the so-called laws of demand and supply.
10. Price theory is most simply developed in the context of a constant price level. Price changes discussed in the theory are changes relative to the average level of all prices. The absolute price of a commodity is its price in terms of money; its relative price is its price in terms of other commodities. In an inflationary period a rise in the *relative price* of one commodity means that its absolute price rises by more than the price level; a fall in its relative price means that its absolute price rises by less than the price level.

TOPICS FOR REVIEW

Quantity demanded and quantity actually bought
Demand schedule and demand curve
Quantity supplied and quantity actually sold
Supply schedule and supply curve
Movement along a curve and shift of a whole curve
Change in quantity demanded and change in demand
Change in quantity supplied and change in supply
Equilibrium, equilibrium price, and disequilibrium
Comparative statics
Laws of supply and demand
Relative price

DISCUSSION QUESTIONS

1. What shifts in demand or supply curves would produce the following results? (Assume that only one of the two curves has shifted.)
   a. The price of pocket calculators has fallen over the past few years, and the quantity exchanged has risen greatly.
   b. As the Canadian standard of living rose, both the prices and the consumption of prime cuts of beef rose steadily.
   c. Summer sublets in Kingston, Ontario, are at rents well below the regular rentals.
   d. Style changes cause the sales of jeans to decline.
   e. Potato blight causes spud prices to soar.
   f. "Gourmet food market grows as affluent shoppers indulge."
   g. Du Pont increased the price of synthetic fibers, although it acknowledged that demand was weak.
   h. The Edsel was a lemon when produced in 1958–1960 but is now a best-seller among cars of its vintage.
   i. Some of the first $10 coins minted in Canada to commemorate the Olympics were imperfectly stamped. These flawed pieces are currently worth as much as $1,000.
   j. Do the same for all the examples given in Box 4-2.
2. Recently the U.S. Department of Agriculture predicted that this spring's excellent weather would result in larger crops of corn and wheat than farmers had expected. But its chief economist warned consumers not to expect prices to decrease since the costs of production were rising and foreign demand for American crops was increasing. "The classic pattern of supply and demand won't work this time," the economist said. Discuss his observation.
3. Compact disk producers find that they are selling more at the same price than they did two years ago. Is this a shift of the demand curve or a movement along the curve? Suggest at least four reasons why this rise in sales at an unchanged price might occur.
4. What would be the effect on the equilibrium price and quantity of marijuana if its sale were legalized?
5. The relative price of personal computers has dropped drastically over time. Would you explain this falling price in terms of demand or supply changes? What factors are likely to have caused the demand or supply shifts that did occur?
6. Classify the effect of each of the following as (i) a decrease in the demand for fish, (ii) a decrease in the quantity of fish demanded, or (iii) other. Illustrate each diagrammatically.
   a. The government of Iceland bars fishermen of other nations from its waters.

b. People buy less fish because of a rise in fish prices.
c. The Roman Catholic Church relaxes its ban on eating meat on Fridays.
d. The price of beef falls, and as a result households buy more beef and less fish.
e. Fears of mercury pollution leads locals to shun fish caught in nearby lakes.
f. It is discovered that eating fish is better for one's health than eating meat.

7. Predict the effect on the price of at least one commodity of each of the following:
a. Winter snowfall is at a record high in Quebec, but drought continues in Rocky Mountain ski areas.
b. A recession decreases employment in Windsor automobile factories.
c. The French grape harvest is the smallest in 20 years.
d. The state of New York cancels permission for citizens to cut firewood in state parks.

8. Are the following two observations inconsistent? (a) Rising demand for housing causes prices of new homes to soar. (b) Many families refuse to buy homes as prices become prohibitive for them.

Appendix to Chapter 4

The Laws of Demand and Supply in an Open Economy

In Chapter 4 we have discussed the determination of price in a single domestic market. But what about all those goods that are traded internationally? A brief look at these may be a useful exercise at this point.

To start we need to define a few terms. An economy that engages in international trade is called an **open economy**. One that does not is called a **closed economy**, and a situation with no international trade is called **autarky**. We shall examine the simple case of a **small open economy**, which is an economy whose exports and imports are small enough in relation to the total volume of world trade that changes in the quantities it imports or exports do not influence the prices of goods established in world markets. For many countries and commodities, this is an empirically applicable assumption.

We also divide all goods into two types. **Nontradables** are goods and services that are produced and sold domestically and do not enter into international trade. Their prices are set on domestic markets by domestic supply and demand. **Tradables** are goods and services that enter into international trade. For a small open economy, the prices of tradables, whether the economy imports or exports them, are given, since they are set on international markets.

FIGURE 4A-1 The Domestic Supply and Demand for Wheat (a Typical Exported Good)

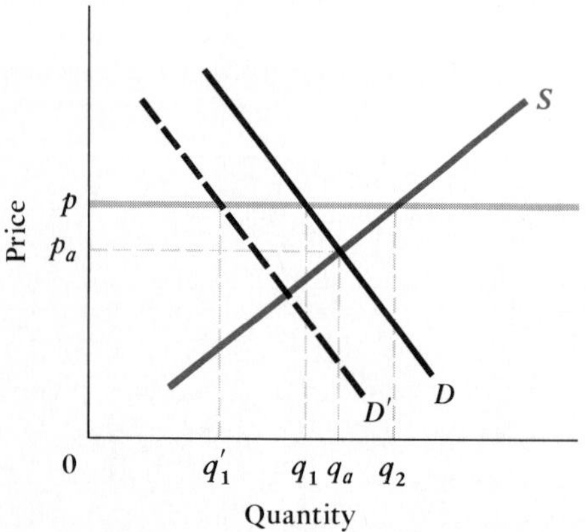

Exports are determined by the domestic excess supply of a tradable good at the world price. D and S are the domestic demand and supply schedules. In autarky, the domestic price would be p_a, and quantity q_a would be produced and consumed domestically. If the world price of wheat, p, exceeds the autarky price, p_a, the country will export wheat. At the world price, p, quantity supplied will be q_2, domestic consumption will be q_1, and q_1q_2 will be exported. A fall in domestic demand to D' increases the quantity exported to $q_1'q_2$.

Nontraded Goods

Equilibrium occurs where the quantity demanded by domestic purchasers is equal to the quantity supplied by domestic producers. In effect, the pricing of nontraded goods is what we have discussed in Chapter 4. The price of nontradables is set by the forces of domestic demand and domestic supply.

Traded Goods

Traded goods prices are set on international markets, while domestic demand and supply determine the quantities that are consumed domestically, produced domestically, and traded at that price.

Exports. Domestic demand and supply would establish a domestic price in the absence of world trade. If, however, the given world price exceeds that domestic price, the good will be exported. Since the small open economy's exports are an insignificant fraction of total world production and consumption of the commodity, the world price will dominate, and the excess of domestic quantity supplied over domestic quantity demanded at that price will be exported. This is analyzed in detail in Figure 4A-1.

Notice that trade raises the price of the exported good above its autarky level. Notice also that the equilibrium is no longer where domestic quantity demanded equals domestic quantity supplied; instead, the equilibrium price is the given world price, and the excess of domestic quantity supplied over domestic quantity demanded is exported.

Imports. If the world price is less than the autarky price, the good will be imported, as shown in Figure 4A-2. Notice that trade lowers the price of the imported good below its autarky level. Notice also that the equilibrium is once again not where domestic quantity demanded equals domestic quantity supplied; price is given by the world price, and the excess of domestic quantity demanded over domestic quantity supplied is met by imports.

For an open economy, equilibrium in markets for traded goods is consistent with domestic demand for those goods being different from domestic supply. If at the world price quantity demanded domestically exceeds quantity supplied domestically, the good will be imported; if quantity supplied domestically exceeds quantity demanded domestically, the good will be exported.

FIGURE 4A-2 **The Domestic Supply and Demand for Cotton Cloth (a Typical Imported Good)**

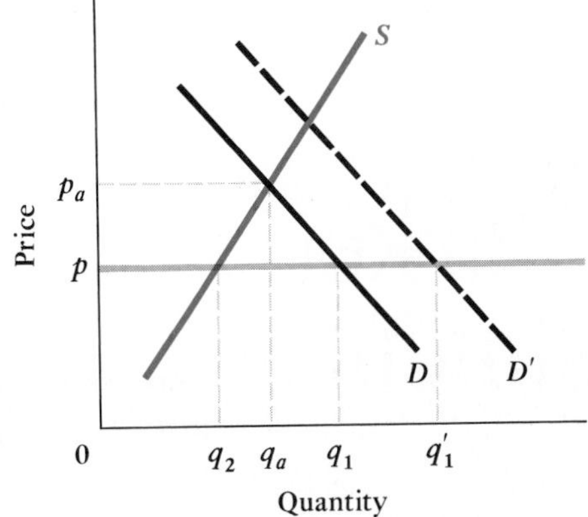

Imports are determined by the excess domestic demand for a tradable good at the world price. D and S are the domestic demand and supply schedules. In autarky, the domestic price would be p_a, and quantity q_a would be produced and consumed domestically. If the world price of cotton cloth, p, is less than the autarky price, p_a, the country will import cotton cloth. At the world price p, quantity supplied will be q_2, domestic consumption will be q_1, and q_2q_1 will be imported. A rise in domestic demand to D' increases the quantity imported to q_2q_1'.

Effects of Changes in Domestic Supply and Demand

Suppose that domestic residents experience a change in tastes. At the same prices, and values of other variables that influence quantity demanded, they decide to consume less of the exported good and more of the imported good. This decision is illustrated in Figure 4A-1, where the demand for the exported good shifts to the left, and in Figure 4A-2, where the demand for imported goods shifts to the right. At the prevailing world prices, these shifts lead to an increase in the quantity of exports and also to an increase in the quantity of imports.

The effects of a change in domestic supply can also be studied. For example, an increase in domestic wages would increase the cost of producing both the imported good and the exported good. This would reduce the quantity that would be supplied domestically at each price; that is, the supply curves shift upward. The reader can verify that, *ceteris paribus*, this would lead to an increase in the quantity of imports and a decrease in the quantity of exports.

In a small open economy, other things being equal, shifts in domestic supply and demand lead to changes in quantities imported and exported rather than to changes in prices.

Since the economy we are studying is assumed to be small relative to the whole world, these changes in domestic demand or supply do not have a noticeable effect on world prices. The result of shifts in domestic demand or supply is a change in the *quantities* of imports and exports. The assumption that world prices are constant means that, in effect, the domestic economy can buy or sell any quantities of tradable goods it wants on world markets.

Note in conclusion that the laws of supply and demand derived in Chapter 4 still apply, but they need modification to cover the case of the horizontal export demand curve characteristic of the tradable goods produced by a small open economy. Shifts in demand have the effects given in the text, while shifts in supply have all of their effects concentrated on quantities and none on prices.

Chapter 5

Elasticity and Market Adjustment

The laws of demand and supply predict the direction of changes in price and quantity in response to various shifts in demand and supply, but usually it is not enough to know merely whether price and quantity each rise or fall; it is also important to know by how much each changes.

When flood damage led to major destruction of the onion crop in the early 1980s, onion prices rose sharply. Not surprisingly, overall consumption of onions fell. The press reported that many consumers stopped using onions altogether and substituted onion salt, sauerkraut, cabbage, and other products. Other consumers still bought onions but in reduced quantities. Was the dollar value (price times quantity) higher or lower? The data do not tell, but the answer is important. A government concerned with the effect of a bad crop on farm income will not be satisfied with being told that food prices will rise and quantities consumed will fall; it will need to know by approximately how much they will change if it is to assess the effects on farmers.

Measuring and describing the extent of the responsiveness of quantities to changes in prices and other variables is often essential if we are to understand the significance of these changes. This is what the concept of *elasticity* does.

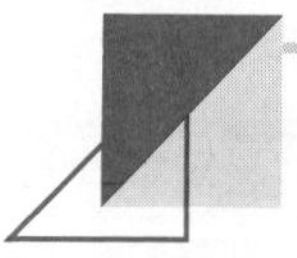

Price Elasticity of Demand

Suppose that there is an increase in a farm crop, that is, a rightward shift in the supply curve. The two parts of Figure 5-1 have the same initial equilibrium, and that equilibrium is disturbed by the same rightward shift in the supply curve. Because the demand curves are different in the two parts of the figure, the new equilibrium position is different, and hence the magnitude of the effects of the increase in supply on equilibrium price and quantity are different.

A shift in supply will have different quantitative effects, depending on the shape of the demand curve.

The difference may be significant for government policy. Consider what would happen if the rightward shift of the supply curve shown in Figure 5-1 occurs because the government has persuaded farmers to produce more of a certain crop. (It might, for example, have paid a subsidy to farmers for producing that crop.)

FIGURE 5-1 **The Effect of the Shape of the Demand Curve**

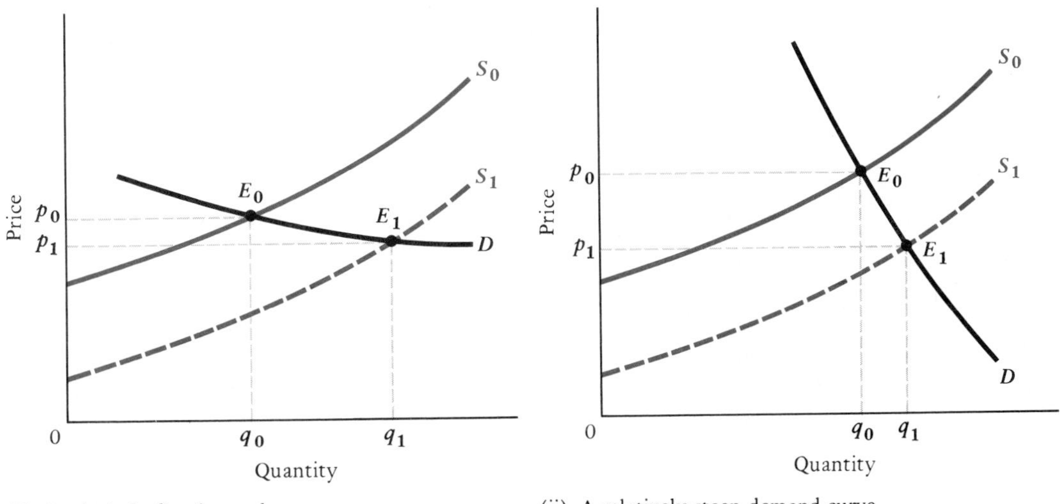

(i) A relatively flat demand curve (ii) A relatively steep demand curve

The more responsive the quantity demanded is to changes in price, the less the change in price and the greater the change in quantity deriving from any given shift in the supply curve. Both parts of the figure are drawn to the same scale. They show the same initial equilibrium and the same shift in the supply curve. In each part initial equilibrium is at price p_0 and output q_0 and the new equilibrium is at p_1 and q_1. In (i) the effect of the shift in supply from S_0 to S_1 is a slight fall in the price and a large increase in quantity. In (ii) the effect of the identical shift in the supply curve from S_0 to S_1 is a large fall in the price and a relatively small increase in quantity.

Part (i) of Figure 5-1 illustrates a case in which the quantity that consumers demand is relatively sensitive to price changes. The rise in production brings down the price, but because the quantity demanded is quite responsive, only a small change in price is necessary to restore equilibrium. The effect of the government's policy, therefore, is to achieve a large increase in the production and sales of this commodity and only a small decrease in price.

Part (ii) of Figure 5-1 shows a case in which the quantity demanded is relatively unresponsive to price changes. As before, the increase in supply at the original price causes a surplus that brings the price down. However, this time the quantity demanded by consumers does not increase much in response to the fall in price. Thus the price continues to drop until, discouraged by lower and lower prices, farmers reduce the quantity supplied nearly to the level that prevailed before they received the subsidy. The effect of the government's policy is to achieve a large decrease in the price of this commodity and only a small increase in the quantity produced and sold.

In both of the cases shown in Figure 5-1, it can be seen that the government's policy has exactly the same effectiveness as far as the farmers' willingness to supply the commodity is concerned—the supply curve shifts are identical. The magnitude of the effects on the equilibrium price and quantity, however, are very different because of the different degrees to which the quantity demanded by consumers responds to price changes. If the purpose of the government's policy is to increase the quantity of this commodity produced and consumed, it will be a great success when the demand curve is similar to the one shown in part (i) of Figure 5-1, but it will be a failure when the demand curve is similar to the one shown in part (ii) of Figure 5-1. If, however, the purpose of the government's policy is to achieve a large reduction in the price of the commodity, the policy will be a failure when demand is as shown in part (i), but it will be a great success when demand is as shown in part (ii).

The Measurement of Price Elasticity

In Figure 5-1, we were able to say that the curve in part (i) showed a demand that was more responsive to price changes than the curve in part (ii) because two conditions were fulfilled. First, both curves were drawn on the same scale. Second, the initial equilibrium prices and quantities were the same in both parts of the figure. Let us see why these conditions matter.

First, by drawing both figures on the same scale, the curve that looked steeper actually did have the larger slope. (The slope of a demand curve tells us the number of dollars by which price must change to cause a unit change in quantity demanded.) If we had drawn the two curves on different scales, we could have concluded nothing about the relative price changes needed to get a unit change in quantity demanded by comparing their appearances on the graph.[1]

Second, because we started from the same price-quantity equilibrium in both parts of the figure, we did not need to distinguish between percentage changes and absolute changes. If the initial prices and quantities are the same in both cases, the larger absolute change is also the larger percentage change. However, when we wish to deal with different initial price-quantity equilibria, we need to decide whether we are interested in absolute or percentage changes.

To see which is relevant, assume that we have the information shown in Table 5-1. Should we conclude that the demand for radios is not as responsive to price changes as the demand for beef? After all, price cuts of 20 cents cause quite a large increase in the quantity of beef demanded but only a small increase in radios.

This discussion raises the issue of absolute versus percentage changes. First, a reduction in the price of 20 cents will be a large price cut for a low-priced commodity and an insignificant price cut for a high-priced commodity. The price reductions listed in Table 5-1 represent different proportions of the total prices. It is usually more revealing to know the percentage change in the prices of the various commodities. Second, by an analogous argument, knowing the quantity by which demand changes is not very revealing unless the initial level of demand is also known. An increase of 7,500 pounds is quite a significant reaction to demand if the quantity formerly bought was 15,000 pounds, but it is insignificant if the quantity formerly bought was 10 million pounds.

Table 5-2 shows the original and new levels of price and quantity. Changes in price and quantity expressed as percentages of the average prices and quantities are shown in the first two columns of Table 5-3.[2] The **price elasticity of demand**, the measure of responsiveness of quantity of a commodity demanded to a change in market price, is symbolized by the Greek letter eta, η. It is defined as

$$\eta = \frac{\textbf{percentage change in quantity demanded}}{\textbf{percentage change in price}}$$

TABLE 5-1 Price Reductions and Corresponding Increases in Quantity Demanded

Commodity	Reduction in price (cents)	Increase in quantity demanded
Beef	20 per pound	7,500 pounds
Men's shirts	20 per shirt	5,000 shirts
Radios	20 per radio	100 radios

The data show, for each of the three commodities, the change in quantity demanded in response to the same absolute fall in price. The data are fairly uninformative about the responsiveness of demand to price because they do not tell us either the original price or the original quantity demanded.

[1] It is misleading to infer anything about the responsiveness of quantity to a price change by inspecting the apparent steepness of a graph of a demand curve. By the same token, it can be misleading to infer anything about the relative responsiveness of two different demands by comparing the appearances of their two curves. The reason is that you can make any curve appear as steep or as flat as you wish by changing the scales. For example, a curve that looks steep when the horizontal scale is 1 inch = 100 units will look much flatter when it is drawn on a graph with the same vertical scale but when the horizontal scale is 1 inch = 1 unit.

[2] The use of averages is designed to avoid the ambiguity caused by the fact that, for example, the 20-cent change in the price of beef is a different percentage of the original price, \$1.70, than it is of the new price, \$1.50 (11.8 percent versus 13.3 percent). We want the elasticity of demand between any two points *A* and *B* to be independent of whether we move from *A* to *B* or from *B* to *A*; as a result, using either original prices and quantities or new prices and quantities would be less satisfactory than using averages. In this illustration 20 cents is unambiguously 12.5 percent of \$1.60 and applies to a price increase from \$1.50 to \$1.70, as well as to the decrease discussed in the text. Further discussion is found in the appendix to this chapter.

TABLE 5-2 Price and Quantity Information Underlying Data of Table 5-1

Commodity	Unit	Original price	New price	Average price	Original quantity	New quantity	Average quantity
Beef	per pound	$ 1.70	$ 1.50	$ 1.60	116,250	123,750	120,000
Men's shirts	per shirt	8.10	7.90	8.00	197,500	202,500	200,000
Radios	per radio	40.10	39.90	40.00	9,950	10,050	10,000

These data provide the appropriate context for the data given in Table 5-1. The table relates the 20-cent-per-unit price reduction of each commodity to the actual prices and quantities demanded.

This measure is frequently called the **elasticity of demand,** or simply *demand elasticity*. Since the variable causing the change in quantity demanded is the commodity's own price, the term *own price elasticity of demand* is also used. **[6]**

Interpreting Numerical Elasticities

Because demand curves have negative slopes, an *increase* in price is associated with a *decrease* in quantity demanded, and vice versa. Since the percentage changes in price and quantity have opposite signs, demand elasticity is a negative number. However, we will follow the usual practice of ignoring the negative sign and speak of the measure as a positive number, as we have done in the illustrative calculations in Table 5-3. Thus the more responsive the quantity demanded (for example, radios relative to beef), the greater the elasticity of demand and the higher the measure (e.g., 2.0 compared to 0.5).

The numerical value of elasticity can vary from zero to infinity. Elasticity is zero when quantity demanded does not respond at all to a price change. As long as the percentage change in quantity is less than the percentage change in price, the elasticity of demand has a value of less than unity (i.e., less than 1). When the two percentage changes are equal, elasticity is equal to unity. When the percentage change in quantity exceeds the percentage change in price, the value for the elasticity of demand is greater than unity.

When the percentage change in quantity is less than the percentage change in price (elasticity less than 1), there is said to be an **inelastic demand.** When the percentage change in quantity is greater than the percentage change in price (elasticity greater than 1), there is said to be an **elastic demand.** This terminology is important, and you should become familiar with it. It is summarized in part A of Box 5-1.

A demand curve need not, and usually does not, have the same elasticity over every part of the curve. Figure 5-2 shows that a negatively sloped, straight-line demand curve does not have a constant elasticity. A straight line has constant elasticity only when it is vertical or when it is horizontal. Figure 5-3 illustrates three special cases of demand curves with constant elasticities.

TABLE 5-3 Calculation of Demand Elasticities

Commodity	(1) Percentage decrease in price	(2) Percentage increase in quantity	(3) Elasticity of demand (2) ÷ (1)
Beef	12.5	6.25	0.5
Men's shirts	2.5	2.50	1.0
Radios	0.5	1.00	2.0

Elasticity of demand is the percentage change in quantity divided by the percentage change in price. The percentage changes are based on average prices and quantities shown in Table 5-2. For example, the 20-cent-per-pound decrease in the price of beef is 12.5 percent of $1.60. A 20-cent change in the price of radios is only 0.5 percent of the average price per radio of $40.

Price Elasticity and Changes in Total Expenditure

In the absence of sales taxes, the total amount spent by purchasers is also the total revenue received by the sellers, so we can use the terms *total (purchaser) expenditure* and *total (seller) revenue* interchangeably.[3]

[3] Allowing for sales taxes complicates the analysis substantially and changes the conclusions in small ways but not in broad outline.

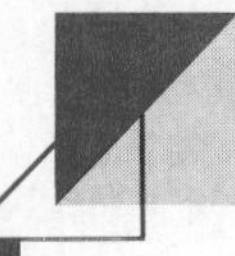

BOX 5-1

Terminology of Elasticity

Term	Symbol	Numerical measure of elasticity	Verbal description
A. Price elasticity of demand (supply)	$\eta(\eta_S)$		
Perfectly or completely inelastic		Zero	Quantity demanded (supplied) does not change as price changes.
Inelastic		Greater than zero, less than one	Quantity demanded (supplied) changes by a smaller percentage than price.
Unit-elastic		One	Quantity demanded (supplied) changes by exactly the same percentage as price.
Elastic		Greater than one but finite	Quantity demanded (supplied) changes by a larger percentage than price.
Perfectly, completely, or infinitely elastic		Infinity	Purchasers (sellers) are prepared to buy (sell) all they can at some price and none at all at an even slightly higher (lower) price.
B. Income elasticity of demand	η_Y		
Inferior good		Negative	Quantity demanded decreases as income increases.
Normal good		Positive:	Quantity demanded increases as income increases:
Income-inelastic		Less than one	Less than in proprotion to the income increase.
Income-elastic		Greater than one	More than in proportion to the income increase.
C. Cross-elasticity of demand	η_{xy}		
Substitute		Positive	Price increase of a substitute leads to an increase in quantity demanded of this good (and less of the substitute).
Complement		Negative	Price increase of a complement leads to a decrease in quantity demanded of this good (as well as less of the complement).

How does this revenue react when the price of a product is changed?

What happens to total revenue depends on the price elasticity of demand. If elasticity is less than unity, the percentage change in price exceeds the percentage change in quantity. The price change will then dominate, so that total revenue will change in the same direction as the price changes. If, however, elasticity exceeds unity, the percentage change in quantity exceeds the percentage change in price. The

FIGURE 5-2 Elasticity Along a Straight-Line Demand Curve

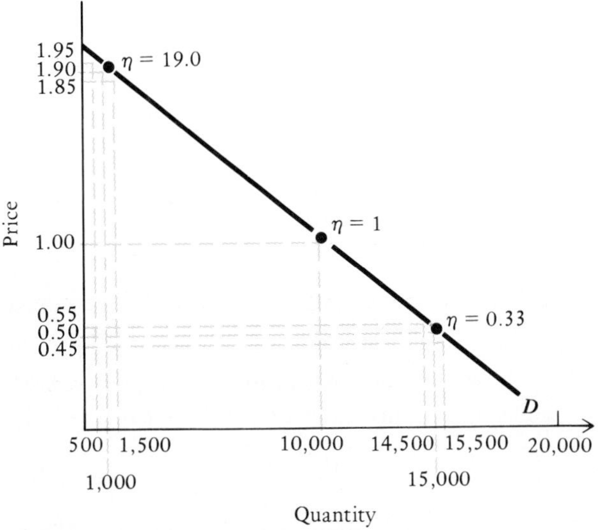

Moving down a straight-line demand curve, elasticity falls continuously. On this straight line a reduction in price of 10 cents always leads to the same increase (1,000 units) in quantity. Near the upper end of the curve, however, where price is $1.90 and quantity is 1,000 units, a reduction in price of 10 cents (from $1.95 to $1.85) is just over a 5 percent price reduction, but the 1,000-unit increase in quantity is a 100 percent quantity increase. Here, elasticity (η) is 19. At the price of 50 cents and quantity of 15,000 units, a price reduction of 10 cents (from 55 to 45 cents) leads to the same 1,000-unit increase in demand. The 20 percent price decrease combines with the 6.67 percent quantity increase to give an elasticity of 0.33.

quantity change will then dominate, so total revenue will change in the same direction as quantity changes (that is, in the opposite direction to the change in price).

The general relationship between elasticity and change in price can be summarized as follows:

1. **If demand is elastic, price and total revenue are negatively related. A fall in price increases total revenue, and a rise in price reduces it.**
2. **If demand is inelastic, price and total revenue are positively related. A fall in price reduces total revenue, and a rise in price increases it.**
3. **If elasticity of demand is unity, total revenue is constant and therefore unrelated to price. A rise or a fall in price leaves total revenue unaffected.**[7]

Figure 5-4 illustrates the relationship between elasticity of demand and total expenditure; the straight-line demand curve from Figure 5-2 is reproduced in part (i), and the total expenditure (equal to the area under the demand curve) corresponding to each possible quantity demanded is shown in part (ii).

Consider two real examples. When a bumper potato crop sent prices down 50 percent, quantity sold increased only 15 percent. Demand was clearly inelastic, and the result of the bumper crop was that potato farmers experienced a sharp *fall* in revenues. When a transit company cut its bus fares by 40 percent for the average journey, the volume of passenger traffic increased from 4.4 million to 14 million journeys within two years. Demand was clearly elastic, and revenues *rose* sharply as a result of the reduction in price.

Other examples can be constructed from Table 5-2. Calculations for what happens to total revenue when the prices of radios, men's shirts, and beef fall are shown in Table 5-4. In the case of beef, the demand is inelastic, and a cut in price lowers the sellers' revenue; in the case of radios, the demand is elastic, and a cut in price raises revenue. The borderline case is men's shirts; here, the elasticity is unity, and the cut in price leaves revenue unchanged.

What Determines Elasticity of Demand?

Table 5-5 shows some estimated price elasticities of demand. Evidently, elasticity can vary considerably. The main determinant of elasticity is the availability of substitutes. Some commodities, such as margarine, cabbage, lamb, and Fords, have quite close substitutes—butter, other green vegetables, beef, and similar makes of cars. A change in the prices of these commodities, *the prices of the substitutes remaining constant,* can be expected to cause much substitution. A fall in price leads consumers to buy more of the commodity and less of the substitutes, and a rise in price leads consumers to buy less of the commodity

FIGURE 5-3 Three Demand Curves

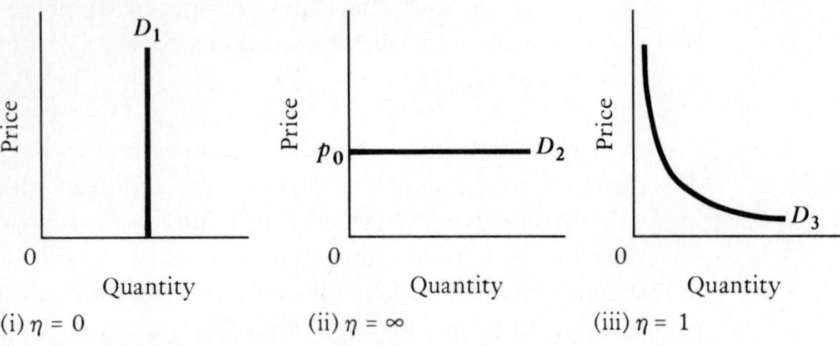

Each of these demand curves has constant elasticity. D_1 has *zero elasticity*: The quantity demanded does not change at all when price changes. D_2 has *infinite elasticity at the price* p_0: A small price increase from p_0 decreases quantity demanded from an indefinitely large amount to zero. D_3 has *unit elasticity*: A given percentage increase in price brings an equal percentage decrease in quantity demanded at all points on the curve.

and more of the substitutes. More broadly defined commodities, such as all foods, all clothing, alcohol, and gasoline, have few, if any, satisfactory substitutes. A rise in their prices can be expected to cause a smaller fall in quantities demanded than would be the case if close substitutes were available.

FIGURE 5-4 Elasticity of Demand and Total Expenditure

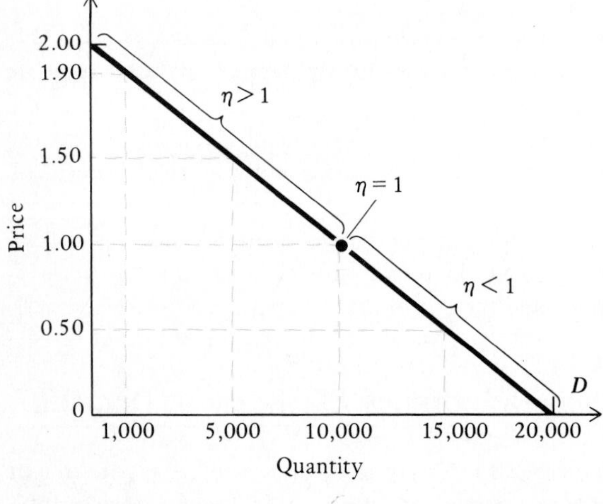

(i) Demand curve

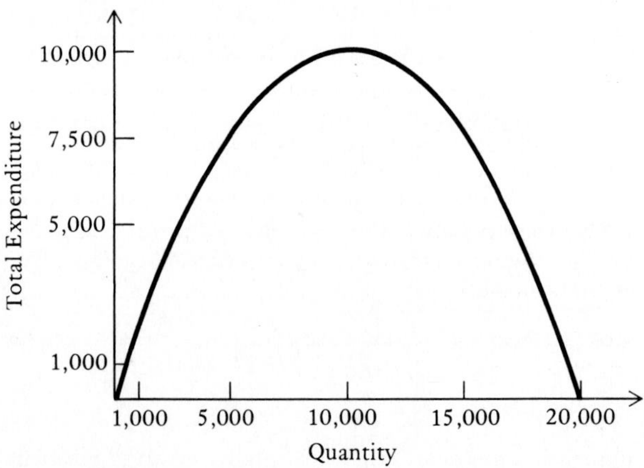

(ii) Total revenue

The change in total expenditure on a commodity in response to a change in price depends upon the elasticity of demand. The linear demand curve in part (i) reproduces Figure 5-2. Part (i) also shows three distinct ranges for the demand curve. Along the upper-left-hand range of the demand curve, elasticity is greater than 1. Along the lower-right-hand range, elasticity is less than 1. At the midpoint, elasticity is exactly equal to 1.

In part (ii), the total expenditure for each possible quantity demanded is plotted. For quantities demanded that are less than 10,000, elasticity of demand is greater than 1, and hence any increase in quantity demanded will be proportionately larger than the fall in price that caused it. In that range total expenditure is increasing. For quantities greater than 10,000, elasticity of demand is less than 1, and hence any increase in quantity demanded will be proportionately smaller than the fall in price that caused it. In that range total expenditure is falling. The maximum of total expenditure occurs where the elasticity of demand equals 1.

TABLE 5-4 Changes in Total Revenue (Total Expenditure) for the Example of Table 5-2

Commodity	Price × quantity (original prices and quantities)	Price × quantity (new prices and quantities)	Change in revenue (expenditure)	Elasticity of demand from Table 5-3
Beef	$ 197,625	$ 185,625	−$12,000	0.5
Men's shirts	1,599,750	1,599,750	0	1.0
Radios	398,995	400,995	+ 2,000	2.0

Whether revenue increases or decreases in response to a price cut depends on whether demand is elastic or inelastic. The $197,625 figure is the product of the original price of beef ($1.70) and the original quantity (116,250 pounds); $185,625 is the product of the new price ($1.50) and quantity (123,750), and so on.

A commodity with close substitutes tends to have an elastic demand; a commodity with no close substitutes tends to have an inelastic demand.

Closeness of substitutes—and thus measured elasticity—depends on both how the commodity is defined and the time period. This is explored next.

Definition of the Commodity

For food taken as a whole, demand is inelastic over a large price range. It does not follow, however, that any one food, such as white bread or beef, is a necessity in the same sense. Individual foods can have quite elastic demands, and they frequently do.

Durable goods provide a similar example. Durables as a whole are less elastic than individual kinds of durable goods. For example, when the price of television sets rises, many households may replace their lawnmower or their vacuum cleaner instead of buying that extra television set. Thus while their purchases of television sets fall, their total purchases of durables do not.

Because most specific manufactured goods have close substitutes, studies show they tend to have elastic demands. Millinery, for example, has been estimated to have an elasticity of 3.0. In contrast, clothing in general tends to be inelastic.

Any one of a group of related products will have a more elastic demand than the group taken as a whole.

Long-Run and Short-Run Elasticity of Demand

Because it takes time to develop satisfactory substitutes, a demand that is inelastic in the short run may prove elastic when enough time has passed. For example, at the time when cheap electric power was first brought to rural areas (long after it had come to cities), few farm households were wired for electricity. The initial measurements showed rural demand for electricity to be very inelastic. Some commentators even argued that it was foolish to invest so much money in bringing cheap electricity to farmers because they would not buy it even at low prices.

TABLE 5-5 Estimated Price Elasticities of Demand[a] *(selected commodities)*

Demand significantly inelastic (less than 0.9)	
Potatoes	0.3
Sugar	0.3
Public transportation	0.4
All foods	0.4
Cigarettes	0.5
Gasoline	0.6
All clothing	0.6
Consumer durables	0.8
Demand of close to unit elasticity (between 0.9 and 1.1)	
Beef	
Beer	
Marijuana	
Demand significantly elastic (more than 1.1)	
Furniture	1.2
Electricity	1.3
Lamb and mutton (U.K.)	1.5
Automobiles	2.1
Millinery	3.0

[a] For the United States except where noted.

The wide range of price elasticities is illustrated by these selected measures. These elasticities, from various studies, are representative of literally hundreds of existing estimates. Explanations of some of the differences are given in the text.

Gradually, however, farm households became electrified and purchased appliances, and measured elasticity steadily increased.

Petroleum provides a more recent example. In the early 1970s the Organization of Petroleum Exporting Countries (OPEC) cartel shocked the world with its first sudden and large increase in the price of oil. At that time the short-run demand for oil proved to be highly inelastic. Large price increases were met in the short run by very small reductions in quantity demanded. In this case the short run lasted for several years. Gradually, however, the high price of petroleum products led to such adjustments as the development of smaller, more fuel-efficient cars, economizing on heating oil by installing more efficient insulation, and replacement of fuel oil in many industrial processes with such other power sources as coal and hydroelectricity. The long-run elasticity of demand, relating the change in price to the change in quantity demanded after all adjustments were made, turned out to have an elasticity of well over 1, although the long-run adjustments took as much as a decade to work out.

The degree of response to a price change, and thus the measured price elasticity of demand, will tend to be greater the longer the time span considered.

Because the elasticity of demand for a commodity changes over time as consumers adjust their habits and substitutes are developed, the demand curve also changes; hence a distinction can be made between short-run and long-run demand curves. Every demand curve shows the response of consumer demand to a change in price. For such commodities as cornflakes and pillowcases, the full response occurs quickly, and there is little reason to worry about longer-term effects, but other commodities are typically used in connection with highly durable appliances or machines. A change in price of, say, electricity and gasoline may not have its major effect until the stock of appliances and machines using these commodities has been adjusted. This adjustment may take a long time to occur.

For commodities whose substitutes are developed over a period of time, it is helpful to identify two kinds of demand curve. A *short-run demand curve* shows the response of quantity demanded to a change in price for a given structure of the durable goods that use the commodity and for the existing sets of substitute commodities. A different short-run demand curve will exist for each such structure.

The *long-run demand curve* shows the response of quantity demanded to a change in price after enough time has passed to ensure that all adjustments to the changed price have occurred. The relationship between long-run and short-run demand curves is shown in Figure 5-5. The principal conclusion, already suggested in our discussion of elasticity, is this:

The long-run demand curve for a commodity will tend to have a substantially higher elasticity than any of the short-run demand curves.

FIGURE 5-5 Short-Run and Long-Run Demand Curves

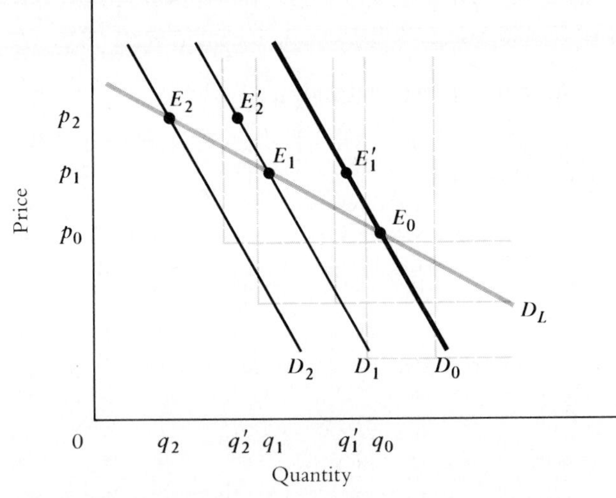

The long-run demand curve is more elastic than the short-run demand curve. D_L is a long-run demand curve. Suppose that consumers are fully adjusted to price p_0. Equilibrium is then at E_0, with quantity demanded q_0. Now suppose that price rises to p_1. In the short run, consumers will react along the short-run demand curve D_0 and reduce consumption to q_1'. Once time has permitted the full range of adjustments to price p_1, however, a new equilibrium at E_1 will be reached with quantity q_1. At E_1 there is a new short-run demand curve D_1. A further rise in price to p_2 would lead first to a short-run equilibrium at E_2' but eventually to a new long-run equilibrium at E_2. The screened long-run demand curve is more elastic than any of the short-run curves.

Market adjustment. The distinction between long-run and short-run demand curves, and hence between long-run and short-run demand elasticity, has important implications for the market response to a shift in supply.

In the short run, when demand is relatively inelastic, a shift in supply leads to a sharp change in the equilibrium price but only a small change in the equilibrium quantity exchanged. However, demand is more elastic in the long run than in the short run. This responsiveness of demand means that in the long run the shift in supply gives rise to a smaller change in the equilibrium price and a larger change in quantity.

Figure 5-6 shows the case of an increase in supply. In the short run, the increase leads to a movement down the relatively inelastic short-run demand curve; it thus gives rise to a large fall in price but only a small increase in quantity. In the long run, demand is more elastic, so long-run equilibrium has price and quantity above those that prevailed in short-run equilibrium.

The fact that price falls more in the short run than in the long run is sometimes referred to as *overshooting* the price. This "overshooting" of price, and the "undershooting" of quantity that is also evident in the figure, is the way in which markets are cleared in the face of demand's being less elastic in the short run than in the long run.

FIGURE 5-6 Short-Run and Long-Run Equilibrium Following an Increase in Supply

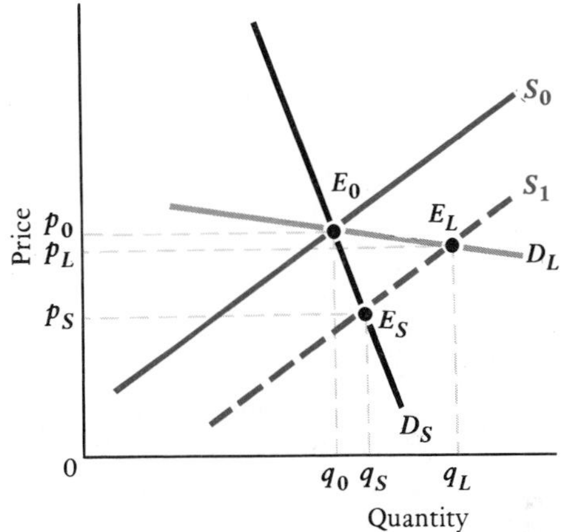

The magnitude of the changes in the equilibrium price and quantity following a shift in supply depends on the time allowed for demand to adjust. The change in the price is greater and the change in quantity is less in the short run than in the long run. The initial equilibrium is at E_0, with price p_0 and quantity q_0. There is then an increase in supply such that the supply curve shifts from S_0 to S_1.

On impact the relevant demand curve is the short-run curve D_S, and the new equilibrium immediately following the supply shock is E_S. Price falls sharply to p_S, and quantity rises only to q_S. In the long run, the demand curve is the more elastic one given by D_L, and equilibrium is at E_L. The long-run equilibrium price is p_L (greater than p_S), and quantity is q_L (greater than q_S).

The "overshooting" of the price is clear, since price initially falls from p_0 to p_S and rises back to p_L. Quantity, however, "undershoots," since it rises first from q_0 to q_S and then again from q_S to q_L.

Although revenue at the new long-run equilibrium (given by the product p_Lq_L) is thus clearly greater than that at the short-run equilibrium (given by the product p_Sq_S), whether it is greater than or less than revenue at the initial equilibrium (given by the product p_0q_0) depends on the elasticity of the long-run demand curve.

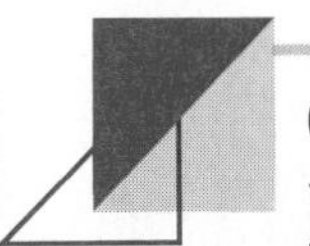

Other Demand Elasticities

Income Elasticity of Demand

One of the most important determinants of demand is the income of the potential customers. When the Food and Agricultural Organization (FAO) of the United Nations wants to estimate the future demand for some crop, it needs to know by how much world income will grow and how much of that additional income will be spent on the particular foodstuff. For example, as a nation gets richer, its consumption patterns change, with relatively more being spent on meat and relatively less being spent on staples such as rice and potatoes.

The responsiveness of demand to changes in income is termed **income elasticity of demand** and may be symbolized η_Y.

$$\eta_Y = \frac{\textbf{percentage change in quantity demanded}}{\textbf{percentage change in income}}$$

For most goods, increases in income lead to increases in demand, and income elasticity will be positive. These are called **normal goods**. Goods for which consumption decreases in response to a rise in income have negative income elasticities and are called **inferior goods**.

The income elasticity of normal goods may be greater than unity (elastic) or less than unity (inelastic), depending on whether the percentage change in the quantity demanded is greater or less than the percentage change in income that brought it about. It is also common to use the terms *income-elastic* and *income-inelastic* to refer to income elasticities of greater or less than unity. (See Box 5-1 for further discussion of elasticity terminology.)

The reaction of demand to changes in income is extremely important. We know that in most Western countries economic growth has caused the level of income to double every 20 to 30 years over a sustained period of at least a century. This rise in income is shared to some extent by most citizens. As they find their incomes increasing, they increase their demands for most commodities, but the demands for some commodities such as food and basic clothing will not increase much, while the demands for other commodities will increase rapidly. In developing countries, such as Ireland and Mexico, the demand for durable goods is increasing most rapidly as household incomes rise, while in North America and Western Europe the demand for services is rising most rapidly. The uneven impact of the growth of income on the demands for different commodites has important economic effects, which are studied at several points in this book, beginning with the discussion of agriculture in Chapter 6.

TABLE 5-6 Estimated Income Elasticities of Demand[a] *(selected commodities)*

Inferior goods (negative income elasticities)	
Whole milk	−0.3
Starchy roots	−0.2
Inelastic normal goods (0.0 to 1.0)	
Coffee (U.S.)	0.0
Wine (France)	0.1
Vegetables	0.2
All food (U.S.)	0.2
Poultry	0.3
Beef and veal	0.4
Housing (U.S.)	0.6
Cigarettes (U.S.)	0.8
Elastic normal goods (greater than 1.0)	
Gasoline (U.S.)	1.1
Wine (U.S.)	1.4
Cream (U.K.)	1.7
Wine	1.8
Consumer durables	1.8
Poultry (Sri Lanka)	2.0
Restaurant meals (U.K.)	2.4

[a] For Canada except where noted.

Income elasticities vary widely across commodities and sometimes across countries. The basic source of food estimates by country is the FAO, but many individual studies have been made. Explanations of some of the differences are given in the text.

What Determines Income Elasticity?

The variations in income elasticities shown in Table 5-6 suggest that the more basic or staple a commodity, the lower its income elasticity. Food as a whole has an income elasticity of 0.2, consumer durables of 1.8. In Canada such starchy roots as potatoes are inferior goods; their quantity consumed falls as income rises.

Does the distinction between luxuries and necessities help to explain differences in income elasticities? The table suggests that it does. The case of meals eaten away from home is one example. Such meals are almost always more expensive, calorie for calorie, than meals prepared at home. It would thus be expected that at lower ranges of income, restaurant meals would be regarded as an expensive luxury, but that the demand for them would expand substantially as households became richer. This is in fact what happens.

Does this mean that the market demand for the foodstuffs that appear on restaurant menus will also have high income elasticities? Generally, the answer is no. When a household eats out rather than prepare meals at home, the main change is not in what is eaten but who prepares it. The additional expenditure on "food" goes mainly to pay cooks and waiters and to yield a return on the restaurateur's capital. Thus when a household expands its expenditure on restaurant food by 2.4 percent in response to a 1 percent rise in its income, most of the extra expenditure on "food" goes to workers in service industries; little, if any, finds its way into the pockets of farmers. This is a striking example of the general tendency for households to spend a rising proportion

FIGURE 5-7 Income-Consumption Curves of Different Commodities

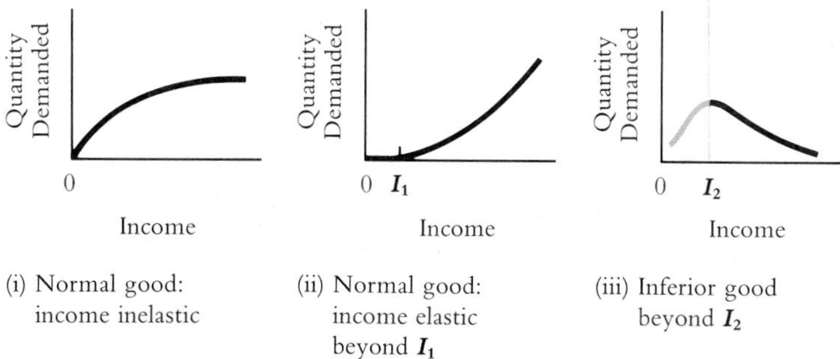

Different shapes of the curve relating quantity demanded to income correspond to different ranges of income elasticity. Normal goods have rising curves; inferior goods have falling curves. Many different patterns of income elasticity have been observed. The good in (i) is a typical normal good that is a necessity. It is purchased at all levels of income; even at high levels of income, some fraction of extra income is spent on it, although this fraction steadily decreases. The good in (ii) is a luxury good that is income-elastic beyond income I_1. The good in (iii) is a necessity at low incomes that becomes an inferior good for incomes beyond I_2.

of their incomes on services and a lower proportion on foodstuffs as their incomes rise.

The more basic is an item in the consumption pattern of households, the lower is its income elasticity.

So far we have focused on differences in income elasticities among commodities. However, income elasticities for any one commodity also vary with the level of a household's income. When incomes are low, households may eat almost no meat and consume lots of starchy foods such as bread and potatoes; when incomes are higher, they may eat cheap cuts of meat and more green vegetables along with their bread and potatoes; when incomes are even higher, they are likely to eat more (and more expensive) meat, to substitute frozen for canned vegetables, and to eat a greater variety of foods.

What is true of individual households is also true of countries. Empirical studies show that for different countries at comparable stages of economic development, income elasticities are similar. However, the countries of the world are at various stages of economic development and so have widely different income elasticities for the same products. Notice in Table 5-6 the different income elasticity of poultry in Canada, where it is a standard item of consumption, and in Sri Lanka, where it is a luxury.

Graphical Representation

Increases in income shift the demand curve to the right for a normal good and to the left for an inferior good. Figure 5-7 shows a different kind of graph, an **income-consumption curve**. The curve resembles an ordinary demand curve in one respect: It shows the relationship of quantity demanded to one other variable, *ceteris paribus*. The other variable is not price, however, but household income. (A change in the price of the commodity, incomes remaining constant, would shift the curves shown in Figure 5-7 downward.)

The figure shows three different patterns of income elasticity. Goods that consumers regard as necessities will have high income elasticities at low levels of income but will show low income elasticities beyond some level. The obvious reason is that as incomes rise, it becomes possible for households to devote a smaller proportion of their income to meeting basic needs and a larger proportion to buying things they have always wanted but could not afford. Some of these necessities may even become inferior goods. So-called luxury goods will not tend to be purchased at low levels of income but will have high income elasticities once incomes rise enough to permit households to sample the better things of life available to them.[4]

Cross-elasticity of Demand

The responsiveness of demand to changes in the price of another commodity is called the **cross-elasticity of demand**. It is often denoted η_{xy} and defined as follows:[5]

$$\eta_{xy} = \frac{\text{percentage change in quantity demanded of one good } (X)}{\text{percentage change in price of another good } (Y)}$$

Cross-elasticity can vary from minus infinity to plus infinity. Complementary commodities, such as cars and gasoline, have negative cross-elasticities. A large rise in the price of gasoline will lead (as it did in Canada in the 1970s) to a decline in the demand for cars, as some people decided to do without a car and others decided not to buy a second (or third) car. Substitute commodities, such as cars and public transport, have positive cross-elasticities. A large rise in the price of cars (relative to public transport) would lead to a rise in the demand for public transport as some people shifted from cars to public transport.

Measures of cross-elasticity sometimes prove helpful in defining whether producers of similar products are in competition. For example, glass bottles and tin cans have a high cross-elasticity of demand. The producer of bottles is thus in competition with the producer of cans. If the bottle company raises its price, it will lose substantial sales to the can producer. Men's shoes and women's shoes have a low cross-elasticity. A producer of men's shoes is not in close competition with a producer of women's shoes. If the former raises its price, it will not lose many sales to the latter. Knowledge of cross-elasticities can be important in anticombines investigations in which the issue is whether a firm in one industry is or is not in active competition with firms in another industry. Whether waxed paper and plastic wrap or aluminum cable and copper cable are or are not substitutes may determine questions of monopoly under the law. The positive or negative sign of cross-elasticities tell us whether or not goods are substitutes.

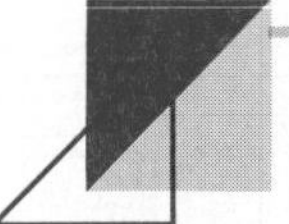

Elasticity of Supply

The concept of elasticity can be applied to supply as well as to demand. **Elasticity of supply** measures the responsiveness of the quantity supplied to a change in the commodity's price. It is denoted η_S and defined as

$$\eta_S = \frac{\text{percentage change in quantity supplied}}{\text{percentage change in price}}$$

This is often called *supply elasticity*.

The supply curves considered in this chapter all have positive slopes: An increase in price causes an increase in quantity sold. Such supply curves all have positive elasticities.

There are important special cases. If the supply curve is vertical—the quantity supplied does not change as price changes—elasticity of supply is zero. This would be the case, for example, if suppliers produced a given quantity and dumped it on the market for whatever it would bring. A horizontal supply curve has an infinitely high elasticity of supply: A small drop in price would reduce the quantity producers are willing to supply from an indefinitely large amount to zero. Between these two extremes, elasticity of supply will vary with the shape of the supply curve.[6]

[4] In Figure 5-7, in contrast to the ordinary demand curve, quantity demanded is on the vertical axis. This follows the usual practice of putting the variable to be explained (called the *dependent variable*) on the vertical axis and the explanatory variable (called the *independent variable*) on the horizontal axis. It is the ordinary demand curve that has the axes "backward." The explanation is buried in the history of economics and dates to Alfred Marshall's *Principles of Economics* (1890), the classic that is one of the foundation stones of modern price theory. **[8]** For better or worse, Marshall's scheme is now used by everybody, although mathematicians never fail to wonder at this further example of the odd ways of economists.

[5] The change in price of good Y causes the *demand curve* for good X to shift. Holding the price of good X constant means that we can measure the shift in the demand curve in terms of the change in quantity demanded of good X at the given price of good X.

[6] Steepness, which is related to absolute rather than percentage changes, is not always a reliable guide. For example, as is shown in the appendix to this chapter, *any* upward-sloping straight line passing through the origin has an elasticity of +1.0 over its entire range.

Determinants of Supply Elasticity

Supply elasticities are important for many problems in economics. Much of the treatment of demand elasticity carries over to supply elasticity. For example, the ease of substitution can vary in production as well as in consumption. If the price of a commodity rises, how much more can be produced profitably? This depends in part on how easy it is for producers to shift from the production of other commodities to the one whose price has risen. If agricultural land and labor can be readily shifted from one crop to another, the supply of any one crop will be more elastic than if they cannot.

Supply elasticity depends to a great extent on how costs behave as output is varied, an issue that will be treated at length in Part 3. If costs of production rise rapidly as output rises, then the stimulus to expand production in response to a rise in price will quickly be choked off by increases in costs. In this case supply will tend to be rather inelastic. If, however, costs rise only slowly as production increases, a rise in price that raises profits will elicit a large increase in quantity supplied before the rise in costs puts a halt to the expansion in output. In this case supply will tend to be rather elastic.

Long-Run and Short-Run Elasticity of Supply

As with demand, length of time for response is important. It may be difficult to change quantities supplied in response to a price increase in a matter of weeks or months but easy to do so over a period of years. An obvious example concerns the planting cycle of crops. Also, new oil fields can be discovered, wells drilled, and pipelines built over a period of years but not in a few months. Thus elasticity of oil supply is much greater over five years than over one year.

The distinction between long-run and short-run supply curves, and hence between long-run and short-run supply elasticity, has important implications for the market response to a shift in demand. In the short run, when supply is relatively inelastic, a shift in demand leads to a sharp change in the equilibrium price but only a small change in the equilibrium quantity exchanged. However, in the long run, when supply is more elastic than in the short run, the shift in demand leads to a smaller change in the equilibrium price and a larger change in quantity.

FIGURE 5-8 Short-Run and Long-Run Equilibrium Following a Shift in Demand

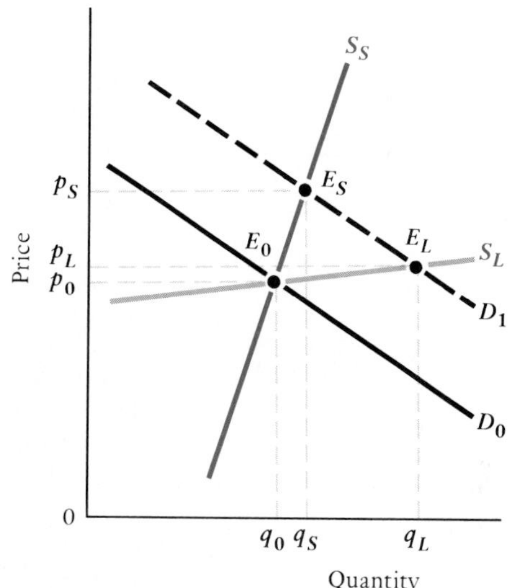

The magnitudes of the changes in the equilibrium price and quantity following a shift in demand depend on the time frame of the analysis. The change in the price is greater and the change in quantity is less in the short run than in the long run. The initial equilibrium is at E_0, with price p_0 and quantity q_0. There is then an increase in demand such that the demand curve shifts from D_0 to D_1.

On impact the relevant supply curve is the short-run curve S_S, and the new equilibrium immediately following the demand shock is E_S. Price rises sharply to p_S, and quantity rises only to q_S. In the long run, the supply curve is the more elastic one given by S_L. In the long run, equilibrium is at E_L; price is p_L (less than p_S), and quantity is q_L (greater than q_S).

The "overshooting" of the price discussed in the text is clear. As we can see also, quantity adjusts only partly on impact, so the long-run change in quantity exceeds the short-run change.

Although revenue at the new long-run equilibrium (given by the product p_Lq_L) is thus clearly greater than that at the initial equilibrium (given by the product p_0q_0), whether it is greater than or less than revenue at the short-run equilibrium (given by the product p_Sq_S) depends on the elasticity of the demand curve D_1.

Figure 5-8 illustrates the case of an increase in demand. The short-run "overshooting" of price, and the "undershooting" of quantity that is evident in the figure, is analogous to that shown in Figure 5-6 in response to a shift in supply. Here it arises following a shift in demand and is the market-clearing response to the fact that supply is less elastic in the short run than in the long run.

SUMMARY

1. *Price elasticity of demand* (also called simply *elasticity of demand*) is a measure of the extent to which the quantity demanded of a commodity responds to a change in its price. It is defined as the percentage change in quantity demanded divided by the percentage change in price that brought it about. Elasticity is defined to be a positive number, and it can vary from zero to infinity.
2. When the numerical measure of elasticity is less than unity, demand is *inelastic*. This means that the percentage change in quantity demanded is less than the percentage change in price that brought it about. When the numerical measure exceeds unity, demand is *elastic*. This means that the percentage change in quantity demanded is greater than the percentage change in price that brought it about.
3. Elasticity and total revenue of sellers are related in the following way: If elasticity is less than unity, total revenue is positively associated with price; if elasticity is greater than unity, total revenue is negatively associated with price; and if elasticity is unity, total revenue does not change as price changes.
4. The main determinant of the price elasticity of demand is the availability of substitutes for the commodity. Any one of a group of close substitutes will have a more elastic demand than the group as a whole.
5. Elasticity of demand tends to be greater the longer the time over which adjustment occurs. Items that have few substitutes in the short run may develop ample substitutes when consumers and producers have time to adapt. Hence a shift in supply will lead to a larger change in price and a smaller change in quantity in the short run than in the long run.
6. *Income elasticity of demand* is the percentage change in quantity demanded divided by the percentage change in income that brought it about. Luxuries tend to have higher income elasticities than necessities. The income elasticity of demand for a commodity will usually change as income varies. For example, a commodity that has a high income elasticity at a low income (because increases in income bring it within reach of the typical household) may have a low or negative income elasticity at higher incomes (because with further rises in incomes it can be replaced by a superior substitute).
7. *Cross-elasticity of demand* is the percentage change in quantity demanded divided by the percentage change in the price of some other commodity that brought it about. It is used to define commodities that are substitutes for one another (positive cross-elasticity) and commodities that complement one another (negative cross-elasticity).
8. *Elasticity of supply* is an important concept in economics. It measures the ratio of the percentage change in the quantity supplied of a commodity to the percentage change in its price. It is the analogue on the supply side to the elasticity of demand.
9. Supply tends to be more elastic in the long run than in the short run, since there are more possibilities for substituting production techniques and uses of inputs. This means that a shift in demand will

lead to a larger change in price and a smaller change in quantity in the short run than in the long run.

TOPICS FOR REVIEW

Elasticity of demand
Significance of elastic and inelastic demands
Difference between inelastic and perfectly inelastic demand and between elastic and infinitely elastic demand
Relationship between demand elasticity and total expenditure
Short-run and long-run demand curves
Income elasticity of demand
Income-elastic and income-inelastic demands
Normal goods and inferior goods
Cross-elasticity of demand
Substitutes and complements
Elasticity of supply
Short-run and long-run supply curves

DISCUSSION QUESTIONS

1. From the following quotations what, if anything, can you conclude about elasticity of demand?
   a. "Good weather resulted in record corn harvests and sent corn prices tumbling. For many corn farmers the result has been calamitous."
   b. "Ridership always went up when bus fares came down, but the increased patronage never was enough to prevent a decrease in overall revenue."
   c. "As the price of compact disk players fell, producers found their revenues soaring."
   d. "Coffee to me is an essential—you've gotta have it no matter what the price."
   e. "Soaring price of condominiums does little to curb the strong demand in Toronto."
2. Advocates of minimal charges for people using doctors' services in Canada hope that this will greatly reduce the cost to the provinces while not denying essential medical services to anyone. Opponents argue that even minimal charges will deny critical services to lower-income Canadians. Use elasticity terminology to restate the views of each of these groups.
3. What would you predict about the relative price elasticity of demand of (a) food, (b) meat, (c) beef, (d) chuck roast, (e) chuck roast sold at the local supermarket? What would you predict about their relative income elasticities?
4. "Avocados have a limited market, not greatly affected by price until the price falls to less than 25 cents a pound. Then they are much demanded by manufacturers of dog food." Interpret this statement in terms of price elasticity.
5. "Home computers were a leader in sales appeal through much of the 1980s. But per capita sales are much lower in Puerto Rico than in Canada and lower in New Brunswick than in Ontario. Manufacturers are puzzled by the big differences." Can you offer an explanation in terms of elasticity?
6. What elasticity measure or measures would be useful in answering the following questions?

a. Will cheaper transport into the central city help keep downtown shopping centers profitable?
b. Will raising the bulk postage rate increase or decrease the postal deficit?
c. Are producers of toothpaste and mouthwash in competition with each other?
d. What effect will rising gasoline prices have on the sale of cars that use propane gas?

7. Interpret the following statements in terms of the relevant elasticity concept.
a. "As fuel for tractors has become more expensive, many farmers have shifted from plowing their fields to no-till farming. No-till acreage increased from 30 million acres in 1972 to 95 million acres in 1982."
b. "Fertilizer makers brace for dismal year as fertilizer prices soar."
c. "When farmers are hurting, small towns feel the pain."

8. It has been observed recently that obesity is a more frequent medical problem for the relatively poor than for the middle-income classes. Can you use the theory of demand to shed light on this observation?

9. Suggest commodities that you think might have the following patterns of elasticity of demand.
a. High income elasticity, high price elasticity
b. High income elasticity, low price elasticity
c. Low income elasticity, low price elasticity
d. Low income elasticity, high price elasticity

10. When the New York City Opera faced a growing deficit, it cut its ticket prices by 20 percent, hoping to attract more customers. At the same time the New York Transit Authority raised subway fares to reduce its growing deficit. Was one of these two opposite approaches to reducing a deficit necessarily wrong?

Appendix to Chapter 5

Elasticity: A Formal Analysis

The verbal definition of elasticity used in the text may be written symbolically in the following form:

$$\eta = \frac{\Delta q}{\Delta p} \times \frac{\text{average } p}{\text{average } q}$$

where the averages are over the arc of the demand curve being considered. This is called **arc elasticity**, and it measures the average responsiveness of quantity to price over an interval of the demand curve.

Most theoretical treatments use a different but related concept called **point elasticity**. This is the measure of responsiveness of quantity to price at a particular point on the demand curve. The precise definition of point elasticity uses the concept of a derivative, which is drawn from differential calculus.

In this appendix we first study arc elasticity, which may be regarded as an approximation of point elasticity. Then we study point elasticity.

Before proceeding, we should notice one further change. In the text of Chapter 5 we reported our price elasticities as positive values and thus implicitly multiplied all our calculations by -1. In theoretical work it is more convenient to retain the concept's natural sign. Thus normal demand elasticities will have negative signs, and statements about "more" or "less" elasticity must be understood to refer to the absolute, not the algebraic, value of demand elasticity.

The following symbols will be used throughout.

$\eta \equiv$ elasticity of demand
$\eta_s \equiv$ elasticity of supply
$q \equiv$ the original quantity
$\Delta q \equiv$ the change in quantity
$p \equiv$ the original price
$\Delta p \equiv$ the change in price

Arc Elasticity As an Approximation of Point Elasticity

Point elasticity measures elasticity at some point (p,q). In the approximate definition, however, the responsiveness is measured over a small range starting from that point. For example, in Figure 5A-1 the elasticity at point 1 can be measured by the responsiveness of quantity demanded to a change in price that takes price and quantity from point 1 to point 2. The algebraic formula for this elasticity concept is

$$\eta = \frac{\Delta q}{\Delta p} \times \frac{p}{q} \qquad [1]$$

This is similar to the definition of arc elasticity except that since elasticity is being measured at a point, the p and q corresponding to that point are used (rather than the average p and q over an arc of the curve).

Equation 1 splits elasticity into two parts: $\Delta q/\Delta p$, the ratio of the change in quantity to the change in price, which is related to the *slope* of the demand curve, and p/q, which is related to the *point* on the curve at which the measurement is made.

Figure 5A-1 shows a straight-line demand curve. To measure the elasticity at point 1, take p and q at that point and then consider a price change, say, to point 2, and measure Δp and Δq as indicated. The slope of the straight line joining points 1 and 2 is $\Delta p/\Delta q$. The term in Equation 1 is $\Delta q/\Delta p$, which is the reciprocal of $\Delta p/\Delta q$. Therefore, the first term in the elasticity formula is the reciprocal of the slope of the straight line joining the two price-quantity positions under consideration.

Although point elasticity of demand refers to a point (p,q) on the demand curve, the first term in Equation 1 still refers to changes over an arc of the curve. This is the part of the formula that involves approximation, and, as we shall see, it has some unsatisfactory results. Nonetheless, some interesting theorems can be derived by using this formula as long as we confine ourselves to straight-line demand and supply curves.

1. *The elasticity of a downward-sloping straight-line demand curve varies from zero at the quantity axis to infinity at the price axis.* First notice that a straight line has a constant slope, so the ratio $\Delta p/\Delta q$ is the same everywhere on the line. Therefore its reciprocal,

FIGURE 5A-1 A Straight-Line Demand Curve

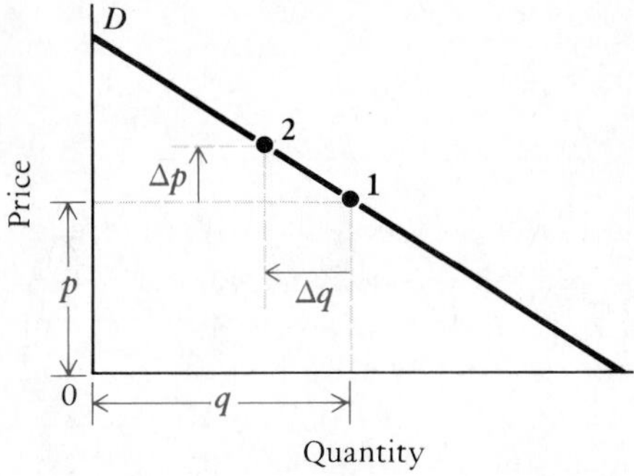

Because p/q varies with $\Delta q/\Delta p$ constant, the elasticity varies along this demand curve; it is high at the left and low at the right.

FIGURE 5A-2 Two Parallel Straight-Line Demand Curves

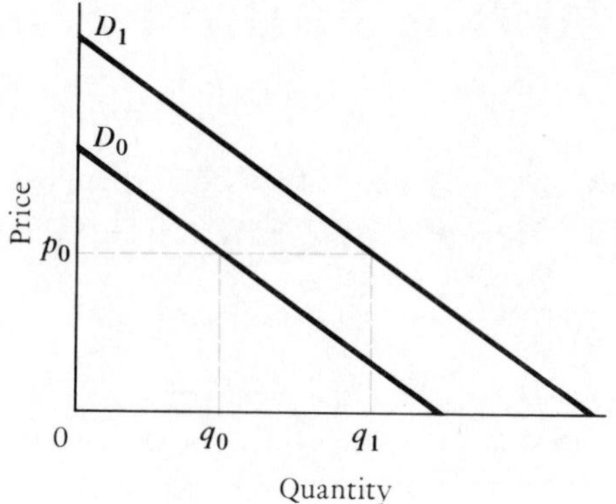

For any given price the quantities are different on these two parallel curves; thus the elasticities are different, being higher on D_0 than on D_1.

$\Delta q/\Delta p$, must also be constant. The changes in η can now be inferred by inspecting the ratio p/q. Where the line cuts the quantity axis, price is zero, so the ratio p/q is zero; thus $\eta = 0$. Moving up the line, p rises and q falls, so the ratio p/q rises; thus elasticity rises. Approaching the top of the line, q approaches zero, so the ratio becomes very large. Thus elasticity increases without limit as the price axis is approached.

2. *Where there are two straight-line demand curves of the same slope, the one farther from the origin is less elastic at each price than the one closer to the origin.* Figure 5A-2 shows two parallel straight-line demand curves. Compare the elasticities of the two curves at any price, say, p_0. Since the curves are parallel, the ratio $\Delta q/\Delta p$ is the same on both curves. Since elasticities at the same price are being compared on both curves, p is the same, and the only factor left to vary is q. On the curve farther from the origin, quantity is larger (i.e., $q_1 > q_0$) and hence p_0/q_1 is smaller than p_0/q_0; thus η is smaller.

It follows from theorem 2 that parallel shifts of a straight-line demand curve lower elasticity (at each price) when the line shifts outward and raise elasticity when the line shifts inward.

3. *The elasticities of two intersecting straight-line demand curves can be compared at the point of intersection merely by comparing slopes, the steeper curve being the less elastic.* In Figure 5A-3 there are two intersecting curves. At the point of intersection, p and q are common to both curves and hence the ratio p/q is the same. Therefore η varies only with $\Delta q/\Delta p$. On

FIGURE 5A-3 Two Intersecting Straight-Line Demand Curves

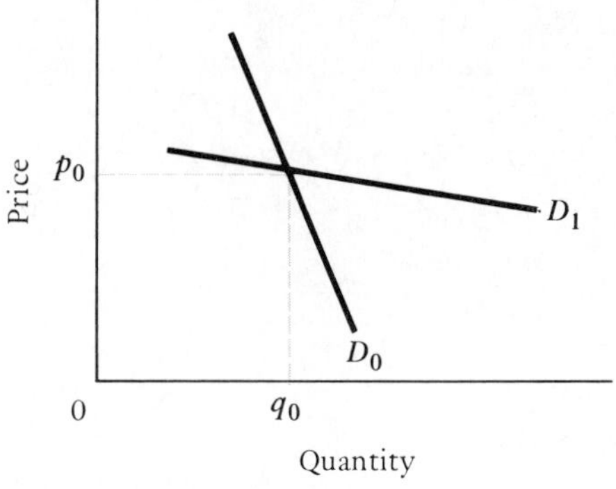

Elasticities are different at the point of intersection of these demand curves because the slopes are different, being higher on D_0 than on D_1. Therefore, D_1 is more elastic than D_0 at p_0.

the steeper curve, $\Delta q/\Delta p$ is smaller than on the flatter curve, so elasticity is lower.

4. *If the slope of a straight-line demand curve changes while the price intercept remains constant, elasticity at any given price is unchanged.* This is an interesting case for at least two reasons. First, when more customers having similar tastes to those already in the market enter the market, the demand curve pivots outward in this way. Second, when more firms enter a market that is shared proportionally among all firms, each firm's demand curve shifts inward in this way.

Consider in Figure 5A-4 the elasticities at point b on demand curve D_0 and at point c on demand curve D_1. We shall focus on the two triangles, abp_0 on D_0 and acp_0 on D_1, formed by the two straight-line demand curves emanating from point a and by the price p_0.

The price p_0 is the line segment $0p_0$. The quantities q_0 and q_1 are the line segments p_0b and p_0c, respectively. The slope of D_0 is $\Delta p/\Delta q = ap_0/p_0b$ and the slope of D_1 is $\Delta p/\Delta q = ap_0/p_0c$.

FIGURE 5A-4 Two Straight-Line Demand Curves with the Same Price Intercept

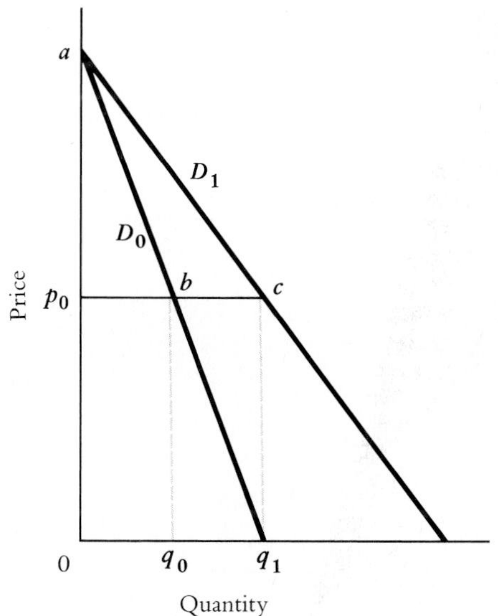

The elasticity is the same on D_0 and D_1 at any price. This situation occurs because the steeper slope of D_0 is exactly offset by the smaller quantity demanded at any price such as p_0.

From Equation 1 we can represent the elasticities of D_0 and D_1 at the points b and c, respectively, as

$$\eta \text{ at point } b = \frac{p_0b}{ap_0} \times \frac{0p_0}{p_0b} = \frac{0p_0}{ap_0}$$

$$\eta \text{ at point } c = \frac{p_0c}{ap_0} \times \frac{0p_0}{p_0c} = \frac{0p_0}{ap_0}$$

The two are the same. The reason is that the distance corresponding to the quantity demanded at p_0 appears in both the numerator and the denominator and thus cancels out.

Put differently, if the straight-line demand curve D_0 is twice is steep as D_1, it has half the quantity demanded at p_0. Therefore in the expression

$$\eta = \frac{\Delta q}{q} \times \frac{p}{\Delta p}$$

the steeper slope (a smaller Δq for the same Δp) is exactly offset by the smaller quantity demanded (a smaller q for the same p).

5. *Any straight-line supply curve through the origin has an elasticity of 1.* Such a supply curve is shown in Figure 5A-5. Consider the two triangles with the sides p, q, and the S curve and Δp, Δq, and the S curve. Clearly, these are similar triangles. Therefore, the ratios of their sides are equal: that is,

$$\frac{p}{q} = \frac{\Delta p}{\Delta q} \quad [2]$$

Elasticity of supply is defined as

$$\eta_s = \frac{\Delta q}{\Delta p} \times \frac{p}{q}$$

which, by substitution from Equation 2, gives

$$\eta_s = \frac{q}{p} \times \frac{p}{q} \equiv 1$$

6. *The elasticity measured from any point (p,q), according to Equation 1, is dependent on the direction and magnitude of the change in price and quantity.* Except for a straight line (for which the slope does not change), the ratio $\Delta q/\Delta p$ will not be the same over different ranges of a curve. Figure 5A-6 shows a demand curve that is not a straight line. To measure the elasticity from point 1, the ratio $\Delta q/\Delta p$—and thus η—will vary according to the size and the direction of the price change.

Theorem 6 yields a result that is very inconve-

FIGURE 5A-5 A Straight-Line Supply Curve Through the Origin

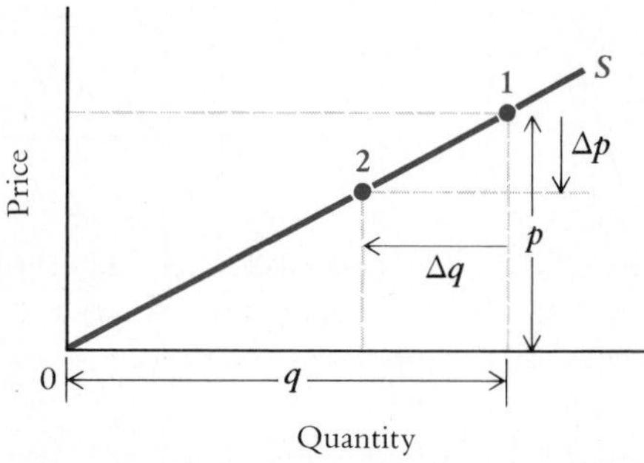

At every point on the curve, p/q equals $\Delta p/\Delta q$; thus elasticity equals unity at every point.

FIGURE 5A-6 Point Elasticity of Demand Measured by the Approximate Formula

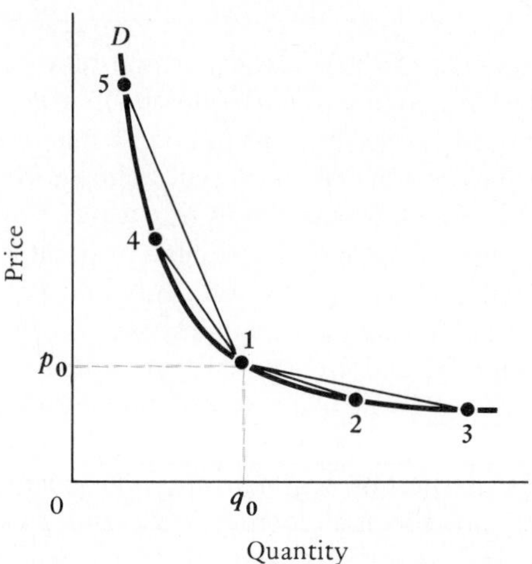

When the approximation of $\eta = \Delta q/\Delta p \times p/q$ is used, many elasticities are measured from point 1 because the slope of the chord between point 1 and every other point on the curve varies.

nient and is avoided by use of a different definition of point elasticity.

Point Elasticity According to the Precise Definition

To measure the elasticity at a point exactly, it is necessary to know the reaction of quantity to a change in price *at that point,* not over a range of the curve.

The reaction of quantity to price change at a point is called dq/dp, and this is defined to be the reciprocal of the slope of the straight line tangent to the demand curve at the point in question. In Figure 5A-7 the elasticity of demand at point 1 is the ratio p/q (as it has been in all previous measures), now multiplied by the ratio of $\Delta q/\Delta p$ measured along the straight line T, tangent to the curve at 1, that is, by dq/dp.

Thus the exact definition of point elasticity is

$$\eta = \frac{dq}{dp} \times \frac{p}{q} \qquad [3]$$

The ratio dq/dp, as defined, is in fact the differential calculus concept of the *derivative* of quantity with respect to price.

This definition of point elasticity is the one normally used in economic theory. Equation 1 is mathematically only an approximation of this expression. It is obvious from Figure 5A-7 that arc elasticity will come closer to point elasticity the smaller the price

FIGURE 5A-7 Point Elasticity of Demand Measured by the Exact Formula

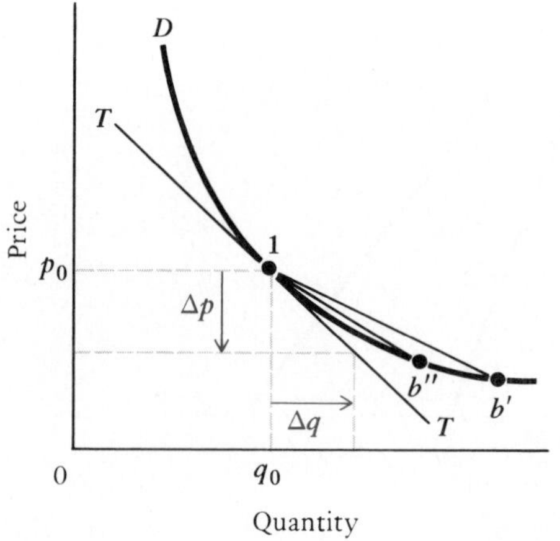

When the exact definition $\eta = dq/dp \times p/q$ is used, only one elasticity is measured from point 1 because there is only one tangent to the demand curve at that point.

change used to calculate the arc elasticity. The $\Delta q/\Delta p$ in Equation 1 is the reciprocal of the slope of the chord connecting the two points being compared. As the chord becomes shorter, its slope gets closer to that of the tangent *T*. (Compare the chords connecting point 1 to b' and b'' in Figure 5A-7.) Thus the error in using Equation 1 as an approximation of Equation 3 tends to diminish as the size of Δp diminishes.

Chapter 6

Supply and Demand in Action: Price Controls and Agriculture

Now that you have mastered the theory of how prices are determined by supply and demand, you have a very powerful tool at your command. However, a full understanding of any theory only comes with practice. This chapter is designed to give you that practice by applying supply and demand to cases drawn from real-world experience. Although we hope that these illustrations are interesting in themselves, the most important reason for studying is to gain mastery of the theory so that you can use it yourself to understand other cases.

This chapter uses the method of comparative statics, first encountered on page 69. In this method, you will recall, we start from a position of market equilibrium and then introduce the event to be studied. The new equilibrium position is then determined and compared with the original one. For example, we might start with an equilibrium in the wheat market and then introduce a reduction in supply due to a failure of this year's crop. A comparison of the price and quantity in the new and the original equilibrium would show the effects of the crop failure.

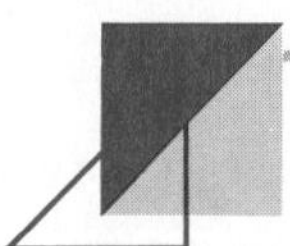

Government-Controlled Prices

Equilibrium in a free market occurs when the quantity demanded equals the quantity supplied. Government **price controls** are designed to hold the actual price at some disequilibrium value that could not be maintained in the absence of the government's intervention. Some controls hold the market price below its equilibrium value. This creates a shortage, with quantity demanded exceeding quantity supplied at the controlled price. Other controls hold price above equilibrium. This creates a surplus, with quantity supplied exceeding quantity demanded at the controlled price.

Disequilibrium Prices

In competitive markets, price changes whenever quantity supplied does not equal quantity demanded. Price then moves toward its equilibrium value, at which point there are neither unsatisfied suppliers nor unsatisfied demanders.

When controls hold price at some disequilibrium value, what determines the quantity actually traded on the market? The key to the answer is the fact that any voluntary market transaction requires both a willing buyer and a willing seller. This means that if quantity demanded is less than quantity supplied, demand will determine the amount actually exchanged, while the rest of the quantity supplied will remain in the hands of the unsuccessful sellers. On the other hand, if quantity demanded exceeds quantity supplied, supply will determine the amount actually exchanged, while the rest of the quantity demanded will represent desired purchases of unsuccessful buyers. This argument is spelled out in more detail in Figure 6-1, which establishes the general conclusion that

At any disequilibrium price, quantity exchanged is determined by the *lesser* of quantity demanded or quantity supplied.

FIGURE 6-1 The Determination of Quantity Exchanged in Disequilibrium

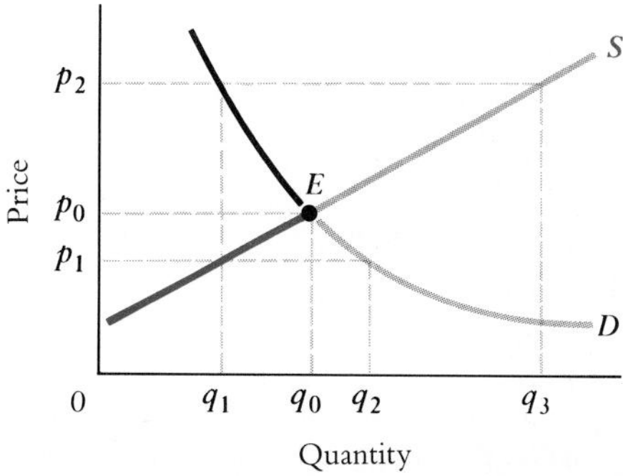

In disequilibrium, quantity exchanged is determined by *whichever is less,* quantity demanded or quantity supplied. At p_0 the market is in equilibrium, with quantity demanded equal to quantity supplied at q_0. For prices below p_0, the quantity exchanged will be determined by the supply curve. For example, the quantity q_1 will be exchanged at the disequilibrium price p_1 in spite of the excess demand of q_1q_2. For prices above p_0, the quantity exchanged will be determined by the demand curve. For example, the quantity q_1 will be exchanged at the disequilibrium price p_2 in spite of the excess supply of q_1q_3. Thus the darker portions of the S and D curves show the actual quantities exchanged at different prices.

Price Floors

The government sometimes establishes a minimum price, or **price floor**, for a good or a service. A price floor that is set at or below the equilibrium price has no effect, because equilibrium remains attainable. If, however, the price floor is set above the equilibrium, it will raise the price, in which case it is said to be *binding* or *effective.*

Price floors may be established by rules that make it illegal to sell the commodity below the prescribed price, as in the case of the minimum wage (examined in Chapter 19). Further, the government may establish a price floor by announcing that it will guarantee a certain price by buying any excess supply of the product that emerges at that price. Such guarantees are a feature of many agricultural support policies (examined later in this chapter).

The effects of binding price floors are illustrated in Figure 6-2, which establishes the following key result:

Effective price floors lead to excess supply. Either an unsold surplus will exist, or someone must enter the market and buy the excess supply.

The consequences of excess supply will, of course, differ from commodity to commodity. If the commodity is labor, subject to a minimum wage, excess supply translates into people without jobs. If the commodity is wheat, and more is produced than can be sold, the surplus wheat will accumulate in grain elevators or government warehouses. These consequences may or may not be "worth it" in terms of the other goals achieved. Whether they are worth it or not, these consequences are inevitable whenever a price floor is set above the market-clearing, equilibrium price.

Why might the government wish to incur these consequences? One reason is that those who actually succeed in selling their commodities at the price floor are better off than if they had to accept the lower equilibrium price. Certain groups of workers, professionals, and farmers are among those who have persuaded the government to establish price floors that enable them to sell their outputs at prices above free market levels.

Price Ceilings

Governments sometimes fix the *maximum prices* at which certain goods and services may be sold. Price controls on oil, natural gas, and rental housing fre-

FIGURE 6-2 A Price Floor

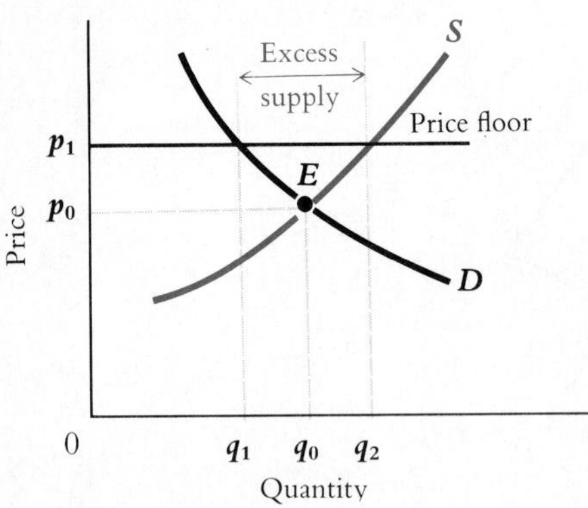

If a price floor is above the equilibrium price, quantity supplied will exceed quantity demanded. The free market equilibrium is at *E,* with price p_0 and quantity q_0. The government now establishes an effective price floor at p_1. Quantity supplied exceeds quantity demanded by q_1q_2.

If the government does nothing else, this excess supply will either go to waste or accumulate in the sellers' inventories. If the government buys the excess supply, q_2 will be sold—q_1 being bought by ordinary purchasers and q_1q_2 by the government, which will have to store it or find some way of disposing of it.

FIGURE 6-3 A Price Ceiling and Black Market Pricing

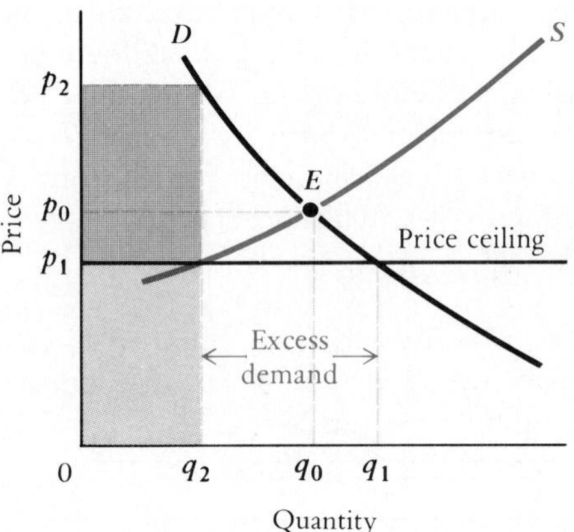

An effective price ceiling causes excess demand and invites a black market. Equilibrium price is at p_0. If a price ceiling is set at p_1, the quantity demanded will rise to q_1 and the quantity supplied will fall to q_2. Quantity actually exchanged will be q_2. Price may not rise legally to restore equilibrium.

If all the available supply of q_2 were sold on a black market, price to consumers would rise to p_2, with black marketeers earning receipts shown by the shaded areas. Since they buy at the ceiling price of p_1 and sell at the black market price of p_2, their profits are represented by the dark shaded area.

quently have been imposed by various levels of government—federal, provincial, or local.

Although sometimes they are referred to as *fixed* or *frozen prices,* most price controls of this type actually specify a **price ceiling**, which is the highest permissible price that producers may legally charge. If the price ceiling is set above the equilibrium price, it has no effect, since the equilibrium remains attainable. If, however, the price ceiling is set below the equilibrium price, the price ceiling lowers the price and is said to be *binding* or *effective.* The effects of price ceilings are shown in Figure 6-3, which establishes the following conclusion:

Effective price ceilings lead to excess demand, with the quantity exchanged being less than its equilibrium amount.

Allocating a Commodity in Short Supply

The free market eliminates excess demand by allowing prices to rise, thereby allocating the available supply among would-be purchasers. Since this does not happen under price ceilings, some other method of allocation must be adopted. Experience shows what we can expect.

If stores sell their available supplies on a first-come, first-served basis, people will rush to those stores that are said to have stocks of the commodity. In most Eastern European and some African countries, where prices of essentials are subject to effective price ceilings, even the rumor that a shop is selling supplies of a scarce commodity can cause a local stampede. Buyers may wait hours to get into the store, only to find that supplies are exhausted before they can be served. This is why standing in lines is a way of life in many command economies.

In market economies first-come, first-served is often the basis for allocating tickets to rock concerts and sporting events when demand exceeds the supply of available seats.

Instead of selling their supplies on a first-come, first-served basis, storekeepers may decide to keep goods "under the counter" and sell only to customers of their own choosing. For example, in the United States in 1978 during a gasoline shortage, some gas station operators sold only to regular customers. When sellers decide to whom they will (and will not) sell scarce supplies, allocation is by **sellers' preferences**.

If the government dislikes this allocation system, there are at least two things it can do. First, it can pass laws requiring suppliers to sell on a first-come, first-served basis. To the extent that this legislation is effective, it leads to allocation according to the buyers' willingness to stand in line.

Second—and more drastic—the government can ration the commodity. To do so, it prints only enough ration coupons to match the available supply and then distributes the coupons to would-be purchasers, who need both money and coupons to buy the commodity. The coupons may be distributed equally among the population or on the basis of some criterion such as age, family status, or occupation.

Rationing substitutes the government's preferences for the sellers' preferences in allocating a commodity that is in excess demand because of an effective price ceiling.

Rationing was used in Canada and most other belligerent countries during both World War I and World War II.

Black Markets

Price ceilings, with or without rationing, usually give rise to black markets. A **black market** is any market in which goods are sold illegally at prices that violate a legal price control.

Many manufactured products are produced by only a few firms but are sold by many retailers. Thus, although it may be easy to police the few producers, it is often impossible to enforce the price at which the many retailers sell to the general public. If the government is able to control the price received by producers but not by retailers, production remains at a level consistent with the price ceiling because the producers receive only the controlled price. At the retail level, however, the opportunity for a black market arises because purchasers are willing to pay more than the price ceiling for the limited amounts of the commodity that are available.

Effective price ceilings create the potential for a black market, because a profit can be made by buying at the controlled price and selling at the black-market price.

Figure 6-3 illustrates the extreme case in which all the available supply is sold on a black market.[1]

Does the existence of a black market mean that the goals sought by imposing price ceilings have been thwarted? The answer depends upon what the goals are. A government might be interested mainly in (1) restricting production (perhaps to release resources for war production); (2) keeping prices down; or (3) satisfying notions of equity in the consumption of a commodity that is temporarily in short supply. When price ceilings are accompanied by a black market, only the first objective is achieved. Black markets frustrate the second objective. Effective price ceilings on manufacturers plus an extensive black market at the retail level may produce the opposite of the third goal. There will be less to go around than if there were no controls, and the available quantities will tend to go to those with the most money or the least social conscience.

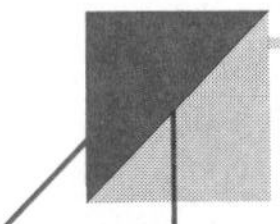

Rent Controls: A Case Study of Price Ceilings

Price ceilings are applied to the rental of houses and apartments for private occupancy in many parts of Canada and the United States. Rent controls have been used worldwide with similar consequences: severe housing shortages, private allocation systems, and black markets.

Rent controls have existed in New York, London, Paris, and many other large cities at least since World War II. In Sweden and in Britain, where rent controls on unfurnished apartments have existed for decades, shortages of rental accommodations are

[1] This case is extreme because there are law-abiding people in every society and because governments ordinarily have considerable power to enforce their price ceilings. Although *some* of a commodity subject to an effective price ceiling will be sold on the black market, it is unlikely that *all* of that commodity will be sold on the black market.

chronic. When British controls were extended to furnished apartments in 1973, the supply of such accommodations dried up, at least until loopholes were found in the law. When rent controls were initiated in Rome in 1978 and in Toronto in 1985, severe housing shortages developed. Such control-induced shortages led University of Chicago Professors George Stigler and Milton Friedman to point to the conflict between the "ceilings" created by controls and the "roofs" provided by housing.

Economic theory is useful in understanding the current experience with rent controls and in predicting further consequences.

General Effects of Rent Controls

Rent controls exist in many parts of North America today. Though of recent vintage in Canada, their effects are already apparent. Economic theory is useful in understanding the current experience with rent controls and in predicting the consequences. Rent controls are just a special case of price ceilings, and Figure 6-3 can be applied to them. It allows us to derive the following predictions, which are straightforward applications to housing of results that apply to any commodity subject to *binding* price ceilings.

1. There will be a housing shortage in the sense that quantity demanded will exceed quantity supplied.
2. The actual quantity of rental housing will be less than if free market rents had been charged.
3. The shortage will lead to alternative allocation schemes. Landlords may allocate by sellers' preferences, or the government may intervene, often through security-of-tenure laws, which protect tenants from eviction and thereby give them priority over prospective new tenants.
4. Black markets will appear. For example, landlords may require large "entrance fees" from new tenants, which reflect the difference in value between the free market rent and the controlled rent. In the absence of security-of-tenure laws, landlords may force tenants out when their leases expire in order to extract a large entrance fee from new tenants.

Specific Effects of Rent Controls

Further effects of rent control arise because housing is a **durable good**, a good that yields its services gradually over an extended period of time. Once it has been built, an apartment can be used for decades or even centuries.

The Supply of Rental Accommodations

The supply of rental accommodations depends on the *stock* of rental housing available, which in any year is composed mainly of buildings put up in the past. The stock is augmented by conversions of housing from other uses and construction of new buildings; it is diminished by conversions to other uses and by demolition or abandonment.

All of these reactions take time, which suggests that we need to use the distinction between short-run and long-run supply that was first introduced in Chapter 5.

Short-run supply. The short-run reaction to changes in rents tends to be quite limited. When rents rise, some conversions from other uses are possible, but it takes years to plan and to build new apartments. When rents fall, some conversions to condominiums and cooperatives may occur, and if rents fall so low that variable cost cannot be covered, buildings will be abandoned, as has happened on a large scale in parts of New York and London. However, wide ranges of variations in rents will be met by quite small changes in the short-run supply of rental accommodations, making the short-run supply curve quite inelastic.

Long-run supply. If the expected return from investing in new apartments falls significantly below what can be earned on other comparable investments, funds will go elsewhere. New construction will be halted, and old buildings will be converted to other uses, or, where this is impossible, they will not be replaced when they wear out. If the return rises significantly above the return on comparable investments, there will be a flow of investment funds into the building of new apartments. It takes years to increase the quantity of housing through new construction; reducing the quantity through nonreplacement takes decades. When all such adjustments are allowed for, the long-run supply curve of rental accommodations (which refers to the quantity supplied after enough time has been allowed for all adjustments) is highly elastic under most market conditions.

The Demand for Rental Accommodations

Does the fact that housing is a basic necessity mean that the demand for rental accommodations is highly inelastic? Although some form of shelter is a necessity, rental accommodations have many close substitutes, and empirical estimates show substantial elasticity in the demand *for a square foot* of rental accommodations.

A rise in the price of rental accommodations will lead to the following types of changes: Some people will stop renting and will buy instead; some will move to smaller, lower-grade rental housing; some will move to other areas where rents are lower; some will stay longer with their parents; and others will find roommates. For example, in response to a dramatic increase during recent decades in the cost of housing—both purchased and rented—the sharing of apartments among middle-income persons is more common today than it was only a few decades ago; they share in larger numbers per apartment, and they remain sharing for more years of their lives.

For all of these reasons, the demand for rental accommodations is quite responsive to changes in its (relative) price.

FIGURE 6-4 Effects of Rent Control in the Short Run and the Long Run

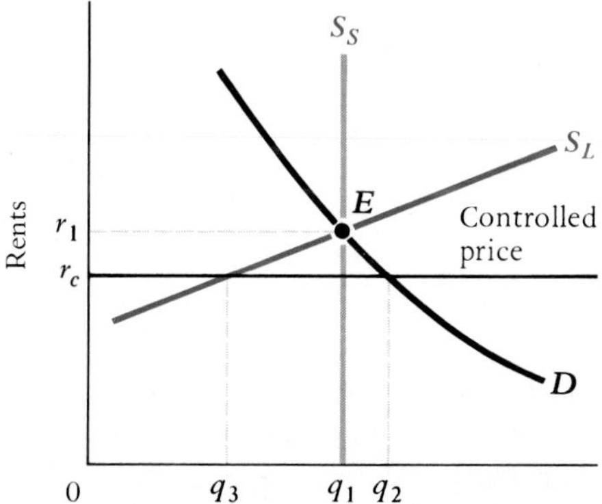

Rent control causes housing shortages that worsen as time passes. The controlled rent of r_c forces rents below their free market equilibrium value of r_1. The short-run supply of housing is shown by the inelastic curve S_S. Thus quantity supplied remains at q_1 in the short run, and the housing shortage is q_1q_2. Over time, the quantity supplied shrinks, as shown by the long-run supply curve S_L. In long-run equilibrium there are only q_3 units of rental accommodations, fewer than when controls were instituted. The housing shortage of q_3q_2, which occurs after supply has fully adjusted, is larger than the initial shortage of q_1q_2.

Rent Control and a Growing Housing Shortage

Because the short-run supply of housing is inelastic, rent controls that hold rentals somewhat below their free market levels cause only a moderate housing shortage in the short run. Indeed, most of the shortage comes from an increase in quantity demanded rather than from a contraction of quantity supplied. As time passes, however, fewer new apartments are built, more conversions take place, and older buildings are not replaced as they wear out. As a result, the quantity supplied shrinks steadily. Furthermore, it is not worthwhile for landlords to spend as much on repairs as under free market conditions because rent controls lower the return on capital invested in rental accommodations. Concern over the deteriorating quality of housing is a recurring theme when effective rent controls have been in place for some time.

Both long-run and short-run effects of rent control are shown in Figure 6-4.

When Rent Controls May Work: Short-Term Shortages

Pressure for rent controls is strongest when prices are rising most rapidly. The case for controlling rising rentals is strongest when the shortages causing the increasing rents are temporary.

Sometimes there is a temporary influx of population into an area. Possibly an army camp is established in wartime, or a pipeline or a nuclear power complex is being built, and many workers are required, even though few will remain behind once the job is done. When the temporary population floods in, market rents will rise. New construction of apartments will not occur, however, because investors recognize that the rise in demand and the rise in rentals is temporary. In such a situation, rent controls may stop existing owners from making large profits and may result in few harmful supply effects, since a long-run supply response is not expected in any case. After the boom is over, demand will fall, and free market equilibrium rents will return to the controlled level (which is also their original level). Rent controls may then be removed with little further effect.[2]

Although under these circumstances the rent controls have no long-run adverse effect, they will have some disadvantages. At controlled rents there will be a severe housing shortage but no *price incentive* for existing tenants to economize on housing or for potential suppliers to find ways to provide extra short-run accommodations. If rents were allowed to rise on the free market, existing tenants would economize on the space they used, and some people would find it profitable to rent out some of their own rooms. Even though the supply of permanent apartments does not change, the supply of temporary accommodations (mobile homes, for example) can increase. Such reactions are encouraged by the signal of rising rents but are inhibited by rent controls.

When Rent Controls Fail: Long-Term Shortages

Long-Run Increases in Demand

Consider what happens when there is a long-term increase in the demand for rental accommodations, as in Vancouver and Toronto, where rapidly increasing population is creating severe local housing shortages and forcing rents to increase. Such increases in rents give the signal that apartments are highly profitable investments. A consequent building boom will lead to increases in the quantity supplied, and it will continue as long as high profits can be earned on rental housing.

If rent controls are imposed in the face of such long-term increases in demand, as they have been in Ontario, they will prevent landlords from earning short-run profits, but they will also prevent the needed long-run construction boom from occurring. Thus controls will convert a temporary shortage into a permanent one. There is also the danger, often realized in practice, that even when increases are granted in the controlled rents to allow for inflation and costs of repairs, they will not fully reflect the resulting rises in costs. When this happens, the discrepancy between the controlled and the equilibrium rents increases, and the housing shortage grows ever more acute as time passes.

Figure 6-5 shows rent controls used successfully to cope with a temporary increase in demand and used unsuccessfully in the face of a permanent increase.

Who Gains and Who Loses

Tenants in rent-controlled accommodations are the principal gainers. As the gap between controlled and equilibrium rents grows, those who are lucky enough to be tenants gain more and more.

If the beneficiaries of rent controls are existing tenants, the losers are the present generation of landlords and those would-be tenants of the future who do not succeed in finding rent-controlled accommodations.

Landlords suffer because they do not get the return that they had expected on their investments. In many cases, the return shrinks to zero. Some landlords are large companies, and others are rich individuals. Neither one of these groups attracts great public sympathy—even though the rental companies' stockholders are not all rich. Nonetheless, they learn from their experience and stop supplying further rental accommodations when the rent controls reduce the return on their capital investment below what could be earned in other lines of activity. Many other landlords are people of modest means who have put their retirement savings into a small apartment or a house or two. They find that the value of their savings is greatly diminished, and often they find themselves in the ironic position of subsidizing tenants who are far better off than they are.

The other major class of people who suffer from rent controls are potential future tenants. The housing shortage hurts them because the rental housing they would require will not be there in the future. The elderly couples who fight to keep rent controls on the apartments that they occupy are behaving in their own best interest. If and when they succeed, they are making life more difficult for the next generation of aged couples, many of whom will not find housing of the same quality if rent controls are continued. The welfare family protected today will have a hard time finding housing if it moves or if its

[2] There is also a risk that political pressure may turn temporary controls into permanent controls.

FIGURE 6-5 Rent Controls in Response to Increasing Demand

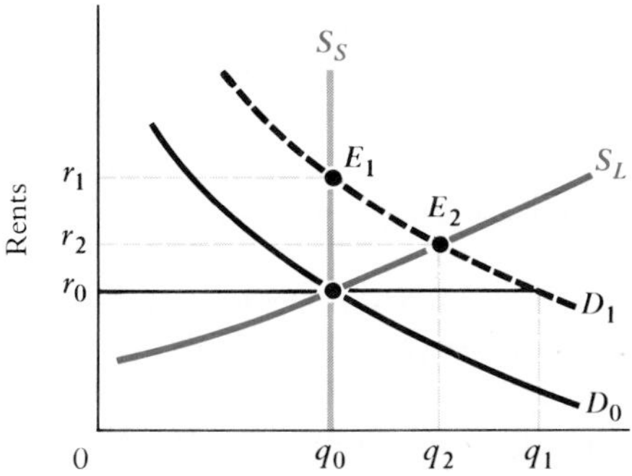

Rent controls prevent a temporary skyrocketing of rents when demand rises but also prevent the long-term supply adjustment where it is required.

Temporary demand fluctuations. The short-run supply curve S_S applies. In the free market a temporary shift in demand from D_0 to D_1 and then back to D_0 will change rents from r_0 to r_1 and then back to r_0. Rent control would hold rents at r_0 throughout; there would be a housing shortage of q_0q_1 due to excess demand, as long as demand was D_1, but rent control would not affect the quantity of housing available.

Permanent changes in demand. The long-run supply curve S_L applies. A permanent rise in demand from D_0 to D_1 will cause free market rents to rise temporarily from r_0 to r_1 and then to fall to r_2 as the quantity of accommodations supplied grows from q_0 to q_2. Controlling the rent at r_0 produces a permanent housing shortage of q_0q_1.

present apartment house is abandoned. Members of minority groups who are existing renters will gain, but those who follow in their footsteps a generation later will find that they are hurt by the steadily shrinking quantity and quality of available rental housing.

Many of these effects are apparent in the Toronto housing market (see Box 6-1).

Alternative Responses to the Rising Costs of Housing

Most rent controls today are meant to protect lower-income tenants, not only against high rents charged by landlords in the face of severe local shortages but also against the steadily rising cost of housing.

The free market solution is to let rents rise sufficiently to cover the rising costs. If people decide that they cannot afford the market price of apartments and will not rent them, construction will cease. Given what we know about past consumer behavior, however, it is more likely that people will make agonizing choices, both to economize on housing and to spend a higher proportion of total income on it, which means consuming less housing and less of other things as well.

If governments do not wish to accept this free market solution, what can be done? Let us consider three important alternatives.

1. Rent controls alone. One alternative is to control rents below the cost of constructing new buildings, which will inevitably result in a housing shortage that grows as the stock of rental accommodations wears out and is not replaced. Rent controls transfer real income from landlords, and future generations of would-be tenants, to the present generation of tenants. This may appeal to present tenants (and to those who want their votes, money, and approval), but it is difficult to find it appealing in terms of a broader sense of social justice that can be applied to the whole society and over time. A further interesting aspect of rent controls is discussed in Box 6-2.

2. Rent controls plus public housing. A second alternative is for government to fill the gap between total demand and private supply with subsidized public housing, financed at the taxpayers' expense (since *someone* must pay the full cost of providing housing).

Because rent controls hold rents below the free market return on capital, public housing supplied at controlled rents must be run at a loss. If the gap between the amount supplied from the private sector and the total amount demanded at the controlled price is large, the burden on the public purse strings may become unacceptable. Few governments in Canada and few authorities elsehere in the world have been willing to pay the enormous costs of providing subsidized public housing to remove fully the shortage created by their own effective controls. Thus the shortage continues, in spite of some efforts to construct public housing. The ones who gain are those who are lucky enough to obtain public housing; the ones who lose are the growing numbers of

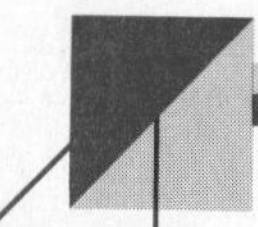

BOX 6-1

Rent Controls in Toronto

The province of Ontario has had some rent controls since 1975. In 1984 these controls were extended to cover all rental units, including high-priced rental properties. Since that time, construction of properties for rental accommodations has dwindled and the housing shortage has become chronic in a number of expanding Ontario cities, especially Toronto.

As the demand for rental accommodations grew while controls held rents down, the gap between demand and supply grew, as did the difference between the controlled rental prices and the prices that would have ruled on the free market. This difference created a valuable asset. For example, if you only have to pay $400 per month for an apartment that would rent on the free market for $700 per month, you have $300 of value per month that you do not pay for.

Naturally, people scramble to appropriate such values. *Key money*—the price charged by landlords to gain access to a rent-controlled flat—became prevalent, and the press reported payments running into many thousands of dollars. (Such lump-sum payments are most burdensome on the low-income persons that the rent control policy is supposed to be aiding.) Subletting became common: A tenant pays the landlord the controlled rent and then sublets at the market rent. This is the worst of both worlds as analyzed in Figure 6-3: The supplier gets the controlled price and hence supplies only a small quantity, while the ultimate user pays the market price, which, because of the control-induced shortage, is higher than the uncontrolled free market price would have been. The gain goes to the tenant who is subletting. It serves no allocative purpose since that person is responsible neither for maintaining the existing building nor for erecting new ones.

The growing housing shortage leads to more and more frantic searches for the available space. A feature article in the *Toronto Star* told of searches involving bribing caretakers, hunting through obituary columns, and finding elderly tenants in the hope of being first on the scene when death makes a flat available. Younger people, particularly those in less skilled jobs, told of landlord preferences for middle-aged, middle-class tenants holding white-collar jobs and earning higher incomes—a predictable allocation by sellers' preferences that tended to discriminate against some of the very groups the policy was supposed to help.

None of these events is a surprise to anyone who has studied the effects of rent controls elsewhere in the world. They are the all-too-predictable consequences of the system. City and provincial politicians and many other rent control advocates, however, express surprise at these events—being understandably unwilling to accept the responsibility that they actually bear for them. Efforts continue to be made to avoid the worst effects that have occurred elsewhere, but as long as rents are held below their long-term market equilibrium level—and there would be no point in having controls otherwise—the consequences analyzed in this chapter will continue to be felt.

those who are not lucky enough to have rent-controlled accommodations or accommodations in subsidized public housing. They are worse off than they would have been under free market conditions.

3. Housing vouchers. A third alternative is for the government to subsidize the housing of citizens who are less well off by providing them with housing vouchers. These would be used to pay rent to a stated value and would be redeemable by landlords in cash paid by the government. Under this scheme taxpayers would be subsidizing the rentals of those who receive the vouchers.

The scheme has the advantage of targeting the expenditures toward those who are judged to be in need. Comprehensive rent controls seek to help the less well off by benefiting all tenants, many of whom are themselves well off. The voucher scheme allows

BOX 6-2

Security of Tenure Through the Economic or the Political Marketplace?

A young couple starting out in life with average income expectations faces a major choice: to rent or to buy their housing. If the couple buys a house, they will have to meet large mortgage payments that will seriously reduce the income they have available to spend on all other items of consumption. In return, they get two important benefits. First, they will gain if they live in an expanding area where the value of their house increases. Second, once their mortgage is paid off, they get security of tenure in their own home for life.

This decision is typical of the many trade-offs between present and future consumption that people face throughout life. Those who save have less to consume now but more later. In comparison, those who do not save but instead consume more now will have to consume less later in life.

If the couple decides to rent, they will have much more money for nonhousing expenditures for the present. However, they will have nothing to gain from increases in local housing values, and they will have no security of tenure. If they are lucky, their city will not grow greatly, and housing and rental costs will stay relatively stable over their lifetimes. If they are unlucky, their city will expand greatly and they will face rapidly rising rents. If this happens later in their lifetimes, they may find themselves evicted from areas where they have lived for decades because they can no longer afford to pay the market price of residing there. This has happened in recent years, for example, to renters in the Kerrisdale district of Vancouver.

When rapid growth of an area causes those who elected to consume more early in life to face rapidly rising rents later in life, they often turn to the political arena to obtain the security of tenure they were unwilling to pay for earlier in life. They petition city hall or the provincial legislature to institute controls to hold rents to levels that they can afford. If they succeed, they have managed to have their cake and eat it too. They had higher living standards when they were young, because they chose to rent, and they get security of tenure at low prices later in life, because of rent controls.

The problem with this solution is that only the first generation of renters gains unambiguously. Later generations will find rental accommodations increasingly hard to find as effective controls reduce the supply of rental housing.

Economics cannot pronounce on the morality of government intervention designed to shield some persons from the consequences of economic decisions that they made earlier in their lives. It can, however, analyze the consequences of doing so. Such intervention is never without economic costs. Those who are given their housing cake through rent controls, having chosen to eat it first by renting rather than buying, gain at the cost of others: landlords, who receive lower rents; the city, which suffers all the consequences of a shrinking supply of rental housing; and future generations of would-be renters, who cannot find sufficient rental accommodations at any price.

the government to target only those whom it feels are really in need of help. The disadvantage, from the political point of view, is that taxpayers must pay the difference between the free market and subsidized rents. With rent controls, the government forces landlords to pay this difference, at least as long as they remain landlords. Rent controls thus transfer income from landlords to tenants at no cost to the government.

The choice. The government's desire to do something, or at least to be seen as trying to do something, while not spending a lot of money doing it may explain why the government usually selects the first alternative, makes only a small effort on the second, and does nothing on the third. Evidence from around the world suggests that relief from high rents is achieved in the short run at the cost of a severe lack of housing in the long run.

Providing rental accommodations has a definite resource cost. If rental housing is to be made available, the only question is who is to pay the cost. Under free market conditions, tenants pay, which is why investors are willing to go on supplying the rental accommodations. Under rent controls, investors are forced to pay some of the cost, which is why they are no longer willing to supply the same quantity of accommodations—so a housing shortage ensues. If the government wishes to avoid a housing shortage while having rent controls, it must fill the gap with public housing. Its tenants then pay a portion of the cost of their housing, but, insofar as the housing is rented below the free market rate, the taxpayers also pay a portion of this cost. The voucher scheme is cheaper, because in this scheme the taxpayers pay only the difference between the market rental and the subsidized rental and because the subsidy is paid only to those who are judged to be in need of it.

The costs of providing additional housing cannot be voted out of existence; these costs can be transferred only from one set of persons to another.

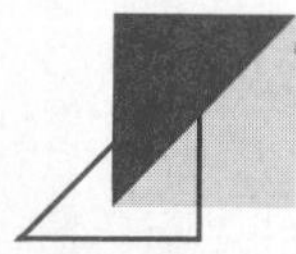

The Problems of Agriculture

When the price system operates freely in agricultural markets, it produces two persistent phenomena. The first is a long-run tendency for farm incomes to fall relative to urban incomes in spite of both an extremely rapid rise in agricultural productivity and a long-term shift of labor from the farms. This latter movement has been dramatic. In 1900 more than 40 percent of the Canadian labor force worked in agriculture, by 1930 it was down to 29 percent, and today it has fallen below 5 percent. The second is wide year-to-year fluctuations in prices, causing much uncertainty about farm income.

To deal with these two problems, governments throughout the Western world have tried a variety of techniques, including price supports, crop insurance, transportation and storage subsidies, and marketing boards. But each of these "solutions" seems to bring problems of its own, sometimes more serious than the original problems they were meant to solve.

Long-Term Trends

Agriculture's long-term problems arise from both the demand and the supply sides of agricultural markets.

Domestic demand. In the twentieth century, output per worker in all Canadian industries has increased at an average rate of almost 2 percent. Such increases in productivity have led to increases in Canadians' real incomes. How did they choose to consume their extra incomes?

The relevant measure is income elasticity of demand, which we studied in Chapter 5. At the levels of income prevailing in Canada and other advanced industrial nations over the past 50 years, most foodstuffs have low income elasticities because most people are already well fed. When people get extra income, they tend to spend much of it on consumer durables and on such services as entertainment and travel.

Income growth causes only a small increase in the demand for agricultural goods.

Large increases in the demand for agricultural goods depend on population growth because all new citizens must spend a significant proportion of their incomes on food.

Domestic supply. If productivity were expanding uniformly among industries, the demands for goods with low income elasticities would be expanding more slowly than output. In such industries, excess supplies would develop, prices and profits would be depressed, and resources would be induced to move elsewhere. Exactly the reverse would happen for industries producing goods with high income elasticities. Demands would expand faster than supplies, prices and profits would tend to rise, and resources would move into the industries producing these goods.

In fact, growth in agricultural productivity has

been well *above* the average for the economy. Encouraged by government-financed research, by subsidies, and by a government-ensured demand for farm output at relatively stable prices, agricultural productivity has increased enormously over the past century. Since 1947, for example, Canadian farm output per agricultural worker has grown at the rate of about 5 percent per year, about twice the rate of growth of total output per worker.

Rapid productivity increases have shifted the supply curves of agricultural goods rapidly to the right.

Export demand. The contribution of export markets to demand for domestic production has been variable over recent decades. Explosive growth of world population in the past half century has provided an expanding demand for foodstuffs, which, over much of the period, translated into a growing export market for North American produce. This tended to alleviate somewhat the domestic pressures just discussed. Throughout the 1970s, however, many less developed countries succeeded in dramatically increasing their own food production. The European agricultural supports turned the countries of the European Community into exporters of agricultural products rather than importers.

By the beginning of the 1980s, international developments tended to exacerbate the domestic problem of agricultural surpluses instead of alleviating it.

For example, the world price of wheat fell from its peak of $6 per bushel in 1981 to less than $3 in 1987. In real terms this is the lowest price of wheat in Canadian history, including the prices at the depth of the Great Depression of the 1930s.

Starting in 1987, however, world consumption of rice and grains began to rise slowly above world production. Accumulated stocks of past production fell slowly, and prices began to recover, although they are still far below the peaks reached in the early 1980s. If this trend continues, world demand will once again help domestic farmers to market their production at satisfactory prices.

Resource reallocation. We have seen that domestic and export demand has been increasing only slowly while supply has been increasing rapidly. If resources had not been reallocated out of farming, there would have been enormous increases in output, resulting in production that could hardly have been sold within Canada or exported at any price that would cover its costs.

Reallocations of resources in a free market economy result from the incentives of low prices, low wages, and depressed incomes in the declining sector and high prices, wages, and incomes in the expanding sector. But incentives of this kind prove painful—indeed, pain is the spur—to people who live and work on farms, especially when resources move slowly in response to market signals. It is one thing for the farmer's son or daughter to move to the city; it is quite another for the farmer and the farmer's parents, who are more set in their ways, to do so.

Notice that analogous problems arise in any industry where growth in demand is low but productivity growth is high. For example, the rapid rise in productivity in automobile production, combined with government subsidies to new auto plants, threatens to create severe excess capacity in the North American auto industry in the 1990s.

Short-Term Fluctuations

The second characteristic agricultural problem lies in the short-term price volatility typical of many agricultural markets. These short-term fluctuations occur mainly because farm crops are subject to variations in output due to factors completely beyond farmers' control. For example, pests, floods, and lack of rain can drastically reduce output, and exceptionally favorable conditions can cause production to exceed expectations. By now you should not be surprised to hear that such unplanned fluctuations in output cause fluctuations in farm prices. There are other, less obvious consequences that shed light on farmers' problems.

Fluctuating Supply with Inelastic Demand

The basic behavior is illustrated in Figure 6-6. Variations in farm output cause price fluctuations in the direction opposite to crop size. A bumper crop sends prices down; a small crop sends them up. The price change will be larger, the less elastic the demand curve.

FIGURE 6-6 The Effect on Price of Unplanned Variations in Output

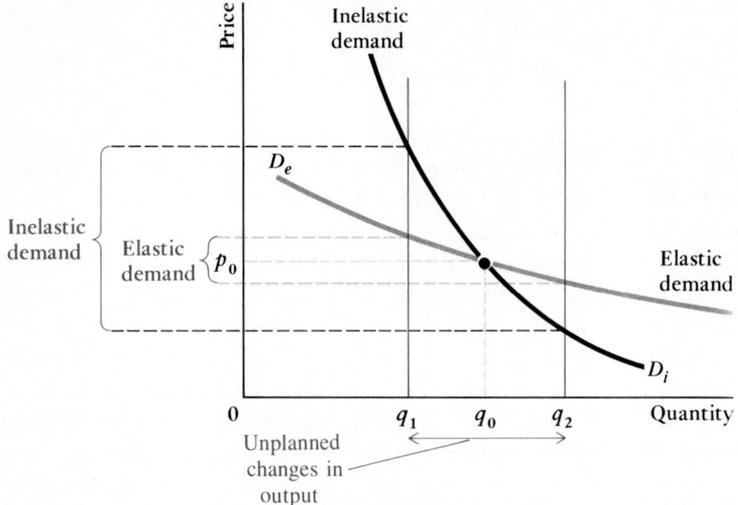

An unplanned fluctuation in output of a given size leads to a much sharper fluctuation in price when the demand curve is inelastic than when it is elastic. Suppose that the expected price is p_0 and the planned output is q_0. The two curves D_i and D_e are *alternative* demand curves. If actual production always equaled planned production, the equilibrium price and quantity would be p_0 and q_0 with either demand curve. Unplanned variations in output, however, cause quantity to fluctuate year by year between q_1 (a bad harvest) and q_2 (a good harvest). When demand is inelastic (shown by the black curve), prices will show large fluctuations. When demand is elastic (shown by the gray curve), price flucations will be much smaller.

Because farm products typically have inelastic demands, price fluctuations tend to be large in response to unplanned changes in production.

What are the effects on the receipts of farmers? If the commodity in question has an elastic demand, increases in the quantity supplied will raise farmers' receipts. If the demand is inelastic, increases in quantity supplied will reduce farmers' receipts.

Wherever demands are inelastic, good harvests will bring reductions in total farm receipts and bad harvests will bring increases.

Most farm products do have inelastic demands. When nature is bountiful and produces a bumper crop, farmers' receipts dwindle; when nature is moderately unkind and output falls unexpectedly, their receipts rise. The interests of the farmer and the consumer are exactly opposed in such cases.

Fluctuating Demand with Inelastic Supply

As the tide of business activity flows and ebbs, demand curves for all commodities rise and fall. The magnitude of the effects on prices and outputs depend on the elasticity of *supply*.

Industrial products typically have rather elastic supply curves, so shifts in demand cause fairly large changes in outputs but only small changes in prices, as Figure 6-7(i) illustrates. In contrast, agricultural commodities typically have rather inelastic supply curves because land, labor, and machinery devoted to agricultural uses is neither quickly transferred to nonagricultural uses when demand falls nor quickly returned to agriculture when demand rises. Given an inelastic supply curve for most agricultural products, farm prices, farm receipts, and farm income will be sensitive to demand shifts, as Figure 6-7(ii) illustrates. A sharp drop in demand (a leftward shift of the demand curve) will cause hardship among those whose income depends on farm crops.

Agricultural Stabilization in Theory

Governments throughout the world intervene in agricultural markets in attempts to stabilize agricultural prices and incomes in the face of short-term and uncontrollable fluctuations in supply and cyclical fluctuations in demand. We shall consider the eco-

FIGURE 6-7 The Effect on Receipts of a Decrease in Demand

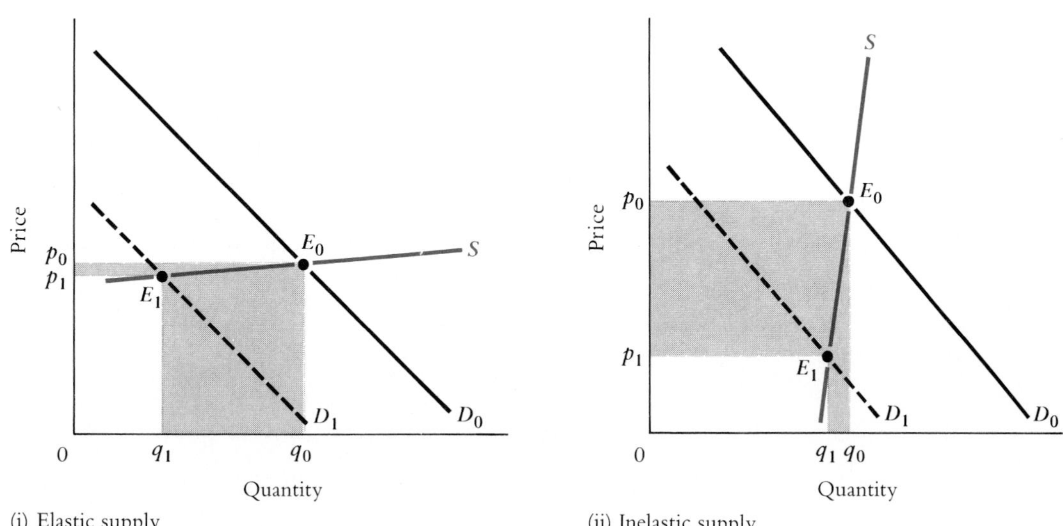

Both elastic and inelastic supply curves can lead to sharp decreases in receipts, but the effects on prices are very different in the two cases. In each part of the figure, when demand decreases from D_0 to D_1, price and quantity decrease to p_1 and q_1 and total receipts decline by the shaded area. In (i) the symptom is primarily the sharp decrease in quantity. Employment and total profits earned fall drastically, though wage rates and profit margins on what is produced may remain close to their former level. In (ii) the symptom is mainly the sharp decrease in price. Output and employment remain high, but the drastic fall in price will reduce or eliminate profits and put downward pressure on wages.

nomics of several of the most common types of schemes.

To start, assume that the supply curve in each case refers to planned (or average) production per year but that actual production fluctuates around that level. In a free market, as we have seen, this causes both prices and farmers' receipts to fluctuate widely from year to year.

We deal with two cases that are relevant to much of Canadian agriculture. In the first case, an agricultural product is produced mainly for export at prices that are determined on international markets. These prices are largely independent of the amount sold by domestic producers because these producers contribute only a small proportion of total world supply. (This is the case discussed in the first section of the Appendix to Chapter 4.) In the second case, an agricultural product is sold mainly on the domestic market, where the price is determined by domestic demand and supply because high transport costs or trade barriers keep out imports.

Exports at World Market Prices

When Canadian production is sold on world markets at prices largely beyond Canadian control, domestic producers face a perfectly elastic demand curve, indicating that they can sell all that they wish at the given world price. A government stabilization policy then faces two key problems: first, how to cope with short-term supply fluctuations at home and, second, how to react to fluctuations in world prices.

Output fluctuations at given world prices. Figure 6-8 illustrates fluctuations in domestic output. It considers sales over several years at a given world price. If the government does nothing in the face of supply fluctuations, farmers will find their incomes fluc-

FIGURE 6-8 Exports at a Given World Price

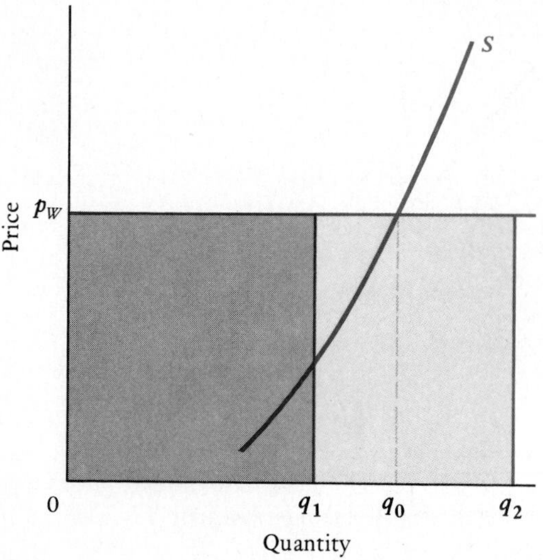

A country that exports only a small portion of the world's supply of some commodity faces a perfectly elastic demand because the world price is not affected by its own sales. The given world price is p_W. The domestic supply curve shows that intended output is q_0 at that price. Unintended fluctuations cause output to vary between q_1 and q_2. When output is at q_1, farm income is given by the dark shaded area. When output is q_2, farm income is given by the total of the light and the dark shaded areas.

tuating in the *same* direction as their outputs. In years of bumper crops, sales will rise, and price will not be driven down, so incomes will rise. In years of poor crops, sales will fall, but price will not rise, so incomes will fall.

Note the contrast with the case where demand is inelastic and farm incomes fluctuate in the direction *opposite* to output. In this case good harvests depress incomes and bad harvests raise them. However, the effect of selling on the international market and being only a small part of total world supply is to make the demand curve that domestic producers face perfectly elastic (even though the world demand curve is inelastic). This reverses the direction of income fluctuations.

When domestic farmers sell at a given world price that is unaffected by their own volume of sales, their incomes fluctuate in the same direction as their short-term fluctuations in output.

The incomes of farmers who produce nonperishable crops could be stabilized if the government developed a scheme allowing farmers to store their outputs in years of bumper crops and to sell from stocks in years of poor crops. Effectively, sales would always be equal to planned output. Any unplanned excess of production would be stored, and any shortfall would be made up out of sales from stocks. But storage costs money and postpones the receipt of revenue until the sales occur. An alternative would be to sell all the crop each year and then save the extra money received in good years to spend in bad years. This is something that farmers can do on their own without assistance from the government.

Fluctuations in world prices. When world prices fluctuate, it may pay to hold stocks. When the government judges that this year's price is unusually low, it can store some of the output in the hope of selling it later at a better price. When the government judges that this year's price is unusually high, it can sell some of the stocks that it put aside in years when the price was low.

In a world in which future prices were known with certainty, the government would merely calculate the extra revenue that could be obtained by selling at some future price higher than the present one and subtract the costs of storage to see if the crop should be sold now or held. In practice, the future is not known, and the government must use its knowledge of market conditions to guess its best policy. The government will be inclined to store a larger amount this year the more it expects prices to rise in future years and to sell more from stocks the more it expects prices to fall in future years. If the government is good at predicting the future state of the market, it will increase farmers' revenues by selling less when prices are low and more when prices are high, as compared with a policy of selling the whole crop each year. If the government's market predictions are wrong, however, the scheme can bring losses.

Sales on the Domestic Market Only

What of commodities that are sold mainly on the domestic market where the main supply comes from domestic production? The difference between this case and the one just considered is that the demand curve facing domestic producers is now negatively sloped and typically inelastic. The analysis of Figure 6-6 now applies, so farm income will fluctuate in the direction opposite to output. Can farm income be stabilized in this case?

Price stabilization. Suppose that the government enters the market, buying and thereby adding to its own stocks when there is a surplus, and selling and thereby reducing its stocks when there is a shortage. If it had enough grain elevators and warehouses, and if its support price were set at a realistic level, the government could stabilize *prices* indefinitely. But this would not stabilize farmers' revenues, which would be high with bumper crops and low with poor crops.

In effect, the government policy imposes a demand curve that is perfectly elastic at the support price. The situation is then analogous to the one analyzed in Figure 6-8: The product can be sold at a given world price, and income fluctuates in the same direction as output.

Government price supports at the equilibrium price would not stabilize revenues. They would, however, reverse the pattern of revenue fluctuation.

Revenue stabilization. Obviously, there must be a government buying and selling policy that will stabilize farmers' receipts. What are its characteristics? As has been seen, too much price stability causes receipts to vary directly with production, and too little price stability causes receipts to vary inversely with production. It appears that the government should aim at some intermediate degree of price stability. If the government allows prices to vary in inverse proportion to variations in production, receipts will be stabilized. A 10 percent rise in production should be met by a 10 percent fall in price, and a 10 percent fall in production by a 10 percent rise in price.

To stabilize farmers' receipts, the government must make the demand curve unit elastic. It must buy in periods of high output and sell in periods of low output, but only enough to let prices change in inverse proportion to farmers' output.

Long-term effects. In practice, stabilization plans, whether they seek to fix prices completely or merely to dampen free market fluctuations, often seek to set an averge price *above* the average free market equilibrium level. This is due to the fact that stabilization is not the only goal; there is also a desire to assure farmers of a standard of living comparable with that of city dwellers. This involves attempting to *raise* farm incomes in addition to stabilizing them.

Here, too, the government buys in periods of high output and sells in periods of low output, but on average it buys much more than it sells, with the result that unsold surpluses accumulate (see Figure 6-9). Taxpayers will generally be paying farmers for producing goods that no one is willing to purchase, at least at prices that come near to covering costs.

This is the route taken by the European Community (EC) with its Common Agricultural Policy (CAP). This policy has supported the existing farm population of Europe by guaranteeing stable, high prices. It has also meant that Western Europe has changed from being a net importer of agricultural

FIGURE 6-9 Price Supports Above the Equilibrium Price

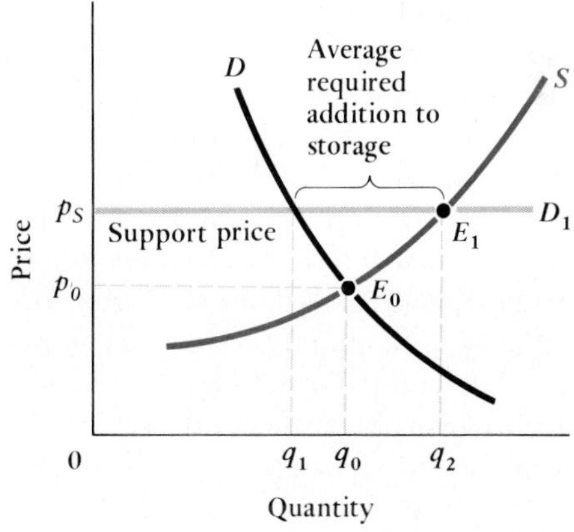

The support price becomes a price floor, and the government must purchase the excess supply at that price. Average annual demand and supply are D and S, respectively. The free market equilibrium is at E_0. If the government will buy any quantity at p_S, the demand curve becomes the gray curve D_1 and equilibrium shifts to E_1. The average addition to storage is the quantity q_1q_2. The government purchases add to farmers' receipts and to government expenditures.

products—which it had been for over a century and would still be under free market determination—into a net exporter. As a result of the CAP, the EC is now faced with mounting stockpiles of many agricultural products. Periodically, it seeks to sell some of the surpluses to outside countries, particularly those in Eastern Europe, charging prices well below the costs of production. The net result is that taxpayers in Western Europe are subsidizing consumers in Eastern Europe by allowing them to buy goods at prices much below their cost of production. Payments under the CAP now account for over half of the EC's entire budget, and concern is mounting that the ever-growing payments to farmers may soon outrun the EC's ability to pay.

FIGURE 6-10 Price Support Through the Use of Quotas

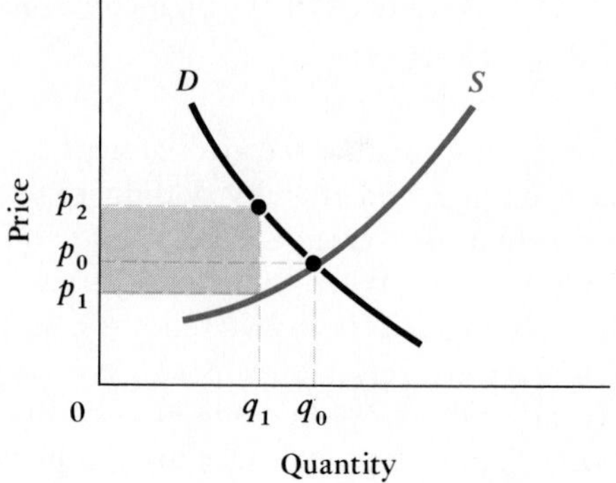

A quota below the equilibrium quantity maintains the price above the equilibrium level without generating surpluses. If a total quota of q_1 is enforced, the price will rise to p_2. Since the supply curve indicates that in a free market producers would be willing to supply q_1 at a lower price p_1, the effect is to provide holders of quotas with additional revenues, represented by the shaded area.

Government quotas. Another way of holding the price above its free market equilibrium level is to reduce the supply through quotas. Under this system, no one can produce the product without having a government-issued quota. Sufficient quotas are issued to hold production at any desired level below the free market output. This drives prices above their free market level. This quota system, which is analyzed in Figure 6-10, has the advantage of not causing the accumulation of massive unsold surpluses. It is widely used in Canada.

The quota system affects both the short-term and the long-term behavior of agricultural markets. Consider short-term fluctuations first. There will still be good crops and poor crops, and other natural disturbances such as outbreaks of disease, that will cause short-term fluctuations in output. A shortfall of output below the quota will drive price upward. Farmers with no crop to sell will lose, but farmers whose outputs fall proportionally less than the price rise will gain. Since most agricultural products have inelastic demands, the typical farmer must gain—the percentage increase in market price will exceed the percentage fall in the aggregate crop.

What about unplanned extra output due to favorable conditions? The farmer is allowed to sell only the amount covered by the quota. The rest must be either destroyed or sold on some secondary market not covered by the quota system. Farm income is stabilized. The quota output is sold at the market price for that output even when there is surplus output (and the rest goes for what it can get). Given that demand is typically inelastic, without quotas the free market price would fall by a larger percentage than output would rise, and producers' incomes would shrink drastically.

A quota system guarantees that farmers will get the free market price of the total quota output when output equals or exceeds the quota and more when output falls short of the quota.

Thus the quota system is superior to many of the systems mentioned earlier in that it really does remove the downside risks caused by unexpected increases in output, and unlike the CAP, it does not lead to accumulating stockpiles of unsold output. The main cost is met by consumers, who on average pay a price that is higher, and consume an output that is lower, than would occur under free market conditions.

Now consider the long term. We have seen that the quota drives price above its free market level by restricting output. For purposes of illustration let us suppose that the quota is for eggs. Those who are producing eggs when the quota system is first instituted must gain. Since production falls, total costs must fall; since demand is inelastic, total revenue must rise. Therefore, egg producers find their profits rising, since they spend less to earn more revenue. No wonder quotas are popular among the original producers!

But do quotas really increase farm income in the long run? Because people leave the industry for such reasons as death and retirement and new people must enter to replace them, the quotas are made transferable. Existing holders can transfer their quotas to new would-be egg producers. But the quota is valuable since it confers the right to produce eggs that earn a large profit as a result of the supply restriction. Therefore, the quota commands a price. The price turns out to be the value of the extra profits that the quota system has produced.[3] The reasons why this is so are spelled out in detail in Chapter 12, where we consider entry into a competitive industry. But to show the common sense of the result now, we argue as follows.

People have alternative ways of investing their money. For example, someone with money to invest could buy an egg farm, a small factory, a share in a large corporation, or a government bond. When returns are relatively high in one line of activity, people will rush to invest funds in it; when returns are relatively low, people will be reluctant to invest in that activity. This search by investors for the most profitable use for their funds tends to force equality in the rates of return in alternative investments that are open to investors (making due allowances for differences in risk).

When the quota system makes production of eggs unusually profitable, there will be a rush to invest in egg production. But to produce eggs one must have a quota. The result is that the rush to enter the egg industry will bid up the price of the egg quota until egg production is no more profitable than other investments with similar risks.

The free market price of a quota to produce some good will be such that the profitability of that good's production will, after deducting the cost of the quota, be no more than the profitability of other lines of activity carrying similar risks.

In other words, the whole extra profitability created by the quota system becomes embodied in the price of the quota. The extra profits created by the quota will just provide an acceptable return on the money invested in buying the quota—if it provided more, the price of the quota would be bid up; if it provided less, the price of the quota would fall.

For this reason, new entrants to the industry will earn no more than the return available in other lines of production. Since that would also be the case under market-determined prices and outputs, the quota does not raise the profitability of producing eggs. What it does do is reduce some of the uncertainty due to unexpected short-term fluctuations of output. Farming becomes a somewhat less risky operation than before.

One other long-run effect must be mentioned. If demand keeps rising after the new producer has bought a quota while the number of quotas is not increased correspondingly, profitability of egg production will rise. Producers will sell the same amount of eggs at a higher price. As a result, the market price of a quota will rise. Thus all producers who bought their quotas before the demand rise was foreseen will gain from an increase in quota prices. They will find that when they come to retire, they can sell out for more than they paid to buy in. This is the typical case in most real-world quota systems, and it gives existing producers, even those who bought in recently, some long-term gain from the system—once again bought at the expense of consumers, who pay more for their eggs than under a free market system. It thus also gives those producers an incentive to fight to preserve the quota system.

Economics alone cannot tell us whether such a system is good or bad. What it can do is show us who will gain and who will lose and also which alleged sources of gain are effective and which are illusory.

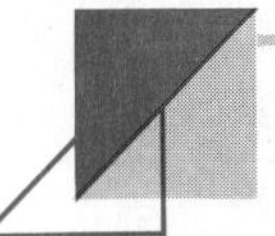

Agricultural Policy in Canada

The main tools of agricultural stabilization in Canada are marketing boards and income supplement pro-

[3] The profits are an ongoing flow that will come to the farmer every year, whereas the price paid for the quota is a once-and-for-all payment. In Chapter 18 we will see how to calculate what is called the *discounted present value* of a flow of future receipts. This is what determines the exact price of the quota. In principle, it is the value to someone today of the claim to the flow of profits that will be received over the future.

grams. Sales through marketing boards account for about half of all farm cash receipts.

Marketing Boards

Basically there are two types of government marketing boards. The first seeks to influence prices by controlling supply. The second accepts prices and acts as a selling agency for producers.

Supply Management

The supply management schemes typically are provincially administered systems that restrict output through quotas issued by provincial marketing boards. They vary from province to province but often cover milk, eggs, cheese, butter, and poultry. The monopoly profits created by these schemes are enormous and can be accurately measured by the prices farmers must pay to purchase quotas. For example, it currently costs $1 million to buy the minimum-size quota needed to operate one family-sized chicken farm in Ontario, and it costs $3 million to buy the quota needed to operate an average-size dairy farm in the Fraser Valley.

All such supply management schemes require federal cooperation to limit imports. Otherwise, the high prices brought about by the restriction of domestic supply would attract a flood of imports. Imports are limited by issuing import quotas. Those who are lucky enough to obtain these quotas, usually the large food companies, can buy at cheap international prices and sell at high domestic prices, thereby reaping large gains, once again at the expense of consumers.

Schemes of this type, analyzed in Figure 6-10, are successful in reducing short-term fluctuations. However, they also greatly increase the cost of becoming a producer because a quota must be purchased in addition to the physical capital needed for production. The schemes are popular among farmers because they reduce risk in the short term and because the value of the quotas often rises over the long term. The gains to farmers and food importers is paid for by consumers in the form of higher prices.

Recently two other important effects of supply management systems have become apparent. First, they harm Canadian manufacturers of food products. Canadian firms producing frozen and canned foods must buy expensive Canadian produce, whereas their foreign competitors can buy their raw foodstuffs at the lower world prices. Second, they reduce competition among users of agricultural products. For example, to allocate scarce supplies of milk, the Fraser Valley Milk Marketing Board channels supplies to selected users of raw milk. These milk processors have no incentive to compete for market share or to introduce new products because a successful competitor could not get the larger supplies of raw milk needed to increase sales.

The persistence of these schemes is evidence of the political power of the small number of well-organized producers who gain from them and of the relative lack of political power of the large number of organized consumers and food producers, who foot the bill. The effect on consumers has been attested by the rising amount of cross-border shopping—Canadian consumers are willing to travel long distances to gain the benefit of low foreign prices of foodstuffs. Canadian producers have sought to maintain their monopoly positions by persuading the Canadian government to stop cross-border shopping, forcing Canadian consumers to buy at the higher Canadian prices.

Orderly Marketing Schemes

The prime example of an orderly marketing scheme is the Canadian Wheat Board, which markets Canadian wheat at prices set on the world wheat market. Canada has a long history of government involvement in marketing wheat, dating back at least to the early 1900s. The Wheat Board was established under the Canadian Wheat Board Act (1935). Each year the board estimates the average price at which it expects the wheat crop to be sold. Seventy-five percent of that price is then paid to each farmer on delivery of the wheat. After the board sells the wheat, any proceeds in excess of the initial payments are distributed to the producers in proportion to the amount of wheat supplied by each.

The goals of the Wheat Board are not to influence world prices. Instead, by paying farmers 75 percent of the estimated average selling price over the year, the board provides farmers with a secure cash flow early in the selling period. The board also serves to secure farmers' incomes aginst intra-year fluctuations in wheat prices. It does this by pooling all of its receipts and paying them out to farmers according to the amount of wheat delivered by each farmer but irrespective of the date within the year of that delivery. So the farmer is relieved of worry about what the spot price of wheat may be on the day of delivery.

These functions of the board appear to be in the farmers' interests and not to be disadvantageous to consumers. Most farmers approve of the annual averaging of receipts, most find the information provided by an early estimate of this year's price useful, and most like the early cash flow of 75 percent of the estimated selling price provided on delivery.

Income Supplements

As market conditions for grain deteriorated during the 1980s, the Canadian government provided substantial, and rising, support to maintain farmers' incomes. Federal direct assistance to farmers, mainly those in grain production, rose from $2.8 billion in 1983 to over $6 billion in 1988! (This is about $500 for every Canadian household.)

The result of this assistance is that in spite of deteriorating world market conditions, net farm income rose every year in the 1980s. In 1981 this income was $3.8 billion, of which 94.5 percent came from sales revenue and 5.5 percent from direct government assistance. By 1988 farm income had risen to $5.2 billion, of which just over 17 percent came from government assistance.

In spite of this, many farmers were still experiencing financial difficulties, partly as a result of heavy borrowing and overinvestment in the face of what turned out to be temporary boom conditions in the 1970s. The Economic Council of Canada estimated that in 1988 some 25 percent of all farmers faced financial difficulties, and 10 percent of all farmers were considered "nonviable" because their incomes (including federal assistance) fell short of their expenses.

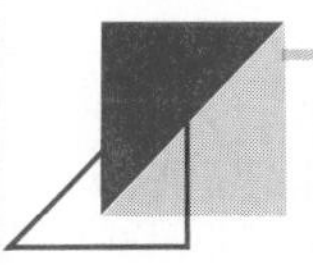

Conclusion: General Lessons About the Price System

We have examined examples of government intervention in markets that might have been left unregulated. Our discussion suggests four widely applicable lessons.

1. Costs May Be Shifted, but They Cannot Be Avoided

Production, whether in response to free market signals or to government controls, uses resources; thus it involves costs to members of society. If it takes 5 percent of the nation's resources to provide housing at some stated average standard, those resources will not be available to produce other commodities. If resources are used to produce unwanted food products, those resources will not be available to produce other commodities. For society there is no such thing as free housing or free food.

The average standard of living depends on the amount of resources available to the economy and the efficiency with which these resources are used. It follows that *costs are real* and are incurred no matter who provides the goods. Rent controls or subsidies to agriculture can change the share of the costs paid by particular individuals or groups, lowering the share for some and raising the share for others, but they cannot make the costs go away.

Different ways of *allocating* the costs may also affect the total amount of resources used and thus the amount of costs incurred. For example, controls that keep prices and profits of some commodity below free market levels will lead to increased quantities demanded and decreased quantities supplied. Unless government steps in to provide additional supplies, fewer resources will be allocated to producing the commodity. If government chooses to supply all the demand at the controlled prices, more resources will be allocated to it, which means that fewer resources will be devoted to other kinds of goods and services.

2. Free Market Prices and Profits Encourage Economical Use of Resources

Prices and profits in a market economy provide signals to both demanders and suppliers. Prices that are high and rising (relative to other prices) provide an incentive to purchasers to economize on the commodity. They may choose to satisfy the want in question with substitutes whose prices have not risen so much (because they are less costly to provide) or to satisfy less of that want by shifting expenditure to the satisfaction of other wants.

On the supply side, rising prices tend to produce rising profits. High profits attract further resources into production. Short-term profits that bear no relation to current costs repeatedly occur in market economies. They cause resources to move into industries with profits until profits fall to levels that are earned elsewhere in the economy.

Falling prices and falling profits provide the opposite motivations. Purchasers are inclined to buy more; sellers are inclined to produce less and to move resources out of the industry and into more profitable undertakings.

The price system responds to need for change in the allocation of resources, say, in response to an external event such as the loss of a source of a raw material or the outbreak of a war. Changing relative prices and profits signal the need for change to which consumers and producers respond.

3. Government Intervention Affects Resource Allocation

Governments intervene in the price system sometimes to satisfy generally agreed social goals and sometimes to help politically influential interest groups. Government intervention changes the allocation of resources that the price system would achieve.

Interventions have allocative consequences because they inhibit the free market allocative mechanism. Some controls, such as rent controls, prevent prices from rising (in response, say, to an increase in demand with no change in supply). If the price is held down, the signal is not given to consumers to economize on a commodity that is in short supply. On the supply side, when prices and profits are prevented from rising, the profit signals that would attract new resources into the industry are never given. The shortage continues, and the movements of demand and supply that would remove it are not set in motion.

Other controls, such as agricultural price supports, prevent prices from falling (in response, say, to an increase in supply with no increase in demand). This leads to excess supply, and the signal is not given to producers to produce less or to buyers to increase their purchases. Surpluses continue, and the movements of demand and supply that would eliminate them are not set in motion.

4. Intervention Requires Alternative Allocative Mechanisms

Intervention typically requires alternative allocative mechanisms. During times of shortages, allocation will be by sellers' preferences, by first-come, first-served, or by some system of government rationing. During periods of surplus, there will be unsold supplies unless the government buys and stores the surpluses. Since long-run changes in demand and costs do not induce resource reallocations through private decisions, the government will have to step in. It will have to force resources out of industries where prices are held too high, as it has tried to do in agriculture, and into industries where prices are held too low, as it can do, for example, by providing public housing.

Intervention almost always has both benefits and costs. Economics cannot answer the question of whether a particular intervention with free markets is desirable, but it can clarify the issues by identifying benefits and costs and who will enjoy or bear them. In doing so it can identify the competing values involved. This will be discussed in detail in Chapter 22.

SUMMARY

1. The elementary theory of supply, demand, and price provides powerful tools for analyzing and understanding some real-world problems and policies.
2. Effective price floors lead to excess supply. Either the potential seller is left with quantities that cannot be sold, or the government must step in and buy the surplus. Effective price ceilings lead to excess demand and provide a strong incentive for black marketeers to buy at the controlled price and sell at the higher free market price.

3. Rent controls are a form of price ceiling. The major consequence of effective rent control is a shortge of rental accommodations that gets worse due to a slow but inexorable decline in the quantity of rental housing.
4. Rent controls can be an effective response to temporary situations in which there is a ban on building or a transitory increase in demand. They will almost surely fail if they are introduced as a response to a long-run increase in demand or to inflation in the costs of providing rental housing.
5. The long-term problems of agriculture arise from a high rate of productivity growth on the supply side and a low income elasticity on the demand side. This means that unless many resources are being transferred out of agriculture, quantity supplied increases faster than quantity demanded year after year.
6. Many agricultural prices and incomes are depressed by chronic surpluses in agricultural markets. At various times and places, government policies to protect farm incomes have included buying farmers' output at above free market prices, and limiting production and acreage by quotas. Such policies tend to inhibit the reallocation mechanism and thus to increase farm surpluses above what they would otherwise be and lead to accumulating stocks.
7. Agricultural commodities are subject to wide fluctuations in market prices, which cause fluctuations in producers' incomes. This is because of year-to-year unplanned fluctuations in supplies combined with inelastic demand and because of cyclical fluctuations in demand combined with inelastic supplies. Where demand is inelastic, large crops tend to be associated with low total receipts and small crops with high total receipts.
8. Canadian agricultural stabilization policies operate in two types of markets. In the first, which covers products such as wheat, the bulk of production is exported at prices set in world markets. In this case there is little that the government can usefully do to stabilize prices or to insulate revenues from fluctuating in response to unplanned fluctuations in output. The government can, however, seek to mitigate fluctuations in revenue that stem from fluctuations in world prices. This is done by storing some of the crop when prices are thought to be unusually low and selling out of stocks when prices are thought to be unusually high.
9. In the second type of market, which includes many products such as milk, eggs, cheese, and chickens, the product is sold in a domestic market that is protected from foreign competition either by natural factors or by government restrictions on imports. This is the case with most provincial supply management schemes. These seek to reduce output by issuing quotas. The effect is that price is not driven down when there is an unplanned increase in supply (because the extra output cannot be sold in the market covered by the quota scheme), and thus actual price exceeds the free market equilibrium price. Farmers gain by the reduction in short-term price fluctuations and by any increase in the values of their quotas after they have purchased them. Since the quota price reflects the additional profits brought about by supply restriction, new entrants into the industry do not earn higher returns on their investments than they could earn in other lines bearing similar risks or that they would have earned if the good were produced under free market conditions.

TOPICS FOR REVIEW

Price floor and price ceiling
Allocation by sellers' preferences, rationing, and black market
The allocative function of profits
Short-run and long-run supply curves
Effects of high productivity growth and low income elasticity
Importance of export demand
Price supports at and above the level of free market equilibrium
Supply management in domestic markets

DISCUSSION QUESTIONS

1. "When a controlled item is vital to everyone, it is easier to start controlling the price than to stop controlling it. Such controls are popular with consumers, regardless of their harmful consequences." Explain why it may be inefficient to have such controls, why they may be popular, and why, if they are popular, the government might nevertheless choose to decontrol these prices.
2. Discuss the following statements about the housing problem in Vancouver.
   a. "Zoning laws that require that most of Vancouver be restricted to single-family dwellings reflect the exploitation of the poor by the middle class."
   b. "The world is awash with agricultural surpluses while land-starved Vancouver is prevented from spreading into much of the adjacent Fraser Valley by government 'land banks' designed to preserve agricultural land from urbanization."
   c. "More than 40 percent of all rented apartments in Vancouver are illegal and would not be permitted if their owners applied for permission to rent their space legally."
3. It is sometimes asserted that the rising costs of construction are putting housing out of the reach of ordinary citizens. Who bears the heaviest cost when rents are kept down by (a) rent controls, (b) a subsidy to tenants equal to some fraction of their rent payments, and (c) low-cost public housing?
4. Discuss the following excerpt from a story that appeared in the *Toronto Star* in October 1986. Toronto landlord Lawrence Smither "says he won't rent his empty apartments until the [Rent Control] Commission gives him permission to charge $400.40 for all his two-bedroom units. Rent review officer Robert Sutherland agrees $400.40 is a 'reasonable rent' for those units, but he says the Commission won't give Smither permission to charge higher rents because they would exceed the allowable annual rent increases."
5. Recently several Liberal and Conservative Ontario politicians were quoted as saying that they did not intend to keep their provinces' rent controls indefinitely; they went on to say that controls would be removed as soon as the vacancy rate for apartments rose to reasonable levels, signaling an end to the housing crisis. Given this condition for their removal, how long would you expect rent controls to persist?
6. "This year the weather smiled on us, God smiled on us, and we made a crop," says Don Marble, a grain and cotton farmer in South Plains, Texas. "But just as we made a crop, the economic situation changed." This quotation brings to mind the old saying, "If you

are a farmer, the weather is always bad." Discuss the sense in which this saying might be true.

7. The Kenya Meat Commission (KMC) decided that it was undemocratic to allow meat prices to be out of the reach of the ordinary citizen. It decided to freeze meat prices. Six months later, in a press interview, the managing commissioner of the KMC made the following statements. Do the facts alleged make sense, given the KMC's policy?

a. "The price of amost everything in Kenya has gone up, but we have not increased the price of meat. The price of meat in this country is still the lowest in the world."

b. "Cattle are scarce in the country, but I do not know why."

c. "People are eating too much beef, and unless they diversify their eating habits and eat other foodstuffs, the shortage of beef will continue."

8. Discuss the following statement by University of Saskatchewan professor of agricultural economics Gary Storey. "One of the sad truths of the agricultural policies in Europe and the United States is that they do very little for the future generations of farmers. Most of the subsidies get capitalized into higher land prices, creating [large] gains for current landowners (i.e., gains that they neither expected nor did anything to earn). It creates a situation where the next generation of farmers require, and ask for, increased government support."

9. Compare the following two headlines that appeared within a week of each other.

a. "Bumper potato crop dashes farmers' hopes."

b. "Record high wheat crop leaves farmers smiling."

10. Discuss the following two statements. Do you see a relation between them?

a. "The current financial crisis is so large that it may be beyond the fiscal capability of governments to solve by subsidies and public assistance. Government assistance has not been able to prevent farm financial problems."—George Brinkman, professor of agricultural economics, University of Guelph

b. "Ironically, the industry is a victim of its own success. Programs [to increase agricultural production in many countries in the 1970s] were so successful that the world is now awash with surplus food. There are mountains of grain, cheese, and beef in storage around the world, and lakes of milk, wine, and olive oil."—Oliver Bertin, journalist

11. Discuss the following recent headlines in terms of the analysis of this chapter.

a. "Huge grain stockpiles blunt price upturn, economist says."

b. "Farm children plan for careers off the family land."

c. "Subsidies for farmers may be intractable dilemma."

d. "If wheat prices fall, so do land prices."

12. Why do you think farmers get government assistance in the face of poor market conditions when producers in other industries are left to sink or swim on their own resources? Is this desirable? Is it equitable?

PART 3

CONSUMPTION, PRODUCTION, AND COST

Chapter 7

Household Consumption Behavior

In Part 2 we saw that demand is an important part of the explanation of market prices and that the shapes of demand curves influence how markets behave. Why do market demand curves have the shapes they do? To address this question, we need to study the behavior of individual households, since that behavior underlies market demand curves.

We start by studying the choices faced by every household that has money to spend and that desires to purchase certain commodities. Later in the chapter we develop theories of how households make their choices.

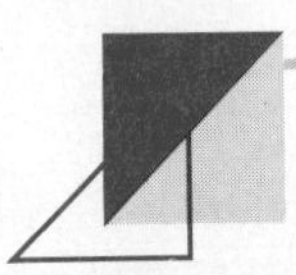

The Choices Households Face

To begin, we reduce the problem to its basics by considering a household that has a specific income that it can spend on just two commodities—food and clothing. (Simplifying the problem by considering only two commodities allows us to see the essential points more easily.) Suppose that the household has a money income of \$360 per week and that the prices for food and clothing are \$12 per unit for food and \$6 per unit for clothing. For the purpose of our example, further suppose that the household does not save; its only choice is in deciding how much of its \$360 to spend on food (F) and how much to spend on clothing (C).

The Budget Line

The household's alternatives are described by the solid line *ab* in Figure 7-1. That line, called a **budget line**, shows all the combinations of food and clothing that the household can buy if it spends a fixed amount of money, in this case all its income, at fixed prices of the commodities. (It is also sometimes called an *isocost line*, since all points on it represent bundles of goods with the same total cost.)

The budget line is given by the equation

$$E = P_F F + P_C C$$

where E is money income, P_F and P_C are the money prices of food and clothing, and F and C are the quantities of food and clothing chosen. It has several important properties.

1. Points on the budget line indicate bundles of commodities that use up the household's entire income. (Try, for example, the point $20C$, $20F$.)

2. Points between the budget line and the origin indicate bundles of commodities that cost less than the household's income. (Try, for example, the point 20*C*, 10*F*.)
3. Points above the budget line indicate combinations of commodities that cost more than the houshold's income. (Try, for example, the point 30*C*, 40*F*.)

The budget line shows all combinations of commodities that are available to the household given its money income and the prices of the goods that it purchases.

FIGURE 7-1 A Budget Line

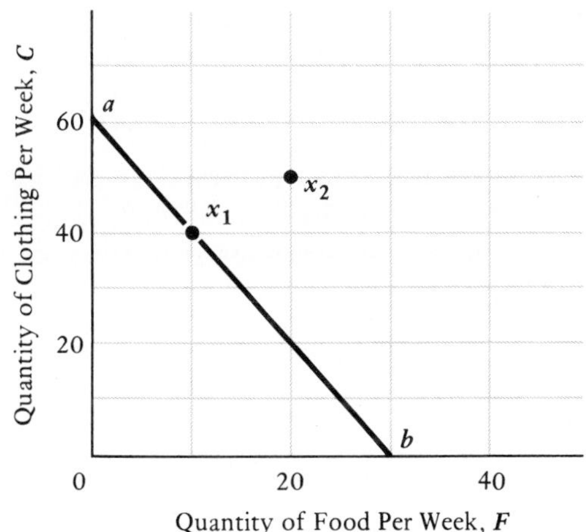

The budget line shows the quantities of goods available to a household given its money income and the prices of goods it buys. Any point in this diagram indicates a combination (or bundle) of so much food and so much clothing. Point x_1, for example, indicates 40 units of clothing and 10 units of food per week.

With an income of $360 a week and prices of $12 per unit for food and $6 per unit for clothing, the household's budget line is *ab*. This line shows all the combinations of *F* and *C* available to a household spending this income at these prices. The household could spend all of its money income on clothing and obtain 60 units of clothing and zero food each week. It could likewise go to the other extreme and purchase only food, buying 30 units of *F* and zero units of *C*. It could also choose an intermediate position and consume some of both goods; for example, it could spend $120 to buy 10 units of *F* and $240 to buy 40 units of *C* (point x_1). Points above the budget line, such as x_2, are not attainable.

Shifts in the Budget Line

Recall from Chapter 4 that the *absolute*, or *money*, price of a commodity is the amount of money that must be spent to acquire one unit of the commodity. We contrasted this with the *relative* price of the commodity, which is the ratio of its absolute price to the absolute price of some other commodity or group of commodities.

We now encounter a similar distinction for income. A household's **money income** is its income measured in monetary units per period of time—so many dollars per week or per year. A household's **real income** is the *purchasing power* of its money income; it is the quantity of goods and services that can be purchased with that money income. The next few paragraphs show this important distinction in terms of the budget line.

Changes in Money Income

What happens to the budget line when money income changes? If the household's money income is halved from $360 to $180 per week, while money prices remain unchanged at $12 per unit for food and $6 per unit for clothing, the amount of goods that the household can buy will also be halved. This causes the budget line to shift inward toward the origin, as shown in Figure 7-2. All possible combinations that are now open to the household appear on budget line *cd*, which is closer to the origin than the original budget line *ab*.

If the household's money income *rises* to $540, while the money prices of food and clothing remain unchanged, it will be able to increase its purchases of both commodities. The budget line shifts outward, as shown by the line *ef* in Figure 7-2.

Variations in the household's money income, with money prices constant, shift the budget line parallel to itself. It shifts inward (toward the origin) when money income falls and outward (away from the origin) when money income rises.

Proportional Changes in All Money Prices

Now return to the initial situation, in which the household has a money income of $360 and faces

FIGURE 7-2 **The Effect on the Budget Line of Changes in Money Income**

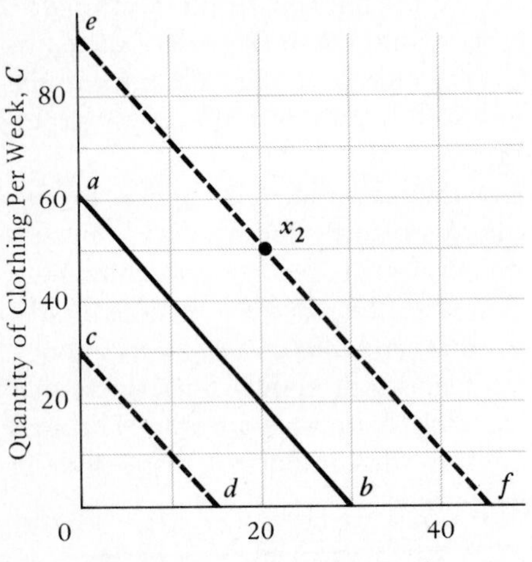

Changes in the household's money income shift the budget line inward toward the origin when money income falls and outward when money income rises. The original budget line *ab* refers to a money income of \$360 and prices of \$12 per unit for *F* and \$6 per unit for *C*. If the household's money income is halved from \$360 to \$180 per week, while prices remain unchanged, the amount of goods the household can buy will also be halved. This causes the budget line to shift inward (toward the origin) to *cd*. If the household spends all its money income on clothing, it will now get 30 units of clothing and zero units of food (point *c* in the figure). If it spends all its money income on food, it will get 15 units of food and zero units of clothing (point *d*).

If the household's money income rises to \$540, while the prices of food and clothing remain unchanged, the budget line shifts outward to *ef*. If the household buys only clothing, it can have 90 units of clothing; if it buys only food, it can have 45 units of food. Point x_2, indicating 50 units of *C* and 20 units of *F*, is now attainable, as shown by the fact that it lies on the new budget line *ef*.

prices of \$12 per unit for food and \$6 per unit for clothing. Let the money prices of food and clothing double to \$24 per unit for food and \$12 per unit for clothing. This halves the quantities of food and clothing that can be bought and so shifts the budget line inward, parallel to itself. These money changes have exactly the same effect as when prices remain constant at \$12 per unit for food and \$6 per unit for clothing but money income falls from \$360 to \$180.

Similarly, a proportional reduction of both money prices causes the budget line to shift outward in exactly the same manner that an increase in money income does.

Proportional changes in the money prices of all goods, if money income remains constant, shift the budget line parallel to itself. It shifts outward (away from the origin) when money prices fall and inward (toward the origin) when money prices rise.

Money Income and Real Income

Clearly, there can be exact offsetting changes in money prices and money incomes that leave the household's real income unchanged. For example, if money income and money prices all rise by 10 percent, the position of the budget line, and hence the choices available to the household, are unchanged.

A proportional change in money income and in all money prices leaves the household neither better nor worse off in terms of its ability to purchase commodities.

The foregoing observations show the importance of the distinction between *money* income and *real* income.

If money prices remain constant, any change in money income will cause a corresponding change in real income. If the household's money income rises by 10 percent (say, from \$10,000 to \$11,000), the household is able to buy 10 percent more of all commodities—its purchase power has risen by 10 percent.

If money prices change, real and money incomes will not change in the same proportion; indeed, they can easily change in *opposite* directions. Consider a situation in which all money prices rise by 10 percent. If money income rises by any amount less than 10 percent, real income falls. If money income also rises by 10 percent, real income will be unchanged. Only if money income rises by more than 10 percent will real income also rise.

A household's ability to purchase goods and services is measured by its real income, not by its money income.

Changes in real income are shown graphically by shifts in the budget line. When the budget line in Figure 7-2 shifts toward the origin, real income falls; when the budget line shifts away from the origin, real income rises.

Changes in Relative Prices

A *relative price* is the ratio of two absolute prices. The statement "The price of *F* is $12" refers to an absolute price; the statement "The price of *F* is twice the price of *C*" refers to a relative price.

A change in a relative price can be accomplished by changing both of the absolute prices in different proportions or by holding one absolute price constant and changing the other. The points we wish to make can be established by studying the case in which changes in relative prices are accomplished by holding one money price constant and changing the other.

Let us return to our illustration in which a household with a money income of $360 faces prices of $12 per unit for food and $6 per unit for clothing. Now let the price of food fall to $6 per unit. This lowers the price of food *relative to the price of clothing* and, as shown in Figure 7-3, changes the slope of the budget line.

The important conclusion is this:

A change in relative prices alters the slope of the budget line.

FIGURE 7-3 The Effect on the Budget Line of Changes in the Price of Food

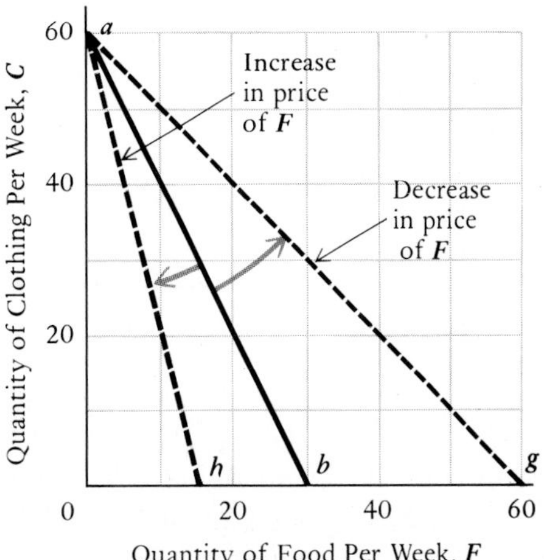

A change in the absolute price of one commodity changes relative prices and thus changes the slope of the budget line. The original budget line *ab* occurred with a money income of $360, with units of *C* priced at $6 and units of *F* at $12. A fall in the price of *F* to $6 doubles the quantity of *F* obtainable for any given quantity of *C* purchased and pivots the budget line outward to *ag*. A rise in the price of *F* to $24 reduces the quantity of *F* obtainable and pivots the budget line inward to *ah*.

The significance of the slope of the budget line for food and clothing is that it reflects the opportunity cost of food in terms of clothing. This is because, as we have just seen, the slope of the budget line reflects the relative prices of the two commodities. In order to increase food consumption while maintaining expenditure constant, one must move along the budget line and therefore consume less clothing.

Return for the moment to the original situation, in which the price of food (p_F) is $12 per unit and the price of clothing (p_C) is $6 per unit. With income fixed, it is necessary to forgo the purchase of two units of clothing to acquire one extra unit of food. The opportunity cost of a unit of food is thus two units of clothing. This opportunity cost can also be stated as p_F/p_C, which is the relative price of food in terms of clothing.

The opportunity cost of food in terms of clothing is measured by the slope of the budget line and also by the relative price ratio, p_F/p_C. [9]

Notice that the relative price (in our example $p_F/p_C = 2$) is consistent with an infinite number of absolute prices. If $p_F = \$40$ and $p_C = \$20$, it is still necessary to sacrifice two units of clothing to acquire one unit of food. This shows that relative, not absolute, prices determine opportunity cost.

When relative prices change, there is a change in the real choices households face. As a result, a change in relative prices has an effect on the household's *real income*. As we shall see in the next section, this effect depends not only on the choices households face but also on the choices they make. For this reason, when relative prices change, the measurement of the effect on real income is more difficult than it is when money income and all absolute prices change in proportion so that relative prices remained constant.

The Choices Households Make

The combination of goods and services that a household chooses to purchase will depend on both what it *can* do and what it *wants* to do. What it can do is shown by its budget line, which we have just studied. What it wants to do is determined by its tastes. Given its budget line and its tastes, what will the household do?

The key assumption about household behavior is that households maximize what is variously called their *satisfactions,* their *welfare,* their *well-being,* or their *utility.*[1] However it is worded, and whatever the theory used to develop it, the important thing is that households are assumed to try to do as well for themselves as they can.

Facing a choice among alternative consumption bundles, each household is assumed to choose the bundle that it prefers—which is the same as saying that the household makes its choices so as to maximize its satisfactions or its welfare.

The popular but misguided criticism that this assumption should be rejected as "unrealistic" is considered in Box 7-1.

Income and Substitution Effects

How does the household react to a change in the price of one good? For purposes of illustration we consider a fall in price.

A fall in the price of one good affects the consumer in two ways. First, relative prices change, providing an incentive to buy *more* of the good in question because it is cheaper. Second, the household's real income increases, because it can buy more of all commodities (as can be seen, for example, by comparing budget lines *ab* and *ag* in Figure 7-3). This rise in real income provides an incentive to buy different amounts of all goods. (Recall from Chapter 5 that when its income rises, the household buys more of all normal goods and less of all inferior goods.)

These two effects are illustrated in Figure 7-3. The household initially has a money income of $360 and faces prices of food and clothing of $12 and $6, respectively. The budget line is shown by line *ab* in the figure; given the household's tastes, it will prefer a combination of goods shown by some particular point on this line. The price of food then falls to $6, which shifts the budget line to *ag* in the figure and makes it possible for the household to buy more of both commodities—which is why we say that its real income has risen. The household then chooses its preferred position on the new budget line. The shift in consumption is partly a response to the change in the *slope* of the budget line, reflecting the change in relative prices. It is also partly a response to an *outward* shift in the budget line, reflecting the increase in the household's real income due to the fall in one money price with money income and all other money prices remaining constant.

The *extent* of the rise in real income depends on the share of total expenditures that the household spends on each good. For example, consider the extreme case of a household that spends all of its income on food; it will find that its real income has doubled because at a price of food of $6, it can now afford to purchase 60 units of food rather than only the 30 units it could afford at the original price of $12. At the other extreme, a household that spends none of its income on food and all of it on clothing finds that its consumption opportunities are unchanged—it can still buy only 60 units of clothing. For the more likely intermediate cases where some of both goods are purchased, there will be some positive effect on real income when the price of food falls, the strength of which will depend on the share of food expenditures in the household's budget.

To make our example precise, we assume that the household chooses the particular combinations shown in Figure 7-4 and Table 7-1. Suppose that at the initial prices, with budget line *ab*, the household chooses to consume 15 units of food and 30 units of clothing. This combination is indicated by the point

[1] In the two appendixes to this chapter we develop two theories of household choice. In Appendix A this assumption is worded in the form that households seek to maximize welfare by reaching the highest attainable indifference curve. In Appendix B this assumption is worded in the form that households seek to maximize utility. In the text we show how far we can get using the budget line alone plus the simple assumption that households are consistent in their decision making.

BOX 7-1

Does Demand Theory Require That Households Always Act Rationally?

The theory of household behavior uses the key assumption that households always act rationally in their pursuit of satisfaction. This assumption of rationality appears in slightly different form in various theories, but it always amounts to assuming that, facing alternatives, each household consistently chooses the one it prefers.

It is tempting to dismiss demand theory with the objection that consumer rationality is an unrealistic assumption. After all, most of us know people who occasionally buy strawberries in spite of a rise in their price, and others who sometimes spend a week's pay on a binge or a frivolous purchase that they afterward regret.

To assess the significance of such observed "irrationalities," it is helpful to distinguish three possible uses of demand theory. The first is to study the aggregate behavior of all households—as illustrated, for example, by the market demand curve for gasoline or carrots. The second use is to make statements about a particular household's probable actions. The third is to make statements about what each household will certainly do.

The criticism that the assumption of rationality is not realistic applies primarily to the third use of demand theory. Observations of unusual or irrational behavior refute only the prediction that *all* households *always* behave as assumed by the theory. To predict the existence of a relatively stable, negatively sloped market demand curve (the first use) or to predict what an individual household will probably do (the second use), we do *not* require that *all* households behave as assumed by the theory all of the time. Consider two illustrations.

First, some households may always behave in a manner inconsistent with the theory. Households whose members have serious emotional disturbances are one obvious example. The erratic behavior of such households will not cause market demand curves to depart from their downward slope, as long as these households account for a minority of total purchasers of any product. Their erratic behavior will be swamped by the normal behavior of the majority of households.

Second, occasional impulse buying or downright irrationality on the part of any household will not upset the downward slope of the market demand curve as long as these isolated inconsistencies do not occur at the same time and in the same way in all households. As long as such inconsistencies are unrelated across households, occurring now in one and now in another, their effects will be offset by the normal behavior of the majority of households.

The downward slope of the demand curve requires only that at any moment in time *most* households are behaving as predicted by the theory. This is compatible with inconsistent behavior on the part of some households all of the time and on the part of all households some of the time.

U.S. President Abraham Lincoln once said, "You can fool some of the people all of the time and all of the people some of the time, but you cannot fool all of the people all of the time." The same holds for irrational behavior: Most people may behave irrationally some of the time; some people behave irrationally all of the time; but all people will not behave irrationally all of the time. Lincoln's observation helps make clear why the assumption of rationality yields correct predictions about the slope of market demand curves.

E_0 in part (i) of Figure 7-4 and is also described in lines (2) and (3) of the table. Following the fall in the price of food, with the new budget line of *ag*, we suppose that the household chooses to consume 25 units of food and 35 units of clothing. This combination is indicated by point E_1 in the figure and is described in lines (5) and (6) of the table.

To isolate the effect of the change in relative price

FIGURE 7-4 The Income and Substitution Effects

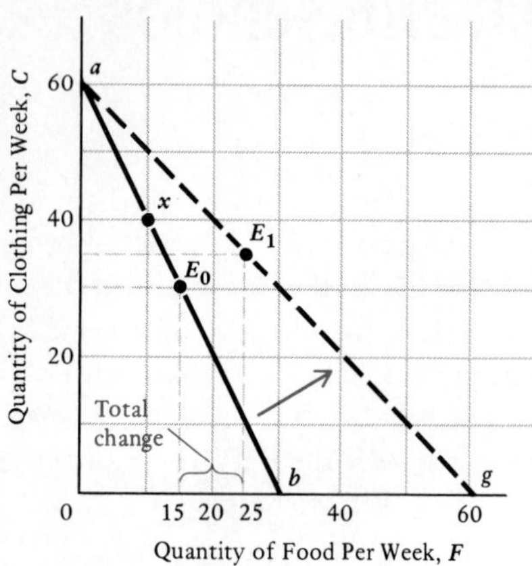

(i) A fall in the price of food

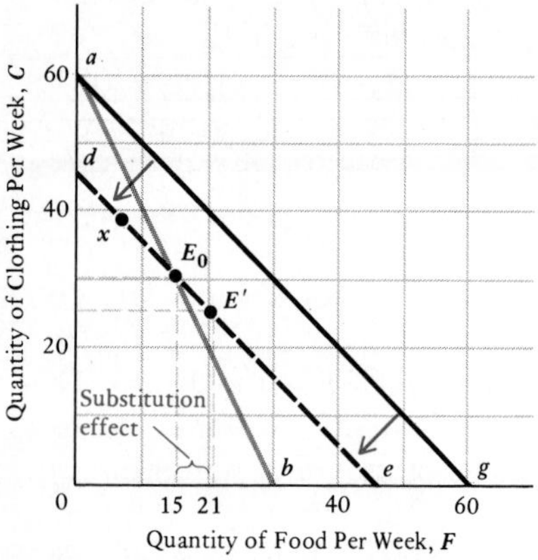

(ii) The substitution effect

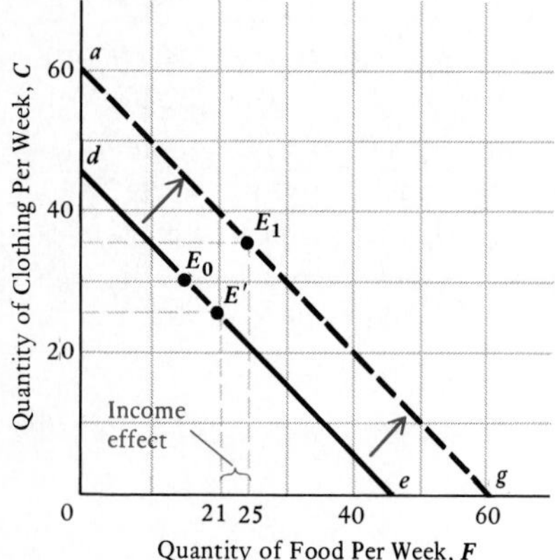

(iii) The income effect

The effect on household choice of a change in price can be broken into (1) a substitution effect measuring the response to a change in relative prices with purchasing power being held constant and (2) an income effect measuring the response to the change in purchasing power caused by the price change. (i) The initial budget line is *ab*, and the household's chosen position is E_0. E_0 corresponds to line (2) of Table 7-1, and at E_0 food consumption is 15 units. The price of food then falls, taking the budget line to *ag* and consumption to the bundle indicated by E_1. E_1 corresponds to line (5) of Table 7-1, and at E_1 food consumption is 25 units. Hence the total change in the demand for food is 10 units.

(ii) The substitution effect is shown by reducing money income so that the original bundle can just be bought at the new prices. Graphically, this shifts the budget line to *de*, where it is parallel to *ag* but passes through E_0. The combined effect of the change in the price and the fall in income is that the budget line rotates through the initial consumption point E_0. The household chooses point E' on *de*, making the substitution effect the movement from E_0 to E'. This corresponds to line (9) of Table 7-1; the substitution effect on the demand for food is 6 units.

(iii) The income effect is measured by restoring money income to its original level. Graphically, this shifts the budget line from *de* to *ag*. The income effect is the change in consumption from E' to E_1. This corresponds to line (13) of Table 7-1; the income effect on the demand for food is 4 units.

The figure also shows why the substitution effect can never cause the household to buy less food when its price falls. Such an outcome would mean that the household had chosen a bundle such as *x*, which lies to the left of E_0 on the budget line *de* in part (ii). However, when the household had budget line *ab*, it could have chosen *x* (by not spending all its income). Instead it rejected *x* in favor of E_0. If the household is consistent, it will not choose now a previously rejected combination. Instead it will choose some position on *de* at, or to the right of, E_0; such points were not available to it when it chose E_0 on budget line *ab*. *Any* point on *de* to the right of E_0 indicates more consumption of food, the good whose price has fallen.

TABLE 7-1 The Income and Substitution Effects: A Numerical Example

	Food	Clothing	Total
	I. Initial position (price of food = $12 per unit)		
(1) Price	$ 12	$ 6	
(2) Quantity	15	30	
(3) Expenditure	$180	$180	$360
	II. New position (price of food = $6 per unit)		
(4) Price	$ 6	$ 6	
(5) Quantity	25	35	
(6) Expenditure	$150	$210	$360
(7) Total effect: Line (5) − Line (2) = 10 additional units of food purchased			
	III. Substitution effect: money income is reduced to $270 so that the initial bundle can still be purchased at the new prices		
(8) Price	$ 6	$ 6	
(9) Quantity	21	24	
(10) Expenditure	$126	$144	$270
(11) Substitution effect: Line (9) − Line (2) = 6 additional units of food purchased			
	IV. Income effect: money income is returned to $360		
(12) Price	$ 6	$ 6	
(13) Quantity	25	35	
(14) Expenditure	$150	$210	$360
(15) Income effect: Line (13) − Line (9) = 4 additional units of food purchased			
	V. Total effect: change in food purchases in response to a change in the price of food		
Substitution effect (from line (11)):	6 units of food		
Income effect (from line (15)):	4 units of food		
Total effect (confirms line (7)):	10 units of food		

The substitition effect measures the response to a change in relative prices when the purchasing power of income is held constant; the income effect measures the response to a change in purchasing power when relative prices are held constant. In the initial position shown in panel I, a consumer with a money income of $360 faces prices of $12 per unit for food and $6 per unit for clothing, buying 15*F* and 30*C*. As shown in panel II, the money price of food then falls to $6 per unit. The consumer now buys 25*F* and 35*C*, so the demand for food rises by 10 units.

Panel III shows the substitution effect. Money income is reduced to $270, so the initial bundle of 15*F* and 30*C* can just be bought at the new prices of $6 each. In this example, the household now purchases 21*F* and 24*C*.

Panel IV shows the income effect. Money income is returned to its original level of $360. As a result, the consumption of *F* and *C* both rise. In this example, *F* rises to 25 and *C* to 35.

As shown in panel V, the total effect is the sum of the income and the substitution effects, so a fall in the price of *F* from $12 to $6 leads to an increase of 10 units in the quantity of *F* demanded, from 15 to 25 units per week.

when the price of food falls, we can consider what would happen if we also reduce the household's money income to restore its original purchasing power. To do this we can reduce money income until the original bundle of food and clothing can just be bought at the new prices. The consumption bundle that the household chooses when it faces this hypothetical situation with the new prices and the reduced money income reflects the effect of the change in relative prices when the purchasing power of income is held constant. The change in the household's choice, compared to its initial preferred combination, is the **substitution effect**, which is the change in quantity demanded as a result of a change in relative prices, with real income held constant.[2] In our example, the new budget line is *de* in part (ii) of Figure 7-4, and the household chooses the combination indicated by point E' in the figure and described in lines (9) and (10) of Table 7-1. The substitution effect causes the household to buy more food, whose relative price has fallen, and less clothing, whose relative prices has risen.

Next we restore the household's money income, which shifts the budget line outward, parallel to itself. Assuming that we are dealing with a normal good, the household will increase its consumption of food. (It will also increase its consumption of clothing.) The change in quantity demanded as a result of the household's reaction to this shift of its budget line is called the **income effect**. It is shown by the change between lines (9) and (13) in Table 7-1 and points E' and E_1 in part (iii) of Figure 7-4.

We have now broken down the reaction to a fall in the price of a commodity (food, in our example) into a substitution effect and an income effect. In our numerical example the substitution effect raises the consumption of food by 6 units, and the income effect raises it by 4 units, making the overall response to the fall in price of food an increase of 10 units. Of course, when the price of food falls, the household moves directly from its initial position to its final position, buying 10 more units of food. By breaking this movement into two parts, however, we are able to study the household's total change in quantities demanded in terms of a response to a change in relative prices and a response to a change in real income.

Notice that the size of the income effect depends on the amount of income spent on the good whose price changes and on the amount by which the price changes. In our simple example, where the household was spending one-half of its income on food, a 50 percent fall in the food price was equivalent (at the new prices) to a 25 percent increase in income. Now consider a different case. Assume that the price of petroleum falls by 20 percent. For a household that was spending only 5 percent of its income on gas and oil, this is equivalent (at the new prices) to only a 1 percent increase in purchasing power (20 percent of 5 percent).

Derivation of a Demand Curve

The demand curve relates the quantity of a particular commodity demanded to the commodity's price. Figure 7-5 shows the derivation of the demand curve for food based on the example in Table 7-1. Part (i) reproduces part (i) of Figure 7-4; it shows the effect of a fall in the price of food on the budget line and on the consumption bundle chosen by the household. Each combination of a price of food and the corresponding quantity of food purchased is then plotted as a point in part (ii) in Figure 7-5. When joined together, such points give rise to the demand curve for food. As shown, the demand curve is negatively sloped.

The Slope of the Demand Curve

The negative slope of the demand curve shows that a fall in price leads to an increase in the quantity demanded. Earlier in this book we merely assumed this slope, but the analysis underlying Figure 7-4 allows us to explain it. As it is drawn in Figure 7-4, the substitution effect leads the household to buy more food, which is the commodity whose price has fallen.

We now ask a fundamental question: Could the substitution effect of a fall in the price of food have led the household to buy less food? Graphically, this would mean that the household would select some bundle that had less food and more clothing than its initial bundle. An example would be the bundle indicated by the point x on budget line *de* in part (ii) of Figure 7-4. When the household faced its original budget line, *ab*, it could have gone to x (by not

[2] This measure, which isolates the substitution effect by holding the household's purchasing power constant, is known as the *Slutsky effect*. An alternative measure that holds the household's level of satisfaction constant is discussed in Appendix A to this chapter.

FIGURE 7-5 Derivation of the Demand Curve for Food

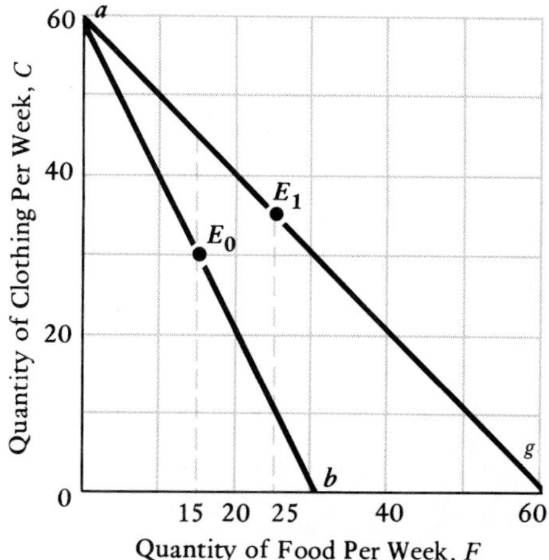

(i) The budget line and consumption bundles

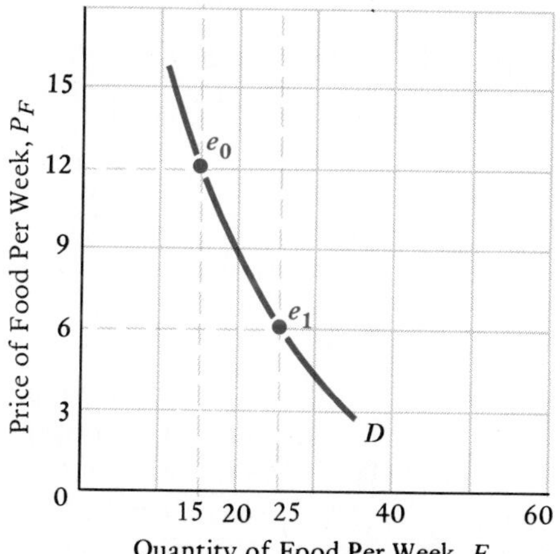

(ii) The demand curve for food

With a given money income, a change in the price of food causes the budget line to rotate and a new bundle of food and clothing to be purchased. This gives the information needed to derive the demand curve for food. Part (i) reproduces part (i) of Figure 7-4. The household has an income of \$360, and prices are initially \$12 per unit of food and \$6 per unit of clothing. The budget line is *ab*, and the household consumes at point E_0, purchasing 15 units of food. When the price of food falls to \$6 per unit, the budget line shifts to *ag*. The household consumes at point E_1, purchasing 25 units of food.

Part (ii) plots the quantity of food demanded against the price of food to yield the demand curve for food. Point e_0 corresponds to point E_0 in (i), where we saw that at a price of \$12 per unit, the household purchases 15 units of food. Point e_1 corresponds to point E_1 in (i); at the lower price of \$6 per unit, the household's demand for food rises to 25 units. Considering other prices would give rise to a series of points that when joined would yield the demand curve *D*.

spending all of its income), but it chose not to do so, going to E_0 instead. So as long as its preferences remain unchanged, the household will not now go to *x*.

This argument, which is laid out more fully in Box 7-2, leads us to an important conclusion:

The substitution effect can *never* lead a household to purchase less of a commodity whose price has fallen.

Now consider the second part of the household's adjustment to the fall in price, the income effect. A rise in income leads the household to buy more of all normal goods. This leads to the second conclusion:

The income effect leads the household to buy more of the commodity whose price has fallen, provided that it is a normal commodity.

BOX 7-2

More About the Slope of Demand Curves

This box gives a more precise treatment of the discussion found in the text and then discusses the implications of the negative income effects that arise with inferior goods. The basic assumption about tastes that is used in this approach is called the *consistency assumption*. It states that if the household chose some bundle of goods that we call *A* over some other bundle that we call *B* in one situation, it would never choose *B* over *A* in some subsequent situation in which *A* and *B* are both available to it.

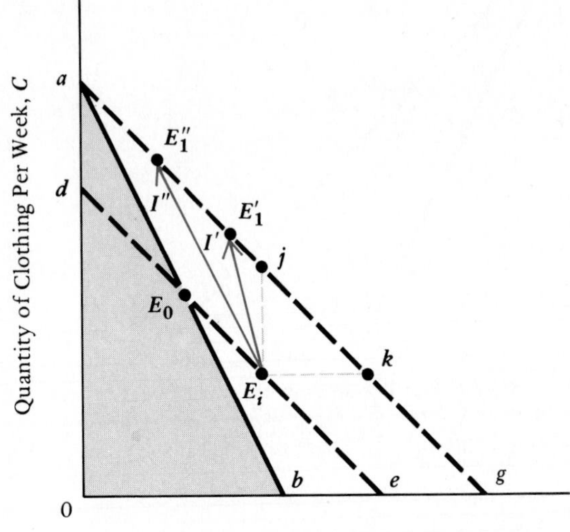

Normal Sloped Demand Curves

Let the initial budget line be *ab* and the chosen position be E_0. This means that the household has chosen the combination indicated by E_0 over all other attainable combinations. The rejected combinations are indicated by the points in the shaded triangle between *ab* and the origin. (Note that when it faces the budget line *ab*, the household can reach any point on *ab* by spending all of its income and can reach any point lying in the shaded area below *ab* by spending less than all its income.) If the household is consistent, it will never choose another bundle within that area when the bundle indicated by E_0 is also available.

Now let the price of *F* fall, taking the budget line to *ag*. To isolate the substitution effect, we also reduce money income so that the budget line becomes *de*. This new budget line is parallel to *ag*, indicating that the household faces the new relative price. The new budget line also passes through E_0, indicating that the household has only its original purchasing power.

Consistency requires that the household cannot choose any point to the left of E_0 on the new budget line *de*, since those points lie within the shaded area that was rejected when E_0 was chosen on the budget

Putting these two effects together gives the following conclusion:

Because of the combined operation of the substitution effect and the income effect, the demand curve for any normal commodity will be negatively sloped, indicating that a fall in price will lead to an increase in quantity demanded.

The Role of Tastes

Earlier we observed that what the household can do depends on its budget line, whereas what it does do depends on its tastes. Yet we appear to have studied the household's reactions to a change in price without saying much about the household's tastes. In fact, we did make use of a simple assumption about tastes. We assumed that households were consistent in the sense that if once they chose bundle of goods *A* over bundle *B*, they would not subsequently choose bundle *B* over bundle *A*. This is what allowed us to say that when the price of food fell and income was adjusted so that the original bundle could just be purchased, the household would never choose a new bundle containing less food because any such bundle could have been chosen in the initial situation. This

line *ab*. The household either stays at E_0 or moves to some point to the right of E_0—let us say it goes to E_i.

The foregoing argument shows that the substitution effect cannot be positive; when the price of food falls, the household cannot buy less food.

Now consider the income effect. Begin by drawing a vertical and a horizontal line from E_i to cut *ag* at *j* and *k*. Points on *ag* between *j* and *k* indicate an increase in the consumption of both commodities when the budget line goes from *de* to *ag*. This is what must happen if both goods are normal goods. This shows that the income effect of a fall in the price of food must lead to an increase in the demand for food, assuming only that it is a normal (noninferior) good.

So we know that if the price of some product falls, the substitution effect cannot lead to less of it being consumed, and, if the good is normal, the income effect leads to more of it being consumed. A fall in the price of any normal good must therefore lead to an increase in its demand; that is, its demand curve has a negative slope.

Positively Sloped Demand Curves

Could the demand curve for F ever be positively sloped? This can happen only if F is an inferior good (a necessary condition). The figure illustrates two cases in which F is inferior. In the first case, the movement of the budget line from *de* to *ag* takes the equilibrium position along the arrow I' to E_1'. In this case, the income effect leads to a fall in the demand for F, but the substitution effect is stronger than the income effect. Hence the overall change in the quantity of F is an increase as the chosen position goes from E_0 to E_1'. In the second case, the negative income effect is stronger, and the equilibrium follows the path I'' from E_i to E_1''. In this case, the income effect of the inferior good outweighs the substitution effect, and the quantity of F demanded falls from that indicated by E_0 to that indicated by E_1'', as a result of a fall in the price of F.

We can now conclude the following:

1. **All normal goods have negatively sloped demand curves.**
2. **All inferior goods for which the substitution effect outweighs the income effect have negatively sloped demand curves.**
3. **A positively sloped demand curve requires an inferior good for which the income effect outweighs the substitution effect.**

assumption is laid out in more detail in Box 7-2 for readers who would like to study it further. In Box 7-2 we also consider the possibility of the unusual case in which the demand curve for an inferior good could be positively sloped.

Can Demand Curves Ever Have Positive Slopes?

What the great English economist Alfred Marshall called the **law of demand** asserts that, other things being constant, the market price of a product and the quantity demanded in the market are negatively associated; that is, the demand curves have negative slopes. Criticisms of the law have taken various forms, focusing on Giffen goods, conspicuous consumption goods, and goods whose demands are perfectly inelastic. Let us consider each of these in turn.

Giffen Goods

Great interest was attached to the nineteenth century English economist Sir Robert Giffen's apparent refutation of the law of demand. He is alleged to have observed that when a rise in the price of imported wheat led to an increase in the price of bread, members of the British working class *increased* their consumption of bread. This meant that their demand curve for bread was positively sloped.

The reasoning discussed in Box 7-2 shows that such an exception to the law of demand could occur. There are two requisites: (1) The good must be an inferior good, and (2) the good must take a large proportion of total household expenditure; that is, its income effect must be large. Bread was indeed a dietary staple of the British working classes during the nineteenth century. A rise in the price of bread would cause a large reduction in their real income. This could lead to increased consumption of bread as households cut out their few luxuries in order to be able to consume enough bread to keep alive. Though possible, such cases are all but unknown in the modern world. The reason is that in all but the poorest societies, typical households do not spend large proportions of their incomes on a single inferior good.

Conspicuous Consumption Goods

Thorstein Veblen in *The Theory of the Leisure Class* noted that some commodities were consumed not for their intrinsic qualities but because they carried a snob appeal. He suggested that the more expensive such a commodity became, the *greater* might be its ability to confer status on its purchaser.

Consumers might buy diamonds, for example, not because they particularly like diamonds per se but because they wish to show off their wealth in an ostentatious but socially acceptable way. They are assumed to value diamonds precisely because diamonds are expensive. Thus a fall in price might lead them to stop buying diamonds and to switch to a more satisfactory object of conspicuous consumption. They may behave in the same way with respect to luxury cars, buying them *because* they are expensive.

Households that behave in this way will have positively sloped *individual demand curves* for diamonds and cars. However, no one has ever observed a positively sloped *market demand curve* for such commodities. The reason for this is easy to discover. A consideration of the countless lower-income consumers who would be glad to buy diamonds or Cadillacs if these commodities were sufficiently inexpensive suggests that positively sloped demand curves for a few individual wealthy households are much more likely than a positively sloped market demand curve for the same commodity.

Perfectly Inelastic Demand Curves

Even if demand curves never had positive slopes, the substantial insight provided by the law of demand would be diminished if there were important commodities for which changes in price had virtually no effect on quantity demanded.

It is surprising how often the assumption of a vertical demand curve is implicit. For example, a common response of urban bus or subway systems to financial difficulties is to propose a percentage increase in fares equal to the percentage increase that they require in their revenues. Even professors are not immune to this type of response. At a meeting of an association of university professors, a motion was introduced "to raise annual dues by 20 percent in order to raise revenues by 20 percent," in spite of the empirical evidence showing that a previous increase in dues had led (as theory would predict) to a drop in membership.

It was once widely argued that the demand for gasoline was almost perfectly inelastic on the grounds that people who had paid thousands of dollars for cars would not balk at paying a few cents extra for gasoline. The events of the past two decades have proved how wrong this argument is: Higher gasoline prices in the early 1980s led to production of smaller cars, to more car pools, to more economical driving speeds, and to less pleasure driving. Falling gasoline prices in the mid 1980s led to a reversal of these trends.

In summary, a mass of accumulated evidence confirms that most demand curves do in fact have a negative slope.

The hypothesis that demand curves are negatively sloped is strongly supported by the evidence.

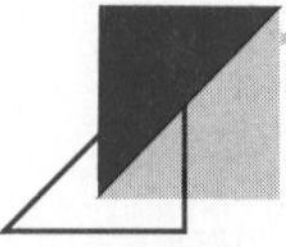

Consumers' Surplus

Imagine yourself facing an either-or choice concerning some particular commodity: You can have the amount you are now consuming, or you can have none of it. Assume that you would be willing to pay as much as $100 per month for that amount rather than do without it. Further assume that you actually buy that amount of the commodity for $60 instead of $100. What a bargain! You have paid $40 less than the top figure you were willing to pay. Yet this sort of bargain is not rare; it occurs every day in any economy in which prices do the rationing. Indeed, it is so common that the $40 "saved" in this example has been given a name: *consumers' surplus*. We will define the term later; first let us look at how this surplus arises.

Consumers' surplus is a direct consequence of negatively sloped demand curves. To illustrate this connection, suppose that we have collected the information in Table 7-2 on the basis of an interview with Mrs. Swartz. Our first question to Mrs. Swartz is, "If you were getting no milk at all, how much would you be willing to pay for one glass per week?" With no hesitation she replies $3.00. We then ask, "If you had already consumed that one glass, how much would you pay for a second glass per week?" After a bit of thought she answers $1.50. Adding one glass per week with each question, we discover that she would be willing to pay $1.00 to get a third glass per week and 80, 60, 50, 40, 30, 25, and 20 cents for successive glasses from the fourth to the tenth glass per week.

TABLE 7-2 Consumers' Surplus on Milk Consumption by One Consumer

(1) Glasses of milk consumed per week	(2) Amount the consumer would pay to get this glass	(3) Consumers' surplus on each glass if milk costs 30 cents per glass
First	$3.00	$2.70
Second	1.50	1.20
Third	1.00	.70
Fourth	.80	.50
Fifth	.60	.30
Sixth	.50	.20
Seventh	.40	.10
Eighth	.30	.00
Ninth	.25	—
Tenth	.20	—

Consumers' surplus on each unit consumed is the difference between the market price and the maximum price the consumer would pay to obtain that unit. The table shows the value that one consumer, Mrs. Swartz, puts on successive glasses of milk consumed each week. Her negatively sloped demand curve shows that she would be willing to pay progressively smaller amounts for each additional unit consumed. As long as she would be willing to pay more than the market price for any unit, she obtains a consumers' surplus on it when she buys it. The marginal unit is the one valued just at the market price and on which no consumers' surplus is earned.

The sum of the values that she places on each glass of milk gives us the *total value* that she places on all 10 glasses. In this case, Mrs. Swartz values 10 glasses of milk per week at $8.55. This is the amount she would be willing to pay if facing the either-or choice of 10 glasses or none. This is also the amount she would be willing to pay if she were offered the milk one glass at a time and if she were charged the maximum she was willing to pay for each.

However, Mrs. Swartz does not have to pay a different price for each glass of milk she consumes each week; she can buy all she wants at the prevailing market price. Suppose the price is 30 cents per glass. She will buy eight glasses per week (one each weekday and two on Sunday) because she values the eighth glass just at the market price but all earlier glasses at higher amounts. She does not buy a ninth glass because she values it at less than the market price.

Because she values the first glass at $3.00 but gets it for 30 cents, she makes a "profit" of $2.70 on that glass. Between her $1.50 valuation of the second glass and what she has to pay for it, she clears a "profit" of $1.20. She clears a "profit" of 70 cents on the third glass, and so on. These "profits" are called her consumer's surplus on each glass. They are shown in column 3 of Table 7-2; the total consumers' surplus is $5.70 per week.

In Table 7-2 we arrive at her consumers' surplus by summing her surpluses on each glass. We arrive at the same total by first summing what she would pay for all eight glasses, which is $8.10, and then by subtracting the $2.40 that she does pay.

The value placed by each household on its total consumption of some commodity can be estimated in at least two ways: The valuation that the household places on each successive unit may be summed, or the household may be asked how much it would pay to consume the amount

FIGURE 7-6 Consumers' Surplus for an Individual

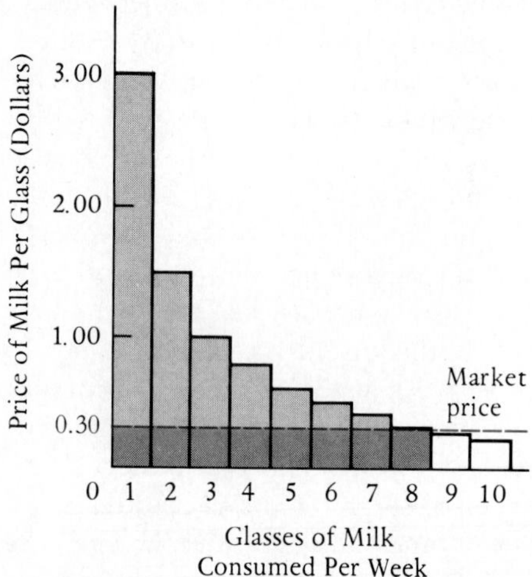

Consumers' surplus is the sum of the extra valuations placed on each unit above the market price paid for each. This figure is based on the data in Table 7-2. Mrs. Swartz will pay the amounts shown in the dark shaded area for the eight glasses of milk she will consume per week when the market price is 30 cents per glass. The total value she places on these eight glasses is the entire shaded area. Hence her consumers' surplus is the light shaded area.

FIGURE 7-7 Consumers' Surplus for the Market

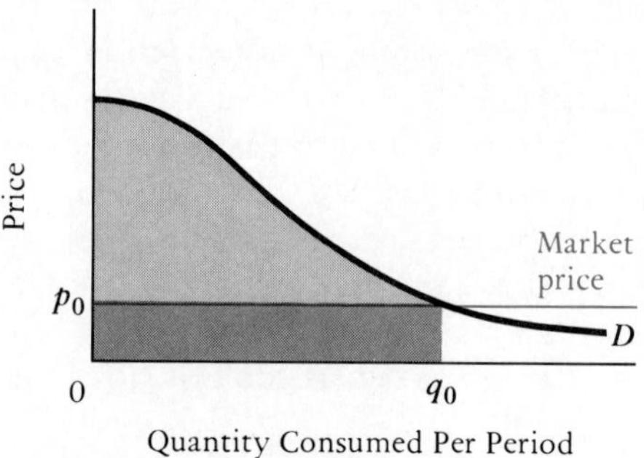

Total consumers' surplus is the area under the demand curve and above the price line. The demand curve shows the amount consumers would pay for each unit of the commodity if they had to buy their units one at a time. The area under the demand curve shows the total valuation that consumers place on all units consumed. For example, the total value that consumers place on q_0 units is the entire shaded area under the demand curve up to q_0. At a market price of p_0, the amount paid for q_0 units is the dark shaded area. Hence consumers' surplus is the light shaded area.

in question if the alternative were to have none of that commodity.[3]

Although other households would put different numerical values into Table 7-2, the negative slope of the demand curve implies that the figures in column 2 would be declining for each household. Since a household will go on buying additional units until the value placed on the last unit equals the market price, it follows that there will be a consumers' surplus on every unit consumed except the last one.

In general, **consumers' surplus** is the difference between the total value that consumers place on all the units consumed of some commodity and the payment they must make to purchase that amount of the commodity.

The data in columns 1 and 2 of Table 7-2 give Mrs. Swartz's demand curve for milk. It is her demand curve because she will go on buying glasses of milk as long as she values each glass at least as much as the market price she must pay for it. When the market price is $3.00 per glass, she will buy only one glass; when it is $1.50, she will buy two glasses; and so on. The total valuation is the area below her demand curve, and consumers' surplus is the part of the area that lies above the price line. This is shown in Figure 7-6.

Figure 7-7 shows that the same relationship holds for the smooth market demand curve that indicates the total amount all consumers would buy at each price.[4]

[3] This is only an approximation, but it is good enough for our purposes. More advanced theory shows that the calculations presented here overestimate consumers' surplus because they ignore the income effect. Although it is sometimes necessary to correct for this bias, no amount of refinement upsets the general result that we establish here: When consumers can buy all units they require at a single market price, they pay much less than they would be willing to pay if facing a choice between having the quantity they consume and having none.

[4] Figure 7-6 is a bar chart because we only allowed Mrs. Swartz to vary her consumption in discrete units of one glass at a time. Had we allowed her to vary her consumption of milk one drop at a time, we could have traced out a continuous curve similar to the one shown in Figure 7-7.

Consumers' surplus is an extremely important and useful concept. Understanding it is the key to understanding the theory of demand. In Chapter 8 we shall see how it helps us to resolve some real-world events that on the surface seem pradoxical. In later chapters consumers' surplus will play a key role in our analysis of certain aspects of the performance of the market system.

A Preview

In this chapter we have presented the minimum amount of demand theory that is needed for the rest of this book. In the next chapter we shall present a number of applications. The two appendixes to this chapter present more formal theories of household tastes that lead to the prediction of negatively sloped demand curves. Some of you will skip both of these appendixes; others will read one or both. Whatever you do, remember that although abstract in its current presentation, modern demand theory grew up to handle a number of real and interesting problems. We shall see how the theory can be applied to real issues both in the next chapter and later in this book.

SUMMARY

1. The budget line shows all combinations of commodities that are available to the household, given its money income and the prices of the goods it purchases.
2. The budget line is shifted parallel to itself by either a change in money income, with all money prices being held constant, or a proportionate change in all money prices, with money income being held constant.
3. Changes in relative prices change the slope of the budget line.
4. The budget line describes what the household *can* purchase; what it *does* purchase depends on its tastes.
5. A change in one money price has an income effect and a substitution effect. The substitution effect is the reaction of the household to the change in relative prices, with real income being held constant. It can be measured by allowing price to change and then by altering money income until the original bundle can just be purchased. In this situation, a consistent household would never reduce its purchases of the commodity whose relative price has fallen. The income effect is then measured by a parallel shift of the budget line to restore its initial money income. The income effect of a fall in one money price will lead to an increase in the purchases of all normal commodities.
6. The combined effect of the income and the substitution effects ensures that the quantity demanded of any normal good will increase when its money price falls, other things being equal. This means that normal goods have negatively sloped demand curves.
7. Three conceivable exceptions to the law of negatively sloped demand curves are a Giffen good, which is an inferior good on which a household spends much of its income; conspicuous consumption goods, which are goods consumed *because* they are expensive; and goods with perfectly inelastic demands. Such exceptions rarely, if ever, cause actual market demand curves to have a positive slope.
8. Consumers' surplus arises because a household can purchase every unit of a commodity at a price equal to the value it places on the last unit purchased. The negative slope of demand curves implies that the value that households place on all other units purchased exceeds the value of the last unit purchased, and hence that all but the last unit purchased yield a consumers' surplus.
9. The total value that consumers place on some quantity of a com-

modity consumed is given by the area under the demand curve up to that quantity. The market value is given by an area below the market price up to that quantity. Consumers' surplus is the difference between the two.

TOPICS FOR REVIEW

Causes of shifts in the budget line
Real income and money income
Absolute (or money) prices and relative prices
Income effect and substitution effect
The law of demand and its possible exceptions
Consumers' surplus

DISCUSSION QUESTIONS

1. Is a household relatively better off if its money income is decreased by 10 percent or if the prices of all the goods it buys are increased by 10 percent? Does it matter in answering this question whether the household spends all its income?
2. Look at Figure 7-4 and see what happened to the quantity of clothing demanded when the price of food fell. Could that change in the quantity of clothing consumed have been in the opposite direction from the one you determine? What would that have implied about the change in the quantity of food? Can you use Figure 7-4 to discover a relationship between the price elasticity of demand for food and the change in the quantity of clothing bought when the price of food changes?
3. A middle-aged business executive reports that she now drinks a lot more French wine than she used to when she first started working for the company, even though imported wine is now much more expensive than it used to be. Do you think she has a positively sloped demand curve for French wine?
4. The measured elasticity of demand for salt is quite low. Why do you think this is so? Does this low elasticity imply that if one firm were to monopolize the sales of salt in the whole country, it could go on raising its revenues indefinitely by continually increasing the price of salt?
5. Between 1980 and 1991 the cost of purchasing a representative bundle of consumers' goods rose by almost 100 percent, as measured by the Consumer Price Index. What else would you need to know to find out what had happened to the average Canadian's real income?
6. When the prices of fuel oil and gasoline rose drastically in the early 1980s, many Canadians reported that they felt worse off. Did this feeling have anything to do with the income effect or the substitution effect? What do you think the income and the substitution effects of these prices were?
7. Compare and contrast the consequences of the income effect of a drastic fall in food prices with the consequences of a rise in money incomes when money prices are constant.
8. In recent years, the price of housing has increased dramatically in Toronto and Vancouver but only slightly in Halifax and Winnipeg. What income and substitution effects would you expect from these changes?
9. Consider a household that, on average, uses 1,500 kilowatt-hours

(kwh) of electricity per month, at a price of 5 cents per kwh. Suppose that the local utility company, the only supplier of electricity, adopts a new policy whereby its customers will be billed $100 per month plus 5 cents for each kwh in excess of 2,000 that it uses in any month. How will this affect the household's demand for electricity? How will this affect the consumers' surplus that it derives from consumption of electricity?

10. Professors Jeff Biddle and Daniel Hamermesch of Michigan State University have recently estimated that a 25 percent increase in wages will cause the average individual to reduce the time that they spend sleeping by about 1 percent. Interpret this in terms of the substitution effect. Would you expect to find an income effect on the amount of time that a person spends sleeping?

11. In an effect to promote responsible drinking and to encourage the use of designated drivers, many campus bars in the country have started offering soft drinks at very low prices, sometimes even free. Describe the results you would expect in terms of the income and substitution effects.

Appendix A to Chapter 7

Indifference Theory

The history of demand theory has seen two major breakthroughs. The first was the marginal utility theory, which assumed that the utility that people received from consuming commodities could be measured objectively. By distinguishing total and marginal values, this theory explained why what seemed like a paradox—necessary goods that cannot be dispensed with often have low market values, while luxury goods that could easily be dispensed with often have high market values—was not a paradox at all. (A further discussion of this so-called paradox of value can be found in Chapter 8.)

The second breakthrough came with the indifference theory, which showed that demand theory could dispense with the dubious assumption of measurable utility on which marginal utility theory was based. All that was needed in this new theory was to assume that households could say which of two consumption bundles they preferred without having to say by how much they preferred it.

Appendix A develops the modern indifference theory, and Appendix B deals with marginal utility theory.

An Indifference Curve

Start with an imaginary household that currently has available to it some specific bundle of goods, say, 18 units of clothing and 10 units of food. Now offer the household an alternative bundle of, say, 13 units of clothing and 15 units of food. This alternative combination of goods has 5 fewer units of clothing and 5 more units of food than the first one. Whether the household prefers this bundle depends on the relative valuation that it places on 5 more units of food and 5 fewer units of clothing. If it values the extra food more than the forgone clothing, it will prefer the new bundle to the original one. If it values the food less than the clothing, it will prefer the original bundle. If the household values the extra food the same as it values the forgone clothing, it is said to be *indifferent between* the two bundles.

Assume that after much trial and error we have identified several bundles among which the household is indifferent. In other words, each bundle gives the household equal satisfaction. They are shown in Table 7A-1.

There will, of course, be combinations of the two commodities other than those enumerated in Table 7A-1 that will give the same level of satisfaction to the household. All of these combinations are shown in Figure 7A-1 by the smooth curve that passes through the points plotted from the table. This curve is an indifference curve. In general, an **indifference curve** shows all combinations of commodities that yield the same satisfaction to the household; the household is indifferent between the combinations indicated by any two points on one indifference curve.

Any points above the curve show combinations of food and clothing that the household would prefer to combinations indicated by points on the curve. Consider, for example, the combination of 20 units of food and 18 units of clothing, represented by point *g* in Figure 7A-1. Although it may not be obvious that this bundle must be preferred to bundle *a* (which has more clothing but less food), it is obvious that it will be preferred to bundle *c* because there is both less clothing and less food represented at *c* than at *g*.

TABLE 7A-1 Alternative Bundles Giving a Household Equal Satisfaction

Bundle	Clothing	Food
a	30	5
b	18	10
c	13	15
d	10	20
e	8	25
f	7	30

These bundles all lie on a single indifference curve. Since all of these bundles of food and clothing give equal satisfaction, the household is "indifferent" among them.

Inspection of the graph shows that *any* point above the curve will be obviously superior to *some* points on the curve in the sense that it will contain both more food and more clothing than those points on the curve. However, since all points on the curve are equal in the household's eyes, any point above the curve must be superior to *all* points on the curve. By a similar argument, all points below and to the left of the curve represent bundles that are inferior to bundles represented by points on the curve.

FIGURE 7A-1 An Indifference Curve

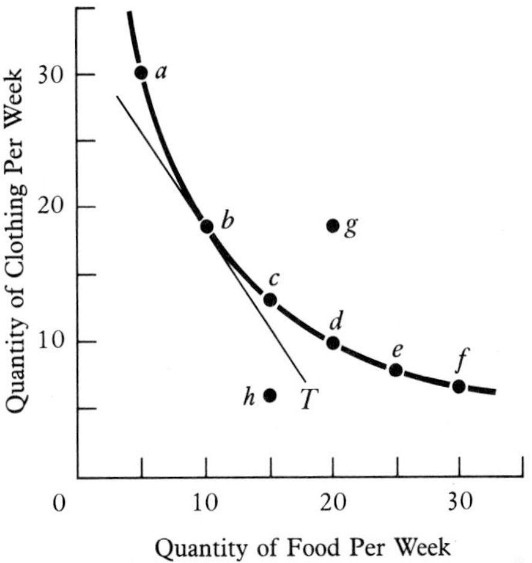

This indifference curve shows combinations of food and clothing that yield equal satisfaction and among which the household is indifferent. Points *a* through *f* are plotted from Table 7A-1. The smooth curve through them is an indifference curve; each combination on it gives equal satisfaction to the household. Point *g* above the line is a preferred combination to any point on the line; point *h* below the line is an inferior combination to any point on the line. The slope of the line *T* gives the marginal rate of substitution at point *b*. Moving down the curve from *b* to *f*, the slope flattens, showing that the more food and the less clothing the household has, the less willing it will be to sacrifice further clothing to get more food.

The Hypothesis of Diminishing Marginal Rate of Substitution

How much clothing would the household be prepared to give up to get one more unit of food? The answer to this question measures what is called the marginal rate of substitution of clothing for food. The **marginal rate of substitution (*MRS*)** is the amount of one commodity that a consumer would be prepared to give up in order to get one more unit of another commodity.

The first basic assumption of indifference theory is that the algebraic value of the *MRS* is always negative.

This means that to gain a positive change in its consumption of one commodity, the household is prepared to incur a negative change in its consumption of a second. The negative marginal rate of substitution is indicated in graphical representation by the negative slope of all indifferences curves. (See, for example, the curve in Figure 7A-1.)

The second basic assumption of indifference theory is that the marginal rate of substitution between any two commodities depends on the amounts of the commodities currently being consumed by the household.

Consider a case in which the household has a lot of clothing and only a little food. Common sense suggests that the household might be willing to give up quite a bit of its plentiful clothing in order to get one unit more of scarce food. It suggests as well that the household with a little clothing and a lot of food would be willing to give up only a little of its scarce clothing in order to get one more unit of already plentiful food.

This example illustrates the hypothesis of diminishing marginal rate of substitution. The less of one commodity, *A*, and the more of a second commodity, *B*, the household has already, the smaller will be the amount of *A* that it will be willing to give up in order to get one additional unit of *B*. The hypothesis says that the marginal rate of substitution changes systematically as the amounts of two commodities presently consumed vary. The graphical expression of this is that the slope of any indifference curve becomes flatter as the household moves downward and to the right along the curve. In Figure 7A-1 a movement downward to the right means that less clothing and more food are being consumed. The decreasing steepness of the curve means that the house-

TABLE 7A-2 The Marginal Rate of Substitution Between Clothing and Food

Movement	(1) Change in clothing	(2) Change in food	(3) Marginal rate of substitution (1) ÷ (2)
From *a* to *b*	−12	5	−2.4
From *b* to *c*	− 5	5	−1.0
From *c* to *d*	− 3	5	−0.6
From *d* to *e*	− 2	5	−0.4
From *e* to *f*	− 1	5	−0.2

The marginal rate of substitution of clothing for food declines as the quantity of food increases. This table is based on Table 7A-1. When the household moves from *a* to *b*, it gives up 12 units of clothing and gains 5 units of food; it remains at the same level of overall satisfaction. The household at point *a* is prepared to sacrifice 12 units of clothing for 5 units of food (i.e., 12/5 = 2.4 units of clothing per unit of food obtained). When the household moves from *b* to *c*, it sacrifices 5 units of clothing for 5 units of food (a rate of substitution of 1 unit of clothing for each unit of food).

hold is willing to sacrifice less and less clothing to get each additional unit of food. [10]

The hypothesis is illustrated in Table 7A-2, which is based on the example of food and clothing in Table 7A-1. The last column of the table shows the rate at which the household is prepared to sacrifice units of clothing per unit of food obtained. At first the household will sacrifice 2.4 units of clothing to get 1 unit more of food, but as its consumption of clothing diminishes and that of food increases, the household becomes less and less willing to sacrifice further clothing for more food.[1]

The Indifference Map

So far we have constructed only a single indifference curve. However, starting at any other point of Figure 7A-1, such as *g*, there will be other combinations that will yield equal satisfaction to the household. If the points indicating all of these combinations are connected, they will form another indifference curve. This exercise can be repeated as many time as we wish, and as many indifference curves as we wish can be generated. The farther any indifference curve is from the origin, the higher will be the level of satisfaction given by any of the combinations of goods indicated by points on the curve.

A set of indifference curves is called an **indifference map**, an example of which is shown in Figure 7A-2. It specifies the household's tastes by showing its rate of substitution between the two commodities for every possible level of current consumption of these commodities. When economists say that a household's tastes are *given*, they do not mean that the household's current consumption pattern is given; rather, they mean that the household's entire indifference map is given.

FIGURE 7A-2 An Indifference Map

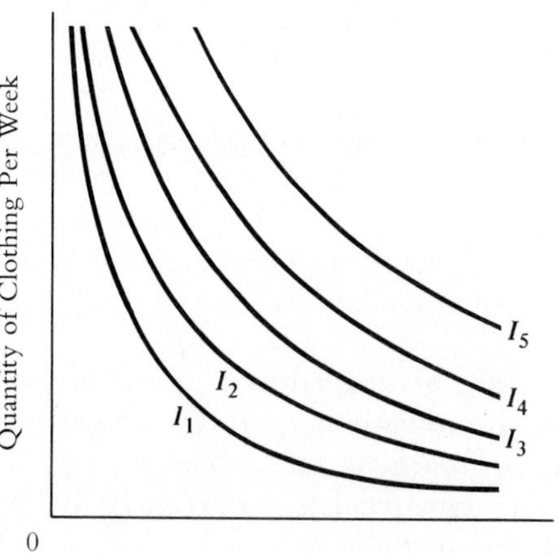

An indifference map consists of a set of indifference curves. All points on a particular curve indicate alternative combinations of food and clothing that give the household equal satisfaction. The farther the curve is from the origin, the higher is the level of satisfaction it represents. For example, I_5 is a higher indifference curve than I_4, which means that all the points on I_5 yield a higher level of satisfaction than do the points on I_4.

[1] Movements between widely separated points on the indifference curve have been examined. In terms of a small movement from any of the points on the curve, the rate at which the household will give up clothing to get food is shown by the slope of the tangent to the curve at that point. The slope of the line *T*, which is a tangent to the curve at point *b* in Figure 7A-1, may thus be thought of as the slope of the curve at that precise point. It tells us the rate at which the household will sacrifice clothing per unit of food obtained when it is currently consuming 18 units of clothing and 10 units of food (the coordinates of point *b*).

FIGURE 7A-3 The Equilibrium of a Household

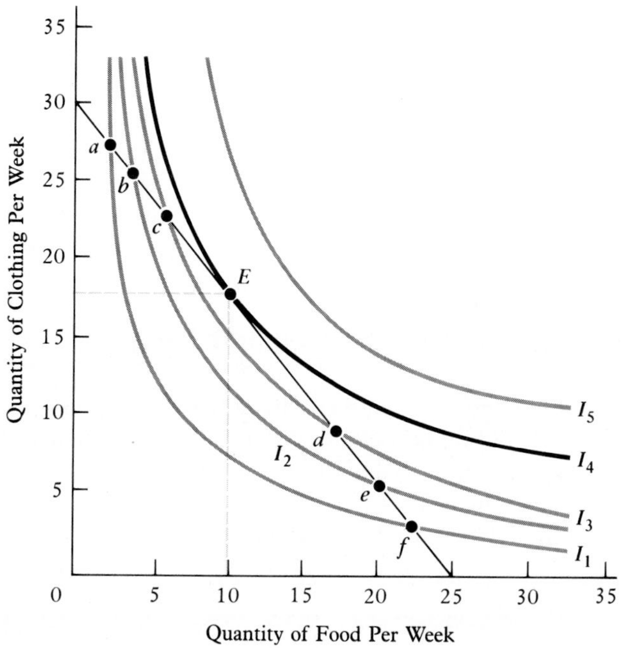

Equilibrium occurs at *E*, where an indifference curve is tangent to the budget line. The household has a money income of $750 per week and faces money prices of $25 per unit for clothing and $30 per unit for food. A combination of units of clothing and food indicated by point *a* is attainable, but by moving along the budget line, higher indifference curves can be reached. The same is true at *b* and at *c*. At *E*, however, where an indifference curve is tangent to the budget line, it is impossible to reach a higher curve by moving along the budget line. If the household did alter its consumption bundle by moving from *E* to *d*, for example, it would move to the lower indifference curve I_3 and thus to a lower level of satisfaction.

The Equilibrium of the Household

Indifference maps describe the preferences of households. Budget lines describe the possibilities open to each household. To predict what households will actually do, both sets of information must be put together. This is done in Figure 7A-3. The household's budget line is shown by the straight line, and the curves from the indifference map are also shown. Any point on the budget line is attainable, but which point will actually be chosen by the household?

Since the household wishes to maximize its satisfaction, it wishes to reach its highest attainable indifference curve. Inspection of Figure 7A-3 shows that if the household purchases any bundle on its budget line at a point cut by an indifference curve, a higher indifference curve can be reached. Only when the bundle purchased is such that the indifference curve is tangent to the budget line is it impossible for the household to alter its purchases and reach a higher curve.

The household's satisfaction is maximized at the point where an indifference curve is tangent to the budget line.

At such a tangency position the slope of the indifference curve (the household's marginal rate of substitution of the goods) is the same as the slope of the budget line (the relative prices of the goods in the market).

Common sense recognizes in this result that if the household values goods differently than the market does, there is room for profitable exchange. The household can give up some of the good it values relatively less than the market does and take in return some of the good it values relatively more than the market does. When the household is prepared to swap goods at the same rate as they can be traded on the market, there is no further opportunity for it to raise its satisfaction by substituting one commodity for the other.

The household is presented with market prices

that it cannot change. It adjusts to these prices by choosing a bundle of goods such that, at the margin, its own subjective evaluation of the goods coincides with the valuations given by market prices.

The Household's Reaction to a Change in Income

We have seen that changes in income lead to parallel shifts of the budget line—toward the origin when income falls and away from the origin when income rises. For each level of income there will be an equilibrium position at which an indifference curve is tangent to the relevant budget line. Each such equilibrium position means that the household is doing as well as it possibly can at that level of income. If we move the budget line through all possible levels of income, and if we join up all the points of equilibrium, we will trace out what is called an **income-consumption line**, an example of which is shown in Figure 7A-4. This line shows how the consumption bundle changes as income changes, with relative prices being held constant.

The Household's Reaction to a Change in Price

We already know that a change in the relative price of the two goods changes the slope of the budget line. Given a price of clothing, for each possible price of food there is an equilibrium consumption position for the household. If we connect these positions, we will trace out a **price-consumption line**, as is shown in Figure 7A-5. Notice that in this example as the relative price of food and clothing changes, the relative quantities of food and clothing purchased also change. In particular, as the price of food falls, the household buys more food.

Derivation of the Demand Curve

If food and clothing were the only two commodities purchased by households, we could derive a demand curve for food from the price-consumption line in Figure 7A-5. This line represents how the quantity of food demanded varies as the price of food changes,

FIGURE 7A-4 The Income-Consumption Line

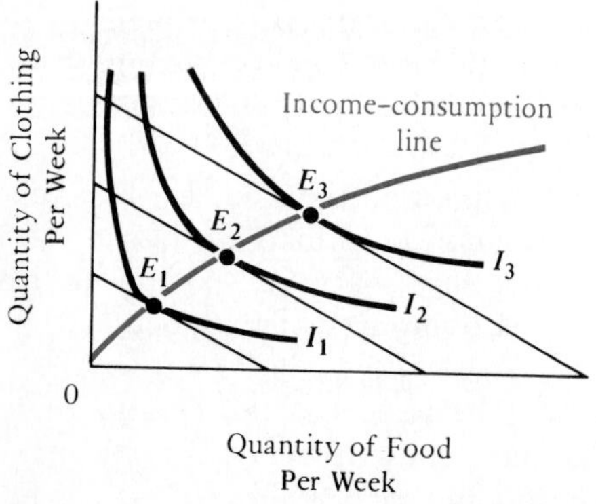

The income-consumption line shows how the household's purchases react to a change in money income with relative prices being held constant. Increases in money income shift the budget line out parallel to itself, moving the equilibrium from E_1 to E_2 to E_3. By joining up all the points of equilibrium, an income-consumption line is traced out.

FIGURE 7A-5 The Price-Consumption Line

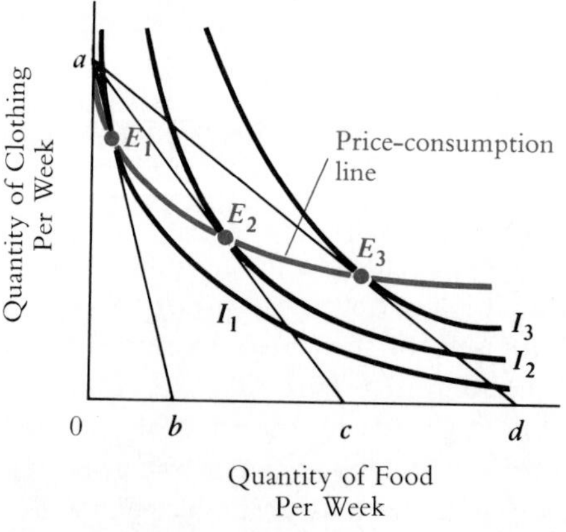

The price-consumption line shows how the household's purchases react to a change in one price with money income and other prices being held constant. Decreases in the price of food (with money income and the price of clothing being held constant) pivot the budget line from *ab* to *ac* to *ad*. The equilibrium position moves from E_1 to E_2 to E_3. By joining up all the points of equilibrium, a price-consumption line is traced out.

with the price of clothing remaining unchanged. This is what we did in Chapter 7 to explain the general idea. Now, however, we can be more precise. To use indifference theory to derive the type of demand curve introduced in Chapter 4, it is necessary to depart from the world of two commodities.

FIGURE 7A-6 Derivation of a Household's Demand Curve

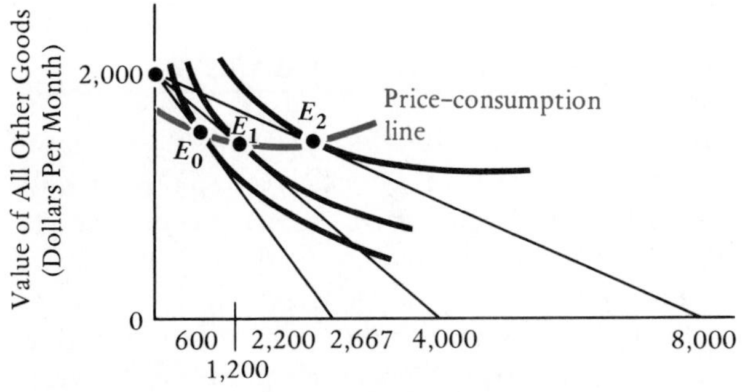

(i)

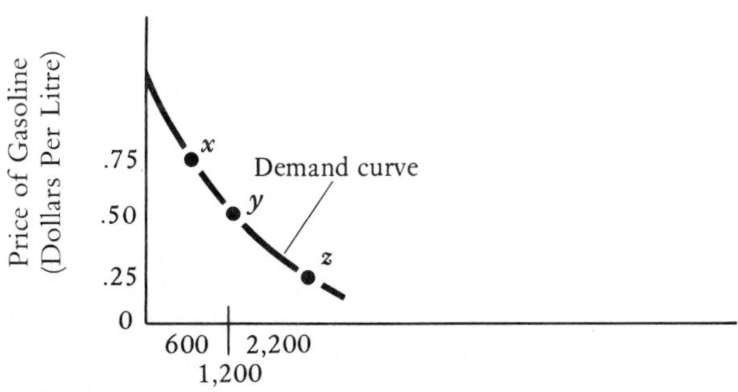

(ii)

Every point on the price-consumption line corresponds to both a price of the commodity and a quantity demanded; this is the information required for a demand curve. In part (i) the household has a money income of $2,000 and alternatively faces prices of 75, 50, and 25 cents per litre of gasoline, choosing positions E_0, E_1, and E_2 at each price. The information for litres demanded at each price is then plotted in part (ii) to yield the household's demand curve. The three points *x*, *y*, and *z* in part (ii) correspond to the three equilibrium positions E_0, E_1, and E_2 in part (i).

What happens to the household's demand for some commodity, say, gasoline, as the price of that commodity changes, *all other prices being held constant?* In part (i) of Figure 7A-6 a new type of indifference map is plotted in which litres of gasoline per month are measured on the horizontal axis and the value of all other goods consumed per month is plotted on the vertical axis. We have in effect used *everything but gasoline* as the second commodity. The indifference curves give the rate at which the household is prepared to substitute gasoline for money (which allows it to buy all other goods) at each level of consumption of gasoline and of all other goods.

To illustrate the derivation of demand curves, we use the numerical example shown in Figure 7A-6. The household is assumed to have an after-tax money income of $2,000 per month. This money income is plotted on the vertical axis, showing that if the household consumes no gasoline, it can consume $2,000 worth of other goods each month. When gasoline costs 75 cents per litre, the household could buy a maximum of 2,667 litres per month. This gives rise to the innermost budget line. Given its tastes, the household reaches equilibrium at point E_0, consuming 600 litres of gasoline and $1,550 worth of other commodities.[2] Next let the price of gasoline fall to 50 cents per litre. Now the maximum possible consumption of gasoline is 4,000 litres per month, giving rise to the middle budget line in the figure. The household's equilibrium is, as always, at the point where the new budget line is tangent to an indifference curve. At this point, E_1, the household is consuming 1,200 litres of gasoline per month and spending $1,400 on all other goods. Finally, let the price fall to 25 cents per litre. The household can now buy a maximum of 8,000 litres per month, giving rise to the outermost of the three budget lines. The household reaches equilibrium by consuming 2,200 litres of gasoline per month and by spending $1,450 on other commodities.

If we let the price vary over all possible amounts, we will trace out a complete price-consumption line, as shown in the figure. The points derived in the

[2] Our household must do a lot of traveling! If we chose more realistic figures for its consumption of gasoline, however, the various equilibrium positions would all be so close to the horizontal axis that the graph would be difficult to read.

preceding paragraph are merely three points on this line.

We have now derived all that we need to plot the household's demand curve for gasoline, since we know how much the household will purchase at each price. To draw the curve, we merely replot the data from part (i) of Figure 7A-6 onto a demand graph, as shown in part (ii) of Figure 7A-6.

Like part (i), part (ii) has quantity of gasoline on the horizontal axis. By placing the two graphs one under the other, we can directly transcribe the quantity determined on the upper graph to the lower one. We first do this for the 600 litres consumed on the innermost budget line. We now note that the price of gasoline that gives rise to that budget line is 75 cents per litre. Plotting 600 litres against 75 cents in part (ii) produces the point x, derived from point E_0 in part (i). This is one point on the household's demand curve. Next we consider the middle budget line, which occurs when the price of gasoline is 50 cents per litre. We take the figure of 1,200 litres from point E_1 in part (i) and transfer it to part (ii). We then plot this quantity against the price of 50 cents to get the point y on the demand curve. Doing the same thing for point E_2 yields the point z in part (ii): price 25 cents, quantity 2,200 litres.

Repeating the operation for all prices yields the demand curve in part (ii). Note that the two parts of Figure 7A-6 describe the same behavior. Both parts measure the quantity of gasoline on the horizontal axes; the only difference is that in part (i) the price of gasoline determines the slope of the budget line, whereas in part (ii) the price of gasoline is plotted explicitly on the vertical axis.

The Slope of the Demand Curve

The price-consumption line in part (i) of Figure 7A-6 indicates that as price decreases, the quantity of gasoline demanded increases. However, one can draw the indifference curves in such a way that the response to a given decrease in price is for *less* to be consumed rather than more. This possibility gives rise to the positively sloped demand curve, referred

FIGURE 7A-7 The Income Effect and the Substitution Effect in Indifference Theory

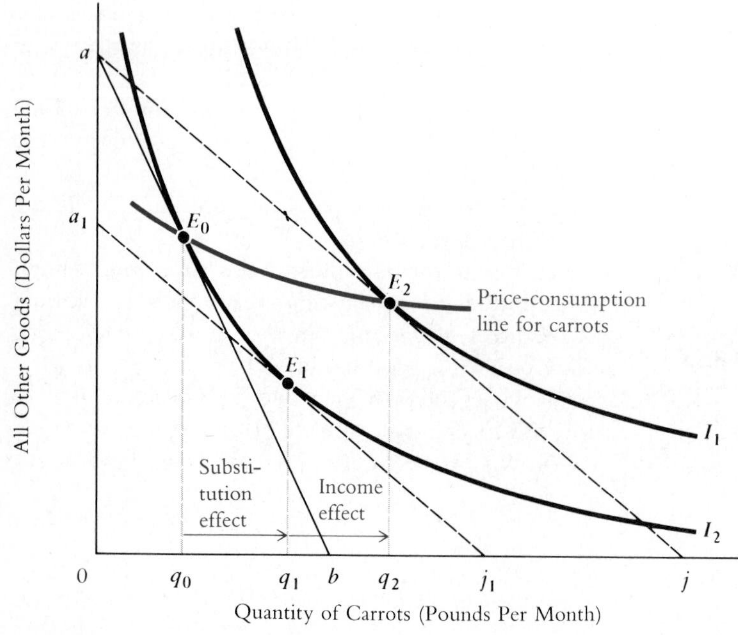

The substitution effect is defined by sliding the budget line around a fixed indifference curve; the income effect is defined by a parallel shift of the budget line. The original budget line is at *ab*, and a fall in the price of carrots takes it to *aj*. The original equilibrium is at E_0 with q_0 of carrots being consumed, and the final equilibrium is at E_2 with q_2 of carrots being consumed. To remove the income effect, imagine reducing the household's money income until it is just able to attain its original indifference curve. We do this by shifting the line *aj* to a parallel line nearer the origin that just touches the indifference curve that passes through E_0. The intermediate point E_1 divides the quantity change into a substitution effect q_0q_1 and an income effect q_1q_2. It can also be obtained by sliding the original budget line *ab* around the indifference curve until its slope reflects the new relative prices.

to as a Giffen good, that was briefly discussed in Chapter 7. Let us see how the conditions leading to this case are analyzed using indifference curves.

Income and Substitution Effects

The key, as we saw in the text, is to distinguish between the income effect and the substitution effect of a change in price. In Chapter 7 we eliminated the income effect by changing money income *until the original bundle of goods could just be consumed*. This is the approach used in the famous Slutsky equation, which is a major tool in empirical studies of demand.

In indifference theory, however, the income effect is removed by changing money income until the original level of *satisfaction*—the original indifference curve—can just be achieved. This results in a slightly different measure of the income effect, but the principle involved in separating the total change into an income effect and a substitution effect is exactly the same as in the text.[3]

The separation of the two effects according to indifference theory is shown in Figure 7A-7. The figure shows in greater detail part of the price-consumption line first drawn in Figure 7A-6. Points E_0 and E_2 are on the price-consumption line for carrots. We can think of the separation occurring in the following way. After the price of the good has fallen, we reduce money income *until the original indifference curve can just be obtained*. This leads the household to move from point E_0 to an intermediate point E_1, and this response is defined as the substitution effect. Then, to measure the income effect, we restore money income. The household moves from the point E_1 to the final point E_2, and this response is defined as the income effect.

Now compare this indifference theory definition with the Slutsky definition used in Chapter 7. In the text we measure the substitution effect of any price change by altering money income until the original bundle of goods can just be purchased. In this appendix we measure the substitution effect by altering money income until the original level of satisfaction—the original indifference curve—can just be attained.

The advantage of the Slutsky definition is that it is operational; the change in money income required to allow the original bundle to be purchased at the new prices can be simply calculated. The disadvantage is that this change does not leave unchanged the household's real income, defined as its level of satisfaction. The advantage of the indifference curve approach is that the change does leave the household's level of satisfaction unchanged and hence defines the substitution effect as the response to changes in relative prices with real satisfaction unchanged. The disadvantage is that the measurement is not easily made operational; we have to know each household's tastes to be able to make the required change in money income.

In Figure 7A-7 the income and substitution effects are in the same direction, both tending to increase quantity demanded when price falls. Is this necessarily the case? The answer is no. Though it follows from the convex shape of indifference curves that the substitution effect is always in the same direction, income effects can be in either direction. The direction depends on the distinction we drew earlier between normal and inferior goods.

Normal Goods

For a normal good, an increase in real income due to a decrease in the price of the commodity leads to its increased consumption, reinforcing the substitution effect. Because quantity demanded increases, the demand curve slopes downward.

Inferior Goods

Figure 7A-8 shows indifference curves for inferior goods. The income effect is negative in each part of the graph. This follows from the nature of an inferior good: As income rises, less of the good is consumed. In each case the substitution effect serves to increase the quantity demanded as price decreases and is offset to some degree by the negative income effect. The final result depends on the relative strengths of the two effects. In part (i) the negative income effect only partly offsets the substitution effect, and thus quantity demanded increases as a result of the price decrease, though not as much as for a normal good. This is the typical pattern for inferior goods, and it

[3] The approach used in the text (see page 128) defines constant real income as constant purchasing power. The introduction of indifference curves allows a slightly more sophisticated concept of constant real income—constant satisfaction as captured by the original indifference curve. However, the two are very similar in practice, and, indeed, in most applications the approach taken in the chapter (the Slutsky equation) is used.

FIGURE 7A-8 Income and Substitution Effects for Inferior Goods

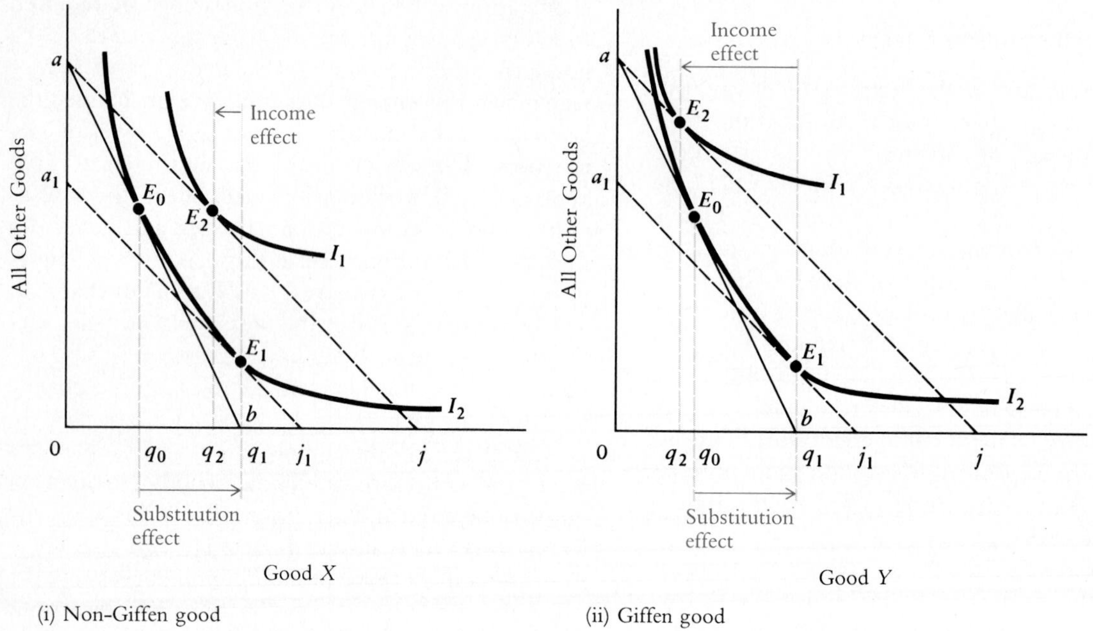

Inferior goods have negative income effects. A large enough negative income effect can outweigh the substitution effect and lead to a decrease in consumption in response to a fall in price. In each part of the figure, the household is in equilibrium at E_0, consuming a quantity q_0 of the good in question. The price then decreases, and the budget line shifts to *aj*, with a new equilibrium at E_2 and quantity consumed being q_2. In each case the substitution effect is to increase consumption from q_0 to q_1. In (i) there is a negative income effect of q_1q_2. Because this is less than the substitution effect, the latter predominates, so good *X* has a normal, downward-sloping demand curve. In (ii) the negative income effect q_1q_2 is larger than the substitution effect, and quantity consumed actually decreases. Good *Y* is thus a Giffen good.

too leads to negatively sloped demand curves, often relatively inelastic ones.

In part (ii) the negative income effect actually outweighs the substitution effect and thus leads to a positively sloped demand curve. This is the Giffen case. For this to happen, the good must be inferior, but that is not enough; the change in price must have a negative income effect *strong enough* to offset the substitution effect. A combination of circumstances that makes this possible is not often expected, and therefore a positively sloped market demand curve is an infrequent exception to the rule that demand curves have negative slopes.

SUMMARY

1. The budget line describes what the household *can* purchase; indifference curves describe the household's tastes and, therefore, refer to what it *would like* to purchase. A single indifference curve joins combinations of commodities that give the household equal satisfac-

tion and among which it is therefore indifferent. An indifference map is a set of indifference curves.

2. The basic hypothesis about tastes is that of a diminishing marginal rate of substitution. This hypothesis states that the less of one good and the more of another the household has, the less willing it will be to give up some of the first good to get an additional unit of the second. This means that indifference curves are downward-sloping and convex to the origin.
3. The household achieves an equilibrium that maximizes its satisfactions, given its budget line at the point at which an indifference curve is tangent to its budget line.
4. The income-consumption curve shows how quantity consumed changes as income changes with relative prices being held constant.
5. The price-consumption curve shows how quantity consumed changes as relative prices change. When prices change, the household will consume more of the commodity whose relative price falls.
6. The price-consumption curve relating the purchases of one particular commodity to all other commodities contains the same information as an ordinary demand curve. The horizontal axis measures quantity, and the slope of the budget line measures price. Transferring this price-quantity information to a diagram whose axes represent price and quantity leads to a conventional demand curve.
7. The effect of a change in price of one commodity, all other prices and money income being held constant, changes not only relative prices but also real incomes. A price decrease can affect consumption through both the substitution effect and the income effect.
8. Demand curves for normal goods have negative slopes because both income and substitution effects work in the same direction, a decrease in price leading to increased consumption.
9. For an inferior good, a decrease in price leads to more consumption via the substitution effect and less consumption via the income effect. In the extreme case of a Giffen good, the negative income effect more than offsets the substitution effect, and the consumption of the commodity decreases as a result of a price decrease. This is a theoretical possibility that has seldom, if ever, been observed in fact.

Appendix B to Chapter 7

Marginal Utility Theory

In this second appendix to Chapter 7 we study the marginal utility theory of household demand.

Marginal and Total Utility

We confine our attention for the moment to the consumption of a single commodity. The satisfaction that a consumer receives from consuming that commodity is called its **utility**. **Total utility** refers to the total satisfaction resulting from the consumption of that commodity by a consumer. **Marginal utility** refers to the change in satisfaction resulting from consuming a little more or a little less of that commodity. For example, the total utility of consuming 14 eggs per week is the total satisfaction that those 14 eggs provide. The marginal utility of the fourteenth egg consumed is the additional satisfaction provided by the consumption of that egg. Thus marginal utility is the difference in total utility gained by consuming 13 eggs and by consuming 14.[1]

The Hypothesis of Diminishing Marginal Utility

The basic hypothesis of utility theory, sometimes called the *law of diminishing marginal utility,* is as follows:

The utility that any household derives from successive units of a particular commodity diminishes as total consumption of the commodity increases while the consumption of all other commodities remains constant.

Consider water. Some minimum quantity is essential to sustain life, and a person would, if necessary, give up all of his or her income to obtain that quantity of water. Thus the marginal utility of that much water is extremely high. More than this bare minimum will be drunk, but the marginal utility of successive glasses of water drunk over a period of time will decline steadily.

Evidence for this hypothesis will be considered later, but you can convince yourself that it is at least reasonable by asking a few questions. How much money would induce you to cut your consumption of water by one glass per week? The answer is very little. How much would induce you to cut it by a second glass? By a third glass? To only one glass consumed per week? The answer to the last question is quite a bit. The fewer glasses you are consuming already, the higher the marginal utility of one more or one less glass of water.

Water has many uses other than for drinking. A fairly high marginal utility will be attached to some minimum quantity for bathing, but much more than this minimum will be used only for more frequent baths or for having a water level in the bathtub higher than is absolutely necessary. The last weekly litre used for bathing is likely to have a low marginal utility. Again, some small quantity of water is necessary for brushing teeth, but many people leave the water running while they brush. The water going down the drain between wetting and rinsing the brush surely has a low utility. When all the extravagant uses of water by the modern consumer are considered, the marginal utility of the last, say, 30 percent of all units consumed is probably very low, even though the total utility of *all* the units consumed is extremely high.

Utility Schedules and Graphs

The schedule in Table 7B-1 is hypothetical. It is constructed to illustrate the assumptions that have been made about utility, using movie attendance as an example. The table shows that total utility rises as the number of movies attended each month rises. Everything else being equal, the more movies the household attends each month, the more satisfaction

[1] Here and elsewhere in elementary economics it is common to use interchangeably two concepts that mathematicians distinguish. Technically, *incremental* utility is measured over a discrete interval, such as from 9 to 10, whereas *marginal* utility is a rate of change measured over an infinitesimal interval. However, common usage applies the word *marginal* when the last unit is involved, even if a one-unit change is not infinitesimal. **[11]**

TABLE 7B-1 Total and Marginal Utility Schedules

Number of movies attended per month	Total utility	Marginal utility
0	0	
1	30	30
2	50	20
3	65	15
4	75	10
5	83	8
6	89	6
7	93	4
8	96	3
9	98	2
10	99	1

Total utility rises, but marginal utility declines as this household's consumption increases. The marginal utility of 20, shown as the second entry in the third column, arises because total utility increases from 30 to 50—a difference of 20—with attendance at the second movie. To indicate that the marginal utility is associated with the change from one rate of movie attendance to another, the figures in the third column are recorded between the rows of the figures in the second column. When plotting marginal utility on a graph, it is plotted at the midpoint of the interval over which it is computed.

FIGURE 7B-1 Total and Marginal Utility Curves

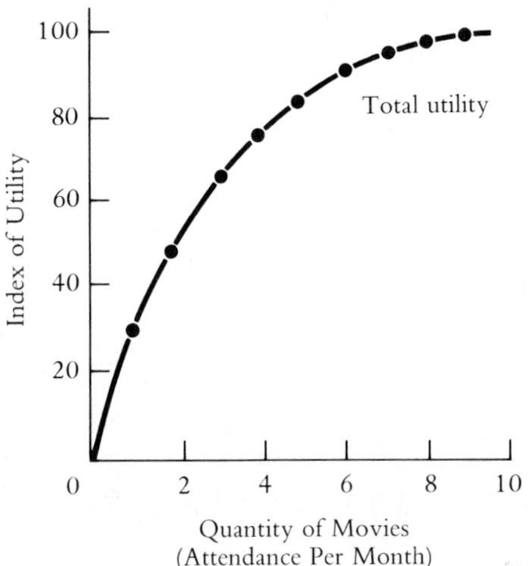

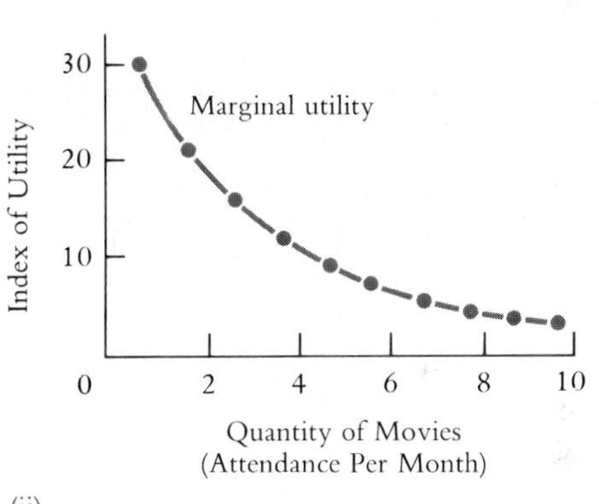

The total utility curve rises, but the marginal utility curve falls as the quantity consumed rises. The dots correspond to the values listed in Table 7B–1; smooth curves have been drawn through them.

it gets—at least over the range shown in the table. However, the marginal utility of each additional movie per month is less than that of the previous one even though each movie adds something to the household's satisfaction. The schedule in Table 7B-1 shows that marginal utility declines as quantity consumed rises. **[12]** The same data are shown graphically in the two parts of Figure 7B-1.

Maximizing Utility

A basic assumption of the economic theory of household behavior is that households try to make themselves as well off as they possibly can in the circumstances in which they find themselves. In other words, the members of a household seek to maximize their total utility.

The Equilibrium of a Household

How can a household adjust its expenditure so as to maximize its total utility? Should it go to the point at which the marginal utility of each commodity is the same, that is, the point at which it would value equally the last unit of each commodity consumed? This would make sense only if each commodity had the same price per unit. However, if a household must spend \$3 to buy an additional unit of one commodity and only \$1 to buy one unit of another, the first commodity would represent a poor use of its money if the marginal utility of each were equal. The household would be spending \$3 to get satisfaction equal to what it would have acquired for only $1.

The household that is maximizing its utility will allocate its expenditures among commodities so that the utility of the last dollar spent on each is equal.

Imagine that the household is in a position in which the utility of the last dollar spent on carrots yields three times the utility of the last dollar spent on brussels sprouts. In this case total utility can be increased by switching a dollar of expenditure from brussels sprouts to carrots and by gaining the difference between the utilities of a dollar spent on each.

The utility-maximizing household will continue to switch its expenditure from brussels sprouts to carrots as long as a dollar spent on carrots yields more utility than a dollar spent on brussels sprouts. This switching, however, reduces the quantity of brussels sprouts consumed and, given the law of diminishing marginal utility, raises the marginal utility of brussels sprouts. At the same time, switching increases the quantity of carrots consumed and thereby lowers the marginal utility of carrots.

Eventually the marginal utilities will have changed enough so that the utility of a dollar spent on carrots is just equal to the utility of a dollar spent on brussels sprouts. At this point there is nothing to be gained by a further switch of expenditure from brussels sprouts to carrots. If the household persists in reallocating its expenditure, it will further reduce the marginal utility of carrots (by consuming more of them) and raise the marginal utility of brussels sprouts (by consuming less of them). Total utility will no longer be at its maximum because the utility of a dollar spent on brussels sprouts will exceed the utility of a dollar spent on carrots.

Let us now consider the conditions for maximizing utility in a more general way. Denote the marginal utility of the last unit of commodity X by MU_x and its price by p_x. Let MU_y and p_y refer, respectively, to the marginal utility of a second commodity Y and its price. The marginal utilty per dollar of X will be MU_x/p_x. For example, if the last unit adds 30 units to utility and costs $2, its marginal utility per dollar is $30/2 = 15$.

The condition required for a household to maximize its utility is, for any pair of commodities,

$$\frac{MU_x}{p_x} = \frac{MU_y}{p_y} \qquad [1]$$

This says that the household will allocate its expenditure so that the utility gained from the last dollar spent on each commodity is equal.

This is the fundamental equation of the utility theory of demand. Each household demands each good (for example, movie attendance) up to the point at which the marginal utility per dollar spent on it is the same as the marginal utility of a dollar spent on another good (for example, water). When this condition is met, the household cannot shift a dollar of expenditure from one commodity to another and increase its utility.

An Alternative Interpretation of Household Equilibrium

If we rearrange the terms in Equation 1, we can gain additional insight into household behavior.

$$\frac{MU_x}{MU_y} = \frac{p_x}{p_y} \qquad [2]$$

The right side of this equation states the *relative* price of the two goods. It is determined by the market and is outside the control of the individual household; the household reacts to these market prices but is powerless to change them. The left side states the relative ability of the goods to add to the household's satisfaction and is within the control of the household. In determining the quantities of different goods it buys, the household also determines their marginal utilities. (If you have difficulty seeing why, look again at part (ii) of Figure 7B-1.)

If the two sides of Equation 2 are not equal, the household can increase its total satisfaction by rearranging its purchases. Assume, for example, that the price of a unit of X is twice the price of a unit of Y ($p_x/p_y = 2$), while the marginal utility of a unit of X is three times that of a unit of Y ($MU_x/MU_y = 3$). Under these conditions it is worthwhile for the household to buy more of X and less of Y. For example, if the household reduces its purchases of Y by two units, enough purchasing power is freed to buy a unit of X. Since one extra unit of X bought yields 1.5 times the satisfaction of two units of Y forgone, the switch is worth making. What about a further switch of X for Y? As the household buys more of X and less of Y, the marginal utility of X

falls and the marginal utility of Y rises. The household will go on rearranging its purchases—reducing Y consumption and increasing X consumption—until, in this example, the marginal utility of X is only twice that of Y. At this point, total satisfaction cannot be further increased by rearranging purchases between the two commodities.

Now consider what the household is doing. It faces a set of prices that it cannot change. The household responds to these prices and maximizes its satisfaction by adjusting the things it can change—the quantities of the various goods it purchases—until Equation 2 is satisfied for all pairs of commodities.

This sort of equation—one side representing the choices that the outside world gives decision makers and the other side representing the effect of those choices on their welfare—recurs in economics. It reflects the equilibrium position reached when decision makers have made the best adjustment that they can to the external forces that limit their choices.

When it enters the market, every household faces the same set of market prices. When all households are fully adjusted to these prices, each will have identical ratios of its marginal utilities for each pair of goods. Of course, a rich household may consume more of each commodity than a poor household. However, the rich and the poor households (and every other household) will adjust their *relative* purchases of each commodity so that the relative marginal utilities are the same for all. Thus if the price of X is twice the price of Y, each household will purchase X and Y to the point at which the household's marginal utility of X is twice its marginal utility of Y. Households with different tastes will, however, have different marginal utility schedules and so may consume differing relative quantities of commodities, even though the ratios of their marginal utilities are the same for all households.

Derivation of the Household's Demand Curve

To derive the household's demand curve for a commodity, it is only necessary to ask what happens when there is a change in the price of that commodity. As an example, let us do this for candy. Take Equation 2 and let X stand for candy and Y for all other commodities. What will happen if, with all other prices remaining constant, the price of candy rises? The household that started from a position of equilibrium will now find itself in a position in which

$$\frac{MU \text{ of candy}}{MU \text{ of } Y} < \frac{\text{price of candy}}{\text{price of } Y} \qquad [3]^2$$

To restore equilibrium, it must buy less candy, thereby raising its marginal utility until once again Equation 2 (where X is candy) is satisfied.[3] The hypothesis of diminishing marginal utility tells us that the marginal utility of candy *per dollar* falls when its price rises. The household began with the utility of the last dollar spent on candy equal to the utility of the last dollar spent on all other goods, but the rise in candy prices changes this. The household buys less candy (and more of other goods) until the marginal utility of candy rises enough to make the utility of a dollar spent on candy the same as it was originally.

This analysis leads to the basic prediction of demand theory:

A rise in the price of a commodity (with income and the prices of all other commodities being held constant) will lead to a decrease in the quantity of the commodity demanded by each household.

If this is what each household does, it is also what all households taken together do. Thus the theory predicts a downward-sloping market demand curve.

[2] The inequality sign (<) points to the smaller of two magnitudes. When the price of candy rises, the right side of Equation 2 increases. Until the household adjusts its consumption patterns, the left side will stay the same. Thus Equation 2 is replaced by Inequality 3.

[3] For most consumers, candy absorbs only a small proportion of their total expenditures. If, in response to a change in its price, expenditure on candy changes by $5 per month, this represents a large change in candy consumption but only a negligible change in the consumption of other commodities. Hence in the text we proceed by assuming that the marginal utilities of other commodities do not change when the price and the consumption of candy change.

SUMMARY

1. Marginal utility theory distinguishes between the total utility gained from the consumption of all units of some commodity and the marginal utility resulting from the consumption of one more unit of the commodity.
2. The basic assumption made in utility theory is that the utility the household derives from the consumption of successive units of a commodity per period of time diminishes as the consumption of that commodity increases.
3. Households are assumed to maximize utility and thus reach equilibrium when the utility derived from the last dollar spent on each commodity is equal. Another way of putting this is that the marginal utilities derived from the last unit of each commodity consumed will be proportional to their prices.
4. Demand curves have negative slopes because when the price of one commodity, X, falls, each household restores equilibrium by increasing its purchases of X sufficiently to restore the ratio of X's marginal utility to its now lower price (MU_x/p_x) to the same level as it has achieved for all other commodities.

Chapter 8

Using Demand Theory

In Chapter 7 we covered some basic material concerning the theory of demand. In this chapter we go further and develop some important applications of this theory. We start by showing the link between the household demand curves that we discussed in Chapter 7 and the market demand curves that we discussed in earlier chapters. We then discuss some issues that arise in demand theory as a result of *uncertainty*.

Market and Individual Demand Curves

Market demand curves tell how much is demanded by all purchasers. For example, in Figure 4-1 (page 59) the market demand for carrots is 90,000 tons when the price is $40 per ton. This 90,000 tons is the sum of the quantities demanded by millions of different households. It may be made up of 4 pounds for the Carsons, 7 pounds for the Chows, 1.5 pounds for the Smiths, and so on. The demand curve in Figure 4-1 also tells us that when the price rises to $60, the total quantity demanded falls to 77,500 tons per month. This quantity too can be traced back to individual households. The Carsons might buy only 3 pounds, the Chows 6.5 pounds, and the Smiths none at all. Notice that we have now described two points not only on the market demand curve but also on the demand curves of each of these households.

The market demand curve is the horizontal sum of the demand curves of individual households.

It is the horizontal sum because we wish to add quantities demanded at a given price, and quantities are measured in the horizontal direction on a conventional demand curve. This is illustrated in Figure 8-1.

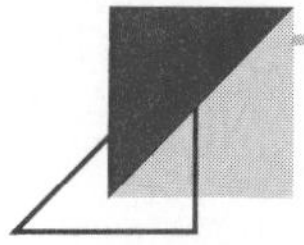

Some Applications of Consumers' Surplus

In subsequent chapters we will find many uses for the concept of consumers' surplus. In this chapter we show how it can be used to resolve some very old problems.

The Paradox of Value

Early economists, struggling with the problem of what determines the relative prices of commodities, encountered what they called the *paradox of value*: Many necessary commodities, such as

FIGURE 8-1 The Relationship Between Household and Market Demand Curves

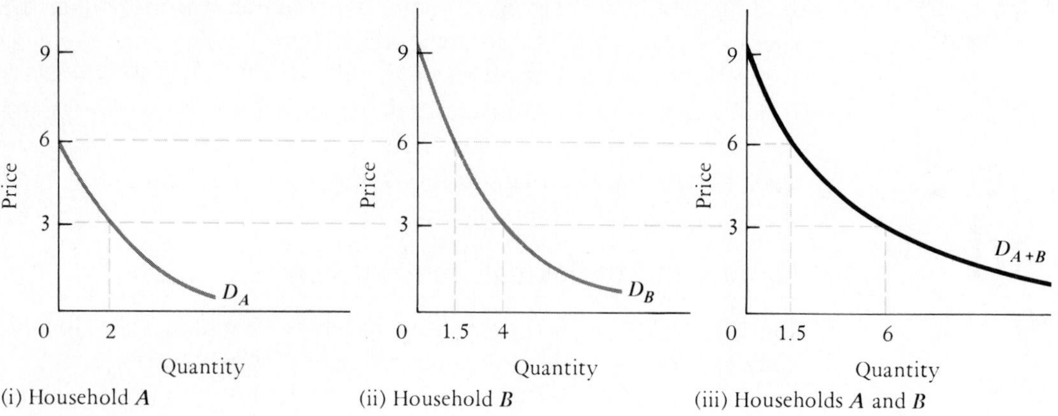

An aggregate demand curve is the horizontal sum of the individual demand curves of all households in the market. The figure illustrates aggregation over only two households. At a price of \$3, household A purchases 2 units and household B purchases 4 units; thus together they purchase 6 units. No matter how many households are involved, the process is the same.

water, have prices that are low compared with the prices of luxury commodities, such as diamonds. Water is necessary to our existence, whereas diamonds are used mostly for frivolous purposes and could disappear from the face of the earth tomorrow without causing any real hardship. Does it not seem odd, then, these economists asked, that water is so cheap and diamonds are so expensive? It took a long time to resolve this apparent paradox, so it is not surprising that even today analogous confusions cloud many policy discussions.

The key to resolving this "paradox" lies in the important distinction between what one would pay to avoid having one's consumption of a commodity reduced to zero and what one would pay to gain the use of one more unit of that commodity. This point involves a distinction between total and marginal values that is frequently encountered in many branches of economics.

We have seen already that the area under the demand curve shows what the household would pay for the commodity if it had to purchase it unit by unit. It is thus a measure of the total value that the household places on *all* of the units it consumes. In Figure 7-7 on page 140 the *total* value of q_0 units is the entire shaded area (light and dark) under the demand curve.

What about the *marginal value* that the household places on one more, or one less, than the q_0 units it is currently consuming? This is given by the commodity's market price, which is p_0 in this case. Facing a market price of p_0, the household buys all the units that it values at p_0 or greater but does not purchase any units that it values at less than p_0. It follows that the household places on the last unit consumed of any commodity a value that is measured by the commodity's price.[1]

Now look at the total market value of the commodity. This is the amount that everyone spends to purchase it. It is price multiplied by quantity. In Figure 7-7 this is the dark shaded rectangle with sides p_0 and q_0.

We have seen that the total value that consumers

[1] In terms of indifference theory (Appendix A to Chapter 7), the price measures the rate at which the household is prepared to substitute the good in question for money—that is, the slope, at the equilibrium point, of the indifference curve drawn with the quantity of the good on one axis and consumption of all other goods, measured in money units, on the other axis. In terms of utility theory (Appendix B to Chapter 7), the price measures the marginal utility of the last unit that the household purchases.

place on a given amount of a commodity, as measured by the relevant area under the demand curve, is different from the total market value of a commodity, as given by the commodity's price multiplied by the quantity consumed. Being different, the two values do not have to be related. Figure 8-2 illustrates a case in which a good with a total high value has a low market value, and vice versa.

The resolution of the paradox of value is that a good that is very plentiful, such as water, will have a low price and will thus be consumed to the point where all households place a low value on the last unit consumed, whether or not they place a high value on their total consumption of the commodity. By contrast, a commodity that is relatively scarce will have a high market price, and consumption will

FIGURE 8-2 Total Value Versus Market Value

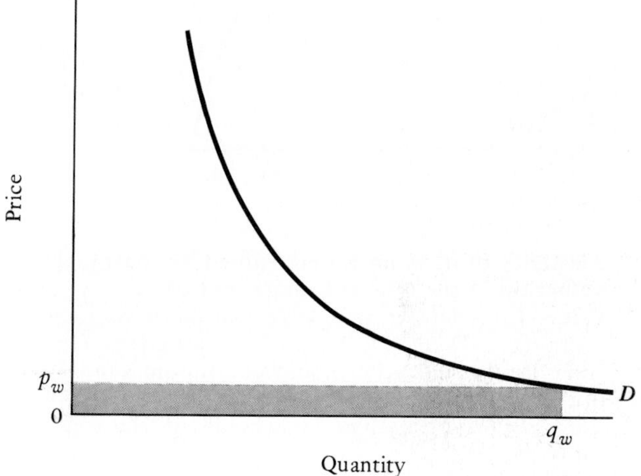

(i) Water

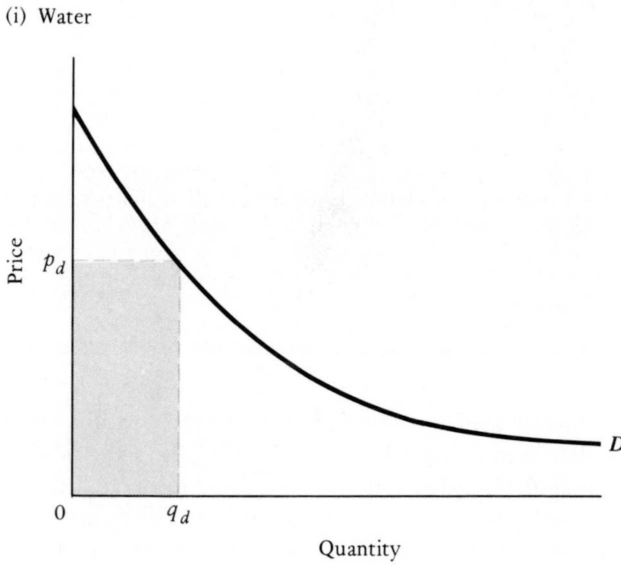

(ii) Diamonds

The market value of the amount of some commodity bears no necessary relationship to the total value that consumers place on that amount. The graph presents hypothetical demand curves for water and diamonds that are meant to be stylized versions of the real curves. The total value that households place on water, as shown by the area under the demand curve, is great—indeed, we do not even show the curve for very small quantities because people would pay all they had rather than be deprived completely of water. The total valuation that households place on diamonds is shown by the area under the demand curve for diamonds. This is clearly less than the total value placed on water.

The low supply of diamonds makes diamonds scarce and keeps diamonds high in price, as shown by p_d in part (ii) of the figure. Thus the total market value of diamonds sold, indicated by the dark shaded area of $p_d q_d$, is high.

The large supply of water makes water plentiful and makes water low in price, as shown by p_w in part (i) of the figure. Thus the total market value of water consumed, indicated by the dark shaded area of $p_w q_w$, is low.

therefore stop at a point where consumers place a high value on the last unit consumed, regardless of the value that they place on their total consumption of the good.

We have now reached an important conclusion:

Because the market price of a commodity depends on demand and supply, there is nothing paradoxical in there being a commodity on which consumers place a high total value selling for a low price and hence having only a small amount spent on it.

Necessities, Luxuries, and Elasticity

In ordinary discussions people often distinguish between necessities and luxuries, necessities being commodities that are difficult to do without and luxuries being commodities that could be fairly easily dispensed with. The distinction is somewhat arbitrary; for example, are eggs a necessity or a luxury? Nonetheless, some sense can be made of the distinction by understanding it in order to compare the *total* values that households place on their consumption of different commodities. Earlier in this chapter we learned to measure these total values by the areas under demand curves. Using this terminology, we would say that a necessity has a very large area under its demand curve; a luxury has a smaller area under its demand curve.

A frequent error occurs when people try to use knowledge of total values to predict demand elasticities. It is sometimes argued that since luxuries can be given up, they have highly elastic demands; when their prices rise, households can stop purchasing them. It is likewise argued that necessities have highly inelastic demands because when prices rise, households have no choice but to continue to buy them.

However, elasticity of demand depends on how consumers value commodities at the margin, not on how much they value the total consumption of the commodity. The relevant question for the determination of elasticity is, "How much do households value a bit more of some commodity?" and not "How much do they value *all* of the commodity that they are now consuming?"

Demand theory leads to the prediction that when the price of a commodity rises, each household will reduce its purchases of that commodity until it values

FIGURE 8-3 The Relationship of Elasticity of Demand to Total Value

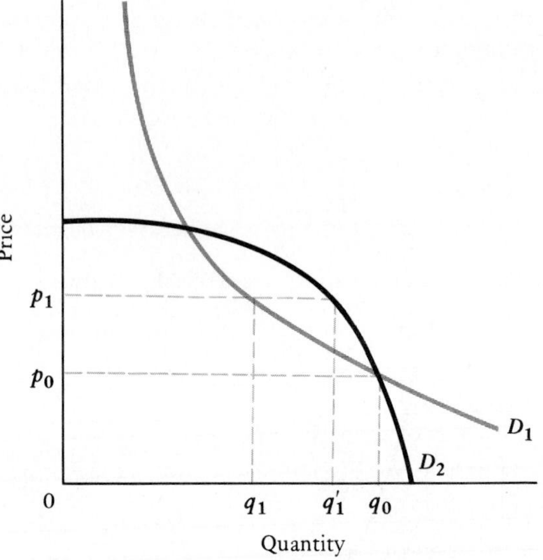

Elasticity of demand is determined by marginal valuation in the relevant range, not total value. Consider two alternative demand curves for a commodity, D_1 and D_2. Suppose that price is p_0. Given either demand curve, the household consumes the quantity q_0, where the last unit consumed is valued at p_0. When the price rises to p_1, households cut their consumption.

If the black line D_2 is the demand curve, consumption falls to only q_1', and the demand for the product is quite inelastic. If, however, the gray line D_1 is the demand curve, consumption falls to q_1, and the demand for the product is less inelastic.

Although the shape of the demand curve in the relevant range is important, its shape outside of this range is irrelevant for determining elasticity. However, total value depends on the whole area under the curve. Depending on the shape of the curve up to q_0, either curve can show more or less total value than the other. Thus total value has no influence on market behavior in response to a change in price from p_0 to p_1.

the last unit consumed of the commodity at the price that it must pay for that unit. Will the reduction in quantity required to raise the valuation be a little or a lot? This depends on the shape of the demand curve in the relevant range. If the demand curve is flat, a large change in quantity is required, and demand will be elastic. If the curve is steep, a small change will suffice, and demand will be inelastic. Figure 8-3 presents two possible responses to a doubling in price. It leads to this important conclusion:

The size of the response of quantity demanded to a change in price depends on the value that households place on having a bit more or a bit less of the commodity and has no necessary relationship to the value that they place on their total consumption of the quantity in question.

Box 8-1 provides an example from outside the field of economics of the importance of distinguishing between the total value that people get from some activity and the value that they would place on doing a bit more or a bit less of it.

Free, Scarce, and Freely Provided Goods

A **free good** is one for which the quantity supplied exceeds the quantity demanded at a price of zero. Such goods therefore will not command positive prices in a market economy. A household can become better off by increasing its consumption of free goods as long as it places a positive value on the extra units consumed. It follows that free goods will be consumed up to the point at which the value that households place on another unit consumed is zero. At some times in some places, air, water, salt, sand, and wild fruit have been free goods. Note that a good may be free at one time or place but not at another.

A **scarce good** is one for which the quantity demanded exceeds the quantity supplied at a price of zero. If all such goods had zero prices, the total amount that people would want to consume would greatly exceed the amount that could be produced. Such goods therefore will command positive prices in a market economy. Most goods are scarce goods.

Many people have strong views about the prices that are charged for certain commodities. These views are often an emotional reaction to the total values of the goods rather than to their marginal values. Here is an example: "Because water is such a complete necessity of life to rich and to poor, it is wrong to make people pay for water. Instead, the government should provide free water for everyone."

When deciding between a zero price and a modest price for water, the relevant question for the consumer is not, "Is water so necessary that we want everyone to be provided with some of it?" but rather "Are the marginal uses of water so important that we are willing to use scarce resources to provide the necessary quantities?" The distinction is important because the two questions will have different answers.

The evidence that we have about the consumption of water at various prices suggests that the demand curve for water is shaped like the curve shown in part (i) of Figure 8-2. If so, the difference in consumption that results from providing water free or charging a modest price for it will be large. The additional water consumed, however, is costly to provide, and its provision requires scarce resources that could have been used to produce other commodities. If the value that households place on the commodities forgone is higher than the value that they place on the extra water consumed, households are worse off as a result of receiving water free. A charge for water would release resources from water production to produce commodities that households value more highly at the margin. Of course, some minimum quantity of water could be provided free to every household, but the effects of this would be quite different from the effects of making all water free.

It follows that neither the gain to consumers of encouraging a little more consumption of some commodity nor the loss from inducing a little less can be inferred from a knowledge of the total value placed on all of the consumption of that commodity.

Similar considerations apply to food, medical services, and a host of other commodities that are necessities of life but that also have numerous low-value uses that will be encouraged if a scarce commodity is provided at a zero price.

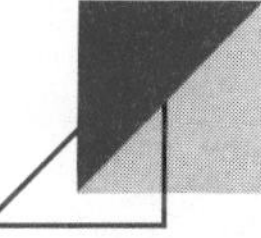

Household Behavior Under Uncertainty[2]

In Chapter 7 we studied how households choose between alternatives that are *certain*. As we have seen earlier in this chapter, the theory of demand that results from this approach is very powerful in explaining many real-world events that we observe.

[2] The remainder of this chapter can be skipped without loss of continuity.

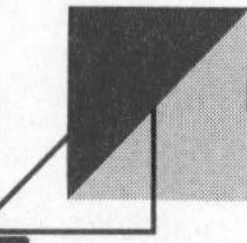

BOX 8-1

What Do Attitude Surveys Measure?

Surveys, popular both in the daily newspapers and in sociology and political science, often take the form of asking such questions as these:

"Do you like the Progressive Conservatives more than the Liberals?"

"In deciding to live in area *A* rather than area *B*, what factors influenced your choice? List the following in order of importance: neighbors, schools, closeness to swimming area, price and quality of housing, play areas for children, general amenities."

"In choosing a university, what factors were important to you? List the following in order of importance: environment, academic excellence, residential facilities, parents' opinion, school opinion, athletic facilities, tuition."

The three survey questions cited, and most of those you might add, attempt to measure the *total* value that households place on some activity rather than the *marginal* value that they would place on a little more or a little less of that activity.

The total value being measured includes the consumers' surplus. Of course, people are free to measure anything that interests them, and in some cases knowledge of total valuation may be useful. But in most cases actual behavior is determined by marginal valuation, and anyone who attempts to predict such behavior from a knowledge of total valuation, even if it is correct, will be hopelessly in error.

Where the behavior being predicted involves an either-or decision, such as a vote for the Progressive Conservatives or the Liberals in a two-party contest, total value attached to each choice will indeed be what matters because the voters are choosing one or the other. However, where the decision is marginal, between a little more and a little less, total value is not what will determine behavior.

A recent poll taken in a large U.S. city showed that two-thirds of the city's voters rated its excellent school system as an important asset. Yet in a subsequent election the voters turned down a school bond issue. Is this irrational behavior, as newspaper editorials charged? Does it show a biased sample in the poll? It demonstrates neither. The poll measured the people's assessment of the total value derived from the school system (high), whereas the school bond issue vote was a result of the people's assessment of the marginal value of a little more money being spent on the school system (low). There is nothing contradictory in anyone's feeling that the total value of the city's fine school system is high but that the city (or the taxpayer) has other needs that have a higher value at the margin than further money being spent on schools.

A recent survey showed—paradoxically, it claimed—that many Canadians are getting more pleasure from their families just at the time that they are electing to have smaller families. There is nothing paradoxical about a shift in tastes that increases the marginal value of one or two children and reduces the marginal value of each additional child, nor is there anything paradoxical about a parent's getting a high total value from the total time being spent with the children but assigning a low marginal value to the prospect of spending additional time with them each evening.

However, many, if not all, of the choices that households make involve *uncertainty*. Of course, for many problems, the role of uncertainty is incidental, and the standard analysis assuming certainty is perfectly adequate. However, there are some situations, such as whether to buy lottery tickets or insurance, in which uncertainty is central to the issue. In the remainder of this chapter we examine how the theory of demand deals with uncertainty.[3]

What are the sources of uncertainty? How does

[3] For the purposes of this chapter we follow convention and use the terms *risk* and *uncertainty* synonymously, although more advanced treatments sometimes distinguish between the two.

uncertainty influence household decisions? How do markets cope with uncertainty? Is the market for insurance different from the market for carrots?

Sources of Uncertainty

Uncertainty arises whenever decisions are made with imperfect information about the alternatives. It is present in virtually all aspects of economic life. Any action, some of the effects of which will be felt in the future, will of necessity have some uncertainty attached to it. It is obviously true of speculative purchases of gold, real estate, or stocks. It is also true when you buy a consumer durable; for example, since you cannot be sure about the reliability and durability of a new automobile, you are uncertain about the value of the services that the car will deliver. Box 8-2 takes up the interesting problems that this poses for the used-car market.

Uncertainty obviously complicates the household's decisions. For example, a household may be uncertain about the quality of the products from among which it is choosing. The household may think that the more expensive Brand Q will last longer and require less maintenance expenditure than the cheaper Brand X. How much longer will Brand Q last, and how much less maintenance is involved? Another household may be deciding between buying a condominium in the ritzy part of town or buying a cheaper one "on the wrong side of the tracks." Buying the expensive one may reduce the chances of being broken into, but by how much?

Consider a household choosing between bundle *A* (10 units of food and 5 units of clothing) and bundle *B* (6 units of food and 12 units of clothing). The household may know with certainty the contents of each bundle, but it may be unsure of what the weather will be or whether relatives might drop by for the weekend. Hence it does not know for certain what the relative merits of each bundle of food and clothing will turn out to be. In this case it knows with certainty what is in each bundle, but it is uncertain about the circumstances that will occur while the goods are being consumed. These circumstances are often called either the *state of the world* or the *state of nature*.

If different commodities or bundles of commodities have different values in different states of the world, then uncertainty about the state of the world introduces an important element of uncertainty into the problem of household choice.

This chapter is about households, so we shall concentrate on household behavior under uncertainty. However, firms also make choices under uncertainty; production takes time and involves spending money now to produce goods that will be sold in the uncertain future. Indeed, all decision makers operate under conditions of significant uncertainty much of the time.

Many of the principles discussed in this chapter were first developed by analyzing games of chance such as roulette or coin tossing. The same principles arise in consumption and production decisions involving uncertainty, but it is often easier to appreciate them in the context of the kind of games that were first studied. The discussion in this chapter gives only an intuitive overview of the principles involved.[4]

The Characterization of Risky Events

Much of what is involved in making risky choices can be captured in two measures: the *expected value* of the choice and the *degree of risk* attached to making the choice.

Expected value. Let us say that you are playing a game in which a fair coin is tossed once every minute. (A fair coin is one for which there is an equal chance that either heads or tails will turn up; that is, a coin with a probability of .5 that it will turn up heads and a probability of .5 that it will turn up tails.) The game is as follows: You win $1 if the result is heads, and you lose $1 if the result is tails.

The expected value of the outcome of any game can be expressed by adding up the various possible outcomes, each multiplied by its probability of occurrence. The amount that you would expect to win in this coin toss game, the *expected value of the game*, is zero. The probability of winning $1 is one-half, and the probability of losing $1 is one-half. Thus, the expected value of any toss of the coin is

$$\$1(0.5) - \$1(0.5) = \$0.5 - \$0.5 = \$0$$

[4] Be forewarned that many of the ideas are quite subtle. To handle them rigorously requires careful definitions and some complex analysis.

BOX 8-2

Used-Car Prices: The Problem of "Lemons"

It is common for people to regard the large loss of value of a new car in the first year of its life as a sign that consumers are overly style-conscious and will always pay a big premium for the latest in anything. Professor George Akerlof of the University of California suggests a different explanation based on the proposition that the flow of services expected from a 1-year-old car that is *purchased on the used-car market* will be lower than those expected from an *average* 1-year-old car on the road. Consider his theory.

Any particular model year of automobiles will include a certain proportion of "lemons"—cars that have one or more serious defects. Purchasers of new cars of a certain year and model take a chance on their car's turning out to be a lemon. Those who are unlucky and get a lemon are more likely to resell their car than those who are lucky and get a quality car. Hence in the used-car market there will be a disproportionately large number of lemons for sale. (Also, not all cars are driven in the same manner; those that are driven for long distances or under bad conditions are much more likely to be traded in or sold as used cars than those that are driven on good roads and for moderate distances.)

Thus buyers of used cars are right to be on the lookout for low-quality cars, while salespeople are quick to invent reasons for the high quality of the cars they are selling ("It was owned by a little old lady who drove it only on Sundays"). Because it is difficult to identify a lemon or a badly treated used car before buying it, the purchaser is prepared to buy a used car only at a price that is low enough to offset the increased probability that it is of poor quality.

This is a rational consumer response to uncertainty and may explain why 1-year-old cars typically sell for a discount that is much larger than can be explained by the physical depreciation that occurs in one year in the *average* car of that model. The large discount reflects the lower services that the purchaser can expect from a used car because of the higher probability that it will be a lemon.

If you play the game for 10 minutes, you may be lucky and win \$10. There is an equal chance that you will be unlucky and lose \$10. It is much more likely, however, that you will get some heads and some tails and end up winning or losing a sum much smaller than \$10. The single most likely outcome is that you will exactly break even; that is, you will receive the expected value of the game. The two next most likely results are that you will win \$2 (six heads and four tails), or that you will lose \$2 (six tails and four heads). Outcomes with larger gains and larger losses become less and less likely until you get to the two least likely results: winning \$10 and losing \$10.

Now consider playing the game repeatedly day after day, for several months. It is still possible that you will end up winning \$10 or losing \$10. After all, if you break even after many days of play, you still may encounter 10 heads in a row in your last 10 plays. As you go on playing, however, it is more likely that your gain or loss will be close to the expected outcome of zero and less likely that your gain or loss will be high.

More generally, the expected value of any choice is the average outcome that would arise from playing the game many times.

Degree of risk. In the game just discussed you stood to win \$1 per toss or to lose \$1 per toss. If you play for 10 minutes, your maximum possible loss is \$10. Now suppose that you play the same game but you win \$100 on heads and lose \$100 on tails. This still seems to be a fair game since it has an expected outcome of zero, but because the stakes are higher, you now risk more if you play it for any given amount of time. There is the same chance that you will encounter an unlucky run of 10 tails, but now you stand to lose \$1,000. Clearly there is more risk attached to the second game than to the first.

Risk refers to the dispersion of the possible results. In the first game the possible results from 10 minutes of play are dispersed over a range running from +\$10 to −\$10; in the second game the possible results are dispersed over a range running from +\$1,000 to −\$1,000.

The risk attached to any choice refers to the dispersion of the possible outcomes resulting from making that choice.[5]

Fair and Unfair Games

The coin toss games that we have considered so far are fair games in the sense that if you play them, you have just as much chance of winning as of losing. A lottery in which all of the ticket revenues are paid out is also a fair game. Say, for example, that 100 lottery tickets are sold for \$1 each and that a draw then determines which of the ticket holders wins \$100. This is called a *fair game,* because each ticket holder has 1 chance in 100 of winning \$99 (the person's own \$1 back and the \$99 in winnings) and 99 chances in 100 of losing \$1. The expected value of buying the lottery ticket is \$99(1/100) − \$1(99/100) = \$0.99 − \$0.99 = \$0. A **fair game** is one for which the expected value of the outcome is zero.

If you play a fair game repeatedly, you may end up winning or losing, depending on the "luck of the toss," but the *average gain or loss per play* will tend to approach zero as the number of times that the game is repeated increases.

Now consider playing the coin toss game under the rule that if you toss heads you win \$2 and if you toss tails you lose \$1. The expected value of the outcome of each toss is \$2(0.5) − \$1(0.5) = \$1 − \$0.50 = \$0.50. If you play the game only once, you will either win \$2 or lose \$1. If you play it repeatedly, however, your average gain will tend toward 50 cents per toss. This is not a fair game; instead, it is biased in your favor (and hence biased against whomever you are playing with).

Finally, consider lotteries. In most cases the organizers—be they a firm, a charity, or the government—take a proportion of the ticket revenue as their profit and distribute the rest as prize money. Such lotteries are *not* fair games. They are biased against the participants, because the expected value of participating in the game is negative.

To illustrate this point, take our example of a lottery in which 100 tickets are sold at \$1 each. Now, however, assume that the organizers take \$50 as their profit and pay the other \$50 to the winning ticket. The expected value of a lottery ticket is now \$49(1/100) − \$1(99/100) = \$0.49 − \$0.99 = −\$0.50. The negative value shows that this is not a fair game; instead, it is biased against anyone who plays it. (Another way of viewing this is to ask yourself what would happen if you bought all the tickets. You would spend \$100 and win \$50, thus incurring a loss of \$50. This is a loss of 50 cents per ticket, which, as we have seen already, is the expected value of each ticket.)

Preferences Toward Risk

How do people behave when they face risky choices? Some people dislike risk and would pay to avoid or eliminate it. Others like risk and, everything else being equal, would choose a more risky alternative over a less risky one. Still others are indifferent about it, so the relative risk of two alternatives will not influence their choice.

Risk-neutral individuals are indifferent about risk. They care only about the average return that a given activity is expected to yield, and they will engage in the activity only if the expected return is positive. Thus they are indifferent about playing a fair game, would willingly play one that is biased in their favor, and would not play one that is biased against them.

Risk-averse individuals do not like risk. They will engage in a risky activity only if the expected return is high enough to compensate them for the risk that they will have to take. (The required increase in the expected return is often called the *risk premium.*) Thus risk-averse individuals will play only games that are sufficiently biased in their favor to overcome their aversion to risk; they will be unwilling to play fair games, let alone ones that are biased against them.

Risk lovers like risk. They will engage in some risky activities simply in order to get some of the pleasure that the risk entails. Thus risk lovers will not only gladly play fair games and games biased in their favor but also willingly play some games that are biased against them, the extent of the love of risk

[5] For many purposes, the dispersion can be satisfactorily measured by the range of possible outcomes; in other situations it can be better measured by what is called the *variance* of the possible results.

being measured by the degree of bias that a person is willing to accept. (No one would knowingly buy a ticket for a lottery in which the prize were zero, but some extreme risk lovers might enter a lottery in which only 10 percent of the ticket money was to be paid out as prize money.)

How do these differences influence the reaction to the fair coin toss game that we studied? Recall that each play offers an equal chance of winning or losing \$1. Risk-neutral people are indifferent about playing the game. Thus they must value the chance of winning \$1 the same as they value the chance of losing \$1; that is, their valuation of a \$1 change in their wealth is the same for small increases or decreases to their wealth. Risk-averse people would choose not to play the game. Thus they value the chance of winning \$1 less than they value the chance of losing \$1; that is, their valuation of a \$1 change in their wealth is larger for decreases than for increases. Risk lovers would choose to play the game. Thus they must value the chance of winning \$1 more than they value the chance of losing \$1; that is, their valuation of a \$1 change in their wealth is larger for increases than for decreases.[6]

The Market for Insurance

What role do preferences toward risk play in the market for insurance? We shall first study household demand for insurance, and then we shall look briefly at the behavior of insurance firms.

The Demand for Insurance

Suppose that there is 1 chance in 100 that some unfavorable outcome will happen in which you will lose some asset (possibly your house) that you value at \$100,000, and suppose that there are 99 chances in 100 that nothing at all will happen to this asset. The most likely outcome is that nothing will happen, but there is a small chance that you will incur a very big loss.

Suppose that someone now offers you an insurance policy that costs \$1,000. If nothing else happens, you simply lose the \$1,000. However, if the disaster occurs and you suffer the loss of \$100,000, you will be fully compensated.

If you buy the policy, you give up \$1,000 for certain, but you are no longer at risk. If you do not buy the policy, you are taking a risk. The possible outcomes from having no insurance are 1 chance in 100 of losing \$100,000 and 99 chances in 100 of losing nothing. This gives an expected value of $-\$100{,}000(1/100) + \$0(99/100) = -\$1{,}000$. The insurance policy represents a "fair game" because the expected values of both courses of action are the same—a loss of \$1,000.

Although the expected values of the two choices are the same, not buying the insurance is a much riskier choice than buying it. If you do not buy the insurance and are lucky, you save the \$1,000 insurance premium; however, if you are unlucky, you lose \$100,000. If you buy the insurance, you lose \$1,000 for certain.

Someone who is risk-averse would buy the policy, whereas someone who is a risk lover would not. Since both courses have the same expected value, a risk-neutral person would be indifferent to either buying the insurance policy or not buying it—if there were no other considerations.

This discussion assumes that the insurance policy offers a fair bet, but insurance companies must themselves make money, so they do not offer their policyholders mathematically fair policies. In the case in which the risk was 1 chance in 100 of losing \$100,000, the policy would actually cost more than \$1,000—say, \$1,200. Now the expected return from holding the policy remains at \$1,000, but the cost of the policy is \$1,200; thus the expected value of buying the policy is negative, and a risk-neutral person would not buy it. If the excess of the cost of insurance over the expected return is not too large, some risk-averse individuals would still buy the insurance.

In a market in which insurance companies must charge a premium that is large enough to provide them with an expectation of profit, neither a risk lover nor a risk-neutral person would buy insurance; only some risk-averse individuals would.

Most people choose to buy insurance for a large number of activities. This can be explained by as-

[6] In terms of the concepts introduced in Appendix B to Chapter 7, risk neutrality arises when there is constant marginal utility of income. Similarly, risk aversion arises when there is diminishing marginal utility of income, and risk loving arises when there is increasing marginal utility of income. The basis for this classification comes from the pathfinding 1940s analysis by two Princeton University professors, John von Neumann and Oscar Morgenstern, who developed the *expected utility hypothesis*. This hypothesis holds that consumer evaluation of a risky prospect can be described by calculating the expected value of the utility that would be obtained in each of the possibilities.

suming that most people are sufficiently risk-averse. Although the cost of the policy exceeds the expected value of the loss without insurance, most people feel that this is compensated for by eliminating the risk that has to be borne if they are uninsured. Box 8-3 explores the problems that arise in reconciling this explanation with the observation that many people engage in the risky activity of gambling.

TABLE 8-1 Incomes When Risks Are and Are Not Pooled

	Risks not pooled		Risks pooled
	John	June	Each
Tails-tails	$ 0	$ 0	$ 0
Tails-heads	0	500	250
Heads-tails	500	0	250
Heads-heads	500	500	500

Pooling of independent risks reduces risk. Each person gets an income of $500 if he or she tosses heads and nothing if he or she tosses tails. There are four possible results. In two of them, one heads and one tails occurs. In the other two, either two tails or two heads occurs. When each accepts his or her own risks, each expects an income of $500 half the time and zero the other half. When the incomes are pooled and then split, only one combination in four gives them zero income, while half of the time they will get $250. The deviations of their monthly incomes from the expected value of $250 is decreased by pooling, but the expected value itself is unchanged.

The Supply of Insurance

When households buy insurance, they are essentially "trading in risk" with those who sell them the insurance. Why are firms willing to supply insurance to households who demand it?

An insurance firm takes your money and agrees to pay out a certain sum should the unlucky event strike you. It expects to make profits on the difference between the premiums it charges and the amount of claims it expects to pay to its customers. These profits, however, are not guaranteed. Conceivably, the insurance firm itself could have a run of bad luck in which many of the people it insures suffer losses at the same time. Indeed, conceivably, it could even incur losses sufficiently large to cause it to go bankrupt.

How can insurance companies afford to absorb their customers' risks? The main explanation of insurance company behavior relies on their ability to engage in *risk pooling* and *risk sharing* in order to reduce the total amount of risk that has to be borne by them and their customers.

Risk pooling. To see what is involved in the pooling of risks, consider two individuals who receive an income that varies according to the toss of a coin. (Once again, the coin toss is simply an example used to illustrate the principles that apply for any source of uncertainty.) Each individual tosses a coin each month. If heads comes up, John receives $500; if tails comes up, he receives nothing. The same applies to June: She receives $500 if she tosses heads and nothing if she tosses tails. The expected value of each person's income is $500(0.5) = $250 per month. Over a long period of time, each person's monthly income will indeed average close to $250, but John and June may not like the possibility of going from $500 to nothing on the toss of a coin each month.

Suppose that they decide to pool their incomes each month and each take one-half of the resulting amount. The expected value of each person's income is still $250 per month.[7] However, the variation from month to month will be diminished. The result is shown in Table 8-1. When they were operating on their own, each person's income deviated from its expected value by $250 each month; in good months it was $250 above the expected value, and in bad months it was $250 below the expected value. When the two incomes are pooled, the expected value is reached whenever one person is lucky and the other is unlucky, which will be about half the time. Only in one-quarter of the outcomes will income be above $250, and only in one-quarter of the outcomes will it be below $250. These results each require that both be lucky or unlucky at the same time.

The key to this result is that the events must be independent. The result of John's coin toss was independent of the result of June's. In the case in which their incomes were not pooled, for either of them the zero-income result occurs whenever they themselves are unlucky. The probability of the zero-income result is less likely when they pool their incomes, be-

[7] This can be seen by evaluating the four possible outcomes: There is a 25 pecent chance of each individual's share of the pool being $500, a 50 percent chance of it being $250, and a 25 percent chance of it being $0. This sums to $500(0.25) + $250(0.5) + $0(0.25) = $125 + $125 + $0 = $250.

BOX 8-3

The Economics of Gambling

Gambling and insurance both represent market activities that involve uncertainty. They differ from each other in that when one buys insurance, one pays a certain sum to avoid the chance of incurring a larger loss, whereas when one gambles, one pays a certain sum to obtain the chance of incurring a larger gain. That is, buying insurance reduces the risk that an individual faces, whereas gambling increases it. Buying insurance and gambling thus appear to be inconsistent; the former requires risk-averse behavior, whereas the latter requires risk-taking behavior. Yet we observe both insurance and gambling in our society. How can we explain this? To answer this question, we must first look at the demand to gamble.

The Demand to Gamble

Consider any situtíon in which one has an option to pay money to purchase the chance of a gain. This could be a lottery ticket, a bet on a football game, an investment of money by a firm in a new technological development that might produce profits in the future, or a purchase by an individual of a share in a firm on the stock market.

Consider first a mathematically fair possibility. You are offered the chance to buy a ticket in a lottery consisting of 100 tickets, each being sold for \$1, with a single prize of \$100 to the winning ticket. As we saw earlier, this is a fair bet; if you are risk-averse, you would not buy a ticket, and if you are risk-neutral, you would be indifferent about it. Only a risk lover would be eager to buy a ticket.

Most gambling games, however, are not mathematically fair. Instead, they are biased against the player. The organizer of the game takes out some of the money wagered as profit (if the game is legal, the government may also take some in the form of a tax); only what is left is distributed as prize money. This is true of lotteries, pari-mutuel betting on horse races, casino gambling, and every commercial or government-operated gambling operation.

Gambling on any event in which the organizers take a profit or on which the government levies a tax has a negative expected value. We would not expect to see risk-averse or risk-neutral individuals take such gambles.

Reconciling Insurance and Gambling

Why is it that we observe both gambling, which appeals only to risk lovers, and insurance, which

cause it requires that both be unlucky at the same time.

If three people pool their incomes, each receives zero only when all three are unlucky at the same time. This case occurs with a probability of 1 chance in 8. (There is 1 chance in 2 that any one will toss a tail but a $(1/2)(1/2)(1/2) = 1/8$ chance that all three will toss tails at once.) If four people pool their incomes, the extreme case of each receiving \$0 income will occur only with a probability of 1/64. By the time 10 people are involved, the extreme case will occur only 1 time in 2^{10}—a very small fraction indeed.

The larger the number of independent events that are pooled, the less and less likely that extreme results will occur.

The same reasoning applies to all kinds of events that may be regarded as chance events, as long as they are independent of one another. Suppose that there is 1 chance in 1,000 that any given house in the country will burn down in any given year, and suppose that an insurance company collects a premium from the owners of these houses and offers them full compensation if their house burns down.

If the company is so small that it can only insure 10 houses, it may be unlucky in having 10 owners who just happen to be careless at the same time and have their houses burn down accidentally. This is unlikely but not impossible. A bad bit of luck that destroys all 10 insured houses would ruin the company, since it could not meet all of its insured risks at the same time. Suppose, however, that the com-

appeals only to risk avoiders? One possibility is that although most people are risk-averse, some people are risk takers. This would explain why the latter make bets that have negative expected values. It would, however, be inconsistent with their buying of insurance policies with negative expected values, so this explanation does not help explain why *the same person* would both buy insurance and gamble.

A second possibility is that people are not risk lovers in terms of their evaluations of the expected monetary gains and losses involved but do get some pleasure simply from playing the game. Betting on the home team or on the sentimental favorite is common, even though the odds offered may not adequately reflect the team's realistic chances; this is often described as "betting with one's heart rather than with one's head." You probably know some people who usually behave in a risk-averse fashion but who bet "irrationally" on their favorite baseball team. Others may bet on horse races because they think that they are good enough handicappers to overcome the odds or because they get real pleasure from watching a horse race in which they have a financial stake. People who get pleasure from *particular* gambles might still buy insurance, as long as their risk aversion was a stronger force than the satisfaction attached to the particular risks of being uninsured.

A third possibility is that even though people are not risk lovers in general, they get some utility from the dreams that they have attached to even a remote possibility of winning a lottery or a similar bet. In this case they know that the average participant will lose, but they are sustained by the mere thought that against all the odds, they might win a sum large enough to transform an otherwise dull, or even hopeless, life. This may go a long way toward explaining why people buy tickets for lotteries in which only a few very large prizes are to be won. It is a less satisfactory explanation of why people bet on horse races, in which winnings, although more frequent, are not enough to change their whole life-style.

A further possibility is of course that people are just badly informed. They may not know the expected value of the gambles that they take. It is probably true that many people do not realize the magnitude of the negative expected value of many of their gambles.

pany is large enough to insure 100,000 houses. Now it is pooling its risks over a large number, and the chances are high that something very close to 1 house in 1,000 insured will burn down. With 100,000 houses insured, the most likely outcome is that 100 houses will burn down. The company might be unlucky and have 110 burn down or lucky and have only 90 burn down, but to have even 150 burn down is very unlikely indeed, as long as the chance of a fire burning down one house is independent of the chance of a fire burning down another. (Insurance companies are careful to spread the houses that they insure over a wide geographic area!)

This requirement of independence is why insurance policies normally exclude wars and other situations in which some common cause acts on all the insured units. A war may lead to a vast number of houses being destroyed. Since the cause of the loss of one house is not independent of the cause of the loss of another, if the insurance company suffers losses on any house because of wear, there is a high probability that it will suffer losses on a large proportion of its insured properties, and this could ruin the insurance company.

The basic feature in insurance is the pooling of independent events, which is what makes extreme outcomes unlikely. A common cause that has a similar effect on all insured items defeats the principle on which insurance is based.

The typical insurance company therefore deals with repeated events such as fires or death in which the probability that any individual insured item will be a subject of a claimant is independent of the probability that any other insured item will be.

Risk sharing. Let us say that a famous concert pianist wants to insure her hands against any event that would end her career as a performer. The amount insured would be colossal, amounting to all the income that she would have earned over her life if her hands had not been harmed. The company can calculate the chances that any randomly chosen person in the population will suffer such a loss. It is not insuring an entire population, however; only one person is involved. If there is no catastrophe, the company will gain its premium; if there is a catastrophe, the company will suffer a large loss.

The trick in being able to insure the pianist, or any unique person or thing posing the risk of a large loss, lies in what is called *risk sharing*. One company writes a policy for the pianist and then breaks the policy up into a large number of subpolicies. Each subpolicy carries a fraction of the payout and earns a fraction of the premium. The company then sells each subpolicy to a different firm.

Assume, for the purposes of illustration, that 100 firms each write one such primary policy, for example, one on a pianist's hands, one on a football player's legs, one on a rare painting being flown to Japan for an exhibit, and so on. Each then breaks its primary policy up into 100 subpolicies and sells each subpolicy to the other 99 firms. Each firm ends up holding risks that are independent of each other, no one of which is large enough to threaten the firm should it give rise to a claim. This is what Lloyd's of London does. It is a syndication of a large number of insurance underwriters. Each one is prepared to insure almost anything as long as a claim would not bankrupt all the firms when the risk is spread over a large number of them.

As with risk pooling, the possibilities for risk sharing require that the events being insured against are independent. An insurance company that takes one-tenth of the risk for each of 10 events that are closely related and hence likely to occur together if they occur at all is no better off than the insurance company that simply insures against one of the events.

Moral Hazard and Adverse Selection

Insurance markets work quite well at reducing the risk that individuals must contend with *and* at reducing the overall risk in the economy. However, there are problems that reduce the ability of insurance companies to exploit the principles of risk pooling and risk sharing to insure households against some risks. Two of the most interesting are *moral hazard* and *adverse selection*.

Having insurance often affects people's behavior. How often have you heard someone say—or have you said yourself—"Don't worry about it; it's insured"? When having insurance leads people to behave less carefully, thus raising the insurance company's expected costs, the situation is described as displaying **moral hazard**. For example, car owners might be much more willing to park their cars in an unsavory part of town where the risk of theft is high and might be less diligent about locking them regularly if their cars are insured against theft. If this effect is strong enough, insurance companies will not find it profitable to offer insurance against the particular event, and hence car owners will have to bear the risk themselves. Often the problem is sufficient to make it impossible for the car owners to obtain complete insurance; the insurance company offers only *partial coverage* by requiring that the car owner pay the first, say, $250 dollars in the event of a claim.

Another problem is that not everyone buys insurance, so the full benefits of risk pooling are not available to the insurance company. In particular, for any policy that is offered, *those most likely to make a claim are also most likely to purchase the policy*. This is referred to as **adverse selection**, since from the insurer's viewpoint the wrong people have chosen to buy the policy.

If insurance companies can distinguish among different potential customers, they can "customize" policies to suit each group's characteristics. For example, life insurance companies usually require that applicants have a medical examination, and they charge higher premiums to those who are thus demonstrated to be higher risks.

When insurance companies cannot distinguish among different potential customers and thus have to make any policy available on the same terms to all potential customers, they will have to charge a high enough premium to allow for the increased risks created by adverse selection. This may mean that potential customers who know themselves to be low-risk individuals will choose not to buy the policy. If these people could convince the insurance company that they are low risks, there is a price at which the insurance company would be able to sell them insurance and still make a profit, but, of course, everybody would like to convince the insurance company that they are low-risk individuals and hence benefit from the lower premiums.

Thus adverse selection can create a situation in which some individuals cannot purchase insurance. One way in which insurance companies deal with this probelm is to identify characteristics—often age, sex, or occupation—that are related to risk and then to offer different policies to individuals with different characteristics; however, in many places legislation has been introduced that makes such discrimination illegal.

This completes our introductory study of the importance of risk. We shall have occasion to return to these problems and to build on the present discussion at several points later in this book.

SUMMARY

1. Market demand curves reflect the aggregate of the consumption behavior of the millions of households in the economy.
2. It is important to distinguish between total and marginal values because choices concerning a bit more and a bit less cannot be predicted from a knowledge of total values. The paradox of value involves a confusion between total value and market value.
3. Elasticity of demand is related to the marginal value that households place on having a bit more or a bit less of some commodity; it bears no necessary relationship to the total value that households place on all of the units consumed of that commodity.
4. Households will consume any good that has a zero price up to the point where the marginal value that they place on further consumption is zero.
5. Risky events can be characterized in terms of their expected value and the degree of risk that they involve. A risky event that has a zero expected value is called a fair game.
6. Risk-neutral individuals are indifferent toward risk and hence are indifferent about participating in a fair game. Risk-averse people avoid risk and would choose not to participate in a fair game. Risk lovers like risk and would participate in a fair game.
7. Risk-averse people would choose to buy insurance as long as the premium does not exceed the expected value of the risky alternative by too much. Insurance companies can absorb risk from such people and then reduce the risk that they themselves bear by exploiting the principles of risk pooling and risk sharing. These principles operate when the risky events being insured are independent of one another.
8. Insurance markets may fail to operate effectively if there are serious problems of moral hazard or adverse selection. Moral hazard arises when having insurance causes people to behave in a manner that increases the chance of bad outcomes occurring, thus reducing the expected profits of the insurance company. Adverse selection arises when potential customers have different risk characteristics and insurance companies cannot easily distinguish the various groups.

TOPICS FOR REVIEW

Market demand and individual household demand curves
The paradox of value
Total value versus marginal value
Necessities and luxuries
Free goods and scarce goods
Expected value and degree of risk
Fair and unfair games
Risk-neutral, risk-averse, and risk-loving behavior
The market for insurance

Risk pooling and risk sharing
Moral hazard and adverse selection

DISCUSSION QUESTIONS

1. Why is market demand the horizontal sum of individual demand curves? Is the vertical sum different? What would a vertical sum of individual demand curves show? Can you imagine any use of vertical summation of demand curves?
2. Which of these implied choices involve a consideration of marginal values, and which involve a consideration of total values?
   a. Parliament debates whether 17-year-olds should be given the vote.
   b. A diet calls for precisely 1,200 calories per day.
   c. My doctor says that I must give up smoking and drinking or else accept an increased chance of heart attack.
   d. When Armand Hammer decided to buy the Rembrandt painting *Juno* for $3.25 million, he called it the "crown jewel of my collection."
   e. I enjoyed my golf game today, but I was so tired that I decided to stop at the seventeenth hole.
3. Explain the transactions described in the following quotations in terms of the value of the commodity. Interpret "worthless" and "priceless" as used here.
   a. "Bob Koppang has made a business of selling jars of shredded U.S. currency. The money is worthless, and yet he's sold 53,000 jars already and has orders for 40,000 more—at $5 a jar. Each jar contains about $10,000 in shredded bills."
   b. "In February 1987 Vincent Van Gogh's priceless painting *Sunflowers* sold at auction for $39 million."
4. How might people's behavior differ in serving themselves at a fixed-price buffet and at a restaurant where orders are taken from an a la carte menu. Discuss the marginal and average values of food consumed in each case.
5. Mary is willing to pay $10 for the first widget that she purchases each year, $9 for the second, $8 for the third, and so on down to $1 for the tenth and nothing for the eleventh. How many widgets will she buy, and what will be her consumers' surplus if widgets cost $3 each? What will happen if the price of widgets rises to $5? Can you state a generalization about the relationship between consumers' surplus obtained and the price of a commodity?
6. What do you think about someone who buys two lottery tickets instead of one and tells you that he does this "to increase my chances of coming out a winner"?
7. Describe the difference in behavior at a cocktail party at which drinks are free between someone who imbibes up to the point where the *marginal* value of more alcohol consumed is zero and someone who imbibes up to the point where the *average* value of alcohol consumed is zero.
8. Bookmakers, or "bookies," often operate by accepting bets at odds that are set by others—for example, in newspapers or by the "Vegas line." What risks do they face? What motivates them sometimes to "lay off" bets with other bookies?

Chapter 9

The Role of the Firm

Ask almost anyone you know to name 10 North American firms. The odds are that the lists will include some of these firms: General Motors Corporation, Bombardier, General Electric, IBM, Bell Canada, Dow Chemical, the T. D. Bank, Du Pont, Canadian Pacific, Air Canada, and the CBC. Drive around Gananoque, Ontario, and note at random 10 firms that come into view. They will probably include a Loblaw's supermarket, Harding's Drugstore, a PetroCan service station, Donevan's Hardware, the Modern Café, and the Bank of Montreal. Drive through Manitoba or Saskatchewan and look around you: Every farm is a business, or firm, as well as a home.

Firms develop and survive because they are efficient institutions for organizing resources to produce goods and services and for organizing their sale and distribution. It is not hard to count ways in which Bell Canada, the Modern Café, and the Saskatchewan wheat farm are different. However, we can gain insight by treating them all under a single heading, that is, by seeing what they have in common. This is what economic theory does. Economists usually assume that the firm's behavior can be understood in terms of a common motivation. Whether the firm is Ma and Pa's Bar and Grill or the Ford Motor Company, and whether a particular decision is made by the board of directors or the owner-manager, are regarded as irrelevant to predicting what decisions are made. Criticisms that economic theory neglects differences among firms will be considered in Chapter 16.

Before studying how the firm is treated in economic theory, we shall examine more closely the firm in North America today.

The Organization of Production

Forms of Business Organization

There are three major forms of business organization in the private sector: the single proprietorship, the partnership, and the corporation. In the **single proprietorship**, one owner makes all the decisions and is personally responsible for all of the firm's actions and debts. In the **partnership**, there are two or more joint owners, each of whom may make binding decisions and may be personally responsible for all of the firm's actions and debts. In the **corporation**, the firm has a legal existence separate from that of the owners. The owners are the firm's shareholders, and they risk only the amount that they put up to purchase their shares. The owners elect a board of directors, which hires managers to run the firm under the board's supervision.

In addition to the three forms of private-sector organization, *crown corporations* play a significant role in the Canadian economy. Also known as *public enterprises,* **crown corporations** are businesses owned by the government. Typically they have a board of directors and a president or chief executive officer, much like private corporations, but their operations are to some extent guided by public policy objectives rather than earning profits for shareholders. In 1988 the Economic Council of Canada identified 236 wholly owned government enterprises in Canada, 43 of them federal and 193 provincial. (Another 23 businesses were identified as effectively controlled by government.) Included in these numbers are some *agency corporations,* which are essentially extensions of government departments that are often financed through appropriations from general government revenues; two examples are the Unemployment Insurance Commission and the Atomic Energy Control Board. Also included are *proprietary corporations* such as the CBC, PetroCanada, and the electric power corporations that operate in most provinces. These organizations engage in various market-related activities and earn a substantial portion of their revenue from the sale of goods and services but often also receive government funds to cover operating deficits.

In most sectors of the Canadian economy, the corporation is the dominant form of organization. In 1990, about 70 percent of manufacturing firms were incorporated; they employed about 90 percent of all workers and accounted for around 95 percent of the value of all shipments. Only in agriculture and in services (such as hairstyling, medicine, and accounting) is the corporation relatively unimportant; yet even here its share of the business is steadily rising.

Professor Christopher Green of McGill University confirms that of the several hundred thousand firms in Canada—over 30,000 in manufacturing alone—a relatively few large ones, including some of the large crown corporations, account for a substantial share of total assets, sales, and employment.[1] We return to the issue raised by such corporate concentration in Chapter 15.

[1] Christopher Green, *Canadian Industrial Organization and Policy,* 3d ed. (Toronto: McGraw-Hill Ryerson, 1990).

The Single Proprietorship and the Partnership

The major advantage of the single proprietorship is that the owner is the boss who maintains full control over the firm. The disadvantages are, first, that the size of the firm is limited by the amount of capital that the owner can personally raise and, second, that the owner is personally responsible by law for all debts of the firm.

The partnership overcomes to some extent the first disadvantage of the single proprietorship but not the second. Ten partners may be able to finance a much bigger enterprise than one owner could, but they are still subject to unlimited liability. Each partner is fully liable for all of the debts of the firm.

Because of unlimited liability, people with substantial personal assets are unwilling to enter into a partnership unless they have complete trust in the other partners and a full knowledge of all the obligations of the firm. Investors may be willing to risk a specific sum but unwilling to jeopardize their entire fortune; if, however, they join a partnership in order to do the former, they may also do the latter.

In certain professions a general partnership is traditional. These include law, medicine, and (until recently) brokerage. Partnerships survive in these professions partly because they depend heavily on a relationship of trust between owners and clients, and the partners' unlimited liability for one another's actions is thought to enhance public confidence in the firm.

The **limited partnership**, which has two classes of partners (general and limited), provides protection against some of the risks of the general partnership. The firm's *general partners* have unlimited liability; the firm's *limited partners* are liable only for the amount that they have invested. Limited partners can neither participate in the running of the firm nor make agreements on its behalf. In effect, the limited partnership permits some division of the functions of decision making and risk taking.

The Corporation

The corporation is regarded by law as an entity separate from the individuals who own it. It can enter into contracts, sue and be sued, own property, contract debts, and generally incur obligations that are the legal obligations of the corporation *but not of its owners.* The corporation's right to be sued may not seem to be an advantage, but it is, because it allows others to enter into enforceable contracts with the corporation.

Although some corporations are owned by just a few persons, who also manage the business, the most important type of corporation is one that sells shares to the general public. The company raises the funds that it needs for the business by selling stock, and those who invest their money by buying its stock, called its **stockholders**, or its **shareholders**, are the company's owners. All profits belong to the stockholders. Profits that are paid out to them are called **dividends**; profits that are retained to be reinvested in the firm's operations are called **undistributed profits**. If the corporation is liquidated, stockholders share any assets that remain after all the debts are paid.

Diffuse ownership of corporate shares means that the owners cannot all be managers. Stockholders, who are entitled to one vote for each share that they own, elect a board of directors. This board of directors defines general policy and hires senior managers whose job it is to translate this general policy into detailed decisions.

Should the corporation go bankrupt, the personal liability of any one stockholder is limited to whatever money that stockholder has actually invested in the firm. This is called **limited liability**.

From a stockholder's viewpoint, the most important aspect of the corporation is its limited liability.

The advantage to the corporation is that it can raise capital from a large number of individuals. Each of these individuals who invest money in the firm shares in the firm's profits but has no personal liability beyond risking the loss of the amount invested. Thus investors know how much they have at risk. Because shares are easily transferred from one person to another, a corporation has a continuity of life that is unaffected by frequent changes in investors.

From the individual investor's point of view, there are some disadvantages in investing in a corporation. First, the investor may have little to say about the management of the firm. For example, if holders of a majority of the shares decide that the corporation should not pay dividends, an individual investor cannot compel the payment of his or her share of the earnings. Second, the income of the corporation is taxed twice. Corporations are taxed on their income before dividends are paid. Dividends are paid out of the after-tax income and are then taxed as part of the stockholders' incomes. Some people view this *double taxation* of corporate income as unfair and discriminatory; others see it as the price to be paid for the advantage of incorporating.[2]

Fifty years ago, most corporations had a physical presence in only one country. Of course, many corporations exported some or even all of their production, and some corporations imported some of their inputs, but they did not produce outside of the country in which they were incorporated. Today a great deal of production takes place in **transnational corporations**, which have a physical presence in more than one country. These corporations are discussed further in Box 9-1.

The Rise of the Modern Corporation

The direct predecessors of the modern corporation were the English chartered companies of the sixteenth century. The Muscovy Company, chartered in 1555; the East India Company, chartered in 1600; and the Hudson's Bay Company, chartered in 1609 and still going strong in Canada nearly 400 years later, are famous examples of early joint-stock ventures with limited liability. Their needs for many investors to finance a ship that would not return with its cargo for years—if it returned at all—made this exceptional form of organization desirable.

In the next three centuries, the need to commit large amounts of capital for long periods of time and to diversify risks were felt in other fields, and charters were granted for insurance, turnpikes and canals, and banks, as well as for foreign trade. Exploiting the new techniques of the Industrial Revolution required the growth of large firms in many branches of manufacturing. The increasing need for large firms led to the passage of laws permitting incorporation with limited liability *as a matter of right rather than as a special grant of privilege*. Such laws became common in England and in North America during the late nineteenth century.

Today incorporation is relatively routine, although it is subject to a variety of provincial laws. Moderate fees are charged for the privilege of incor-

[2] Some adjustment for this, referred to as integration of the personal and corporate tax systems, is made through the dividend tax credit.

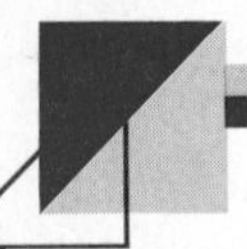

BOX 9-1

Transnational Corporations*

Over the past half century, the concept of a *national* economy has become less precise as a growing portion of production has been undertaken by firms with production facilities in more than one country. Such firms used to be called *multinational corporations,* but they are now officially designated by the United Nations as *transnational corporations (TNCs).* TNCs encourage global competition as well as provide a means of transferring technological know-how among countries.

In 1985 some 600 TNCs had sales of more than U.S.$1 billion each. A dominant group of 74 of these accounted for half of the group's total sales. More than 75 percent of the total sales of all 600 TNCs occurred in the petroleum, chemicals, machinery and equipment, and motor vehicle industries. Fully 45 percent of the 600 firms in the "billion-dollar club" are based in the United States, and just over 45 percent are in eight other developed nations—Switzerland, the Netherlands, Canada, the United Kingdom, Sweden, France, Japan, and Germany.

The 1980s saw many changes in the behavior of TNCs. The United States changed from being the leading provider of foreign investment through its TNCs to being the world's leading recipient of investment from foreign TNCs. Japan has become a leading foreign investor through TNCs. The Japanese transnationals have demonstrated a superior ability to innovate in high-tech activities such as the application of microelectronics-based technologies to manufacturing systems and to the handling of information in the service sector. Finally, the less developed countries (LDCs) have suffered large reductions in the amount of foreign capital that they import through foreign TNCs. (As a result, most of the LDCs have reduced their anti–foreign capital rhetoric and instead adopted policies designed to attract such investment.)

The world is still in the phase of what the United Nations calls the "continuing transnationalization of world economic activity." TNCs in the United States now seem to have reached a plateau of size after strong expansion in earlier decades. Rapid expansion of TNCs from Japan, Western Europe, Australia, Canada, and Korea suggests, however, that although the location of expanding TNCs may have changed, the overall expansion continues.

The TNCs' primary instrument for developing foreign operations has been foreign direct investment (FDI)—acquiring the controlling interest in

* The material in this box draws on *Transnational Corporations in World Development: Trends and Prospects* (New York: United Nations, 1988).

porating, and a company can usually choose whether to incorporate federally or under the regulations of one of the provinces.

Financing of Firms

The money that a firm raises for carrying on its business is sometimes called its **financial** (or *money*) **capital**. This is distinct from its **real** (or *physical*) **capital**, the physical assets of the firm that constitute plant, equipment, and inventories. Money capital may be broken down into **equity capital**, which refers to funds provided by the owners of the firm, and **debt**, which refers to the funds that have been borrowed from persons or institutions who are not owners of the firm.

The use of the term *capital* to refer to both an amount of money and a quantity of goods can be confusing, but it is usually clear from the context which is being referred to. The two uses are not independent, for much of the money capital raised by a firm will be used to purchase the capital goods that the firm requires for production.

Equity Financing

We have seen that the owners of the firm are its stockholders. They make their money available to

foreign production facilities either by purchasing existing facilities or by building new ones. During the 1980s, however, FDI fell dramatically, and other instruments have become more common. The most important of these are joint ventures with domestic firms located in countries where the TNCs wish to develop an interest and licensing arrangements whereby a domestic firm produces a TNC's product locally.

There are many reasons for a company to transfer some of its production beyond its home base (thus becoming a TNC) rather than producing everything at home and then exporting the output. First, local conditions matter. As products become more sophisticated and differentiated, locating production in large local markets allows more flexible responses to local needs than can be achieved through centralized production "back home." Second, nontariff barriers to trade make location in large foreign markets, such as the United States and the European Community, less risky than sending exports from the home base. Third, many of the TNCs are now in rapidly developing service industries such as advertising, marketing, public management, accounting, law, and financial services. In these service industries, the option of producing everything at home and then exporting the output does not exist. To produce a service in some country, a physical presence is needed in that country. Fourth, the computer and communications revolutions have allowed production to be "disintegrated" on a global basis. Components of any one product are often manufactured in many countries, each component being made where its production is cheapest. This globalization of production has been a boon to many less developed countries that have gained increasing employment at wages that are low by world standards but high by their own. In contrast, however, many TNCs that transferred assembly operation abroad in the 1970s have recently been repatriating them to the home country, particularly in North America.

As a result of "transnationalization," TNCs account for a large proportion of the foreign trade of many developed countries. This has long been so for the United States and is now becoming true for several other countries, in particular Japan. While all types of TNCs have grown, much of the growth in recent years has been concentrated in small and medium-size TNCs, including some based in less developed countries. As the United Nations puts it: "This dynamic aspect of the growth of TNCs is one of the major channels by which economic change is spread throughout the world."

the firm and risk losing it in return for a share of the firm's profits. Stockholders usually have the right to one vote for each of their shares in the election of a board of directors. The board of directors in turn set broad company policy and select senior management personnel.

The firm can raise equity capital in two ways. One is to sell newly issued shares. The other is to reinvest, or plow back, some of its own profits. Although shareholders do not receive reinvested profits directly as their dividend income, they benefit from the rise in value of their shares (called *capital gains*) that occurs if the funds are reinvested profitably. Reinvestment has become an important source of funds in modern times. In Canada, over $15 billion per year is obtained for investment in this fashion.

Debt Financing

Firms can also raise money by issuing debt, either by selling bonds or by borrowing from financial institutions. A **bond** is a promise to pay interest each year and to repay the principal at a stated time in the future (say, 20 years hence). Bank loans are often short-term; sometimes the firm even commits to repaying the principal *on demand*. Debtholders are creditors, not owners, of the firm: They have loaned money to the firm in return for the firm's promise to pay interest on the loan and, of course, to repay the principal. The commitment to make interest payments is a legal obligation that must be met whether or not profits have been made. Many a firm that would have survived a temporary crisis had all its capital been equity-financed has been forced to liquidate its assets because it could not meet its contractual obligations to pay interest to its debtholders. Debtholders, and all other creditors, have the first claims on the firm's funds. Only when they have been repaid in full can the stockholders attempt to recover anything for themselves.

The Firm in Economic Theory

Obviously, IBM and the Main Street Deli make decisions differently. Within a single large corporation, not all decisions are made by the same people or in the same way. For example, someone at IBM decided to introduce a small computer in 1981. Someone else decided to call it the IBM Personal Computer and market it for home use. Someone else decided how and where to produce it. Someone else decided its price. Someone else decided how best to promote its sales. The common aspect of these decisions is that all were in pursuit of the same goal—to earn profits for IBM.

Economic theory assumes that the same principles underlie each decision made within a firm regardless who makes it. The assumption that a single theory of decision making can be applied to all firms is discussed further in Box 9-2.

Motivation: Profit Maximization

In building a theory of how firms behave, economists usually assume that firms try to make their profits as large as possible. In other words, firms are assumed to *maximize their profits,* which are the difference between the value of sales and the costs to the firm of producing what is sold.

Why is this assumption made? First, it is necessary to make *some* assumption about what motivates decision makers if the theory is to predict how they will act. Second, a great many of the predictions of theories based on this assumption have been confirmed by observation. Third, no single alternative assumption has yet been shown to yield more accurate predictions. However, the assumption has been criticized, and alternatives have been suggested (see Chapter 16).

The assumption of profit maximization provides a principle by which firms' actions can be predicted.

Economists predict the behavior of firms by studying the effect that making each choice available to the firm would have on profits. They then predict that firms will select the alternative that yields the largest profits.

This theory does not say that profit is the *only* factor that influences the firm's behavior; rather, it says that profits are important enough that assuming profits to be the firm's sole objective will produce predictions that are substantially correct.

Factors of Production

Firms seek profits by producing and selling commodities. Production may be compared to a sausage machine. Certain elements, such as raw materials and the services of capital and labor, are fed in at one end, and a product emerges at the other end. The materials and services of factors of production, called **factor services**, that are used in the production process are called **inputs**, and the goods and services that result from the production process are called **outputs**. One way of looking at the production process is to regard the inputs as being combined to produce the outputs. Another equally useful way is to regard the inputs as being used up, or sacrificed, to gain the outputs.

Hundreds of inputs enter into the output of most goods and services. Among the inputs entering into the output of automobiles are sheet steel, rubber, spark plugs, electricity, machinists, cost accountants, forklift operators, managers, and painters. These inputs can be grouped into four broad classes: (1) those that are inputs to the automobile manufacturer but outputs to some other manufacturer, such as spark plugs, electricity, and sheet steel; (2) those that are provided directly by nature, such as the land used by the automobile plant; (3) those that are provided directly by households, such as the services of workers; and (4) those that are provided by machines, such as drill presses and robots.

Inputs in the first group just mentioned are called **intermediate products**. They are goods that are

BOX 9-2

Kinds of Firms

In economic theory the firm is defined as the unit that makes decisions with respect to the production and sale of commodities. This single definition covers a variety of business organizations, from the single proprietorship to the corporation, and a variety of business sizes, from inventors operating in their garages and financed by whatever they can extract from reluctant bank managers to vast undertakings with tens of thousands of stockholders and creditors. We know that in large firms decisions are actually made by many different individuals. We can nonetheless regard the firm as a single, consistent decision-making unit because of the assumption that all decisions are made to achieve the common goal of maximizing the firm's profits.

Whether a decision is made by a small independent proprietor, a plant manager, or a board of directors, that person or group is the firm for the purposes of that decision. This is a truly heroic assumption; it amounts to saying that for purposes of predicting the aspects of their behavior that interest us, we can treat a farm, a corner grocery, a department store, a small law partnership, and General Motors all under the umbrella of a single theory of the behavior of the firm. If this turns out to be even partly correct, it will prove enormously valuable in revealing some unity in behavior where to the casual observer there is only bewildering diversity.

We should not be surprised, therefore, if at the first encounter the theory seems rather abstract and out of touch with reality. To generalize over such a wide range of behavior, the theory must ignore many familiar features that distinguish the farmer from the grocer and each of them from Bell Canada. Any theory that generalizes over a wide range of apparently diverse behavior necessarily has this characteristic because it ignores the most obvious factors that create the appearance of diversity. If it were not possible to do this, it would be necessary to have dozens of different theories, one for each type of firm. The task of learning economics would then be much more complex than it is now!

produced by other firms. They appear as inputs only because the stages of production are divided among different firms so that at any one stage, a firm is using as inputs goods produced by other firms. If these products are traced back to their sources, all production can be accounted for by the services of only three kinds of inputs, which are called *factors of production*: Economists call all gifts of nature, such as land and raw materials, **land**; all physical and mental contributions that are provided by people, **labor**; and all manufactured aids to further production, such as machines, **capital**.

Extensive use of capital is one distinguishing feature of modern production. Instead of making consumer goods with only the aid of simple natural tools, productive effort goes into the manufacture of tools, machines, and other goods that are desired not in themselves but as aids to making other goods.

The Meaning of Cost

Profits are the difference between the value of the goods that a firm sells and the cost of producing these goods. In later chapters we will look at the firm's sales revenues. Here we are concerned with cost. **Cost**, to the producing firm, is the value of inputs used to produce its output.

Notice the use of the word *value* in the definition. A given output produced by a given technique, say, 6,000 cars produced each week by General Motors with its present production methods, has a given set of inputs associated with it—so many working hours of various types of laborers, supervisors, managers, and technicians; so many tons of steel, glass, and aluminum; so many kilowatt-hours of electricity; and so many hours of the time of various machines. The cost of each can be calculated, and the sum of these separate costs is the total cost to GM of producing 6,000 cars per week.

Opportunity Cost

Although the details of economic costing vary, they are governed by a common principle that is sometimes called *user cost* but is more commonly called *opportunity cost*, a concept introduced in Chapter 1.

The opportunity cost of using something in a particular venture is the benefit forgone by not using it in its best alternative use.

Box 9-3 considers some general applications of the principle of opportunity cost.

The Measurement of Opportunity Cost

To measure opportunity cost, the firm must assign to each input that it uses a monetary value equal to what it has sacrificed to use the input. Applying this principle to specific cases is not quite as easy as it may seem at first.

Purchased and Hired Factors

Assigning costs is a straightforward process when inputs purchased in one period are used up in the same period and when the price that the firm pays is determined by forces beyond its control. Inputs of intermediate products purchased from other firms fall into this category. If a firm pays $110 per ton for coal, it has sacrificed its claims to whatever else the $110 can buy, and thus the purchase price is a reasonable measure of the firm's opportunity cost of using 1 ton of coal.

Inputs of hired factors of production are also in this category. Firms hire labor, and the opportunity cost is the price that must be paid for these labor services. This includes the wage rate and all related expenses, such as contributions to pension funds, unemployment and disability insurance, and other fringe benefits. Firms also use borrowed money. Interest payments measure the opportunity cost of borrowed funds because the money paid out as interest could have been used to buy something else of equivalent monetary value.

Imputed Costs

Some of the inputs that the firm uses are neither purchased nor hired for current use. Their use requires no payment to anyone outside the firm, so the costs of using them are not obvious. Nonetheless, their use does entail a cost. The opportunity cost of these inputs is the amount that the firm would earn if it were to shift the inputs to their next best use. When these costs are calculated, they are called **imputed costs**, costs that must be inferred because they are not made as money payments. The following examples all involve imputed costs.

Using the firm's own money. Consider a firm that uses $100,000 of its own money, which instead it could have loaned out at 10 percent per year, yielding $10,000 per year. This amount should be deducted from the firm's revenue as the cost of funds used in production. If, to continue the example, the firm earns only $6,000 over all other costs, one should not say that the firm made a profit of $6,000 but that it lost $4,000. If it had closed down completely and merely loaned out its money to someone else, it could have earned $10,000.

Costs of durable assets. The costs of using assets owned by the firm, such as buildings, equipment, and machinery, include a charge, called **depreciation**, for the loss in value of an asset over a period of time because of its use in production, due to physical wear and tear and to obsolescence. The economic cost of owning an asset for a year is the loss in value of the asset during the year.

Accountants use several conventional methods to show depreciation based on the price originally paid for the asset, which is called its *historical cost*. One of the most common is *straight-line depreciation*, in which the same amount of historical cost is deducted in every year of useful life of the asset. Although historical cost is often a useful approximation, in some cases it may differ substantially from the depreciation required by the opportunity-cost principle. Consider two examples.

Assets that may be resold. A woman buys a new automobile for $12,000. She intends to use it for six years and then sell it for $6,000. She may think that, using straight-line depreciation, this will cost her $1,000 per year. If after one year, however, the value of her car on the used-car market is $10,000, it has cost her $2,000 to use the car during the first year. Why should she charge herself $2,000 depreciation during the first year? After all, she does not intend to sell the car for six years. The answer is that one

BOX 9-3

Opportunity Cost Beyond Economics

Opportunity cost plays a vital role in economic analysis, but it is also a fundamental principle that applies to a wide range of situations. It is one of the great insights of economics. Consider some examples:

George Bernard Shaw, on reaching his ninetieth birthday, was asked how he liked being 90. He is reputed to have said, "It's fine, when you consider the alternative."

Llewelyn Formed likes to watch both Peter Mansbridge and Lloyd Robertson. If he finally decides to watch Mansbridge, what is the opportunity cost of this decision?

Lisa Heartthrob, 31 years old and single, is thinking about marrying. Although she thinks Ray Gular is a great guy, she realizes that if she marries him, she will give up the chance of wedded bliss with another guy she may meet next year, so she decides to wait awhile. What other information do you need to determine the opportunity cost of this decision?

Serge Ginn, M.D., complains that now that he is earning large fees, he can no longer afford to take the time for a vacation trip to Europe. In what way does it make sense to say that the opportunity cost of his vacation depends on his fees?

Retired U.S. General Robert Russ, who is married to a wealthy woman, has decided to contribute $5,000 to the campaign of a political candidate. His lawyer points out to him that since in the U.S. political contributions earn a credit against his tax liabilities, the real cost of his contribution is the same as if he were giving an extra $3,200 to his spendthrift stepson (who refers to him as Gen. R. Russ). Is the opportunity cost of the political contribution $5,000 or $3,200?

of the purchaser's alternatives is to buy a one-year-old car and operate it for five years. Indeed, that is the position she is in after the first year. Whether she likes it or not, she has paid $2,000 for the use of the car during the first year of its life. If the market had valued her car at $11,500 after one year (instead of $10,000), the correct depreciation would have been only $500.

Sunk costs. In the example just given, an active used-asset market was available. At the other extreme, consider an asset that has no alternative use. This is sometimes called a *sunk cost.* Assume that a firm has a set of machines that it purchased a few years ago for $100,000. These machines were expected to last 10 years, and the firm's accountant calculates the depreciation costs of these machines by the straight-line method at $10,000 per year. Assume also that the machines can be used to make one product and nothing else. Suppose, too, that they are installed in the firm's plant, they cannot be leased to any other firm, and their scrap value is negligible. In other words, the machines have no value except to this firm in its current operation. If the machines are used to produce the product, assume that the cost of all other factors used will amount to $25,000, and the goods produced can be sold for $29,000.

Now, if the accountant's depreciation "costs" of running the machines are added in, the total cost of operation comes to $35,000; with revenues at $29,000, this yields an annual loss of $6,000 per year. It appears that the goods should not be made!

The fallacy in this argument lies in the adding in of a charge based on the sunk cost of the machines as one of the costs of current operations. The machines have no alternative uses whatsoever. Clearly, their *opportunity cost is zero.* The total cost of producing this line of goods is thus only $25,000 per year (assuming that all other costs have been correctly assessed), and the line of production shows an annual return over all relevant costs of $4,000, not a loss of $6,000.

To see why the second calculation leads to the correct decision, we notice that if the firm abandons this line of production as unprofitable, it will have no money to pay out and no revenue received on this account. If the firm takes the economist's advice and pursues the line of production, it will pay out $25,000 and receive $29,000, thus making it $4,000 per year better off than if it had not done so. Clearly, the production is worth undertaking. The amount that the firm happens to have paid out for the machines in the past has no bearing whatever on deciding on the correct use of the machines once they are installed on the premises.

Because they involve neither current nor future costs, sunk costs should have no influence on deciding what is currently the most profitable thing to do.

The principle of "let bygones be bygones" extends well beyond economics and is often ignored in poker, in war, and in love. Because you have invested heavily in a poker hand, a war, or a courtship does not mean that you should stick with it if the prospects of winning become very small. At every moment of decision making, maximizing behavior should be based on how benefits from this time forward compare with current and future costs.

Risk taking. One difficulty in imputing costs has to do with risk taking. Business enterprise is often a risky affair. Uninsured risks are borne by the owners of the firm, who, if the enterprise fails, may lose the money that they have invested in the firm.

Risk must be borne by someone. When the firm bears the risk, it will not carry on production unless it is compensated for the risk. If a firm does not yield a return that is sufficient to compensate for the risks involved, it will not be able to persuade people to invest in it. Those who buy the firm's shares expect a return that exceeds what they could have obtained if they had invested their money in a virtually riskless manner, say, by buying a government bond.

Suppose that a businesswoman invests $100,000 in a class of risky ventures and expects that most of the ventures will be successful but that some will fail. In fact, she expects that about $10,000 will be a total loss. (She does not know which specific ventures will be the losers; if she did, she would not invest in them.) Suppose further that she requires a 20 percent return on her total investment. To earn a $20,000 profit and recover the $10,000 expected loss, she needs to earn a $30,000 profit on the $90,000 of successful investment. This is a rate of return of 33⅓ percent. She charges 20 percent for the use of the capital plus 13⅓ percent for the risk she takes.

Patents, trademarks, and other special advantages. Suppose that a firm owns a valuable patent or a highly desirable location or produces a popular brand-name product such as Coca-Cola or Labatt's Blue. Each of these involves an opportunity cost to the firm in production (even if it was acquired free) because if the firm does not choose to use the special advantage itself, it could sell or lease it to others.

The Meaning and Significance of Profits

Economic profits, sometimes also called *pure profits*, are the difference between the revenues received by the firm from the sale of output and the opportunity cost of all the inputs used to make the output. If costs are greater than revenues, such "negative profits" are called *losses*.

This definition *includes* in costs (and thus *excludes* from profits) the imputed returns to capital and to risk taking. By doing so, it gives a special meaning to the words *profits* and *losses*—a meaning that differs somewhat from everyday usage. Table 9-1 illustrates how the terms *cost* and *profit* are used by economists.

Other Definitions of Profits

Firms define *profits* as the excess of revenues over costs as measured by the conventions of accounting. Economists' definition of profits differs from one based on pure accounting conventions in a number of ways. Accountants do not charge for risk taking and use of the owner's own capital as costs, and thus these items are recorded by the firm as part of its profits. When a firm says it needs a certain amount of profits to stay in business, it is making sense within its definition, for its "profits" must be large enough to pay the costs of those of its inputs that accounting conventions do not include as costs.

Economists would express the same notion by saying that the firm needs to cover *all* of its costs, including those that are not used in accounting. If the firm is covering all of its opportunity costs, it could not do better by using its resources in any other line of activity than the one currently being followed.

The term *profit* is sometimes used in a different way. Some economists use the term **normal profits** to refer to the opportunity costs of capital and risk taking. When this definition is used, we would say that the firm must earn normal profits if it is to be willing to stay in the industry. Whatever we call the

TABLE 9-1 The Calculation of Economic Profits: An Example

Gross revenue from sales	$1,000
Less: direct cost of production (materials, labor, electricity, etc.)	– 650
"Gross profits" (or "contributions to overhead")	350
Less: indirect costs (depreciation, overhead, management salaries, interest on debt, etc.)	– 140
"Net profits"	210
Income taxes payable	– 74
After-tax "net profits"	136
Less: normal profits (i.e., imputed charges for own capital used and for risk taking)	– 130
Economic profits	$ 6

Economic profits are less than net profits. The main difference between economic profits and what a firm calls its net profits is in the subtraction of normal profits, which are the imputed charges for use of capital owned by the firm and for risk taking. Income tax is levied on whatever definition of profits the taxing authorities choose, usually closely related to net profits. Although economic profits are necessarily less than net profits, they can be greater or less than normal profits. (In this example they are much less.)

opportunity costs of capital and risk taking—costs or normal profits—they must be covered if the firm is to remain in production in that industry.

A situation in which revenues equal costs (economic profits of zero) is satisfactory because all factors, hidden as well as visible, are being rewarded at least as well as they would be in their *best* alternative uses.

The income tax authorities have yet another definition of *profits*, which is implicit in the thousands of rules as to what may and may not be included as a deduction from revenue in arriving at taxable income. In some cases the taxing authorities allow more for costs than accountants recommend; in other cases they allow less than accountants recommend.

It is important to be clear about different meanings of the term *profits*, not only to avoid fruitless semantic arguments but also because a theory that predicts that certain behavior depends on *profits* defined in one way will not necessarily predict behavior accurately if *profits* is defined in another way. For example, the prediction that new firms will seek to enter an industry whenever profits are earned will not stand up if it is tested against the accountants' definition of *profits*. Firms may be recording accounting profits but economic losses because they are not covering the full opportunity costs of their capital. In this case the tendency will be for firms to leave rather than enter the industry.

The definition of *economic profits* as an excess over all opportunity costs is for many purposes the most useful, but in order to apply it to business behavior or to tax policy, appropriate adjustments must be made. Conversely, to apply accounting or tax data to particular economic theories requires the reverse set of adjustments. Henceforth, when we use the word *profits*, unless otherwise noted, we mean *economic profits*.

Profits and Resource Allocation

When resources are valued by the opportunity cost principle, their costs show how much these resources would earn if used in their best alternative uses. If there is an industry in which revenues exceed opportunity costs, the firms in that industry will be earning profits. Thus the owners of factors of production will want to move resources into that industry because they could earn more there than in their present uses. Conversely, if in some other industry firms are incurring losses, resources in that industry could earn more revenues in other uses, and their owners will want to move them to those other uses. Only when economic profits are zero is there no incentive for resources to move into or out of an industry.

Profits and losses play a crucial signaling role in the workings of a free market system.

SUMMARY

1. The firm is the economic unit that produces and sells commodities. The economist's definition of the firm abstracts from real-life differences in size and form of the organization of firms.
2. The single proprietorship, the partnership, and the corporation are the major forms of business organization in Canada today. The

corporation is by far the most common wherever large-scale production is required. The corporation is recognized as a legal entity; the liability of its owners, or shareholders, is limited to the amount of money that they have invested in the organization. Corporate ownership is readily transferred by the sale of shares of the company's stock in securities markets.

3. Firms can raise money through equity financing or debt financing. A firm's owners provide equity capital both when they purchase newly issued shares and when the firm reinvests its profits. The firm obtains debt financing from creditors either by borrowing from financial institutions or by selling bonds to the public.
4. Economic theory assumes that the same principles underlie each decision made within the firm and that the actual decision is uninfluenced by who makes it. The key behavioral assumption is that the firm seeks to maximize its profit.
5. Production consists of transforming inputs (the services of factors of production) into outputs (goods and services). It is often convenient to divide factors of production into categories. One common classification is land, labor, and capital. Land includes land and natural resources, labor means all human services, and capital denotes all manufactured aids to further production. An outstanding feature of modern production is the use of capital goods.
6. The opportunity cost of using a resource is the value of that resource in its best alternative use. If the opportunity cost of using a resource in one way is less than or equal to the gain from using the resource in this way, there is no better way of using it.
7. Measuring opportunity cost to the firm requires imputing the cost of resources not purchased or hired for current use. Among these imputed costs are those for the use of the owners' money, depreciation, risk taking, and any special advantages, such as trademarks, that the firm possesses.
8. A firm that is maximizing profits, defined as the difference between revenue and the opportunity cost of all the resources that it uses, is making the best allocation of the resources under its control, according to the firm's evaluation of its alternatives.
9. When a firm is earning zero *economic profits,* its revenue is covering all of its opportunity costs. This means that it could do no better by using its resources in other ways.
10. Economic profits and losses provide important signals concerning the reallocation of resources. Profits earned in an industry provide a signal that more resources can profitably move into the industry. Losses show that resources have more profitable uses elsewhere and serve as a signal that some of these resources should be transferred out of that industry.

TOPICS FOR REVIEW

Role of profit maximization
Single proprietorship, partnership, corporation, and crown corporation
Advantages of the corporation
Debt and equity financing
Inputs and factors of production
Opportunity costs
Imputed costs

Alternative definitions of profits
Profits and resource allocation

DISCUSSION QUESTIONS

1. Can the economic theory of the firm be of any help in analyzing the decisions of such nonprofit organizations as governments, churches, and colleges? What role, if any, does the notion of opportunity cost play for them?
2. "There is no such thing as a free lunch." Can anything be free? In earlier decades, gasoline stations routinely provided many free services, including windshield cleaning, tire inflation, and road maps. Now many sell road maps and have discontinued free services. Indeed, self-service stations are becoming increasingly popular with motorists who like the lower gasoline prices at these stations. Under what conditions will profit-maximizing behavior lead to the coexistence of full-service and self-service gasoline stations? What would determine the proportions in which each occurred?
3. What is the opportunity cost of the following?
   a. Fining a politician \$10,000 and sending her to prison for one year
   b. Lending \$500 to a friend
   c. Not permitting a \$116 million electric power dam to be built because it would destroy a rare 3-inch-long fish found only in that particular river
   d. Towing icebergs to Saudi Arabia to provide drinking water at the cost of 50 cents per cubic meter
4. According to *Forbes* magazine (June 13, 1988), "Unredeemed frequent-flyer coupons, the bright promotional idea dreamed up first by American Airlines in 1981 and subsequently copied by just about everyone else . . ." mean that ". . . the industry owes passengers about 25 billion miles of free travel . . . [and] if all the miles earned were cashed in, it would cost the airlines \$1.7 billion." How would you go about estimating the cost to the airlines of the 25 billion frequent-flyer miles that are now outstanding?
5. Having bought a used car from Smiling Sam for \$2,000, you drive it for two days, and it stops. You now find that it requires an extra \$1,500 before it will run. Assuming that the car is not worth \$3,500 fixed, should you make the repairs?
6. "To meet the legislated standard of 3.4 grams of carbon monoxide per mile driven, General Motors has calculated that it will cost \$100 million and prolong 200 lives by one year each, thus costing \$500,000 per year of extra life. Human lives are precious, which is why it is so sad to note another use of that money. It has been estimated that the installation of special cardiac-care units in ambulances could prevent premature deaths each year at an average cost of only \$200 for each year of extra life."

   Assume that the facts in this quotation are correct. If the money spent on carbon monoxide control would have been spent on cardiac-care units instead, what is the opportunity cost of the carbon monoxide requirement? If the money would not have been so spent but simply reduced automobile companies' costs, what is the opportunity cost? In either case, do the facts tell us whether the regulation of carbon monoxide to the 3.4-gram level is desirable or undesirable?
7. Which concept of profits is implied in the following quotations?
   a. "Profits are necessary if firms are to stay in business."

b. "Profits are signals for firms to expand production and investment."
c. "Accelerated depreciation allowances lower profits and thus benefit the company's owners."

8. Discuss ways in which the operations of proprietary crown corporations such as Air Canada and the CBC might differ from their private-sector competitors Candian International Airlines and CTV.

Chapter 10

Production and Cost in the Short Run

Every firm knows that its total costs of production are positively related to its output. If it produces more, it must pay more to hire additional workers and to buy more of other inputs. Perhaps, more interestingly, many firms also find that their costs *per unit of output* are systematically related to their outputs. Both very low and very high levels of output are usually associated with high unit costs, while intermediate levels that are near the plant's normal output capacity are typically associated with lower unit costs of production.

In Chapter 9 we defined costs of production. In this chapter we see how and why costs vary with the level of production and with changes in factor prices.

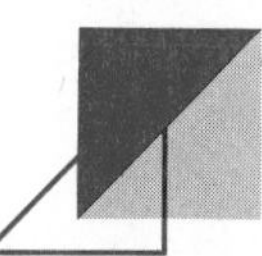

Choices Open to the Firm

Consider a firm that is producing a single product in a number of plants. If its rate of sales has fallen off, should production be reduced correspondingly, or should production be held at the old rate and the unsold amounts stored up against an anticipated future rise in sales? If production is to be reduced, should a single plant be closed, or should some plants be operated for shorter periods of time? Such decisions concern how best to use *existing* plants and equipment. They involve time periods that are too short in which to build new plants or to install more equipment.

Rather different decisions must be made when managers make their long-range plans. Should the firm adopt a highly automated process that will greatly reduce its wage bill, even though it must borrow large sums of money to buy the necessary equipment. Or, should it continue to build new plants that use current techniques? These matters concern what a firm should do when it is changing or replacing its plant and equipment. Such decisions may take a long time to put into effect.

In the examples just given, managers make decisions from known possibilities. Large firms also have research and development (R&D) staffs whose job it is to discover new products and new methods of production. Such firms must decide how much money to devote to R&D and in what areas the payoff for new development will be largest. If, for example, a shortage of a particular labor skill or raw material is anticipated, the research staff can be told to try to find ways to economize on that input or even to eliminate it from the production process.

Time Horizons for Decision Making

Economists organize the decisions that firms make into three classes: (1) how best to employ existing plant and equipment—the *short run*; (2) what new plant and equipment and production processes to select, given the framework of known technical possibilities—the *long run*; and (3) how to encourage, or adapt to, the invention of new techniques—the *very long run*.

The Short Run

The **short run** is a time period in which the quantity of some inputs, called **fixed factors**, cannot be increased.[1] A fixed factor is usually an element of capital (such as plant and equipment), but it might be land, the services of management, or even the supply of skilled labor. Inputs that can be varied in the short run are called **variable factors**.

The short run does not correspond to a specific number of months or years. In some industries it may extend over many years; in others it may be a matter of months or even weeks.

In the electric power industry, for example, it takes three or more years to acquire and install a steam turbine generator. An unforeseen increase in demand will involve a long period during which the extra demand must be met with the existing capital equipment. In contrast, a machine shop can acquire new equipment or sell existing equipment in a few weeks. An increase in demand will have to be met with the existing stock of capital for only a brief time, after which the stock can be adjusted to the level made desirable by the higher demand.

The Long Run

The **long run** is a time period in which all inputs may be varied but in which the basic technology of production cannot be changed. Like the short run, the long run does not correspond to a specific length of time.

The long run corresponds to the situation the firm faces when it is planning to go into business, to expand the scale of its operations, to branch out into new products or new areas, or to change its method of production. The firm's *planning decisions* are long-run decisions because they are made from given technological possibilities but with freedom to choose from a variety of production processes that will use factor inputs in different proportions.

The Very Long Run

Unlike the short run and the long run, the **very long run** is a period of time in which the technological possibilities available to a firm will change. Modern industrial societies are characterized by continuously changing technologies that lead to new and improved products and production methods.

Some of these technological advances are made by the firm's own research and development efforts. For example, much of the innovation in cameras and films has been made by Kodak and Polaroid. Other firms adopt technological changes developed by others. For example, the transistor and the electronic chip have revolutionized dozens of industries that had nothing to do with developing them. Firms must regularly decide how much to spend in efforts to change technology either by developing new techniques or by adapting techniques that have been developed by others.

Connecting the Runs: The Production Function

The various runs are simply different aspects of the same basic problem: getting output from inputs efficiently. They differ in terms of what the firm is able to change.

The **production function** describes the precise physical relationship between factor inputs and output. A simplified production function in which there are only two factors of production, labor and capital, will be considered here, but the conclusions apply equally when there are many factors. (Capital is taken to be the fixed factor, and labor is taken to be the variable one.) This chapter deals with the short-run situations in which output and cost change as

[1] Sometimes it is physically impossible to increase the quantity of a fixed factor in a short time. For instance, there is no way to build a hydroelectric dam or a nuclear power plant in a few months. At other times it might be physically possible but prohibitively expensive to increase the quantity of a fixed factor in a short time. For example, a suit-manufacturing firm could conceivably rent a building, buy and install new sewing machines, and hire a trained labor force in a few days if money were no consideration. Prohibitive costs, along with physical impossibility, are both sources of fixed factors.

different amounts of the variable input, labor, are used. Long-run situations in which both factors can be varied, and very long run situations in which the production function changes, are both covered in Chapter 11.

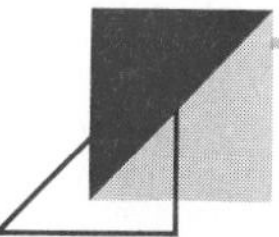

Short-Run Choices

Total, Average, and Marginal Products

Assume that a firm starts with a fixed amount of capital (say, 4 units) and contemplates applying various amounts of labor to it. Table 10-1 shows three different ways of looking at how output varies with the quantity of the variable factor. As a first step, some terms need defining.

Total product (*TP*) is the total amount that is produced during a given period of time. If the inputs of all but one factor are held constant, total product will change as more or less of the variable factor is used. This variation is shown in columns 1 and 2 of Table 10-1, which gives a total product schedule. Figure 10-1(i) shows such a schedule graphically. (The shape of the curve will be discussed shortly.)

Average product (*AP*) is the total product divided by the number of units of the variable factor used to produce it. If we let the number of units of labor be denoted by L, the average product can be written as

$$AP = \frac{TP}{L}$$

Notice in column 3 of Table 10-1 that as more of the variable factor is used, average product first rises and then falls. The level of output at which average product reaches a maximum (34 units in the example) is called the **point of diminishing average productivity**. Up to that point, average productivity is increasing; beyond that point, average productivity is decreasing.

Marginal product (*MP*), sometimes called *incremental product* or **marginal physical product (*MPP*)**, is the change in total product resulting from the use of one unit more of the variable factor:[2] **[13]**

$$MP = \frac{\Delta TP}{\Delta L}$$

Computed values of marginal product are shown in column 4 of Table 10-1. The figures in this column are placed between the other lines of the table to stress that the concept refers to the *change* in output caused by the *change* in quantity of the variable factor. For example, the increase in labor from 3 to 4 units ($\Delta L = 1$) raises output by 12 from 48 to 60 ($\Delta TP = 12$). Thus the MP equals 12, and it is recorded between 3 and 4 units of labor. Note that the MP in the example first rises and then falls as output increases. The level of output at which marginal product reaches a maximum is called the **point of diminishing marginal productivity**.

Figure 10-1(ii) plots average product and marginal product curves. Although three different schedules are shown in Table 10-1 and three different curves are shown in Figure 10-1, they are all aspects of the same single relationship described by the production function. As we vary the quantity of labor, with capital being fixed, output changes. Sometimes

TABLE 10-1 Variation of Output with Capital Fixed and Labor Variable

(1) Quantity of labor (L)	(2) Total product (TP)	(3) Average product (AP)	(4) Marginal product (MP)
0	0	—	
			15
1	15	15.0	
			19
2	34	17.0	
			14
3	48	16.0	
			12
4	60	15.0	
			2
5	62	12.4	

The relationship between changes in output and changes in the quantity of labor can be looked at in three ways. Capital is assumed to be fixed at 4 units. As the quantity of labor increases, the level of output (the total product) increases. Average product increases at first and then declines. The same is true of marginal product.

Marginal product is shown between the lines because it refers to the *change* in output from one level of labor input to another. When graphing the schedule, marginal products are plotted at the midpoint of the interval. For example, the marginal product of 12 would be plotted to correspond to quantity of labor of 3.5.

[2] Δ is read "change in." For example, ΔL is read "change in quantity of labor."

FIGURE 10-1 Total Product, Average Product, and Marginal Product Curves

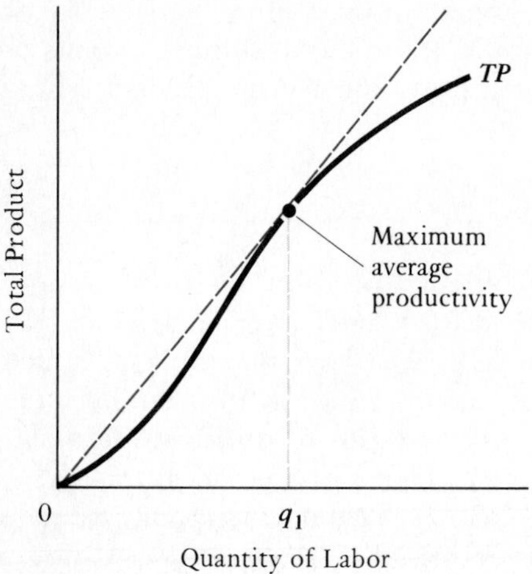

(i) Total product curve

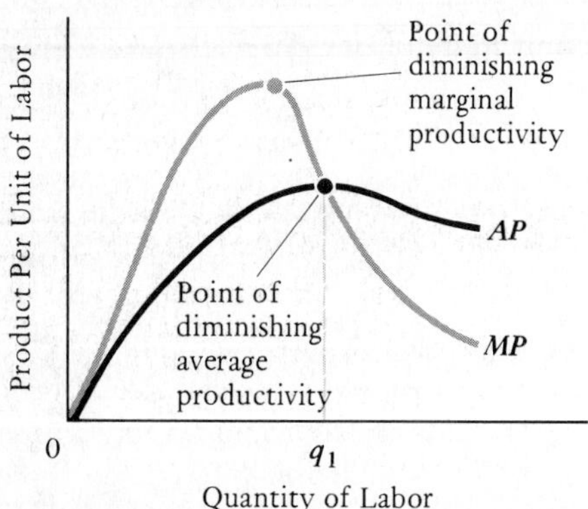

(ii) Average and marginal product curves

Total product (*TP*), average product (*AP*), and marginal product (*MP*) curves often have the shapes shown here. The total product curve in (i) shows the total product steadily rising, first at an increasing rate and then at a decreasing rate. This causes both the average and the marginal product curves in (ii) to rise at first and then to decline. The point of diminishing average productivity (also called the point of maximum average productivity) is q_1. At this point $MP = AP$.

it is interesting to look at total output, sometimes at the average output, and sometimes at the marginal change in output.

Finally, bear in mind that the schedules in Table 10-1 and the curves in Figure 10-1 all assume a specified quantity of the fixed factor. If the quantity of capital were, say, 10 units instead of the 4 that were assumed, there would be a different set of total product, average product, and marginal product curves. The reason is that if for any specified amount of labor there is more capital to work with, labor can produce more output; that is, the total product will be greater.

The Shape of Marginal Product and Average Product Curves

The Law of Diminishing Returns

The variations in output that result from applying more or less of a variable factor to a given quantity of a fixed factor are the subject of a famous economic hypothesis. Usually it is called the **law of diminishing returns**. (Sometimes it is also called the *law of variable proportions*.)

The law of diminishing returns states that if increasing amounts of a variable factor are applied to a given quantity of a fixed factor, eventually a situation will be reached in which each additional unit of the variable factor adds less to total product than did the previous unit; that is, the marginal product of the variable factor will decline.

The commonsense explanation of the law of diminishing returns is that as output is increased in the short run, more and more of the variable factor is combined with a given amount of the fixed factor. As a result, each unit of the variable factor has less and less of the fixed factor to work with. When the fixed factor is capital and the variable factor is labor, each unit of labor gets a declining amount of capital to assist it as the total output grows. It is not surprising, therefore, that sooner or later equal increases in labor eventually begin to add diminishing amounts to total output.

It is possible that marginal product might diminish from the outset, so that the first unit of labor contributes most to total production and each successive unit contributes less than the previous unit. It is also possible for the marginal product to rise at first and to decline only at some higher level of output. In this case the law of diminishing marginal returns might more accurately be described as the law of *eventually diminishing marginal returns*.

To illustrate this second case, consider the use of workers in a manufacturing operation. If there is only one worker, that worker must do all the tasks, shifting from one to another and becoming competent in each. As a second, third, and subsequent workers are added, each laborer can specialize in one task, becoming expert at it. This process, as we noted in Chapter 1, is called the *division of labor*. If additional workers allow for more efficient divisions of labor, marginal product will rise: Each newly hired worker will add more to total output than did each previous worker. However, according to the law of diminishing returns, the scope for such economies must eventually disappear, and sooner or later the marginal products of additional workers must decline. When this happens, each additional worker that is hired will increase total output by less than did the previous worker. This case, in which marginal product rises at first and then declines, is the one illustrated in Figure 10-1.

Eventually, as more and more of the variable factor is employed, marginal product may reach zero and then become negative. It is not hard to see why, if you consider the extreme case in which there would be so many workers in a limited space that additional workers would simply get in the way.

So far we have spoken of diminishing marginal returns, but average returns also are expected to diminish. The *law of diminishing average returns* states that if increasing quantities of a variable factor are applied to a given quantity of fixed factors, the average product of the variable factor will eventually decrease. Both diminishing marginal and average products are illustrated in Table 10-1. **[14]**

The Significance of Diminishing Returns

Empirical confirmation of both diminishing marginal and diminishing average returns occurs frequently. Some examples are illustrated in Box 10-1. One might wish that it were not so. There would then be no reason to fear a food crisis caused by the population explosion in less developed countries. If the marginal product of additional workers applied to a fixed quantity of land were constant, food production could be expanded in proportion to population growth merely by keeping a constant fraction of the population on farms. With fixed techniques, however, diminishing returns dictate an inexorable decline in the marginal product of each additional laborer because an expanding population has a fixed supply of agricultural land.

Thus unless there is a steady improvement in the techniques of production, continuous population growth will bring with it, according to the law of diminishing returns, declining average living standards and eventually widespread famine. This gloomy prediction of the nineteenth century English economist Thomas Malthus is discussed further in Box 11-2.

The Relationship Between Marginal and Average Curves

Notice that in Figure 10-1(ii) the *MP* curve cuts the *AP* curve at the *AP*'s maximum point. It is important to understand how these curves are related. **[15]**

The average product curve slopes upward as long as the marginal product curve is *above* it; whether the marginal product curve is itself *sloping* upward or downward is irrelevant. This makes sense because if an additional worker is to raise the average product of all workers, that additional worker's output must be greater than the average output of all the other workers. It is immaterial whether the new worker's contribution to output is greater or less than the contribution of the worker hired immediately before; all that matters is that the new worker's contribution to output exceeds the average output of *all workers hired previously*. (The relationship between marginal and average measures is illustrated further in Box 10-2.)

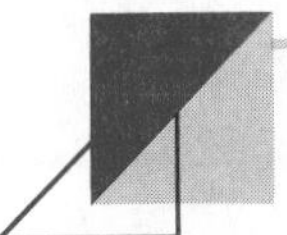

Short-Run Variations in Cost

We now shift our attention from the firm's production to its costs. The majority of firms cannot influence the prices of the inputs that they employ; instead they must pay the going market price for their inputs. For example, a shoe factory in Winnipeg, a candy manufacturer in Montreal, a rancher in Alberta, and a boat builder in Halifax are each too small a part of the total demand for the factors that they use to be able to influence their prices significantly. The firms must pay the going rent for the land that they need, the going wage rate for the labor that they employ, and the going interest rate that

BOX 10-1

Diminishing Returns

The law of diminishing returns operates in a wide range of circumstances.

When Southern California Edison was required to modify its Mojave power plant to reduce the amount of fly ash emitted into the atmosphere, it discovered that a series of filters applied to the smokestacks could do the job. A single filter eliminated one-half of the discharge. Five filters in series reduced the fly ash discharge to the 3 percent allowed by law. When a state senator proposed a new standard that would permit no more than 1 percent fly ash emission, the company brought in experts who testified that this would require at least 15 filters per stack and would triple the cost.

British Columbia's Campbell River, a noted sport fishing area, has become the center of a thriving, well-promoted tourist trade. As fishing has increased, the total number of fish caught has steadily increased, but the number of fish per person fishing has decreased and the average hours fished for each fish caught have increased.

Public opinion pollsters, as well as all students of statistics, know that you can use a sample to estimate characteristics of a very large population. Even a relatively small sample can provide a useful estimate—at a tiny fraction of the cost of a complete enumeration of the population. However, sample estimates are subject to sampling error. If, for example, 38 percent of a sample approves of a certain policy, the percentage of the population that approves of it is likely to be close to 38 percent, but it might well be anywhere from 36 to 40 percent. The theory of statistics shows that the size of the expected sampling error can always be reduced by increasing the sample size. A 4 percent interval could be cut in half—to 2 percent—by *quadrupling the sample size*; that is, if the original sample had been 400, a new sample of 1,600 would halve the chance of an error of any given size from occurring. To reduce the interval to 1 percent, the new sample would have to be quadrupled again—to 6,400. In other words, increasing the sample size leads to diminishing marginal returns in terms of accuracy.

banks charge for loans. As it is with these firms, so it is with most other firms.[3] Given these prices and the physical returns summarized by the product curves, the costs of different levels of output can be calculated.

Cost Concepts Defined

The following brief definitions of several cost concepts are closely related to the product concepts just introduced.

[3] The firm that is a large enough employer of labor or user of land or capital that it is able to affect the prices of its factor services is the exception rather than the rule. The exceptions are very large firms such as General Motors and firms in one-company towns. (Even such firms cannot set just any wage they wish because their workers always have the option of moving to another town.) The important problems that arise when a firm can influence the wage rate that it pays to its employees are considered in Chapter 19.

Total cost (*TC*) is the total cost of producing any given level of output. Total cost is divided into two parts, *total fixed cost* and *total variable cost*. **Total fixed cost (*TFC*)** does not vary with the level of output; it is the same whether output is 1 unit or 1 million units. Such a cost is also referred to as an *overhead cost* or an *unavoidable cost*. A cost that varies directly with output, rising as more output is produced and falling as less output is produced, is called a **total variable cost (*TVC*)** (also a *direct* or *avoidable cost*). In the example in Table 10-1, since labor is the variable factor of production, wages are a variable cost.

Average total cost (*ATC*), also called **average cost (*AC*)**, is the total cost of producing any given number of units of output divided by that number. Average total cost can be separated into **average fixed costs (*AFC*)**, fixed costs divided by quantity

BOX 10-2

Mario Lemieux's Goal-scoring Record

The relationship between the concepts of marginal and average measures is very general. An interesting example comes from Mario Lemieux's goals-per-season record for the first six years after he joined the NHL's Pittsburgh Penguins for the 1984–1985 season, as shown in the table.

For each season, the first column shows the total number of NHL goals that Lemieux had scored as of the start of the season. In the second column, that total is divided by the number of seasons he had played to calculate his career *average* goals per season. The third column gives the number of goals he scored that season—that is, his *marginal* goals-per-season production. The fourth column then gives his new *average* goals per season as of the end of the season. It is calculated as his new career total goals scored, the sum of columns 1 and 3, divided by his total number of seasons. Column 4 is transferred to column 2 for the next season.

Note that in each of his first five seasons, Lemieux's marginal production exceeded his start-of-season average, and as a result his average rose. *Whenever his performance during a season is better than his career average at the start of the season, his career average rises.* For example, Lemieux entered the 1987–1988 season having averaged 48.33 goals per season in his first three years. That year he scored 70 goals, so his *marginal* production exceeded his average. Thus the average that he carried forward from the 1987–1988 season rose to 53.75.

In 1989–1990, the last year shown, Lemieux missed a lot of the season due to injury, and as a result he had a below-average year. He entered the season with a career average of 60 goals per season, but his production that year was only 45 goals, so at the end of the season his career average had fallen to 57.5. *Whenever his performance during a season is worse than his career average at the start of the season, his career average falls.*

This illustrates the important relationship between marginal (in this case, current-season) and average (in this case, career) measures:

If the average is to rise, all that matters is that the marginal be above the average; if the average is to fall, all that matters is that the marginal be below the average.

Mario Lemieux's Goals Per Season

		Old average	*Marginal*	*New average*
Season	**(1) Career total at start of season**	**(2) Career average at start of season**	**(3) Goals scored during season**	**(4) Career average at end of season**
1984–1985	—	—	43	43.00
1985–1986	43	43.00	48	45.50
1986–1987	91	45.50	54	48.33
1987–1988	145	48.33	70	53.75
1988–1989	215	53.75	85	60.00
1989–1990	300	60.00	45	57.50

TABLE 10-2 Variation of Costs with Capital Fixed and Labor Variable

		Total cost ($)			Marginal cost ($ per unit)	Average cost ($ per unit)		
(1) Labor (*L*)	(2) Output (*q*)	(3) Fixed (*TFC*)	(4) Variable (*TVC*)	(5) Total (*TC*)	(6) (*MC*)	(7) Fixed (*AFC*)	(8) Variable (*AVC*)	(9) Total (*ATC*)
0	0	100	0	100		—	—	—
					0.67			
1	15	100	10	110		6.67	0.67	7.33
					0.53			
2	34	100	20	120		2.94	0.59	3.53
					0.71			
3	48	100	30	130		2.08	0.62	2.71
					0.83			
4	60	100	40	140		1.67	0.67	2.33
					5.00			
5	62	100	50	150		1.61	0.81	2.42

The relationship of cost to level of output can be looked at in several ways. These cost schedules are computed from the product schedule of Table 10-1, given the price of capital of $25 per unit and the price of labor of $10 per unit. Marginal cost (in column 6) is shown between the lines of total cost because it refers to the *change* in cost divided by the *change* in output that brought it about. For example, the *MC* of 71 cents is the $10 increase in total cost (from $120 to $130) divided by the 14-unit increase in output (from 34 to 48). In constructing a graph, marginal costs should be plotted midway in the interval over which they are computed. The *MC* of 71 cents would be plotted at an output of 41.

of output, and **average variable costs (*AVC*)**, total variable cost divided by quantity of output.

Although average *variable costs* may rise or fall as production is increased (depending on whether output rises more rapidly or more slowly than total variable costs), it is clear that average *fixed costs* decline continuously as output increases. A doubling of output always leads to a halving of fixed costs per unit of output. This is a process popularly known as *spreading one's overhead.*

Marginal cost (*MC*), sometimes called *incremental cost,* is the increase in total cost resulting from raising the rate of production by one unit. Because fixed costs do not vary with output, marginal fixed costs are always zero. Therefore, marginal costs are necessarily marginal variable costs, and a change in fixed costs will leave marginal costs unaffected. For example, the marginal cost of producing a few more potatoes by farming a given amount of land more intensively is the same, whatever the rent paid for the land. [16]

Short-Run Cost Curves

Using the production relationships found in Table 10-1, assume that the price of labor is $10 per unit and that the price of capital is $25 per unit. The cost schedules that result from these values are shown in Table 10-2.

Figure 10-2 shows cost curves that are similar in shape to those arising from the data in Table 10-2. Notice that the marginal cost curve cuts the average total cost curve and the average variable cost curve at their lowest points. This is another example of the relationship between a marginal and an average curve. The *ATC* curve, for example, slopes downward as long as the *MC* curve is below it; it makes no difference whether the *MC* curve is itself sloping upward or downward.

To see this, consider an example in which 10 units are produced each week at an average cost of $5 per unit (total cost equals $50). The average cost of producing 11 units will exceed $5 if the eleventh unit adds more than $5 to the output (*MC* exceeds *AC*) and will be less than $5 if the eleventh unit adds less than $5 to the cost (*MC* is less than *AC*). The marginal cost of the tenth unit does not matter for this calculation. (It could be above, below, or equal to the eleventh unit's marginal cost.)[4]

Short-run average variable cost. In Figure 10-2 the average variable cost curve reaches a minimum and

[4] If you do not see where any of the numbers come from, review Table 10-1 and the definitions of cost just given.

FIGURE 10-2 Total Cost, Average Cost, and Marginal Cost Curves

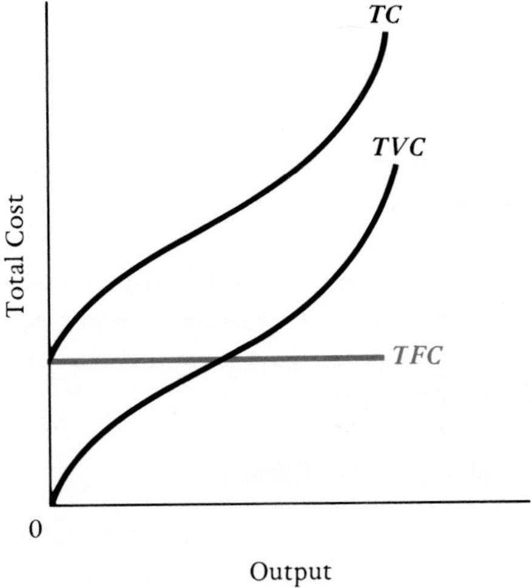

(i) Total cost curves

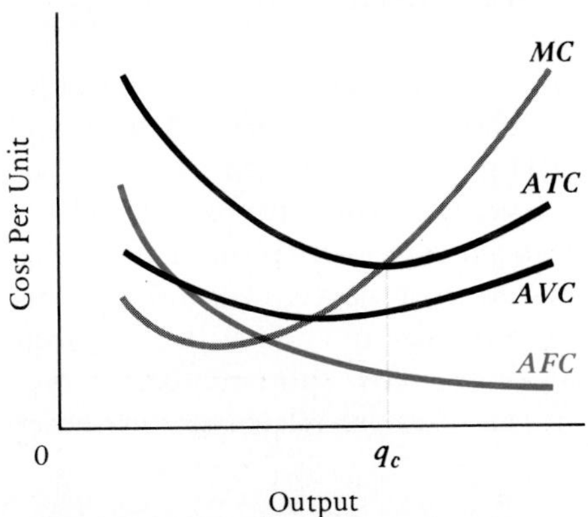

(ii) Marginal and average cost curves

Total cost (*TC*), average cost (*AC*), and marginal cost (*MC*) curves often have the shapes shown here. Total fixed cost does not vary with output. Total variable cost and the total of all costs ($TC = TVC + TFC$) rise with output, first at a decreasing rate and then at an increasing rate. The total cost curves in (i) give rise to the average and marginal curves in (ii). Average fixed cost (*AFC*) declines as output increases. Average variable cost (*AVC*) and average total cost (*ATC*) fall and then rise as output increases. Marginal cost (*MC*) does the same, intersecting *ATC* and *AVC* at their minimum points. Capacity output is q_c, the minimum point on the *ATC* curve.

then rises. With fixed factor prices, when average product per worker is at a maximum, average variable cost is at a minimum. [17] Common sense tells us that each additional worker adds the same amount to cost but a different amount to output, and when output per worker rises, the cost per unit of output must fall, and vice versa.

Eventually diminishing average productivity implies eventually increasing average variable costs.

Short-run average total cost curve. Short-run *ATC* curves are often U-shaped. This reflects the assumptions that (1) average productivity increases when output is low but that (2) at some level of output, average productivity begins to fall fast enough to cause average variable costs to increase faster than average fixed costs are falling. When this happens, *ATC* increases.

Marginal cost curves. In Figure 10-2(ii) the marginal cost curve is shown as a declining curve that reaches a minimum and then rises. This is the reverse of the shape of the marginal product curve in Figure 10-1(ii). The reason for the reversal is as follows. If extra units of a variable factor that is bought at a fixed price per unit result in increasing quantities of output (marginal *product rising*), the cost per unit of extra output must be falling (marginal *cost falling*). However, if marginal product is falling, marginal cost will be rising. Thus the hypothesis of eventually diminishing marginal product implies eventually increasing marginal cost. [18]

Total variable cost. In Figure 10-2(i) total variable cost is shown as an upward-sloping curve, indicating that total variable cost rises with the level of output. This is true as long as marginal cost is positive, since the total variable cost of producing any given level of output is the area under the marginal cost curve up to that level of output. [19]

Definition of Capacity

The level of output that corresponds to the minimum short-run average total cost is often called the **capacity** of the firm. In this sense capacity is the largest output that can be produced without encountering rising average costs per unit. In Figure 10-2(ii) ca-

FIGURE 10-3 The Effect of a Change in Input Prices

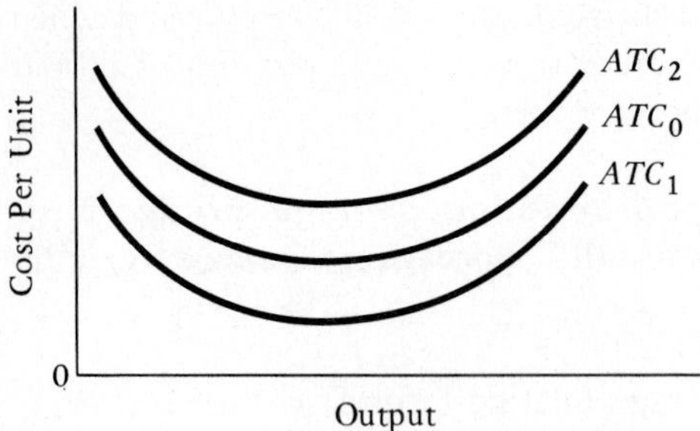

A change in any input price shifts the entire average total cost curve. The original average total cost curve is shown by ATC_0. A rise in the price of a variable input used by the firm must raise the price of producing each level of output. In the figure it shifts the average total cost curve upward to ATC_2. Conversely, a fall in the price of a variable input used by the firm shifts the average total cost curve downward; in the figure this shift is to ATC_1.

pacity output is q_c units, but higher outputs can be achieved, provided that the firm is willing to accept the higher per unit costs that accompany any level of output that is "above capacity." A firm that is producing at an output less than the point of minimum average total cost has **excess capacity**.

The technical definition gives the word *capacity* a meaning that is different from the one used in everyday speech, in which it often means an upper limit that cannot be exceeded. The technical definition is, however, a useful concept in economic and business discussions.

Shifts in Short-Run Cost Curves

So far we have seen how costs vary as output varies, with input prices being held constant. Figure 10-3 shows the effect on a firm's cost curves of a change in the price of any variable input. A rise in the price of any input used by the firm must raise the price of producing any given quantity of output. A fall in the price of any input has the opposite effect. This is a very simple relationship but important nonetheless.

A change in the price of any variable input used by the firm will shift its variable and total cost curves—upward for a price increase and downward for a price decrease.

A Family of Short-Run Cost Curves

A short-run cost curve shows how costs vary with output for a given quantity of the fixed factor, say, a given size of plant.

There is a different short-run cost curve for each given quantity of the fixed factor.

A small plant that manufactures nuts and bolts will have its own short-run cost curve. A medium-size plant and a large plant will each have its own short-run cost curve. If a firm expands and replaces its small plant with a medium-size plant, it will move from one short-run cost curve to another. This change from one plant size to another is a long-run change. We shall discuss how short-run cost curves of plants of different sizes are related to each other in Chapter 11.

SUMMARY

1. A firm's production decisions can be classified into three groups: (a) how best to employ existing plant and equipment—the short run; (b) what new plant and equipment and production processes to select, given the framework of known technical possibilities—the long run; and (c) how to encourage or to adapt to technological changes—the very long run.
2. The short run involves decisions in which one or more factors of production are fixed. The long run involves decisions in which all factors are variable but technology is given. The very long run involves decisions in which technology can change.
3. The production function shows the output that results from each possible combination of inputs. Short-run and long-run situations

can be interpreted as implying different kinds of constraints on the production function. In the short run the firm is constrained to use no more than a *given* quantity of some fixed factor; in the long run it is constrained only by the available techniques of production.

4. The theory of short-run costs is concerned with how output varies as different amounts of the variable factors are combined with given amounts of the fixed factors. The concepts of total, average, and marginal product represent alternative relationships between output and the quantity of the variable factor of production.
5. The hypothesis of diminishing returns asserts that if increasing quantities of a variable factor are combined with given quantities of fixed factors, the marginal and the average products of the variable factor will eventually decrease. If factor prices are fixed, this hypothesis implies that marginal and average costs will eventually rise.
6. Given physical productivity schedules and the prices of inputs, it is a matter of simple arithmetic to develop the whole family of short-run cost curves, one for each quantity of the fixed factor.
7. Short-run average total cost curves are U-shaped. Average productivity increases at low levels of outputs but eventually declines sufficiently and rapidly to offset advantages of spreading overheads. The output corresponding to the minimum point of a short-run average total cost curve is called the plant's capacity.
8. Changes in factor prices shift the short-run cost curves—upward when prices rise and downward when prices fall. Thus there is a whole family of short-run curves, one for each set of factor prices.

TOPICS FOR REVIEW

Short run, long run, and very long run
Total product, average product, and marginal product
The law of diminishing returns
Marginal product curves and average product curves
Relationship between productivity and cost
Total cost, marginal cost, and average cost
Short-run cost curves
Capacity and excess capacity

DISCUSSION QUESTIONS

1. Does the short run consist of the same number of months for increasing output as for decreasing it? Must the short run in an industry be the same length for all firms in the industry? Under what circumstances might the short run actually involve a longer time span than the very long run for one particular firm?
2. Use the distinction between long run and short run to discuss each of the following.
   a. A guaranteed annual employment contract of at least forty-eight 40-hour weeks of work for all employees
   b. A major economic recession during which there is substantial unemployment of labor and in which equipment is being used at well below capacity levels of production
   c. A speeding up of delivery dates for new easy-to-install equipment
3. In 1921 experimenters who were working with chemical fertilizers at the Rothampsted Experimental Station, an agricultural research institute in Hertfordshire, England, applied different amounts of a particular fertilizer to 10 apparently identical quarter-acre plots of land. The results for one test, using identical seed grain, are listed in

the following table. Compute the average and marginal product of fertilizer, and identify the (approximate) points of diminishing average and marginal productivity.

Plot	Fertilizer dose	Yield index*
1	15	104.2
2	30	110.4
3	45	118.0
4	60	125.3
5	75	130.2
6	90	132.4
7	105	131.9
8	120	132.3
9	135	132.5
10	150	132.8

*Yield without fertilizer = 100.

4. Indicate whether each of the following conforms to the hypothesis of diminishing returns and, if so, whether it refers to marginal returns, average returns, or both.
a. "The bigger they are, the harder they fall."
b. "As more and more of the population receives smallpox vaccinations, the reduction in the smallpox disease rate for each additional 100,000 vaccinations becomes smaller."
c. "Five workers produce twice as much today as 10 workers did 40 years ago."
d. "Diminishing returns set in last year when the rising rural population actually caused agricultural output to fall."

5. Consider the education of a human being as a process of production. Regard years of schooling as one variable factor of production. What are the other factors? What factors are fixed? At what point would you expect diminishing returns to set in? For an Einstein, would diminishing returns set in during his lifetime?

6. Suppose that each of the following news items is correct. Discuss each in terms of its effects on cost. (You will have to decide which concept of cost is most likely to be affected.)
a. A provincial board of education reports that the increasing level of education of youth has led both to higher productivity and to increases in the general level of wages.
b. During the winter of 1977, many factories were forced by fuel shortages to reduce production and to operate at levels of production far below capacity.
c. NASA, the U.S. space agency, reports that the space program has led to the development of electronic devices that have brought innovations to many industries.

7. "Because overhead costs are fixed, increasing production lowers costs. Thus small businesses are sure to be inefficient. This is a dilemma of modern society, which values both smallness *and* efficiency." Discuss.

8. Look again at the examples of diminishing returns given in Box 10-1. Indicate for each whether it refers to marginal returns, average returns, or both, and identify what is being held constant and what is varying.

Chapter 11

Production and Cost in the Long Run and the Very Long Run

In this chapter we shall look first at *long-run* behavior, in which firms are free to vary all factors of production. Should firms use a great deal of capital and only a small amount of labor? Should they use less capital and more labor? What effects do these decisions have on firms' costs?

In the second part of the chapter we shall examine the *very long run*. The discussion concerns the improvements in technology and productivity that have dramatically increased output and incomes in all industrial countries during the past 100 years.

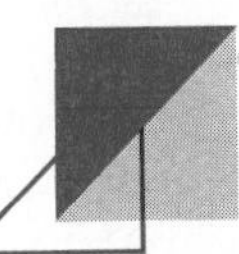

The Long Run: No Fixed Factors

In the short run, in which only one factor varies, the only way to produce a given output is to adjust the input of the variable factor until the desired level of output is achieved. Thus once the firm has decided on a rate of output, there is only one possible way of achieving it. In the long run, all factors can be varied, so there are numerous technically possible ways to produce any given output. Thus the firm must decide both on a level of output *and* on how to produce that output. Specifically, this means that firms in the long run must choose the nature and amount of plant and equipment, as well as the size of their labor force.

In making this choice, the firm will wish to avoid being technically inefficient, which means using more of *all* inputs than are necessary. Being technically efficient is not enough, however. To be economically efficient, the firm must choose from among the many technically efficient options the one that produces a given level of output at the lowest possible cost. (The distinction among various types of efficiency sometimes causes confusion, particularly when engineers and economists are involved in the same decision-making process. Box 11-1 elaborates on this distinction for readers who wish to study it further.)

Long-run planning decisions are important. A firm that decides to build a new steel mill and to invest in machinery that will go into it will choose among many alternatives. Once installed, that equipment is fixed for a long time. If the firm makes a wrong choice, its survival may be threatened; if it estimates shrewdly, it may be rewarded with large earnings.

Long-run decisions are risky because the firm must anticipate what methods of production will be efficient not only today but also for many years in the future, when the costs of labor and

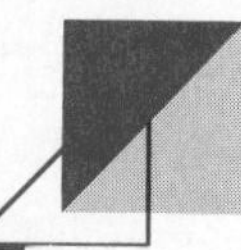

BOX 11-1

Various Concepts of Efficiency

In popular discussion, in business decision making, and in government policies, three different types of efficiency concepts are encountered. These are engineering, technical, and economic efficiency. Each is a valid concept, and each conveys useful information. However, the use of one concept in a situation in which another is appropriate is a potential source of error and waste.

Engineering efficiency refers to the *physical* amount of some *single key input* that is used in production. It is measured by the ratio of that input to output. For example, the engineering efficiency of an engine refers to the ratio of the amount of energy in the fuel burned by the engine to the amount of usable energy produced by the engine. The difference goes in friction, heat loss, and other unavoidable sources of waste. Saying that a steam engine is 40 percent efficient means that 40 percent of the energy in the coal that is burned in the boiler is converted into work that is done by the engine, while the other 60 percent is lost.

Technical efficiency (or technological efficiency) is related to the *physical* amount of *all factors* used in the process of producing some commodity. The production of a given output is technically inefficient if there exist other ways of producing the output that will use less of at least one input while not using more of any others. Production is technically efficient if there is no alternative that uses less of all inputs. (Economists often call technical inefficiency *X-inefficiency.*)

Economic efficiency is related to the *value* of all inputs used in producing a given output. The production of a given output is economically efficient if there is no other way of producing the output that will use a smaller total value of inputs.

What is the relationship between economic efficiency and these other two concepts? Technical efficiency is desirable as long as inputs are costly to the firm in any way. If a technically inefficient process is replaced by a technically efficient process, there is a saving. We do not need to put a precise value on the cost of inputs to make this judgment. All we need to know is that inputs have a positive cost to the firm, so that saving on these costs is desirable.

Usually, however, any given output may be produced in any one of many alternative, technically efficient ways in the long run. Avoiding technical inefficiency is clearly a necessary condition for producing any output at the least cost. The existence of technical inefficiency means that costs can be reduced by reducing some inputs and not increasing any others. Avoiding technical efficiency is not, however, a sufficient condition for producing at lowest possible cost. The firm must still ask which of the many technically efficient methods it should use. This is where the concept of economic efficiency comes in. The appropriate method is the one that uses the smallest value of inputs. This ensures that the firm spends as little as possible on its given output; in terms of opportunity cost, the firm sacrifices the least possible value with respect to other things that it might do with those inputs.

We have seen that engineering efficiency measures the efficiency with which a single input is used. Although knowing the efficiency of any given steam, electric, or diesel engine is interesting, increasing this efficiency is not necessarily economically efficient, because doing so usually requires the use of other valuable resources. For example, the engineering efficiency of a steam engine can be increased by using more and stronger steel in the firebox and the boiler. Similar gains can be made in all types of engines in existence today. Raising the engineering efficiency of an engine saves on fuel, but at the cost of using more of other inputs. To know whether this is worth doing, the firm must compare the value of the fuel saved with the value of the other inputs used. The optimal level of engineering efficiency is achieved by increasing efficiency, as long as the value of the input saved exceeds the value of the extra resources used, but not by increasing efficiency into the range where the costs exceed the value of the input saved.

raw materials will no doubt have changed. The decisions are risky, too, because the firm must estimate how much output it will want to produce. Is the industry to which it belongs growing or declining? Will new products emerge to render its existing products, such as typewriters or records, less useful than an extrapolation of past sales suggests?

Profit Maximization and Cost Minimization

Any firm that is trying to maximize its profits should in the long run select the economically efficient method, which is the method that produces its output at the lowest possible cost. This implication of the hypothesis of profit maximization is called **cost minimization**: From the alternatives open to it, the profit-maximizing firm will choose the least costly way of producing whatever specific output it chooses.

Choice of Factor Mix

If it is possible to substitute one factor for another to keep output constant while reducing total cost, the firm is not using the least costly combination of factors. In such a situation the firm should substitute one factor for another factor, as long as the marginal product of the one factor *per dollar* expended on it is greater than the marginal product of the other factor *per dollar* expended on it. The firm cannot minimize its costs as long as these two magnitudes are unequal. For example, if an extra dollar spent on labor produces more output than an extra dollar spent on capital, the firm can reduce costs by spending less on capital and more on labor.

If we use K to represent capital, L to represent labor, and p to represent the price of a unit of the factor, the necessary condition of cost minimization may be stated as follows:

$$\frac{MP_K}{p_K} = \frac{MP_L}{p_L} \qquad [1]$$

Whenever the two sides of Equation 1 are not equal, there are possibilities for factor substitutions that will reduce costs.[1]

To see why this equation must be satisfied if costs of production are to be minimized, suppose that the left side of Equation 1 is equal to 10, showing that the last dollar spent on capital added 10 units to output, while the right side of Equation 1 is equal to 4, showing that the last dollar spent on labor added only 4 units to output. In such a case, the firm, by using \$2.50 less of labor, would reduce output by 10 units. It could regain that lost output, however, by spending \$1.00 more on capital. Making such a substitution of capital for labor would leave output unchanged and reduce costs by \$1.50. Thus the original position was not cost-minimizing.[2]

By rearranging the terms in Equation 1, we can look at the cost-minimizing condition a bit differently.[3]

$$\frac{MP_K}{MP_L} = \frac{p_K}{p_L} \qquad [2]$$

The ratio of the marginal products on the left side of the equation compares the contribution to output of the last unit of capital and the last unit of labor. If the ratio is 4, this means that 1 unit more of capital will add 4 times as much to output as 1 unit more of labor. The right side of the equation shows how the cost of 1 unit more of capital compares to the cost of 1 unit more of labor. If the ratio is also 4, the firm cannot reduce costs by substituting capital for labor or vice versa. Now suppose that the ratio on the right side of the equation is 2. Capital, though twice as expensive, is four times as productive. It will pay the firm to switch to a method of production that uses more capital and less labor. If, however, the ratio on the right side is 6 (or *any* number more than 4), it will pay to switch to a method of production that uses more labor and less capital.

How much should inputs be changed? We have seen that when the ratio MP_K/MP_L is 4, while the ratio P_K/P_L is 2, the firm will substitute capital for labor. How far does the firm go in making this substitution? There is a limit, because as the firm uses more capital, its marginal product falls, while as it uses less labor, the marginal product of labor rises. Thus the ratio MP_K/MP_L falls. When it reaches 2, the firm need substitute no further. The ratio of

[1] Readers who read Appendix B to Chapter 7 should notice that Equation 1 is analogous to the condition for the utility-maximizing household, given on page 156, in which the household equated the ratio of the marginal utilities of each pair of goods with the ratio of their prices.

[2] The argument in this paragraph assumes that the marginal products do not change when expenditure changes by a small amount.

[3] The appendix to this chapter provides a graphical analysis of this condition, which is similar to the analysis of household behavior in Appendix A to Chapter 7.

the marginal products is equal to the ratio of the prices.

Equation 2 shows how the firm can adjust the elements over which it has control (the quantities of factors used, and thus the marginal products of the factors) to the prices of the factors given by the market.

Long-Run Equilibrium of the Firm

The firm will have achieved long-run equilibrium factor proportions when there is no opportunity for cost-reducing substitutions. This occurs when the marginal product per dollar spent on each factor is the same (Equation 1) or, equivalently, when the ratio of the marginal products of factors is equal to the ratio of their prices (Equation 2).

The Principle of Substitution

Suppose that a firm is meeting the cost-minimizing conditions shown in Equations 1 and 2 and that the cost of labor increases while the cost of capital remains unchanged. The least-cost method of producing any output will now use less labor and more capital than was required to produce the same output before the factor prices changed.

Methods of production will change if the relative prices of factors change. Relatively more of the cheaper factor and relatively less of the more expensive factor will be used.

This is called the **principle of substitution**, and it follows from the assumption that firms minimize their costs.

The principle of substitution plays a central role in resource allocation, since it relates to the way in which individual firms respond to changes in relative factor prices that are caused by the changing relative scarcities of factors in the economy as a whole. Individual firms are motivated to use less of factors that become scarcer to the economy and more of factors that become more plentiful. Here are two examples of the principle of substitution in action.

In recent decades, construction workers' wages have risen sharply relative to the wages of factory labor and the cost of machinery. In response, many home builders have shifted from on-site construction to panelization, a method of building that uses standardized modules. The wiring, plumbing, insulation, and painting of these standardized modules are all done at the factory. The bulk of the factory work is performed by machinery and by assembly line workers whose wages are only half those of on-site construction workers.

Some countries have plentiful land and small populations. Their land prices are low, and because their labor is in short supply, their wage rates are high. In response, their farmers make lavish use of the cheap land while economizing on expensive labor; thus their production processes use low ratios of labor to land. Other countries are small in area but have large populations. The demand for land is high relative to its supply, and land is relatively expensive while labor is relatively cheap. In response, farmers economize on land by using much labor per unit of land; thus their production processes use high ratios of labor to land.

Once again we see the price system functioning as an automatic control system. No single firm needs to be aware of national factor surpluses and scarcities. These are reflected by market prices, so individual firms that never look beyond their own profits are led to economize on factors that are scarce to the nation as a whole.

This discussion suggests why methods of producing the same commodity differ among countries. In Canada, where labor is highly skilled and expensive, a farmer with a large farm may use elaborate machinery to economize on labor. In China, where labor is abundant and capital is scarce, a much less mechanized method of production is appropriate. The Western engineer who believes that the Chinese are inefficient because they are using methods long ago discarded in the West is missing the truth about efficiency in the use of resources. The notion that to aid underdeveloped countries we have only to export Western "know-how" is misleading.

Cost Curves in the Long Run

There is a best (least-cost) method of producing each level of output when all factors are free to be varied. In general, this method will not be the same for different levels of output. If factor prices are given, a minimum achievable cost can be found for each possible level of output; if this cost is expressed as a quantity per unit of output, we can obtain the long-run average cost of producing each level of output. When this least-cost method of producing each output is plotted on a graph, the result is called a **long-run average cost (*LRAC*) curve.** Figure 11-1 shows one such curve.

This cost curve is determined by the technology of the industry (which is assumed to be fixed) and by the prices of the factors of production. It is a "boundary" in the sense that points below it are unattainable; points on the curve, however, are attainable if sufficient time elapses for all inputs to be adjusted. To move from one point on the *LRAC* curve to another requires an adjustment in all inputs, which may, for example, require building a larger, more elaborate factory.

The *LRAC* curve is the boundary between cost levels that are attainable, with known technology and given factor prices, and those that are unattainable.

The Shape of the Long-Run Average Cost Curve

The *LRAC* curve shown in Figure 11-1 first falls and then rises. This curve is often described as U-shaped, although "saucer-shaped" might be more accurate.

Decreasing costs. Over the range of output from zero to q_m the firm has falling long-run average costs: An expansion of output permits a reduction of costs per unit of output. These are referred to as **economies of scale**. (Of course, when output is increased, such economies of scale will be realized only after enough time has elapsed to allow changes in all factor inputs.) Since the prices of factors are assumed to be constant, the reason for the decline in long-run average cost must be that output is increasing *more than* in proportion to inputs as the scale of the firm's production expands. Over this range of output the decreasing-cost firm is often said to enjoy long-run **increasing returns.**[4]

Increasing returns may occur as a result of increased opportunities for specialization of tasks made possible by the division of labor. Adam Smith's classic discussion of this important point is given in Box 3-1 on page 44. Even the most casual observation of the differences in production techniques used in large and small plants will show that larger plants use greater specialization.

These differences arise because large, specialized equipment is useful only when the volume of output that the firm can sell justifies employment of that equipment. For example, assembly line techniques, body-stamping machinery, and multiple-boring en-

[4] Economists shift back and forth between speaking in physical terms (i.e., *increasing returns to scale*) and cost terms (i.e., *decreasing costs of production*). As we have seen in the text, the same relationship can be expressed in either terms.

FIGURE 11-1 A Long-Run Average Cost Curve

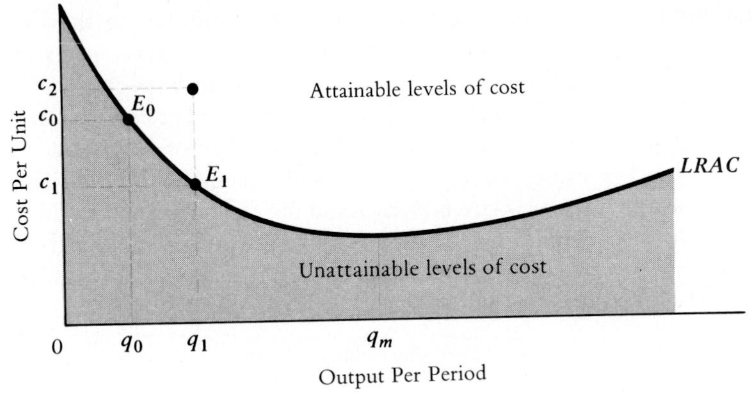

The long-run average cost (*LRAC*) curve provides a boundary between attainable and unattainable levels of costs. If the firm wishes to produce output q_0, the lowest attainable cost level is c_0 per unit. Thus point E_0 is on the *LRAC* curve. E_1 represents the least-cost method of producing q_1. Suppose that a firm is producing at E_0 and desires to increase output to q_1. In the long run a plant optimal for output q_1 can be built, and the cost of c_1 can be attained. However, in the short run it will not be able to vary all factors, and thus costs will be above c_1, say, c_2. At output q_m the firm attains its lowest possible per unit cost of production for the given technology and factor prices.

gine-block machines in automobile production are economically efficient only when individual operations are repeated thousands of times. Use of elaborate harvesting equipment (which combines many individual tasks that would otherwise be done by hand and by tractor) provides the least-cost method of production on a big farm but not on a few acres.

Typically, as the level of planned output increases, capital is substituted for labor and complex machines are substituted for simpler machines. Robotics is a contemporary example. Electronic devices can handle huge numbers of operations quickly, but unless the level of production requires such a large volume of operations, robotics or other forms of automation will not provide the least-cost method of production.

The foregoing discussion refers to the technology of production, which is one major source of increasing returns to scale. A second source lies in the geometry that is intrinsic to the three-dimensional world in which we live. To illustrate how geometry may matter, consider a firm that wishes to store a gas or a liquid. The firm is interested in the *volume* of storage space. However, the materials cost of a storage container is related to the *area* of its surface. When the size of a container is increased, the storage capacity, which is determined by its volume, increases faster than its surface area.[5] This is a genuine case of increasing returns—the output, in terms of storage capacity, increases more proportionately than the increase in the costs of the required construction materials.

A third source of increasing returns is inputs that do not have to be increased as the output of a product is increased, even in the long run. For example, there are often large fixed costs in developing new products, such as a new generation of airplanes or a more powerful computer. These R&D costs have to be incurred only once for each product and hence are independent of the scale at which the product is subsequently produced.

Even if the product's total *production costs* increase in proportion to output in the long run, average total costs, including *product development costs,* will fall as the scale of output rises. This phenomenon is popularly referred to as "spreading one's overhead." It is similar to what happens in the short run when averaged fixed costs fall with output. The difference is that fixed short-run production costs are variable long-run production costs. If the firm increases its scale of output for some product, it will incur more capital costs in the long run as a larger plant is built. However, its costs of developing that product are not affected. The influence of such once-and-for-all costs is, other things being equal, that they cause average total costs to be falling over the entire range of output. (The significance of such once-and-for-all costs is discussed in several places in Chapter 14.)

Increasing costs. Over the range of outputs greater than q_m the firm encounters rising long-run costs. An expansion in production, even after sufficient time has elapsed for all adjustments to be made, will be accompanied by a rise in average costs per unit of output. If costs per unit of input are constant, the firm's output must be increasing *less than* in proportion to the increase in inputs. When this happens, the increasing-cost firm is said to encounter long-run **decreasing returns**.[6] Decreasing returns imply that the firm suffers some diseconomy of scale. As its scale of operations increases, diseconomies are encountered that increase its per unit cost of production.

These diseconomies may be associated with the difficulties of managing and controlling an enterprise as its size increases. For example, planning problems do not necessarily vary in direct proportion to size. At first, there may be scale economies as the firm grows, but sooner or later planning and coordination problems may multiply more than in proportion to the growth in size. If so, management costs per unit of output will rise. Other sources of scale diseconomies concern the possible alienation of the labor force as size increases and the difficulties of providing appropriate supervision as more and more tiers of supervisors and middle managers come between the

[5] For example, consider a cubic container with metal sides, bottom, and lid, all of which measure 1 foot by 1 foot. To build this container, 6 square feet of metal is required (six sides, each 1 square foot), and it will hold 1 cubic foot of gas or liquid. Now increase all of the lengths of each of the container's sides to 2 feet. Fully 24 square feet of metal is now required (six sides, each 4 square feet), and the container will hold 8 cubic feet of gas or liquid (2 feet × 2 feet × 2 feet). So increasing the amount of metal in the container's walls fourfold has the effect of increasing its capacity eightfold.

[6] Long-run decreasing returns differ from the short-run diminishing returns. In the short run at least one factor is fixed, and the law of diminishing returns ensures that returns to the variable factor will eventually diminish. In the long run all factors are variable, and it is possible that physically diminishing returns would never be encountered—at least as long as it was genuinely possible to increase inputs of all factors.

person at the top and the workers on the shop floor. Control of middle-range managers may also become more difficult. As the firm becomes larger, managers may begin to pursue their own goals rather than devote all of their efforts to making profits for the firm. (This is the principal-agent problem that is discussed in detail in Chapter 16.)

Constant costs. In Figure 11-1 the firm's long-run average costs fall until output reaches q_m and rises thereafter. Another possibility should be noted. The firm's *LRAC* curve might have a flat portion over a range of output around q_m. With such a flat portion, the firm would be encountering constant costs over the relevant range of output. This means that the firm's long-run average costs per unit of output do not change as its output changes. Since factor prices are assumed to be fixed, the firm's output must be increasing *exactly in proportion to* the increase in inputs. A firm in this situation is said to be encountering **constant returns**.

FIGURE 11-2 Long-Run Average Cost and Short-Run Average Cost Curves

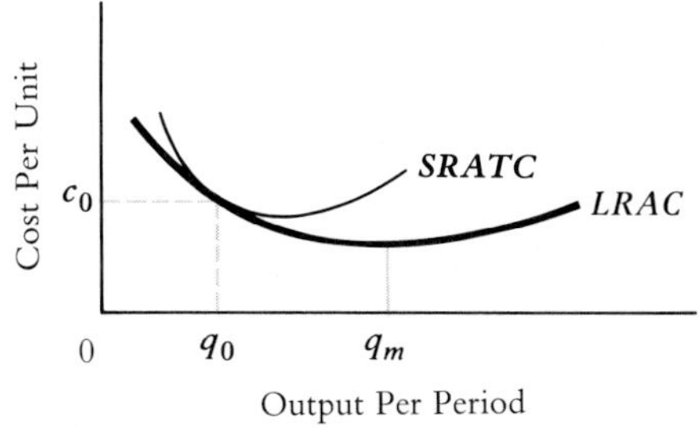

The short-run average total cost (*SRATC*) curve is tangent to the long-run average cost (*LRAC*) curve at the output for which the quantity of the fixed factors is optimal. If output is varied around q_0 units with plant and equipment fixed at the optimal level for producing q_0, costs will follow the short-run cost curve. Whereas *SRATC* and *LRAC* are at the same level for output q_0, where the fixed plant is optimal for that level, for all other outputs there is too little or too much plant and equipment, and *SRATC* lies above *LRAC*. If some output other than q_0 is to be sustained, costs can be reduced to the level of the long-run average cost curve when sufficient time has elapsed to adjust the plant and equipment.

Relationship Between Long-Run and Short-Run Costs

The short-run cost curves mentioned at the conclusion of Chapter 10 and the long-run curve studied in this chapter are all derived from the same production function. Each curve assumes given prices for all factor inputs. In the long run all factors can be varied; in the short run some must remain fixed. The long-run average cost (*LRAC*) curve shows the lowest cost of producing any output when all factors are variable. Each short-run average total cost (*SRATC*) curve shows the lowest cost of producing any output when one or more factors are held constant at some specific level.

No short-run cost curve can fall below the long-run curve because the *LRAC* curve represents the lowest attainable cost for each possible output. As the level of output is changed, a different-size plant is normally required to achieve the lowest attainable cost. This is shown in Figure 11-2, where the *SRATC* curve lies above the *LRAC* curve at all outputs except q_0.

As we observed at the end of Chapter 10, an *SRATC* curve, such as the one shown in Figure 11-2, is one of many such curves. Each curve shows how costs vary as output is varied from a base output, holding the fixed factor at the quantity most appropriate to that output. Figure 11-3 shows a family of short-run average total cost curves, along with a single long-run average cost curve. The long-run average cost curve sometimes is called an **envelope** because it encloses a series of short-run average total cost curves by being tangent to them. Each *SRATC* curve is tangent to (touches) the long-run average cost curve at the level of output for which the quantity of the fixed factor is optimal and lies above it for all other levels of output.[7]

Shifts in Cost Curves

The cost curves derived so far show how cost varies with output, given constant factor prices and fixed technology. Changes in either technological knowledge or factor prices will cause the entire family of short-run and long-run average cost curves to shift. Loss of existing technological knowledge is rare, so

[7] Notice that since all costs are variable in the long run, we do not need to distinguish between *AVC*, *AFC*, and *ATC*, as we did in the short run; in the long run there is only one *LRAC* for any given set of input prices.

FIGURE 11-3 The Envelope Relationship Between the Long-Run Average Cost Curve and All the Short-Run Average Cost Curves

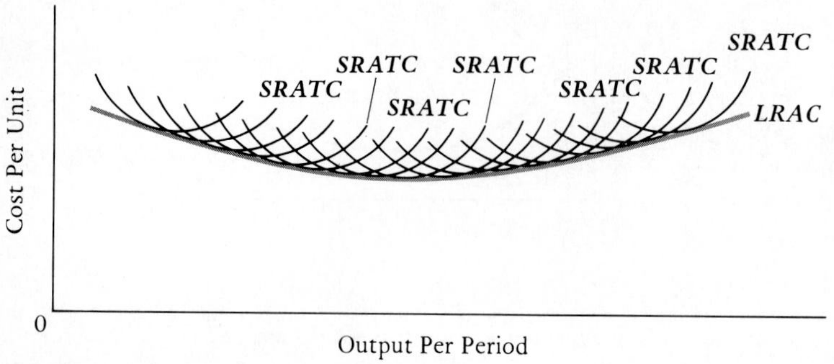

To every point on the long-run average cost (*LRAC*) curve there is an associated short-run average total cost (*SRATC*) curve tangent at that point. Each short-run curve shows how costs vary if output varies, with the fixed factor being held constant at the level that is optimal for the output at the point of tangency.

technological change normally causes change in only one direction, shifting cost curves downward. Improved ways of making existing commodities mean that lower-cost methods of production become available. (Technological change will be discussed in more detail later in this chapter.)

Changes in factor prices can exert an influence in either direction. If a firm has to pay more for any factor that it uses, the cost of producing each level of output will rise; if the firm has to pay less for any factor that it uses, the cost of producing each level of output will fall.

A rise in factor prices shifts the family of short-run and long-run average cost curves upward. A fall in factor prices, or a technological advance, shifts the entire family of average cost curves downward.

Although factor prices usually change gradually, sometimes they change suddenly and drastically. For example, in the mid 1980s oil prices fell dramatically; the effect was to shift downward the cost curves of all users of oil and oil-related products.

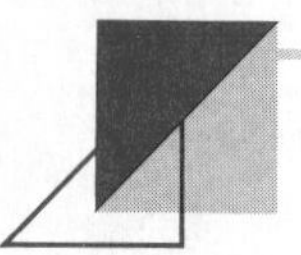

The Very Long Run

In the long run, profit-maximizing firms do the best they can to produce known products with the techniques and the resources currently available. This means being *on*, rather than above, their long-run cost curves. In the very long run the techniques and resources that are available change. Such changes cause *shifts* in long-run cost curves. These shifts, along with the development of new products, are major sources of economic growth—the long-run rise in output that accounts for rising living standards.

The decrease in costs that can be achieved by choosing widely among available factors of production, known techniques, and alternative levels of output is necessarily limited, since a firm can never do better in the long run than to select the best available technique. Improvements by invention and innovation are potentially limitless, however, and for this reason sustained growth in living standards is critically linked to technological change.

Kinds of Technological Change

Three kinds of change dominate production and cost in the very long run. All are related to technology, broadly defined.

New techniques. Throughout the twentieth century, changes in the techniques available for producing existing products have been dramatic. About the same amount of coal is produced in North America today as was produced 50 years ago, but the number of coal miners is less than one-tenth what it was then. Eighty years ago roads and railways were built by gangs of workers who used buckets, spades, and draft horses. Today bulldozers, steam shovels, giant trucks, and other specialized equipment have banished the workhorse completely from construction sites and to a great extent have displaced the pick-and-shovel worker. Generally, capital has been substituted for labor.

An important new production technique, called *lean production,* is rapidly replacing the long-established *mass-production, assembly-line* techniques in many industries. *Lean* production is a more flexible, lower-cost method of production that produces higher-quality products and reduces the cost of developing new products. Lean production typically has a lower long-run cost curve than conventional mass production, and a more rapidly downward shifting cost curve in the very long run. Lean production is discussed further in Box 11-2.

New products. New goods and services are constantly being invented and marketed. Color television, polio vaccine, synthetic fabrics, personal computers, and many other current consumer products did not exist a mere generation or two ago. Other products have changed so dramatically that the only connection they have with the "same" commodity that was produced in the past is the name. A 1990 Ford automobile is very different from a 1920 Ford. It is even different from a 1970 Ford in size, safety, and gasoline consumption. Modern jets are revolutionary compared with the DC-3, which was the workhorse of the airlines during the 1930s and 1940s. The DC-3 itself bore little resemblance—beyond having wings and an engine—to the Wright brothers' airplane, which made history's first flight during the lifetime of some living Canadians.

Improved inputs. Improvements in such intangibles as health and education raise the quality of labor services. Today's workers and managers are healthier and better educated than their grandparents. Many of today's unskilled workers are literate and competent in arithmetic, and their managers are apt to be trained in modern scientific methods of business management and computer science.

Similarly, improvements in raw materials occur. For example, the type and quality of metals have changed. Steel has replaced iron, and aluminum substitutes for steel in a process of change that makes a statistical category such as "primary metals" seem unsatisfactory. Even for a given category, say, steel, today's product is lighter, stronger, and more flexible than the "same" product manufactured only 20 years ago.

Sources of Technological Change

Technological change refers to all changes in the available techniques of production. To measure its extent, economists use the notion of **productivity**, defined as a measure of output produced per unit of resource input. The rate of increase in productivity provides a measure of the progress caused by technological change. Growth in productivity highlights society's ability to get more and better output from given resources. The significance of such growth is explored further in Box 11-3. We shall discuss some of the major historical sources of productivity increase.

One widely used measure of productivity is output *per hour* of labor. This is the measure that we shall use. Other possible measures include output *per worker*, output *per person*, and output *per unit* of inputs, measured by an index number.

Substitution of Capital for Labor

Manufacturing, transportation, communications, mining, and agriculture have all seen a steady substitution of capital for labor over the years. This substitution is measured by changes in the **capital-labor ratio**—the amount of capital per worker in an economy—which has increased continually for more than 100 years.

Three reasons for this substitution can be identified. First, the price of labor has risen relative to capital goods. As predicted by the principle of substitution, this has led to the use of more capital and less labor per unit of output. Second, machines have become more and more productive over time, so a laborer working with a typical machine will produce much more now than in the past. Third, growing demand—due to a rising population and a rising per capita income—has allowed each industry to produce larger outputs by using more capital, thereby taking advantage of economies of scale.

Energy Substitution

Related to the substitution of capital for labor has been the increasing reliance on inanimate energy for production. Energy to plow fields, to turn machines, to move goods, to provide heat, and to transform

BOX 11-2

The Lean Production Revolution

Production techniques are currently being revolutionized by the introduction, in many industries and in many countries, of *lean production techniques*. This is the most fundamental change to occur since the introduction of mass production—a technique brought to full development by Henry Ford early in the twentieth century. To understand the "lean production revolution," pioneered by the Japanese, one must distinguish the three types of production methods used today.

Craft methods employ highly skilled workers to make nonstandardized products that are often tailor-made for individual purchasers. The result is usually an expensive product of high quality, made by artisans who get considerable job satisfaction.

Mass production methods are based on specialization and division of labor, as first analyzed by Adam Smith in the eighteenth century (see Box 3-1 on page 44). They use skilled personnel to design the products and the production methods. They then employ relatively unskilled labor to produce standardized parts and to assemble them with the aid of highly specialized, single-purpose machines. The parts are usually manufactured in separate locations, often by distinct companies, and then assembled on a central production line, often called an *assembly line*. The design of the product is centralized, and manufacturers bid competitively to produce parts to the specifications provided to them. The cost of changing the specialized equipment from the production of one product variant to another is high, and thus specific product types are produced for as long as possible. The result is a standardized product, made in a fairly small number of variants, produced at low cost and with moderate quality. The work is repetitive, and workers are regarded as variable costs to be laid off or taken on as the desired rate of production varies.

Lean production methods combine the flexibility and high quality standards of craft production with the low cost of mass production techniques. They are lean because they use less of all inputs, including time, labor, capital, and inventories compared with either of the other techniques. They are flexible because the costs of switching from one product line to another are minimized.

In lean production, workers are organized as teams; each worker is encouraged to do all of the tasks assigned to the team, using equipment that is less highly specialized than is used in mass production techniques. This emphasizes individuality and initiative rather than a mind-numbing repetition of one unskilled operation. It also helps workers to identify places where improvements can be made and encourages them to follow up on these. Finally, it reduces the costs of switching equipment from production of one product variant to another.

In mass-production plants, stopping an assembly line to correct a problem at one point stops everyone from working at all points. So stopping the line is regarded as a serious matter, and keeping the assembly line running is the sole responsibility of a senior line manager. To reduce stoppages, large stocks of each part are held, and defective parts are discarded. Faults in assembly, which are treated as random events, are left to be corrected after the product has been assembled—often an expensive procedure. Stops are nonetheless frequent to correct materials supply and coordination problems. In lean production, every worker has the ability to stop production whenever a fault is discovered. Parts are delivered by the suppliers to the work stations "just

natural resources is a major determinant of the productive power of an economy. In 1900 more than half of all North American energy requirements was supplied by human beings, horses, mules, and oxen. By 1990 human and animal power provided well under 10 percent of all energy that was consumed; they have been replaced by coal, oil, gas, nuclear, and hydroelectric power.

Invention and Innovation

Invention is the discovery of something new, such as a production technique or a product. **Innovation**

in time." Defective parts are put aside for their source to be identified, and any defects are treated as events with patterns of causes that need to be understood. When lean methods are first introduced, work stoppages are frequent as problems are identified and investigated. As the sources are found and removed, work stoppages diminish, and the typical mature lean production line—wherein any worker can stop the line—stops much less frequently than the typical mass-production assembly line, where only the line foreman can press the stop button.

The result for labor is much more worker identification with the job and much more worker satisfaction than under mass production techniques. Employers find that their labor force develops substantial skills, and they try to hold on to workers rather than treating them as strictly variable factors. (Some union leaders feel that workers lose when they and management form a cooperative rather than an adversarial relation and consequently oppose the introduction of lean production methods.)

Product design is expensive. Mass-production firms try to reduce the costs by using specialist designers. For example, one person may spend his or her life trying to improve window-opening mechanisms. The specialization creates problems both in coordinating the work of various designers and in getting good feedback from parts producers and assembly line workers to designers. The best theoretical design is of little use if it poses costly production problems. Lean producers use design teams that are nonspecialized and work closely with production engineers and parts producers. This creates more flexibility and better feedback, from the practical problems that arise in production to the basic design of products. It also allows parts producers to be presented with broad specifications of the required parts while they do their own R&D to develop the detailed specifications.

The use of design teams also cuts product development time dramatically. In the specialized design techniques, the designing must be done in a linear manner: The product design must be worked out in detail before the machine makers begin to design the specialized equipment needed to do the work. In the lean design team, everyone is working together. As the new product begins to take shape, the tool designers can begin to work on their outline plans; as the product design becomes better specified, the design of the tools can likewise be more fully developed.

Although lean production methods still have scale economies—unit costs fall as the volume of output increases—their main effect is to shift the whole long-run cost curve dramatically downward. Lean methods are also effective in the very long run, especially in developing successful new products that can be produced efficiently and cheaply.

Japanese automobile firms using lean methods have been able to achieve unit costs of production below those of mass-production-based North American car factories that have twice their volume of output. They have also been able to lead in international competition to design new products efficiently and rapidly. Lean production methods are a major source of the Japanese competitive advantage, both in automobiles and in a range of other manufactured goods. The ability of firms in other countries to compete succesfully with these Japanese firms may depend on the speed with which they can institute lean methods in their own production processes.

is the introduction of an invention into methods of production. Invention is thus a precondition to innovation.

Invention is cumulative in effect. A useful invention is adopted; a useless one is discarded. The cumulative impact of many small, useful devices and techniques may be as great as the impact of one occasional dramatic mechanism such as the steam engine, the cotton gin, or the sewing machine. Indeed, few famous inventions have sprung from a single act of creative inspiration; usually each builds on the contributions of prior inventors. The backlog

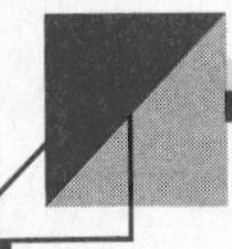

BOX 11-3

The Significance of Productivity Growth

Economics used to be known as "the dismal science" because some of its predictions were dismal. Malthus and other classical economists predicted that the pressure of more and more people on the world's limited resources would cause a decline in output per person due to the operation of the law of diminishing returns. Human history would see more and more people living less and less well and the surplus population that could not be supported dying off from hunger and disease.

This prediction has proved wrong for the developed countries, for two main reasons. First, their populations have not expanded as rapidly as foreseen by early economists, who were writing before birth control techniques were widely used. Second, pure knowledge and its applied techniques have expanded so rapidly during the past 150 years that the ability to squeeze more out of limited resources has expanded faster than the population. We have experienced sustained growth in productivity that has permitted increases in output per person.

Growth in productivity permits increases in output per person and thus contributes to rising standards of living.

Productivity increases are a powerful force for increasing living standards. Our great-grandparents would have regarded today's standard of living in most industrialized countries as unattainable. An apparently modest rate of increase in productivity of 2 percent per year leads to a doubling of output per hour of labor every 35 years. Productivity in Canada has increased at a rate somewhat greater than this throughout most of the twentieth century.

The growth rates of other countries have been even higher. Between 1945 and 1980 German productivity increased at 5 percent per year, doubling its output every 14 years. In Japan it increased at more than 9 percent per year, a rate that doubles output per hour of labor approximately every 8 years! In many countries, a stable rate of productivity growth came to be taken for granted as an automatic source of ever-increasing living standards.

During the 1970s the rate of productivity growth in most industrialized countries dropped sharply below its historical trend, and the slowdown was particularly acute in Canada and the United States. Since 1982, however, productivity growth has resumed at almost 2 percent per year. It remains to be seen whether the slowdown was a onetime occurrence or whether the accustomed doubling of productivity in every generation is a thing of the past.

A permanent slowdown in productivity growth would have severe consequences. Declining productivity growth means that living standards rise more slowly.

of past inventions constitutes society's technical knowledge, and that backlog in turn feeds innovation.

Innovation depends on a steady supply of new inventions. However, new methods, machines, materials, and products do not come into use simply because they have been invented. They are introduced if and when it appears profitable to do so, and they flourish if their production proves to be profitable.

The Endogenous Nature of Technological Change

Technological change once was thought to be mainly a random process, brought about by inventions made by crackpots and eccentric scientists working in garages or basements. We now know better.

Changes in technology are often *endogenous responses* to changing economic signals; that is, they are responses to the same things that induce the substitution of one factor for another in a given technology. In our discussion of long-run demand curves in Chapter 5, we looked at just such technological changes in response to rising relative prices when we spoke of the development of smaller, more fuel-efficient cars in the wake of rising gasoline prices. Similarly, much of the move to substitute capital for labor in industry in response to rising wage rates has taken the form of inventing new labor-saving methods of production.

Invention can frequently be produced on demand; the development of the atomic bomb in the 1940s is a dramatic example of this. Money and determination can buy invention. Major technological changes are often the result of expenditures on research and development.

Current evidence indicates that to a significant degree, productivity growth is a response to investment in research. Countries whose industries have stepped up R&D expenditures, particularly Germany and Japan, have experienced much higher levels of productivity growth than countries such as the United States, Canada, and the United Kingdom, whose industries have let such expenditures lag. Similarly, industries that are major R&D spenders (e.g., chemicals, electrical equipment, air transport) have maintained productivity growth at much higher levels than industries that do little research (e.g., steel and construction). Some sectors that do little research, such as coal mining and farming, may buy their inputs (equipment, fertilizer, seed) from industries that do much R&D, achieving gains in productivity as a result. These sectors buy invention and innovation through the price they pay for inputs.

Innovation has an unmistakably endogenous component, rising as profit incentives increase, declining as they fall. Profit incentives are in turn affected by many aspects of the economic climate, among them the rate of growth of the economy, the cost and availability of money for investment, and all sorts of government policies from taxes to regulations. Some of the important lessons that can be learned from the slackening in productivity growth at the start of the 1970s are discussed in Box 11-4.

In proportion to its gross domestic product, Canada spends less on R&D activities than many other industrialized countries. This is due partly to Canada's specialization in many industries that do not typically do a lot of R&D and partly to the fact that Canadian subsidiaries of transnational corporations have direct access to the R&D done by their companies in other countries. When these and other similar factors are allowed for, the question of whether Canada still does less R&D than is needed to achieve good long-run growth performance is the subject of a controversy that we encounter several times in this book.

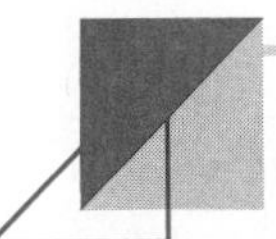

How Much Productivity Growth Do We Want?

An important question about social values remains. Progress has come to mean growth, and growth has usually meant industrialization. Applied to the economy as a whole, industrialization, and its accompanying changes in productivity, has changed our material well-being vastly and has permitted ever more people to escape hunger and poverty.

Paradoxically, however, slowdowns in productivity growth are sometimes a part of the growth process itself. The current shift to the provision of services with relatively high income elasticities but low productivity levels is the most obvious example. People spend much of the increases in their income that growth has provided on entertainment, travel, education, and other services and less and less on manufactured products.

Few things in this world come without some cost. Growth in productivity is often accompanied by increased pollution and more industrial accidents. The gasoline engine, the steel mill, the jet airplane, DDT, plastics, and the skyscraper with its hundreds of thousands of electric lights are the artifacts of our progress over the past century. In some ways such innovations have lowered the quality of life even while raising the standard of living. Expenditures to control pollution or to increase safety may decrease measured productivity growth but improve the quality of life.

Just as members of a society can benefit (at some stage of economic development) from more luxuries and fewer basic necessities, so, too, they may sometimes benefit from more amenities and a lower productivity growth. To the extent that they can, a slower rate of productivity growth may reflect a better life, not a worse one.

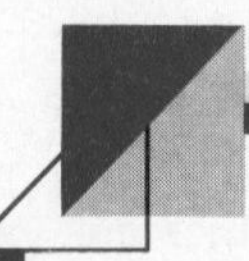

BOX 11-4

Causes of Decline in Productivity Growth

The rate of productivity growth in North America slackened in the 1970s and early 1980s. Not surprisingly, this raised fears that the slowdown might be permanent. The partial recovery of productivity growth in the mid 1980s showed that the more extreme views of the end of productivity-driven growth were unfounded. Here we shall discuss some of the possible sources of such a slowdown in productivity growth.

Decline of growth opportunities. When a country starts to industrialize, labor is generally employed in labor-intensive, low-productivity industries. As labor shifts into high-productivity, capital-intensive industries, productivity rises. As a country becomes industrialized, there is less possibility for further gains in productivity, since most of the labor has already shifted from low- to high-productivity sectors.

Abundance of energy. Falling energy prices assisted Canadian and American productivity growth for a century. Each worker was supplied with more and more of ever-cheapening energy, so each could produce more output. In the early 1970s oil became scarce and expensive. Rising energy costs slowed productivity increases by reducing the amount of energy that it was profitable to combine with each worker. Now that energy costs are again falling, productivity is rising.

Demographic changes. Growth of per capita income is easier to achieve in a moderately increasing population than in a static or a declining one. When relatively few industries and firms are expanding, less investment will take place, and firms will tend to keep existing plant and equipment in place. Every time a firm undertakes new investment, it is likely to adopt the most modern technology available. A growing industry often has profitable opportunities for investment geared to a larger scale of output.

Similarly, it is easier for labor to adapt to the changing requirements of growth when the population is growing than when it is remaining static. It is harder to retrain existing workers than to train new workers in newly needed skills—and the faster the population is growing, the more new workers there will be in any one year. Moreover, a fall in the growth rate also causes a fall in the rate at which new occupations and promotion opportunities are being developed. This may in turn discourage young people from acquiring the fresh skills that contribute to further productivity growth.

Shifts in the composition of output. During recent decades in North America there has been a major

SUMMARY

1. There are no fixed factors in the long run. Profit-maximizing firms choose from the alternatives open to them the least-cost method of achieving any specific output. A long-run cost curve represents the boundary between attainable and unattainable levels of cost for the given technology.
2. The principle of substitution says that efficient production will use cheaper factors lavishly and more expensive ones economically. If the relative prices of factors change, relatively more of cheaper factors and relatively less of more expensive ones will be used.
3. The shape of the long-run cost curve depends on the relationship of inputs to outputs as the whole scale of a firm's operations changes. Increasing, constant, and decreasing returns lead, respectively, to decreasing, constant, and increasing long-run average costs.

shift of demand from high-productivity manufacturing to lower-productivity services. Fast food and other services—such as garbage collection, clean air, police protection, libraries, and medical and hospital care—tend to have a lower value of output per worker than is typical in manufacturing industries. The shifts of labor from sectors with relatively high levels of productivity (largely due to abundant capital per worker) to those with much lower levels has decreased average productivity. This has nothing to do with the skill or dedication of the librarian compared to the factory worker; it is related to the nature of their tasks and the tools at their disposal. In the librarian's production of services there is no counterpart to the highly automated assembly line where automobiles are produced.

Low saving and investment. Despite a high *private* savings rate, large government deficits have meant that Canada has had a low *national* savings rate. Thus a significant amount of investment has had to be financed out of foreign-owned funds. This in itself need not reduce the growth rate, although it will, over the years, increase the proportion of Canadian income accruing to foreign residents. Of more importance to the growth rate is the declining amount of investment. The decline in productivity growth in the late 1970s and early 1980s was accompanied by low investment (as a share of national income), and the modest recovery in the later 1980s was accompanied by a relatively strong investment performance.

Institutional climate. The profits from innovation depend on tax laws and regulatory requirements, among other things. If innovators are allowed to reap large gains from successful innovations, they will be more likely to take the risks of innovating. Innovation can be encouraged by investment tax credits, strong patent laws, low tax rates, government subsidies, and government-assisted R&D. It can be discouraged by regulatory burdens such as environmental impact statements, safety regulation, and the delays involved in meeting government requirements.

Many believe that the institutional climate became increasingly hostile to private innovation during the 1960s and 1970s and that high taxes, government regulations, and economic protection all added to the forces inhibiting innovation and growth. Part of the support for economic deregulation in the 1980s was an attempt to make the economic climate more favorable to innovation.

4. The long-run and short-run cost curves are related. Every long-run cost corresponds to *some* quantity of each factor and is thus on some short-run cost curve. The short-run cost curve shows how costs vary when that particular quantity of a fixed factor is used to produce outputs greater than or less than the output for which it is optimal.
5. Cost curves shift upward or downward in response to changes in the prices of factors or changed technology. Increases in factor prices shift cost curves upward. Decreases in factor prices, or technological advances, shift cost curves downward.
6. Over extended periods, the most important influence on costs of production and on standards of living has been the very long run increases in output made possible by new technology, which has led to new techniques, new products, and improved inputs.

7. Major sources of productivity growth in industrializing countries include the substitution of capital for labor (an increasing capital-labor ratio), increased energy use, and invention and innovation.
8. Innovation is the key to productivity growth. It requires invention but also profitable opportunities for the introduction of available knowledge. Thus innovation and the changes in technology it brings are partly endogenous. The state of the economy, the institutional climate, and differences in technological possibilities in sectors where demand is growing and declining all affect the opportunities for innovation.
9. Material progress leads both to more goods and services per person and to opportunities for better living. Yet such progress is a mixed blessing; pollution and an increased number of injuries and accidents accompany growth in productivity. Expenditures to control pollution and increase safety are examples of things that may decrease measured productivity while improving the quality of life.

TOPICS FOR REVIEW

Implication of cost minimization
Interpretation of $MP_K/MP_L = p_K/p_L$ and $MP_K/p_K = MP_L/p_L$
The principle of substitution
Increasing, decreasing, and constant returns
Economies of scale
Envelope curve
Distinction between production and productivity
Level of productivity and rate of growth of productivity
Sources of increasing productivity
Invention and innovation
Determinants of innovation
Causes of slowdowns in productivity growth

DISCUSSION QUESTIONS

1. Why does the profit-maximizing firm choose the least-cost method of producing any given output? Might a non-profit-maximizing organization such as a university, church, or government intentionally choose a method of production other than the least-cost one?
2. The chairman of an American multinational oil company recently said, "Our government has adopted a gratuitously hostile attitude. Industry has been compelled to spend more and more of its research dollars to comply with environmental, health, and safety regulations—and to move away from longer-term efforts aimed at major scientific advance." If this is true, is it necessarily a sign that government policies are misguided?
3. Use the principle of substitution to predict the effect of each of the following.
   a. During the 1960s salaries of professors rose much more rapidly than those of teaching assistants. During the 1970s salaries of teaching assistants rose more than those of professors. During the 1980s the relative salaries of these two groups did not change greatly.
   b. The cost of land in big cities increases more than the cost of high-rise construction.
   c. Gold leaf is produced by pounding gold with a hammer. The thinner it is, the more valuable it is. The price of gold is set on the world market, but the price of labor varies among countries.

d. Wages of textile workers and shoe machinery operators rise more in Ontario than in Quebec.

4. The long-run average cost curve can be thought of as consisting of a series of points, one pulled from each of a number of short-run average total cost curves. Explain in what sense any point on the long-run average cost curve is also on some short-run average total cost curve. What is the meaning of a move from one point on a long-run average cost curve to another point on the same curve? Contrast this with a movement along a short-run average total cost curve.

5. During the "energy crisis" of the 1970s, the director of U.S. federal energy programs urged the American people to make necessary "long-run adjustments to the energy shortage by reducing energy input per unit of output." How exactly might this be done? Is this use of *long run* also the economists' use of *long run*? During the 1980s the price of many types of energy fell relative to the general price level. What effects would this have?

6. Israel, a small country, imports the "insides" of its automobiles, but it manufactures the bodies. If this makes economic sense, what does it tell us about cost conditions of automobile manufacturers?

7. Name five important modern products that were not available when you were in grade school. Make a list of major products that you think have increased their sales at least tenfold during the past 30 years. Check your judgment by consulting the *Canada Year Book* or a similar source. Consider to what extent the growth in each list may reflect product or process innovation.

8. Each of the following is a means of increasing productivity. Discuss which groups within a society might oppose each one.

a. A labor-saving invention that permits all goods to be manufactured with less labor than before

b. Rapidly increasing growth of population in the economy

c. Removal of all government production safety rules

d. Reduction in corporate income taxes

e. Reduction in production of services and increase in agricultural production

Appendix to Chapter 11

Isoquants: An Alternative Analysis of the Firm's Input Decisions

The production function gives the relationship between the factor inputs that the firm uses and the output that it obtains. In the long run the firm can choose among many different combinations of inputs that will yield the same output. The production function and the long-run choices open to the firm can be represented graphically using what are called *isoquants*.

A Single Isoquant

Table 11A-1 illustrates a hypothetical example in which several combinations of two inputs (labor and capital) can produce a given quantity of output. The data from Table 11A-1 are plotted graphically in Figure 11A-1. A smooth curve is drawn through the points to indicate that there are additional ways, which are not listed in the table, of producing 6 units.

This curve is called an **isoquant**. It shows the whole set of technologically efficient factor combinations for producing a given level of output—6 units in this case. This is an example of graphing a relationship among three variables in two dimen-

TABLE 11A-1 Alternative Methods of Producing 6 Units of Output: Points on an Isoquant

Method	K	L	ΔK	ΔL	Rate of substitution $\Delta K/\Delta L$
a	18	2			
			−6	1	−6.00
b	12	3			
			−3	1	−3.00
c	9	4			
			−3	2	−1.50
d	6	6			
			−2	3	−0.67
e	4	9			
			−1	3	−0.33
f	3	12			
			−1	6	−0.17
g	2	18			

An isoquant describes the firm's alternative methods for producing a given output. The table lists some of the methods indicated by a production function as being available to produce 6 units of output. The first combination uses a great deal of capital (K) and very little labor (L). As we move down the table, labor is substituted for capital in such a way as to keep output constant. Finally, at the bottom, most of the capital has been replaced by labor. The rate of substitution between the two factors is calculated in the last three columns of the table. Note that as we move down the table, the absolute value of the rate of substitution declines.

FIGURE 11A-1 An Isoquant for Output of 6 Units

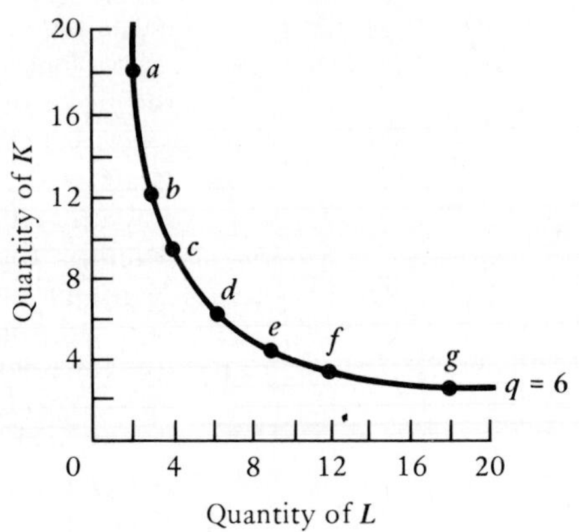

Isoquants are downward-sloping and convex. The downward slope reflects the requirement of technical efficiency. A method that uses more of one factor must use less of the other factor if it is to be technically efficient. The convex shape of the isoquant reflects a diminishing marginal rate of substitution. The lettered points on the graph are plotted from the data in Table 11A-1. Starting from point *a*, which uses relatively little labor and much capital, and moving to point *b*, 1 additional unit of labor can substitute for 6 units of capital (while holding production constant). However, from *b* to *c*, 1 unit of labor substitutes for only 3 units of capital This diminishing rate is expressed geometrically by the flattening of the slope of the isoquant.

sions. It is analogous to the contour line on a map, which shows all points of equal altitude, and to an indifference curve (discussed in Appendix A to Chapter 7), which shows all combinations of commodities that yield an equal utility.

As we move from one point on an isoquant to another, we are *substituting one factor for another* while holding output constant. If we move from point *b* to point *c*, we are substituting 1 unit of labor for 3 units of capital. The marginal rate of substitution measures the rate at which one factor is substituted for another with output being held constant. Graphically, the marginal rate of substitution is measured by the slope of the isoquant at a particular point. Table 11A-1 shows the calculation of some rates of substitution between various points of the isoquant. [20]

The marginal rate of substitution is related to the marginal products of the factors of production. To see how, consider an example. Assume that at the present level of inputs of labor and capital, the marginal product of 1 unit of labor is 2 units of output, while the marginal product of capital is 1 unit of output. If the firm reduces its use of capital and increases its use of labor to keep output constant, it needs to add only ½ unit of labor for 1 unit of capital given up. If, at another point on the isoquant with more labor and less capital, the marginal products are 2 for capital and 1 for labor, then the firm will have to add 2 units of labor for every unit of capital it gives up. The general proposition is this:

The marginal rate of substitution between two factors of production is equal to the ratio of their marginal products.

Isoquants satisfy two important conditions: They are downward-sloping, and they are convex viewed from the origin. What is the economic meaning of these conditions?

The downward slope indicates that each factor input has a positive marginal product. If the input of one factor is reduced and that of the other is held constant, output will be reduced. Thus if one input is decreased, production can be held constant only if the other factor input is increased. The marginal rate of substitution has a negative value. Decreases in one factor must be balanced by increases in the other factor if output is to be held constant.

To understand convexity, consider what happens as the firm moves along the isoquant of Figure 11A-1 downward and to the right. Labor is being added and capital reduced to keep output constant. If labor is added in increments of exactly 1 unit, how much capital may be dispensed with each time? The key to the answer is that both factors are assumed to be subject to the law of diminishing returns. Thus the gain in output associated with each additional unit of labor added is *diminishing*, whereas the loss of output associated with each additional unit of capital forgone is *increasing*. It therefore takes ever-smaller reductions in capital to compensate for equal increases in labor. This implies that the isoquant is convex viewed from the origin.

An Isoquant Map

The isoquant of Figure 11A-1 is for 6 units of output. There is another isoquant for 7 units, another for 7,000 units, and a different one for every rate of output. Each isoquant refers to a specific output and connects combinations of factors that are technologically efficient methods of achieving that output. If we plot a representative set of these isoquants from the same production function on a single graph, we get an **isoquant map** like that in Figure 11A-2. The

FIGURE 11A-2 An Isoquant Map

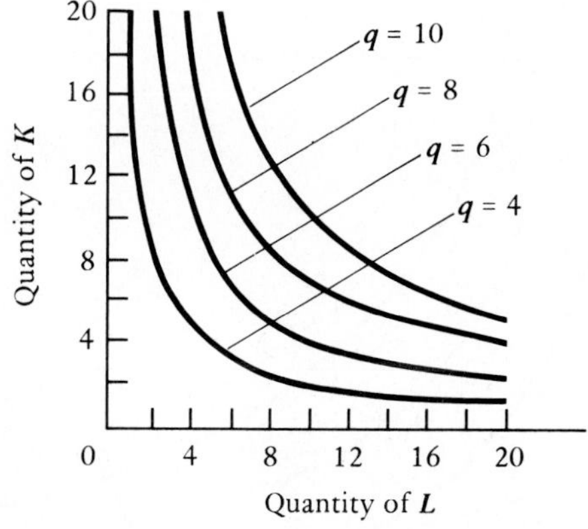

An isoquant map shows a set of isoquants, one for each level of output. The figure shows four isoquants drawn from the production function and corresponding to 4, 6, 8, and 10 units of production.

FIGURE 11A-3 Isocost Lines

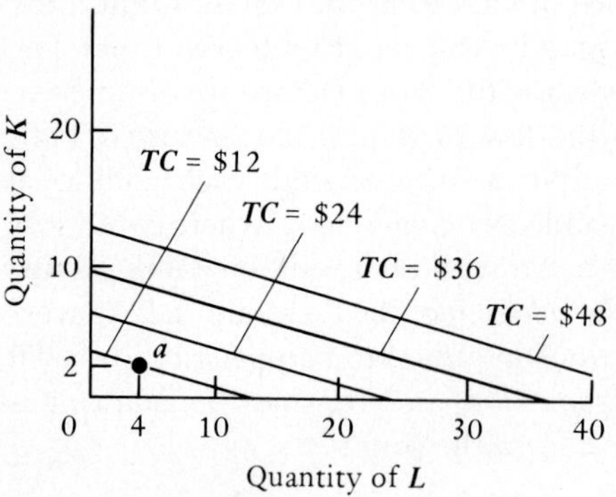

Each isocost line shows alternative factor combinations that can be purchased for a given outlay. The graph shows the four isocost lines that result when labor costs $1 per unit and capital $4 per unit and when expenditure is held constant at $12, $24, $36, and $48, respectively. The line labeled TC = $12 represents all combinations of the two factors that the firm could buy for $12. Point *a* represents 2 units of K and 4 units of L.

higher the level of output along a particular isoquant, the farther the isoquant is from the origin.

Conditions for Cost Minimization

Finding the efficient way of producing any output requires finding the least-cost factor combination. To do this requires that when both factors are variable, factor prices be known. Suppose, to continue the example, that capital is priced at $4 per unit and labor at $1 per unit. In Chapter 7 a budget line was used to show the alternative combinations of goods that a household could buy; here an *isocost line* is used to show alternative combinations of factors that a firm can buy for a given outlay. Four different isocost lines appear in Figure 11A-3. The slope of each reflects *relative* factor prices, just as the slope of the budget line in Chapter 7 represented relative product prices. For given factor prices, a series of parallel isocost lines will reflect the alternative levels of expenditure on factor purchases that are open to the firm. The higher the level of expenditure, the farther the isocost line is from the origin.

In Figure 11A-4 the isoquant and isocost maps

FIGURE 11A-4 The Determination of the Least-Cost Method of Output

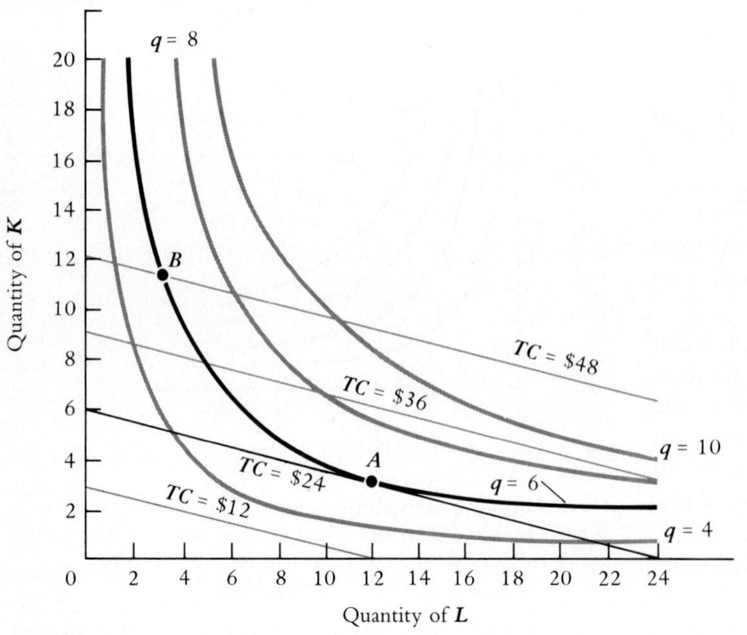

Least-cost methods are represented by points of tangency between isoquant and isocost lines. The isoquant map of Figure 11A-2 and the isocost lines of Figure 11A-3 are brought together. Consider point *A*. It is on the 6-unit isoquant and the $24 isocost line. Thus it is possible to achieve the output q = 6 for a total cost of $24. There are other ways to achieve this output, for example, at point *B*, where TC = $48. Moving along the isoquant from point *A* in either direction increases cost. Similarly, moving along the isocost line from point *A* in either direction lowers output. Thus either move would raise cost per unit.

are brought together. The economically most efficient method of production must be a point on an isoquant that just touches (i.e., is tangent to) an isocost line. If the isoquant cuts the isocost line, it is possible to move along the isoquant and reach a lower level of cost. Only at a point of tangency is a movement in either direction along the isoquant a movement to a higher cost level. The lowest attainable cost of producing 6 units is \$24. This cost level can be achieved only by operating at *A*, the point where the \$24 isocost line is tangent to the 6-unit isoquant. The lowest average cost of producing 6 units is thus \$24/6 = \$4 per unit of output.

The least-cost position is given graphically by the tangency point between the isoquant and the isocost lines.

Notice that point *A* in Figure 11A-4 indicates not only the lowest level of cost for 6 units of output but also the highest level of output for \$24 of cost. Thus we find the same solution if we set out *either* to minimize the cost of producing 6 units of output *or* to maximize the output that can be obtained for \$24. One problem is said to be the "dual" of the other.

The slope of the isocost line is given by the ratio of the prices of the two factors of production. The slope of the isoquant is given by the ratio of their marginal products. When the firm reaches its least-cost position, it has equated the price ratio (which is given to it by the market prices) with the ratio of the marginal products (which it can adjust by varying the proportions in which it hires the factors). In symbols,

$$\frac{MP_K}{MP_L} = \frac{p_K}{p_L}$$

This is equivalent to Equation 2 on page 203. We have now derived this result by use of the isoquant analysis of the firm's decisions. [21]

FIGURE 11A-5 The Effects of a Change in Factor Prices on Costs and Factor Proportions

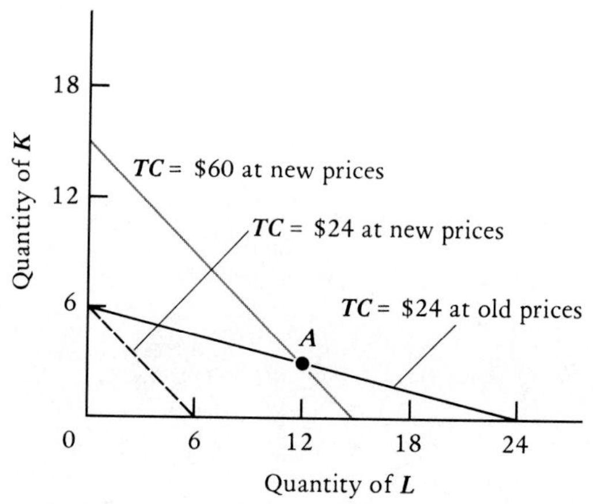

(i) The effect on the isocost line of an increase in the price of labor

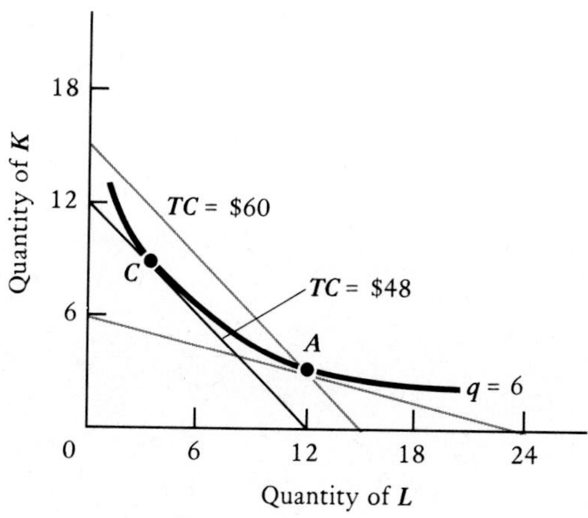

(ii) Substitution of capital for labor resulting from an increase in the price of labor

An increase in the price of labor pivots the isocost line inward and thus increases the cost of producing any output. It also changes the slope of the isocost line and thus changes the least-cost method of producing. (i) The rise in the price of *L* from \$1 to \$4 per unit (with the price of *K* being held constant at \$4) pivots the \$24 isocost line inward to the dashed line. Any output previously produced for \$24 will cost more at the new prices if it uses any amount of labor. The new cost of producing *A* rises from \$24 to \$60. (ii) The steeper isocost line is tangent to the isoquant at *C*, not *A*. Costs at *C* are \$48, higher than they were before the price increase, but not as high as they would be if the factor substitution had not occurred.

The Principle of Substitution

Suppose that with technology unchanged, that is, with the isoquant map being held fixed, the price of one factor changes. Suppose that with the price of capital unchanged at $4 per unit, the price of labor rises from $1 to $4 per unit. Originally, the efficient factor combination for producing 6 units was 12 units of labor and 3 units of capital. It cost $24. To produce that same output in the same way would now cost $60 at the new factor prices. Figure 11A-5 shows why this is not efficient. The slope of the isocost line has changed, which makes it efficient to substitute the now relatively cheaper capital for the relatively more expensive labor.

This illustrates the principle of substitution.

Changes in relative factor prices will cause a partial replacement of factors that have become relatively more expensive by factors that have become relatively cheaper.

Of course, substitution of capital for labor cannot fully offset the effects of a rise in cost of labor, as Figure 11A-5(i) shows. Consider the output attainable for $24. In the figure there are two isocost lines representing $24 of outlay—at the old and new prices of labor. The new isocost line for $24 lies inside the old one (except where no labor is used). The isocost line must therefore be tangent to a lower isoquant. This means that if production is to be held constant, higher costs must be accepted. However, because of substitution, it is not necessary to accept costs as high as those that would accompany an unchanged factor proportion. In the example, 6 units can be produced for $48 rather than the $60 that would be required if no change in factor proportions were made.

This leads to the following predictions:

A rise in the price of one factor with all other factor prices being held constant will (1) shift upward the cost curves of commodities that use that factor and (2) lead to a substitution of factors that are now relatively cheaper for the factor whose price has risen.

Both of these predictions were stated in Chapter 11; now they have been derived formally by using the isoquant technique.

PART 4

MARKETS AND PRICING

Chapter 12

Competitive Markets

Market Structure and Firm Behavior

Does Imperial Oil compete with PetroCan in the sale of gasoline? Does American Express compete with Diners Club? Does a wheat farmer from Biggar, Saskatchewan, compete with a wheat farmer from Brandon, Manitoba? If we use the ordinary meaning of the word *compete,* the answer to the first two questions is plainly yes, and the answer to the third is probably no.

The Imperial Oil Company and PetroCan both advertise extensively to persuade car drivers to buy *their* product. Everything from new mileage-stretching additives to free dishes is used to tempt drivers to buy one brand of gasoline rather than another. A host of world travelers in various tight spots attest on television to the virtues of American Express, while discreet ads in many magazines tell us that the Diners Club card is *the* prestigious credit card to carry.

When we shift our attention to firms producing wheat, however, we see that there is nothing that the Saskatchewan farm family can do to affect either the sales or the profits of the Manitoba farm family. There would be no point in doing so even if they could, since the sales and profits of the Manitoba farm have no effect on those of the Saskatchewan farm.

Behavior and Market Structure

To sort out the questions of who is competing with whom and in what sense, it is useful to distinguish between the *behavior* of individual firms and the *type of market* in which they operate. In everyday use, the word *competition* usually refers to competitive behavior. Economists, however, are interested both in the competitive behavior of individual firms and in a quite distinct concept, competitive market structure.

The term **market structure** refers to all the features of a market that may affect the behavior and performance of the firms in that market. Examples are the number of firms in the market and the type of product that they sell.

Competitive market structure. The competitiveness of the market refers to the extent to which individual firms have power to influence market prices or the terms on which their product is sold. The less power an individual firm has to influence the market in which it sells its product, the more competitive that market is.

• KEY IDEAS IN •

MICROECONOMICS

This section provides important diagrams and captions from the text as reminders of basic economic concepts at a glance. If you need to refresh your memory concerning a principle being shown here, look in the appropriate chapter for a full explanation.

CHAPTER 1 A Production Possibility Boundary

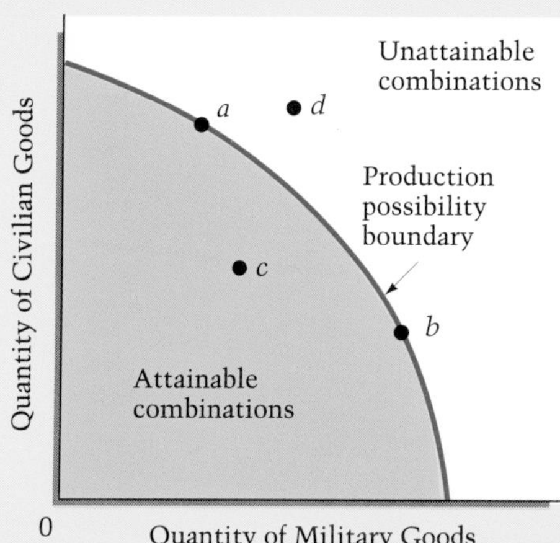

The negatively sloped boundary shows the combinations that are just attainable when all of the society's resources are efficiently employed.

CHAPTER 4 The Equilibrium Price

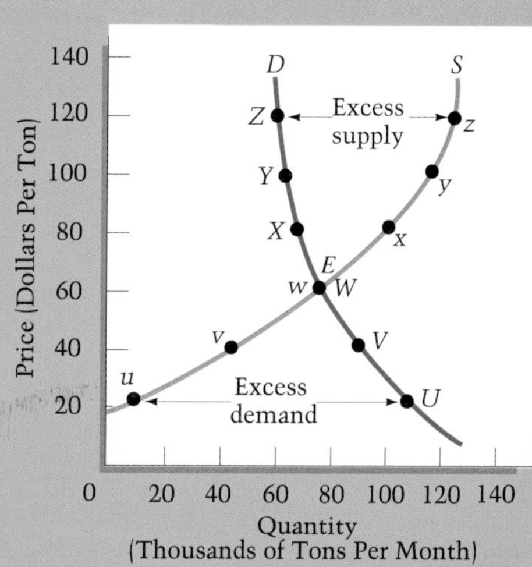

The equilibrium price is at *E*, where the demand and supply curves intersect.

CHAPTER 4 The Laws of Demand and Supply

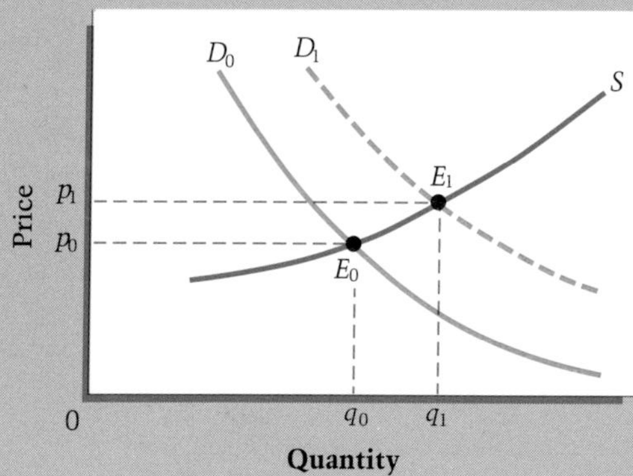

(i) The effects of shifts in the demand curve

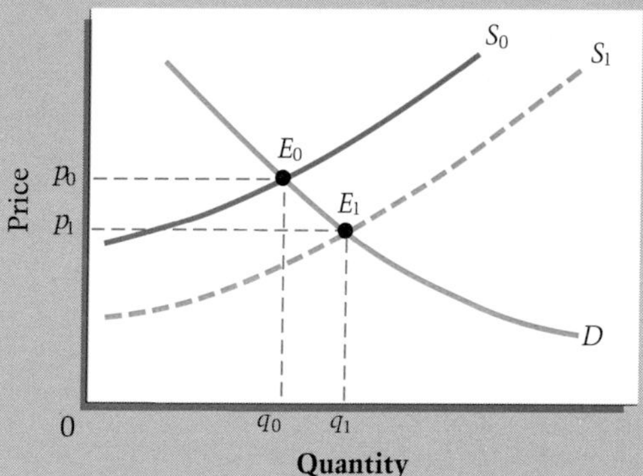

(ii) The effects of shifts in the supply curve

The effects on equilibrium price and quantity of shifts in either demand or supply are called the *laws of demand and supply*. Price and quantity change in the *same* direction when demand shifts and in the *opposite* direction when supply shifts.

CHAPTER 5 Elasticity of Demand and Total Expenditure

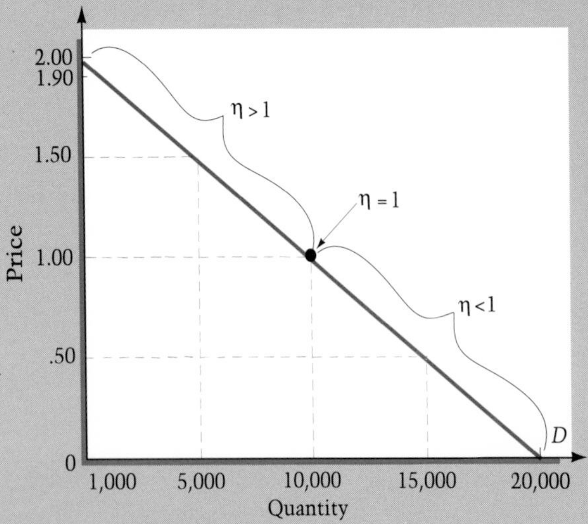

(i) Demand curve

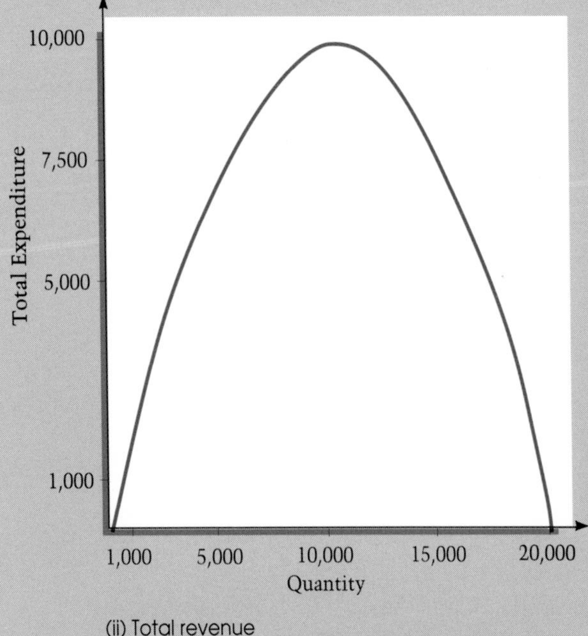

(ii) Total revenue

The change in total expenditure on a commodity in response to a change in price depends upon the elasticity of demand.

CHAPTER 6 The Effect of Unplanned Variations in Output

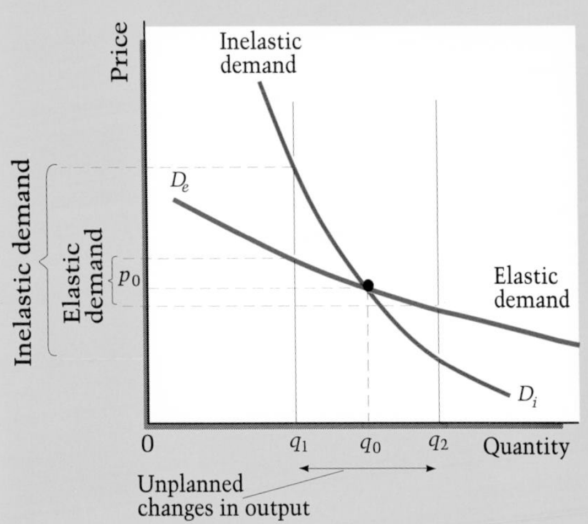

Unplanned fluctuations in output lead to larger fluctuations in price when the demand curve is inelastic than when it is elastic.

CHAPTER 7 Consumers' Surplus

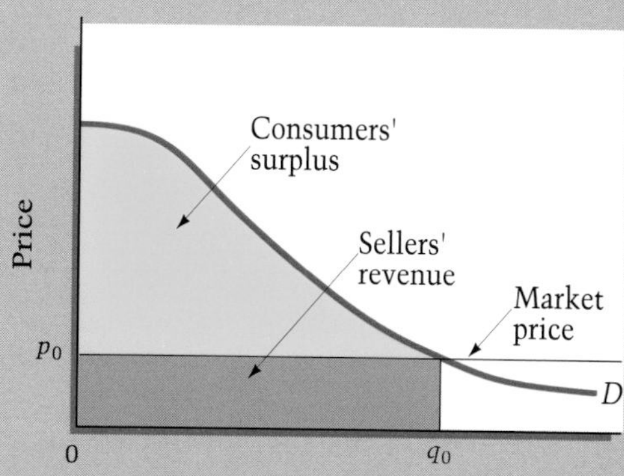

Total consumers' surplus is the area under the demand curve and above the price line.

CHAPTER 7 The Income and Substitution Effects

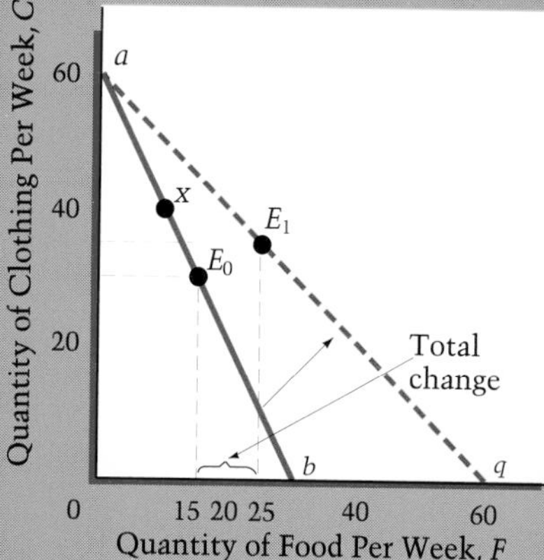

(i) A fall in the price of food

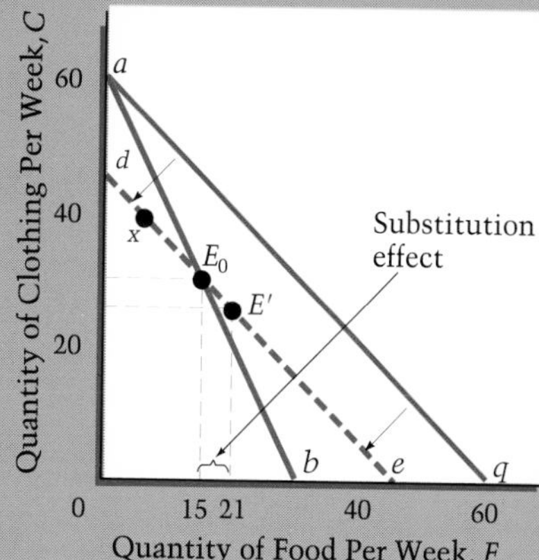

(ii) The substitution effect

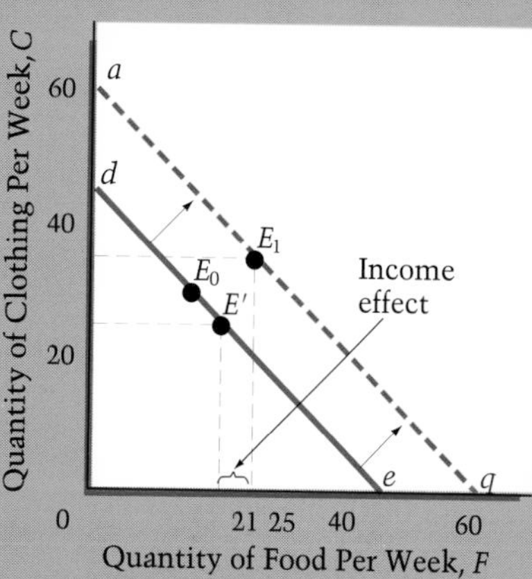

(iii) The income effect

The effect on household choice of a change in price can be broken into (1) a substitution effect measuring the response to the change in relative prices with purchasing power being held constant, and (2) an income effect measuring the response to the change in purchasing power caused by the price change.

CHAPTER 10 Total Product, Average Product, and Marginal Product Curves

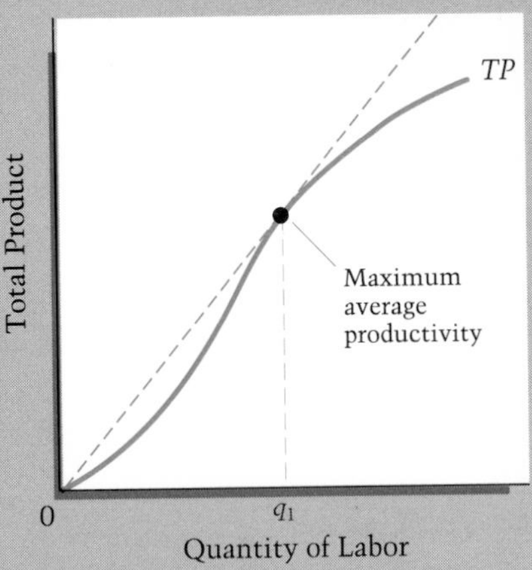

(i) Total product curve

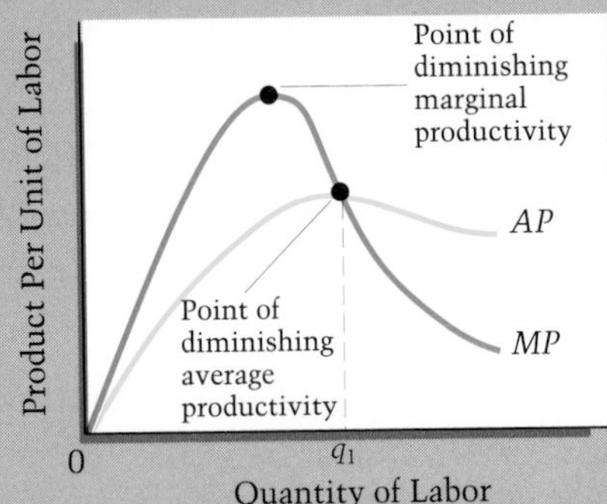

(ii) Average and marginal product curves

Total product (*TP*), average product (*AP*), and marginal product (*MP*) curves often have the shapes shown here.

CHAPTER 10 Total Cost, Average Cost, and Marginal Cost Curves

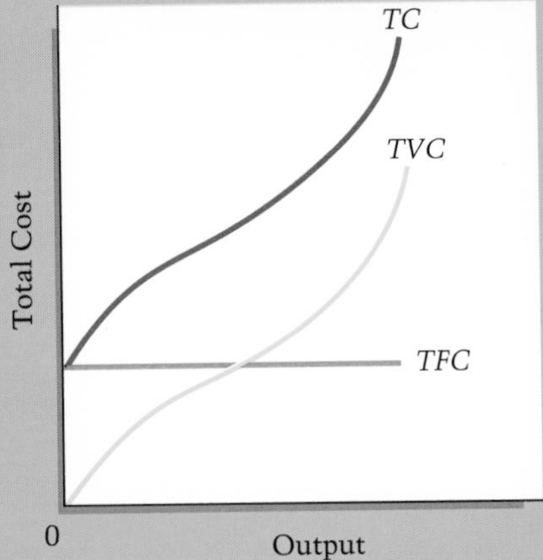

(i) Total cost curves

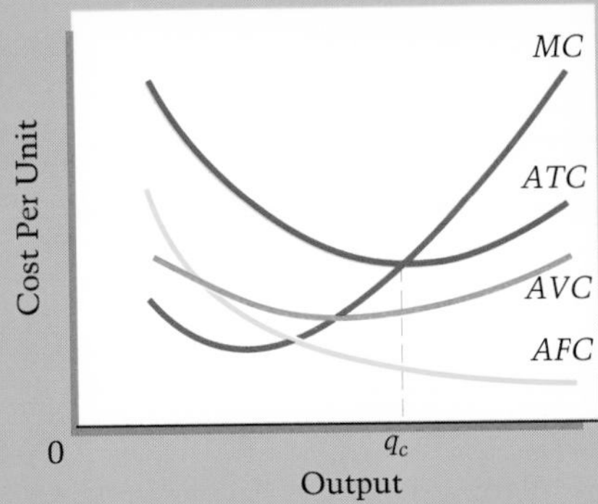

(ii) Marginal and average cost curves

Total cost (*TC*), average cost (*AC*), and marginal cost (*MC*) curves often have the shapes shown here.

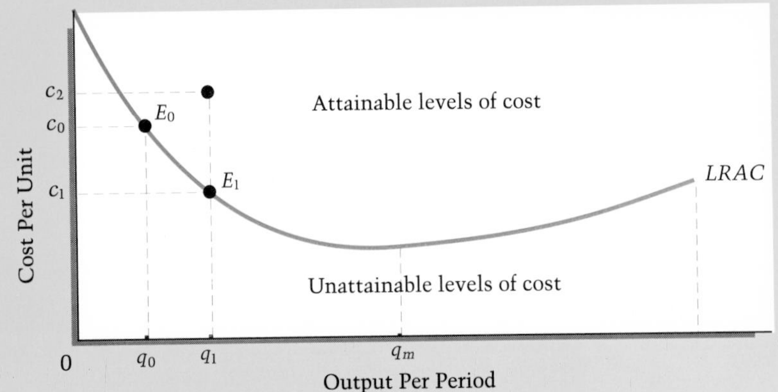

CHAPTER 11 A Long-Run Average Cost Curve

The long-run average cost (*LRAC*) curve provides a boundary between attainable and unattainable levels of cost when all long-run adjustments have been made.

The extreme form of competitiveness occurs when each firm has zero market power. In such a case, there are so many firms in the market that each must accept the price set by the forces of market demand and market supply. The firms perceive themselves as being able to sell as much as they choose at the prevailing market price and as having no power to influence that price. If the firm charged a higher price, it would obtain no sales; so many other firms would be selling at the market price that buyers would take their business elsewhere.

This extreme is called a *perfectly competitive market structure*. In it there is no need for individual firms to compete actively with one another, since none has any power over the market. One firm's ability to sell its product does not depend on the behavior of any other firm. For example, the Saskatchewan and the Manitoba wheat farmers do not engage in active *competitive behavior* with each other. They operate in a perfectly competitive market over which they have no power. Neither can change the market price for its wheat by altering its own behavior, so neither needs to indulge in competitive behavior against the other.

Competitive behavior. In everyday language, the term *competitive behavior* refers to the degree to which individual firms actively compete with one another. For example, Imperial and PetroCan certainly engage in competitive behavior. It is also true, however, that both companies have real power over their market. Either firm could raise its prices and still continue to attract customers. Each has the power to decide, within limits set by buyers' tastes and the prices of competing products, the price that drivers will pay for their gasoline and oil. So even though they compete actively with each other, they do so in a market that is not perfectly competitive.

Behavior versus structure. The distinction that we have just made explains why firms in perfectly competitive markets (e.g., the Saskatchewan and the Manitoba wheat producers) do not actively compete with each other, while firms that do compete actively with each other (e.g., Imperial and PetroCan) do not operate in perfectly competitive markets.

The Significance of Market Structure

Imperial and PetroCan are two of several large firms in the oil *industry*. They produce petroleum products and sell them in various *markets*. The terms *industry* and *market* are familiar from everyday use. However, economists give them precise definitions that we need to understand.

We noted earlier that a *market* consists of the firms from which a well-defined product can be purchased, while from the point of view of firms, it consists of the buyers to whom a well-defined product can be sold. A group of firms that produces a well-defined product or a closely related set of products constitutes an **industry**. In earlier chapters we have developed and used market demand curves. Notice that the market demand curve for any particular product is the demand curve for the *industry* that produces the product.

When the managers of a firm make their production and sales decisions, they need to know what quantity of a product their firm can sell at various prices that it could charge for the product. Their concern is therefore not so much with the *market* demand curve for their industry's product as with their firm's *own* demand curve for that product. If they know the demand curve that their own firm faces, they know the sales that their firm can make at each price it might charge, and thus they know its potential revenues. If they also know their firm's costs for producing the product, they can calculate the profits that would be associated with each rate of output and can therefore choose the output that maximizes profits.

We have seen that economists define market structure to mean the characteristics that affect the behavior and performance of firms that sell in that market. These characteristics determine, among other things, the relationship between the market demand curve for the industry's product and the demand curve for each firm in that industry.

To reduce the analysis of market structure to manageable proportions, economists focus on four theoretical market structures that cover a high proportion of actual cases. These are called perfect competition, monopoly, monopolistic competition, and oligopoly. Perfect competition will be dealt with in the rest of this chapter; the others will be dealt with in the chapters that follow.

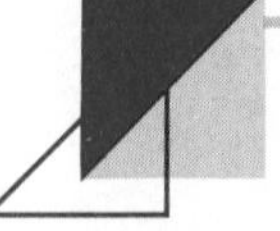

Elements of the Theory of Perfect Competition

The perfectly competitive market structure—usually referred to simply as perfect competition—applies

BOX 12-1

Demand Under Perfect Competition: Firm and Industry

Since all products have negatively sloped market demand curves, *any* increase in the industry's output will cause *some* fall in the market price. As the calculations in the table show, however, any conceivable increase that one wheat farm could make in its output has such a negligible effect on the industry's price that the farmer correctly ignores it. (For our purposes, the farm is a firm producing wheat.)

The table calculates in two steps the elasticity of demand for one wheat farmer. Step 1 shows that a 200 percent variation in the firm's output leads to only a very small percentage variation in the world price. Thus, as step 2 shows, the firm's elasticity of demand is very high: 71,428!

Although the arithmetic used in reaching these measures is unimportant, understanding why the wheat farmer is a price taker in these circumstances is vital.

Here is the argument that the table summarizes. The market elasticity of demand for wheat is approximately 0.25. This means that if the quantity of wheat supplied in the world increased by 1 percent, the price would have to fall by 4 percent to induce the world's wheat buyers to purchase the entire increase in the crop.

Even huge farms produce a very small fraction of the total world crop. In a recent year, one large farm produced 1,750 metric tons of wheat. This was only 0.0035 percent of the world production of 500 million metric tons. Suppose that the farm decided in one year to produce nothing and in another year managed to produce twice its normal output of 1,750 metric tons. This is an extremely large variation in one farm's output.

The increase in output from zero to 3,500 metric tons is a 200 percent variation that is measured around the farm's average output of 1,750 metric tons. Yet the percentage increase in world output is only (3,500/500 million)100 = 0.0007 percent. The table shows that this increase would lead to a decrease in the world price of 0.0028 percent (2.8 cents in $1,000) and give the firm's own demand curve an elasticity of over 71,000! This is an enormous elasticity of demand; the farm would have to increase its output by over 71,000 percent to bring about a 1 percent decrease in the price of wheat! Because the farm's output cannot be varied this much, it is not surprising that the farmer regards the price of wheat as unaffected by any change in output that this one farm could conceivably make. For all intents and purposes, the wheat-producing firm faces a perfectly elastic demand curve for its product; *it is a price taker.*

directly to a number of real-world markets. It also provides an important benchmark for comparison with other market structures.

Assumptions of Perfect Competition

The theory of **perfect competition** is built on a number of key assumptions relating to the firm and to the industry.

Assumption 1: All the firms in the industry sell an identical product. Economists describe this by saying that the firms sell a **homogeneous product**.

Assumption 2: Customers know the nature of the product being sold and the prices charged by each firm.

Assumption 3: The level of a firm's output at which its long-run average total cost reaches a minimum is small relative to the industry's total output (when price is such that firms are covering all costs).

Assumption 4: The *firm* is assumed to be a **price taker**. This means that the firm can alter its rate of production and sales without significantly affecting the market price of its product. Thus, as stated earlier, a firm that is operating in a perfectly competitive market has no power to influence that

The Calculation of the Firm's Elasticity of Demand (η_F) from Market Elasticity of Demand (η_M)

Given:

$\eta_M = 0.25$

World output = 500 million metric tons

A large farm with an average output of 1,750 metric tons varies its output between 0 and 3,500 tons.

The variation of 3,500 tons on the farm's average output of 1,750 metric tons = 200 percent.

This causes world output to vary by (3,500/500 million)100 = 0.0007 percent.

Step 1. Find the percentage change in world price.

$$\eta_M = -\frac{\text{percentage change in world output}}{\text{percentage change in world price}}$$

$$\text{Percentage change in world price} = \frac{\text{percentage change in world output}}{\eta_M} = -\frac{0.0007}{0.25} = -0.0028$$

Step 2. Compute the firm's elasticity of demand.

$$\eta_F = -\frac{\text{percentage variation in firm's output}}{\text{percentage change in world price}}$$

$$= -\frac{+200}{-0.0028} = +71{,}428$$

market through its own individual actions. It must passively accept whatever happens to be the ruling price, but it can sell as much as it wants at that price.[1]

Assumption 5: The *industry* is assumed to be characterized by *freedom of entry and exit*; that is, any new firm is free to set up production if it so wishes, and any existing firm is free to cease production and leave the industry. Existing firms cannot bar the entry of new firms, and there are no legal prohibitions or other artificial barriers to entering or exiting the industry.

[1] To emphasize its importance, we identify price taking in a separate assumption, although, strictly speaking, it is implied by assumptions 1, 2, and 3.

An Illustration

The Saskatchewan and the Manitoba wheat farmers whom we considered earlier provided us with good illustrations of firms that are operating in a perfectly competitive industry.

Since each individual wheat farmer is just one of a very large number of producers who are all growing the same product, one firm's contribution to the industry's total production is only a tiny drop in an extremely large bucket. Each firm will correctly assume that variations in its output have no significant effect on the world price of wheat. Thus each firm, knowing that it can sell as much or as little as it chooses at that price, accepts the market price of wheat. Furthermore, anyone who has the capital can become a wheat farmer. There is nothing that existing farmers can do to stop another farmer from growing wheat, and there are no legal deterrents to becoming a wheat farmer.

The difference between the wheat farmers and the Imperial Oil Company is in *degree of market power.* Each firm that is producing wheat is an insignificant part of the whole market and thus has no power to influence the price of wheat. The oil company does have power to influence the price of gasoline because its own sales represent a significant part of the total sales of gasoline in the Canadian market.

Box 12-1 explores further the reasons why each firm that is producing wheat finds the world price of wheat to be beyond its influence.

Demand and Revenue for a Firm in Perfect Competition

A major distinction between firms operating in perfectly competitive markets and firms operating in any other type of market is in the shape of the firm's own demand curve.

The demand curve for a single firm in perfect competition is horizontal, because variations in the firm's output over the range that it needs to consider have no noticeable effect on price.

The horizontal (perfectly elastic) demand curve does not mean that the firm could actually sell an infinite amount at the going price. It means, rather, that the variations in production *that it will normally be possible for the firm to make* will leave price virtually unaffected because its effect on total industry supply will be insignificant.

Figure 12-1 contrasts the demand curve for a competitive industry and that for a single firm in that industry.

Total, average, and marginal revenue. To study the revenues that firms receive from the sales of their products, we define three concepts—total, average, and marginal revenue—that are the revenue counterparts of the concepts of total, average, and marginal cost that we considered in Chapter 10.

Total revenue (*TR*) is the total amount received by the seller from the sale of a product. If q units are sold at p dollars each,[2] $TR = p \cdot q$.

[2] Three common ways of indicating that any two variables such as p and q are to be multiplied are $p \cdot q$, $p \times q$, and pq.

FIGURE 12-1 The Demand Curve for a Competitive Industry and for One Firm in the Industry

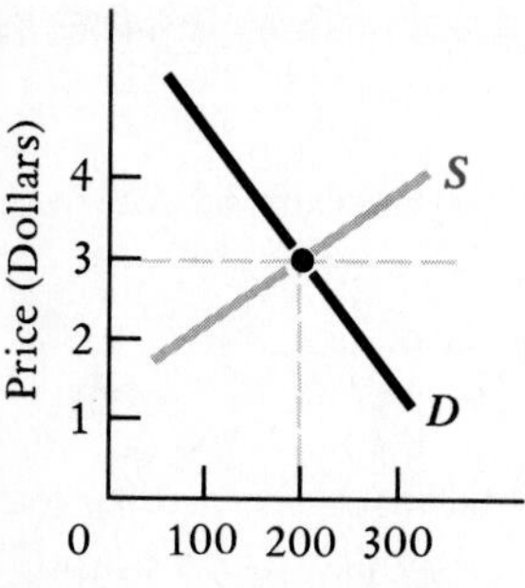

(i) Competitive industry's demand curve

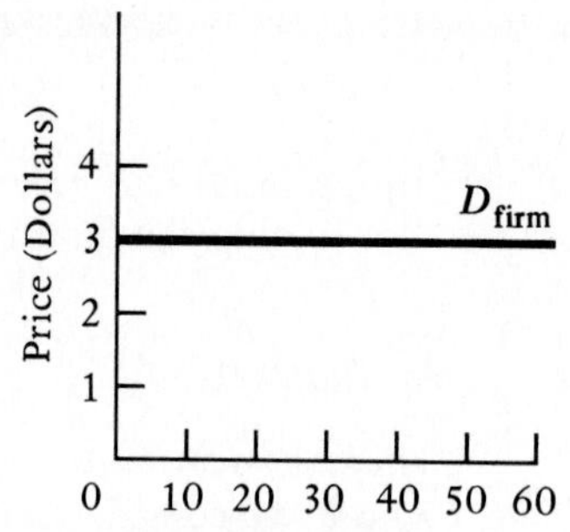

(ii) Competitive firm's demand curve

The industry's demand curve is negatively sloped; the firm's demand curve is virtually horizontal. Notice the difference in the quantities shown on the horizontal scale in each part of the figure. The competitive industry has output of 200 million tons when the price is \$3. The individual firm takes that market price as given and considers producing up to, say, 60,000 tons. The firm's demand curve in (ii) appears horizontal because of the change in the quantity scale compared to the industry's demand curve in (i). The firm's output variation has only a tiny percentage effect on industry output. If we plotted the industry demand curve from 199,970,000 tons to 200,030,000 tons on the scale used in (ii), the D curve would appear virtually horizontal.

Average revenue (*AR*) is the amount of revenue *per unit sold*. This is equal to the price at which the product is sold.

Marginal revenue (*MR*), sometimes called *incremental revenue*, is the change in a firm's total revenue resulting from a change in its rate of sales by one unit. Whenever output changes by more than one unit, the change in revenue must be divided by the change in output to calculate marginal revenue. For example, if an increase in output of three units per month is accompanied by an increase in revenue of $1,500, the marginal revenue resulting from the sale of *one extra unit* per month is $1,500/3, or $500. At any existing level of sales, marginal revenue shows what revenue the firm would gain by selling one unit more and what revenue it would lose by selling one unit less. [22]

To illustrate each of these revenue concepts, consider a firm that is selling an agricultural commodity in a perfectly competitive market at a price of $3 per ton. Total revenue rises by $3 for every ton sold. Since every ton brings in $3, the average revenue per ton sold is clearly $3. Furthermore, since each *additional* ton sold brings in $3, the marginal revenue of an extra ton sold is also $3. Table 12-1 shows calculations of these revenue concepts for a range of outputs between 10 and 13 tons.

The important point that is illustrated in Table 12-1 is that as long as the firm's output does not affect the price of the product it sells, marginal revenue is equal to average revenue (which is always equal to price). Graphically, as shown in part (i) of Figure 12-2, average revenue and marginal revenue are the same horizontal line drawn at the level of market price. Since the firm can sell any quantity it chooses at this price, the horizontal line is also the *firm's demand curve*; it shows that any quantity that the firm chooses to sell will be associated with this same market price.

TABLE 12-1 Revenue Concepts for a Price-taking Firm

Price p	Quantity q	$TR = p \cdot q$	$AR = TR/q$	$MR = \Delta TR/\Delta q$
$3	10	$30	$3	
				$3
3	11	33	3	
				3
3	12	36	3	
				3
3	13	39	3	

When the firm is a price taker, $AR = MR = p$. Marginal revenue is shown between the lines because it represents the change in total revenue (e.g., from $33 to $36) in response to a change in quantity (from 11 to 12 units): $MR = (36 - 33)/(12 - 11) = \$3$ per unit.

FIGURE 12-2 Revenue Curves for a Price-taking Firm

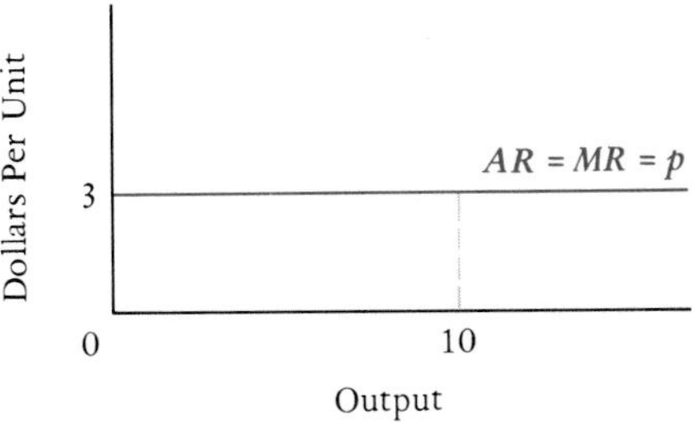

(i) Average and marginal revenue

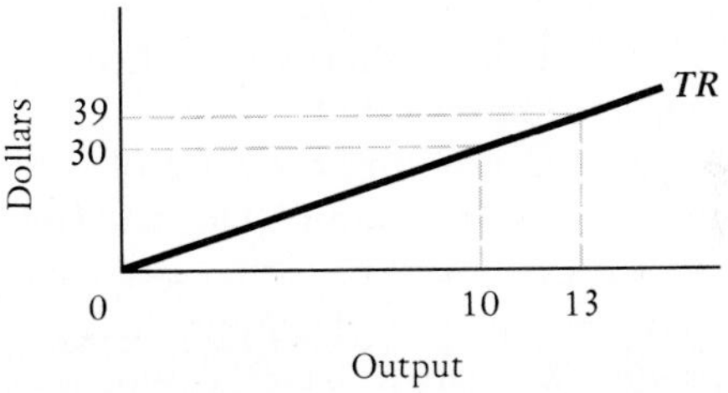

(ii) Total revenue

This is a graphical representation of the revenue concepts in Table 12-1. Because price does not change, neither marginal revenue nor average revenue varies with output. When price is constant, total revenue is an upward-sloping straight line starting from the origin.

If the market price is unaffected by variations in the firm's output, then the firm's demand curve, its average revenue curve, and its marginal revenue curve all coincide in the same horizontal line.

This result can be stated in a slightly different way that turns out to be important for our later study:

For a firm in perfect competition, price equals marginal revenue.

This means, of course, that total revenue rises in direct proportion to output, as shown in part (ii) of Figure 12-2.

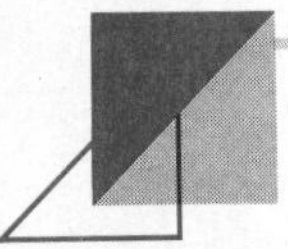

Short-Run Equilibrium

The Firm's Equilibrium Output

We learned in Chapter 11 how each firm's costs vary with its output. In the short run the firm has one or more fixed factors, and the only way in which it can vary its output is by using more or less of the factors that it can vary. Thus the firm's short-run cost curves are relevant to its decision regarding output.

We have just learned how the revenues of each price-taking firm vary with its output. The next step is to combine information about the firm's costs and revenues to determine the level of output that will maximize its profits. We start by stating two rules that apply to *all* profit-maximizing firms, whether or not they operate in perfectly competitive markets. The first determines whether or not the firm should produce at all, and the second determines how much it should produce.

Rules for All Profit-maximizing Firms

Should the firm produce at all? The firm always has the option of producing nothing. If it exercises this option, it will have an operating loss that is equal to its fixed costs. If it decides to produce, it will add the variable cost of production to its costs and the receipts from the sale of its product to its revenue. Therefore, it will be worthwhile for the firm to produce as long as it can find some level of output for which total revenue exceeds total variable cost. However, if total revenue is less than total variable cost at *every* level of output, the firm will actually lose more by producing than by not producing.

Rule 1: **A firm should not produce at all if for *all* levels of output the total variable cost of producing that output exceeds the total revenue derived from selling it or, equivalently, if the average variable cost of producing the output exceeds the price at which it can be sold. [23]**

How much should the firm produce? If a firm decides that (according to Rule 1) production is worth undertaking, it must decide how much to produce. Common sense dictates that on a unit-by-unit basis, if any unit of production adds more to revenue than it does to cost, producing and selling that unit will increase profits. However, if any unit adds more to cost than it does to revenue, producing and selling it will decrease profits. Using the terminology introduced earlier, a unit of production raises profits if the marginal revenue obtained from selling it exceeds the marginal cost of producing it; it lowers profits if the marginal revenue obtained from selling it is less than the marginal cost of producing it.

Now let the firm with some existing rate of output consider increasing or decreasing that output. If a further unit of production will increase the firm's profits, the firm should expand its output. However, if the last unit produced reduced profits, the firm should contract its output. From this it follows that the only time the firm should leave its output unaltered is when the last unit produced adds the same amount to costs as it does to revenue.

If we put the results in these two paragraphs together, we will get the following important result:

Rule 2: **Assuming that it is worthwhile for the firm to produce, the firm should produce the output at which marginal revenue equals marginal cost. [24]**

The two rules that we have stated refer to each firm's own costs and revenues, and they apply to all profit-maximizing firms, whatever the market structure in which they operate.[3]

Rule 2 Applied to Price-taking Firms

Rule 2 tells us that any profit-maximizing firm that produces anything will produce at the point where marginal cost equals marginal revenue. However, we have already seen that for price-taking firms, marginal revenue is the market price. This conclusion can be drawn:

[3] A third rule is needed to distinguish between profit-*maximizing* and profit-*minimizing* positions: The marginal cost curve must cut the marginal revenue curve from below. This rule is not, however, needed for the discussion that follows, so we say nothing further about it. We only consider situations in which it is met.

FIGURE 12-3 The Short-Run Equilibrium of a Competitive Firm

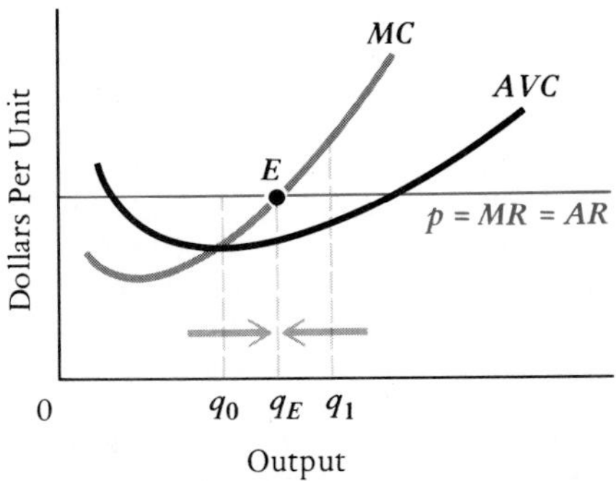

The firm chooses the output for which $p = MC$ above the level of AVC. When $p = MC$, as at q_E, the firm would decrease its profits if it changed its output. At any point to the left of q_E, say, q_0, price is greater than the marginal cost, and it is worthwhile for the firm to increase output (as indicated by the arrow on the left). At any point to the right of q_E, say, q_1, price is less than the marginal cost, and it is worthwhile for the firm to reduce output (as indicated by the arrow on the right). The short-run equilibrium output for the firm is q_E.

A firm that is operating in a perfectly competitive market will produce the output that equates its marginal cost of production with the market price of its product (as long as price exceeds average variable cost).

Equilibrium Output

In a perfectly competitive industry, the market determines the price at which the firm sells its product. The firm then picks the quantity of output that maximizes its profits. We have seen that this is the output for which price equals marginal cost.

When the firm is maximizing profits, it has no incentive to change its output. Therefore, unless prices or costs change, the firm will continue to produce this output because it is doing as well as it can do, given the market situation. The firm is in *short-run equilibrium,* as illustrated in Figure 12-3.

In a perfectly competitive market, each firm is a quantity adjuster. It pursues its goal of profit maximization by increasing or decreasing quantity until it equates its short-run marginal cost with the price of its product that is given to it by the market.

Short-Run Supply Curves

We have seen that in a perfectly competitive market, the firm responds to a price that is set by the forces of demand and supply. By adjusting the quantity it produces in response to the current market price, the firm helps to determine the market supply. The link between the behavior of the firm and the behavior of the competitive market is provided by the *market supply curve.*

The supply curve for one firm. The firm's supply curve is derived in part (i) of Figure 12-4, which shows a firm's marginal cost curve and four alternative prices. The horizontal line at each price is the firm's demand curve when the market price is at that level. The firm's marginal cost curve gives the marginal cost corresponding to each level of output. We require a supply curve that shows the quantity that the firm will supply at each price. For prices below average variable cost, the firm will supply zero units (Rule 1). For prices above average variable cost, the firm will equate price and marginal cost (Rule 2, modified by the proposition that $MR = p$ in perfect competition). This leads to the following conclusion:

In perfect competition the firm's supply curve is its marginal cost curve above average variable cost.

The supply curve of an industry. Figure 12-5 illustrates the derivation of an industry supply curve for only two firms. The general result is as follows:

In perfect competition the industry supply curve is the horizontal sum of the marginal cost curves (above the level of average variable cost) of all firms in the industry.

The reason for this is that each firm's marginal cost curve shows how much that firm will supply at each given market price, and the industry supply curve is the sum of what each firm will supply.

This supply curve, based on the short-run marginal cost curves of all the firms in the industry, is

FIGURE 12-4 **Derivation of the Supply Curve for a Price-taking Firm**

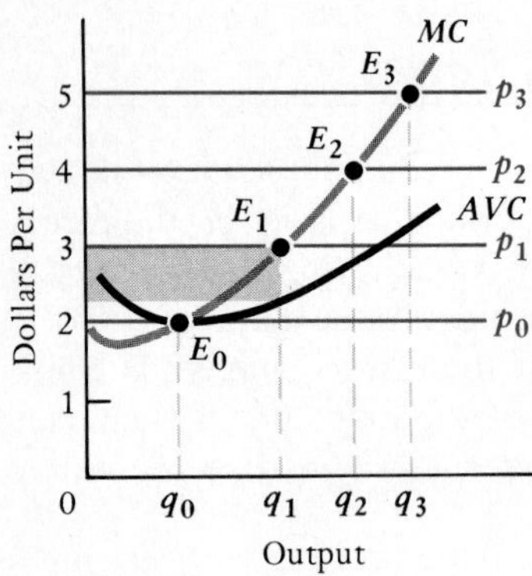

(i) Marginal cost and average variable cost curves

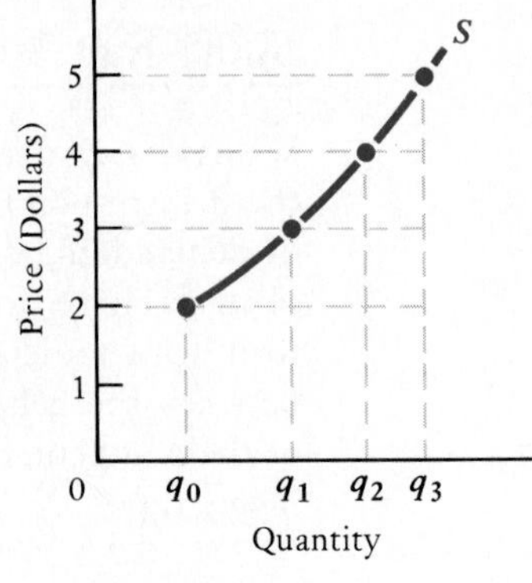

(ii) Supply curve

The supply curve of the price-taking firm, shown in part (ii), is the same as its *MC* curve, shown in part (i). For prices below \$2, output is zero, because there is no output at which *AVC* can be covered. Thus the point E_0, where the price of \$2 is just equal to *AVC*, is the point at which the firm will shut down. As price rises to \$3, \$4, and \$5, equilibrium shifts to E_1, E_2, and E_3, taking output to q_1, q_2, and q_3. At any of these prices, the firm's revenue exceeds its variable costs of production. An example of the excess is shown in part (i) of the figure by the shaded area associated with price p_1 and output q_1. This amount is available to help cover fixed costs and, once these are covered, to provide a profit.

the industry's supply curve that was first introduced in Chapter 4. We have now established the profit-maximizing behavior of individual firms that underlies this curve. It is sometimes called a **short-run supply curve** because it is based on the short-run, profit-maximizing behavior of the firms in the industry. This distinguishes it from a *long-run supply curve,* which relates quantity supplied to the price that rules in long-run equilibrium (which we will study later in this chapter).

FIGURE 12-5 **Derivation of the Supply Curve for a Competitive Industry**

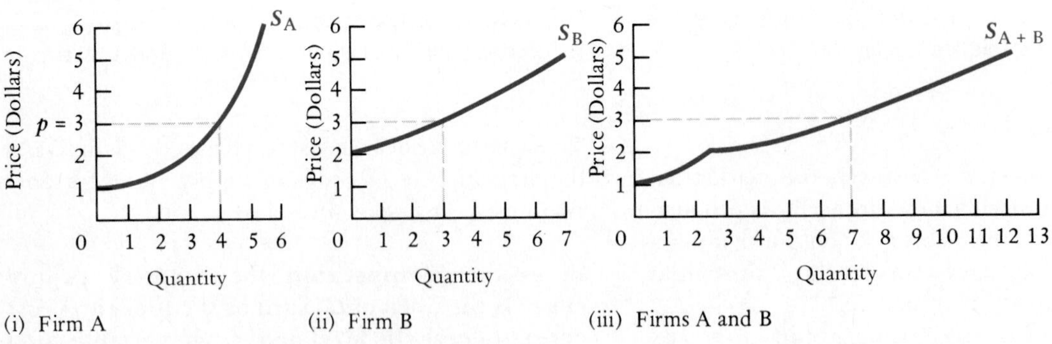

(i) Firm A (ii) Firm B (iii) Firms A and B

The industry's supply curve is the horizontal sum of the supply curves of each of the firms in the industry. At a price of \$3, Firm A would supply 4 units and Firm B would supply 3 units. Together, as shown in (iii), they would supply 7 units. If there are hundreds of firms, the process is the same. Each firm's supply curve (derived as in Figure 12-4) shows what the firm will produce at any given price *p*. The industry supply curve relates the price to the sum of the quantities produced by each firm. In this example, because Firm B does not enter the market at prices below \$2, the supply curve S_{A+B} is identical to S_A up to price \$2 and is the sum of $S_A + S_B$ above \$2.

Short-Run Equilibrium Price

The market price of a product sold in a perfectly competitive market is determined by the interaction of the industry's short-run supply curve and the market demand curve. Although no one firm can influence the market price significantly, the collective actions of all firms in the industry (as shown by the industry supply curve) and the collective actions of households (as shown by the market demand curve) together determine the equilibrium price. This occurs at the point where the market demand curve and the industry supply curves intersect.

At the equilibrium price, each firm is producing and selling a quantity for which its marginal cost equals price. No firm is motivated to change its output in the short run. Since total quantity demanded equals total quantity supplied, there is no reason for market price to change in the short run; the market and all the firms in the industry are in short-run equilibrium.

Short-Run Profitability of the Firm

We know that when an industry is in short-run equilibrium, each firm is maximizing its profits. However, we do not know *how large* these profits are. It is one thing to know that a firm is doing as well as it can, given its particular circumstances; it is another thing to know how well it is doing.

Figure 12-6 shows three possible positions for a firm in short-run equilibrium. In all cases the firm is maximizing its profits by producing where price equals marginal cost, but in part (i) the firm is suffering losses, in part (ii) it is just covering all of its costs (breaking even), and in part (iii) it is making profits because revenues exceed costs. In part (i) we could say that the firm is minimizing its losses rather

FIGURE 12-6 Alternative Short-Run Equilibrium Positions of a Competitive Firm

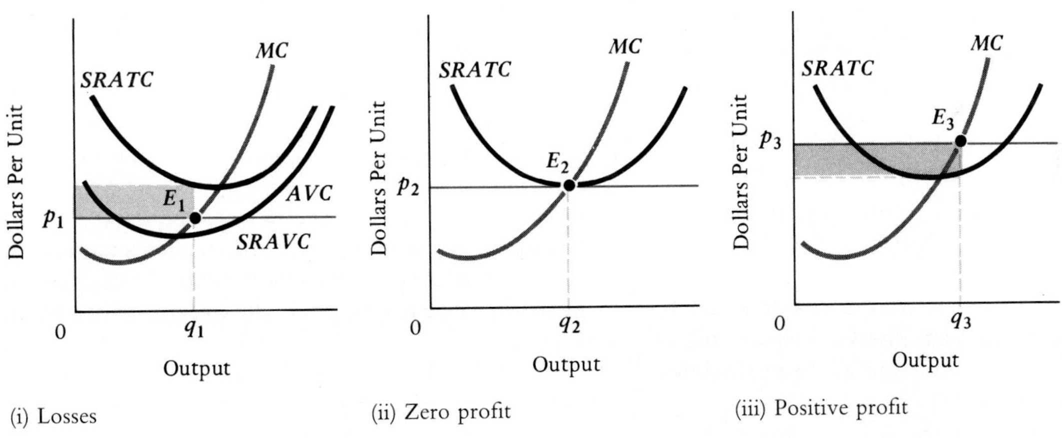

When it is in short-run equilibrium, a competitive firm may be suffering losses, breaking even, or making profits. The diagrams show a firm with given costs that faces three alternative prices p_1, p_2, and p_3. In each part of the figure, equilibrium occurs at the point where $MC = MR =$ price. Since in all three cases price exceeds AVC, the firm is in short-run equilibrium at E_1 in part (i), E_2 in part (ii), and E_3 in part (iii).

In (i) price is p_1 and the firm is suffering losses, shown by the color-shaded area, because price is below average total cost. Since price exceeds average variable cost, it is worthwhile for the firm to keep producing, but it is *not* worthwhile for it to replace its capital equipment as the capital wears out.

In (ii) price is p_2 and the firm is just covering its total costs. It is worthwhile for the firm to replace its capital as it wears out, since it is covering the full opportunity cost of its capital.

In (iii) price is p_3 and the firm is earning profits, shown by the gray-shaded area.

than maximizing its profits, but both statements mean the same thing. The firm is doing as well as it can, given its costs and the market price.

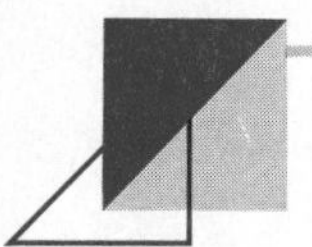

Long-Run Equilibrium

Although Figure 12-6 shows three possible short-run equilibrium positions for the firm in perfect competition, not all of them are possible long-run equilibrium positions.

The Effect of Entry and Exit

The key to long-run equilibrium under perfect competition is entry and exit. We have seen that when firms are in *short-run equilibrium,* they may be making profits, suffering losses, or just breaking even. Since costs include the opportunity cost of capital, firms that are just breaking even are doing as well as they could do by investing their capital elsewhere. Thus there will be no incentive for such firms to leave the industry, and there will be no incentive for new firms to enter the industry, since capital can earn the same return elsewhere in the economy. If, however, existing firms are earning profits over all costs, including the opportunity cost of capital, new capital will enter the industry to share in these profits. If existing firms are suffering losses, capital will leave the industry because a better return can be obtained elsewhere in the economy. Let us now consider this process in a little more detail.

First, let all firms in the competitive industry be in the position of the firm shown in part (iii) of Figure 12-6. New firms, attracted by the profitability of existing firms, now will enter the industry. Suppose that in response to the high profits that 100 existing firms are making, 20 new firms enter the industry. The market supply curve that formerly added up the outputs of 100 firms must now add up the outputs of 120 firms. At any price, more will be supplied because there are more producers.

This shift in the short-run industry supply curve, with an unchanged market demand curve, means that the previous equilibrium price will no longer prevail. The shift in supply will lower the equilibrium price, and both new and old firms will have to adjust their output to this new price. This is illustrated in Figure 12-7. New firms will continue to enter, and the equilibrium price will continue to fall, until all firms in the industry are just covering their total costs. Firms will then be in the position of the firm shown in part (ii) of Figure 12-6, which is called a *zero-profit equilibrium.*

FIGURE 12-7 The Effect of New Entrants

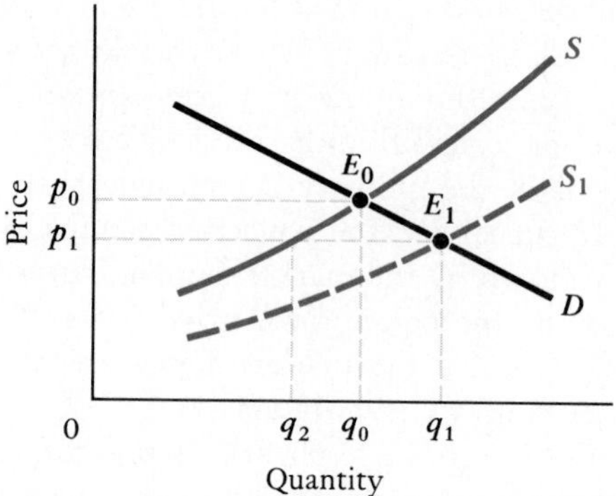

New entrants shift the supply curve to the right and lower the equilibrium price. Initial equilibrium is at E_0. The entry of new firms shifts the supply curve to S_1. Equilibrium price falls to p_1, while output rises to q_1. Before the entry of new firms, only q_2 would have been produced had the price been p_1. The extra output is supplied by the new productive capacity.

Profits in a competitive industry are a signal for the entry of new firms; the industry will expand, pushing price down until the profits fall to zero.

Now let the firms in the industry be in the position of the firm shown in part (i) of Figure 12-6. Although the firms are covering their variable costs, the return on their capital is less than the opportunity cost of this capital. They are not covering their total costs. This is a signal for the exit of firms. Old plants and equipment will not be replaced as they wear out. As a result, the industry's short-run supply curve shifts leftward, and the market price rises. Firms will continue to exit, and the market price will continue to rise, until the remaining firms can cover their total costs, that is, until they are all in the zero-profit equilibrium illustrated in part (ii) of Figure 12-6. The exit of firms then ceases.

Losses in a competitive industry are a signal for the exit of firms; the industry will contract, driving the market price up until the remaining firms are covering their total costs.

Since firms exit because they are motivated by their losses and enter because they are motivated by their profits, this conclusion follows:

The long-run equilibrium of a competitive industry is a zero-profit equilibrium.

In all of this we see profits serving the function of providing signals that guide the allocation of scarce resources among the economy's industries.

Conditions for Long-Run Equilibrium

There are four conditions for a competitive industry to be in long-run equilibrium.

First, existing firms must be doing as well as they can, given their existing capital. This means that short-run marginal costs of production must be equal to market price.

Second, existing firms must not be suffering losses. If they are suffering losses, they will not replace their capital. In this case the size of the industry will shrink over time.

Third, there must be no incentive for new firms to enter the industry. The absence of an incentive for entry requires that existing firms are not earning profits on their existing plants; if they were, new entrants could duplicate these facilities and earn profits themselves.

Fourth, existing firms must not be able to increase their profits by changing the size of their production facilities. This implies that each existing firm must be at the minimum point of its long-run cost curve. This is a new condition; to understand it, assume that it does not hold and see that firms could then increase their profits. This is shown in Figure 12-8. Although the firm is in short-run equilibrium, where it is just covering all of its costs, there are unexploited economies of scale. By increasing its size (for example, by building a new plant with a larger capacity than its existing plant), the firm can reduce its average cost. Since in its present position average cost is just equal to price, any reduction in average cost must yield profits.

FIGURE 12-8 Short-Run Versus Long-Run Equilibrium of a Competitive Firm

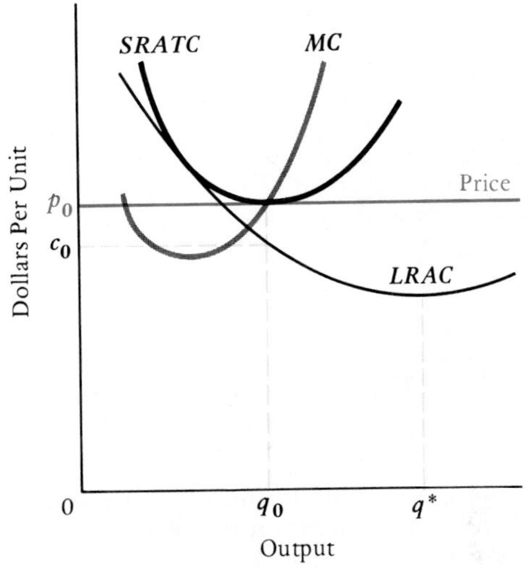

A competitive firm that is not at the minimum point on its *LRAC* curve cannot be in long-run equilibrium. A competitive firm with short-run cost curves *SRATC* and *MC* faces a market price of p_0. The firm produces q_0, where *MC* equals price and total costs are just being covered. However, the firm's long-run cost curve lies below its short-run curve at output q_0. The firm could produce output q_0 at cost c_0 by building a larger plant so as to take advantage of economies of scale. Profits would rise, because average total costs of c_0 would then be less than price p_0. The firm cannot be in long-run equilibrium at any output below q^* because, with any such output, average total costs can be reduced by building a larger plant. The output q^* is the *minimum efficient scale* of the firm.

The only way in which a price-taking firm can be in long-run equilibrium with respect to its size is by producing at the minimum point on its *LRAC* curve.

The level of output at which *LRAC* reaches a minimum is known as the firm's **minimum efficient scale (*MES*)** or its *minimum optimal scale*.

When all firms in the industry are producing at the minimum point of their long-run average cost curve and just covering costs (i.e., they are in the position shown in Figure 12-9), the whole industry is in equilibrium. Because marginal cost equals price,

FIGURE 12-9 The Equilibrium of a Firm When the Industry Is in Long-Run Equilibrium

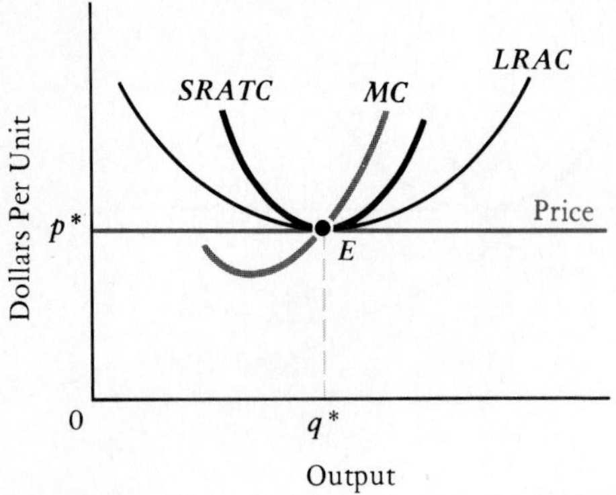

In long-run competitive equilibrium the firm is operating at the minimum point on its *LRAC* curve. In long-run equilibrium each firm must be (1) maximizing short-run profits, $MC = p$; (2) earning profits of zero on its existing plant, $SRATC = p$; and (3) unable to increase its profits by altering the scale of its operations. These three conditions can be met only when the firm is at E, the minimum point on its *LRAC* curve, with price p^* and output q^*.

no firm can improve its profits by varying its output in the short run. Because *LRAC* is above price at all possible outputs except the current one, where it is equal to the price, there is no incentive for any existing firm to move along its long-run cost curve by altering the scale of its operations. Because there are neither profits nor losses, there is no incentive for entry into or exit from the industry.

In long-run competitive equilibrium, the firm's cost is the lowest attainable cost, given the limits of known technology and factor prices.

To summarize, the conditions for long-run equilibrium for a competitive industry are as follows: (1) Existing firms produce at the point where marginal cost equals price; (2) existing firms have no incentive to exit (existing firms are not making losses); (3) potential new firms have no incentive to enter (existing firms are not making profits); and (4) existing firms produce at the minimum point on their long-run average cost curve.[4] This is the position shown in Figure 12-9. (Note that conditions 2 and 3 can be combined into a single condition that the total revenues of existing firms should exactly equal their total costs.)

The Long-Run Industry Supply Curve

Consider a competitive industry that is in the type of long-run equilibrium that we have just studied. The market demand for the industry's product then increases. The reactions to this demand shift are a familiar story by now. First, price will rise, and, in response, existing firms will increase their outputs and earn profits. New firms, attracted by the profits, will enter the industry. As the industry's capacity expands, price will fall, and this process will continue until profits have been eliminated. At that time, existing firms will once again be just covering their full costs.

This is familiar ground, but there is one further question that we could ask. When all the dust has settled, will the new long-run equilibrium price be higher than, lower than, or the same as the original price? A similar analysis could be made for a fall in demand, and the same question could be asked.

The adjustment of a competitive industry to the types of changes that we have just discussed is shown by the **long-run industry supply (*LRS*) curve**. This curve shows the relationship between the market price and the quantity supplied by a competitive industry when it is in long-run equilibrium. Note, however, that the curve does not take very long run reactions into account and so is drawn on the assumption that technological knowledge is constant. (Very long run changes in technology will *shift* the *LRS* curve.) The derivation of this curve, and its various possible shapes, are shown in Figure 12-10.

In part (i) of the figure, the *LRS* curve is horizontal. This indicates that the industry will adjust its size to provide at a constant price whatever quantity is demanded . An industry with a horizontal *LRS* curve is said to be a *constant-cost industry*. This situation occurs when the long-run expansion of the industry, due to the entry of new firms, leaves the

[4] Since all costs are variable in the long run, there is no need to distinguish long-run average variable cost from long-run average total cost. They are identical, and we refer to them merely as long-run average costs *(LRAC)*.

FIGURE 12-10 Long-Run Industry Supply Curves

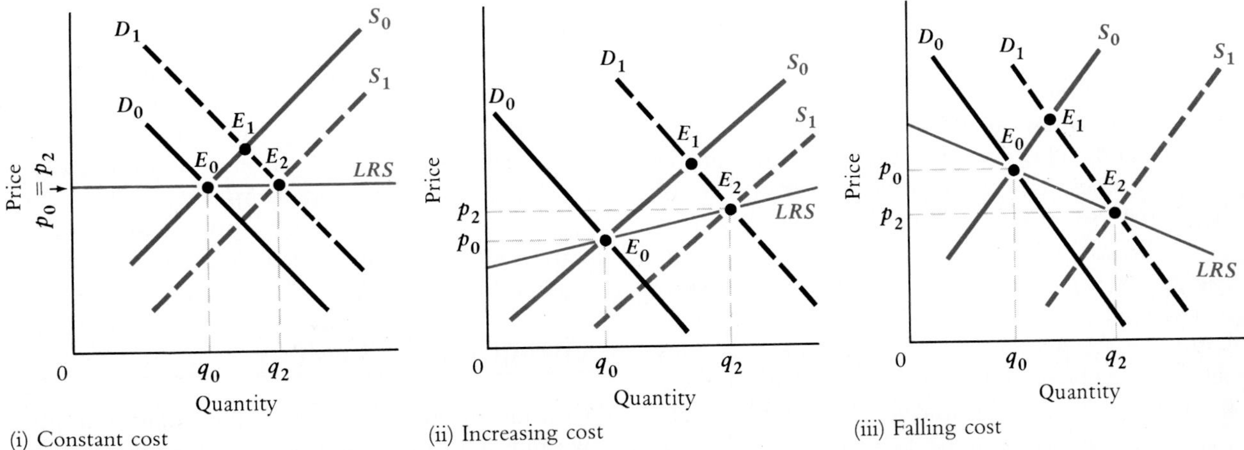

(i) Constant cost (ii) Increasing cost (iii) Falling cost

The long-run industry supply curve may be horizontal, positively sloped, or negatively sloped. In all three parts, the initial curves are at D_0 and S_0, yielding equilibrium at E_0, with price p_0 and output q_0. A rise in demand shifts the demand curve to D_1, taking the short-run equilibrium to E_1. New firms now enter the industry, shifting the supply curve outward, pushing down price until pure profits are no longer being earned. At this point the supply curve is S_1 and the new equilibrium is E_2, with price at p_2 and output q_2.

In (i) price returns to its original level, making the long-run supply curve horizontal. In (ii) profits are eliminated before price falls to its original level, giving the *LRS* curve a positive slope. In (iii) the price falls below its original level before profits are eliminated, giving the *LRS* curve a negative slope.

long-run cost curves of existing firms unchanged. Since new firms have access to the same technology and face the same factor prices as existing firms, their cost curves will be the same as those of existing firms. It follows that the cost curves of all firms, new or old, will be unaffected by expansion (or contraction) of the industry. Thus long-run, zero-profit equilibrium can be reestablished only when price is returned to its original level—which was, and still is, equal to each firm's unchanged minimum long-run average total cost. In other words, since cost curves are unaffected by the expansion or contraction of the industry, each firm must start from, and return to, the long-run equilibrium position shown in Figure 12-9—*which means that market price must do the same*.

Changing factor prices and rising long-run supply curves. When an industry expands its output, it needs more inputs. The increase in demand for these inputs may bid up their prices.[5]

If costs rise with increasing levels of industry output, so too must the price at which the producers are able to cover their costs. As the industry expands, the short-run supply curve shifts outward, but the firms' *SRATC* curves shift upward because of rising factor prices. The expansion of the industry comes to a halt when price is equal to minimum *LRAC* for existing firms. This must occur at a higher price than ruled before the expansion began, as illustrated in part (ii) of Figure 12-10. A competitive industry with rising long-run supply prices is often called a *rising-cost industry.*

[5] In a fully employed economy, the expansion of one industry implies the contraction of some other industry. What happens to factor prices depends on the proportions in which the expanding and the contracting industries use the factors.

Can the long-run supply curve decline? So far we have suggested that the long-run supply curve may be constant or rising. Could it ever decline, thereby indicating that higher outputs were associated with lower prices in long-run equilibrium?

It is tempting to answer yes, because of the opportunities of more efficient scales of operation using greater mechanization and more effective specialization of labor. However, this answer would not be correct for perfectly competitive industries, because each firm in long-run equilibrium must already be at the lowest point on its *LRAC* curve. If a firm could lower its costs by building a larger, more mechanized plant, it would be profitable to do so without waiting for an increase in demand. Since any single firm perceives that it can sell all it wishes at the going market price, it will be profitable for the firm to expand the scale of its operations as long as its *LRAC* is falling.

The scale economies that we have just considered are within the control of the firm; they are said to be **internal economies of scale**. A perfectly competitive industry might, however, have falling long-run costs if industries that supply its inputs have increasing returns to scale. Such effects are outside the control of the perfectly competitive firm and are called **external economies of scale**. Whenever expansion of an industry leads to a fall in the prices of some of its inputs, the firms will find their cost curves shifting downward as they expand their outputs.

As an illustration of how the expansion of one industry could cause the prices of some of its inputs to fall, consider the early stages of the growth of the automobile industry. As the output of automobiles increased, the industry's demand for tires grew greatly. This, as is well known, increased the demand for rubber and tended to raise its price, but it also provided the opportunity for tire manufacturers to build larger plants that exploited the scale economies available in tire production. These economies were large enough to offset any factor price increases, and tire prices charged to automobile manufacturers fell. Thus automobile costs fell because of lower prices of an important input. This case is illustrated in part (iii) of Figure 12-10. An industry that has a declining long-run supply curve is often called a *falling-cost industry*.

Notice that although the economies were external to the automobile industry, they were internal to the tire industry. This in turn requires that the supplying industry not be perfectly competitive. If it were, all its scale economies would already have been exploited, so this case refers to a perfectly competitive industry that uses an input produced by a non-perfectly competitive industry whose own scale economies have not yet been fully exploited because demand is insufficient. Another example is provided by perfectly competitive agricultural industries who buy their farm machinery from an industry that is dominated by a few large firms.

We can now use our long-run theory to understand two commonly encountered but often misunderstood real-world situations.

Changes in Technology

Consider an industry in long-run equilibrium. Since the industry is in equilibrium, each firm must be in zero-profit equilibrium. Now assume that technological development lowers the cost curves of newly built plants. Since price is just equal to the average total cost for the existing plants, new plants will be able to earn profits, and some of them will now be built. The resulting expansion in capacity shifts the short-run supply curve to the right and drives price down.

The expansion in capacity and the fall in price will continue until price is equal to the short-run average total cost of the *new* plants. At this price, old plants will not be covering their long-run costs. As long as price exceeds their average variable cost, however, such plants will continue in production. As the outmoded plants wear out, they will gradually be closed. Eventually, a new long-run equilibrium will be established in which all plants will use the new technology.

What happens in a competitive industry in which technological change occurs not as a single isolated event but more or less continuously? Plants built in any one year will tend to have lower costs than plants built in any previous year.[6] This common occurrence is illustrated in Figure 12-11.

Industries that are subject to continuous technological change have a number of interesting characteristics. One of them is that plants of different ages and at different levels of efficiency exist side by side.

[6] This statement refers to real resource costs, which tend to fall due to technological change. Of course, in times of general inflation, *money costs* of plants may well be rising. In the comparisons made here, we are assuming that costs have been adjusted for changes in the general price level.

FIGURE 12-11 Plants of Different Vintages in an Industry with Continuous Technological Progress

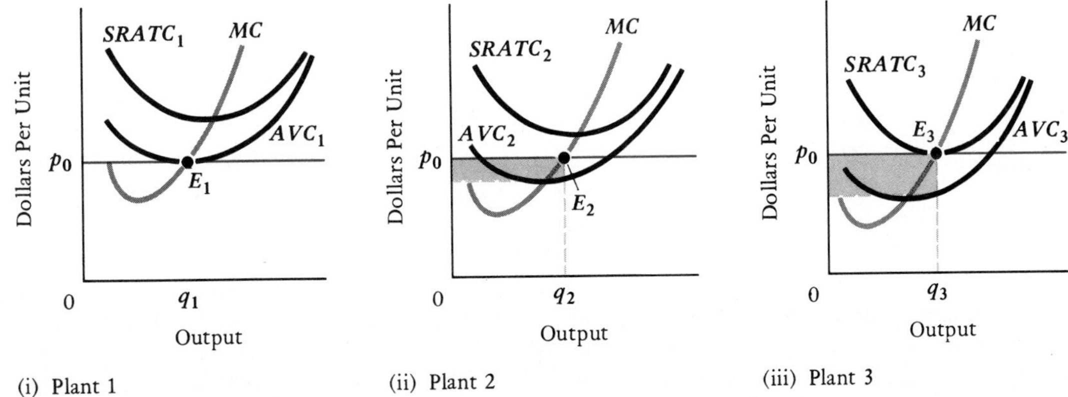

(i) Plant 1 (ii) Plant 2 (iii) Plant 3

Entry of progressively lower-cost firms forces price down, but older plants with higher costs remain in the industry as long as price covers average variable cost. Plant 3 is the newest plant with the lowest costs. Long-run equilibrium price will be determined by the average total costs of plants of this type, since entry will continue as long as the owners of the newest plants expect to earn profits from them. Plant 1 is the oldest plant in operation. It is just covering its *AVC*, and if the price falls any further, it will be closed down. Plant 2 is a plant of intermediate age. It is covering its variable costs and earning some contribution toward its fixed costs. In parts (ii) and (iii), the excess of revenues over variable costs is indicated by the shaded area.

This characteristic is dramatically illustrated by the variety of vintages of steam turbine generators found in any long-established electric utility.

Critics who observe the continued use of older, less efficient plants and urge that something be done "to eliminate these wasteful practices" miss the point of economic efficiency. If the plant is already there, the plant can be profitably operated as long as its revenues more than cover its variable costs. As long as a plant can produce goods that are valued by consumers at an amount above the value of the resources currently used up for their production (variable costs), the value of society's total output is increased by using that plant to produce goods.

A second characteristic of a competitive industry that is subject to continuous technological change is that price is governed by the *minimum ATC* of the most efficient plants.[7] Entry will continue until plants of the latest vintage are just expected to earn normal profits over their lifetimes. The benefits of the new technology are passed on to consumers because all of the units of the commodity, whether produced by new or old plants, are sold at a price that is related solely to the *ATC*s of the new plants. Owners of older plants find that their returns over variable costs fall steadily as more and more efficient plants drive the price of the product down.

A third characteristic is that old plants are discarded (or "mothballed") when the price falls below their *AVC*s. This may occur well before the plants are physically worn out. In industries with continuous technological progress, capital is usually discarded because it is *economically obsolete,* not because it is physically worn out. Old capital is obsolete when the market price of output does not even cover its average variable cost of production.

Declining Industries

What happens when a competitive industry in long-run equilibrium begins to suffer losses due to a per-

[7] Price will not necessarily equal minimum *ATC*. If firms anticipate the future changes, they will install new capital only when they expect to cover costs over the lifetime of the capital. This means that there must be sufficient profits in early years to match the losses in later years. Thus price will exceed average costs in the most efficient plants.

manent and continuing decrease in the demand for its products? As market demand declines, market price falls, and firms that were previously covering average total costs are no longer able to do so. They find themselves in the position shown in part (i) of Figure 12-6. Firms suffer losses instead of breaking even; the signal for the exit of capital is sounded, but exit takes time.

The Response of Firms

The economically efficient response to a steadily declining demand is to continue to operate with existing equipment as long as its variable costs of production can be covered. As equipment becomes obsolete because it cannot cover even its variable cost, it will not be replaced unless the new equipment can cover its total cost. As a result, the capacity of the industry will shrink. If demand keeps declining, capacity must keep shrinking.

Declining industries typically present a sorry sight to the observer. Revenues are below long-run total costs, and as a result, new equipment is not brought in to replace old equipment as it wears out. The average age of equipment in use thus rises steadily. The untrained observer, seeing the industry's plight, is likely to blame it on the old equipment.

The antiquated equipment in a declining industry is often the effect rather than the cause of the industry's decline.

An interesting illustration of the importance of the distinction between fixed and variable costs—one that is familiar to most hotel users—is given in Box 12-2.

The Response of Governments

Governments are often tempted to support declining industries because they are worried about the resulting job losses. Experience suggests, however, that propping up genuinely declining industries only delays their demise—at significant national cost. When the government finally withdraws its support, the decline is usually more abrupt and hence more difficult to adjust to than it would have been had the industry been allowed to decline gradually under the market force of steadily declining demand.

Once governments recognize the decay of certain industries and the collapse of certain firms as an inevitable aspect of economic growth, a more appropriate response is to provide welfare and retraining schemes that cushion the impacts of change. These can moderate the effects on the incomes of workers who lose their jobs and make it easier for them to transfer to expanding industries. Intervention that is intended to increase mobility and reduce the social and personal costs of mobility is a viable long-run policy; trying to freeze the existing industrial structure by shoring up an inevitably declining industry is not.

A striking example of the confusion of cause and effect in a declining industry occurred during the debate over the nationalization of the coal industry in Great Britain during the period between World Wars I and II. The widely held view that public control was needed to save the industry from the hands of third-rate, unenterprising private owners was undoubtedly a factor that led to its eventual nationalization. Sir Roy Harrod, a leading British economist from the 1920s to the 1960s, shocked many people by taking the opposite view, arguing that the run-down state of the coal industry in some parts of the country represented the correct response of the owners to the signals of the market. He wrote:

> Economic efficiency does not consist in always introducing the most up-to-date equipment that an engineer can think of. . . . In not introducing new equipment, the managements may have been wise, not only from the point of view of their own interest, but from that of national interest, which requires the most profitable application of available capital. . . . It is right that as much should be extracted from the inferior mines as can be done by old-fashioned methods [with equipment already installed] and that they should gradually go out of action.[8]

The general point that Harrod makes is important. Capital resources are scarce; to install new plant and equipment in a genuinely declining industry is to use the nation's scarce resources where they will not lead to the largest possible increases in the value of national output. It is in the public and private interest for methods that appear to be antiquated to be employed in declining industries.

[8] Roy Harrod, *The British Economy* (New York: McGraw-Hill, 1963), p. 54.

BOX 12-2

Parable of the Seaside Inn

Why do some resort hotels stay open during the off-season, even though to do so they must offer bargain rates that do not even cover their "full costs"? Why does the management of other hotels allow them to fall into disrepair even though they are able to attract enough customers to stay in business? Are the former being overly generous, and are the latter being irrational penny pinchers?

To illustrate what is involved, consider an imaginary resort hotel called the Seaside Inn. Its revenues and costs of operating during the four months of the season and during the eight months of the off-season are shown in the table. When the profit-maximizing price for its rooms is charged, the hotel earns a return over its total variable costs of $22,000 during the season, as shown in the table. This surplus goes toward meeting the hotel's fixed costs of $24,000.

If it were to charge the same rates during the off-season, it could not attract enough customers even to cover its costs of maids, bellhops, and managers. The hotel discovers, however, that by charging lower rates during the off-season, it can rent some of its rooms and earn revenues of $20,000. Its costs of staying open are $18,000, and if it allocates the same portion of its fixed costs of $24,000 to each month that it stays open, it will not be covering its total costs (fixed plus variable costs) in the off-season, but it will be earning a surplus of $2,000 over variable costs. This surplus, though relatively small, can go toward covering some part of the fixed costs. Therefore, the hotel stays open during the whole year by offering bargain rates to grateful guests. (Indeed, if it were to close during the winter months, it would not be able to cover its total fixed and variable costs solely through its season operations.)

Now assume that the off-season revenues fall to $19,000 (everything else remaining the same). The short-run condition for staying open, $TR > TVC$, is met both for the season and for the off-season. However, the long-run condition is not met, since the TR over the whole year of $77,000 is less than the total costs of $78,000, all of which are variable in the long run. The hotel will remain open as long as it can do so with its present capital—it will produce in the short run. However, it will not be worthwhile for the owners to replace the capital as it wears out.

It will become one of those run-down hotels about which guests ask, "Why don't they do something about this place?"—but the owners are behaving rationally. They are operating the hotel as long as it covers its variable costs, but they are not putting any more investment into it, since it cannot cover its fixed costs. Sooner or later, the fixed capital will become too old to be run, or at least to attract customers, and the hotel will be closed.

The Seaside Inn ***(total costs and revenues)***

	Total revenue	*Total variable cost*	*Contribution to fixed costs*	
Season	***TR***	***TVC***	***TR − TVC***	**Total fixed costs**
Season	$58,000	$36,000	$22,000	
Off-season	$20,000	$18,000	$ 2,000	
Total	$78,000	$54,000	$24,000	$24,000

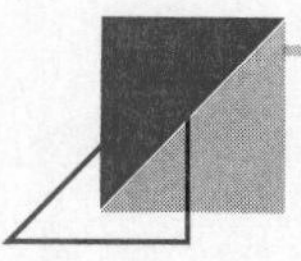

The Appeal of Perfect Competition

Consider an economy in which all markets are perfectly competitive. In this economy there are many firms and many households. Each is a price taker, responding as it sees fit to signals that are sent to it by the market. No single firm or consumer has any power over the market; instead, each is a passive quantity adjuster who merely responds to market signals. Yet the impersonal force of the market produces an appropriate response to all changes. If tastes change, for example, prices will change, and the allocation of resources will change in the appropriate direction. Throughout the entire process, no one firm will have any power over any other firm. Dozens of firms will react to the same price changes, and if one firm refuses to react, countless other profit-maximizing firms will be eager to make the appropriate changes.

Market reactions, not public policies, eliminate shortages or surpluses. There is need neither for regulatory agencies nor for bureaucrats to make arbitrary decisions about who may produce what, how to produce it, or how much it is permissible to charge for the product. If there are no government officials to make such decisions, no bribes will be necessary to influence one decision rather than another.

In the impersonal decision-making world of perfect competition, neither private firms nor public officials wield economic power. The market mechanism, like an invisible hand, determines the allocation of resources among competing uses.

The theory of perfect competition is an intellectual triumph in showing how a price system can work to coordinate decentralized decision making by allowing all necessary adjustments to occur, in spite of the fact that no one foresees them or provides any overall plan for them.

Lord Acton once observed, "Power tends to corrupt; absolute power corrupts absolutely." To someone who fears power either in the hands of the state or in such private organizations as large firms, the perfectly competitive model has a strong appeal. It describes an economy that functions efficiently without any private or public group exercising any significant market power.

Economic and social policy would be much simplified if the entire economy were perfectly competitive. Although the price system often allocates resources in ways that are quite similar to the perfectly competitive economy, and although some markets are indeed perfectly competitive, in our world many groups have power over many markets. Large firms often set prices, determine what will be produced, and decide what research will take place. Labor unions often influence wages by offering or withdrawing their labor services. Governments influence many markets by being the dominant purchaser, as well as by regulating many others. As it is, those who fear the concentration of market power can only regret that the perfectly competitive model does not describe the world in which we live; so many problems would disappear if only it did.

SUMMARY

1. Market behavior is concerned with the degree to which individual firms compete against one another; market structure is concerned with the type of market in which firms operate. Market structure affects the degree of power that individual firms have to influence such market variables as the price of the product. Under the market structure known as perfect competition, individual firms are price takers.
2. Five key assumptions of the theory of perfect competition are these: (a) All firms produce a homogeneous product; (b) purchasers know the nature of the product and the price charged for it; (c) each firm's minimum efficient scale occurs at a level of output that is small relative to the industry's total output; (d) firms are price takers; and (e) the industry displays freedom of entry and exit. A firm that is a price taker will adjust to varying market conditions by altering its output.

3. A profit-maximizing firm will produce at a level of output at which (a) price is at least as great as average variable cost and (b) marginal cost equals marginal revenue. In perfect competition, firms are price takers, so marginal revenue is equal to price. Thus a profit-maximizing firm operating in a perfectly competitive market equates marginal cost to price.
4. Under perfect competition, each firm's short-run supply curve is identical with its marginal cost curve above average variable cost. The perfectly competitive industry's short-run supply curve is the horizontal sum of the supply curves of the individual firms (i.e., the horizontal sum of the firms' marginal cost curves).
5. If a profit-maximizing firm is to produce at all, it must be able to cover its variable cost. However, such a firm may be suffering losses (price is less than average total cost), making profits (price is greater than average total cost), or just breaking even (price is equal to average total cost).
6. In the long run, profits or losses will lead to the entry or the exit of capital from the industry. This entry or exit of capital will push a competitive industry to a long-run, zero-profit equilibrium and move production to the level that is consistent with minimum average total cost.
7. The long-run response of a competitive industry to steadily changing technology is the gradual replacement of less efficient plants and machines by more efficient ones. Older plant and equipment will be employed as long as price exceeds average variable cost; only when average variable costs rise above price will they be discarded and replaced by more modern ones. The long-run response of a declining industry will be to continue to satisfy demand by employing its existing machinery as long as price exceeds average variable cost. Despite its antiquated appearance, it is correct to use the existing machinery when faced with a steadily falling demand.
8. The great appeal of perfect competition as a means of organizing production lies in the decentralized decision making of myriad firms and households. No individual firm or household exercises power over the market. At the same time, it is not necessary for the government to intervene to determine resource allocation and prices. Although some markets in modern economies are perfectly competitive, overall these economies are not perfectly competitive.

TOPICS FOR REVIEW

Competitive behavior and competitive market structure
Rules for maximizing profits
Perfect competition
Price taking and a horizontal demand curve
Average revenue, marginal revenue, and price under perfect competition
Relationship of supply curves to marginal cost curves
Short-run and long-run equilibrium of firms and industries
Entry and exit in achieving long-run equilibrium

DISCUSSION QUESTIONS

1. A number of agricultural products, such as milk, eggs, and chickens, were once produced in Canada under conditions coming close to perfect competition. What were the main features of these industries that made them perfectly competitive? Use the theory you have learned in this chapter to predict the consequences of the introduction

of provincial marketing boards that attempted to raise farmers' incomes by restricting total output through a system of quotas.

2. It is often alleged that when all firms in an industry are charging the same price, this indicates the absence of competition and the presence of some form of price-setting agreement. Discuss.
3. Which of the following observed facts about an industry are inconsistent with its being a perfectly competitive industry?
   a. Different firms use different methods of production.
   b. The industry's product is extensively advertised by a trade association.
   c. Individual firms devote 5 percent of their sales receipts to advertising their own product brands.
   d. There are 24 firms in the industry.
   e. The largest firm in the industry makes 40 percent of the sales, and the next largest firm makes 20 percent of the sales, but the products are identical, and there are 61 other firms.
   f. All firms made large profits in 1989.
4. Suppose entry into an industry is not artificially restricted but takes time because of the need to build plants, to acquire technical knowhow, and to establish a marketing organization. Can such an industry be characterized as perfectly competitive? Does ease of entry imply ease of exit, and vice versa?
5. What, if anything, does each one of the following tell you about ease of entry into or exit from an industry?
   a. Profits have been very high for two decades.
   b. No new firms have entered the industry for 20 years.
   c. The average age of the firms in the 40-year-old industry is less than 7 years.
   d. Most existing firms are using obsolete equipment alongside newer, more modern equipment.
   e. Profits are low or negative; many firms are still producing, but from steadily aging equipment.
6. In the 1970s prices obtained for Canadian wheat rose substantially relative to other agricultural products. Explain how each of the following may have contributed to this result.
   a. Crop failures caused by unusually bad weather around the world in several years
   b. Rising demand for beef and chickens because of rising population and rising per capita income
   c. Great scarcities in fishmeal, a substitute for grain in animal diets, because of a mysterious decline in the anchovy harvest off Peru
   d. Increased Soviet purchases of grain on the world market
7. In the late 1980s the prices obtained for Canadian wheat fell dramatically relative to other agricultural products. Explain how each of the following may have contributed to the result.
   a. The green revolution has made more and more countries self-sufficient in food.
   b. Reforms in Russian agricultural production led to bumper harvests in the late 1980s.
   c. Agricultural subsidies in the European Community (EC) have turned it from a net importer to a net exporter of agricultural produce.

Chapter 13

Monopoly

Is Québec Hydro a monopoly? How about Bombardier, Algoma Steel, the National Hockey League, provincial liquor boards, or the Post Office? The word *monopoly* comes from the Greek words *monos polein*, which mean "alone to sell." In economics, a **monopoly** is a market structure in which the output of an entire industry is produced and sold by a single firm. The firm itself is called a **monopolist** or a *monopoly firm*.

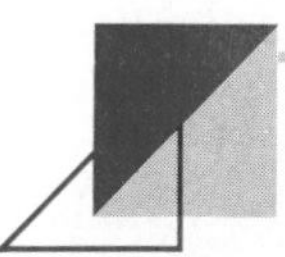

A Single-Price Monopolist

In the first part of this chapter we shall deal with a monopoly firm that charges a single price for everything that it sells. The firm's profits, like those of all firms, will depend on the relationship between its production costs and its sales revenues.

Cost and Revenue in the Short Run

We saw in Chapter 10 that U-shaped short-run cost curves are a consequence of the law of diminishing returns. Since this law applies to the conditions under which goods are produced rather than to the market structure in which they are sold, monopoly firms have U-shaped short-run cost curves no different from those of perfectly competitive firms.

What distinguishes a monopoly firm from a firm that operates under any other market structure is the firm's demand curve. Because the monopoly firm is the sole producer of a particular product, its demand curve is identical with the market demand curve for that product. The market demand curve, which shows the total quantity that buyers will purchase at each price, also shows the quantity that the monopolist will be able to sell at each price that it might set. Thus the monopoly firm, unlike the perfectly competitive firm, faces a negatively sloped demand curve. This means that it faces a trade-off between price and quantity: Sales can be increased only if price is reduced, and price can be increased only if sales are reduced.

Average and Marginal Revenue

Starting with the market demand curve, the monopoly firm's average and marginal revenue curves can be readily derived. When the monopoly firm charges the same price for all units sold, average revenue per unit is identical with price. Thus the market demand curve is also the firm's *average revenue curve*.

TABLE 13-1 Relationship Between Average Revenue and Marginal Revenue: A Numerical Example

Price $p = AR$	Quantity q	$TR = p \cdot q$	$MR = \Delta TR/\Delta q$
$9.10	9	$81.90	
			$8.10
9.00	10	90.00	
			7.90
8.90	11	97.90	

Marginal revenue is less than price because price must be lowered to sell an extra unit. In this example, to increase sales from 10 to 11 units, the monopolist must reduce the price on all units sold from $9.00 to $8.90. The extra unit sold brings in $8.90, but the firm sacrifices 10 cents on each of the 10 units that it could have sold at $9.00 had it not wanted to increase sales. The net addition to revenue is the $8.90, minus 10 cents times 10 units, or $1.00, making $7.90 altogether. Thus the marginal revenue resulting from the increase in sales from 9 to 10 units is $7.90, which is less than the price at which the 10 units are sold.

Marginal revenue is shown displaced by half a line to emphasize that it represents the effect on revenue of the *change* in output between the two amounts shown in the first column.

Now consider the monopoly firm's *marginal revenue* resulting from the sale of an additional (or marginal) unit of production. Because its demand curve is negatively sloped, the monopoly firm must lower the price that it charges on *all* units in order to sell an *extra* unit. [25] It follows that the addition to its revenue resulting from the sale of an extra unit is less than the price that it receives for that unit (less by the amount that it loses as a result of cutting the price on all the units that it was selling already).

The monopoly firm's marginal revenue is less than the price at which it sells its output.

This proposition, which is explored numerically in Table 13-1 and graphically in Figure 13-1, provides an important contrast with perfect competition (in which, you will recall, the firm's marginal revenue from selling an extra unit of output is equal to the price at which that unit is sold). The reason for the difference is not difficult to understand. The perfectly competitive firm is a price taker, selling all it wants at the given market price; the monopoly firm faces a negatively sloped demand curve and drives the market price down when it increases its sales.

Marginal Revenue and Elasticity

The top part of Figure 13-2 illustrates the average and marginal revenue curves for a monopoly firm that faces a negatively sloped, straight-line demand curve.[1] In Chapter 5 we discussed the relationship between the elasticity of the market demand curve and the total revenue derived from selling the product. Figure 13-2 summarizes this earlier discussion and extends it to cover marginal revenue:

When the demand curve is elastic, total revenue rises as more units are sold; marginal revenue must therefore be positive. When the demand curve is inelastic, total revenue falls as more units are sold; marginal revenue must therefore be negative.

Short-Run Monopoly Equilibrium

To show the profit-maximizing position of a monopoly firm, we bring together information about its revenues and its costs and then apply the two rules developed in Chapter 12. Recall that these two rules are (1) the firm should not produce at all unless there is some level of output for which price is at least equal to total variable cost, and (2) if the firm does produce, its output should be set at the point where marginal cost equals marginal revenue.

When the monopoly firm equates marginal cost with marginal revenue, it reaches the equilibrium shown in Figure 13-3. Because marginal revenue is less than price for the monopoly firm, when marginal revenue is equated with marginal cost, both are less than price.

Marginal revenue equals price for the perfectly competitive firm, but it is less than price for the monopoly firm; marginal cost equals price in a perfectly competitive equilibrium, but it is less than price in a monopolistic equilibrium.

The relationship between elasticity and revenue just discussed has an interesting implication for the monopoly firm's equilibrium. Since marginal cost is

[1] It is helpful when you are drawing these curves to remember that if the demand curve is a downward-sloping straight line, the *MR* curve also slopes downward but is twice as steep. Its price intercept (where $q = 0$) is the same as that of the demand curve, and its quantity intercept (where $p = 0$) is one-half that of the demand curve.

FIGURE 13-1 Effect on Revenue of an Increase in Quantity Sold

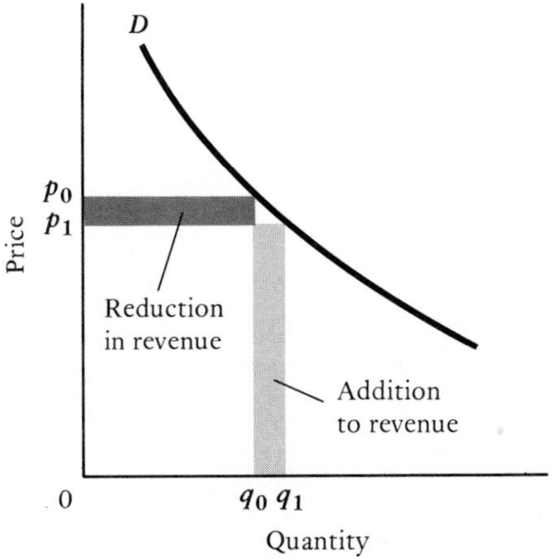

For a negatively sloped demand curve, marginal revenue is less than price. A reduction of price from p_0 to p_1 increases sales by one unit from q_0 to q_1. The revenue from the extra unit sold is shown as the lighter shaded area. To sell this unit, however, it is necessary to reduce the price on all of the q_0 units previously sold. The loss in revenue is shown as the darker shaded area. The marginal revenue associated with increasing output from q_0 to q_1 is equal to the *difference* between the two areas.

FIGURE 13-2 Relationship Between Total, Average, and Marginal Revenue and Elasticity of Demand

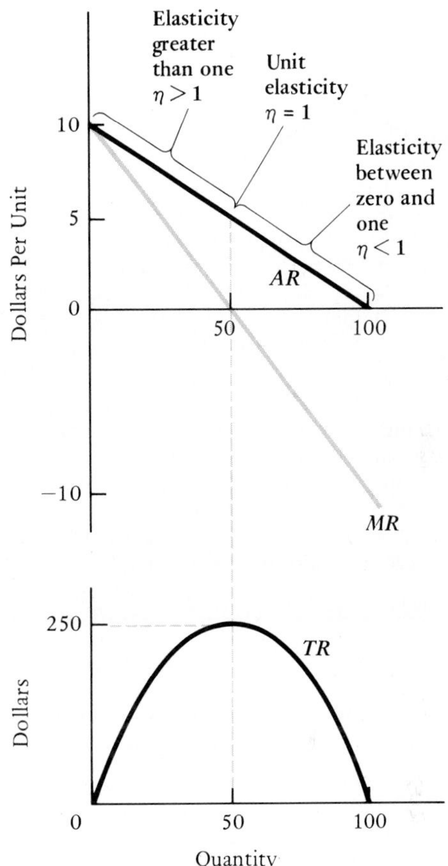

For a monopolist, *MR* is always less than price; when *TR* is rising, *MR* is greater than zero and elasticity is greater than one. The monopoly firm's demand curve is its *AR* curve; the *MR* curve is below the *AR* curve because the demand curve has a negative slope.

In the example shown, for outputs from 0 to 50, marginal revenue is positive, elasticity is greater than one, and total revenue is rising. For outputs from 50 to 100, marginal revenue is negative, elasticity is less than one, and total revenue is falling.

always greater than zero, a profit-maximizing monopoly (which produces where $MR = MC$) will always produce where marginal revenue is positive, that is, where demand is elastic. If the firm were producing where demand was inelastic, it could reduce its output, thereby both increasing its total revenue and reducing its total costs.

A profit-maximizing monopoly will never sell in the range where the demand curve is inelastic.

Monopoly profits. The fact that a monopoly firm produces the output that maximizes its profits tells us nothing about how large these profits will be or even whether there will be any profits at all. Profits may exist, as shown in part (i) of Figure 13-3. As part (ii) of Figure 13-3 shows, however, the profit-maximizing monopolist may break even or suffer losses. Nothing guarantees that a monopoly firm will make profits in the short run, but if it suffers persistent losses, it will eventually go out of business.

No supply curve for a monopoly. In describing the monopolist's profit-maximizing behavior, we did

FIGURE 13-3 Profit-maximizing Position of a Monopolist

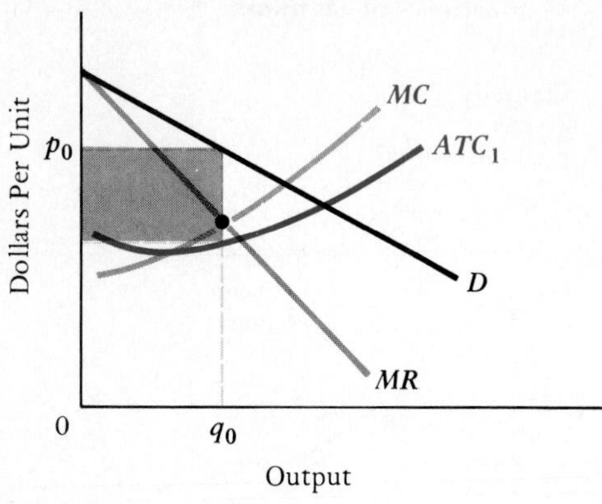

(i) Positive profits

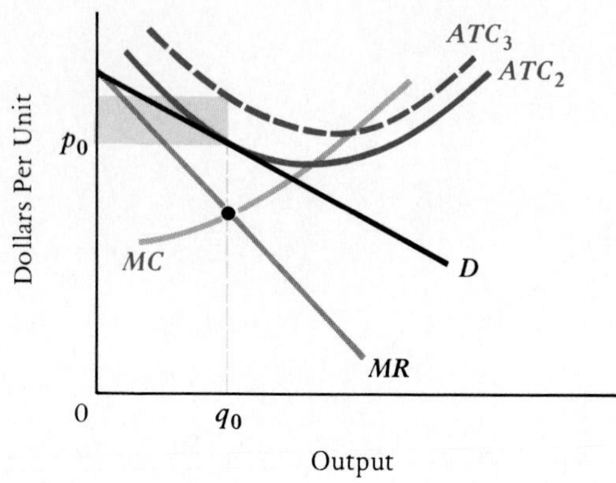

(ii) Zero profits

Profit-maximizing output is q_0, where $MR = MC$; price is p_0, which is above MC at that output. The rules for profit maximization require $MR = MC$ and $p > AVC$. (AVC is not shown in the graph, but it must be below ATC.) Whether or not there are profits depends on the position of the ATC curve. In (i), where average total cost is ATC_1, there are profits, as shown by the gray-shaded area. In (ii), where average total cost is ATC_2, profits are zero. If average total costs were ATC_3, the monopolist would suffer the losses shown by the color-shaded area.

not introduce the concept of a supply curve, as we did in the discussion of perfect competition. In perfect competition the industry short-run supply curve depends only on the marginal cost curves of the individual firms. This is because under perfect competition profit-maximizing firms equate marginal cost with price. Given marginal costs, it is possible to know how much will be produced at each price. This is not the case, however, with a monopoly.

In a monopoly there is no unique relationship between market price and quantity supplied.

Let us see why this is so. Like all profit-maximizing firms, a monopoly firm equates marginal cost with marginal revenue, but unlike firms in perfect competition, the monopoly firm's marginal revenue does not equal its price. Because marginal revenue depends on the slope of the demand curve and not on the price, a given price can be associated with many different demand curves and hence many different levels of output. If the same output can be associated with different prices, there is no unique relationship between price and output that is required for a supply curve.

Firm and industry. Since the monopolist is the only producer in an industry, there is no need for separate theories about the firm and the industry, as is necessary with perfect competition. The monopolist *is* the industry. Thus the short-run, profit-maximizing position of the firm, as shown in Figure 13-3, is also the short-run equilibrium of the industry.

Long-Run Monopoly Equilibrium

In a monopolized industry, as in a perfectly competitive one, losses and profits provide incentives for exit and entry.

If the monopoly firm is making losses in the short run, it will continue to operate as long as it can cover its variable costs. In the long run, however, it will leave the industry unless it can find a scale of operations at which its full opportunity costs can be covered.

If the monopoly firm is making profits, other

firms will wish to enter the industry in order to earn more than the opportunity cost of their capital. If such entry occurs, the equilibrium position shown in part (i) of Figure 13-3 will change, and the firm will cease to be a a monopolist.

Entry Barriers

Impediments that prevent entry are called **entry barriers**; they may be either natural or created.

If a monopoly's profits are to persist in the long run, the entry of new firms into the industry must be prevented by effective entry barriers.

Natural Barriers

Natural barriers most commonly arise as a result of economies of scale. When the long-run average cost curve is negatively sloped over a large range of output, big firms have significantly lower average total costs than small firms.

You will recall from Chapter 12 that the *minimum efficient scale (MES)* is the smallest-sized firm that can reap all of the economies of large-scale production. It occurs at the level of output where the firm's long-run average total cost curve reaches a minimum.

Now suppose that the technology of an industry is such that one firm's *MES* would be 10,000 units per week at an average total cost of $10 per unit. Further assume that at a price of $10, the total quantity demanded is 11,000 units per week. Under these circumstances, only one firm can operate at or near its *MES*.

A **natural monopoly** occurs when the industry's demand conditions allow only one firm, at most, to cover its costs while producing at its *MES*. In a natural monopoly, there is no price at which two firms can both sell enough to cover their total costs.

Another type of natural barrier is *set-up cost*. If a firm could be catapulted fully grown into the market, it might be able to compete effectively with the existing monopolist. The cost to the new firm of entering the market, developing its products, and establishing such things as its brand image and its dealer network may, however, be so large that entry would be unprofitable.

Created Barriers

Some barriers to entry can be created by the conscious action of governments and are therefore condoned by it. Patent laws, for instance, may prevent entry by conferring on the patent holder the sole right to produce a particular commodity. A firm may also be granted a charter or a franchise that prohibits competition by law.

Other barriers can be created by the firm or firms already in the market. In extreme cases, the threat of force or sabotage can deter entry. The most obvious entry barriers of this type are encountered in organized crime, where operation outside of the law makes available an array of illegal but potent barriers to new entrants. Legitimate firms must use legal tactics. These may range from the threat of price cutting, designed to impose unsustainable losses on a new entrant, to heavy brand-name advertising, intended to increase a new entrant's set-up costs. (These and other created entry barriers will be discussed in much more detail in Chapter 14.)

The Significance of Entry Barriers

Because there are no entry barriers in perfect competition, profits cannot persist in the long run.

Profits attract entry, and entry erodes profits.

In monopoly, however, profits can persist in the long run whenever there are effective barriers to entry.

Entry barriers frustrate the adjustment mechanism that pushes profits to zero in the long run.

Absence of Entry Barriers in the Very Long Run: "Creative Destruction"

In the very long run, technology changes. New ways of producing old products are invented, and new products are created to satisfy both familiar and new wants. What has this to do with entry barriers? The answer is that a monopoly that succeeds in preventing the entry of new firms that can produce its commodity will sooner or later find its barriers circumvented by innovations. One firm may be able to use new processes that avoid some patent or other barrier that the monopolist relies on to bar entry of competing firms. Another firm may compete by producing a new product that satisfies the same need as the monopoly firm's product. Yet another firm might get around a natural monopoly by inventing a technology that produces at a low *MES* and ultimately allows several firms to enter the market and still cover costs.

The distinguished Austrian-born American economist Joseph Schumpeter took the view that entry barriers were not a serious problem in the very long run. He argued that monopoly profits provide one of the major incentives for people who risk their money by financing inventions and innovations. In his view, the large, short-run profits of a monopoly provide a strong incentive for others to try to usurp some of these profits for themselves. If a frontal attack on the monopolist's barriers to entry is not possible, the barriers will be circumvented by such means as the development of similar products against which the monopolist will not have protection from another firm's entry.

Schumpeter called the replacing of one monopoly by another through the invention of new products or new production techniques the *process of creative destruction*. He argued that this process precludes the very long run persistence of barriers to entry into industries that earn large profits.

He pushed this argument further and argued that because creative destruction thrives on innovation, the existence of monopoly profits is a major incentive to economic growth. A key part of his argument can be found in the following words:

> What we have got to accept is that it [monopoly] has come to be the most powerful engine of progress and in particular of the long-run expansion of total output not only in spite of, but to a considerable extent through, this strategy [i.e., creating monopolies], which looks so restrictive when viewed in the individual case and from the individual point of time. In this respect, perfect competition is not only impossible but inferior, and has no title to being set up as a model. It is hence a mistake to base the theory of government regulation of industry on the principle that big business should be made to work as the respective industry would work in perfect competition.[2]

Schumpeter was writing at a time when the two dominant market structures studied by economists were perfect competition and monopoly. His argument easily extends, however, to any market structure that allows profits to exist in the long run. Today there are few examples of pure monopolies, but there are many industries in which profits can be earned for long periods of time. Such industries, which are called *oligopolies*, are candidates for the operation of the process of creative destruction. We study these industries in detail in Chapter 14.

Examples of creative destruction abound. In the nineteenth century, railways began to compete with wagons and barges for the carriage of freight. In the twentieth century, trucks operating on newly constructed highways began competing with trains. During the 1950s and 1960s, airplanes began to compete seriously with trucks and trains.

The slide rule is an example of a product that had its market destroyed by a new one, which resulted in the elimination of a firm's monopoly power. Keuffel & Esser had achieved a dominant position in the manufacture and the sale of slide rules, which were essential tools for engineers and applied scientists. Its dominant position and highly profitable operations were wiped out, not by a better slide rule, but by the pocket calculator. When they were first introduced in the early 1970s, pocket calculators were relatively expensive, often costing over $100. They were also relatively crude in their capabilities. Nonetheless, they proved to be popular; sales and profits rose, and firms rushed to enter the lucrative new field. Competition led simultaneously to product improvements and price reductions. Today calculators that perform basic calculations can be bought for a few dollars, and sophisticated scientific and programmable pocket calculators can be bought for under $50. Few of today's college students have heard of Keuffel & Esser, but most of them know about Texas Instruments.

In recent years the development of facsimile transmission and electronic mail eliminated the natural monopoly of the Post Office in delivering hardcopy (as opposed to oral) communications. In their myriad uses, microcomputers for the home and the office swept away the markets of many once-thriving products and services. For instance, in-store computers answer customer questions, decreasing the need for salespeople. Aided by computers, "just in time" inventory systems greatly reduce the investment in inventories required of existing firms and new entrants alike. Computer-based flexible manufacturing systems allow firms to switch production easily and inexpensively from one product line to another, thereby reducing the minimum scale at

[2] Joseph Schumpeter, *Capitalism, Socialism, and Democracy*, 3d ed. (New York: Harper & Row, 1950), p. 106.

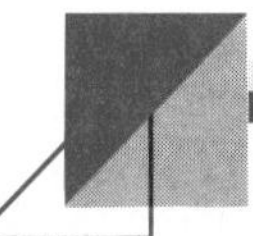

BOX 13-1

Erosion of a Monopoly

The great strength of the incentive to share in a monopoly's profits can be illustrated by the case of the ball-point pen, in which a monopoly was created by product innovation and quickly destroyed by imitators.

In 1945 Milton Reynolds developed a new type of pen that wrote with a ball bearing rather than with the then-conventional nib. He formed the Reynolds International Pen Company, which he capitalized at $26,000, and began production on October 6, 1945.

The Reynolds pen was introduced with a good deal of fanfare by Gimbels, which guaranteed that the pen would write for two years without needing refilling. The price was set at $12.50. Gimbels sold 10,000 pens on October 29, 1945, the first day that they were on sale. In the early stages of production the cost of producing the pens was estimated to be around 80 cents per pen.

The Reynolds International Pen Company quickly expanded its production. By early 1946 it employed more than 800 people in its factory and was producing 30,000 pens per day. By March 1946 it had $3 million in the bank.

Macy's, Gimbels' traditional rival, introduced an imported ball-point pen from South America. Its price was $19.98 (production costs are unknown).

The heavy sales of this pen quickly elicited a response from other pen manufacturers. Eversharp introduced its first model in April 1946, priced at $15.00. In July 1946 *Fortune* magazine reported that Sheaffer was planning to sell a pen for $15.00, and Eversharp announced its plan to produce a "retractable" model that would be priced at $25.00 Reynolds introduced a new model but kept the price at $12.50. Costs were estimated at 60 cents per pen.

The first signs of trouble now emerged. The Ball Point Pen Company of Hollywood put a model for $9.95 on the market, and a manufacturer named David Kahn announced his plans to introduce a pen that would sell for less than $3.00. *Fortune* reported that there were fears in the industry of an impending price war in view of the growing number of manufacturers and the low cost of production. In October Reynolds introduced a new model, priced at $3.85, that cost about 30 cents to produce.

By late December 1946 approximately 100 manufacturers were in production, some of whom were selling pens for as little as $2.98. By February 1947 Gimbels was selling a ball-point pen that was made by the Continental Pen Company for 98 cents. Reynolds introduced a new model that was priced to sell at $1.69, but Gimbels sold it for 88 cents in a price war with Macy's. Reynolds felt betrayed by Gimbels. Reynolds introduced a new model that was listed at 98 cents. By this time ball-point pens had become economy rather than luxury items, but they were still a highly profitable item to sell.

In mid 1948 ball-point pens were selling for as little as 39 cents and costing about 10 cents to produce. In 1951 prices of 25 cents were common. Within six years the power of the monopoly was gone forever. Since that time the market has been saturated with a wide variety of models and prices of pens ranging from 19 cents and up. The firms that manufacture them cover the full opportunity costs of their capital, but they have long since ceased to earn pure profits.

Of course there can still be strong incentives to gain monopoly power and profits, even if the effort is sure to fail eventually. The lag between an original monopoly and its subsequent erosion by competition may be long enough to ensure large profits to the monopolist. It is estimated, for example, that Milton Reynolds earned profits as high as $500,000 in a single month—about 20 times his original investment.

which each can be produced profitably. One day computers may even displace the college textbook.

Another example of this process of creative destruction is discussed in more detail in Box 13-1.

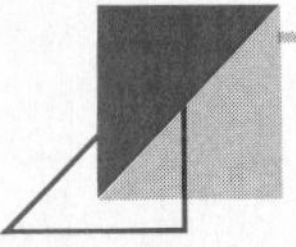

Cartels As Monopolies

To this point in this chapter a monopoly has meant a firm that is the only seller of a product in an industry. A second way in which a monopoly can arise is for many firms in an industry to agree to cooperate with one another, to behave as if they were a single seller, in order to maximize joint profits, thus eliminating competition among themselves. Such a group of firms is called a **cartel**. A cartel that includes *all* firms in the industry can behave in the same way as a single-firm monopoly that owned all of these firms. The firms can agree among themselves to restrict their total output to the level that maximizes their joint profits.[3]

The Effects of Cartelization

The incentive for firms to form a cartel lies in the cartel's ability to restrict output, thereby creating profits.

It is *always* profitable for all of the firms in perfectly competitive equilibrium to increase their profits by means of an agreement that restricts output.

The intuitive reasoning behind this result is as follows. Because perfectly competitive firms are price takers, they accept the market price as given and increase their production until their marginal cost equals price. The monopoly firm, however, faces a market demand curve that is its own demand curve and as a result knows that increasing output forces the market price downward. To take account of this, the monopolist stops increasing output when marginal revenue is equal to marginal cost. If all the firms in a perfectly competitive industry get together in a cartel, they too will be able to take account of the effect of their *joint output* on price. They can agree to restrict industry output to the level that maximizes their joint profits (where the industry's marginal cost is equal to the industry's marginal revenue).

When a perfectly competitive industry is cartelized, the firms can agree to restrict their joint output to the profit-maximizing level. One way to do this is to establish a quota for each firm's output. Say that the profit-maximizing output is two-thirds of the perfectly competitive output. When the cartel is formed, each firm could be given a quota equal to two-thirds of its competitive output. The effect of cartelizing a perfectly competitive industry and of reducing its output through production quotas is shown in more detail in Figure 13-4.

Problems That Cartels Face

Cartels encounter two characteristic problems. The first is how to ensure that each firm in the industry follows the behavior that will maximize the firms' *joint* profits, and the second is how to prevent these profits from being eroded by the entry of new firms.

Enforcement of output restrictions. The managers of any cartel want the industry to produce its profit-maximizing output. Their job is made more difficult if individual firms either stay out of the cartel or enter and then cheat on their output quotas. Any one firm, however, does have an incentive to do just this: to be either the one that stays out of the organization or the one that goes in and cheats. For the sake of simplicity, assume that all firms enter the cartel, so enforcement problems are concerned strictly with the cheating of its members.

If Firm X is the only firm to cheat, it is in the best of all possible situations. All other firms restrict output and hold the industry price near its monopoly level. They earn profits but only by restricting output. Firm X can then reap the full benefit of the other firms' restraint and sell all that it wishes at the high price that has been set by the cartel's actions. However, if all of the firms cheat, the price will be pushed back to the competitive level, and all of the firms will return to their zero-profit position.

This conflict between the interests of the group and the interests of the individual firm is the cartel's dilemma. Provided that enough people cooperate in restricting output, all firms are better off than they

[3] In this chapter we deal with the simple case in which all of the firms in a perfectly competitive industry form a cartel in order to act as if they were a monopoly. Cartels are sometimes formed by a group of firms that account for a significant part, but not all, of the total supply of some commodity. The effect is to create what is called an *oligopoly*. We shall return to this type of cartel in Chapter 14.

FIGURE 13-4 Effect of Cartelizing an Industry in Perfectly Competitive Equilibrium

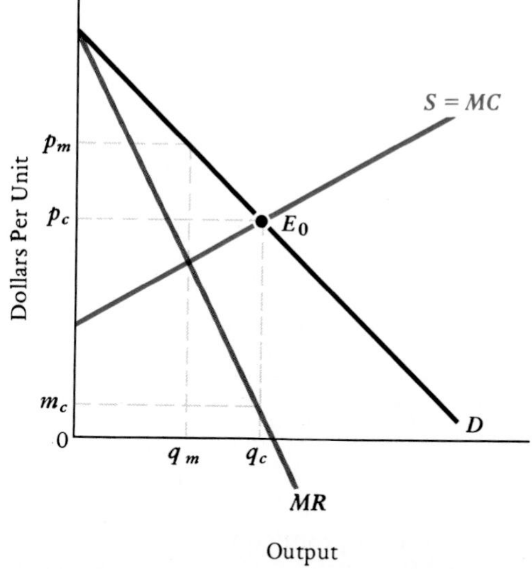

Cartelization of a perfectly competitive industry can always increase that industry's profits. Equilibrium for a perfectly competitive industry occurs at E_0, where the supply and the demand curves intersect. Equilibrium price and output are p_c and q_c. Because the industry demand curve is negatively sloped, marginal revenue is less than price. In the graph, marginal revenue is m_c at the competitive equilibrium output of q_c.

If the industry is cartelized, profits can be increased by reducing output. All units beween q_m and q_c add less to revenue than to cost—the marginal revenue curve lies below the marginal cost curve. (Recall from Figure 12-5 that the industry's supply curve is the sum of the supply curves, and hence of the marginal cost curves, of each of the firms in the industry.) If the units between q_m and q_c are not produced, output is reduced to q_m and price rises to p_m. This price-output combination maximizes the industry's profits because it is where marginal revenue equals marginal cost.

would be if the industry remained perfectly competitive. Any one firm, however, is even better off if it remains outside or enters and cheats. However, if all firms act on this incentive, all will be worse off than if they had joined the cartel and restricted output.

Cartels tend to be unstable because of the incentives for individual firms to violate the output quotas that are needed to enforce the monopoly price.

The conflict between the motives for cooperation and for independent action is analyzed in more detail in Figure 13-5.

Cartels and similar output-restricting arrangements have a long history. For example, schemes to raise farm incomes by limiting crops bear ample testimony to the accuracy of the predicted instability of cartels. Industry agreements concerning crop restriction often break down, and prices fall as individual farmers exceed their quotas. This is the reason why most crop restriction plans are now operated by governments rather than by private cartels. Government marketing boards of the type discussed in Chapter 6, backed by the full coercive power of the state, can force monopoly behavior on existing producers and can effectively bar the entry of new ones.

Restricting entry. A cartel must not only police the behavior of its members but also be able to prevent the entry of new producers. An industry that can support a number of individual firms must have no overriding natural entry barriers. Thus if it is to maintain its profits in the long run, a cartel of many separate firms must create barriers that prevent the entry of new firms that are attracted by the cartel's profits. Successful cartels are often able to license the firms in the industry and to control entry by restricting the number of licenses. At other times the government has operated the quota system and has given it the force of law. If no one can produce without a quota and the quotas are allocated among existing producers, entry is precluded. Box 13-2 provides an example of the typical fate of a cartel that cannot control entry.[4]

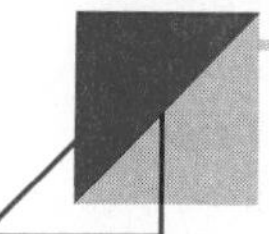

A Multiprice Monopolist: Price Discrimination

So far in this chapter we have assumed that the monopoly firm charges the same price for every unit of its product, no matter to whom or where it sells. However, other situations are common. Raw milk is often sold at one price when it is to be used as fluid milk but at a lower price when it is to be used to make ice cream or cheese. Doctors in private prac-

[4] The rest of this chapter may be omitted without loss of continuity.

FIGURE 13-5 **Conflicting Forces Affecting Cartels**

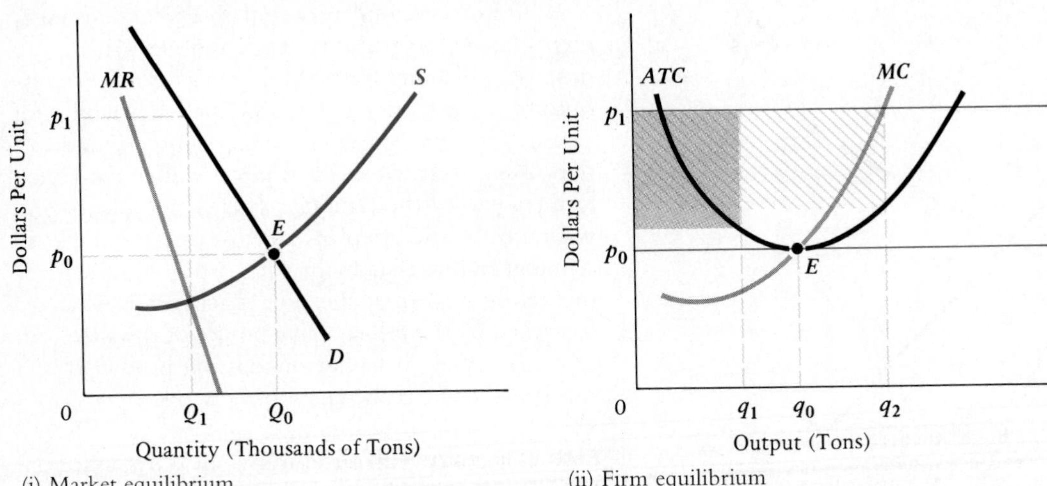

(i) Market equilibrium (ii) Firm equilibrium

Cooperation leads to the monopoly price, but individual self-interest may lead to production in excess of the monopoly output. Market conditions are shown in part (i), and the situation of a typical firm is shown in part (ii). (Note the change of scale between the two graphs.) Initially, the market is in competitive equilibrium with price p_0 and quantity Q_0. The individual firm is producing output q_0 and is just covering its total costs.

The cartel is formed and then enforces quotas on individual firms that are sufficient to reduce the industry's output to Q_1, the output where the supply curve cuts the marginal revenue curve. Q_1 is thus the output that maximizes the joint profits of the cartel members. Price rises to p_1 as a result. The typical firm's quota is q_1. The firm's profits rise from zero to the amount shown by the gray-shaded area in part (ii). Once price is raised to p_1, however, the individual firm would like to increase output to q_2, where marginal cost is equal to the price set by the cartel. This would allow the firm to earn profits, shown by the diagonally striped area. However, if all firms increase their outputs above their quotas, industry output will increase beyond Q_1, and the profits earned by all firms will fall.

tice often charge for their services according to the incomes of their patients. Movie theaters may have lower admission prices for children than for adults. Railroads charge different rates per ton per mile for different products. Electric companies sell electricity at one rate to homes and at another, lower rate to firms. Airlines often charge less to people who stay over a Saturday night than to those who come and go within the week.

Price discrimination occurs when a producer charges different prices for different units of the same commodity for reasons not associated with differences in cost. Not all price *differences* represent price *discrimination*. Quantity discounts, differences between wholesale and retail prices, and prices that vary with the time of day or the season of the year may not represent price discrimination, because the same product sold at a different time, in a different place, or in different quantities may have different costs. If an electric power company has unused capacity at certain times of the day, it may be cheaper for the company to provide service at those hours than at peak demand hours. If price differences reflect cost differences, they are not discriminatory.

When a price difference is based on different buyers' valuations of the same product, it is discriminatory. It does not cost a movie theater operator less to fill seats with children than with adults, but it may be worthwhile for the movie theater to let the children in at a discriminatory low price if few of them would attend at the full adult fare and if they take up seats that otherwise would be empty.

BOX 13-2

The Importance of Entry

Assume that there are many barber shops and that anyone who qualifies can set up as a barber. Assume also that the going price for haircuts is $20 and that at this price all barbers believe their incomes are too low. The barbers hold a meeting and decide to form a cartel (which they euphemistically call a trade association). They agree on the following points: First, all barbers in the city must join the association and abide by its rules; second, any new barbers who meet certain professional qualifications will be required to join the association before they are allowed to practice their trade; third, the association will recommend a price for haircuts that no barber shall undercut.

The barbers intend to raise the price of haircuts in order to raise their incomes. You are called in as a consulting economist to advise them of the probable success of their plan. Suppose you are persuaded that the organization does have the requisite strength to enforce a price rise to, say, $25. What are your predictions about the consequences?

You now need to distinguish between the short-run and the long-run effects of an increase in the price of haircuts. In the short run the number of barbers is fixed. Thus in the short run the answer depends only on the elasticity of the demand for haircuts.

If the demand elasticity is less than 1, total expenditure on haircuts will rise and so will the incomes of barbers; if demand elasticity exceeds 1, the barbers' revenues will fall. Thus you need some empirical knowledge about the elasticity of demand for haircuts.

Suppose that on the basis of the best available evidence you estimate the elasticity of demand over the relevant price range to be 0.45. You then predict that barbers will be successful in raising income in the short run. A 25 percent rise in price will be met by an 11.25 percent fall in business, so the total revenue of the typical barber will rise by about 11 percent.*

* Let p and q be the price and quantity before the price increase. Total revenue after the increase is then given by $TR = (1.25p)(0.8875q) = 1.108375pq$.

Now what about the long run? If barbers were just covering costs before the price change, they will now be earning profits. Barbering will become an attractive trade relative to others requiring equal skill and training, and there will be a flow of barbers into the industry. As the number of barbers rises, the same amount of business must be shared among more and more barbers, so the typical barber will find business—and thus profits—decreasing. Profits may also be squeezed from another direction. With fewer customers coming their way, barbers may compete for the limited number of customers. The association does not allow them to compete through price cuts, but they can compete in service. They may spruce up their shops, offer their customers expensive magazines to read, and so forth. This kind of competition will raise operating costs.

Such changes will continue until barbers are just covering their opportunity costs, at which time the attraction for new entrants will vanish. The industry will settle down in a new long-run equilibrium in which individual barbers make incomes only as large as they did before the price rise. There will be more barbers than there were in the original situation, but each barber will be working for a smaller fraction of the day and will be idle for a larger fraction (the industry will have excess capacity). Barbers may prefer this situation; they will have more leisure. Customers may or may not prefer it: They will have shorter waits even at peak periods, and they will get to read a wide choice of magazines, but they will pay more for haircuts.

You were hired, however, to report to the barbers with respect to the effect on their incomes, not the effect on their leisure. The report that you finally present will thus say, "You will succeed in the short run (because you face a demand curve that is inelastic), but your plan is bound to be self-defeating in the long run unless you are able to prevent the entry of new barbers."

Why Price Discrimination Is Profitable

Why should a firm want to sell some units of its output at a price that is well below the price that it receives for other units of its output? The simple answer is because it is profitable to do so. Why should it be profitable?

Persistent price discrimination is profitable either because different buyers are willing to pay different amounts for the same commodity or because one buyer is willing to pay different amounts for different units of the same commodity. The basic point about price discrimination is that in either of these circumstances sellers may be able to capture some of the consumers' surplus that would otherwise go to buyers. (Review the discussion of consumers' surplus on pages 138–141.)

Discrimination among units of output. Look back to Table 7-2 on page 139, which showed the consumers' surplus received by one consumer when she bought eight glasses of milk at a single price. If the firm could sell her each glass separately, it could capture this consumers' surplus. It would sell the first unit for \$3.00, the second unit for \$1.50, the third unit for \$1.00, and so on until the eighth unit was sold for 30 cents. The firm would get total revenues of \$8.10 rather than the \$2.40 obtained from selling eight units at the single price of 30 cents each. In this example the firm is able to discriminate perfectly and to extract the entire consumers' surplus.

Perfect price discrimination occurs when the entire consumers' surplus is obtained by the firm. This usually requires that each unit be sold at a separate price. In practice, perfect discrimination is seldom possible. Suppose, however, that the firm could charge two different prices, one for the first four units sold and one for the next four units sold. If it sold the first four units for 80 cents and the next four units for 30 cents, it would receive \$4.40—less than it would receive if it could discriminate perfectly but more than it would receive if it sold all units at any single price.

Discrimination among buyers. Think of the demand curve in a market that is made up of individual buyers, each of whom has indicated the maximum price that he or she is prepared to pay for a single unit. Suppose, for the sake of simplicity, that there are only four buyers, the first of whom is prepared to pay any price up to \$4, the second of whom is prepared to pay \$3, the third, \$2, and the fourth, \$1. Suppose that the product has a marginal cost of production of \$1 per unit for all units. If the seller is limited to a single price, it will maximize its profits by charging \$3, sell two units, and earn profits of \$4. If the seller can discriminate among units, it could charge the first buyer \$4 and the second \$3, thus increasing its profits from the first two units to \$5. Moreover, it could also sell the third unit for \$2, thus increasing its profits to \$6. It would be indifferent about selling a fourth unit because the price would just cover marginal cost.

Price discrimination more generally. Demand curves have a negative slope because different units are valued differently, either by one individual or by different individuals. This fact, combined with a single price for a product, gives rise to consumers' surplus.

The ability to charge multiple prices gives a seller the opportunity to capture some (or, in the extreme case, all) of the consumers' surplus.

In general, the larger the number of different prices that can be charged, the greater the firm's ability to increase its revenue at the expense of consumers. This is illustrated in Figure 13-6.

It follows that if a seller is able to discriminate through price, it can increase revenues received (and thus also profits) from the sale of any given quantity. **[26]** However, price discrimination is not always possible, even if there are no legal barriers to its use.

When Is Price Discrimination Possible?

Discrimination among units of output sold to the same buyer requires that the seller be able to keep track of the units that a buyer consumes in each period. Thus the tenth unit purchased by a given buyer in a given month can be sold at a price that is different from the fifth unit *only* if the seller can keep track of who buys what. This can be done by an electric company through its meter readings or by a magazine publisher by distinguishing between renewals and new subscriptions. It can also be done by a firm's distributing of certificates or coupons that allow, for example, a car wash at a reduced price on a return visit.

Discrimination among buyers is possible only if

FIGURE 13-6 Price Discrimination

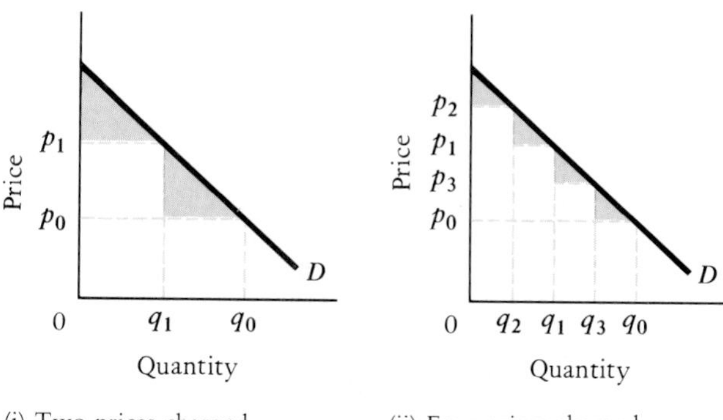

(i) Two prices charged

(ii) Four prices charged

Multiple prices permit a seller to capture consumers' surplus. Suppose in either graph that if a single price were charged, it would be the price p_0. Quantity q_0 would be sold, and consumers' surplus would be the entire area above p_0 and below the demand curve. In part (i) two prices are charged: p_1 for the first q_1 units and p_0 for the remaining q_1q_0 units. Consumers' surplus is reduced to the two shaded areas, and the seller's revenue is increased accordingly. In part (ii) four prices are charged: p_2 for the first q_2 units, p_1 for the units between q_2 and q_1, and so on. Consumers' surplus is further reduced to the shaded areas, and the seller's revenue is increased accordingly. At the extreme, if a different price could be charged for each unit, producers could extract every bit of the consumers' surplus, and the price discrimination would be perfect.

the buyers who face the low price cannot resell the goods to the buyers who face the high price. However, even though the local butcher might like to charge the banker twice as much for buying his steak as he charges the taxi driver, he cannot succeed in doing so. The banker can always shop for meat in the supermarket, where her occupation is not known. Even if the butcher and the supermarket agreed to charge her twice as much, she could hire the taxi driver to shop for her. The surgeon, however, may succeed in discriminating (especially if other reputable surgeons do the same) because it will not do the banker much good to hire the taxi driver to have her operation for her.

Price discrimination is possible if the seller can either distinguish individual units bought by a single buyer or separate buyers into classes such that resale among classes is impossible.

The ability to prevent resale tends to be associated with the character of the product or the ability to classify buyers into readily identifiable groups. Services are less easily resold than goods; goods that require installation by the manufacturer (e.g., heavy equipment) are less easily resold than movable goods such as household appliances. An interesting example of nonresalability occurs in the case of plate glass. Small pieces of plate glass are much cheaper to buy per square foot than bigger pieces, but the person who needs glass for a picture window that is 6 by 10 feet cannot use four pieces of glass that are 3 by 5 feet. Transportation costs, tariff barriers, and import quotas separate classes of buyers geographically and may make discrimination possible.

Of course, it is not enough to be able to separate buyers or units into separate classes. The seller must also be able to control the supply to each group. This is what makes price discrimination an aspect of the theory of monopoly.

Consequences of Price Discrimination

The consequences of price discrimination are summarized in the following two propositions.

Proposition 1: **For any given level of output, the most profitable system of discriminatory prices will provide higher total revenue to the firm than the profit-maximizing single price.**

This proposition was illustrated in Figure 13-6. All that it requires is a negatively sloped demand curve. To see that the proposition is reasonable, remember that a monopolist with the power to discriminate *could* produce exactly the same quantity as a single-price monopolist and charge everyone the same price. Therefore, it need never receive *less* revenue, and it can do better if it can raise the price on even one unit sold.

***Proposition 2:* Output under price discrimination will generally be larger than under a single-price monopoly.**

Remember that a monopoly firm that must charge a single price for a product will produce less than would all the firms in a perfectly competitive industry because producing and selling more of the product would drive down the price against itself. Price discrimination allows it to avoid this disincentive. To the extent that the firm can sell its output in separate blocks, it can sell another block without spoiling the market for the block that is already being sold. In the case of *perfect price discrimination,* in which every unit of output is sold at a different price, the profit-maximizing monopolist will produce every unit for which the price charged is greater than or equal to its marginal cost. It will therefore produce the same quantity of output as the firm in perfect competition does.

Normative Aspects of Price Discrimination

The predicted combination of higher average revenue and higher output does not in itself have any *normative* significance. It will typically lead to a different distribution of income and a different level of output than when the seller is limited to a single price. The ability of the discriminating monopolist to capture some of the consumers' surplus will seem undesirable to consumers but not to the monopolist. How outsiders view the transfer may depend on who gains and who loses. For instance, when railroads discriminated against small farmers, the results aroused public anger. However, when doctors in private practice discriminate by giving low-priced service to poor patients, it is taken to be necessary since lower-income people would not be able to afford medical care if doctors charged all their patients the same fees. Not everyone will judge it to be bad for airlines to discriminate by giving senior citizens and vacationers lower fares than business travelers. Further examples are explored in Box 13-3.

There are two quite separate issues involved in evaluating any particular example of price discrimination. One concerns the effect of discrimination on the level of output, and the other concerns the effect of discrimination on the distribution of income. Discrimination usually results in a higher output than would occur if a single price were charged. Often, however, it is the effect of discrimination on income distribution that accounts for people's strong emotional reactions to it. By increasing the monopoly's profits, price discrimination transfers income from buyers to sellers. When buyers are poor and sellers are rich, this may seem undesirable. However, as in the case of doctors' fees and senior citizens' discounts, discrimination sometimes allows lower-income people to buy a product that they would be unable to afford if it were sold at the single price that maximized the producers' profits.

Systematic and Unsystematic Price Discrimination

So far the discussion has been concerned with persistent, systematic price discrimination. Systematic price discrimination most often consists of classifying buyers according to age, location, industry, income, or the use they intend to make of the product and then charging different prices to the different "classes" of buyers. It may also take other forms, such as charging more for the first unit bought than for subsequent units.

Another sort of price discrimination is common. Any firm that occasionally gives a favorite customer a discount or reduces its price to land a new account is also engaged in price discrimination. If these practices are used irregularly, they are called *unsystematic* discrimination. Such discrimination is not really part of the equilibrium structure of prices, but it does play a major role both in the dynamic process by which prices change in response to changing market conditions and in rivalrous behavior among competing firms. For example, a tacit agreement among a number of producers to refrain from competing with each other may begin to break down when firms offer discriminatory price reductions to favored customers. If this signals the outbreak of competition among firms that were previously behaving as if they were a monopoly, it may be in the public interest to allow such discriminatory behavior.

BOX 13-3

Is Price Discrimination Bad?

The consequences of price discrimination differ from case to case. No matter what an individual's values are, he or she is almost bound to evaluate individual cases differently from one another.

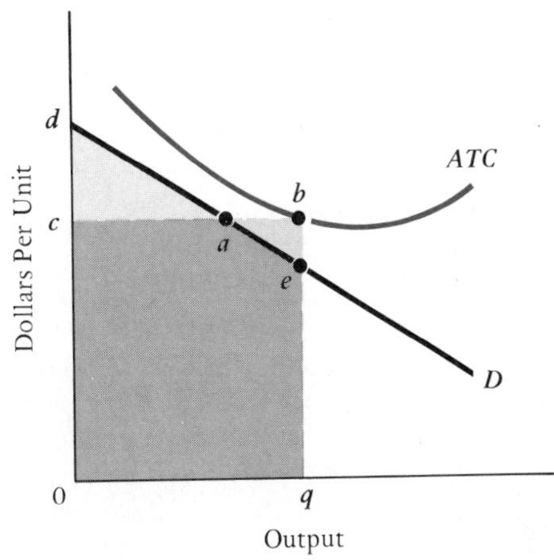

Secret rebates. A large oil-refining firm agrees to ship its product to market on a given railroad, provided that the railroad gives the firm a secret rebate on the transportation cost and does not give a similar concession to rival refiners. The railroad agrees and is thereby charging discriminatory prices. This rebate gives the oil company a cost advantage that it uses to drive its rivals out of business or to force them into a merger on dictated terms. (John D. Rockefeller was accused of using such tactics in the early years of the Standard Oil Company.)

Use of product. When the Aluminum Company of America (ALCOA) had a virtual monopoly on the production of aluminum ingots, it sold both the raw ingots and the aluminum cable that was made from the ingots. At one time ALCOA sold aluminum cable at a price that was 20 percent *below* its price for ingots. (Of course, the cable price was above ALCOA's variable cost of producing the cable.) It did so because users of cable could substitute copper cable, but many users of ingots had no substitute for aluminum. In return for its "bargain price" for cable, ALCOA made the purchasers of cable agree to use it only for transmission purposes. (Without such an agreement, any demander of aluminum might have bought cable and then melted it down.)

Covering costs. A product that many people want to purchase has a demand and a cost structure such that there is no single price at which a producing firm can cover total costs. However, if the firm is allowed to charge discriminatory prices, it will be willing to produce the product and it may make a profit. This is illustrated in the figure.

Because the average total cost (*ATC*) curve is everywhere higher than the demand curve (*D*), no single price would lead to revenues equal to costs. A price-discriminating monopolist may be able to cover total costs. The total cost of output *q* is the area *0cbq*. The maximum revenue attainable at any output by perfect discrimination is the area under the demand curve. For output *q* this area, shown as the dark and light gray shaded areas, exceeds total cost, since the light gray shaded triangle *cda* is greater than the color-shaded triangle *abe*.

Equitable fares. For many years British railways were not allowed to discriminate among passengers in different regions. To prevent discrimination, a fixed fare per passenger mile was specified and charged on all lines, whatever their passenger traffic and whatever the elasticity of demand for the services of the particular line. In the interests of economy, branch lines that could not cover costs were closed. Some lines stopped operating, even though their users preferred rail transport to any alternatives and the strength of their preference was such that they would have willingly paid a price that would have been sufficient for the line to yield a profit. However, the lines were closed because it was thought to be inequitable to discriminate against the passengers on these lines.

The causes and consequences of systematic price discrimination are very different from those of unsystematic price discrimination.

The legal system is generally unable to distinguish between systematic and unsystematic price discrimination and so hits at both. Legislation, motivated solely by a desire to attack systematic discrimination, may have unforeseen and possibly undesired effects on unsystematic discrimination. Because unsystematic price discrimination is important for market adjustment and the process of competition, prohibiting it may slow market adjustments and help to maintain the power of the monopoly.

SUMMARY

1. Monopoly is a market structure in which an entire industry is supplied by a single firm. The monopoly firm's own demand curve is identical with the market demand curve for the product. The market demand curve is the monopoly firm's average revenue curve, and its marginal revenue curve always lies below its demand curve.
2. When a single-price monopoly is maximizing its profits, marginal revenue is positive and thus elasticity of demand is greater than unity. The amount of profits that a monopoly earns may be large, small, zero, or negative in the short run, depending on the relationship between demand and cost. For monopoly profits to persist in the long run, there must be effective barriers to the entry of other firms. Entry barriers can be natural or created.
3. Monopoly power is limited by the presence of substitute products, the development of new products, and the entry of new firms. In the very long run it is difficult to maintain entry barriers in the face of the process of creative destruction—the invention of new processes and new products to attack the entrenched position of an existing monopolist.
4. A group of firms may form a cartel by agreeing to restrict their joint output to the monopoly level. Cartels tend to be unstable because of the strong incentives for each individual firm to cheat by producing more than its quota allows.
5. A price-discriminating monopolist can capture some of the consumers' surplus that exists when all of the units of a product are sold at a single price. Successful price discrimination requires that the firm be able to control the supply of the product offered to particular buyers and to prevent the resale of the product.
6. For any given level of output, the best system of discriminatory prices will provide larger profits and higher output than occur under a single-price monopoly.

TOPICS FOR REVIEW

Relationship between price and marginal revenue for a monopolist
Relationships among marginal revenue, total revenue, and elasticity for a monopolist
Potential monopoly profits in perfectly competitive equilibrium
Natural and created entry barriers
Cartels as monopolies
The instability of cartels
Systematic and unsystematic price discrimination
Causes and consequences of price discrimination

DISCUSSION QUESTIONS

1. Suppose that only one professor teaches economics at your university. Would you say that this professor is a monopolist who can exact any "price" from her students in the form of readings assigned, tests given, and material covered? Suppose now that two additional professors have been hired. Has the original professor's monopoly power been decreased?
2. Imagine a monopoly firm that has fixed costs but no variable or marginal costs, for example, a firm that owns a spring of water that can produce indefinitely once certain pipes are installed in an area where no other source of water is available. What would be the firm's profit-maximizing price? What elasticity of demand would you expect at that price? Would this seem to be an appropriate pricing policy if the water monopoly were municipally owned?
3. Which of these industries—licorice candy, copper wire, outboard motors, coal, or the local newspaper—would you most like to monopolize? Why? Does your answer depend on several factors or on just one or two? Which would you as a consumer least like to have monopolized by someone else? If your answers to the two questions are different, explain why.
4. A movie exhibitor, Aristotle Murphy, owns movie theaters in two towns of roughly the same size, 50 miles apart. In Monopolia he owns the only chain of theaters; in Competitia there is no theater chain, and he is but one of a number of independent operators. Would you expect movie prices to be higher in Monopolia than in Competitia in the short run? In the long run? If differences occur in his prices, would Murphy be discriminating in price?
5. Liquor retailing is a government monopoly in most Canadian provinces but a competitive industry in most American states. What differences would you expect to find in the industry in the two countries?
6. Airline rates to Europe are higher in summer than in winter. Some railroads charge lower fares during the week than on weekends. Electric companies charge consumers lower rates, the more electricity they use. Are these all examples of price discrimination? What additional information would you like to have before answering this question?
7. Discuss whether each of the following represents price discrimination. In your view, which are the most socially harmful?
   a. Weekend airline fares that are less than full fare
   b. Cheap fares available only to bona fide students under 22 years of age
   c. First-class fares that are 50 percent greater than tourist fares, recognizing that two first-class seats use the space of three tourist seats
   d. Discounts negotiated from list price, for which sales personnel are authorized to bargain and to get as much in each transaction as the traffic will bear
   e. Higher tuition for out-of-state students at state-supported colleges and universities
   f. Higher tuition for law students than for history students

Chapter 14

Patterns of Imperfect Competition

The two market structures that we have studied so far are important "polar" cases. They define the extremes of market power over an industry, just as the North and the South Poles define the limits of "traveling north" and "traveling south." Under perfect competition, firms are price takers; price is driven to the level of marginal cost; and profits are zero, which means that firms are just covering the opportunity cost of their capital. The monopoly firm is a price setter; it sets price above marginal cost; and it may earn more than the opportunity cost of its capital. Although they provide important insights, these two polar market structures are insufficient for an understanding of the behavior of all firms. For example, in the many industries that contain enough firms to be perfectly competitive, each firm sells its own distinctive set of products. As a result, each firm has some control over the price that it charges, unlike a perfect competitor. This is true in many branches of retailing and in some branches of manufacturing, such as clothing and fabrics. It is also true that most industries in which a few large firms have market power contain more than one firm. These firms compete vigorously, so they cannot be monopolies. Most of the major manufacturing industries, such as automobiles, aircraft, and household appliances, fall into this category.

Before we study other theoretical market structures, we need to look in a bit more detail at the structure of the Canadian economy.[1]

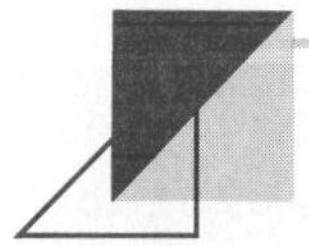

The Structure of the Canadian Economy

Canada is a large, resource-rich country with a small population. In area, it is the second largest in the world; in population, it is one of the smallest of the developed industrial nations. Much of Canadian industry is devoted directly to exploiting its rich resources, among them lumber, minerals, and power, and to producing products that depend on these resources, such as plywood, steel, and aluminum (an enormous user of power).

Because of the Canadian market's small size, many Canadian firms cannot grow to efficient size unless they can export a substantial part of their production. In the past, many inefficient

[1] This section relies heavily on the excellent discussion of these topics in Christopher Green's *Canadian Industrial Organization and Policy* (Toronto: McGraw-Hill/Ryerson, 1990).

small firms have survived only because of tariffs on imported goods. For this reason, Canadian industry has always had three main market sectors. The exporting sector is efficient enough to compete in foreign markets and thus achieve the scale of output needed to reap available economies of scale. The import-competing sector produces mainly for the local market, sometimes behind tariff protection and always in competition with foreign producers. The nontraded sector serves a local market that is protected from foreign competition by natural barriers of transport costs and perishability. (In this context, *traded* and *nontraded* refer to *foreign* trade.)

Over the whole of the twentieth century, reductions in transport costs, plus technological developments to reduce perishability, have steadily shrunk the nontraded goods sector until today there are few goods (and a shrinking number of services) that are not open to potential competition from imports.

Over the last half of the twentieth century, Canadian tariffs have been steadily reduced. As a result, industries that could not survive foreign competition have shrunk in size, while those that could compete have grown. Canadian industry is now able to compete in world markets in a wide range of goods. This expansion of sales through exports has caused falling costs, rising per capita outputs, and rising real wages for the typical employee.

The nontraded sector has often been characterized by large numbers of small competing firms. The industries in the (now shrinking) protected part of the economy have usually each been restricted to a few large, often foreign-owned firms that came to Canada to serve the tariff-protected home market. Many of the exporting industries contain only a few large firms, but these are often in active competition with firms in other countries. These large firms are often the major firms in older industries, usually producing established products but sometimes developing new ones. In other cases, exporters are small or medium-size firms.

Box 14-1 elaborates further on the globalization of both production and competition that has affected all trading nations in the last two decades.

Turnover of Firms

One characteristic of market economies is constant change. As a result, new firms are continually coming into existence to produce new products. Typically, an entrepreneur will have a bright idea for a new product and raise money to finance the necessary research and development (R&D). This will be a "start-up" firm. *If* the entrepreneur succeeds (most fail), the firm will grow. Hence at any one time in the manufacturing sector, small and middle-size firms coexist with large ones. Some of them are new and growing, while some of them are stable, having reached the size that can be supported by the market for the products that they produce.

Turnover of firms is high in market economies. Even in stable industries—at least those that have many firms—existing firms grow, prosper, and decay only to be replaced by other, younger, more dynamic firms. The great English economist and observer of industry, Alfred Marshall, likened this process to the life cycle of *trees* (firms) through birth, growth, and decay while the *forest* (the industry) remained stable in size. In growing industries, however, the process of firm turnover will result in a net addition to the size of the industry and possibly also to the number of firms. In declining industries, the reverse holds true. The important point to notice is the continual turnover of firms and jobs. In the Canadian economy, as in all market economies, firms are constantly being born and constantly dying. This means that jobs are constantly being created and constantly being destroyed.[2]

Industrial Concentration

An industry that is highly concentrated contains few firms, whereas an industry that has a low degree of concentration contains many firms. You will recall that monopoly and perfect competition lie at the two extremes of concentration. A monopoly is an industry with only one firm, and perfect competition is an industry with so many firms that no one of them has any influence on market price. Most industries lie between these two extremes of concentration.

[2] This large turnover of firms and jobs makes it difficult to discern the effects of any change in government policy on the numbers of firms and jobs. The net effect cannot be determined merely by observing the number of firms and jobs that go out of existence over any period of time since the policy was put in place. Many of these firms and jobs would have gone out of existence anyway, and many of the new firms and jobs that come into existence would have done so anyway. What is needed, but is hard to do, is to discern the *net change* in both firm and job destruction and firm and job creation resulting from the policy change being studied.

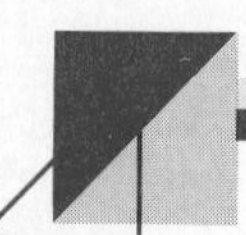

BOX 14-1

Globalization of Production and Competition

A mere 100 years ago, people and news traveled by sailing ship, so that it took months to communicate across various parts of the world. Advances in the first 60 years of the twentieth century sped up both communications and travel, and people came to take them for granted. In the past two decades, the pace of change in communication technology has accelerated. The world has witnessed a communication revolution that has dramatically changed the way business decisions are made and implemented.

Three decades ago, telephone links were laboriously and unreliably connected by operators, satellites were newfangled and not especially useful toys for rocket scientists, photocopying and telecopying were completely unknown, mail service to overseas destinations took weeks, computers were in their infancy, and jets were just beginning to replace the much slower and less reliable propeller aircraft. Today direct dialing is available to most parts of the world, at a fraction of what long distance calls cost 30 years ago, while faxes, satellite links, fast jet travel, computer networks, cheap courier services, and a host of other developments have made communication that is reliable, and often instantaneous, available throughout the world.

The communication revolution has been a major contributor to the development of what has become known as the "global village," a term first used by Canadian author Marshall McLuhan in his writing about the social implications of changes in communication technology.

Three important characteristics of the global village are a *disintegration* of production, an increase in competition, and a decline in the power of the nation-state.

Production

The communication revolution has allowed many large international companies, known as transnational corporations (TNCs), to decentralize their production process. They are now able to locate their research and development (R&D) where the best scientists are available. They can produce various components in dozens of places, locating each activity in a country where costs are cheapest for that type of production. They can then ship all the parts, as they are needed, to an assembly factory where the product is "made."

The globalization of production has brought employment, and rising real wages, to people in many less developed countries. At the same time, it has put less skilled labor in the developed countries under strong competitive pressures.

Competition

The communications revolution has also caused an internationalization of competition in almost all in-

Concentration Ratios

When measuring whether an industry has power concentrated in the hands of only a few firms or dispersed over many, it is not sufficient to count the number of firms. For example, an industry with one enormous firm and 29 minute ones is more concentrated in any meaningful sense than an industry with only five firms, all of which are of equal power. To get around the problem that number of firms is not a good criterion, economists calculate what is called a **concentration ratio**, which shows the fraction of total market sales controlled by the largest group of sellers. Common types of concentration ratios cite the share of total market sales made by the largest four or eight firms.

A problem in using concentration ratios is to define the market with reasonable accuracy. On the one hand, the market may be much smaller than the whole country. For example, concentration ratios in national cement sales are low, but they understate the market power of cement companies because high transportation costs divide the cement *industry* into a

dustries. National markets are no longer protected for local producers by high costs of transportation and communication or by the ignorance of foreign firms. Walk into a local supermarket or department store today, and you will have no trouble finding products representing most of the United Nations.

Consumers gain by being able to choose from an enormous range of well-made, low-priced goods and services. Firms that are successful gain worldwide sales. Firms that fall behind even momentarily may, however, be wiped out by competition coming from many quarters. Global competition is fierce competition, and firms need to be fast on the uptake—either of other people's ideas or of new ones of their own—if they are to survive.

A few short decades ago, many Canadian industries contained a few large firms that had little to worry about if they could restrain their urges to compete with each other. Today there are few such industries. If Canadian producers slack off, they are likely to lose market shares to a host of foreign imports.

Economic Policy

The international character of TNCs means that national economic policies have been seriously constrained. Much international trade takes place between segments of single TNCs. This gives them the chance, through their accounting practices, to localize their profits in countries where corporate taxes are lowest and their costs in countries where cost write-offs are highest.

The disintegration of production also allows TNCs to shift production around the world. So tough national policies that reduce profitability may be self-defeating as firms move production elsewhere. Generous policies that seek to attract production may only succeed in attracting small and specialized parts of it. For example, Sweden has given generous tax treatment to R&D expenditures, seeking to attract firms to do their high-tech, high-wage production in that country. Instead, however, many firms have come to Sweden to do their R&D and then have transferred the knowledge to countries where production costs are lower. The net result is that Swedish taxpayers are subsidizing world consumers by paying for R&D that is generating production in other countries.

The examples given here illustrate an important development: globalization of production, and consequently of competition, means a great reduction in the scope for relatively small countries, such as Canada, to implement distinctive economic policies.

series of regional *markets,* in each of which there are relatively few firms. On the other hand, the market may be larger than one country. This is a particularly important consideration in a small trading country such as Canada. For example, a single Canadian firm in one industry does not have a monopoly if it is in competition with five U.S. firms that can easily sell in the Canadian market. When appropriately used, however, concentration ratios tell us how much production for a given market is concentrated in the hands of a few firms.

Concentration in Canada

According to McGill University professor Christopher Green, the concentration ratios that are typical of various sections of the Canadian economy differ greatly from one another. In agriculture, concentration ratios are very low. The market structure is close to perfect competition, except where government supply management has created cartels. In forestry, four firms account for 20 percent of the total sales, but the remainder is accounted for by numerous small firms. Most of these firms, large and small, sell in highly competitive international markets. In manufacturing, the degree of concentration ranges from very high to very low. In approximately half of all Canadian manufacturing industries, the top four firms control over 50 percent of the sales. In transportation, communications, and energy utilities, the degree of concentration is even higher. There are two firms in rail transportation and two main firms (with some fringe competitors) in air transport and in television networks. There is either monopoly, or publicly owned firms, in telecommunication, electric energy, and water and natural gas pipelines. Various parts of the wholesale trade have low to medium degrees of concentration, while in the retail trades, the ratios range from low to high. In community, business, and personal services, concentration tends to be quite low (except in small towns, where there are many natural monopolies). Finally, in insurance and real estate, concentration is quite low, while in the financial industries concentration is often high.

This is quite a varied story, and we can gain further insight into this experience of concentration by examining the manufacturing sector in greater detail.

Concentration in Canadian Manufacturing

Table 14-1 shows the four-firm concentration ratios in selected Canadian manufacturing industries. The table makes it clear that few, if any, of these industries come close to either perfect competition or monopoly. There are no industries with a concentration ratio of 100 percent for four firms, let alone for one. At the other extreme, there are quite a few industries with low concentration ratios. The perfectly competitive model could conceivably fit some of these industries.

Even here, however, there are doubts. Manufacturers of women's clothing have some control over price, contrary to the conditions of perfect competition, because of style and fashion. Metal stamping

TABLE 14-1 Four-Firm Concentration Ratios for Selected Canadian Manufacturing Industries

Industries	Number of firms in 1982	Percentage of shipments accounted for by the leading four firms		
		1985	1980	1965
Petroleum refining	16	64.0	61.7	84.8
Pulp and paper mills	57	—	30.9	36.9
Motor vehicle manufacturers	14	95.1	93.7	93.3
Slaughtering and meat processors	426	35.9	43.3	61.8
Iron and steel mills	37	—	77.9	78.8
Sawmills and planing mills	1,081	17.4	19.2	16.8
Motor vehicle parts and accessories	286	—	44.6	54.2
Manufacturers of industrial chemical and organic products	30	65.1	64.2	—
Communications equipment manufacturers	400	—	52.4	—
Aircraft and aircraft parts manufacturers	143	—	75.0	76.8
Feed industry	450	23.1	25.7	28.8
Electric industrial equipment manufacturers	195	—	46.8	64.3
Men's clothing factories	412	—	20.6	11.1
Fish products industry	277	47.1	44.7	35.6
Agricultural implement industry	187	—	61.9	71.6
Women's clothing factories	517	—	6.4	6.4
Fruit and vegetable canners and preservers	134	40.7	39.0	—
Breweries	8	97.7	99.0	94.5
Household furniture manufacturers	885	—	17.6	—
Manufacturers of pharmaceuticals and medicines	114	27.2	27.1	26.1

Source: Christopher Green, *Canadian Industrial Organization and Policy* (Toronto: McGraw-Hill/Ryerson, 1990), p. 80.

firms, print shops, and soft drink bottlers, though numerous nationally, operate in small regional and local markets in which a small number of sellers, in direct rivalry, do not regard themselves as price takers.

Although similarities in standard of living, consumption patterns, and education in Canada and the United States have led to many similarities in industrial structure, the Canadian manufacturing sector is substantially more concentrated than the American. This is partly because the small size of the Canadian economy leaves room for fewer firms operating at minimum efficient scale than the larger American economy does. But the Canadian economy is a very open economy, and for many industries the relevant market is the combined Canadian-American market.

Three economists, John Baldwin of Queen's University, Paul Gorecki of the Economic Council of Canada, and John McVey of Statistics Canada, have taken up this point, arguing that Canadian concentration ratios significantly overstate the amount of effective concentration in Canadian manufacturing industries. They suggest a number of corrections to the published data. First, the published data assign all of the output of each plant to the industry to which the largest proportion of its output belongs. They separate output streams from multiple output plants and assign each to its appropriate industry. Second, no account is taken of imports in the published concentration ratios. The three economists correct for this fault by adding to each firm's output any imports that it brings in for sale in Canada and by adding to the size of the Canadian market any sales made by firms that only import. Thus the market size is estimated on the basis of what is sold, whether or not it is produced in Canada, and the importance of one firm in that market is estimated on the basis of what it sells in that market no matter where these goods were produced.

Table 14-2 gives the results based on the published four-firm concentration ratios for Canada and the corrected figures derived by the three economists. It shows that when the corrections are made, the number of Canadian industries that have low concentration ratios rises and the number that have high ratios falls.

The table shows that even with the corrected data, in about 70 percent of Canadian manufacturing industries, the four largest firms control over 25 percent of the value of sales. Such industries are not monopolies because there are several firms in the industry, and these firms engage in rivalrous behavior. Residents even of small towns will find more than one drugstore, garage, barber, and dress shop competing for their patronage. Similarly, manufacturers of computers, television sets, and chemicals belong to industries in which there are several close domestic rivals (and often foreign competitors). But neither are these firms in perfectly competitive markets. Often there are only a few major rival firms in an industry, but even when there are many, *they are not price takers.* Virtually all consumer goods are differentiated products, and any one firm will typically have several lines of a product that differ more or less from one another and from competing lines produced by other firms. To explain and predict behavior in these markets, we need theories of market structures other than the two polar cases studied so far.

TABLE 14-2 Distribution of Concentration Ratios for 140 Canadian Manufacturing Industries

Concentration ratio categories	Industry count	
	Unadjusted ratio	Adjusted ratio
0–24.9	17	41
25–49.9	50	58
50–74.9	45	34
75–100	28	7
All industries	140	140

Source: John Baldwin, Paul Gorecki, and John McVey, Economic Council of Canada, manuscript.

The standard concentration ratios overstate the degree of concentration in Canadian industries. The first column shows the four-firm concentration ratio. For example 0–24.9 indicates a low degree of concentration since the four largest firms account for less than 25 percent of the sales, whereas 75–100 indicates a high level of concentration with the four largest firms accounting for more than 75 percent of all sales. The second column gives the number of industries in each concentration ratio class according to the standard figures. The last column gives the distribution of the same industries when corrections are made for plants with multi-industry outputs and for the importance of imports in the Canadian market. When the corrected figures are substituted for the usual ones, the fall in measured concentrations of the typical Canadian industry is striking.

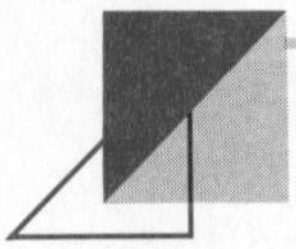

Imperfectly Competitive Market Structures

Neither the theory of perfect competition nor of monopoly can explain the behavior of firms that compete actively. (Recall the discussion in Chapter 12.) Intermediate market structures that are designed to help us understand such behavior are called *imperfectly competitive*. The word *competitive* emphasizes that we are not dealing with monopoly, and the word *imperfect* emphasizes that we are not dealing with perfect competition (in which firms are price takers and do not need to compete actively).

Before studying specific market structures that are imperfectly competitive, we note certain patterns of behavior that are more or less common patterns to all such industries.

Firms Select Their Products

If a new farmer enters the wheat industry, the full range of products that can be produced is already in existence. If a new firm enters the cigarette industry, that firm must decide on the characteristics of the new cigarettes that it is to produce. It will not produce cigarettes that are identical to those already in production. Rather, it will develop, possibly at substantial cost, one or more new cigarettes, each of which will have its own distinctive characteristics. As a result, firms in the cigarette industry sell an array of differentiated products, no two of which are identical.

Differentiated product refers to a group of commodities that are similar enough to be called the same product but dissimilar enough that they can be sold at different prices. For example, although one brand of soap is similar to all others, soaps differ from each other in their chemical composition, color, smell, softness, brand name, reputation, and a host of other characteristics that matter to customers. So face soap is a distinct product from detergents, and all face soaps taken together are one differentiated product.

Most industries in imperfectly competitive market structures sell differentiated products. In such industries, the firm itself must decide on what characteristics to give the products that it will sell. Having done so, it must then develop such a product and market it.

Firms Administer Their Prices

Because firms in perfect competition sell a homogeneous product, they face a market price that they are quite unable to influence. So they adjust their quantities to this price (firms are price takers and quantity adjusters).

In perfect competition, changes in market conditions are signaled to firms by changes in the market prices that they face.

In all other market structures, firms have negatively sloped demand curves and thus face a tradeoff between the price that they charge and the quantity that they sell. Whenever different firms' products are not perfect substitutes, the firms must decide on a price to quote. If they are unsatisfied with the sales that they achieve at this price, they can change their quote, but quote a price they must. In such circumstances, economists say that firms *administer* their price. An **administered price** is a price set by the conscious decision of an individual firm rather than by impersonal market forces.

No market sets a single price for razor blades or television sets, for example, by equating overall demand with overall supply. Instead, it is in the nature of such products that each producer must state a price at which it is willing to sell each of its own products. (Of course, a certain amount of haggling is possible, particularly at the retail level, but this is usually within well-defined limits that have been set by the price that was initially quoted by the seller.) What is true for razor blades and for television sets is also true for virtually all consumer goods—they are *differentiated products*. Any one firm will typically have several product lines that differ more or less from each other and from the competing product lines of other firms. Each product has a price that must be set by its seller. Of course, the firm has some idea of how much it can sell at each price that it might set. Unexpected market fluctuations will nonetheless take the form of unexpected variations in the quantities that are sold at the administered prices.

In market structures other than perfect competition, firms set their prices and then let demand

determine their sales. Changes in market conditions are signaled to the firm by changes in the quantity that the firm can sell at its current administered price.

The changed conditions may or may not then lead firms to change their prices.

Other Aspects of the Behavior of Firms

Several other important aspects of the observed behavior of firms in imperfect competition are inconsistent with either perfect competition or monopoly.

Unexploited scale economies. Many firms in industries that contain more than one firm appear to be operating on the downward-sloping portion of the long-run average cost curves for many of their products. For example, following the two major rounds of tariff reductions in the 1970s (the Kennedy Round) and the 1980s (the Tokyo Round), many Canadian manufacturing firms that were able to increase their export sales found that their average costs were reduced. Although this is possible under monopoly, firms in perfect competition must, in the long run, be at the minimum point of their long-run average cost curves. (See Figure 12-9 on page 236.)

Prices are sticky in the short term. Many firms do not alter their prices in response to every shift in demand or costs. Their prices change less frequently than prices in perfectly competitive markets.

Nonprice competition. Many firms spend large sums of money on advertising. They do so in an attempt both to shift the demand curves for the industry's products and to attract customers from competing firms. Any kind of advertising is inconsistent with perfect competition; advertising directed at competing firms in the same industry is, by definition, inconsistent with monopoly.

Many firms engage in a variety of other forms of nonprice competition, such as giveaway contests, variation in quality, and varying product guarantees.

Entry prevention. Firms in many industries engage in activities that appear to be designed to hinder the entry of new firms, thereby preventing existing pure profits from being eroded by entry.

The market structures of monopolistic competition and oligopoly, which will be discussed in the rest of this chapter, are designed for industries that are neither in monopoly situations nor in perfect competition.

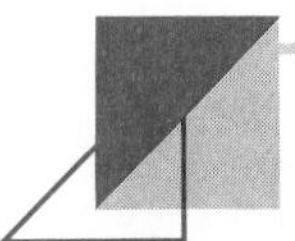

Monopolistic Competition

The theory of **monopolistic competition** was originally developed to deal with the phenomenon of product differentiation.[3] This market structure is similar to perfect competition in that the industry contains many firms and exhibits freedom of entry and exit. It differs, however, in one important respect. Whereas firms in perfect competition sell a *homogeneous product* and are price takers, firms in monopolistic competition sell a differentiated product and have some power over the price of their own product.

Product differentiation leads to, and is enhanced by, the establishment of brand names and advertising, and it gives each firm a degree of monopoly power over its own product. Each firm can raise its price, even if its competitors do not, without losing all its sales. This is the monopolistic part of the theory. Each firm's monopoly power is severely restricted, however, by the presence of similar products that are sold by many competing firms and by easy entry and exit. As a result, each firm's demand curve is much flatter than the industry's demand curve. This is the competition part of the theory.

Assumptions of Monopolistic Competition

The theory of monopolistic competition is based on three key assumptions.

1. *Each firm produces one specific variety, or brand, of the industry's differentiated product.* Each firm thus faces a demand curve that, although it is negatively sloped, is highly elastic, because other va-

[3] This theory was first developed by the American economist Edwin Chamberlin in his pioneering book *The Theory of Monopolistic Competition* (Cambridge, Mass.: Harvard University Press, 1933).

rieties of the same product that are sold by other firms provide many close substitutes.

2. *The industry contains so many firms, each of which is in close competition with many others, that each one ignores the possible reactions of its many competitors when it makes its own price and output decisions.* In this way, firms in monopolistic competition are similar to firms in perfect competition. They make decisions based on their own demand and cost conditions and do not consider interdependence between their own decisions and those of the other firms in the industry. (There are too many firms for it to be possible for any one firm to try to take the other firms' separate reactions into account.)
3. *There is freedom of entry and exit in the industry.* If profits are being earned by existing firms, new firms have an incentive to enter. When they do, the demand for the industry's product must be shared among more brands, and this is assumed to take demand equally from all existing firms. Entry continues until profits fall to zero, just as they do under perfect competition.

Predictions About Behavior

The only thing that makes monopolistic competition different from perfect competition is the differentiated product. However, product differentiation has important consequences for behavior in both the short and the long run.

The Short-Run Equilibrium of the Firm

In the short run, a firm that is operating in a monopolistically competitive market structure is similar to a monopoly. It faces a negatively sloped demand curve and maximizes its profits by equating marginal cost with marginal revenue. If the demand curve cuts the average total cost curve, as is shown in part (i) of Figure 14-1, the firm can make pure profits over and above the opportunity cost of its capital.

The Long-Run Equilibrium of the Industry

The existence of profits, as shown in part (i) of Figure 14-1, provides an incentive for new firms to enter the industry. As they do so, the total demand for the industry's product must be shared among this larger number of firms, so each gets a smaller share of the total market. This shifts the demand curve for each existing firm's product to the left. Entry, and the consequent leftward shifting of the existing firms' demand curves, continues until profits are eliminated. When this has occurred, each firm is in the position shown in part (ii) of Figure 14-1. Its demand curve has shifted to the left until the curve is *tangent* to the average total cost curve. At this output, the firm is just covering all of its costs. At any other output, it would be suffering losses, because average total costs would exceed average revenue.[4]

The excess capacity theorem. Part (i) of Figure 14-1 makes it clear that monopolistic competition results in a long-run equilibrium of zero profits, even though each individual firm faces a negatively sloped demand curve. It does this by forcing each firm into a position in which it has excess capacity; that is, each firm is producing to the left of the lowest point on its average total cost curve. If the firm were to increase its output, it would reduce its cost per unit, but it does not do so, because selling more would reduce revenue by more than it would reduce cost. This result is called the **excess capacity theorem**.

In monopolistic competition, commodities are produced at a point where average total costs are falling, in contrast to perfect competition, where they are produced at their lowest possible cost.

Evaluation of the Theory of Monopolistic Competition

Alleged inefficiency. The excess capacity theorem once aroused passionate debate among economists because it seemed to show that all industries that sell differentiated products would produce them inefficiently at a higher cost than was necessary. Since product differentiation is a characteristic of virtually all modern consumer goods industries, this suggested that modern market economies were systematically inefficient. A few decades ago, many critics of market economies called for state intervention to eliminate unnecessary product differentiation, thus ensuring efficient (i.e., cost-minimizing) levels of production in consumer goods industries.

[4] If the demand curve *nowhere touched* the average total cost curve, there would be no output at which costs could be covered, and exit would occur. If the demand curve were to *cut* the average total cost curve, there would be levels of output at which profits could be earned, and entry would occur. Thus the only possible long-run equilibrium consistent with there being neither entry nor exit is one where the demand curve is tangent to the average total cost curve (i.e., the demand curve just touches the average total cost curve at one output and lies below it at all other outputs).

FIGURE 14-1 Equilibrium of a Firm in Monopolistic Competition

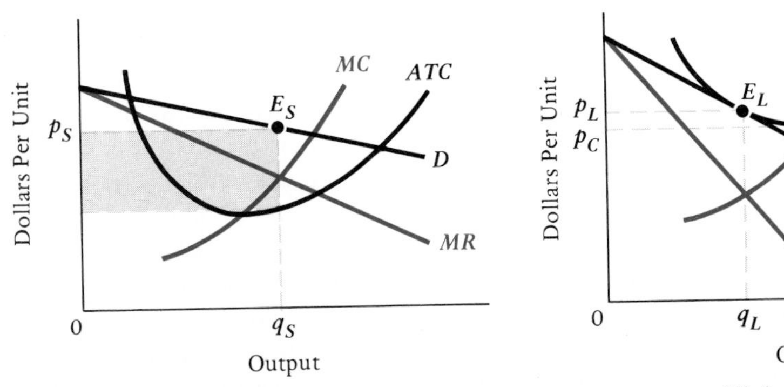

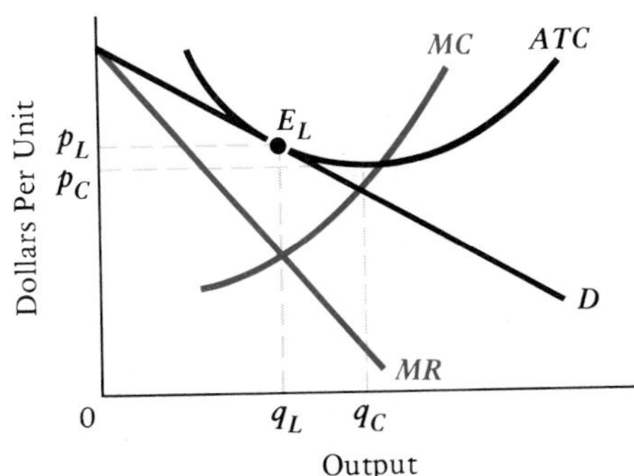

(i) Short-run equilibrium

(ii) Long-run equilibrium

Short-run equilibrium for a monopolistically competitive firm is the same as for a monopolist. In the long run, a monopolistically competitive industry has zero profits and excess capacity. Short-run equilibrium occurs in part (i) at E_S, the output for which $MR = MC$. Price is p_S and quantity is q_S. Profits may exist; in this example they are shown by the shaded area. Starting from the short-run equilibrium shown in part (i), entry of new firms shifts the firm's demand curve to the left and eliminates profits. In part (ii), point E_L, where demand is tangent to ATC, is the long-run equilibrium. Price is p_L and quantity is q_L. Price is greater and quantity is less than the perfectly competitive equilibrium price and quantity (p_C and q_C). At equilibrium, the monopolistically competitive firm has excess capacity of q_Lq_C.

A more modern analysis by economists such as William Baumol, Kelvin Lancaster, and Joseph Stiglitz has shown that the charge of inefficiency has not been proved. The "excess capacity" of monopolistic competition does not necessarily indicate inefficiency (and hence waste of resources) because when firms can choose the characteristics of their own products, minimizing costs of producing a given set of products is not necessarily the most efficient thing to do. Differentiated products provide consumers with a choice among a variety of products, and it is clear that consumers have different tastes with respect to differentiated products. For example, each brand of breakfast food, running shoes, personal computers, and cameras has its devotees.

From society's point of view, there is a tradeoff between producing more brands to satisfy diverse tastes and producing fewer brands at a lower cost per unit.

Monopolistic competition produces a wider range of products but at a somewhat higher cost per unit than perfect competition. It cannot be proved, however, that consumers will necessarily be worse off with ten brands of a differentiated product to choose from than with one standard brand, or vice versa. Since consumers clearly value variety, the extra cost that variety imposes must be matched against the benefits of variety in judging the social efficiency of monopolistic competition in order to find the *optimum amount* of product differentiation. Product differentiation is wasteful only if the costs of providing variety exceed the benefits conferred by providing that variety.

The optimum number of varieties of a differentiated product is attained when the gain to consumers from adding one more variety equals the loss from having to produce each existing variety at a higher cost because less of each is produced.

Empirical relevance. Controversy raged for decades as to the empirical relevance of monopolistic competition. Of course, product differentiation is an almost universal phenomenon in consumer goods and in many other industries. Nonetheless, many economists maintain that this market structure is almost never found in practice.

To see why, we need to distinguish between products and firms. In many manufacturing industries, numerous differentiated products are produced by only a few firms. In breakfast foods, for example, a vast variety of products is produced by three major firms (Kellogg's, Nabisco, and General Foods). Similar circumstances exist in soap, chemicals, cigarettes, consumer electronics, and numerous other industries in which many more or less competing products are produced by a few very large firms. Clearly, these industries are neither perfectly competitive nor monopolies. Are they monopolistically competitive? The answer is no, because they contain only a few firms that often take account of one another's reactions when they are determining their own behavior. Furthermore, they often earn large profits without attracting new entries. In fact, these firms operate under a market structure that is called *oligopoly,* which we shall consider next.

While accepting that many differentiated products are produced by industries that are not monopolistically competitive, some economists find that the theory of monopolistic competition is useful for analyzing industries where concentration ratios are low and the product is differentiated.

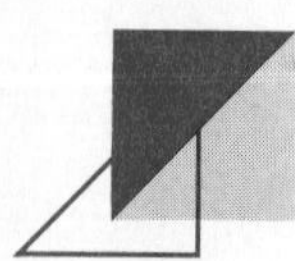

Oligopoly

The data in Tables 14-1 and 14-2 show that many Canadian industries are characterized by a small number of firms, each of which accounts for a significant fraction of each industry's production. These firms—typically, from 3 to 12—tend to dominate such industries, and newcomers find it hard to establish themselves. The market structure that embraces such industries is called *oligopoly,* from the Greek words *oligos polein,* meaning "few to sell." An **oligopoly** is an industry that contains two or more firms, at least one of which produces a significant portion of the industry's total output. Whenever there is a high concentration ratio for the firms that are serving one particular market, that market is oligopolistic.

Characteristics of Oligopoly

An oligopolistic firm faces a downward-sloping demand curve. It is large enough to realize that its competitors may respond to anything that it does. In other words, oligopolists are aware of the interdependence among the decisions made by the various firms in the industry, and they engage in the type of rivalrous behavior discussed on page 225.

Oligopolistic industries are of many types. In some such industries there are only a few firms (three, in the case of cigarettes). In others there are many firms, but only a few dominate the market. For example, there are 16 petroleum refiners, but the 13 smallest firms together account for only about one-third of the aggregate value of output. There are 38 manufacturers of mixed fertilizers, of which the largest 4 account for 70 percent of total sales. Oligopoly is consistent with a large number of small sellers, called a "competitive fringe," as long as a "big few" dominate the industry's production.

In oligopolistic industries, prices are typically administered. Products are usually differentiated. The intensity and the nature of rivalrous behavior vary greatly from industry to industry and from one period of time to another. This variety has invited extensive theoretical speculation and empirical study.

Why Bigness?

Why are so many industries dominated by a few large firms? It turns out that there is more than one answer to this question.

Economies of scale. Much factory production uses the principle of the division of labor that we first studied in Chapter 1. The production of a commodity is broken up into hundreds of simple, repetitive tasks. This type of division of labor was the basis of the assembly line, which revolutionized the production of many goods in the early twentieth century, and it still underlies economies of large-scale production in many industries. Such division of labor is, as Adam Smith observed long ago, dependent on the size of the market (see Box 3-1 on page 44). There is no point in dividing the production of a commodity into a number of tasks, each of which can be done in a few minutes, if only a few units of the product can be sold each day.

Economies of scope. Modern industries produce many differentiated products that give rise to a different type of scale economy. To develop a new product is costly, and it may be only a matter of a few years before it is replaced by some superior version of the same basic product. These fixed costs of product development must be recovered in the revenues from sales of the product. The larger the firm's sales, the less the cost that has to be recovered from each unit sold. Consider a product that costs $1 million to develop and to market. If 1 million units are to be sold, $1 of the selling price of each unit must go toward recovering the development costs. If, however, the firm expects to sell 10 million units, each unit need only contribute 10 cents to these costs, and the market price that will cover the total costs of development and production will be lowered accordingly. With the enormous development costs of some of today's "high-tech" products, firms that can sell a large volume have a distinct pricing advantage over firms that sell a smaller volume.

Other scope economies are related to financing and to marketing. It is costly to enter a market, to establish a sales force, and to make consumers aware of a product. These costs are often nearly as high when a small volume is being marketed as when a large volume is being marketed. Thus the smaller the volume of the firm's sales, the higher the price must be if the firm is to cover all of these costs. Notice that these economies relate to the size of the firm rather than to the amount it produces of any one of its differentiated products or to the size of any one of its plants. Economies that depend on the overall size of the *firm* rather than on the size of its *plants* or the volume of production of any one commodity are called the **economies of scope**.

Where size confers a cost advantage either through economies of scale or of scope, there may be room for only a few firms, even when the total market is quite large. This cost advantage of size will dictate that the industry be an oligopoly unless government regulation prevents the firms from growing to their efficient size.

In other cases, as we shall see later in this chapter, the existing firms in the industry may create barriers to entry where natural ones do not exist. The industry will then be dominated by a few large firms only because they are successful in preventing the entry of new firms that would lower the industry's concentration ratio.

The Basic Dilemma of Oligopoly

Oligopolists face a basic dilemma between competing and cooperating.

The firms in an oligopolistic industry will make more profits as a group if they cooperate; any one firm, however, may make more profits for itself if it competes.

This result is similar to the one established in Chapter 13 for the cartelization of a perfectly competitive industry. In a perfectly competitive industry, however, there are so many firms that they cannot reach the cooperative equilibrium unless some central governing body is formed, by either themselves or the government, to force the necessary behavior on all firms. In contrast, the few firms in an oligopolistic industry cannot help but recognize their mutual interdependence. As a result, they see the possibility of tacitly agreeing to avoid competitive behavior.

The Cooperative Equilibrium

If the firms in an oligopolistic industry cooperate, either overtly or tacitly, to produce among themselves the monopoly output, they can maximize their joint profits. If they do this, they will reach what is called the **cooperative equilibrium**, which is the equilibrium that a single monopoly firm would reach if it owned all the firms in the industry.

The Noncooperative Equilibrium

If all the firms in an oligopolistic industry are at the cooperative equilibrium, it will usually be worthwhile for any one of them to cut its price or to raise its output, as long as the others do not do so. However, if everyone does the same thing, they will be worse off as a group and may all be worse off individually. An equilibrium that is reached by firms when they proceed by calculating only their own gains, without worrying about the reactions of others, is called **noncooperative equilibrium**.

An Example from Game Theory

A typical situation of this sort is illustrated in Figure 14-2 for the case of a two-firm oligopoly, called a **duopoly**. This figure shows what is called a *payoff matrix*. It takes us into the realm of *game theory*, which

FIGURE 14-2 The Oligopolist's Dilemma: To Cooperate or to Compete

		A's Output	
		One-half monopoly output	Two-thirds monopoly output
B's Output	One-half monopoly output	B: 20, A: 20	B: 15, A: 22
	Two-thirds monopoly output	B: 22, A: 15	B: 17, A: 17

Cooperation to determine the overall level of output can maximize joint profits, but it leaves each firm with an incentive to alter its production. The figure gives what is called a payoff matrix for a two-firm duopoly game. Only two levels of production are considered in order to illustrate the basic problem oligopolists face. A's production is indicated across the top of the matrix, and its profits (measured in millions of dollars) are shown in the white circles within each square. B's production is indicated down the left side of the matrix, and its profits (in millions of dollars) are shown in the colored circles within each square. For example, the top right square tells us that if B produces one-half, while A produces two-thirds, of the output that a monopolist would produce, A's profits will be $22 million, while B's will be $15 million.

If A and B cooperate, they can each produce one-half the monopoly output and can each earn profits of $20 million. This is shown in the upper left box. However, at that position, known as the cooperative equilibrium, each firm can raise its profits by producing two-thirds of the monopoly output, provided that the other firm does not do the same.

Now assume that A and B make their decision noncooperatively. A may reason that whether B produces either one-half or two-thirds of the monopoly outout, A's best output is two-thirds. B may reason similarly. In this case they reach the noncooperative equilibrium, as shown in the bottom right square. Each produces two-thirds of the monopoly output, and each makes less than it could if they had cooperated.

analyzes optimal strategies for games in which players compete while knowing that they need to take account of each other's reactions.

When game theory is applied to oligopoly, the players are firms, their game is played in the market, their strategies are their price or output decisions, and the payoffs are their profits.

Look closely at the payoff matrix in Figure 14-2, which shows a simplified version of an oligopoly game. The simplified game, adopted for the purposes of illustration, allows only two strategies for each firm: produce an output equal to one-half of the monopoly output or two-thirds of that output. Even this simple game, however, is sufficient to illustrate several key ideas in the modern theory of oligopoly.

The data in the matrix show that if both sides cooperate, each producing one-half of the monopoly output, they achieve the cooperative equilibrium and jointly earn the monopoly profits by jointly producing the output that a monopolist would produce. As a group, they can do no better.

Once the cooperative position is attained, the data in the figure show that if A cheats and produces more, its profits will increase. However, B's profits will be reduced: A's behavior drives the industry's prices down, so B earns less from its unchanged output. Since A's cheating takes the firms away from the joint profit-maximizing, monopoly output, their joint profits must fall, which means that B's profits will fall by more than A's will rise.

Figure 14-2 shows that similar considerations also apply to B: It is worthwhile for B to depart from the joint maximizing output, as long as A does not. So both A and B have an incentive to depart from the joint profit-maximizing level of output.

Finally, Figure 14-2 shows that when either firm does depart from the joint maximizing output, the other has an incentive to do so as well. As a result of such "selfish" behavior, they reach a noncooperative equilibrium at which they jointly produce one and one-half times as much as the monopolist would so that each has profits that are lower than at the cooperative equilibrium.

Nash equilibrium. The noncooperative equilibrium shown in Figure 14-2 is called a *Nash equilibrium*, after the American mathematician John Nash, who developed it in the 1950s. A **Nash equilibrium** is one in which each firm's best strategy is to maintain its present behavior *given the present behavior of the other firm*. It is easy to see that there is one Nash equilibrium in Figure 14-2. In the bottom right square, the best decision for each firm, given that the other firm is producing two-thirds of the monopoly output, is to produce two-thirds of the monopoly output itself. Neither player has a self-interest in departing from this position, except through cooperation with the other.

The basis of a Nash equilibrium is rational decision making in the absence of cooperation. Its particular importance in oligopoly theory is that it is the only self-policing equilibrium. If it is established—by any means whatsoever—the individual firms have no incentive to depart from it by altering their own individual behavior.

Recognition of interdependence. We have seen how the Nash equilibrium in Figure 14-2 can be arrived at when firms cheat on an agreement to reach the cooperative equilibrium. The same equilibrium will be attained if each firm decides independently what its optimal strategy will be, taking into account what the other firm may do. Let us see how this works.

First, assume that firm A reasons as follows: "What if B produces one-half of the monopoly output? If I do the same, I receive a profit of 20, but if I produce two-thirds of the monopoly output, I receive 22." Next A asks itself: "What if B produces two-thirds of the monopoly output? If I produce one-half of the monopoly output, I receive a profit of 15, whereas if I produce two-thirds, I receive 17. Clearly, my best strategy is to produce two-thirds in either case." B reasons in the same way. As a result, they end up producing $1\frac{1}{3}$ times the monopoly output between themselves, and each earns a profit of 17.

We have now seen in detail that oligopolists have an incentive to cooperate but may be driven, through their own individual decisions, to produce more and earn less than they would at a cooperative equilibrium. Our next step is to look in more detail at the types of cooperative and rivalrous behavior that oligopolists may adopt. We can then go on to study the forces that influence the balance between cooperation and competition in actual situations.

Types of Cooperative Behavior

When firms agree to cooperate in order to restrict output and to raise prices, their behavior is called **collusion**. Collusive behavior may occur with or without an actual agreement to collude. Where explicit agreement occurs, economists speak of *overt* or *covert collusion*, depending on whether the agreement is open or secret. Where no explicit agreement actually occurs, economists speak of *tacit collusion* (lawyers call it *conscious parallel action*). In this case, all firms behave cooperatively without an explicit agreement to do so. They merely understand that it is in their mutual interests to restrict output and to raise prices. In terms of Figure 14-2, Firm A decides to produce one-half of the monopoly output, hoping that Firm B will do the same. Firm B does what A expects, and they achieve the cooperative equilibrium without ever explicitly cooperating.

Explicit Cooperation

The easiest way for firms to ensure that they will all maintain their joint profit-maximizing output is to make an explicit agreement to do so. Such collusive agreements have occurred in the past in Canada, although they have been illegal for a long time. When they are discovered today, they are rigorously prosecuted. We shall see, however, that such agreements are not illegal everywhere in the world, particularly when they are supported by national governments.

We saw in Chapter 13 that when a group of firms gets together to act in this way, it is called a *cartel*. Cartels show in stark form the basic conflict between cooperation and competition that we just discussed. Full cooperation always allows the industry to achieve the result of monopoly. It also always presents individual firms with the incentive to cheat. The larger the number of firms, the greater the temptation for any one of them to cheat. After all, the cheating of one small firm may not be noticed, since it will have a negligible effect on price. The problems all cartels face are seen most vividly, therefore, in the case that we studied in Chapter 13, in which the number of firms is so large that most of them are price takers. This is why cartels that involve firms in industries that would otherwise be perfectly competitive tend to be unstable. Cartels may also be formed by a group of firms that would otherwise be in an oligopolistic market. The smaller the group of firms that forms a cartel, the more likely that the firms will let their joint interest in cooperating guide their behavior. Although cheating may still occur, the few firms in the industry can easily foresee the outcome of an outbreak of rivalrous behavior among themselves.

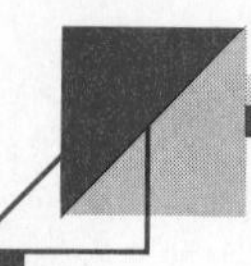

BOX 14-2

Explicit Cooperation in OPEC

The experience of the Organization of Petroleum Exporting Countries (OPEC) in the 1970s and 1980s illustrates the power of cooperative behavior to create short-run profits, as well as the problems of trying to exercise long-run market power in an industry without substantial entry barriers.

OPEC did not attract worldwide attention until 1973, when its members voluntarily restricted their output by negotiating quotas among themselves. In that year, OPEC countries accounted for about 70 percent of the world's supply of crude oil and 87 percent of the world's oil exports. So, although it was not a complete monopoly, the cartel came close to being one. By reducing output, the OPEC countries were able to drive up the world price of oil and to earn massive profits both for themselves and for non-OPEC producers, who obtained the high prices without having to limit their output. After several years of success, however, OPEC began to experience the typical problems of cartels.

New Entry

New entry became a problem. The high price of oil encouraged the development of new supplies, and within a few years new productive capacity was coming into use at a rapid rate in non-OPEC countries.

Long-Run Adjustment of Demand

There was not too much that consumers could do in the short run, and the short-run demand for oil proved to be highly inelastic. Over time, however, adaptations to reduce the demand for oil were made within the confines of existing technology. Homes and offices were insulated more efficiently, and smaller, more fuel-efficient cars became popular. This is an example of the distinction between the short-run and long-run demand for a commodity, first introduced in Chapter 5.

Innovation in the Very Long Run

Innovation further reduced the demand for oil in the very long run. Over time, technologies that were more efficient in their use of oil, as well as alternative energy sources, were developed. Had the oil prices stayed up longer than they did, major breakthroughs in solar and geothermal energy would surely have occurred.

This experience in both the long run and the very long run shows the price system at work, signaling the need for adaptation and providing the incentives for that adaptation. It also provides an illustration of Schumpeter's concept of creative destruction, which we first discussed in Chapter 13. In order to share in the profits generated by high

The most famous modern example of a cartel that engages in explicit cooperative behavior is the Organization of Petroleum Exporting Countries (OPEC). This cartel is discussed in more detail in Box 14-2.

Tacit Cooperation

While collusive behavior that affects prices is illegal in Canada, a small group of firms that recognize the influence that each has on the others may act without any explicit agreement to achieve the cooperative equilibrium. In such *tacit* agreements, the two forces that push toward cooperation and competition are still evident.

First, firms have a common interest in cooperating to maximize their joint profits at the cooperative equilibrium. Second, each firm is interested in its own profits, and any one of them can usually increase its profits by behaving in a rivalrous fashion. Although the most obvious way in which to do this is for one firm to produce more than its share of the joint profit-maximizing output, there are, as we shall soon see, other ways in which rivalrous behavior may break out.

energy prices, new technologies and new substitute products were developed, and these destroyed much of the market power of the original cartel.

Cheating

At first, there was little incentive for OPEC countries to violate quotas. Members found themselves with such undreamed-of increases in their incomes that they found it difficult to use all of their money productively. As the output of non-OPEC oil grew, however, OPEC's output had to be reduced to hold prices high. Incomes in OPEC countries declined sharply as a result.

Many OPEC countries had become used to their enormous incomes, and their attempts to maintain them in the face of falling output quotas brought the instabilities inherent in all cartels to the surface. In 1981 the cartel price reached its peak of U.S. $35 per barrel (oil prices are traditionally quoted in U.S. dollars). In real terms, this was about five times as high as the 1972 price, but production quotas were less than one-half of OPEC's capacity. Eager to increase their oil revenues, many individual OPEC members gave in to the pressure to cheat and produced in excess of their production quotas. In late 1984, Saudi Arabia indicated that it would not tolerate further cheating by its partners and demanded that others share equally in reducing their quotas yet further. However, agreement proved to be impossible. In December 1985, OPEC decided to eliminate production quotas and let each member make its own decisions about output.

After the Collapse

OPEC's collapse as an output-restricting cartel led to a major reduction in world oil prices. Early in 1986, the downward slide took the price to $20 per barrel, and it fell to $11 per barrel later in the year. Allowing for inflation, this was around the price that had prevailed just before OPEC introduced its output restrictions in 1973. Prices have been volatile since then. For the rest of the 1980s, they oscillated between about $10 per barrel, which is close to the perfectly competitive price, and $20 per barrel, which seems to be all that can be sustained under the modest output restrictions that can currently be obtained.

Only after the outbreak of the Kuwait crisis in 1990 did prices rise above $20. The interruption of supplies from Kuwait and Iraq, plus stockpiling in anticipation of worse shortages to come, led to high and volatile prices.

Even if *joint* profits are maximized, there is the problem of market shares. How is the profit-maximizing level of sales to be divided among the competing firms? Competition for market shares may upset the tacit agreement to hold to joint maximizing behavior. In an industry that has many differentiated products and in which sales are often by contract between buyers and sellers, cheating may be covert rather than overt. Secret discounts and rebates can allow a firm to increase its sales at the expense of its competitors while appearing to hold to the tacitly agreed monopoly price.

Another reason why the monopoly level of profits may not be achieved, even if the monopoly price is maintained, is that firms often compete for market shares through various forms of nonprice competition, such as advertising and variations in the quality of their product. Such costly competition may reduce industry profits.

Very long run considerations may also be important. In a world in which technology and product characteristics change constantly, a firm that chooses to behave in a rivalrous way may be able to maintain a larger market share and to earn larger profits than it would if it behaved in a cooperative way, even though all the firms' joint profits are lower. In such a world of constant change, a firm that thinks it can *keep* ahead of its rivals has an incentive to compete even if that competition lowers the joint profits of the whole industry.

For these and for other reasons, there are often strong incentives for oligopolistic firms to compete rather than to maintain the cooperative equilibrium, even when they understand the inherent risks to their joint profits.

Cooperation or Competition?

Empirical research by such economists as Jo Bain and Nobel Laureate Herbert Simon suggests that the relative strengths of the incentives to cooperate and to compete vary from industry to industry in a systematic way, depending on observable characteristics of firms, markets, and products. What are some of the characteristics that will affect the strength of the two incentives?

1. *The tendency toward joint maximization of profits is greater for smaller numbers of sellers than for larger numbers of sellers.* This involves both motivation and ability. When there are few firms, they will know that one of them cannot gain sales without inducing retaliation by its rivals. Also, a few firms can tacitly coordinate their policies with less difficulty than can many firms.

2. *The tendency toward joint maximization of profits is greater for producers of similar products than for producers of sharply differentiated products.* The more nearly identical the products of sellers, the closer the direct rivalry for customers and the less able one firm is to gain a lasting advantage over its rivals. Such sellers will tend to prefer joint efforts to achieve a larger pie to individual attempts to increase their own shares.

3. *The tendency toward joint maximization of profits is greater in a growing market than in a contracting market.* When demand is growing, firms can produce at full capacity without any need to "steal" customers from their rivals. When firms have excess capacity, they are tempted to give price concessions to attract customers. When their rivals retaliate, price cuts become general.

4. *The tendency toward joint maximization of profits is greater when the industry contains a dominant firm rather than a group of more or less equal competitors.* A dominant firm may become a *price leader,* a firm that sets the industry's price while all other firms fall into line. Even if a dominant firm is not automatically a price leader, other firms may look to it for judgment about market conditions, and its decisions may become a tentative focus for tacit agreement.

5. *The tendency toward joint maximization of profits is greater when nonprice rivalry is absent or limited.* When firms seek to suppress their basic rivalry by avoiding price competition, rivalry will tend to break out in other forms unless it is expressly curtailed. Firms may seek to increase their market shares through extra advertising, changes in the quality of the product, the establishment of new products, giveaways, and a host of similar schemes that leave their prices unchanged but increase their costs and so reduce their joint profits.

6. *The tendency toward joint maximization of profits is greater when the barriers to entry of new firms are greater.* The high profits of existing firms attract new entrants, who will drive down price and reduce profits. The greater the barriers to entry, the less this will occur. Thus the greater the entry barriers, the closer the profits of existing firms can be to their joint maximizing level without being reduced by new entrants.

Short-Run Price Stickiness

We have seen that all firms that sell differentiated products, whether under monopolistic competition, oligopoly, or monopoly, must administer their prices. One striking contrast between perfectly competitive markets, on the one hand, and markets for differentiated products, on the other hand, concerns the behavior of prices. In perfect competition, prices change continually in response to changes in demand and supply. In markets where differentiated products are sold, prices change less frequently. Manufacturers' prices for radios, automobiles, television sets, and men's suits do not change with anything like the frequency that prices change in markets for basic materials or stocks and bonds.

Since the bulk of manufacturing industries that sell differentiated products are oligopolies, this phenomenon is often referred to as the *stickiness* of oligopolistic prices.

Before considering possible explanations of why

prices may be sticky, it is important to recognize that administered prices do change.

Changing Prices

Oligopolistic prices usually change when there are major changes in costs of production. Sometimes a specific set of costs will rise, as when the two OPEC oil shocks pushed up the prices of oil, gasoline, and all oil-related products. Sometimes most costs will be rising, as with a general inflation. Whatever the case, increases in input costs are passed on quite quickly by means of rises in output prices. This is because such increases in costs threaten to eliminate profits unless they are passed on, at least in part, in the form of higher prices. By the same token, major reductions in costs, as when a new product such as the personal computer is being developed, are usually followed by reductions in prices. This is because of the rivalry among oligopolistic firms. If one firm fails to cut prices when costs fall, another firm will do so, seeking thereby to increase its market share.

Oligopolistic prices also often change in response to large, unexpected shifts in demand. If an industry finds itself facing an apparently permanent downward shift in demand, firms will often cut prices in an attempt to retain their markets until long-term adjustments can be made. For example, the North American automobile industry faced declining demand from 1980 to 1982 due to its lag in developing small, fuel-efficient cars that would be competitive with Japanese imports. It offered big rebates that slashed prices to levels that could not have been maintained in the long run.

Sticky Prices

The stickiness of administered prices occurs mainly in the face of cyclical and seasonal fluctuations in demand. The existence of business cycles (i.e., alternating periods of high and low demand for output) is well known to firms, even if the precise course of each cycle cannot be predicted in advance. Oligopolistic (and monopoly) firms tend to adjust to these changes more by varying quantities than by varying prices.

Price stickiness is short-term behavior that need not affect our long-term view of how the economy functions. Nonetheless, stickiness is an interesting problem in its own right, and it also has important implications for macroeconomics.[5]

Flat Cost Curves

Maintaining sticky prices in the face of fluctuating demand and output would cause large losses to firms whose costs varied greatly with output, as shown by the U-shaped curve in Figure 14-3. However, a firm with a flat cost curve of the type that also is shown in Figure 14-3 can maintain prices without suffering large losses. Part of the explanation of sticky prices in the presence of the costs of price adjustments is found, therefore, in the rather flat cost curves that

[5] A major problem of macroeconomics is understanding why in the short run it is mainly output, rather than price, that responds to changes in the total demand for goods and services across the whole economy. The oligopolistic behavior that we have studied in this section provides one part of the explanation of this phenomenon.

FIGURE 14-3 U-shaped Versus Saucer-shaped Cost Curves

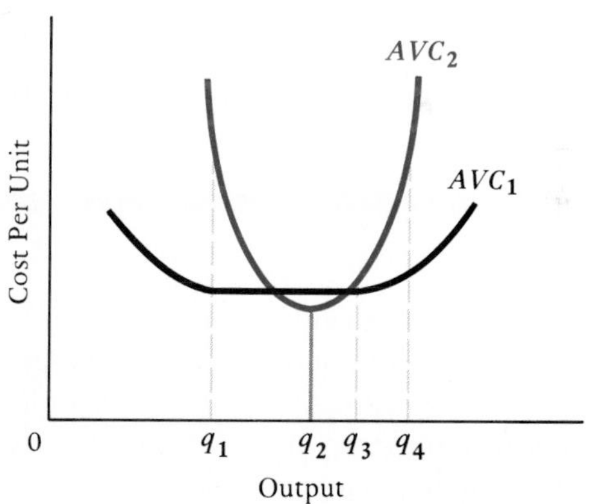

A firm that anticipates fluctuating output may choose a plant with a flat-bottomed cost curve. AVC_1 and AVC_2 are alternatives based on how a plant is designed and built. AVC_2 achieves lower unit costs than AVC_1 if output is very close to q_2, but it is much less adaptable to either higher or lower outputs. If the firm could count on producing q_2 in every period, it would prefer the plant yielding AVC_2. However, if it anticipates outputs ranging from q_1 to q_4, it would prefer AVC_1.

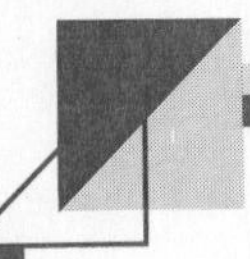

BOX 14-3

Saucer-shaped Industry Cost Curves

Ever since economists began measuring the cost curves of manufacturing firms half a century ago, they have reported flat, short-run variable cost curves. The evidence is now clear that in most manufacturing industries, and in some others, cost curves are shaped like the black curve (AVC_1) shown in Figure 14-3, with a long, flat portion in the middle and sharply rising sections at each end. For such a saucer-shaped curve, there is a large range of output over which average variable costs are constant. Over this range, marginal costs are equal to average variable costs, and thus they, too, are constant per unit of output.

Why are many cost curves saucer-shaped rather than U-shaped? The answer is that firms design plants to have this property so that they can accommodate the inevitable seasonal and cyclical swings in demand for their products. As Professor George Stigler, the 1982 Nobel Laureate in Economics, pointed out, a firm that faces two possible average variable cost curves, such as those shown in Figure 14-3, might well prefer to build a plant that results in the saucer-shaped curve if it anticipates widely fluctuating demand. The saucer-shaped curve then leads *on average* to lower costs, even if at some output the U-shaped cost curve dips below it.

To see why a firm can choose the shape of its short-run average cost curve, consider again the law of diminishing returns that we first encountered in Chapter 10. The U-shaped, short-run cost curve arises when a variable amount of one factor, say, labor, is applied to a fixed amount of a second factor, say, capital. Imagine starting from zero output and zero use of the variable factor and then increasing output. As more of the variable factor is used, a more nearly optimal combination with the fixed factor is achieved. Once the optimal combination is arrived at, the use of further units of the variable factor leads to too much of the variable factor being used in combination with the fixed factor. This causes average variable costs to begin to rise. Only one quantity of labor leads to the least-cost factor proportions.

These changing combinations of fixed and variable factors must occur in the short run whenever all of the fixed factor must be used all of the time; in other words, when the fixed factor is *indivisible*. This is not always the case, however. Even though

are encountered by many manufacturing firms: monopolistic competitors, oligopolists, and monopolists.

Cost curves that are steep at either extreme and flat over a long middle portion are often referred to as being *saucer-shaped*. Box 14-3 discusses the reason for this shape.

Although the saucer-shaped cost curves that are typically found in manufacturing do not *force* firms to adopt sticky pricing policies, they do make it possible for such policies to be profitable.

Costly Price Changes

One reason why producers of differentiated products do not change their prices with the frequency that prices change in perfectly competitive markets is that it is costly to change prices. In a perfectly competitive market, producers must accept whatever price is set by the impersonal forces of demand and supply. With differentiated products, each firm must list the price at which it is prepared to supply each of its products. Modern firms that sell differentiated products typically have hundreds, and sometimes even thousands, of distinct products on their price lists. Changing such a long list of administered prices, at the same frequency that competitive market prices change, would be physically impossible. Changing them at all is costly. These include the costs of printing new list prices and notifying all customers, the difficulty for accounting and billing to keep track of frequently changing prices, and the loss of customer and retailer goodwill due to the uncertainty caused by frequent

the firm's plant and equipment may be fixed in the short run, so that *no more* than what exists is available, it is often possible to use *less* than this amount. For this reason, the flat cost curve is not inconsistent with the law of diminishing returns. The divisibility of the fixed factor means that diminishing returns does not apply, because variations in output below full capacity are accomplished by reducing the input of both labor and capital.

Consider, as a simple example, a factory that consists of 10 sewing machines in a shed, each of which has a productive capacity of 20 units per day when operated by 1 operator for 1 shift. If 200 units per day are required, then all 10 machines would be operated by 10 workers on a normal shift. If demand falls to 180, then 1 operator could be laid off. There is no need, however, to have the 9 remaining operators dashing about trying to work 10 machines. Clearly, 1 machine could be "laid off" as well, and the ratio of *employed* labor to *employed* machines could be held constant. Production could go from 20 to 40 to 60 all the way to 200 units per day without any change in the proportions in which the employed factors would be used. In this case, we would expect the factory to have constant marginal and average variable costs from 20 to 200 units per day. Only beyond 200 units per day would it begin to encounter rising costs, since production would have to be extended by overtime and other means of combining more labor with the maximum available supply of 10 machines.

In such a case, the fixed factor is *divisible*. Since some of it can be left unemployed, there is no need to depart from the most efficient ratio of *labor used* to *capital used* as production is decreased. Thus average variable costs can be constant over a large range, up to the point at which all of the fixed factor is used.

A similar situation occurs when a firm has many plants. For example, a plywood manufacturer with 10 plants may choose to reduce its output by temporarily closing one or more plants (or operating them on a limited-time basis) while operating the rest at normal-capacity output. The *firm's* short-run variable costs tend to be constant over a large range of output because there is no need to depart from the optimal combination of labor and capital in the plants that are kept in operation.

changes in prices. These costs are often a significant consideration to multiproduct firms.

Because producers of differentiated products must administer their own prices, the frequency with which they change these prices is one of the firm's decision variables. In making this decision, the firm will balance the cost of making price changes against the revenue lost by not making price changes. Clearly, the firm will be more likely to make costly price changes the larger the disturbance to which it is adjusting and the greater the probability that the disturbance will not be reversed.

Thus transitory fluctuations in demand may be met by changing output with prices constant, while changes in costs that accompany inflation are passed on through price increases. Since few firms expect inflationary price increases to be reversed, they know that they must raise their prices to cover them. Even in these cases, however, they do so periodically, rather than continuously, because of the costs incurred in making such changes.

Whether or not further explanations of short-term price stickiness are required has been a matter of debate among economists for a long time. Some of the competing explanations that have been offered are discussed in the appendix to this chapter.

Long-Run Behavior: The Importance of Entry Barriers

Suppose that firms in an oligopolistic industry succeed in raising prices above long-run average total costs and earn substantial profits that are not completely eliminated by nonprice competition. In the absence of significant barriers to entry, new firms will enter the industry and erode the profits of existing firms, as they do in monopolistic competition.

Natural barriers to entry were discussed in Chapter 13. Where such natural barriers do not exist, oligopolistic firms can earn profits in the long run only if they can create entry barriers. To the extent to which this is done, existing firms can move toward joint profit maximization without fear that new firms, attracted by the high profits, will enter the industry. We discuss next some types of created barriers.

Brand Proliferation

By altering the characteristics of a differentiated product, it is possible to produce a vast array of variations on the general theme of that product. Think, for example, of cars with a little more or a little less acceleration, braking power, top speed, cornering ability, gas mileage, and so on, compared with existing models. Although the multiplicity of existing brands is no doubt partly a response to consumers' tastes, it can have the effect of discouraging the entry of new firms.

To illustrate why brand proliferation may be a formidable barrier to a small, potential entrant, assume that the product is the type for which there is a substantial amount of brand switching by consumer. In this case, the larger the number of brands sold by existing firms, the smaller the expected sales of a new entrant. Say that an industry contains 3 large firms, each selling one brand of cigarettes, and say that 30 percent of all smokers change brands in a random fashion each year. If a new firm enters the industry, it can expect to pick up 25 percent of the smokers who change brands (the smoker has available 1 out of the new total of 4 brands). This would give the new firm 7.5 percent (25 percent of 30 percent) of the total market the first year merely as a result of picking up its share of the random switchers, and it would keep increasing its share thereafter. If, however, the existing 3 firms have 5 brands each, there would be 15 brands already available, and a new firm selling 1 new brand could expect to pick up only one-sixteenth of the brand switchers, giving it less than 2 percent of the total market the first year, with smaller gains also in subsequent years. This is an extreme case, but it illustrates a general result.

The larger the number of differentiated products that are sold by existing oligopolists, the smaller the market share available to a new firm that is entering with a single new product.

Set-up Costs

Existing firms can create entry barriers by imposing significant fixed costs on new firms that enter their market. This is particularly important if the industry has only weak natural barriers to entry, because the minimum efficient scale occurs at an output that is low relative to the total output of the industry.

Advertising is one means by which existing firms can impose heavy set-up costs on new entrants. Advertising, of course, serves purposes other than that of creating barriers to entry. Among them, it performs the useful function of informing buyers about their alternatives, thereby making markets work more smoothly. Indeed, a new firm may find that advertising is essential, even when existing firms do not advertise at all, simply to call attention to its entry into an industry in which it is unknown.

Nonetheless, advertising can also operate as a potent entry barrier by increasing the set-up costs of new entrants. Where heavy advertising has established strong brand images for existing products, a new firm may have to spend heavily on advertising to create its own brand images in consumers' minds. If the firm's sales are small, advertising costs *per unit sold* will be large, and price will have to be correspondingly high to cover those costs.

Figure 14-4 illustrates how heavy advertising can shift the cost curves of a firm with a low minimum efficient scale (*MES*) to make it one with a high *MES*. In essence, what happens is that a high *MES* of advertising is added to a low *MES* of production, with the result that the overall *MES* is raised:

A new entrant with small sales but large set-up costs finds itself at a substantial cost disadvantage relative to its established rivals.

Any once-and-for-all cost of entering a market has the same effect as a large initial advertising expenditure. For example, with many consumer goods, the cost of developing a new product that is similar, but not identical, to existing products may be quite substantial. Even if there are few economies

FIGURE 14-4 **Advertising Cost As a Barrier to Entry**

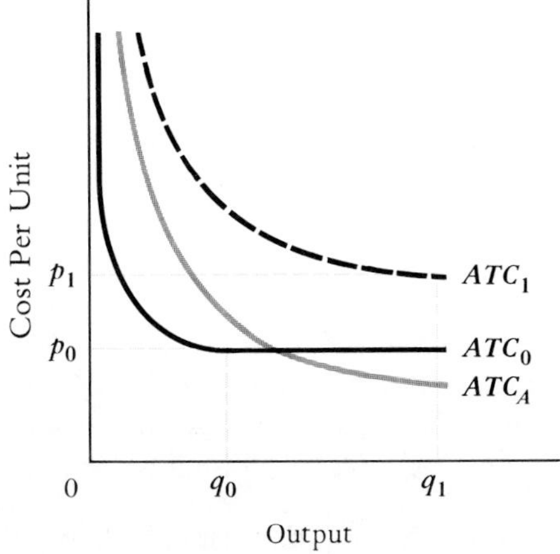

Large advertising costs can increase the minimum efficient scale (*MES*) of production and thereby increase entry barriers. The ATC_0 curve shows that the *MES* without advertising is at q_0. The curve ATC_A shows that advertising cost per unit falls as output rises. Advertising increases total cost to ATC_1, which is downward sloping over its entire range. Advertising has given a scale advantage to large sellers and has thus created a barrier to entry.

of scale in the production of the product, its large fixed development cost can lead to a falling long-run average total cost curve over a wide range of output.

An Application

The combined use of brand proliferation and advertising as an entry barrier can help to explain one apparent paradox of everyday life—that one firm often sells multiple brands of the same product, which compete directly against one another as well as against the products of other firms.

The soap and cigarette industries provide classic examples of this behavior. Since all available scale economies can be realized by quite small plants, both industries have few natural barriers to entry. Both contain a few large firms, each of which produces an array of heavily advertised products. The numerous existing products make it harder for a new entrant to obtain a large market niche with a single new product. The heavy advertising, although it is directed against existing products, creates an entry barrier by increasing the set-up costs of a new product that seeks to gain the attention of consumers and to establish its own brand image.

Predatory Pricing

A firm that is considering entry will not do so if it expects losses after entry. One way in which existing firms can create such a situation is to cut prices below costs whenever entry occurs and to keep them there until the entrant goes bankrupt. The existing firms sacrifice profits while doing this, but they send a discouraging message to potential future rivals, as well as to present ones. Economists use the term *reputation effects* to refer to the effects of a strategy of predatory price cutting against new entrants. Even if this strategy is costly in terms of lost profits in the short run, it may pay for itself in the long run by deterring the entry of new firms at other times or in other markets that the firm controls.

Predatory pricing is controversial. Some economists argue that pricing policies that appear to be predatory can be explained by other motives and that existing firms only hurt themselves when they engage in such practices instead of accommodating new entrants. Others argue that predatory pricing has been observed and that it is in the long-run interests of existing firms to punish the occasional new entrant even when it is costly to do so in the short run.

The courts have taken the position that predatory pricing does occur. A number of firms have been convicted of using it as a method of eliminating competition.

Oligopoly and the Functioning of the Economy

Oligopoly is found in many industries and in all advanced economies. It typically occurs in industries where both perfect and monopolistic competition are made impossible by the existence of major economies of scale or of scope (or both). In such industries, there is simply not enough room for a large number of firms all operating at or near their minimum efficient scales.

Two questions are important for the evaluation of the performance of the oligopolistic market structure. First, in their short-run and long-run price-output behavior, where do oligopolistic firms typically settle between the extreme outcomes of monopoly and perfect competition? Second, how much do oligopolists contribute to economic growth by encouraging innovative activity in the very long run?

Short-Run Price-Output Decisions

We have seen that under perfect competition, prices are set by the impersonal forces of demand and supply, whereas firms in oligopolistic markets administer their prices. The market signaling system works slightly differently when prices are administered rather than determined by the market. Changes in the market conditions for both inputs and outputs are signaled to the perfectly competitive firm by changes in the prices of its inputs and its outputs. Changes in the market conditions for inputs are signaled to oligopolistic firms by changes in the prices of their inputs. Changes in the market conditions for the oligopolist's output are typically signaled, however, by changes in the sales at administered prices.

Increases in costs of inputs will shift cost curves upward, and oligopolistic firms will be led to raise prices and lower outputs. Increases in demand will cause the sales of oligopolistic firms to rise. Firms will then respond by increasing output, thereby increasing the quantities of society's resources that are allocated to producing that output. They will then decide whether or not their administered prices need to be altered.

The market system reallocates resources in response to changes in demands and costs in roughly the same way under oligopoly as it does under perfect competition.

Some oligopolies succeed in coming close to joint profit maximization. Others compete so intensely among themselves that they come close to achieving competitive prices and outputs. The consequences for the behavior of the economic system vary accordingly. Box 14-4 discusses one recent theory that outlines some of the conditions under which oligopoly can be pushed toward the competitive equilibrium by potential, rather than actual, entry.

Innovation

An important defense of oligopoly relates to Schumpeter's concept of creative destruction (see pages 249–252). Some economists have theorized that intermediate market structures, such as oligopoly, would lead to more innovation than would occur in either perfectly competitive or monopolistic industries. They argue that the oligopolist faces clear and present competition from existing rivals and cannot afford the more relaxed life of the monopolist. At the same time, however, the oligopolistic firm expects to keep a good share of the profits that it earns from any innovative activity that it undertakes. The empirical evidence is broadly consistent with this view. Professor Jesse Markham of Harvard University concluded a survey of empirical findings thusly:

> If technological change and innovational activity are, as we generally assume, in some important way a product of organized R&D activities financed and executed by business companies, it is clear that the . . . payoffs that flow from them can to some measurable extent be traced to the doorsteps of large firms operating in oligopolistic markets.

Everyday observation provides some confirmation of this finding. Leading North American firms that operate in highly concentrated industries, such as Bombardier, IBM, Alcan, Xerox, General Electric, and Lumonics, have been highly innovative over many years.

A Final Word

Oligopoly is an important market structure in modern economies because there are many industries in which the minimum efficient scale is simply too large to support a large group of competing firms. Although oligopoly will usually not achieve the same static efficiency as perfect competition, rivalrous oligopoly may be effective in producing very long run adaptations that develop both new products and cost-reducing methods of producing old ones.

The defense of oligopoly as a market structure is that it may be the best of the available alternatives when minimum efficient scale is large. The challenge to public policy is to keep oligopolists competing, rather than colluding, and using their competitive energies to improve products and to lower costs, rather than merely to erect entry barriers.

BOX 14-4

Contestable Markets

Professors William Baumol of Princeton University, Robert Willig of Princeton University, and John Panzer of Northwestern University have recently developed a theory of what they call **contestable markets**. This theory holds that markets do not have to contain many firms or to experience actual entry for profits to be held near the competitive level. Potential entry can do the job just as well as actual entry, as long as (1) entry can be easily accomplished and (2) existing firms take potential entry into account when making price and output decisions.

Entry is usually costly to the entering firm. It may have to build a plant, it may have to develop new versions of the industry's differentiated product, or it may have to advertise heavily in order to call attention to its product. These and many other initial expenses are often called *sunk costs of entry*. A sunk cost of entry is a cost that a firm must incur to enter the market and that cannot be recovered if the firm subsequently exits. For example, if an entering firm builds a product-specific factory that has no resale value, this is a sunk cost of entry. However, the cost of a factory that is not product-specific and that can be resold for an amount that is close to its original cost is not a sunk cost of entry.

A market in which new firms can enter and leave without incurring any sunk costs of entry is called a *perfectly contestable market*. A market can be perfectly contestable even if the firm must pay some costs of entry, as long as these can be recovered when the firm exits. Since all markets require at least some sunk costs of entry, contestability must be understood as a variable. The lower the sunk costs of entry, the more contestable the market.

In a contestable market, the existence of profits, even if they are due to transitory causes, will attract entry. Firms will enter to gain a share of these profits and will exit when the transitory situation has changed.

Consider, for example, the market for air travel in the lucrative Montreal-Toronto-Ottawa triangle. It will be quite contestable as long as counter and loading space is available to new entrants at the three cities' airline terminals. An airline that is not currently serving the cities in question can shift some of its existing planes to the market with little sunk costs of entry. Some training of personnel will be needed for them to become familiar with the route and the airport. This is a sunk cost of entry that cannot be recovered if the cities in question are no longer to be served. However, most of the airline's costs are not sunk costs of entry. If it subsequently decides to leave a city, the rental of terminal space will stop, and the airplanes and the ground equipment can be shifted to another location.

Sunk costs of entry constitute a barrier to entry, and the larger these are, the larger the profits of existing firms can be without attracting new entrants. The flip side of this coin is that firms operating in markets without large sunk costs of entry will not earn large profits because if they do, firms will enter to capture the profits while they last and then exit.

Contestability, where it is possible, is a force that limits the profits of existing oligopolists. Even if entry does not occur, the ease with which it can be accomplished will keep oligopolists away from the cooperative equilibrium.

Contestability is just another example, in somewhat more refined form, of the key point that the possibility of entry is the major force preventing the exploitation of market power to restrict output and to raise prices. There is reason to think, however, that many oligopolistic markets are not highly contestable because of large sunk costs of entry. In these cases, potential entry cannot be relied on to hold profits close to zero.

SUMMARY

1. Some Canadian industries fit the perfectly competitive model, but almost none are pure monopolies. Most have intermediate market structures that are called imperfectly competitive.
2. Most of the firms operating in these market structures sell differentiated products whose characteristics they chose themselves. They also administer their prices, sometimes have unexploited economies of scale, do not change their prices as often as prices in perfectly competitive markets change, engage in nonprice competition, and sometimes take actions designed to prevent the entry of new firms.
3. Monopolistic competition is a market structure that has the same characteristics as perfect competition, except that the firms sell a differentiated product rather than a homogeneous one. Firms face negatively sloped demand curves and may earn monopoly profits in the short run. In the long run, new firms enter the industry whenever profits can be made and the equilibrium requires that each firm earns zero profits. Each firm's demand curve is tangent to its average total cost curve, which means that each firm is producing less than its minimum-cost level of output.
4. Monopolistic competition does not necessarily result in inefficiency. Even though each firm produces at a cost that is higher than the minimum attainable cost, the resulting product choice is valued by consumers and so may be worth the extra cost.
5. Oligopolies are dominated by a few large firms that usually sell differentiated products and have significant market power. They can maximize their joint profits if they cooperate to produce the monopoly output. By acting individually, each firm has an incentive to depart from this cooperative equilibrium, but rivalrous behavior reduces profits and may lead to a noncooperative Nash equilibrium from which no one firm has an incentive to depart.
6. Tacit cooperation is possible but often tends to break down as firms struggle for market share, indulge in nonprice competition, and seek advantages through the introduction of new technology. Oligopolistic industries are likely to come closer to the joint profit-maximizing, cooperative position (a) the smaller the number of firms in the industry, (b) the less differentiated their products, (c) when the industry's demand is growing rather than shrinking, (d) when the industry contains a dominant firm, (e) the less the opportunity for nonprice competition, and (f) the smaller the barriers to entry.
7. Oligopolistic prices do not change continually in the way that free market prices do. As a result, the first effect of a change in demand is a change in output rather than a change in price. This price stickiness applies to most differentiated products and is partly explained by the fact that firms face flat cost curves and find it costly to change prices.
8. Oligopolistic industries will exhibit profits in the long run only if there are significant barriers to entry. Natural barriers relate to scale economies in production and in entry costs. Firm-created barriers can relate to proliferation of competing brands, heavy brand-image advertising, and the threat of predatory pricing when new entry occurs. Contestable market theory holds that potential entry may be sufficient to hold profits down and emphasizes the importance of sunk costs as an entry barrier.
9. In the presence of major scale economies, oligopoly may be the best of the feasible alternative market structures. Evaluation of oligopoly

depends on how much interfirm competition (a) drives the firms away from the cooperative, profit-maximizing equilibrium and (b) leads to innovations in the very long run.

TOPICS FOR REVIEW

Concentration ratios
Reasons for the persistence of large firms
Administered prices
Product differentiation
Imperfect competition
Monopolistic competition
The excess capacity theorem
Types of collusion
The cooperative, joint profit-maximizing equilibrium
The noncooperative equilibrium
OPEC as a cartel
Firm-created entry barriers
Contestable markets

DISCUSSION QUESTIONS

1. It is sometimes said that there are more drugstores and gasoline stations than are needed. In what sense might that be correct? Does the consumer gain anything from this plethora of retail outlets?

2. Are any of the following industries monopolistically competitive? Explain your answer.
   a. Textbook publishing (*Fact:* Over 50 elementary economics textbooks are in use somewhere in North America this year.)
   b. Postsecondary education
   c. Cigarette manufacturing
   d. Restaurant operation
   e. Automobile retailing

3. What bearing did each of the following have on the eventual inability of OPEC to maintain a monopoly price for oil?
   a. Between 1979 and 1985, OPEC's share of the world oil supply decreased by half.
   b. "Saudi Arabia's interest lies in extending the life span of oil to the longest possible period," said Sheik Yamani.
   c. The Soviet Union, in order to earn Western currency to pay for grain, increased its oil exports to the West during the late 1970s, becoming the world's second largest oil exporter.
   d. The Iran-Iraq war decreased oil production in the Middle East from 1979 to 1981 by 4.5 million barrels a day.
   e. Government policies during the 1970s protected consumers from oil price shocks by holding domestic prices well below OPEC levels.
   f. In the late 1980s, Iran became increasingly concerned to maximize its oil revenues in order to pay for its war with Iraq.
   g. Iraq invaded Kuwait in 1990 after a prolonged dispute related to Kuwait's continued violation of its OPEC production quota.

4. Do the following groups stand to gain or to lose if oil prices fall over the next five years?
   a. Canadian consumers
   b. Coal miners in North America
   c. People who have invested in companies developing synthetic fuels

d. Indonesia, an oil-exporting country with small oil reserves and a large population
e. U.S. drillers of wildcat oil wells
f. Saudi Arabia

5. "The decade from 1975 to 1985 proved to the world that there were many available substitutes for gasoline, among them bicycles, car pools, moving closer to work, cable TV, and Japanese cars." Discuss how each of these may be a substitute for gasoline.

6. Compare the effects on the automobile and the wheat industries of each of the following. In the light of your answers, discuss general ways in which oligopolistic industries fulfill the same general functions as perfectly competitive industries.
a. Large rise in demand
b. Large rise in costs of production
c. Temporary cut in supplies coming to market due to a three-month rail strike
d. Rush of cheap foreign imports

7. Most Canadian provinces have laws requiring a company to produce beer in the province if it wishes to sell there. What do you think this does to the price of beer? What would be the consequences of repealing these laws? Why can small, high-cost local beers exist in open competition with large, low-cost, nationally sold beers?

8. Evidence suggests that the profits earned by all the firms in many oligopolistic industries are less than the profits that would be earned if the industry were monopolized. What are some reasons why this might be so?

Appendix to Chapter 14

Oligopolistic Price Stickiness

Chapter 14 discussed the sense in which oligopoly prices are and are not sticky. This appendix outlines the three main explanations of oligopolistic price stickiness that have been offered: tacit collusion, fear of competitors' reactions, and the cost of changing prices. Each may have validity in certain circumstances.

Tacit Collusion

We have seen that it is worthwhile for oligopolistic firms to avoid price competition and therefore maximize their joint profits by achieving the monopoly price and output for the industry as a whole. We have also seen that such agreements will be fragile because of the incentive for individual firms to cheat.

Realizing this, oligopolistic firms that do have some effective tacit cooperation on price and output will be reluctant to alter prices or outputs in response to small or temporary changes in demand. They will fear that other firms will misinterpret their actions and react in a rivalrous way, causing an outbreak of competitive behavior that will reduce everyone's profits.

FIGURE 14A-1 The Kinked Demand Curve

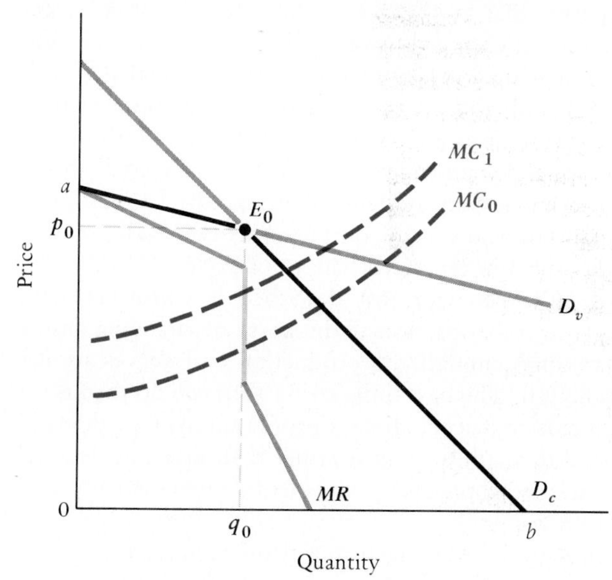

Price stickiness in the case of varying costs can result if the firm assumes that its competitors will match its price reductions but not its price increases. The firm is in equilibrium at E_0 by charging a price of p_0 and selling at q_0. Its demand curve, drawn on the assumption that all other firms follow any price changes it makes, is the curve D_c. The firm's market share is constant along this curve. (This *c* subscript stands for *constant* market share.) The firm's demand curve, drawn on the assumption that all other firms hold their prices constant, is D_v. Along this curve the firm's market share varies negatively with the price it charges: The higher its price, the lower its market share. (The *v* subscript stands for *variable* market share.)

Since the firm assumes that its competitors will match its price cuts but not its price increases, its demand curve is given by D_c below E_0 and D_v above E_0. Thus the whole demand curve runs from *a* to E_0 to *b* with a kink at E_0, where the change in the demand curve is relevant to the duopolist's decisions. The marginal revenue curve for this kinked demand curve takes a jump at quantity q_0. For lower quantities, where the demand curve D_v is relevant, its *MR* curve is high and relatively flat. For larger quantities, where the demand curve D_c is relevant, its *MR* curve is lower and steeper.

The marginal cost curves of MC_0 and MC_1 both give equilibrium output at q_0 with price p_0 because both pass through the point where the marginal revenue curve "jumps."

Where rivalrous price and output behavior is being restrained by tacit cooperation, caution may restrain firms from changing prices as a result of changes in demand that might otherwise lead them to alter prices.

This theory may explain some price stickiness in situations in which firms are tacitly cooperating and fear rivalrous competitive behavior. It does not explain the observed price stickiness on the part of monopolists who have no competitors to worry about, oligopolists who either feel that their cooperation is secure or do not cooperate at all and so are already in the noncooperative equilibrium, or monopolistic competitors who are by definition unconcerned about the reaction of the numerous firms in their industry.

Fear of Competitors' Reactions: The Kinked Demand Curve

A second explanation also considers each firm's anticipation of its competitors' reactions. This time, however, the competitors are assumed to react in a very specific manner.

According to this theory, each oligopolist conjectures that its rivals will match any price decreases that it makes but will not match any price increases that it makes. If one firm raises its price and no one follows, it will lose its market share, and its sales will fall off rapidly. Thus its demand curve for price *increases* will be rather flat. In contrast, if one firm lowers its price and everyone follows, it will not increase its market share. Its sales will expand only in proportion to the expansion in the industry's sales. Thus the demand curve for price *reductions* will be steeper than the demand curve for price increases. The resulting **kinked demand curve** is shown in Figure 14A-1.

Whenever oligopolists make these assumptions about their competitors' reactions, they will be reluctant to change prices in response to shifts in costs or demand. Their profit-maximizing strategy will be to hold prices constant in the face of significant shifts in marginal costs, even though the cooperative equilibrium calls for a rise in price and a fall in output.

This theory may well explain oligopolistic price stickiness in specific circumstances in which oligopolists make the stated assumptions about their competitors' reactions. The earlier discussion makes it clear, however, that oligopolists' assumptions about their competitors' reactions may vary with the market circumstances in which they find themselves. Thus a theory based on the assumption of one particular reaction is unlikely to explain all cases. It does not, for example, explain price stickiness when oligopolists are cooperating with each other, either tacitly or overtly. Also, the theory has the same limitations as those discussed in connection with tacit collusion: It does not explain the observed price stickiness among monopolies and monopolistic competitors.

Cost of Changing Prices

We saw in Chapter 14 that firms often have cost curves that are flat up to full capacity output. We also noted that multiproduct firms selling differentiated products find it costly to change their quoted prices.

The explanation of sticky prices based on flat cost curves and the cost of changing prices is illustrated in Figure 14A-2. Firms estimate their *normal* demand curve, that is, the average of what they can expect to sell at each price over booms and slumps. Having built a plant consistent with this normal demand, and with the expected fluctuations in output, they adopt the profit-maximizing price derived from their normal demand curve as their "normal price." Short-run fluctuations in demand are met by holding price constant and varying output. This avoids all the costs involved in repeated changes of prices.

The behavior just described is consistent with profit maximization if the costs of changing prices are high enough and production cost curves are flat enough. The best thing that a firm can do then is set the price that maximizes profits for average demand and then adjust output rather than price, as demand varies over the cycle. The theory applies equally well to firms in oligopoly, monopolistic competition, and monopoly. Manufacturing firms in all of these market structures find it costly to change prices and usually have saucer-shaped cost curves. Furthermore, the theory predicts stickiness in the face of short-term shifts in demand, which clearly does occur, while allowing price changes in the face of shifts in costs, which also seems to conform with available evidence.

FIGURE 14A-2 A Theory of Sticky Prices in the Face of Fluctuating Demand

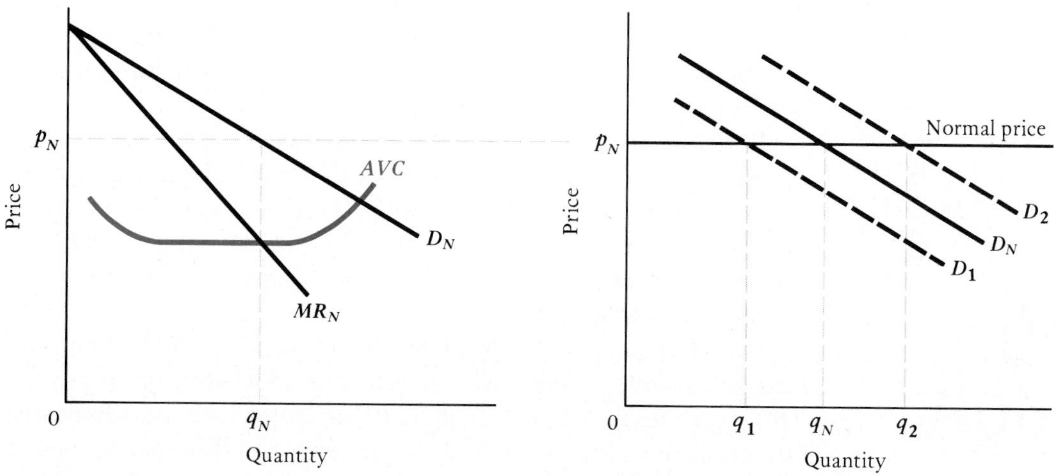

(i) Determining normal price

(ii) Adjusting to demand fluctuations

If it is costly to make price changes, a profit-maximizing firm may fix a price based on average sales and vary quantity in the face of fluctuating demand. In part (i), the firm with normal capacity q_N and a normal (average) demand curve D_N with a marginal revenue curve MR_N sets p_N as the profit-maximizing price, where $MR_N = MC$ (which equals AVC, because average variable cost is constant at q_N). This price becomes its normal price. As shown in part (ii), when demand slumps to D_1, the firm reduces output to q_1 but keeps price unchanged. When demand peaks at D_2, it also maintains prices and increases output to q_2.

Chapter 15

Public Policy Toward Monopoly and Competition

Monopoly has long been regarded with suspicion. In *The Wealth of Nations* (1776), Adam Smith developed a stinging attack on monopolists. Since then, most economists have criticized monopoly and advocated competition.

In this chapter we first consider what economic theory has to say about the relevant advantages of the two polar market structures of monopoly and competition. Next we examine intermediate market forms and then go on to observe some details of public policy that are directed at encouraging competition and discouraging monopoly.

Part of the appeal of competition and the distrust of monopoly is noneconomic, being based on a fear of concentration of power. This was discussed in Chapter 12 on page 242. Much of the attraction of competition and the dislike of monopoly, however, has to do with the understanding that competition is efficient in ways that monopoly is not. This argument over *efficiency* constitutes the classic case against monopoly. To understand the arguments, we must first define *efficiency*.

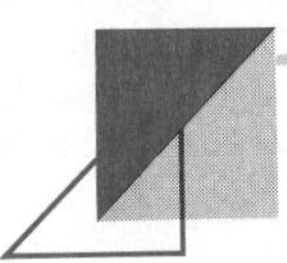

Economic Efficiency

Economic efficiency requires avoiding the waste of resources. When labor is unemployed and factories lie idle (as occurs in serious recessions), their potential current output is lost. If these resources could be employed, total output would be increased and hence everyone could be made better off. However, full employment of resources by itself is not enough to prevent the waste of resources. Even when resources are being fully used, they may be used inefficiently. Let us look at three examples of inefficiency in the use of resources.

1. If firms do not use the least costly method of producing their chosen outputs, they waste resources. For example, a firm that produces 30,000 pairs of shoes at a resource cost of \$400,000 when it could have been done at a cost of only \$350,000 is using resources inefficiently. The lower-cost method would allow \$50,000 worth of resources to be transferred to productive uses.
2. If some firms produce at high cost while other firms produce at low cost, the industry's overall cost of producing its output is higher than necessary.

3. If too much of one product and too little of another product are produced, resources are being used inefficiently. To take an extreme example, suppose that so many shoes are produced that every consumer has all the shoes he or she could possibly want and so places a zero value on obtaining an additional pair of shoes. Further assume that fewer coats are produced relative to demand, so that each consumer places a positive value on obtaining an additional coat. Now each consumer can be made better off by reallocating resources from shoe production (where the last shoe produced has a low value in the eyes of consumers) to coat production (where one more coat produced would have a higher value to consumers).

These examples suggest that we must refine our ideas of the waste of resources beyond the simple notion of ensuring that all resources are employed. The sources of inefficiency just outlined suggest important conditions that must be fulfilled if economic efficiency is to be attained. These conditions are conveniently collected into two categories, called *productive efficiency* and *allocative efficiency,* which were studied long ago by the great Italian economist Vilfredo Pareto (1848–1923). Indeed, efficiency in the use of resources is often called *Pareto-optimality* or *Pareto-efficiency* in his honor.

Productive Efficiency

Productive efficiency has two aspects, one concerning production within each firm and one concerning the allocation of production among the firms in an industry.

The first condition for **productive efficiency** is that each firm should produce any given output at the lowest possible cost. In the short run, with only one variable factor, the firm has no problem of choice of technique. It merely uses enough of the variable factor to produce the desired level of output. In the long run, however, more than one method of production is available. Productive efficiency requires that the firm use the least costly of the available methods of producing any given output. This means that firms will be located on, rather than above, their long-run average cost curves.

In Chapter 11 we studied the condition for productive efficiency within the firm:

Productive efficiency requires that each firm produce its given output by combining factors of production in such a way that the ratios of the marginal products of each pair of factors is made equal to the ratio of their prices.

This is the same thing as saying that $1 spent on every factor should yield the same output. If this is not so, the firm can reduce the resource costs of producing its given output by substituting the input for which $1 of expenditure yields the higher output for the input for which $1 of expenditure yields the lower output.[1]

The second condition for productive efficiency ensures that the total output of each industry is allocated among its individual firms in such a way that the total cost of producing the industry's output is minimized. If an industry is productively inefficient, it would be possible to reduce the industry's total cost of producing any given total industry output by reallocating production among the industry's individual firms.

Productive efficiency requires that all firms in an industry must produce output levels at which they have the same level of marginal cost

To see the importance of this condition, assume that it is not fulfilled. Suppose that the Jones Brothers shoe manufacturing firm has a marginal cost of $40 for the last shoe of some standard type that it produces, while Gonzales, Inc., has a marginal cost of only $35 for the same type of shoe. If the Jones plant produces one less pair of shoes while the Gonzales plant produces one more, total shoe output is unchanged, but total industry costs are reduced by $5. Thus $5 worth of resources will be freed to increase the production of other commodities.

Clearly, this cost saving can go on as long as the two firms have different marginal costs. However, as the Gonzales firm produces more shoes, its marginal cost rises, and as the Jones firm produces fewer

[1] As we saw in Box 11-1, producing at least cost within the firm also involves a more obvious type of efficiency, called *technical efficiency*. Technical efficiency means that the firm does not adopt any method of production when there exists another method that uses less of all inputs. Productive (economic) efficiency then ensures that the firm chooses the one method that uses the lowest *value* of resources from among the technically efficient methods. Professor Harvey Leibenstein has developed a theory of why firms, particularly those in less developed countries, may often adopt technically inefficient methods. When a firm is technically inefficient for any one of the reasons given in his theory, he speaks of it as being *X-inefficient* rather than technically inefficient.

shoes, its marginal cost falls. (By producing more, the Gonzales firm is moving upward to the right along its given *MC* curve, while by producing less, the Jones firm is moving downward to the left along its given *MC* curve.) Say, for example, that after Gonzales, Inc., increases its production by 1,000 shoes per month, its marginal cost *rises* to $37, while when Jones Brothers reduces its output by the same amount, its marginal cost *falls* to $37. Now there is no further cost saving to be obtained by reallocating production between the two firms.

Figure 15-1 shows a production possibility curve of the sort that was first introduced in Figure 1-2. Productive inefficiency implies that the economy is at some point inside the curve. In such a situation it is possible to produce more of some goods without producing less of others.

Productive efficiency implies being on, rather than inside, the economy's production possibility curve.

Allocative Efficiency

Productive efficiency ensures that any given volume of an industry's output is produced at the lowest possible cost. Allocative efficiency concerns the relative quantities of the commodities to be produced. Achieving allocative efficiency ensures that the bundle of goods actually produced is an efficient one. **Allocative efficiency** refers to a situation in which it is impossible to change the allocation of resources in such a way as to make someone better off without making someone else worse off. Changing the allocation of resources implies producing more of some goods and less of others, that is, changing the mix of production.

From an allocative point of view, resources are said to be used *inefficiently* when using them to produce a different bundle of goods would make it *possible* for at least one person to be better off while making no other person worse off. Conversely, resources are said to be used *efficiently* when it is *impossible*, by using them to produce a different bundle of goods, to make any one person better off without making at least one other person worse off.

Reallocating resources to produce a different bundle of goods means moving from one point on the economy's production possibility curve to another point. This is also shown in Figure 15-1.

FIGURE 15-1 Productive and Allocative Efficiency

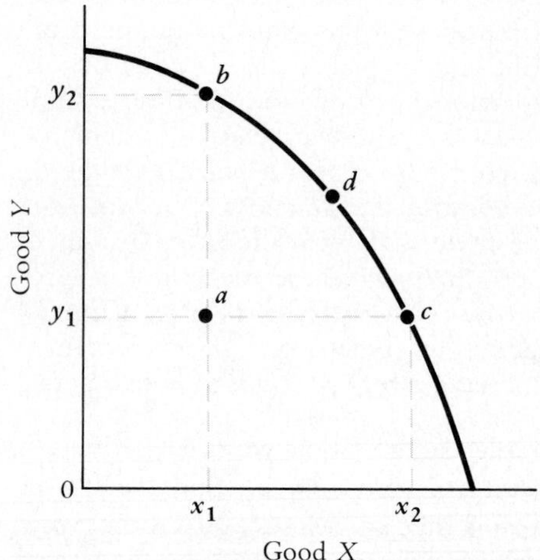

Any point on the production possibility curve is productively efficient; not all points on this curve are allocatively efficient. The curve shows all combinations of two goods *X* and *Y* that can be produced when the economy's resources are fully employed and being used with productive efficiency.

Any point inside the curve, such as *a*, is productively inefficient. If the inefficiency exists in industry *X*, production could be reallocated among firms in that industry in such a way as to raise production of *X* from x_1 to x_2. This would take the economy from point *a* to point *c*, raising production of *X* without any reduction in production of *Y*. Similarly, if the inefficiency exists in industry *Y*, production of *Y* could be increased from y_1 to y_2, which would take the economy from point *a* to point *b*. If both industries are allocatively inefficient, production can be increased to take the economy to some point on the curve *between* *b* and *c*, thus increasing the production of *both* commodities.

Allocative efficiency concerns being at the most efficient point on the production possibility curve. Assessing allocative efficiency means judging among points on the curve, such as *b*, *c*, and *d*. Usually only one such point will be allocatively efficient, while all others will be inefficient.

This tells us what is meant by allocative efficiency, but how is it achieved? How do we find the efficient point on the production possibility curve? For example, how many shoes should be produced to achieve allocative efficiency? How many dresses should be produced? How many hats should be produced?

The answer is as follows:

The economy's allocation of resources is efficient when, for every good produced, marginal cost of production is equal to its price.

To understand the reasoning behind this answer, we need to recall a point that was established in our discussion of consumers' surplus in Chapter 7. The price of any commodity indicates the value that each consumer places on the last unit of that commodity that is consumed. Facing the market price of some commodity, the consumer goes on buying units until the last one is valued exactly at its price. Consumers' surplus arises because the consumer would be willing to pay more than the market price for all but the last unit that is bought. On the last unit bought (i.e., the marginal unit), however, the consumer only "breaks even," because the valuation placed on it is just equal to its price.

Now assume that some commodity, say, shoes, sells for $30 per pair but has a marginal cost of $40. If one less pair of shoes were produced, the value that all households would place on the pair of shoes not produced would be $30. Using the concept of opportunity cost, however, we see that the resources that would have been used to produce that last pair of shoes could instead produce another good (say, a coat) valued at $40. If society can give up something that its members value at $30 and get in return something that its members value at $40, the original allocation of resources is inefficient. Someone can be made better off, and no one need be worse off.

This is easy to see when the same household gives up the shoes and gets the coat, but it follows even when different households are involved, for the gaining household could compensate the losing household and still come out ahead.

Assume next that shoe production is cut back until the price of a pair of shoes rises from $30 to $35, while its marginal cost falls from $40 to $35. Efficiency is achieved in shoe production because $p = MC =$ $35. Now if one less pair of shoes were produced, $35 worth of shoes would be sacrificed, while, at most, $35 worth of other commodities could be produced with the freed resources.

In this situation the allocation of resources to shoe production is efficient because it is not possible to change it to make someone better off without making someone else worse off. If one household were to sacrifice the pair of shoes, it would give up goods worth $35 and would then have to obtain for itself all of the new production of the alternative commodity produced just to break even. It cannot gain without making another household worse off. The same argument can be repeated for every commodity, and it leads to the conclusion that we have stated already: The allocation of resources is efficient when each commodity's price equals its marginal cost.

Allocative efficiency is assured for the whole economy if price equals marginal cost in all industries.

Efficiency in Perfect Competition and in Monopoly

We now know that for productive efficiency, marginal cost should be the same for all firms in any one industry and that for allocative efficiency, marginal cost should be equal to price in all industries. Do the market structures of perfect competition and monopoly lead to productive and allocative efficiency?

Perfect Competition

Productive efficiency. We saw in Figure 12-9 that in the long run under perfect competition, all firms produce at the lowest point on their long-run average cost curves. Therefore, no one firm could lower its costs by altering its own production.

We also know that in perfect competition, all firms in an industry face the same price of their product and that they equate marginal cost to that price. It follows immediately that marginal cost will be the same for all firms. Because all firms in the industry have the same cost of producing their last unit of production, no reallocation of production among the firms could reduce the total industry cost of producing a given output.

Productive efficiency is achieved under perfect competition because all firms in an industry face the same price and so have identical marginal costs at all times and achieve the same level of minimized costs in long-run equilibrium.

Allocative efficiency. We have seen already that perfectly competitive firms maximize their profits by equating marginal cost to price. Thus when perfect competition is the market structure for the whole economy, price is equal to marginal cost for all production.

Allocative efficiency is achieved when perfect competition prevails across the whole economy because price will be equal to marginal cost in all industries.

Monopoly

Productive efficiency. Monopolists have an incentive to be productively efficient because their profits will be maximized when they adopt the lowest-cost method that can be used to produce the level of output that is chosen. Thus profit-maximizing monopolists will operate on their *LRAC* curves. Furthermore, when they have more than one plant producing the same product, they will allocate production among those plants so that the cost of producing the last unit of output is the same in all plants.

Allocative efficiency. Although any profit-maximizing monopoly is productively efficient, its level of output will be too low to achieve allocative efficiency. We have seen that the monopolist chooses an output at which the price charged is greater than marginal cost. This violates the conditions for allocative efficiency because the amount that consumers pay for the last unit of output exceeds the opportunity cost of producing it.

Consumers would be prepared to buy additional units for an amount that is greater than the cost of producing these units. Some consumers could be made better off, and none need be made worse off, by shifting extra resources into production of the monopolized commodity, thus increasing the production of the product. As a consequence, the monopolist produces an output that is *not* allocatively efficient.

From this follows the classic efficiency-based preference for competition over monopoly.

Monopoly is not allocatively efficient, since the monopolist's price always exceeds its marginal cost.

This result has important policy implications for economists and for policymakers, as we shall see later in this chapter.

Efficiency in Other Market Structures

Note that the result just stated extends beyond the case of a simple monopoly. Whenever a firm has any power over the market in the sense that it faces a negatively sloped rather than a horizontal demand curve, its profit-maximizing behavior will lead it to produce where *MC* equals *MR,* not where *MC* equals price. Thus, strictly speaking, both oligopoly and monopolistic competition are allocatively inefficient.

Oligopoly is an important market structure in today's economy because in many industries the minimum efficient scale is simply too high to support a large group of competing firms. Although oligopoly does not achieve the conditions for allocative efficiency, it may produce more satisfactory results than monopoly. As we observed in Chapter 14, oligopoly may also be effective in generating very long run adaptations that result in both new products and cost-reducing methods of producing old ones.

The defense of oligopoly as a market form is that it may be the best of the available alternatives when minimum efficient scale is large. As we observed at the end of Chapter 14, the challenge to public policy is to keep oligopolists competing and using their competitive energies to improve products and to lower costs rather than to restrict interfirm competition and to erect entry barriers. As we shall see later in this chapter, much public policy has just this purpose. What economic policymakers call *monopolistic practices* include not only output restrictions operated by firms with complete monopoly power but also anticompetitive behavior among firms that are operating in oligopolistic market structures.

Allocative Efficiency: An Elaboration

We have established a basic understanding of productive and allocative efficiency. A fuller interpretation of the normative significance of allocative efficiency can be given by using the concepts of consumers' and producers' surplus.

Consumers' and Producers' Surplus

We saw in Chapter 7 that consumers' surplus is the difference between the total value that consumers

FIGURE 15-2 Consumers' Surplus and Producers' Surplus

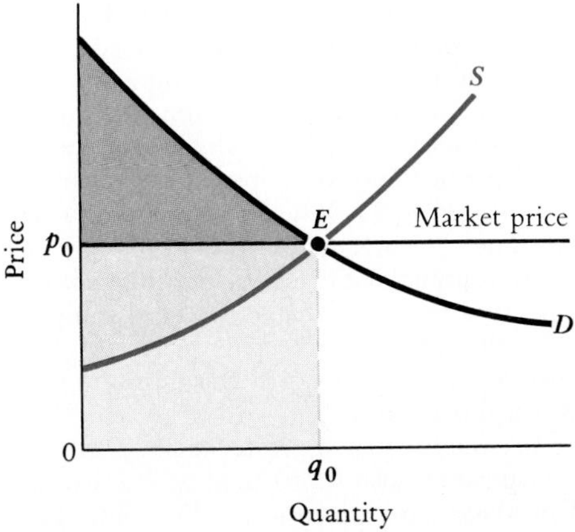

Consumers' surplus is the area under the demand curve and above the market price line. Producers' surplus is the area above the supply curve and below the market price line. The equilibrium price and quantity in this competitive market are p_0 and q_0, respectively. The total value that consumers place on q_0 of the commodity is given by the sum of the three shaded areas. The amount that they pay is p_0q_0, the rectangle that consists of the two lighter shaded areas. The difference, shown as the dark shaded area, is *consumers' surplus*.

The receipts to producers from the sale of q_0 units are also p_0q_0. The area under the supply curve, the color-shaded area, is total variable cost, the minimum amount that producers require to supply the output. The difference, shown as the light gray shaded area, is *producers' surplus*.

place on all the units consumed of some commodity and the payment that they actually make for the purchase of that commodity. Consumers' surplus is shown once again in Figure 15-2.

Producers' surplus is analogous to consumers' surplus. It occurs because all units of each firm's output are sold at the same market price, while, given a rising supply curve, each unit except the last is produced at a marginal cost that is less than the market price.

Producers' surplus is defined as the amount that producers are paid for a commodity less their total variable cost of producing the commodity. The total variable cost of producing any output is shown by the area under the supply curve up to that output.[2] Thus producers' surplus is the area above the supply curve and below the line giving market price. Producers' surplus is also shown in Figure 15-2.

The Allocative Efficiency of Perfect Competition Revisited

If the sum of consumers' and producers' surplus is not maximized, the industry could be moved to the point where it was, and the extra surplus that is available could be used to make some household better off without making anyone worse off.

Allocative efficiency occurs at the point where the sum of consumers' and producers' surplus is maximized.

The point where the sum of consumers' and producers' surplus is maximized is where the demand curve intersects the supply curve, that is, the point of equilibrium in a competitive market. This is shown graphically in Figure 15-3. For any output that is less than the competitive output, the demand curve is above the supply curve, which means that consumers value the last unit at an amount that is greater than its marginal cost of production. Suppose, for example, that the current output of shoes is such that consumers value at $45 an additional pair of shoes that adds $35 to costs. If it is sold at any price between $35 and $45, both producers and consumers gain; there is $10 of potential surplus to be divided between the two groups. In contrast, the last unit produced and sold at competitive equilibrium adds nothing to either consumers' or producers' surplus, since consumers value it at exactly its market price, and it adds the full amount of the market price to producers' costs.

If production were pushed beyond the competitive equilibrium, the sum of the two surpluses would

[2] The marginal cost shows the addition to total cost caused by producing one more unit of output. Summing these additions over each unit of output, starting with the first, yields the total variable cost of output. For example, the sum of the marginal costs of producing the first 10 units of output is the total variable cost associated with 10 units of output. Graphically, this process of summation is shown by the whole area under the marginal cost curve. Since, as we have already seen, the industry supply curve is merely the sum of the marginal cost curves of all the firms in the industry, the area under that supply curve up to some given output is the total of all the firms' variable costs of producing that output.

FIGURE 15-3 **The Allocative Efficiency of Perfect Competition**

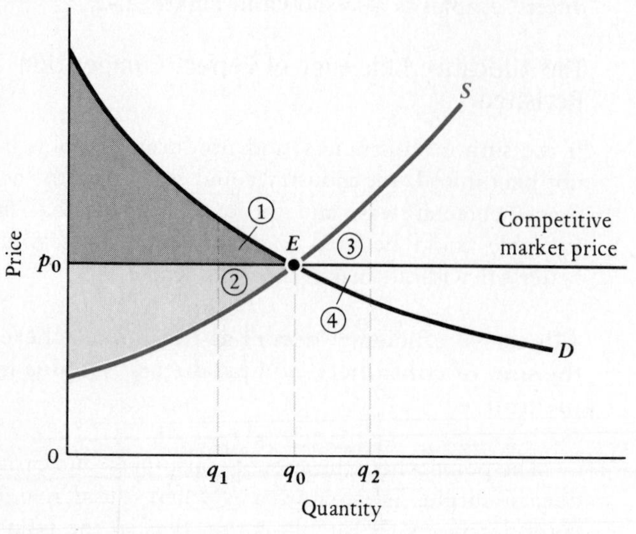

Competitive equilibrium is allocatively efficient because it maximizes the sum of consumers' and producers' surplus. The competitive equilibrium occurs at the price-output combination p_0q_0. At this equilibrium, consumers' surplus is the dark shaded area above the competitive market price line, while producers' surplus is the light shaded area below the competitive market price line.

For any output that is less than q_0, the sum of the two surpluses is less than at q_0. For example, reducing output to q_1 but keeping price at p_0 lowers consumers' surplus by area 1 and lowers producers' surplus by area 2.

For any output that is greater than q_0, the sum of the surpluses is also less than at q_0. For example, if producers are forced to produce output q_2 and to sell it to consumers, who are in turn forced to buy it at price p_0, producers' surplus is reduced by area 3 (the amount by which variable costs exceed revenue on those units), while the amount of consumers' surplus is reduced by area 4 (the amount by which expenditure exceeds consumers' satisfactions on those units).

Only at the competitive output, q_0, is the sum of the two surpluses maximized.

be diminished. Assume, for example, that firms were forced to produce and sell further units of output at the competitive market price and that consumers were forced to buy these extra units at that price. (Note that neither group would do so voluntarily.) Firms would lose producers' surplus on those extra units because their marginal costs of producing the extra output would be above the price that they received for it. Purchasers would lose consumers' surplus because the valuation that they placed on these extra units, as shown by the demand curve, would be less than the price that they would have to pay.

The sum of producers' and consumers' surplus is maximized *only at the competitive output,* which is thus the only output that is allocatively efficient.

The Allocative Inefficiency of Monopoly Revisited

Since, as we have just seen in Figure 15-3, the perfectly competitive equilibrium output maximizes the sum of consumers' and producers' surplus, it follows immediately that the lower monopoly output must result in a smaller total of consumers' and producers' surplus.

Why would producers and consumers agree to reduce their surpluses? The answer is that the monopoly equilibrium is not the outcome of voluntary agreement between the one producer and the many consumers. Instead, it is imposed by the monopolist by virtue of the power it has over the market. When the monopolist reduces output below the competitive level, market price rises. As a result, consumers' surplus is diminished, and producers' surplus is increased. In this way the monopoly firm gains at the expense of consumers. This is not the whole story, however.

When output is lowered from the competitive level, there is always a *net* loss of surplus. More is given up by consumers than is gained by the monopolist. Some surplus is lost, because output between the monopolistic and the competitive levels is not produced. This loss of surplus is called the *dead-*

FIGURE 15-4 The Allocative Inefficiency of Monopoly

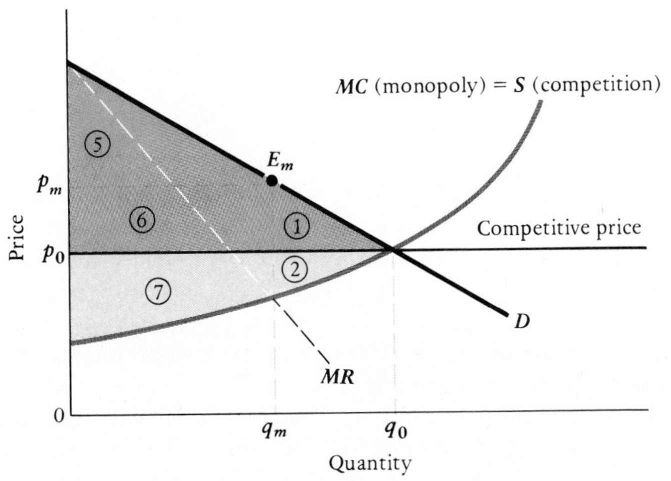

Monopoly is allocatively inefficient because it produces less than the competitive output and thus does not maximize the sum of consumers' and producers' surplus. If this market were perfectly competitive, price would be p_0, output would be q_0, and consumers' surplus would be the sum of areas 1, 5, and 6 (the dark shaded area). When the industry is monopolized, price rises to p_m, and consumers' surplus falls to area 5. Consumers lose area 1 because that output is not produced; they lose area 6 because the price rise has transferred it to the monopolist.

Producers' surplus in a competitive equilibrium would be the sum of areas 7 and 2 (the light shaded area). When the market is monopolized and price rises to p_m, the surplus area 2 is lost because the output is not produced. However, the monopolist gains area 6 from consumers (6 is known to be greater than 2 because p_m maximizes profits).

While area 6 is transferred from consumers' to producers' surplus by the price rise, *areas 1 and 2 are lost.* They represent the deadweight loss resulting from monopoly and account for its allocative inefficiency.

weight loss of monopoly. This is illustrated in Figure 15-4.

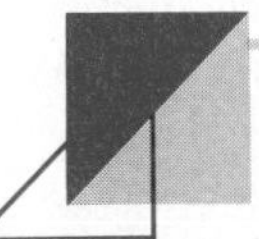

Major Policy Issues

Monopolies, cartels, and price-fixing agreements among oligopolists, whether explicit or tacit, have met with public suspicion and official hostility for over a century. These and other noncompetitive practices are collectively referred to as *monopoly practices.* Note that such practices go far beyond what actual monopolists do and include noncompetitive behavior of firms that are operating in other market structures. The laws and other instruments that are used to prevent monopoly practices make up **competition policy.** In addition, governments at all levels employ *economic regulations,* which precribe the rules under which firms can do business and in some cases determine the prices that businesses can charge for their output. Electric power and local telephone service are examples of services that are subject to this kind of regulation.

The goal of economic efficiency provides rationales both for competition policy and for economic regulation. Competition policy can be used in an attempt to promote efficiency by increasing competition in the marketplace. Where effective competition is not possible (as in the case of a natural monopoly, such as an electric power company), economic regulation of privately owned firms or public ownership can be used as a substitute for competition. Consumers can then be protected from the high prices and reduced output that result from the use of monopoly power.[3]

As we shall see in the remainder of this chapter, public policies are indeed used in these ways, but they are often used in ways that reduce economic efficiency. Why? The answer is partly that economic

[3] A second kind of regulation, *social regulation,* involves a government's rules that require firms to consider the health, safety, environmental, and other social consequences of their behavior. Social regulation will be discussed in Chapter 23.

efficiency is not the only thing that policymakers have been concerned with in the design and implementation of competition policy. Partly it is an example of a more general phenomenon that we shall discuss in Chapter 22: When public policies that have the potential to redistribute income and wealth are available, various private interests will try to use them for private gain, regardless of their original public purpose. We shall see in the remainder of this chapter that competition policy and economic regulation have often been used in ways that reduce efficiency by protecting firms from the consequences of competition. Protection of Canadian firms from competition comes in many forms, including protection of firms from foreign competition, protection of less efficient firms from their more efficient domestic rivals, and protection of firms generally from "unfair" competition.

In the remainder of this chapter we shall look at a variety of ways in which Canadian policymakers have chosen to intervene in the workings of the market economy through competition policy and economic regulation.

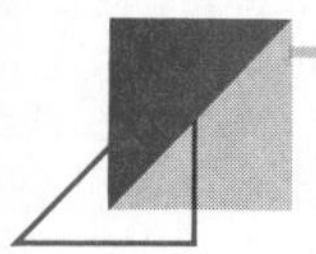

Canadian Competition Policy

Competition policy refers to public policy designed to encourage competition and discourage monopoly practices. This can be done by influencing either the market structure or the behavior of individual firms. By and large, Canadian competition policy has sought to create more competitive market structures where possible, to discourage monopolistic practices, and to encourage competitive behavior where competitive market structures could not be established.

We shall study three aspects of Canadian competition policy: first, the direct control of natural monopolies; second, the direct control of oligopolies; and, third, the creation of competitive conditions. The first is a necessary part of any competition policy, the second has been important in the past but is less so now, and the third constitutes the main current thrust of Canadian competition policy.

Direct Control of Natural Monopolies

The most apparent case for public intervention arises with a natural monopoly, an industry in which scale effects are so dominant that there is room for only one firm to operate at the minimum efficient scale. Canadian policymakers have not wanted to compel the existence of several smaller, less efficient producers whenever a single firm would be much more efficient; neither have they wanted to give a natural monopolist the opportunity to restrict output, raise prices, and reap the profits from large-scale production.

One response to natural monopoly is for government to assume *ownership* of the single firm, setting it up as a crown corporation. (In Canada, any government-owned firm is called a *crown corporation*.) The government appoints managers who are supposed to set prices guided by their understanding of the national interest.

Another response, common in Canada and the United States since the late nineteenth century, has been to allow private ownership but to *regulate* the monopoly firm's behavior.

Price Setting

Whether the state nationalizes or merely regulates privately owned, natural monopolies, the industry's pricing policy is determined by the government. Usually, the industry is asked to follow some policy other than profit maximization.

Marginal cost pricing. Sometimes the government dictates that the natural monopoly should try to set price equal to short-run marginal cost in an effort to maximize consumers' plus producers' surpluses in that industry. According to economic theory, this policy, which is called **marginal cost pricing**, provides the efficient solution.

Marginal cost pricing does, however, create some problems. The natural monopoly may still have unexploited economies of scale and may hence be operating on the falling portion of its average total cost curve. In this case, marginal cost will be less than average total cost, and pricing at marginal cost will lead to losses. This is shown in part (i) of Figure 15-5.

A falling-cost, natural monopoly that sets price equal to marginal cost will suffer losses.

Demand, however, may be sufficient to allow the firm to produce on the rising portion of its average total cost curve, that is, where output exceeds what

FIGURE 15-5 Pricing Policies for Natural Monopolies

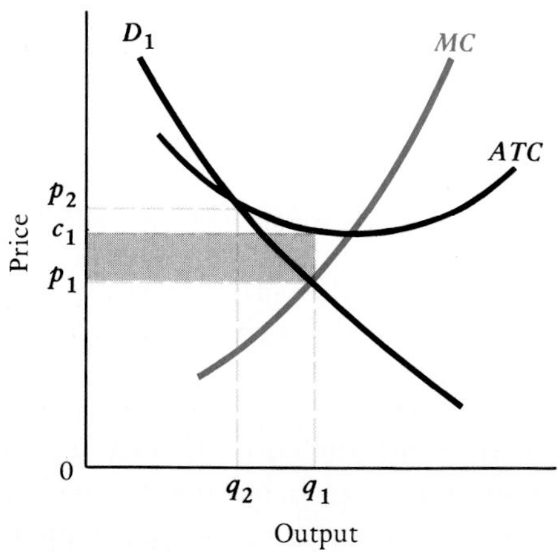

(i) Losses in a falling-cost industry

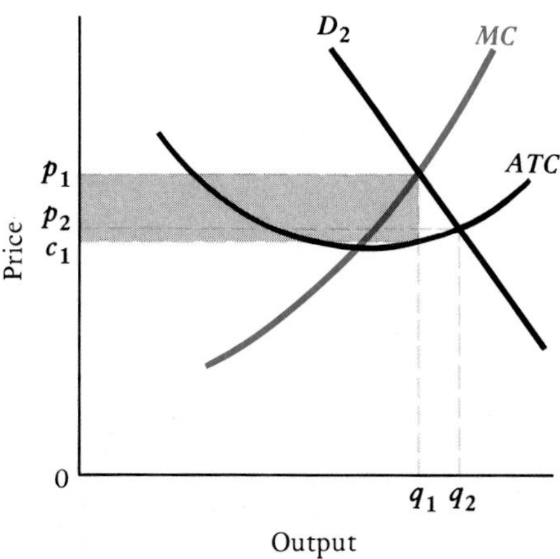

(ii) Profits in a rising-cost industry

Marginal cost pricing leads to profit or losses, whereas average cost pricing violates the efficiency condition. In each part, the output at which marginal cost equals price is q_1 and price is p_1.

In part (i), average costs are falling at output q_1, so marginal costs are less than the average cost of c_1. There is a loss of $c_1 - p_1$ on each unit, making a total loss equal to the shaded area.

In part (ii), average cost of c_1 is less than price at output q_1. There is a profit of $p_1 - c_1$ on each unit sold, making a total profit equal to the shaded area.

In each part of the diagram, the output at which average cost equals price is q_2 and price is p_2. In part (i), marginal cost is less than price at q_2, so output is below its optimal level. In part (ii), marginal cost exceeds price at q_2, so output is greater than its optimal level.

is needed to achieve the minimum efficient scale. At any such output, marginal cost exceeds average total cost. If the firm is directed to equate marginal cost to price, it will earn profits. This is shown in part (ii) of the figure.[4]

When a rising-cost, natural monopoly sets price equal to marginal cost, it will earn profits.

Average cost pricing. Sometimes natural monopolies are directed to produce the output that will just cover total costs, thus earning neither profits nor losses. This means that the firm produces to the point where average revenue equals average total cost, which is where the demand curve cuts the average total cost curve. Part (i) of Figure 15-5 shows that for a falling-cost firm, this pricing policy requires producing at less than the optimal output. The losses that would occur under marginal cost pricing are avoided by producing less than the efficient output.[5] Part (ii) shows that for a rising-cost firm, the policy requires producing at more than the optimal output. The profits that would occur under marginal cost pricing are dissipated by producing more than the efficient output.

Generally, average cost pricing will not result in allocative efficiency.

[4] Sometimes a natural monopoly is defined as one where long-run costs are falling when price equals marginal cost. This, however, is only *sufficient* for a natural monopoly; it is not *necessary*. Demand may be such that one firm is producing, when price equals marginal cost, on the rising portion of its long-run cost curve, while there is no price at which two firms could both cover their costs. For example, if a firm's minimum efficient scale is 1 million units of output and demand is sufficient to allow the firm to cover costs at 1.2 million units, there may be no price at which two firms, with their combined *MES* of 2 million units, can cover their full costs.

[5] Note that the losses are financial losses, not social welfare losses. Every unit produced between the points where *AC* equals price and *MC* equals price adds to consumers' surplus but brings private financial loss to the producer.

Investment Policies

The optimal pricing policy makes price equal to short-run marginal cost. The position of the short-run marginal cost curve (as well as the short-run average cost curve) depends, however, on the amount of fixed capital that is currently available to be combined with the variable factor. What should determine the long-run investment decision to accumulate fixed capital?

The efficient answer, if marginal cost pricing is being followed, is to compare the current market price with the long-run marginal cost. The former expresses the value consumers place on one additional unit of output. The latter expresses the full resource cost of providing an extra unit of output including capital costs.[6] If price exceeds long-run marginal cost, capacity should be expanded. If it is less, capacity should be allowed to decline as capital wears out.

The efficient pricing system rations the output of existing capacity by setting price equal to the short-run resource cost of producing another unit. It also adjusts capacity in the long run until the full marginal cost of producing another unit of output is equal to the price.

Provincial Hydro Authorities: An Example

The use of average cost pricing tends to distort investment decisions. Assume, for example, that there are three methods of generating electricity: cheap hydroelectric plants, medium-cost plants using fossil fuels, and expensive nuclear power stations. All of the hydroelectric sites have been used, and further fossil fuel plants are considered undesirable on environmental grounds, so new capacity must come from nuclear energy plants. The provincial hydro authority uses average cost pricing, so users pay more than the cost of the cheap hydroelectricity and less than the costs of expensive nuclear power. The hydro authority finds that there is excess demand for electricity at its current market price and proposes to install new capacity. Should it do so?

The relevant test is not, however, the existence of excess demand at the current price because the long-run cost of providing more electricity exceeds that price. The cost is, in fact, the full long-run marginal cost of providing electricity from atomic plants. On efficiency grounds, another plant should be built only if there is excess demand at a price that equals that full long-run cost.

This case illustrates the inefficient policies often adopted by nationalized and regulated industries that face rising long-run costs. If they priced at marginal cost, they would make profits, so they price at average cost. As a result, market price does not then provide the correct signal about the social value of further investment.

If a rising-cost firm installs enough capacity to meet all the demand when price is set equal to average cost, it will create more capacity than is socially optimal.

Such socially wasteful policies have been adopted by several provincial hydro authorities, including Ontario Hydro. On the one hand, they have resisted recommendations that they price at marginal cost because that would mean making profits at consumers' expense. On the other hand, they have increased capacity whenever demand exceeded supply at a price equal to average cost; they thus require that consumers pay enough in electricity costs to cover the building of new plants whose output consumers would be unwilling to buy if asked to pay its full costs of production.

The Very Long Run

Natural monopoly is a long-run concept, meaning that *given existing technology,* there is room for only one firm to operate profitably. In the very long run, however, technology changes. Not only does today's competitive industry sometimes become tomorrow's natural monopoly, but today's natural monopoly sometimes becomes tomorrow's competitive industry.

A striking example is the telecommunications industry. Fifteen years ago, message transmission was a natural monopoly. Now technological developments such as satellite transmission, electronic mail, and fax machines have made this activity highly competitive. In many countries an odd circumstance has now arisen: Nationalized industries seek to maintain their profitability by prohibiting entry into what

[6] To make the correct comparison, the cost of capital must be expressed at its current rental price so that it can be added to such other costs as wages and fuel.

would otherwise become a fluid and competitive industry. Since it has the full force of the legal system behind it, the public firm may be more successful than the privately owned firm in preserving its monopoly long after technological changes have destroyed its "naturalness."

Market economies change continually under the impacts of innovation and growth; to be successful, government policy must also be adopted continually to keep it relevant to the ever-changing existing situation.

Direct Control of Oligopolies

Governments have from time to time intervened in industries that were oligopolies, rather than natural monopolies, seeking to enforce the type of price and entry behavior that was thought to be in the public interest. Such intervention has typically taken two distinct forms. In the United Kingdom, it was primarily nationalization of whole oligopolistic industries such as railways, steel, and coal mining, which were then to be run by government-appointed boards. In the United States, firms such as airlines, railways, and electric power companies were left in private hands, but their decisions were regulated by government-appointed bodies that set prices and regulated entry. As so often happens, Canada followed a mixture of the British and the American practices. Many Canadian crown corporations, which are in effect nationalized firms, were set up, and many firms that were left in private hands were regulated. For example, in the regulated railway industry, the CPR was privately owned, while the CNR was a crown corporation.

Skepticism About Direct Control

In recent times, policymakers have become increasingly skeptical of their ability to improve the behavior of oligopolistic industries by having the state control the details of their behavior either through ownership or regulation. Several experiences have been important in determining this skepticism.

First, oligopolistic market structures have provided much of the economic growth since World War II. New products, and new ways of producing old products, have followed each other in rapid succession, all leading to higher living standards and higher productivity. Many of these innovations have been provided by firms in oligopolistic industries such as automobiles, agricultural implements, steel, petroleum refining, chemicals, and telecommunications. As long as governments can keep oligopolists competing with each other, rather than cooperating to create monopoly profits, most economists see no need to regulate such things as the prices at which oligopolists sell their products and the conditions of entry into oligopolistic industries.

Second, many regulatory bodies have imposed policies that were not related to the cost of each of the services being priced. These prices involved what is called *cross subsidization,* whereby profits that are earned in the provision of one service are used to subsidize the provision of another at a price below cost. Typically, regulators have required that long-distance telephone calls subsidize local calls, first-class mail subsidize third-class mail, and long-haul airline rates subsidize short-haul rates. These pricing policies have forced users of the profitable service to subsidize users of the unprofitable service. When these users are firms that compete with firms in other countries where regulators do not require cross subsidization, international competitiveness can be reduced. For example, firms using long-distance telephones in Canada are placed at a disadvantage with respect to firms using similar services in the United States, where competition holds long-distance rates close to the cost of providing the service.

Third, the record of postwar government intervention into regulated industries seemed poorer in practice than its supporters had predicted. When industries were *nationalized,* antagonism often persisted between management, concerned with financial viability, and workers, concerned with take-home pay. As a result, it was not long before the unexpected became commonplace: strikes against the industries that the people themselves owned. When industries were *regulated,* the results were often less beneficial to consumers than had been expected. Research by economists slowly established that in many industries, regulatory bodies were captured by the very firms that they were supposed to be regulating. As a result, the regulatory bodies that were meant to ensure competition often acted to enforce monopoly practices that would have been illegal if instituted by the firms themselves.

This last point, which entails the use of regulatory policy to protect firms from too much competition rather than to protect consumers from too little, will be discussed in more detail.

Protection *Against* Competition

Regulatory bodies have frequently protected firms rather than consumers. For example, Canadian and American railroad rates were originally regulated in order to keep profits down by establishing schedules of *maximum* rates. By the 1930s, however, concern had grown over the depressed economic condition of the railroads and the emerging vigorous competition from trucks and barges. The regulators then became the protectors of the railroads, permitting them to establish *minimum* rates for freight of different classes, allowing price discrimination, and encouraging other restrictive practices. Moreover, the regulators became leading advocates of including trucking under the regulatory umbrella. Restricting entry into trucking and setting minimum rates for trucks was unmistakably protectionist. The only reason for regulating the large carriers was to control their competition with the railroads. The big road carriers were limited in where they could go and how low a price they could quote. As a result, they became targets for small, unregulated truckers, who could cut rates and thus draw away customers without fear of retaliation. To eliminate the rate competition, regulation was extended to small truckers.

Airline regulation in Canada and the United States provided another example. When airline routes and fares were first regulated, there was arguably so little demand that competition could not have been effective. By the mid 1960s, however, the regulation was plainly protectionist and designed to shield the major carriers from competition in both countries. Supporters of regulation argued that unrestricted competition would be so intense that it might ruin the industry and even invite cost-cutting practices that endangered public safety. Critics argued that competition might destroy some existing airlines but would prepare the ground for an efficient industry, while regulation could still be used to enforce such things as minimum safety standards on private airline firms.

For decades, Canadian regulation of airline prices consistently blocked price competition. Foreign airlines wishing to cut fares between Canada and Europe have been barred from doing so. Until recently, airlines other than Air Canada and CAI were prevented from introducing cheap transcontinental fares. In the circumstances, it is hard to see Canadian airline regulation as protecting the interests of passengers against the predatory behavior of the carriers.

Why did regulatory bodies shift from protecting consumers to protecting firms? One thesis championed by the American professor George Stigler is that the regulatory commissions were gradually captured by the firms they were supposed to regulate. In part, this capture was natural enough. When regulatory bodies were hiring staff, they needed people who were knowledgeable in the industries they were regulating. Where better to go than to people who had worked in these industries? Naturally, these people tended to be sympathetic to firms in their own industries. Also, since many of them aspired to go back to those industries once they had gained experience within the regulatory bodies, they were not inclined to arouse the wrath of industry officials by imposing policies that were against the firms' interests.

Deregulation and Privatization

The 1980s witnessed a movement in many advanced industrial nations to reduce the level of government control over industry. A number of forces had been pushing in this direction: (1) the experience that regulatory bodies often sought to reduce, rather than increase, competition; (2) the dashing of the unreasonable hopes that nationalized industries would work better than private firms in the areas of efficiency, productivity growth, and industrial relations; (3) the realization that replacing a private monopoly with a publicly owned one would not greatly change the industry's performance and that replacing privately owned oligopolists by a publicly owned monopoly might actually worsen the industry's performance; (4) the awareness that falling transportation costs and revolutions in data processing and communications exposed local industries to much more widespread international competition than they had previously experienced domestically; and (5) concern over the cross subsidization often required by regulatory bodies.

The natural outcome of these revised views were deregulation, intended, among other things, to leave prices and entry free to be determined by private decisions, and the privatization of crown corporations.

Privatization went a long way in the United Kingdom in the 1980s. Most of the nationalized industries, both those containing a few large firms and those containing many smaller firms, were returned to private ownership. In Canada, hundreds of crown corporations that the government had acquired for a variety of reasons but were neither natural monopolies nor operating in highly concentrated oligopolistic industries were sold off.[7] Other firms, such as airlines and gas and oil, were deregulated. Prices were freed, to be set by the firms in the industry, and entry was no longer restricted by government policy.

Once the government decides to sell off a crown corporation, a decision has to be made between short-run and long-run benefits. On the one hand, the industry can earn most profits, and thus sell for the highest price, if it remains a monopoly. However, the government may then face renewed regulatory pressures when the monopoly position is exploited by the private owners in later years. On the other hand, competition can be encouraged if the industry is broken into as many parts as possible and then sold to different owners. The sale price will then be less because a competitive industry will earn lower profits than the monopolized one. Many economists urged governments to enhance the long-run public interest by selling off their industries in as competitive a form as possible. The U.K. government has not done this and has often chosen to get the maximum revenue—which can be used to generate a temporary reduction in its budget deficit—by selling off industries in a monopolized form. It remains to be seen if the Canadian government will be more far-sighted or whether it will give in to the temptation to get the maximum sale price when it comes to privatizing some of its own large crown corporations.

In the United States, the movement to reduce government intervention took the form of deregulation. Airlines, motor carriers, banks, natural gas producers, and long-distance telephone companies are among those that have been substantially unleashed from close regulatory supervision of both prices and entry. The effects, and thus the wisdom, of these changes are the subject of both economic analysis and political debate. A considerable lapse of time is needed, however, before the industry settles into a stable postregulation pattern. For example, when the airline industry was first deregulated, competition became fierce as many small entrants challenged the existing giants. Fares fell, and travelers enjoyed numerous bargains. Slowly, however, a series of mergers produced larger and larger companies, and the lowest cut-rate fares gradually disappeared. Nonetheless, average fares per mile traveled still remain substantially lower than in Europe, where governments are still inching slowly toward airline deregulation. Where the industry will finally settle, and whether that result will be judged to be more in the consumers' interests than the regulation situation, remains to be seen.

[7] It has always been difficult to estimate the number of government-owned corporations in Canada since these are underrepresented on many official lists. Marsha Gordon, in *Government in Business* (Montreal: C. D. Howe Institute, 1981, p. 3), gives the number as 464 federal corporations in 1981; numerous others were either wholly or partly owned by provincial governments. Since that time, the number has been reduced significantly through the government's privatization policy.

Intervention to Keep Firms Competing

The least stringent form of government intervention is designed neither to force firms to sell at particular prices nor to regulate the conditions of entry and exit; it is designed, instead, to create conditions of competition by preventing firms from merging unnecessarily or from engaging in certain anticompetitive practices such as colluding to set monopoly prices. Here the policy seeks to create the most competitive market structure possible and then to prevent firms from reducing competition by engaging in certain forms of cooperative behavior.

The Thrust of Canadian Policy

Laws designed for these purposes are called **combine laws** in Canada. They have provided the main thrust of Canadian competition policy since its inception in the nineteenth century. They prohibit monopolies, attempts to monopolize, and conspiracies in restraint of trade. Throughout the history of Canadian competition policy, legislation has been directed chiefly at the misuse of market power by single firms or groups of firms and only rarely at mergers per se. In introducing legislation in 1910, the minister of labor, stated: "This measure seeks to afford the means of conserving to the public some of the benefits which arise from large organizations of capital."

This acceptance of the need for relatively large

firms in the business sector was partly a function of the small size of the Canadian economy in the days when most production was for the domestic market. In small markets such as Canada's, firms that were large enough to exploit the available economies of scale were likely to be large in relation to the total market. This meant that there would be fewer firms in Canadian industries dominated by scale effects than would be found in similar industries in such relatively large economies as the United States'.

The Development of Canadian Policy

The first Canadian combine laws were adopted in 1889 and 1890 when legislation made it an offense to combine, to agree to lessen competition unduly, or to restrain trade. Because the proscribed behavior was illegal, an offense was a criminal act to be handled by the criminal justice system. The laws have been changed frequently since that time, but their basic procompetition stance still prevails in current legislation.

The Combines Investigation Act of 1910 empowered the minister of labor to appoint a board of three commissioners to carry out a full inquiry into specific allegations and publish a report of its findings. This legislation relied strongly on the publicity attached to an investigation as a deterrent to restrictive trade practices. The Combines Investigation Act of 1923 provided punishment for past participation in the formation or operation of a combine. In 1935 the legislation was amended to prohibit discriminatory pricing that substantially lessened competition or eliminated a competitor, and in 1951 resale price maintenance was added to the list of proscribed practices.

With these amendments, the first major development of competition policy was completed. The laws made illegal three broad classes of activity: (1) combinations, such as price-fixing agreements that unduly lessen competition; (2) mergers or monopolies that may operate to the detriment of the public interest; and (3) unfair trade practices.

Many cases of unfair trade practices were successfully pursued under these laws, but compared to the United States, few cases were brought against mergers, and none of those that were brought were successful. The reason most often cited for this lack of success was the inability of criminal legislation to cope with complex economic issues. Under criminal law, the government must prove beyond a reasonable doubt that the accused has committed the offense.

As an added complication, Canadian courts have been much less willing than American courts to assess economic evidence. For example, Justice Spence in *R.* v. *Howard Smith Paper Mills* (1959) reemphasized the courts' difficulty:

> Surely the determination of whether or not an agreement to lessen competition was "undue" by a survey of one industry's profits against profits of industry generally, and a survey of the movement of the prices in that one industry against the movement of prices generally, would put the Court to the essentially non-judicial task of judging between conflicting political theories. It would entail the Court's being required to conjecture—and by a Court it would be nothing more than mere conjecture, since a Court is not trained to act as an arbitrator of economics—whether better or worse results would have occurred to the public if free and untrammelled competition had been permitted to run its course.

Current Canadian Policy

A major review of Canadian legislation was undertaken in the late 1960s by the Economic Council of Canada. Its recommendations, published in a report in 1969, together with those of a committee of experts appointed by the Department of Consumer and Corporate Affairs, formed the basis of the amendments to the Combines Investigation Act that are still in force. Of the recommendations that were accepted, some were put into practice in 1976 and the remainder in 1986.

Amendments of 1976. The first set of amendments, proclaimed in 1976, included several provisions: (1) extending the Combines Investigation Act to service industries, (2) allowing *civil* (rather than criminal) actions to be brought for damages resulting from contravention of the act, and (3) strengthening legislation against misleading advertising. Also, the Restrictive Trade Practices Commission was given the power to order suppliers to halt certain practices. Customers were protected by prohibiting suppliers from (1) refusing to supply without good reason, (2) requiring exclusive dealerships, (3) restricting the way a good is sold, or (4) requiring tied sales. As a result, retailing practices for many goods have changed considerably.

Misleading advertising is also dealt with. Claims about product quality must now be based on adequate tests. Advertising a product at a bargain price when the supplier does not or cannot supply the product in reasonable quantities and supplying a product at a price higher than the advertised price are both prohibited.

Amendments of 1986. In 1986, after four previous attempts had failed, the final set of amendments to the act were passed. The resulting act has three central themes: to promote economic efficiency to allow firms to adapt to changing circumstances and to recognize that competition and monopoly must no longer be judged on purely national grounds but in the context of rapidly globalizing international trade. Its stated goals are as follows:

> [To] maintain and encourage competition in Canada in order to promote the efficiency and adaptability of the Canadian economy, in order to expand opportunities for Canadian participation in world markets while at the same time recognizing the role for foreign competition in Canada, in order to ensure that small and medium-sized enterprises have an equitable opportunity to participate in the Canadian economy and in order to provide consumers with competitive prices and product choices.

The new act creates a specialized Competition Tribunal to deal with civil matters now that competition policy has been taken out of the sphere of the criminal law. This tribunal is empowered to hear applications and issue orders in respect of reviewable practices contained in the act.

The tribunal can also accept consent orders from the director of investigations on terms agreed on by the parties involved without hearing further evidence. When this happens, Canadian procedures, which used to be very public ones (what economists call *transparent*), now go on very much behind the scenes in private negotiations between the firms involved and the director of investigations. Furthermore, in the important case of the takeover of Texaco Oil Company by Imperial Oil, a carefully worked out agreement among the parties and the director of investigations was seriously amended by the tribunal. This showed that the tribunal was unwilling merely to rubber-stamp agreements worked out behind the scenes under the auspices of the director.

Under the new act, mergers are also placed under civil law, the statutory test being whether or not the merger "substantially lessens competition." For the first time in Canada, economic considerations are stated to be directly relevant in judging the acceptability of a merger. When reviewing a merger, the director is to consider such things as effective competition after the merger, the degree of foreign competition, barriers to entry, the availability of substitutes, and the financial state of the merging entities. Furthermore, an allowable defense of a merger is that the gains in efficiency more than offset any reductions in competition.

This new merger legislation seems to have had some substantial effect on business mergers for the first time in the history of Canadian competition policy. Many firms have consulted with the director before effecting a merger. As a result, some proposed mergers have been amended, and a few have been abandoned. Many mergers that have gone forward have been investigated, and the terms of some have been substantially modified.

Conclusion

The new act will not be the end of the history of the evolution of Canadian combine legislation, but it may be the end of a major chapter. Canadian legislation has for a long time provided substantial protection to consumers against the misuse of market power by large firms. For the first time, it now also seems to provide some substantial protection against the creation, through mergers, of market power that is not justified by gains to efficiency or international competitiveness. Many observers are cautiously optimistic that these laws, no doubt to be further refined in the future, will provide more protection to consumers than direct government intervention did—either through government ownership of particular firms or through government control of prices and conditions of entry.[8]

[8] Since writing this passage there have been three successful court challenges to provisions in the new act. If the Supreme Court sustains these and other challenges now before the courts, the hopes that a chapter of Canadian competition policy had been closed may be dashed.

SUMMARY

1. Resources are said to be used efficiently when it is impossible, by using them differently, to make any one household better off without making at least one other household worse off. We distinguish two kinds of efficiency: productive and allocative.
2. Productive efficiency exists for given technology when whatever output is being produced is being produced at the lowest attainable cost for that level of output. This requires, first, that firms be on, rather than above, their relevant cost curves and, second, that all firms have the same marginal cost. Profit-maximizing behavior ensures that productive efficiency will be achieved.
3. Allocative efficiency is achieved when it is impossible to change the mix of production in such a way as to make someone better off without making someone else worse off. The allocation of resources will be efficient when each commodity's price equals its marginal cost.
4. Whereas an economy that contains both monopolies and perfect competition can be productively efficient, allocative efficiency is achieved in an economy composed solely of perfect competitive market structures but not in an economy with monopolies.
5. The classical economic appeal of perfect competition is that it achieves both productive and allocative efficiency. Productive efficiency is achieved because the same forces that lead to long-run equilibrium lead to production at the lowest attainable cost. Allocative efficiency is achieved because in competitive equilibrium, price equals marginal cost for every product. The classical economic case against monopoly rests on its allocative inefficiency, which arises because price exceeds marginal cost.
6. The classical argument for the superiority of perfect competition should be interpreted with four qualifications in mind: (a) Efficiency is not the only goal, (b) private costs may be a poor measure of society's costs, (c) perfect competition throughout the economy may be incompatible with productive efficiency, and (d) in the very long run, cost curves may shift downward faster in market structures other than competition.
7. Levels of cost are not independent of market structures. If there are economies of scale or of scope, the minimum efficient size of the firm may be too large to be compatible with conditions of perfect competition. In such cases a shift from competition to a more concentrated market structure may lead to lower costs and increased efficiency.
8. Very long run considerations, such as the effect of market structure on innovation and the incentive effects of monopoly profits, are important in evaluating market structures. Joseph Schumpeter advocated the view that the incentive to innovate is so much greater under monopoly that monopoly is to be preferred to perfect competition, despite its allocative inefficiency. Though few modern economists go that far, the empirical evidence suggests that technological change and innovation can to a measurable extent be traced to the efforts of large firms in concentrated industries.
9. Canadian competition policy is designed to encourage competitive practices and discourage monopolistic ones. It seeks to regulate natural monopolies either by running them as state-owned crown corporations or leaving them in private hands and regulating them. Regulation of oligopolistic industries involves controlling their

prices and conditions of entry. Competition policy seeks to prevent unnecessary combines and the exploitation of market power where such power is made necessary by the efficiencies of large size.

10. Efficiency of natural monopolies requires that price be set equal to short-run marginal cost and that investment be undertaken whenever that price exceeds the full long-run marginal cost of providing another unit of output. Average cost pricing results in too much output in the short run and too much investment in the long run in rising-cost industries and too little output and too little investment in falling-cost industries.
11. Direct control of pricing and entry conditions of some key oligopolistic industries has been common in the past, but deregulation is reducing such control. The move to deregulation is largely the result of the experiences that oligopolistic industries are a major engine of growth, as long as their firms are kept competing; that direct control of such industries has produced disappointing results in the past; and that forced cross subsidization can have serious consequences for some users.
12. Canadian combine laws have always recognized the need for firms that are large in relation to the domestic market if size efficiencies are to be exploited. Such laws seek to restrict growth in size through mergers where the size is not justified by efficiencies and seek to prevent the unwarranted exploitation of market power where such power is necessary. Recently, such laws have been removed from the criminal code, where enforcement proves difficult, and placed in the civil code, where enforcement appears to be easier.

TOPICS FOR REVIEW

Productive and allocative efficiency
Consumers' and producers' surplus
Classical preference for competition over monopoly
Pareto-optimality
Economies of scale and of scope
Effect of costs on market structure
Effect of market structure on costs
Marginal and average cost pricing
Deregulation
Privatization
Canadian competition policy

DISCUSSION QUESTIONS

1. "Suppose that allocative inefficiency of some economy amounts to 5 percent of the value of production." What does this statement mean? If it is true, would consumers be better off if policy measures succeeded in eliminating the allocative inefficiency? Why or why not?
2. If the many plants producing a given product were built at different times, have different levels of capacity, and have different cost curves, is it possible that producing the industry's output using all of them is productively efficient? Show why or why not.
3. Consider an innovation that lowers the marginal cost of production by the same amount in two industries, one of which is perfectly competitive and the other a single-firm monopoly. Show that prices will fall as a response to a change in marginal costs in each industry but that prices and quantities will change less in monopoly than in competition.

4. "Canadian air travellers opting for U.S. carriers were [partly] responsible for Canadian airlines deregulation"—C. D. Howe Institute

   "Canadian consumers crossing the border to buy cheap U.S. groceries may be responsible for the end of supply management in Canada."—Canadian business economist

   What market forces are behind these quotations? What difficulties do they reveal for the regulation of particular industries?
5. Is the consumer benefited by lower prices, by higher quality, by more product variety, by advertising? If trade-offs are necessary (more of one means less of another), how would you evaluate their relative importance with respect to the following products?
   a. Vitamin pills
   b. Beer
   c. Cement
   d. Bath soap
   e. Women's dresses
   f. Television programs
6. Would competition laws be necessary in an economy of perfect competition? Would they be beneficial in an economy of natural monopoly?
7. What are the arguments for and against exemption from prosecution under the competition laws of the following?
   a. Labor unions
   b. Farmers
   c. American professional baseball teams (but not professional football teams)
8. Price-fixing agreements are (with some specific exemptions) violations of government laws. Consider the effects of the following. In what way, if at all, should they be viewed as being similar to price-fixing agreements?
   a. A manufacturer "recommends" minimum prices to its dealers.
   b. A manufacturer publishes a product price list that is changed only every three months.
   c. A trade association publishes "average industry total costs of production" every month.
9. "In a competitive market, the least-cost production techniques are revealed by entry and exit, whereas in public utility regulation, they are revealed by commission rate hearings. It is easier to fool the commission than the market. Therefore, wherever possible, competition should be permitted." Discuss.

Chapter 16

Market for Corporate Control: Takeovers, Foreign Investment, and Profit Maximization

How are we to judge the record number of takeovers and buyouts of large firms during the past 15 years? Do takeovers of some domestic firms by other domestic firms significantly reduce competition in Canadian markets? Do takeovers of Canadian firms by foreign firms threaten Canadians' economic and political independence? Should government encourage, discourage, or ignore such activities? Is profit maximization a good description of what firms actually do or of what they should do?

Few of these questions can be answered, or even easily discussed, using the simple theory of the firm that we have developed so far. In that theory, firms are users of factors of production and producers of commodities. They face cost and demand curves that are largely determined by forces beyond their control. They seek to maximize their profits by keeping their costs as low as possible and by producing to satisfy consumers' demands. Managers care only about profits, and their decisions are uninfluenced by the way in which their firms are organized to do business. Thus they contribute to our high living standards by producing, as cheaply as possible, goods that satisfy consumers' demands.

In this chapter we examine the great takeover boom of the last 10 years, played out in what came to be known as the *market for corporate control*. We also look *inside* the firm and examine the standard assumption that firms always maximize profits by introducing a number of alternative *behavioral* models of firms. The two sets of issues are related; the internal organization and the day-to-day behavior of firms are greatly influenced by the market for corporate control. In particular, a firm that deviates too far from profit maximization becomes an attractive candidate for takeover.

Later in this chapter we will study nonmaximizing behavior in detail. In the meantime we merely observe that there are many reasons why the people who run firms may not maximize the firms' profits. For example, managers may be inefficient, or they may look after their own interests rather than the interests of their firm's shareholders.

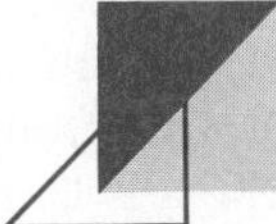

Mergers, Takeovers, and Buyouts

A **takeover** occurs when Company A buys Company B (which then becomes a part of A). A **merger** occurs when Companies A and B join together, often combining even their names. A **buyout** occurs when a group of investors, rather than a firm, buys up a firm.

Three types of merger are commonly distinguished: horizontal mergers, vertical mergers, and conglomerate mergers. When mergers are among companies producing the same product, they are termed *horizontal mergers.* An example was the merger of Texaco and Imperial Oil, both producers of petroleum products. Mergers among businesses at different stages of the production process are termed *vertical mergers,* which may be "forward" or "backward." Forward integration involves merger toward the market in which the product is sold, for example, the acquisition of retail gas stations by the oil refining companies. Backward integration involves acquisition of suppliers of inputs to the firm, for example, the purchase of a printing company by a publishing company. A third type of merger, known as a *conglomerate merger,* is between firms without obvious common interests in production. Insofar as lower costs result from conglomerate mergers, they are usually associated with managerial, marketing, or financial economies or with risk reduction through diversification.

Buyouts, mergers, and takeovers can be interpreted as transactions in a **market for corporate control**. This market, like any other, has both buyers (those who would acquire the rights to control a firm) and sellers (the current owners of stock in the firm). Also, as in other markets, the expected outcome is that the resource (control) winds up in the hands of those who value it most. In the market for corporate control, the value of the firm will be maximized when the firm is in the control of the best possible managers.

The wave of buyouts and takeovers that began during the 1980s and extended into the 1990s has been interpreted in just this light—as an efficiency-enhancing response to unrealized profit opportunities that improves the overall quality of management and the productivity of the target firms. It has also been interpreted as a speculative binge of no intrinsic value that poses a number of longer-term threats to the health of the economy. When takeovers involve foreign firms, they are often also assumed to pose a threat because of loss of control over the domestic economy to foreigners. We shall summarize the debate and its implications for public policy.

A *takeover* begins when the management of the acquiring firm makes a **tender offer** to the stockholders of the target firm. Tender offers are promises to purchase stock at a specified price for a limited period of time, during which the acquiring firm hopes to gain control of the target company. Typically, the prices offered are considerably higher than the prevailing stock market price. The takeover is called a *hostile takeover* when the current management of the target firm does not approve of it. Box 16-1 provides a discussion of how takeovers can sometimes be resisted.

The Effects of Takeovers

The heart of the argument in favor of takeovers is that after a takeover, new management can make more efficient use of the target firm's assets. The acquiring firm should be able to exploit profit opportunities that target management is not exploiting. This can be done by such means as operating the target firm more efficiently, providing funds that the target firm could not obtain, or providing access to markets that would be too expensive for the target firm to open up on its own.

If this is true, the value of the target firm will rise in response to a takeover, reflecting the new profits to come.[1] Further, if the *acquiring* firm's managers are acting in the best interest of *their* stockholders, the value of the acquiring firm should also rise when it is successful in a takeover bid.

Returns to Shareholders of Target Companies

Evidence on the effects of takeovers strongly supports the proposition that they benefit the stockholders of target firms. Estimates of the magnitude of the gains vary, but even the low estimates exceed 20 percent of pretakeover stock value during the period from 1962 through 1985. Estimates of the average gains in successful tender offers during the 1980s range from about 30 percent to more than 50 percent.

Returns to Stockholders of Acquiring Companies

The benefits to stockholders in the acquiring firms vary greatly from takeover to takeover. Sometimes the benefit is large; at other times it is negative (the takeover *lowers* the acquiring firm's profits). Indeed,

[1] Any takeover bid is likely to raise the value of a firm on the stock market. A profitable takeover raises these values permanently; a misjudged takeover does so only temporarily.

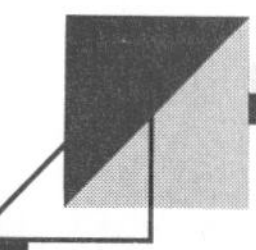

BOX 16-1

Accepting or Resisting Takeovers

When a takeover bid is made, the management of the target firm may respond in a number of ways. It can recommend that stockholders accept the tender offer. It can look for or organize an alternative buyer—one that would be more sympathetic to management's interests. It can promise to implement reforms that improve the operation of the firm, thus increasing its profits and removing the motivation for takeover. It can resist the takeover by employing financial devices that make the target firm unattractive for takeover.

Acceptance. In many cases, target management will decide that the takeover bid is in the best interests of its stockholders, and they will choose to work with the acquiring firm in reorganizing the target firm's operation. (Note that such agreement is almost always desirable. Target management will always possess a good deal of information that can help new management to improve the firm's operations.) In this case, the takeover is no longer hostile and becomes indistinguishable from a merger.

Acceptance of takeover bids by target management can be facilitated by *golden parachutes*. These are contracts that ensure that, in the event of successful takeovers, managers of the target firms will receive generous severance pay. Properly implemented, they can reduce the conflict between managers, who want to keep their jobs, and stockholders, who want to see the price of their stock rise—something that the acquiring management promises. Improperly implemented, they can reduce incentives for management to run the firm well: If a manager knows that after the takeover he or she will be set for life, why should the manager work hard to prevent the firm from becoming a takeover target? Finally, with or without golden parachutes, target management sometimes will approve the takeover in accordance with an ancient economic principle: "If you can't lick 'em, join 'em."

Resistance. There are two basic ways in which target management can resist a takeover. One is to look for a takeover on terms that are more favorable to management (and, perhaps, to the stockholders). Often this will involve searching for a *white knight,* a company that the target management finds to be a more congenial merger partner. Sometimes management may use the technique of the *leveraged buyout (LBO)* and take over the firm itself. The second form of resistance is to make the target firm unattractive to the acquiring firm. A number of financial mechanisms, loosely called *poison pills,* can be used for this purpose. The idea behind a poison pill is implicit in its name. It is a device that makes the target firm difficult or impossible to digest. One form of poison pill works by requiring that after a successful takeover, the new firm must buy back stock from existing shareholders at well above the market price. Such a commitment would make the target firm very unattractive to new owners (it would have a contractual commitment to buy assets for more than they are worth) and thus discourage a takeover bid. To the extent that poison pills are legal, they very much reduce the vulnerability to takeovers of firms that employ them.

Reform. By the time a tender offer is made, it is unlikely that target management can implement profit-enhancing reforms in time to resist the takeover bid. However, the threat of takeover may work as an incentive for existing management to implement the changes that would have been implemented after a takeover. Indeed, it is this unseen effect (no takeover bid will take place because current management is acting in the best interests of stockholders) that is at the heart of the argument in favor of takeover activity. The argument is that the activity that we see serves to discipline the behavior of corporate managers in general.

some evidence suggests that the *average benefit* in the 1980s was slightly negative. How could this be? One possibility, suggested by University of Chicago professors Andrei Schleifer and Robert Vishny, is that the unprofitable takeovers result from non-profit-maximizing motivations on the part of the *acquiring* firms' management.

Consider the position of the top management of a firm in an industry that is slowly declining. The firm may be highly profitable. Indeed, to the extent that the slow decline allows the firm to forgo some investments to replace old equipment, the firm may be very profitable in an accounting sense and may have a good deal of cash on hand. In this case, optimal behavior of the firm on behalf of the stockholders will often be to pay large dividends or to repurchase stock—either of which strategies transfers the firm's cash to its owners. However, if management is also interested in its own perquisites and power, it may want to move into areas that are growing, even if it has no expertise in these areas. Moreover, management may be willing to pay a high premium to get into new areas, thus reducing the value of the acquisition for its stockholders while increasing it for the stockholders of the target firm. Notice the irony here. The threat of takeover acts as a disciplining device on one set of managers who are not maximizing their profits. At the same time, the takeover provides an opportunity for another set of managers to engage in behavior that does not benefit their stockholders.

Benefits to the Economy

Much criticism of the recent takeover movement is based on the possibility that acquiring firms are incurring risks to the economy as a whole in excess of the risks that they themselves bear. Whether this problem will be as serious as some observers believe was still unclear at the start of the 1990s.

Most economists believe that takeovers provide a useful discipline on the ability of managers to act in nonmaximizing ways, but the case is not conclusive, and many of the potential costs of takeover activity will not be measurable for 5 to 10 years. In the absence of evidence to show that takeovers do not increase efficiency, however, most economists would probably favor leaving the market for corporate control free of further government intervention.

Leveraged Buyouts

A **leveraged buyout (LBO)** refers to the buying of a firm by new owners where the required funds are raised by bonds sold to the public. (*Leverage* is nothing more than a financial term for *debt,* so a "highly leveraged firm" is one that has much debt relative to equity.) The group wishing to take over the firm borrows most of the money needed to buy up the existing shares. When the deal is completed, a public company, owned by many shareholders, has been turned into a private one, owned by a few buyers who financed their purchase by issuing debt.

Junk bonds are bonds sold to finance leveraged buyouts. They involve a relatively high risk, since the new management must make profits sufficient to meet the large interest payments on these bonds in bad times as well as in good times. In contrast, when finance is by equities, a year of low profits can be a year of low dividend payments without threatening the financial solvency of the firm. Junk bonds carry high interest rates, and the amounts by which these exceed the interest on a safe government bond reflect the market's assessment of the risks involved in the newly financed enterprises.

Leveraged buyouts occur for many reasons, but two of the most important in recent years have been to dismantle unprofitable conglomerates formed in an earlier wave of mergers and to provide a defense of existing management against hostile takeover bids.

Dismantling Conglomerates

The 1970s saw a wave of what were called **conglomerate mergers**. These were the merging into a single conglomerate firm of several firms producing quite different products and operating in quite different industries. One important idea behind these mergers was risk sharing. Typically, as economic growth proceeds, some industries decline while others grow. If a firm is in an industry that is declining, there may be little it can do to stem its own decline no matter how progressive its management. But if a firm straddles many industries, so went the argument, it may spread its risks among them. Since it is unlikely that all of the industries in which it is involved will be declining at the same time, the conglomerate firm may "win with the swings while losing with the roundabouts." Other reasons associated with these takeovers were to gain economies of scope. For example, a large conglomerate might find it easier to raise cash from outside lenders or to move cash from one enterprise to another within its structure, or it might be able to share its marketing expertise across its firms.

In practice, many conglomerate mergers proved ill-founded. In an impressive demonstration of the virtues of the division of labor, management based in one industry proved to be ill-equipped to assist in the management of firms based in other industries. Neither did the expected economies of scope emerge in any large way. Much marketing and financial expertise proved to be industry-specific, and any economies that could be realized often turned out to be smaller than the inefficiences of trying to unite firms across industries. (To the extent that the separate units of the conglomerate were left to behave completely independently, there was no advantage in having the conglomerate in the first place.)

Investors also found problems with conglomerates. By buying the stock of a conglomerate, they were forced to take a stake in *all* of its enterprises. They could not sell off their ownership in one of the conglomerate's parts whose performance they disliked while holding on to a share of another part whose performance they did like.

For these and other reasons, many of the conglomerates formed in the 1970s were judged to be failures by the mid 1980s. The result of this failure was that the current value of the whole firm was less than the potential value of the sum of its individual parts, if they could be allowed to operate independently. Smart operators perceived this. They decided to buy up the conglomerates, break them up into their constituent parts, allow them to operate long enough so that their profits would be seen to rise, and then sell the parts for more in total than they had paid for the whole firm.

When buyers make the correct assessment, they pay off the junk bonds out of the proceeds of the sales and pocket the balance as a return for perceiving that efficiency could be increased by breaking up the conglomerates. The new purchasers finance much of their acquisition by issuing equities so that the firm is no longer fully debt-financed.

When buyers guess wrong, either because there is no advantage in breaking up the conglomerate or, more usually, because establishing the advantage takes longer than expected, they have to default on their junk bond payments, and the investors lose their money.

In spite of the great publicity attached to the failure of some leveraged buyouts and the consequent default of their junk bonds, the great majority of such buyouts have been successful. The conglomerates have been broken up, the individual parts sold at a profit, and the junk bondholders paid off. The failures show only, as the high interest rate on junk bonds attests, that leveraged buyouts are risky. If there had been no failures, the market would have been wrong in demanding a junk bond risk premium in the first place.

Leveraged buyouts and junk bonds got a bad name in the press. Undoubtedly, as with any new idea, there were excesses. Nonetheless, we can see in this development that the market for corporate control is doing what it is supposed to do.

Someone who perceives that a firm's current management practices, or its internal organization, are inefficient can make a gain by buying the firm at its current value and then selling at an increased value after the firm's efficiency has been increased.

Defense Against Takeovers

Leveraged buyouts have also been used by the current management of a firm as a defense against hostile takeover bids. If the current managers feel that they can run the firm as well as a prospective new management that is making a hostile takeover bid, they can raise money on the junk bond market and make the buyout themselves. If they succeed, and if they are right in assuming that they can operate the firm well enough to justify the amounts paid for its purchase, they will be able to show a profit above the price that they pay for the firm.

Notice, however, that the current management cannot have been maximizing profits in the first place, or there would have been no incentive for a takeover. To buy the firm themselves in order to prevent the takeover, they must know how to maximize profits in the future.

The 1980s saw the development of a number of tactics designed to protect target firms from hostile takeovers and buyouts. These tactics are known collectively as *poison pills*. For example, the target firm can acquire a firm that competes with the potential buyer, thus increasing the possibility of running afoul of the competition laws. Also, the target firm may make a highly leveraged acquisition of another firm, thus leaving it with few liquid funds and much debt—a financial position that is likely to deter potential leveraged buyers. These are both market tactics. A political tactic is to attempt to get the laws changed to make takeovers more difficult. Popular hostility to takeovers and junk bonds has made this political route attractive to firms, and a number of U.S. states have adopted legislation that strongly deters all hostile takeovers and buyouts. Such legislation has the effect of shielding inefficient management from market disciplines. Major investors, such as pension fund managers, complain that this prevents them from maximizing the returns from their investment, and many economists fear that it will make it harder for the market to correct major inefficiencies in the operations of firms.

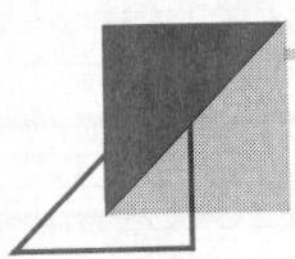

Foreign Investment

When takeovers, buyouts, and mergers involve a domestic firm being taken over by a foreign firm, a further consideration is added: How much should we worry about the nationality of the owners of firms that operate in our country? This question arises most dramatically when a foreign takeover occurs. It pertains more generally to all foreign investment, whether it is the formation of a new, foreign-owned firm in Canada, new investment by an existing foreign-owned firm, or a takeover of a Canadian-owned firm by a foreign-owned firm.

Foreign Investment in Developing Countries

Foreign investment—investment in one country by firms owned in a foreign country or by individuals resident in a foreign country—has long been a major factor in world development. The residents of newly settled areas, such as North and South America in the seventeenth, eighteenth, and nineteenth centuries, could not hope to generate enough savings to finance the rapid development of their vast potential. Investment funds were required in large amounts to build *infrastructure* (such as roads, dams, city halls, post offices, and bridges), *private productive facilities* (such as factories, machines, and offices), and *housing* both for rental and for ownership. In the first instance, the economic growth of all such countries was financed by foreign investment.

As these economies grew, they produced larger and larger flows of their own domestic savings. These savings financed an increasing proportion of domestic investment, they helped buy back much of the foreign ownership in their country, and they provided a flow of foreign investment going to other, newer countries. This was the pattern in the United States, which was a net importer of capital from abroad until the early part of the twentieth century but became, as the century advanced, a net exporter of capital.[2]

The same pattern has been observed in Canada, but it has not yet gone as far as in the United States. This is due mainly to Canada's smaller size in relation to the investment needed to exploit its huge resources. Canada has always been a recipient of a great deal of foreign investment. As the Canadian economy grew, however, the flow of domestic savings increased. This had several effects. First, a larger and larger proportion of new investment in Canada has been financed by domestic rather than by imported capital. Second, the share of total capital investment located in Canada that is foreign-owned rose more and more slowly, until it peaked at about 40 percent in 1972, after which it fell until the late 1980s.[3] Third, Canada became a rising source of foreign investment in other countries as successful Canadian firms expanded into foreign markets and private Canadian investors added foreign investments to their portfolios of assets.

World Attitudes to Transnationals

World attitudes toward foreign investment were fairly tolerant throughout most of the period since the Industrial Revolution. Most people saw such investment as a benign force leading to more rapid growth in both total population and output per person than could be financed through domestic savings alone. Then, in the late 1950s and the 1960s, attitudes became more hostile to foreign investment. This change was partly the result of the growth of what

[2] In the 1980s this pattern was reversed, with the United States once again becoming a net importer of capital until by 1990 it held more foreign capital than any other country in the world. The reasons are discussed in Chapters 42 and 43.

[3] More recently the share has risen, for reasons that will be discussed shortly.

was then called the *multinational enterprise,* now called the *transnational corporation* (*TNC*). (See Box 9-1 on page 178.) These are firms that are present in many countries: A domestic firm may engage in international trade by selling in many countries; a transnational has production facilities in many countries.

TNCs may be highly centralized, with head offices, research and development, and all major policy determination located in the home country. They may also be quite decentralized, with research, product development, and policy determination being done in many different countries.

TNCs have become increasingly important over the years and now account for the majority of international trade and foreign investment. Indeed, much international trade is between different units of the same TNC (intra-TNC trade). Also, the typical organization of a TNC has undergone changes. Although all types have always existed, the typical form in earlier times was a highly centralized firm. Today, with the demands for specialized products carefully tailored to the specific needs of each country and with the ability to produce small runs of each product variation efficiently thanks to computer-assisted production, decentralized organizations are becoming increasingly prevalent.

In the 1950 and 1960s, however, the rise of the TNC was seen as an ominous development. People correctly perceived that TNCs would make it more difficult for individual countries to maintain economic policies that differed from those of their trading partners. For example, TNCs have the ability, through internal accounting, to shift costs to areas where local tax laws permit the greatest cost write-offs and to shift profits to areas where profit taxes are lowest. They can also shift R&D to where tax advantages or subsidies are largest and then make the results of this R&D available throughout their entire organization—which often means throughout the entire world.

TNCs are able to arbitrage country-specific economic policies.

This ability represented an inevitable weakening of the power of the individual state. It also provided a pressing reason for the creation of larger political units such as the European Community (EC) to provide the political scope necessary to exercise some control over TNCs.

The rise of TNCs aroused worldwide concerns over American economic imperialism. Since many of the most successful early TNCs were American, many observers in other countries feared the spread of American economic dominance and cultural influence. Influential books in Europe and Canada decried the growth of U.S. economic imperialism and urged that TNCs be kept out as a defense. Today, with North American firms all too often on the defensive against Japanese and European firms, the fear of U.S. dominance seems but a quaint reminder of the human tendency to think that whatever is now happening will always happen.

By the 1980s, attitudes toward TNCs had softened again. Several developments were responsible. First, it was clear to industrial nations that TNCs were here to stay. As world trade become more and more globalized under the impact of the communication and computer revolutions, TNCs became increasingly important until it became apparent that no advanced country could do without them. Second, less developed countries came to the same realization and put out a welcome mat. As the executive director of the United Nations Center on TNCs recently said:

> The 1980s have witnessed major changes in the world production system, with TNCs being the principal forces shaping the future of technological innovation. At the same time, a more pragmatic and businesslike relationship between host governments and TNCs has emerged within the past decade. Many developing countries, burdened by debt and economic stagnation, have liberalised their policies towards TNCs while these corporations have displayed greater sensitivity to the development and economic goals of host countries. The era of confrontation has receded and been replaced by a practical search for a meaningful and mutually beneficial accommodation of interests.[4]

Canadian Attitudes to Transnationals

Official Canadian views have matched these swings in world views. Until the 1960s, Canada welcomed foreign investment as a means to achieving economic growth that would have been impossible if it had to be financed by domestic savings alone. Then, in the 1960s, suspicion of foreign (particularly American) investment grew. This resulted in the formation of

[4] United Nations Center on Transnational Corporations, *Transnational Corporations in World Development: Trends and Prospects* (New York: United Nations, 1988), p. iii.

the Foreign Investment Review Agency (FIRA) in the 1970s. This agency had the right to screen all new foreign investment in Canada. It turned down about 5 percent of the applications that it reviewed—quite a high rejection rate by international standards. It imposed requirements with respect to domestic production and exports on many of the investments that it did accept. Its presence also discouraged some unknown number of other firms from applying in the first place, so its overall effect in limiting foreign investment in the country is hard to discern.

In line with the change in world opinion about TNCs, in 1984 the new Conservative government replaced FIRA with an organization called Investment Canada. With this new body, Canadian officials announced that Canada once again welcomed foreign investment. Although Investment Canada still has the power to review foreign takeovers of Canadian firms, it has turned down no applications since it came into existence. It has, however, insisted on some conditions before approving some deals. For example, when the Canadian laser company Lumonics was taken over by the Japanese conglomerate Sumitomo (because Lumonics could not raise sufficient capital in Canada), Investment Canada insisted on a number of assurances designed to keep the creative activities of Lumonics located in Canada.

In the Canada-U.S. Free Trade Agreement (FTA), Canada agreed to raise the threshold of review of U.S. takeovers of Canadian firms from a firm size of $5 million to $150 million. Critics decried this reduction in ability to screen foreign takeovers of Canadian firms. Supporters pointed out, first, that fully 80 percent of nonfinancial capital in Canada was located in firms larger than $150 million and so was still subject to review and, second, that in return for this Canadian concession, the United States had in effect exempted Canadian firms wishing to operate in that country from any review that the United States might subsequently initiate.[5]

[5] When the FTA was signed in 1988, the United States had no review mechanism for foreign investment, but the growing concern over such investment makes such a review possible in the future. By conferring national treatment on Canadian investors in the United States, the agreement effectively exempts Canada from any new U.S. practices that discriminate between foreign and domestic investors. (See Chapter 21 for a full discussion of national treatment, which in effect means that whatever laws, rules, and regulations—no more and no less—apply to domestic units also apply to foreign units to whom national treatment is extended.)

Foreign Investment in and by Canada: Some Facts

Canada is heavily reliant on foreign investment; about 22 percent of its total economy was foreign-owned in 1986. The percentages vary greatly among industries, being about 50 percent in manufacturing and over 90 percent in the car and rubber industries.

The United States has traditionally accounted for about 75 percent of all foreign direct investment stock in Canada, although this share is gradually declining. It stood at about 70 percent in 1989. Canada is also the largest single host country for U.S. foreign investment—just over $60 billion in 1988.

Canadian foreign direct investment in the United States totaled nearly $30 billion in 1990. The gap between the two countries' investment positions has been steadily narrowing since 1975. In recent years, Canadian TNCs have been far more aggressive investors in the United States than vice versa. As a result, Canadian direct investment in the United States grew by an annual average of 20 percent in the period 1977–1987, while U.S. direct investment in Canada grew by only 8 percent per year. If present trends continue, Canadian investors will own as much of the U.S. stock of investment as U.S. investors own of the Canadian stock of investment shortly after the start of the twenty-first century.

Foreign Investment in Canada: The Debate

By and large, but with some notable exceptions, economists have been skeptical of the view that Canada loses by foreign investment. Among the alleged benefits of foreign investment are (1) more total investment than could be possible if all investment had to be financed by domestic savings, hence a larger population than could otherwise be supported by the full infrastructure; (2) a higher rate of growth due to a more rapid rise in the capital available for each worker; and (3) participation in the world's division of labor as brought about by TNCs. Among the alleged costs are (1) profits earned by foreigners rather than domestic capitalists, (2) loss of control over resource development, (3) loss of control over one's own economy, and (4) loss of good managerial and research jobs to foreign locations favored by TNCs.

Potential Benefits

The first two advantages listed have already been discussed in our treatment of economic growth of countries that have not yet generated domestic savings large enough to finance their own domestic economic growth. The third point is key in today's globalized world. The growth of global production and globalized competition, with its attendant growth of the TNCs, means that many individual firms are developing a presence over the entire trading world. If ownership of TNCs is spread evenly over the whole advanced world, no single country can expect to own the majority of the capital in all the TNCs that are operating within its borders. This important point can be illustrated by a numerical example.

Assume that 60 percent of the production of goods and services in each country is done by local firms serving the domestic market, while 40 percent is done by TNCs serving the world market. This means that a typical country can expect to own the 60 percent of its capital that is devoted to domestic production alone, plus *its share* of the 40 percent that is owned by TNCs. If the country in question is similar to Canada, domestic output will account for about 4 percent of the world production of internationally traded commodities. If it owns its share of the TNC capital involved in this production, it will own 4 percent of the 40 percent of the capital in its country that is owned by TNCs. (It will also own 4 percent of the TNC capital that is producing in other countries.) This means that the country will own 61.6 percent of the total capital producing within its borders (the 60 percent that is local capital, plus 4 percent of the 40 percent that is owned by TNCs, which is 1.6 percent of the country's total capital). The percentage owned by foreigners will be 38.4.

In such a world, to insist that the majority of the TNC production facilities located in Canada should be owned in Canada is to insist that Canada own the majority of the world's TNCs (which would require an amount vastly in excess of all Canadian wealth). The only other alternative would be to insist that production in Canada should be by domestically owned companies serving the domestic market alone and not by TNCs, which would condemn Canada to inefficient local production of most of its internationally traded goods.[6] The point is that when production is in the hands of TNCs, no one country can hope to own the bulk of TNC capital located within its borders; instead, if TNC ownership is spread more or less evenly throughout the developed world, each country will own a small proportion of the capital within its own borders—and a small proportion of the capital located in each of the other countries.

Another aspect of this point concerns the growth of firms that develop new products. Many new products are developed by TNCs. Others, however, are invented and developed by entrepreneurs starting out in their own firms—firms that grow as their new products catch on. There comes a critical point in the development of such firms when they must decide how to market their products internationally, which today effectively means over much of the world. A few manage to handle this themselves and grow to become new TNCs. More often, however, the costs and risks of creating world market links and developing the international know-how that goes with being a large TNC are just too great to be acceptable to the still small firm.

So the entrepreneur sells the firms to an existing TNC that can develop its potential. No one has been exploited. The successful entrepreneur sells out for a handsome profit, and the TNC gets a new product that its world network allows it to market efficiently. Typically, however, the TNC will be foreign-owned, since, as we just determined, most TNCs operating within any one country will be foreign-owned. Public policy critics are likely to perceive a national loss when the home entrepreneur is "forced" to sell out (no matter how willingly the sale was made). The point is, however, that it may be both profitable and efficient for the small entrepreneur to sell to a TNC that already has the needed world marketing capacity rather than to develop it over again, at great cost and risk. Furthermore, if public policy prevents selling out to a TNC, future entrepreneurs may be less willing to develop new products because they cannot be sold to firms capable of marketing on a world scale.

[6] Canada could do this by imposing high tariff barriers, but not only would this be forbidden under our commitments to such international organizations as the GATT, but it would also be extremely harmful to our living standards, as shown in Chapter 20.

Alleged Costs

Loss of profits to foreigners. Insofar as the industries are competitive, profits are merely normal returns on capital. If foreigners provide capital that Canadians cannot provide, they get only the normal return. Employment, wages, and many other benefits stay in Canada.

More recently, however, economists have been interested in the pure profits that accompany innovations in oligopolistic industries. In oligopolies, profits can persist well into the long run, and the owners of the firm may make more than the normal return on capital. If so, ownership matters. The owners are gaining more than is being made by investors in other industries who earn just the normal return on capital. How large such profits are, and whether or not they provide a reason for public intervention to hold the profits at home, is a subject of current debate.

Loss of control over industry. All industries in Canada are subject to Canadian law. Canada can, for example, regulate the rate of resource extraction in oil and gas and impose that regulation equally on Canadian and foreign-owned firms operating in Canada. It can also have tough environmental laws and any others that impose requirements on all firms in Canada.

TNCs, however, do pose a serious problem called *extraterritoriality,* which is the extension of the laws of the country where the TNC is owned to activities of that firm in other countries. The usual international principle is *national treatment,* under which foreign-owned TNCs operating in a host country are governed by the host country's laws. The United States, however, has championed the principle of extraterritoriality by sometimes trying to make U.S. multinationals that operate in other countries follow U.S. rather than host-country laws. Thus, for example, if the United States has prohibitions against trading with Cuba or China, it tries to apply these laws not only to foreign TNCs operating within the United States but also to U.S. TNCs operating in such foreign countries as Canada. Host countries have resisted these American attempts to extend its legal jurisdiction beyond its own borders, and the issue remains unresolved. The solution lies in attempts to limit the operation of extraterritoriality; solving the problem by banning TNCs would be like cutting off one's leg to cure a boil on it, since TNCs are a key part of the international trading scene.

Many people worried that the Canada-U.S. Free Trade Agreement eroded Canadian sovereignty with respect to control over TNCs. Defenders of the agreement argued that such concerns were based on a misunderstanding of the principle of national treatment, which allows Canada and the United States each to impose its own requirements on firms operating within their borders. These requirements may differ between the two countries; all that is required by national treatment is that foreign and domestic firms be treated equally in any one country. The only thing one country or the other cannot do is use its laws to discriminate by applying tougher laws to foreign-owned than to domestically owned firms. So the FTA would appear to have introduced no new reason why foreign investment should limit Canada'a ability to control its economy and its environment as it wishes.

Loss of key activities. Some industries are firmly rooted in a country by virtue of natural advantages. For example, Canadian oil must be extracted in Canada, and Canadian lumber must be cut in Canada. Thus the oil and lumber industries are firmly rooted in Canada as long as supplies of the important natural resources exist. Other industries—high-tech ones are important examples—are much more footloose. They can be moved among countries to wherever the economic climate and economic policies are most favorable to them. The key characteristic of these industries is that they are knowledge-intensive.[7] When head offices determine the location of R&D and other knowledge-intensive activities, they make decisions that influence the course of a country's economic development. They could conceivably direct the types of production with the highest values to their home countries and keep lower-value production, which produces lower wages, in host countries.

A similar issue relates to what are called *key industries*. Some observers believe that certain key industries have important *spillovers* to the rest of the economy. Keeping these key industries at home will favorably affect the value of economic activity elsewhere in the economy. If a TNC takes over one of these key industries, it may relocate the industry to

[7] This issue is considered more fully in Chapters 20 and 21.

its home country, thereby harming the economies of the other country. Shipbuilding and steel production were thought to be key industries in the 1960s, and many people believe that automobiles and such high-tech industries as chips and computers are key industries today.

These are important and unresolved issues. No one is sure how important these possibilities are. Furthermore, it is not easy to see what practical policy measures should be recommended if these possibilities were shown to be important. This latter issue is discussed next.

What Could Be Done?

Say that foreign investment was thought to be harmful. What could be done?

It would be impractical to prohibit all, or even most, foreign investment. First, this would greatly reduce the amount of capital available in Canada, with adverse effects on Canadian economic growth. Second, this would deny Canada's participation in the large segment of international trade that is dominated by TNCs, most of which cannot be owned by Canadians. For a small trading nation such as Canada, with about 30 percent of its GDP generated by exports, that would be a serious matter.

Given the volume of Canadian savings, the most that could be done would be to redirect foreign investment from some industries into others. This would be done by discouraging investment in some industries and hoping both that Canadian investment would flow into them and that foreign investment would fill in the gaps where the Canadian investment would otherwise have gone. For such a policy to be successful, bureaucrats must be able to discern the areas where it is advantageous to prevent foreign investment, Canadian capital must flow into these areas, and foreign capital must fill the gaps created by the reallocation of Canadian investment. Such a policy is full of risks, of which the following are merely illustrative.

First, because Canadian investment did not flow into the "designated" activities in the first place, there is a risk that it may not do so after the restrictions are imposed. Second, there is a risk that the activities will be transferred abroad if foreign TNCs are prevented from engaging in them in Canada. In this case, the substitution is not of Canadian-owned for foreign-owned activity in Canada but of foreign-located for Canadian-located activity. Third, politicians and administrators must be able to identify and promote the activities that are best held in Canadian ownership. Large firms, such as the CPR, CIL, CAI, and Noranda, are the ones that would cause the most political problems if they were taken over by foreigners. Unfortunately, these most visible and best-known companies are not necessarily the ones with the greatest potential payoff from restricting foreign ownership, since they are likely to be only normally profitable. If there is indeed a case to hold ownership at home, it is likely to be stronger for small and mid-size industries that are not household names but are at the forefront of industrial development. Yet it is not clear that these are the industries that the political process would hold at home if foreign investment were once again to be seriously controlled.

Conclusion

The worldwide debate about the value of foreign investment is not as heated as it was a decade or two ago. Most countries are aware of the value of foreign investment in economic growth and of the need in today's globalized world for TNCs, most of which cannot be owned by any one small country. There is debate about the need to encourage domestic ownership of certain key industries and about the need to control the activities of TNCs within one country by such means as requiring local R&D expenditure. There is also an awareness of how easy it is to kill the goose that lays the golden egg by passing laws that drive TNCs to relocate abroad.

The prevailing view in the Canadian government during the 1980s and early 1990s has been that foreign investment is beneficial on balance and that it should be subject to only a minimum of controls. According to this view, TNCs are profit maximizers who will locate activities where it is most profitable to do so rather than hold them in their home country as a matter of course. In that case the market activities of TNCs will produce the most efficient international allocation of resources and the highest possible living standards in both home and host countries. Furthermore, according to this view, the international economy with globalized competition is so complex and sophisticated that investment-regulating intervention is all too likely to do more harm than good. Critics are not so sure. They advocate controls to hold certain key industries under domestic ownership and certain key activities, such as R&D, in home locations.

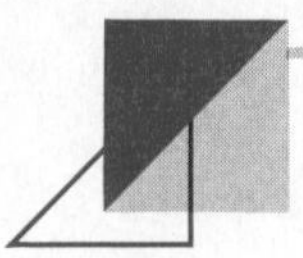

What Do Firms Maximize?

One reason why a firm may be taken over by another is that the first firm is not maximizing its profits. The new management may believe that, after the takeover, it can exploit profitable opportunities that are being ignored by the present management.

The view that many firms maximize something other than profits is made plausible by the nature of the modern corporation. One hundred years ago the single-proprietor firm, whose manager was its owner, was common in many branches of industry. In such firms the single-minded pursuit of profits would be expected. Today, however, ownership is commonly diversified among thousands of stockholders, and the firm's managers are rarely its owners. Arranging matters so that managers always act in the best interests of stockholders is, as we shall see, anything but straightforward. Thus there is potential for managers to maximize something other than profits.

The Separation of Ownership from Control

Writing in 1932, A. A. Berle and Gardiner Means hypothesized that because of diversified ownership and the difficulty of assembling or organizing stockholders, the managers, rather than the stockholders or the directors, exercise effective control over the corporation.

The hypothesis of the separation of ownership from control is that managerial control exists and leads to different behavior than would direct control by the firm's owners.

In corporations, the stockholders elect directors, who appoint managers. Directors are supposed to represent stockholders' interests and to determine broad policies that the managers will carry out. In order to conduct the complicated business of running a large firm, a full-time professional management group must be given broad powers of decision. Although managerial decisions can be reviewed from time to time, they cannot be supervised in detail. The links between the directors and the managers are typically weak enough so that top management often truly controls the corporation over long periods of time.

As long as directors have confidence in the managerial group, they accept and ratify their proposals, and stockholders elect and reelect directors who are proposed to them. If the managerial group does not satisfy the directors' expectations, it may be removed and replaced, but this is a disruptive and drastic action that is seldom employed.

Within wide limits, then, effective control of the corporation's activities resides with the managers. Although the managers are legally employed by the stockholders, they remain largely unaffected by them. Indeed, the management group typically asks for, and gets, the *proxies* of enough stockholders to elect directors who will reappoint it, and thus it perpetuates itself in office. (A *proxy* authorizes a person who is attending a stockholders' meeting to cast a stockholder's vote. In the vast majority of cases, nearly all votes cast are in the form of proxies.)

None of this matters unless the managers pursue different interests from those of the stockholders. Do these interests in fact diverge?

Principal-Agent Analysis

If you (the *principal*) hire the youngster down the block (your *agent*) to mow your lawn while you are away, all you can observe is how the lawn looks when you come back. She *could* have mowed it every 10 days, as you agreed, or she could have waited until two days before you were due home and mowed it only once. By prevailing on a friend or a neighbor to *monitor* her behavior, you could find out what she did, in fact, but only at some cost.

When you hire a physician to diagnose and to treat your lower back pain, it is almost impossible for you to monitor the physician's effort and diligence on your behalf. You have not been to medical school, and much of what the physician does will be a mystery to you. This situation is close to the relationship that exists between stockholders and managers. The managers have information and expertise that the stockholders do not—indeed, that is *why* they are the managers. The stockholders can observe profits but cannot directly observe the managers' efforts. To complicate matters further, even when the managers' behavior can be observed, the stockholders do not generally have the expertise to evaluate whether that behavior was the best available. Everyone can see how the firm does do, but it takes very detailed knowledge of the firm and the industry to know how well it *could* do. Boards of directors, who represent the firm's stockholders, can acquire some of the relevant expertise and monitor managerial behavior, but, again, this is costly.

These examples illustrate the **principal-agent problem**: the problem of designing mechanisms that will induce *agents* to act in their *principals'* interests. In general, unless there is costly monitoring of the agent's behavior, the problem cannot be completely solved. Hired managers (like hired gardeners) will generally wish to pursue their own goals. They cannot ignore profits because if they perform badly enough, they will lose their jobs. Just how much latitude they have to pursue their own goals at the expense of profits will depend on many things, including the degree of competition in the industry and the possibility of takeover by more profit-oriented management.

Principal-agent analysis shows that when ownership and control are separated, the self-interest of agents will tend to make profits lower than in a "perfect," frictionless world in which principals act as their own agents.

Sales maximization. Even though we may know that the corporation is unlikely always to maximize profits, this does not tell us what *is* maximized. Whatever may be maximized, managers are not entirely free to pursue their own private ends. Instead, their goals, whatever they are, will be maximized as long as profits are high enough that stockholders will not revolt and others will not be tempted to take over the firm.

Suppose that the managers need to make some minimum level of profits to keep the stockholders satisfied. Beyond this they are free to maximize something else unhampered by profit considerations. One theory is that managers will seek to maximize their firm's sales revenue. This is a sensible policy on the part of management, the argument runs, because salary, power, and prestige all rise with the size of a firm as well as with its profits. Generally, the manager of a large, normally profitable corporation will earn a salary that is considerably higher than the salary earned by the manager of a small but highly profitable corporation.

The sales maximization hypothesis says that managers of firms seek to maximize their sales revenue, subject to a profit constraint.

Sales maximization subject to a profit constraint leads to the prediction that firms will sacrifice some profits by setting price below and output above their profit-maximizing levels (see Figure 16-1).

Failure to minimize costs. The sales maximization hypothesis implies that the firm's managers will choose to produce more than the profit-maximizing level of output. As was noted in Chapter 15, it is also possible that firms will produce their chosen output at greater than minimum cost. Why would a firm fail to minimize costs? There are many possible answers, but the most straightforward one is that minimizing costs can demand a great deal of detailed managerial attention, and if management can avoid doing so, it would prefer not to make the necessary effort. Moreover, as we shall see later in this chapter, it may be costly for a firm to change its routine behavior. If this is so, one firm may operate at a higher cost than another, but it will still not be worthwhile for the first firm to copy the behavior of the second firm. The *transactions costs* of making the change could outweigh the benefits. As with sales maximization, stockholders and competition will limit the extent to which economic or technological inefficiency can survive, but they may not eliminate inefficiency.

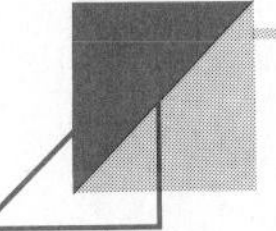

Nonmaximizing Theories

Many students of corporate behavior criticize the profit maximization assumption from a perspective different from that given by principal-agent theory. They argue that there are other reasons for doubting that modern corporations are "simple profit-maximizing computers." They believe that corporations are profit-oriented in the sense that, other things being equal, more profits are preferred to less profits.

They do not believe, however, that corporations are profit maximizers.

Full-Cost Pricing

Most manufacturing firms sell differentiated products and are price setters. As we saw in Chapter 14, they must quote a price for each of their products rather than accept a price that has been set in some impersonal competitive market. Simple profit-maximizing theory predicts that these firms will change their prices in response to every change in demand and cost that they experience. Yet students of large firms have long observed that except during periods of rapid inflation, such price flexibility rarely is observed. In the short run, prices of manufactured goods do not appear to vary in response to every shift in demand. They appear to change less often.

This short-run behavior is consistent with the hypothesis of **full-cost pricing**, originally advanced in the 1930s by Robert Hall, a British economist, and Charles Hitch, an American economist, following a series of detailed case studies of actual pricing decisions. Case studies in the intervening decades have continued to reveal the widespread use of full-cost pricing procedures.

The full-cost pricer, instead of equating marginal revenue with marginal cost, sets price equal to average cost at normal-capacity output plus a fixed markup.

The full-cost pricing firm changes its prices when its average costs change substantially (as a result of such events as a new union contract or a sharp change in the prices of key raw materials), and it may occasionally change its markup. However, its short-run pricing behavior is rather unresponsive to changes in demand.

A nonmaximizing interpretation of full-cost pricing. Some modern critics of profit-maximizing theory hold that the prevalence of conventional full-cost practices shows that prices are tyically not at their profit-maximizing level. They also hold that full-cost pricing shows that firms are creatures of custom that make only occasional profit-oriented changes at fairly infrequent intervals.

A profit-maximizing interpretation of full-cost pricing. We saw in Chapter 14 that the short-term stickiness of oligopolistic prices can be accounted for under profit-maximizing theory by the combination of saucer-shaped cost curves and the costs for a multiproduct firm to change its list prices. The possible conflict between full-cost and profit-maximizing theory then concerns only the setting of the markup that relates prices to costs. If markups are arbitrary and only rarely revised, there is conflict. If, however, the markup is the profit-maximizing one for normal-capacity output, full-cost pricing can be consistent with profit maximization.

Organization Theory

A common criticism of profit-maximizing theory is that the behavior of firms is influenced seriously by their organizational structure. **Organization theory** argues that the size and form of the internal organization of firms affects the substance of the decisions. One way in which the decision-making process varies among firms is the extent to which this process is centralized. Some firms require that everything be approved by "headquarters." Other firms allow smaller operating units to make decisions. Firms of the first type generally respond to new situations more slowly, but also more consistently, than firms of the second type.

The central prediction of organization theory is that in any given situation, different decisions will result from different forms of organization.

One proposition that follows from this theory is that large and diffuse organizations find it necessary to develop standard operating procedures to help them in making decisions. These rules for decision making arise as compromises among competing points of view and, once adopted, are changed only reluctantly. Even if a particular compromise were the profit-maximizing strategy in the first place, it would not remain so when conditions changed. Thus it is predicted that profits will usually not be maximized.

Another prediction is that decision making by means of compromise will lead firms to adopt conservative policies that avoid large risks. Smaller firms that do not face the necessity of compromising competing views will take bigger risks than large firms.

Organization theorists have suggested an alternative to profit maximization that they call **satisficing**. The theory of satisficing was first put forward by Professor Herbert Simon of Carnegie-Mellon

University, who in 1978 was awarded the Nobel Prize in Economics for his work on the behavior of firms. He wrote, "We must expect the firm's goals to be not maximizing profits but attaining a certain level or rate of profit, holding a certain share of the market or a certain level of sales." In general, a firm is said to be satisficing if it does not change its behavior, provided that a *satisfactory* (rather than optimal) level of performance is achieved.

According to the satisficing hypothesis, firms will strive to achieve certain target levels of profits, but, having achieved them, they will not strive to improve their profit position further. This means that the firm could produce any one of a range of outputs that yield at least the target level of profits rather than the unique output that maximizes profits. An example of this behavior is sales maximization, which is illustrated in Figure 16-1.

The theory of satisficing predicts not a unique equilibrium output but a range of possible outputs that includes the profit-maximizing output.

FIGURE 16-1 Output of the Firm Under Profit Maximizing, Sales Maximizing, and Satisficing

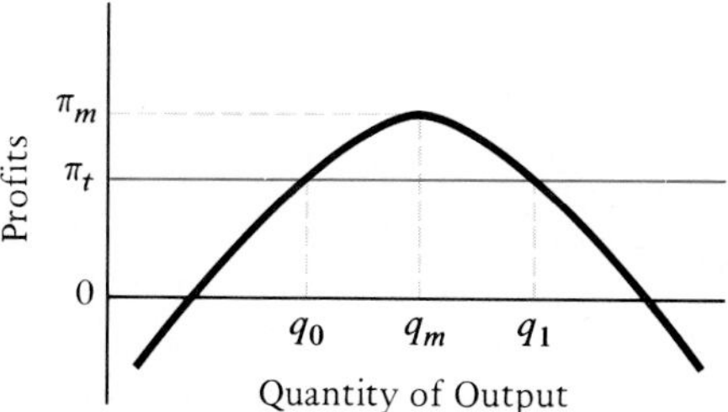

The "best" level of output depends on the motivation of the firm. The curve shows the level of profits associated with each level of output. A profit-maximizing firm produces output q_m and earns profit π_m. A sales-maximizing firm, with a minimum profit constraint of π_t, produces the output q_1.

A satisficing firm with a target level of profits of π_t is willing to produce any output between q_0 and q_1. Thus satisficing allows a range of outputs on either side of the profit-maximizing level, whereas sales maximization results in a higher output than profit maximization.

Evolutionary Theories

The modern evolutionary theories advanced by such economists as Richard Nelson and Sidney Winter of Yale University build on the earlier theories of full-cost pricing and satisficing. Nelson and Winter argue that firms do not—indeed, could not—behave as profit-maximizing theory predicts. They see firms operating cautiously with imperfect information in an uncertain world and so making only gradual changes toward the profit-maximizing position. However, since the conditions are constantly changing, firms are best seen as evolving toward a moving target that they never reach. Thus, even though firms are profit-oriented, they never, except by accident, succeed in maximizing their profits, either locally or globally.

Evolutionary theorists have gathered much evidence to show that tradition seems to be important in firms' planning. The basic effort at the early stages of planning is directed, they argue, toward the problem of performing reasonably well in established markets and maintaining established market shares. They quote evidence to show that suggestions that are made in preliminary planning documents to do something entirely new in some areas, even on a 10-year horizon, are usually weeded out in the reviewing process. They believe that most firms spend little effort on plans to enter entirely new markets and still less on plans to leave or even to reduce their share in long-established markets. These attitudes were illustrated by one firm that, although faced with obviously changing circumstances, reported that "we have been producing on the basis of these raw materials for more than 50 years with success, and we have made it a policy to continue to do so."

The evolutionary theory of the firm draws many analogies with the biological theory of evolution. Here are two.

Genes. In biological theory, some behavior patterns are transmitted by genes. Rules of behavior fulfill the same function in the evolutionary theory of the firm. In Professor Winter's words, "A great deal of firm decision behavior is routinized. Routinized decision procedures cover decision situations from pricing practices in retail stores to such 'strategic' decisions as advertising or R and D effort, or the question of whether or not to invest abroad." Winter talks of firms "remembering by doing" according to repetitive routines. He adds that government policymakers tend to have unrealistic expectations about firms' flexibility and responsiveness to changes in market incentives. These expectations arise from the maximizing model, whose fatal flaw, Winter alleges, is to underestimate the difficulty "of the task of merely continuing the routine performance, i.e., of preventing undesired deviations."

Mutations. In the theory of biological evolution, mutations are the vehicle of change. In the evolutionary theory of the firm, this role is played by innovations. Some innovations are the introduction of new products and new production techniques. However, a further important class of innovations in evolutionary theory is the introduction of new rules of behavior. Sometimes innovations are thrust on the firm; at other times the firm consciously plans for and creates innovations.

According to maximizing theory, innovations are the result of incentives—the "carrot" of new profit opportunities. In evolutionary theory, the firm is much more of a satisficer, and it usually innovates only under the incentive of the "stick" of unacceptably low profits or some form of external prodding. Firms change routines when they get into trouble, not when they see a chance to improve an already satisfactory performance. For example, in the growing markets of the 1960s, many firms continued all sorts of wasteful practices that they shed fairly easily when their profits were threatened in the more difficult economic climate of the 1970s and 1980s.

Profit Maximization As an Evolutionary Equilibrium

The American economist Armen Alchian has suggested that in long-run equilibrium, firms will evolve to become profit maximizers. The basic argument is based in the principle of "survival of the fittest." In a competitive environment, firms that pursue goals or adopt rules that are inconsistent with profit maximization will be unable to stay in business; firms that either choose or happen upon rules that are closer to profit maximization will undersell and displace those that do not. Eventually, only the profit-maximizing firms will survive in the marketplace.

A similar kind of argument can be applied to firms that operate in oligopolistic or monopolistic markets. Here it is not competition that forces the firm toward profit maximization in the long run but the possibility of a takeover. A firm that does not maximize profits will be less valuable than one that does maximize profits. Thus the nonmaximizing firm can be bought by maximizing managers, who will increase its value as they increase its profits, as described earlier in this chapter.

Alchian's argument suggests the following conclusion:

Even if no firm starts out with the intention of maximizing profits, in the long run each firm that survives in the marketplace will be a profit-maximizing firm.

This view provides an apparent synthesis of maximizing and evolutionary theories of the firm. The distinction between the theories is not so stark as it might seem. In contrast, many organization theorists point out that evolutionary equilibrium is unlikely ever to be achieved. As technology and tastes change over time, so too does profit-maximizing behavior. Without a fixed target, a firm's behaviors will continually evolve (generally toward profit maximization) but will never reach an equilibrium. The target refuses to stay put.

Should Firms Maximize Profits?

The foregoing discussion has operated under the implicit assumption that by maximizing profits, firms are acting in the best interests of society. There are at least two reasons why profit maximization might not be desirable, however. One is that firms may use their power to manipulate consumer tastes. If they are successful in doing so, one of the basic ideas of standard economics—that of consumer sovereignty—is called into question. We treat this possibility, which is associated with the writings of John Kenneth Galbraith, in Box 16-2. Another line of thought argues that firms should take the public interest into account, especially with regard to the environmental consequences of their production. (We shall discuss pollution at some length in Chapters 22 and 23.)

Consumerism, which is growing in influence in Canada, is a movement that asserts that there is a conflict between the interests of firms and the public interest and that the conflict should be removed by reforming firms so that they are motivated by the public interest rather than by their stockholders' desires for maximum profits. Consumerists believe, for example, that General Motors' directors should be made to recognize that automobiles pollute and cause accidents and that GM's resources should be invested in the development and installation of safety and antipollution devices. This, they argue, would be a proper use of GM's funds, even if GM's stockholders do not agree and even if automobile purchasers do not want to pay for the extra safety and antipollution devices.

What are the main arguments *for* this view? First, only the company can know the potentially adverse effects of its actions. Second, by virtue of holding a corporate charter, the corporation assumes the responsibility to protect the general welfare while pursuing private profits.

What are the main arguments *against* the consumerist view? Managers of companies have neither the knowledge nor the ability to represent the general public interest; they are largely selected, judged, and promoted according to their ability to run a profit-oriented enterprise, and the assumption that they are especially competent to decide broader *public* questions is unjustified. Moral, as distinct from economic, decisions—such as whether to use nuclear power, to make or use internal combustion engines, to manufacture or smoke cigarettes, and to manufacture or use insecticides or aerosol sprays—cannot properly be delegated to corporations or their executives. Some are individual decisions; others require either the expertise or the authority of a public regulatory agency. Whoever makes decisions on behalf of the public must be potentially responsible to the public. Neither corporate managers nor consumer activists meet this criterion.

Those who oppose the consumerist view hold that required changes in corporate behavior should be accomplished not by exhorting business leaders to behave responsibly or by placing consumer representatives on a corporation's board of directors but by regulations or incentives that force or induce the desired corporate behavior. Let corporations pursue their profits but be subject to public laws. For example, Parliament can require that all cars have seat belts or air bags or have antipollution devices or meet specific standards of emission levels. It can prohibit the use of DDT; it can fine companies that pollute above a specified level; it can regulate the use of nuclear power and aerosols. Parliament can also make it easier for private parties to bring lawsuits that would either enjoin certain behavior or force corporations to pay for the damages that their products cause. By adopting strategies like these, the profit motive itself can be harnessed on behalf of public policy goals. Firms that do not act in accordance with the law will lose profits through the fines and damages that they must pay.[8]

The Importance of Nonmaximizing Theories

An impressive array of empirical and theoretical evidence can be gathered in support of various non-profit-maximizing theories. What would be the implications if they were accepted as being better theories of the behavior of the economy than the "standard model," which is based on the assumption of profit maximization?

To the extent that existing non-profit-maximizing theories are correct, the economic system does not perform with the delicate precision that follows from profit maximization. Firms will not always respond quickly and precisely to small changes in market signals from either the private sector or government policy. Nor are they certain to make radical changes in their behavior even when the profit incentives to do so are large.

Generally, the nonmaximizing theories imply that in many cases firms' responses to changes in market signals will be of uncertain speed and direction.

There are limits, however, to the extent that the nonmaximizing behavior can survive in the marketplace. According to all of the existing theories, maximizing and nonmaximizing, firms will tend to sell more when demand goes up and less when it goes down. They will also tend to alter their prices and their input mixes when they face sufficiently large changes in input prices. Moreover, failure to respond to profit opportunities can lead to takeover by a more profit-oriented management. While this does not mean that profits are being precisely maximized at all times, it does put real limits on the extent to which firms can ignore profits.

[8] The costs of enforcing laws and regulations are discussed in Chapters 23 and 24.

BOX 16-2

Do Firms Control the Market?

John Kenneth Galbraith has argued that it is *not* consumers' wants that create the market signals that provide profit opportunities and motivate business behavior. On the contrary, Galbraith argues, large corporations have the power to create and to manipulate demand in the interest of reducing their own uncertainty.

The key to Galbraith's hypothesis is the power of advertising, whereby corporations persuade consumers to buy what the corporations want them to buy rather than what the consumers themselves want. Being responsive to consumers, he argues, would require more investment. It is much safer and cheaper merely to make consumers into corporate puppets through the power of advertising. Corporations are also alleged to manipulate the government in order to provide a favorable environment in which to control the market.

There is much superficial support for this view. Large corporations spend a good deal of money on advertising, and they also exert considerable influence on all levels of government. There have been many cases in which this influence has been blatantly corrupt.

Still, the bulk of the evidence, both theoretical and empirical, suggests that in the end, it is consumers who dictate what firms must do to survive, rather than the other way around. Consider the recent history of the U.S. automobile industry. In spite of the industry's enormous financial and political power and in spite of billions of dollars of advertising, the advent of the small, fuel-efficient car, introduced by foreign competitors, nearly brought the industry to its knees. The cars of today are safer, more comfortable, and more efficient than those of 10 or 15 years ago, at least in part because the industry had to meet the competition and to serve the desire of its customers.

Turnover in the list of leading North American companies is revealing. Only one company, Exxon (Standard Oil of New Jersey), was in the top 10 both in 1910 and in 1985. Consider these giants of 1910, none of which are among the largest 250 today: International Mercantile Marine (today United States Lines), United States Cotton Oil, American Hide and Leather, American Ice, Baldwin Locomotive, Cudahy, International Salt, and United Shoe Machinery. They have slipped or disappeared from the marketplace largely because of the relative decline in the demand for their prod-

Profits are a potent force in the life and death of firms. The resilience of profit-maximizing theory and its ability to predict the economy's reactions to many major changes (such as the dramatic variations in energy prices that have occurred over the past two decades) suggest that firms are at least strongly motivated by the pursuit of profits.

In the past decade or so, the question of how firms behave in detail has received renewed attention from both economists and organization theorists. Almost everyone in the field agrees that firms do not exactly maximize profits. At the same time, almost everyone agrees that firms cannot stray too far from the goal of profit maximization. Just how far is too far depends on the circumstances in which firms operate and the mechanisms that firms' owners can use to influence managers. These areas are at the frontier of current economic research.

SUMMARY

1. In the market for corporate control, would-be buyers of firms deal with would-be sellers (in friendly takeovers, mergers, and buyouts) as well as with reluctant sellers (in hostile takeovers). Buyers who believe that they can operate a firm more profitably than its present

ucts. Today's giants include automobile, oil, airline, computer, and electric power companies, for the obvious reason that demand for these products is strong.

Are these shifts in demand explained by the corporate manipulation of consumers' tastes through advertising or by more basic changes? Advertising has two major aspects: It seeks to inform consumers about available products, and it seeks to influence consumers by altering their demands. The first aspect, informative advertising, plays an important part in the efficient operation of any free market system; the second aspect is one through which firms seek to control the market rather than be controlled by it.

About the second aspect, there can be no question—advertising *does* influence consumers' demand. If GM were to stop advertising, it would surely lose sales to Ford, Chrysler, and imports, but it is hard to believe that the automotive society was conjured up by advertisers. When you are persuaded to take advantage of Nation Air's low-priced services, your real alternative is not a covered wagon, a bicycle, or even a Greyhound bus; more likely you are forgoing Air Canada or CAI.

Careful promotion can influence the success of one rock group over another, but could it sell the waltz to today's teenager? Taste making through advertising unquestionably plays a role in shaping demand, but so do more basic human attitudes, psychological needs, and technological opportunities. When existing companies are cautious about adopting new technologies, new companies will take the risk in order to make a profit. The personal computer is an excellent example. A small number of unknown entrepreneurs invented and successfully marketed the first personal computers. When they did so, advertising was irrelevant. What mattered was that they took a technology and developed a product that they could sell at a price that would earn them a profit. When they had done so, a whole industry followed their lead. Only then did advertising begin to play a role.

The evidence suggests that the allocation of resources among major product groups owes far more to the tastes and the values of consumers than it does to corporate advertising and related activities.

management or than its present organization allows can afford to pay more than the present market value of the firm's equities to acquire it. The possibility of such purchases provides an incentive for current managers to come close to maximizing the firm's profits and encourages their replacement by new buyers when they do not.

2. Leveraged buyouts, financed by junk bonds, have been a means of buying out firms whose organization is too large and cumbersome—often as a result of conglomerate mergers of earlier decades. If the deal is successful, the firm is broken up into its constituent parts, which are sold for a total exceeding the purchase price of the whole. The junk bonds are then retired, with a profit left over for the purchasers. This is the market system working to undo an earlier experiment (conglomerate mergers) that proved to be a failure.
3. Foreign investment has played a large part in opening up less developed countries over the past few centuries. In their time, Canada and the United States were less developed than the United Kingdom and some other European countries and were the recipients of foreign investment that flowed from Europe to the New World.

4. As the countries of the New World grew, they were able to generate a rising flow of domestic savings, which reduced their need for new investment, repatriated some old foreign investment, and provided a flow of investment to newer, less developed countries. The United States has experienced this entire cycle. Canada, having a smaller population in a larger geographical area, still needs foreign investment. However, the flow is a much smaller proportion of total investment than it has been in the past, and since 1975 Canada has been a net exporter of capital, sending more abroad to buy foreign assets than it takes in from foreigners who buy Canadian assets.
5. The growth of transnational corporations means that no country can hope to own a majority of the capital that is devoted to the production within its borders of internationally traded commodities. The TNCs also have the power to arbitrage national policies, thereby reducing the effectiveness of many policies designed to give advantages to the initiating country.
6. There is debate in Canada about the benefits and costs of foreign investment, but such investment could not be dispensed with since the wealth involved vastly exceeds Canadians' ability to buy it. The most that can be expected from an active policy to influence foreign investment is to redirect such investment out of some industries and into others. Economists and others do not agree, however, on which sectors should be targeted for reducing the degree of foreign ownership (and which should increase as a result of redirecting that investment).
7. Principal-agent theory gives support to the idea that corporate managers will not always operate corporations in the best interests of the stockholders; that is, the managers will pursue their own interests rather than simply maximizing profits. Sales maximization is an example of such a pursuit.
8. An alternative set of hypotheses denies that firms seek to maximize any well-defined objective:
   a. Some theories hold that firms do not have sufficient information to maximize their profits. Other theories hold that firms consciously choose to do something other than maximize their profits.
   b. The full-cost hypothesis states that firms determine price by adding a customary—and infrequently changed—markup to full costs. This also makes pricing behavior relatively insensitive to short-term fluctuations in demand.
   c. Organization theorists see firms as insensitive to short-term fluctuations in market signals. The reason lies in the decision-making structure of large organizations, which must rely on routines and rules of thumb rather than on fresh calculations of profitability as each new situation presents itself. Organization theorists also emphasize that different decision-making structures will lead to different responses to market signals.
   d. Evolutionary theorists build on full-cost and organizational theories. They see the firm as a profit-oriented entity in a world of imperfect information, making small changes in response to new information but being more resistant to large "structural changes."
9. In recent years serious concern has developed over whether corporations should represent the interests of their owners and managers or whether they should be responsible to a broader public interest.

Consumerism argues for the latter point of view; others prefer to rely on markets and government control to protect the public interest.

10. Firms that are not run in stockholders' interests—that do not maximize profits—are attractive targets for takeover because their value is below their potential, profit-maximizing value. This possibility will limit the ability of managers to pursue their own ends instead of maximizing profits.

TOPICS FOR REVIEW

Mergers, takeovers, and buyouts
Tender offer
Poison pills
Junk bonds
Leveraged buyouts
Transnational corporations
Sales maximization
Full-cost pricing
Organization theory
Satisficing
Evolutionary theories

DISCUSSION QUESTIONS

1. In light of principal-agent theory, why might physicians and lawyers be required to subscribe to professional codes of ethics that prevent (or at least limit) their ability to sell unneeded services to their clients? Why do we not see similar codes of ethics for automobile mechanics?
2. Comment on the following quote from the *New York Times* on October 26, 1988:

   "While many stockholders are rejoicing at the flurry of huge corporate takeover attempts, bondholders are wincing at the damage inflicted on their holdings. . . . Buyers of new and old industrial bonds are balking because, when companies are taken over by buying out shareholders with huge amounts of new debt, existing bondholders are left holding securities that are not as safe as before. Suddenly, the chance of an economic downturn could make it impossible for the company to pay interest on all the debt it owes."
3. *The Economist* ran the following on October 29, 1988, under the headline "Someone's Wrong":

   "Notice the curious paradox involved in the biggest and third biggest takeover deals in history? Kohlberg Kravis Roberts is offering $20.3 billion so RJR Nabisco can split its tobacco companies away from the food-making parts of its empire by taking Winston, Camel and Salem private, while selling off Nabisco and Del Monte. [*Note:* Kohlberg's eventual winning bid was billions higher.] Over at Philip Morris, the exact opposite is going on: The company is willing to pay $11.5 billion to add another food company, Kraft, to its existing tobacco and food business (Marlboro, Benson and Hedges, General Foods). More than $30 billion is therefore riding on two flatly contradictory views of the best future for the food and tobacco business. LBOs may be fashionable, but no one can accuse the American investors of herd instinct."

   a. Why does *The Economist* find these behaviors so puzzling?
   b. Think of some explanations for the puzzle and discuss them.

4. Assume that each of the following assertions is factually correct. Taken together, what would they tell you about the prediction that big business is increasing its control of the Canadian economy?
   a. The share of total manufacturing assets owned by the 100 largest corporations has been rising over the past 25 years.
   b. The number of new firms begun each year has increased over the past 25 years.
   c. The share of manufacturing in total production has been decreasing for 40 years.
   d. Profits as a percentage of national income are no higher now than half a century ago.
5. In 1988, de Haviland aircraft, makers of the famous Dash series of commuter airplanes, was taken over by Boeing, only to be offered for sale a few years later to another foreign firm. In 1989, Lumonics, a state-of-the-art laser firm, was taken over by the Japanese conglomerate Sumitomo. In the same year Connaught laboratories, famous as the base for the discovery of insulin, was bought by a consortium based in France. In all three cases the sale was made only after strenuous efforts to find Canadian buyers had failed. In what ways might these transactions be, or not be, in Canada's best interests?
6. "The business of the businessman is to run his business so as to make profits. If he does so, he will serve the public interest better than if he tries to decide what is good for society. He is neither elected nor appointed to that task." Discuss.
7. "Our list prices are really set by our accounting department: They add a fixed markup to their best estimates of fully accounted cost and send these to the operating divisions. Managers of these divisions may not change those prices without permission of the board of directors, which is seldom given. Operating divisions may, however, provide special discounts if necessary to stay competitive." Does this testimony by the president of a leading manufacturing company support the full-cost pricing hypothesis?
8. The leading automobile tire manufacturers sell original equipment (OE) tires to automobile manufacturers at a price below the average total cost of all the tires they make and sell. This happens year after year. Is this consistent with profit-maximizing behavior in the short run? In the long run? If it is not consistent, what does it show? Do OE tires compete with replacement tires?
9. In his article "Which Is Us?" Robert Reich criticizes American (and by implication Canadian) policy for giving assistance to domestically *owned* rather than domestically *located* TNCs. Why, he asks, should an American (or Canadian) owned firm get R&D assistance for research done in Taiwan to produce goods in Singapore which is denied to a Japanese-owned firm doing research in California (or Toronto) to develop new products to be produced in Kentucky (or Winnipeg)? Who gains the benefits from subsidies provided by governments (and paid for by taxpayers) to each of these types of firms?

PART

5

THE DISTRIBUTION OF INCOME

Chapter 17

Factor Mobility and Factor Pricing

Are the poor getting poorer and the rich getting richer, as Karl Marx thought they would? Are the rich becoming relatively poorer and the poor becoming relatively richer, as Alfred Marshall hoped they would? Is the distribution of income affected by social changes, such as the increased participation of women in the labor force? Is it affected by changes in public policy toward poverty? Should we reject the view held by the great Italian economist Vilfredo Pareto (inventor of indifference curves and student of income distribution) that inequality of income is a social constant determined by forces that are possibly beyond human understanding and probably beyond human influence?

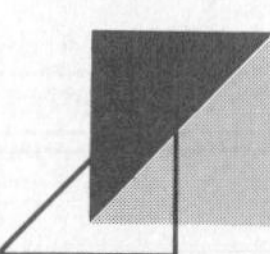

Functional Distribution and Size Distribution

The founders of classical economics, Adam Smith and David Ricardo, were concerned with the distribution of income among what were then the three great social classes: workers, capitalists, and landowners. They defined three factors of production as labor, capital, and land. The return to each factor was treated as the income of the respective social class.

Smith and Ricardo were interested in what determined the income of each class relative to the total national income. Their theories predicted that as society progressed, landlords would become relatively better off and capitalists would become relatively worse off. Karl Marx had a different theory. He predicted that as growth occurred, capitalists would become relatively better off and workers would become relatively worse off (at least until the whole capitalist system collapsed).

These nineteenth century debates focused on what is now called the **functional distribution of income**, defined as the distribution of total income among the major factors of production. Table 17-1 shows data for the functional distribution of income in Canada in 1988.

Although functional distribution categories (wages, rent, profits) pervade current statistics, economists have shifted to another way of looking at differences in incomes. At the beginning of the century, Pareto studied what is now called the **size distribution of income**, the distribution of income among different households without reference to the source of the income or the social class of the household. He discovered that inequality in income distribution was substantial in all countries and, more surpris-

TABLE 17-1 Functional Distribution of National Income in Canada, 1988

Type of income	Billions of dollars	Percentage of total
Employee compensation	326.0	69.0
Corporate profits	62.3	13.2
Proprietor's income, including rent	38.8	8.2
Interest	45.6	9.6
Total	472.7	100.0

Source: Bank of Canada Review, January 1990.

Total income is classified here according to the nature of the factor service that earned the income. Although these data show that employee compensation accounts for nearly 70 percent of national income, this does not mean that workers and their families receive only that proportion of national income. Many households will have income in more than one category listed in the table.

TABLE 17-3 Inequality in Family Income Distribution, 1988

Family income rank	Percentage share of aggregate income
Lowest fifth	6.5
Second fifth	12.4
Middle fifth	17.9
Fourth fifth	24.0
Highest fifth	39.2
	100.0

Source: Statistics Canada, 13–207.

Though far from showing overall equality, income distribution is relatively equal for the middle 40 percent of the distribution. If the income distribution were perfectly equal, each fifth of the families would receive 20 percent of aggregate income.

ingly, that the degree of inequality was quite similar from one country to another. Tables 17-2 and 17-3 show that in Canada in 1988 there was substantial inequality in the size distribution of income.

Inequality in the distribution of income is shown graphically in Figure 17-1. This curve of income distribution, called a **Lorenz curve**, shows how much of total income is accounted for by given proportions of the nation's families. (The farther the curve bends away from the diagonal, the more unequal is the distribution of income.) Today the bottom 20 percent of all Canadian households receive only 6.5 percent of all income earned. The present size distribution of income is virtually unchanged from what it was 25 years ago.

There are good reasons why much of the attention of modern economists is devoted to the size, rather than the functional, distribution of income. After all, some capitalists (such as the owners of small retail stores) are in the lower part of the income scale, while some wage earners (such as skilled athletes) are at the upper end of the income scale. Moreover, if someone is poor, it matters little whether that person is a landowner or a worker.

To understand the distribution of income, we must first study how the income of households is determined. Superficial explanations of differences in income, such as "People earn according to their ability," are clearly inadequate. Incomes are distributed much more unequally than any *measured* index of ability, be it IQ, physical strength, or typing skill. In what sense is Nick Faldo five times as able a golfer as Dave Barr? His average score is only 1 percent better, yet he earns five times as much. However, if answers couched in terms of worth and ability are easily refuted, so are answers such as "It's all a matter of luck" or "It's just the system."

TABLE 17-2 Incomes of Canadian Families, 1988

Income class	Percentage of families
Less than $9,999	3.8
$10,000–$19,999	13.7
$20,000–$29,999	15.4
$30,000–$39,999	16.4
$40,000–$49,999	15.1
$50,000–$59,999	12.1
$60,000 and over	23.5

Source: Statistics Canada, 13–208.

Although median family income in 1988 was just over $40,000, many families received much less than this, and some received a great deal more. While nearly one-fourth of Canadian families had very comfortable incomes of more than $60,000, almost one-fifth had to subsist on incomes below $20,000, less than half the national average.

FIGURE 17-1 A Lorenz Curve of Family Income in Canada

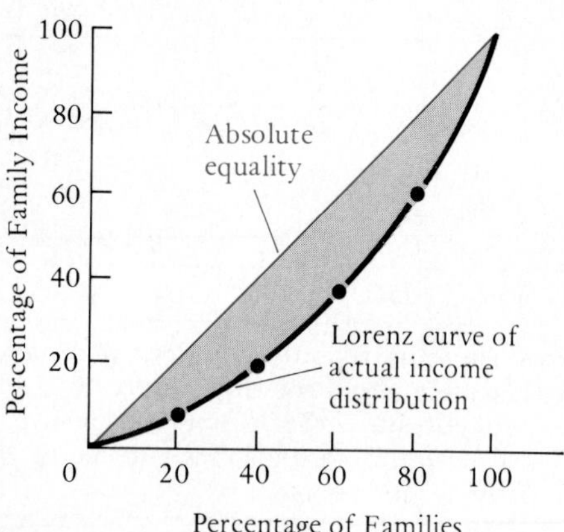

The size of the shaded area between the Lorenz curve and the diagonal is a measure of the inequality of income distribution. If there were complete income equality, the bottom 20 percent of income receivers would receive 20 percent of the income, and so forth, and the Lorenz curve would coincide with the diagonal line. Because the lowest 20 percent receive only 5 percent of the income, the Lorenz curve lies below the diagonal line. The extent to which it bends away from the straight line indicates the amount of inequality in the distribution of income.

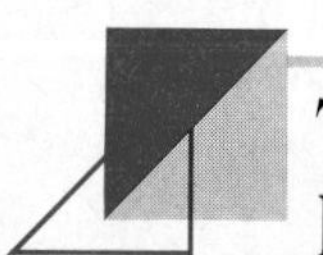

The Theory of Income Distribution

How does economic theory explain the distribution of income more satisfactorily than these superficial explanations? In this chapter, using the basic tools of supply and demand, we provide an answer to this question.

Factor Markets and Factor Incomes

Workers' incomes depend on their wage rates and on the hours that they work. Similarly, all incomes have two components: prices paid and quantities supplied. We look at each of these.

Factor prices. Consider the money wage of $5 per hour. Does someone who earns this money wage expect to get a large or a small share of the nation's total production? In 1930, when a bus ride cost 5 cents in many cities and a restaurant meal could be bought for 25 cents, $5 per hour offered command over what most people would have regarded as a very satisfactory share of the nation's output. In 1990, when a bus ride costs over $1 in many cities and even a modest restaurant meal costs over $5, a wage rate of $5 per hour offers command over what most people would regard as a quite unsatisfactory share of the nation's output.

What this example illustrates is that a factor's real income depends on the price that it can command *relative to* all the other prices in the economy. "Expensive" and "cheap" are relative concepts. A factor becomes more expensive and commands a larger share of the nation's total income when its price rises relative to most other prices. It becomes cheap and commands a smaller share of the nation's total income when its price falls relative to most other prices. The theory of factor pricing is concerned with relative prices, with what makes a factor become more or less expensive relative to the prices of other goods and services in the economy, so that the factor will command a larger or smaller share of the nation's total output.[1]

Factor quantities. There is no point in being offered a high wage rate if little or no work can be found at that rate. This emphasizes that a factor's share of the national income depends not only on the price that its services command but also on the quantity of those services that are sold.

Factor income. To discover a factor's income, we need to know the price of its services and the amount of them that are sold. This is something that we have done already for final goods and services that are sold in competitive and in monopolistic markets.

According to the neo-Classical theory of distribution, *determining* a factor's income is just a particular application of price theory.

[1] The theory of inflation is concerned with why all prices change; that is, it is concerned with the absolute level of all prices. The theory of market prices of goods and factor services is concerned with why some prices change relative to others; that is, it is concerned with relative prices. If we assume that all prices other than the one under consideration are constant, then a change in a factor's money price is a change in its relative price. If all other prices are rising, then a change in relative price requires that the factor's money price rise faster or slower than the average of all prices. A fuller discussion was given in Chapter 4.

This determination is shown for a competitive market in Figure 17-2. (Look again at Figure 4-8 on page 68 to see why this analysis is familiar.) This is all there is to the essence of the neo-Classical theory of distribution in competitive markets. The theory applies to all factors that are priced and sold in any market. To apply it to any particular factor, such as plumbers, we need only to allow for any special forces that influence the demand or the supply of plumbers. To apply the theory of noncompetitive markets, we need merely to apply what we have learned already about pricing in markets under monopoly or oligopoly.

In this chapter and the next, we shall study some interesting applications of this theory that can be made to competitive markets. In Chapter 19, we shall study the market for labor in some detail; to do so, we consider now a number of special forces that influence the demand and the supply of labor, and we extend the theory to cover noncompetitive market structures.

FIGURE 17-2 The Determination of Factor Price and Income in a Competitive Market

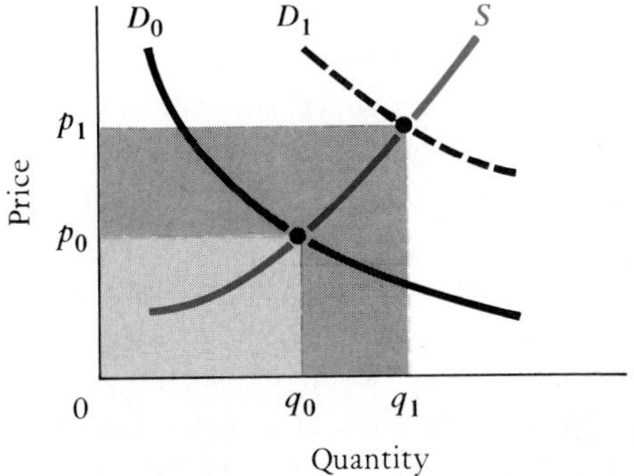

In competitive factor markets, demand and supply determine factor prices, quantities of factors used, and factor incomes. With demand and supply curves D_0 and S, the price of the factor will be p_0 and the quantity employed will be q_0. The total income earned by the factor is the light gray shaded area. A shift in demand from D_0 to D_1 raises equilibrium price and quantity to p_1 and q_1, respectively. The income earned by the factor rises by an amount equal to the dark gray shaded area.

The Demand for Factors

Firms require inputs not for their own sake but as a means to produce goods and services. For example, the demand for computer programmers and technicians is growing as we use more and more computers. The demand for carpenters and building materials rises and falls with the amount of housing construction. Anything that increases the demand for new housing—population growth, lower interest rates on mortgages, and so on—will increase the demand for the inputs that are required to build the houses. The demand for any input depends on the existence of a demand for the goods or services that it helps to produce; the demand for a factor of production is therefore called a **derived demand**.[2] Typically, one input will be used in making many commodities. Steel is used in dozens of industries, as are the services of carpenters.

The total demand for an input will be the sum of the derived demands for it in every activity in which it is used.

The theory of income distribution rests in part on the demand by firms for land, labor, and capital to be used as inputs. Firms also use products that are produced by other firms as their inputs, such as steel, plastics, and electricity. If we investigate the production of these inputs, we will find that they, too, are made by using land, labor, capital, and other produced inputs. If we continue following through the chain of outputs used as inputs, we will find that we can account for all of the economy's output in terms of inputs of the three basic factors of production—land, labor, and capital.

The Total Supply of Factors

To what extent do economic forces determine the *total supply* of a factor to the whole economy? To what extent do economic forces determine the *supply available to a particular industry*?

In this section we look at total supply. At any one time, the total supply of each factor of production is given. For example, in each country the labor force is of a certain size, there is so much arable land available, and there is a given known supply of petroleum. However, these supplies can and do change

[2] In Chapter 18, we shall look in detail at the role of marginal productivity theory in understanding the derived demand for the services of factors of production.

in response to both economic and noneconomic forces. Sometimes the change is very gradual, as when a climatic change slowly turns arable land into desert or when a medical discovery lowers the rate of infant mortality and hence increases the rate of population growth, thereby eventually increasing the supply of adult labor. Sometimes the changes can be quite rapid, as when a boom in business activity brings retired persons back into the labor force, a rise in the price of oil greatly encourages the discovery of new oil supplies, or a rise in the price of agricultural produce encourages the draining of marshes to add to the supply of arable land.

Although people worry about depleting natural resources, complete exhaustion of a given resource is quite rare. Frequently, newly discovered or previously unexploited sources of a resource maintain the supply, though perhaps at a higher cost than existing supplies. Ultimately, of course, there is an upper limit, and resources can be exhausted; worse, they can be contaminated or otherwise despoiled before they are consumed. However, even when the supply of one resource is exhausted, substitutes are usually developed. The exhaustion of high-grade iron ore reserves in the Mesabi Range of northern Michigan did not end steel production in the United States, partly because ways to use low-grade iron ores once thought worthless were discovered and partly because new supplies in Labrador and in the Caribbean were developed.

Shortages often lead to their own correction. When oil became scarce over a decade ago, its price rose; users turned to substitutes to meet their demands; synthetic oil was developed; and oil companies explored for new sources.

Time is an important element in the determination of the total supply of a factor. The longer the time period, the more responsive the total supply of any factor to economic forces.

Now consider the total supply of each of the three key factors of production.

Total Supply of Capital

The supply of capital in a country consists of the stock of existing machines, plant, equipment, and so on. Capital is a manufactured factor of production, and its total supply is in no sense fixed, although it changes only slowly. Each year the stock of capital goods is diminished by the amount that becomes physically or economically obsolete and is increased by the amount that is produced. On balance, the trend has been for the capital stock to grow over the past decades. In Chapter 18 we shall consider the theory of investment that deals with long-term changes in the stock of capital.

Total Supply of Land

The total area of dry land in a country is almost completely fixed, but the supply of *fertile* land is not fixed. Considerable care and effort are required to sustain the productive power of land. If the return to land is low, its fertility may be destroyed within a short time. Moreover, scarcity and high prices may make it worthwhile to increase the supply of arable land by irrigation and other forms of reclamation.

Total Supply of Labor

The *total supply of labor* is the total number of hours of work that the population is willing to supply. This quantity is often also called the **supply of effort**. It has many obvious determinants, such as the rewards for working, the ages at which people enter the labor force and retire from it, and the length of the conventional work week. It also has many less obvious ones. For example, a social trend, such as the women's liberation movement, affects labor force participation. For another, the whole pattern of tax rates, unemployment insurance, and welfare payments affects the relative advantages of working and not working.

As is discussed in Chapter 25, the evidence shows some small adverse effects of taxes on the supply of effort. However, welfare schemes have sometimes been a severe disincentive to work. Although most people prefer working to being on welfare, it is not surprising that they respond rationally to an incentive system that severely penalizes any work done by welfare recipients.

The Supply of Factors for a Particular Use

Most factors have many uses. A given piece of land can be used to grow any one of several crops, or it can be subdivided for a housing development. A computer programmer in Halifax can work for one of several firms, for the government, or for Dalhousie University. A lathe can be used to make many different products, and it requires no adaptation when it is turned for one use or another. Plainly, it is easier for any one user to acquire more of a scarce factor of production than it is for all users to do so simultaneously. One user can bid resources away from another user, even though the total supply may be fixed.

The total supply of any factor must be allocated among all the different uses to which it can possibly be put.

Factor Mobility

When we are considering the supply of a factor for a particular use, the most important concept that we should keep in mind is *factor mobility.* A factor that shifts easily between uses in response to small changes in incentives is said to be *mobile.* It will be in elastic supply in any one of its uses, because a small increase in the price offered will attract many units of the factor from other uses. A factor that does not shift easily from one use to another, even in response to large changes in remuneration, is said to be *immobile.* It will be in inelastic supply in any one of its uses, because even a large increase in the price offered will attract only a small inflow from other uses. Often a factor may be immobile in the short run but mobile in the long run.

An important key to factor mobility is time. The longer the time interval, the easier it is for a factor to convert from one use to another.

Consider the factor mobility among particular uses of each of the three key factors of production.

Capital. Some kinds of capital equipment—lathes, trucks, and computers, for example—can be shifted readily among uses; many others are comparatively unshiftable. A great deal of machinery is utterly specific: Once built, it must be used for the purpose for which it was designed, or it cannot be used at all. (It is the immobility of much fixed capital equipment that makes the exit of firms from declining industries the slow and difficult process described in Chapter 12.)

In the long run, however, capital is highly mobile. When capital goods wear out, a firm may simply replace them with identical goods, or it may exercise other options. It may buy a newly designed machine to produce the same goods, or it may buy machines to produce totally different goods. Such decisions lead to changes in the long-run allocation of a country's stock of capital among various uses.

Land. Land, which is physically the least mobile of factors, is one of the most mobile in an economic sense. Consider agricultural land. Within one year, one crop can be harvested and a totally different crop can be planted. A farm on the outskirts of a growing city can be sold for subdivision and development on short notice.

Once land is built on, its mobility is much reduced. A site on which a hotel has been built can be converted into an office building site, but it takes a large differential in the value of land use to make it worthwhile, because the hotel must be torn down.

Although land is highly mobile among alternative uses, it is completely immobile as far as location is concerned. There is only so much land within a given distance of the center of any city, and no increase in the price paid can induce further land to be located within that distance. This locational immobility has important consequences, including high prices for desirable locations and the tendency to build tall buildings to economize on the use of scarce land, as in the center of large cities.

Labor. Labor is unique as a factor of production in that the supply of the service requires the physical presence of the person who supplies it. Absentee landlords, while continuing to live in the place of their choice, can obtain income from land that is located in remote parts of the world. Investment can be shifted from iron mines in South Africa to mines in Labrador, while the owners commute between Vancouver and Hawaii. However, when a worker who is employed by a firm in Regina decides to supply labor service to a firm in Toronto, the worker must physically travel to Toronto. This has an important consequence.

Because of the need for labor's physical presence, nonmonetary considerations are much more important in the allocation of labor than in the allocation of other factors of production.

People may be satisfied with or frustrated by the kind of work that they do, where they do it, the people with whom they do it, and the social status of their occupations. Since these considerations influence their decisions about what they will do with their labor services, they will not always move just because they could earn a higher wage. Nevertheless, occupational and job movement do occur when there are changes in the wage structure.

The mobility that does occur depends on many forces. For example, it is not difficult for a secretary to shift from one company to another in order to take a job in Winnipeg instead of in Vernon, British Columbia, but it can be difficult for a secretary to become an editor, a model, a machinist, or a doctor in a short period of time. Workers who lack ability, training, or inclination find certain kinds of mobility to be difficult or impossible.

Some barriers may be virtually insurmountable once a person's training has been completed. It may be impossible for a farmer to become a surgeon or for a truck driver to become a professional athlete, even if the relative wage rates change greatly. However, the children of farmers, doctors, truck drivers, and athletes, when they are deciding how much education or training to obtain, are not nearly as limited in their choices as their parents, who have already completed their education and are settled in their occupations.

Thus the labor force as a whole is mobile, even though many individual members in it are not. At one end of the age distribution are people who enter the labor force directly from school; at the other end are those who leave it through retirement or death. The turnover in the labor force due to these causes is 3 or 4 percent per year. Over a period of 10 years, a society could create a quite different occupational distribution merely by directing new entrants to jobs other than the ones that were left vacant by workers who left the labor force, without a single individual ever changing jobs. The role of education in helping people to adapt to available jobs is great. In a society in which education is provided to all, it is possible to achieve large increases in the supply of any needed labor skill within a decade or so.

Factor Price Differentials

If every laborer were the same, and if all benefits were monetary, then the price of labor would tend to be the same in all uses. Workers would move from low-priced jobs to high-priced ones. The quantity of labor supplied would diminish in occupations in which wages were low, and the resulting labor shortage would tend to force those wages up; the quantity of labor supplied would increase in occupations in which wages were high, and the resulting surplus would force wages down. The movement would continue until there were no further incentives to change occupations, that is, until wages were equalized in all uses.[3]

In fact, however, wage differentials commonly occur. These differentials may be divided into two distinct types: those that exist only in disequilibrium situations and those that persist in equilibrium.

Disequilibrium Differentials

Some factor price differentials reflect a temporary state of disequilibrium. They are brought about by circumstances such as the growth of one industry and the decline of another. The differentials themselves lead to reallocation of factors, and such reallocations in turn act to eliminate the differentials.

Consider the effect on factor prices of a rise in the demand for air transport and a decline in the demand for rail transport. The airline industry's demand for factors increases while the railroad industry's demand for factors decreases. Relative factor prices will go up in airlines and down in railroads. The differential in factor prices causes a net movement of factors from the railroad industry to the airline industry, and this movement causes the differentials to lessen and eventually to disappear. How long this process takes will depend on how easily factors can be reallocated from one industry to the other, that is, on the degree of factor mobility.

Equilibrium Differentials

Some factor price differentials persist in equilibrium, without generating any forces that will eliminate them. These **equilibrium differentials** can be explained by intrinsic differences in the factors themselves, by differences in the cost of acquiring skills, or by different nonmonetary advantages of different occupations.

Intrinsic differences. If various units of a factor have different characteristics, the price that is paid may

[3] Similar remarks also apply to all other factors of production.

differ among these units. If intelligence and dexterity are required to accomplish a task, intelligent and manually dexterous workers will earn more than less intelligent and less dexterous workers. If land is to be used for agricultural purposes, highly fertile land will earn more than poor land. These differences will persist even in long-run equilibrium.

Acquired differences. If the fertility of land can be increased by costly methods, then that land must command a higher price than less fertile land. If it did not, landlords would not incur the costs of improving fertility. The same holds true for labor. It is costly to acquire most skills. For example, a mechanic must train for some time, and unless the earnings of mechanics remain sufficiently above what can be earned in less skilled occupations, people will not incur the cost of training.

Nonmonetary advantages. Whenever working conditions differ among various uses for a single factor, that factor will earn different equilibrium amounts in its various uses. The difference between a test pilot's wage and a chauffeur's wage is only partly a matter of skill; the rest is compensation to the worker for facing the higher risk of testing new planes as compared to driving a car. If both were paid the same, there would be an excess supply of chauffeurs and a shortage of test pilots.

Academic researchers commonly earn less than they could earn in the world of commerce and industry because of the substantial nonmonetary advantages of academic employment. If chemists were paid the same in both sectors, many chemists would prefer academic to industrial jobs. Excess demand for industrial chemists and excess supply of academic chemists would then force chemists' wages up in industry and down in academia until the two types of jobs seemed equally attractive on balance.

The same forces account for equilibrium differences in regional earnings of otherwise identical factors. People who work in remote logging or mining areas are paid more than people who do jobs requiring similar skills in large cities. Without higher pay, not enough people would be willing to work at sometimes dangerous jobs in unattractive or remote locations. Similarly, if enough people prefer living in the Atlantic provinces to living in Hamilton, Ontario, equilibrium wages in comparable occupations will be lower in the Atlantic provinces than in Hamilton. Box 17-1 discusses the implications of trying to remove equilibrium differentials among Canadian provinces.

Differentials and Factor Mobility

The distinction between equilibrium and disequilibrium differentials is closely linked to factor mobility.

Disequilibrium differentials lead to, and are eroded by, factor movements; equilibrium differentials are not eliminated by factor mobility.

Equalizing net advantage. The behavior that causes the erosion of disequilibrium differentials is summarized in the assumption of the *maximization of net advantage*: The owners of factors of production will allocate them to uses that maximize the net advantages to themselves, taking both monetary and nonmonetary rewards into consideration. If net advantages were higher in occupation A than in occupation B, factors would move from B to A. The increased supply in A and the lower supply in B would drive factor earnings down in A and up in B until net advantages would be equalized, after which no further movement would occur. This prediction is summarized in the hypothesis of *equal net advantage*: In equilibrium, units of each kind of factor of production will be allocated among alternative possible uses in such a way that the net advantages in all uses are equalized.

Although nonmonetary advantages are important in explaining differences in levels of pay for labor in different occupations, they tend to be quite stable over time. As a result, monetary advantages, which vary with market conditions, lead to changes in *net advantage*.

A change in the relative price of a factor between two uses will change the net advantages of the uses. It will lead to a shift of some units of that factor to the use whose relative price has increased.

This implies a rising supply curve for a factor in any particular use. When the price of a factor rises in that use, more will be supplied to that use. This factor supply curve (like all supply curves) can *shift* in response to changes in other variables. For example, a change in laws that relate to safety or a new union agreement that alters working conditions will shift the curve of labor to that use, showing a new quantity supplied at each wage.

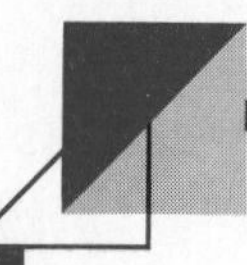

BOX 17-1

Could Per Capita Incomes and Unemployment Rates Be Equalized Across Canadian Provinces?

The answer to the question posed in the title is almost certainly no—at least when we consider the kinds of policy tools likely to be available to any foreseeable Canadian government.

This answer comes from a simple application of the hypothesis of *equal net advantage*. As long as provinces differ in their nonmonetary attractiveness, there will be equilibrium differences in their per capita incomes and/or unemployment rates. Why is this so?

Consider low levels of income. Suppose that Province A—despite strong physical, climatic, and social attractions—has a set of natural endowments that will not produce as high an income per person employed as Province B. Deficiencies in economic opportunities in a particular province might arise for many reasons: An inadequate resource base, technological backwardness, slow growth in demand for one region's products, and rapid natural growth of the labor force are just a few.

Suppose that because of migration costs, cultural and language differences, climatic advantages, or other local amenities, many people choose to live in Province A even though they earn lower incomes there. Markets can adjust to such regional differences in two basic ways.

If wages and prices are flexible, real wages and incomes will fall in Province A for the kinds of workers who are in excess supply. The falling real wages will give the province an advantage in new lines of production. Real wages will continue to fall until everyone who is willing to stay at the lower wage has a job and those who are not have migrated. In long-run equilibrium, Province A is a low-wage, low-income province, but it has no special unemployment problem. Those who do not value its amenities as much as they value the higher incomes to be earned in Province B, or who are subject to lower migration costs, will have left. What the price system does is equalize net advantages. It does not equalize economic advantage, because the noneconomic advantages of living in Province A exceed those of living in Province B.

The second possibility arises because wages are not totally flexible. Minimum wage laws, national unions, and nationwide pay scales for the federal

Policy issues. The distinction between equilibrium and dynamic factor price differentials raises an important consideration for policy. Trade unions, governments, and other bodies often have explicit policies about earnings differentials, often seeking to eliminate them in the name of equity. The success of such policies depends to a great extent on the kind of differential that is being attacked.

Consider a policy that resists a disequilibrium differential. Only a short time ago, large differentials opened up between earnings in the Prairie oil patch and those in the industrial center. These were disequilibrium differentials that were associated with a boom in the oil industry. The wage differentials could have been narrowed by imposing similar wages for similar jobs done everywhere in the country—as is done by national unions in some countries and has been proposed by some advocates of equal pay legislation. If successful, such policies would have slowed the movement of labor to the oil patch and thus would have prolonged the period during which there would be excess labor in Alberta and a shortage in the center.

Policies that attempt to eliminate equilibrium differentials will encounter even more severe difficulties. A recent example is legislation requiring *equal pay for work of equal value*, or *pay equity*. Whatever the social value of such laws, they run into trouble whenever they require equal pay for jobs that have different nonmonetary advantages.

civil service put substantial restraints on possible interprovincial wage differentials. People who prefer Province A remain there, yet wages do not fall to create a wage incentive to move to B. Instead, unemployment rates in A rise until (1) the extra uncertainty of finding a job and (2) the lower lifetime income expectations because of bouts of unemployment just balance both the nonpecuniary advantages that A enjoys over B and the costs of moving from A to B. In the long run, those who are willing to stay in spite of the higher unemployment remain, and the others leave.

In these circumstances, increasing local demand, even where that is possible, will lower the rate of out-migration but *not* the unemployment rate. This is because in the long run A's unemployment rate must remain sufficiently high relative to B's to balance the relative amenity and migration-cost advantages that Province A enjoys over B.

In these circumstances, trade restrictions, such as laws that require the employment of local labor only and labor market policies such as employment subsidies, will not reduce unemployment, although they will increase employment. As new jobs are created, the rate of out-migration slows so that the rate of unemployment is unchanged. Unless the province's policies are sufficient to create jobs for everyone entering its labor force, all that will happen when more jobs are created is that fewer people will migrate. The local supply rises as fast as the local demand for labor, and the unemployment rate is left unchanged.

The foregoing argument does not imply that nothing can be done for regions that have lower incomes or higher unemployment rates. There are many reasons why we might wish to make income transfers to poorer regions. However, it is important to realize that if the differential is an equilibrium phenomenon, no amount of policy intervention will remove it. If the policies continue to be strengthened as long as these differentials in unemployment persist, expenditures will rise and rise and rise, and the ultimate goal of equalization will continue to prove elusive.

Say that two jobs demand equal skills, training, and everything else that is taken into account when deciding what is work of equal value but that, in a city with an extreme climate, one is an outside job and the other is an inside job. If some pay commission requires equal pay for both jobs, there will be a shortage of workers who work outside and an excess of people who want to work inside. Employers will seek ways to compensate those who work outside through monetary advantages. Higher pensions, shorter hours, longer holidays, overtime paid for but not worked, and better working conditions may be offered. If these are allowed, they will achieve the desired result but will defeat the original purpose of equalizing the monetary benefits of the inside and outside jobs; they will also cut down on the number of outside workers that employers will hire, since the total cost of an outside worker to an employer will have risen. If the jobs are unionized, or if the pay commission prevents such "cheating," the shortage of workers for outside jobs will remain. The issue of equal pay for work of equal value is further considered in Chapter 19. The main point is that policies designed to achieve this concept of equality run into a series of problems—which may or may not be surmountable—whose existence is to be understood by the hypothesis of equal net advantage.

Factor price differentials are a natural market consequence of conditions of supply and demand. Mobility of factors tends to establish equilibrium levels of factor prices at which dynamic differentials are eliminated and equilibrium differentials are restored.

Policies that seek to eliminate factor price differentials without consideration of what caused them or how they affect the supply of the factor are likely to have perverse results.

FIGURE 17-3 **The Determination of Rent in Factor Payments**

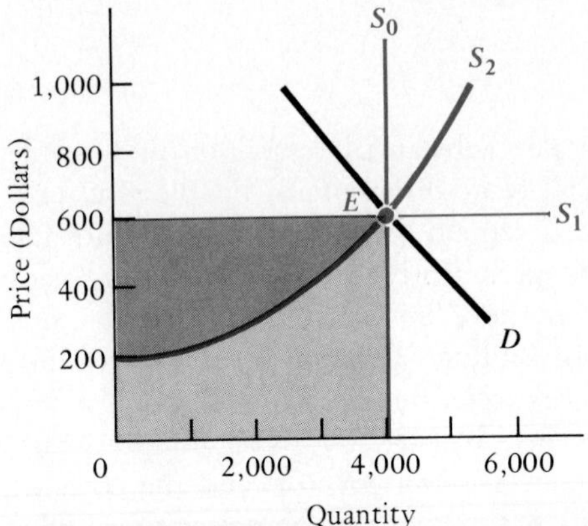

The amount of rent in factor payments depends on the shape of the supply curve. A single demand curve is shown with three different supply curves. In each case the competitive equilibrium price is \$600, and 4,000 units of the factor are hired. The total payment (\$2.4 million) is represented by the entire shaded area.

When the supply curve is vertical (S_0), the whole payment is economic rent, because a decrease in price would not lead any unit of the factor to move elsewhere.

When the supply curve is horizontal (S_1), none of the payment is rent, because even a small decrease in price offered would lead all units of the factor to move elsewhere.

When the supply curve is positively sloped (S_2), part of the payment is rent. As shown by the height of the supply curve, at a price of \$600 the 4,000th unit of the factor is receiving just enough to persuade it to offer its services in this market, but the 2,000th unit, for example, is earning well above what it requires to stay in this market. The aggregate of economic rents is shown by the dark gray shaded area, and the aggregate of what must be paid to keep 4,000 units in this market is shown by the light gray shaded area.

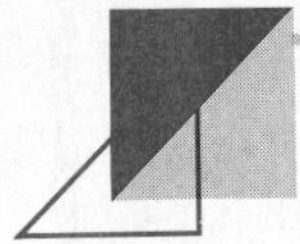

Economic Rent

One of the most important concepts in economics is that of *economic rent*. A factor must earn a certain amount in its present use to prevent it from moving to another use.[4] If there were no nonmonetary advantages in alternative uses, the factor would have to earn its opportunity cost (what it could earn elsewhere) to prevent it from moving elsewhere. This is usually true for capital and land. Labor, however, gains important nonmonetary advantages in various jobs, and what it must earn in one to prevent it from moving to another is enough to equate the two jobs' total advantages—monetary and nonmonetary. *Any excess that it earns over this amount* is called its **economic rent**.

Economic rent is analogous to the economists' concept of profit as a surplus over the opportunity cost of capital. The concept of economic rent is crucial in predicting the effects that changes in earnings have on the movement of factors among alternative uses. However, the terminology of rent is confusing because economic rent is often called simply *rent*, which can of course also mean the price paid to hire something, such as a machine or a piece of land. How the same term came to be used for these two different concepts is explained in Box 17-2.

The Division of Factor Earnings

In most cases, economic rent makes up part of the actual earnings of a factor of production. The distinction is most easily seen, however, by examining two extreme cases. In one, everything a factor earns is rent; in the other, none is rent.

The possibilities are illustrated in Figure 17-3. When the supply curve is perfectly inelastic (vertical), the same quantity is supplied, whatever the price. Evidently, there is no minimum that the factor needs to be paid to keep it in its present use, since the quantity supplied does not decrease, no matter how low the price goes. In this case, the whole of the payment is economic rent. The price actually paid allocates the fixed supply to those who are most willing to pay for it.

When the supply curve is perfectly elastic (hori-

[4] Alfred Marshall called this amount the factor's *transfer earnings*.

BOX 17-2

Origin of the Term *Economic Rent*

In the early nineteenth century, there was a public debate about the high price of wheat in England. The price was causing great hardship because bread was a primary source of food for the working class. Some people argued that wheat had a high price because landlords were charging high rents to tenant farmers. To pay these rents for land, the prices that farmers charged for their wheat also had to be raised to a high level. In short, it was argued that the price of wheat was high because the rents of agricultural land were high. Some of those who held this view advocated restricting the rents that landlords could charge.

David Ricardo, a great British economist who was one of the originators of Classical economics, argued that the situation was exactly the reverse. The price of wheat was high, he said, because there was a shortage, which was caused by the Napoleonic Wars. Because wheat was profitable to produce, there was keen competition among farmers to obtain land on which to grow wheat. This competition in turn forced up the rent of wheat land. Ricardo advocated removing the tariff so that imported wheat could come into the country, thereby increasing its supply and lowering both the price of wheat and the rent that could be charged for the land on which it was grown.

The essentials of Ricardo's argument were these: The supply of land was fixed. Land was regarded as having only one use, the growing of wheat. Nothing had to be paid to prevent land from transferring to a use other than growing wheat because it had no other use. No landowner would leave land idle as long as some return could be obtained by renting it out. Therefore, all the payment to land, that is, rent in the ordinary sense of the word, was a surplus over and above what was necessary to keep it in its present use.

Given a fixed supply of land, the price of land depended on the demand for land, which depended on the demand for wheat. *Rent,* the term for the payment for the use of land, thus became the term for a surplus payment to a factor over and above what was necessary to keep it in its present use.

Later, two facts were realized. First, land often had alternative uses, and, from the point of view of any one use, part of the payment made to land would necessarily have to be paid to keep it in that use. Second, factors of production other than land also often earned a surplus over and above what was necessary to keep them in their present use. Television stars and great athletes, for example, are in short and fairly fixed supply, and their potential earnings in other occupations often are quite moderate. However, because there is a huge demand for their services as television stars or athletes, they may receive payments greatly in excess of what is needed to keep them from transferring to other occupations. This surplus is now called *economic rent*, whether the factor is land, labor, or a piece of capital equipment.

zontal), none of the price paid is economic rent. If any lower price is offered, nothing whatsoever will be supplied. All units of the factor will transfer to some other use.

The more usual situation is that of a gradually rising supply curve. A rise in the factor's price serves the allocative function of attracting more units of the factor into the market in question, but the same rise provides additional economic rent to all units of the factor that are already employed. We know that the extra pay that is going to the units already employed is economic rent because the owners of these units were willing to supply them at the lower price. The general result for a positively sloped supply curve is stated as follows:

If the demand for a factor in any of its uses rises relative to the supply available to that use, its price will rise in that use. This will serve the allocative function of attracting additional units

into that use. It will also increase the economic rent to all units of the factor already in that use.

Determinants of the Division

The proportion of a given payment to a factor that is economic rent varies from situation to situation. We cannot point to a factor of production and assert that some fixed fraction of its income is always its economic rent. The proportion of its earnings that is rent depends on the alternatives that are open to it.

Focus first on a narrowly defined use of a given factor, say, its use by a particular firm. From that firm's point of view, the factor will be highly mobile, since it could readily move to another firm in the same industry. The firm must pay the going wage or risk losing that factor. Thus from the perspective of the single firm, a large proportion of the factor payment is a transfer payment.

Focus now on a more broadly defined use, for example, the factor's use in an entire industry. From the industry's point of view, the factor is less mobile, because it would be more difficult for it to gain employment quickly outside the industry. From the perspective of the particular *industry* (rather than the specific *firm* within the industry), a larger proportion of the payment to a factor is economic rent.

From the even more general perspective of a particular *occupation,* mobility is likely to be less, and the proportion of the factor payment that is economic rent is likely to be more. It may be easier, for example, for a carpenter to move from the construction industry to the furniture industry than to retrain as a computer operator.

As the perspective moves from a narrowly defined use of a factor to a broadly defined use of a factor, the mobility of the factor decreases; as mobility decreases, the share of the factor payment that is economic rent increases.

Application to Factors of Production

We now illustrate how these considerations apply to each of the key factors of production.

Labor. How much has to be paid to keep labor in its present use depends on the use of that labor.

First, consider movement *among firms in one industry.* Assume, for example, that carpenters receive $160 for working a normal eight-hour day. To a construction firm, none of the $160 is economic rent; if it were not paid, carpenters would not remain with that firm.

Second, consider movement *among industries.* Assume that there is a decline in demand for buildings and that all construction firms reduce the wages that are offered to carpenters. Now carpenters cannot move to other construction firms to get more money. If the most that they can earn in other industries is $125 per day (and nonmonetary advantages are the same in the two uses), they will not begin to leave the construction industry until wages there fall below $125 per day. When carpenters were receiving $160, the additional $35 per day was economic rent from the point of view of the construction *industry.*

Third, consider movement *among occupations.* Assume that there is a decline in the demand for carpenters in all industries. The only option that a carpenter has is to move to another occupation, say, truck driving. If no carpenters are induced to leave carpentry until the wage falls to $110 per day, then $110 is what must be paid to keep people in the occupation. From the point of view of that occupation, any payment over $110 is economic rent.

Consider how this applies to the often controversial large salaries that are received by some highly specialized types of laborers, such as superstar singers and professional athletes. These performers have a style and a talent that cannot be duplicated, whatever the training. The earnings that they receive are mostly economic rent from the viewpoint of the occupation: These performers enjoy their occupations and would pursue them for much less than the high remuneration that they actually receive. For example, Wayne Gretzky would choose hockey over other alternatives even at a much lower salary. However, because of Gretzky's amazing skills as a hockey player, most NHL teams would pay handsomely to have him on their rosters, and he is able to command a high salary from the team he does play for. From the perspective of the firm, the Los Angeles Kings, most of Gretzky's salary is required to keep him from switching to another team and hence is not economic rent. From the point of view of the hockey "industry," however, much of his salary is economic rent.

Land. The analysis for land is similar to the analysis for labor. In order to have the use of a particular piece of land, an *individual* wheat farmer must pay the land's going price to prevent it from being transferred to another wheat farmer. From this point of view, therefore, none of the payment is economic rent. In order for the wheat *industry* to secure land for wheat production, it will be necessary to offer at least as much as the land could earn when put to other uses. From the industry point of view, only the payment made for land that is above what the land could earn in its next most remunerative use is economic rent. Finally, consider the choice between *agricultural* and *urban uses*. Land is highly mobile among agricultural uses because its location is usually of little importance. For urban uses, however, location is critical. From this point of view, land is, of course, completely immobile. If there is a shortage of land in Montreal, any land that is available will command a high price, but no matter what the price, land in rural areas will not move into Montreal. The high payments made to urban land are thus well in excess of what is necessary to prevent it from being transferred back to agricultural uses; much of the payment is thus economic rent.

Capital. If a piece of capital equipment has several uses, the analysis of land or labor can be repeated. Much equipment, however, has only one use. For capital that is virtually immobile, any income arising from its use is economic rent.

Assume, for example, that when some machine was installed, it was expected to earn $5,000 per year in excess of all its operating costs, and assume also that the machine has no scrap value. If the demand for the product falls so that the machine can earn only $2,000 per year, it will still be worthwhile to keep it in operation rather than to scrap it. Indeed, it will be worthwhile to do so as long as it yields any return at all over its operating costs. Thus all the return that is earned by the installed machine is economic rent because it will still be allocated to its present use—it has no other—as long as it yields even $1 above its operating costs. *Once the machine has been installed*, any net income that it earns is economic rent.

The machine will, however, wear out eventually, and it will not be replaced unless it is expected to earn a return over its lifetime that is sufficient to make it a good investment for its owner. Thus in long-run equilibrium, the revenue earned by the machine is not economic rent; if the revenue is not earned, a machine will not continue to be allocated to that use.

Do Factors Move in Response to Changes in Earnings?

The theory that has been developed in this chapter predicts that factors move among uses, industries, and places, taking both monetary and nonmonetary rewards into account. It predicts that they will move in such a way as to maximize the net advantages to the owners of factors.

Does the world behave in the way that theory predicts? Because there are impediments to the mobility of factors, there may be lags in the response of factors to changes in relative prices, but the question remains: Do adjustments occur even though there are impediments?

Land and Capital

The most casual observation reveals to us that the allocative system works pretty much as described by the theory with respect to land and capital. Land is transferred from one crop to another in response to changes in the relative profitabilities of the crops. Land on the edge of town is transferred from rural to urban uses as soon as it can earn substantially more as a building site than as a cornfield. Materials and capital goods move from use to use in response to changes in relative earnings in those uses.

This is hardly surprising. Nonmonetary benefits do not loom large for factors other than labor, and the theories of both competition and monopoly predict that quantities supplied will respond to increases in earnings generated by increased demand.

In the case of nonhuman factors—land and capital—there is strong evidence that factors move in response to earnings differentials.

Labor

Labor can be mobile in many ways, moving among occupations, industries, firms, skill categories, and regions. These categories are not exclusive; in order to change occupation from a farm laborer to a steelworker, for example, a person will also have to change industry and probably place of residence.

There are, of course, barriers to labor mobility. Unions, pension funds, and other institutions inhibit labor mobility in various ways. Provincial governments have erected barriers to mobility in the form

FIGURE 17-4 The Changing Composition of the Nonagricultural Labor Force

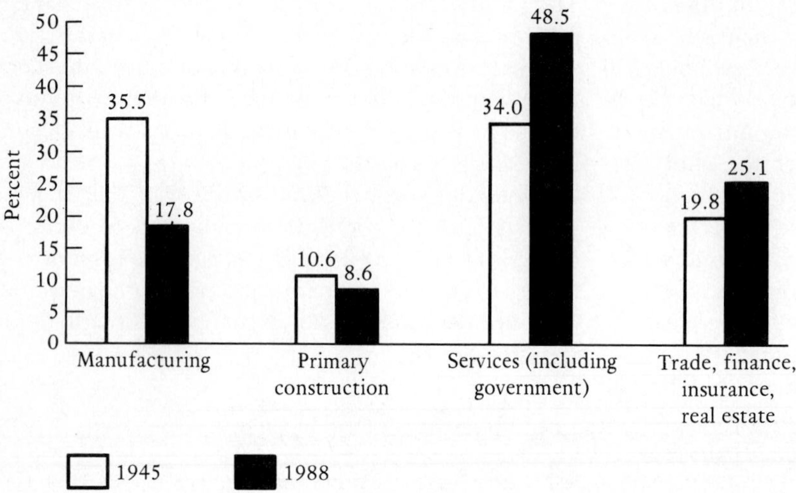

In less than half a century, a major shift has occurred in labor utilization. The figure shows the percentage of the nonagricultural labor force employed in each of four sectors; for each sector, the first bar shows the percentage in 1945 and the second bar shows the percentage in 1988. Looking at the first two categories, it can be seen that in 1945, over 46 percent of the nonagricultural labor force was employed in heavy industrial (largely blue-collar) sectors, but by 1988 this percentage had decreased to 26 percent. The shift was to the service-oriented (largely white-collar) sectors shown in the last two sets of bars: government, trade, finance, insurance, and other services. (*Source:* Statistics Canada, 71-201.)

of occupational licensing, differential training requirements, and the like.

Nevertheless, the documented mobility of labor is impressive. When wages in manufacturing areas soared during World War II, workers flocked to those areas to take lucrative jobs in the rapidly expanding industries producing aircraft, ships, and other materials of war. When new oil fields were discovered in northern Alaska and Canada, high wages attracted welders, riveters, and the many other types of labor that the oil fields required.

Figure 17-4 illustrates another dimension of labor mobility. The shifts among sectors that have occurred during the postwar period indicate the substantial adaptability of the labor force to changing patterns of demand for the outputs of various sectors.

One process that is evident from the figure is that of "deindustrialization"; there has been a significant shift in employment away from the goods-producing sectors—agriculture, manufacturing, mining, and construction—toward the service sector. That trend toward services has been going on for over 100 years in all advanced industrial societies, including Canada. At the start of the twentieth century, over 70 percent of the Canadian labor force worked in the goods sector; today that ratio has fallen to less than 30 percent. In 1990, the Economic Council of Canada published a major study of the service sector, called *Good Jobs, Bad Jobs.* The study shows that while many new jobs created in the economy are "good jobs" with high pay and excellent working conditions, many others are "bad jobs" characterized by low pay and little security. Many of the latter are part-time jobs found primarily, but not exclusively, in the service sector. The process of deindustrialization is discussed further in Box 17-3.

From decade to decade, labor is highly mobile in response to changes in demand.

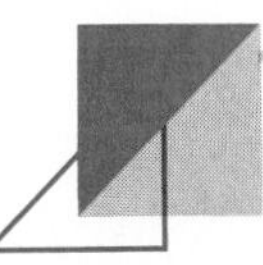

The Pricing of an Exhaustible Resource

So far we have discussed the pricing of factors, such as labor and capital, that can be replaced as they wear out. As older people leave the labor force due to retirement and death, young persons, seeking their first jobs, enter. As existing capital equipment is retired due to depreciation or obsolescence, it is replaced by new capital. Such resources are called **renewable resources**.

We now consider factors of production that are available in fixed amounts. For each such factor, the total stock is given, and every unit that is used today permanently reduces the stock that is available for future use. Such a factor is called a **nonrenewable resource** or an **exhaustible resource**. (It is usually a subclass of the broadly defined factor of production that economists call *land*.)

In practice, few, if any, resources are completely nonrenewable. Although there is only a fixed stock of oil, coal, or iron ore that is known to exist at any moment in time, new discoveries add to the known stock, while extraction subtracts from it. It is, however, possible to imagine exhausting all of the world's supplies of oil, natural gas, or coal. In this sense, these are closer to being exhaustible resources than renewable resources.

An Example

To focus on the basic issues, it is easiest to think of an imaginary resource that is completely nonrenewable: There is just so much "zube oil" in existence, and every unit that is used permanently diminishes the available stock by one unit.

Assume that many firms own the land that contains the zube oil supply. They have invested money in discovering the oil, drilling wells, and laying pipelines. Their current extraction costs are virtually zero; all they have to do is turn their taps on, and the oil flows at any desired rate to the zube oil markets.[5]

Optimal Firm Behavior

What should each firm do? It could extract all of its oil in a great binge of production this year, or it could husband the resource for some future rainy day and produce nothing this year. In practice, it is likely to adopt some intermediate policy, producing and selling some oil this year and holding stocks of it in the ground for extraction in future years. But *how much* should it extract this year and *how much* should it carry over for future years? What will the decision imply for the price of oil over the years?

The firms that own the zube oil land are holding a valuable resource. Holding it, however, has an opportunity cost: It could have been extracted and sold this year, yielding revenue to the firms (and value to consumers) in the same year. The firms will be willing to leave the resource in the ground only if it earns a return equal to what the firm can earn in other investments. This is measured by the interest rate. So if next year's price is expected to rise by less than the interest rate, the firms will extract more oil this year. Because the demand curve has a negative slope, raising the extraction rate will lower this year's price. Production will be curtailed, and the price will fall until the expected price rise between this year and next year is equal to the interest rate. The firms will then be indifferent at the margin between producing another barrel this year and holding it for production next year. If, conversely, next year's price is expected to rise over this year's price by more than the interest rate, the firms will produce less oil this year. They will prefer to leave more barrels in the ground, where they earn a higher return than could be earned by selling the oil this year and investing the proceeds at the current interest rate. This will raise this year's price until the gap between the current price and next year's expected price is equal to the interest rate.

[5] It is, of course, a simplification of any real case to assume that current production costs are actually zero. The assumption, however, is not too far from reality in the case of such a resource as oil, where the fixed costs of discovery, extraction, and distribution account for the bulk of total costs. When extraction costs are nonzero, all statements about prices in the text refer to the margin by which price *exceeds* the current opportunity cost of extraction.

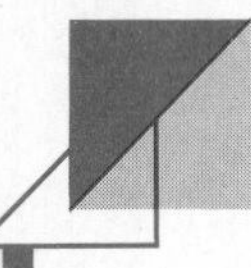

BOX 17-3

Deindustrialization and the Growth of the Service Sector

The growth of employment in services and the retail trade over the past decades has been dramatic in all industrialized nations. The growth has been concentrated in several areas: transportation and communication, eating and drinking, health care, education, retail services such as hotels and entertainment, and a host of business services. In Canada in 1990, *total* employment in the manufacturing of durable goods (about 11 million persons) was equal to the *increase* in employment in services over the previous two decades.

In one sense this is good news, for without these new job opportunities, overall unemployment would have been high. But many people worry about the effects of deindustrialization on the economy.

Some fear that productivity is lower and the opportunities for growth are much more limited in service industries than in goods-producing industries. They argue that the possibilities for using more capital per unit of labor employed, which raises labor productivity, are less in selling hamburgers than in manufacturing. Another concern, stressed by the Economic Council of Canada in *Good Jobs, Bad Jobs,* is that many of the new jobs in the service sector are "bad jobs" characterized by low pay and little security.

However, there are reasons to be cautious about accepting some of the pessimism concerning the growth of services. First, we need to keep a sense of perspective about the emergence of low-paying service jobs. As noted in the text, the trend toward services has been going on for over a century. Yet disposable income per employed person has been rising throughout this period; as a nation, we are getting wealthier, not poorer. Further, the size distribution of income has not changed dramatically over this period, so the increased wealth has been experienced by individuals in all income classes.

Second, to a considerable extent, the decrease in the share of manufacturing in total employment is a result of that sector's dynamism. More and more manufactured goods have been produced by fewer and fewer workers, leaving more workers to produce services. This movement is analogous to the one out of agriculture earlier in the century. At the turn of the century, nearly 50 percent of the Canadian labor force worked on farms. Today less than 5 percent of the employed work in farming, yet they produce more total output than did the 50 percent in 1900. (A similar shift also occurred in the United States.) This "deagriculturalization" freed workers to move into manufacturing, raising our living standards and transforming our way of life. In like manner, deindustrialization is freeing workers to move into services, and by replacing the grimy blue-collar jobs of pollution-creating smokestack industries with white-collar jobs in the relatively clean service industries, it will once again transform our way of life.

Third, to a considerable extent, the decrease in the share of manufacturing in total employment also follows from consumers' tastes. Just as consumers in the first half of the century did not want to go on consuming more and more food products as their incomes rose, today's consumers do not wish to spend all of their additional income on manufactured products. Households have chosen to spend a high proportion of their increased incomes on services, thus creating employment opportunities in that sector.

Fourth, although some service industries—particularly personal services and fast foods—do generate low-paying jobs, so do many manufacturing industries. Two decades ago, pessimists worried that the new industrial revolution of automation and computerization was going to destroy most of the jobs for the unskilled. But the growth in the service sector fully compensated for the lost low-skilled jobs in manufacturing.

Finally, it is easy to underestimate the scope for quality, quantity, and productivity increases in services. As one example of productivity increases, compare your local bank with what you see in a movie filmed in a bank no more than 20 years ago. As another, note that since 1950, output per full-time worker has grown about twice as fast in the communications industry as it has in manufacturing. In its study, the Economic Council of Canada stresses that the service sector is changing quickly. There has been some trend toward the mass production techniques that provided much of the basis for productivity growth in the goods sector earlier in this century. Services are also becoming globalized, so international trade will provide more opportunity for specialization and hence increased productivity. Also, much of the recent growth in demand for services comes as an input into goods-producing industries—either indirectly in the form of "bundling" sales with, say, maintenance contracts, or directly through productivity-enhancing management skills, inventory control methods, and the like. These contribute to the value added of the goods sector and hence to real national income.

It is also the case that many quality improvements in services go unrecorded. Today's hotel room is vastly more luxurious than a hotel room of 40 years ago, yet this is unlikely to show up in our national income statistics as a quality improvement. All that the statistics are likely to reflect is that the price of "a hotel room" has risen.

Measuring such technological improvements is even more difficult when they take the form of entirely new products. Airline transportation, telecommunications, fast-food chains, and financial services are prominent examples. The resulting increase in output is not always properly captured in our existing statistics.

It is easy to become concerned when looking at the official statistics, which show slow growth rates and low wages earned in some service jobs. Indeed, the council's report confirms that the shift in employment toward services is, like most changes that hit the economy, a mixed blessing. It entails a significant increase in the number of "bad" service-sector jobs with low pay, low job security, and sometimes poor working conditions. However, if we look at the growth in real standards of living, there is little reason to think that the shift in employment from industries to services in the second half of the twentieth century—which, after all, is driven by our rising real incomes—will be any less beneficial to industrialized nations than the shift from agriculture to manufacturing in the first half of the century.

In a perfectly competitive industry, the profit-maximizing equlibrium for a nonrenewable resource occurs when the last unit produced would have earned just as much for each firm as if it had been left in the ground.

Say, for example, that a barrel produced this year sells for $1.00 and that next year's price is expected to be $1.05. If the rate of interest is 5 percent, zube oil producers make the same amount of money whether they leave $1.00 worth of oil in the ground to be worth $1.05 next year or they sell the oil for $1.00 this year and invest the proceeds at a 5 percent interest rate.

Optimal Social Behavior

Zube oil is a valuable social resource, and the value to consumers of one more barrel produced now is the price that they would be willing to pay for it, which is the current $1.00 market price of the oil. If the oil is extracted this year and the proceeds are invested at the rate of interest (they might be used to buy a new capital good), they will produce $1.05 worth of valuable goods next year. If that barrel of oil is not produced this year and is left in the ground for extraction next year, its value to consumers at that time will be next year's price of oil. It is not socially optimal, therefore, to leave the oil in the ground unless it will be worth $1.05 to consumers next year. More generally, society obtains increases in the value of what is available for consumption by conserving units of a nonrenewable resource to be used in future years only if the price of these units is expected to rise at a rate that is at least as high as the interest rate.

This answer to the question "How much of a nonrenewable resource should be consumed now?" was provided many years ago by the American economist Harold Hotelling. His answer is very simple, yet it specifically determines the optimal profile of prices over the years. It is interesting that the answer applies to all nonrenewable resources. It does not matter whether there is a large or a small demand or whether that demand is elastic or inelastic. In all cases the answer is the same:

The rate of extraction of any nonrenewable resource should be such that its rate of price increase is equal to the interest rate.

Hotelling also argued that this is the rate of extraction that will be produced by a competitive industry.

The Amount of Extraction

Now, what about the actual rate at which the resource is extracted? The answer to this question *does* depend on market conditions. Specifically, it depends on the position and the slope of the demand curve. If the quantity demanded at all prices is small, the rate of extraction will be small. The larger the quantity demanded at each price, the higher the rate of extraction will tend to be.

Now consider the influence of the slope of the demand curve. A steep demand curve suggests that there are few substitutes and that purchasers are prepared to pay large sums rather than do without the resource. This will produce a relatively even rate of extraction, with small reductions in each period being sufficient to drive up the price at the required rate. A relatively flat demand curve suggests that people can easily find substitutes once the price rises. This will encourage a great deal of consumption now and a rapidly diminishing amount over future years, since large reductions in consumption are needed to drive the price up at the required rate.

Figure 17-5 illustrates this working of the price mechanism with a simple example in which the whole stock of zube oil must be consumed in only two periods, this year and next year. The general point illustrated is this:

The steeper the demand curve, the more even the rate of extraction (and hence the rate of use) over the years; the flatter the demand curve, the more uneven the rate of extraction over the years.

A flat demand curve will lead to a large consumption now and a rapid fall in consumption over the years. A steep demand curve will lead to a smaller consumption now and a less rapid fall in consumption over the years.

Resource Rents

The incomes earned by the owners of the zube oil resources are *rents*: The owners would be willing to produce the oil at any price that covers the direct

FIGURE 17-5 The Extraction Rate for a Nonrenewable Resource

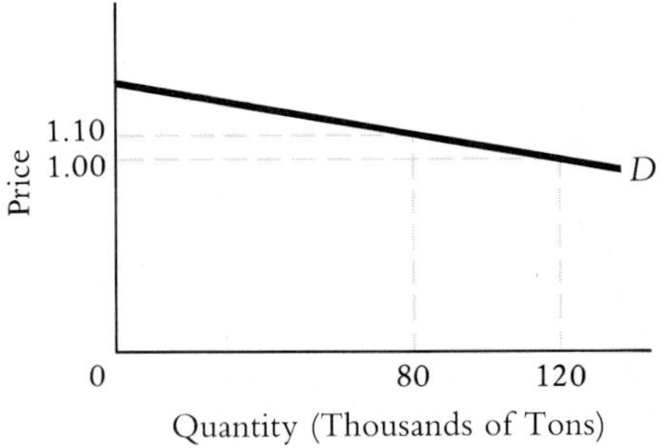

(i) Relatively flat demand curve

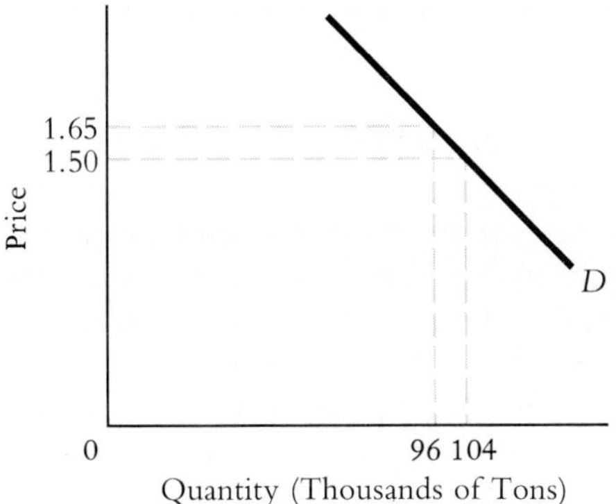

(ii) Relatively steep demand curve

The shape of the demand curve determines the extraction profile over time. In the example in this figure, the interest rate is assumed to be 10 percent, and there is a fixed supply of 200,000 tons of zube oil that can be extracted from the ground at zero variable cost. (All costs are fixed costs.) The zube oil is available for extraction either in the current period or in the next period, after which it spoils.

In part (i) of the figure, the demand curve is relatively flat. The two conditions—that the whole supply be used over two periods and that the price rise by 10 percent between the two periods—dictate that the quantities be 120,000 tons in the first period, with a price of $1.00 per ton, and 80,000 in the second period, with a price of $1.10 per ton.

In part (ii), the demand curve is rather steep. The same two conditions now dictate that the quantities be 104,000 tons in the first period, with a price of $1.50 per ton, and 96,000 tons in the second period, with a price of $1.65 per ton.

costs of extraction, which in this example is zero.[6] Although these incomes serve no function in getting the product produced, since any nonzero price would do the job, they do fulfill an *intertemporal* allocative function. As we have seen, the price profile determines the use of the resource and hence the amount of resources allocated to its production *over time*.

The Price System As a Conservation Mechanism

In the entire preceding discussion we see the price system playing its now familiar role of coordinator. By following private profit incentives, firms are led to conserve the resource in a manner that is consistent with people's needs.

The Role of Rising Prices

The optimal profile for a totally nonrenewable resource is for its price to rise at a constant rate each year. This may seem unsatisfactory to the casual observer, but if price is prevented from so rising, the resource will be depleted much faster. The rising price fulfills a number of useful functions.

First, the rising price encourages conservation. As the resource becomes scarcer and its price rises, users will be motivated to be more and more economical in its use. Uses with low yields may be abandoned altogether, and uses with high yields will be pursued only as long as their value at the margin is enough to compensate for the high price.

Second, the rising price encourages the discovery of new sources of supply—at least in cases in which the world supply is not totally fixed and known.

Third, the rising price encourages innovation. New products that will do the same job may be developed, as well as new processes that use alternative resources.

How Might the Price System Fail?

There are three basic ways in which the price system might fail to produce the optimal rate of resource extraction: First, firms may not know enough to make the correct calculations; second, deficiencies in property rights may result in firms having incentives

[6] In real cases, the direct cost of extracting the resource is positive, and the rent is the income earned above that amount.

to extract the resource too fast; and third, markets may not correctly reflect social values. We look at examples of each of these and ask if they justify government intervention.[7]

Ignorance. Private owners might not have enough knowledge to estimate the rate at which prices will rise. If they do not know the world stocks of their commodity and the current extraction rate, they may be unable to estimate the rate of the price rise and so will not know when to raise or lower their current rates of production. For example, if all firms mistakenly think that prices will not rise greatly in the future, they will all produce too much now and conserve too little for future periods.

There is no reason to think that the government could do better, unless it has some special knowledge that private firms do not have. If it does have such knowledge, the government needs only to make it public; further intervention is unnecessary. In practice, what knowledge does exist about both the proven reserves of nonrenewable resources and their current extraction rates is usually freely and openly available.

Inadequate property rights. Some nonrenewable resources have the characteristics of what is called *common property*. This is property that cannot be exclusively owned and controlled by one person or firm. For example, one person's oil-bearing land may be adjacent to another person's, and the underground supplies may be interconnected. In such a case, if one firm holds off producing now, the oil may end up being extracted by its neighbor. In such cases, which are sometimes encountered with petroleum, there is a tendency for a firm to extract the resource too fast, because a firm's oil that has been left in the ground may not be available to that firm at a future date.

This is a problem of inadequate property rights. Since the resource will be worth more in total value when it is exploited at the optimal extraction rate than when overly small firms exploit it too quickly, there will be an incentive for individual owners to combine until each self-contained source of supply is owned by only one firm. After that, the problem of overexploitation will no longer arise. Government ownership is not necessary to achieve this result. What is needed, at most, is intervention to ensure that markets can work to provide the optimal size of individual units so that proper extraction management can be applied by the private owners.

Political uncertainty can provide another source of inadequate property rights. For example, the owners of the resource may fear that a future election or a revolution will establish a government that is determined to confiscate their property. They will then be motivated to exploit the resource too quickly, on the grounds that certain revenue now is more valuable than highly uncertain revenue in the future. The current rate of extraction will tend to increase until the expected rate of price rise exceeds the interest rate by a sufficient margin to compensate for the risks of future confiscation of supplies left in the ground.

Divergences between market and social values. Normally, in a competitive world, the market interest rate indicates the rate at which it is optimal to discount the future over the present. Society's investments are valuable if they earn the market rate of return and are not valuable if they earn less (because the resources could be used in other ways to produce more value to consumers). In certain circumstances, however, the government may have reasons to adopt a different rate of discount. It is then said that the *social rate of discount*—the discount rate that is appropriate to the society as a whole—differs from the privte rate, as indicated by the market rate of interest. In such circumstances, there is reason for the government to intervene to alter the rate at which the private firms would exploit the resource.

Critics are often ready to assume that profit-mad producers will despoil most exhaustible resources by using them up too quickly. They argue for government intervention to conserve the resource by slowing its rate of extraction. Yet unless the social rate of discount is clearly below the private rate, there is no clear social gain in investing by holding resources in the ground where they only will yield, say, a 2 percent return when, say, 5 percent can be gained on other investments.

Since governments must worry about their short-term popularity and their chances of reelection, there is no presumption that government intervention will slow down the rate of extraction. Instead, governments might extract a resource faster than market

[7] This discussion partly anticipates some of the analysis in Part 7, which investigates market successes and market failures in more general terms.

forces alone would. Many economists think that the federal government's decision in September 1990 to subsidize the development of the Hibernia oil fields off the Newfoundland coast is a case in point. At that time, extraction costs could only be covered with the aid of a government subsidy paid at the taxpayers' expense; if the oil were left in the ground, the price could rise enough to eventually cover its extraction costs.

Actual Price Profiles

Many nonrenewable resources do not seem to have the steadily rising profile of prices that the theory predicts. The price of oil, having been raised artificially by the OPEC cartel, returned in the late 1980s to an inflation-adjusted level that was not far from where it was in 1970. Indeed, it has since been held somewhat above that price only insofar as the producing countries have succeeded in intermittently enforcing some output restrictions. The price of coal has not soared; neither has the price of iron ore. In many cases, the reason for this lies in the discovery of new supplies, which have prevented the total known stocks of many resources from being depleted. In the case of petroleum, for example, the ratio of known reserves to one year's consumption is no lower now than it was two or even four decades ago. Furthermore, most industry experts believe that large quantities of undiscovered oil exist under both the land and the sea.

In other cases, the invention of new substitute products has reduced the demand for some of these resources. For example, plastics have replaced metals in many uses, and fiber optics are rapidly replacing copper wire in many types of message transmission.

In yet other cases, the reason is to be found in government pricing policy. An important example of this type is water for irrigation in much of the United States. Vast underground reserves of water lie in aquifers beneath many areas of the United States. Although these reserves were accumulated over millennia, they are being used up at a rate that will exhaust them in a matter of decades. The water is often supplied by government water authorities at a price that covers only a small part of its total cost and that does not rise steadily to reflect the dwindling stocks.

Such a constant price policy for any nonrenewable resource creates three characteristic problems. First, the resource will be exhausted much faster than if price were to rise over time. A constant price will lead to a constant rate of extraction to meet the quantity demanded at that price until the resource is completely exhausted. Second, no signals will go out to induce conservation, innovation, and exploration. Third, when the supply of the resource is finally exhausted, the adjustment will have to come all at once. If the price had risen steadily each year under free market conditions, adjustment would have taken place little by little each year. The controlled price, however, gives no signal of the ever-diminishing stock of the resource until all at once the supplies run out. The required adjustment will then be much more painful than it would have been if it had been spread over time in response to steadily rising prices.

The dwindling water supplies under much of the continent would long ago have led to price rises close to those predicted by Hotelling's theory and hence to a series of gradual adjustments, had the price been set on a free market.

In the United States, the present generation of water users is, in effect, obtaining a subsidy from future water users, who, if present policies continue, will have to make many adjustments abruptly while paying much higher prices for their water.

SUMMARY

1. The functional distribution of income refers to the shares of total national income going to each of the major factors of production; it focuses on sources of income. The size distribution of income refers to the shares of total national income going to various groups of households; it focuses only on the size of income, not its source.
2. The income of a factor of production is composed of two elements: the price paid per unit of the factor and the quantity of the factor used. The determination of factor prices and quantities is an application of the same price theory that is used to determine product prices and quantities.

3. The demand for any factor of production is a derived demand because the factor is used as an input into the production of goods and services. The total demand for a factor of production will be the sum of the individual derived demands for it in each activity in which it is used. The total supply of any factor must be allocated among all the uses to which it can possibly be put.
4. Factor mobility is the ease with which a factor can move to alternative uses. Land is mobile between uses but cannot change its geographical location. Capital equipment is durable, but firms regularly replace discarded or worn-out machinery with totally different machines and so change the composition of the nation's capital stock gradually but steadily. Labor mobility is greatly affected by nonmonetary considerations. The longer the period of time, the more mobile a factor.
5. In competitive factor markets, prices are determined by demand and supply, and factor price differentials often occur. Disequilibrium differentials in the earnings of different units of factors of production induce factor movements that eventually remove the differentials. Equilibrium differentials reflect differences among units of factors as well as nonmonetary benefits of different jobs; they can persist indefinitely.
6. The hypothesis of equal net advantage is a theory of the allocation of the total supply of factors to particular uses. Owners of factors will choose the use that produces the greatest net advantage, allowing for monetary and nonmonetary advantages of a particular employment. In so doing, they will cause dynamic factor price differentials to be eliminated.
7. Some amount *must* be paid to a factor in order to prevent it from transferring to another use. Economic rent is the difference between that amount and a factor's actual earnings. Whenever the supply curve is upward-sloping, part of the factor's total pay is transfer earnings, and part of it is rent. The proportion of each depends on the mobility of the factor. The more narrowly defined the use, the larger the fraction that is transfer earnings and the smaller the fraction that is economic rent.
8. Factor mobility is typically greater for nonhuman factors than it is for labor. Even where impediments to mobility exist, factors (including labor) tend to move in response to persistent differences in earnings or employment opportunities.
9. The socially optimal rate of exploitation for a nonrenewable resource occurs when its price rises at a rate that is equal to the rate of interest. This is also the rate that will be established by a profit-maximizing, competitive industry.
10. Resources for which the demand is highly elastic will have a high rate of exploitation in the near future and a fairly rapid falloff over time. Resources for which the demand is highly inelastic will have a lower rate of exploitation in the near future and a smaller falloff over time.
11. Rising prices act as a conservation device by rationing consumption over time according to people's preferences. As prices rise, conservation, discovery of new sources of supply, and innovation to reduce demand are all encouraged.
12. The price system can fail to produce optimal results if (a) people lack the necessary knowledge, (b) property rights are inadequate to

protect supplies left for future use by their owners, or (c) the social rate of discount differs significantly from the market rate.

13. Controlling the price of an exhaustible resource at a constant level speeds up the rate of exploitation and removes the price incentives to react to the growing scarcity until the resource is completely exhausted.

TOPICS FOR REVIEW

Functional distribution and size distribution of income
Derived demand
Factor mobility
Disequilibrium and equilibrium differentials
Hypothesis of equal net advantage
Economic rent
Exhaustible resources
Resource rents and intertemporal resource allocation

DISCUSSION QUESTIONS

1. Other things being equal, how woud you expect each of the following to affect the size distribution of after-tax income? Do any of them lead to clear predictions about the functional distribution of income?
   a. An increase in unemployment
   b. Rapid population growth in an already crowded city
   c. An increase in food prices relative to other prices
   d. An increase in social insurance benefits and taxes
   e. Elimination of the personal income tax deduction for interest paid on mortgages
2. Consider the effects on the overall level of income inequality of each of the following.
   a. Increasing participation of women in the labor force as many women shift from work in the home to full-time jobs
   b. Increasing use by Nova Scotia produce growers of migrant workers who are in the country illegally
   c. Increasing numbers of minority group members studying law and medicine
   d. Cuts in the rates of income tax, together with the elimination of some personal income tax deductions
3. How much of the following payments for factor services is likely to be economic rent?
   a. The $750 per month that a landlord receives for an apartment leased to students
   b. The salary of the prime minister
   c. The $1 million annual salary of Kelly Gruber
   d. The salary of a window cleaner who says, "It's dangerous, dirty work, but it beats driving a truck."
4. Which of the following are disequilibrium differentials and which are equilibrium differentials in factor prices?
   a. Differences in earnings of hockey coaches and wrestling coaches
   b. A "bonus for signing on" offered by a construction company seeking carpenters in a tight labor market
   c. Differences in monthly rental charged for three-bedroom houses in different parts of the same metropolitan area
   d. Higher prices per square foot of condominium space in Vancouver compared with St. Catharines

5. Equal pay for work of equal value is a commonly held goal, but "equal value" is hard to define. What would be the consequences of legislation that enforces equal pay for what turns out to be work of unequal value?
6. Rent controls often succeed in reducing rents paid by tenants in the short run but at the cost of a growing housing shortage in the long run. What does this tell us about the nature of the earnings of landlords in the short and the long run?
7. Look again at the data in Figure 17-4. What economic forces might have given rise to the labor movements described there? What would you predict about the pattern of wages in the various categories in the figure? (Check the facts to see if your predictions were correct.) For occupations that saw an increase in wages, did the increases represent increased transfer payments or economic rents?
8. Can you think of any resources that are renewable if they are exploited at one rate and nonrenewable if they are exploited at other, higher rates?
9. Vacant lots, or unpaved parking lots, in the middle of cities, adjacent to otherwise identical pieces of land on which stand office towers generating large revenues, seem to represent a real economic waste. Are the owners of these lots necessarily underutilizing their resource?
10. A recent book written by two economists and two geologists called *Toward a New Iron Age?* addresses the optimistic view of the former (that markets will give rise to efficient husbanding of exhaustible resources) with the pessimistic view of the latter that low-cost sources of many minerals will be exhausted within the foreseeable future and that the resulting switch to high-cost sources will be devastating for economic growth. What might be the basis for the economists' optimism?

Chapter 18

More on Factor Markets

Why is the demand for steel quite inelastic, while the demand for cedar shakes and shingles is highly elastic? Why is the relative price of oil quite volatile, while the relative price of construction workers has remained relatively stable? To deal with these and many related subjects, we need to inquire further into the determinants of the demand for and supply of factors of production.

The Demand for Factors of Production

We saw in Chapter 17 that the demand for any factor depends on the demand for the goods that it helps to produce. For this reason, the demand for a factor is called a *derived demand.* What are the economic forces that influence this demand?

Marginal Productivity Theory

All profit-maximizing firms, whether they are selling under conditions of perfect competition, monopolistic competition, oligopoly, or monopoly, produce to the point at which marginal cost equals marginal revenue. Similarly, all profit-maximizing firms hire units of the variable factor up to the point at which the last unit employed adds as much to revenue as it does to cost. Thus it is a simple implication of profit maximization that *firms* hire units of a variable factor up to the point at which the marginal cost of the factor (i.e., the addition to the total cost resulting from the employment of one more unit) equals the marginal revenue produced by the factor.

Because we use the term *marginal revenue* to denote the change in revenue that results when the rate of product sales is increased by one unit, we shall use another term, **marginal revenue product (*MRP*)**, to refer to the change in revenue caused by the sale of the increased output resulting from using *an additional unit of the variable factor.* [27] Using this term, the implication of profit maximization, which was stated in the preceding paragraph, can be written as follows:

Marginal cost of the variable factor = **marginal revenue product of that factor**

If the firm does not influence the price of the variable factor by buying more or less of it (i.e., if the firm is a price taker when it is *buying factors*), the marginal cost of the factor is its price. The cost, for example, of adding an extra worker to such a firm's work force is the wage that must be paid to that worker. The firm will continue to add workers to its labor force until the marginal revenue product of the last worker added is equal to the wage that the firm pays to that last worker.

A profit-maximizing firm that is a price taker in factor markets hires a factor up to the point at which the price of the factor equals the factor's marginal revenue product.

If we let w stand for the market-determined price of the variable factor, we can write this as

$$w = MRP$$

For example, if the wage rate is $10 per hour, it will be profitable for a firm to take on more workers as long as each additional worker adds more than $10 to its revenue per hour. Once an additional hour worked adds only $10, the firm will stop hiring more workers. It will be in equilibrium.

The proposition that in equilibrium factors will be paid the value of their respective marginal products is often called the **marginal productivity theory of distribution.**[1] This is nothing more than an implication of profit maximization. Over the years, however, the theory has been the subject of many emotional attacks and defenses and has often been seriously misunderstood.

Slope of the Derived Demand Curve

So far we have drawn all factor demand curves to indicate that the price of a factor and its quantity demanded are negatively related. Three reasons for this are worth noting.

Diminishing Returns

Because of the operation of the law of diminishing returns, each equal additional unit of a variable factor that is combined with a given amount of a fixed factor adds smaller and smaller amounts to total output. Thus if a factor's price rises, each firm will reduce the amount of factors that it hires until the marginal revenue product of the last unit is large enough to cover the now higher price of hiring it. Similarly, if a factor's price falls, each firm will hire more factors until the *MRP* of the last unit hired is reduced to the now lower price of hiring it.

Substitution

A second influence operates by means of the principle of substitution. When the price of one factor goes up, other relatively cheaper factors will be substituted. For example, if carpenters' wages rise relative to those of factory workers, some factory-prefabricated door and window frames will be used to replace on-the-job carpenters.

Derived Demand

A third influence arises because the demand for a factor of production depends on the demand for the commodity that it helps to make (i.e., it is a *derived* demand). A negatively sloped demand for a commodity implies a negatively sloped demand for the factors that help to make it.

For example, a rise in carpenters' wages will raise the cost of producing houses, thus shifting the supply curve of houses to the left. This leads to a rise in the price of houses and, because of the negatively sloped demand curve for houses, to a decrease in the number of houses sold. If fewer houses are sold, fewer will be built, and fewer carpenters will be needed. A decrease in carpenters' wages has the opposite set of effects: The cost of producing houses falls; the supply curve shifts to the right; more houses are built; and more carpenters are demanded.

Elasticity of Factor Demand

The elasticity of demand for a factor measures the *degree* of the response of the quantity demanded to a change in its price. The three influences that were discussed in the preceding sections explain the *direction* of the response; that is, the quantity demanded is negatively related to price. You should not be surprised, therefore, to hear that the degree of the response depends on the strength with which these three influences operate.

Diminishing Returns

The first influence on the slope of the demand curve is the diminishing marginal productivity of a factor.

[1] The way in which marginal productivity theory can be used to derive the demand curve for a factor is discussed in the appendix to this chapter.

If marginal productivity declines rapidly as more of a variable factor is employed, a fall in the factor's price will not induce many more units to be employed. Conversely, if marginal productivity does not fall rapidly as more of a variable factor is employed, there will be a large increase in quantity demanded as price falls.

Substitution

The second influence on the slope of the demand curve is the ease with which one factor can be substituted for another. The greater the ease of substitution, the greater the elasticity of demand for the factor. The ease of substitution depends on the substitutes that are available and on the technical conditions of production. Even in the short run it is possible to vary factor proportions in surprising ways. For example, in automobile manufacturing and in building construction, glass and steel can be substituted for each other simply by varying the dimensions of the windows. Another example is that construction materials can be substituted for maintenance labor in the case of most durable consumer goods. This is done by making the product more or less durable and more or less subject to breakdowns by using more or less expensive materials in its construction.

Such short-run substitutions are not the end of the story. In the long run, plant and equipment are being replaced continually, which allows more or less capital-intensive methods to be built into new plants in response to changes in factor prices. Similarly, engines that use less gasoline per mile tend to be developed when the price of gasoline rises severely.

Derived Demand

The third influence on the slope of the demand curve is related to derived demand. Since the demand for a factor of production is derived from the demand for the product that it helps to produce, two separate influences affect the elasticity of demand for the factor: how much the supply curve of a commodity shifts when a factor's price changes and how much this shift affects the output of the commodity that the factor helps to make.

Importance of the factor. The larger the fraction of the total costs of producing some commodity that are made up of payments to a particular factor, the greater the elasticity of demand for that factor. To see this, suppose that wages account for 50 percent of the costs of producing a good and raw materials account for 15 percent. A 10 percent rise in the price of labor raises the cost of producing the commodity by 5 percent (10 percent of 50 percent), but a 10 percent rise in the price of raw materials raises the cost of the commodity by only 1.5 percent (10 percent of 15 percent). The larger the increase in cost, the larger the shift in the commodity's supply curve and hence the larger the decreases in the demand for the commodity and for the factors that were used to make it.

Elasticity of demand for the commodity produced. Other things being equal, the more elastic the demand for the commodity that the factor helps to make, the more elastic the demand for the factor. If an increase in the price of the commodity causes a large decrease in the quantity demanded—that is, if the demand for the commodity is elastic—there will be a large decrease in the quantity of a factor needed to produce it in response to a rise in the factor's price. However, if an increase in the price of a commodity causes only a small decrease in the quantity demanded—that is, if the demand for the commodity is inelastic—there will be only a small decrease in the quantity of the factor required in response to a rise in its price.[2]

Let us summarize the effect that works through derived demand.

An increase in the price of a factor that produces a particular commodity causes the supply curve for that commodity to shift to the left, which reduces its equilibrium quantity and in turn reduces the quantity of the factor that is demanded. The fall in quantity of the factor demanded will be greater (1) the greater the proportion of total costs accounted for by that factor, since this proportion determines the

[2] All of these propositions are qualified by the usual condition of other things being equal. For example, the smaller the proportion of a commodity's total costs that is accounted for by the cost of one particular factor, the lower the elasticity of demand for that factor, *other things being equal*. Other things are not equal, for example, if we compare two factors, both of which account for small parts of total cost but one of which can easily be dispensed with because it has many good substitutes while the second has few good substitutes. The first will have elasticity of demand (the ease of substitution will be what matters), while the second will have a low elasticity (its unimportance in total cost will be what matters).

amount that the commodity's supply curve shifts, and (2) the more elastic the demand curve for the commodity, since this elasticity determines the amount by which the commodity's output falls when its supply curve shifts to the left.

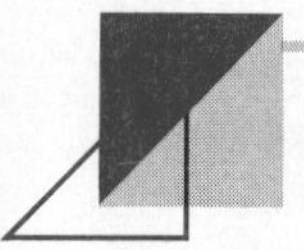

Distribution Theory: Some Evidence

Does the theory of distribution satisfactorily explain the allocation process in our economy? In Chapter 17, we reviewed the impressive array of evidence that showed that despite the presence of impediments to factor mobility—such as licensing and union restrictions for labor, safety requirements for capital equipment, and zoning laws for land—factors do move in response to changes in factor prices. Here we examine whether market forces do in fact determine factor prices and factor earnings.

Capital and Land

Many nonhuman factors are sold on competitive markets. The theory predicts that changes in the earnings of these factors will be associated with changes in market conditions. The evidence overwhelmingly supports this prediction, as illustrated by the following examples.

The prices of plywood, tin, rubber, cotton, and hundreds of other materials fluctuate daily in response to changes in their demand and supply. The responses of factor markets to the many shortages that characterized the Canadian economy during the 1970s and early 1980s provide dramatic confirmation of this. When the price of agricultural commodities shot up following a grain shortage, farm income soared. When oil became scarce, prices rose, and oil producers and owners of oil properties found their profits and incomes rising rapidly. Not only did the relative prices of oil products rise, but the relative prices of numerous other commodities, such as chemical fertilizers and air travel, which make use of petroleum products, rose as well. When oil became abundant in the mid 1980s, these trends were reversed.

Land in the heart of growing cities provides another example. Such land is fixed in supply, and values rise steadily in response to increasing demand for it.[3] Land values may even be high enough to make it worthwhile for people to destroy durable buildings in order to convert the land to more productive uses. The high rise is a monument to the high value of urban land. The increase in the price of land on the periphery of every growing city is an observable example of the workings of the market.

Similar results occur in markets that are far from being perfectly competitive. In 1979 the price of power in virtually all its forms rose sharply in response to the energy shortage that caused a doubling of the price of oil. Oligopolists producing key metals such as zinc, molybdenum, steel, and aluminum raised prices when their costs of production rose. Further examples can be found in almost every issue of the *Financial Post* and the *Globe and Mail,* but the point should now be clear.

The prices and earnings of nonhuman factors are successfully predicted by market theories of factor pricing.

Labor

When we apply the theory of distribution to labor, we encounter two important complications. First, because labor is the human factor of production, nonmonetary considerations loom large in its incentive patterns, and this may redirect the effect of market signals. Second, the competitive and noncompetitive elements of labor markets occur in different proportions from market to market. These complications make it harder to see if market conditions determine factor earnings. Nevertheless, there is a mass of evidence to support the view that they do.

Market Fluctuations

The evidence shows that earnings often respond to normal fluctuations of demand and supply. For example, with the advent of the automobile, skilled carriage makers saw the demand for their services decline rapidly. Earnings fell, and many older workers found that they had been earning substantial economic rents for their scarce but highly specific skills. They suffered large income cuts when they moved to other industries. Workers who acquired skills that

[3] A friend is fond of saying, "Nobody buys land anymore; its price is too high."

were wanted in the newly expanding automotive industry found that the demand for their services and their incomes rose rapidly.

More recently there has been a large increase in the earnings of premier professional athletes. In part this has resulted from rising demand due to an expansion in the number of major league teams. In part it has resulted from increased revenues to the teams and leagues from televising sports, which has increased the marginal revenue product of the athletes. Further, in part it has resulted from athletes' acquiring the right to offer their services to more than one employer, thereby reducing the ability of employers to hold down wages by eliminating competition among themselves.

One group that has been suffering the consequences of factor price determination on competitive markets is college graduates. In recent years the earnings of college graduates have fallen relative to other workers as employment opportunities have dropped sharply, especially for new graduates. The downturn is explained partly by slackening demand and partly by continued growth of supply as the "baby boomers" finish college.

Wage changes induced by market conditions have little to do with abstract notions of justice or merit. If you have some literary talent, why is it that you can make a lot of money writing copy for an advertising agency but very little money writing poems? It is not because an economic dictator or a group of philosophers has decided that advertising is more valuable than poetry. It is because in the economy there is a large demand for advertising but a small demand for poetry.

Monopoly Elements

A strong union—one that is able to bargain effectively with management and to control entry of labor into its market—can raise wages well above the competitive level. These high earnings attract others to the occupation or the industry, and the privileged position can be maintained only if the supply of labor can be restricted effectively. Highly skilled plasterers, plumbers, and electricians have all managed to restrict entry into their trades and, as a result, maintain wages well above what they would be in a competitive market. Many similar cases have been documented.

Not only can monopoly elements raise incomes above their competitive levels, but they can also prevent wages from falling in response to decreases in demand. (Of course, if the demand disappears more or less overnight, there is nothing any union can do to maintain incomes.)

For example, from 1945 to 1965 the production of coal declined as oil, gas, and electricity were steadily substituted for it. The coal that was produced was mined by ever more capital-using and labor-saving techniques. Both these forces led employment to shrink steadily. Coal mining was plainly a declining labor market from 1945 until 1965. Competitive theory would predict relatively low wages and low incomes, followed by exit of the most mobile coal miners and hard times for those who decided to stick it out.

Precisely this happened in Canada. Average wages, which in 1945 had been 36 percent above those in manufacturing, fell steadily until in 1965 they were 8 percent below those in manufacturing, and employment declined to 35 percent of its previous level. In the United States, however, this was *not* the pattern. Facing a similar decline in production, relative wages actually rose in U.S. coal mining, from 18 percent above manufacturing in 1945 to 34 percent above it in 1965. Employment did fall—indeed, by 1965 employment was only 30 percent of the 1945 level—but those who kept jobs did relatively well.

What happened was that a powerful American union, the United Mine Workers, prevented wages from falling. By raising wages despite falling demand, the union actually accelerated the decline in employment. The lower employment that accompanied the "high wage" policy of the United Mine Workers discouraged the young from waiting for jobs in the industry. As workers left the industry because of retirement, ill health, or death, they were not replaced.

In the 1970s, the demand for coal miners rebounded as the demand for coal to produce electricity surged. As a result, as theory predicts, employment and relative wages in coal mining rose sharply in Canada and other countries and more moderately in the United States.

All of these examples support the following general proposition:

Earnings of labor respond to significant changes in market conditions.

Implications for Economic Efficiency

The theory and evidence presented so far can be summarized in two important propositions.

1. **Factors will move between alternative uses in order to maximize the net advantage to the factors' owners.**
2. **Profit-maximizing employers will hire any factor up to the point at which the last unit hired adds as much to revenue as it does to cost (i.e., its *MRP* equals its *MC*).**

Together these two propositions have an important implication for economic efficiency. To see this implication, we present the case of labor, but the argument applies equally to all factors.

Absence of nonmonetary advantages. Suppose—to consider the simplest case first—that workers of one type all derive the same satisfaction (or dissatisfaction) from all jobs; the only thing that distinguishes one job from another is the wage rate. Whenever wage rates differ among jobs, workers move from low-paying to high-paying jobs. This movement continues until the wages paid for that type of labor have been equalized among the various jobs.

Since competitive firms equate the wage rate with labor's marginal revenue product (proposition 2), the *MRPs* of this type of labor are equalized in all its uses. When this is true, the value of total output cannot be increased by reallocating labor. If a worker were to move from one firm to another, the value that the workers would add to the output of the new firm would be exactly equal to the value of the fall in output in the old firm.

If the nonmonetary advantages are the same in all possible uses of a factor, competitive markets equalize that factor's marginal revenue products in all uses; as a result, the value of total output is maximized.

Effect of nonmonetary advantages. We can now allow for the fact that workers derive different levels of satisfaction from different jobs. When workers compare different jobs, they compare both the wage rates and the other satisfactions (or dissatisfactions) that the jobs offer. They then move among jobs until the net advantages of each—both monetary and nonmonetary—are equalized. As a result, wages are higher in jobs with low levels of nonmonetary satisfaction than they are in jobs with high satisfaction levels.

In the presence of nonmonetary advantages, the competitive market does not equalize wage rates.

It follows that when competitive firms equate wage rates with marginal revenue products, *MRPs* are not equalized in all the jobs that are occupied by this type of labor. As a result, output does not achieve its maximum possible value. Instead, it is possible to increase output by moving labor from a job where its wage and the value of its *MRP* are low (because the job has a high nonmonetary advantage) to a job where its wage and the value of its *MRP* are high (because the job has a low nonmonetary advantage). However, the increase in output of goods and services would be offset by the "psychic" cost to the worker in moving from a more preferred activity to a less preferred one. For example, a carpenter in Victoria may earn a lower wage and have a lower marginal product than one in Dawson City. If the carpenter moves to the Yukon, the economy's value of output of carpentry services would go up. But if the initial differences in wages, and hence in marginal products, reflected the net nonmonetary advantage to the carpenter of living in Victoria, the increase in value of output of carpentry services will be exactly matched by the decrease in nonmonetary returns to the carpenter.

The message is that factor prices reflect the value of factors in alternative uses and thus play a key role in their efficient allocation.

If factors are not priced according to their scarcity, there will be no easy means of allocating them efficiently among competing uses.

This is not just idle speculation. In the early years of the communist experiment in the Soviet Union, interest, which is the price paid for capital, was banned for ideological reasons. The resulting misallocation of capital among its various uses led to such serious waste that the policy had to be abandoned.

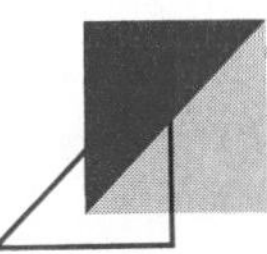

Capital and Interest

We begin by exploring an important complication that arises because factors of production are durable—a machine lasts for years, a laborer for a lifetime, and land more or less forever. It is convenient to think of a factor's lifetime as being divided into shorter periods that we refer to as *production periods* or *rental periods*.

The durability of factors makes it necessary to distinguish between the factor itself and the flow of services that it provides in a given production period. We can, for example, rent the use of a piece of land for some period of time, or we can buy the land outright. This distinction is just a particular instance of the general distinction between flows and stocks that we first encountered in Chapter 2.

Although what follows applies to any durable factor, applications to capital are of most importance, so we confine the remainder of our text discussion to capital. Box 18-1 discusses some of these issues as they apply to labor.

Two Prices of Capital

If a firm hires the use of a piece of capital equipment for some period of time, for example, one truck for one month, it pays a price for the privilege of using that piece of capital equipment. If the firm buys the truck outright, it pays a different (and higher) price for the purchase. Consider each of these prices—rental price and purchase price—in turn.

Rental Price

The *rental price of capital* is the amount that a firm pays to obtain the services of a capital good for a given period of time. The rental price of one week's use of a piece of capital is analogous to the weekly wage rate and the weekly rent bill that are the prices of hiring the services of labor and land.

Just as a profit-maximizing firm continues to hire labor until its *marginal revenue product* (*MRP*) equals its wage, so will the firm go on hiring capital until its *MRP* equals its rental price, *R*. Since in a competitive market all firms will face the same rental price, all firms that are in equilibrium will have the same *MRP* of capital.

As a result of profit maximization, the rental price of capital will be equated with its *marginal revenue product* (*MRP*), which is the net addition to the firm's revenue that is contributed by the use of the capital services over the rental period.

A capital good may also be used by the firm that owns it. In this case the firm does not pay out any rental fee. However, the rental price is the amount that the firm could charge if it leased its capital to another firm. It is thus the *opportunity cost* to the firm of using the capital good itself. This rental price is the *implicit* price that reflects the value to the firm of the services of its own capital that it uses during the current production period.

Whether the firm pays the rental price explicitly or calculates it as an implicit cost of using its own capital, the rental price of a capital good over the production period is equal to its marginal revenue product, which in turn is the stream of net income that the capital good produces over that period.

Purchase Price

The price that a firm pays to buy a capital good is called the *purchase price of capital*. When a firm buys a capital good outright, it obtains the use of the good's services over the whole of that good's lifetime. What the capital good will contribute to the firm is a flow that is equal to the expected marginal revenue product of the good's services over the good's lifetime. The price that the firm is willing to pay is, naturally enough, related to the total value that it places now on this stream of *expected* receipts to be received over future time periods.

The term *expected* emphasizes that the firm is usually uncertain about the prices at which it will be able to sell its outputs in the future. For the sake of simplicity, we confine ourselves to the special case in which the firm knows the future *MRP*s.

Present Value of Future Returns

The amount that the stream of future income that is provided by a capital good is worth *now* is called the good's *present value*. In general, **present value (*PV*)** refers to the value *now* of one or more payments to be received *in the future*.

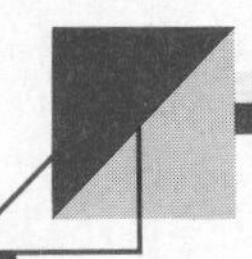

BOX 18-1

The Rental and Purchase Price of Labor

If you wish to farm a piece of land, you can buy it yourself, or you can rent it for a specific period of time. If you want to set up a small business, you can buy your office and equipment, or you can rent them. The same is true for all capital and all land; a firm often has the option of buying or renting.

Exactly the same would be true for labor if we lived in a slave society. You could buy a slave to be your assistant, or you could rent the services either of someone else's slave or of a free person. Fortunately, slavery is illegal throughout most of today's world. As a result, the labor markets that we know deal only in the services of labor; no one goes to a labor market to buy a worker body and soul. However, one can buy the services of a laborer for a long period of time. In professional sports, multiyear contracts are common, and 10-year contracts are not unknown. Some symphony orchestras have appointed their famous conductors for life. Herbert von Karajan, for example, was appointed conductor for life of the Berlin Philharmonic Orchestra. Publishers sometimes tie up their authors in multibook contracts, and entertainment firms, such as movie and television production units, often sign up their actors on long-term contracts. In all cases of such *personal services contracts*, the person is not a slave, and his or her personal rights and liberties are protected by law. The purchaser of the long-term contract is nonetheless buying ownership of the factor's services for an extended period of time. If the contract is transferable, the owner can sell these services for a lump sum or rent them out for some period. As with land and capital goods, the price paid for this *stock* of labor services is the present value of the expected rental prices over the contract period.

Present Value of a Single Future Payment

One period hence. To learn how to find the present value, we start with the simplest possible case. How much would a firm be prepared to pay *now* to purchase a capital good that will produce a single marginal revenue product of \$100 in one year's time, after which time the good will be useless? One way to answer this question is to discover how much the firm would have to lend out in order to have \$100 a year from now. Suppose for the moment that the interest rate is 5 percent, which means that \$1.00 invested today will be worth \$1.05 in one year's time.[4]

If we use PV to stand for this unknown amount, we can write $PV(1.05)$ = \$100 (which means PV *multiplied by* 1.05). Thus PV = \$100/1.05 = \$95.24. This tells us that the present value of \$100, receivable in one year's time, is \$95.24 when the interest rate is 5 percent. Anyone who lends out \$95.24 for one year at 5 percent interest will receive \$95.24 back plus \$4.76 in interest, which makes \$100 in total. When we calculate this present value, the interest rate is used to *discount* (i.e., reduce to its present value) the \$100 to be received one year hence. The maximum price that a firm would be willing to pay for this capital good is \$95.24 (assuming that the relevant interest rate is 5 percent).

To see why, let us start by assuming that firms are offered the capital good at some other price. Say that the good is offered at \$98. If, instead of paying this amount for the capital good, a firm lends its \$98 out at 5 percent interest, it would have at the end of one year more than the \$100 that the capital good will produce. (At 5 percent interest \$98 yields \$4.90 in interest, which, together with the principal, makes \$102.90.) Clearly, no profit-maximizing firm would pay \$98—or, by the same reasoning, any sum in excess of \$95.24—for the capital good. It could do better by using its funds in other ways.

Now say that the good is offered for sale at \$90.

[4] The analysis in the rest of this chapter assumes *annual* compounding of interest.

A firm could borrow \$90 to buy the capital good and could pay \$4.50 in interest on its loan. At the end of the year, the good yields \$100. When this is used to repay the \$90 loan and the \$4.50 in interest, \$5.50 is left as profit to the firm. Clearly, it would be worthwhile for a profit-maximizing firm to buy the good at a price of \$90 or, by the same argument, at any price less than \$95.24.

The actual present value that we have calculated depended on our assuming that the interest rate is 5 percent. What if the interest rate had been 7 percent? At that interest rate, the present value of the \$100 receivable in one year's time would be \$100/1.07 = \$93.46.

These examples are easy to generalize. In both cases we have found the present value by dividing the sum that is receivable in the future by 1 plus the rate of interest.[5] In general, the present value of R dollars one year hence at an interest rate of i per year is

$$PV = \frac{R}{1 + i} \qquad [1]$$

Several periods hence. Now we know how to calculate the present value of a single sum that is receivable one year hence. The next step is to ask what would happen if the sum were receivable at a later date. What, for example, is the present value of \$100 to be received *two* years hence when the interest rate is 5 percent? This is \$100/(1.05)(1.05) = \$90.70. We can check this by seeing what would happen if \$90.70 were lent out for two years. In the first year the loan would earn an interest of (0.05)(\$90.70) = \$4.54, and hence after one year the firm would receive \$95.24. In the second year the interest would be earned on this entire amount; interest earned in the second year would equal (0.05)(\$95.24) = \$4.76. Hence in two years the firm would have \$100. (The payment of interest in the second year on the interest income earned in the first year is known as *compound interest*.)

In general, the present value of R dollars after t years at i percent is

$$PV = \frac{R}{(1 + i)^t} \qquad [2]$$

[5] Notice that in this type of formula, the interest rate is expressed as a decimal fraction where, for example, 7 percent is expressed as 0.07, so $(1 + i)$ equals 1.07.

All that this formula does is discount the sum, R, by the interest rate, i, repeatedly, once for each of the t periods that must pass until the sum becomes available. If we look at the formula, we see that the higher i or t is, the higher the whole term $(1 + i)^t$ is. This term, however, appears in the denominator, so PV is *negatively* related to both i and t.

The formula $PV = R/(1 + i)^t$ shows that the present value of a given sum payable in the future will be smaller the more distant the payment date and the higher the rate of interest.

Present Value of a Continuous Stream of Payments

Finally, consider the present value that the firm would place on a capital good that is producing a stream of marginal revenue products that continues forever. In effect, this means that the capital good is not subject to depreciation. This simplifies the argument while still retaining the essence of the nature of capital.

Say that some capital good will produce \$100 each year forever and that the interest rate is 10 percent. To find the present value of \$100 payable every year in the future, we ask how much money would have to be invested now at an interest rate of 10 percent per year to obtain \$100 every year in the future. This present value is simply $0.1(PV) = \$100$, where PV is the sum required. In other words, $PV = \$100/0.1 = \$1{,}000$. This tells us that \$1,000 invested at 10 percent interest forever would yield a constant stream of income of \$100 per year; put the other way around, when the interest rate is 10 percent, the present value of \$100 per year forever is \$1,000.

To generalize for any interest rate, we merely write i for the interest rate and R for the revenue to be received each year. Now we wish to find the amount PV that, invested at i, will yield R per year forever. This is $i(PV) = R$, or

$$PV = \frac{R}{i} \qquad [3]$$

Here, as before, PV is related to the rate of interest: The higher the interest rate, the less the (present) value of any stream of future receipts and hence the lower the price that the firm would be prepared to pay to purchase the capital good.

Conclusions

From the foregoing discussion we can put together the following important propositions about the rental and purchase prices of capital.

1. **The rental price of capital is the flow of net receipts that the capital good is expected to produce over the rental period, that is, the marginal revenue product of the capital good.**
2. **The maximum purchase price that a firm would pay for a capital good is the discounted present value of the flow of net receipts, that is, rental values, that the good is expected to produce over its lifetime.**
3. **The maximum purchase price that a firm would pay for a capital good is positively associated with its rental price and negatively associated with the interest rate and amount of time that the owner must wait for payments to accrue.**

Equilibrium of the Firm

An individual firm faces a given interest rate and a given purchase price of capital goods. The firm can vary the quantity of capital that it employs, and, as a result, the marginal revenue product of its capital varies; the law of diminishing returns holds that the more capital the firm uses, the lower is its *MRP.*

The Decision to Purchase Capital

Price exceeds present value. Suppose that for $8,000 a firm can purchase a machine that yields $1,000 per year into the indefinite future. Also suppose that the firm can borrow (and lend) money at an interest rate of 10 percent. The present value of the income stream earned by the machine is R/i = $1,000/0.10 = $10,000. It is profitable for the firm to purchase the machine, since it obtains something worth $10,000 for a price of only $8,000.

It is always worthwhile for a firm to buy another unit of capital whenever the present value of the stream of *MRP*s that the capital provides exceeds its purchase price.

Marginal efficiency exceeds the interest rate. Another way to see the profitability for the firm of the purchase of a unit of capital is to suppose that the firm has only two uses for its money: to buy the machine or to lend out the $8,000 at 10 percent interest. It will be worthwhile for the firm to buy the machine, because the firm can do so and earn $1,000 per year, whereas if it lends the $8,000 at 10 percent interest, it will earn only $800 per year. In this example, each dollar invested in the machine yields a return of 12.5 percent ($1,000/$8,000 = 0.125), whereas each dollar lent out produces a return of only 10 percent. The concept of the **marginal efficiency of capital (*MEC*)** generalizes this result. It is defined as the return on capital per dollar invested in that capital. For the type of capital that we are considering—one that produces a perpetual stream of net revenue of R per period—

$$MEC = \frac{R}{P} \qquad [4]$$

It is always worthwhile for the firm to buy another unit of capital whenever the *MEC* exceeds the interest rate.

The two preceding statements in color are just two ways of stating the same condition for a profitable purchase of capital. To say that the present value, which is R/i, should exceed the purchase price, P, is the same as saying that the MEC, which is R/P, should exceed the interest rate, i. So now we know when it is worthwhile for a firm to buy capital, but how much will it buy?

The Size of the Firm's Capital Stock

Since the *MRP* declines as the firm's capital stock rises, the firm will eventually reach an equilibrium with respect to its capital stock. The firm will go on adding to its capital until the present value of the flow of *MRP*s conferred by the last unit added is equal to the purchase price of the capital. If we continue to use R for the *MRP* per period, we can write it as

$$PV = \frac{R}{i} = P$$

The equilibrium capital stock of the firm is such that the present value of the stream of net income that is provided by the marginal unit of capital is equal to its purchase price.

A second way of stating the same result is that the firm will go on adding to its capital until the *MEC* falls to the level of the rate of interest; that is,

$$MEC = i$$

Saying that R/P (the *MEC*) should equal i in equilibrium is the same as saying that R/i (the *PV* of the capital's stream of marginal revenue products) should equal P.[6]

The negative relationship between the *MRP* and the stock of capital implies that the firm's desired capital stock falls when the rate of interest rises and that it rises when the rate of interest falls.

FIGURE 18-1 The Marginal Efficiency of Capital

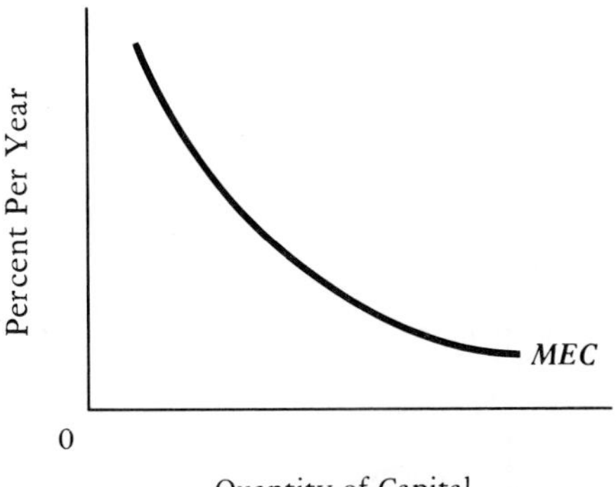

The marginal efficiency of capital (*MEC*) curve shows the relationship between the size of the capital stock and the rate of return on the marginal unit of capital. Because of diminishing returns, each successive unit of capital adds less to output than each previous unit. Thus the *MEC* curve, which relates the value of the additional output of each additional dollar's worth of capital added to the capital stock, is negatively sloped.

Equilibrium for the Economy

The term **capital stock** refers to some aggregate amount of capital. The *firm's capital stock* has a marginal revenue product, showing the increase in the firm's revenue when another unit of capital is added to its capital stock. The *economy's capital stock* also has a marginal revenue product. This is the addition to total national output (GDP) that is caused by adding another unit of capital to the economy's total stock. This capital stock also has an average product, which is total output divided by the total capital stock (i.e., the amount of output per unit of capital).[7]

If the industries that produce capital goods are perfectly competitive, the price of these goods will equal their marginal cost of production. We take this as it is given by the cost conditions in these industries and beyond the control of the firms that purchase and use capital goods. Thus there is a given price of producing one more unit of capital.

The *MEC* Schedule

Now consider how the marginal efficiency of capital varies for the whole economy as the existing capital stock is varied. The law of diminishing returns tells us that the larger the capital stock that is applied to the economy's given supplies of land and labor, the lower will be the marginal revenue product of a marginal unit of capital. Thus as we vary the size of the capital stock, the *MRP* in Equation 4 varies and so, therefore, does the *MEC*. Specifically, as the capital stock grows, the *MEC* falls. This negative relationship between these two magnitudes is shown in Figure 18-1.

Short-Run Equilibrium

In the short run, the economy's capital stock is given, but for the economy as a whole, the interest rate is variable. Whereas the firm reaches equilibrium by altering its capital stock, the whole economy reaches equilibrium through variations in the interest rate. Let us see how this comes about.

For the economy as a whole, the condition that *MEC* = *i* determines the equilibrium interest rate.

[6] In this chapter we assume that the rate of interest reflects the opportunity cost of capital to the firm. We saw in Chapter 9 that this may not always be the case. When the market rate of interest and the firm's own opportunity cost of capital diverge, the *MEC* must be equated with the latter, not the former.

[7] The idea of a capital stock being measured by a single number is a simplification (as is the idea of a total quantity of labor being measured by a single number). Society's stock of capital goods is made up of a diverse array of aids to production such as factories, machines, bridges, and roads. Also, the marginal and average products referred to in the text relate to the *flow of services* provided by the capital goods rather than to the goods themselves.

FIGURE 18-2 The Equilibrium Interest Rate

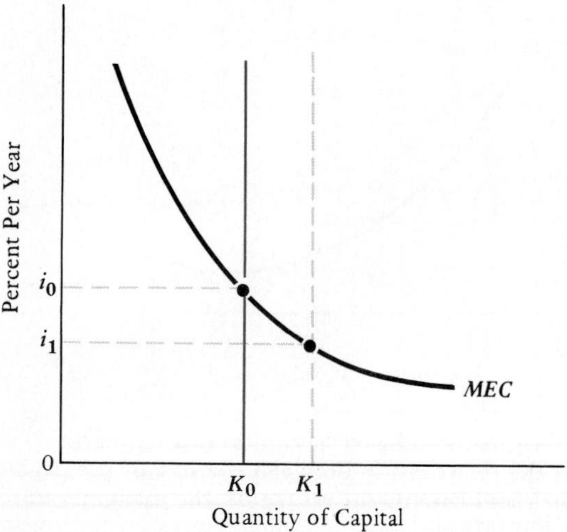

The economy's equilibrium interest rate is negatively related to the quantity of capital. The *MEC* curve is reproduced from Figure 18-1. If the capital stock is K_0, the equilibrium interest rate is i_0. If the actual rate were below i_0, all firms would wish to borrow in order to invest in capital, and this would drive the interest rate upward to i_0. If the actual rate were above i_0, no firm would wish to borrow in order to invest in capital, and this would drive the interest rate down to i_0.

An increase in the capital stock to K_1 lowers the equilibrium interest rate to i_1.

FIGURE 18-3 The Effect of Changing Technology and Capital Stock

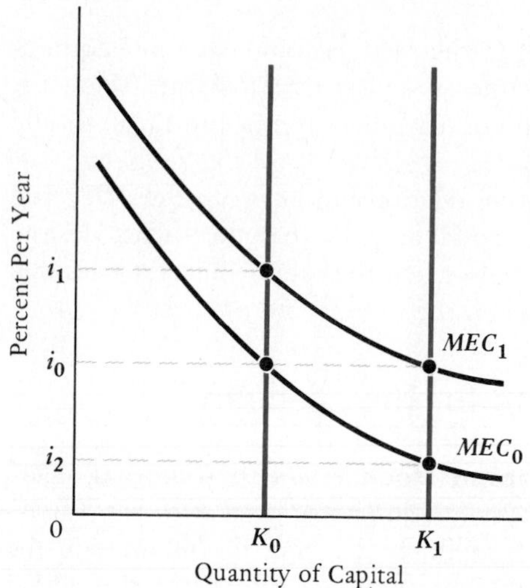

Increases in technological knowledge and in the capital stock have opposite effects on the equilibrium interest rate. The original capital stock is K_0, and the original state of technology gives rise to the marginal efficiency of capital schedule MEC_0. Thus the equilibrium interest rate is i_0. Technological improvements shift the marginal efficiency of capital curve to MEC_1 and, with a constant stock of capital, would raise the interest rate to i_1. Suppose that in addition the capital stock increases to K_1. If the *MEC* had remained at MEC_0, the equilibrium interest rate would have fallen to i_2. In the figure, the two effects exactly offset each other, and i remains unchanged at i_0, where K_1 and MEC_1 intersect.

If the market interest rate were below the *MEC*, which is the same thing as saying that the price of capital is less than the present value of its stream of future *MRP*s, it would be worthwhile for all firms to borrow money to invest in capital. For the economy as a whole, however, the stock of capital cannot change quickly, so the effect of this demand for borrowing would be to push up the interest rate until it equaled the *MEC*. Conversely, if the *MEC* were below the interest rate—that is, if the price of capital were above its present value—no one would wish to borrow money to invest in capital, and the rate of interest would fall. This is illustrated in Figure 18-2.

Accumulation of Capital in the Long Run

As more capital is accumulated over time, the economy's stock of capital grows slowly. As this happens, the *MEC* falls. This will cause the equilibrium interest rate to fall over time, as shown in Figure 18-2.

Changing Technology in the Very Long Run

In the very long run, technology changes. As a result, capital becomes more productive, shifting the *MEC* curve outward. This tends to increase the equilibrium interest rate associated with any one stock of capital. The accumulation of capital moves the economy downward to the right along any given *MEC* curve, and that tends to lower the interest rate associated with any one *MEC* curve. The net effect on the interest rate of both of these changes may be to raise it, to lower it, or to leave it unchanged, as shown in Figure 18-3. The very long run effects of changing technology, combined with a growing capital stock, are studied further in Chapter 38.

SUMMARY

1. The demand for any factor is derived from the demand for the commodities that the factor is used to make. Factor demand curves have negative slopes for two reasons. First, an increase in a factor's price will raise the cost of production of goods that use the factor in their production; this will increase the price of those goods and thus reduce the amount demanded. Second, an increase in a factor price will create incentives for producers to substitute cheaper factors for more expensive ones.
2. A profit-maximizing firm will hire units of any variable factor until the last unit that is hired adds as much to costs as it does to revenue. If factors are bought in a competitive market, the addition to cost will be the price of a unit of a factor. From this comes the important condition that in competitive equilibrium, the price of a factor will equal its marginal revenue product. This is the marginal productivity theory of distribution.
3. The elasticity of factor demand will tend to be greater (a) the greater the elasticity of demand of the products it makes, (b) the greater the ease of substitution of one factor for another, and (c) the greater the proportion of the total cost of production accounted for by the factor.
4. Market conditions exert a powerful influence on factor earnings. This is most evident for nonhuman factors such as raw materials and land, but it is also true for labor, despite the greater role of nonmonetary considerations and the greater importance of noncompetitive markets.
5. The marginal productivity theory of factor demands has the important implication that factors will be allocated efficiently among competing uses.
6. Because capital goods are durable, we distinguish between the stock of capital goods and the flow of services provided by them and thus between their purchase price and their rental price. The linkage between them relies on the ability to assign a present value to future returns. The present value of a future payment will be lower when the payment is more distant and the interest rate is higher.
7. The rental price of capital, equal to its marginal revenue product, is the amount that is paid to obtain the flow of services that a capital good provides for a given period. The purchase price is the amount that is paid to acquire ownership of the capital, and in equilibrium it is equal to the present value of the future income stream generated by the capital.
8. The marginal efficiency of capital (*MEC*) is the ratio of the value of the additional income stream to the value of the additional capital stock that is needed to produce the increased income stream. In equilibrium, the *MEC* will equal the interest rate.
9. An individual firm will invest in capital goods as long as the *MEC* exceeds the interest rate or, equivalently, as long as the present value of the stream of future net incomes that are provided by another unit of capital exceeds its purchase price; thus the condition that $MEC = i$ determines the firm's equilibrium capital stock. In the economy as a whole, the size of the total capital stock and hence the *MEC* changes only slowly; hence the condition that $MEC = i$ determines the interest rate.

TOPICS FOR REVIEW

Derived demand
Marginal revenue product
Marginal productivity theory of distribution
Elasticity of factor demand
Efficient allocation of factors
Rental price and purchase price of durable goods
Present value
Marginal efficiency of capital
The interest rate and the capital stock

DISCUSSION QUESTIONS

1. The demands listed here have been increasing rapidly in recent years. What derived demands would you predict have risen sharply? Where will the extra factors of production that are demanded be drawn from?
   a. Demand for electric power
   b. Demand for medical services
   c. Demand for international and interregional travel
2. Can the following factor prices be explained by the marginal productivity theory of distribution?
   a. The actor James Garner is paid $25,000 for appearing in a 10-second commercial. The model who appears in the commercial with him is paid $500.
   b. The same jockey who is riding the same horse is paid 50 percent more money for winning a $\frac{3}{4}$-mile race with a $150,000 first prize than a $1\frac{1}{2}$-mile race with a $100,000 first prize.
   c. The manager of the New York Yankees is paid *not* to manage during the third year of a three-year contract.
   d. The Los Angeles Kings lure hockey superstar Wayne Gretzky away from the Edmonton Oilers, which he has led to several Stanley Cup titles, by an offer that the Oilers—one of the richest clubs in the National Hockey League—are unwilling to match.
3. "One of the interesting side effects of the women's liberation movement has been a growing shortage of nurses." Why might women's liberation and the shortage of nurses be linked? Under what circumstances would the shortage persist? Under what circumstances would it be eliminated fairly quickly?
4. Consider the large-scale substitution of jumbo jets, each of which has a seating capacity of about 350, for jets with a seating capacity of about 125. What kinds of labor service would you predict will experience an increase in demand, and what kinds will experience a decrease? Under what conditions would airplane pilots (as a group) be made better off economically by virtue of this substitution?
5. A recent study has shown that after differences in education, age, hours worked per week, weeks worked per year, and the like are taken into account, professionally trained people earn approximately 15 percent less if they work in universities than if they work in government service. Can this be accounted for by the theory of distribution that we have been studying?
6. Discuss the implications of the suggestion that the Canadian federal government should change its policy of paying all its secretaries according to the same salary scale, regardless of location, to one that adapts the salary scale to local market conditions.
7. Stock market analysts are fond of evaluating the attractiveness of investing in a particular stock in terms of its *price-earnings ratio* and

in using the average P-E ratio to determine whether they think the stock market is overvalued or undervalued. How does this compare to the criteria in Equations 1 through 4? What is the current P-E ratio on the Toronto Stock Exchange? Does it make sense at current interest rates?

8. Suppose that you are offered, free of charge, either one of each of the following pairs of assets. What considerations would determine your choice?
   a. A perpetuity that pays $20,000 a year forever or an annuity that pays $100,000 a year for five years
   b. An oil-drilling company that earned $100,000 after corporate taxes last year or Canada Savings Bonds that paid $100,000 in interest last year
   c. A 1 percent share of a new company that has invested $10 million in a new cosmetic that is thought to appeal to middle-income women or a $100,000 bond that has been issued by the same company

9. How would you go about evaluating the present value of each of the following?
   a. The existing reserves of a relatively small oil company
   b. The total world reserves of an exhaustible natural resource whose completely fixed supply is known
   c. A perpetuity, issued by a very shaky third-world government, in which it promises to pay the bearer $1,000 per year forever
   d. A lottery ticket that your neighbor bought for $10, which was one of 1 million tickets sold for a drawing that is to be held in one year's time and will pay $2 million to the single winning ticket

Appendix to Chapter 18

The Firm's Demand for Factors

In Chapter 18 we saw that all profit-maximizing firms will hire units of the variable factor up to the point at which the marginal cost of the factor equals the marginal revenue that is produced by the factor. For a firm that is a price taker in factor markets, this means that it hires a factor up to the point at which the factor's price equals its marginal revenue product. Consider a single firm with only one variable factor, labor, and one fixed factor, capital. Assume that the average and marginal revenue products of the labor are those shown in Figure 18A-1. The firm wishes to hire the quantity of labor that will maximize its profits.

The demand curve for a factor is the negatively sloped portion of the marginal revenue product curve where it is below the average revenue product curve.

To see why this statement is correct, let us first ask a number of questions.

Why do points on the negatively sloped portion of *MRP*, such as *a* and *b* in Figure 18A-1, belong on the demand curve? If the wage rate (the price of the variable factor) is w_2, the profit-maximizing firm will hire the factor up to the point where $w = MRP$, that is, up to q_2. This is point *a*. If the wage rate is w_1, the firm will hire up to q_1. This is point *b*. Points *a* and *b* are thus on the firm's demand curve for the factor.

What is the maximum wage rate that the firm will pay? In Chapter 12 we saw that it will never be worthwhile for the firm to produce a product when its price is below the level of average variable cost. We also saw that where average product is a maximum, average variable cost is a minimum. For any wage rate above w_3, such as w_4, the average revenue that is generated by a unit of labor (shown by *ARP*) would be less than the variable cost of the unit of labor (its wage rate). For such a wage rate, it is not worthwhile for the firm to hire any workers. In other words, w_3, where average revenue product is a maximum, is the highest factor price that a firm could pay and still cover its variable costs.

Why is the negatively sloped, not the positively sloped, portion of *MRP* the demand curve? Consider the wage rate w_2. Here $w = MRP$ at both q_4 (point *c*) and q_2 (point *a*). We have already seen that point *a* is on the demand curve. What about point *c*? For every unit of labor that is hired up to q_4, *MRP* is less than the wage rate. In other words, each unit of labor is contributing less to revenue than to cost. Thus a profit-maximizing firm would be better off if it hired

FIGURE 18A-1 The Demand for a Factor and Marginal Revenue Product

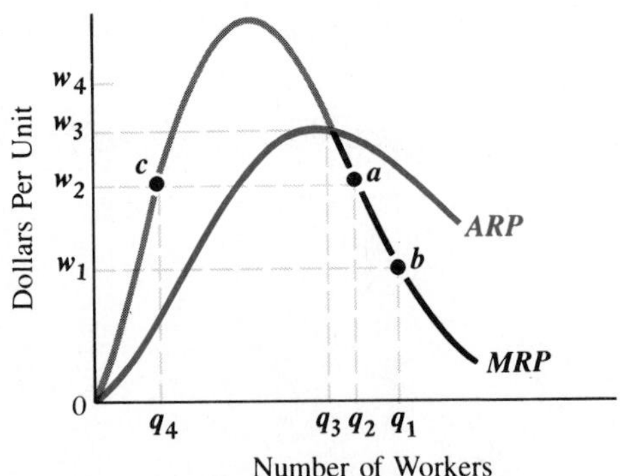

The derived demand curve for a factor is the negatively sloped portion of the *MRP* curve below the *ARP* curve as indicated by the black portion of the *MRP* curve. Suppose that the factor in question is labor. The average revenue generated by a unit of labor, the average revenue product of labor, is shown by the curve *ARP*, while the revenue generated by a marginal increase in the labor force, the marginal revenue product of labor, is shown by the curve *MRP*. Only points on the black portion of the *MRP* curve are on the firm's demand curve for the factor.

zero units rather than q_4 units. For every unit of labor from q_4 to q_2, *MRP* exceeds the wage rate. Thus if a firm were hiring q_4 units, it would find each additional unit beyond q_4 (up to q_2) worth hiring. Point *c*, where *MRP* is rising when it equals the wage rate, is a point of *minimum* profit, not maximum profit. [28] A firm at point *c* would improve its profitability by moving in either direction—to hiring zero workers or to hiring q_2 workers. (We already know that q_2 is better than zero because at that quantity *ARP* is greater than the wage rate.) Only points where *MRP* cuts the wage rate from above, that is, where *MRP* is downward-sloping, are possible profit-maximizing quantities.

Will There Be a Negatively Sloped Portion of *MRP*?

Having shown that only negatively sloped portions of *MRP* are relevant to the demand curve for the factor, we may now ask whether we have any reason to believe that *MRP* will have a negative slope. The presence of diminishing returns is sufficient to ensure this result, as we can easily show. Marginal revenue product depends on two things: (1) the physical increase in output that an additional unit of the variable factor makes possible, multiplied by (2) the increase in revenue derived from that extra output. The first of these is called the *marginal product* (*MP*); the second of these is called *marginal revenue* (*MR*), which by now is a familiar concept:

$$MRP = MP \times MR$$

The hypothesis of diminishing marginal returns was introduced in Chapter 10. This hypothesis says that *MP* has a declining section over some range of output. If marginal revenue is constant (as it is in perfect competition), *MRP* will have the same shape as *MP* and must also decline.

Marginal revenue, however, may not be constant. If *MR* declines as output increases (as it does in monopoly and in any other situation in which the firm's demand curve declines), *MRP* must decline even more sharply. The hypothesis of diminishing marginal productivity thus implies diminishing *MRP* and a negatively sloped demand curve for the factor.

Chapter 19

Labor Markets and Discrimination

The competitive theory of factor price determination tells us a great deal about factor prices, factor movements, and the distribution of income. Indeed, for the pricing and employment of many nonhuman factors, there is little need to modify the competitive model. Much of what is observed about labor markets is also consistent with the theory of competitive markets, but not all of it is.

The owners of capital or land need not be present when the services of factors are used. We observed in Chapter 18, however, that the need for workers to be physically present when their labor services are used differentiates labor from these other factors of production. As a result, nonmonetary factors, such as location of employment and other working conditions, are likely to be more important in the labor market than in markets for other factors of production.

Considerations other than material advantage enter the relationship between employer and employee, for it is a relationship that involves loyalty, fairness, appreciation, and justice along with paychecks and productivity. It is also a relationship that may involve discrimination on the basis of such things as gender, race, and age. The performance of labor markets will be affected by all of these "noneconomic" considerations and more.

Labor unions, employers' associations, collective bargaining, and government intervention in free market wage determination are important features of the real world. They influence wages and working conditions and affect the levels of employment and unemployment in many industries.

The theory of factor price determination must therefore be modified somewhat before it can be applied to the full range of problems concerning the determination of wages.

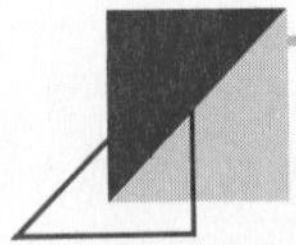

Theoretical Models of Wage Determination

If all workers were identical and labor markets were perfectly competitive, in equilibrium everyone would earn the same wage.[1] We know that in the real world this is hardly the case. Some people work full-time and are in poverty; others are able to live

[1] Remember that unless otherwise specified, we are dealing with real wages, that is, wages relative to the price level. For a review, see Chapter 4, pages 70–72.

very well on their wages or salaries. Generally, the more education and experience a worker has, the higher his or her wages will be. Given equal education and experience, blacks currently earn less than whites (on average), and women currently earn less than men (on average). Workers in highly unionized industries tend to get paid more than workers with similar skills and experience in nonunionized industries. These differentials arise both because all workers are not identical and because many important noncompetitive forces operate in labor markets. We shall look more systematically at the reasons why different labor groups earn different incomes.

Wage Differences in Competitive Labor Markets

Where there are many employers (buyers) and many nonunion workers (sellers), there is a competitive factor market of the kind discussed in Chapter 17. Under competitive conditions, the wage rate and level of employment are set by supply and demand. No worker or group of workers and no firm or group of firms would be able to affect the market wage. Indeed, if all workers and all jobs were identical, there would be only one market wage.

Of course, there are many kinds of workers and many kinds of jobs. Some jobs require highly specialized skills; some do not. Some jobs require that workers take great risks or work in unpleasant environments, while others can be performed in safety and comfort. In competitive equilibrium without discrimination, there will be three major sources of differences in pay.

Luck

Skills that are essentially impossible to teach and that are highly valued, for example, the physical ability to play professional hockey, will earn large incomes. In this case, there is a small and inelastic supply of the relevant kind of labor and a large enough demand so that the market-clearing wage is high. There are also less extreme cases. Some people are endowed with the ability to make others feel good—they make superior salespersons and therapists. Some people enjoy working hard more than others; they are thus more valuable on the job and often get paid more. In general, people's inheritance and early environment, both of which depend on luck, can have important effects on their ability to earn income as adults.

Human Capital

Investment in capital is usually discussed in terms of tangible assets such as buildings or machines. Much modern production, however, requires another type of investment. Skills and attitudes that can only be acquired through education are needed for many of today's skilled jobs. When people invest in acquiring these skills, they are investing in a sort of capital.

Consider a high school graduate who could get and keep a job. Instead of taking a job, however, she elects to go to university and possibly to graduate or professional school. During her university career, her contribution to society's current output is small (only a summer job, perhaps), but because of her education, her lifetime contribution to production (and her lifetime earnings) may be substantially larger than they would have been had she taken a job after high school.

The choice of whether to take a job immediately or to continue one's education has all the basic elements of an investment decision, and it is useful to regard this situation as if the student were making an investment to acquire capital. Because the value derived from such an investment is embodied in a person—in terms of greater skills, more knowledge, better health, and the like—rather than in a machine, it is known as **human capital**. Major elements of human capital are health, training, and education of all sorts. An extended education program requires, for example, that resources be withdrawn from the production of goods for current consumption. The resources include materials in the school, services of teachers, and the time and talents of pupils. The education of an individual is a good investment if the difference between the value of the lifetime output of the trained worker and the lifetime output of the individual without that training exceeds the value of the incremental resources that are used in the education process. If it does, the education increases the value of total production of the economy.

Skills that can be learned will be rewarded in the market. Thus engineers are highly paid, in part as compensation for undergoing many years of arduous training. During their training years, their pay is much *lower* than it would have been in some other line of work. Their high wages must compensate them both for the training itself and for the opportunity cost of acquiring it. So one cause of wage differentials is the return on human capital necessary to persuade people to acquire it. These differentials will persist in equilibrium.

Notice that in this case an increase in wages above their equilibrium value will induce an increase in the number of people choosing to become engineers. Where wages are high in order to compensate for human capital acquisition, the supply curve will be at least somewhat elastic—a further rise in the wage will encourage others to acquire the capital that is needed to earn that wage.

Notice also that experience can be an important form of human capital. An experienced worker is often more able than an inexperienced one. This will increase the experienced worker's wage relative to that of the inexperienced worker.

Compensating Differentials

Given identical skills, workers will be rewarded for working under relatively onerous or risky conditions. Thus construction workers who work the "high iron," assembling the frames for skyscrapers, are paid more than workers who do similar work at ground level. Other things being equal, risk and unpleasantness will reduce the supply of labor, raising the wage above what it would otherwise be.

Because workers and jobs differ greatly, the labor market is best thought of as many related markets—one for each type of worker in each kind of job—rather than as a single market.

In competitive labor markets, supply and demand set the equilibrium wage, but the wage will differ according to the characteristics of the worker and the nonmonetary advantages of the job.

The Influence of Market Structure

One major reason for wage differences is found in the different types of market in which various groups of labor sell their services. In Chapters 12–14 we distinguished different structures for the markets in which firms sell their outputs. The inputs that firms use are also bought in markets that can have different structures. Although some markets are perfectly competitive, many show monopoly elements on either the demand or the supply side.

To study the influence of different labor market structures (as well as to keep the analysis simple), we consider the case of an industry that employs only one kind of worker for one kind of job. Furthermore, we assume that all of the workers involved have the same level of skill.

Monopoly: A Union in a Competitive Market

For the purposes of our discussion of labor markets, a **union** (or *trade union* or *labor union*) is an association that is authorized to represent workers in negotiations with their employers.

Suppose that a union enters a competitive labor market to represent all of the workers. As the single seller of labor for many buyers, the union is a monopoly. If it uses its power, it will negotiate a wage above the competitive level. By doing so it is establishing a minimum wage below which no one will work. This changes the supply curve of labor. The industry can hire as many units of labor as are prepared to work at the union wage but no one at a lower wage. Thus the industry (and each firm) faces a supply curve that is horizontal at the level of the union wage up to the maximum quantity of labor that is willing to work at that wage.

This is shown in Figure 19-1, where the intersection of this horizontal supply curve and the demand curve establishes a higher wage rate and a lower level of employment than the competitive equilibrium.

There will be some workers who would like to obtain work in the industry or occupation but cannot. This presents a problem for the union, which seeks to represent *all* the employees in the industry. A conflict of interest has been created between serving the interests of the union's employed and unemployed members. Pressure to cut the wage rate may develop among the unemployed, but the union must resist this pressure if the higher wage is to be maintained.

An alternative way to achieve the higher wage level *without* the resulting unemployment is to shift the supply curve to the left. The union may do this by restricting entry into the occupation by methods such as lengthening the required period of apprenticeship and reducing openings for trainees. Alter-

FIGURE 19-1 Effect on Wages of Union Entry in a Competitive Labor Market

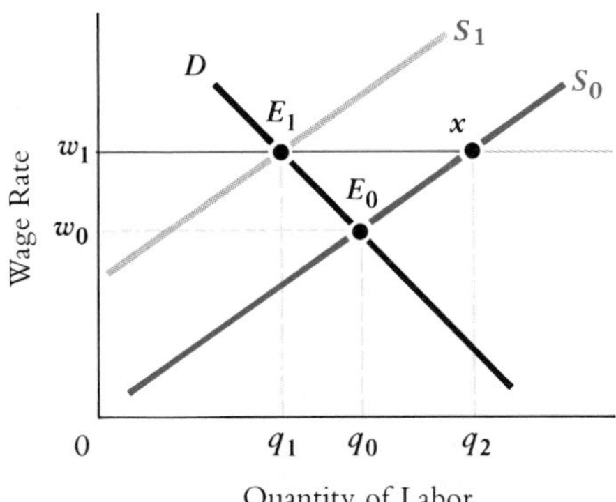

A union can raise the wages of those who continue to be employed in a competitive labor market at the expense of the level of employment. The competitive equilibrium is at E_0, the wage is w_0, and employment is q_0. If a union enters this market and sets a wage of w_1, a new equilibrium will be established at E_1. The supply curve has become w_1xS_0. At the new wage, w_1, employment will be q_1, and there will be q_1q_2 workers who would like to work but whom the industry will not hire. The decrease in employment due to the wage increase is q_1q_0.

The wage w_1 can be achieved without generating a pool of persons who are seeking but unable to find work in the occupation. To do so, the union must restrict entry into the occupation and shift the supply curve to the left to S_1. Employment will again be q_1.

This figure can also be used to illustrate the effect of government's imposing a minimum wage of w_1 on the market where the competitive equilibrium is at E_0. The q_1 workers who remain employed benefit by the wage increase. The q_1q_0 workers who lose their jobs in this industry suffer to the extent that they fail to find new jobs at a wage of w_0 or more.

natively, the union may shift the supply curve by persuading the government to impose restrictive licensing or certification requirements on those who would work. Either way, the result is less efficient than the competitive labor market. Workers who *could* do the work at the competitive wage are not doing it. However, these potential workers in the industry are unable to offer their services at the lower wage because of the entry restrictions.

Raising wages without restricting supply will give rise to a pool of unemployed workers who would like to work in the industry but cannot find jobs. Restricting supply will raise wages without creating a group of workers who are unemployed in the occupation at the going wage.

Raising wages by restricting entry is not, of course, limited to unions. Consider the profession of medicine. Because professional standards have long been regarded as necessary to protect the public from incompetent practitioners, doctors have found it publicly acceptable to control supply by limiting entry into their profession. Physicians' incomes are among the highest of any profession partly because of barriers to entry, including the difficulties of getting into an approved medical school, the high costs of creating new medical schools, and various certification requirements applying to students, schools, and practitioners.

Monopsony: A Single Buyer in the Market

A **monopsony** is a market where there is only one buyer; it is to the buying side of the market what monopoly is to the selling side. Although pure monopsony is rare, it is not uncommon to see labor markets in which there are only a few firms. Analysis of the case of a pure monopsony can shed considerable light on such cases. Imagine, then, that the firms in an industry form an employers' hiring association in order to act as a single buying unit.

Monopsonistic labor markets in the absence of unions. Suppose that there are many potential employees and that they are not members of a union. The employers' association can offer any wage rate that it chooses, and the workers must either accept employment at that rate or find a different job.

Suppose that the monopsonist decides to hire some specific quantity of labor. The labor supply curve shows the wage that it must offer. To the monopsonist, this wage is the *average cost curve* of labor. In deciding how much labor to hire, however, the monopsonist is interested in the marginal cost of hiring additional workers. The monopsonist wants to know how much its costs will rise if it takes on more labor.

Whenever the supply curve of labor slopes upward, the marginal cost of employing extra units will exceed the average cost. It exceeds the wage paid (the average cost) because the increased wage rate necessary to attract an extra worker must also be paid to *everyone already employed.* [29] For example, assume that 100 workers are employed at $8.00 per hour and that in order to attract an extra worker, the wage must be raised to $8.01 per hour. The marginal cost of the 101st worker is not the $8.01 per hour paid to the worker, but $9.01 per hour—made up of the extra 1 cent per hour paid to the 100 existing workers and $8.01 paid to the new worker. Thus the marginal cost is $9.01; the average cost, $8.01.

The profit-maximizing monopsonist will hire labor up to the point where the marginal cost just equals the amount that the firm is willing to pay for an additional unit of labor. That amount is determined by the marginal revenue product of labor and is shown by the demand curve. This is illustrated in Figure 19-2.

FIGURE 19-2 Monopsony in a Labor Market

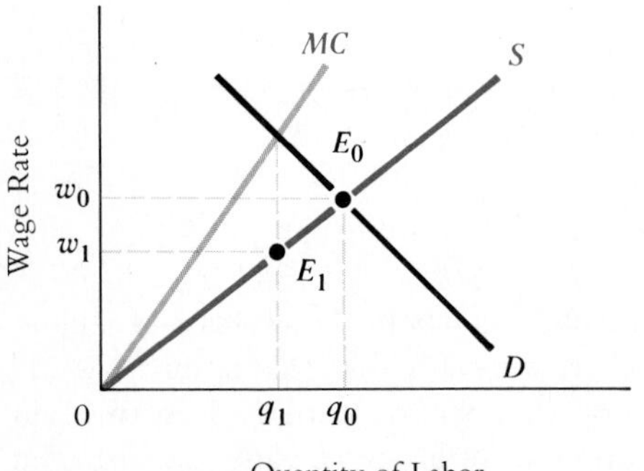

A monopsonist lowers both the wage rate and employment below their competitive levels. *D* and *S* are the competitive demand and supply curves. In competition, equilibrium is at E_0, the wage rate is w_0, and the quantity of labor hired is q_0. The marginal cost of labor (*MC*) to the monopsonist is above the average cost. The monopsonistic firm will maximize profits at E_1. It will hire only q_1 units of labor. At q_1 the marginal cost of the last worker is just equal to the value to the firm of that worker's output, as shown by the demand curve. The wage that must be paid to get q_1 workers is only w_1.

Monopsonistic conditions in a labor market will result in a lower level of employment and a lower wage rate than would rule when labor is purchased under competitive conditions.

The common sense of this result is that the monopsonistic employer is aware that by trying to purchase more, it is responsible for driving up the wage. It will therefore stop short of the point that is reached when the wages are negotiated by many separate firms, no one of which can exert an influence on the wage rate.

Monopoly versus monopsony: A union in a monopsonistic market. What if a wage-setting union now enters the monopsonistic market and sets a wage below which labor will not work? There will then be no point in the employer's holding off hiring for fear of driving the wage up or of reducing the quantity demanded in the hope of driving the wage rate down. Here, just as in the case of a wage-setting union in a competitive market, the union presents the employer with a horizontal supply curve (up to the maximum number of workers who will accept work at the union wage). As demonstrated in Figure 19-3, the union can raise wages and employment above the monopsonistic level.

Because the union turns the firm into a price taker in the labor market, it can prevent the exercise of the firm's monopsony power and thus raise both wages and employment to the competitive levels.

The union may not be content merely to neutralize the monopsonist's power. It may choose to raise wages further. If it does, the outcome will be similar to that shown in Figure 19-1. If the wage is raised above the competitive level, the employer will no longer wish to hire all the labor that is offered at that wage. The amount of employment will fall, and unemployment will develop. This is also shown in Figure 19-3. Notice, however, that the union can raise wages substantially above the competitive level before employment falls to a level as low as it was in the preunion monopsonistic situation.

Minimum Wage Laws

When unions set wages for their members, they are in effect setting a minimum wage. Governments can

FIGURE 19-3 Effects of Union Entry in a Monopsonistic Labor Market

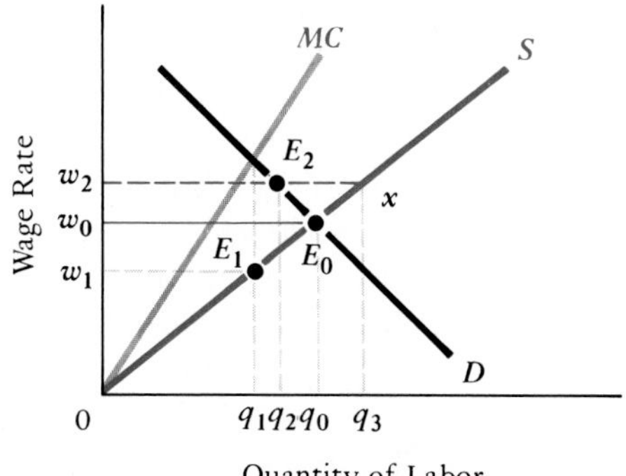

By presenting a monopsonistic employer with a fixed wage, the union can raise both wages and employment over the monopsonistic level. The monopsony position before the union enters is at E_1 (from Figure 19-2), with a wage rate of w_1 and q_1 workers hired. A union now enters and sets the wage at w_0. The supply curve of labor becomes w_0E_0S, and wages and employment rise to their competitive levels of w_0 and q_0 without creating a pool of unemployed workers. If the wage is raised further, say, to w_2, the supply curve will become w_2xS, the quantity of employment will fall below the competitive level, to q_2, and a pool of unsuccessful job applicants of q_2q_3 will develop.

This figure can also be used to illustrate the effect of the government's imposing a minimum wage of w_0 or w_2 on a monopsonistic labor market, where the equilibrium wage would be w_1.

cause similar effects by legislating specific **minimum wages**, wage rates that are the lowest that may legally be offered.

In Canada, industries under federal jurisdiction are subject to the Canadian Labour Code, which in 1989 had a minimum wage of $4.00 per hour. The major coverage, however, is provided by provincial legislation that in 1989 set minimum wages for adult workers ranging from $4.25 per hour in Newfoundland to $5.00 in Ontario and Quebec.

For a large proportion of all employment covered by the law, the minimum wage is below the actual market wage. In such cases, the minimum wage is said to be *not binding*. However, some workers are in occupations or industries in which the free market wage rate would be below the legal minimum, and there the minimum wage is said to be *binding* or *effective*.[2]

Although minimum wages are an accepted part of the labor scene, economists view their effects as less obviously beneficial than do many other observers. To the extent that they are effective, they raise the wages of employed workers. However, as our analysis in Chapter 6 indicated, an effective floor price (which is what a minimum wage is) may well lead to a market surplus—in this case, unemployment. Thus minimum wages will benefit some groups while hurting others.

The problem is more complicated than the analysis of Chapter 6 would suggest, both because not all labor markets are competitive and because minimum wage laws do not cover all employment. Moreover, some groups in the labor force, especially youths and minorities, are affected more than the average worker.

A Comprehensive Minimum Wage

Suppose that minimum wage laws apply uniformly to all occupations. The occupations and the industries in which minimum wages are effective will be the lowest-paying in the country; they usually involve unskilled or at best semiskilled labor. In most of them, the workers are not members of unions. Thus the market structures in which minimum wages are likely to be effective include both those in which competitive conditions pertain and those in which employers exercise monopsony power. The effects on employment are different in the two cases.

Competitive labor markets. The consequences for employment of an effective minimum wage are unambiguous when the labor market is competitive. By raising the wage employers face, minimum wage legislation leads to a reduction in the quantity of labor that is demanded and an increase in the quantity of labor that is supplied. As a result, the actual level of employment falls, and unemployment is generated. This situation is exactly analogous to the one that arises when a union succeeds in setting a wage above the competitive equilibrium wage, as illus-

[2] Whether minimum wages are effective is not always easy to determine. For example, one response of employers to minimum wage legislation might be to reduce fringe benefits so that total compensation remains constant.

trated in Figure 19-1. The excess supply of labor at the minimum wage also creates incentives for people to evade the law by working below the legal minimum wage.

In competitive labor markets, effective minimum wage laws raise the wages of those who remain employed but also create some unemployment.

Monopsonistic labor markets. By effectively flattening out the labor supply curve, the minimum wage law can simultaneously increase both wages and employment in monopsonistic labor markets. The circumstances in which this can be done are the same as those in which a union that is facing a monopsonistic employer succeeds in setting a wage above the wage that the employer would otherwise pay, as shown in Figure 19-3. Of course, if the minimum wage is raised above the competitive wage, employment will start to fall, as in the union case. When it is set at the competitive level, however, the minimum wage can protect workers against monopsony power *and* lead to increases in employment.

A Noncomprehensive Minimum Wage

Suppose that a minimum wage covers only 50 percent of all jobs and that applying the minimum wage to the covered jobs does cause some unemployment in that sector. The workers displaced can move to the uncovered sector. If they do, they will shift the supply curve in the uncovered sector to the right. This will lead to lower wages and increased employment in the uncovered sector. As a general rule, the increase in employment in the uncovered sector will not be large enough to offset the decrease in the covered sector.[3]

Overall Effect

Researchers have devoted a great deal of effort to studying the effect of minimum wages on employment. The studies show that the adverse employment effects of minimum wages fall most heavily on those who have the least education and training. This group, which includes many teenagers, women, and visible minorities, has fewer job opportunities as the wage rate rises. Many of those affected could have found jobs at lower wages. Estimates of the effect of a 10 percent increase in the minimum wage on teenage unemployment rates vary from 0.75 to 3.00 percentage points. Even a 0.75 percent effect on the unemployment rate is not small, but it must be evaluated against an overall teenage unemployment rate of about 20 percent for the past decade. The minimum wage also adversely affects the employment of young adults (aged 20 to 24), to a lesser extent. Females suffer a disproportionately greater loss of employment due to minimum wages than males.

These job losses could have important long-term effects. Much acquisition of skill occurs on the job. Employees in occupations in which on-the-job training occurs frequently "pay" for their education by receiving low wages in the initial stages of their employment. Minimum wage legislation makes this more difficult. Instead of being able to apprentice in jobs that will lead to productive careers, some workers may become trapped either in unemployment or in low-skill, short-term, or part-time employment. Just how important these effects are in practice is not known.

Several Canadian provinces have responded to the employment problems caused by minimum wages by allowing lower minimum wages for young or inexperienced workers and for workers demonstrably in a "learning period."[4] The United States also has a lower minimum wage (85 percent of the general minimum wage) for students, but the provision is rarely used.

The adverse employment effect is, however, only one element in deciding whether minimum wages are beneficial or harmful overall. It is clear that minimum wage laws raise the incomes of many workers at the very lowest levels of pay. Some of those who benefit most are members of groups that are chronically poor and whom the government is eager to aid by income redistribution. However, the lowest paid are not the only ones who gain. Because union wage structures maintain differentials between skill

[3] Only if the demand curve in the uncovered sector is horizontal (infinitely elastic) or if the supply curve is vertical (completely inelastic) will every displaced worker from the covered sector find employment. But these are not likely circumstances.

[4] It may be objected that such exceptions are discriminatory, but, as we saw earlier, labeling something "discriminatory" does not necessarily mean that it is bad. The argument favoring a minimum wage for youth is that it is better to be employed at a lower wage than unemployed at a higher one.

classes, an increase in minimum wages also raises wages in many occupations that are already above the minimum.

Thus there are gainers and losers from minimum wage laws. Labor union members as a whole are gainers, as are white males. Females and teenagers are net losers, because the loss of earnings resulting from less employment is larger than the gains resulting from higher wage rates. Of course, there are gainers and losers in each group. The losers are the ones without jobs; the gainers are those who receive higher wages than they otherwise would. Again, recent empirical work on the subject tends to suggest that the distributional effects of the minimum wage, like the employment effects, are fairly small. An article by Charles Brown, reviewing the literature on minimum wages, concludes that "the minimum wage is overrated: by its critics as well as its supporters."[5]

Given its mixed economic effects, support for and opposition to the minimum wage may best be understood as arising largely from political and sociological motives. Organized labor has consistently pressed for a broad, relatively high minimum wage. There is some economic reason for this, in that there is evidence that the minimum wage "trickles up" to higher-wage workers, both unionized and not. Arguably, however, the support dates back to the 1930s, when organized labor was still fighting for its position in North Americn society. Enactment of a minimum wage was then a great political victory, and the minimum wage still has symbolic significance.

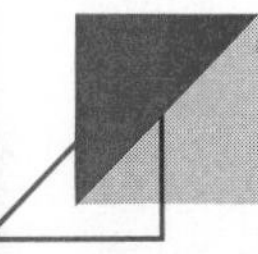

The Nature and Evolution of Modern Labor Unions

Unions today represent only about 28 percent of the workers in the private sector and less than 40 percent of all workers, but union influence is greater than these percentages suggest. One reason is the impact that union wage contracts have on other labor markets. When, for example, the Canadian Auto Workers negotiate a new contract, its provisions set a pattern that directly or indirectly affects other labor markets, both in Ontario and in other provinces. A second reason is the major leadership role that unions have played in the past 50 years in the development of labor market practices and in lobbying for legislation that applies to all workers.

[5] For this and much of the preceding discussion, see Charles Brown, "Minimum Wage Laws: Are They Overrated?" *Journal of Economic Perspectives*.

Labor Market Institutions

The process by which unions and employers (or their representatives) arrive at and enforce their agreements is known as **collective bargaining**. This process has an important difference from the theoretical models with which we began this chapter. There we assumed that the union set the wage and the employer decided how much labor to hire. In collective bargaining, the wage is negotiated. In terms of Figure 19-3, it may be that the employer wants the wage to be w_1 and the union wants the wage to be w_2. Depending on each side's market power, the final wage that is agreed on may be anywhere in between. In collective bargaining, there is usually a substantial range over which an agreement can be reached, and the actual result in particular cases will depend on the strengths of the two bargaining parties and on the skill of their negotiators.

Unions today are an accepted part of economic life, especially in manufacturing industries and in much of government service. It was not always so. Within the lifetime of many of today's members, unions were fighting for their lives, and union organizers and members were risking theirs. In the 1930s the labor movement evoked the loyalties and passions of people as a great liberal cause in ways that seem quite extraordinary today. Indeed, some unions today appear to many people as conservative, even reactionary, groups. Why and how did the change come about?

The Urge to Organize

Trade unionism had its origin in the pitifully low wages and brutal working conditions in nineteenth century factories. Box 19-1 provides a vivid picture of factory conditions at the turn of the twentieth century. Out of these conditions and other grievances of working men and women came the full range of radical political movements. Out of the same conditions also came a pragmatic form of collective action called **bread-and-butter unionism**, whose

BOX 19-1

Factory Life in 1903

Stories of workers' very real suffering during the Industrial Revolution and the years that followed could fill many volumes, but an example will illustrate some of the horrors that lay behind the drive for change and reform. The quotation, about conditions in the American South, comes from *Poverty* by Robert Hunter, published in 1904.

In the worst days of cotton-milling in England the conditions were hardly worse than those now existing in the South. Children—the tiniest and frailest—of five and six years of age rise in the morning and, like old men and women, go to the mills to do their day's labor; and when they return home, they wearily fling themselves on their beds, too tired to take off their clothes. Many children work all night—"in the maddening racket of the machinery, in an atmosphere insanitary and clouded with humidity and lint." It will be long before I forget the face of a little boy of six years, with his hands stretched forward to rearrange a bit of machinery, his pallid face and spare form showing already the physical effects of labor. This child, six years of age, was working twelve hours a day in a country which has established in many industries an eight-hour day for men. The twelve-hour day is almost universal in the South, and about twenty-five thousand children are now employed on twelve-hour shifts in the mills of the various Southern states. The wages of one of these children, however large, could not compensate the child for the injury this monstrous and unnatural labor does him; but the pay which the child receives is not enough, in many instances, even to feed him properly. If the children fall ill, they are docked for loss of time. . . . The mill-hands confess that they hate the mills, and no one will wonder at it. A vagrant who had worked in a textile mill for sixteen years once said to a friend of mine: "I done that [and he made a motion with his hand] for sixteen years. At last I was sick for two or three days with a fever, and when I crawled out, I made up my mind that I would rather go to hell than go back to the mill."

goals were higher wages and better working conditions rather than political reform.

The early industrial organizer saw that 10 or 100 employees acting together had more influence than one acting alone and dreamed of the day when all workers would stand solid against the employer. (The word *solidarity* occurs often in the literature and songs of the labor movement.) However, employers did not sit by idly; they too knew that in union there was strength. "Agitators" who tried to organize workers were fired and blacklisted; in some cases, they were beaten and killed.

The union movement showed its first real power among small groups of relatively skilled workers. Why? First, it was easier to control the supply of skilled workers than unskilled ones; employers could easily find replacements when unskilled labor threatened to strike. But skilled workers—the coopers (barrelmakers), the bootmakers, the shipwrights—controlled access to their trades by means of apprenticeships. The original craft unions were, in effect, *closed shops*: One had to belong to the union to hold a job in the craft, and the union set the rules of admission.

Second, employers were often vulnerable to the demands of a union of workers whose skills might be indispensable to the production process.

Third, because labor in a particular skilled occupation is likely to account for a relatively low proportion of total costs, the effect on the employer's overall costs of giving in to a small group's demand for a wage increase is likely to be small. The difficulty of substituting other factors for skilled labor and a relatively small contribution to total costs combined to create an inelastic demand. This gave the unions of skilled workers an advantage in fighting the employer that was not enjoyed by other groups of workers.

The Historical Development of Canadian Unions

The present structure of Canadian trade unionism can be traced to the latter half of the nineteenth century. Its development has been strongly dominated by the influence of international unions, which had their headquarters and an overwhelming proportion of their membership outside Canada. The creation of Canadian locals of American unions began in the 1860s, and in 1911, the earliest date for which figures are available, international unions had 90 percent of total union membership.

Two facets dominated the history of Canadian trade unionism in the first half of the twentieth century. One was the movement toward a single national federation; the other was the struggle to achieve autonomy from American unions. The issues became intertwined when conflicts in the United States arose between craft and industrial unions. Until the 1930s, craft unions were the characteristic form of collective action in the United States. In Canada, meanwhile, trade unionists were attracted to the principle of industrial unions that embraced unskilled workers as well as skilled craftsmen.

Because of the impossibility of establishing bargaining strength by controlling the supply of unskilled workers, the rise of industrial unionism in Canada was associated with political action as an alternative means of improving the lot of the membership. In general, social and political reform were given much more emphasis by Canadian unionists than by their American counterparts. Political action here extended to the support for socialist political parties: first, the Cooperative Commonwealth Federation (CCF), established in 1932, and later its successor, the New Democratic Party (NDP), formed in 1961.

The dominance of international (American) unions in the Canadian labor movement has long been a source of public concern in Canada. Some people regard it as inconsistent with Canadian sovereignty and dangerous to Canadian interests. However, Senator Eugene Forsey, a former director of research for the Canadian Labour Congress, views the unification of the bulk of Canadian unions under the CLC in 1956 as the beginning of virtual autonomy for Canadian locals—the CLC has guidelines for the conduct of international unions operating in Canada. Throughout the postwar period, the percentage of total union membership represented by international unions fell: In the mid 1950s it was about 70 percent, and by 1990 it was only 32 percent.

One factor in the increased share of national unions is the growth of membership in the two unions representing government workers, the Canadian Union of Public Employees and the Public Service Alliance. Public-sector unions are discussed further in Box 19-2. Another major component of noninternational union membership has arisen out of the distinct aspirations of French-Canadian workers. More recently, the formation of the Canadian Auto Workers, independent of the American Auto Workers, represented a significant further reduction of membership in international unions.

Public Policy Toward Collective Bargaining

Rapid gains in union membership occurred in the years during and immediately after World War II. This led to pressure for the rights of workers to organize and to elect an exclusive bargaining agent. These rights were established by provisions of the Wartime Labour Relations Regulations Act of 1944.

Government intervention in industrial disputes in Canada has a history dating back to the early years of the twentieth century. The earliest legislation applied only to public utilities and coal mining. It provided that before a strike or a lockout could be initiated, the parties were required to submit any dispute to a conciliation board. This system of compulsory conciliation and compulsory delay in work stoppage was extended to a much larger segment of the economy under special emergency powers adopted by the government of Canada during World War II. In the postwar period, jurisdiction over labor policy reverted to the provinces, but the principles established have been carried over into provincial legislation.

Objectives of Modern Unions

Unions seek many goals when they bargain with management. They may push for higher wages, higher fringe benefits, more stable employment, or less onerous working conditions. Whatever their specific goals, unless they face a monopsonist across the bargaining table, they must deal with a fundamental dilemma.

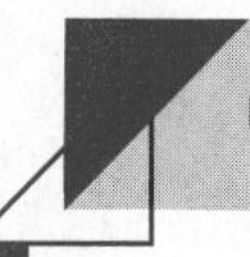

BOX 19-2

Unionism in the Public Sector

Whatever the reason, the scope of union activity within the public sector has expanded rapidly since the 1960s. Indeed, the rapid growth in union membership in Canada noted in the text arises primarily from this increase in union membership in the public sector.* In addition, because most public service unions are Canadian, their growth has diminished the role of international unions in Canada.

Since 1965, public-sector unions have had the right to strike, and strikes in the public sector have not been infrequent. Canadians have often experienced interruptions in the postal service or have had to cancel holidays because of the disruption of airport services.

It is often argued that such withdrawals of services are unfair for several reasons. First, they affect large numbers of people who are not party to the labor-management dispute. Second, government often has a monopoly in the provision of the services being withheld, and hence there are no alternatives. Third, public-sector employers are not restrained by market forces from conceding excessive wages. Government services are not typically sold in the marketplace but are paid for out of general tax revenues. Further, politicians have a strong incentive to avoid unpopular strikes.

Professor Morely Gunderson of the University of Toronto has estimated that during the six-year period beginning in 1965 (the year of the institution of the right to strike in the public sector), there developed a public service wage advantage of about 6 percent for males and 8 percent for females, relative to comparable jobs in the private sector. Other studies confirm the maintenance of, if not an increase in, this advantage over the next few years for all but the most senior public employees.

Some economists believe that the public sector has become a wage leader and a source of inflation in the economy. However, studies have called into question the evidence confirming a spillover, and the issue is still hotly contested.

Furthermore, many observers feel that a major reason for the introduction of wage and price controls by the federal government in 1975 was to

* Under Canadian law, municipalities are treated as private corporations, and their employees are governed by labor legislation applicable to the private sector.

There is an inherent conflict between the level of wages and the size of the union itself.

The more successful a union is in raising wages, the more management will attempt to reduce the size of its work force, substituting capital for labor. This will lead to lower union membership. However, if the union does not provide some wage improvement for its members, they will have little incentive to stay around.

Wages Versus Employment

A union that sets wages above the competitive level is making a choice of higher wages for some and unemployment for others. Should the union strive to maximize the earnings of the group that remains employed? If it does, some of its members will lose their jobs, and the union's membership will decline. Should it instead maximize the welfare of its present members? Or should it seek to expand employment opportunties (perhaps by a low-wage policy) so that the union membership grows? Different unions decide these questions differently.

Severe strains developed between Canadian and American members of international unions as a result of different views of how to respond to the difficult economic conditions of the 1980s. Two key differences typified a range of differences in attitudes.

American unions were willing to reopen contracts and accept wage cuts when the alternative seemed to be plant closures or company liquidations. They were also willing to consider schemes designed

appeal to an external force to regain control over wage settlements with their own employees. Public-sector unions, in this view, had become so powerful that the federal government was unable, or unwilling, to control wages in the federal civil service through the usual negotiating and bargaining procedures. In 1982, the federal government introduced temporary wage controls on wages under federal government jurisdiction, with its 6 & 5 Program. These provided guidelines for the moderation of wage demands while the inflation rate was expected to fall.

In the last half of the 1980s, with increased foreign competition in the private sector and pressure to hold down costs in the public sector, the major bargaining issues became job security and the maintenance of working conditions rather than wage increases. A postal strike in 1987 was a case in point. Faced with a directive from Ottawa to remove its large deficit, the post office sought concessions from unions that would reduce the number of jobs (by attrition, not by direct firing) and alter working conditions so that more of the hours actually paid for would be spent on the job. The union opposed the proposals for their content but also because it saw the post office's suggestions as the thin edge of the wedge for many additional cost-reducing demands in other public-sector occupations.

It is useful to compare the Canadian situation with that prevailing elsewhere. In the United States, federal and state government workers are prohibited from striking over pay. In Britain, the normal means of determining government pay levels is strict adherence to private-sector comparability guidelines. Canadian public-sector labor policy is now among the most liberal in the world.

Some economists believe that government employees do not need collective bargaining or the strike weapon to ensure that they are paid adequately; in the long run, the supply of labor to the public sector is a function of the price paid for labor by the public employer, relative to what workers can earn elsewhere. This offers considerable insurance that public employees, with or without collective bargaining, will not long be underpaid, at least at entry job levels.

to move away from the traditional pattern where wages are relatively stable over the cycle while employment does most of the adjusting to fluctuating demand. The alternative is to have wages vary more over the cycle in order to maintain a more stable employment pattern. One way of doing this is to move toward the Japanese arrangement whereby wages are to some extent linked to profits.

Canadian unions have been more inclined to stick with traditional approaches. First, a contract should not be reopened before it expires. Even if the agreed wages threaten to cause plant closures, the sanctity of the contract is a more important principle than the saving of specific jobs. Second, profit sharing means selling out to the bosses. The traditional system should be maintained in which wages are stable over the cycle and most of the adjustment to variations in demand occurs through variations in employment.

Under the dynamic leadership of Bob White, the Canadian Automobile Workers (CAW) split with the United Automobile Workers (UAW) over these and related issues. A separate Canadian union was set up, and its different approach to bargaining soon became apparent.

Many American union leaders tend to see their Canadian colleagues as trying to live in a world that is quickly fading. They worry that practices appropriate to the 1960s will not be in the best interests of labor in the 1990s. Many Canadian union leaders tend to see their American counterparts as having sold out to management. By reopening contracts and considering profit sharing, the traditional interests of the working class have, in their view, been seriously compromised.

Since the breakaway, the CAW has been significantly more hostile to changes in work organization than the UAW has been. The CAW's National Policy Statement issued in October 1989 explicitly rejects innovations such as flexible job classifications and supervisor-worker interchanges that appear to have contributed greatly to productivity in the Japanese automobile industry. (Recall the discussion in Box 11-2.) Because the North American automobile industry is under immense challenges from Japanese and other foreign producers, this statement seemed to many observers to be an open invitation to automobile firms to invest in the United States rather than Canada. However, the policy statement and the actual policies adopted by the CAW may differ: Faced with the real possibility of the closure of a major plant in Ste. Thérèse, Quebec, the union was considerably more flexible in agreeing to a number of changes in work arrangements.

Job Security

One method of seeking job security is through *seniority rules* that require employers to lay off and to rehire on the basis of years of service. This protects existing workers, and many unions have been willing to accept lower wages in order to build seniority provisions into their contracts.

A second method of seeking job security is to resist the introduction of labor-saving innovations. During a period of heavy unemployment, the installation of a labor-saving machine in a factory is likely to mean unemployment for those whose jobs are lost by the change. It is little wonder that during and after the Great Depression, new machines were opposed bitterly and that job-saving restrictive practices were adhered to with tenacity.

In the long run, however, this strategy would not work. Mechanization increases productivity and consequently the wages and profits that are earned. After World War II, the attitude of many unions slowly changed from one of resisting technological change to one of embracing it and trying to reduce some of its costs to individuals who would be adversely affected by it.

The 1980s saw a major change in union attitudes toward job security. Many of the current generation of leaders see the increased efficiency of Japanese, Korean, and German firms, rather than the increased mechanization of their own employers, as the principal threat to union workers' jobs. Improving the ability of North American employers to compete with foreign firms is now one way in which unions attempt to increase job security for their members.

Canadian unions have not always followed the Americans in these ways. They have sometimes put their reliance in traditional modes of behavior and have regarded flexible approaches to industries by foreign competition as unacceptable.

Fringe Benefits

Indirect or **fringe benefits**, such as company contributions to union pension and welfare funds, sick leave, and vacation pay, as well as required payments toward social insurance and unemployment compensation, are estimated to make up almost one-third of the total compensation of industrial workers. Why do unions and employers not simply agree to a wage and let it go at that? Why should an employed automobile worker who earns $40,000 cost the company $60,000?

Fringe benefits appeal to employees in part because they are often not subject to income taxes. Pension funds and medical benefits let employees provide for their future and that of their families more cheaply than they could by purchasing them privately, and these benefits often protect them even when they lose their jobs. A package that includes high wages and job security for the employed and unemployment benefits for those squeezed out by high wages appeal to union leaders because it provides something for everyone.

The use of fringe benefits also offers some advantages to employers. For example, pension funds tend to bind the worker more closely to the company, thereby decreasing the turnover rate among employees. If employees stand to lose part of their benefits by changing jobs, they will not be so ready to move.

Two-Tier Pricing

A recent U.S. innovation that is designed to resolve the wage-employment dilemma for the present generation of union members is called *two-tier pricing*. The objective of a two-tier wage structure is to protect the high wages of existing employees who have seniority in their unions but at the same time to permit employers to lower their labor costs by hiring new workers on a lower wage scale. This benefits the union—so goes the argument—because it ensures a flow of new members who would otherwise not be hired. It benefits new employees *if* they would not otherwise have been hired, and it does not hurt existing union members. In many cases, however, two-tier pricing has led to significant friction between workers in the two tiers. It also encourages management to replace old workers with new ones.

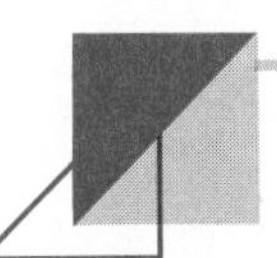

Discrimination in Labor Markets

There have been, and continue to be, large differences between the earnings of women and men. If we create an index of median wage and salary earnings with males equal to 100, females equal about 65. These disparities in earnings have multiple causes, but they raise a concern about the existence of labor market discrimination and the extent to which discriminatory employment practices give rise to the differences in earnings.

The economic effects of discrimination against minorities and women take many forms. Labor market discrimination does not wholly explain, but surely contributes to, lower wages and higher unemployment rates for those discriminated against. Both lower wages and greater unemployment lead to lower incomes for the workers involved.

Discrimination may also have powerful indirect effects on attitudes toward the workplace and toward society. It affects not only the workers discriminated against but also their children, whose ability, aspirations, and willingness to undertake the education or training required to succeed may be adversely affected. Indeed, it may change their definition of success. There are many subtle ways in which discrimination can become part of the way in which a society functions, and these can be as important in their effects as overt (and now generally illegal) direct discrimination.

A Model of Labor Market Discrimination

To isolate the effects of discrimination, we begin by building a simplified picture of a nondiscriminating labor market, and then we introduce discrimination between two sets of workers who are in every sense equally qualified. We phrase our discussion in terms of male versus female, but it applies equally to any form of discrimination in labor markets.

Suppose there are two groups of equal size in a society. One is male; the other, female. Each group has the same proportion who are educated to various levels, each has identical distributions of talent, and so on. Suppose also that there are two occupations. Occupation E (for elite) requires people of above average education and skills, and occupation O (for ordinary) can use anyone, but if wages in the two occupations are the same, employers in occupation O will prefer to hire above average workers. There is no discrimination, and the nonmonetary advantages of the two occupations are equal.

The competitive theory of distribution suggests that the wages in E occupations will be bid up slightly above those in O occupations in order that the E jobs attract the workers of above average skills. Men and women of above average skill will flock to E jobs, while the others, male and female alike, will have no choice but to seek O jobs. Because skills are equally distributed, each occupation will have half male and half female workers.

Now we introduce discrimination in its most extreme form. All E occupations are hereafter open only to males; all O occupations are open to either males or females. The immediate effect is to reduce by 50 percent the supply of job applicants for E occupations (applicants must be *both* male and above average) and, potentially, to increase by 50 percent the supply of applicants for O jobs (this group includes all women and the below average men).

Wage Level Effects

Suppose that labor is perfectly mobile among occupations, that everyone seeks the best job that he or she is eligible for, and that wage rates are free to vary so as to equate supply and demand. The analysis is shown in Figure 19-4. Wages rise in E occupations and fall in O occupations. The take-home pay of those in O occupations falls, and the O group is now approximately two-thirds female.

Discrimination, by changing supply, can decrease the wages and incomes of a group that is discriminated against.

In the longer run, further changes may occur. Notice that total employment in the E industries falls. Employers may find ways to use slightly below

FIGURE 19-4 Economic Discrimination: Wage Level Effects

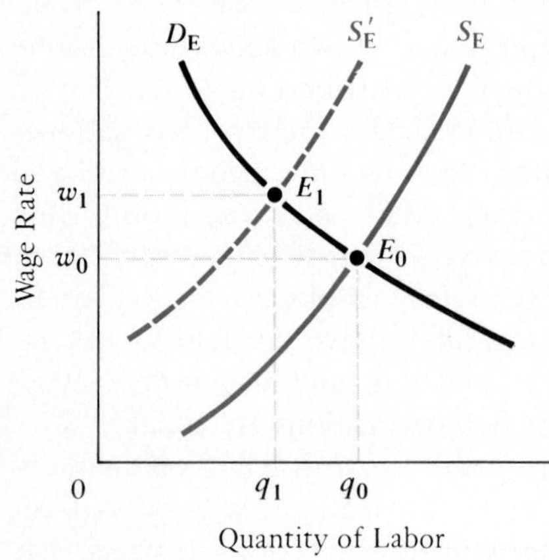

(i) Elite market (E)

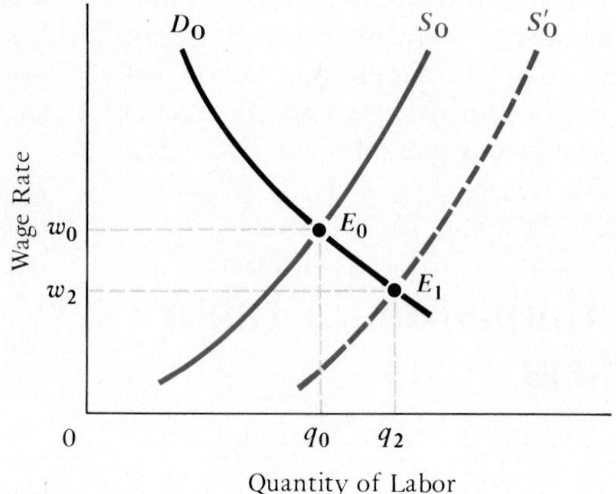

(ii) Ordinary market (O)

If market E discriminates against one group and market O does not, the supply curve will shift to the left in E and to the right in O. Market E requires above average skills, while market O requires only ordinary skills. When there is no discrimination, demand and supply are D_E and S_E, respectively, in market E and D_O and S_O in market O. Initially, the wage rate is represented by w_0 and employment by q_0 in each market. (The actual wage in market E will be slightly higher than the wage in market O.) When all females are barred from E occupations, the supply curve shifts to S'_E, and the wage earned by the remaining workers, all of whom are males, rises to w_1. Females put out of work in the E occupation now seek work in the O occupation. The resulting shift in the supply curve to S'_O brings down the wage to w_2 in the O occupations. Since all females are in O occupations, they have a lower wage rate than many males. The average male wage is higher than the average female wage.

average labor and thus lure the next best qualified males out of O occupations. This will raise O wages slightly, but it will also make these occupations increasingly "female occupations." If discrimination has been in effect for a sufficient length of time, females will learn that it does not pay to acquire above average skills. Regardless of ability, females are forced by discrimination to work in unskilled jobs.

Now suppose that a long-standing discriminatory policy is reversed. Because they will have responded to discrimination by acquiring fewer skills than males, many females will be locked into O occupations, at least for a time. Moreover, if both males and females come to expect that females will have less education than males, employers will tend to look for males to fill the E jobs. This will reinforce the belief of females that education does not pay. This, and other kinds of subtle discrimination, can persist for a very long time, making the supply of females to O jobs higher than it would be in the absence of discrimination, thus depressing the wages of females.

Discrimination in competitive labor markets. We have seen that in the absence of discrimination, competitive markets will tend to equalize the wages of the two groups. Some economists go further than this and argue that in equilibrium, discrimination cannot be sustained. This theory, propounded by Professors Gary Becker of the University of Chicago and Thomas Sowell of the Hoover Institution, works like this: Employers of workers in E jobs who pay high wages (w_1) can increase their profits if they hire qualified females at any lower wage. If females have the same distribution of qualifications as males, under discrimination there will be plenty of workers who will be willing to work in E jobs at any wage that is greater then the low wage level in the O market (w_2)—much less than the going wage for males. If some employers take advantage of this opportunity, there will be competitive pressure that, all other things being equal, works against the maintenance of discrimination. As firms that hire qualified females at wages below w_1 (but above w_2) earn profits, they will grow, and other firms will have to imitate them or go out of business. Eventually, the discrimination will disappear in competitive equilibrium.

This theory shows the important pressures that act against discrimination in competitive markets. The idea, however, that competitive equilibrium is completely inconsistent with the practice of discrimination fails to take into account a number of important phenomena. One of these is the indirect effect of discrimination on both the acquisition of skill and on the expectations of employers. Further, the taste for discrimination, presumably arising in part from a dislike of females on the part of males, will inhibit at least some firms from maximizing profits if doing so requires breaking social norms that reinforce discrimination. It is also possible that tastes for discrimination will have direct market effects. For example, consumers who dislike females may refrain from buying the products of firms that employ females in E occupations; prejudiced workers may be less productive if females are treated as equal in the workplace. In any event, the history of both race and sex discrimination in the North American economy suggests that whatever competitive forces do work against discrimination, they are not strong enough to *eliminate* it. In *Understanding the Gender Gap*, Professor Claudia Goldin notes, for example, that never in U.S. history has an all-female firm been established in a male-intensive industry.

Employment Effects

For a number of reasons, labor market discrimination may have adverse employment effects that are even more important than effects on wage levels. Labor is not perfectly mobile, wages are not perfectly flexible downward, and not everyone who is denied employment in an E occupation for which he or she is trained and qualified will be willing to take a "demeaning" O job. We continue the graphical example in Figure 19-5.

If wages do not fall to the market-clearing level, possibly because of minimum wage laws, the increase in supply of labor to O occupations will cause excess supply, which will result in unemployment in O occupations. Since females dominate these occupations, they will bear the brunt of the extra unemployment, as illustrated in Figure 19-5(i).

A similar result will occur if labor is not fully mobile between occupations. For example, many of the O occupation jobs might be in places to which the females are unable or unwilling to move. See Figure 19-5(ii). Potential O workers who cannot move to places where jobs are available become unemployed or withdraw from the labor force. Quite apart from any discrimination, long-term technological changes tend to decrease the demand for less skilled labor of the kind that is required in O occupations. Occupation O then becomes increasingly oversupplied. This possibility is outlined in Figure 19-5(iii).

The kind of discrimination that we have considered in our model is extreme. It is similar to the South African apartheid system, in which blacks are excluded by law from prestigious and high-paying occupations. In North America, labor market discrimination against a particular group usually occurs in somewhat less obvious ways. First, it may be difficult (but not impossible, as in our model) for members of the group to get employment in certain jobs. Second, members of groups subject to discrimination may receive lower pay for a given kind of work than members of groups not subject to discrimination.

Indeed, the first type of discrimination may encourage the second type! How might this happen? First, if discrimination makes it difficult for a qualified person to get a good job, she may be more willing to accept such a job even if the pay and working conditions are poorer than those given to others in the same job. Even under relatively unfavorable terms, the job will still be better than the alternative (an O job). Second, employers who are seeking to fill E jobs and who have no taste for discrimination nonetheless will be able to hire qualified females at wages that, although higher than O wages, are lower than E wages. As long as there is some discrimination of the first type (in the extreme, apartheid), there will be pressures coming from both the supply and the demand sides of the labor market for discrimination of the second type.

In the long term, these unemployment effects

FIGURE 19-5 Economic Discrimination: Employment Effects

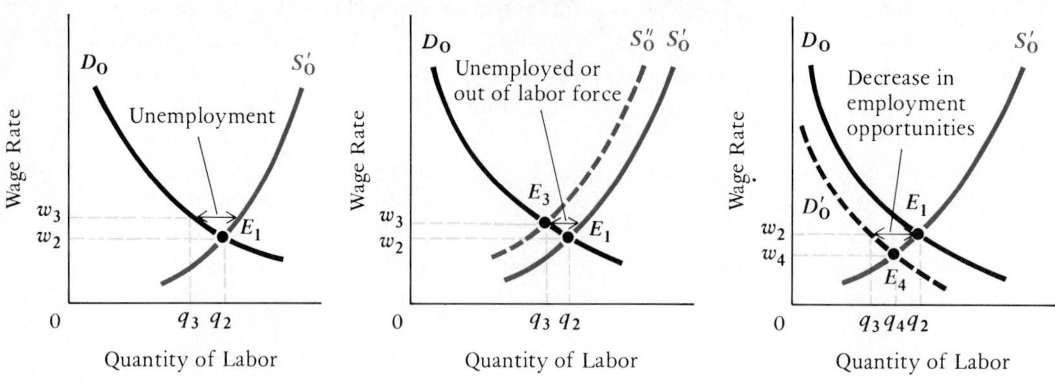

(i) Wage rigidities (or minimum wage)

(ii) Immobile labor (or withdrawal from labor force)

(iii) Declining demand

Increasing supply or decreasing demand in occupations in which those discriminated against are the major sources of labor can increase unemployment. In each part of the figure, the curves D_O and S'_O are those from Figure 19-4(ii); they show the market for O workers after the discriminatory policies are put into effect. Equilibrium is at E_1. In each case, the wage w_2 would clear the market and provide employment of q_2.

(i) If the wage rate cannot fall below w_3, perhaps because of a miniumum wage law, employment will fall to q_3, and unemployment will occur in the amount shown by the arrows.

(ii) If some of the potential workers in O occupations are unable or unwilling to take employment in O jobs, the supply curve will not be S'_O but S''_O. Equilibrium will be at E_3. Though O wages will rise somewhat to w_3, employment will be only q_3, and a number of workers, shown by the arrows, will not be employed. Whether they are recorded as unemployed or as having withdrawn from the labor force will depend on the official definitions.

(iii) If demand is declining in O occupations over time, say, from D_O to D'_O, either wages and employment will fall to the new equilibrium E_4 with w_4 and q_4, or wages will be maintained but employment will fall to q_3. The arrows illustrate the latter case, where the fall in employment is q_3q_2.

may be increased by sociological and economic forces. Female children of women who are discriminated against may take as role models women who have made a life outside the labor force. Technological changes in the economy tend to decrease the demand for less skilled labor of the kind required in O occupations, which become increasingly oversupplied. This possibility is sketched in Figure 19-5(iii).

These theoretical possibilities have their counterparts in the real world. We shall discuss them briefly.

Female-Male Differentials

Although high unemployment is often a feature of labor market discrimination, it is not the key to female/male differentials. The labor force participation of women doubled from 28 percent in 1956 to over 56 percent in 1988. This occurred without any increase in the unemployment rate of females, which is approximately equal to that of males.

Getting jobs is, of course, not the whole story. It has long been clear that women and men make, and are offered, different occupational choices. But even here there is notable progress. Over the past two decades, women have steadily increased their participation in supposedly higher-status occupations, including managerial, sales, scientific, and technical jobs. For example, in 1966 women accounted for 16 percent of the professional labor force; by 1985 that figure had risen significantly.

Despite these rather dramatic changes, average earned income of females in the labor force is well below that of males of similar ages. The female-to-male earnings ratio has narrowed slightly from approximately 0.59 in 1960 to about 0.65 in 1990. The persistence of the remaining "salary gap" for females is due to a combination of causes: Women are still underrepresented in high-status occupations, proportionately fewer women than men reach higher-paying jobs in the occupations in which both work, and those who do reach higher-paying jobs do so more slowly. Do these facts reflect discrimination?

Discrimination within occupations. To what extent do differences in pay levels of men and women *within* an occupation reflect direct discrimination against women, and to what extent do they reflect other sex-linked characteristics, the most important of which is the persistent difference in lifetime patterns of labor force participation? The evidence shows that, on average, women have fewer years of work experience than men of the same age. The average working female is less mobile occupationally and geographically than her male counterpart. These facts reflect, at least in part, *labor market attachment*. For example, many women withdraw from the labor force or work only part-time in order to have and raise children.

The causes of gender differences in labor market attachment have attracted attention from both social psychologists and economists. There is ample evidence that *sex-role socialization* is an important factor. To the extent that women and men are socialized to accept the view that women should be the primary caretakers of young children, some social scientists argue that differences in labor market attachment arise from a form of indirect discrimination. However important this may be, it arises from differences in the way in which boys and girls are raised, not from the direct behavior of the labor market.

The extent of direct discrimination in an occupation may be measured by comparing the pay status of groups with similar characteristics. Professors Mary Corcoran and Greg Duncan analyzed pay differences between men and women in the United States and found that less than half (44 percent) of the differences could be explained by differences in education, work experience, and labor market attachment. Other studies show much the same thing and conclude that from 10 to 25 percent of the pay differences are *not* explained by these variables.[6] Analysts attribute this part of male-female pay differentials to direct discrimination.

Interoccupational discrimination. Women may tend to be employed in a different set of occupations from men. They have been refused admission, or have been discouraged from seeking entry into, certain occupations; for example, traditionally they have been urged into nursing rather than medicine, social work rather than law, and secretarial schools rather than managerial training programs. The result of this is called *occupational segregation*. Similarly, girls who have been raised in a culture in which their education seems less important than that of their brothers or in which they are trained to think of themselves as potential homemakers are less likely to acquire the skills for many high-paying occupations that are wholly within their capabilities. This is a form of sex-role socialization.

Differences in pay among occupations reflect, as we have seen, differences in supply and demand, including nonmonetary factors. Might they not also reflect discrimination, if one occupation is predominantly female and the other predominantly male? This is certainly possible, and a number of studies have shown that such an effect exists; that is, if one uses the characteristics of workers (education, training, experience, etc.) to explain their wages, the fraction of female workers in the occupation has a significant negative effect. Moreover, this effect exists for both men and women. Men (and women) who work in predominantly female occupations are paid less than men (and women) with the same training and experience in predominantly male occupations. For this reason, many have urged that attention be paid to interoccupational pay differences under the general term *pay equity*. Determining how much observed differences reflect discrimination is extremely difficult, because so many different considerations affect the pay levels of, say, firefighters and librarians.

Government Policies to Redress Discrimination

Governments have long had policies to eliminate discrimination between men and women doing the

[6] Much of this literature is summarized in University of Toronto economist Morley Gunderson's "Male-Female Wage Differentials and Policy Responses," *Journal of Economic Literature* 27 (1989): 46–72.

same job. These policies are relatively easy to administer. They require that a man and a woman doing a job with the same job description must receive the same pay.

A much harder case arises when an attempt is made to remove alleged discrimination between jobs. If one job is staffed primarily with women and another primarily with men, do differences between the wages paid in the two jobs represent differences in market conditions, or are they due to discrimination?

There is no doubt that some discrimination does occur. For example, psychologists have conducted many studies that suggest a bias against women that could easily lead to discriminatory pay differences. In one experiment, department heads were given identical files, one with a male name and the other with a female name. They were 10 percent more likely to select the male for a job offer than the female with the identical résumé. In another experiment, female college students were asked to rank paintings on a scale from 1 to 10. The same picture consistently got a higher rating when it had a male name attached than when it was ascribed to a female artist.

Most empirical studies of male-female wage differentials show that much of the differences between jobs is due to differences in such objective factors as educational requirements and years of experience in the work force and on the job. When all such factors have been allowed for, however, there remains a residual that is consistent with some direct sex discrimination.

Much of the persistence of male-female pay differentials results from wages in male-dominated occupations exceeding those in female-dominated ones. As a result, the federal government and many of the provinces have enacted legislation that mandates wage adjustments to eliminate disparities between jobs of "comparable worth" or "equal value." Initially such policies applied only to public-sector employment, but in 1987, pay equity legislation in Ontario expanded the coverage to the private sector as well.[7]

Comparable worth policy relies on a job evaluation program that measures the *intrinsic* value of different occupations. In practice, this involves assigning "worth points" to various attributes of a given job (typically effort, initiative, skill, training, responsibility, and conditions of work). These points can then be summed to obtain a "total job score"; comparing scores for different jobs allows a comparison of their intrinsic values. Pay equity requires that two jobs of equal value receive equal pay.

Needless to say, pay equity policies have been very controversial. Supporters argue that they do not go far enough and that significant differentials will persist even after full implementation. Many critics argue that the evaluation schemes are often arbitrary and always imperfect. Simple schemes are easy to administer but give poorer results; more complex schemes are, in principle, more accurate but harder to administer. Implementation problems such as definition of an establishment, determination of criteria to include in the evaluation program and the weights to assign to them, and definition of gender dominance plague most schemes currently in place.

Economists are often concerned that the policies fail to distinguish between equilibrium and disequilibrium differentials as stressed throughout this discussion. They fear that misguided attempts to eliminate equilibrium differentials will lead to the emergence of excess demand in some occupations and excess supply in others, with associated efficiency costs for the economy. This issue is taken up further in Box 19-3.

Supporters of pay equity policy often argue that job evaluation and comparison play an important role in any big firm's employment policy, implicitly and often explicitly. Hence, they argue, pay equity legislation merely formalizes in the law procedures that already play an important role in labor markets. Economists point out, however, that market-oriented job evaluation policies, whether explicit or implicit, have the major advantage of reacting quickly to market forces. Such evaluations are only a guideline to determining wages. If changes occur to make previously determined evaluations no longer consistent with market balance and surpluses or shortages arise, firms will respond quickly by altering their guidelines and changing relative wages. Legislated comparisons determining wages may cause shortages or surpluses to persist for long periods of time. This too is illustrated in Box 19-3.

A preliminary assessment of pay equity legislation in Canada has recently been put forward by

[7] As of mid 1990, the Ontario legislation applied only to within-firm comparisons in the private sector, and individual firms were given considerable freedom to design their own evaluation schemes.

BOX 19-3

Pay Equity and Equilibrium Differentials

When pay equity legislation serves to eliminate wage differentials that arose due to pure discrimination, they do not cause any economic problems as "side effects." Indeed, they serve to improve economic efficiency. However, problems can arise when such laws are imposed on a situation where the original wage differential reflects what we have earlier called *equilibrium differentials*—differences due to nonmonetary advantages or job requirements that imply that demand and supply can be balanced in two jobs only when their wages are unequal.

Suppose that two groups of city employees, call them librarians and firefighters, have the supply and demand curves shown here. In competitive equilibrium, librarians would earn a wage of w_1 and firefighters, w_2; that is, there is an equilibrium differential in the market-clearing wages. Now, as a result of a comparable worth study, the city is ordered to pay equal wages to the two groups.

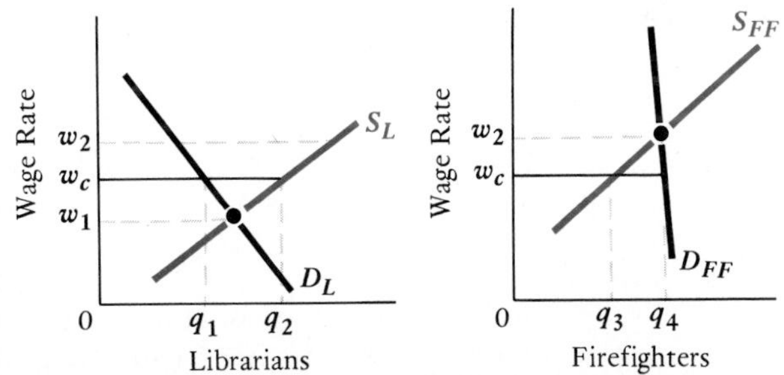

The mayor proposes to comply by paying both groups a compromise wage, w_c, somewhat higher than the wage librarians have been receiving but lower than that of firefighters. Librarians are pleased, and, indeed, the mayor begins to get extra applications from persons who seek to be librarians once the new wage goes into effect. (There is an excess supply of librarians, q_1q_2, at w_c.) But the head of the Firefighters' Union is burned up: "You can't cut our pay. We'll quit." Indeed, some of the firefighters do quit. (At wage w_c, there is an excess demand of q_3q_4.) The fire chief warns the mayor that he won't be able to fill the firehouse or meet all the calls for putting out fires. The mayor decides to go back to the court with her dilemma. The judge is unsympathetic: "All your problems come from the proposed cut in firefighters' pay. You may pay anything you like to firefighters; just be sure to pay the librarians the same."

The mayor then tells the state compensation director that he should raise librarians' pay to w_2, the firefighters' competitive rate.

In order to meet the extra wage bill, the city council orders libraries closed two days a week and lays off some librarians. The firefighters do not complain, but the laid-off librarians do, and so do the citizens, who want the libraries open on Fridays and Saturdays. Meanwhile, the head of libraries is besieged with applications for the newly attractive library jobs.

Professor Roberta Robb of Brock University.[8] She identifies three potential costs: economic efficiency losses (including allocation distortions and implementation costs), private costs of employers (including higher wages for some female employees and administration costs), and private costs of employees (including adverse employment effects for females as illustrated in Box 19-3). Potential benefits include increased productivity of females (resulting from the incentive effects of increased earnings) and a reduced male-female wage differential. The latter is viewed as an objective in its own right, and it has been suggested that current legislation may succeed in reducing the differential from its current 40 percent to 25 percent.

Is pay equity "progressive pragmatism," as one

[8] "The Costs and Benefits of Canadian Pay Equity Policy" in *Pay Equity Legislation*, ed. Richard Chaykowski (Kingston, Ont.: Queen's University Industrial Relations Centre, 1990).

supporter put it, or is it "a profoundly flawed concept," as a critic pronounced? The answer will depend on the magnitude of the resource misallocation caused by setting relative wages through a system that does not attempt to balance demand and supply and on one's view of whether this lost efficiency is a price worth paying in the name of equity. As Robb concludes, "This kind of legislation is likely to have a very significant impact on individual perceptions of what women's jobs are worth. This result is clearly important if one believes that part of the role of this policy is to break the cycle of systematically undervaluing women's jobs."

Who Loses from Discrimination?

Obviously, the victims lose as a result of labor market discrimination, but it is a mistake to think that they are the only losers. Society loses, too, because of the losses in efficiency that discrimination causes and in other ways.

Efficiency losses arise for several reasons. If females and males are not given equal pay for equal work, the labor force will not be allocated so as to get the most out of society's resources. When people are kept from doing the jobs at which they are most productive and must instead produce goods or services that society values less, the total value of goods and services produced is reduced. More obviously, when prejudice increases unemployment, it reduces the nation's total output.

The gainers from discrimination are those who earn the higher pay that comes from limiting the supply of jobs in their occupations, those who get the jobs that others might have held, and the bigots who gain pleasure from not having to work with or consume services provided by members of the discriminated-against group. But if the total output of society is less, the net losses will be borne by the society as a whole.

Beyond the efficiency losses that discrimination imposes on society are further economic and social costs. Increased welfare or unemployment payments may be required, and the costs of enforcing antidiscrimination laws must be paid.

The costs of discrimination also include increased crime, hostility, and violence. These things are all by-products of unemployment, poverty, and frustration. Discrimination, if it is not attacked and rolled back, has one more cost, perhaps the most important: a sense of shame in a society that does not do what is necessary to eliminate the barriers to equal treatment.

SUMMARY

1. In a competitive labor market, wages are set by the forces of supply and demand. Differences in wages will arise because some skills are more valued than others and because some jobs are more onerous than others.
2. A union entering a competitive market can raise wages, but only at the cost of reducing employment and creating a pool of unemployed who would like to work at the going wage but are unable to gain employment in that market.
3. If the union can limit entry into the field, it can shift the supply curve to the left and achieve a higher wage without creating unemployment in the occupation.
4. A union entering a monopsonistic market may increase both employment and wages over some range. If, however, it sets the wage above the competitive level, it will create a pool of workers who are unable to get the jobs that they want at the going wage.
5. Governments set some wages above their competitive levels by passing minimum wage laws. The overall effects of minimum wages have now been studied extensively. It is clear that they raise the incomes of many employees, but they cause unemployment for some of those with the lowest levels of skills.
6. Labor markets have developed a wide variety of institutions, including labor unions and employers' associations. Such institutions greatly affect wage determination.

7. North American unionism developed first in the skilled trades, along craft lines, where it was possible to control supply and prevent non-union members from undercutting union wages. Widespread organization of the unskilled did not occur until later. The emergence of mature collective bargaining is a relatively recent development in the stormy history of North American labor unions.
8. Unions face a basic conflict between the goals of raising wages and preserving employment opportunities for members and potential members. Other trade-offs concern wages and job security, and wages and fringe benefits.
9. Discrimination has played a role in labor markets. Direct discrimination affects wages and employment opportunities in part by limiting labor supply in the best-paying occupations and by increasing it in less attractive occupations.
10. Indirect discrimination has had an effect through limiting the opportunities for education and training available to those who are subject to discrimination and through lowering people's career aspirations.
11. Discrimination imposes costs on the victims of discrimination. In addition, it leads to inefficiency and loss of output and is costly in other ways.

TOPICS FOR REVIEW

Competitive wage differences
Monopsony power
Power of unions
Effects of minimum wages
Collective bargaining
Goals of unions
Labor market attachment
Effects of economic discrimination on wages and employment
Direct and indirect discrimination
Pay equity

DISCUSSION QUESTIONS

1. A union that has bargaining rights in two plants of the same company in different provinces may insist on "equal pay for equal work" in the two plants, but not on equal pay for men and women in the same jobs. Can you see any economic reasons for such a distinction?
2. U.S. unions have traditionally supported laws restricting immigration, expelling illegal aliens, and raising the minimum wage and extending its coverage. How do each of these positions benefit or hurt the following groups: (a) consumers, (b) workers as a whole, (c) unionized workers with seniority in their jobs?
3. One critic of pay equity legislation argues that it leads to distortions because it confuses "value determined at the *margin* by supply and demand" with a "job evaluator's concept of the *average* value of the inputs required to do the job." Reread the discussion of the paradox of value in Chapter 8, and then comment on this criticism.
4. "The great increase in the number of women entering the labor force for the first time means that relatively more women than men earn beginning salaries. It is therefore not evidence of discrimination that the average wage earned by females is less than that earned by males." Discuss.

5. The American Cyanamid Corporation once had a policy of removing women of child bearing age from, or not hiring them for, jobs that expose them to lead or other substances that could damage a fetus. Is this sex discrimination? Whether it is or is not, debate whether this sort of protective hiring rule is something that the government should require, encourage, or prohibit.
6. "One can judge the presence or absence of discrimination by looking at the proportion of the population in different occupations." Does such information help? Does it suffice? Consider each of the following examples. Relative to their numbers in the total population, there are
   a. Too many blacks and too few Jews among professional athletes
   b. Too few male secretaries
   c. Too few female judges
7. Consider the consequences of applying the notion of equal pay for work of equal value to compensation of:
   a. Football coaches and cross-country coaches
   b. University presidents and network anchors
   c. Fashion models and poets
   d. Police in large cities and police in small towns
8. Compare the following policies designed to reduce pay differentials due to occupational segregation of women in lower-paying jobs.
   a. Making pay adjustments based on an analysis of the purported comparable worth of occupations
   b. Removing barriers to women's employment in traditionally male jobs
   c. Setting quotas based on the relevant population statistics for minimum fractions of females in each occupation
9. Actuaries are among the highest-paid people of all professionals. According to *Forbes* magazine, "The biggest drag on finding new actuaries is the rarefied mathematical talents the job requires. Like fiction writing or figure skating, this is a profession you join not for the money but because you love the work." Compare the market for actuaries with that for insurance agents. How do demand and supply conditions differ? What might account for the high salaries of actuaries?
10. According to *Fortune* magazine, the Vatican doubled its spending between 1981 and 1986. "In the 1960s and 1970s a docile non-union work force settled for low wages and . . . members of the clergy earned less than lay employees. . . . Some 1700 of the Holy See's 2300 employees are members of the clergy." In 1980, lay workers threatened to strike over the right to unionize, and by 1985, members of the clergy were receiving equal pay.
    a. How might the change in compensation have been a response to the supply of clergy (priests and nuns)?
    b. Now that clergy earn the same as lay workers, what would you expect to happen to the composition of the work force at the Vatican?
    c. Would you expect the Vatican to employ inputs in the same way as a profit-maximizing firm? Why or why not?

PART 6

INTER-NATIONAL TRADE

Chapter 20

The Gains from Trade

Canadians buy Volkswagens, Germans take holidays in Italy, Italians buy spices from Tanzania, Africans import oil from Saudi Arabia, Arabs buy Japanese cameras, and the Japanese buy Canadian lumber. *International trade* refers to exchanges of goods and services that take place across international boundaries.

The founders of modern economics were concerned with international trade problems. The great eighteenth century British philosopher and economist David Hume, one of the first to work out the theory of the price system as a control mechanism, developed his concepts mainly in terms of prices in foreign trade. Adam Smith in *The Wealth of Nations* attacked government restriction of trade. David Ricardo in 1817 developed the basic theory of the gains from trade that is studied in this chapter. The repeal of the Corn Laws—tariffs on the importation of grains into Great Britain—and the transformation of that country during the nineteenth century from a country of high tariffs to one of completely free trade were, to a significant extent, the result of agitation by economists whose theories of the gains from trade led them to condemn tariffs.

In this chapter we explore the fundamental question of what is gained by international trade; in Chapter 21 we will deal with the pros and cons of interfering with the free flow of such trade.

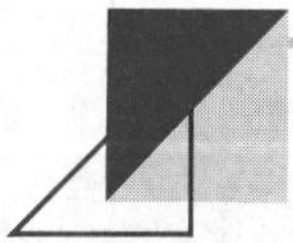

Sources of the Gains from Trade

The increased output realized as a result of trade is called the **gains from trade**. The source of such gains is most easily visualized by considering the differences between a world with trade and a world without it. Although politicians often regard foreign trade differently from domestic trade, economists from Adam Smith on have argued that the causes and consequences of international trade are simply an extension of the principles governing domestic trade. What is the advantage of trade among individuals, among groups, among regions, or among countries?

Interpersonal, Interregional, and International Trade

Consider trade among individuals. Without trade, each person would have to be self-sufficient; each would have to produce all the food, clothing, shelter, medical services, entertainment, and luxuries that he or she consumed. A world of individual self-sufficiency would be a world with extremely low living standards.

Trade among individuals allows them to specialize in activities that they can do well and to buy from others the goods and services that they cannot easily produce. A good doctor who is a bad carpenter can provide medical services not only for her own family but also for an excellent carpenter who does not possess either the training or the ability to practice medicine. Thus trade and specialization are intimately connected. Without trade, individuals must be self-sufficient. With trade, individuals can specialize in what they do well and satisfy other needs by trading.

The same principles apply to regions. Without interregional trade, each region would be forced to be self-sufficient. With trade, each region can specialize in producing commodities for which it has some natural or acquired advantage. Plains regions can specialize in growing grain, mountain regions can specialize in mining and forest products, regions with abundant power can specialize in heavy manufacturing, and regions with highly skilled labor can specialize in knowledge-intensive, high-tech goods. Cool regions can produce wheat and other crops that thrive in temperate climates, and hot regions can grow such tropical crops as bananas, sugar, and coffee. The living standards of the inhabitants of all regions will be higher when each region specializes in products in which it has some natural or acquired advantage and obtains other products by trade than when all regions seek to be self-sufficient.

The same principle also applies to nations. A national boundary seldom delimits an area that is naturally self-sufficient. Nations, like regions or persons, can gain from specialization and from the international trade that must accompany it. Specialization means that each country produces more of some goods than its residents wish to consume and less of others.

International trade is necessary to achieve the gains that international specialization makes possible.

This discussion suggests one important possible gain from trade:

With trade, each individual, region, or nation is able to concentrate on producing goods and services that it produces efficiently while trading to obtain goods and services that it does not produce.

Specialization and trade go hand in hand because there is no motivation to achieve the gains from specialization without being able to trade the goods that are produced for goods that are desired. Economists use the term *gains from trade* to embrace the results of both.

We shall examine two sources of the gains from trade. The first source consists of differences among regions of the world in climate and resource endowment that lead to advantages in producing certain goods and disadvantages in producing others. These gains occur even though each country's costs of production are unchanged by the existence of trade. The second source is the reduction in each country's costs of production that results from the greater scale of production that specialization brings.

Gains from Trade with Given Costs

In order to focus on differences in countries' conditions of production, suppose that there are no advantages arising from either economies of large-scale production or cost reductions that are the consequence of learning new skills. In these circumstances, what leads to gains from trade? To examine this question, we use an example involving only two countries and two products, but the general principles apply as well to the cases of many countries and many commodities.

A Special Case: Absolute Advantage

The gains from trade are clear when there is a simple situation involving absolute advantage. **Absolute advantage** concerns the quantities of a single product that can be produced using the same quantity of resources in two different regions. One region is said to have an absolute advantage over another in the production of commodity X when an equal quantity of resources can produce more X in the first region than in the second.

Suppose that region A has an absolute advantage over B in one commodity and that region B has an absolute advantage over A in another. This is a case of *reciprocal absolute advantage*: Each country has an absolute advantage in some commodity. In such a situation, the total production of both regions can be increased (relative to a situation of self-sufficiency) if each specializes in the commodity in which it has the absolute advantage.

Table 20-1 provides a simple example. Total

TABLE 20-1 Gains from Specialization with Absolute Advantage

A. Amounts of wheat and cloth that can be produced with one unit of resources in Canada and England

	Wheat (bushels)	Cloth (yards)
Canada	10	6
England	5	10

B. Changes resulting from the transfer of one unit of Canadian resources into wheat and one unit of English resources into cloth

	Wheat (bushels)	Cloth (yards)
Canada	+10	− 6
England	− 5	+10
World	+ 5	+ 4

When there is a reciprocal absolute advantage, specialization makes it possible to produce more of both commodities. Part A shows the production of wheat and cloth that can be achieved in each country by using one unit of resources. Canada can produce 10 bushels of wheat or 6 yards of cloth; England can produce 5 bushels of wheat or 10 yards of cloth. Canada has an absolute advantage in producing wheat, England in producing cloth. Part B shows the changes in production caused by moving one unit of resources out of cloth and into wheat production in Canada and moving one unit of resources in the opposite direction in England. There is an increase in world production of 5 bushels of wheat and 4 yards of cloth; worldwide, there are gains from specialization. In this example, the more resources transferred into wheat production in Canada and cloth production in England, the larger the gains.

world production of both wheat and cloth increases when each country produces more of the good in which it has an absolute advantage. A rise in the production of all commodities entails a rise in average living standards.

The gains from specialization make the gains from trade possible. When specialization occurs, England produces more cloth and Canada more wheat than if they were self-sufficient. Canada is producing more wheat and less cloth than Canadian consumers wish to buy, and England is producing more cloth and less wheat than English consumers wish to buy. If consumers in both countries are to get cloth and wheat in the desired proportions, Canada must export wheat to England and import cloth from England.

A First General Statement: Comparative Advantage

When each country has an absolute advantage over the other in the production of one commodity, the gains from trade are obvious. What, however, if Canada can produce both wheat and cloth more efficiently than England? In essence this was David Ricardo's question, posed over 170 years ago. His answer underlies the theory of comparative advantage and is still accepted by economists as a valid statement of the potential gains from trade.

To start with, assume that Canadian efficiency increases tenfold above the levels recorded in the example, so that one unit of Canadian resources can produce either 100 bushels of wheat or 60 yards of cloth. English efficiency remains unchanged (see Table 20-2). It might appear that Canada, which is now better at producing both wheat and cloth than England, has nothing to gain by trading with such an inefficient foreign country, but it *does* have something to gain, as shown in Table 20-2. Even though Canada is 10 times as efficient as in the situation of Table 20-1, it is still possible to increase world production of both wheat and cloth by having Canada produce more wheat and less cloth and by having England produce more cloth and less wheat.

What is the source of this gain? Although Canada has an *absolute* advantage over England in the production of both wheat and cloth, the *margin* of advantage differs in the two commodities. Canada can produce 20 times as much wheat as England by using the same quantity of resources, but only 6 times as much cloth. Canada is said to have a **comparative advantage** in the production of wheat and a comparative disadvantage in the production of cloth. (This statement implies another: England has a comparative disadvantage in the production of wheat, in which it is one-twentieth as efficient as Canada, and a comparative advantage in the production of cloth, in which it is only one-sixth as efficient.)

A key proposition in the theory of international trade is this:

The gains from trade depend on the pattern of comparative, not absolute, advantage.

TABLE 20-2 Gains from Specialization with Comparative Advantage

A. Amounts of wheat and cloth that can be produced with one unit of resources in Canada and England

	Wheat (bushels)	Cloth (yards)
Canada	100	60
England	5	10

B. Changes resulting from the transfer of one-tenth of one unit of Canadian resources into wheat and one unit of English resources into cloth

	Wheat (bushels)	Cloth (yards)
Canada	+10	− 6
England	− 5	+10
World	+ 5	+ 4

When there is comparative advantage, specialization makes it possible to produce more of both commodities. The productivity of English resources is left unchanged from Table 20-1; that of Canadian resources is increased tenfold. England no longer has an absolute advantage in producing either commodity. Total production of both commodities can nonetheless be increased by specialization. Moving one-tenth of one unit of Canadian resources out of cloth and into wheat and moving one unit of resources in the opposite direction in England causes world production of wheat to rise by 5 bushels and cloth by 4 yards. Reciprocal absolute advantage is not necessary for gains from trade.

TABLE 20-3 Absence of Gains from Specialization When There Is No Comparative Advantage

A. Amounts of wheat and cloth that can be produced with one unit of resources in Canada and England

	Wheat (bushels)	Cloth (yards)
Canada	100	60
England	10	6

B. Changes resulting from the transfer of one unit of Canadian resources into wheat and 10 units of British resources into cloth

	Wheat (bushels)	Cloth (yards)
Canada	+100	−60
England	−100	+60
World	0	0

When there is no comparative advantage, no reallocation of resources within each country can increase the production of both commodities. In this example, Canada has the same absolute advantage over England in each commodity (tenfold). There is no comparative advantage, and world production cannot be increased by reallocating resources in both countries. Therefore, specialization does not increase total output.

A comparison of Tables 20-1 and 20-2 refutes the notion that the absolute *levels* of efficiency of two areas determine the gains from specialization. The key is that the margin of advantage that one area has over the other must differ between commodities. As long as this margin differs, total world production can be increased when each area specializes in the production of that commodity in which it has a comparative advantage.

Comparative advantage is necessary, as well as sufficient, for gains from trade. This is illustrated in Table 20-3, which shows a case in which Canada has an absolute advantage in both commodities but neither country has a comparative advantage in the production of either commodity. Canada is 10 times as efficient as England in the production of wheat and in the production of cloth. Now there is no way to increase the production of both wheat and cloth by reallocating resources. Part B of the table provides one example of a resource shift that illustrates this.

Absolute advantage without comparative advantage does not lead to gains from trade.

A Second General Statement: Opportunity Costs

Much of the foregoing argument uses the concept of a unit of resources. It assumes that units of resources can be equated across countries, so that statements such as "Canada can produce 10 times as much wheat with the same quantity of resources as England" are meaningful. Measurement of the real resource cost of producing commodities poses many difficulties. If, for example, England uses land, labor, and capital in proportions that are different from those used in Canada, it may not be clear which country gets more

TABLE 20-4 Opportunity Cost of Wheat and Cloth in Canada and England

	Wheat (bushel)	Cloth (yard)
Canada	0.60 yard cloth	1.67 bushels wheat
England	2.00 yards cloth	0.50 bushel wheat

Comparative advantages can be expressed in terms of opportunity costs that differ between countries. These opportunity costs can be obtained from Table 20-1 or Table 20-2. The English opportunity cost of one unit of wheat is obtained by dividing the cloth output of one unit of English resources by the wheat output. The result shows that 2 yards of cloth must be sacrificed for every extra unit of wheat produced by transferring English resources out of cloth production and into wheat. The other three cost figures are obtained in a similar manner.

TABLE 20-5 Gains from Specialization with Differing Opportunity Costs

Changes resulting from each country's producing one more unit of a commodity in which it has the lower opportunity cost

	Wheat (bushels)	Cloth (yards)
Canada	+1.0	−0.6
England	−0.5	+1.0
World	+0.5	+0.4

Whenever opportunity costs differ between countries, specialization can increase the production of both commodities. These calculations show that there are gains from specialization, given the opportunity costs of Table 20-4. To produce one more bushel of wheat, Canada must sacrifice 0.6 yard of cloth. To produce one more yard of cloth, England must sacrifice 0.5 bushel of wheat. Making both changes raises world production of both wheat and cloth.

output per unit of resource input. Fortunately, the proposition about the gains from trade can be restated without reference to so fuzzy a concept as units of resources.

To do this, go back to the examples of Tables 20-1 and 20-2. Calculate the *opportunity cost* of wheat and cloth in the two countries. When resources are fully employed, the only way to produce more of one commodity is to reallocate resources and produce less of the other commodity. Table 20-1 shows that one unit of resources in Canada can produce 10 bushels of wheat *or* 6 yards of cloth. From this it follows that the opportunity cost of producing one unit of wheat is 0.60 unit of cloth, whereas the opportunity cost of producing one unit of cloth is 1.67 units of wheat. These data are summarized in Table 20-4. The table also shows that in England the opportunity cost of one unit of wheat is 2.0 units of cloth forgone, while the opportunity cost of one unit of cloth is 0.50 unit of wheat. Table 20-2 also gives rise to the opportunity costs in Table 20-4.

The sacrifice of cloth involved in producing wheat is much lower in Canada than in England. World wheat production can be increased if Canada rather than England produces it. Looking at cloth production, we can see that the loss of wheat involved in producing one unit of cloth is lower in England than in Canada. England has the lower (opportunity) cost as a producer of cloth. World cloth production can be increased if England, rather than Canada, produces it. This situation is shown in Table 20-5.

The gains from trade arise from differing opportunity costs in the two countries.

The conclusions about the gains from trade arising from international differences may be summarized as follows:

1. Country A has a comparative advantage over country B in producing a commodity when the opportunity cost (in terms of some other commodity) of production in country A is lower. This implies, however, that it has a comparative disadvantage in the other commodity.
2. Opportunity costs depend on the relative costs of producing two commodities, not on absolute costs. (Notice that the examples in Tables 20-1 and 20-2 each give rise to the opportunity costs in Table 20-4.)
3. When opportunity costs are the same in all countries, there is no comparative advantage and hence no possibility of gains from specialization and trade. (You can illustrate this for yourself by calculating the opportunity costs implied by the data in Table 20-3.)
4. When opportunity costs differ in any two countries and both countries are producing both commodities, it is always possible to increase total world production of both commodities by a suitable reallocation of resources within each country. (This proposition is illustrated in Table 20-5.)

Why Opportunity Costs Differ

We have seen that the sources of the gains from trade are comparative advantages, which themselves arise from differences in opportunity costs among nations. Why do different countries have different opportunity costs?

Different factor proportions. The traditional answer to this question was provided early in the twentieth century by two Swedish economists, Eli Heckscher and Bertil Ohlin. According to their theory, differences in factor endowments among nations result in different opportunity costs. For example, a country that is well endowed with fertile land but has a small population will find that land is cheap but labor is expensive. It will therefore produce land-intensive goods, such as wheat and corn, cheaply and labor-intensive, manufactured goods, such as watches and silicon chips, only at a high cost. The reverse will be true for a second country that is small in size but possessed with abundant and efficient labor. As a result, the first country will have a comparative advantage in land-intensive goods, the second in labor-intensive goods. Another country that is unusually well endowed with energy will have low energy prices and will thus have a comparative advantage in energy-intensive goods, such as chemicals and aluminum.

According to the Heckscher-Ohlin theory, countries have comparative advantages in the production of commodities that are intensive in the use of the factors of production with which their endowments are relatively abundant.

This is often called the *factor endowment theory of comparative advantage*. It assumes that all countries have the same production functions such that equal inputs of factor services produce equal outputs in all countries but that the supplies of factors, and hence relative factor prices, differ among nations.

Different climates. Research suggests that this theory explains much, but not all, of observed comparative advantages. One obvious additional influence comes from all the natural factors that can be called *climate* in the broadest sense. If we combine land, labor, and capital in the same way in Nicaragua and in Iceland, we will not get the same output of most agricultural goods. Sunshine, rainfall, and average temperature also matter. If we seek to work with wool or cotton in dry and damp climates, we will get different results. (We can, of course, artificially create any climate that we wish in a factory, but it costs money to create what is freely provided elsewhere.)

***Climate*, interpreted in the broadest sense, undoubtedly helps to determine comparative advantages.**

This explanation assumes that climatic conditions cause nations to have different production functions so that the same inputs of factor services will produce different outputs in different climates. Countries will tend to have comparative advantages in goods for whose production their climates are particularly favorable.

Gains from Trade with Variable Costs

So far we have assumed that unit costs are the same, whatever the scale of output, and have seen that there are gains from specialization and trade as long as there are interregional differences in opportunity costs. If costs vary with the level of output or as experience is acquired via specialization, *additional* sources of gain are possible.

Economies of Scale

Over some range of outputs, unit costs of production usually fall as the scale of output increases. The larger a firm's output, the greater its opportunities to employ efficient, large-scale machinery and to effect a detailed division of tasks among its workers. Countries such as Canada, France, and Israel, whose domestic markets are not large enough to exploit all available economies of scale, would find it prohibitively expensive to become self-sufficient. They would have to produce a little bit of everything at very high cost.[1]

Trade allows smaller countries to specialize in producing a limited range of commodities at high enough levels of output that they will reap the available economies of scale.

[1] Economies of scale are discussed in Chapter 11. The classic discussion of this effect is quoted in Box 3-1 on page 44.

FIGURE 20-1 Scale and Learning Effects

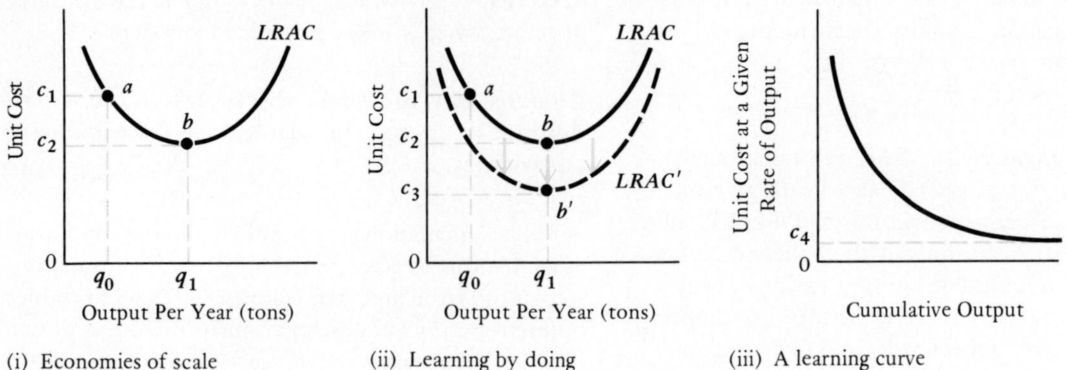

Specialization may lead to gains from trade either by permitting economies of scale or by leading to downward shifts of cost curves, or both. Consider a country that wishes to consume the quantity q_0 of some product. Suppose that it can produce that quantity at a unit cost of c_1. Suppose further that the country has a comparative advantage in producing this commodity and can export the quantity q_0q_1 if it produces q_1. This may lead to cost savings in two ways. In part (i), the increased level of production of q_1 compared to q_0 permits it to *move along* its cost curve, *LRAC,* from *a* to *b,* thus reaching the *MES* and reducing unit costs to c_2. This is an economy of scale. In part (ii), as workers and management become more experienced, they may discover means of increasing productivity that lead to a downward shift of the cost curve from *LRAC* to *LRAC'*. This is learning by doing. The downward *shift,* shown by the arrows, lowers the cost of producing any rate of output. At output q_1, costs per unit fall to c_3. The movement from *a* to *b'* incorporates both economies of scale and learning by doing.

Part (iii) shows a learning curve, which is another way of showing the effects of learning by doing. This curve shows the relation between the costs of *producing a given output per period* and the total output over the whole time during which production has taken place, called *cumulative output.* Growing experience with making the product causes costs to fall as more and more is produced. When all learning possibilities have been exploited, costs reach a minimum level, shown by c_4 in the figure. Moving the rate of output from q_0 to q_1 in part (i) causes the firm to move faster along its learning curve in part (iii).

Economies of scale are illustrated in part (i) of Figure 20-1.

Big countries such as the United States and the USSR have markets that are large enough to allow the production of most items at home at a scale of output that is great enough to obtain the available economies of scale. For them the gains from international trade arise mainly from specializing in commodities in which they have a comparative advantage. Yet even for such countries, a broadening of their markets permits achieving economies of scale in subproduct lines, such as specialty steels or blue jeans.

The importance of product diversity and specialization in specific subproduct lines has been one of the lessons learned from changing patterns of world trade since World War II. When the European Common Market (now called the European Community) was set up in the 1950s, economists expected that specialization would occur according to the Classical theory of comparative advantage, with one country specializing in cars, another in refrigerators, another in fashion clothes, another in shoes, and so on. This is not the way it has worked out. Today one can buy French, English, Italian, and German fashion goods, cars, shoes, appliances, and a host of other goods in London, Paris, Bonn, and Rome. Ships loaded with Swedish furniture bound for London pass ships loaded with English furniture bound for Stockholm, and so on.

What European free trade did was allow a proliferation of differentiated products, with different countries each specializing in different subproduct lines. Consumers have shown by their expenditures that they value this enormous increase in the range of choice among differentiated products. As Asian countries have expanded into North American markets with textiles, cars, and electronic goods, North American manufacturers have increasingly specialized their production, and we now export textiles, cars, and electronics equipment to Japan while importing similar but differentiated products from Japan.

Learning by Doing

The discussion so far has assumed that costs vary only with the *level* of output. They may also vary with the length of time that a product has been produced.

Early economists placed great importance on a phenomenon that we now call *learning by doing*. They believed that as countries gained experience in particular tasks, workers and managers would become more efficient in performing them. As people acquire expertise, costs tend to fall. There is substantial evidence that such learning by doing does occur in a wide range of industries. It is particularly important in many of today's knowledge-intensive, high-tech products.

Learning by doing is a phenomenon quite unlike anything we have studied so far in this book. Care must be taken to distinguish it from the familiar cost curves that relate a firm's costs to its current rate of output.

When learning by doing occurs, the *LRAC* curve shifts downward.

This shift, which is shown in part (ii) of Figure 20-1, means that any given rate of output is associated with a lower average total cost than before. The shift occurs because of increased productivity due to learning from experience gained over all past production. As a result, costs fall as the total of all cumulative *past* output rises.

This important phenomenon can be shown by a **learning curve**. This curve, which is shown in part (iii) of Figure 20-1, shows how the cost of producing a *given rate of output* falls as the total output accumulates.

An example may help to illustrate learning by doing. Suppose that a firm starts operations on January 1, 1990, producing at a rate of 10,000 units per month. On January 1, 1991, the total of all past output is 120,000 units, and by January 1, 1992, the total is 240,000 units. Now suppose that the unit cost associated with the monthly production of 10,000 units was $5.00 on January 1, 1990, $4.00 on January 1, 1991, and $3.50 on January 1, 1992. This sequence of events allows us to identify three points on the firm's learning curve: The unit cost of producing the given rate of output is $5.00 when past output is zero, $4.00 when past output is 120,000 units, and $3.50 when past output is 240,000 units. The firm has moved along its learning curve. The costs associated with producing 10,000 units a month have fallen as its labor and management have learned from the accumulated experience of producing more and more output.

Now assume that the firm had been able to produce at a faster rate, say, 20,000 units per month. Its unit costs might now have been different because it would be at a different point on its long-run average cost curve. To illustrate the learning effect simply, however, assume that the average total cost curve is flat for outputs between 12,000 and 24,000 units per month. Thus unit costs of producing at the higher rate of 24,000 units per month are $5.00 per unit when the firm starts operations on January 1, 1990. However, the firm will move down its learning curve faster as a result of having a higher rate of output. By January 1, 1991, it will have a cumulative past output of 240,000, and its unit costs will have fallen to $3.50, the level it took two years to reach when the firm was producing only 10,000 units a month.

Where learning by doing is important, the higher a firm's current rate of output, the faster its unit costs associated with a *given* rate of output will fall.

This tendency for costs to fall as the total of all past output accumulates confers large advantages on firms that are first into the market with a new product as well as on firms that have a large domestic market that will support a high initial rate of output.

The distinction between economies of large-scale production, which are associated with the *current rate of output,* and learning by doing, which is associated with the *total of all past output,* is illustrated in Figure 20-1. The distinction provides one more example of the difference between a movement along a curve and a shift of a curve.

Recognition of the opportunities for learning by doing leads to an important implication: Policymakers need not accept *current* comparative advantages as given. Through such means as education and tax incentives, they can seek to develop new comparative advantages.[2] Moreover, countries cannot complacently assume that an existing comparative advantage will persist. Misguided education policies, the wrong tax incentives, or policies that discourage risk taking can lead to the rapid erosion of a country's comparative advantage in a particular product. So, too, can competitive developments elsewhere in the world.

A changing view of comparative advantage. The Classical theory of the gains from trade, which still has many adherents, assumes that there are given cost structures, based largely on a country's natural endowments. This leads to a given pattern of international comparative advantage. It leads to the policy advice that a government, interested in maximizing its citizens' material standard of living, should encourage production to be specialized in goods in which it currently has a comparative advantage.

There is today a competing view. In extreme form, it says that comparative advantages certainly exist but are typically acquired, not nature-given—and they change. This view of comparative advantage is *dynamic* rather than static. New industries are seen as depending more on human capital than on fixed physical capital or natural resources. The skills of a computer designer, a videogame programmer, a sound mix technician, or a rock star are acquired by education and on-the-job training (which contribute to the negative slope of their industry's learning curve). Natural endowments of energy and raw materials cannot account for Britain's prominence in modern pop music, the United States' leadership in computer software, or Japan's success in the automobile and silicon-chip industries. When a country such as the United States finds its former dominance (based on comparative advantage) declining in such smokestack industries as automobiles and steel, its firms need not sit idly by. Instead, they can begin to adapt by developing new areas of comparative advantage.

There are surely elements of truth in both extreme views. It would be unwise to neglect resource endowments, climate, culture, and social and institutional arrangements. However, it also would be unwise to assume that all sources of comparative advantage are innate and immutable.

To some extent these views are reconciled in the theory of human capital that we discussed in Chapter 19. Comparative advantages that depend on human capital are consistent with the traditional Heckscher-Ohlin theory. The difference is that human capital is acquired by making conscious decisions relating to such matters as education and technical training.

Is comparative advantage obsolete? In the debate preceding the signing of the Canada-U.S. Free Trade Agreement, some opponents argued that the agreement relied on an outdated view of the gains from trade based on comparative advantage. The theory of comparative advantage was said to have been made obsolete by the new theories that we have just discussed.

In spite of such assertions, comparative advantage remains an important economic concept. At any one time, the operation of the price system will result in trade that follows the current pattern of comparative advantage. This is because comparative advantage is reflected in international relative prices, and these relative prices determine what goods a country will import and what it will export. For example, if Canadian costs of producing steel are particularly low, Canada's price of steel will be low by international standards, and steel will be a Canadian export (which it is). If Canada's costs of producing textiles are particularly high, Canada's price of textiles will be high by international standards, and Canada will import textiles (which it does—as much as Canadian tariffs and quotas permit). So there is no reason to change the view that Ricardo long ago expounded: Current comparative advantage is a major determinant of trade under free market conditions.

What has changed, however, is economists' views

[2] Of course, they might foolishly use the same policies to develop industries in which they do not have, and will never achieve, comparative advantage. See the discussion in Chapter 21.

about the *determinants* of comparative advantage. It now seems that current comparative advantage may be more open to change by private entrepreneurial activities and by government policy than used to be thought. Thus what is obsolete is the belief (to the extent that it was ever held) that a country's current comparative advantages, and hence its current pattern of imports and exports, must be accepted as given by nature.

The theory that comparative advantage determines trade flows is not obsolete, but the theory that comparative advantage is fully determined by forces beyond the reach of public policy has been discredited.

It is one thing to observe that governments may be able to influence comparative advantage. It is another thing to conclude that it is advisable for them to try. As we shall see in Part 7, the case for a specific government intervention requires that (1) there is scope for governments to improve on the results achieved by the free market, (2) the costs of the intervention be less than the value of the improvement to be achieved, and (3) governments will actually be able to carry out the required interventionist policies (without, for example, being sidetracked by considerations of electoral advantage). These conditions are considered in detail in Part 7.

The Terms of Trade

So far we have seen that world production can be increased when countries specialize in the production of the commodities in which they have or can acquire a comparative advantage and then trade with one another. We now ask, How will these gains from specialization and trade be shared among countries? The division of the gain depends on the terms under which trade takes place. The **terms of trade** measure the quantity of imported goods that can be obtained per unit of goods exported and are measured by the ratio of the price of exports to the price of imports.

A rise in the price of imported goods, with the price of exports remaining unchanged, indicates a *fall in the terms of trade*; it will now take more exports to buy the same quantity of imports. Similarly, a rise in the price of exported goods, with the price of imports remaining unchanged, indicates a *rise in the terms of trade*; it will now take fewer exports to buy the same quantity of imports. Thus the ratio of prices is a measure of the amount of exported goods that are needed to acquire a given quantity of imports.

In the example of Table 20-4, the Canadian domestic opportunity cost of one unit of cloth is 1.67 bushels of wheat. In other words, if in Canada resources are transferred from wheat to cloth, 1.67 bushels of wheat are given up for every yard of cloth gained. However, if Canada can obtain its cloth by trade on more favorable terms, it is worthwhile for the nation to produce and export wheat to pay for cloth imports. Suppose, for example, that international prices are such that 1 yard of cloth exchanges for (i.e., is equal in value to) 1 bushel of wheat. At these prices, Canadians can obtain 1 yard of cloth for 1 bushel of wheat exported. They get more cloth per unit of wheat exported than they can by moving resources out of wheat into cloth production at home. Therefore, the terms of trade favor specializing in the production of wheat and trading wheat for cloth in international markets.

Similarly, in the example of Table 20-4, English consumers gain when they can obtain wheat abroad at any terms of trade that are more favorable than 2 yards of cloth per unit of wheat. If the terms of trade permit exchange of 1 bushel of wheat for 1 yard of cloth, the terms of trade favor English traders' buying wheat and selling cloth in international markets. Here, both England and Canada gain from trade. Each can obtain the commodity in which it has a comparative disadvantage at a lower opportunity cost through international trade than through domestic production. How the terms of trade affect the gains from trade is shown graphically in Box 20-1.

Because actual international trade involves many countries and many commodities, a country's terms of trade are computed as an index number:

$$\text{Terms of trade} = \frac{\text{index of export prices}}{\text{index of import prices}} \times 100$$

A rise in the index is referred to as a *favorable* change in a country's terms of trade. A favorable change means that more can be imported per unit of goods exported than previously. For example, if the export price index rises from 100 to 120 while the import price index rises from 100 to 110, the terms-of-trade index rises from 100 to 109. At the new

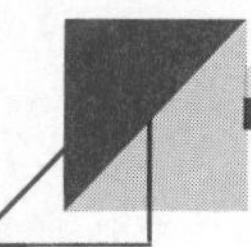

BOX 20-1

The Gains from Trade Illustrated Graphically

International trade leads to an expansion of the set of goods that can be consumed in the economy in two ways: by allowing the bundle of goods consumed to differ from the bundle produced and by permitting a profitable change in the pattern of production. The key to these gains is that international trade allows the separation of production decisions from consumption decisions. Without international trade, the choice of which bundle of goods to produce would be the same as the choice of which bundle to consume. With international trade, the consumption and production bundles can be altered independently to reflect the relative value placed on goods by international markets.

This proposition is illustrated graphically here for a simplified world in which there are only two goods, *X* and *Y*. The illustration is in two stages.

Stage 1: Fixed Production

In each part of the figure, the black curve is the economy's production possibility boundary (such a boundary was introduced in Figure 1-2 on page 5).

If there is no international trade, the economy must consume the same bundle of goods that it produces. Thus the production possibility boundary is also the consumption possibility boundary. Suppose that the economy produces and consumes

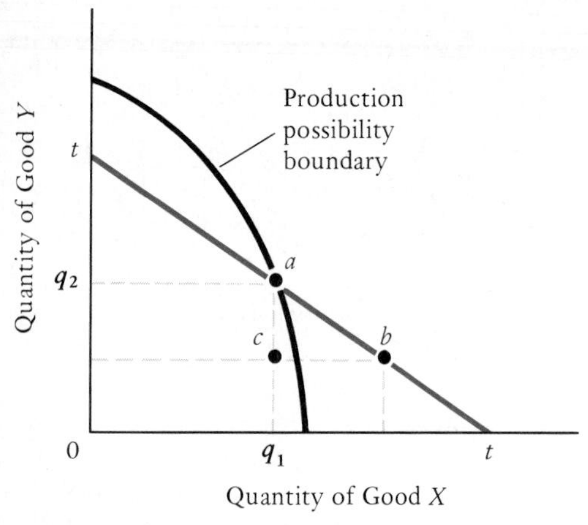

(i) Stage 1: Fixed production

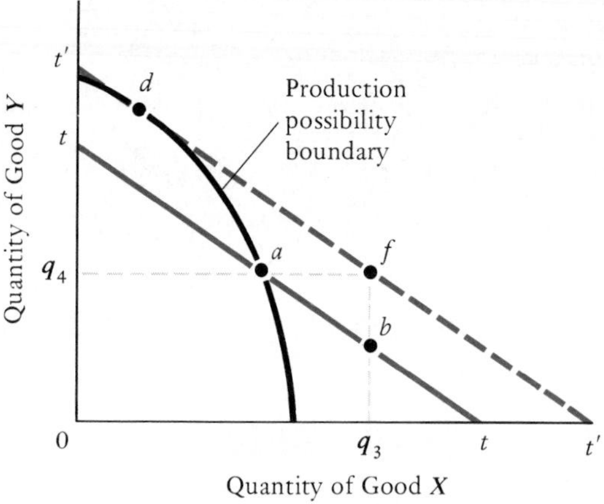

(ii) Stage 2: Variable production

terms of trade, a unit of exports will buy 9 percent more imports than at the old terms.

A decrease in the index of the terms of trade, called an *unfavorable* change, means that the country can import less in return for any given amount of exports or, what is the same, that it must export more to pay for any given amount of imports. For example, reductions in the international prices of wood and mineral products in the early 1980s hit the Canadian economy particularly hard. The terms of trade turned against Canada as the same amount of exports of mineral and wood products paid for much smaller amounts of imports. Later in the decade, sharp reductions in the international prices of agricultural products, particularly grains, hit the Prairie provinces, causing unfavorable changes in their terms of trade.

Many of Canada's exports are heavily concentrated in primary products whose prices tend to vary over the business cycle much more than prices of

at point a, with q_1 of good X and q_2 of good Y, as in part (i) of the figure.

Next, suppose that while production stays at point a, good Y can be exchanged for good X in international markets. The consumption possibilities are now enhanced, as is shown by the line tt drawn through point a. The slope of this line indicates the world terms of trade and reflects the quantity of good Y that can be exchanged for a unit of good X on the international market.

Although production is fixed at a, consumption can now be anywhere on the line tt to the right of a. For example, the consumption point could be at b. This could be achieved by exporting ac units of good Y and importing cb units of good X. Since point b (and all others on line tt to the right of a) lies outside the production possibility boundary, there are potential gains from trade. Consumers are no longer limited by *their* country's production possibilities. Suppose that consumers prefer point b to point a. They have achieved a gain from trade by being allowed to exchange some of their production of good Y for some quantity of good X and thus to consume more of good X than is produced at home.

Stage 2: Variable Production

In stage 1, production was constant at a. An additional opportunity for the expansion of the country's consumption possibilities arises because, with trade, the production bundle may be profitably altered in response to international prices. The country may produce the bundle of goods that is most valuable in world markets, which is represented by the bundle d in part (ii) of the figure. The consumption possibility set is shifted to the line $t't'$ by changing production from a to d and thereby increasing the country's degree of specialization in good Y. For every point on the original consumption possibility set, tt, there are points on the new set, $t't'$, that allow more consumption of both goods. Compare, for example, points a and f. Notice also that except at the zero-trade point, d, the new consumption possibility set lies everywhere above the production possibility curve.

Many consumption bundles that cannot be produced domestically are made available by trade. The benefits from moving from a no-trade position, such as a, to a trading position, such as b or f, are the *gains from trade* to the country. When the production of good Y was increased and the production of good X was decreased, the country was able to move to point f by producing more of good Y, in which the country has a comparative advantage, and by trading the additional production for good X. Economists refer to such production changes as "exploiting the country's comparative advantage."

manufactured goods. Thus the Canadian terms of trade tend to vary quite significantly over the cycle, turning favorably in boom times and unfavorably in recessions. These swings are often accompanied by swings in optimism and pessimism about the long-run future of the Canadian economy among commentators and policymakers who misinterpret reversible cyclical fluctuations as permanent long-term changes.

SUMMARY

1. One country (or region or individual) has an absolute advantage over another country (or region or individual) in the production of a commodity when it can produce more of the commodity than the other can with the same input of resources in each country.

2. In a situation of absolute advantage, total production of both commodities will be raised if each country specializes in the production of the commodity in which it has the absolute advantage. However, the gains from trade do not require absolute advantage on the part of each country, only comparative advantage.
3. Comparative advantage is the relative advantage that one country enjoys over another in the production of various commodities. World production of all commodities can be increased if each country transfers resources into the production of the commodities in which it has a comparative advantage.
4. Comparative advantage arises from countries' having different opportunity costs of producing particular goods. This creates the opportunity for all nations to gain from trade.
5. The most important proposition in the theory of the gains from trade is that trade allows all countries to obtain the goods in which they do not have a comparative advantage at a lower opportunity cost than they would face if they were to produce all commodities for themselves. This allows all countries to have more of all commodities than they could have if they tried to be self-sufficient.
6. As well as gaining the advantages of specialization arising from comparative advantage, a nation that engages in trade and specialization may realize the benefits of the economies of large-scale production and of learning by doing.
7. Classical theory regarded comparative advantage as largely determined by natural resource endowments and climatic factors and thus as difficult to change. Economists now believe that comparative advantage can be acquired and thus can be changed either by private entrepreneurial activity or by government policy.
8. The terms of trade refer to the ratio of the prices of goods exported to the prices of goods imported, which determines the quantities of exports needed to pay for imports. The terms of trade determine how the gains from trade are shared. A favorable change in terms of trade, that is, a rise in export prices relative to import prices, means that a country can acquire more imports per unit of exports.

TOPICS FOR REVIEW

Interpersonal, interregional, and international specialization
Absolute advantage and comparative advantage
Gains from trade: specialization, scale economies, learning by doing, and learning curves
Opportunity cost and comparative advantage
Dynamic comparative advantage
Terms of trade

DISCUSSION QUESTIONS

1. Adam Smith saw a close connection between the wealth of a nation and its willingness "freely to engage" in foreign trade. What is the connection?
2. Suppose that the situation described in the accompanying table exists. Assume that there are no tariffs and no government intervention and that labor is the only factor of production. Let X take different values—say, \$10, \$20, \$40, and \$60. In each case, in what direction will trade have to flow in order for the gains from trade to be exploited?

	Labor cost of producing one unit of	
Country	Artichokes	Bikinis
Inland	\$20	\$40
Outland	\$20	\$$X$

3. Suppose that Canada had an absolute advantage in all manufactured products. Should it then ever import any manufactured products?
4. Suppose that the Quebec referendum had passed and Canada had become two separate countries in 1980. What predictions would you make about the standard of living compared with what it is today? Does the fact that Canada, the United States, and Mexico are separate countries lead to a lower standard of living in the three countries than if they were united into a new country called Northica?
5. Studies of Canadian trade patterns have shown that high-wage sectors of industry are among the largest and fastest-growing export sectors. Does this contradict the principle of comparative advantage?
6. Predict what each of the following events would do to the terms of trade of the importing country and the exporting country, other things being equal.
   a. A blight destroys a large part of the coffee beans produced in the world.
   b. The Koreans cut the price of the steel they sell to Canada.
   c. General inflation of 10 percent occurs around the world.
   d. Violation of OPEC output quotas leads to a sharp fall in the price of oil.
7. Heavy Canadian borrowing abroad has several times led to a high value of the dollar and thus a rise in the ratio of export prices to import prices. Although this is called a favorable change in the terms of trade, are there any reasons why it may not have been a good thing for the Canadian economy?
8. Business people often worry that if their country's inflation rate exceeds the rates their major trading partners are experiencing, they will be priced out of foreign markets; they worry that exports will then dwindle away, while imports of ever-more-competitive foreign goods will boom. Is this worry founded?

Chapter 21

Barriers to Free Trade

Conducting business in a foreign country is always difficult. Differences in language, in local laws and customs, and in currency all complicate transactions. Our concern in this chapter is not, however, with these difficulties but with the government's policy toward international trade, which is called its **commercial policy**. At one extreme is a policy of **free trade**, which means an absence of any form of government interference with the free flow of international trade. **Protectionism** refers to any departure from free trade designed to give some protection to domestic industries from foreign competition.

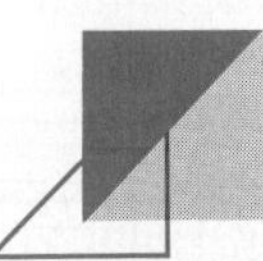

The Theory of Commercial Policy

Today debates over commercial policy are as heated as they were 200 years ago, when the theory of the gains from trade was still being worked out. Should a country permit the free flow of international trade, or should it seek to protect its local producers from foreign competition? Such protection may be achieved either through **tariffs**, which are taxes designed to raise the prices of foreign goods, or through **nontariff barriers**, which are devices other than tariffs designed to reduce the flow of imported goods. Examples include quotas and customs procedures that are deliberately made more cumbersome than necessary.

The Case for Free Trade

The case for free trade is based on the analysis presented in Chapter 20, in which we saw that whenever opportunity costs differ among countries, specialization and trade will raise world living standards. Free trade allows countries to specialize in producing commodities in which they have a comparative advantage.

Free trade allows the maximization of world production, thus making it *possible* for every household in the world to consume more goods than it could without free trade.

This does not necessarily mean that everyone will indeed be better off with free trade than without it. Protectionism could allow the citizens of some countries to obtain a larger share of a smaller world output so that they would benefit even though on average everyone would lose. If we ask whether it is *possible* for free trade to be advantageous to everyone, the answer is yes. But if we ask whether free trade is, in fact, *always* advantageous to everyone, the answer is not necessarily.

There is abundant evidence to show that significant differences in opportunity costs exist and that large gains are realized from international trade because of these differences. What needs explanation is the fact that trade is not wholly free. Why do tariffs and nontariff barriers to trade continue to exist two centuries after Adam Smith and David Ricardo stated the case for free trade? Is there a valid case for protectionism? Before addressing these questions, let us examine the methods that are used in protectionist policy.

Methods of Protection

The two main types of protectionist policy are illustrated in Figure 21-1. Both cause the price of the imported good to rise and its quantity to fall. They

FIGURE 21-1 Methods of Protecting Domestic Producers

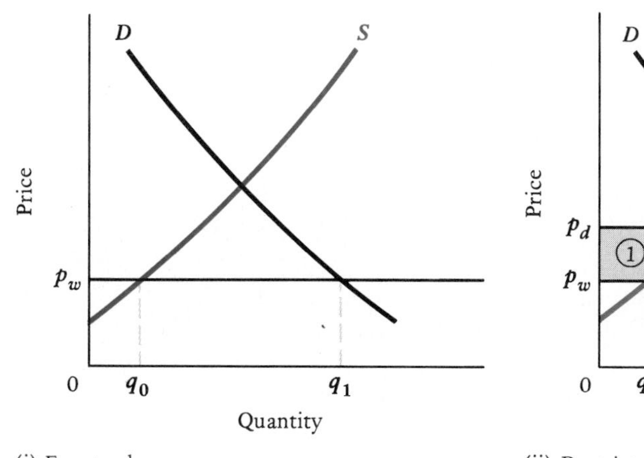

(i) Free trade

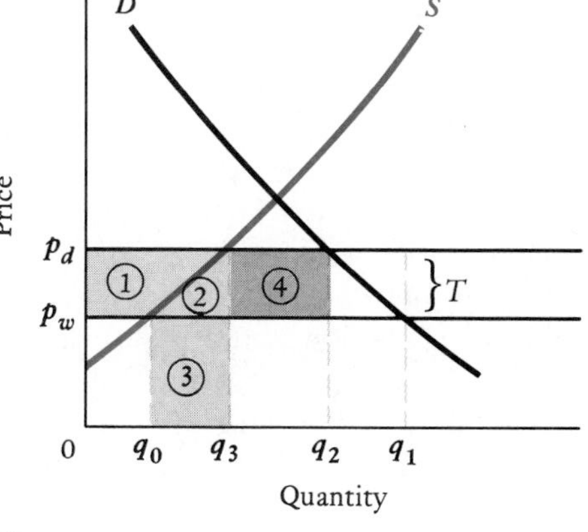

(ii) Restricted trade

The same reduction in imports and increase in domestic production can be achieved by using either a tariff or a quantity restriction. In both parts of the figure, D and S are the domestic demand and supply curves, respectively, and p_w is the world price of some commodity that is both produced at home and imported.

Part (i) of the figure shows the situation under free trade. Domestic consumption is q_1, domestic production is q_0, and imports are q_0q_1.

Part (ii) shows what happens when protectionist policies restrict imports to the amount q_3q_2. When this is done by levying a tariff of T per unit, the price in the domestic market rises by the full amount of the tariff to p_d. Consumers reduce consumption from q_1 to q_2 and pay an extra amount, shown by the shaded areas 1, 2, and 4, for the q_2 that they now purchase. Domestic production rises from q_0 to q_3. Since domestic producers receive the domestic price, their receipts rise by the three light shaded areas, labeled 1, 2, and 3. Area 3 is revenue that was earned by foreign producers under free trade, while areas 1 and 2 are paid by domestic consumers because of the higher prices that they must now pay. Foreign suppliers of the imported good continue to get the world price, so the government receives as tariff revenue the extra amount paid by consumers for the q_3q_2 units that are still imported (shown by the dark shaded area, 4).

When the same result is accomplished by a quantity restriction, the government—either through a quota or a *voluntary export agreement (VER)*—reduces imports to q_3q_2. This drives the domestic market price up to p_d and has the same effect on domestic producers and consumers as the tariff. Since the government has merely restricted the quantity of imports, both foreign and domestic suppliers get the higher price in the domestic market. Thus foreign suppliers now receive the extra amount paid by domestic consumers (represented by the shaded area labeled 4) for the units that are still imported.

differ, however, in how they achieve these results. The caption to Figure 21-1 analyzes the general effects of these policies.

Policies That Initially Raise Price

The first type of protectionist policy initially raises the *price* of the imported commodity. A tariff, also often called an *import duty*, is the most common policy of this type. Other such policies are any rules or regulations that fulfill three conditions: They are costly to comply with; they do not apply to competing, domestically produced commodities; and they are more than is required to meet any purpose other than restricting trade.

Tariffs come in two main forms: **specific tariffs**, which are levied as a specific amount of money on *each unit* of the product, and **ad valorem tariffs**, which are levied as *a percentage of the price* of the product. Tariffs raise revenues, as well as provide protection. For some less developed countries which have limited sources of revenue, tariffs can be an important revenue source. For developed countries, such as Canada, the revenue-raising function is relatively unimportant.

As shown in part (ii) of Figure 21-1, tariffs affect both foreign and domestic producers, as well as domestic consumers. The initial effect is to raise the domestic price of the imported commodity above its world price by the amount of the tariff. Imports fall, and as a result, foreign producers sell less and so must transfer resources to other lines of production. The price received on domestically produced units rises, as does the quantity produced domestically. On both counts domestic producers earn more. However, the extra production is achieved at a cost that is higher than the price at which the commodity could be purchased on the world market. Thus the benefits to domestic producers come at the expense of domestic consumers, who must pay the extra cost of production in terms of higher prices. Indeed, domestic consumers lose on two counts: First, they consume less of the product because its price rises, and second, they pay a higher price for the amount that they do continue to consume. Their extra spending ends up in two places: The extra that is paid on all units produced at home goes to domestic producers, and the extra that is paid on units still imported goes to the government as tariff revenue.

Policies That Initially Lower Quantities

The second type of protectionist policy initially restricts the *quantity* of the imported commodity. A common example is the **import quota**, whereby the importing country sets a maximum of the quantity of some commodity that may be imported each year. Increasingly popular, however, is the **voluntary export restriction (VER)**, an agreement by an exporting country to limit the amount of a good that it sells to the importing country.

The European Community (EC) and the United States have used VERs extensively, and the EC also makes frequent use of import quotas. Japan has been pressured into negotiating several VERs with the EC, Canada, and the United States in order to limit sales of some of the Japanese goods that have had the most success in international competition. For example, in 1983 the United States and Canada negotiated VERs whereby the Japanese government agreed to restrict total sales of Japanese cars to these two countries for three years. When the agreements ran out in 1986, the Japanese continued to restrain their automobile sales by unilateral voluntary action. This episode is further considered in Box 21-1.

As shown in part (ii) of Figure 21-1, a quantity restriction of the appropriate size can have the same effects as a tariff both on the domestic price and on the quantities produced and consumed domestically. This means that its effects on domestic consumers and producers are the same as a tariff that has the equivalent effect in limiting imports. The major difference is in who gets the additional money that domestic consumers pay for the quantities that are still imported. When the government levies a tariff, it gets the revenue. When the government imposes (or negotiates) an import restriction, the same sum of money is transferred as additional revenue to foreign producers. This is because the quantity restriction drives up the domestic price and all of the extra amount that purchasers pay for the imported units of the commodity go to the foreign suppliers.

In addition to devices that are designed to restrict imports for protectionist purposes, there is also a series of devices that are designed to prevent what are called "unfair trade practices" by foreign firms or governments. The two most common of these are *antidumping duties* and *countervailing duties*. Laws relating to these measures are often called **fair trade**

laws or **trade remedy laws**. Although they are not intended as tools of protectionism, they are often used as such. They are considered later in this chapter.

Nominal and Effective Rates of Tariff

The rate of tariff charged on each imported commodity, called the **nominal rate of tariff**, does not necessarily show the degree of protection given to that commodity. Nominal rates of tariff frequently understate the degree of protection offered to domestic manufacturing industries, and a better measure is provided by what is called the *effective tariff rate*.

The distinction between nominal and effective rates of tariff arises whenever imported raw materials or semifinished goods carry a lower rate of duty than imports of the final manufactured goods that embody these intermediate products. If the final good is made abroad, the duty for manufactured goods is applied to the entire price of that good, even though the price includes the values of the raw materials and semifinished goods that it embodies. If the final good is produced domestically, the raw materials and semifinished goods enter at the lower rate of tariff. For this reason, a tariff of, say, 10 percent on the final good will protect a domestic producer that is much more than 10 percent less efficient than its foreign competitor.

To illustrate this important point, consider an example. A product, using a Canadian raw material, is manufactured in both Canada and the United States. Assume that the raw material enters the United States duty-free but that the manufactured good is subject to a 10 percent tariff. Further assume that when the product is manufactured in Canada, the raw material accounts for one-half the cost of the final product; the other half is value added by the Canadian manufacturer. Because of the 10 percent tariff, one unit of output that costs $1.00 to produce in Canada—50 cents for raw materials and 50 cents for manufacturing cost—will sell in the United States for $1.10.

Now consider the position of a U.S. manufacturer that in this particular industry is less efficient than the Canadian manufacturer. (If the U.S. producer were not less efficient, there would be no need for protection.) Let the U.S. firm's production costs be 20 percent higher than those of the Canadian firm. Thus to produce one unit of output, the raw material costs the U.S. firm 50 cents, but its other costs—including the opportunity costs of its capital—are 60 cents (i.e., 20 percent higher than the Canadian manufacturer's costs of 50 cents). This gives the U.S. firm a final price of $1.10, which is just low enough to compete against the tariff-burdened Canadian import.

In this example, a tariff of 10 percent on the value of the final product is sufficient to protect a U.S. firm that is 20 percent less efficient than its Canadian competitor. To measure this effect, the **effective rate of tariff** expresses the tariff as a percentage of the *value added* by the exporting industry in question. Thus the effective American rate of tariff on the Canadian manufacturing industry in the example is 20 percent, whereas the nominal tariff on manufactured goods is only 10 percent.

Although nominal U.S. tariffs on Canadian goods were quite low even before the Canada-U.S. Free Trade Agreement came into effect, effective rates on goods manufactured using Canadian raw materials were significantly higher for the reason just studied. One reason for wishing to eliminate the U.S. tariffs was to end the bias this created toward exporting Canadian raw materials for manufacture in the United States rather than manufacturing the products in Canada and then exporting them.

The Case for Protectionism

Two kinds of arguments for protection are commonly offered. The first concerns national objectives other than national income; the second concerns the desire to increase domestic national income, possibly at the expense of total world income.

Objectives Other Than Maximizing National Income

It is quite possible to accept the proposition that national income is higher with free trade and yet rationally to oppose free trade because of a concern with policy objectives other than maximizing per capita national income. For example, comparative advantage might dictate that a country should specialize in producing a narrow range of commodities. The government might decide, however, that there

BOX 21-1

Import Restrictions on Japanese Cars: Tariffs or Quotas?

In the early 1980s, imports of Japanese cars seriously threatened the automobile industries of the United States, Canada, and Western Europe. While continuing to espouse relatively free trade as a long-term policy, the American and Canadian governments argued that the domestic industry needed short-term protection. This protection was needed in order to tide it over the period of transition that it faced as smaller cars became the typical North American household's vehicle. Once the enormous investment needed to transform the North American automobile industry had been made and new models had gained acceptance, it was hoped that free trade could be restored and the North American industry could be asked to stand up to foreign competition.

How was this protection to be achieved? Voluntary export restrictions (VERs) seemed the easiest route. An agreement was reached whereby the Japanese government agreed to limit severely the number of Japanese cars that could be exported to North America.

What does economic theory predict about the effects of VERs and tariffs? In both cases, imports are restricted, and the resulting scarcity supports a higher market price. With a tariff, the extra market

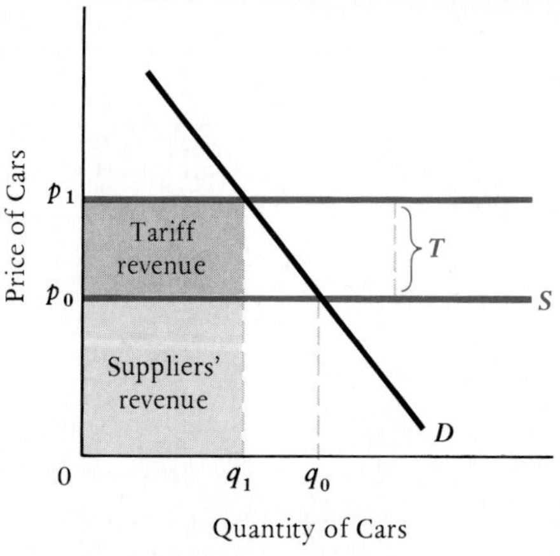

(i) Tariff of T dollars per car

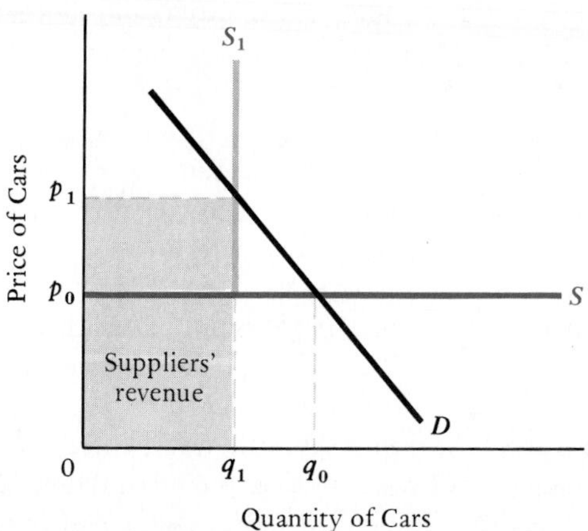

(ii) Quota of q_1 cars

are distinct social advantages to encouraging a more diverse economy. Citizens would be given a wider range of occupations, and the social and psychological advantages of diversification would more than compensate for having living standards, say, 5 percent below what they could be with full specialization of production according to comparative advantage.

For a very small country, specializing in the production of only a few commodities—though dictated by comparative advantage—may involve risks that the country does not wish to take. One such risk is that technological advances may render its basic product obsolete. Another risk is that cyclical fluctuations in the prices of basic commodities may cause a country to face depressed prices for years at a time

value is appropriated by the government of the importing country—in this case the Canadian or U.S. government. With a VER, the extra market value accrues to the goods' suppliers—in this case the Japanese car makers and their North American retailers.

Both cases are illustrated in the accompanying figure. We assume that the North American market provides a small enough part of total Japanese car sales to leave the Japanese willing to supply all the cars that are demanded in Canada and the United States at their fixed list price. This is the price p_0 in both parts of the figure. Given the North American demand curve for Japanese cars, D, q_0 cars are sold before restrictions are imposed.

In part (i), Canada and the United States place a tariff of T per unit on Japanese cars, raising their price in North America to p_1 and lowering sales to q_1. Suppliers' revenue is shown by the light-shaded area. Tariff revenue accruing to the governments of Canada and the United States is shown by the dark-shaded area.

In part (ii), a VER of q_1 is imposed, making the supply curve vertical at q_1. The market-clearing price is p_1. The suppliers' revenue is the whole shaded area (p_1 times q_1).

In both cases, the shortage of Japanese cars drives up their price, creating a substantial margin over costs. Under a tariff, the North American governments capture the margin. Under a VER policy, however, the margin accrues to the Japanese manufacturers.

Although this is a simplified picture, it captures the essence of what actually happened. First, while sellers of North American cars were keeping prices as low as possible and sometimes offering rebates on slow-selling models, Japanese cars were listed at healthy profit margins. Second, while it was always possible for the buyer of a North American car to negotiate a good discount off the list price, Japanese cars usually sold for their full list price. Third, since Japanese manufacturers were not allowed to supply all of the cars that they could sell in North America, they had to choose which types of cars to supply. Not surprisingly, they tended to satisfy fully the demand for their more expensive cars, which have larger profit margins, and to restrict exports of the less expensive cars, which have lower profit margins.This change in the "product mix" of Japanese cars exported to North America raised the average profit per car exported. The VERs were thus very costly to Canadian and American consumers and an enormous profit boon to Japanese car manufacturers. Indeed, it was estimated that North American consumers paid about $150,000 per year for each job that was saved in the U.S. and Canadian car industries and that most of this went to Japanese producers.

and then enjoy periods of very high prices. Everyone understands these risks, but there is debate about what governments can do about them. The protariff argument is that the government can encourage a more diversified economy by protecting industries that otherwise could not compete. Opponents argue that governments, being naturally influenced by political motives, are, in the final analysis, poor judges of which industries can be protected in order to produce diversification at a reasonable cost.

Another noneconomic reason for protectionism concerns national defense. It is sometimes argued, particularly in large countries, that because an experienced merchant marine is needed in case of war, a merchant marine should be sheltered by protectionist policies in times of peace even though it is inefficient. The Jones Act provides this protection for U.S. shipping by requiring that all cargoes moving between U.S. ports be carried in U.S. ships.

Although most people would agree that, other things being equal, they would prefer more income to less, a nation may rationally choose to sacrifice some income in order to achieve other goals. Economists can do three things when they are faced with such reasons for imposing tariffs. First, they can see if the proposed tariff really does achieve the goals suggested. Second, they can calculate the cost of the tariff in terms of lowered living standards. Third, they can check policy alternatives to see if there are other means of achieving the stated goal at a lower cost in terms of lost output.

The Objective of Maximizing National Income

Next we consider five important arguments for the use of tariffs when the objective is to make national income as large as possible.

To alter the terms of trade. Trade restrictions can sometimes be used to turn the terms of trade in favor of countries that produce and export a large fraction of the world's supply of some commodity. They can also be used to turn the terms of trade in favor of countries that constitute a large fraction of the world demand for some commodity that they import.

When the OPEC countries restricted their output of oil in the 1970s, they were able to drive the price of oil up relative to the prices of other traded goods. This turned the terms of trade in their favor; for every barrel of oil exported, they were able to obtain a larger quantity of imports. When the output of oil grew greatly in the mid 1980s, the relative price of oil fell dramatically, and the terms of trade turned unfavorably for the oil-exporting countries. These are illustrations of how changes in the supply of exports can affect the terms of trade.

Now consider a country that provides a large fraction of the total demand for some product that it imports. By restricting its demand for that product through tariffs, it can force the price of that product down. This turns the terms of trade in its favor, because it can now get more units of imports per unit of exports.

Both of these techniques lower world output. They can, however, make it possible for a small group of countries to gain, because they get a sufficiently larger share of the smaller world output. However, if foreign countries retaliate by raising their tariffs, the ensuing trade war can easily leave every country with a lowered income.

To protect against "unfair" actions by foreign firms and governments. Tariffs may be used to prevent foreign industries from gaining an advantage over domestic industries through the use of predatory practices that will harm domestic industries and hence lower national income. Two common practices are the payment of subsidies by foreign governments to their exporters and dumping by foreign firms. Such practices are called *unfair trade practices*, and the laws that deal with them are called *fair trade laws*. The circumstances under which foreign subsidization and dumping provide a valid argument for tariffs are considered in detail later in this chapter.

To protect infant industries. The oldest valid argument for protectionism as a means of raising living standards concerns economies of scale. It is usually called the **infant industry argument**. If an industry has large economies of scale, costs and prices will be high when the industry is small but will fall as the industry grows. In such industries, the country first in the field has a tremendous advantage. A newly developing country may find that in the early stages of development its industries are unable to compete with established foreign rivals. A trade restriction may protect these industries from foreign competition while they grow. When they are large enough, they may be able to produce as cheaply as foreign rivals and thus be able to compete without protection.

To encourage learning by doing. Learning by doing, which we discussed in Chapter 20, suggests that the existing pattern of comparative advantage need not be taken as immutable. If a country can learn enough by producing commodities in which it is currently at a comparative disadvantage, it may gain in the long run by specializing in those commodities and developing a comparative advantage in them as the learning process helps to lower their costs.

Learning by doing is an example of what in Chapter 20 we called *dynamic comparative advantages*. The successes of such *newly industrialized countries* (*NICs*) as Brazil, Hong Kong, South Korea, Singapore, and Taiwan seemed to many observers to be based on acquired skills and government policies that created favorable business conditions. This helped to support the theory that comparative advantages can change and can be developed by suitable government policies.

Protecting a domestic industry from foreign competition may give its management time to learn to be efficient and its labor force time to acquire needed skills. If so, there may be a long-term payoff to protecting the industry against foreign competition while a dynamic comparative advantage is being developed.

Similarly, protecting the entire industrial sector may give time for a rural labor force to move to the city, learn new skills, and develop new attitudes. After some decades, the industrial sector may have become competitive and be able to engage in freer foreign trade. The argument here is that increasing returns to scale and learning by doing may apply to the *entire industrial sector* just as it can apply to a single industry within that sector.

Some countries have clearly succeeded in developing strong comparative advantages in targeted sectors and specific industries, but others have failed. One reason such policies have sometimes failed is that protecting local industries from foreign competition may make the industries unadaptive and complacent. Another reason is that it is difficult to identify the industries that will eventually succeed. All too often the protected infant industry grows up to be a weakling that requires permanent tariff protection for its continued existence, or else its rate of learning is slower than that of similar industries in countries that do not provide protection from the chill winds of international competition. In these instances the anticipated comparative advantage never materializes.

To create or to exploit a strategic trade advantage. A major new argument for tariffs or other trade restrictions is to create a strategic advantage in producing or marketing some new product that is expected to generate pure profits. To the extent that all lines of production earn normal profits, there is no reason to produce goods other than ones for which a country has a comparative advantage. Some goods that are produced under oligopolistic conditions may, however, yield pure profits. Where such industries are already well established, there is little chance that a new firm will replace one of the existing oligopolistic giants. The situation is more fluid with new products, however. The first firm to develop and to market a new product successfully may earn a substantial excess profit over all of its opportunity costs and become one of the few established firms in the industry. If protection of the domestic market can increase the chance that one of the protected domestic firms will become one of the established oligopolists in the international market, the protection may pay off. This is the general idea behind the modern concept of strategic trade policy, and it is treated in more detail in the next section.

Strategic Trade Policy

Implications of high development costs. Many of today's high-tech industries have falling average total cost curves due to their large fixed costs of product development. They also often have steep learning curves. For a new generation of civilian aircraft, silicon chips, computers, artificial intelligence machines, and genetically engineered food products, a high proportion of each producer's total costs are for product development. These are fixed costs of entering the market, and they must be incurred before a single unit of output can be sold. In such industries, the actual factory costs of producing each unit of an already developed product may be quite small. Even if average variable costs are constant, the large fixed development costs mean that the average total cost curve has a significant negative slope over a large range of output. It follows that the larger the sales that the firm expects, the lower the price that it can charge and still recover its full costs. These characteristics of many modern high-tech products have several important consequences.

First, the markets for such products are extremely risky. Vast sums must often be spent before any product is tested on purchasers. If the product fails in the market, the fixed development costs are lost.

Second, there may be room for only a few firms in the industry. The large fixed costs of entry create the conditions of natural oligopoly and sometimes even natural monopoly. A large number of firms, each of which has a relatively small output, could not recover their fixed costs. A small number of firms, each of which has a high output, could do so.

Third, a small number of firms may make large profits. Say, for example, that two firms could make large profits but three would make losses. In this case the first two firms that become established in the market will control it and will earn the profits.[1]

The production of full-sized commercial jets provides an example of an industry that possesses many of these characteristics. The development costs of commercial jet aircraft have risen greatly with each new generation. If the aircraft manufacturers are to recover these costs, each of them must have large sales. Thus the number of firms that the market can support has diminished steadily until today there is room for only two or three firms in the industry.

Argument for subsidies. The characteristics that we have just listed are used to provide arguments for subsidizing the development of such industries. Say, for example, that there is room in the aircraft industry for only two major producers of the next round of passenger jets. If the government subsidizes a domestic firm, this firm may become one of the two that succeed. In this case the profits that are subsequently earned may more than repay the cost of the subsidy. Furthermore, a third country's firm, which was not subsidized, may have been just as good as the two that succeeded. Without the subsidy, however, this firm may lose out in the battle to establish itself as one of the two firms in the market. Having lost this one battle, it loses its entire fight for existence. The firm and the country's chances of being represented in the industry are gone for the foreseeable future.

The competition between the Boeing 767 and the Airbus, which is produced by a European consortium, illustrates the importance of subsidies. The European producers received large direct subsidies (and they charge that Boeing received many indirect ones). Whatever the merits of the argument about who got most subsidies, several things are well established: The civilian long-range jet aircraft industry remains profitable; there is room for only two or three major producers; and one of these would not have been the European consortium if it had not been for very substantial government assistance.

Argument for tariffs. The argument for tariffs is that a protected domestic market greatly reduces the risks of product development and allows successful firms to achieve sufficient scale on the domestic market to be able to sell at competitive prices abroad. The classic example here is the victory of the Japanese semiconductor producers over their American rivals. From the beginning of the industry, American firms held a large competitive edge over all others. Then the Japanese decided to develop their industry. To do so, they shielded their domestic market from penetration by U.S. firms while encouraging intense competition among a few Japanese firms. At first well behind the American firms, the Japanese caught up and were then able to penetrate the open U.S. market. In the end the Japanese succeeded with their newest generation of silicon chips, and the once dominant U.S. industry has been eclipsed.

A combination of domestic competition and tariff protection allowed the Japanese semiconductor industry to score a major victory in terms of market share over its U.S. competitors. The strategy, however, entailed large costs, for both product development and aggressive, below-cost pricing policies. Currently, there is debate as to whether the long-run profits resulting from this policy will be sufficient to cover all these costs.

Debate over strategic trade policy. Generalizing from this and similar cases, some economists advocate that Canada and the United States should adopt a *strategic trade policy*, which means, for high-tech industries, government protection of the home market and government subsidization (either openly or more subtly) of the product development stage. These economists say that if North American firms do not follow their advice, they will lose out in industry after industry to the more aggressive Japanese and European competition, which is adept at combining private innovative activity with government assistance.

Opponents argue that strategic trade policy is nothing more than a modern version of the age-old justifications for tariff protection. They argue that once all countries try to be strategic, they will all waste vast sums trying to break into industries in which there is no room for most of them. Consum-

[1] The reason for this is found in the *indivisibility* of product development costs. If, say, $500 million is required to develop a marketable product, the firm that spends $300 million gets nothing. To see why this creates the potential for profits, assume that the market is large enough for the product to be sold at a price that would cover variable costs of production and also pay the opportunity costs of $1.25 billion worth of capital. Further assume that the capital required for actual production is negligible. In this case two firms with a total of $1 billion of capital invested in development costs will enter the market and earn large profits. However, if a third firm entered, making the industry's total invested capital $1.5 billion, all three firms would incur losses.

ers would benefit most, they say, if their governments let other governments engage in this game. Consumers could then buy the cheap, subsidized foreign products and export traditional, lower-tech products in return.

Opponents of strategic trade policy also argue that democratic governments that enter the game of picking and backing winners are likely to make as many bad choices as good ones. One bad choice, with *all* of its massive development costs written off, would require many good choices in order to generate sufficient profits for taxpayers to break even overall. For example, if the rate of return were 25 percent, one bad choice would require four good ones for there to be a zero profit overall. Furthermore, eight successes and one failure makes the overall return only a modest 11 percent.[2] Many observers doubt that democratic governments could have such a success rate.

Advocates of strategic trade policy reply that a country cannot afford to stand by while others play the strategic game. They argue that there are key industries that have major "spillovers" into the rest of the economy. If a country wants to have a high living standard, it must, they argue, compete with the best. If a country lets all of its key industries migrate to other countries, many of the others will follow. The country then risks being reduced to the status of a less developed nation.

This is a debate about dynamic comparative advantage and the effects of key industries on growth and living standards. It is a difficult issue, and one that is vigorously debated in North America today. It is important because it concerns nothing less than the place of the North American economy in the world of the future. Over the next few decades, will North America maintain its place as a leading industrial producer and innovator and as one of the world's highest-income regions? Will it instead go the way other leading countries have gone in the past—from a burst of dynamism, when its society was young and vibrant, to a period of relative stagnation? This happened to Spain in an earlier century and to the United Kingdom in this century. Will Canada and the United States be next? What is the best way to ensure a negative answer to this question? Should unaided market forces or government assistance through strategic trade policy be relied on?

[2] Let each investment be $100 and, when successful, return $125, for a 25 percent return. Nine investments cost $900, and eight successes and one total loss yield $1,000, making an overall profit of $100 on a $900 investment, for a rate of return of 11.1 percent.

How Much Protectionism?

So far we have seen that there is a strong case for allowing free trade in order to realize the gains from trade but that there are also some reasons for departing from completely free trade.

It is not necessary to choose between free trade, on the one hand, and absolute protectionism, on the other. A country can have some trade and some protectionism, too.

Free Trade Versus No Trade

Undoubtedly, it would be possible to grow coffee beans in Prince Edward Island greenhouses and to synthesize all of the oil that we consume (as Germany did during World War II). However, the cost in terms of other commodities forgone would be huge, because these artificial means of production require lavish inputs of factors of production. It would likewise be possible for a tropical country, currently producing foodstuffs, to set up industries to produce all the manufactured products that it consumes. However, for a small country without natural advantages in industrial production, the cost would also be huge. It is thus clear that there is a large gain to all countries in having the kind of specialization and trade that we discussed in Chapter 20. The real output and consumption of all countries would be very much lower if each of them chose to produce domestically all of the goods that it consumed.

In an all-or-nothing choice, almost all countries would choose free trade over no trade.

A Little More Trade Versus a Little Less Trade

Today we have trade among nations, but this trade is not perfectly free. Table 21-1 shows the levels of tariffs on selected commodities in force today.

Would we be better off if today's barriers to trade were reduced or increased? This question shifts the focus of our discussion considerably, for it is quite a jump from the proposition that free trade is better than no trade to the proposition that a little less trade restriction than we have at present is better than a little more. The General Agreement on Tariffs and

TABLE 21-1 Current Tariffs on Industrial Products by Sector: Canada, United States, and All Industrial Countries (*percentage*)[a]

Sector	Canada	United States	All industrial countries
Textiles	16.7	9.2	8.5
Wearing apparel	24.2	22.7	17.5
Leather products	6.3	4.2	3.0
Footwear	21.9	8.8	12.1
Wood products	3.2	1.7	1.9
Furniture and fixtures	14.3	4.1[b]	7.3
Paper and paper products	6.7	0.2	4.2
Printing and publishing	1.0	0.7	1.5
Chemicals	7.5	2.4	6.7
Rubber products	6.7	2.5	4.1
Nonmetal mineral products	6.4	5.3	4.0
Glass and glass products	7.2	6.2	7.9
Iron and steel	5.4	3.6	4.4
Nonferrous metals	2.0	0.7	1.6
Metal products	8.5	4.8	6.3
Nonelectrical machinery	4.5	3.3	4.7
Electrical machinery	5.8	4.4	7.1
Transportation equipment	1.6	2.5	6.0
Miscellaneous manufactures	5.4	4.2	4.7
All industries	5.2	4.3	5.8

Source: A. V. Deardorff and R. M. Stern, "Economic Effects of Complete Elimination of Post–Tokyo Round Tariffs," in *Trade Policy in the 1980s*, ed. W. R. Cline (Washington, D.C.: Institute for International Economics, 1983), pp. 674–675.

[a] Weighted by own-country imports, excluding petroleum.

[b] Estimated from incomplete data.

Canada remains a relatively high tariff country. These Canadian and U.S. tariffs apply to trade with third countries. Tariffs on trade between Canada and the United States are being phased out under the Canada-U.S. Free Trade Agreement over the period 1989–1999. In spite of having cut its tariffs significantly in rounds of GATT negotiations over the past several decades, Canada remains a relatively high tariff country compared to both the United States, its largest trading partner, and the average of all industrial countries. Note that a few Canadian tariffs are still over 20 percent. The data show tariff rates in effect after the last round of tariff negotiations had been phased in at the end of 1986. They will remain in place until the cuts agreed to during the Uruguay Round are phased in during the 1990s.

Trade (GATT) has concentrated on reducing the levels at each round of talks. The Canada-U.S. Free Trade Agreement removes all tariffs on trade between the two countries but leaves in place many nontariff barriers on Canada-U.S. trade and all existing barriers to trade with other countries. To determine the gains for such partial elimination of tariffs, we need to know the losses resulting from existing tariffs.

Constant costs. Most early measurements of the cost of the Canadian tariff assumed that the costs of producing all commodities would remain unchanged when tariffs were removed. Under this assumption, the cost of the tariff was typically measured to be somewhere between 1 and 2 percent of total Canadian output as measured by the country's gross domestic product (GDP). The losses from tariffs were then just the losses from failing to produce according to comparative advantage under conditions of constant costs (as studied in the first part of Chapter 20).

To gain some insight into these figures, compare the effects of a 20 percent uniform effective rate of tariff with those of free trade. Tariffs of 20 percent will protect industries that are up to 20 percent less efficient than foreign competitors. If the costs of the various tariff-protected industries were spread out evenly, some would be 20 percent less efficient than their foreign competitors and others only 1 percent less efficient. Their average inefficiency would be about half the tariff rate, so they would be on average about 10 percent less efficient than their foreign competitors.

Suppose that as a result of tariffs, approximately 15 percent of a country's resources are allocated to industries different from the ones to which they would be allocated if there were no tariffs. If the average protected industry is 10 percent less efficient than its foreign rival, approximately 15 percent of a country's resources are producing on average about 10 percent less efficiently than they would be if there were no tariffs. This causes a reduction in national income on the order of 1.5 percent as a result of tariff protection.

Scale effects. Most manufacturing industries produce a wide range of differentiated products; for example, the paper industry produces over 300 types and grades of paper products. Furthermore, technological developments are constantly changing the products that can be produced.

Associated with each differentiated product are fixed costs for product development and for product-specific machinery. Like all fixed costs, they give rise to a range of falling unit costs as the overheads are spread over more units when output rises. Total unit costs will start to rise only when scale diseconomies in production are strong enough to offset the effect of these falling overheads per unit of output. As a result, associated with each line of differentiated goods is a minimum efficient scale that is often quite large.

The consequences of this large *MES* for firms serving the Canadian market were analyzed in an important study by Professors Harry Eastman and Stephen Stykholt of the University of Toronto. They argued, as shown in Figure 21-2, that the Canadian market is often not large enough to allow each differentiated product to be produced at minimum efficient scale when each Canadian industry produces the whole range of products for the domestic market alone. Thus when tariffs protect Canadian firms selling solely for the home market, costs are considerably higher than they would be if the market were large enough to allow production to reach *MES* in each product line, as it often does in the large U.S. markets.

When tariffs are removed, the Canadian firms specialize in a reduced number of product lines, which they produce at their *MES*s, selling some of the output in the domestic market and exporting the rest. As a result, cost-reducing economies are

FIGURE 21-2 Product Line Specialization by a Canadian Firm

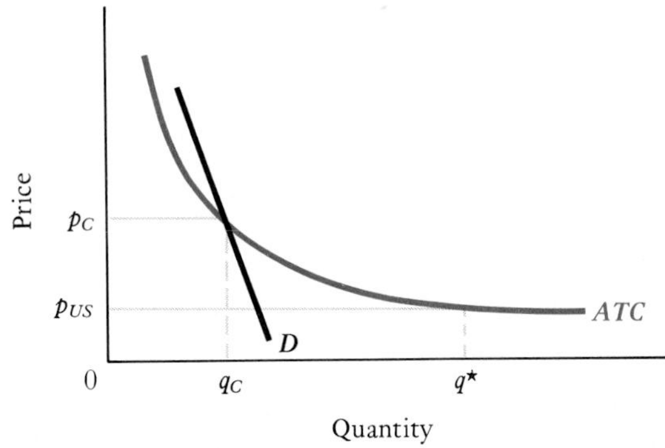

The Canadian market is often too small to allow Canadian firms to reach minimum efficient scale in a wide range of differentiated goods. The figure shows the average total cost curve for one product type in a firm producing many types of some differentiated product. The Canadian demand curve for the product is D. The lowest price at which costs can be covered is p_C, where sales are q_C.

The U.S. market is so large that firms selling a range of differentiated products in that market can produce an output of each product that is at least as large as the *MES* of q^*. They thus achieve the price p_{US}.

If Canadian firms gain access to the U.S. market, they will specialize in a few product lines and produce at a volume sufficient to reach the *MES* of each. The outputs of these products will be q^* or more. This will allow cost to be covered at the price prevailing in the American market, which is p_{US}.

achieved. Exports of some product lines go up, as do imports of other product lines. So trade increases on an intra-industry basis, and the advantages of efficiency in production are achieved without losing the advantages of diversity in consumption. This specialization in a narrowed range of product lines, with the resulting increase in intra-industry trade, is often referred to as *rationalization* of the domestic industry.

Such rationalization has occurred when tariffs have been reduced on Canadian-American trade as a result of successive rounds of negotiations under the GATT. It has often resulted from simple profit-maximizing reactions to changing market circumstances. It has sometimes resulted from conscious decisions made by transnational corporations to allow foreign subsidiaries to specialize in particular product lines, which they export to markets throughout the world. One other very important rationalization within an industry resulted from a specific agreement covering the Canadian and American automobile industries, known as the Auto Pact. It rationalizes the auto industries in the two countries, allowing the North American producers to behave as if they were in a single country. Several safeguards were built into the pact, ensuring that production would not be transferred to the United States. The provisions of the pact have now been included in the broader Canadian-U.S. Free Trade Agreement, which is discussed later in this chapter.

Calculations allowing for these scale effects have been made by such Canadian economists as Richard Harris of Queen's University and David Cox of the University of Toronto. They suggest a cost of the Canadian tariff of between 4 and 8 percent of Canadian GDP.

Suppose that the cost of the Canadian tariff is 5 percent of GDP. That may not seem like a very large number, especially when one realizes that is the increase in GDP that economic growth produces on average every three or four years. Yet at 1989 prices, it is over $20 billion. That amount each year forever could buy a lot of hospitals, schools, medical research, and new energy supplies.

Fallacious Trade Policy Arguments

We have seen that there are gains to be had from a high volume of international trade and specialization. We have also seen that there can be valid arguments for a moderate degree of protectionism. There are also many claims that do not advance the debate. Fallacious arguments are heard on both sides, and they color much of the popular discussion. These arguments have been around for a long time, but their survival does not make them true. We examine them now to see where their fallacies lie.

Fallacious Free Trade Arguments

Free trade always benefits all countries. This is not necessarily so. We have just seen that some countries may gain by restricting trade in order to get a sufficiently favorable shift in their terms of trade. Such countries would lose if they gave up these tariffs and adopted free trade unilaterally.

Infant industries never abandon their tariff protection. It is argued that granting protection to infant industries is a mistake, because these industries seldom admit to growing up and will cling to their protection even when they are fully grown. However, infant industry tariffs are a mistake *only* if these industries never grow up. In this case, permanent tariff protection would be required to protect a weak industry that would never be able to compete on an equal footing in the international market. However, if the industries do grow up and achieve the expected scale economies, the fact that, like any special interest group, they cling to their tariff protection is not a sufficient reason for denying protection to other genuine infant industries. When economies of scale are realized, the real costs of production are reduced and resources are freed for other uses. Whether or not the tariff or other trade barriers remain, as they sometimes do, or are removed, as they often are, a cost saving has been effected by the scale economies.

Fallacious Protectionist Arguments

Prevent exploitation. According to the exploitation theory, trade can never be mutually advantageous; one trading partner *must* always reap a gain at the other's expense. Thus the weaker trading partner must protect itself by restricting its trade with the stronger partner. However, the principle of comparative advantage shows that it is possible for both parties to gain from trade and thus refutes the exploitation doctrine of trade. When opportunity cost ratios differ in two countries, specialization and the accompanying trade make it possible to produce more of all commodities and thus make it possible for both parties to consume more as a result of trade than they could get in its absence.

Keep the money at home. This argument says, "If I buy a foreign good, I have the good and the foreigner has the money, whereas if I buy the same good locally, I have the good and our country has the money, too."

The argument is based on a misconception. It assumes that domestic money actually goes abroad physically when imports are purchased and that trade flows only in one direction. However, when Canadian importers purchase Italian-made goods, for example, they do not send dollars abroad. They (or their financial agents) buy Italian lire and use them to pay the Italian manufacturers. They purchase the lire on the foreign exchange market by giving up dollars to someone who wishes to use them for expenditure *in Canada*. Even if the money did go abroad physically—that is, if an Italian firm accepted a shipload of Canadian dollars—it would be because that firm (or someone to whom it could sell the dollars) wanted them to spend in the only country where they are legal tender, Canada.

Currency ultimately does no one any good except as a form of purchasing power. It would be miraculous if engraved pieces of paper could be exported in return for real goods; after all, the Bank of Canada has the power to create as much new money as it wishes. It is only because the paper can buy Canadian commodities and assets that people want it.

Protect against low-wage foreign labor. Surely, the argument says, the products of low-wage countries will drive U.S. and Canadian products from the market, and our high standard of living will be dragged down to that of our poor trading partners. Arguments of this sort have swayed many voters over the years.

As a prelude to considering them, stop and think about what the argument would imply if it were taken out of the international context and put into a local one, where the same principles govern the gains from trade. Is it really impossible for a rich person to gain from trading with a poor person? Would the local millionaire be better off is she did all her own typing, gardening, and cooking? No one believes that a rich person cannot gain from trading with those who are less rich. Why, then, must a rich group of people lose from trading with a poor group? "Well," you say, "the poor group will price its goods too cheaply." Does anyone believe that consumers lose from buying in a discount house or a supermarket just because the prices are lower there than at the old-fashioned corner store? Consumers gain when they can buy the same goods at a lower price. If the Koreans pay low wages and sell their goods cheaply, *Korean* labor may suffer, but we will gain because we obtain their goods at a low cost in terms of the goods that we must export in return. The cheaper our imports are, the better off we are in terms of the goods and services that are available for domestic consumption.

Stated in more formal terms, the gains from trade depend on comparative, not absolute, advantages. World production is higher when any two areas, say, North America and Japan, specialize in the production of the goods for which they have a comparative advantage than when they both try to be self-sufficient.

Might it not be possible, however, that Japan will undersell Canadian and U.S. industries in all lines of production and thus appropriate all, or more than all, the gains for itself, leaving the North American countries no better off, or even worse off, than if they had no trade with Japan? The answer is no. The reason for this depends on the behavior of exchange rates, which we shall study in Chapter 41. As we shall see, equality of demand and supply in foreign exchange markets ensures that trade flows in both directions.

Imports can be obtained only by spending the currency of the country that makes the imports. Claims to this currency can be obtained only by exporting goods and services or by borrowing. Thus, lending and borrowing aside, imports must equal exports. All trade must be in two directions; countries can buy only if they can also sell.

In the long run, trade cannot hurt a country by causing it to import without exporting.

Trade, then, always provides scope for international specialization, with each country producing and exporting goods for which it has a comparative advantage and importing goods for which it does not.

Exports raise living standards; imports lower them. Exports add to aggregate demand; imports subtract from it. Thus, other things being equal, exports tend to increase national income and imports tend to reduce it. Surely, then, it is desirable to encourage exports and to discourage imports. This is an appealing argument, but it is incorrect.

Exports raise national income by adding to the value of domestic output, but they do not add to the value of domestic consumption. In fact, exports are goods produced at home and consumed abroad, while imports are goods produced abroad and consumed at home. The standard of living in a country depends on the goods and services available for *consumption,* not on what is produced.

If exports were really good and imports were really bad, then a fully employed economy that managed to increase exports without a corresponding increase in imports ought to be better off. Such a change, however, would result in a reduction in its current standards of living, because when more goods are sent abroad and no more are brought in from abroad, the total goods available for domestic consumption must fall.

The living standards of a country depend on the goods and services *consumed* in that country. The importance of exports is that they permit imports to be made. This two-way international exchange is valuable because more goods can be imported than could be obtained if the same goods were produced at home.

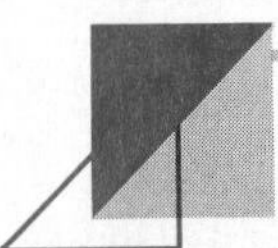

Current Trade Policy

International Agreements on Trade and Tariffs

In the past, any country could impose any desired tariffs on its imports. However, when one country increases its tariffs, the action may trigger retaliatory actions by its trading partners. Just as an arms race can escalate, so can a tariff war. Extended negotiations may then be required to undo the damage.

The General Agreement on Tariffs and Trade (GATT)

In the 1930s, a high-water mark of world protectionism was reached as each country sought to raise its employment by raising its tariffs. The end result was lowered efficiency and less trade but no additional employment. One of the most notable achievements of the post–World War II era was the creation of the General Agreement on Tariffs and Trade (GATT). Under this agreement, member countries meet periodically to negotiate general cuts in tariffs that apply to them all, currently close to 100 countries. The GATT prevents countries from raising tariffs barriers unilaterally. It also has a code of conduct regulating unfair trade practices. Disputes involving allegations that a member has violated a GATT rule are adjudicated by a panel of experts drawn from other member countries. Although there is no enforcement mechanism, the need to remain within GATT has meant that no country has failed to abide by a GATT panel decision—although sometimes reluctantly and after much procrastination.

The two most recent rounds of GATT negotiations have each reduced world tariffs by about one-third. The Kennedy Round of negotiations was completed in 1967, and new rates were phased in over a five-year period, ending in 1972. The Tokyo Round of negotiations was completed in 1979, and the reductions were phased in between 1981 and 1986. At the completion of the Uruguay Round in 1990, a further set of reductions may be agreed on and phased in over the first half of the 1990s.

Ironically, as that new round of reductions began, pressure was mounting in many countries to protect jobs at home through trade restrictions. Protectionist policies grew alarmingly in the EC and many other areas. As time passed, even the GATT itself came under attack. The worldwide recession that began in late 1981 was undoubtedly an important source of this pressure. In addition, protectionist sentiment in many countries was stirred up by the decline in the international competitiveness of traditional industries due to sharp changes in terms of trade. Also, under the impact of the persistent U.S. trade deficit, protectionist pressures grew through the first half of the 1980s in the United States.

The Uruguay Round of GATT negotiations began in 1986. It addressed five key issues: (1) the growing worldwide use of nontariff barriers to trade; (2) the need to develop rules for liberalizing trade in services, which is the most rapidly growing component of foreign trade; (3) the distorting effect on trade in agricultural products caused by heavy domestic subsidization of agriculture; (4) the need to develop more effective methods of settling disputes that arise from violations of GATT rules; and (5) the desire of developed nations to gain better copyright protection for intellectual property—a desire that pitted the rich, innovating nations against the poorer nations with a self-interest in gaining access to intellectual property on terms as favorable as possible. (Intellectual property is a property right resulting from mental effort, such as discovery, product development, or the creation of a work of art, and resulting in a right of ownership conferred by a document such as a patent or a copyright.) The final result of the negotiations will be known by the time this book is published.

Common Markets

A **common market** is an agreement among a group of countries to eliminate barriers to free trade among themselves and to present a common barrier to trade with the rest of the world. The most important example of this came into being in 1957, when the Treaty of Rome brought together France, Germany, Italy, the Netherlands, Belgium, and Luxembourg in what was first called the European Common Market (ECM), then the European Economic Community (EEC), and now just the European Community (EC). The original six countries were joined in 1973 by the United Kingdom, the Republic of Ireland, and Denmark; Greece entered in 1983; and Spain and Portugal entered in 1986.

This organization is dedicated to bringing about free trade, complete mobility of factors of production, and the eventual harmonization of fiscal and monetary policies among the member countries. Many tariffs on manufactured goods have been eliminated, and much freedom of movement of labor and capital has been achieved. Substantial monetary integration has also been achieved, and it is expected that Europe will have a single currency by the end of the century. At the time of writing this book, a major push was under way to remove most of the remaining restrictions by the end of 1992. How far it will succeed was uncertain at the beginning of 1990. Its full success, however, would make the EC into a genuine common market with enormous economic potential.

Other common markets have been formed, among them the Central American Common Market and the East African Community, but none has yet achieved the success of the EC, and some have collapsed.

Most federal countries, such as Australia and Germany, provide one common market among the constituent states or provinces. Canada is an exception. Provincial governments create many restrictions to trade in goods and services as well as to the free movement of labor among the provinces. For example, most provinces require that Canadian beer sold in the province be manufactured in the province. As a result, Canada has many small, inefficient breweries that have trouble competing with imported beers and in selling at competitive prices abroad. Free movement of labor and professions around the country is hindered partly by provincial regulations and partly by union rules protected by provincial laws. In these and many other ways, Canada is far from being a common market within its own borders.

Free Trade Associations

A **free trade association** allows for tariff-free trade between the member countries, but unlike a common market, it leaves each member free to levy its own tariffs on imports from other countries. As a result, members must maintain customs points at their common border (if they have one) to make sure that imports into the free trade area do not all enter through the country that is levying the lowest tariff on each item.

The first important free trade association in the modern era was the European Free Trade Association (EFTA). It was formed in 1960 by a group of European countries that was unwilling to join the European Common Market because of its all-embracing character. They removed all tariffs on trade among themselves. Each of the EFTA countries also signed a free trade area agreement with the Common Market. This makes the EC-EFTA market the largest market in the industrialized world (over 300 million people) in which goods can move unhindered by tariff barriers.

In 1988, Canada and the United States signed a sweeping agreement instituting free trade on all goods and many services, covering what is the largest flow of international trade between any two countries in the world. Australia and New Zealand have also entered into an association that removes restrictions on trade in goods and services between the two countries. In 1990, the United States and Mexico began negotiations that may end in an agreement for free trade, at least in goods. At the time of writing in late 1990, it appeared that Canada would join in these negotiations.

Trade Remedy Laws and Nontariff Barriers

Before 1980, negotiations under the GATT had concentrated on the reduction of tariffs. As these were lowered, countries that wished to protect domestic industries began using a series of trade restrictions that came to be known as nontariff barriers (NTBs). Most NTBs are ostensibly levied for purposes other than protectionism, often called *trade relief purposes*.

An effort to control the growing use of NTBs was made in the Tokyo Round of GATT negotiations. These measures were classified, and the circumstances under which their use was legitimate were laid down. The ironic result is that by making all countries aware of these measures and by making their use respectable under some circumstances, these GATT agreements seem to have led to an increase in the use of NTBs for purposes of trade restriction.

Escape clause. One procedure that can be used as an NTB is the so-called escape clause action. A rapid surge of imports may temporarily threaten the existence of domestic producers. These producers may then be given temporary relief by raising tariff rates over and above those agreed to during the GATT negotiations. The trouble is that once imposed, these "temporary" measures are hard to eliminate.

One "temporary" measure that is still in force provides a cautionary tale. In the late 1950s, the textile and clothing industries in many advanced industrial nations saw their market shares reduced by a rising volume of trade from Hong Kong, South Korea, the Philippines, and other newly industrializing nations. The response of the developed countries was to negotiate *multifiber agreements* (MFAs) that provided maximum annual quotas for each exporting textile-producing country for a 20-year period. Starting in 1981, many of these soon-to-expire agreements were renegotiated, generally leading to more, rather than less, restrictive policies. At the start of the 1990s they were still in effect.

Dumping. When a commodity is sold in a foreign country at a price that is lower than the price in the domestic market for reasons not related to cost, this is called **dumping**. Dumping is a form of price discrimination of the kind studied in the theory of monopoly (see Chapter 13). Most governments have antidumping duties, which protect their own industries against unfair foreign pricing practices.

Dumping, if it lasts indefinitely, can be a gift to the receiving country whose consumers get goods from abroad at less than their real cost. Dumping is more often a temporary measure, designed to get rid of unwanted surpluses, or a predatory attempt to drive competitors out of business. In either case, domestic producers complain about unfair foreign competition. In these cases it is accepted international practice to levy *antidumping duties* on foreign imports. These duties are designed to eliminate the discriminatory elements in their prices.

Unfortunately, antidumping laws have been evolving over the past two decades in ways that allow antidumping duties to become barriers to trade rather than redresses for unfair trading practices. The United States and Canada have been leaders in making these changes, but many other countries, including those of the EC, have been quick to follow.

Two features of the antidumping system that is now in effect in many countries make it highly protectionist. First, *any* price discrimination is classified as dumping and hence subject to penalties. Thus prices in the producer's domestic market become, in effect, minimum prices below which no sales can be made in foreign markets, regardless of the circumstances. Second, following an alteration in the U.S. law in the early 1970s, many importing countries' laws now calculate the "margin of dumping" as the difference between the price that is charged in that country's market and the foreign producers' "full allocated cost" (average total cost). This means that when there is global excess demand such that the profit-maximizing price for all producers is below average total cost (but above average variable cost), foreign producers can be convicted of dumping. This gives domestic producers enormous protection whenever the market price falls temporarily below *ATC*. They are permitted to sell at these prices, but their foreign competitors are not. Furthermore, it is very difficult to allocate overheads among individual products in many multiproduct industries. This is particularly true in industries such as chemicals, where fixed costs are a high proportion of total costs and there are many individual products that have widely differing development costs.

Countervailing duties. Countervailing duties provide another case in which a trade relief measure can sometimes become a covert NTB. The countervailing duty is designed to act not as a tariff barrier but rather as a means of creating a "level playing field" on which fair international competition can take place. This "trade remedy" is most commonly used by the United States and most feared by Canadian exporters. (As of mid 1990, only once has a Canadian countervailing duty been levied on a U.S. export to Canada.)

American firms rightly complain that they cannot compete against the bottomless purses of foreign governments. Subsidized foreign exports can be sold indefinitely in the United States at prices that are below the exports' full costs of production. The original object of countervailing duties was to counteract the effect on price of the presence of such foreign subsidies.

If a U.S. firm suspects the existence of such a subsidy and registers a complaint, the American government is then required to make an investigation. For a countervailing duty to be levied, the investigation must find, first, that the foreign subsidy to the specific industry in question does exist and, second, that it is large enough to cause significant injury to competing American firms.

There is no doubt that countervailing duties have sometimes been used to remove the effects of "unfair" competition that are caused by foreign subsidies. Other governments complain, however, that countervailing duties are often used as a thinly disguised barrier to trade. At the early stages of the development of countervailing duties, only subsidies whose prime effect was to distort trade were subject to countervail. Even then, however, the existence of equivalent domestic subsidies was not taken into account when decisions were made to put countervailing duties on subsidized imports. Over time, the type of subsidy that is subject to countervail has evolved to the point that almost any government program that affects industry now qualifies. Since all governments have many programs that provide some direct or indirect assistance to industry, the potential for the use of countervailing duties as thinly disguised trade barriers is enormous.

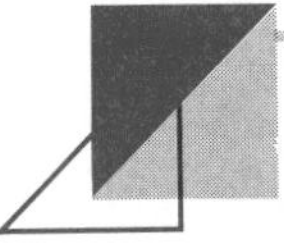

Canadian Trade and Trade Policy

Foreign trade accounts for a large part of the Canadian economy. In 1989, exports were over 25 percent of GDP, compared to about 9 percent for the United States. The most important explanation of these figures is the relative size of the two countries. The world as a whole cannot undertake any "foreign" trade (at least until other planets are colonized). As a general rule, the larger the country, the larger its interregional trade and the less its international trade.

Figure 21-3 shows Canadian merchandise exports and imports as a percentage of GDP for the years 1947–1989. As can be seen, both ratios have consistently been in the 20 to 30 percent range.

The data in Figure 21-3 underestimate the international exposure of the Canadian economy in two important ways. First, because government expenditure on goods and services accounts for more than 20 percent of Canadian GDP, exports represent virtually *half* the goods produced in the private sector! Second, the figures represent goods actually imported and exported. Many imported goods face competition in domestic markets from close substitutes produced in Canada, called import-competing goods. Similarly, goods identical or very similar to those exported are also produced and consumed in Canada. Hence the fractions of *importables* and *exporables* are much larger than the fractions of actual imports and exports.

The Canadian economy is dependent on foreign trade and open to foreign competition because exports generate a large part of private-sector Canadian national income.

Canada's climate and resource endowments help to determine its trade patterns. Severe winters cause Canadians to spend money on foreign vacations and on imports of fresh fruits and vegetables. Canada has an abundance of arable land, timber, minerals, and energy in the form of both fossil fuels and hydroelectric power. As a consequence, Canada's exports

FIGURE 21-3 Exports and Imports As a Percentage of GDP, 1947–1989

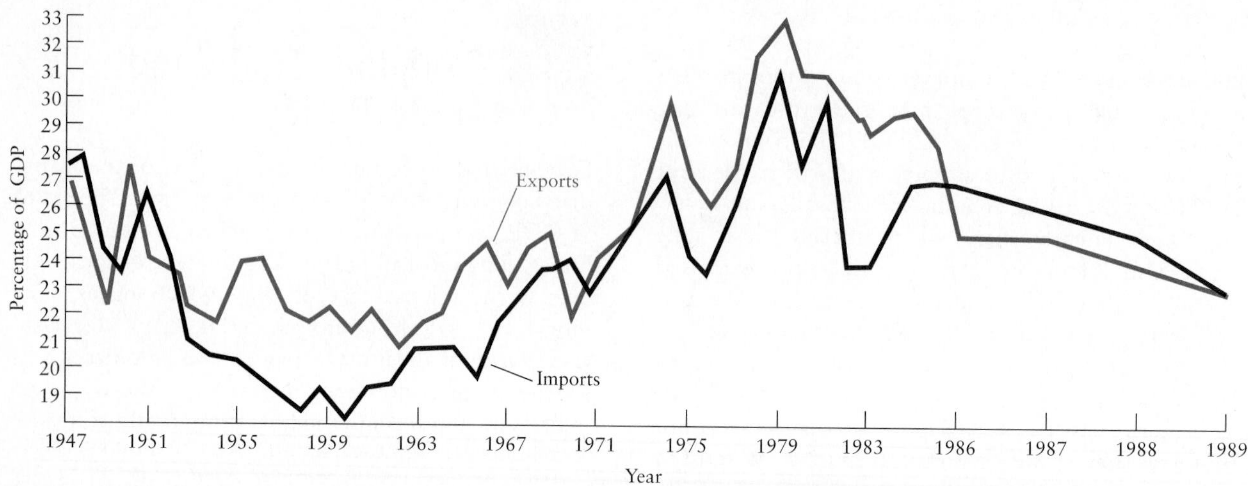

Exports and imports have each been a relatively constant fraction of GDP in the post–World War II period. Exports and imports are plotted as a percentage of national income. Although exports, imports, and GDP all fluctuate considerably, the three series tend to be correlated fairly closely, and thus their ratios are relatively stable. Fluctuations in exports cause fluctuations in GDP, so the two series tend to move together. Fluctuations in GDP cause fluctuations in expenditure on imports, so these two series tend to move together as well.

are heavily concentrated in *primary products* and in manufactured goods that require large amounts of these resources in their production. A further important resource is human capital. A literate, numerate, relatively sophisticated Canadian population gives Canada a comparative advantage in many skill-intensive commodities.[3]

Trade and Trade Policy in the Past

The Staples Thesis

The central role of primary product exports in Canada's economic development is illustrated by the experience with prairie wheat, which emerged as an important export between the years 1886 and 1914.

[3] This is one reason why economists worry so much about the current decline in educational standards. If the education of Canadians and Americans who become average members of the labor force declines seriously relative to what is obtained by Europeans and Japanese, Canadian and American comparative advantages will shift toward lower-skill, lower-income-producing activities.

During this "wheat boom" period, real GDP increased by 150 percent and population grew from 5.1 to 7.9 million. Much of this growth was tied closely to the wheat sector. For example, over 10,000 miles of railway track were laid in order to transport agricultural products from the prairies to the lakehead at Thunder Bay and to the west coast. With the expansion of the railways came construction of grain elevators and investment in farm equipment and food-processing industries.

Based in part on Canada's experience during the wheat boom, Professors Harold Innis of the University of Toronto and W. A. MacIntosh of Queen's University developed the *staples thesis.* According to this thesis, economic growth in Canada has been tied to a sequence of exports of staple products, primary products for which Canada has had a comparative advantage. The important staple industries in the seventeenth and eighteenth centuries were the fur trade and the east coast fishery; during the nineteenth century, timber and wheat from Upper Canada were the important staples; and in the twentieth century, staples have been prairie wheat, pulp and paper, minerals, and oil and natural gas. These staples have been important not only as exports but also as stimuli to growth in other sectors of the economy.

Reciprocity: 1854–1866

In 1854, British North America and the United States signed a reciprocity treaty, and until 1866, when the treaty was abrogated by the United States, many commodities (including all primary products) crossed the border duty-free. After confederation, the Canadian government maintained low tariffs as it tried to persuade the United States to renew the reciprocity treaty. In the mid 1870s, however, the Canadian economy was hit with a recession, and, as often happens during recessions, manufacturers pressed for more protection.

High Tariffs and the National Policy: 1878–1935

Partly in response to this pressure, Sir John A. MacDonald introduced his National Policy in 1878. This policy was presented as a program for long-run economic development and included subsidies for building railways, support for farm settlement, and emphasis on the export of a few primary products. However, the cornerstone was increased tariff protection for Canadian manufacturing. This protectionist policy remained essentially unchanged until 1935.

Although economic historians still debate the overall benefits to Canada of the National Policy, it clearly influenced different regions differently. Manufacturing industries in Ontario and Quebec gained from tariff protection, but the remaining provinces, which mainly exported primary goods and imported manufactured goods, lost by it. The National Policy raised the prices of the manufactured goods they bought. They had either to buy expensive, tariff-protected Canadian-produced goods or else pay the tariff-burdened price for imported goods.

Falling Tariffs: 1935 to the Present

The enormous increase in world protectionism in the 1920s and early 1930s demonstrated how vulnerable Canadians were to trade restrictions imposed by other countries. As a result, Canadian policy switched from pursuing trade restrictions to promoting trade liberalization.

This historic shift to a policy of promoting trade liberalization began with two tariff-reducing treaties negotiated with the United States in 1935 and 1937. It was confirmed in 1947 when Canada became a charter member of the General Agreement on Tariffs and Trade (GATT).

As a result of the tariff cuts negotiated between 1935 and 1980, Canadian tariffs have fallen from high to more moderate levels. In the process, much Canadian manufacturing has been integrated into the world economy, and Canada has become an exporter of many manufactured goods (while also remaining an important exporter of primary products). Table 21-2 gives some relevant data.

Analysis of Canada's trade and industrial performance by the Economic Council of Canada indicated that trade liberalization in the 1970s and 1980s resulted in more trade *within* each industry. Canadian firms rationalized by reducing the number of their product lines, attaining competitive costs on a much smaller range of products. Many of these products proved to be exportable, and the abandoned lines were now imported. The net effect was an increased amount of intra-industry foreign trade between Canada and the United States.

Some industries did experience growth in imports relative to exports, although exports grew even in these industries—they just grew less than imports. Since these industries experienced a decline in net exports as a proportion of total production, some shrinkage in their relative size did occur.

In other industries the reverse happened. Resource-based industries such as wood products and paper, which were already substantial net exporters, experienced modest increases in their net exports. The most dramatic increase in exports occurred in industries such as chemicals, machinery, and rubber and plastic products, all of which had been significant net importers during the 1960s.

Thus as trade barriers have been reduced, both Canadian exports and Canadian imports have increased in virtually all sectors. Whole industries have not disappeared in either Canada or the United States. Instead, each industry has specialized in *particular product lines* in each country so that both Canadian *and* American exports have increased in each industry. The shift in *net* export positions has been modest for most industries. This is just as it was in Europe when trade was liberalized after formation of the Common Market, and for just the same rea-

TABLE 21-2 Commodity Composition of Canadian Exports, 1960–1986

	1960	1970	1980	1989
Food and agriculture	18.8	11.4	11.1	7.1
Crude materials	21.2	18.8	19.8	12.9
Fabricated materials	51.9	35.8	39.4	33.4
Manufactured end products	7.8	33.8	29.4	46.3
Special transactions	0.3	0.2	0.3	0.3
Total	100.0	100.0	100.0	100.0

Source: Statistics Canada, *Summary of External Trade.*

son—because the adjustment was intra-industry.

The foregoing discussion explains why many economists believe that a misunderstanding of the adjustment process has led some people to overestimate the difficulties of adjusting to tariff cuts. The evolution from 1935 to 1986 that removed something like three-quarters of Canadian trade barriers created far more jobs than it destroyed. This "creation" and "destruction" of jobs is another way of saying that labor was being reallocated out of tariff-protected jobs into jobs where Canada has a comparative advantage. The gains from this more efficient specialization accrued to a great extent to labor because of the higher wages and increased job security that could be offered in the more efficient lines of production. The reallocation also caused far fewer adjustment difficulties than might have been expected because so much of the reallocation of resources was intra-industry. For example, it is far easier to reallocate resources from producing one type of paper product to another type or from producing one type of fashion good to another than it is to reallocate resources from, say, the fashion goods industry to the paper products industry.

The development of a competitive manufacturing sector in Canada was aided by a sectoral free trade agreement called the Auto Pact. This introduced free trade in automobiles and auto parts with some safeguards to ensure that production remained divided between the two countries.

Increasing Dependence on the United States

In 1938, some 40 percent of Canada's exports went to the United Kingdom and only 23 percent to the United States. By 1960, a mere 17 percent went to the U.K. while 57 percent went to the U.S. In 1986, the figures were 2 percent and 78 percent, respectively. In part the causes of this shift were beyond Canadian control. For example, the United Kingdom's entry into the European Economic Community in 1973 ended any major trading relation between Canada and the U.K. In part the shift represents a major victory for Canadian business. In the 1980s, with the European economies stagnant and the less developed countries trying to cut imports (because of their need to free foreign exchange to pay interest on their large foreign debts), the American market was the only *growing* market open to international traders. Firms from all over the world tried to sell more in that market, and Canada succeeded better than almost any other country in gaining a share of the great growth in American demand. Table 21-3 tells us the story of the changes.

Many Canadians worried about these changes; many wished that Canada were not so dependent on its enormous neighbor to the south. But no Canadian government, Liberal or Conservative, has been able to develop an effective policy to reduce that dependence.

The Current Setting

As it always has, Canada exports far more primary products than it imports. In return, in spite of the growth of Canadian manufacturing, Canada imports more manufactured goods than it exports.

As we have seen, Canada, along with the rest of the industrialized world, embarked in 1947 on a policy of tariff reduction under the newly formed GATT. As a result of these tariff reductions and of the Auto Pact, many Canadian manufacturing industries have developed to the extent that they can export successfully, and several Canadian firms, such

TABLE 21-3 Composition of Canada's Trade, Selected Years (*percentage*)

	Exports			Imports		
	1960	1983	1989	1960	1983	1989
United States	57	73	73	70	72	64
United Kingdom	17	3	2	11	2	4
Other EC	8	5	7	5	6	12
Japan	3	5	6	2	6	6
All other countries	15	14	12	12	14	14

Source: Statistics Canada, *Summary of External Trade.*

as Northern Telecom, Alcan, and Brascan, have developed into highly successful transnational corporations. Although resource-based industries will continue to be important, Canada's future prosperity may be linked more and more to its ability to export manufactured and service-related products. But the world markets for manufactured goods and services are fiercely competitive, and Canada's access to these markets is not assured. Policymakers are concerned not only to gain better access but also simply to preserve existing access.

Canadian industry is also under competitive pressure from newly industrialized countries (NICs), especially in lower-wage, lower-value-added commodities. Canadians need to adjust to this, just as Japan did, by reallocating resources out of lower-wage, lower-value-added lines of production and into higher-wage, higher-value-added lines.

Canada and the Rise of World Protectionism

An important feature of the recent rise in protectionism, particularly in the United States and the European Community, is that nontariff barriers (NTBs), rather than tariffs, have been raised. As mentioned earlier, GATT rules constrain the use of tariffs and also codify (as a result of negotiations in the 1970s) the circumstances under which NTBs can be used. However, the GATT authorities have had little success in constraining the growing use of NTBs. This is discussed further in Box 21-2.

Growing U.S. protectionism not only threatened the access to the American market of many of Canada's exports, but it also threatened to cause an exodus of Canadian capital to the United States. Many successful Canadian exporters were motivated to set up plants in the United States in order to avoid existing U.S. trade barriers and threatened new ones. Such relocations occurred in large numbers throughout the 1980s, and surveys of investment intentions, conducted by Canadian economists Don Daly and D. C. McCharles, showed an increase in the intention to do so in the 1990s.

The Canada-U.S. Free Trade Agreement

The Canada-U.S. Free Trade Agreement (FTA) was proposed by many as a natural response to the economic problems just described. On the positive side, it was pointed out that about three-quarters of the trade barriers that existed in 1935 had already been dismantled and Canadian industry had prospered with steadily increasing employment, exports, and real wages. Business leaders were mainly confident that they could benefit from open, global competition without tariff protection.[4] On the negative side, the fear of mounting U.S. protectionism led many to look for ways of preserving Canada's access to its most important foreign market, the United States.

After nearly two years of negotiations, an agreement was signed in October 1987. There followed a year of intense debate in Canada on the economic,

[4] In the 1960s, well over half of the members of the Canadian Manufacturers' Association, which represents middle-size business, were opposed to further tariff cuts. By the mid 1980s, after having responded successfully to the Tokyo Round tariff cuts, Canadian leaders had undergone a major shift of attitude. By 1986, the Business Council on National Issues, which represents large businesses in Canada; the Canadian Manufacturers' Association; and the Small Business Association had all polled their members and found strong majorities in favor of free trade with the United States.

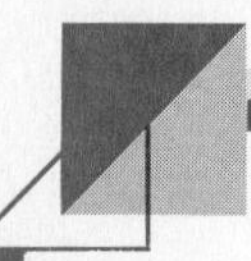

BOX 21-2

The Crisis in the Multilateral Trading System

At the end of World War II, the United States took the lead in forming the GATT and in pressing for reductions in world tariffs through successive rounds of negotiations. Largely as a result of this U.S. initiative, the world's tariff barriers have been greatly reduced, and the volume of world trade has risen steadily.

The 1980s saw a serious crisis evolve in this multilateral trading system. The most important single force that led toward this was a shift in the attitudes of many Americans toward protectionism. There are at least two key reasons for this shift.

The Growth of Protectionist Sentiment

First, under the impact of the persistent trade deficit, which is further discussed in Chapters 42 and 43, many influential U.S. leaders have become protectionist for the first time since the early 1930s. Second, the stiff competition coming from Japanese and European industry has led many Americans to fear a loss of U.S. competitiveness. Many seem to feel that American industry cannot compete effectively in the free market. This concern leads some to support *managed trade* as a protectionist device.

The growth of protectionist sentiment is not confined to the United States. Similar changes have been occurring in Europe for similar reasons. The great success of Japanese exporters in penetrating the EC market while helping consumers has caused trouble for many producers and has led to a search for ways to protect firms in the EC. The EC has made use of quotas, antidumping duties, and VERs. Since fighting an antidumping case can be time-consuming and expensive, the mere registering of an antidumping complaint can often lead a foreign firm to raise its prices to the levels that are charged by domestic producers. This has the effect, desired by the domestic producers, of preventing a more efficient foreign supplier from underselling them.

As a small trading country, Canada'a self-interest lies in preserving the multilateral trading system and in minimizing protectionist sentiment. The classic Canadian problem is to be unintentionally, but nonetheless painfully, sideswiped in a trade restriction war between trading giants. The United States may put a restriction against imports of product *X* aimed at European exporters, and the EC may retaliate with a restriction on product *Y* sold by the United States to the EC. Neither the United States nor the EC may notice that Canada exports both *X* and *Y* and is hit hard by the measures they are aiming at each other.

The Pressure to Manage Trade

In the free market system, competitive prices determine what is imported and what is exported.

social, and political consequences of the proposed FTA. In November 1988, a federal election, fought mainly on the free trade issue, returned to power the Progressive Conservative Party, which supported the FTA (both the Liberal Party and the NDP opposed it). On January 1, 1989, the first round of tariff cuts took place, and firms began to restructure their investment and other decisions in the expectation of tariff-free flows of all trade across the Canada–United States border before the end of the twentieth century.

The Terms

The main terms of the Free Trade Agreement were as follows:

1. All tariffs are to be removed from all trade between the two countries over the next 10 years. By agreement of the industries involved, some tariffs were removed immediately, and many others in five annual increments. The remainder will see their tariffs go in 10 equal annual steps.

Under managed trade, the state has a major influence in determining the direction and magnitude of the flow of trade. The voluntary export agreement discussed earlier in this chapter is a typical example of the tools of managed trade. To fulfill a VER, the government of the exporting country must form its exporting firms into a cartel so that they can divide up the portion of the foreign market that they are allowed to serve and to ensure that they do not violate the export ceiling.

Another current example of the tools of managed trade is the suggestion that trade balances be judged bilaterally rather than multilaterally. Many authorities would manage trade to reduce large bilateral balances; some would impose strict bilateral trade balances between pairs of countries. The essence of the multilateral trading system is that one country does not have to buy the same amount from another country as it sells to it, just as one country does not have to buy the same amount from each of its domestic suppliers as it sells to it. Enforcing bilateral balances would impose this requirement on each pair of trading countries. Such a requirement makes no more economic sense, however, than requiring that the barber should only cut the butcher's hair to the value of the meat that the barber buys from the butcher, and so on for each supplier with whom the barber deals. To achieve bilateral balances, the state must intervene in the market to regulate exports and imports.

Regional Trading Blocks

The current trading world is dominated by the *triad countries.* These three great trading areas are (1) the countries of the European Community (EC) and the European Free Trade Area (EFTA); (2) the countries of North America (the United States, Canada, and Mexico); and (3) Japan.

Some observers are concerned with the possible growth of more and more formally negotiated regional trading blocks. Such agreements need not conflict with the multilateral trading system. The U.S.-Canadian agreement, for example, is consistent with increased trade between these two countries *and* the rest of the world. Such regional trading arrangements can, however, be inward-looking, in the sense that they encourage trade between members while discouraging trade with the rest of the world. If the growth of protectionist sentiment in the United States and the EC were to leave the countries of other areas, such as the Pacific Rim, feeling excluded from the markets of Europe and North America, some of them might form their own trading block, in which they could at least trade freely with each other.

2. The agreement removes a number of nontariff barriers, such as quotas and some "buy local" government procurement policies. Quotas remain, however, where they are required to support the supply management schemes of the Canadian provincial governments. (See Chapter 6 for a discussion of these schemes.) By providing for a closer (voluntary) harmonization of standards, the FTA seeks to control another potent nontariff barrier.
3. The FTA institutionalizes the present regime of free trade in energy products, although all foreign (including U.S.) takeovers of Canadian energy firms are still subject to government review and approval. It contains a controversial clause that requires energy sharing in times of national shortage. This clause has no effect in normal times, when markets will set the prices and quantities of energy being marketed. The clause comes into effect only if the exporting country decides that there is some emergency sufficient to justify introducing production and export controls that in-

terfere with existing commercial contracts. The agreement then requires that exports should be restricted no more than in proportion to restrictions on total output. For example, Canada could not impose a reduction in production of 30 percent and then impose the entire reduction on foreign consumers. The clause does *not* require that once some amount of energy is sold to the United States, it must always be sold in the future. If in the normal evolution of the Canadian economy, Canada requires a larger proportion of its energy supplies for home consumption, normal commercial contracts will be negotiated selling more to home users and less abroad. The only thing that the FTA prevents is *government intervention* to cut off supplies going to the partner country on the grounds of emergency if similar restrictions are not placed on domestic consumers.

4. The FTA allows for freer trade in services by having each country extend the principles of *right of establishment* and *national treatment* to the other country's firms that sell services. This means that firms selling services in one country have the right to establish themselves in the other country and be treated the same as local service firms.
5. The FTA prevents discrimination against each country's investment in the other country by extending the principle of national treatment to all such investment.
6. The FTA provides a number of imaginative mechanisms for settling disputes related to the agreement, including an alternative to the GATT mechanism for settling disputes arising out of the application of trade remedy laws in each country. (The complaining country can elect to take its dispute either to the GATT or to the bilateral dispute settlement mechanism.)
7. The FTA mandates a five- to seven-year period for negotiations to draw up a convention on subsidy practices that would reduce or eliminate the need for countervailing duties and to agree on ways of curtailing the use of antidumping laws.

Evaluation

The FTA caused great debate in the period leading up to its signing, and it still arouses strong passions today. Disagreement raged over its economic, social, and political manifestations. By and large, supporters saw it as primarily an economic agreement, one among many such agreements in place throughout the world, whose impact would be small except for its beneficial economic effects. By and large, opponents saw it as a broad politicoeconomic agreement that would have profound political and social effects extending well beyond its harmful economic effects.

Economic effects. Supporters say that the FTA is merely a continuation of the Canadian trend toward liberalizing trade that was begun in 1935. They say that there is every reason to expect this round of tariff reductions to bring effects similar to those that followed all earlier rounds—a growing number of jobs, growing exports (and imports), growing real incomes, relatively minor adjustment problems, and a growing attractiveness of Canada for foreign investment (since the entire U.S.-Canadian market can be served, duty-free, from Canada).

Opponents say that the results of this new round of tariff reduction will be quite different from the results of previous rounds—more jobs destroyed by new import competition than are created by new exports, falling exports and rising imports, falling real incomes, and a flight of foreign capital (now that there is no protected Canadian market to keep foreign firms in Canada, producing solely for domestic demand).

If the critics prove to be correct, the results of this set of tariff reductions will be very different from the results of all reductions since 1935. Furthermore, the results will be different from those predicted by economic theory, which predicts that there are gains from trade and hence from bilateral tariff reductions.

Disappointments. One major disappointment for Canadian policymakers was failure to gain fully secure access to the U.S. market by stopping the use of countervailing and antidumping duties as nontariff barriers to trade. No agreement was reached, however, and all that was obtained was a commitment to go on negotiating over the next five to seven years. Since Canada and the United States always have the option of taking a dispute to the GATT, the only purpose of the negotiations is to see if better protection can be agreed bilaterally than can be agreed within the GATT framework. Thus the bilateral negotiations will start seriously after the results of the Uruguay Round of GATT negotiations are known. Canadians had also hoped to make more gains on the government procurement issue than were in fact agreed. They had also hoped to end restrictions on trucking and shipping, but U.S. protectionist interests proved too strong in these industries.

BOX 21-3

National Treatment

The Canadian-U.S. FTA is based on the fundamental principle of *national treatment,* which means that each country treats the other country's goods, firms, and investors when they are within its own borders just as it would its own goods, firms, and investors. This principle, which is also embedded in the GATT, is intended to give maximum policy independence to each country while preventing it from using its laws to discriminate on the basis of the nationality of individuals and firms. According to the FTA's national treatment clause, all *new* government policies, rules, or regulations that do not directly inhibit trade are permissible as long as they meet a single key test: that they apply with equal force to foreign and to domestic entities.* All that national treatment rules out is using as concealed trade barriers laws designed for other purposes. For example, Canadian laws designed to protect food quality can be as tough as Canadians wish them to be, but they cannot be made tougher on food products imported from the United States than on those produced in Canada. Thus Canadians can have environmental protection laws, social services, or any other laws, rules, and regulations that differ greatly from their U.S. counterparts as long as these apply equally to both Canadian and foreign firms operating in Canada.

The alternative to national treatment is *extraterritoriality.* This principle, discussed in Chapter 16 (see page 320), is sometimes asserted by the United States when it holds that U.S.-owned companies operating in foreign countries should be subject to certain U.S. laws, rules, and regulations. More generally, extraterritoriality makes firms subject to the rules of the country of their ownership rather than the country of their location. This principle would, if accepted, be cause for serious Canadian concern. It would exempt U.S. firms operating in Canada from Canadian environmental or social laws that applied to Canadian-owned competitors operating in Canada.

* Already existing policies, rules, and regulations are exempt from the national treatment obligation.

Although some Canadian critics were unhappy about the terms of the energy portion, they were not disappointments to the firms and governments in the energy-producing provinces. Alberta oil producers, and the provincial government, welcomed the FTA as protection against a new national energy policy that would force them to sell their energy within Canada below world market prices.

The biggest American disappointment was over the so-called cultural industries. The United States wanted free competition in media industries such as publishing, radio, and television. In spite of strong U.S. pressure, Canada maintained its right to protect these industries from foreign ownership and, in many cases, from foreign competition. Americans were also disappointed that Canada would not give up its right to review, and reject if necessary, U.S. takeovers of Canadian firms larger than $150 million. They did get national treatment (see Box 21-3) for all U.S. firms that are operating in Canada but failed to get completely open flows of capital into Canada (although there are no restrictions on Canadian capital flowing into the United States). Americans were also upset about the exemption of the beer industry and about certain restrictions that remain on textiles.

Although there were disappointments and compromises on both sides, the FTA was a success viewed as a trade-liberalizing measure. It covers the world's largest bilateral trade flow, and it has fewer exemptions from the principle of free trade in goods and services than almost any other existing regional trade-liberalizing agreement.

Policy Constraints

Much of the debate over the FTA concerned allegations that Canada has given up too much sovereignty by constraining itself explicitly or implicitly with respect to many economic and social policies that it might want to adopt in the future.

Economic policy. Does the FTA seriously constrain future Canadian economic policy? It certainly institutionalizes free market competition in energy between Canada and the United States. Furthermore, it would be impossible under the FTA to go back to higher tariffs or increased trade restrictions against the United States. Although the ability to do so is already greatly constrained by Canada's membership in the GATT, the FTA goes further. The FTA also makes it difficult to institute tougher controls on U.S. foreign investment or a revised national energy policy. By tying Canada into market competition, the FTA seems beneficial to people who believe that market forces tend to produce good results on balance. By the same token, it seems harmful to those who distrust market forces.

The FTA does nothing, however, to prevent interference by either country's government into market forces by any desired degree as long as the interference is operated on a national treatment basis. National treatment, which is the key to understanding why the FTA does not impose legal pressures for policy harmonization, is discussed further in Box 21-3.

Social policy. A major charge of the agreement's critics was that it will force a harmonization of Canadian social and economic policies with those of the United States. It was argued that the closer competition between firms in the two countries would cause firms in Canada to push for reductions in all social services and tax burdens to their American levels (and that governments would accede to these demands).

Supporters pointed out that the principle of national treatment, which is the guiding principle of the FTA, provides no legal pressure for harmonization of social policies. As for market pressures, they argued that since Canada's distinctive social policies had evolved during the period from 1947 to 1985 when Canada was dismantling most of its tariff protection, eliminating the last of the tariffs would cause no more harmonization pressures than the earlier tariff reductions did. They accepted that harmonization pressures are strong but argued that they are related to the mobility of factors of production rather than to the mobility of goods. Countries must worry, for example, about getting their levels of personal and corporate taxes out of line with other countries for fear of inducing a flight of capital and highly talented labor to the lower-tax jurisdiction. These pressures not to get policies out of line, which have always been very strong between Canada and the United States, are caused by the fear of factor movements, and economic theory does not suggest that they will be greater when tariffs are 10 percent than when they are zero.

Political sovereignty. Many people feared increasing dominance of the United States as a result of closer economic ties with that country. Some went so far as to predict the end of Canada as an independent country within 10 years.

Supporters of the FTA argued that other countries had survived free trade arrangements without losing their political sovereignty and that the principle of national treatment was designed to encourage national sovereignty in all areas other than trade restrictions. They also noted that Canada had lived in close proximity with the United States for a long time and that removing the last of the already greatly reduced tariffs was unlikely to have such dramatic political effects.

The Results

Economists who have studied the effects of the Treaty of Rome, which brought the European Community into existence in 1958, agree that the major effects could not be discerned by so early a date as 1960. Similarly, in spite of the understandable desire of supporters and critics to get strong evidence, many years must go by before the changes due to the FTA can be firmly established. One reason for this is that most of the changes expected from the FTA are not large in relation to other changes that are occurring all the time. For example, the 10 percent rise in the value of the Canadian dollar from 78 U.S. cents to 86 U.S. cents had the same unfavorable effect over two years on the Canadian firms competing with imports as will result from the entire removal of a 10 percent tariff over 10 years.

A recent United Nations study of transnational investment behavior did give some preliminry judgment on the investment effects of the agreement.[5]

[5] United Nations Center on Transnational Corporations, *Regional Economic Integration and Transnational Corporations in the 1990s: Europe 1992, North America, and Developing Countries* (New York: United Nations, 1990).

After first noting pre-FTA plans of U.S. TNCs to *reduce* investment in Canada (as noted earlier in this discussion), they referred to surveys taken after the FTA was in place showing an *increase* in planned U.S. investment expenditure in Canada (by 11 percent in 1989 and 20 percent in 1990). The study then went on to say:

> Perhaps the most significant long-term impact of the Free Trade Agreement on FDI [foreign direct investment] will be to increase investment by third countries in the integrated North American market, particularly in Canada. . . . Free trade between the United States and Canada appears to have triggered a wave of restructuring of Canadian industry, as companies retreat from activities that are likely to prove unsustainable in a free-trade environment, and enter businesses that are slated for growth.

The Outlook for Canadian Trade

The breakup of the world into a set of trading blocs that do more and more trade within the bloc and less and less with outside countries would be to the disadvantage of most countries, particularly the smaller ones. Bilateral bargaining between nations tends to involve large countries, with the smaller ones left on the sidelines. For these two reasons, among many others, Canada, as a small trading country with nearly 50 percent of its private-sector GDP generated by exports, has an enormous stake in the preservation of the liberalized, multilateral trading system.

This means that Canadian policymakers will continue to regard the GATT as Canada's best friend in pushing for more liberalized international trade and as its best defense against protectionist pressures. The FTA, however, also gives Canada increased access to what is by far its largest market and shields that access to some extent against growing protectionist sentiment in the United States. The FTA does not provide a perfect shield, but it is difficult to argue that Canadian access to the U.S. market would be better shielded without the FTA than with it.

Canada prospers or suffers as its trading sector prospers or suffers. For this reason, maintaining a healthy trading sector will remain, as it has been for decades, a prime concern of Canadian policymakers, who wish to maintain and enhance the country's material prosperity.

SUMMARY

1. The case for free trade is that world output of all commodities can be higher under free trade than when protectionism restricts regional specialization.
2. Domestic industries may be protected from foreign competition by tariffs and other policies, which affect the prices of imports, or by import quotas and voluntary export agreements, which affect the quantities of imports. Both sets of policies end up increasing prices in the domestic market and lowering the quantities of imports. Both harm domestic consumers and benefit domestic producers of the protected commodity. The major difference is that the extra money paid for imports goes to the government under tariffs and to foreign producers under quantity restrictions.
3. Protection can be urged as a means to ends other than maximizing world living standards. Examples of such ends are to produce a diversified economy, to reduce fluctuations in national income, to retain distinctive national traditions, and to improve national defense.
4. Protection also can be urged on the grounds that it may lead to higher living standards for the protectionist country than a policy of free trade would. Such a result might come about by using a monopoly position to influence the terms of trade or by developing a dynamic comparative advantage by allowing inexperienced or uneconomically small industries to become efficient enough to compete with foreign industries.

5. Almost everyone would choose free trade if the only alternative were *no* trade. Cutting existing tariff barriers offers gains that may seem small when expressed as a percentage of GDP but are large in terms of the total of goods and services involved.
6. Some fallacious free trade arguments are that (a) because free trade maximizes world income, it will maximize the income of every individual country, and (b) because infant industries seldom admit to growing up and thus try to retain their protection indefinitely, the whole country necessarily loses by protecting its infant industries.
7. Some fallacious protectionist arguments are that (a) mutually advantageous trade is impossible because one trader's gain must always be the other's loss; (b) buying abroad sends our money abroad, while buying at home keeps our money at home; (c) our high-paid workers must be protected against the competition from low-paid foreign workers; and (d) imports are to be discouraged because they lower national income and cause unemployment.
8. As tariff barriers have been reduced over the years, they have been replaced in part by nontariff barriers. Voluntary export agreements are strightforward restrictions on trade. Antidumping and countervailing duties can provide legitimate restraints on foreign unfair trading practices, but they can also be used as nontariff barriers to trade.
9. The General Agreement on Tariffs and Trade, whereby countries agree to reduce trade barriers through multilateral negotiations and not to raise them unilaterally, has brought great reductions in world tariffs since its inception in 1947. The European Free Trade Area and the European Community are regional arrangements for free trade in goods among their members.
10. International trade has always been important to the Canadian economy. Canadian trade policy supported relatively free trade until 1878, when the National Policy was introduced. This was a high-tariff policy that sought to encourage Canadian manufacturing industries to serve the Canadian market. Since 1935, Canadian trade policy has supported trade liberalization, first with reciprocal agreements with the United States, then through the GATT, and more recently with the Canada-U.S. Free Trade Agreement.
11. Reductions in tariffs on Canadian-American trade have led mainly to intra-industry specialization, with both countries' imports and exports tending to increase in each industry as firms specialized in particular product lines.
12. The Canada-U.S. Free Trade Agreement provides for the complete elimination of tariffs on all trade in goods between the two countries by 1999, the liberalization of trade in services and some government procurement, and the removal of some nontariff barriers (and mandated major negotiations on other nontariff barriers over a period of five years). It also provides for freer movement of capital between the two countries. It institutionalized free trade in energy and contains a controversial energy-sharing agreement for use in times of energy crisis. A number of sectors, including the Canadian cultural industries—broadly defined to include the mass media—are exempt from the terms of the agreement.
13. The FTA's fundamental principle is *national treatment,* which allows either of the two countries to have policies on any issue that differ

from those in the other country as long as the policies are applied equally within one country to all individuals, products, and firms irrespective of the nationality of their origin or ownership.

TOPICS FOR REVIEW

Free trade and protectionism
Tariff and nontariff barriers to trade
Countervail and voluntary export agreements
Fallacious arguments for free trade
Fallacious arguments for protectionism
Countervailing duties
Dumping and antidumping duties
General Agreement on Tariffs and Trade (GATT)
Common markets, customs unions, and free trade associations
Canada-U.S. Free Trade Agreement (FTA)
National treatment

DISCUSSION QUESTIONS

1. It has been calculated that the voluntary export agreement to reduce Japanese car imports into the North American market cost Canadian and American consumers more than $150,000 per job saved. Who gained and who lost from this agreement?
2. The policy of "aggressive reciprocity" has recently been urged on the Canadian and American governments. Under it, every time a foreign government introduced a new barrier to trade, Canada and the United States would reciprocate aggressively by introducing a new barrier of their own. Discuss the likely outcome of such a policy. What are some alternative policies for enhancing world trade?
3. Look at the Canadian tariffs shown in Table 21-1. What economic and political reasons can you see for duties on some commodities being above the average rate of duty charged and for others being below it? What other forms of protectionism could make some duties misleading?
4. Suppose that Quebec formed a separate state and refused to trade with the rest of Canada. What predictions would you make about the standard of living in Quebec and in the rest of Canada compared to what it is today? What if the separate state of Quebec formed a free trade area with the rest of Canada and the United States?
5. Suppose that each of the Canadian provinces was a separate country. If free trade were permitted among them, would you expect a pattern of production different from the one that exists now? If Manitoba put high tariffs on all trade with its Canadian trading partners, what would be the effect on Manitoba and on the other nine countries? Suppose that all ten countries seriously restricted imports from one another in order to foster local industries. What would be the result?
6. If the developments in Europe in 1992 cause such a rise in efficiency that the price of every good produced in Germany, France, and Italy fell below the prices of the same good manufactured in Canada, what would happen? Would Canadians gain or lose because of this?
7. Discuss the following statements made during the Canadian free trade debate. Three of the four can be challenged using points of economic theory.
   a. "Tariff reductions, which should help both countries, disproportionately benefit the United States because average Canadian tariffs

are higher."—Jeff Simpson, *Toronto Globe and Mail,* October 9, 1987.

b. "The historical records show that the concerns expressed two decades ago about the Auto Pact were not entirely misplaced. In only 9 years of the Pact's 22 years of operation has Canada been in a surplus position in Auto Pact trade."—Glen Williams, *Toronto Globe and Mail,* November 28, 1987.

c. "We would like to think we are about to get the best of both worlds—Canadian stability and a more caring society, [combined with] U.S. markets—but what if instead, we get their crime rates, health programs, and gun laws and they get our markets, or what is left of them?"—Margaret Atwood, testimony to parliamentary committee on free trade, November 4, 1987.

d. "The complete removal of tariffs doesn't help Canadian exporters as much as the devaluation of our dollar, because the key to breaking into the U.S. market is to be able to flog it with cheaper goods than they have at home."—Edgar Benson, former Liberal minister of finance, *Toronto Star,* October 10, 1987.

8. Some Canadians opposed trying to negotiate a Canadian free trade agreement with Mexico on the grounds that Canadian firms could not compete with the goods produced by cheap Mexican labor, which, at the 1980 exchange rate, was earning an average of about C$0.60 per hour. Comment on the following points in relation to the above argument:

a. Many Mexican goods already enter Canada free of tariffs, and where tariffs are levied, the average Canadian rate is less than 10 percent.

b. Not only are Mexican wages low, but the average productivity of Mexican workers is also low.

c. The theory of the gains from trade says that rich, high-productivity countries can profitably trade with poor, low-wage countries.

d. A situation in which Mexico undersold all Canadian tradable goods and services could not be one of international trade equilibrium.

PART

7

THE MARKET ECONOMY: PROBLEMS AND POLICIES

Chapter 22

Benefits and Costs of Government Intervention

There are two caricatures of the Canadian economy. One pictures Canada as the last stronghold of free enterprise, with millions of Canadians in a mad and brutal race for the almighty dollar. In the other, Canadian business people, workers, and farmers are seen as strangling slowly in a web of red tape spun by the spider of government regulations. Neither is realistic.

Many aspects of economic life in Canada are determined by the operation of a free market system. Private preferences, expressed through private markets and influencing private profit-seeking enterprises, determine much of what is produced, how it is produced, and the incomes of productive factors.

But even casual observation makes it clear that public policies and public decisions play a large role in the nation's economic life. Laws restrict what people and firms may do, and taxes and subsidies influence their choices. Much public expenditure is not market-determined, and this influences the distribution of national product. Canada's is in fact a mixed economy.

The general case for some reliance on free markets is that allowing decentralized decision making is more efficient in a number of ways than having all economic decisions made by a centralized planning body. This is a lesson that the governments of the USSR, the People's Republic of China, and Eastern Europe have learned the hard way.

The general case for some public intervention is that almost no one wants to let the market decide everything about our economic affairs. Most people's moral and practical sense argues for some state intervention to mitigate the disastrous results that the market deals out to some. Most people believe that there are areas in which the market does not function well and in which state intervention can improve the general social good. Indeed, even when there is maximum reliance on the market economy, government is needed to enforce contracts and prevent theft. For such reasons, there is no known economy in which the people have opted for complete free market determination of all economic matters and against any kind of government intervention.

Although many nineteenth century economists advocated a policy of **laissez faire**—the minimizing of government interference with the operation of markets—the operative choice is not between an unhampered free market economy and a fully centralized command economy. It is rather the choice of what mix of markets and government intervention best suits a nation's hopes and needs. Although all economies are mixed, the mixture varies greatly among economies and over time. Whether the existing mixture is wrong—and, if so, in which direction—is debated continually.

Even the most passionate advocates of free markets agree that government must provide for enforcement of the rules under which private firms and individuals make contracts. Without well-defined property rights, the enforcement of contracts, and a reasonable assurance that goods and services will not be stolen, market economies cannot function. In the modern, mixed economy, however, government does a great deal more than act as a "traffic cop" for the private sector.

One reason that there are mixed economies lies in what an unkind critic once called the economists' two great insights: *Markets can work,* and *markets can fail.* A second reason is what the critic might have called the political scientists' two great insights: *Government intervention can work,* and *government intervention can fail.*

In this chapter we discuss the role of the government in market-based economies. Why is it there at all? What does it do well, and what does it do badly? Do we need more or less government intervention?

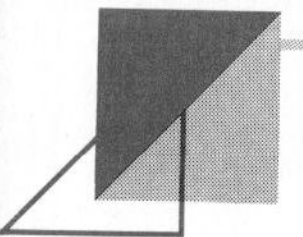

How Markets Coordinate

Any economy consists of thousands of individual markets. There are markets for agricultural goods, for manufactured goods, and for consumers' services; there are markets for intermediate goods such as steel and pig iron, which are outputs of some industries and inputs of others; there are markets for raw materials such as iron ore, trees, bauxite, and copper; there are markets for land and for thousands of different types of labor; there are markets in which money is borrowed and in which securities are sold.

An economy is not a series of markets functioning in isolation but an interlocking system in which an occurrence in one market affects many others.

Any change, such as an increase in demand for a product, requires many further changes and adjustments. Will the quantity produced change? If it does, by how much and by what means? Any change in the output of one product will generally require changes in other markets and will start a chain of adjustments. Someone or something must decide what is to be produced, how, and by whom and what is to be consumed and by whom.

The essential characteristic of the market system is that its coordination occurs in an unplanned, decentralized way. Millions of people make millions of independent decisions concerning production and consumption every day. Most of these decisions are not motivated by a desire to contribute to the social good or to make the whole economy work well but by fairly immediate considerations of self-interest.

The price system coordinates decentralized decisions, making the whole system fit together and respond to the wishes of individual consumers and producers.

The basic insight into how a market system works is that decentralized, private decision makers, acting in their own interests, respond to such signals as the prices of what they buy and sell. Economists have long emphasized price as a signaling device. When a commodity becomes scarce, its market price rises. Firms and households that use the commodity are led to economize on it and to look for alternatives. Firms that produce it are led to produce more of it. How the price system informs these decisions has been examined at several places in this book (for example, with respect to carrots and brussels sprouts in Chapter 3 and with respect to agriculture in Chapter 6). When a shortage occurs in a market, price rises and profits develop; when a glut occurs, price falls and losses develop. These are *signals,* for all to see, that arise from the overall conditions of market supply and demand. An appreciation for the coordination performed by the price system and an anticipation of some of the problems involved in interfering with it can be found in Box 22-1.

The Role of Profits and Losses

Although the free market economy often is described as a *price system,* the basic engine that drives the economy is economic profits. Except when there is monopoly, economic profits and losses are symptoms of *disequilibrium,* and they are the driving force in the adaptation of the economy to change.

A rise in demand or a fall in production costs creates profits for that commodity's producers. Prof-

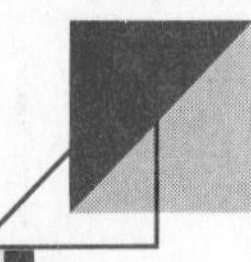

BOX 22-1

A View from the Outside of the Inside of Upside Down*

The operation of the price system, and the effectiveness with which it helps coordinate decisions, is often taken for granted. Some insight can be gleaned by examining what can happen when governments try to intervene in its operations. In the early 1970s, in an attempt to reduce inflation, the U.S. government under President Richard Nixon tried directly to control the millions of individual prices of goods, services, and factors of production. Here Jackson Grayson, Nixon's "price administrator," tells of some of the problems he encountered:

On the 18th of October, 1971, I assumed responsibility for the Price Commission in the conduct of Phase II of President Nixon's Wage and Price Control program. . . . I want to relate something about my view of policy-making at the national level. I want to explain why it is inherently a confused sort of occupation and I want to imbue the reader with a healthy skepticism for the ability of central control to solve economic problems.

One of the main reasons why the policy-making process in general and wage and price controls in particular are inherently difficult is because they are attempting to regulate the most sophisticated information system that the world has ever seen—namely the North American market economy. . . . The information system is the network formed by free people buying and selling, and the signals are the variations in and the levels of wages, prices, interest rates, rents and, unfortunately, taxes. . . .

Most of the products and services that we take for granted in our everyday lives can be taken for granted only because there is a functioning price system. A system that, despite its imperfections, delivers just the right quantity of California lettuce to Montana or Alberta, Canada, and decides the relationship between raw log prices in California and the price of finished lumber in Boston. As we discovered when we tampered with, and effectively suspended, the operation of the price system, we could no longer rely on the system itself and were forced to get more and more involved with what were, before controls, essentially automatic functions.

The problem that policy-makers must cope with, if they are determined to control the system, is the endless detail that is involved in the operation of the system. To control the system and yet keep it running smoothly, the authorities must intercept all of the signals coming from the system (and there are hundreds of millions), interpret them, appropriately change them (assuming they know how) and retransmit them.

What we at the Price Commission continuously found was that everything is related to everything else and there was, accordingly, no such thing as one intervention. We were drawn inevitably and progressively deeper into the system, and the temptation to limit the necessity for our involvement by arbitrarily changing the system was very great. . . .

The difficulty of taking over the wage-price signaling mechanism is indicated by the fact that during the first three weeks of Phase II there were nearly 400,000 inquiries about the program. In terms of getting down to the nitty gritty, had the Dow Chemical Company and the Commission not agreed to an across-the-board increase of 2 percent, we would have had to examine nearly 100,000 submissions on different products for that company alone.

*Excerpted from an article of the same title by Jackson Grayson, dean of the School of Business, Southern Methodist University, in *The Illusion of Wage and Price Control*, ed. M. Walker (Vancouver: Fraser Institute, 1976).

its make an industry attractive to new investment. They signal that there are too few resources devoted to that industry. In search of these profits, more resources enter the industry, increasing output and driving down price, until profits are driven to zero. A fall in demand or a rise in production costs creates losses. Losses signal the reverse and an excess of resources devoted to the industry. Resources will leave the industry until those that remain are no longer suffering losses.

The importance of profits and losses is that they set in motion forces that tend to move the economy toward a new equilibrium.

Individual households and firms respond to common signals according to their own best interests. There is nothing planned or intentionally coordinated about their actions, yet when, say, a shortage causes price to rise, individual buyers begin to reduce the quantities that they demand, and individual firms begin to increase the quantities that they supply. As a result, the shortage begins to lessen. As it does, price begins to come back down, and profits are reduced. These signals are in turn noted and responded to by firms and households. Eventually, when the shortage has been eliminated, there are no profits to attract further increases in supply. The chain of adjustments to the original shortage is completed.

Notice that in the sequence of signal-response-signal-response no one has to foresee at the outset the final price and quantity, nor does any government agency have to specify who will increase production and who will decrease consumption. Some firms respond to the signals for more output by increasing production, and they keep on increasing production until the signals get weaker and weaker and finally disappear. Some buyers withdraw from the market when they think that prices are too high, and perhaps they reenter gradually, as prices seem to them to become more reasonable. Households and firms, responding to market signals, not to the orders of government bureaucrats, decide who will increase production and who will limit consumption. No one is forced to do something against better judgment. Voluntary responses collectively produce the end result.

Because the economy is adjusting to shocks continuously, a snapshot of the economy at any given moment reveals substantial positive profits in some industries and substantial losses in others. A snapshot at another moment also will reveal windfall profits and losses, but in different places.

The price system, like an *invisible hand* (Adam Smith's famous phrase), coordinates the responses of individual decision makers who seek only their own self-interests. Because they respond to signals that reflect market conditions, their responses are coordinated without any conscious planning.

Coordination in the Absence of Perfect Competition

To say that the price system coordinates is not to imply that it always leads to the results that perfect competition would produce. The price system coordinates responses even to prices that are "rigged" by monopolistic producers or that are altered by government controls. The signal-response process occurs in a price system even when the prices have not been determined in freely competitive markets.

When an international cartel of uranium producers decided to reduce production and raise the price of uranium, they created a shortage (and a fear of worse future shortages) among electric utilities that depend on uranium to fuel nuclear power plants. The price of uranium shot up from under $10 per pound to over $40 in less than a year. This enormous price rise greatly increased efforts among producers outside the cartel to find more uranium and to increase their existing production by mining poorer-grade ores previously considered too costly to mine.

The increases in production from these actions slowly began to ease the shortage. On the demand side, high prices and short supplies led some utilities to cancel the construction of planned nuclear power plants and to delay the construction of others. Such actions implied a long-run substitution of oil or coal for uranium. Only the fact that the OPEC cartel had also sharply raised the price of oil prevented an even more rapid reversal of the previous trend from oil to nuclear powered generators. With the prices of both uranium and oil quadrupling, the demand for coal increased sharply, and its price and production rose. Thus the market mechanism generated adjustments to the relative prices of different fuels, even though some prices were set by cartels rather than by the free market forces of supply and demand. It also set in motion reactions that placed limits on the power of the cartel.

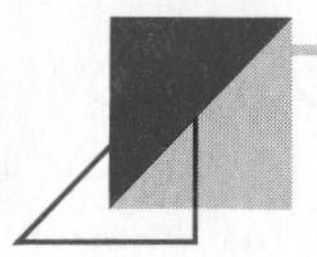

The Case for the Market System

In presenting the case for free market economies, economists have used two different approaches. One of these may be characterized as the formal case. It is based on showing that a free market economy consisting of nothing but perfectly competitive industries would lead to an optimal allocation of resources. The case was discussed in Chapter 15.

The other approach is at least as old as Adam Smith and is meant to apply to market economies whether they are perfectly competitive or not. It is based on variations and implications of the theme that the market system is an effective coordinator of decentralized decision making. The case is intuitive in that it is not laid out in graphs or equations representing a complete, formal model of an economy, but it does follow from some hard reasoning, and it has been subjected to much intellectual probing. What is the nature of this defense of the free market?

Flexible and Automatic Coordination

Defenders of the market economy argue that compared with the alternatives, the decentralized market system is more flexible and leaves more scope for adaptation to change at any moment in time and for quicker adjustment over time.

Suppose, for example, that the price of oil rises. One household might prefer to respond by maintaining a high temperature in its house and economizing on its driving, while another might drive as much as ever but lower the home thermostat a few degrees. A third household might give up air conditioning instead. This flexibility can be contrasted with centralized control, which would force the same pattern on everyone, say, by rationing heating oil and gasoline, by regulating permitted temperatures, and by limiting air conditioning to days when the temperature exceeded 26°C.

Furthermore, as conditions change over time, prices will change, and decentralized decision makers can react continually. In contrast, government quotas, allocations, and rationing schemes are much more difficult to adjust. As a result, there are likely to be shortages and surpluses before adjustments are made. The great value of the market is that it provides automatic signals as a situation develops, so all of the consequences of some major economic change need not be anticipated and allowed for by a body of central planners. Millions of adaptations to millions of changes in tens of thousands of markets are required every year, and it would be a herculean task to anticipate and plan for them all.

A market system allows for coordination without *anyone* needing to understand how the whole system works.

As Professor Thomas Schelling put it:

> The dairy farmer doesn't need to know how many people eat butter and how far away they are, how many other people raise cows, how many babies drink milk, or whether more money is spent on beer or milk. What he needs to know is the prices of different feeds, the characteristics of different cows, the different prices . . . for milk . . . , the relative cost of hired labor and electrical machinery, and what his net earnings might be if he sold his cows and raised pigs instead.[1]

It is, of course, an enormous advantage that all the producers and consumers of a country can collectively make the system operate without any one of them, much less all of them, having to understand how it works. Such a lack of knowledge becomes a disadvantage, however, when people have to vote on schemes for interfering with market allocation. This contrast lies at the heart of the intuitive argument in favor of market systems.

Stimulus to Innovation and Growth

Technology, tastes, and resource availability are changing all the time, in all economies. Twenty-five years ago there was no such thing as a personal computer or a digital watch. Front-wheel drive was a curiosity. Students carried their books in briefcases or in canvas bags that were anything but waterproof. Manuscripts existed only as hard copy, not as com-

[1] *Micromotives and Microbehavior* (New York: Norton, 1978).

puter records. To change one word in a manuscript, one often had to retype every word on a page. Videocassettes did not exist. The next 20 years will surely also see changes great and small. New products and techniques will be devised to adapt to shortages, gluts, and changes in consumer demands.

In a market economy, individuals risk their time and money in the hope of earning profits. Many fail, but some succeed. New products and processes appear and disappear. Some are passing fads or have little impact; others become items of major significance. The market system works by trial and error to sort them out and allocates resources to what prove to be successful innovations.

In contrast, planners in more centralized systems have to guess which are going to be productive innovations or products that will be in demand. Planned growth may achieve wonders by permitting a massive effort in a chosen direction, but central planners may also guess wrong about the direction and put far too many eggs in the wrong basket or reject as unpromising something that will turn out to be vital. It is striking that the two largest centrally planned economies in the world, the Soviet Union and mainland China, have dramatically increased their use of markets.

Relative Prices Reflect Relative Costs

A market system tends to drive prices toward the average total costs of production. When markets are close to perfectly competitive, this movement occurs quickly and completely; but even where there is substantial market power, new products and new producers respond to the lure of profits, and their output drives prices down toward the costs of production.

The advantage of having relative prices reflect relative costs was discussed in Chapter 15. When prices are equal to marginal costs, there will be allocative efficiency, because market choices are then made in the light of opportunity costs.[2] Firms will choose methods that minimize their own cost of producing output and in so doing will automatically minimize the opportunity cost of the resources that they use. Similarly, when households choose commodity A over commodity B, even though A uses resources of twice the total value of the resources used to produce B, they will have to pay the (difference in) price. They will only do so when they value A correspondingly more than B at the margin.

When relative prices reflect relative costs, producers and consumers use the nation's resources in a manner that is consistent with allocative efficiency.

Self-correction of Disequilibrium

Equilibrium of the economic system is continually disrupted by change. If the economy does not "pursue" equilibrium, there would be little comfort in saying that things would be bright indeed if only it reached equilibrium.

An important characteristic of the price system is its ability to set in motion forces that tend to correct disequilibrium.

To review the advantages of the price system in this respect, imagine operating without a market mechanism. Suppose that planning boards make all market decisions. The Board in Control of Men's Clothing hears that pleated shirts are all the rage in neighboring countries. It orders a certain proportion of clothing factories to make pleated shirts instead of the traditional men's dress shirt. Conceivably, the quantities of pleated shirts and traditional shirts produced could be just right, given shoppers' preferences. But what if the board guesses wrong and orders too many traditional shirts and not enough pleated shirts to be produced? Long lines would appear at pleated-shirt counters, while mountains of traditional shirts would pile up. Once the board sees the lines for pleated shirts, it could order a change in quantities produced. Meanwhile, it could store the extra traditional shirts for another season or ship them to a country with different tastes.

Such a system can correct an initial mistake, but it is usually slow in doing so. It uses a lot of resources in planning and administration that could instead be used to produce commodities. Further, many consumers may be greatly inconvenienced if the board is slow to correct its error. In such a system the members of the board may have no incentive to admit and correct a mistake quickly. Indeed, if the

[2] Of course, the mechanism in the text only ensures that prices tend to equal average costs, not marginal costs. Except when there is natural monopoly, long-run average costs will be near long-run marginal costs, and the mechanism in the text will generate allocations that are nearer to being efficient.

authorities do not like pleated shirts, the board may get credit for having stopped the craze before it went too far![3]

In contrast, suppose that in a market system a similar misestimation of the demand for pleated shirts and traditional shirts is made by the men's clothing industry. Lines develop at pleated-shirt counters, and inventories of traditional shirts accumulate. Stores raise the prices of pleated shirts and at the same time lower them for traditional shirts. Consumers who care more about price than fashion could get bargains by buying traditional shirts. Pleated-shirt manufacturers could earn profits by raising prices and running extra shifts to increase production. Some traditional-shirt producers would be motivated to shift production quickly to pleated shirts and to make traditional shirts more attractive to buyers by cutting prices. Unlike the planning board, the producers in a market system would be motivated to correct their initial mistakes as quickly as possible. Those who would be slowest to adjust would lose the most money and might even be forced out of business.

Decentralization of Power

Another important part of the case for a market economy is that it tends to decentralize power and thus requires less coercion of individuals than any other type of economy. Of course, even though markets tend to diffuse power, they do not do so completely; large firms and large unions clearly do have and do exercise substantial economic power.

Though the market power of large corporations and unions is not negligible, it tends to be constrained both by the competition of other large entities and by the emergence of new products and firms. This is the process of creative destruction that was described by Joseph Schumpeter (see page 250). In any case, say defenders of the free market, even such aggregations of private power are far less substantial than government power.

Governments must coerce if markets are not allowed to allocate people to jobs and commodities to consumers. Not only will such coercion be regarded as arbitrary (especially by those who do not like the results), but the power surely creates major opportunities for bribery, corruption, and allocation according to the tastes of the central administrators. If at the going prices and wages there are not enough apartments or coveted jobs to go around, the bureaucrats can allocate some to those who pay the largest bribe, some to those with religious beliefs, hairstyles, or political views that they like, and only the rest to those whose names come up on the waiting list. This line of reasoning has been articulated forcefully by the conservative economist and Nobel Prize winner Milton Friedman, who argues that economic freedom—the ability to allocate resources through private markets—is essential to the maintenance of political freedom. Many other economists and social theorists contend that this proposition has not been demonstrated empirically.

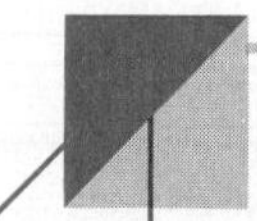

The Case for Intervention

Free markets do all of the good things that we have just discussed and more; yet there are many circumstances in the workings of the free market that do not result in the most desirable outcomes. When this happens, we say that markets have *failed*. The case for intervening in free markets turns in large part on identifying the conditions that lead to **market failure**. Much of the following discussion is devoted to this task.

The word *failure* in this context may convey the wrong impression.

Market failure does not mean that nothing good has happened but that the *best attainable outcome* has not been achieved.

The phrase *market failure* is used to apply to two quite different sets of circumstances. One is the failure of the market system to achieve efficiency in the allocation of society's resources. The other is the failure of the market system to serve social goals other than efficiency, such as a desired distribution of income or the preservation of value systems. We treat each in turn.

Failure to Achieve Efficiency

Market economies can fail to be efficient for any one of four broad types of reasons. The first is *monopoly*, which we discussed in Chapter 15. Monopoly pro-

[3] Less abstractly, this view is the basis for many economists' opposition to "equal pay for work of equal value" legislation, as discussed in Chapter 19.

ducers will maximize profits at an output where price exceeds marginal cost, leading to inefficiency. Although some monopolies are maintained through artificial barriers to entry, others arise naturally because in some industries the least costly way to produce a good or a service is to have a single producer. The standard government remedies are competition policy and public utility regulation, which, as discussed in Chapter 15, present problems of their own.

The three other broad types of phenomena that lead to inefficient market outcomes are called *externalities, collective consumption goods,* and *information asymmetries.*

As in the case of monopoly, externalities, collective consumption goods, and information asymmetries cause inefficiency to arise because in market equilibrium the marginal revenue for the producer is not equal to the marginal cost to society.

This violates the conditions for allocative efficiency that were discussed in Chapter 15.

Externalities

Costs, as economists define them, concern the value of resources used in the process of production. According to the opportunity cost principle, value is the benefit that resources would produce in their best alternative use. But who decides what resources are used when and what their opportunity cost is?

Consider the case of a student who is thinking of extending a party for one more hour at 1:00 A.M. For this student, the opportunity cost includes the psychological value of getting an extra hour of sleep, the money cost of the electricity to run the stereo, whatever will be eaten and drunk, and the value of repairs to the apartment. However, another resource is also used when the party runs for an extra hour—the neighbors' sleep—and the student may not consider it when making the decision to keep the stereo blasting.

Private and social costs. The difference in the viewpoint of the party thrower and the neighbors illustrates the important distinction between *private cost* and *social cost.* **Private cost** measures the best alternative use of the resource available to the private decision maker. The party thrower incurs private costs equal to her best alternative use of the resources that go into an extra hour of partying. The party thrower cannot make any use of the neighbors' sleep and so may value the sleep at zero. The **social cost** includes the private cost but also includes the best use of *all* resources available to society. In this case, social cost includes the cost imposed on the neighbors by an extra hour of partying.

Discrepancies between private and social cost lead to market failure.

The reason for this is that efficiency requires that prices cover social cost, but private producers and consumers, adjusting to private costs, will neglect the elements of social cost that are incurred by others. This is shown in Figure 22-1, which illustrates the case of a firm whose production process generates harmful smoke. Individuals who live and work in the neighborhood of the firm bear real costs due to the firm's production. In addition to the disutility of enduring the smoke and of any adverse health effects, they may invest in air conditioners to keep the noxious fumes out. None of the resources that are used to remove the pollution are available to the firm. Therefore, the value of these resources will not be taken into account when the firm decides how much to produce. The element of social cost that the firm is ignoring in its decision is external to its decision-making process.

In general, discrepancies between social and private cost occur when there are **externalities**, which are the costs or benefits of a transaction that are incurred or received by other members of the society but not taken into account by the parties to the transaction. They are also called *third-party effects*, because parties other than the two primary participants in the transaction (the buyer and the seller) are affected. Externalities arise in many different ways, and they may be beneficial or harmful.

When I paint my house, I enhance my neighbors' view and the value of their property. When an Einstein or a Rembrandt gives the world a discovery or a work of art whose worth is far in excess of what he is paid to produce it, he confers an external benefit. Private producers will tend to produce too little of commodities that generate beneficial externalities because the producers bear all of the costs themselves, while others reap some of the benefits.

Other externalities are harmful. Before we consider several examples, we can observe that private producers will tend to produce too much of com-

FIGURE 22-1 Private and Social Cost

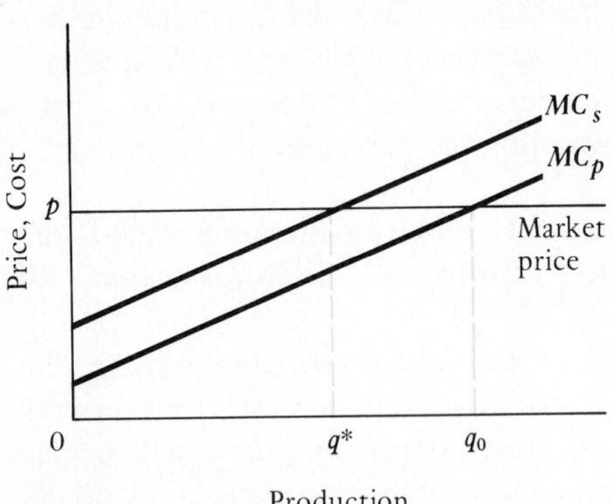

A competitive firm will produce output to the point where its private marginal cost equals the market price. In this case, every unit of output produced imposes *external costs,* equal to the distance between MC_p (private marginal cost—the marginal cost curve the firm faces) and MC_s (social marginal cost). The profit-maximizing competitive firm chooses to produce q_0, the output where price equals private marginal cost. If the full social cost of production were taken into account, only q^* would be produced. Notice that for each unit of output between q^* and q_0, the cost borne by all members of society exceeds the value to consumers, which is the market price. Over this range, social cost exceeds private revenue, implying allocative inefficiency.

modities that generate harmful externalities because the producers themselves bear none of the extra costs that are suffered by others.

Externalities, whether adverse or beneficial, cause market outcomes to be inefficient because they cause marginal private revenue to differ from marginal social cost.

Pollution. When firms use resources that they do not regard as scarce, they fail to consider the cost of those resources. This is a characteristic of most examples of pollution, including the case that is illustrated in Figure 22-1. When a paper mill produces pulp for the world's newspapers, more people are affected than its suppliers, employees, and customers. Its water-discharged effluent hurts the fishing boats that ply nearby waters, and its smog makes many resort areas less attractive, thereby reducing the tourist revenues that local motel operators and boat renters can expect. The firm neglects these external effects of its actions because its profits are not affected by them.[4]

Dumping of hazardous wastes, air pollution, and water pollution may occur as a result of calculated decisions as to what and how to produce or consume. They may also occur because private producers are willing to take excessive risk when they bear only part of the costs should things go wrong. Thus undesired and unplanned accidents, such as an oil blowout or the breakup of a tanker, may occur more frequently because private firms devote insufficient resources to avoiding risk.

Common-property resources. The world's oceans once teemed with fish, but today overfishing has caused a worldwide fish shortage. How could this happen?

Fish are an example of what is called a **common-property resource**, a resource that is owned by no one and may be used by anyone. No one owns the oceans' fish until they are caught. The world's international fishing grounds are common property for all comers. If by taking more fish, one person reduces the catch of others, the fisher does not count this as a cost, but it is a cost to society.

It is socially optimal to add to a fishing fleet until marginal social revenue (the increase in the value of the fleet's total catch from adding the last boat) just equals the marginal social cost (the value of the resources used to operate the last boat). This is the size of the fishing fleet that a benevolent social planner would choose.

The free market will not, however, produce this result. Potential new entrants will judge entry to be profitable if the value of their own catch is greater than the cost of operating their boats. However, a new entrant's catch is *partly* an addition to total catch and *partly* a reduction of the catch of others—because of congestion, each new boat reduces the catch of all other boats. Thus under free entry there will be too many boats in the fleet. Boats will continue to enter until there are no longer any profits for the marginal boat. In other words, boats will enter until the *av-*

[4] We consider the economics of pollution and the environment in more detail in Chapter 23.

erage value of the catch of a typical boat is equal to the cost of running that boat. At this point, however, the net addition to the *total* catch brought about by the last boat will be substantially less than the cost of operating the boat.

With common-property resources, the level of activity will be too high because each new entrant will gain revenue not only from the amount that it adds to total product but also from the amount that it takes away from the outputs of other producers.

This is not an untested theory. Fishing grounds and other common-property resources show a typical pattern of overexploitation. As a result, governments often use quotas and other restrictions in an attempt to hold the industry to its socially optimal size. At the start of the 1990s, the problems arising from overexploitation of the east coast fisheries, by foreign as well as domestic fleets, posed a threat to the bases of the economies of the Atlantic provinces.

Congestion. The externality arising from common-property resources often takes the form of *congestion.* When a commuter drives to work during the morning rush hour, she incurs the cost of driving her car, including the opportunity cost of spending her time in traffic rather than doing something else. She is also imposing a social cost on other commuters. Because her trip adds to traffic congestion, she is making everyone else's trip on the same road take a little bit longer. If she is just indifferent between taking the trip and not, her private cost will just equal her private benefit.

The social costs imposed on others will not be taken into account by any individual commuter. At the optimum, there would be less traffic—the time and money cost of the marginal commuter plus the extra time costs imposed on all other drivers would add up to the commuter's benefit from the trip.

Congestion externalities arise in highway traffic, air traffic (where the externality is the added risk of collision that another plane imposes on all others in the sky), and city sidewalks at lunch hour. They also occur, in the form of brownouts, when people consider only the money cost of using their air conditioners. As we shall see, some congestion externalities are relatively easy to ameliorate through government intervention, and others are not.

Myopia. Private producers and consumers making decisions today often fail to account fully for the effects that their behavior will have in the future. The externalities imposed can, again, be either positive or negative, but it is generally thought that negative cases, where current behavior imposes future costs that are not taken into account, are the more prevalent. Long-term environmental damage may arise from failure to take the well-being of future citizens into account. *Myopia* is especially likely to lead to misallocation of resources when *collective consumption goods*, such as environmental quality, are involved.

Collective Consumption Goods

Collective consumption goods, sometimes called **public goods**, have the peculiar property that the total cost of providing them does not increase as the number of consumers increases. The classic case is national defense. Adding to the population of a country does not diminish the extent to which each citizen is defended by a given size and quality of the armed forces. Information is also a public good. Suppose that a certain food additive causes cancer. The cost of discovering this needs to be borne only once. The information is then of value to everyone who might have used the additive, and the cost of making the information available to one more consumer is essentially zero.

Both of these examples raise what is called the *free-rider* problem. In neither case will the private market produce efficient amounts of the public good, because in both cases, once the good is produced, it is virtually impossible to make people pay for its use. Indeed, it is quite possible that markets will fail to produce collective consumption goods at all. The obvious remedy in these cases is government provision of the good, paid for by taxes.

How much of a public good should the government provide? It should provide up to the point where the *sum of everyone's individual valuations* of the good is just equal to the marginal cost of providing the good. To see why we must add up everyone's marginal valuation, consider a simple example. Suppose that Andy, Barbara, Carol, and Dick are all thinking of renting a videotape. Watching the video will be a collective consumption good for the four of them, because the cost will be the same no matter how many of them decide to watch. Suppose that each of them honestly sets a personal value on watching the tape: It is worth $1 to Andy, $2 each to Barbara and Carol, and 50 cents to Dick. If the rental charge for the tape is $5.50 or less, it is worth renting, because the total value to all consumers will be at least equal to the cost.

This example can also illustrate the free-rider problem. If the cost of renting the tape is only $3, each person will have an incentive to understate the value placed on watching the tape, hoping to get the others to pay enough to permit him or her a "free ride."

Inefficient exclusion. Sometimes it is possible to eliminate the free-rider problem by charging a fee for using a public good. In our video example, the tape rental would have been covered if each member of the group were charged $1. That, however, would have been inefficient. Dick, who would be willing to pay 50 cents to see the video, would refuse to pay $1 and thus be excluded. However, considering that the marginal benefit of letting Dick see the video is 50 cents and the marginal cost is zero, it is plainly inefficient to exclude him.

Parks, roads, and bridges often are financed through fees or tolls that lead to inefficient exclusion. For an uncongested road, efficiency requires that users pay marginal cost, which is very close to zero. (Gasoline taxes typically cover maintenance costs.) Charging a toll that pays for construction of a road, as is done on some bridges and roadways, excludes users who value its use at more than marginal cost but less than the toll. There is another inefficiency involved in charging tolls. They are expensive to collect, and, as anyone who has ever driven on toll roads in large cities knows, they cause congestion of their own.

Even where getting around the free-rider problem is technically possible, it is usually inefficient. As in cases in which the private market would not produce a public good at all, the obvious remedy is government provision.

Efficient provision of public goods requires that consumers pay the marginal cost of their consumption—zero. Private markets will never provide goods at a price of zero and thus will always underprovide collective consumption goods.

Asymmetric Information

The role of information in the economy has received increasing attention from economists in recent years. Information is, of course, a valuable commodity, and markets for information and expertise are well developed, as every college student is aware. Markets for expertise are conceptually identical to markets for any other valuable service. They can pose special problems, however. One of these we have already discussed: Information is often a public good and thus will tend to be underproduced by the private sector, because once the information is known to anyone, it is extremely cheap to make it available to others.

Even where information is not a public good, markets for expertise are prone to market failure. The reason for this is that one party to a transaction can often take advantage of special knowledge in ways that change the nature of the transaction itself. Here are some important examples.

Moral hazard. As we saw in Chapter 8, *moral hazard* problems often occur as a result of insurance. In general, we say that there is moral hazard when one party to a transaction has both the incentive and the ability to shift costs onto the other party. The classic example is the homeowner who does not bother to shovel snow from his walk because he knows that his insurance will cover the cost if the mail carrier should twist an ankle. The costs of the homeowner's lax behavior will be borne largely by others, including the mail carrier, the insurance company, and, indirectly, others who purchase insurance. Individuals and firms who are insured against loss will generally take less care to prevent that loss than they would in the absence of insurance. They do so because they do not bear all of the marginal cost imposed by the risk, whereas they do bear all of the marginal cost of taking action to reduce the risk.

As in all of the cases of market failure that we have considered, the failure arises because the marginal private benefit of an action is not equal to the marginal social cost of that action. The existence of insurance markets, which ideally merely spread risk, will also increase total risk because of moral hazard.

Insurance is not the only context in which moral hazard problems arise. Another example is professional services. Suppose that you ask a physician whether you are sick or an attorney whether you need legal assistance. The doctor and the lawyer both face moral hazard in that they both have a financial interest in giving you answers that will encourage you to buy their services, and it is difficult for you to find out if their advice is trustworthy. A similar situation occurs when you ask your mechanic what is wrong with your engine. In all of these cases, one party to the transaction has special knowledge that could be used to change the nature of the transaction in that party's favor. As long as the auto mechanic is merely selling his expertise in repairing cars, there is no problem, but when he uses his expertise to persuade the consumer to demand more repairs than are warranted, there is a moral hazard problem. Codes of professional ethics and licensing and certification practices, both governmental and private, are reactions to concerns about this kind of moral hazard.

Adverse selection. Closely related to moral hazard is the problem of *adverse selection*—the tendency of people who are most at risk to buy the most insurance. A man who is suffering from a heart condition may seek to increase his life insurance coverage by purchasing as much additional coverage as is available without a medical examination. People who buy insurance almost always know more about themselves as individual insurance risks than their insurance companies do. The company can try to limit the variation in risk by setting up broad categories based on variables, such as age and occupation, over which actuarial risk is known to vary. The rate charged is then different across categories and is based on the average risk in each category, but there must always be much variability of risk *within* any one category.

People who know that their risk is well above the average for their category are offered a bargain and will be led to take out more car, health, life, or fire insurance than they otherwise would. Also, their insurance premiums will not cover the full expected cost of the risk that they are insuring against. Once again, their private cost is less than social cost. On the other side, people who know that they are at low risk and pay higher prices than warranted by their risk are motivated to take out less insurance than they otherwise would. In this case, the private cost is more than the social cost. In both cases, resources are allocated inefficiently because the marginal private benefit of the action (taking out insurance) is not equal to the social cost.

More generally, whenever either party to a transaction lacks information that the other party has or is deceived by claims made by the other party, market results will tend to be changed, and such changes may lead to inefficiency. Economically (but not legally) it is but a small step from such unequal knowledge to outright fraud. The arsonist who buys fire insurance before setting a building on fire and the business person with fire insurance who decides that a fire is preferable to bankruptcy are extreme examples of moral hazard.

Asymmetric information is involved in many other situations of market failure. The *principal-agent* problem, which was discussed in Chapter 16, is an example. In its classic form, the firm's managers act as agents for the stockholders, who are the legal principals of the firm. The managers are much better informed than the principals are about what they do and what they can do. Indeed, the managers are hired for their special expertise. Given that it is expensive to monitor what the agents do, they have latitude to pursue goals other than the firms' profits. The private costs and benefits of their actions will thus be different from the social costs and benefits, with the usual consequences for the efficiency of the market system. Another example of market failure due to asymmetric information is the apparent overdiscounting of the prices of used cars because of the buyer's risk of acquiring a "lemon." (See the discussion of this in Box 8-2.)

Government remedies to problems that arise from moral hazard, adverse selection, and principal-agent problems are relatively rare. One is the provision of government health insurance for the elderly. Without government insurance, it would be impossible for elderly consumers to obtain insurance coverage for serious illness. Why? Because insurance companies are quite aware of the problem of adverse selection. They fear that only the elderly who know themselves to be bad risks would buy health insurance. At the price that the companies need to charge to break even while covering the worse risks, no one would want insurance at all! By providing mandatory insurance, paid for by payroll taxes, the government can get around the adverse-selection problem. Furthermore, whether they are good or bad risks, all the elderly can be required to buy hospital insurance. Thus the insurance can be provided without any adverse selection.

Failure to Achieve Other Social Goals

Notwithstanding the real problems that are generated by externalities, information asymmetries, and public goods, the great strength of market systems is their ability to generate reasonably efficient outcomes, in a great many cases, using very decentralized organization. It should not be surprising that markets do less well at fostering goals that are held for society as a whole rather than derived from individuals' desires to improve their private circumstances. Some of these goals, for example, the desire for an "equitable" income distribution, are basically economic. Some, especially notions that people in a given society should have shared values, such as patriotism or a belief in civil liberties, are basically noneconomic. In either set of cases, however, markets are not very effective, precisely because the goods in question are not of the kind that can be exchanged in decentralized transactions. (Indeed, if we stretch the definition a bit, these are collective consumption goods, and we know that markets tend to underproduce such goods.)

Income Distribution

An important characteristic of a market economy is the *distribution* of the income that it determines. People whose services are in heavy demand relative to supply, such as television anchors and superior football players, earn large incomes, while people whose services are not in heavy demand relative to supply, such as Ph.D.'s in classics and high school graduates without work experience, earn much less.

The distribution of income produced by the market can be looked at in equilibrium or in disequilibrium. In equilibrium, in an efficiently operating free market economy, similar efforts of work or investment by similar people will tend to be similarly rewarded everywhere in the economy. Of course, dissimilar people will be dissimilarly rewarded.

In disequilibrium, similar people making similar efforts are likely to be dissimilarly rewarded. People in declining industries, areas, and occupations suffer the punishment of low earnings through no fault of their own. Those in expanding sectors earn the reward of high earnings through no extra effort or talent of their own.

These rewards and punishments serve the important function in decentralized decision making of motivating people to adapt. The advantage of such a system is that individuals can make their own decisions about how to alter their behavior when market conditions change; the disadvantage is that temporary rewards and punishments are dealt out as a result of changes in market conditions that are beyond the control of the affected individuals.

Moreover, even equilibrium differences in income may seem unfair. A free market system rewards certain groups and penalizes others. Because the workings of the market may be stern, even cruel, society often chooses to intervene. Should heads of households be forced to bear the full burden of their misfortune if, through no fault of their own, they lose their jobs? Even if they lose their jobs through their own fault, should they and their families have to bear the whole burden, which may include starvation? Should the ill and the aged be thrown on the mercy of their families? What if they have no families? Both private charities and a great many government policies are concerned with modifying the distribution of income that results from such things as where one starts, how able one is, how lucky one is, and how one fares in the free market world.

Often the goal of a more equitable distribution conflicts with the goal of a more efficient economy.

Some of the problems that this can create in policy debates are further discussed in Chapter 25.

Preferences for Public Provision

Police protection and even justice might be provided by private-market mechanisms. Security guards, private detectives, and bodyguards all provide policelike protection. Privately hired arbitrators, "hired guns," and vigilantes of the Old West represent private ways of obtaining "justice." Yet the members of society may believe that a public police force is *preferable* to a private one and that public justice is preferable to justice for hire.

As another example, public schools may be better or worse than private schools; either way they are likely to be different, particularly because persons other than parents, teachers, and owners influence their policies. Much of the case for public education rests on the advantages of having other people's children educated in a particular kind of environment that is *different* from what a private school would provide. In these cases, the fact that markets provide individual choice is viewed by some as a major social problem.

Protecting Individuals from Others

People can use and even abuse other people for economic gain in ways that the members of society find offensive. Child labor laws and minimum standards of working conditions are responses to such actions. Yet direct abuse is not the only example of this kind of market failure. In an unhindered free market, the adults in a household would usually decide how much education to buy for their children. Selfish parents might buy no education, while egalitarian parents might buy the same education for all of their children, regardless of their abilities. The members of society may want to interfere in these choices, both to protect the child of the selfish parent and to ensure that some of the scarce educational resources are distributed according to the ability and the willingness to use them rather than according to a family's wealth. All households are forced to provide a minimum of education for their children, and a number of inducements are offered—through public universities, scholarships, and other means—for talented children to consume more education than they or their parents might choose if they had to pay the entire cost themselves.

Paternalism

Members of society, acting through the state, often seek to protect adult (and presumably responsible) individuals not from others but from themselves. Laws prohibiting the use of heroin, cocaine, and other drugs and laws prescribing the installation and use of seat belts are intended primarily to protect individuals from their own ignorance or shortsightedness. This kind of interference in the free choices of individuals is called **paternalism**. Whether such actions reflect the wishes of the majority in the society or whether they reflect the actions of overbearing governments, there is no doubt that the market will not provide this kind of protection. Buyers do not buy what they do not want, and sellers have no motive to provide it.

Protection and paternalism are often closely related to **merit goods**. Merit goods are goods that society deems to be especially important and that individuals should be required or encouraged to consume. Housing, education, and health care are prime examples of merit goods.

Social Obligations

In a free market system, you can pay another person to do many things for you. If you persuade someone else to clean your house in return for $35, presumably both parties to the transaction are better off: You prefer to part with $35 rather than to clean the house yourself, and the person you hire prefers $35 to not cleaning your house. Normally society does not interfere with people's ability to negotiate mutually advantageous contracts.

Most people do not feel this way, however, about activities that are regarded as social obligations. For example, when military service is compulsory, contracts similar to the one between you and a housekeeper could also be negotiated. Some persons faced with the obligation to do military service could no doubt pay enough to persuade others to do their tour of service for them.[5] By exactly the same argument as we just used, we can presume that both parties will be better off if they are allowed to negotiate such a trade. Yet such contracts are usually prohibited. They are prohibited because there are values to be considered other than those that can be expressed in a market. In times when it is necessary, military service by all healthy males is usually held to be a duty that is independent of an individual's tastes, wealth, influence, or social position. It is felt that everyone *ought* to do this service, and exchanges between willing traders are prohibited.

Military service is not the only example of a social obligation. Citizens cannot buy their way out of jury duty or legally sell their votes to another, even though in many cases they could find willing trading partners.

[5] During the U.S. Civil War it was a common practice for a man to avoid the draft by hiring a substitute to serve in his place.

Even if the price system allocated goods and services with complete efficiency, members of a society may not wish to rely solely on the market if they have other goals that they wish to achieve.

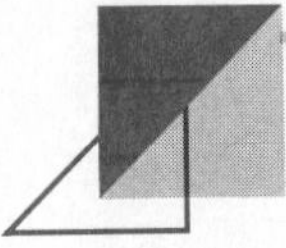

Government Intervention

Private collective action can sometimes remedy the failures of private individual action. (Private charities can help the poor; volunteer fire departments can fight fires; insurance companies can guard against adverse selection by more careful classification of clients.) However, by far the most common remedy for market failure is government intervention.

Our earlier discussion made clear that markets *do* fail, thereby providing scope for governments to intervene in beneficial ways. Whether government intervention is warranted in a given case will depend both on the magnitude of the market failure that the intervention is designed to correct and on the costs of the government action itself. The benefits of some types of government intervention (e.g., the social advantages of having a publicly provided justice system) are both difficult to quantify and potentially very large. For many types of government activity, however, **benefit-cost analysis**, developed by economists to consider what sorts of economic projects ought to be undertaken by governments, can be helpful in considering the general question of when and to what extent governments ought to intervene.

The idea behind benefit-cost analysis is transparently simple: Add up the (opportunity) costs of a given action, then add up the benefits, and take the action if the benefits outweigh the costs. In practice, benefit-cost analysis can be difficult for three reasons. First, it may be difficult to ascertain what will happen when an action is undertaken. Second, many government actions involve costs and benefits that will take place only in the distant future. Just how to *discount* future events raises both technical and normative problems for the analyst. Third, some benefits and costs (e.g., the benefits of prohibiting actions that would harm members of an endangered species) are at best very hard to quantify. Indeed, many people would argue that they cannot be and should not be quantified, as they involve values that are not commensurate with money. The practice then is to use benefit-cost analysis to measure the things that can be measured and to be sure that the things that cannot be measured are not forgotten when collective decisions are made. By narrowing the range of things that must be determined by informal judgment, benefit-cost analysis can still play a useful role.

In this chapter we have been working toward a benefit-cost analysis of government intervention. We have made a general case against it (free markets are great economizers on information and coordination costs). We have made a general case for it (free market will fail to produce efficiency when there are public goods, externalities, or information asymmetries and will fail to produce other social goals as well). We now turn to the more specific questions of what governments do when they intervene, what the costs of government intervention are, and under which circumstances government interventions are likely to fail to improve on even imperfect private markets.

Tools of Government Intervention

The legal power of the government to intervene in the workings of the economy is limited only by the Constitution (as interpreted by the courts), the willingness of Parliament to pass laws, and the willingness of the government to enforce them. There are numerous ways in which one or another level of government can prevent, alter, complement, or replace the workings of the unrestricted market economy.

Public provision. National defense, the criminal justice system, the public schools, the highway system, air traffic control, and the national parks are all examples of goods or services that are directly provided by governments in Canada. Public provison is the obvious remedy for market failure to provide collective consumption goods, but it is also often used in the interest of redistribution (e.g., public hospitals) and other social goals (e.g., public schools). In Chapter 24 we shall consider public spending in detail.

Redistribution and social insurance programs. Taxes and spending are often used to provide a distribution of income that is different from that generated by the private market. In Chapter 24 we shall examine the distributive effects of the tax and transfer system.

That chapter also contains a discussion of the effect of redistributive spending on government budgets.

Proscriptive rules. Proscriptive rules take the form "Thou shalt . . ." or "Thou shalt not . . .": They tell people and firms what they can and cannot do. Such rules require parents to send their children to school and to have them inoculated against measles and diphtheria. Laws that prohibit gambling and pornography attempt to enforce a particular moral code on the whole society. In Chapter 15 we discussed an important form of policy by prohibition—competition policy.

There are many other examples. Children cannot be served alcoholic drinks legally. Prostitution is prohibited in many places, even between a willing buyer and a willing seller. In some provinces you must buy automobile insurance. A person who offers goods for sale, including his or her own house, cannot refuse to sell to someone because of a dislike for the customer's appearance or dress. There are rules against fraudulent advertising and the sale of substandard, adulterated, or poisonous foods.

Notice that proscriptive rules are used to deal with a wide range of types of market failure. In the examples just given, the rules requiring that all drivers have automobile insurance and prohibiting the selling of poisonous food are designed to prevent negative externalities. Rules against housing discrimination support a social value of equal opportunity. Rules against serving alcohol to minors are basically paternalistic. Competition laws, at least some of the time, directly proscribe a type of market imperfection.

Prescriptive rules. Prescriptive rules substitute the rule maker's judgment for the firm's or the household's judgment about such things as prices charged, products produced, and methods of production. Prescriptive regulation tends to restrict private action more than proscriptive regulation because it *replaces* private decision making rather than simply *limiting* the set of acceptable private decisions. Regulation of public utilities is an important example of prescriptive regulation (see Chapter 15), but prescriptive regulation goes far beyond the natural monopoly regulation that we have discussed. Indeed, much economic regulation, especially regarding pollution control, safety, and health, comes in the form of prescriptive rules (see Chapter 23).

As is the case with proscriptive rules, prescriptive rules are used to deal with essentially all types of market failure. Public utility regulation is designed to ameliorate the consequences of natural monopoly; some health and safety regulation reduces negative externalities, and some is arguably paternalistic. Some states require that private firms provide specific fringe benefits (the consequences here are primarily redistributive). Many localities require real estate developers to donate and to develop parkland when they build certain types of projects. The resulting parks are collective consumption goods that are privately provided.

Problems with rule making. Rule making often appears to be a cheap, easy, and direct way of compelling desirable behavior in the face of market failure, but this appearance is deceptive. Rules must be enforceable and enforced, and once enforced, they must be effective in obtaining the hoped-for results. These conditions are often difficult and expensive to achieve. Moreover, difficulties in enforcement can lead to inequities.

Consider a requirement for the installation of an antipollution device that will meet a certain standard in reducing automobile exhaust emissions. Such a law may be the outcome of parliamentary debate on pollution control—and having passed the bill, Parliament will turn to other things. Yet certain problems must be solved before the law can achieve its purpose. Even with perfect compliance by the manufacturer, the device may not work well unless it is kept in working order by the owner. Yet the owner has no private incentive to maintain it, and it would be expensive to inspect every vehicle regularly and to force owners to keep the devices at the standard that is set by law.

Even a well-designed rule will work only to the extent that the people subject to it cannot figure out a way to evade its intent while obeying its letter.

There will be a substantial incentive to find loopholes in regulations. Resources that could be used elsewhere will be devoted by the regulated to the search for such loopholes and then, in turn, by the regulators to counteract such evasion.

Structuring incentives. Almost all government actions, including the kinds that we have discussed here, change the incentives that households and firms face. If the government provides a park, people will have a weakened incentive to own large plots of land of their own. If the government proscribes a certain type of behavior, the penalty that is imposed will influence people to do something else. Fixing minimum or maximum prices (as we saw in the discussion of agriculture and rent control in Chapter 6) affects privately chosen levels of output.

The government can adjust the tax system to provide subsidies to some kinds of behavior and penalties to others (see Chapter 24). Deductible mortgage interest and real estate taxes, for example, would make owned housing relatively more attractive than other assets that a household might purchase. Such tax treatment sends the household different signals from those sent by the free market. Scholarships to students to become nurses or teachers may offset barriers to mobility into those occupations. Fines and criminal penalties for violating the rules that are imposed are another part of the incentive structure. By providing direct or indirect fines or subsidies, the government can correct externalities, induce private production of public goods, change the income distribution, and encourage behavior that is deemed socially valuable.

The government has many tools at its disposal and can use them singly or in combination to address different kinds of market failure.

Costs of Government Intervention

Consider the following argument: The market system is working imperfectly; government has the legal means to improve the situation; therefore, the public interest will be served by government intervention.

This appealing argument is deficient because it neglects two important considerations. First, government intervention is costly. For this reason, not every market failure is worth correcting. Second, government intervention may be imperfect. Just as markets sometimes succeed and sometimes fail, so government intervention sometimes succeeds and sometimes fails. In this section we consider costs of intervention, neglecting government failure. Later we consider the added problem imposed by imperfect government intervention.

The *benefits* of government intervention are the value of the market failures averted. To evaluate government intervention, it is necessary to consider the costs of the intervention and compare costs with benefits.

Large potential benefits do not necessarily justify government intervention, nor do large potential costs necessarily make it unwise. What matters is the balance between benefits and costs.

There are several kinds of costs of government intervention.

Internal Costs

Government intervention uses real resources that could be used elsewhere. Civil servants must be paid. Paper, photocopying, and other trappings of bureaucracy, the steel in the navy's ships, the fuel for the army's tanks, and the pilot of the prime minister's plane all have valuable alternative uses. The same is true of the accountants who administer the social insurance system and of the educators who retrain displaced workers.

Similarly, when government inspectors visit plants to monitor compliance with federally imposed standards of health, industrial safety, or environmental protection, they are imposing costs on the public in the form of the salaries and expenses of the inspectors. When regulatory bodies develop rules, hold hearings, write opinions, or have their staff prepare research reports, they are incurring costs. The costs of the judges, clerks, and court reporters who hear, transcribe, and review the evidence are likewise costs imposed by government regulation. All these activities use valuable resources that could have provided very different goods and services.

Whatever the form of government intervention, it will impose direct internal costs.

This type of cost is fairly easy to see, as it almost always involves expenditure of public budgets. Other costs of intervention are less apparent but no less real.

External Costs

Most government interventions in the economy impose some costs on firms and households. The nature and the size of the extra costs borne by firms and households subject to government intervention vary with the type of intervention. A few examples are worth noting.

Changes in costs of production. Federal safety and emission standards for automobiles have raised the costs of both producing and operating cars. These costs are much greater than the direct budgetary costs of administering the regulations. Taxes used to finance the provision of collective consumption goods must be paid by producers and consumers and typically increase the cost of producing or selling goods and services.

Costs of compliance. Government regulation and supervision generate a flood of reporting and related activities that often are summarized in the phrase *red tape*. The number of hours of business time devoted to understanding, reporting, and contesting regulatory provisions is enormous. Affirmative action, occupational safety, and environmental control have all increased the size of nonproduction payrolls. The legal costs alone of a major corporation can run into tens or hundreds of millions of dollars per year. While all this provides lots of employment for lawyers and economic experts, it is costly because there are other tasks such professionals could do that would add more to the production of consumer goods and services.

Losses in productivity. Quite apart from the actual expenditures, the regulatory climate may reduce the incentive for experimentation, innovation, and the introduction of new products. Requiring advance government clearance before a new method or product may be introduced (on grounds of potential safety hazards or environmental impact) can eliminate the incentive to develop it. Requiring advance approval by a regulatory commission before entry is permitted into a regulated industry can discourage potential competitors. Tax policy can also have an effect. An income tax may make it less profitable to invest in specialized training that will yield a high income.

Government "Imperfection"

Our conceptual benefit-cost analysis of government intervention is almost complete. First, we calculate the social cost of each market failure. This cost is the potential benefit of intervention. Then we make our best estimate of the actual effect of the intervention—in most cases, the best that we can do is less than the maximum potential benefit. Then we calculate the costs of the intervention, as just outlined. If the benefits exceed the costs, the intervention is warranted. Unfortunately, things are never this simple. For one thing, as we have just explained, many of the benefits of government intervention are extremely difficult to quantify. Even in the "easy" cases, however, where the benefits and the direct costs of intervention can be measured, governments, like private markets, are imperfect. Often they will fail, in the same sense that markets do, to achieve their potential.

Causes of Government Failure

The reason for government failure is not that public-sector employees are less able, honest, or virtuous than people who work in the private sector. Rather, the causes of government failure, like the causes of market failure, are by and large natural ones. Indeed, as we show in Box 22-2, some of them are inescapable costs of democratic decision making.

Governments as monopolists. Governments face the same problems of cost minimization that private firms do but often operate in an environment where they are monopoly producers without stockholders. Large governments (provinces, big cities, the federal government) face all of the organizational problems faced by large corporations. They tend to use relatively rigid rules and thus to respond only slowly to change. Building codes are an example of this type of problem. Most local governments have detailed requirements regarding the materials that must go into a new house, factory, or office. When technology changes, the codes often lag behind. For example, plastic pipe, which is cheaper and easier to use than steel pipe, was prohibited by building codes for decades after its use became feasible. Similarly, much antipollution regulation specifies the type of control equipment that must be employed. Changes in technology may make a regulation inefficient, but the regulation may stay in place for some time.

Like those of large private enterprises, a government's "organization chart" will often be out of date. In Chapter 15 we discussed the example of the regulatory commission that was charged with maintain-

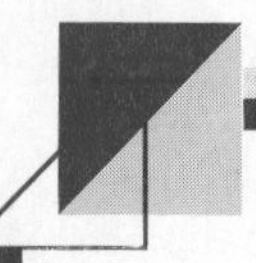

BOX 22-2

Social Choice Theory: The Economic Analysis of Government Behavior

Economics is the study of the allocation of scarce resources. Given that many of these resources, even in market-oriented economies such as Canada's, are allocated by government, economists have spent a good deal of effort in the study of government provision of goods and services. Social choice theory asks what the relationship is between the rules that governments use to reach decisions and the way in which society's real resources are allocated.

Logrolling

At the core of most people's idea of democracy is the idea that each citizen's vote should count the same. Social choice theory demonstrates that resource allocation based on the principle of one person, one vote is generally inefficient because it fails to take into account the *intensity of preferences*. Consider three farmers, A, B, and C, who are contemplating building access roads. Suppose that the road to A's farm is worth $7,000 to A and that the road to B's farm is worth $7,000 to B. (C's farm is on the main road, which already exists.) Suppose that under the tax rules in effect, each road would cost each of the three farmers $2,000. It is plainly efficient to build both roads, since each generates net benefits of $1,000 ($7,000 gross benefits to the farmer helped, less $6,000 total cost). But each would be defeated 2-1 in a simple majority vote. (B and C would vote against A's road; A and C would vote against B's road.)

Now suppose that we allow A and B to make a deal: "I will vote for your road if you will vote for mine." Such deals, often decried by political commentators, are examples of *logrolling*. In this case, the deal enhances efficiency: Both roads now get 2-1 majorities, and both roads get built. However, logrolling can sometimes reduce efficiency. If we make the gross value of each road $5,000 instead of $7,000 and let A and B roll their logs, each road will still command a 2-1 majority, but building the roads will now be inefficient. (The gross value of each road is now only $5,000, while the cost is still $6,000.) In either case A and B are using democracy to appropriate resources from C.

"Special interests." This latter case can be interpreted in a different way. Instead of being the third farmer, C might be all of the voters in the county. Instead of bearing one-third of the costs, A and B each might bear only a small portion of the costs. To the extent that A and B are able to articulate forcefully the benefits that they would derive from the roads, they may be able to use democracy to appropriate resources from taxpayers in general. Much of the concern with the power of "special interests" stems from the fact that the institutions of representative democracy tend to be responsive to benefits (or costs) that focus on particular, identifiable, and articulate groups. Often, costs that are borne diffusely by taxpayers or voters in general are hardly noticed. This potential bias applies to regulations as well as to direct government provisions. For example, as we saw in Chapter 6, rent controls can be interpreted, at least in part, as benefiting existing tenants at the expense of future potential tenants; the latter group tends to have no political power at all.

Arrow's Impossibility Theorem

Nobel Laureate Kenneth Arrow has shown that it is generally impossible to construct a set of rules for making social choices that is at once comprehensive, democratic, efficient, and consistent. Arrow's theorem has led to decades of work on the part of economists, philosophers, and political scientists, who have tried to find conditions under which choices made by democratic vote yield efficient allocations of resources. The news is generally not good. Unless individual preferences or their distribution in the population meet fairly unlikely criteria, either democracy or efficiency must be sacrificed in the design of social choice mechanisms.

The Arrow theorem can be illustrated by a familiar and simple case, depicted in the table. Again we have a society that consists of three voters. This time they are choosing how many trees to plant in the local park. There are three possibilities: (1) Plant very few trees in one corner. This would make the park suitable for Frisbee and soccer but not for walks in the woods. (2) Plant trees in moderate density throughout the park. In this case, the park would be nice for jogging but not usable for most sports. (3) Plant trees densely everywhere. This would make the park a pleasant place to get away from it all (for whatever reasons) but not a good place to jog in. Voter A loves jogging, hates Frisbee and the noise that Frisbee players make, and likes walking in the woods. His ranking of the alternatives is 2-3-1. Voter B likes the wide-open spaces. His ranking is 1-2-3. Voter C likes to play Frisbee, likes solitude even more, and has little taste for a park that provides neither. Her ranking is 3-1-2.

Suppose that the electorate gets to choose between alternatives that are presented two at a time. What does majority rule do? It depends on which two alternatives are presented. In a choice of 1 versus 2, 1 wins. When the choice is between 2 and 3, 2 wins. When 3 is pitted against 1, 3 wins. Thus the *social choice mechanism of majority rule* is inconsistent. It tells us that 1 is preferred to 2, 2 is preferred to 3, and 3 is preferred to 1.

	Voter		
Density of trees	**A**	**B**	**C**
Sparse	3	1	2
Medium	1	2	3
Thick	2	3	1

Bureaucracy and "Leviathan"

Social choice theorists also stress that government agencies are not subject to the disciplines of the marketplace. Economist William Niskanen has proposed that bureaucrats will act like revenue-maximizing monopolists, trying to make their agencies as large as possible. Other economists have noted that competition among agencies will limit but not eliminate the power of government agencies to do this. Another limitation arises from the fact that politicians who give too much power to bureaucrats reduce their chances of being reelected.

An extreme model, in which neither of these three checks on bureaucracy is assumed to apply, was proposed by Gerald Brennan and Nobel Laureate James Buchanan. Brennan and Buchanan argue that the bureaucrat-politicians' ability to gain control over economic resources only can be limited by the taxing power granted to them in the Constitution. This leads Brennan and Buchanan to advocate limiting the range of activities that the government may tax and to advocate the requirement of balanced budgets.

The "New" Political Economy

The rise of social choice theory has added to the economist's ability to analyze the institutions that affect the allocation of resources. From the economist's perspective, once it is recognized that there is a role for government, it follows that even within government, economic incentives will matter. In order to make an informed choice about what should be privately and publicly provided in a society, one must look at the nonmarket mechanisms that determine public resource allocation. Political scientists have known this for years, but they have not had available to them the economist's tools for undertaking the investigation. The application of these tools has revealed much, not the least of which is that social institutions have a profound effect on the allocation of economic resources.

ing a healthy telecommunications system. With the advent of new technologies, the commission's mandate will have become much broader, including control over satellites and fax machines. The same kind of problem might well arise when the purchasing division in a large corporation, which uses typewriters exclusively, is confronted with modern word processing technology. In the private sector, there are usually market forces pushing the corporation into revising its view of the problem at hand. Usually there is no market mechanism tending to force governments toward the use of relatively efficient rules of thumb and organizational structures. Put in the language of Chapter 16, the scope for satisficing governments to depart from optimal behavior is generally greater than that for satisficing firms. Put in another way, much government failure arises precisely because governments do not have competitors.

Principal-agent problems in government. Governments face the same kinds of *principal-agent problems* (see Chapter 16) that firms do, but the problem in the case of governments can be more serious for two reasons. First, the possibility of a hostile takeover, although quite powerful as applied to elected officials (they can be removed from office), is very weak as applied to bureaucracies. Second, the principal in the case of government is all of its citizens, and this group will in general be unable to agree on what government *should* do. Stockholders can all agree that the firm should maximize stock value. Citizens who vote, by contrast, are not expected to agree on any simple mission for their elected representatives. This lack of agreement makes it that much more difficult for the agents to serve their principals and that much easier for agents who do not perform well to get away with it.

Rent seeking. A different kind of problem arises from the mere existence of government and its potential to use its tools in ways that affect the distribution of economic resources. The example of the railroads will serve again. Once the government is in the business of setting prices for private firms, it will be rational for these firms to spend real resources trying to influence the regulators. The opportunity cost of these resources might be the development of cost-saving technology in the industry. Similar cases arise with collective consumption goods, externalities, and taxes. Given that the government *can* act in ways that transfer resources to private entities and given that government's behavior can be influenced, whether by voting, campaign contributions, lobbying, or bribes, real resources will be used in trying to influence government behavior. Taken to its logical conclusion, this argument suggests that the mere existence of government imposes a negative externality. More practically, some people have used the problem raised by rent-seeking behavior as an argument for limiting the size and scope of government.

The Effect of Government Failure

Suppose, for any of the reasons that we have just discussed, that the government makes a mistake in regulation. Say the government mistakenly specifies a method of pollution control that is less effective than the best method. This will increase the cost of achieving any given level of prevention. If the government insists on the level of control that is appropriate to the correct method but requires the incorrect method, it can convert a social gain from control into a social loss.

To generalize from the specific example, it is clear that any form of government failure adds to the costs of or decreases the benefits of government intervention. Thus the lower the public's confidence in government's ability to do the right thing, the lower will be its willingness to have government intervention.

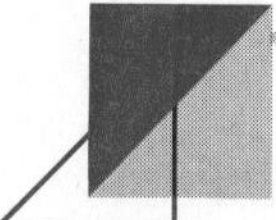

How Much Should Government Intervene?

The theoretical principles for determining the optimal amount of government intervention are individually accepted by almost everyone. What they add up to, however, is more controversial. Does government intervene too little or too much in response to market failure? This question reflects one aspect of the ongoing argument about the role of government in the economy.

Much of the rhetoric of our concern with ecology urges government intervention against heartless, profit-hungry, giant corporations that destroy the environment for their own crass purposes. Such feelings lead to the demand for more—and more stringent—government regulation.

At the same time, others see the heavy hand of government regulation as burdening private companies with regulations that add to costs and impede innovation and thus keep prices and wages artificially high. Even perfect intervention would be costly, but imperfect intervention makes it much too costly. In this view, the deregulation movement that started during the 1980s was long overdue.

Evaluating the costs and the effectiveness of government intervention requires a comparison of the unregulated economic system as it is working (not as it might work ideally) with the pattern of government intervention as it is likely to perform (not as it might perform ideally).

The Role of Analysis

Economic analysis and measurement can help to eliminate certain misconceptions that cloud and confuse the debate on the "proper" role of government. One mistake is the notion that the invisible hand of free markets will always lead to an efficient allocation of resources. Externalities, public goods, and moral hazard problems are features of real market economies, and they lead to inefficiency whenever they appear.

Another mistake is to equate market failure with the greed of profit-motivated corporations. Externalities do not require callous, thoughtless, or deliberately deceptive practices of private, profit-seeking firms; they occur whenever the signals to which decision makers respond do not include social as well as private benefits and costs. Such situations are not limited to private firms in a capitalist system. Cities and nationalized industries pollute just as much as privately owned industries when they neglect externalities in their operations, as they often do. As the economies of Eastern Europe opened up in the late 1980s, observers were shocked not only by the low levels of income but also by pollution far worse than any found in free market economies of similar size and structure.

A third mistake is to think that the profits of a corporation tell something about neglected externalities. It is possible for either a profitable firm or an unprofitable one to spend too little on pollution control or on safety, but it is also possible for it to spend too much. The existence of profits provides no clue as to which is the case.

The Role of Ideology

Although positive analysis has a role to play, there are several reasons why ideology plays a bigger role in evaluating government intervention than in other areas. First, much of what government does is in the realm of "other social goals," rather than economics. Economic analysis can be useful in helping to find ways to achieve such goals, but at bottom political and social ideology must always play a large role in defining the shape and the role of government.

Second, measuring the costs of government intervention is difficult, particularly with respect to external costs, because some of the trade-offs are inherently uncertain. How important and how unsafe is nuclear power? Does the ban on some pesticides cause so much malnutrition as to offset the environmental gains that it brings? Costs that cannot be measured readily can be alleged to be extremely high (or low) by opponents (or supporters) of intervention. The numerous findings by scholars on both sides of each of these subjects has led one economist to the cynical conclusion that "believing is seeing."

Third, classifying the actual pattern of government intervention as successful or not is in part subjective. Has government safety regulation been useful if imperfect, virtually ineffective, or positively adverse? All three views have been expressed and "documented."

Fourth, specifying what constitutes market failure is difficult. Does product differentiation represent market success (by giving consumers the variety they want) or failure (by foisting expensive and useless variations on them)?

What government actually *does* should have some bearing on the debate, regardless of ideology. In Chapter 15 we discussed government action that is designed to affect monopoly and competition. In Chapters 23 and 24 we shall discuss in some detail three other important types of intervention in the Canadian economy today: environmental and safety regulation, taxation, and public spending.

SUMMARY

1. The various markets in the economy are coordinated in an unplanned, decentralized way by the price system. Profits and losses play a key role in achieving a coordinated market response. Changes in prices and profits, resulting from emerging scarcities and surpluses, lead decision makers to adapt to a change in any one market of the economy. Such responses tend to correct the shortages and surpluses as well as to change the market signals of prices and profits.
2. Important features of market coordination include voluntary responses to market signals, the limited information required by any individual, and the fact that coordination will occur under any market structure.
3. A widely held argument in favor of the free market goes beyond its ability to provide automatic coordination. Many observers believe that its flexibility and adaptability make it the best coordinator and also encourage innovation and growth. The tendency of the market to push relative prices toward the costs of production fosters efficient allocation of resources and self-correction of disequilibrium. Furthermore, the market economy tends to be impersonal, to decentralize power, and to require relatively little coercion of individuals.
4. Markets do not always work perfectly. Dissatisfaction with market results often leads to government intervention. Four main kinds of market failure are (a) externalities arising from differences between private and social costs and benefits, (b) the inability of markets to produce collective consumption goods, (c) information asymmetries, and (d) failure to achieve social goals other than efficiency.
5. Pollution is an example of an externality. An important source of pollution is producers' use of resources such as water and air that they do not regard as scarce. Since they do not pay all of the costs of using these resources, they are not motivated to avoid the costs. Individual use of common-property resources causes congestion and also gives rise to externalities.
6. National defense is an example of a collective consumption good, often called a public good. Markets fail to produce collective consumption goods because the benefits of such goods are available to people whether they pay for them or not.
7. Information asymmetries cause market failure when one party to a transaction is able to use his or her expertise to manipulate the transaction in his or her own favor. Moral hazard, adverse selection, and principal-agent problems are all consequences of information asymmetries.
8. Changing the distribution of income is one of the roles for government intervention that members of a society desire. Others include values that are placed on public provision for its own sake, on protection of individuals from themselves or from others, and on recognition of social obligations.
9. Microeconomic policy concerns activities of the government that alter the unrestricted workings of the free market system in order to affect either the allocation of resources or the distribution of income. Major tools of microeconomic policy include (a) public provision, (b) redistribution, (c) rule making, and (d) structuring incentives. (The first two are the subject of Chapter 24.) Both

prescriptive and proscriptive rules occur in a variety of forms. Incentives can be structured in a number of ways, including the use of fines, subsidies, taxes, and effluent charges (which are discussed in Chapter 23). Each of these is a means of internalizing externalities and thus of avoiding market failure.

10. The costs and benefits of government intervention must be considered in deciding whether, when, and how much intervention is appropriate. Among the costs are the direct costs that are incurred by the government, the direct and indirect costs that are imposed on the people who are regulated, and the costs that are imposed on third parties. These costs are seldom negligible and are often large.

11. If government intervention fails, the costs of intervention are incurred without realizing the benefits of avoiding market failure. The possibility of government failure must be balanced against the potential benefits of removing market failure. It is neither possible nor efficient to correct all market failure; neither is it always efficient to do nothing.

TOPICS FOR REVIEW

Market coordination
Differences between private and social valuations
Market failure
Rule making
Externalities
Collective consumption goods
Benefit-cost analysis
Information asymmetries
Benefits and costs of government intervention
Government failure

DISCUSSION QUESTIONS

1. Should the free market be allowed to determine the price for the following, or should government intervene? Defend your choice for each.
   a. Transit fares
   b. Plastic surgery for victims of fires
   c. Garbage collection
   d. Postal delivery of newspapers and magazines
   e. Fire protection for churches
   f. Ice cream
2. The following activities have known harmful effects. In each case, identify any divergence between social and private costs.
   a. Cigarette smoking
   b. Driving a car at 120 kph
   c. Private ownership of guns
   d. Drilling for offshore oil
3. Suppose that the following statements are true. Should they trigger government intervention? If so, what policy alternatives are available?
   a. Hospital costs have been rising at about four times the rate of increase of personal income, and proper treatment of a serious illness has become extraordinarily expensive.
   b. The cost of an average one-family house in Ottawa is now over $200,000—an amount beyond the reach of many government employees.

   c. Cigarette smoking tends to reduce the life expectancy of the smoker by eight years.
   d. Saccharin in large doses has been found to cause cancer in mice.

4. Consider the possible beneficial and adverse effects of each of the following forms of government intervention.
   a. Charging motorists a tax for driving in the downtown areas of large cities and using the revenues to provide peripheral parking and shuttle buses
   b. Prohibiting juries from awarding large malpractice judgments against doctors
   c. Mandating no-fault automobile insurance, in which the automobile owner's insurance company is responsible for damage to his or her vehicle no matter who causes the accident
   d. Requiring automobile manufacturers to warrant the tires on cars that they sell instead of (as at present) having the tire manufacturer be the warrantor
5. The president of Goodyear Tire and Rubber Company complained that government regulation had imposed $30 million per year in "unproductive costs" on his company, as listed here. How would one determine whether these costs were "productive" or "unproductive"?
   a. Environmental regulation, $17 million
   b. Occupational safety and health, $7 million
   c. Motor vehicle safety, $3 million
   d. Personnel and administration, $3 million
6. Your local government probably provides, among other things, a police department, a fire department, and a public library. What are the market imperfections, if any, that each of these is designed to correct? Which of these are closest to being collective consumption goods? Which are furthest?
7. What market failure(s) does public support of higher education seek to remedy? How would you go about evaluating whether the benefits of this support outweigh the costs?

Chapter 23

Environmental and Safety Regulation

In almost everything we do, we are subject to some form of government regulation. The system of criminal law regulates our interactions with people and property. Local zoning ordinances regulate the ways in which the land that we own may be used. Public utility commissions set rates for electricity, natural gas, local telephone service, and a host of other goods and services. Seat belts, brake lights, turn signals, air bags, internal door panels, bumpers, and catalytic converters are all subjects of regulation in just one industry. The number of electrical outlets per room, the material used for plumbing, and the spacing of the vertical supports in an interior wall are dictated by local building codes. The list goes on and on. A good case can be made that governments in Canada have more effect on the economy through regulation than through taxing and spending.

In Chapter 22 we identified a number of types of market failure that might be addressed by government policy. Regulation of economic activity is used to address each of them. Market failure arising from *natural monopoly* has led to public utility regulation, as discussed in Chapter 15. *Externalities,* especially the negative externalities of industrial pollution, are the motivation for environmental regulation, a major topic of this chapter.

Regulation of advertising and much health and safety regulations are designed to deal with market failures arising from *information asymmetries*. There is no easy way for a consumer to know whether the paint on a child's toy can cause lead poisoning, so the Department of Consumer Affairs regulates the market for children's toys. Occupational licensing is defended on the same grounds; in most provinces, professionals as different as barbers and psychiatrists must undergo specified courses of training before they are allowed to ply their trade. The idea is to prevent "just anyone" from claiming and abusing alleged expertise.

Information about a professional's training is a *public good*: Once the information is available to one consumer, it can be made available to all very cheaply. Occupational licensing is a way to produce this public good—in the form of the familiar diploma that hangs on the wall of the barbershop, physician's office, or repair garage.

Regulations can also be used to change the *distribution of income*. This is the purpose of, among other regulations, rent controls, minimum wages, and agricultural pricing rules. Finally, the laws and regulations that enforce private contracts are a pure public good that is essential to the operation of a market economy. Without reliably enforceable contracts, many transactions would be so risky that they would not take place.

The principal topic of this chapter might be called *social regulation*. Social regulation does not mean the regulation of social behavior (e.g., dress and speech). Rather, it is the regulation of economic behavior to advance social goals in circumstances in which neither competition nor economic regulation can be expected to do the job.

In this chapter we consider both the market failures that social regulation addresses and the effectiveness of different kinds of regulation in correcting these market failures. We start by extending Chapter 22's analysis of negative externalities to the problem of environmental pollution.

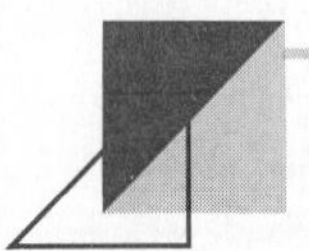

Pollution and Pollution Control

Pollution is a negative externality. As a result of producing or consuming goods and services, "bads" are produced as well. Steel plants produce heat and benzene in addition to steel. Farms produce chemical runoff as well as food. Households produce human waste and garbage as they consume goods and services. In all of these cases, the technology of production and consumption automatically generates pollution. Indeed, there are few human endeavors that do not give rise to negative pollution externalities.

The Economic Rationale for Regulating Pollution

Figure 23-1 illustrates a typical case. A profit-maximizing competitive firm sets its marginal cost equal to the market price of output. When the firm's production generates pollution, however, there is an *external cost* that is not borne by the firm. If we add the marginal private cost that the firm bears (MC_p) and the external cost that it imposes on others (EC), we get the *marginal social cost curve* of the firm's production (MC_s).

Allocative efficiency requires that the price (the value that consumers place on the marginal unit of output) be just equal to the marginal social cost (the value of resources that society gives up to produce the marginal unit of output).

By producing where price equals marginal private cost and thereby ignoring the externality, the firm is maximizing profits. However, from the social viewpoint, the firm is producing too much output. The price that consumers pay covers the marginal private cost but does not pay for the external damage. The **social benefit** of the last unit of output (the market price) is less than the social cost (MC_s). Reducing output by one unit would reduce social benefit by p and reduce social cost by MC_s for a net gain just equal to the pollution externality. The unregulated market fails to achieve efficiency because of the externality.

Making the firm bear the entire social cost of its

FIGURE 23-1 Pollution Externalities

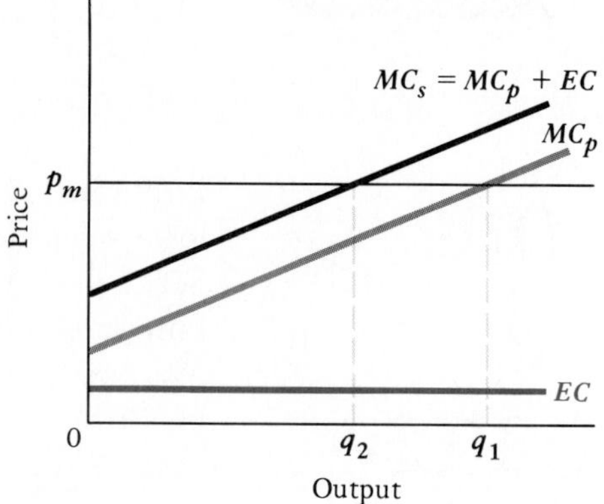

Internalizing an externality can correct market failure. The private marginal cost curve, MC_p, is the conventional marginal cost for a firm that is producing output in a competitive market. The horizontal external cost curve, EC, depicts marginal cost that the firm's production imposes on people other than its owners, employees, and customers. Since the firm is maximizing profits, it will ignore EC and produce output q_1, where the market price p_m equals marginal cost. Adding EC and MC_p yields *social marginal cost,* MC_s. The socially optimal level of output is q_2, where price is equal to MC_s. Here the price is sufficient to pay for the private marginal cost of production, MC_p, *and* to compensate others for the external marginal cost imposed on them, EC.

Suppose that the firm is required to pay a tax of EC dollars per unit of output. Its MC_p curve will now become the MC_s curve. The externality will be *internalized,* and the profit-maximizing firm will be motivated to reduce its output to the socially optimal level, q_2. It does this because with the tax added to its private marginal cost, q_2 is the profit-maximizing level of output.

production is called **internalization** of the externality. This will cause it to produce at a lower output. Indeed, at the optimal output, consumer prices would just cover all of the marginal social cost of production—marginal private cost plus the externality. We would have the familiar condition for economic efficiency that marginal benefits to consumers are just equal to the marginal cost of producing these benefits. The difference here is that some of the marginal cost takes the form of an externality that has been internalized.

Suppose that Warthog Industries, Inc., manufactures kitchen cabinets and that residue from painting the cabinets is washed into a stream that runs outside the plant. The stream is part of the municipal water supply, which is treated at a water purification plant before it is sent into people's homes. Suppose that each cabinet produced increases the cost of running the water treatment plant by 1 cent. Then, in terms of the foregoing analysis, *EC* is 1 cent, and MC_s will be exactly 1 cent above MC_p.

In practice, the external cost (*EC*) is often quite difficult to measure. This is especially true in the case of air pollution, where the damage is often spread over hundreds of thousands of square miles and can have real but small effects on millions of people. Another difficulty arises because the cost that is imposed by pollution will generally depend on the mechanisms used to undo the damage that it causes. Control mechanisms are themselves costly, and their costs must also be counted as part of the social cost of pollution. Nevertheless, the basic analysis of Figure 23-1 applies to these more difficult cases.

The socially optimal level of output is the quantity where *all* marginal costs, private plus external, equal the marginal benefit to society.

Notice that the optimal level of output is not the level at which there is *no* pollution. Rather, it is the level at which the beneficiaries of pollution (the consumers and producers of Warthog Industries' kitchen cabinets, in our example) are just willing to pay the marginal social cost that is imposed by the pollution.

Unregulated markets will generally produce excessive amounts of environmental damage. Zero environmental damage, however, is neither technologically possible nor economically efficient.

Pollution Control in Theory and Practice

Figure 23-2 depicts the benefits and costs of pollution control. The figure might be thought of as applying, say, to water pollution in a specific watershed. It is drawn from the perspective of a public authority that has been charged with maximizing social welfare. The horizontal axis shows the amount of *pollution abated* (or prevented). Thus zero on the horizontal axis represents the amount of pollution that would occur in an unregulated market. The greater the distance from the origin, the greater the amount of pollution that has been prevented and the smaller the amount of pollution remaining. The reason that we

FIGURE 23-2 The Optimal Amount of Pollution Abatement

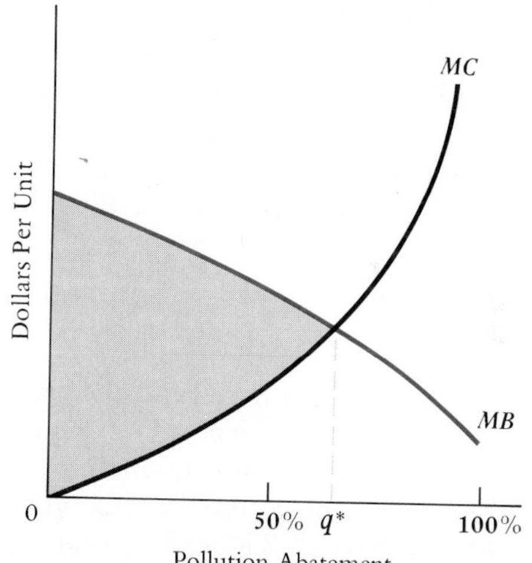

The optimal amount of pollution abatement occurs where the marginal cost of reducing pollution is just equal to the marginal benefits from doing so. *MB* represents the marginal benefit that is achieved by pollution prevention in some activity. *MC* represents the marginal cost of preventing pollution; it rises sharply as more and more pollution is eliminated. The optimal level of pollution control is q^*, where $MB = MC$. *Notice that not all pollution is eliminated.* For all units up to q^*, the marginal benefits derived from pollution abatement exceed the marginal costs. Net benefits are shown by the total shaded area. Any further reductions in pollution would add more to costs than to benefits.

put pollution that has been prevented on the horizontal axis is that pollution abatement is a good of economic value, and we are used to looking at supply and demand analyses for such goods.

The marginal cost curve is the marginal cost of preventing pollution. It is shown as starting low and rising steeply. There are two reasons for believing that this shape is generally accurate. First is the familiar logic behind increasing marginal costs. For each firm that pollutes, there will be some antipollution measures that can be taken fairly easily, so the first portion of pollution reduction will be cheap relative to later portions. In addition, it is likely that pollution reduction of any degree will be easier for some firms than for others. New facilities are likely to run cleaner than old ones, for example. Reducing pollution from a factory that was designed in the era of environmental concern may be much easier than obtaining similar reductions from an older factory. After some point, however, the easy plants and the easy fixes are exhausted, and the marginal cost of reducing pollution further rises steeply.

The marginal benefit of pollution reduction is depicted as falling, for much the same reason that the typical demand curve slopes downward. Starting at any nonlethal level of pollution, people will derive some benefit from reducing the level of pollution, but the marginal benefit from a given amount of reduction will be lower, the lower the level of pollution.[1]

The optimal amount of pollution reduction occurs where the marginal benefit is equal to the marginal cost—where "supply" and "demand" in Figure 23-2 intersect. In trying to reach this optimum, the pollution control authority faces three serious problems. First, although Figure 23-2 looks like a supply and demand graph, we have already seen that the private sector will not create a market in pollution control. Thus the authority must intervene in private-sector markets if the optimal level of control that is shown in Figure 23-2 is to be attained.

The second problem is that q^* is generally not easily known because the marginal benefit and the marginal cost curves that are shown in Figure 23-2 are generally not observable. In practice, the relevant authority can only estimate these curves, and accurate estimates are often difficult to obtain, especially when the technology of pollution control is changing rapidly and the health consequences of various pollutants (e.g., chemicals that are new to the marketplace) are not known.

Determining the optimal level of pollution control in the real world is often very difficult.

The third problem is that the available techniques for regulating pollution are themselves imperfect. Even when the optimal level of pollution control is known, there are both technical and legal impediments to achieving that level through regulation.

Direct Controls

Direct control is the form of environmental regulation that is used most often. Automobile emissions standards are direct controls that are familiar to most of us. The standards must be met by all new cars that are sold in Canada. They require that emissions per mile of a number of noxious chemicals and other pollutants be less than certain specified amounts. The standards are the same no matter where the cars are driven. The marginal benefit of reducing carbon monoxide emissions in rural Alberta, where there is relatively little air pollution, is almost certainly much less than the marginal benefit in Toronto, where there is already a good deal of carbon monoxide in the air. Yet the standard is the same in both places.

Direct controls also often require that specific techniques be used in order to reduce pollution. Thus coal-fired utility plants are often required to use devices called "scrubbers" in order to reduce sulfur dioxide emissions.

Another form of direct control is the simple prohibition of certain polluting behaviors. Many cities and towns, for example, prohibit the private burning of leaves and other trash because of the air pollution problem that the burning would cause. A number of communities have banned the use of wood stoves. Similarly, the government has gradually reduced the amount of lead that is allowed in leaded gasoline.

[1] This argument does not work in the case of toxic pollutants. There the marginal benefit of pollution reduction is small or zero if the level of emissions remains above some dangerous threshold and is very large when pollution is reduced below the threshold. The marginal benefit curve in these cases would be sharply kinked at the threshold. The health consequences of most pollution, however, are of a kind that is consistent with the shape of the "demand" curve that is shown in Figure 23-2.

Problems with direct controls. Economists have consistently criticized the use of direct controls on efficiency grounds. Suppose that pollution of a given waterway is to be reduced by a certain amount. Regulators will typically apportion the required reduction among all polluters according to some roughly equitable criterion. The regulators might require that every polluter reduce its pollution by the same percentage. Alternatively, every polluter might be required to install a certain type of control device or to ensure that each gallon of water that is dumped into the watershed meets certain quality criteria. Although any of these rules might seem reasonable, unless the polluters face identical pollution abatement costs, each of them will be inefficient.

To see this, consider two firms that face different costs of pollution abatement, as depicted in Figure 23-3. Suppose that Firm A's marginal cost of pollution abatement is everywhere below Firm B's. Such a circumstance is quite likely when one recalls that in the real world, pollution comes from many different industries. It may be easy for one industry to cut back on the amount of some pollutant that it produces; in another industry the pollutant may be an unavoidable by-product of the production process. Clearly, the most efficient way to reduce pollution would be to have Firm A cut back on its pollution until the marginal cost of further reductions is just equal to Firm B's marginal cost of reducing its first (and cheapest to forgo) unit of pollution. Once their marginal costs of reducing pollution are equalized, *further* reductions in pollution will be efficient only if this equality is maintained. To see this, suppose that the marginal costs of abatement are different for the two firms. By reallocating some pollution abatement from the high-marginal-cost

FIGURE 23-3 Inefficiency of Direct Pollution Controls

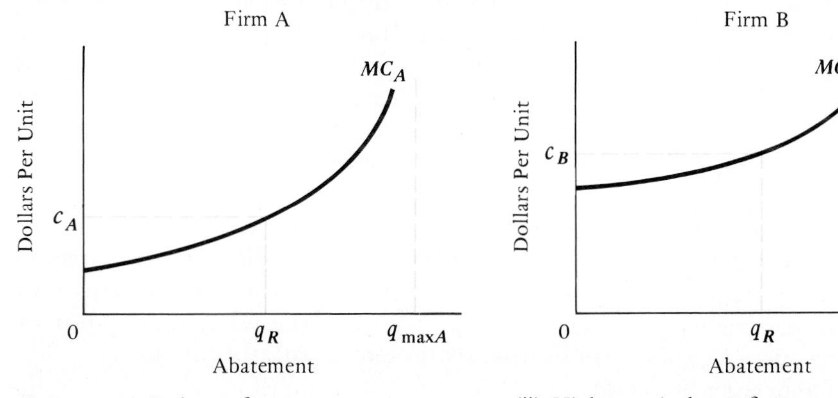

(i) Low-marginal-cost firm

(ii) High-marginal-cost firm

Requiring equal amounts of pollution abatement from different polluters is likely to be inefficient. Firm A is able to reduce its emissions according to the marginal cost curve MC_A. Firm B, which operates at the same scale but in a different kind of factory, has a higher marginal cost of abatement, MC_B. Suppose that a regulatory authority requires that the two firms reduce pollution by the same amount, q_R. Firm A will have a marginal cost of pollution abatement of c_A, while Firm B's marginal cost will be c_B, a greater amount.

To see that this outcome is inefficient, consider what happens if Firm A increases its pollution abatement by one unit, while Firm B is allowed to pollute one unit more. Total pollution remains the same, but total costs fall. Firm A incurs added costs of c_A, and Firm B saves a greater amount c_B. Since the total amount of pollution is unchanged, the total social cost of pollution and pollution abatement would fall.

firm to the low-cost firm, total pollution abatement could be kept constant while the real resources used to abate pollution would be reduced. Alternatively, one could hold the resource cost constant and increase the amount of abatement.

Direct pollution controls are usually inefficient in that, for any given expenditure, they do not maximize the amount of pollution abatement achieved.

When direct controls require that firms adopt specific techniques of pollution abatement, a second type of inefficiency arises. Regulations of this kind tend to change only slowly: The regulators will often mandate today's best techniques tomorrow, even if something more effective has come along.

Both of these sources of inefficiency in direct controls are examples of government failure, as discussed in Chapter 22. In both cases, the government does not do as well as it could in pursuing its valid social objectives. In terms of Figure 23-2, government failure would add to the marginal cost of pollution reduction. Thus the socially optimal level of pollution will be higher, the less efficient the method used to control pollution.

A final problem that arises with direct controls in practice is that they are expensive to monitor and to enforce. The regulatory agency has to check, factory by factory, farm by farm, how many pollutants of what kinds are being emitted. It then also needs a mechanism for penalizing offenders. Accurate monitoring of all potential sources of pollution requires a level of resources that is much greater than has ever been made available to the relevant regulatory agencies. Moreover, the existing system of fines and penalties, in the view of many critics, is not nearly harsh enough to have much effect. A potential polluter, required to limit emissions of a pollutant to so many pounds or gallons per day, will take into account the cost of meeting the standard, the probability of being caught, and the severity of the penalty before deciding how to behave. If the chances of being caught and the penalties for being caught are small, the direct controls may have little effect.

Monitoring and enforcement of direct pollution controls is costly, which reduces the effectiveness of the controls.

Emissions Taxes

An alternative method of pollution control is to levy a tax on emissions at the source. The great advantage of such a procedure is that it internalizes the pollution externality so that decentralized decisions can lead to efficient outcomes. Again, suppose that Firm A can reduce emissions cheaply, while it is more expensive for Firm B to reduce emissions. If all firms are required to pay a tax of t on each unit of pollution, profit maximization will lead them to reduce emissions to the point where the marginal cost of further reduction is just equal to t. This means that Firm A will reduce emissions much more than Firm B and that in equilibrium, both will have the same marginal cost of further abatement, which is required for efficiency. This is illustrated in Figure 23-4.

Note that if the regulatory agency is able to obtain a good estimate of the marginal damage that is done by pollution, it could set the tax rate just equal to that amount. In such a case, polluters would be forced by the tax to internalize the full pollution externality.

A second great advantage of using emissions taxes is that they do not require the regulators to specify anything about *how* polluters should abate pollution. Rather, polluters themselves can be left to find the most efficient abatement techniques. The profit motive will lead them to do so, because they will want to avoid paying the tax.

Emissions taxes can, in principle, perfectly internalize pollution externalities so that profit-maximizing behavior on the part of firms will lead them to produce the efficient amount of pollution abatement at minimum cost.

Box 23-1 provides an example of a pollution tax that seems to be both economically and politically successful. In this case, the polluters are ordinary households, and the pollution is ordinary household trash. Yet the principles we have discussed are very much in evidence. By using an emissions tax, an externality is internalized; individual decision makers are forced to take social costs into account.

Difficulties in using emissions taxes. Emissions taxes can only work if it is possible to measure emissions accurately. For some types of pollution, this does not pose much of a problem, but for many other types

FIGURE 23-4 A Tax on Pollution

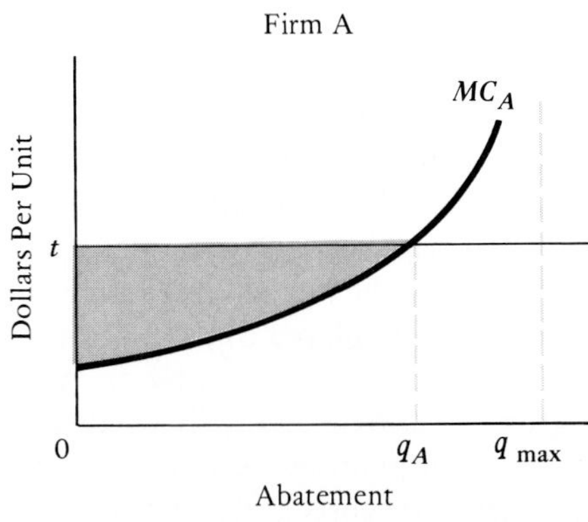

(i) Low-marginal-cost firm

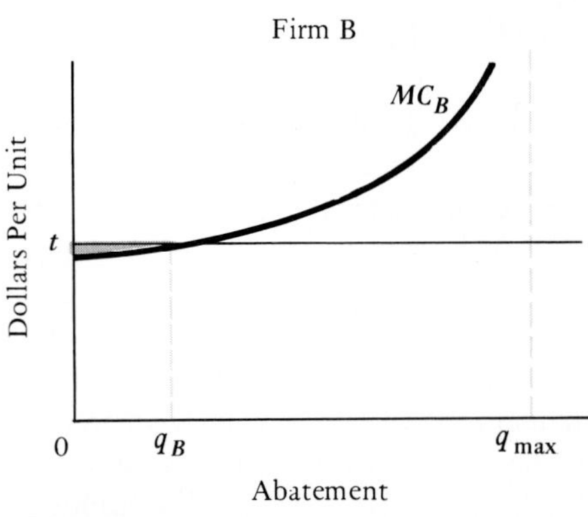

(ii) High-marginal-cost firm

Taxes on pollution can lead to efficient pollution abatement. As in Figure 23-3, Firm A faces a lower marginal cost of pollution abatement than Firm B. Suppose that the regulatory authority imposes a tax of t per unit of pollution. Firm A will choose to reduce its pollution by q_A. Up to this point, the tax saved by reducing pollution exceeds the marginal cost of reducing pollution. If Firm A chooses not to abate pollution at all, it would pay t times q_{max} in pollution taxes, where q_{max} is the firm's total pollution if it does nothing to prevent pollution. By reducing its pollution to $q_{max} - q_A$ (the same thing as abating pollution by q_A), Firm A saves an amount that is given by the shaded area in part (i).

Firm B chooses to abate only a small amount of pollution, q_B, shown in part (ii). Any further abatement would require that the firm incur costs along MC_B, which would be greater than the taxes saved, t.

Note that in equilibrium, both firms have the same marginal cost of abatement, and marginal reallocation of abatement between firms would not affect total social costs of pollution plus abatement.

If the regulatory agency wished to reduce pollution further, it could raise the tax rate; there would still be equality of marginal abatement costs between firms.

of pollution, accurate measuring devices that can be installed at reasonable cost do not exist. Obviously, in these cases emissions taxes cannot work. One important example of such a case is automotive pollution. It would be very expensive to attach a reliable monitor to every car and truck and then to assess taxes due based on readings from the monitor. In this case, as in many others, direct controls are the only feasible approach.

When there is good reason to prohibit a pollutant altogether, direct controls are obviously better than taxes. Municipal bans on burning of leaves fall in this category, as do the occasional emergency bans on some kinds of pollution that are invoked during an air pollution crisis in cities such as Los Angeles and Denver.

Another problem with emissions taxes involves setting the tax rate. Ideally, the regulatory agency would obtain an estimate of the marginal social damage caused per unit of each pollutant and set the tax equal to this amount. This would perfectly internalize the pollution externality. However, the information that is needed to draw the curves shown in Figures 23-1 and 23-4 is often difficult to obtain. If society is currently far away from the optimum, it may be very difficult to estimate what the marginal social damage *will be* at the optimum. If the regulatory agency sets the tax rate too high, too many resources will be devoted to pollution control—the equilibrium will be beyond q^* in Figure 23-2. If the tax is set too low, there will be too much pollution. In many practical cases, regulators may have a much

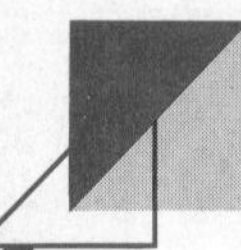

BOX 23-1

Charging for Emissions at Home*

Nov. 21—Tossing out the household trash here requires care and ingenuity these days, because residents of this town of 4,000 must now pay for garbage disposal by the bag.

In an effort to control disposal rates that have soared across most of the nation, High Bridge has stopped charging households a flat $280 annual fee for garbage collection. In January, the town began charging for the amount of trash residents actually discard.

Each 30-gallon can or 30-gallon bag set out at curbside each week must carry a town sticker. Households are charged $140 for 52 stickers, and additional stickers cost $1.25 each.

Environmental Result

The switch to billing by the bag has also had an environmental impact, reducing High Bridge's residential trash volume by 25 percent, officials say.

* This article, by Robert Harley, originally ran under the headline "Pay-by-Bag Trash Disposal Pays, New Jersey Town Discovers." *New York Times,* November 24, 1988, nat. ed., p. 8. © 1988 by The New York Times Company. Reprinted by permission.

At a time when the United States throws away more trash than any nation in the world, the switch has heightened awareness of recycling programs for newspapers, aluminum cans and glass bottles and has ended careless ways at the kitchen trash bin.

The new system has also placed this hilly town 16 miles east of the Pennsylvania border in the forefront of a growing movement. About three dozen New Jersey communities—all anguished about soaring trash-disposal costs as the state closes landfills—have called the High Bridge Town Clerk, Claire Knapp, to hear how its system works. Centerville, Utah, and Afton, Minn., have also expressed interest.

People here quickly began sorting and recycling their trash.

"I've been doing it for years, but many of my friends and neighbors said they couldn't be bothered," said Emily Bruton, who has seven children. "But now they bother because it's hitting them in the pocketbook."

Neighborly Sharing

Some people whose garbage can is only two-thirds full on the eve of the weekly collection share their

better idea of the acceptable level of pollution than of the tax rate that would lead to that result.

A potentially serious problem with emissions taxes is that information necessary to determine the optimal tax rate is usually unavailable.

Further, experience in a number of countries has shown that as conditions change and hence *optimal* taxes change, actual tax rates change only very slowly in response.

A final argument against pollution taxes is more political than economic, but it is certainly important in explaining why such taxes are so rare. The argument is that by taxing pollution, rather than by outlawing it above some amount, the government is selling licenses to commit crimes against society. Direct controls, according to this argument, have much greater normative force, because they say that violating the standards is simply wrong. Most economists find arguments of this kind unpersuasive. An absolute ban on pollution is impossible, and in choosing how much pollution to allow, society must trade pollution abatement against other valuable things. Economic analysis has a good deal to say about how a society might minimize the cost of *any* degree of pollution abatement.

Tradable Emissions Permits

The great advantage of direct controls is that the regulators can set the standards to limit the total

empty space with neighbors whose can is overflowing.

"I've heard of people taking bags of garbage home from parties to help the hostess out," said Mary Briggs, the Town Council member who organized the new collection system.

Trash compactors are going into more and more kitchens. And outdoor compost piles, common generations ago, are popping up in many yards.

Sixteen-year-old Peter Butkosky tends his family's compost on Wood Glen Drive. Anything that's biodegradable goes on the pile, including potato peels, melon rinds, spoiled fruits and vegetables, even the innards of fish that Peter and his father catch in the Atlantic.

"We let it all rot in sections for a year and then use it as fertilizer for the lawn," Peter said.

Volume of Trash Declines

Since billing by the garbage bag started, the trash collected by the town truck has dropped to an average of 6.3 tons a day from 8.5, according to William Newell, a Town Councilman.

The town's 4,000 residents include many older people on fixed incomes. Many are retirees of a now-defunct iron foundry that manufactured weapons for all the nation's wars since the Revolution. Most retirees, said Miss Knapp, the Town Clerk, produce far less trash than young families with children. But under the old system, everybody paid the same flat rate.

Under the new system, households that put out just one can a week pay only \$140; those that put out more buy more stickers in strips of 10 for \$12.50.

Extra stickers are required for bulky disposable items, like stuffed chairs (2) and sofa beds (6).

The value of the stickers appears to be inspiring some communal sacrifice.

"We wanted to throw out an old sofa, and they wanted four stickers on it," said Janet Nazif. "We didn't want to part with them, so we looked extra hard and found a school that wanted a used couch for a classroom."

quantity of pollution in a given geographic area. This can be done without knowing the details of either the marginal benefit or the marginal cost curve in Figure 23-2. The great advantage of emissions taxes is that they allow for decentralized decision making, providing firms with an incentive to internalize the negative externality of pollution. *Tradable emissions permits* can combine both of these advantages.

In Figure 23-3 we noted that direct pollution controls would generally be inefficient because the marginal cost curves for pollution abatement would vary across firms. Tradable permits can solve this problem. To see how, we must first figure out how much pollution to allow. This involves reformulating the regulator's problem. Start with the same conditions as those in Figure 23-3, and permit each firm to pollute exactly the same amount as would be allowed by the direct controls in the figure. Instead of saying to each firm, "Thou shalt abate pollution by q_R," however, the regulators say, "Thou shalt not pollute more than you would if you abated by q_R." The statements are identical in meaning; all that we have done is describe a glass that is two-thirds empty as one-third full.

Now suppose that the firms are allowed to buy and sell **tradable emissions permits**—rights to pollute. At the initial permitted amounts of pollution (q_R), the marginal cost of pollution for Firm A is lower than that for Firm B. Firm B would be willing to pay up to c_B for the right to pollute one more unit, and Firm A would be willing to sell that right for any amount that exceeded c_A. Notice that if such a trade were made, the total amount of pollution would be unchanged, the total cost of abating pollution would fall (by $c_B - c_A$), and both firms would be at least as well off as before. We would thus have a clear efficiency improvement. No one is made worse off, and at least one party is made better off.

Once the firms are allowed to exchange rights to pollute, they will do so until their marginal abatement costs are equalized. At this point there is no further gain from trading permits. Notice that the new equilibrium is identical to that depicted in Figure 23-4, with the equilibrium *price* of an emissions permit just equal to the emissions *tax* shown in that figure.

Tradable emissions permits can be used to achieve the same allocation of resources as would occur with emissions taxes.

Tradable emissions permits in practice. Although Canada has not had any direct experience with the use of tradable permits, in the United States both the Environmental Protection Agency (EPA) and a number of state agencies have. According to a recent study, such trading programs have had no adverse effect on environmental quality. The study estimates that savings in pollution control costs from these programs amounted to over $4 billion in the period of 1974–1985. Although this is a considerable sum, many economists who specialize in environmental economics would argue that it is but a small percentage of the savings that could be realized if trading in emissions permits were more widespread.

Two American episodes that are the source of much of the optimism about tradable permits are noteworthy.[2] First, the EPA has allowed trading in the right to emit carbon monoxide, sulfur dioxide, and nitrous oxides. The cost savings from this are thought to be very large; in particular, considerable efficiency is gained by allowing firms some flexibility in offsetting increased emissions in one plant or of one type by reductions elsewhere. Second, as the allowable lead content in gasoline has been reduced, refineries have been issued tradable permits related to their production capacity and the allowable lead content. Refineries that do not use all their permits can sell them. Trading activity has been substantial, as have been the estimated refinery cost savings. Tradable permits seem to be an idea whose time may be coming.

Tradable permits and emissions taxes pose formidable problems of implementation. Some of these involve technical difficulties in measuring pollution and in designing mechanisms to ensure that firms and households comply with regulations. Furthermore, the potential efficiency gains arising from tradable permits cannot be realized if regulatory agencies are prone to change the rules under which trades may take place. This has been a problem in the past, but one that can be corrected.

Governmental creation of a "market" in "bads" may become one of the most promising strategies for efficiently overcoming the market failure that leads to environmental pollution.

Much environmental pollution is caused by the failure of markets to account for externalities. At the same time, marketlike mechanisms can be effective in internalizing the externalities. Pollution is an example of a problem in which markets themselves can be used to correct market failure. The basic case for market-based solutions rests on their efficiency and their flexibility. They provide the maximum environmental improvement for any *given* amount spent, and they provide the most responsive solution, with private incentives ensuring that the amount of resources devoted to environmental control responds to the needs of the current situation. Box 23-2 discusses some of the sources of opposition to the use of markets to address environmental issues.

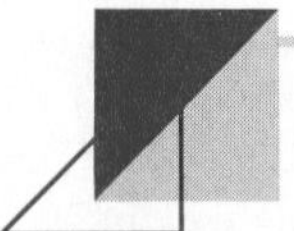

Regulation for Health and Safety

The Department of Consumer and Corporate Affairs must approve the marketing of both prescription and nonprescription drugs in Canada. The National Transport Agency requires that automobiles have brake lights and seat belts, and a requirement that new automobiles be equipped with air bags has been a source of controversy for a decade. Consumer and Corporate Affairs can remove dangerous goods from

[2] For a detailed discussion, see the chapter by Professor Don McFetridge in *The Environmental Imperative,* ed. G. Bruce Doern (Toronto: C. D. Howe Institute, 1990).

• KEY IDEAS IN •
MICROECONOMICS

This section provides important diagrams and captions from the text as reminders of basic economic concepts at a glance. If you need to refresh your memory concerning a principle being shown here, look in the appropriate chapter for a full explanation.

CHAPTER 12 Derivation of the Supply Curve for a Price-taking Firm

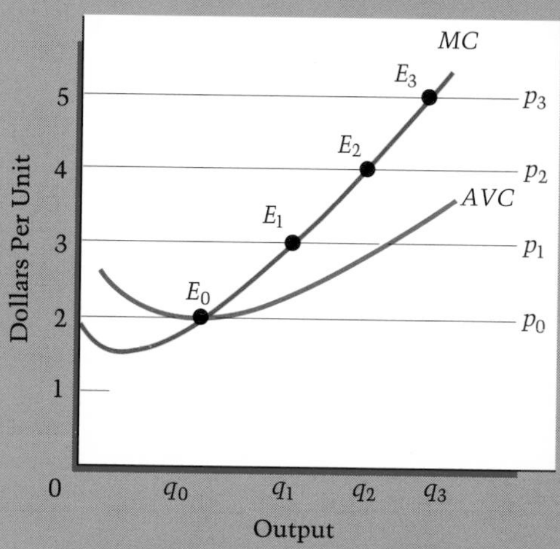

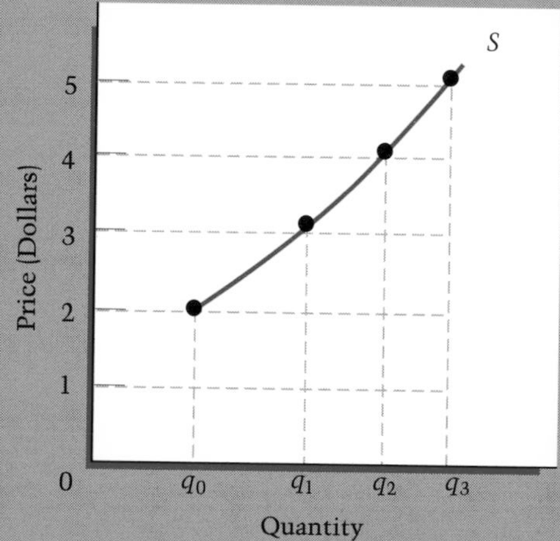

Above the *AVC* curve, the supply curve of the price-taking firm, shown in part (ii), is the same as its *MC* curve, shown in part (i).

CHAPTER 12 Equilibrium of a Firm When a Perfectly Competitive Industry is in Long-Run Equilibrium

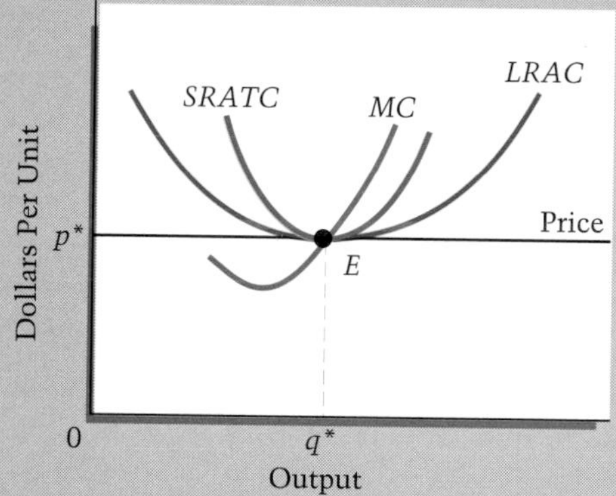

In long-run, perfectly competitive equilibrium, the firm is operating at the minimum point on its *LRAC* curve.

CHAPTER 13 Equilibrium Under Monopoly

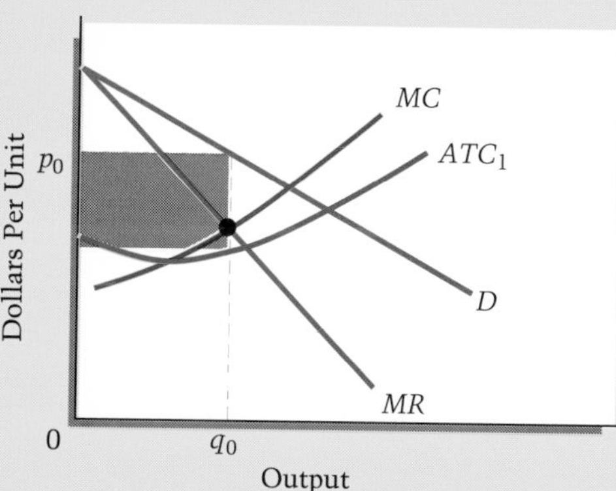

Profit-maximizing output is q_0, where $MR = MC$; price is p_0, which is above *MC* at that output.

CHAPTER 14 Equilibrium Under Monopolistic Competition

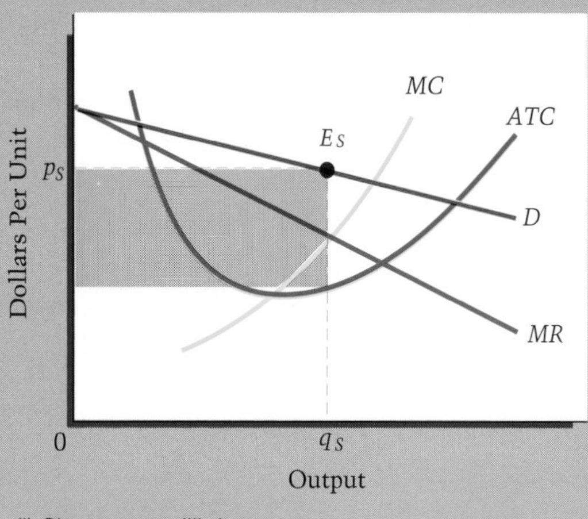

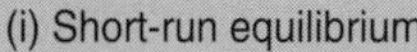

(i) Short-run equilibrium

(ii) Long-run equilibrium

Short-run equilibrium of a monopolistically competitive firm is the same as for a monopolist. In the long run, a monopolistically competitive industry has zero profits and excess capacity.

CHAPTER 14 The Oligopolist's Dilemma: To Cooperate or to Compete

Cooperation to determine the overall level of output can maximize joint profits, but it leaves each firm with an incentive to alter its production. (B's profits are represented by orange circles; A's profits are represented by green circles.)

B's output	A's output: One-half monopoly output	A's output: Two-thirds monopoly output
One-half monopoly output	20 / 20	15 / 22
Two-thirds monopoly output	22 / 15	17 / 17

CHAPTER 15 The Allocative Efficiency of Perfect Competition

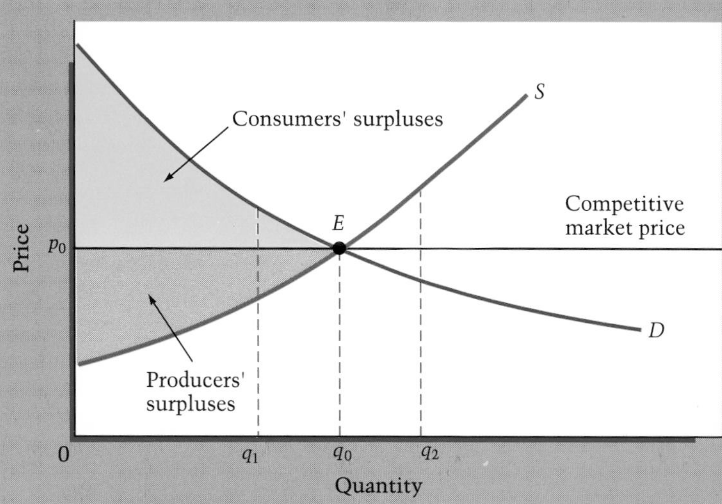

Competitive equilibrium is allocatively efficient, because it maximizes the sum of consumers' plus producers' surplus.

CHAPTER 17 The Determination of Factor Price and Income in a Competitive Market

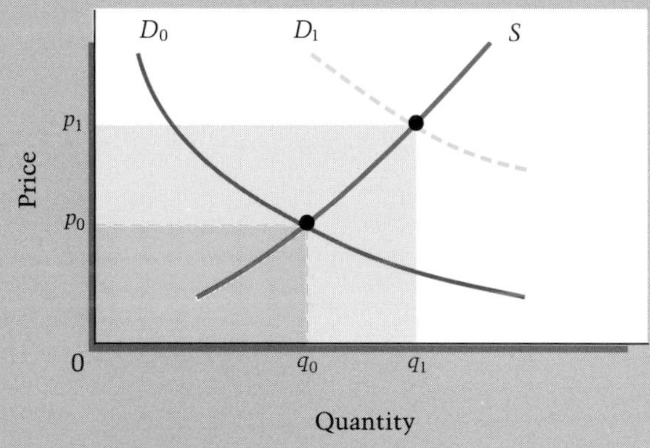

In competitive factor markets, demand and supply determine factor prices, quantities of factors used, and factor incomes.

CHAPTER 17 The Determination of Rent in Factor Payments

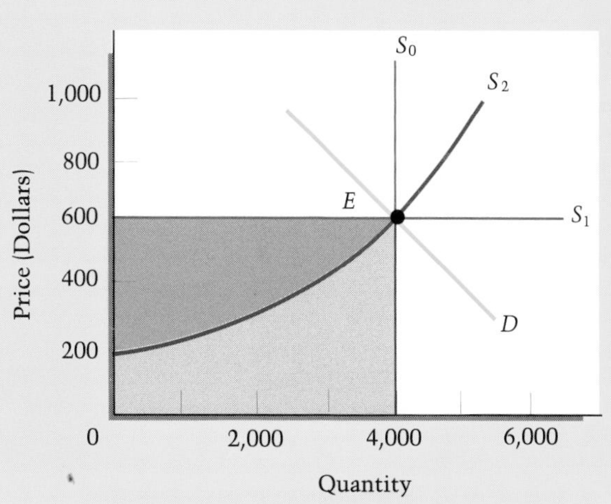

The amount of rent in factor payments depends on the shape of the supply curve.

CHAPTER 20 The Gains from Trade

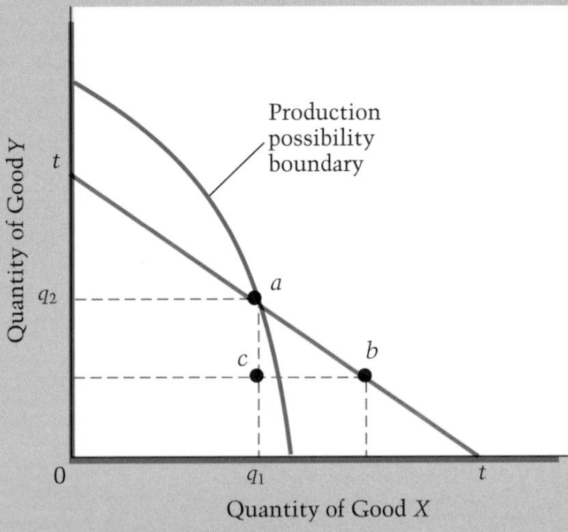

(i) Stage 1: Fixed production

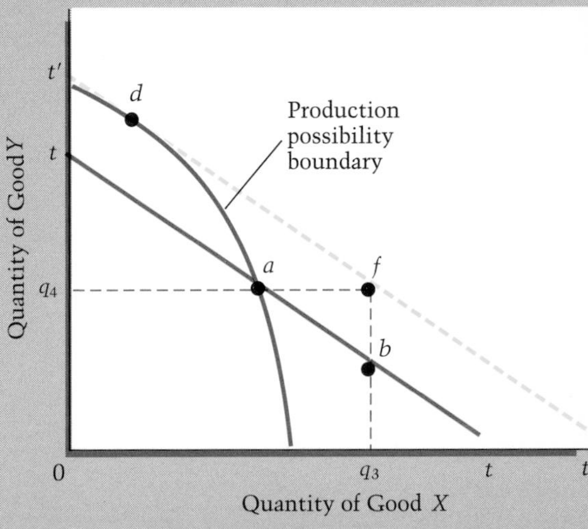

(ii) Stage 2: Variable production

International trade makes it possible to trade: (1) either from the *existing production point, a* in part (i), to points beyond the production possibility boundary, such as *b* in part (i), or (2) by altering production to, say, point *d* in part (ii), to make available a set of points totally outside what could be achieved by domestic production, such as point *f* in part (ii).

CHAPTER 23 Pollution Externalities

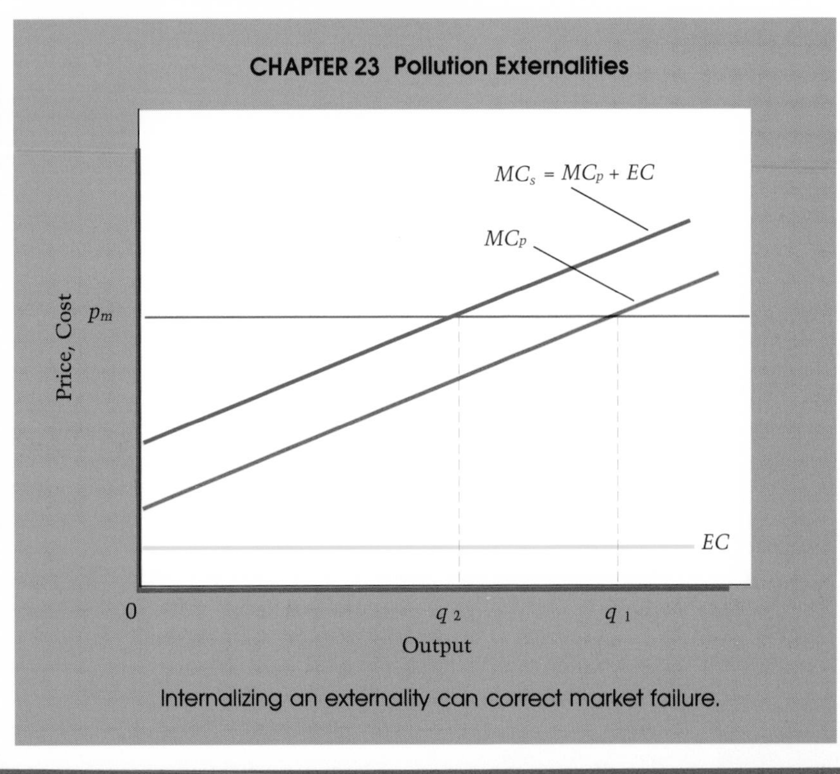

Internalizing an externality can correct market failure.

the marketplace. It can also set standards for product safety, such as requiring "dead man" controls that automatically stop engines in lawn mowers when the operator lets go of the handle. It also regulates "truth in advertising." The Workmen's Compensation Board is broadly responsible for health and safety in the workplace. It sets detailed standards designed to reduce workers' exposure to injury and to health risks, such as asbestos.

What all of these examples have in common is that the market failure that they address is in the market for information. A consumer has no way of knowing if a cold remedy has dangerous side effects, what the effect of brake lights is on the chances of having an accident, or how likely a child's pajamas are to catch fire. An individual worker may be in no position to assess the risks of working on a given machine and may not be able to find out easily whether there are toxic chemicals in the workplace.

Health and Safety Information As a Public Good

In Chapter 22 we saw that information is likely to be underproduced in private markets because information is an example of a (nearly) *pure public good.* Once the flammability of different materials that are used in children's pajamas is known, making the information available to interested parents can be done at negligible marginal cost. A private firm that develops the information would be unable to recoup its investment. Unless the government intervenes, product information would tend to be either unavailable or available only at inefficiently high prices. Most economists would agree that information about safety in the workplace and product safety is a public good; this provides a rationale for the government either to produce or to require private firms to produce such information.[3]

[3] People who do not agree would rely on the legal system to compel private producers and employers to develop the information. If someone is hurt by an unsafe product, the person can sue the manufacturer for damages. If the manufacturer has provided accurate information about the risks inherent in using the product, the consumer's chance of winning the lawsuit is much reduced. Thus the manufacturer has an interest in developing accurate information. A similar case can be made regarding worker health and safety. In practice, however, many lawsuits of this kind are defended on the grounds that manufacturers had no knowledge of or reason to be concerned about their products' hazards. That such defenses often succeed suggests that there is an incentive to *fail* to develop relevant information about health and safety.

Is Good Information Enough?

In practice, most health and safety regulation goes well beyond the simple provision of information. Rather, firms are required to meet standards of workplace and product safety. Many economists have argued that given good information, private markets will assure efficient levels of workplace safety. In order to evaluate this argument, we present here a very simple example of what would happen if there were no standards and everyone had accurate information about safety risks.

Consider a worker who can take a job at either Firm A or Firm B. The worker knows that accidents at Firm A will lead the typical worker to miss two weeks of work per year, while the average time lost to injury at Firm B is one week per year. There is no compensation paid for the time spent at home due to injury. In order to keep the example simple, suppose that lost pay is the only cost of accidents that is borne by workers. (These must be pretty trivial accidents!)

Equilibrium in the labor market can only occur if workers at Firm A have a higher wage than workers at Firm B. Assume that full-time work in both firms is 50 weeks per year. Workers in Firm A can expect to be laid up and unable to work for an average of one week per year more than those at Firm B. They will thus require a wage that is 50/49 times the wage paid to workers in Firm B (assuming that they get no pleasure from spending a week at home in bed).

Notice that in this example all that is required for equilibrium to occur is that the workers know the probability of accidents at each firm and that markets respond to conditions of demand and supply. No government standard needs to be set. Rather, workers who work in the firm that is less safe will demand a compensating wage differential in order to work there. Thus the greater the chance of an accident at work, the higher the wages that a firm must pay. This is illustrated by the positively sloped curve shown in Figure 23-5 on page 484. From the perspective of the employer, the curve represents the marginal wage cost (per worker) of increasing the probability of accidents. As accidents become more likely (moving along the horizontal axis), the firm must pay higher wages.

The firm also faces a corresponding marginal benefit curve. Returning to our example, suppose that Firm A could be just as safe as Firm B if it spent

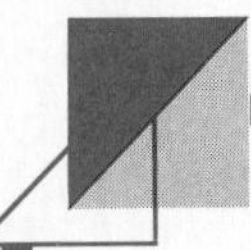

BOX 23-2

Resistance to Market-based Environmental Policies

Despite the many advantages that can be identified for market-based approaches to the environment, this approach encounters much resistance from firms, ordinary members of the public, and environmentalists. Why?

Producers

Opposition to market-based solutions sometimes comes from management. Several reasons may be suggested.

Some firms object to the costs that they are asked to pay in terms of emissions taxes or the purchase prices of pollution rights. However, there is no reason why payments to government under any market-based scheme need to be a tax grab. Taxes need not be in excess of the costs imposed on society by the industry's activities. If government uses the introduction of a market-based scheme to raise *general revenue,* firms can oppose the *extra* tax burden without opposing the market-based scheme itself.

The introduction of market-based measures may signal the end of a free ride that producers have been taking at society's expense. If an industry was bearing none of the cost of its pollution, almost any antipollution scheme will impose a burden on producers—but only to the extent of forcing them to bear a cost of their own activities that they have previously been passing on to the society at large. Firms need to accept that *any* move to clean up their industry's pollution will impose costs on them. The difference between the command solution and the market-based solution, however, is that the former will cost the industry, and hence the average firm in the industry, more than the market solution.

Market-based schemes do not ensure, however, that *all* firms pay less than under a common scheme, only that the *average* firm does. When some firms pay more, they may oppose the measures out of a feeling of injustice that they must pay more than under alternative schemes or more than some of their competitors. However, command solutions also have differential impacts on firms.

Finally, under market-based schemes, many firms feel a sense of unfairness because their competitors continue polluting while they must clean up. Their complaints, however, ignore the fact that those who continue to pollute have paid for the right to do so, either by paying effluent taxes or by buying pollution rights, and that the complaining firm could do the same if it wished (it does not do so because cleaning up is cheaper for it than paying to pollute, as the neighbors are doing).

This points to a key issue in assessing market-based solutions: Such solutions must not be judged in isolation. Given a government's decision to reduce pollution, the market solution must be compared with its alternatives. When this is done, much of the producer opposition fades away because the reasons for opposition are usually all less in the market-based than in the command solution. (If this is not the case, at least for the vast majority of firms, the designers of the proposed market-based solution should think again; it is almost certain that they can do better.)

The Public

Opposition from the public can develop for a number of reasons, including the oft-encountered general hostility to market-based solutions and preference for government-imposed solutions.

One source of public opposition is a moral reaction to giving anyone a right to pollute. Since it involves human survival, dealing in rights to pollute seems especially evil. This view makes difficult the rational evaluation of alternative plans for dealing with a serious social problem.

A further important source of opposition is found in the market-based solution's characteristic of allowing those who have the highest costs of cleaning up to go on polluting while those with the lowest costs do the cleaning up. It may be futile to point out that it is efficient to have those who can clean up most cheaply do so; morality may dictate to many observers that the biggest polluters should do the cleaning up. (In response to this reaction, economists cannot show it to be wrong; they can only point out the cost in terms of the higher prices, lower employment, unnecessary resource use, and less overall pollution abatement that follow from adopting such a moral position.)

Environmentalists

Many environmentalists are skeptical about the efficiency of markets. Some do not understand economists' reasoning as to why markets can be, and often are, efficient in their use of resources. Others understand the economists' case but reject it, although few environmentalists bother to complete the argument by trying to demonstrate that command-type allocation by government will be more efficient.

Second, many environmentalists do not like the use of self-interest incentives to solve social issues. Economists who point to the voluminous evidence of the importance of self-interest incentives are often accused of ignoring higher motives such as social duty, self-sacrifice, and compassion. Although such motives are absent from the simple theories that try to explain the everyday behavior of buyers and sellers (because it has not been found necessary to introduce such motives into these theories), economists since Adam Smith have been aware that these higher motives often do exert strong influences on human behavior.

Such higher motives are very powerful at some times and in some situations, but they do not govern many people's behavior in the course of day-to-day living. If we want to understand how people behave in the aftermath of a flood or an earthquake, we will need motives in addition to self-interest; if we want to understand how people behave day after day in their buying and selling, we need little other than a theory of the self-interested responses to market incentives. Since control of the environment requires influencing the mass of small decisions, as well as a few large ones, the appeal to self-interest is the only currently known way to induce the behavior that is required.

Another reason why many environmentalists reject market-based solutions is their belief that the market cannot be relied on to get the trade-off between present and future right. As we saw in Chapter 17, conservationists, fearful that relying on the free market to set production rates for resource products will cause a resource to be exploited too quickly, argue that government intervention is necessary to conserve the resource for the future. Although market failures in rates of extraction are possible, no one has succeeded in proving a general tendency for the market to extract resources too quickly. Further, the assumption that governments, dominated as they so often are by considerations of the next election, will nonetheless take a longer view than the market can only be described as a touching act of faith. One has to look no further than the Hibernia project for an example of the Canadian federal government's proposing to extract now a resource that would someday be valuable but that is today worth a negative amount—an amount that taxpayers will have to put up before firms will be willing to extract the oil.

Finally, some environmentalists have a somewhat mystical view that resources are above mere monetary calculation and should thus be treated in special ways. The economist can point out that the use of the mystical view to justify departing from market solutions and from solutions based on calculations of market failures (which are measured in terms of failure to provide maximum economic value) ensures that measured material living standards will be lowered. If that is the understood and accepted price of regarding resources as mystical entities, then so be it!

FIGURE 23-5 The "Market" for Occupational Safety

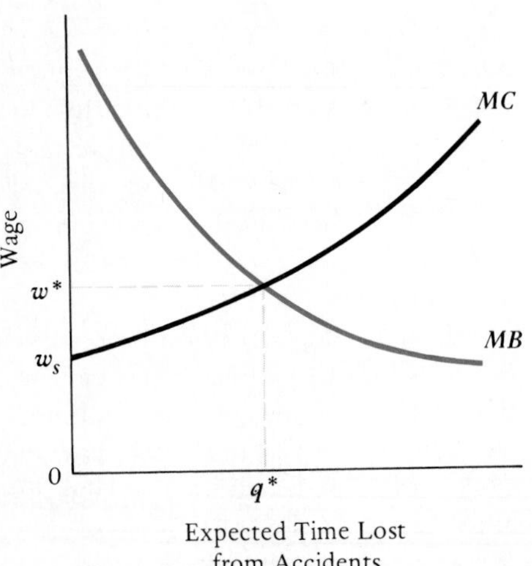

The labor market can induce firms to provide workplace safety. Suppose that a perfectly safe workplace would have to pay a wage of only w_s. As the expected time lost because of accidents increases, the required wage rises in order to compensate workers for the risk of injury. The curve that shows the higher wages is labeled *MC*, because it gives the marginal cost to the firm (per worker) of letting the workplace become less safe.

The marginal benefit to the firm of reducing safety is given by the *MB* curve, which shows the *savings* (per worker) that the firm can obtain by reducing safety-related expenditures. At the axis, time that is lost through accidents is zero; the workplace is perfectly safe. The *MB* curve starts very high because the cost of making an already safe workplace even safer is likely to be very high. Thus reducing safety by a small amount from perfect safety would sharply reduce the firm's costs.

Where the two curves intersect, the marginal cost of making the workplace safer is just equal to the marginal benefit from doing so. Given that the *MC* curve is derived from the preferences of workers who are well informed about workplace risks, the market solution of q^* and w^* will be cost-minimizing for the firm and socially efficient.

c dollars per year per worker on improved lighting and more frequent cleanup of potentially hazardous debris on the shop floor. If c is greater than one week's pay, the extra costs would not be worth it. The firm would be spending c per worker per year and saving less than c. If the costs of reducing the probability of lost time at work by one week per worker (c) were less than one week's pay, however, a cost-minimizing firm would incur those costs. In general, the marginal benefit to the firm of increasing the probability of accidents is the savings in safety-related costs. This is shown as the negatively sloped *MB* curve in Figure 23-5.

In equilibrium, firms will choose a level of safety such that the savings in nonwage costs of reducing safety a little bit is just equal to the increase in the wages that the firm would have to pay. Notice that the optimal rate of accidents, much like the optimal level of pollution, is not zero. Rather, it depends on the cost of reducing the level of accidents.

In the oversimplified world of Figure 23-5, there is no need for safety standards; if workers are perfectly informed about the risk of accidents (and about the costs that they would bear when accidents occur) and firms minimize costs, the private market will generate efficient solutions. This argument can also be extended to product safety, given the strong assumption that consumers are perfectly informed about the risks inherent in consuming the products that they buy.

With perfect information, private markets will produce efficient levels of occupational and product safety.

In spite of this, there are a number of arguments for government intervention to promote health and safety.

Perfect information may be impossible to obtain or to evaluate. Our example of Firm A and Firm B could work quite well for, say, an experienced machinist who is comparing two machine shops. Such a worker will have a good sense of what can be expected on the shop floor and may be able to estimate quite accurately the chances of injury. If the government requires all firms to publish their accident histories every year, the worker can make an informed choice. Such a choice may be impossible, however, when the cause of harm in the workplace is a chemical that might cause cancer. Evaluation of carcinogens often takes many years, the medical literature is likely to be unclear or tentative, and it is quite probable that the typical worker will have a difficult time interpreting the information even if it is made easily available.

Information about safety risks in offices is also unlikely to be available, at least in some cases. Most white-collar workers have no idea what their buildings are made of, how quickly the buildings would burn, or what kind of emergency lighting would be available in case of a fire. Further, it would not be easy for them to decode the blueprints of different buildings to make informed choices about fire safety.

Similar problems arise with product safety. The typical automobile driver is not able to make informed choices about the benefits of collapsing steering columns, reinforced door panels, or dual braking systems. A complete maintenance report on each airplane that you fly on would probably be of little help to you in assessing the safety of the airplane. Less dramatically, it would be prohibitively expensive for the government to develop accident data for every consumer product and then to let consumers sift through the information as they decided what to buy.

Safety standards can free workers and consumers from making difficult calculations that they are ill equipped to make. When information is costly or impossible to process, standards can enhance efficiency.

Paternalism and merit goods. One of the most cost-effective regulations in existence involves collapsing steering columns in automobiles. (In a front-end collision, the steering column breaks before impaling the driver.) According to a recent estimate, the protection afforded by the collapsing steering column saves about 1,300 lives per year at a cost (in 1985) of $100,000 per life. On pure efficiency grounds, matters might be further improved if automobile manufacturers offered the collapsing steering column as an option and were required to provide data on the hazards of noncollapsing steering columns. Only very ardent proponents of laissez faire would argue for such a policy.

Another safety regulation requires that children's sleepwear meet a nonflammability standard. (The standard requires that the fabric not burst into flame when it is lit.) This regulation is less cost-effective than the requirement for collapsing steering columns. In 1985 the cost *per life saved* was estimated to be about $1.3 million. Still, few people would wish to permit parents to choose flammable pajamas at somewhat lower cost. It is hard to think of a government regulation that is more literally paternalistic!

Health and Safety Regulation in Practice

In Chapter 22 we noted that even when there is market failure, the case for government intervention is weakened by the possibility of government failure. Many widely cited examples of government failure arise in the area of health and safety regulation.

A notorious example of regulatory failure is the short-lived ban on saccharin in the United States. Saccharin was banned under the Delaney Amendment, which requires that the Food and Drug Administration ban any product that has been shown to cause cancer in laboratory animals. When huge doses of saccharin caused rats to get cancer, the FDA followed the law. Saccharin was so popular that Congress passed a special law exempting it from the Delaney Admendment. But the Delaney Amendment still applies generally, and it is used to ban products from the marketplace even when the risk of cancer is very low and the cost of alternative products is high.[4] Box 23-3 discusses a surprising and controversial challenge to a form of health regulation that most people accept as being obviously beneficial.

As with pollution, health and safety regulators often take an engineering approach to their task. Rather than specifying a particular outcome or providing incentives for increased safety, they mandate that certain kinds of equipment be used to perform certain functions. Many Canadian cities, for example, have building codes involving detailed specifications that limit the choices that consumers can make and substantially increase construction costs.

In principle, the case for the engineering approach may be stronger for safety regulation than it is for pollution control because the alternative of a "safety tax" generally is not feasible. Unfortunately, the problems inherent in all engineering standards—that they may become obsolete and that they may be much more effective in some settings than in others—remain. To the extent possible, efficiency dictates that standards be expressed in terms of required performance rather than required design and materials. The reason for this is that it provides an

[4] The Delaney Amendment does not apply to tobacco products, which are not officially considered to be either foods or drugs. Thus tobacco is permitted to be sold even though "normal doses" are known to cause cancer in humans.

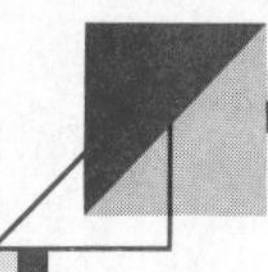

BOX 23-3

Licensing of Physicians: Regulation for Health or Profit?

In Canada, physicians are licensed by the government, and with the government's support, they set the standards of medical practice and determine the qualifications for people entering this field. Most people accept that such regulation is necessary because of the complexities involved in health care and the serious consequences for health if unskilled persons were allowed to practice medicine. The argument is that the only way to avoid the disasters that would be caused by unqualified practitioners is to give physicians the power to police their own industry. Many people further believe that self-regulation will lead physicians to act so as best to promote the public welfare. This is in line with the conventional view of industrial and professional regulation, which sees lower prices, better quality, reduction of monopoly power, or some other aspect of the public good as the natural outcome.

An alternative analysis of medical regulation reflects a very different view of why such regulations exist, building on the influential ideas of Nobel Laureate George J. Stigler. Stigler's thesis is that whatever its stated purpose, much economic regulation serves the interests of those who are regulated. In Stigler's view, the main effect of most regulations and licensing requirements is to erect barriers against entry into the regulated industry or profession and thereby create a cartel, with all of its attendant gains in income, power, and prestige for members. The Stigler theory implies that instead of an enhanced quality of medicine, wealth maximization is the implicit goal—and the frequent result—of the self-regulation of physicians.

In a recent Fraser Institute book titled *Canadian Medicine: A Study on Restricted Entry,* Professor Ronald Hamowy of the University of Alberta examined the economic effects of medical licensing in Canada. The study does not pretend to be an evenhanded examination of these two opposing theories of regulation. Rather, it is an attempt to provide a counterbalance to the wide acceptance of the conventional view, and it should be appraised in conjunction with other evidence and opinions. Professor Hamowy identifies a number of policies that the Canadian medical establishment has at one time pursued and are consistent with the alternative view:

It banned price and other advertising for licensed doctors.

It set minimum price schedules.

It acted to prevent "overcrowding," or an oversupply of physicians, by setting up irrelevant criteria for licensing, such as a knowledge of mathematics, Latin, philosophy, and other academic studies, and language and citizenship requirements.

It outlawed the uncontrolled study of medicine, even for people who do not intend to practice.

It placed roadblocks in the path of foreign doctors who wish to practice in Canada, where they would compete with domestic physicians.

It imposed examinations only at the time the doctor starts practice and required no reexaminations during the doctor's career.

It opposed doctors testifying for plaintiffs in medical malpractice suits and discouraged charity work as undermining minimum fee schedules and professional prestige.

Some of these policies provide obvious evidence in favor of the Stigler alternative. For others, the reasoning is more subtle. Consider the use of entry examinations only. If certification of quality were the true goal of these exams, they would more likely be required of practicing physicians every decade or so; there is obviously no guarantee—certainly not on the basis of testing—that a doctor of 70 years of age is still qualified merely for having passed an examination 40 years earlier. According to Hamowy, as a result of these and other practices, physicians have succeeded in raising their income levels beyond those of other, equally skilled professionals in Canada.

The analysis does not condemn individual doctors. The typical doctor in this country is not involved in limiting entry into the field as a means of feathering his or her own nest. On the contrary, the average physician works long, hard hours and is concerned about his or her professional practice, not the financial exploitation of patients. The motivation of most doctors is not notably different from that of the average participant in the other sectors of the economy protected by government-erected barriers to entry. For example, airline pilots and truck drivers, safeguarded by regulations protecting their respective industries, and farmers, protected by marketing boards, are almost solely concerned with their day-to-day activities and not with the regulations that seal them off from competition.

However, there is little doubt that the leadership of the medical profession—in conjunction with well-meaning, though paternalistic, bureaucrats—do actively restrict competition. Consider the potential for an increased role of paramedics—people with some medical training but much less than licensed physicians—as a way of reducing costs in the health care sector. Many public policy analysts argue that physicians perform many tasks that less qualified persons could do at a fraction of the cost. If these paramedics were allowed to do these things, public costs could be greatly cut, and the only real losers would be doctors, whose monopoly will have been eroded.

The following statement by Dr. Robert Gourdeau, ex-president of the Canadian Medical Association, reveals the nature of the medical profession's position on paramedics: "It's time Canadian doctors did something to end the 'continuous and systematic erosion' of their territory by a horde of other allied health workers." The report of Dr. Gourdeau's speech went on to say that he argued "that for many years an increasing number of paramedical bodies—for reasons of ambition, prestige, autonomy, economics and other professional or personal reasons, not always related to the common good of the public—have been pressuring to increase their responsibility," that doctors could face "a 'painful tomorrow if we do not give this problem the time and energy necessary to develop appropriate means toward this invasion,' " and that "medicine must ensure that those who practise the profession are appropriately trained and licensed to do so." The report concluded by noting that Dr. Gourdeau called on doctors to educate their patients "to confound those who strive to expropriate for their own profit, a greater share of our domain."*

Challenging as Professor Hamowy's arguments are, they seem unlikely to have much influence on medical regulation in Canada. But his research identifies some real costs that may be associated with the current method of regulation. Furthermore, the insights, when applied to as vital a field as medicine, may contribute to regulatory reform in other areas in the economy.

* *London Free Press,* June 21, 1978, p. A9.

incentive for firms to find inexpensive ways of meeting the standards, thus reducing the cost of complying with them. An example is the standard requiring that riding lawn mowers be equipped with "dead man" controls. Basically, the requirement is simply that the controls must work; the manufacturers may choose the design.

The overall record on health and safety regulation is mixed. Formal studies and public opinion both suggest that while some regulations appear to be very effective at achieving their objectives, many others simply lead to a waste of time and energy, and some are even counterproductive. While there is much that can be said, the problems involved in carefully evaluating the effects of most regulations are considerable.

Many observers think that regulatory reform should be a government priority in the next decade. Commenting on a 1986 report by his Task Force on Program Review, Deputy Prime Minister Erik Nielsen stated, "Canada is both overregulated and badly regulated."

Regulatory Reform[5]

Growing concern about a variety of perceived problems with Canada's regulatory structure—including obsolescence in the face of rapid changes in technology and world markets, high compliance costs, and inefficiencies in the regulatory process—has led to a number of developments in Canada. (There have been similar developments in the United States, Europe, and Japan as well.) We have already encountered the deregulation trend in Chapter 15 in the context of competition policy, but the current debate and trend concerning regulation of the economy extends beyond the direct regulation of industry.

Over a decade ago, the Economic Council of Canada published two major reports on regulation: *Responsible Regulation* (1979) presented a critical appraisal of the regulatory process, and *Reforming Regulation* (1981) put forward a number of specific recommendations. In its 1979 report, the council proposed that an extensive consultative process be part of any major government attempt at regulatory change, that any major new regulatory proposals be subjected to formal benefit-cost analysis, and that the government review existing regulations and operations of regulatory agencies on a regular basis.

In its 1981 report, the council made proposals that touched on a wide range of regulated activities—trucking, airlines, telecommunications, agriculture, occupational health and safety, and the environment. The general thrust of its proposals was to "streamline the regulatory process and where possible to reduce the extent of regulation."[6] Increased competition and increased application of market forces and financial incentives were also stressed.

When the Progressive Conservative government took office in 1984, it took up this theme of regulatory reform as a key part of its agenda. It established the office of Regulatory Reform, later to become the Office of Privatization and Regulatory Affairs, and the report of the Nielsen task force stressed many of the themes found in the Economic Council reports. In 1986 the government announced its Regulatory Reform Strategy—although it did not endorse comprehensive deregulation, the government committed itself not only to limit the proliferation of new regulations but also "to 'regulate smarter' through greater efficiency, greater accountability, and greater sensitivity to those affected by federal regulations."[7] The strategy invoked a number of principles, including these:

- Recognition of the role of the marketplace;
- Continued use of regulation to achieve social and economic objectives;
- Use of benefit-cost analysis to screen new initiatives; and
- Increased public access and participation in the process.

Many of the new procedures have now found their way into practice, and regulatory hearings have become a regular part of the public policy landscape. Whether the new procedures have in fact met the stated objectives is not yet clear; many critics argue that the new processes, though open, are inefficient. For example, consider the hearings that commenced in May 1990 on the challenge by Canadian Pacific and Ted Rogers (of cable television fame) to Bell

[5] This section draws on a detailed discussion by Professor John Strick of the University of Windsor, *The Economics of Government Regulation: Theory and Canadian Practice* (Toronto: Thompson, 1990).

[6] Strick, p. 109.

[7] Strick, p. 111.

Canada's monopoly on long-distance phone service. These hearings were expected to last over 18 months, and one estimate was that Bell would spend over $35 million dollars representing itself at the hearings.

Most economists would support the principles of the Regulatory Reform Strategy. Even if it is fully adopted, however, difficult social choices and difficult technical problems, of both measurement and program design, will remain. Moreover, when health, life, and safety are at stake, there are many who will never be comfortable with the results of decentralized decision making, no matter how well informed the parties to private transactions may be. The desire to protect people from the negative consequences of their actions extends well beyond an interest in internalizing externalities or providing efficient levels of information.

Economic analysis can help society to examine the costs and the consequences of social regulation. Most important, it can help regulators to achieve desired consequences at minimum cost and thus reduce the level of government failure. It can help us to decide how best to intervene in the interest of health and safety, but it cannot tell us how much we should intervene.

SUMMARY

1. Almost all economic activity is subject to at least some government regulation. Government regulation is used to deal with every type of market failure—public goods, externalities, natural monopoly problems, information asymmetries, and social values.
2. Economic regulation refers to the regulation of natural monopoly, which was discussed in Chapter 15. Social regulation is the regulation of economic behavior to advance social goals where neither competition nor economic regulation can be expected to do the job.
3. Most pollution problems can be analyzed as negative externalities. Polluting firms and households going about their daily business do harm to the environment and fail to take account of the costs that they impose on others.
4. The economically efficient level of pollution in any activity is generally not zero; it is the level where the marginal cost of further pollution reduction is just equal to the marginal damage done by a unit of pollution. If a firm or a household faces incentives that cause it to internalize the costs that pollution imposes, it will choose the economically efficient level of pollution.
5. Pollution can be regulated either directly or indirectly. Direct controls are used most often. Direct controls are often inefficient because they require that all polluters meet the same standard regardless of the benefits and costs of doing so. Indirect controls, such as taxes on emissions, are more efficient; ideally, they cause firms to internalize perfectly the pollution externality. Tradable emissions permits could have the same effect.
6. Health and safety regulation covers workplace health and safety and product safety. Some economists have argued that regulation of this kind is unnecessary because if people are well informed about health and safety risks, the level of resources devoted to safety and health will be efficient.
7. Perfect information about health and safety risks is often difficult to obtain or to evaluate. Society may also choose not to permit people to face certain kinds of risks. In either of these cases, health and safety regulation addresses a real market failure. Government failure is common in the area of health and safety regulation.

8. Increased use of benefit-cost analysis could reduce the social costs imposed by social regulation. Alternatively, holding social cost constant, it could increase the benefits from social regulation. Economics, however, cannot tell society what should and should not be regulated.

TOPICS FOR REVIEW

Costs and benefits of pollution abatement
Emissions taxes
Direct controls
Efficient level of pollution
Tradable emissions permits
Regulatory failure
Cost-effectiveness analysis
Regulatory reform

DISCUSSION QUESTIONS

1. Many occupations are licensed, either by governments or by professional organizations. Are economists licensed? Should they be? Why or why not?
2. "Pollution is wrong. When a corporation pollutes, it commits assault on the citizens of the country, and it should be punished." Comment on the quotation in light of the discussion in this chapter.
3. Assume that the following statements are true. What do they imply about the argument that health and safety regulations are necessary to promote economic efficiency?
    a. Welders who work on the upper stories of unfinished skyscrapers are paid more than welders who work only indoors.
    b. Following a commercial airplane crash, the stock market value of the airline company tends to fall.
    c. City housing of a given structural quality tends to sell for less, the greater the health risk posed by air quality in the neighborhood.
    d. For decades, asbestos was widely used as insulation. Installers of asbestos insulation routinely breathed asbestos fiber in concentrations that are now known to be potentially lethal. For some years, asbestos producers were aware that asbestos was dangerous but did not share this information with installers.
    e. Until recently, the upholstery in airline seats emitted lethal fumes when burning.
4. Consider the following (alleged) facts about pollution control and indicate what, if any, influence they might have on policy determination.
    a. In the mid 1980s, the cost of meeting federal pollution requirements was about $100 per person per year.
    b. More than one-third of the world's known oil supplies lie under the ocean floor, and there is no known blowout-proof method of recovery.
    c. Sulfur removal requirements and strip-mining regulations have led to the tripling of the cost of a ton of coal used in generating electricity.
    d. Every million dollars that is spent on pollution control creates 67 new jobs in the economy.

5. During a Pittsburgh air pollution alert, a 69-year-old retired steelworker was interviewed. He said, "I've got a heart condition myself, and I know that when I look out the window and see the air like it was this morning, I've got to stay inside. Yesterday, I tried to drive to the store, and I couldn't see 50 feet ahead of me, it was so thick, so I just came home. I remember that when I was young, we never thought about pollution. Everybody was working, and everybody had money, and the smokestacks were smoking, and the air was dirty, and we were all happy. I think the best air we ever had in Pittsburgh was during the Depression. That's when nobody was working." Comment on this statement in terms of the issues discussed in this chapter.
6. Suppose that you were given the job of drafting a law to regulate water pollution over the entire length of some river.
   a. How would you determine how much total pollution to permit?
   b. What control mechanism would you use to regulate emissions into the river? Why?
   c. Would you impose the same rules on cities as on farms?
   d. Would the answers to (a), (b), or (c) depend on the quality of information that would be available to you? How and why?
7. One critic of environmental policy argued that the policy had perverse effects in one industry since new firms using modern technology were induced to limit their pollution, but old established firms continued to pour black smoke into the atmosphere. Drawing on the analysis in this chapter, how might this policy be defended?

Chapter 24

Taxation and Public Expenditure

All governments spend money, and they must raise revenue to do so. Governments in Canada—whether federal, provincial, or municipal—are no exception. But government spending and government taxation today go far beyond the minimum required to provide such essentials as a justice system and protection against foreign enemies. Spending and taxation are also key tools of economic policy.

In Chapter 22 we saw that there were a number of reasons why the scope of government is so extensive. Public spending is the obvious way to provide collective consumption goods. It is also one way to change the distribution of income. Taxation is needed to raise money for public spending, and it can also play a policy role in its own right. Taxes can affect the distribution of income—some people get taxed more than others. Moreover, by taxing some activities heavily and others lightly or not at all, the tax system can influence the allocation of resources. In some cases tax policy is carefully designed with such effects in mind; in other cases the effects are unintentional by-products of policies pursued for other purposes.

In this chapter we are concerned with taxation and public expenditure. We ask how these activities of government affect the allocation of resources and the distribution of income. We also ask about the extent to which they are effective tools of public policy. We also consider the question of which governmental services, and which taxes, should be the responsibility of which levels of government.

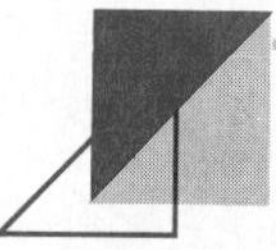

Taxation

There is a bewildering array of taxes, some highly visible (such as sales taxes and income taxes) and others all but invisible because they are imposed on producers of raw materials and intermediate products.

People are taxed on what they earn, on what they spend, and on what they own. Firms are taxed as well as households. Not only are taxes numerous, but they take a big bite. Aggregate taxes amount to more than one-third of the total value of goods and services produced in Canada each year. The diversity and yield of various taxes are shown in Table 24-1.

TABLE 24-1 Government Tax Revenues by Source, 1989

	Revenue		Percentage division		
Kind of tax	Billions of dollars	Percentage	Federal	Provincial	Municipal
Income tax, persons	112.8	44	62	38	—
Income and other taxes, corporations	15.3	6	70	30	—
General sales taxes	58.6	23	46	54	—
Customs duties (est.)	5.0	2	100	—	—
Property tax	21.0	8	—	—	100
All other taxes	42.9	17	—	—	—
Total	255.6	100	44	39	17

Source: National Income and Expenditure Accounts, Statistics Canada, 13-001.

Income taxes are the major source of revenue for the federal and provincial governments. Substantial yields are also obtained from the federal manufacturers' sales tax (to be replaced with the Goods and Services Tax in 1991) and the provincial retail levies that make up the sales tax category. Municipal governments rely entirely on property taxes.

Progressivity of Taxation

When the government taxes one group in society more heavily than it taxes another, it influences the distribution of income. The effect of taxes on the distribution of income can be summarized in terms of *progressivity*. A **progressive tax** system takes a larger percentage of income from people the higher their income. A **proportional tax** system takes amounts of money from people in direct proportion to their income. A **regressive tax** system takes a larger percentage of income from people the lower their income.[1]

A tax system is said to be progressive if it decreases the inequality of income distribution and regressive if it increases the inequality, other things being equal.

The differences can be illustrated by an example. Suppose that we have a very small town with 100 taxpayers, half of whom earn $20,000 a year and half of whom earn $40,000 a year. The town's budget for street repair is $10,000 per year.

Now consider three alternative tax systems. First, if the tax system were simply to assess $100 per year from each taxpayer, the outcome would be regressive: Lower-income taxpayers would be paying 0.5 percent of their incomes, and the higher-income taxpayers would be paying only 0.25 percent of theirs. Second, if the repairs were paid for by a proportional tax, everyone would pay 0.33 percent of income: This would amount to $66.67 for the low-income households and $133.33 for the high-income households. Finally, a scheme whereby the first $20,000 of income would be subject to a 0.1 percent tax rate and all income above $20,000 would be subject to a 0.8 percent tax rate would be progressive. The low-income taxpayers would pay only 0.1 percent of their incomes ($20), while taxes would average 0.45 percent for the high-income group ($180). Note that in all three cases the total tax revenues add up to the requisite $10,000.

[1] While our interest is ultimately in the progressivity of the tax system as a whole, it will also be useful to identify the progressivity of particular features of the tax system, such as income taxes or sales taxes.

Tax Expenditures

Sometimes taxes are used in ways that are similar to spending programs. For example, one way to deal with polluted rivers is to spend public funds to clean them up. An alternative, as we saw in Chapter 23, is to use taxes to penalize polluters or to give tax concessions to firms that install pollution-abating devices. Tax concessions that seek to induce market responses are called **tax expenditures**—tax revenue forgone to achieve purposes that the government believes are desirable.

TABLE 24-2 The Rate Structure of the Canadian Personal Income Tax, 1989

	Federal				Provincial		Combined		
Taxable income	Gross tax	Tax credit	Net tax	Marginal rate	Tax	Marginal rate	Tax	Marginal rate	Average rate
$ 6,066	$ 1,031	$1,031	$ 0	17%	$ 0	9.4%	$ 0	26.4%	0.0%
20,000	3,400	1,031	2,369	17	1,303	9.4	3,672	26.4	18.4
27,803	4,726	1,031	3,695	17	2,032	9.4	5,727	26.4	20.6
40,000	7,897	1,031	6,866	26	3,776	14.3	10,643	40.3	26.6
55,604	11,955	1,031	10,924	26	6,008	14.3	16,932	40.3	30.5
70,000	16,130	1,031	15,099	29	8,304	16.0	23,403	45.0	33.4
100,000	24,830	1,031	23,799	29	13,089	16.0	36,888	45.0	36.9

Both the marginal and the average tax rates rise with taxable income; thus the income tax is progressive in structure. Gross federal tax is equal to 17 percent of the first $27,803 of taxable income, plus 26 percent of the next $27,801, plus 29 percent of all additional taxable income. The federal tax credit is nonrefundable. Its size depends on the circumstances of the individual taxpayer; for a single person with no dependents, the credit is $1,031. Thus that person could earn up to $6,066 without owing any net federal taxes.

The typical provincial tax is 55 percent of net federal taxes payable. Thus the combined marginal tax rate rises from 26.4 percent to a maximum of 45 percent, while the combined average rate climbs steadily with taxable income.

The difference between a tax expenditure and an ordinary budgetary expenditure is that a tax expenditure reduces the revenue side of the budget instead of increasing the expenditure side. As a practical matter, tax expenditures often receive little scrutiny from Parliament. Their effects are usually harder to discern and harder to evaluate than those of direct spending programs.

In many cases, tax expenditures are difficult to distinguish from tax "loopholes." The distinction is often in the eye of the beholder. For example, until recently the federal government allowed an *investment tax credit* on private investment. The credit meant that some designated investments would permit certain taxpayers to reduce their income taxes by a fraction of the investment. Many people, especially in the business community, considered the investment tax credit a means of enhancing economic growth by encouraging investment. Others viewed it as a way of allowing the richest and most successful businesses (and, indirectly, their stockholders) to avoid paying taxes that they were plainly able to pay.

The Canadian Tax System

The term *Canadian tax system* is something of a misnomer. Taxes are collected by the federal government, by each of the 10 provinces, and by thousands of cities, townships, and villages. As can be seen in Table 24-1, the federal government collects about as much revenue as all other governments put together. The provinces, in turn, collect about twice as much as local governments. The federal government gets over 70 percent of its revenues from taxes paid directly by individuals and corporations (called income taxes) and over 20 percent from taxes collected on the sale of goods and services (called sales taxes). The provinces get only about 50 percent from income taxes and over 40 percent from sales taxes. The municipalities rely exclusively on property taxes for their tax revenues.[2]

Personal Income Taxes

Personal income taxes are paid directly to the government by individuals. The amount of tax any individual pays is the result of a fairly complicated series of calculations; indeed, the complicated nature of the calculations is itself a source of cost and irritation to many taxpayers.

First, individuals have to calculate their *tax base*, called their taxable income. All types of income,

[2] Table 24-1 shows *tax* revenues; as we shall see, each of the lower levels of government also receives revenue in the form of transfer payments from more senior governments.

including wages, dividends, interest, rents, and capital gains, are included in what is called total income, although certain types of income qualify for total or partial exemption.[3] Then a number of allowable deductions are subtracted from total income to determine taxable income.

Taxes payable are then calculated from a schedule relating taxable income to taxes due. The tax schedule takes into account the facts that the personal tax rate changes as taxable income changes and that gross taxes are reduced by nonrefundable tax credits to determine net taxes. The essential features of the 1989 Canadian tax schedule are shown in Table 24-2.[4] Table 24-3 presents some illustrative calculations for the case of a hypothetical single taxpayer with no dependents.

The **average tax rate** paid by a taxpayer is his or her total income tax payment divided by total income. The taxpayer's **marginal tax rate** is the amount of tax he or she would pay on an additional dollar of income. As can be seen from Table 24-2, the combined marginal tax rate rises as income rises; this *progressive marginal tax rate* contributes to the progressivity of the income tax system.

However, it is misleading to draw conclusions about the progressivity of the income tax system by looking only at the progressivity of the tax rates in the tax schedule. As we have seen, taxes payable are calculated from taxable income, which, because of the presence of deductions and exemptions, can differ substantially from income earned. The progressivity of tax *rates* means that a deduction is worth more the higher the taxpayer's income is.

TABLE 24-3 A Hypothetical Income Tax Return, 1989 Income Tax Schedule

Employment income		$28,000
Investment income		2,500
Total income		30,500
Deductions		
RRSP contributions		3,500
Interest expenses		500
Taxable income		26,500
Gross federal tax	4,405	
Personal tax credit	1,031	
Federal tax payable		3,474
Federal surtax		139
Net federal tax		3,613
Provincial tax		1,987
Total taxes due		$ 5,600

Taxable income, or the tax base, equals total income less allowable deductions; federal taxes payable equals gross tax, calculated on the basis of taxable income, less tax credits, which depend on the individual taxpayer's circumstances. For this individual, total income is $30,500, made up of $28,000 employment income and $2,500 investment income. In calculating taxable income, the individual is allowed to deduct $3,500 that he or she has deposited in a Registered Retirement Savings Plan, plus $500 in interest expenses incurred on a loan that was used to finance the investment that gave rise to the $2,500 investment income. Since the individual has taxable income of less than $27,803 (the threshold level above which the marginal tax rates rises to 26 percent), gross federal tax is 17 percent of taxable income, or $4,405. The basic personal tax credit, which is all that our single taxpayer with no children qualifies for, is $1,031, so federal tax payable is $3,474. In 1989 there was a 4 percent federal surtax, adding another $139 (4 percent of $3,474) to federal taxes. Provincial taxes are then 55 percent of net federal taxes, so total taxes due are $5,600.

Exemptions and deductions generally make the income tax system less progressive.

For example, for many years Canadians were allowed to deduct the first $1,000 of interest income that they earned. As can be seen from Table 24-2, a $1,000 deduction from taxable income would reduce taxes for someone in the lowest tax bracket by $264 (equal to the combined marginal tax rate times the deduction), while for someone in the top bracket, taxes would fall by $450. As a result, the after-tax incomes of the two would be further apart than if

[3] Until 1972 most capital gains were not taxable in Canada, but beginning in that year taxpayers were required to include one-half of gains received in their taxable income. In his May 1985 budget, Federal Minister of Finance Michael Wilson introduced a $500,000 personal lifetime exemption for capital gains. In the June 1987 tax reform, the lifetime exemption was reduced to $100,000. In 1989 the inclusion rate was raised to 75 percent.

[4] The provinces also collect income taxes; Quebec runs its own income tax system, and the other nine provinces simply use the federal tax base (and federally distributed tax forms) and essentially "top up" federal taxes. The Quebec system is discussed in Chapter 25. For now, we can understand the total system by looking at the federal system augmented by the typical provincial top-up, which we take to be 55 percent.

For simplicity, the table ignores the role of the federal surtax (which is levied as a fraction of net federal taxes due) and of the "clawback," which recaptures benefits received by high-income Canadians from the family allowance, unemployment insurance, and old age security.

the deduction were not allowed; it is in this sense that deductions make the tax system less progressive.[5]

1987 tax reform. Prior to 1987, the federal personal income tax contained 11 tax brackets with the marginal rate rising from 16 percent to 43 percent; thus the combined federal-provincial marginal rate ranged from about 24 percent to over 64 percent. However, the presence of a large number of eligible deductions and exemptions made the overall effect of the income tax system less progressive than suggested by the rising marginal tax rates.

In June 1987, Finance Minister Michael Wilson introduced a major reform of the personal income tax system. The theme of the reform was to *broaden the tax base* by eliminating a number of exemptions and deductions and to *lower marginal tax rates*. The new system appears considerably simpler, as there are now just three tax brackets. The conversion of the basic personal exemption to a personal tax credit—worth the same to each taxpayer regardless of income level—contributes to, rather than detracts from, the progressivity of the system. Further, marginal rates have been reduced for most Canadians, and many other low-income Canadians now pay no taxes.

Although the changes introduced in 1987 were substantial and were intended to be part of a comprehensive reform of the tax system, the personal income tax system continues to change. In the two budgets immediately following the introduction of the reforms, Finance Minister Wilson made further changes—increasing the federal surtax shown in Table 24-3 (which had been scheduled to expire) and introducing a special levy on high income earners intended to "claw back" social benefits such as family allowances. These effectively raise marginal tax rates and add to the complexity of the tax system, and thus both initiatives run counter to the principles that guided the earlier attempts at reform.

Corporate Income Taxes

The federal corporate income tax is, for practical purposes, a flat-rate tax on profits as defined by the taxing authorities—which includes the return on capital as well as pure economic profits. In 1986 the rate was reduced from 50 to 36 percent, and as part of the tax reform of 1987 it was reduced further to 28 percent, effective 1988.

As with the personal income tax, the 1987 reform not only lowered tax rates but also broadened the tax base, and on the whole the changes tended to raise taxes paid by corporations. Base broadening was accomplished primarily by eliminating tax concessions, called investment tax credits, that had been used to encourage investment. Some other changes were also introduced in order to curb tax avoidance and hence to encourage investment decisions made on the basis of sound economic prospects rather than merely "on the advice of tax lawyers and accountants."

It is difficult to determine the effect of corporate taxation on income distribution, for there is great controversy over the extent to which it is "shifted" to consumers. (The question of tax shifting is called the problem of *tax incidence,* that is, who really pays a tax imposed on any one group. Incidence is discussed in detail later in this chapter.)

Excise and Sales Taxes

An excise tax is levied on a particular commodity (such as liquor); a sales tax is levied on all or most sales. These taxes are often referred to as *indirect taxes* to contrast them with income taxes, which are levied directly on individuals.

If two families spend the same proportion of their income on a certain commodity that is subject to a sales or an excise tax, the tax is proportional in its effects on them. If the tax is on a commodity, such as food, that takes a larger proportion of the income of lower-income families, it is regressive. If it is on a commodity, such as jewelry, on which the rich spend a larger proportion of their income than the poor, it is progressive.

Commodities with inelastic demands provide attractive sources of revenue. In many countries commodities such as tobacco, alcohol, and gasoline are singled out for high rates of excise taxation. Because these commodities usually account for a much greater proportion of the expenditure of lower-income than higher-income groups, the taxes on them are regressive.

All provinces except Alberta impose a retail sales tax, and the federal government also imposes a sales

[5] Whether the decline in progressivity is undesirable depends not only on value judgments but also on the purpose of the deduction. We take this up later in this chapter when we discuss horizontal equity.

tax. Although the tax bases of these various sales taxes differ, all are collected on a wide range of goods and services. A general sales tax is regressive because poorer families tend to spend a larger proportion of their incomes than richer families.

For example, suppose there is a 7 percent comprehensive sales tax. A family earning $25,000 a year that saves nothing will pay 7 percent of its income on sales taxes; a family earning $70,000 a year that saves $10,000 will pay 6 percent.

Sales and excise taxes in Canada today are generally regressive.

The GST. When reforms to the direct personal and corporate tax systems were introduced in 1987, the federal government also proposed a major overhaul of the nation's sales tax system. Initially the federal government proposed a national sales tax that would integrate the federal and provincial sales taxes into one unified tax with a common base and rate structure. The efficiency gains in both administration and elimination of distortions would have been substantial. However, the necessary agreement with the provincial governments could not be reached, and the federal government subsequently announced its intention to replace its existing federal sales tax (FST) with a new, radically different goods and services tax (GST) effective January 1, 1991.

The GST is designed to be a neutral tax with regard to resource allocation because, in principle, all activities that produce goods and services would be taxed at the same rate. It seeks to achieve this neutrality by taxing each firm's **value added**, which is the value of its output minus the value of inputs that it has purchased from other firms. Thus the GST is like the value added tax (VAT) common in most European countries.

In practice the GST works by taxing firms on the total value of their output and then allowing a tax credit equal to the taxes paid on its inputs that were produced by other firms. The operation of the GST for the case of the stages leading from the mining of iron ore to the manufacture of a washing machine is illustrated in Figure 24-1.

The GST is a *multistage* tax. Unlike provincial sales taxes that apply only at the time of final retail sale, a multistage tax is levied on and collected from businesses in stages as goods move from primary producers and processors to wholesalers, retailers, and consumers. One important feature of the GST relates to its treatment of internationally traded goods. If a good produced in Canada is exported, no tax is collected on that stage; since a firm that produces for export can still claim a credit for taxes on its inputs, this means that exports are tax-free. The GST is levied on goods produced abroad and imported into Canada. These features enhance the ability of Canadian manufacturers to compete with foreign producers.

FIGURE 24-1 The Operation of a Value Added Tax

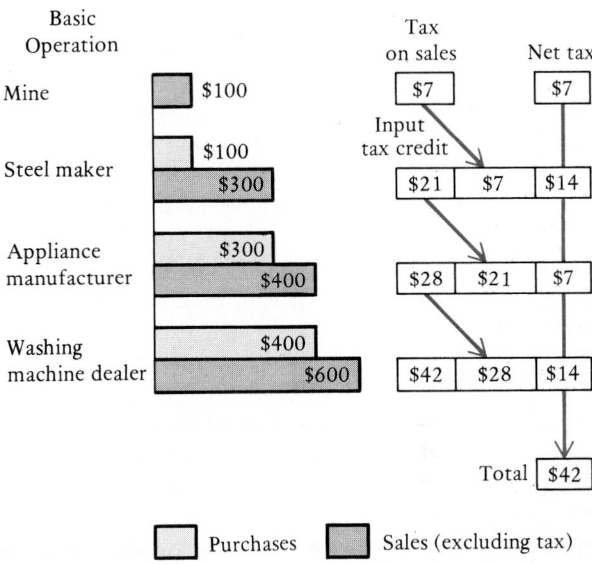

A tax on value added is the same as a tax on the value of total output produced by a firm with a credit allowed for the tax paid by other firms from which it has purchased produced inputs. The example is for the stages involved as iron ore is mined and then sold to a steel maker, the steel then sold to an appliance manufacturer, and a washing machine sold to a retailer and then to a homeowner. The example makes the simplifying assumption that no produced inputs are used in the mining operation; at all further stages, the use of produced inputs makes the firm's value added less than the value of final output at that stage. The steel maker's value added is $200, and its tax is thus $14; this equals $21 on the total value of its output less the $7 credit on the taxes already paid by the mine on the value of the ore. Total taxes paid equal $42, which is 7 percent of the $600 value of the final product (the washing machine); each firm pays 7 percent of its share in creating that $600 value.

The fact that the GST is a sales tax was itself a source of controversy. To people concerned about the apparent ability of the rich to exploit loopholes in the income tax system and pay little or no income taxes, this was a plus, since a sales tax is difficult to avoid. To others, however, this was a serious drawback, since sales taxes are potentially regressive. Because of this concern, the GST proposal exempts food and includes a refundable sales tax credit to compensate lower- and middle-income people for the increased tax burden they would bear as a result of the shift to the GST.

Further controversies surrounding the GST are discussed in more detail in Box 24-1.

Property Taxes

An indirect tax that is an important source of revenue for municipalities is the property tax. Property taxes are based on the value of taxable property.

The property tax is the only important tax in Canada that is based on wealth. It is different from any other important tax because taxpayers do not have to buy or sell anything in order to incur a tax liability.

Taxing the value of existing property leads to two recurring problems with property taxes. First, someone has to assess what the property is worth. Because the assessment is only an estimate, it is always subject to challenge. Most municipalities have an appeal process by which an individual property owner can try to have an assessment reduced, and sometimes large classes of owners (of certain types of properties or in certain neighborhoods) mount group protests. Second, sometimes owners of property that is quite valuable have very low incomes—elderly, retired homeowners, for example—and thus have great difficulty in paying the tax.

The progressivity of the property tax has been studied extensively. It is well known that the rich live in more expensive houses than the poor, but all that this establishes is that the rich tend to pay more in property tax than the poor. Because the rich tend to live in different communities from the poor and thus pay taxes at different rates and because they tend to spend a different proportion of their income for housing, the question of the progressivity of the property tax is difficult. Most studies have shown that the proportion of income spent for housing tends to decrease with income. Many, but not all, public finance experts believe that the property tax tends to be mildly regressive in its overall effect.

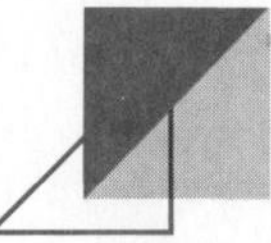

Evaluating the Tax System

Many people use a very simple rule for evaluating taxes: The lower the better. But this does not provide a very helpful guide for designing a tax system. If governments are to spend money to provide services and make transfer payments, they must be able to collect taxes. Therefore, the important question is this: Holding constant the amount of revenue to be raised, what makes one tax system better or worse than another?

Economists answer this question by considering two aspects of taxation—efficiency and equity. The notion of economic efficiency has played a major part of most discussions in this book, and our use of the term here should now seem familiar to you. Taxes affect efficiency by affecting the allocation of resources. We will discuss the efficiency of the Canadian tax system in some detail later in this chapter.

Taxes and Equity

Debate about income distribution and tax policy invokes the important but hard-to-define concepts of *equality* and *equity*.

Equality

Equality is a straightforward concept—or is it? To tax everyone equally can mean several things. It might mean that everyone should pay the same amount—which would be hard on the unemployed worker and easy on Paul Coffey. It might mean that everyone should pay the same proportion of income, say, a flat 20 percent, whether rich or poor, living alone or supporting eight children, healthy or suffering from a disease that requires expensive treatment. It might mean that each should pay an amount of tax such that everyone's income after taxes is the same—which would remove any incentive to earn an above average income. Or it might mean none of these things.

Equity

Equity—fairness—is a normative concept; what one group thinks is fair may seem outrageous to another. Two principles—ability to pay and benefits received—can be helpful in assessing equity.

The ability-to-pay principle. Most people view an equitable tax system as being based on people's *ability to pay taxes.* In considering equity that is based on ability to pay, two concepts need to be distinguished.

Vertical equity concerns equity across income groups; it focuses on comparisons between individuals or families with different levels of income.

This concept is central to discussions of the progressivity of taxation. Proponents of progressive taxation argue as follows. (1) Taxes should be based on ability to pay. (2) The greater one's income, the greater the percentage of income that is available for goods and services beyond the bare necessities. (3) Thus the greater one's income, the greater the proportion of income that is available to pay taxes. (4) Thus an ability-to-pay standard of vertical equity requires progressive taxation.

Horizontal equity concerns equity within a given income group; fundamentally, it is concerned with establishing just who should be considered equal to whom in terms of ability to pay taxes.

Two households with the same income may have different numbers of children to support. One of the households may have greater dental expenses, leaving less for life's necessities and for taxes. One of the households may incur greater expenses that are necessary for earning income (e.g., requirements to buy uniforms or to pay union dues). There is no objective way to decide how much these and similar factors affect the ability to pay taxes. In practice, the income tax law makes some allowance for some factors that create differences in ability to pay by permitting taxpayers to exempt some of their income from tax. However, the corrections are rough at best. We consider the issue of horizontal equity in more detail in Chapter 25.

The benefit principle. According to the *benefit principle,* taxes should be paid in proportion to the benefits that taxpayers derive from public expenditure.[6] From this perspective, the ideal taxes are *user charges,* such as those that would be charged if private firms provided the government services. The benefit principle is the basis for the gasoline tax, since gasoline usage is closely correlated to the services obtained from using public roads. There is also a special excise tax on airline tickets that is used for airport operations, air traffic control, and airport security. Although there are other examples, especially at the local level, the benefit principle has historically played only a minor role in the design of the Canadian tax system.

An interesting example of the conflict between the two principles comes from the controversies surrounding the introduction of a "poll tax," called the community charge, in Great Britain in early 1990. The Thatcher government replaced some existing property taxes, based on property values, with a flat tax per person. The former system could be understood as being based on the ability-to-pay principle; rich owners of valuable property paid more than low-income people with only modest incomes. The new system can be understood as being based on the benefits principle whereby taxes are related to the amounts of the public services consumed—which are roughly equal for any given person. The controversy stemmed from the obvious regressivity of the new system: Many cases of dramatic falls in taxes paid by Britain's upper class (including royalty) were published alongside reports of tax increases faced by low-income households.

How Progressive Is the Canadian Tax System?

It is more difficult to assess the overall impact of the tax system than the impact of any particular tax. The effect of the tax system on the distribution of income depends on the mix of taxes of different kinds. Fed-

[6] It is difficult to see how the benefit principle could be applied to many of the most important categories of government spending. Who gets how much benefit from national defense or from the interest on the national debt? It is even more difficult to imagine applying the benefit principle to programs that redistribute income.

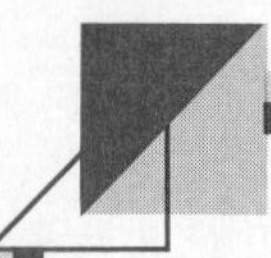

BOX 24-1

The Goods and Services Tax

The goods and services tax (GST) is scheduled to replace the federal sales tax (FST) in January 1991. To some extent, this change could be seen as an extension of the theme of broadening the tax base and lowering the tax rate that had been featured in the reform of the direct tax system. Under the FST, services were excluded—the tax was also known as the manufacturers' sales tax (MST), since it was levied only on manufactured goods. Further, many industries were exempt, so manufactured goods were treated in a discriminatory fashion. The GST broadened the base to include almost all goods and services produced in Canada (food and some financial services are notable exceptions), and the tax rate was to fall from the 13.5 percent FST rate to 7 percent under the GST.

Much of the rationale for the change stemmed from dissatisfaction with the FST. The narrow base of the FST created a sense of unfairness that threatened the integrity of the tax system; there were about 22,000 special provisions for the FST that were the result of industries or firms negotiating special treatment for themselves. The narrow base also created distortions by treating various industries differently, leading to an inefficient allocation of resources. Finally, the continual erosion of the base as new industries negotiated special treatment meant that the FST no longer provided a stable revenue source.

In addition to the problems created by the narrow base, economists identified two other undesirable features of the FST. First, it taxed goods produced for export but not imports; this put Canadian industries at a competitive disadvantage both at home and abroad. Second, since many manufactured capital goods are used as inputs by other industries, the FST raised the price of those inputs and thus again damaged the competitiveness of Canadian producers. These two problems were addressed by the *multistage* nature of the GST.

One advantage of using a multistage tax is that it reduces *tax cascading,* which is the term used to describe the fact that under the FST some commodities effectively get taxed more than once. For example, consider the production of a washing machine illustrated in Figure 24-1. If a sales tax were levied on all transactions, with no offsetting tax credits applied to inputs in the manufacturing process, the ore would be taxed three times: when it is sold to the steel maker, when the steel is sold to the appliance manufacturer, and when the appliance is sold to the consumer. Analogously, the steel would be taxed twice. The GST eliminates this cascading: Once the tax on the ore is collected when it is sold to the steel maker, its value is not taxed again, since further purchasers are given a tax credit for the tax embodied in their purchases.

The elimination of tax cascading is especially important when considering investment and international trade. When a firm invests in a new machine or builds a new plant, much of its purchases will be subject to sales tax. Under a single-stage tax, this is the end of the story, and the sales tax clearly raises the cost of investment to the firm. With a multistage tax, the firm gets a credit for the taxes already paid on its purchases of goods and machines. This reduces the cost of investment to the firm.

Now consider the implications for exports and imports. Again, we refer to the washing machine example in Figure 24-1. Suppose first that the washing machine is produced in Canada but that the dealer sells it in a foreign country. No GST would be paid on the final sale; however, the exporter would be able to collect a credit for the $28 in taxes embodied in the purchases from the appliance manufacturer. Compared to the situation with the FST, the Canadian-made washing machine would be taxed less heavily and thus be more competitively priced in foreign markets. Now suppose that the washing machine were produced abroad and imported into Canada; the GST woud apply, but no credits would be available to offset any taxes collected in the production process—which, after all, would have been collected by a foreign government. As a result, Canadian-made washing machines, on which the GST would also be charged but for which tax credits would be allowed for purchases of inputs, would be able to compete more effectively with the imports.

In a detailed study of the GST, the Economic Council of Canada argued that the replacement of the 13.5 percent FST with a GST at a lower rate would have a number of important effects. Since the effective tax on manufactured goods would fall and that on services (for example, restaurant meals and legal advice) would rise, total output of the former would rise relative to the output of the latter. The council also argued that exports would rise, imports would fall, savings and investment woud both rise, and a process of capital upgrading would occur, leading to increased productivity and growth.

Most economists believe that the FST was a source of considerable inefficiency, and as a result, the move to the GST would be an improvement. Nevertheless, the GST proved to be an extremely unpopular initiative. Part of the problem was that most Canadians were not aware of the existence of the FST, much less of its deficiencies. Unlike provincial sales taxes, the FST is "invisible"; it is applied before the retail transaction, and hence its presence is hidden in retail selling prices. Many people also feared the increase in inflation that the GST would cause; although some prices would fall, many would rise, and there was general agreement among experts that the introduction of the GST would cause an increase of 1 to 2 percent in the general price level. Many Canadians, including most labor leaders, feared that this would contribute to increases in inflation, and hence the prospects of the GST put a strain into many labor contract negotiations during the summer of 1990. Much of the opposition came from small business, farmers, fishermen, and professionals, who feared the burden of record keeping and paperwork that such a complicated system entails. Others feared that the GST would become a "money machine" for the government: Once the GST was introduced, it might prove easy for governments to raise more revenue simply by increasing the GST rate.

Some economists felt that the complications introduced by the GST were not worthwhile. They were concerned not only about the compliance costs that worried most small businesses but also about the complicated interaction that the GST would have with the provincial sales taxes. Since the tax bases for the taxes would not be the same, some goods would be taxable under both, some under one or the other, and some under neither. (And these categories would vary from province to province, since the base for the provincial sales taxes vary from province to province.) Further, some cascading with provincial sales taxes occurs, since those taxes are typically levied after the GST has been. These critics suggested that if a coordinated sales tax system with the provinces is not possible, a better approach would be for the federal government to scrap the FST *and* to abandon the sales tax field altogether. In return, the federal government could take an increased share of direct tax revenues, and the provinces could raise their sales tax rates.

BOX 24-2

The Negative Income Tax

A tax is negative when the government pays the taxpayer instead of the other way around. The so-called **negative income tax (NIT)** is designed to increase progressivity and combat poverty by making taxes *negative* at very low incomes. Such a tax would extend progressivity to the very lowest incomes.

Many versions of the NIT have been proposed; the one described here illustrates the basic idea. The underlying principle is that a family of a given size should be allowed a minimum annual income. The aim is to guarantee this income without eliminating the incentive to become self-supporting. This is done by combining a grant (often called a refundable tax credit) with a tax.

As an example (illustrated in the figure), consider a system in which each household is guaranteed a minimum annual income of $12,000 and the marginal tax rate is 50 percent. For each dollar earned, the household loses 50 cents. The household breaks even at $24,000. If the household earns an income below this level, it receives money from the government (equal to the $12,000 guarantee less 50 percent of its earnings); that is, the family pays a negative tax. If the family earns exactly $24,000, it pays no taxes; its after-tax income is also $24,000. Above this level, it pays a positive tax equal to 50 percent of its earnings in excess of $24,000; for

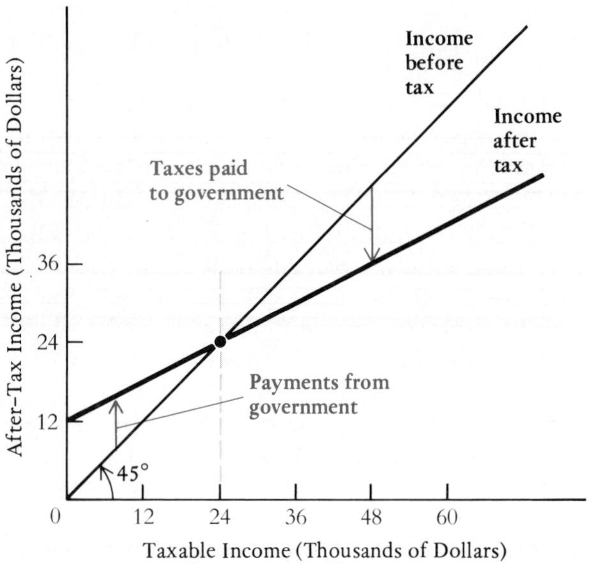

eral taxes tend to be somewhat progressive; the progressivity of the income tax system and the use of a low-income tax credit offset the regressivity of the federal sales tax. Provincial and municipal governments rely heavily on property and sales taxes and thus have tax systems that are probably slightly regressive.

The difficulty of determining progressivity is increased by the fact that income from different sources is taxed at different rates. For example, in the federal personal income tax, income from royalties on oil wells is taxed more lightly than income from royalties on books, and profits from sales of assets (capital gains) are taxed more lightly than wages and salaries. To evaluate progressivity, one needs to know the way in which different levels of income correlate with different sources of income.

The offsetting effects of the various elements of the tax system have led many writers to conclude that overall the tax system has very little net effect on the distribution of income, except for very low-income persons.

The tax system tends to be roughly proportional for most income classes and mildly progressive for low-income persons.

One widely supported proposal for increasing the progressivity of the income tax is discussed in Box 24-2.

The relation of taxes to spending programs. In evaluating the progressivity of the tax system, how the

example, if its earnings are $36,000, it pays $6,000 in taxes, so its after-tax income is $30,000.

The figure shows the operation of this scheme by relating earned income on the horizontal axis to after-tax income on the vertical axis. The 45° line shows what after-tax income would be if there were no taxes. The heavy black line shows the operation of the negative income tax. It starts at the guaranteed annual income, it rises 50 cents for every dollar increase in earned income, and it cuts the 45° line at the break-even level. The vertical distance between the two black lines shows the net transfers between the individual and the government: Below the break-even level, the government makes payments to the individual; above the break-even level, the individual makes payments to the government.

Supporters of the negative income tax believe that it would be an effective tool for reducing poverty. It provides a minimum level of income as a matter of right, not of charity, and it does so without removing work incentives for people who are eligible for payments; every dollar earned adds to the after-tax income of the family.

As a potential replacement for many other relief programs, it promises to avoid the most pressing cases of poverty with much less administrative cost and without the myriad exceptions that are involved in most programs. An incidental advantage is that it removes whatever incentive people might have to migrate to provinces with better welfare programs, but it does not discourage migration to places where work may be available.

One step toward an NIT was taken with the tax reform of 1987, which replaced most personal exemptions with personal tax credits. Recall that an exemption reduces an individual's tax base relative to his or her earned income, whereas a tax credit reduces taxes due by the amount of the credit. At present, the credit is not refundable; it can be used to reduce taxes payable to zero, but any remaining credit cannot be claimed back from the government. If the credit were refundable, someone whose taxes on earned income were less than the credit would receive the difference from the government; that is, the person would pay a negative income tax. Many advocates of the negative income tax argue that the government should take the next step of making the personal tax credit refundable.

money is spent is just as important as how it is collected. A regressive tax may nevertheless provide funds for increased welfare payments, and thus the combined effect of the tax system and government spending may be progressive since it may ultimately redistribute income to the poor.

The purely political barriers to tax reform are formidable. Any single reform is likely to impose large costs on a relatively well identified group, while the benefits it gives would be more widely diffused. The 10 people who would each lose a million dollars from a particular tax reform are much more interested in the issue than the 10 million people who would each gain a dollar. The 10, not the 10 million, hire lobbyists and make campaign contributions. Hence it may be easier for those who want to redistribute income to get the government to undertake more progressive expenditure programs than to adopt more progressive taxes.

Political considerations often tend to make redistribution by expenditures more feasible than redistribution by tax reform.

Efficiency

The tax system influences the allocation of resources by changing the *relative* prices of various goods and factors and the *relative* profitability of various industries and various uses of factors of production.

Although it is theoretically possible to design a neutral tax system—one that leaves all relative prices unchanged—actual tax policy leads to a different allocation of resources than would occur without it.

The reason for this is that the taxes themselves change the relationship between prices and marginal costs and shift consumption and production toward goods and services that are taxed relatively lightly and away from those that are taxed more heavily. Usually, this distortion of free market outcomes causes economic inefficiency. In a world without taxes (and without other market imperfections), prices would equal marginal costs, and society's resources could be allocated efficiently.

Of course, in a world without taxes, there would be other problems—it would be impossible to pay for any government programs or public goods desired by society. In practice, then, the relevant objective for tax policy is to design a tax system that minimizes inefficiency, given the amount of revenue to be raised. In designing such a tax system, a natural place to start would be with taxes that both raise revenue and enhance efficiency. Examples are the fines and emissions taxes that we discussed in Chapter 23. When taxes are imposed on negative externalities, marginal social benefit is moved closer to marginal social cost, *and* government revenue is raised. Unfortunately, such taxes cannot raise nearly enough revenue to finance all of government expenditure.

In the absence of externalities, a tax normally does two things. It takes money from the taxpayers, and it changes their behavior. Taxpayers are typically made worse off by both. Economists call the first, the revenue collected, the **direct burden** of the tax. The additional costs that result from the induced changed behavior is called the **excess burden**. The excess burden is hard to measure in practice but easy to measure in principle. It is the amount of money that the taxpayers would have to be given, *over and above the tax paid,* in order to be just as well off as if there were no tax.

An example, using an excise tax may make help illustrate. Suppose that your city imposes a $2 excise tax on the purchase of compact disks. If you still buy your usual five CDs a month, you pay $10 in taxes and you therefore have to reduce your consumption of other goods by $10. However, there is no excess burden on you; if you were given an additional $10 a month in income, you would be exactly as well off as you were before the tax was imposed. Thus the total burden on you is equal to the direct burden, $10 a month. There is also no economic inefficiency; the cost of raising $10 a month for the city is just the $10 a month that you pay in taxes.

Suppose that your friend down the block is also a music fan but not quite so fanatical. The tax leads her to cut back on her consumption of CDs from two a month to none. In this case, your friend pays no taxes, but she is clearly worse off. She has given up the satisfaction that she would have derived from two new CDs a month. She would have to be given some amount of money greater than zero (in fact, exactly her consumer surplus from buying two untaxed CDs per month) in order to make her as well off as she was before the tax was imposed. Thus in this case there is no direct burden, but there is an excess burden.

When a tax is imposed, some people behave like the music buff and do not change their consumption of the taxed good at all, others cease consuming the taxed good altogether, and still others simply reduce consumption. There will be an excess burden for members of both of the latter two groups. This means that the revenue collected will understate the total cost to taxpayers, actual and potential, of generating that revenue. Since we are holding the total revenue raised, and hence the direct burden, constant, an efficient tax system will be one that minimizes the amount of excess burden.

The excess burden is minimized when taxes are imposed on goods for which the price elasticity of demand is least; the extreme case is illustrated by the music fan, whose price elasticity of demand is zero. A good with perfectly inelastic demand (one that has a vertical demand curve) can be taxed with no excess burden at all. Unfortunately, many of life's necessities (such as food) have very price inelastic demand curves, so a tax system that taxed only goods that had inelastic demand curves would prove to be very regressive.

Efficiency and equity are often competing goals in the design of tax systems.

"Supply-Side" Effects of Taxation

In principle, taxes on some activities can be so high that reducing the tax rate would actually increase tax revenue. This is the idea behind the **Laffer curve**, named for economist Arthur Laffer, whose views on income taxes were influential with U.S. President Ronald Reagan. Its essential feature is that tax revenues reach a maximum at some income tax rate well below 100 percent (see Figure 24-2).

The general shape of the Laffer curve is argued

FIGURE 24-2 A Laffer Curve

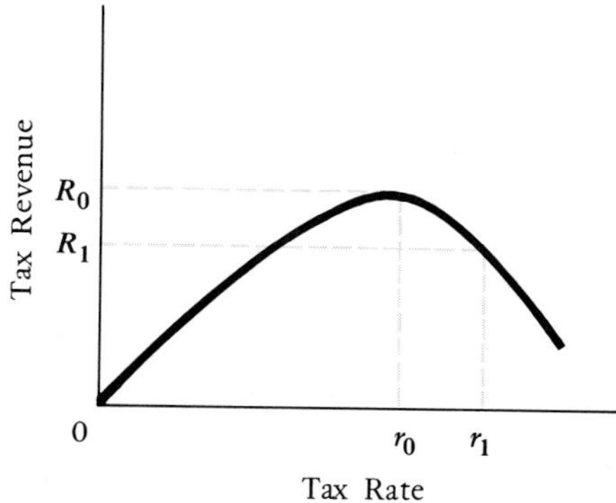

Increases in tax rates beyond some level will decrease rather than increase tax revenue. The curve relates the government's tax revenue to the tax rate. As drawn, revenue reaches a maximum level of R_0 at average tax rate r_0. If tax rates were r_1, *reducing* them to r_0 would increase revenue to the government from R_1 to R_0.

as a matter of simple logic. At a zero tax rate, no revenue would be collected. Similarly, at a 100 percent tax rate, revenue again would be zero because no one would bother to earn taxable income just to support the government. At intermediate rates, people would both earn income and pay taxes. Government tax revenue would reach an upper limit at some rate of taxation below 100 percent. For rates higher than the rate that produces this maximum, every increase in tax rates will lead to a decrease in tax revenue.

Just where this maximum occurs—whether at average tax rates of 40 percent or 80 percent or 95 percent—is an important empirical matter. Laffer believed that by the 1970s the United States had already increased taxes past the point where higher tax rates yielded more revenue. As a result, he argued, any attempt to increase progressivity by raising income tax rates would be self-defeating.

Many other economists disagreed. They might have conceded that some countries had reached such a point, but they argued that this had not happened in the United States or in Canada. A number of careful studies showed that the then top U.S. marginal tax rate of 50 percent was still short of being self-defeating in terms of tax revenue. These studies suggest that Laffer identified a potential rather than an actual problem.

Tax Incidence

One major unresolved question about taxes and resource allocation is empirical: Just how different is the allocation because of tax policy? Perhaps surprisingly, there is no consensus on this question. The reason is that we are not sure who really pays the taxes that are levied. **Tax incidence**, the identification of who ultimately bears the burden of a tax, is currently an active area of economic research and is also a key part of the controversy surrounding the introduction of the GST.

When a tax is imposed on a firm, do its owners bear the burden of the tax, or do they pass it on to its consumers in the form of higher prices? To see why this is a difficult question to answer, consider two examples.

Do Landlords or Tenants Pay the Property Tax?

Landlords characteristically protest that the crushing burden of property taxes makes it impossible for them to earn a reasonable living from renting buildings to tenants, who as often as not abuse the property. Tenants are likely to reply that landlords typically shirk their responsibilities for building maintenance and that the whole burden of the tax is passed on to the tenants in the form of higher rents. Both sides cannot be right in alleging that each bears the entire burden of the tax!

To examine the incidence, suppose that a city imposes a property tax. The thousands of landlords in the city decide to raise rents by the full amount of the tax. This scenario is shown graphically in Figure 24-3. There will be a decline in the quantity of rental accommodations demanded as a result of the price increase.

The decline in the quantity demanded without any change in the quantity supplied will cause a surplus of rental accommodations at the higher prices. Landlords will find it difficult to replace tenants who move out, and the typical unit will remain empty longer between tenancies. Prospective tenants will find alternative sites from which to choose and will become very particular about what they expect from landlords.

Some prospective tenants, seeing vacant apart-

FIGURE 24-3 The Incidence of a Tax on Rental Housing

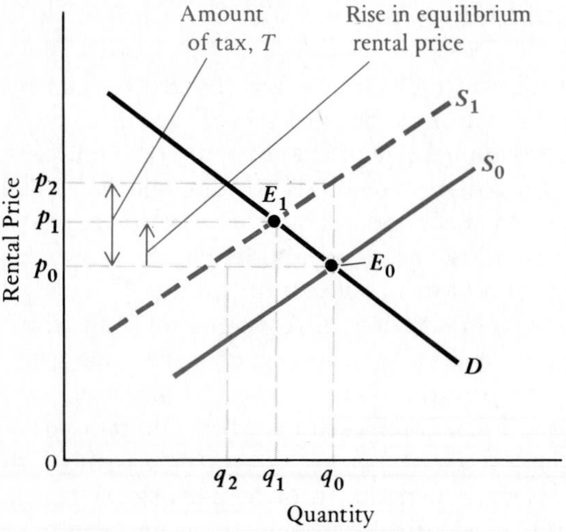

Since the equilibrium rent rises by less than the amount of the tax, landlords and tenants share the burden. The supply schedule S_0 reflects the landlords' willingness to supply rental housing at different levels of rents received. Before the tax, equilibrium is at E_0. When a tax of T is imposed on landlords, the supply curve shifts up by the full amount of the tax to S_1. Suppose that landlords attempt to raise rents by the full amount of the tax, from p_0 to p_2. There will be an excess supply of housing of q_2q_0 at p_2, and rents will fall. At the new equilibrium E_1, with rental price p_1, landlords have succeeded in raising the rental price by p_0p_1, less than p_0p_2, the full amount of the tax. Thus landlords are paying p_1p_2 of the total tax on each unit that is rented.

ments, will offer to pay rents below the asking rent. Some landlords will accept such offers rather than earn nothing from vacant premises. Once some landlords cut rents, others will have to follow suit or find their properties staying unrented for longer periods of time.

Eventually rentals will reach a new equilibrium at which the quantity demanded equals the quantity supplied. The equilibrium rental price will be higher than the original before-tax rent but lower than the rent that passes the entire tax on to the tenants.

The incidence of the property tax is shared by landlords and tenants.

Just how it is shared by the two groups will depend on the elasticity of the demand and supply curves.[7] These elasticities will in turn depend on how quickly landlords and tenants can react to changes.

Notice that the question of incidence is not answered by knowing who writes the cheque to pay the tax bill. In many European countries, the tenant rather than the landlord is sent the tax bill and pays the tax directly to the city; even in this case, however, the landlord bears part of the burden. As long as the existence of the tax reduces the quantity of rental accommodations demanded below what it would otherwise be, the tax will depress the amount received by landlords. In this way landlords will bear part of its burden.

Notice also that this result emerges whether landlords and tenants realize it or not. Because rents are changing for all sorts of other reasons, no one will have much idea of what equilibrium rentals would be in the absence of the tax. It does not do much good just to look at what happens immediately after tax rates are changed because, as we have already seen, landlords may begin by raising rents by the full amount of the tax. Although they think they have passed the tax on, this creates a disequilibrium. In equilibrium, prices will have risen by less than the full amount of the tax.

Do Profit Taxes Affect Prices?

Economic theory predicts that a percentage tax on *economic* profits will have no effect on price or output, and thus the full incidence of such a tax will fall on producers. To see this, suppose that one price-quantity combination gives the firm higher pretax profits than any other. If the government imposes a 20 percent profit tax, the firm will have only 80 percent as much profits after tax as it had before; this will be true for each possible level of output. The firm may grumble, but it will not be profitable for it to alter its price or its output.

Notice that this argument is independent of the tax rate. **[30]** It applies equally whether the tax rate is 10 percent or 75 percent.

[7] We suggest that you draw a series of diagrams with demand and supply curves of different slopes to see how this works. In each case, shift the supply curve up by the same vertical amount—to represent the property tax—and see what proportion of the increase is reflected in the new equilibrium price.

A tax on corporation income. Corporate income taxes are taxes on profits *as defined by the tax laws.* The definitions make them a tax on a combination of economic profits plus some of the return to the factors of production, capital, and risk taking. Because such a profit tax will reduce the returns to these important factors of production, it can have significant effects on the allocation of resources and hence cause some inefficiency.

Just who pays the corporate income tax is much less clear. The tax could be paid, in whole or in part, by owners of capital (which includes most people who have contributed to a private pension fund), by labor (if corporate taxes cause firms to pay lower wages), or by consumers (if prices rise). Research on the incidence of the corporate income tax continues, but no strong consensus has yet emerged.

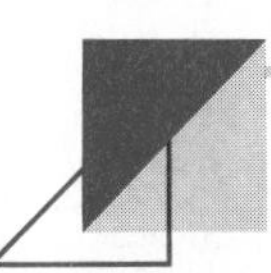

Public Expenditure

Public expenditure is large and growing. It affects both the distribution of income and the allocation of resources. In recent years, spending by the consolidated public sector—which includes federal, provincial, and municipal governments—has amounted to about 40 percent of Canadian national income. Table 24-4 gives the distribution of consolidated government spending across a number of major functions. As can be seen, health care, education, and social welfare are the largest items; collectively they make up about half the total. Defense, transportation and communication, and interest on the public debt add up to another 25 percent of the total. The remainder covers everything else, from police protection and sanitation to general administration of government and scientific research. About 40 percent of public expenditure is made by the federal government.

Types of Government Expenditures

In addition to classifying budget expenditures by function, as in Table 24-4, we may classify them by type of expenditure. This is done for the federal and provincial governments in Table 24-5. For each level of government, total expenditures are equal to the sum of program expenditures and debt service payments; program expenditures include purchases of goods and services and various transfer payments. Figure 24-4 shows the changing importance of different types of federal government program expenditures.

Provision of goods and services. As Table 24-5 indicates, over a quarter of combined federal and pro-

TABLE 24-4 Expenditures of All Governments by Function, 1989

Category	Expenditures (billions of dollars)	Percentage distribution	Average annual rate of growth 1979–1989 (percent)
Health	35.4	13	10
Social welfare	64.2	23	10
Education	36.7	12	8
Defense	10.5	4	9
Transportation and communication	13.1	5	4
Interest on the public debt	43.9	16	14
All other	76.2	27	9
Total	280.0	100	9

Source: Statistics Canada, 68–202.

Health, social services, and debt service charges were the fastest-growing categories of government expenditure in the 1980s. The table shows combined expenditures for federal, provincial, and municipal governments. The category "All other" includes sanitation and waste removal, natural resources, general government, police and fire protection, recreation, and cultural activities.

TABLE 24-5 Federal and Provincial Expenditures by Type, 1989

	Federal		Provincial	
Type	Expenditures (billions of dollars)	Percentage of total	Expenditures (billions of dollars)	Percentage of total
Purchases of goods and services	26.8	19	39.3	31
Transfers to persons	37.9	28	24.7	20
Interest on the public debt	37.3	27	16.9	13
Transfers to other levels of government	25.8	19	40.2	32
Other transfers	9.8	7	6.4	4
Total	137.6	100	127.5	100

Source: Statistics Canada, 13-001.

Purchases of goods and services constitute less than one-quarter of federal government expenditures and less than one-third of provincial government expenditures. The table shows total expenditures by type for each of the federal and provincial governments. Transfer payments constitute the majority of expenditures. For the federal government, transfers to persons plus interest on the debt account for about 55 percent of its total expenditures, while transfers to governments (mostly the provinces) account for another 20 percent. For the provinces, transfers to municipalities account for 32 percent of total expenditures (excluding hospitals).

vincial government spending was for the provision of goods and services. Such spending is the dominant type for provincial (and municipal) governments, as it was for the federal expenditure until 1971 (see Figure 24-4).

Among the goods and services provided by government are defense, transportation facilities, education, and municipal services. In these activities the government acts in much the same way as a firm acts, using factors of production to produce outputs. By and large these are outputs of collective consumption goods, goods with strong third-party effects, or services whose benefits are not marketable.

Public opinion polls show that the majority of Canadians support public provision of such services as basic education, hospital care, and medical care. Nonetheless, rising costs of such services are becoming a serious problem.

Transfer payments. Recall that transfer payments are defined as payments that do not arise out of the production or sale of goods and services. They include intergovernmental transfers, that is, transfers from one level of government to another, but by convention they do not include interest on the national debt. Some federal transfers are made to foreigners as part of foreign aid programs. Transfers are also made by provincial and municipal governments, often using funds they have received as transfers from the federal government. (Some transfer payments are private, such as private pensions and charitable contributions by individuals and corporations; these are not included in Table 24-5.)

Although federal government purchases of goods and services are large (almost $27 billion in 1989), they have remained roughly constant in real terms since the early 1960s. They have been overtaken by transfer payments as the largest form of federal government expenditure.

Transfer payments have been steadily increasing in importance, and this has led to significant effects on both the distribution of income and the allocation of resources.

Fiscal Federalism

Under the British North American Act, Canada was established as a federal state with governing powers divided between the central authority and the 10 provinces. Municipalities provide a third level of government whose powers are determined by the provincial legislatures.

A number of economic considerations bear on the distribution of functions among governments. Since revenue sources do not always match revenue

FIGURE 24-4 The Changing Form of Major Federal Expenditures, 1950–1989

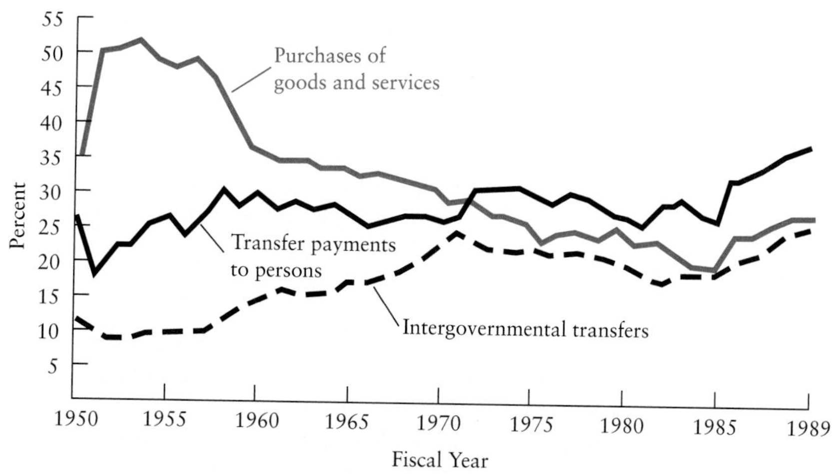

Transfer payments to persons and to provincial and municipal governments have been growing steadily in importance. In 1951 half of all federal expenditures were for purchases of goods and services. By 1980 the fraction was less than one-fourth. Transfer payments to persons in Canada and to provincial and municipal governments have increased from less than 30 percent to more than half the total. The three categories of expenditure graphed account for about 70 percent of total federal expenditures. The largest item not shown on the graph is net interest paid by the government.

needs at each level, a large volume of *intergovernmental transfers* is required, as shown in Table 24-5. They allow the various functions to be distributed among governments in a manner not dictated by revenue sources.

The Intergovernmental Division of Activities

Our discussion in Chapter 22 of reasons for government intervention suggested a number of principles that ideally should determine the distribution of activities among levels of government.

Geographic extent of externalities. Because the government of a province or a municipality is unlikely to be responsive to the needs of citizens outside its jurisdiction, public services that involve geographic spillovers may not be provided adequately unless responsibility for them is delegated to a higher level of government. For example, national defense is normally delegated to the central government for this reason. Control of pollution is another obvious case, since contamination of air and water often literally spills over provincial and municipal boundaries. In Canada the third-party effects involved in both examples are not even confined within national boundaries, as evidenced by ongoing negotiations with the United States over control of acid rain.

At the other extreme is fire protection. If fire protection is to be effective, it is necessary that there be fire stations serving fairly small geographic areas. Accordingly, responsibility for fire stations lies with municipal governments. A national fire station, with an enormous building and thousands of firefighters working at one location, makes very little sense.

Regional differences in preferences. The delegation of some functions to lower levels of government may provide a political process that is more responsive to regional differences in preferences for public versus private goods. Some people may prefer to live in communities with higher-quality schools and police protection, and they may be prepared to pay the higher taxes required. Another important issue at the local level is the extent to which industry should be attracted in order to broaden the property tax base; individual valuations of the social costs in terms of aesthetic or environmental effects are bound to differ, and different local governments will develop different policies in this regard.

At the provincial level, the distinct aspirations of French Canada are a primary consideration in the distribution of functions between Ottawa and the provinces. Indeed, dissatisfaction with the present arrangements, not only in Quebec but also in other provinces, has been a major political problem in Canada throughout its history, and the failure of the

Meech Lake Accord in July 1990 was expected to create the potential for a dramatic devolution of powers to the provinces.

Redistribution of income. An important activity of government is the redistribution of income by taxing the relatively well off and channeling the funds to citizens in need by means of transfer payments. Clearly, the federal government must concern itself with this issue, unless per capita income happens to be the same in all regions. This is of course not the case in Canada, and alleviating regional disparities is a major concern of the federal government. At the same time, provincial governments also actively pursue redistributive policies within their jurisdictions.

Administrative efficiency. Administrative efficiency demands that duplication of the services provided at different levels of government be minimized and that related programs be coordinated. On the revenue side, it is desirable that a particular tax be collected by only one level of government. This consideration has led to the negotiation of federal-provincial tax agreements that provide for efficient collection and revenue sharing. One concern that a number of commentators have expressed about the federal government's GST initiative is that by expanding its role in the sales tax field, it will be contributing to a decline in the degree of tax harmonization that Canada enjoys. Many of the GST's strongest opponents argue that the federal government will be contributing to a "tax jungle."

Intergovernmental Transfers

In addition to the federal government and the 10 provincial governments, there are two territories, more than 4,000 municipalities, and thousands of townships in Canada. Moreover, a large number of overlapping counties or districts are responsible for such local authorities as school boards. Each of these governmental units spends public money, and each must get the money in order to spend it. Not all units have access to revenue that matches the division of responsibilities; this creates a need for intergovernmental financial flows.

A second reason for intergovernmental transfers arises from the spillover effects of activities, both public and private, from one region or locality to others. If, for example, most local roads in one municipality get about 20 percent of their use from people who live outside that municipality, a provincial government grant that pays the municipality 20 percent of its road expenditures will internalize the spillover. The analysis, shown in Figure 24-5, is the same as the analysis of externalities presented in Chapters 22 and 23. In this case, however, the preferred policy is a subsidy rather than a tax because the spillover (externality) is a beneficial one. The 20 percent subsidy reduces the marginal cost of building roads and will cause local governments to build more roads.

Another reason for intergovernmental transfers results from the use of the federal government's *spending power.* For example, Section 36 of the Constitution Act (1982) stipulates that the federal government share responsibility with the provinces for the pursuit of interpersonal equity. Since many of the policy instruments for addressing equity (e.g., health and education) are the responsibility of the provinces, the only way the federal government can fulfill its responsibility is to collect sufficient taxes and then transfer them to the provinces on the condition that provincial spending in the designated areas satisfy national objectives.

The transfer of funds from higher to lower levels of government has been an important aspect of the Canadian federal system since confederation. Transfers are also the focus of much of the continuing controversies surrounding federal-provincial relations.

The scope and nature of intergovernmental grants has changed dramatically in the postwar period. Federal transfers to provincial governments expanded from $200 million in 1950 to over $25 billion in 1989, a more than 126-fold increase. This represented an increase from 6.8 percent to 22 percent of federal revenues; for the provincial governments, federal transfers as a share of their revenues increased, on average, from 20 percent to over 35 percent. For some provinces, federal transfers now represent more than half their total revenues. The transfers occur under four basic programs: revenue sharing, equalization payments, conditional grants, and established programs financing (EPF). Whereas the revenue-sharing and equalization payments transfers are intended largely for income distribution, the conditional grants and EPF have perhaps their main impact on resource allocation. Federal payments for 1989

FIGURE 24-5 Benefit Spillovers and Intergovernmental Transfers

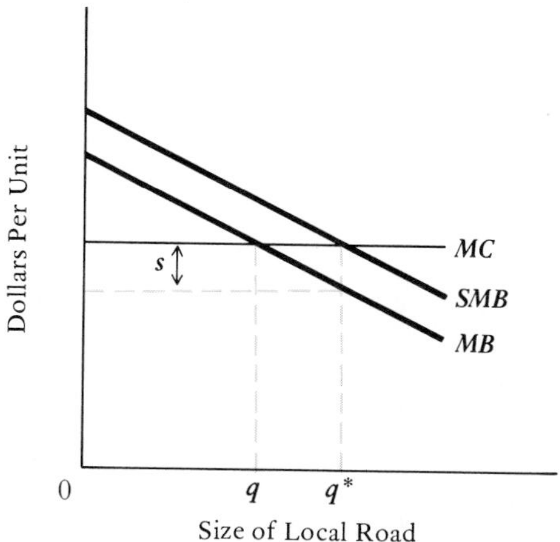

Intergovernmental transfers can internalize benefit spillovers. The figure depicts a local government's demand and cost of adding to the size of a road. The *MB* curve shows the marginal benefit to the residents of the locality. *MC* is the marginal cost of making the road larger. Left to its own devices, the municipal government will choose a road of size q, where marginal benefit equals marginal cost. This neglects the *SMB* curve, which adds the demands of *nonresident* users of the road to that of local users, yielding the social marginal benefit. If the provincial government offers a subsidy of s per unit of road built, the local government will choose q^*, where marginal benefit equals the marginal cost it faces, $MC - s$. If s is chosen optimally by the provincial government, this will be the size of road at which social marginal benefit equals social marginal cost.

TABLE 24-6 Estimated Federal Payments to Provinces and Municipalities, Fiscal 1988–1989

Category	Payments (millions of dollars)
Unconditional payments	
Revenue equalization	7,289
Other	1,362
Total	8,651
Conditional grants (established programs)	
Hospital insurance	5,407
Medicare	1,270
Postsecondary education	2,227
Total	8,904
Conditional grants (other)	
Canada Assistance Plan	4,583
Municipal grants in lieu of taxes	842
Other health and welfare	149
Total	5,574
Total payments	23,129

Source: The National Finances, 1989.

Unconditional grants comprise the fastest-growing category of federal payments to provinces and municipalities. The table shows the transfers of revenue from the federal government other than those arising from income tax abatements. Equalization payments make up the bulk of the unconditional grants and are made to the lower-income provinces.

under the variety of transfers are shown in Table 24-6.

Revenue sharing. Under the terms of the Constitution, the federal government may levy any tax it likes, but the provinces are restricted to *direct taxes.* This has been interpreted rather broadly by the courts to mean that the provinces may levy personal and corporate income taxes, property taxes, and taxes on retail sales.

Since the 1940s, most provinces have entered into **tax-rental arrangements** whereby the federal government collected income taxes and made a per capita payment to the provinces for that right. In 1990, with the exception of the Quebec personal income tax and the Ontario and Quebec corporate levies, all income taxes in Canada were collected by the federal government.

Federal income tax rates are set at levels that allow substantial "tax room" to the provinces. Outside Quebec, the provincial income tax is calculated as a percentage of the federal tax payable at rates determined by the individual provinces. A similar arrangement applies to the corporate income tax.

Equalization payments. To ensure that citizens in all regions of the country have access to a reasonable level of public services, **equalization payments** are made out of federal government general revenues to provinces with below average tax capacity. It is important to note that this is not a revenue-sharing program (provinces with above average tax capacity do not pay in), nor is it a conditional grant program. These grants are calculated by a complicated formula that involves, at last count, 29 revenue sources.

Equalization payments are a relatively new phenomenon in Canada, but they have exhibited rapid growth. From their inception with the 1957 Tax-sharing Act to the time of the 1977 Fiscal Arrangements Act, they expanded from $130 million to $2.2 billion. Equalization payments for 1989 are shown in Table 24-6.

Conditional grants. Conditional grants are transfers made to the provinces to enable them to provide services in a specified area at some minimum national standard. These shared-cost programs have long been a central part of federal-provincial fiscal arrangements. Their increasing number and extent were a source of considerable friction between the provinces and the federal government during the early 1970s. Participation was optional, but a province that declined to participate in a particular scheme forfeited the revenues that would otherwise have been transferred to it. This led to considerable dispute over constitutional issues and to the development of complicated schemes for compensating provinces that opt out. These programs thus became a focal point in the protracted debate over the constitutional division of powers in Canada.

A major concern to the federal government was the open-ended nature of its commitments to shared-cost programs that were controlled by the provincial governments. The provinces complained that they had initiated projects on the basis of federal sharing of the costs—often referred to disparagingly as "50-cent federal dollars"—and then faced the threat of withdrawal of federal support.

Under the Fiscal Arrangement Act of 1977, the system of relating federal contributions to provincial expenditures was discontinued in favor of a system under which federal contributions rise each year in accordance with the overall growth in the economy. The contributions are administered under a program that will be discussed shortly. The major remaining conditional grants relate to regional development programs; the projected breakdown of conditional grants for fiscal year 1988–1989 is given in Table 24-6.

Established programs financing (EPF). The 1977 Fiscal Arrangements Act placed on a new basis federal financing of three major programs previously treated as conditional grants: hospital insurance, medicare, and postsecondary education. They are referred to as established programs to indicate that their existence is not conditional on federal involvement. That federal contributions are independent of the costs of the programs reestablishes federal control over its own contribution. The provinces have gained, for they need not now be confined by narrowly defined federal program conditions.

Prospects for Federal-Provincial Fiscal Relations

The rapid growth in federal transfers to the provinces is part of a trend toward decentralization of activities and responsibilities away from the federal government toward the provinces over the past quarter century. It has been reinforced by the transfer to the provinces of claims on tax revenues and spending responsibilities. A number of commentators have argued that this trend risks potential conflict with the federal government's increased responsibility under the Constitution Act of 1982 to pursue equity as a national objective. This potential for conflict means that federal-provincial fiscal relations will remain in the policy limelight for the next few years; two major events in 1990 promised to complicate negotiations further.

First, in February, the federal government brought down a budget that hit hard at the financial positions of the provinces: It froze EPF payments to the provinces for two years and capped their growth in subsequent years; it capped payments to British Columbia, Alberta, and Ontario for the Canada Assistance Plan (CAP); and it reiterated the federal government's commitment to a goods and services tax, thus encroaching on the province's sales tax territory. In June the British Columbia Supreme Court ruled that the CAP initiative was unconstitutional, although this ruling was being appealed. Many provincial officials and other commentators argued that the combined effects of the reduced transfers and the increased federal competition in the sales tax area would create reactions from the provinces that would lead to disruption and loss of harmonization of federal-provincial fiscal relations.

Second, the process of constitutional renewal, in particular the failure of the Meech Lake Accord, created enormous uncertainty about the future political structure in Canada and about federal spending power. The Meech Lake Accord represented an agreement whereby provinces could opt out of federal programs but still receive the federal transfer provided that they mounted programs of their own that "satisfied the national objectives." However, the accord failed to be ratified, and a new round of arduous negotiations over federal-provincial fiscal relations appears inevitable.

Public Expenditure and the Distribution of Income

As Table 24-1 indicates, the federal government raises most of its revenues by income-related taxes. When these federal receipts are transferred back to individuals or to provincial and municipal governments, they have a substantial redistributive effect.

Federal Transfer Payments to Individuals

In 1970 a federal government white paper on income security classified transfers to individuals according to four types: demogrants, guaranteed income, social insurance, and social assistance. Old age security and family allowance payments are in the first group, guaranteed income supplements and child tax credits are examples of the second, the Canada Pension Plan and unemployment insurance are examples of the third, and the fourth includes special programs for widows, single parents, and others who have no recourse to other support programs.

Transfers to individuals by the federal government have grown as a proportion of expenditures from about 15 percent in 1930 to about 28 percent by the early 1990s. These transfers are often intended as a form of insurance or as an incentive for individuals to redirect expenditures toward specific items such as housing or health. Many of them are part of income maintenance programs. The net effect of the transfers is to reduce inequality in the distribution of income.[8]

There are several reasons for the growth of transfer payments. First, both the number of people eligible for them and the amounts they receive have increased. For example, there has been a general liberalization of the eligibility requirements for unemployment insurance benefits. Second, persistent unemployment during the 1970s and early 1980s greatly increased unemployment compensation payments.

Though some transfer payments go to people with above average incomes, most do not. Transfer payments have thus tended to reduce the inequality of the distribution of income.

The percentage of all personal income received in the form of government transfer payments has increased sharply, from about 9 percent in 1965 to more than 12 percent in 1989.

The Overall Redistributive Effects of Public Expenditures

Since the tax system tends to be roughly proportional in its effect, the overall progressivity of government policies depends on the progressivity of government expenditures. The large and growing role of transfer payments to the poor and of federal-provincial transfers probably assured that from the mid 1950s until 1990 there was some net redistribution of income from high- and middle-income groups to the poor. But such redistribution was never large.

Changes in the degree of income inequality from decade to decade have been small.

Why does government expenditure not have a bigger effect on income distribution? One view is that government programs overall are less progressive than observers once thought because progressive programs are offset by regressive ones. Another view is that market forces exert steady pressure toward more inequality, which government programs merely offset.

To help understand the second view—that one must run hard just to stay even with inequality—imagine that the government today created complete equality in wealth and income. Inevitably, market forces would produce inequality by next year, as some people and firms did well because they worked hard and long, were lucky, or invested wisely, while others did poorly or failed because they took it easy, were unlucky, or squandered their resources on a binge.

Most economists agree that there is a limit to how much inequality can be eliminated. There is

[8] The relative importance of the federal government in making transfers to individuals has been declining since the early 1960s, and that of the provinces has been increasing. We shall discuss the related issue of growth in intergovernmental transfers shortly.

controversy as to how close we are to that limit. And beyond that there is controversy as to how close it is desirable to get to "as much equality as possible," both on ethical grounds of justice and economic grounds of incentives.

Public Expenditure and the Allocation of Resources

Governments in Canada spent over $66 billion in 1989 to provide goods and services. In these activities, government units act like firms, using factors of production to produce outputs. Governments produce some commodities rather than leave production to the free market because Canadians—acting through their municipal councils, provincial legislatures, and the federal parliament—have expressed a desire for government provision in response to the sources of dissatisfaction with market outcomes discussed in Chapter 22.

Whether the government should be attempting to influence the allocation of resources directly is usually a subject of debate when a major new or expanded program is proposed. A central debate of the 1970s, concerning the role of government in providing medical care to the population, is discussed in more detail in Box 25-5 in the next chapter.

By and large, the government produces collective consumption goods, goods with strong externalities, or services whose benefits are not marketable. Governments make both current consumption and investment expenditures, and thus they directly influence the economy's accumulation of capital.[9] In so doing, governments are plainly changing the allocation of resources.

Changes in the Relative Shares of Government Expenditure

Total government expenditures on goods and services increased almost 75-fold over the period 1950–1990, indicating a near doubling in the ratio of government expenditures to total goods and services produced in the economy, from 22 to over 40 percent. In the period since 1960, increases in expenditures have been largest in such areas of provincial and municipal responsibility as health and education. As a result, the federal share of total government expenditures has been falling and that of provincial and municipal governments has been rising. For example, the ratio of federal to provincial government spending on goods and services was about 1.7 in 1950; it has fallen steadily ever since, so that by the late 1980s it was about 0.7, less than half the 1950 value. An even more dramatic picture of the increased decentralization that has occurred is seen by looking at the revenue side: The tax revenue of the federal government is now about equal to that of the provincial governments; in 1950 it was triple!

Several reasons for the changing distribution of government size can be mentioned.

Rising demand for local government services. One of the reasons provincial and municipal government expenditures have been rising more rapidly than their residents' incomes is the high income elasticity of demand for city services. As societies become wealthier, their residents want more parks, more police protection, more and better schools and universities, and more generous treatment of their less fortunate neighbors. This alone, combined with the limited tax sources available, would create budgetary problems for provincial and local governments in a period of rising incomes and rising expectations. Taxpayers increasingly want the social services that governments provide, but they do not always want to pay the taxes required to meet the cost. Elected officials arouse the people's wrath when they fail to provide wanted programs, but they sometimes do the same when they provide the services and then raise taxes.

Rising relative cost of municipal government services. Government services tend to use much labor of a kind whose productivity (output per hour of work) has increased much less rapidly than its cost, and thus cost per unit of output has risen. While average output per hour of work in manufacturing has risen about 50 percent in a decade, the size of the beat covered by a police officer, the number of students taught by each schoolteacher, the number of families that can be effectively handled by a social worker, or the number of temperatures that can be taken by one hospital nurse have not risen in proportion. Because wage levels tend to rise with national average productivity, the unit costs of services in sectors with

[9] Tax expenditures are an important force in this regard. One major tax expenditure is the program of Registered Retirement Savings Plans, which allows some personal savings as a tax-deductible expense, thereby encouraging saving in the private sector.

low productivity growth have risen; such a rise in relative prices tends, other things being constant, to lead to a decline in the quantity demanded, and hence one might expect to have seen a decline in the number of government employees. However, the increased demand for government services due to rising national income has been strong enough to offset this effect, and employment has not fallen significantly at any level of government despite the rising cost of labor. (As discussed in Box 25-5, similar forces have driven up the costs of health care, which falls under provincial jurisdiction.)

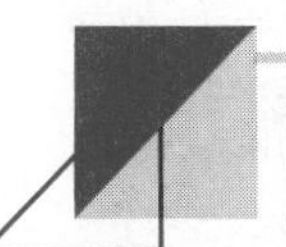

Evaluating the Role of Government

Almost everyone would agree that the government has some role to play in the economy because of the many sources of possible market failure. Yet there is no consensus that the present level and role of government intervention is about right.

One aspect of the contemporary debate about the efficient level of government intervention was discussed at the end of Chapter 22. There we asked when and to what degree government is justified in attempting to modify private market behavior—say, by affecting the way a paper mill discharges its wastes. Other issues arise when government provides goods and services that the private sector does not and will not provide.

Do Benefits of Public Programs Exceed Costs?

As discussed at the end of Chapter 23, governments use benefit-cost analysis to analyze various spending programs. For some government programs, such as flood control, there are well-defined benefits and costs, and it is relatively easy to decide whether the project is beneficial.

However, consider the evaluation of a program such as the great American space adventure of the 1960s—placing a man on the moon before the end of the decade. The budgetary costs were easily defined. At its peak in 1966, the program absorbed (in 1989 U.S. dollars) about $20 billion per year. Unmistakably, the project succeeded; it met its stated objective. But was the "giant step for mankind" worth the billions it cost? The benefits certainly included the psychological lift the moon walks gave the American people and the substantial advances in technology and knowledge that the space program spawned. The opportunity costs are the things that the expenditure replaced.

What Is the Correct Balance Between Private and Public Sectors?

When the government raises money by taxation and spends it on an activity, it increases the spending of the public sector and decreases that of the private sector. Since the public sector and the private sector spend on different things, the government is changing the allocation of resources. Is that good or bad? How do we know if the country has the right balance between the public and private sectors? Should there be more schools and fewer houses or more houses and fewer schools?

Because automobiles and houses are sold on the market, consumer demand has a significant influence on the relative prices and quantities produced of these commodities and thus on the allocation of the nation's resources. This is true for all goods that are produced and sold on the market. But no market provides relative prices for private houses versus schools; thus the choice between allowing money to be spent in the private sector and allowing it to be spent for public goods is a matter to be decided by Parliament and other legislative bodies.

John Kenneth Galbraith's best-seller *The Affluent Society* proclaimed the "liberal" message that a correct assignment of marginal utilities would show them to be higher for an extra dollar's worth of expenditure on parks, clean water, and education than for an extra dollar's worth of expenditure on television sets and deodorants. In this view, the political process often fails to translate preferences for public goods into effective action; thus more resources are devoted to the private sector and fewer to the public sector than would be the case if the political mechanism were as effective as the market.

The alternative, "conservative" view has many supporters who agree with Professor James Buchanan that society already has gone beyond the point where the value of the marginal dollar spent by government is greater than the value of that dollar left in the hands of households or firms that would have spent it had it not been taxed away. The conservatives argue that because bureaucrats are spending other people's money, they don't care very much about a few million or billion dollars here or there. They have only a weak sense of the opportunity cost of public expenditure and thus tend to spend beyond the point where marginal benefits equal marginal costs.

One of the most difficult problems for the student of the Canadian economic system is to maintain perspective about the scope of government activity in the market economy. There are literally tens of thousands of laws, regulations, and policies that affect firms and households. Many people believe that significant additional deregulation would be possible and beneficial.

But private decision makers still have an enormous amount of discretion about what they do and how they do it. One pitfall is to become so impressed (or obsessed) with the many ways in which government activity impinges on the individual that one fails to see that these only make changes—sometimes large, but often small—in market signals in a system that basically leaves individuals free to make their own decisions. It is in the private sector that most individuals choose their occupations, earn their living, spend their incomes, and live their lives. In this sector too, firms are formed, choose products, live, grow, and sometimes die.

A different pitfall is to fail to see that some (perhaps most) of the amounts paid by the private sector to the government as taxes also buy goods and services that add to the welfare of individuals. By and large, the public sector complements the private sector, doing things the private sector would leave undone or do very differently. To recognize this is not to deny that there is often waste, and sometimes worse, in public expenditure policy. Nor does it imply that whatever is is just what people want. Social policies and social judgments evolve and change.

A related pitfall is to believe that the government's alleged inability to improve efficiency also implies an inability to improve equity. Throughout the world, governments are placing more reliance on markets in order to improve economic efficiency and prospects for growth. Accepting the market for efficiency reasons does not, however, mean accepting an increase in the hardships borne by the poor. Promoting social justice through government interventions directed at equity is quite compatible with promoting efficiency, provided that appropriate means are carefully chosen.

Yet another pitfall is failing to recognize that the public and private sectors compete in the sense that both make claims on the resources of the economy. Government activities are not without opportunity costs, except in those rare circumstances in which they use resources that have no alternative use.

Public policies in operation at any time are not the result of a single master plan that specifies precisely where and how the public sector shall seek to complement or interfere with the workings of the market mechanism. Rather, as individual problems arise, governments attempt to meet them by passing ameliorative legislation. These laws stay on the books, and some become obsolete and unenforceable. This is true of systems of law in general.

Many anomalies exist in our economic policies; for example, laws designed to support the incomes of small farmers have created some agricultural millionaires, and commissions created to ensure competition often end up creating and protecting monopolies. Neither individual policies nor whole programs are above criticism.

In a society that elects its policymakers at regular intervals, however, the majority view on the amount and type of government interference that is desirable will have some considerable influence on the interference that actually occurs. This has become a major political issue. Fundamentally, a free market system is retained because it is valued for its lack of coercion and its ability to do much of the allocating of society's resources. But we are not mesmerized by it; we feel free to intervene in pursuit of a better world in which to live. We also recognize, however, that sometimes intervention has proved ineffective or even counterproductive.

SUMMARY

1. Two of the most powerful tools of microeconomic policy are taxation and public expenditure.
2. Although the main purpose of the tax system is to raise revenue, tax policy is potentially a powerful device for income redistribution

because the progressivity of different kinds of taxes varies greatly. Personal income tax rates have traditionally been highly progressive, but their effect on progressivity is reduced by other provisions of the tax law. Sales and excise taxes are likely to be regressive.

3. Tax expenditures are provisions in the tax law that provide favorable tax treatment for certain economic behavior. They are called tax expenditures because their effects could usually be achieved by appropriating money on the spending side of the budget instead of by reducing revenues on the tax side. Tax expenditures in the income tax reduce the progressivity of the tax system.
4. Any tax system involves using a variety of types of taxes. Evaluating the tax system involves evaluating the efficiency and progressivity of the entire system; for a given amount of revenue to be raised, these can be altered by changing the mix of the various taxes used. The total Canadian tax structure is roughly proportional, except for very low income groups (for whom it is mildly progressive). The 1987 tax reforms increased progressivity at low income levels but reduced it at high income levels.
5. Evaluating the effects of taxes on resource allocation requires first determining tax incidence, that is, determining who really pays the taxes. For most taxes, the incidence is shared. Excise taxes, for example, affect prices and are thus partly passed on and partly absorbed by producers. The actual incidence depends on such considerations as demand and supply elasticities.
6. A large part of public expenditure is for the provision of goods and services. Other types of expenditures, including subsidies, transfer payments to individuals, and intergovernmental transfers, are all rising sharply. The four major types of federal-provincial transfers are revenue sharing, equalization payments, conditional grants, and established program financing.
7. The major redistributive activities of the federal government take the form of direct transfer payments to individuals and to provincial and municipal governments for economic welfare payments and regional adjustments. Although the public sector has a tendency to redistribute some income from high- and middle-income groups to the poor, the change in income inequality from decade to decade has been relatively small.
8. Government expenditure of all kinds has a major effect on the allocation of resources. The government determines how much of our total output is devoted to national defense, education, and highways. It is also influential in areas where private provision of goods and services is common; health care is a notable example.
9. Intergovernmental transfers are a key form of public expenditure policy; they lead to a different allocation of resources than would occur without them. The need for such transfers is dramatically revealed by regional differences in Canada.
10. Evaluating public expenditures involves reaching decisions about the absolute merit of government programs (do benefits exceed costs?) and about the relative merit of public and private expenditures.
11. The Canadian economy is a mixed economy and a changing one. Each generation faces anew the choice of which activities to leave to the unfettered market and which to encourage or discourage through public policy.

TOPICS FOR REVIEW

Tax expenditures
Progressive, proportional, and regressive taxes
Vertical and horizontal equity
Tax incidence
Transfer payments to individuals
Intergovernmental transfers
Choosing between private and public expenditures

DISCUSSION QUESTIONS

1. The Canadian taxpayer faces dozens of different taxes with different incidences, different progressivities, and different methods of collection. Discuss the case for and against a single taxing authority that would share the revenue with all levels of government.
2. Consider a change in the tax law that lowers every taxpayer's marginal tax rate, with the maximum rate dropping from 50 percent to 33 percent, but with an increase in the tax base that leaves total tax revenue unchanged.
   a. Is it possible that everyone's average tax *rate* will fall?
   b. Is it possible that everyone's tax *bill* will fall?
   c. Suppose that contributions to universities and colleges are tax-deductible under the original tax law but not under the revised one. Would you predict that such contributions would increase, decrease, or remain the same?
   d. If such contributions are fully deductible under both the original and revised tax laws, would the amount of such contributions be expected to increase, decrease, or remain the same?
   e. Consider now taxpayers whose marginal tax rate falls from 50 percent to 33 percent *and* whose tax bills are less after the revision. Repeat the question in *d*.
3. How might each of the following affect the incidence of a real estate property tax imposed on central-city rental property?
   a. The residents of the community are largely blacks who face racial discrimination in neighboring areas.
   b. The city installs a good, cheap rapid transit system that makes commuting to the suburbs less expensive and more comfortable.
   c. Rent control is imposed; no rent presently being charged may be increased.
4. In reaction to Finance Minister Michael Wilson's 1987 proposal to convert the basic personal exemption and some deductions to tax credits, the *Toronto Star* ran a column, under the sensational headline "Sneaking Some Socialism Through the Back Door," that argued that the proposed changes would "replace measures which allow the rich to shield their income with provisions that raise the income level of the poor." How would the measures proposed accomplish this?
5. In Canada each individual has a lifetime $100,000 exemption for capital gains income, and subsequent capital gains are taxed at three-quarters the rates applicable to other income. Who benefits from this provision? What are its effects on the distribution of income and the allocation of resources?
6. "Taxes on tobacco and alcohol are nearly perfect taxes. They raise lots of revenue and discourage smoking and drinking." In this statement, to what extent are the two effects inconsistent? How is the incidence of an excise tax related to the extent to which it discourages use of the product?

7. The benefit principle is often used to justify excise taxes on particular commodities when their use depends on the availability of government-provided services or facilities. In such cases the tax provides a means of placing the burden of financing expenditures on those who benefit from them. Can you think of any examples where this principle applies? Can it be used to justify the use of property taxes as a major source of revenue by municipal governments?
8. *a.* Suppose that it is agreed to spend $1 billion in programs to provide the poor with housing, better clothing, more food, and better health services. Argue the case for and against assistance of this kind rather than giving the money to the poor to spend as they think best.
   b. Should federal transfers to the provinces be conditional grants or grants with no strings attached? Is this the same issue raised in *a*, or is it a different one?
9. Develop the case for and against having the federal government (rather than provincial and municipal governments) provide each of the following:
   a. Police protection
   b. Teachers' salaries
   c. Highways
   d. Welfare payments to the poor
10. Medical and health costs were 4.5 percent of GDP in 1950 and over 11 percent in 1990. Is 11 percent necessarily too much? Is it necessarily a sign that we are providing better health care? How might an economist think about what is the right percentage of GDP to devote to medical care?

Chapter 25

Social Policy

Controversies over Canada's social programs have been major news items in recent years. Canadian governments have been urged to reexamine and redesign these programs with the twin objectives of improving the benefits delivered to the intended beneficiaries and reducing costs wherever possible. The relevant concept of cost is *social cost,* encountered in Chapter 22, which is broader than just the direct cost of financing the programs.

Some social policy critics argue that the "social safety net" must be expanded to deliver more benefits to less advantaged citizens. Others express concern that existing social programs are already too expensive and ask if the country can afford such generous social programs—programs that absorb almost 60 percent of government program (i.e., noninterest) expenditures. Given the concern over the $30 billion federal budget deficit, it is natural that such a large and important category of spending should come under scrutiny.

Assessing program effectiveness and evaluating proposals for reform of Canada's social policies are not simple matters. One-line evaluations, such as "Nothing needs to be changed" or "The whole system needs to be swept away," are too simplistic but all too common. In this chapter we review some of the issues in the debate over Canada's social programs, showing the need for a careful approach to reforming it.

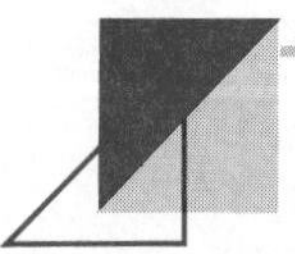

Canada's Social Programs in Perspective

Spending by all levels of government on social programs has grown as a share of national income from just over 20 percent in 1950 to about 45 percent in 1990. In addition, in keeping with the trends noted in Chapter 24, there has been a steady increase in the relative importance of spending by the provincial governments; their spending has roughly tripled as a share of national income, growing from just over 5 percent in 1950 to about 15 percent in 1990.

The Variety of Social Programs

Some social programs are *universal,* in the sense that they pay benefits to anyone meeting only such minimal requirements as age or residence. These are called **demogrants**. Other programs are selective, in the sense that they pay benefits only to people

TABLE 25-1 Federal Spending on Social Programs in 1990–1991 (*estimated in billions of dollars*)

	Direct spending	Tax expenditures[a]	Total
Child benefits	2.7	1.7	4.4
Elderly benefits	17.0	−0.5	16.5
Income security			
Unemployment insurance	12.7	−2.0	10.7
Canada Assistance Plan	4.8	—	4.8
Registered savings plans[b]	—	6.5	6.5
Human resources	5.0	3.0	8.0
Health care	7.0	5.5	12.5
Totals	49.2	14.2	63.4

Sources: Treasury Board and Department of Finance.

[a] Includes federal component only. The provinces also collect revenues on such programs as family allowance, old age security, and unemployment insurance and contribute tax revenues forgone for others, including child and elderly tax credits and registered savings plans.

[b] Registered Retirement Savings Plans and registered pension plans.

Of the more than $63 billion spent on social programs by the federal government in 1990–1991, nearly 80 percent came from direct spending and 20 percent was delivered through the tax system. Child and elderly benefits, each of which include both demogrant and income-tested components, accounted for over $20 billion of the total. Three key programs—unemployment insurance, the Canada Assistance Plan (provincially administered welfare programs), and registered savings plans—accounted for about $22 billion. Human resource development—including contributions to postsecondary education and to labor market schemes—amounted to about $8 billion, and transfers to the provinces for health care accounted for more than $12 billion.

who qualify by meeting specific conditions. These conditions are usually related to income, in which case the term **income-tested** (or *income-related*) **benefits** is used. Some benefits are taxable, so net after-tax receipts decline as income rises; others are not taxable, so net receipts are independent of income. Some are expenditure programs (including direct transfers to persons), while others are delivered through the tax system in the form of special tax concessions called *tax expenditures*. Some programs are administered by the federal government, some by the provincial governments, and still others by the municipalities.

Table 25-1 gives a breakdown of the more than $63 billion spent by the federal government on all social programs in 1990–1991. The table shows both the division of the $63 billion total into direct spending and tax expenditures as well as the allocation of federal spending across six main categories of social programs.

Fiscal, Economic, and Demographic Setting

Figure 25-1 shows projections of social spending under alternative assumptions about future economic and demographic trends. After falling in the short term, social spending is projected to climb as a proportion of GDP after 2010 and, according to the pessimistic scenario, eventually takes a larger proportion of GDP than in 1980.

Three major challenges must be met by any Canadian social spending policy that is to succeed in these future decades. These are the challenges posed by government deficits, technological changes, and demographic trends.[1]

[1] We have adopted this trilogy, and much of the discussion, from T. J. Courchene, *Social Policy in the 1990s: Agenda for Reform* (Toronto: C. D. Howe Institute, 1987). An update appears in Courchene's chapter on social policy in *Getting It Right* (Toronto: C. D. Howe Institute, 1990).

FIGURE 25-1 Two Projections for Social Spending

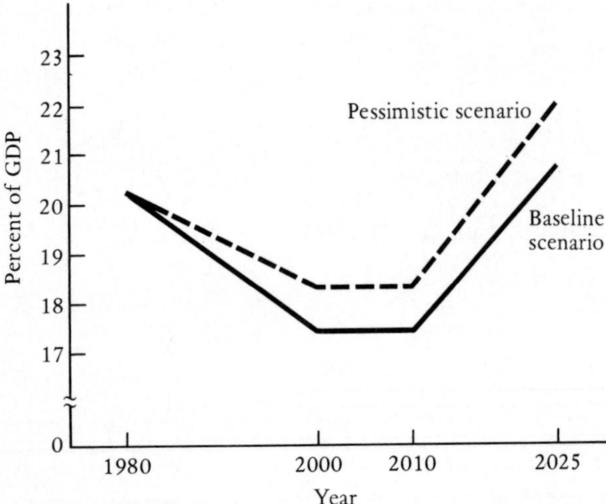

Social spending is expected to fall, stay stable, and then rise as a percentage of GDP over the next 30 years. The pessimistic scenario assumes a slower rate of economic growth and a more rapidly aging population. In both cases the percentage of GDP devoted to social spending falls until 2000, remains steady until 2010, then rises until the end of the projection period in 2025. According to the pessimistic scenario, the proportion of GDP absorbed by social spending is higher at the end of the projection period than it is today; according to the baseline scenario, the proportion is about the same. *Source: Long-Term Trends in Social Expenditures in the Group of Seven Major Industrialized Countries* (Washington, D.C.: International Monetary Fund, 1985).

The fiscal challenge. The fiscal challenge to social programs is a serious one. With the federal deficit running at about $30 billion in 1990, and with $50 billion, or 48 percent of total federal program expenditures, being spent each year on social programs and another $14 billion annually in tax expenditures, it is inevitable that social programs be reviewed carefully.

Fiscal constraints are also severe at the provincial level. Health care expenditures alone account for over 30 percent of total provincial expenditures and are rising. In 1990, fully 8 of the 10 provinces, some economically depressed and some booming, were running budget deficits.

Anyone who would leave social spending untouched while still seeking to reduce the deficit substantially must look to tax increases. However, many critics hold that taxes are already too high in Canada relative to those in our major trading partners (especially the United States) and that it would be hard for Canada to increase tax rates significantly without creating pressures on firms and higher-income individuals to move to the United States.

The need to reduce budget deficits and the desire to avoid tax increases create pressure to reform social policy to meet its objectives at lower cost.

The adjustment challenge. Many recent studies of the Canadian economy, including those done by the Macdonald Royal Commission, have stressed the fierce competition and the rapid change that characterize the international trading world.

To improve or even maintain living standards in a competitive and changing world, countries need to adjust continuously to changing market conditions.

This is especially true for small countries such as Canada that are heavily dependent on international trade. As Courchene puts it:

> The challenge to social policy is twofold: first, to ensure that the incentives within the social policy network will encourage, rather than inhibit, the required adjustment on the economic front; second, to ensure that the social safety net evolves in a manner that reflects the changing needs of citizens as they adapt to the new economic order.

For example, if the economic system requires that people change jobs more frequently than in the past, it is important that pensions be fully portable (that is, that workers be able to take their pension rights with them when they change jobs).

The demographic challenge. Important demographic developments that are already under way imply that social policies designed for the 1960s will not always be well suited to the needs of the 1990s and subsequent decades. Consider just a few of these developments:

An increasingly aging population is putting stresses on the health system. Expenditure on health care is large and growing; demographic trends suggest that this growth will continue, and possibly even accelerate, unless changes are made in the current system.

The increasingly aging population will also put stress on the pension system. Although the federal government is currently taking in more in pension contributions than it is paying out as benefits, the situation will reverse before the end of the century, after which time the excess of benefits paid over contributions received will grow steadily.

A rise in single-parent families, particularly those with women at their head, is causing an increase in the number of working poor whose needs are different from those of the unemployed or the unemployable poor.

The rise in two-worker households brings a demand for expanded day-care facilities.

Many workers are finding that after 20 or 30 years of working in the same job, their skills become obsolete. Retraining facilities and organized assistance in finding new jobs are needed if such workers are to remain gainfully employed. Otherwise, they face a decade or more of unemployment before they reach normal retirement age.

The Federal-Provincial Perspective

Canada's constitution originally granted all authority in social policy to the provinces. As social policy became increasingly important, agreements between the two levels of government gave the federal government responsibility for a large amount of social spending. In some cases this involves direct federal spending, as with the old age security and family allowance programs, and in other cases it involves transferring funds to the provincial governments. (The latter were discussed in Chapter 24.) Some federal payments to provinces are then distributed directly to persons; this is the case with the federal government's Canada Assistance Plan, which is used by the provinces to finance their own welfare programs. Other payments, such as those related to health and postsecondary education, are used by the provinces to finance various expenditures.

Although we focus on federal programs in most of this chapter, a number of reasons why the provinces are important players in determining the cost and effectiveness of Canadian social policy warrant mention.

First, as we have already observed, a large amount of federal spending is in the form of transfer payments to the provinces. Though some transfer payments are nominally earmarked for specific purposes (in particular, postsecondary education and health), the provinces are not required to match changes in their spending in these areas to changes in federal transfers received. In recent years growth in provincial spending in these areas has often been less than the growth in transfers from the federal government. Hence to analyze the efficacy of social programs in these areas, it is not sufficient to focus only on federal transfers. Further, since each province allocates over 60 percent of its spending to social policy, any dramatic change in provincial spending would also represent a significant change in total national spending.

Second, Canada's regional pressures play a major role in shaping federal-provincial fiscal relations. Equalization payments, discussed in Chapter 24, are relevant here. Although they are not considered part of federal social spending, they are a transfer to the provinces whose explicit purpose is to compensate for any shortfall in the fiscal capacity of the relatively poorer provinces to provide a minimum level of government services, primarily social services.

Finally, since the multitude of federal and provincial social programs overlap in their effects, any program change made by one level of government will have one effect if it is offset by the other level and another effect if it is not offset. For example, when in its May 1985 budget the federal government enriched the child tax credit to increase the after-tax income of very poor families with children, a number of provinces reacted by cutting back on their welfare programs. In those provinces, benefits delivered to the poor were not changed in aggregate, but the burden of financing those benefits was shifted to the federal government, and the distribution of benefits was shifted from families without children to those with children.

Experiences such as this illustrate an important point:

Effective reform of Canadian social policy requires changes that are coordinated and sweeping, not piecemeal. The inherent difficulties of such coordination are aggravated by the never easy and often stormy nature of federal-provincial relations in Canada.

The International Perspective

Recently two major international organizations, the International Monetary Fund in Washington and the

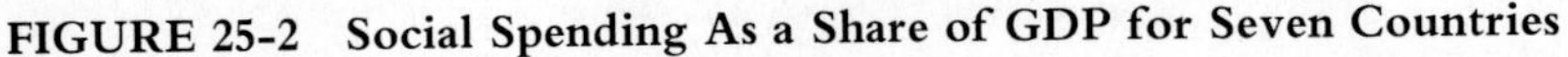

FIGURE 25-2 Social Spending As a Share of GDP for Seven Countries

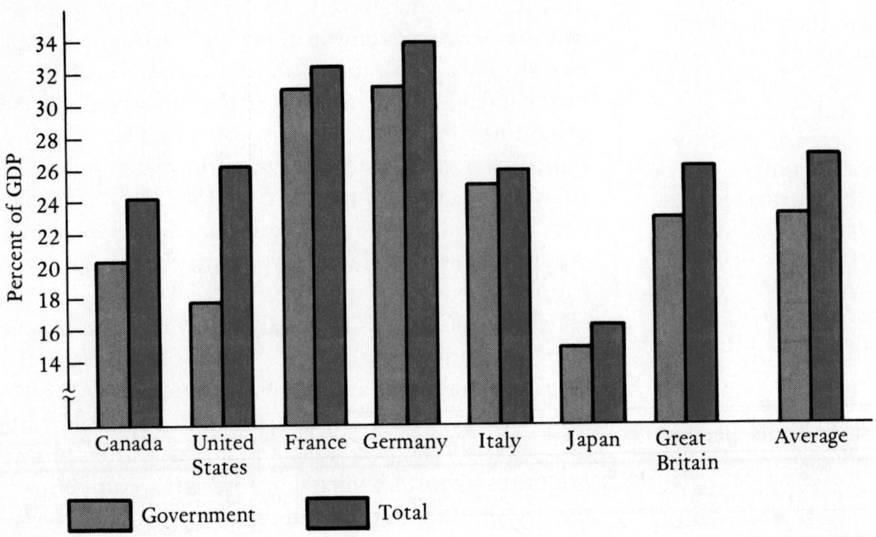

Canada devotes a comparatively low proportion of its GDP to social spending. The figure shows the percentage of GDP accounted for by both government and total (government plus private) social spending for the seven largest industrial countries. Included are spending on medical care, education, welfare payments, public pension plans, and unemployment insurance; excluded are direct housing expenditures and tax expenditures. In government expenditures Canada is lower than all countries except the United States and Japan; in total expenditure Canada is lower than all except Japan. (Note that in the United States, a great deal of expenditure on health care occurs in the private sector.) *Source: Long-Term Trends in Social Expenditures in the Group of Seven Major Industrialized Countries* (Washington, D.C.: International Monetary Fund, 1985).

Organization for Economic Cooperation and Development in Paris, have published studies comparing spending on social programs for a number of countries. Figure 25-2 presents data from the IMF study. Although the data are for 1980, the latest year available on an internationally consistent basis, they are still useful because changes in these percentages occur quite slowly over the years. Both studies show that Canada is below the average of industrialized nations in terms of the share of national income devoted to social spending.

These international comparisons help put the most extreme calls for drastic cuts in Canada's social policies into perspective. However, differences in circumstances among the countries studied—including differences in the age distribution of the population,[2] income levels, and the role of tax expenditures (not included in the data)—make comparisons based on numbers such as those in the table difficult and potentially misleading.

[2] For example, Canadian governments spend 3.5 percent of GDP on pension payments to retired people, whereas France spends 8.0 percent and Germany 8.7 percent.

Issues in Assessing Social Programs

The complex array of Canadian social programs raises a number of issues that must be addressed before their impact can be analyzed or proposals for their reform assessed.

Policy Interactions

The various programs interact to such an extent that the effects of any one cannot be judged in isolation.

For a meaningful analysis of the current state of any social program and proposed changes in it,

the program must be viewed in the context of the overall system.

Interactions between schemes are important not only at the federal-provincial level but also within one level of government. For example, the unemployment insurance program clearly interacts with federal job creation and job training programs as well as with other social programs designed to direct resources to needy families and regions.

Policy Objectives

Given the wide array of programs, each directed at a narrow goal but each interacting with other programs, policy objectives must be clearly understood if policies are to be evaluated intelligently.

Policy evaluation usually involves trade-offs among objectives.

The need for normative judgments. A primary objective of most social policies is to redistribute income away from people least in need toward those most in need. Evaluating need requires making value judgments, which are expressed in the political rather than the economic arena. Economists can, of course, play a role in measuring the distribution of income (as discussed in Chapter 24) and in measuring need once criteria have been established.

Vertical and horizontal equity. As noted in Chapter 24, *vertical equity* concerns equity across income classes and *horizontal equity* concerns equity within a given income class. One example concerns the appropriate treatment of children in the tax system: Two families with the same income but different numbers of children are usually treated differently on the grounds of horizontal equity. This is taken up in more detail later in this chapter.

Distribution versus efficiency. A major issue in the design of social policy is the potential conflict between achieving some desired distribution of income and ensuring that the economy operates efficiently so as to produce the maximum possible total income.

When a person who receives income-tested benefits earns enough income to have the benefits reduced, there is an implicit tax-back rate on that income because the person's disposable income increases by less than the newly earned income. For example, consider a person earning no income and receiving income-tested benefits of $8,000 who takes a part-time job paying $2,000. If, as a result, her income-tested benefits are reduced by $1,000, her implicit tax rate is 50 percent. If a second person in the same situation has his income-tested benefits reduced by $2,000, he faces an implicit tax rate of 100 percent.

When people pay income taxes and also receive income-tested social benefits, the explicit income tax rate on their income and the implicit tax-back rate on their benefits are said to be *stacked,* and the combined rate is called the **effective marginal tax rate**. For example, if a person earns an extra dollar and pays 25 cents in income tax while having her benefits reduced by 30 cents, her effective marginal tax rate is 55 percent.

Because of the high tax-back rates that apply to many income-tested benefits, many beneficiaries face very high effective marginal tax rates, even 100 percent or greater! It should come as no surprise that beneficiaries may reject the opportunity to work when their net income would be no more, or even *less,* than their net income when they choose not to work but receive full benefits. The stacking and disincentive problems associated with a number of Canada's existing social programs are discussed further in Box 25-1.

Some of the most serious efficiency effects of the tax and transfer system follow from its creation of high effective marginal tax rates that discourage beneficiaries from actions that would improve the performance of the economy and increase their own self-reliance.

In a background study for the Quebec White Paper of 1984, Bernard Fortin and Henri-Paul Rousseau of Laval University estimated that the average *efficiency cost* of Quebec's tax and transfer system was 27 cents per dollar. This means that, on average, for every dollar of tax revenue raised by the government, 27 cents is lost due to efficiency costs associated with the distortion of incentives by the tax system. More important, they estimate that the marginal *social cost* of the tax and transfer system was 56 cents. This means that for each additional dollar raised from a proportional increase in Quebec taxes, the private sector lost $1.56 in income. Even though the generosity of Quebec's social programs means that their estimates probably overstate the case for Canada as a whole, they nevertheless make it clear

BOX 25-1

Stacking and Disincentives

A study prepared for the Quebec government in 1984 presented some explicit calculations of the effective marginal tax rate for beneficiaries of major Quebec social programs. These provide striking evidence of the extent of the stacking problem and the disincentives that it creates.

Consider the case of a single man between 30 and 64 years of age with no employment income during the course of the year. (All calculations are based on the tax and transfer programs as they existed in 1983.) He would have received $4,932 in social assistance (including a refundable property tax credit). Suppose that he had the opportunity to work full-time at the then prevailing minimum wage rate of $4 per hour, thus earning $8,000 in employment income (a full working year is about 2,000 hours). Although this $8,000 is by no means a princely sum, it would appear to represent a significant increase in income.

Of course, his employment income would be taxable, but only at the relatively low tax rate that applies at the low end of the income scale. As a result of working and earning this modest income, however, he would no longer qualify for some of the social assistance that he had been receiving. On some forms of social assistance that he would be receiving, benefits are reduced by a dollar for every dollar of income earned, making the implicit tax rate 100 percent. Other benefits, including the refundable tax credit, would be substantially reduced even if not eliminated altogether. Under the provisions of the Quebec tax and transfer system, the individual's disposable income would have risen by only $2,560 as a result of working for the whole year. Because of the stacking of the implicit tax rates on the social benefits with the explicit income tax rate, this individual had an effective marginal tax rate of 68 percent, higher than the highest marginal income tax rate for the country's wealthiest people!

Now consider the situation of an unemployed couple with two young children. They receive more total assistance, because each parent qualifies for some of the programs, and the family receives additional assistance for the children. However, if either parent were to return to work, there are more benefits to be taxed back, and hence their effective marginal tax rate is even higher than that for the single person. The Quebec study calculated the effective marginal tax rate in this case to be 79 percent: Of every dollar earned from work, 79 cents will go in taxes or benefit reductions!

These are realistic cases that represent the situation for many thousands of Canadians. It is not difficult to think of situations—perhaps less common but certainly not rare—where the effective tax rate is even higher, much higher. A single mother of two on welfare, living in subsidized housing and sending her children to subsidized day care, could, if she wanted to improve her lot in life, go to a technical school for 18 months and train as a word processor. She could then earn considerably more than the minimum wage. She would, however, then face an effective marginal income tax rate of

---

that the social costs of Canada's social programs are far from trivial. This is reinforced when we note that the study did not include the direct costs of raising tax revenues, enforcing tax laws, or distributing social benefits.

The social costs arising from disincentives in the tax and transfer system hurt everyone in the economy, including the people that the social programs are designed to help.

Open-economy considerations. In a small open economy such as Canada's, a further efficiency issue relates to the international mobility of labor and capital. The issue can be seen by considering a more extreme case that applied for many years in the

over 150 percent! No wonder when people fall into poverty they find it hard to escape. In our efforts to help such people, we have designed a system that severely penalizes them if they try to become more self-reliant by substituting earned income for social assistance payments.

It is not just people of working age who are affected by these disincentives. The elderly poor who receive the guaranteed income supplement (GIS) also face a marginal tax rate that is higher than that faced by the very rich. In their case benefits are reduced by 50 cents for every dollar of income earned. When combined with a positive rate of income tax, the overall effective rate of tax is well over 50 percent. This means, for example, that elderly single persons who earned $7,000 of private pension income cound face a marginal effective tax rate of over 70 cents on the dollar. Furthermore, this figure does not take account of provincial top-ups that are usually reduced when income rises and could combine with the factors already discussed to make the effective tax rate over 100 percent.

One might think that this is not much of a problem because work disincentives are not likely to have much effect on the nonworking elderly. However, since income from capital is included in taxable income, there are strong disincentives to work and save in the preretirement years, because any accumulated savings will just reduce postretirement social benefits.

The tax and transfer system has been built up over the years in a piecemeal fashion; the resulting lack of integration is the major source of the stacking problem. Each program has its own threshold level at which benefits start to get taxed back; benefits from other programs are often included in that threshold level, and each has its own tax-back rate, which is then stacked on the other tax-back rates and on the explicit income tax rate. Effective reform of the system means more than reform of the individual programs; reforms must be integrated and rationalized so as to eliminate many of the undesirable and avoidable interactions.

The Quebec White Paper of 1984 proposed the principle that anyone who receives transfers should not pay any income tax and that anyone who paid income tax should not receive any transfers. This dramatic change from the system now in force would amount to a negative income tax system as discussed in Chapter 24. The Newfoundland Royal Commission on Unemployment reported in 1986 that despite the huge income transfers that the social security system was generating—particularly in the form of unemployment insurance payments—the disincentive effects of the system were destroying the economic viability (one could almost hear them saying the moral fiber) of the province. In saying so in spite of the enormous financial advantage to Newfoundland of the existing system, it must go down as one of the most remarkably honest documents of the decade.

United Kingdom. In the 1960s and 1970s, marginal rates of income tax, running over 80 percent, encouraged a brain drain of successful people leaving the United Kingdom for lower-tax countries such as the United States. (Many entertainers, including the Beatles, were among the emigrants.) If these high-income earners had remained at home under a regime of, say, 40 to 45 percent maximum income tax rates, then for any given level of tax-financed spending, lower-income persons would have to pay less taxes than if the high-income earners had emigrated.

Similar considerations apply to capital. Is it better to have capital in one's own country paying 30 or 40 percent income tax or abroad in order to avoid an 80 percent domestic tax rate and thus paying no domestic taxes? Egalitarianism may argue for the high rates, but the loss of revenue and other benefits from the location of industry at home must be set against this perceived gain in equity.

If Canada lets its rates of taxes and benefits get seriously out of line with those in the United States, it risks suffering a significant brain and capital drain to that country. Thus there are always substantial "harmonization pressures" between Canadian and American policies.

Of course, Canadian policies need not be identical to those in the United States, but if they get out of line in a way that labor and capital regard as undesirable, there is a risk of inducing an emigration of factors that will do harm to the Canadian economy.

Security versus adjustment. In addition to redistributing income, a goal of social policies is usually the provision of economic security, a kind of safety net in the form of social "insurance" to cushion economic shocks. Indeed, some commentators argue that this motivation has been more important than income distribution in the historical development of Canadian social policies and that this explains the importance of universality in the Canadian debate.

We have already discussed the importance of adjustment to the Canadian economy. It is possible to cushion people against shocks without inhibiting adjustment; retraining and relocation grants are examples. It is also possible to cushion them in ways that inhibit adjustment; shoring up declining industries and providing government jobs for declining occupations are examples.

Many people accept that in today's fiercely competitive world, assistance should be provided to those most hurt by economic shocks and that it should encourage rather than inhibit adaptation.

It is not always easy to stick to this general principle. Many specific, politically motivated interventions that were designed to increase security have reduced adaptability. It is important that such antiadjustment assistance mechanisms not be built into the statutory part of the social system.

Intergenerational issues. Many aspects of social policy are targeted at retired persons. Many of today's retired started their working lives during the Great Depression of the early 1930s, a time when there were few pensions and when saving was difficult, given the low incomes then prevailing. Thus today's elderly tend on average to be low-income persons, and transfers from younger to older citizens seem appropriate.

Of course, many of those who were poor when young will remain poor when they are old, but many of tomorrow's elderly will not be in this category. In light of the high incomes that were earned during the last half of the twentieth century and the generous pension plans that have been established, the outlook is that many of tomorrow's elderly will be well off. Furthermore, the population is slowly aging, and in the early part of the twenty-first century the proportion of the population that is elderly will be much higher than it is today. These considerations suggest the following conclusion:

On grounds of equity and fiscal capacity, help for the elderly and the retired should be more focused on lower-income groups than it is at present.

We return to this issue later in the chapter.

Universality

Controversy has raged over the universality of Canada's social policies. Supporters feel that many of the programs should be available to all Canadians regardless of their incomes or other circumstances. This is the concept of universality. Critics argue that programs should be made more selective, targeted toward people in real need, as the best way of preserving the high standard of the Canadian system at an affordable cost.

The universality principle arouses great passions. Indeed, preserving this characteristic of the Canadian social policy system was described in the 1980s by Prime Minister Mulroney as a "sacred trust." However, the issue of universality is not so clear-cut as the prime minister's comments may have suggested.

Because the benefits paid by most universal programs are taxable, their net after-tax yield depends on the income of the recipient. Hence gross payments may be universal, but net benefits are not.

In the words of Queen's University political scientist Keith Banting: "There really are no universal programs in Canada. So the debate over universality, as conducted in this country, has all the marks of a red herring which, of course, is the best possible subject for political controversy."[3]

As Banting points out, the early Canadian system was modeled on the British system of local relief, which was a means-tested system of delivering relief to people in real, often desperate need. The 1930s showed this system to be inadequate in dealing with the major economic disaster of the Great Depression. Benefits were provided, when they were provided at all, on a grudging and demeaning basis. In the 1940s the flight from selectivity was confirmed. At first this involved more humane but still means-tested forms of relief. Later, however, the system involved the establishment of universal programs for selected groups, such as the elderly or the unemployed, or for specific purposes, such as health insurance.

As well as dealing with the inadequacies of the system of delivering relief to the needy in the 1930s, the idea of universality came to be accepted as the best way of providing security. In the 1940s the Marsh report put it this way: "The general sense of security which would result from such programs would provide a better life for the great mass of people and a potent antidote to the fears and worries and uncertainties of the times." Generalizing from the experience of the 1930s, economic risks were assumed to be felt by everyone. The need was for mass and guaranteed protection, rather than for conditional systems that produced benefits at the whim of the granting body. What was required was a *right* to social security for every citizen.

Universality was also thought to provide better protection from tampering than selective systems. It was thought that if everyone benefited, there would be a powerful constituency to protect the system should any future politician try to dismantle it. A selective system targeted at the poor would be much more vulnerable to such an attack, since the poor have a weaker political voice than the middle class. As the designer of much of the original American social security system, President Franklin Roosevelt, put it: "We put those payroll contributions there so as to give the contributors a legal, moral, and political right to collect their pensions and unemployment benefits. With those taxes in there, no damn politician can ever scrap my social security program." The importance of this consideration can be seen in the ease with which President Ronald Reagan dismantled much of the American antipoverty program—a program directed solely at the poor. Little complaint was heard at the curtailment of food stamps and other income-tested measures, a change that allowed the number of people living in poverty to double in the United States in less than a decade. The contrast with the outcry when Reagan tried to tamper even slightly with the universal old age pension scheme is striking.

These reasons for universality suggest that this aspect is not likely to be dropped from many of Canada's social welfare schemes. Greater targeting and cost effectiveness are likely to be obtained, however, by ensuring that more of the benefits are taxable, by making greater use of tax credits instead of tax deductions, and by a fuller integration of the tax and transfer system so as to avoid stacking and associated disincentives.

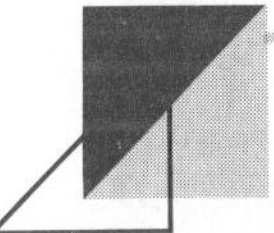

An Assessment of Selected Programs

Now we shall look in some detail at the various elements of Canada's existing social programs and at some suggestions for reform.

Human Resource Development Programs

A survey published by the Canadian Labour Market and Productivity Centre in January 1990 showed that Canadian business and labor leaders regard the top priority for improving Canada's international competitiveness as training and education. This was ranked above all other factors, including lower interest rates, lower government deficit, and increased spending on research and development. Queen's University economist Thomas Courchene adds that education and skills development are also key to understanding economic inequality *within* Canada.

Public education, one of the earliest types of so-

[3] "Universality and the Development of the Welfare State," in A. Green and N. Olewiler, *Report of the Policy Forum on Universality and Social Policies in the 1980s* (Kingston, Ont.: John Deutsch Institute for the Study of Public Policy, 1985). Our discussion relies heavily on Banting's excellent treatment of the universality issue.

cial expenditure in Canada, remains one of the most important. It has been supplemented over the years by numerous other programs aimed at developing human resources.

Basic Education

Primary and secondary schools teach literacy and numeracy—the skills that are needed before further marketable skills can be acquired. Studies show that many Canadian adults (some estimates say as many as one-quarter) are functional illiterates—people who cannot comprehend simple written instructions well enough to carry them out. One educational target should be to reduce illiteracy and innumeracy, deficiencies that are lifetime handicaps.

Basic education is supplemented by further education and training. This occurs in postsecondary institutions, technical schools, and universities, as well as in the workplace. In 1990 the federal government operated about a dozen nonuniversity job creation and training schemes, enrolling nearly half a million people and costing nearly $2 billion. Although few doubt that these schemes are of great value, the critics have noted many deficiencies in the programs and recommended major changes.

Postsecondary Education

Postsecondary education is a provincial responsibility in Canada. As a result of tax-sharing arrangements discussed in Chapter 24, the federal government makes large grants to the provinces—amounting to nearly $2.2 billion in 1990—which are nominally geared to financing the necessary expenditures. However, in 1990 five provinces were spending less money on their universities than the federal high-education grants that they received.

In Canada all universities are public institutions, and university education is heavily subsidized by government, with student fees accounting for only about 15 percent of total costs. Two arguments can be advanced for subsidizing higher education; one is an efficiency argument, and one is redistributional. First, there are externalities for the whole country from higher education. In many cases these externalities cannot be internalized by the students receiving the education, so, left to their own maximizing decisions, students who had to pay the whole cost of their education would choose less than is socially optimal. Second, charging anything like the full cost would make education prohibitively expensive to low- and even middle-income families. Government subsidies help provide training according to ability rather than according to income.

Arguments to reduce the subsidy to higher education, and thus to finance a larger fraction of the costs of running universities from tuition fees, start with the observation that the value of many kinds of education can be internalized and recaptured in higher incomes earned by the recipients in their later life. This is particularly true of professional training in such fields as law, medicine, dentistry, higher education, and computer science. Yet students in these fields typically pay a smaller part of their real education costs than students in the arts, where the argument for externalities is greatest. Also, the subsidized education does represent a significant income transfer from taxpayers to students.

A major question about the subsidization of higher education is this: Does the transfer from lower-income, non-university-trained taxpayers to potentially higher-income-earning university students satisfy our ideas of equity?

People who worry about the equity issue in this context often argue for a system of student loans, whereby more of the cost of education would be recouped from the students themselves later in their lifetimes. People opposed to loans argue, among other things, that loans will discourage children in lower-income families from continuing on to higher education because, from the vantage point of their family's current low income, the liability to be taken on by the student will seem enormous. Some further issues are taken up in Box 25-2.

Job Creation Programs

People with few skills and little job experience often find themselves in a catch-22 situation:

Employers are reluctant to hire inexperienced persons, but the only way to gain experience is to be employed.

To address this problem, the federal government operates a number of job creation programs that attempt to provide the long-term unemployed and new labor market entrants with job experience and basic labor market skills. Job training plus mobility assistance can also encourage the regional movement of labor out of areas of high unemployment into areas with better employment opportunities.

People receiving unemployment insurance anywhere in Canada can enroll in job training programs, completing apprenticeship or journeyman requirements while still receiving unemployment insurance benefits. The federal government has recently announced that funds will be set aside for job creation for people on social assistance. The Quebec government is experimenting with a program that gives supplementary benefits to welfare recipients who voluntarily accept on-the-job training. These examples illustrate a major point on which many experts agree:

To reduce unemployment and raise the earning power of the labor force, job creation programs must be coordinated with both the unemployment insurance program and provincial welfare programs to produce a unified scheme that overcomes the serious disincentive effects of those programs.

Income Transfer and Security Programs

Income transfer and security programs provide assistance for people in financial need due to unemployment, injury, or inadequate wages. (The last group constitutes the working poor.) These programs—which comprise the so-called social safety net—include welfare, unemployment insurance, and family benefits. They make payments to approximately 9 million adult Canadians each year and cost the federal government about $20 billion.

As is evident from its variety of schemes, the income transfer and security system has many goals. One of the most important is to reduce poverty. Though nothing like the serious problem it was in Canada's past and still is in many other countries, poverty remains a matter of real concern to Canadian policymakers. Not the least cause for concern is that the majority of the poverty that can be eliminated by economic growth may have already been eliminated, meaning that much of the remaining poverty may represent the "hard core" that will persist no matter how wealthy the society becomes and can only be alleviated by active public policy. The problem of poverty is discussed in more detail in Box 25-3.

Unemployment Insurance (UI)

Unemployment insurance is the single most costly program administered by the federal government, accounting for almost $11 billion of payments in 1990. Originally instituted in 1940 as an insurance scheme against temporary bouts of unemployment, it was extended in scope and generosity by changes instituted in the 1970s; many of those changes have been the object of criticism, and further reforms designed to meet some of those criticisms were proposed in 1990.

Changes to UI in the 1970s. Critics argue that a number of changes to the UI system introduced in the 1970s caused it to depart from its original purpose of insuring against temporary bouts of involuntary unemployment.

Canada is one of the few countries that provide benefits to those who quit jobs voluntarily, and the incentive for abuse is obvious.

Benefits are provided after as little as 10 weeks of work each year, so the scheme has effectively become a subsidy for seasonal employment.

In an effort to help depressed regions, *extended regional benefits* were introduced, whereby individuals living in regions with high unemployment rates could qualify for extended benefits (for as much as 40 weeks) after working only a brief qualifying period (as short as 10 weeks). Researchers have shown that this discourages labor mobility, both toward occupations and toward places offering more stable employment prospects, and contributes to persistent high regional and national unemployment rates.

Proposals for reform of UI. In 1985 the Macdonald Royal Commission severely criticized the UI system and suggested many reforms. Subsequently, the federal government set up a commission of inquiry under Quebec economist Claude Forget to make further recommendations.

The main thrust of the reports by Macdonald and Forget was that the system had become overbur-

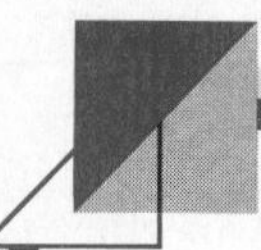

BOX 25-2

Financing Universities

By the start of the 1990s, many Canadian universities were in serious financial trouble. In Ontario, for example, government grants per student fell 25 percent in real terms over the 15-year period from 1972 to 1987. Tuition fees fell about 25 percent over the same period and covered only 15 percent of operating costs, half the fraction they covered at the start of the period.

This deterioration in financial position was being reflected in the quality of the education. Average class sizes and student-teacher ratios were rising. As a result, many students felt deprived of meaningful direct interaction with faculty and increasingly felt part of an impersonal factory system. Writing skills deteriorated as lengthy assignments became too time-intensive to grade; they were either returned with little or no comment or were replaced with short-answer tests that were easier to score. Laboratory equipment was out-of-date and poorly maintained, and as a result, the hands-on experience necessary in many of the sciences was given short shrift. Not only were instructional duties often poorly performed, but also research opportunities were increasingly unavailable to students.

University officials argued that these developments were the inevitable consequence of shrinking real budgets and rising enrollments. A number of initiatives were undertaken in response. Many universities turned to the private sector with capital campaigns, but they all recognized that in the Canadian context of exclusively public institutions, increased private support was only a small part of the solution. In Ontario, Queen's University Vice-Principal Rod Fraser mounted a "Blueprint for Action" that argued for substantial increases in tuition fees, to be phased in over a period of several years, matched by increased contributions from the provincial government. Despite active promotion, the blueprint failed to win the support of either provincial or national student organizations—both of whom maintain a policy in favor of zero tuition fees—although it did get support from student organizations in some Ontario universities.

At the beginning of the 1990s, prospects for future university financing looked rather dim. They looked even dimmer as a result of the 1990 federal budget, which cut back on transfers to the provinces, thus reducing the available funding for universities even more. Some observers saw a signal in that federal budget: If the provinces and especially the users (i.e., the students) don't pay more, the federal government was going to reduce funding. This again put tuition fee increases on the agenda, and many observers expected that substantial fee increases might well be introduced following the next round of provincial budgets. With this prospect, three other proposals began to attract attention, although all seemed far from finding their way into actual government policy.

dened by being used for too many, often conflicting objectives. It should, they argued, be returned to its prime objective of providing insurance against temporary bouts of involuntary unemployment, and other schemes should be used to achieve other objectives. Neither report advocated reform of UI in isolation; both saw UI reform as part of a larger package of reform, with any hardship introduced by making UI more effective strictly as an insurance program being alleviated by other measures to help people with very low incomes.

In the debate that followed the publication of the Forget report, many participants did not distinguish the positive observation that people respond rationally to incentives from the normative judgment that various responses might be deemed morally good or bad. UI gives incentives to remain in seasonal jobs and in areas with poor employment prospects and to take UI-financed holidays. Rational people respond by doing so, thus increasing the national unemployment rate. This does not mean that these individuals are immoral.

Discriminatory Tuition

As argued in the text, the case for subsidizing education is strongest for programs in which the student stands the least chance of capturing most of the social benefits as private income and is weakest in those in which the student might be expected to reap financial rewards commensurate with the social benefits. On this reasoning, fees in the professions (medicine, law, business) should be raised dramatically, but any increases for the liberal arts and humanities should be more modest. Under the current fee structure, a student with high enough grades and enough luck to gain admission to medical school has fallen heir to a large and relatively secure private income, the training for which is largely paid by the public purse.

Contingent Student Loans

A proposal motivated by the same concerns as discriminatory tuition is to raise fees and simultaneously offer student loans that are paid back on a basis contingent on the individual's postgraduation earnings. (The university, in its role as lender, might be viewed as holding equity in the graduate's performance rather than debt backed by the graduate's degree.) Doctors, lawyers, and accountants who go on to earn high postgraduate earnings will pay back much more than those trained in the arts and humanities who go on to perhaps very satisfying but nevertheless only moderately paid white-collar jobs. Those who profit the most from their training pay the most for it.

Vouchers

A third possibility is for universities to be free to charge whatever fees they wish and for the government to issue vouchers directly to students to pay some given amount of fees per year. Some proponents of this view would have the federal government bypass the provinces altogether and issue vouchers directly to students, while others would maintain the present system of federal-provincial transfers and then have the provinces issue the vouchers to students. In either case, universities would receive government support only by attracting students. As Thomas Courchene argues, the result would be a university system competing on both price and quality in response to student demand. Courchene also argues that vouchers would have the benefit of moving the enormous subsidy currently being given to university students into the open and thus would improve the chances for further reform that would enhance the social policy aspects of government financing of universities.

Saying that the UI system encourages behavior that increases unemployment and reduces regional mobility does *not* say that the unemployed themselves are responsible for the "abuses" of the system that lead to these results.

The responsibility lies with the people who designed the incentives and those who strive to preserve them. It is they who can alter the system to make it deliver the intended benefits with fewer incentives for undesired behavior. Some of the political problems involved in the potential reform of the UI system are discussed in Box 25-4.

The McDougall Proposals of 1990. In 1989, Barbara McDougall, minister of employment and immigration, tabled legislation that introduced a number of key changes to the UI system. Some of the changes were clearly in response to the criticisms we have noted. For example, rules for qualifying to receive benefits were tightened up, and extended coverage and additional assistance were provided for individ-

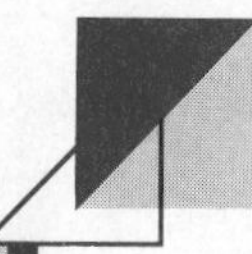

BOX 25-3

Poverty in Canada

What is poverty, and whom does it affect? One definition says that one lives in poverty if one is poorer than most of one's fellow citizens. Since there will always be a bottom 10 percent of any income distribution who are poorer than the remaining 90 percent, poverty in this sense will always be with us. If a completely relative definition is not very revealing, neither is an unchanging absolute definition. The living standards of Canadians regarded as poor would have looked more than adequate to Canadians of 100 years ago and would look princely to citizens of many countries even today.

To meet both of these concerns, economists define poverty as some given level of income, rather than just in relative terms, but they also recognize that as average living standards rise over time, so will our ideas of what constitutes poverty.

Statistics Canada defines the poverty level as the level of income at which a household spends on average more than 58.5 percent of its income on the three basic necessities of food, shelter, and clothing. In 1988, for a family of four, the Canadian poverty level in 1986 ranged from $17,303 in rural areas to $23,521 in the largest cities.

The levels of income just mentioned, low though they seem by our standards, are above the average level of income of all Canadians in 1890 and also above the income of three-quarters of the families in the world today. Neither of these comparisons, however, should lead you to underestimate the hardship of being poor in Canada today. Although $17,303 will buy enough food, shelter, and clothing for a family of four to get by, it does not provide enough money for the full range of commodities that most of us take for granted, such as having a refrigerator, a TV set that works, constant hot water, and an occasional night out at a movie. Many of the poor are understandably bitter and resentful that they and their children are outsiders looking in on the comfortable way of life

Incidence of Poverty Among Canadian Families by Selected Characteristics, 1988

Characteristics	Percentage of families falling below the poverty line
All families	12.3
Place of residence	
Metropolitan	13.7
Other urban	11.9
Rural	9.3
Region	
Atlantic	13.0
Quebec	16.2
Ontario	8.6
Prairies	13.2
British Columbia	12.1
Number of children under 16 years of age	
0	9.4
1 or 2	17.7
3 or more	19.4
Age of head of family	
Under 25	34.3
25–54	10.7
55–64	11.1
65 and over	13.4
Sex of head of family	
Male	8.9
Female	38.7
Employment status of head of family	
In labor force	7.6
Not in labor force	26.6

Source: Statistics Canada, 13-207.

shown in ads and on television. "I'd like, just once," one of the poor said to a magazine interviewer, "to buy Christmas presents the children want instead of presents they need."

Who Are the Poor?

According to the criterion just outlined, 12.3 percent of Canadian families and 34.3 percent of unattached individuals were living in poverty in 1986.

There are poor among all ages, races, and educational levels, employed as well as unemployed. Yet some groups have much higher incidences of poverty than others. For example, the table shows that you are more likely to be poor if you live in the Atlantic provinces, if you are a member of a large family, or if you are an unattached individual over 65 years of age.

Poverty is, however, by no means restricted to these groups. More than half the poor families live in urban areas, live in Ontario and the western provinces, have no more than one child, and are headed by persons of working age. Furthermore, about one-fourth of those in poverty work full-time (the so-called working poor), and over half work at least part-time. These facts help to dispose of two superficial caricatures: the slothful father who feigns a disability because he is too lazy to do an honest day's work and the family with so many children that an ordinary decent wage is spread so thin that the entire household is reduced to poverty. Individual households that come close to these extremes can be found, but most poor households do not.

The Historical Experience

Between 1969 and 1986 the proportion of Canadians living in poverty fell by 35 percent. In part this reflected a variety of government initiatives of the sort discussed in this chapter. But in large measure it resulted from the growth in average income, which has always been the greatest source of relief from poverty.

Today's Poverty: Causes and Cures

It would be a mistake, however, to expect growth to eliminate all poverty. The source of today's poverty problem is no longer low average income but particular groups who are left behind in the general rise in living standards caused by economic growth. It is little consolation—indeed, it must add to the gall—that they are poor in an increasingly affluent society.

There is no single answer to the question of what causes poverty in the midst of plenty. It is partly a result of mental and physical handicaps, partly of low motivation, partly of the raw deal that fate gives to some, partly the result of changing market conditions when industries and occupations can no longer prosper, partly a result of unwillingness or inability to invest in the kind of human capital that does pay off in the long run, and partly the result of the market's valuing the particular abilities an individual does have at such a low price that even in good health and with full-time employment, the income that can be earned leaves that person below the poverty line.

Just as there is no single reason for poverty, there is no single cure. Many of the social programs outlined in this chapter attempt to get at various causes. If poverty has fallen steadily in Canada, the two main reasons are economic growth and social programs that seek to provide assistance for those who cannot help themselves and to assist those who can to learn to do so.

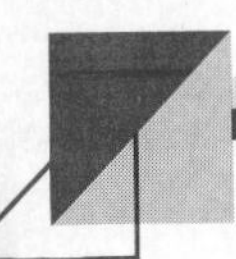

BOX 25-4

Social Policy Reform: A Case Study of Unemployment Insurance

Many economic policies, particularly those directed at redistributing income, concentrate significant benefits on a relatively small fraction of the population while spreading the costs across the entire population. As a result, the costs borne by any particular individual for any particular policy are trivial—though neither the total costs borne by all members of society of any given policy nor the total costs for all policies borne by each member of society are trivial.

Because the beneficiaries have a significant vested interest in maintaining the policies, they will protest strongly when any proposed change threatens to reduce their benefits. At the same time, each taxpayer will be relatively indifferent, since the personal implications of reform of any one program will be trivial. Hence, although the majority of the population may have a preference for reform, the vocal minority who opposes change will tend to dominate the political debate. Not surprisingly, politicians and public administrators are reluctant to change any such program (other than occasionally to enrich it).

This problem applies particularly to social policies, since the *raison d'être* of such policies is the redistribution of income. In Canada these issues are further complicated by regional economic disparities—the benefits from given programs are often highly concentrated in particular regions or provinces. Political sensitivities are particularly strong when the cries of protest are concentrated in particular regions. Those who would lose directly are often joined by other residents of the region who feel a particular personal interest in the program because of the benefits it brings to the regional economy. Also, provincial politicians have an interest in speaking out on behalf of the province when threatened by federal policies. Federal politicians will naturally be reluctant to reform policies in a manner that costs them support in entire regions or provinces.

These issues are vividly illustrated by recent Canadian attempts to reform unemployment insurance. No policy has been studied more frequently or more thoroughly. Though there is disagreement over the details of beneficial reforms, there is a

uals attending approved training courses. At the same time, other aspects of the proposed changes worked in the opposite direction of expanding coverage into areas some critics had argued were bettered handled outside of the UI program (for example, expanded parental and sickness benefits). As of mid 1990, this legislation had been passed by the House of Commons but, in a controversial political move, was being held up in the Senate.

Public Assistance Programs

Social assistance for individuals below retirement age, usually called welfare, is mainly a provincial and municipal responsibility in Canada. Under the Canada Assistance Plan (CAP), however, the federal government contributes half of the costs of eligible provincial social assistance programs. In 1990 the federal government's contribution under the CAP was about $5 billion, and the amount has been rising steadily over the years.

Although the existing welfare system is accepted as necessary by most Canadians, many observers believe that it could be substantially improved. Suggested reforms take two main forms. First, remove the disincentives to work implied by the present stacking of reductions in income-tested benefits and income taxes on earnings, as we have already discussed. Second, provide positive incentives to self-help by increasing benefits for recipients who accept work or training for work.

broad consensus on the general thrust of the necessary reform. Yet until 1990 UI survived virtually untouched; indeed, if anything, the disincentives and inefficiencies in the system got worse.

UI is now clearly much more than a labor market policy. It is a social program that involves huge transfers that are regionally focused. But even though UI does target benefits toward the poorest regions, it does not target benefits at all well toward the neediest within the region. It does nothing, for example, to help the poverty-stricken, destitute individuals and families who are unemployable and who have left the labor force. It is a generous subsidy to the "working poor," particularly those with seasonal jobs.

Because UI as currently constituted is a substantial regional transfer or subsidy program, politically acceptable reform must, in the first instance, maintain those transfers. Any attempt to cut the transfers would cause such a political storm that all hope of political acceptance would be lost. The solution is to maintain the transfers but to alter the incentives attached to them. Instead of creating anti-adjustment incentives to stay in the region or industry or skill group (causing what is called "transfer dependency"), incentives should be created that will reduce the need for the transfer. These include retraining and relocation allowances and other forms of adjustment assistance.

Not the least of the problems involved in such policy changes is that the incentives might, in many cases, greatly reduce the population of some region or even depopulate it altogether. This would pose obvious political difficulties, since it cuts to the very heart of Canadian political and economic issues. This perspective is borne out by the opposition that was mounted to the government's 1990 legislation to reform UI in a way that reduced transfers to seasonal workers in some of Canada's less well-off regions.

Child Benefits System

Benefits related to children cost the federal government about $4.4 billion in 1990. The Canadian tax system includes three elements in its child benefits system. The first is the family allowance scheme, which is a universal, or demogrant, scheme paid directly to beneficiaries. The second is a nonrefundable personal tax credit for each child for whom a taxpayer receives family allowance payments. The third is a refundable child tax credit, also delivered via the tax system.

Not only does the child benefits system influence vertical equity, but elements of it are also intended to improve horizontal equity in the tax system—that is, they recognize that a family with children has a lesser ability to pay taxes than a family with the same income but no children.

Family allowance (FA). Under the family allowance plan, a cheque is mailed monthly to mothers according to the number of children they have (and in Alberta and Quebec, according to the age structure of their children). The family allowance is taxable in the hands of the spouse with the higher income. The net cost of the system is about $2 billion, which is the total value of the cheques distributed less the income taxes collected by the federal government as a result of the increased disposable income of the recipients.

Some supporters of the scheme see as an advantage the fact that the cheque goes directly to the mother. In many households, mothers do not work outside the home and thus have no discretionary income of their own other than the monthly family allowance cheque.

The gross family allowance received is independent of income—it depends only on the number of children in the family. Thus the family allowance scheme is a universal program. Because families with the same levels of income receive more benefits the more children they have, the FA provides a large measure of horizontal equity. Further, because the family allowance is taxable, after-tax benefits decline with income; it thus contributes to progressivity.

The family allowance contributes to both the horizontal and the vertical equity of the tax and transfer system.

In the 1990 federal budget, the government introduced a special social benefits repayment (commonly referred to as a *clawback*) providing for the complete taxing back of family allowance payments (as well as unemployment insurance payments and old age security payments) at high levels of income. The clawback may increase equity and save well over $1 billion of net federal expenditures, but it has the inefficient aspect of paying out the funds with one hand and recovering them with the other.

Personal tax credit. In calculating nonrefundable personal tax credits to be netted against gross federal taxes (see Tables 24-2 and 24-3), taxpayers who receive family allowance payments qualify for a credit for dependent children. This credit was introduced in the tax reform of 1987, replacing a child tax exemption (CTE) that allowed a reduction in taxable income for each child. The value of the CTE benefit depended on both the number of children and the family's income. The higher the spouse's income, the higher the value of the exemption; thus the operation of the CTE was perceived to be regressive. The use of a tax credit preserves the horizontal equity feature of providing tax relief for families with children but eliminates the perception of regressivity.

The personal tax credit for dependent children serves the purpose of horizontal equity.

Refundable child tax credit (CTC). The third element of the child benefits package is the child tax credit. Like the personal credit, the CTC reduces one's tax bill by the amount of the credit; a given credit is thus of equal value to all people who qualify, regardless of their income. However, the CTC is refundable—if taxes are negative as a result of the credit, a refund is due; in some circumstances it can be paid in advance.

The child tax credit is an income-tested program designed to reduce the tax liabilities only of lower-income groups. It does not accrue automatically; it must be applied for. The entire credit can be received by low-income families; when family income reaches $25,000, the CTC starts to be phased out at a rate such that when family income reaches $45,000, the value of the CTC is zero.

The CTC provides a major source of vertical equity.

The phase-out of the child tax credit as the beneficiaries' taxable income rises means that the effective marginal tax rate is increased for families in the phase-out range—a classic stacking problem.

Day care. The great rise of two-income families in which both husband and wife work has led to a growth of day-care facilities. Working couples with pre-school-age children who cannot afford to pay someone to come to their own home must rely on day-care facilities. There is considerable demand for a universal program to provide such facilities either free or at a heavily subsidized rate.

Advocates argue that the state ought to provide such care just as it provides free medical and hospital care. Women's groups also argue that affordable day care is a necessary part of women's liberation. Without it, they say, many women will not be allowed to fulfill themselves by taking on meaningful work outside the home. There is also an externality argument that goes like this: If people are determined to put their children into day-care facilities, it is in society's interest to see that these facilities are fully adequate to the job of caring for children at a very formative stage in their lives. Regulations will not be able to do the job, since high-quality care implies high costs. If many parents are unable or unwilling to pay that cost, their children may end up in inadequate facilities, and society at large will be the long-run loser.

Opponents argue on efficiency grounds that if the second income earner cannot earn enough to pay for day care, it is inefficient for that person to work. Total income would be higher if he or she stayed home, freeing the resources that would have been used to keep the family's children in day care. Opponents also argue on equity grounds that there is no reason why two-income parents with children in day care should be subsidized by funds collected from single persons, married couples who elect to have a parent stay at home to look after the children, and two-income families without children of day-care age. On present evidence, it is not clear whether the average income of the group that pays the subsidy will be higher or lower than the average income of the group that receives the subsidy. It is clear, however, that many individuals who pay the subsidy will have incomes below those of many individuals who receive it. Day care is not, therefore, a simple system for transferring income from richer to poorer households.

Proposals for reform. Most proposals for reform of the family benefits program focus on reducing its demogrant component and redirecting more expenditure to the CTC. (Alternatively, some of the savings from the reduced demogrant could be redirected to other objectives, including day care or deficit reduction.)

Criticism of this type of reform is often based on the increased emphasis it puts on the mechanism of tax credits. The main fault with that mechanism is that the credit, being related to one's income tax return and hence based on last year's income, is delivered only once a year and then only with a considerable lag after filing a return. This lag means that the credit is insensitive to current economic conditions and hence provides no safety net against current exigencies. As a source of help for the newly poor, it will often come too late, even if it is not too little.

Benefits for the Elderly

Over the next decades, a larger and larger fraction of Canadians will be retired, and thus the working people who will be directly or indirectly supporting the retired will constitute a smaller and smaller fraction of the population.

Canada's present youthful age structure may make us think we are richer as a nation than we actually are. When only a small proportion of the population consists of retirees, it is easy to be generous to them because the burden is spread over so many working persons. However, the Canadian population is aging. If overly generous schemes are established, they may become difficult to honor when a large proportion of the population is retired. This crunch is projected to come for Canada sometime early in the twenty-first century.

In the next decade Canadians may adopt obligations toward the small retired population that become hard to honor a decade or two later when the retired population increases.

Registered Retirement Savings Plans (RRSPs). RRSPs provide an incentive for individuals to provide for their own retirement, either because they are not covered by a company plan or because they wish to supplement their company plan. Funds contributed are deductible from taxable income but become fully taxable when they are withdrawn. It is thus a tax deferral plan, and as such it is more valuable the higher one's current taxable income and the lower one's expected future income. Although RRSPs are often criticized as being a "rich person's tax benefit," it is interesting to note that almost one-third of the labor force contributes to such plans, and of those who contribute, about 25 percent have incomes below $20,000.

Tax reform introduced in 1987 included a proposal to increase limits for RRSP contributions, in part to maintain the limit in real terms in the face of inflation and in part to move the personal direct tax system a little bit close to one with a consumption (or expenditure) base rather than one with an income base. However, the scheduled date for implementing the increased limits has been postponed twice since the initial proposal.

The Canada Pension Plan (CPP). The CPP provides a basic level of retirement income for all Canadians who have contributed to it over their working lives. (A separate but similar scheme exists in Quebec.) Unlike some private programs, the pension provided by the CPP is "portable"—changing jobs does not cause any loss of eligibility.

The most important concern about the plan is that it subsidizes the generation currently receiving pensions. Rates were very low when these people were young, and as a result they will receive pensions more than five times as large as what their contributions would actually have bought. This makes the plan a very good deal for those presently retired, but it means that any increase in future benefits will have to be paid for on top of the existing subsidy to those already retired. To make the scheme self-supporting, the government currently plans for contributions nearly to double between 1985 and 2011.

Private-sector pensions. Problems with private-sector pensions include portability, since often some or all eligibility is lost when a worker changes employers; the minimum period of employment needed to qualify, which is often quite long; and vestibility, how soon the pension contributions made by employer and employee belong to the employee.

Recent changes to the Federal Pension Benefits Standards Act have significantly changed the requirements on these matters. This legislation covers approximately 1 million employees under federal labor jurisdiction, and it is also expected to serve as a model for provincial pension reforms. These amendments will permit individuals to accumulate pension credits after only two years of employment and to transfer these benefits easily as they move among jobs. In addition, there is some significant extension of eligibility to part-time workers—an important matter since part-time work is increasing in many sectors of the economy.

Retirement income security programs. The existing public benefits system for the elderly is in many ways analogous to the child benefits system. There are three programs, each similar to a corresponding program in the child benefits system.

First, a universal benefit, or demogrant, called the old age security (OAS) program, acts much like the family allowance. Under the OAS program, the government sends out about 2.5 million monthly benefit cheques of about $330 each, one to each Canadian over the qualifying age of 65. After unemployment insurance, the OAS is the single most expensive program administered by the federal government, accounting for almost $12 billion in 1989. However, as we noted in Chapter 24, since 1989, OAS payments to relatively wealthy individuals have been recaptured by means of a tax claw-back.

Second, in calculating the personal nonrefundable tax credit, provisions available to the elderly serve to reduce their taxes payable. These include a credit available to anyone 65 or older and a pension income credit that offsets the taxes due on the first $1,000 of pension income.

Third, an income-tested program, called the guaranteed income supplement (GIS), provides benefits targeted to the low-income elderly. (In some provinces this is supplemented by further target assistance.) The GIS provides for most of the progressivity that arises in the elderly benefits system.

As with most social programs, the elderly benefits system started out as a pure income-tested benefit scheme and then evolved its current mixture of universal and income-tested elements. Many currently debated proposals for reform focus on the mix of universal and tested elements. The increased emphasis on universality took place during a period when most elderly people were in lower income categories. Recently, more and more people who receive these payments are in income brackets that are higher than that of the average taxpayer who finances them.

Although the average income of the elderly has improved, and will continue to do so in the future, the elderly population is still currently concentrated at the relatively low end of the income scale. Hence very little revenue can be transferred from the high- to the low-income elderly because there is too little total income at the top to be redistributed to the many people at the bottom.

There is very little scope for expenditure-neutral redistribution within the current elderly benefits system, but pressures on the system are mounting.

Thus suggestions for reform focus more on longer-term structural changes in the system.

One suggestion is to index the GIS fully while deindexing the OAS. Inflation would then slowly phase out the OAS by reducing its real value, while the fully indexed GIS would protect the elderly from genuine poverty. This might be politically more palatable than removing the program from the statute books—although economists tend to oppose letting inflation bring in implicitly policies that people are unwilling to let in explicitly.

Another proposal is to follow the United States in gradually raising the eligibility age for full OAS benefits. In the United States the age is to rise from 65 to 66 between the years 2000 and 2009 and then to 67 between 2017 and 2027.

A third proposal is to reduce (or even eliminate) the special provisions for pension income and age in the calculation of the personal tax credit. Some reform was accomplished in 1987 when these credits replaced analogous tax exemptions that were felt to be regressive in their effects. Many social policy analysts feel that any special provisions are anachronisms. They may have served useful functions when they were introduced, given the low incomes of the elderly and the sparsity of other programs. However, they are anomalies in a world of enriched pensions, health benefits, and OAS and GIS programs.

Health Care

Taking federal and provincial payments into account, Canada's public health care system is the country's single most expensive social policy expenditure. In 1989 health expenditures accounted for about 9 percent of Canadian GDP. The annual cost of the part of health care that is paid for by government amounted in that year to about $1,250 for every man, woman, and child in the country—or about $2,500 for every person who pays income taxes. It has also been rising rapidly in recent years.

One major possibility of cost containment is to move away from the present system of fee for service. In the system used in most of Canada, the physician and the hospital charge a prescribed fee for each service that is performed. Since under any provincial health scheme the doctor's and hospital's collection rate is 100 percent, there is no reason for the provider of health services to economize on those services. Indeed, much research shows that the rate of elective surgery—operations that are not necessary for survival but may be useful—rises with the ratio of physicians to the population. In areas where there are many physicians, the typical physician has time on his hands, and the rate of elective surgery goes up. In areas where doctors are in short supply, much less elective surgery is performed.

This illustrates a general point. The case for the free market is strongest when consumers are the best judges of their own needs. The case for market efficiency is greatly weakened when suppliers can influence the demand for the product they supply. But most people do not have the knowledge to second-guess their medical adviser. Thus in the many cases where judgment is needed to decide among several courses of action, all of which have something to recommend them, the evidence is that doctors create their own demand. This does not imply dishonesty on the part of doctors, merely that where judgment calls must be made, the amount of spare time available to doctors will influence their decisions, possibly unconsciously.

Health maintenance organizations (HMOs) provide a possible way around this problem. Large hospitals and large groups of doctors work on what is called a *capitation* basis. This means that the HMO is paid an annual fee for each person registered with it. Since payment is on a per capita basis rather than on a services-rendered basis, there is no incentive to prescribe more care than is needed. The HMO at Sault Ste. Marie, pioneered by the steelworkers' union and their employers, is an early and successful Canadian example of such an organization.

As with all social institutions, there are pros and cons to HMOs. They have their strong supporters and their strong detractors. No doubt their value in holding costs down while maintaining the quality of health services will be debated for a long time to come. Aspects of the health care system and the role of the market in reforming it are discussed further in Box 25-5.

Conclusions

We have seen that Canada's social policy is made up of a complex system of benefits and tax expenditures. There is no doubt that it achieves many of its goals. There is also no doubt that the system could be improved by an integrated set of reforms. Some critics also accuse it of being run by an often impersonal bureaucracy that is frequently overrun with red tape. They would like to see decentralization and more funds provided for private-sector experimentation. We say little about such complaints here, not because we believe them to be unfounded but because they are not easy to assess. A more detailed treatment would, however, have to pay them considerable attention.

Reforming the system is unpopular because people who run the risk of losing some net benefits tend to be very vocal and to find ready political champi-

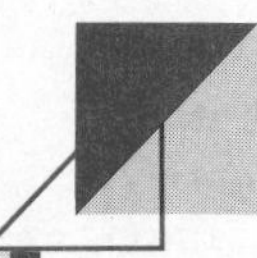

BOX 25-5

The Rising Cost of Health Care

The high and rising cost of health care is an emotional and provocative issue. Almost everyone would agree that in a wealthy society such as Canada, some minimum level of health care should be available to all citizens by right. Economic analysis shows that these two elements—the belief in the right to free medical care and the clamor over its high social cost—are not unrelated.

Explaining the High Cost

Without health insurance, a single major operation or a prolonged illness could impoverish even the most prudent middle-income household. Why has health care become so costly?

One reason is that the wages of nurses, laboratory technicians, and other medical service personnel has risen substantially relative to their productivity (the number of temperatures taken, beds made, and meals served per employee do not increase much over time).

A second reason is the steadily rising quality of medical care. Available knowledge and equipment have improved, and it is now possible not only to provide quicker, surer cures for common ailments but also to prevent and treat less common ailments and complications. Moreover, as per capita income has risen, people have been prepared to pay for more and better health. The demand for health care has proved to be income-elastic.

However, most economists argue that the main reason for rising medical costs is that the way medical care is provided and paid for weakens incentives to economize on its use or to keep costs down.

Free public provision and comprehensive prepaid health insurance lead to higher costs.

Doctors often prescribe expensive medical care, which they or other doctors provide. Will the patient contradict the doctor?

Since most insurance and publicly provided medical programs do not include significant *marginal charges* to the patient for the incremental medical or hospital care consumed, an individual has no incentive to economize on the quantity or quality of elective care. In the market system, individuals would choose medical care (as they choose housing) from a wide variety of price-quality alternatives. If patients had to pay their own bills, and if they could make fully informed choices, many might prefer to pay less and not have the best available treatment in all circumstances. But at zero marginal cost, patients will naturally prefer to have the extra benefits of the best possible care, no matter what the extra cost to the insurance company, employer, or government.

Doctors and hospitals can pass along the higher costs of advanced modern techniques to insurers in higher fees, especially if they do not have to worry that those higher fees may cause a reduction in the quantity of their services demanded. They may well reason, "Our job is to give the best treatment; let others worry about the costs." Further, unscrupulous doctors can prescribe unnecessary surgery or other medical care to increase the demand for their services. Of course, the insurer will pass on the higher claims in the form of higher premiums and so may exercise some cost control. But if the government pays most of the bill (as it does for many patients), there may not be much resistance to rising insurance rates, at least for a long time.

What Are the Right Quantity and Quality of Medical Care?

No doubt the acceptable minimum level of health care, to be provided by public support if necessary, has risen over time; accordingly, public intervention in the health sector has increased. The issue provokes more emotion than a discussion of housing or clothing. After all, human lives are at stake.

However, much (although, of course, not all) medical and hospital care is elective and has almost nothing to do with life or death. By way of analogy, to say that no one should starve is not to say that all people should receive all the free food they want to eat. Nonvital attention accounts for a large part of our demand for health care. If it is offered at little or no marginal cost to users, it will be consumed beyond the point where marginal benefits are equal to the cost of providing it.

But even where life is at stake, do we really always want the very best? Suppose that the extra cost of the very best at all times does pay off in an increased probability of survival. How much would we pay to have, say, only 9 instead of 10 people in 10,000 die from a particular disease? Surely few would want to spend a billion dollars per life saved; most would say that the opportunity cost was too high. Yet doctors in hospitals often make a different decision implicitly by ordering the best of everything. They then pass the costs on to society as a whole through increased resource allocation to the health sector. The issue is not whether to save lives but the opportunity cost of doing so. Money spent to save lives here is money not available to save lives (or improve the quality of life) elsewhere.

In adopting a policy toward health care there are at least three separable decisions: how much care to provide, how to allocate the cost of that care, and how to ration the supply. In the market system, prices do all three. When we elect to have the government intervene because we do not like the free market results, someone has to make these decisions. In health care, as elsewhere, if the price paid by users is kept below the marginal cost of providing the services, the private market will have excess demand. The government must either provide the services demanded directly or subsidize others to do so, or some way must be found to limit the demand to the quantity available. In countries with national health services, rationing is accomplished in part by long lines at doctors' offices and long waits for hospital admissions and in part by a lower average quality of medical services, which then reduces demand.

Controlling the Cost

Neither providers nor patients have sufficient incentive under many present schemes to keep down the costs of medical care. One solution is to place enough of a marginal charge on users that they will ask themselves whether this doctor's visit, this extra day in the hospital, or this use of the most advanced health monitoring system is worth the cost to them.

New institutional arrangements are emerging with incentives to control costs. Ontario and Alberta have experimented, apparently successfully, with privatization of hospital management. Quebec has almost 200 *centres locaux de service communautaires,* which are community-run and where physicians are retained on a salaried, not fee-for-service, basis. Ontario has over 60 health service organizations (HSOs) that also retain physicians on a salaried basis. Other developments include capitation arrangements whereby physicians agree to provide specified levels of care for a fixed fee per patient per year. These institutions all have incentives to keep their costs down.

ons. Other opponents of reform fear that any changes will begin a process of eroding the whole social policy system, which many regard as one of Canada's outstanding accomplishments. It remains to be seen whether any Canadian government will attempt a major overhaul of the system—an overhaul that many observers feel could make the system fairer, less costly, yet more effective but would cause a short-term political outcry.

SUMMARY

1. Canadian governments have been urged to reexamine and redesign social programs with the twin objectives of improving their ability to deliver benefits to the intended beneficiaries and reducing costs wherever possible.
2. Some social programs, called demogrants, are universal, paying benefits to anyone meeting such minimal requirements as residence or age. Other programs are selective, which usually means that they are income-tested. Some are taxable and thus provide net receipts that decline as income rises; others are not taxable and thus have net benefits that are independent of income. Some are expenditure programs (including direct transfers to persons), and others are delivered through the tax system in the form of special tax concessions (called tax expenditures). Some programs are administered by the federal government, some by the provincial governments, and still others by the municipalities.
3. Three major challenges must be met by a successful Canadian social spending policy for the 1990s. These are the challenges posed by government deficits, technological changes, and demographic trends. In the absence of major new revenue sources, it is not a question of whether social programs should be rationalized but of how this should be done.
4. Social programs, and proposed changes to them, must be understood in the context of the overall tax and transfer system.
5. Social policies cannot be evaluated without value judgments about desirable goals and trade-offs among objectives. In evaluating social policies, attention must be paid to vertical and horizontal equity and to the effective marginal tax rate implied by the terms of any program. When a person simultaneously pays income taxes and receives income-tested social benefits, the explicit income tax rate and the implicit tax-back rate applied to the social benefits are said to be stacked. Because of the high rate at which many income-tested benefits are reduced as income rises, the effective marginal tax rate—equal to the sum of the tax-back rates on social benefits received and the marginal income tax rate—of many beneficiaries can become very high. These high effective tax rates create disincentives, such as encouraging people to withhold labor services from the market.
6. In open economies it is also necessary to consider the effect of the tax and transfer system on the movement of mobile labor and capital.
7. In changing economies it is also necessary to ensure that measures designed to increase economic security do not seriously inhibit adjustment to change.
8. Although there has been much concern about preserving the universality of Canada's social welfare system, the facts that many schemes are income-tested and that many benefits are taxable mean that the whole system is progressive, with net benefits tending to fall as income rises.

9. The two major categories of programs are human resource development programs, which include postsecondary education, job creation, and unemployment insurance, and income transfer and security programs. This second category includes unemployment insurance, public assistance programs (welfare), child benefits schemes, benefits for the elderly, and health care, which, when provincial and federal expenditures are counted, is the single most expensive social program in the country, accounting for almost 9 percent of total national income.

TOPICS FOR REVIEW

Fiscal, economic, and demographic pressures
Vertical and horizontal equity
Universal versus selective programs
Demogrants
Tax exemptions and tax credits
Adjustment versus security
Disincentives and social costs

DISCUSSION QUESTIONS

1. Discuss the concept of universality as it applies to the family allowance system.
2. In a recent conference volume, Queen's University professor Keith Banting wrote the following: "The issue is not whether we want a universal or selective welfare state. Rather the questions are: What is the basic structure of the universal programs which we must maintain, and what is the appropriate supplement of selective programs which can be woven in and around that basic universal structure or framework." Discuss this quotation.
3. Discuss the implications for social policy objectives of basing social programs on family rather than individual income.
4. Is the deduction allowed for contributions to RRSPs regressive?
5. In a 1985 book about Britain, Hermione Parker listed 10 reasons why the British tax and benefit system must be changed:
   It is incomprehensible.
   It is uncoordinated.
   It is unnecessarily expensive to administer.
   It is a system of pauperization, not a welfare state.
   It is a major cause of unemployment.
   It is deteriorating, not improving.
   It is discriminatory, arbitrary, and unfair.
   It penalizes marriage and subsidizes family breakup.
   It destabilizes and divides society.
   It undermines the rule of law.

   Assess several of these in the context of the Canadian system.
6. In the February 1986 federal budget, Finance Minister Michael Wilson identified four objectives for reform of social policy:
   Maintaining universal access
   Directing more resources to the people most in need
   Improving opportunities for individuals to become self-reliant
   Reducing the after-tax value of benefits to higher-income Canadians who do not need assistance

   Examine a couple of existing programs (or recent reforms) in terms of these criteria.

7. How would converting the basic personal income exemption to a tax credit affect the disincentives faced by one spouse entering the labor market when the other spouse is already working and earning a much higher wage?
8. "As currently constituted, the unemployment insurance program has very little to do with either unemployment or insurance." Discuss.

PART 8

NATIONAL INCOME AND FISCAL POLICY

Chapter 26

An Introduction to Macroeconomics

Inflation, unemployment, recession, and economic growth are everyday words. Governments worry about how to prevent recessions, reduce inflation, and stimulate growth. Households are anxious to avoid the unemployment that comes with recessions, to protect themselves against the hazards of inflation, and to obtain the rising incomes that are brought about by economic growth. Firms are concerned about how inflations and recessions affect their profits.

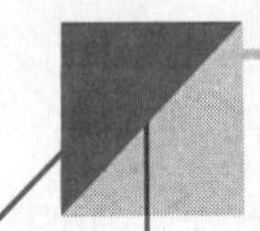

What Is Macroeconomics?

Each of the concerns just mentioned plays a major role in macroeconomics.

Macroeconomics is the study of how the economy behaves in broad outline without dwelling on much of its interesting, but sometimes confusing, detail. In contrast, *microeconomics* deals with the detailed behavior of individual markets, such as the market for wheat, coal, or strawberries.

The difference between the two branches of economics can be illustrated by different aspects of changes in oil prices.

Microeconomic issues. For decades oil prices fell in relation to the prices of most other commodities. Beginning in the 1970s this trend was reversed. Oil became increasingly expensive relative to many other goods and services. Then, in the mid 1980s, oil prices fell dramatically—although they remained somewhat above their pre-1970s levels relative to other prices. In mid 1990 they rose sharply again. These *relative* price changes had an impact on countless individual markets, from those for fertilizers and plastics, which are made from petroleum, to cars and air travel, which use it as fuel. Explaining the causes and effects of such changes are microeconomic issues.

Macroeconomic issues. The average of all prices is called the **price level**. As well as changing relative to other prices, oil prices have tended to follow the rising trend of all prices. Dramatic rises in oil prices helped to accelerate inflation in 1974–1975 and 1979–1980. In both cases inflation was followed by a major recession, with a rise in the nation's rate of unemployment. Explaining the causes and consequences of changes in the general price level, the overall level of business activity, and the rate of unemployment are macroeconomic issues.

Major Macroeconomic Issues

The economy tends to move in a series of ups and downs, called *business cycles,* rather than in a steady pattern. Why did the 1930s see the greatest economic depression in recorded history, with up to one-fifth of the labor force unemployed and with massive unemployment in all major industrial countries? Why were the 25 years following World War II a period of sustained economic growth, with only minor interruptions from modest recessions? Why did the early 1980s see the onset of the worst worldwide recession since the 1930s? What fueled the recovery of the mid 1980s?

Why, during the 1970s and early 1980s, did inflation reach levels never before seen in peacetime in many advanced Western nations? Has our attitude toward inflation permanently changed? In the early 1970s, when inflation crept up to 4 percent, concern was so great that emergency measures were adopted by the U.S. government. By the mid 1980s the Canadian and U.S. governments were claiming credit for having *reduced* inflation to 4 percent!

Earlier in the century, alternating bouts of inflationary boom and deflationary recession caused many headaches for policymakers. Booms still tend to be accompanied by inflationary pressures, but it can no longer be assumed that recessions will bring deflations. Why were the recessions of the 1970s and early 1980s accompanied not only by their familiar companion, high unemployment, but also by an unexpected fellow traveler, rapid inflation? Will **stagflation**—simultaneous high unemployment and rapid inflation—return?

Both total output and output per person have risen for many decades in most industrial countries. These long-term trends have meant rising average living standards. Did the slowdown in worldwide growth rates in the 1970s and 1980s represent a basic change in underlying trends, or was it just a reflection of a prolonged downturn? Can governments do anything to influence growth rates?

At the start of the 1990s, Canada is plagued with the problem of the "twin deficits." The first deficit is the enormous discrepancy between what the federal government spent and what it raised in taxes. This *budget deficit* had to be financed by borrowing funds, thus adding to the national debt. The second deficit is the *trade deficit*—the difference between the value of what Canadian producers sell abroad and what Canadian purchasers buy from abroad.

Did the high trade deficit reflect an underlying loss of Canada's international competitiveness, as some economists believe? Is the trade deficit primarily the consequence of the government's budget deficit, as other economists insist?

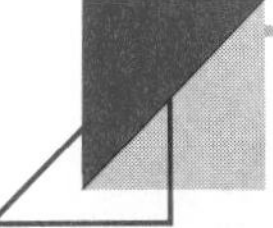

Key Macroeconomic Variables

The price level, employment, total output, and the interest rate are key macroeconomic variables for the domestic side of the economy. The exchange rate and the balance of payments are key variables on the international side. We hear about them on the nightly news and read about them in newspapers; politicians give campaign speeches about them; economists theorize about them. Why are so many people concerned about them? How have these variables behaved over time?

The Price Level and Inflation

Everyone knows what inflation is. Most people complain about its effects when the inflation rate is high and worry that it is just around the corner when the inflation rate is low. To most of us inflation means that prices are going up—not just the price of gasoline, blue jeans, or chewing gum, but all prices.

To study inflation, economists use two concepts. The first is the *price level,* which refers to the average level of all prices in the economy and is given the symbol *P*. The second is the *rate of inflation,* which is the rate at which the price level is rising. The price level and the inflation rate are measured by an index number, and to understand them we must study the meaning and interpretation of index numbers in some detail.

Calculating Index Numbers

Macroeconomists frequenty ask such questions as "How much have prices risen this year?" There is no perfectly satisfactory way to answer such questions, because all prices do not move together. Yet these are not foolish questions. There are trends in prices, trends that can be measured.

If you want to know about the trend in prices over some period of time, it is not helpful to be given a list of changes in, say, 4,682 individual prices.

Index numbers are statistical measures that are used to give summary answers to the inherently complex questions of the kind that have just been suggested; they measure the percentage change that has occurred in some broad average or aggregate over some particular time span. They point to overall tendencies or general drifts, not to detailed facts. They are an essential tool of macroeconomics.

A **price index** measures the average of some group of prices at a specific time, called the *given period,* relative to what it was at some initial time, called the *base period.* Price indexes provide measures of the price level and the rate of inflation. Later we shall use other indexes. Although each index measures something different, the principles of their construction are the same in all cases.

Two important questions must be answered when any price index is to be constructed. First, what group of prices should be used? The **Consumer Price Index (CPI),** which is calculated by Statistics Canada, covers prices of commodities that are commonly bought by households. Changes in the CPI are meant to measure changes in the typical household's *"cost of living."* Other indexes, such as the wholesale price index, cover the prices of different groups of commodities.

Second, what kind of average should be used? If all prices change in the same proportion, this would not matter: A 10 percent rise in each and every price would mean a 10 percent rise in the average of all prices, no matter how the average was constructed. However, different prices usually change in different proportions. It then matters how much importance we give to each price change. Changes in the price of bread, for example, are much more important to the average consumer than changes in the price of caviar. In calculating a price index, each price is given a *weight* that reflects its importance.

Let us see how this is done for the CPI. Every four years, Statistics Canada conducts a nationwide Family Expenditure Survey to see how consumers spend their incomes. The average bundle of goods that is bought is determined, along with the proportion of expenditure that is devoted to each good. These proportions become the weights attached to the individual prices in calculating the CPI. As a result, the CPI weights rather heavily the prices of commodities on which consumers spend much of their income and weights rather lightly the prices of commodities on which consumers spend only a little of their income. Table 26-1 provides a simple example of how these weights are calculated.

Once the weights have been chosen, the average price can be calculated for each period. This is done, as shown in Table 26-2, by multiplying each price by its weight and summing the resulting figures. However, a single average price is not informative. Suppose that you were told that last year the average price of all goods that were brought by consumers was $89.35. "So what?" you might well ask; indeed, by itself, this statistic tells you nothing of value. Now suppose that you are told that this year's average price for the same set of consumer purchases is $107.22. Now you do know something. You

TABLE 26-1 Calculation of Weights for a Price Index

Commodity	Price	Quantity	Expenditure (price × quantity)	Proportional weight
A	$5	60	$300	0.50
B	1	200	200	0.33
C	4	25	100	0.17
Total			$600	1.00

The weights are the proportions of total expenditure that are devoted to each commodity. This simple example lists the prices of three commodities and the quantities bought by a typical household. Multiplying price by quantity gives expenditure on each, and summing these gives the total expenditure on all commodities. Dividing expenditure on each good by total expenditure gives the proportion of total expenditure that is devoted to each commodity, as shown in the last column. These proportions become the weights for the price indexes that are calculated in Table 26-2.

TABLE 26-2 Calculation of a Price Index

Commodity	Weight	Price 1990	Price 1991	Price 1992	Price × weight 1990	Price × weight 1991	Price × weight 1992
A	0.50	$5.0	$6.0	$14.0	$2.50	$3.000	$7.00
B	0.33	1.0	1.5	2.0	0.33	0.495	0.66
C	0.17	4.0	8.0	9.0	0.68	1.360	1.53
Total	1.00				$3.51	$4.855	$9.19

Index 1990 $\frac{3.51}{3.51} \times 100 = 100$

1991 $\frac{4.855}{3.51} \times 100 = 138.3$

1992 $\frac{9.19}{3.51} \times 100 = 261.8$

A price index expresses the weighted average of prices in the given year as a percentage of the weighted average of prices in the base year. The prices of the three commodities in each year are multiplied by the weights from Table 26-1. Summing the weighted prices for each year gives the average price in that year. Dividing the average price in the given year by the average price in the base year and multiplying by 100 gives the price index for the given year. The index is, of course, 100 when the base year is also taken as the given year.

know that, on average, prices paid by consumers have risen sharply over the year. In fact, the increase is 20 percent.[1]

The average for each period is divided by the value of the average for the base period and multiplied by 100. The resulting series is called an index number series; by construction, the base period value in this series equals 100. If prices in the next period average 20 percent higher, the index number for that period will be 120. A simple example of how these calculations are carried out is given in Table 26-2.

Price indexes are constructed by assigning weights to reflect the importance of the individual items being combined. The value of the index is set equal to 100 in the base period.

There is one added complication with respect to the CPI. As Table 26-2 shows, the CPI is an example of what is called a *fixed-weight* index. The weights are the proportion of income that is spent on the three goods in the first year. These weights are then applied to the prices in each subsequent year. Problems arise with a fixed-weight index because consumption patterns change over the years. The fixed weights then less and less represent the importance that consumers *currently* place on each of the commodities. To deal with this problem, Statistics Canada updates its Family Expenditure Survey every four years. The survey conducted in 1990 will be reflected in new weights in the CPI applied by 1992.

[1] The change is $17.87, which is 20 percent of the initial average price of $89.35.

Interpreting Price Indexes

A price index is meant to reflect the broad trend in prices rather than the details. It gives valuable information, but it must be interpreted with care. People often treat index numbers as though they had an accuracy and a significance that their compilers do not claim for them, but being aware of their limitations should not lead people to neglect index numbers for the useful information that they can give: the average changes over time.

Although the weights reflect the average importance of each commodity across the nation, they cannot reflect how each and every household spends its money. Rich, poor, young, old, single, married, urban, and rural households typically consume goods in different proportions. An increase in air fares, for example, will raise the cost of living of a middle-income traveler but will have no effect on that of a nontraveling member of a poor household.

In the hypothetical example of Table 26-2, from 1990 to 1991 the cost of living would have risen by 20 percent, 50 percent, and 100 percent, respectively, for three different families, one of which consumed only commodity *A*, one of which consumed only *B*, and one of which consumed only *C*. The index in the table shows, however, that the cost of living went up by 38.3 percent for a family that consumed all three goods in the proportions indicated.

The more an individual household's consumption pattern conforms to the typical pattern used to weight the index, the better the index will reflect changes in that household's cost of living.

Measuring the Rate of Inflation

At the end of 1989 the CPI was 153.6 (1981 = 100). This means that at the end of 1989 it cost just over 53 percent more to buy a representative bundle of goods than it did in the base period, 1981. In other words, the price level increased by 53.6 percent over the period 1981–1989 as measured by the CPI. The *percentage change* in the cost of purchasing the bundle of goods that is covered by any index is thus the level of the index minus 100.

The *inflation rate* between any two periods of time is measured by the percentage increase in the relevant price index from the first period to the second period. In the rare event of a drop in the price level, we speak of *deflation*. When the rise in the price level is being measured from the base period, all that needs to be done is to subtract the two indexes, as we have just done. When two other periods are being compared, we must be careful to express the change as a percentage of the index in the first period.

If we let P_1 indicate the value of the price index in the first period and P_2 its value in the second period, the inflation rate is merely the difference between the two, expressed as a percentage of the value of the index in the first period:

$$\textbf{Inflation rate} = \frac{P_2 - P_1}{P_1} \times 100$$

(When P_1 is the base period, its value is 100, and the expression reduces to $P_2 - 100$.) In other cases the full calculation must be made. For example, the index went from 145.7 in October 1987 to 153.2 in October 1988, indicating a rate of inflation of 5.1 percent over the year because the rise of 7.5 points in the index reflects a 5.1 percent rise over its initial value of 145.7.

If the two values being compared are not exactly a year apart, it is common to convert the result to an *annual rate*. For example, the CPI stood at 146.8 in January 1989 and at 147.8 in February 1989. This is an increase of 0.68 percent over one month (1.0/146.8 × 100). It is also an *annual rate* of approximately 8.2 percent (0.68 × 12) over the year.[2] This means that *if* the rate of inflation that occurred between January and February 1989 persisted for a full year, the price level would rise by approximately 8.2 percent.

Inflation: The Historical Experience

Figure 26-1 shows one measure of the price level and the inflation rate from 1930 to 1990. The price level is measured by the Consumer Price Index, and the inflation rate is measured by the annual rate of change in that index. What can we learn from Figure 26-1? First, we learn that the price level is constantly changing. Second, we learn that in only 2 of the 60 observations did the price level fall; in the other 58 years the inflation rate was positive. The cumulative effect of this sequence of small but repeated price increases is quite dramatic; in 1980 the price level was six times higher than it was in 1930.

Third, we learn that whereas the long-term increasing trend stands out when we look at the price level, the short-term fluctuations stand out when we look at the inflation rate. From 1965 to 1974 inflation averaged 4.7 percent; from 1975 to 1984 it averaged 9.1 percent! The sharp swings in the inflation rate in the late 1970s and the early 1980s were even more dramatic. The increases in the inflation rate to double-digit levels in 1974 and again in 1979 were associated with major shocks to the world prices of oil and foodstuffs, and the declines in inflation that followed were delayed responses to major recessions. (Note that even when the inflation rate *falls*, as it did in 1982, for example, the price level continues to rise as long as inflation remains *positive*.)

[2] We say *approximately* because a 0.68 percent rise each month *compounded* for 12 months will give rise to an increase over the year that is greater than 8.2 percent. The appropriate procedure is to increase the index in January by 0.68 twelve times rather than just to multiply it by 12. The two results are the difference between simple and compound interest rates.

FIGURE 26-1 The Canadian Price Level and Inflation Rate, 1930–1990

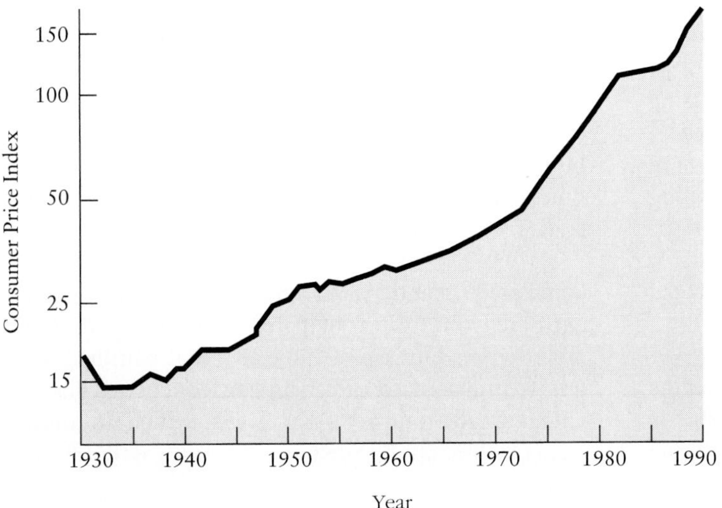

(i) Price level (1981 = 100)

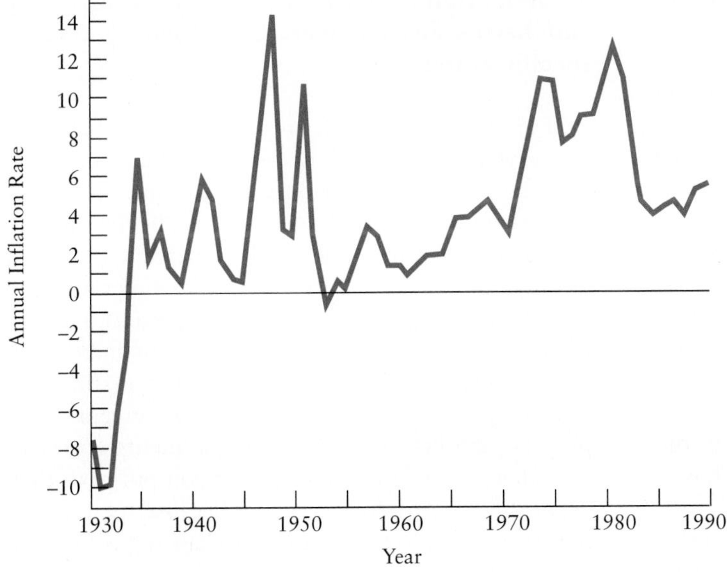

(ii) Annual inflation rate

(i) The overwhelming trend movement in the price level since 1930 has been upward. The data reflect the Consumer Price Index from 1930 to 1990, with 1981, as the base year, equal to 100. They are plotted on a semilog scale on which equal vertical distances represent equal percentage changes. Any acceleration in the rate of increase in the price level shows up as increasing steepness of the curve.

(ii) The rate of inflation has varied from −10 percent to +14 percent since 1930. Prices fell dramatically at the onset of the Great Depression. They rose sharply during and after World War II and during the Korean War. For about a decade thereafter, no trend in the inflation rate was discernible. Starting in the mid 1960s, however, inflation experienced a strong upward trend, interrupted by short-term fluctuations. Finally, in 1983 inflation fell to its lowest level since the early 1970s, and it has averaged around 4 to 5 percent ever since.

Sources: M. C. Urquhart, ed., *Historical Statistics of Canada*; Department of Finance, *Economic Review*; 1990 data are for June.

Why Inflation Matters

Money is the universal yardstick in our economy. We measure economic values in terms of money, and we conduct our economic affairs by using money. Things as diverse as wages, bank balances, the value of a house, and a university's endowment all are stated in terms of money. We value money, however, not for itself but for what we can purchase with it. The term **purchasing power of money**, also known as the *real value of money*, refers to the amount of goods and services that can be purchased with a given amount of money.

A change in the price level affects us because it changes the real value of money.

The purchasing power of money is negatively related to the price level.

For example, if the price level doubles, a dollar will buy only half as much, whereas if the price level halves, a dollar will buy twice as much. Figure 26-1 shows that inflation has reduced the purchasing power of money over each of the past five decades.

If inflation reduces the real value of a given sum of money, it also reduces the real value of anything else whose price is *fixed* in money terms. Thus the real value of a money wage, a savings account, or the balance that is owed on a student loan is reduced by inflation.

Fully anticipated inflation. It is possible to imagine inflation that has no real effects of any kind. What is required for this to happen is, first, that everyone who is making any sort of financial arrangement should know what the inflation rate will be over the life of the contract and, second, that *all* financial obligations be stated in real terms. The real behavior of the economy then would be exactly the same with and without inflation. Say that both sides of a wage contract agree that wages should go up by 3 percent in real terms. If the inflation rate is expected to be zero, they would agree to an increase in money wages of 3 percent. If a 10 percent inflation is expected, however, they would agree to an increase in money wages of 13 percent. Ten percent would be needed to maintain the purchasing power of the money wages that would be paid, and 3 percent would be needed to bring about the desired increase in purchasing power.

Loan contracts would specify that the amount of a loan to be repaid would be increased over the amount borrowed by the rate of inflation. Thus if $100 is borrowed and the price level rises by 10 percent, $110 would have to be returned (apart from any interest that might be paid on the loan). This would ensure that the real value of what is borrowed stays equal to the real value of what is returned.

The result would be a 10 percent increase in everyone's money incomes and money assets, combined with a 10 percent increase in all money prices and all money liabilities. Nothing real would have changed. People's higher money incomes would buy the same amount as before, and the real value of their assets and liabilities would be unchanged.

Another way of making this point is to observe that the economy can function just as well with a price level of 110—or, for that matter, of 200—as with a price level of 100.

Once everything has been adjusted, any one price level is as good as any other price level.

This is just as it ought to be, since it would indeed be magic if altering the number of zeros that we use when stating monetary values could change anything real.

Completely unanticipated inflation. At the opposite extreme from fully anticipated inflation is completely unanticipated inflation. No one sees it coming, so no one is prepared to offset its consequences. The real value of all contracts that are specified in money terms will change unexpectedly. Who will gain and who will lose?

Unexpected inflation benefits anyone who has an obligation to pay specific amounts of money and harms anyone who is entitled to receive specific amounts.

For example, consider a wage contract that specifies a wage increase of 3 percent on the assumption that the price level will remain constant. Both employers and employees expect that the purchasing power of wages paid will rise by 3 percent as a result of the new contract. Now assume, however, that the price level unexpectedly rises by 10 percent over the life of the wage contract. The 3 percent increase in money wages now means a reduction in the purchasing power of wages of about 7 percent. Employers gain because their wage payments represent a smaller part of the value of their output than they expected them to. Workers lose because their wages represent a smaller receipt of purchasing power than they expected to get.

People who have borrowed money will pay back a smaller real amount than they borrowed. By the same token, people who have lent money will receive a smaller real amount than they lent. Suppose that Sylvia lends Jean enough money to buy a medium-size house. The price level subsequently doubles; then Jean pays back the money that he borrowed. Sylvia now finds herself with only one-half of what is required to buy the house.

Wage earners and lenders will be able to adjust

to the new price level when they make new contracts, but some people will be locked into their old money contracts for the rest of their lives. The extreme case is suffered by those who live on fixed money incomes. For example, pensions that are provided by the private sector often promise to pay a fixed money income for life. On retirement, this sum may look adequate, even generous. Twenty years later, however, inflation may have reduced its purchasing power to the poverty level. A family that retired on a fixed money income in 1970 would find the purchasing power of that income reduced year by year, until in 1990 it would have been worth only about 26 percent of its original value.

Intermediate cases. There are several reasons why actual inflation almost always falls somewhere between the two extremes that we have just discussed.

First, the inflation rate is usually variable and seldom foreseen exactly, even though its general course may be anticipated. Thus the actual rate will sometimes be higher than expected—to the benefit of those who have contracted to pay money. At other times the inflation rate will be lower than expected—to the benefit of those who have contracted to receive money. Given the lack of certainty, different people will have different expectations.

Because it is hard to foresee accurately, inflation adds to the uncertainties of economic life. Highly variable inflation rates cause great uncertainty.

Second, even if the inflation rate is foreseen, all adjustments to it cannot occur at the same speed. As a result, inflation redistributes income and does so in a haphazard way. Losers are those whose money incomes adjust more slowly than prices are rising; gainers are those whose money incomes keep ahead of the inflation.

Third, even if the inflation rate is foreseen, the full set of institutions that would be needed for everyone to take full avoiding action do not exist. For example, many private pension plans are stated in money terms. Employees have little choice but to take the only plan that their employers make available to them.

Fourth, much of the tax system is defined in nominal money terms, causing its effects to vary with the price level. For example, if someone sells an asset for more money than was paid for it, the difference is called a capital gain. Under present Canadian tax laws, such gains are essentially regarded as income and are taxed as such.[3] If there is no inflation, a capital gain does represent a real increase in purchasing power. The tax will absorb part of the increase, leaving the rest for the investor. In inflationary circumstances, however, the capital gain may be a purely nominal gain that does not represent a real increase in purchasing power. Consider an investor who buys $1,000 worth of stock in a company. The price level then doubles, after which the stock is sold for $2,000. The investor has made no real gain from the investment. The $2,000 received will buy no more than the original $1,000 that was paid out. The tax authorities will, however, call the $1,000 increase in nominal value a capital gain. If the gain is subject to a 33 percent income tax, the investor will net only $1,667. This is less real value than was invested, and the capital gains tax has turned out to be a tax levied on the real value of capital rather than the income earned by capital.

During inflationary periods, capital gains taxes that are levied on nominal money gains are taxes on the real value of capital rather than taxes on current income.

Indexation. Some of the real effects of inflation can be avoided by indexing. **Indexation** means linking the payments that are made under the terms of a contract to changes in the price level. For example, a retirement pension might pay the beneficiary $15,000 per year starting in 1990, and it might specify that the amount paid will increase each year in proportion to the increase in the CPI. Thus if the CPI rises by 10 percent between 1990 and 1991, the pension that is payable in 1991 would rise by 10 percent, to $16,500. This holds the real purchasing power of the pension constant.

Indexing is valuable as a defense against unforeseen changes in the price level, as a method of reducing uncertainty, and as a way of adapting institutions so that contracts can be made in real terms.

[3] Current Canadian tax laws allow for a partial exemption of capital gains. The first $100,000 earned in the taxpayer's lifetime is tax-free, and after that only 75 percent of any capital gains are included in taxable income. However, the basic point of the example in the text remains valid.

Output and Income Variables

The value of a nation's total production of goods and services is called its *national product*. Since all the value that is produced must ultimately belong to someone in the form of a claim on that value, the national product is equal to the total income claims generated by the production of goods and services. Hence when we study national product, we are also studying *national income*.

In fact, there are several related measures of the nation's total output and total income. Their various definitions and the relationships among them are discussed in detail in Chapter 27. In this chapter we use the generic term *national income* to refer to both the value of total output and the value of the income generated by the production of that output.

Aggregating Total Output

To measure total output, quantities of various goods are *aggregated*. To construct such totals, we add up *values of the various products*. We cannot add tons of steel to loaves of bread, but we can add the money value of steel production to the money value of bread production. Hence by multiplying the physical output of a good by its price per unit and then summing this value for each good produced in the nation, we can find the quantity of total output *measured in dollars*.

Real and Nominal Values

The total that was just described gives the *money value* of national output, often called **nominal national income**. This measure can change because of a change in either the physical quantities or the prices on which it is based. To discover the extent to which any change is due to quantities or to prices, economists calculate **real national income**. This is a measure of total output in which the value of individual outputs is not measured at current prices but at the prices that prevailed in some base period that was chosen for this purpose.[4]

[4] Nominal national income is often referred to as *money national income* or *current-dollar national income*. Real national income is often called *constant-dollar national income*.

Real national income is denoted by the symbol Y. It tells us the value of current output measured at base period prices, that is, the sum of the quantities valued at prices ruling in the base period. Comparing real national incomes of different years provides a measure of the change in real output that has occurred during the interval between the years.

Since its calculation holds prices constant, real national income changes only when quantities change.

Since our interest is primarily in the *real* output of goods and services, we shall use the term *national income* (and output) to refer to *real national income* unless otherwise specified. (An example illustrating this important distinction is given in Box 27-3 on page 582.)

National Income: The Historical Experience

To study national income, we look at one of its most commonly used measures, called *gross domestic product* (GDP). GDP can be measured in either real or nominal terms; we focus here on real GDP. The details of its calculations will be discussed in Chapter 27.

Part (i) of Figure 26-2 shows real GDP produced by the Canadian economy since 1930; part (ii) shows its annual percentage change for the same period. The GDP series in Figure 26-2(i) shows two kinds of movement. The major movement is an upward trend that increased real output more than sevenfold in the half century from 1939 to 1989. Because the trend has generally been upward in the modern era, it is referred to as *economic growth*.

Long-term growth in real national income is reflected in the upward trend in real GDP.

Not only has national income grown throughout this century, but real income per person (also called *per capita real income*) has increased as well. Indeed, it has almost tripled in the past 60 years.

The growth in real per capita GDP is the basis of the enormous increase in living standards that Canadians have enjoyed throughout the twentieth century.

FIGURE 26-2 Canadian Real National Income and Growth Rate, 1930–1990

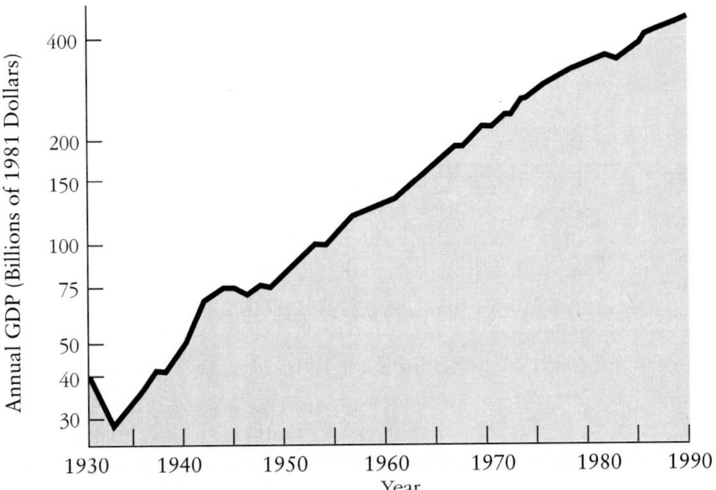

(i) Annual national income in constant (1981) dollars

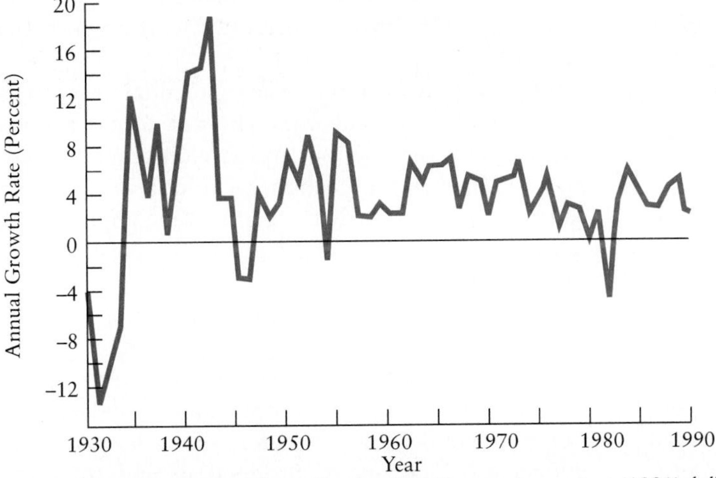

(ii) Annual percentage rate of growth of national income in constant (1981) dollars

(i) Real national income, which measures the total production of goods and services produced in the economy over the period of a year, has grown steadily since 1930, with only a few interruptions. In (i) we see the long-term growth of the economy reflected in the upward trend of real national income. Shorter-term fluctuations are obscured by this trend in (i) but are highlighted in (ii).

(ii) Real growth in the economy, as measured by the annual rate of change of real national income, has fluctuated considerably but has been mostly positive. In (ii) the short-term fluctuations are readily apparent, but the long-term upward trend still shows up because the majority of observations are positive.

(Data prior to 1947 are based on GNP, thereafter on GDP, which is now the standard measure of real national income.) *Sources:* M. C. Urquhart, ed., *Historical Statistics of Canada*; Department of Finance, *Economic Review*; 1990 data are for June.

A second feature of the real GDP series is the short-term fluctuations around the trend, often described as cyclical fluctuations. Overall growth so dominates the real GDP series that the fluctuations are hardly visible in Figure 26-2(i). However, as can be seen in part (ii) of the figure, cyclical fluctuations in real GDP have been significant in the past.

The cyclical behavior of real national income is reflected in the annual fluctuations in the growth rate of real GDP.

The business cycle. The **business cycle** refers to the continual ebb and flow of business activity that occurs around the long-term trend after seasonal ad-

FIGURE 26-3 A Stylized Business Cycle

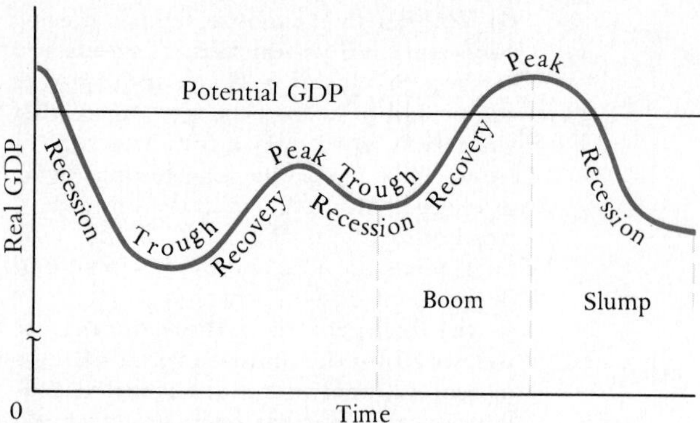

Although the phases of business fluctuations are described by a series of commonly used terms, no two cycles are the same. Starting from a lower turning point, a cycle goes through a phase of recovery, or expansion, reaches an upper turning point, and then enters a period of recession. Cycles differ from one another in the severity of their troughs and peaks and in the speed with which one phase follows another. Sometimes the entire rising half of the cycle is loosely referred to as a *boom* and the entire falling half is called a *slump*.

justments have been made.[5] Such cyclic fluctuations can be seen in many economic series; they are particularly apparent in the continual oscillations in GDP that we observed in Figure 26-2.

Although recurrent fluctuations in economic activity are neither smooth nor regular, a vocabulary has developed to denote their different stages. Figure 26-3 shows stylized cycles that illustrate some useful terms, and Box 26-1 further discusses this terminology.

It is important to realize that no two cycles are exactly the same. There are variations in duration and magnitude. Some expansions are long and drawn out, as was the one that began in 1983; others come to an end before high employment of labor and industrial capacity is reached. Nonetheless, fluctuations are systematic enough that it is useful to identify common factors in the four phases, which are outlined in Box 26-1.

Potential Income and the Output Gap

Actual national income is what the economy does, in fact, produce. An important related concept is *potential* national income. It measures what the economy could produce if all resources—land, labor, the productive capacity—were fully employed at their normal levels. It is usually referred to as just **potential income**, but it is also sometimes called *high-employment income*.[6] We give it the symbol Y^*, to distinguish it from actual national income, which is indicated by Y.

The **output gap**, also called the *GDP gap*, measures the difference between what would have been produced if potential, or high-employment, national income had been achieved and what is actually produced. It is calculated by subtracting actual national income, as measured by current GDP, from potential income ($Y^* - Y$).

The gap is positive when potential income is greater than actual income. The gap then measures the market value of goods and services that *could have been produced* if the economy's resources had been fully employed but that actually went unproduced. This is sometimes referred to as the *deadweight loss* of unemployment.

Recessions are associated with large positive output gaps. In booms the gap may become negative, indicating that actual national income *exceeds* potential income. A negative output gap is possible because potential income is defined for a *normal rate of utilization* of factors of production, and there are many ways in which these normal rates can be exceeded temporarily. Labor may work longer hours than normal; factories may operate an extra shift or not close for routine repairs and maintenance. Although these expedients are only temporary, they are effective in the short term.

Figure 26-4(i) shows potential income for the

[5] When economists wish to analyze monthly or quarterly data, they often remove fluctuations that can be accounted for by a regular seasonal pattern. This *seasonal adjustment* is made because many economic series show a marked seasonal pattern over the year. For example, logging activity tends to be low in the winter months and high in the summer months, whereas sales of fuel oil tend to have the reverse seasonal pattern.

[6] The words *real* and *actual* have similar meanings in everyday usage. In national income theory, however, their meanings are quite distinct. *Real* national income is distinguished from *nominal* national income, and *actual* national income is distinguished from *potential* national income. The latter both refer to real measures, so that the full descriptions are actual real national income and potential real national income.

BOX 26-1

The Terminology of Business Cycles

Economics is a developing subject, and the terms that are used to describe economic fluctuations are constantly evolving. The meanings of some of the main terms that you are likely to encounter are outlined here.

Trough

A trough is characterized by high unemployment and a level of output that is low in relation to the economy's capacity to produce. There is thus a substantial amount of unused productive capacity. Business profits are low; for some individual companies they are negative. Confidence about economic prospects in the immediate future is lacking, and as a result, many firms are unwilling to risk making new investments.

Recovery

The symptoms of a recovery, or expansion, are many: Run-down equipment is replaced; employment, income, and consumer spending all begin to rise; and expectations become more favorable as a result of increases in production, sales, and profits. Investments that once seemed risky may now be undertaken as the climate of business opinion starts to change from one of pessimism to one of optimism. As demand rises, production can be increased with relative ease merely by reemploying the existing unused capacity and unemployed labor.

Peak

A peak is the top of a cycle. At the peak there is a high degree of utilization of existing capacity; labor shortages may develop, particularly in categories of key skills; and shortages of essential raw materials are likely. As shortages develop in more and more markets, a situation of general excess demand develops. Costs rise, but since prices rise also, business remains profitable.

Recession

A **recession**, or contraction, is a downturn in economic activity. Common usage defines a recession as a fall in the real GDP for two quarters in successsion. Demand falls off, and as a result, production and employment fall. As employment falls, so does household income. Profits drop, and some firms get into difficulties. Investments that looked profitable with the expectation of continual rising demand now appear uprofitable. It may not even be worth replacing capital goods as they wear out, because unused capacity is increasing steadily. In historical discussions, a recession that is deep and long-lasting is often called a **depression**.

Booms and Slumps

Two nontechnical but descriptive terms are often used. The whole falling half of the cycle is often called a *slump,* and the whole rising half is often called a *boom*. These are useful terms for us to use when we do not wish to be more specific about the economy's position in the cycle.

years 1967 through 1989. The rising trend reflects the growth in the productive capacity of the Canadian economy over this period. The figure also shows actual real national income, which has kept approximately in step with potential income. The distance between the two, which is the output gap, is plotted in Figure 26-4(ii). Fluctuations in economic activity are apparent from fluctuations in the size of the gap. The deadweight loss from unemployment over any time span is indicated by the overall size of the gap over that time span. It is shown in part (ii) of Figure 26-4 by the shaded area between the curve and the horizontal axis, which represents the level at which actual output equals potential output.

FIGURE 26-4 Potential National Income and the Output Gap, 1967–1989

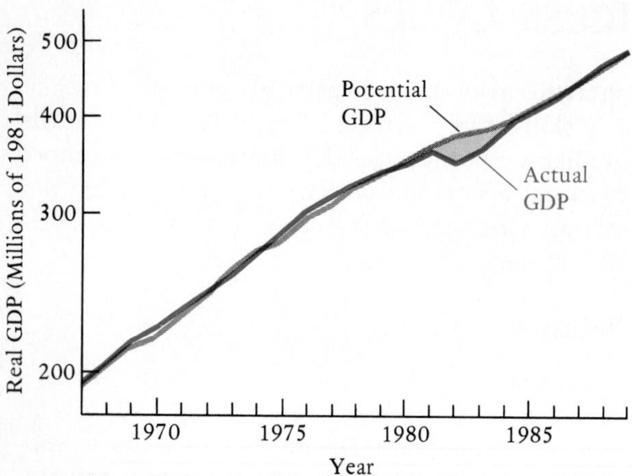

(i) Potential GDP

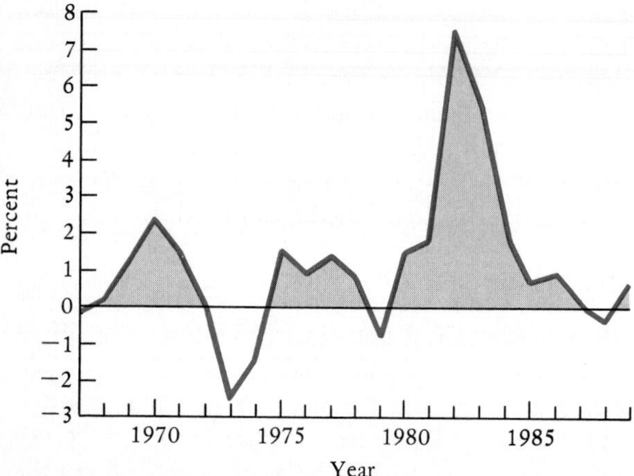

(ii) The output gap

(i) Potential and actual GDP have both displayed an upward trend in recent years. Growth in the economy has been such that both potential and actual GDP have more than doubled since 1967. The two series are plotted in semilog form, so that equal vertical distances represent equal *percentage* changes. Both series are in real terms and are measured in 1981 dollars. The distance between the two represents the output gap. The shaded areas represent periods when there has been a positive output gap.

(ii) The output gap, however, has fluctuated, since it measures the difference between the economy's potential output and its actual output. The cyclical behavior of the economy is apparent from the behavior of the output gap. Slumps in economic activity produce large output gaps, and booms reduce them. The zero line indicates that potential and actual output are the same. The shaded area above the zero line indicates the deadweight loss that arises from unemployment during periods when there is a positive output gap. *Source:* Department of Finance, *Quarterly Economic Report.*

Why National Income Matters

Policymakers care about short-term fluctuations in national income. Recessions cause unemployment and lost output. A large output gap means that actual national income falls short of potential, and it thus signals economic waste and human suffering as a result of a failure to use the economy's resources (including its human resources) at their normal intensity of use.

Booms, although associated with high employment and high output, can bring problems of their own. A negative output gap, indicating that actual national income exceeds potential income, usually signals the outbreak of strong inflationary pressures. These will cause serious concern for any government that is committed to keeping the inflation rate low.

The long-run trend in real national income is even more important than its short-term fluctuations. When income per person grows, each generation can expect, on average, to be substantially better off than preceding ones. For example, if real income per capita grows at the relatively modest rate of 1.5 percent per year, the average person's lifetime income expectancy will be *twice* that of his or her grandparents. Indeed, the low living standards that prevailed at the start of the Industrial Revolution are no longer with us, primarily because economic growth has resulted in more and more output for less and less work over the past century. (It is important to remember, however, that although growth makes people better off on average, it does not necessarily make every individual better off.)

Labor Force Variables

Employment denotes the number of adult workers (defined in Canada as all workers aged 15 and over) who hold jobs. **Unemployment** denotes the number of adult workers who are not employed and are actively searching for a job. The **labor force** is the total number of the employed and the unemployed. The **unemployment rate**, usually represented by the symbol U, is unemployment expressed as a percentage of the labor force:

$$U = \frac{\textbf{unemployed}}{\textbf{labor force}} \times \textbf{100 percent}$$

The number of unemployed persons in Canada is estimated from a sample survey conducted each month by Statistics Canada. Persons who are currently without a job but who say they have searched actively for one during the sample period are recorded as unemployed. The total number of estimated unemployed is then expressed as a percentage of the labor force (employed plus unemployed) to obtain the figure for percentage unemployment. Some problems connected with this measurement are discussed in Box 26-2.

Consideration of employment and unemployment suggests another concept, that of *full employment* or *high employment*. One confusing thing about full employment is that it does *not* mean an absence of unemployment. This is why the concept is now often called *high employment,* although the long history of the use of the term *full employment* in economics guarantees that it will be heard for some time to come. There are two main reasons why full employment is always accompanied by some unemployment.

First, there is a constant turnover of individuals in given jobs and a constant change in job opportunities. New members enter the work force; some people quit their jobs, and others are fired. It may take some time for these people to find jobs. So, at any point in time, there is unemployment due to the normal turnover of labor. Such unemployment is called **frictional unemployment**.

Second, because the economy is constantly changing and adapting, at any moment in time there will always be some mismatching between the characteristics of the labor force and the characteristics of the available jobs. This is a mismatching between the structure of the supplies of labor and the structure of the demands for labor. The mismatching may occur, for example, because labor does not have the skills demanded or because labor is not in the part of the country where the demand is located. Unemployment that occurs because of a mismatching of the characteristics of the supply of labor and the demand for labor, even when the overall demand for labor is equal to the overall supply, is called **structural unemployment**. We will have more to say about these two types of unemployment in Chapter 37.

Full employment is said to occur when the only existing unemployment is frictional and structural. At less than full employment, other types of unemployment are present as well. One major reason for lapses from full employment lies with the business cycle. During recessions, unemployment rises above the minimum avoidable amount of frictional and structural unemployment. This excess amount is called **cyclical unemployment** (or, sometimes, *deficient-demand unemployment*).

The measured unemployment rate when the economy is at full employment is often called the **natural rate of unemployment** or the **NAIRU**.[7] Estimates of this rate are difficult to obtain and are often a source of disagreement among economists. Nevertheless, such estimates are a useful benchmark against which economists can gauge the current performance of the economy, as measured by the actual unemployment rate. Estimates indicate that the natural rate of unemployment rose throughout the 1970s from around 5.5 percent to a high of around 7.5 percent in the late 1970s, and it has now fallen to

[7] *NAIRU* is an acronym for *nonaccelerating inflationary rate of unemployment*. The reasons for the use of this term will become clear in Chapter 36.

BOX 26-2

How Accurate Are the Unemployment Figures?

No measurements of unemployment are completely accurate. The unemployment figures that are calculated by Statistics Canada, however, have a number of shortcomings that tell us much about the concept of unemployment itself.

The measured figure for unemployment may overstate or understate the number of people who are involuntarily unemployed. On the one hand, the measured figure overstates unemployment by including people who are not involuntarily unemployed. For example, unemployment insurance provides protection against genuine hardship, but it also induces some people to stay out of work and collect unemployment benefits for as long as the benefits last. Such people have, in fact, voluntarily withdrawn from the labor force, although, in order to remain eligible for unemployment payments, they must make a show of looking for a job by registering at the local employment center. Such people usually are included in the ranks of the unemployed because, for fear of losing their benefits, they tell the person who surveys them that they are actively looking for a job.

On the other hand, the measured figure understates involuntary unemployment by omitting some people who would accept a job if one were available but who did not actively look for one during the week in which the sample was taken. For example, people who have not found jobs after searching for a long time may become discouraged and stop seeking work. Such people have withdrawn voluntarily from the labor force and will not be recorded as unemployed. They are, however, unemployed in the sense that they would willingly accept a job if one were available. People in this category are referred to as *discouraged workers*. They have voluntarily withdrawn from the labor market because they believe that they cannot find a job under current conditions.

In addition, there are part-time unemployed people. If some workers are working six hours instead of eight hours per day because there is insufficient demand for the product that they help to make, these workers are suffering 25 percent unemployment even though none of them are reported as unemployed. Twenty-five percent of the group's potential labor resources are going unused. Involuntary part-time work is a major source of unemployment of labor resources, which are not reflected in the overall unemployment figures reported in the press.

The official figures for unemployment are useful, particularly because they tell us the direction of *changes* in unemployment. It is unlikely, for example, that they will be rising significantly when unemployment is really falling. For all of the reasons that we have just discussed, however, they can at times give serious under- or overestimates of the total number of persons who would be genuinely willing to work if they were offered a job at the going rate of pay.

between 5 and 6 percent. (We shall discuss the reasons for these changes in Chapter 37.)

Unemployment: The Historical Experience

Figure 26-5(i) shows the trends in the labor force, employment, and unemployment since 1930. Despite booms and slumps, employment has grown roughly in line with the growth in the labor force and the total population. In the 1980s, however, the labor force and employment grew faster than the total population in response to the increasing participation of youths and women in the labor force.

Although the long-term growth trend dominates the employment figures, some unemployment is always present. Figure 26-5(ii) shows that the short-term fluctuations in the unemployment rate have been quite marked. The unemployment rate has been as low as 1.4 percent in 1944 and as high as 19.3

FIGURE 26-5 Canadian Labor Force, Employment, and Unemployment, 1930–1990

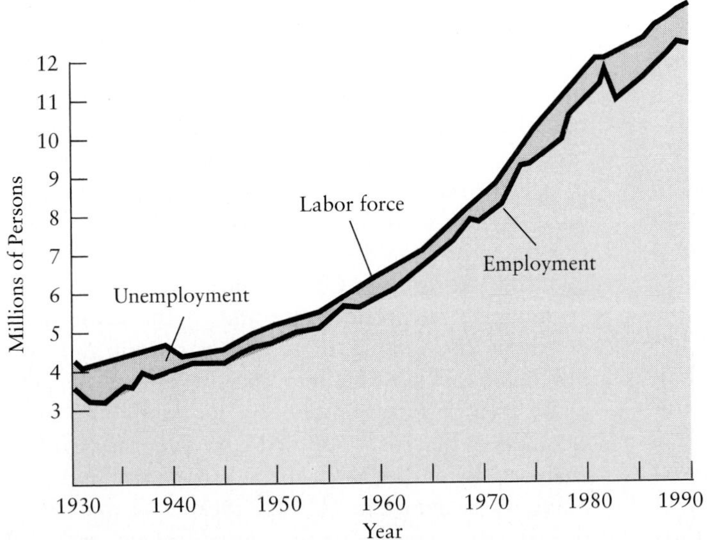

(i) Labor force, employment, and unemployment

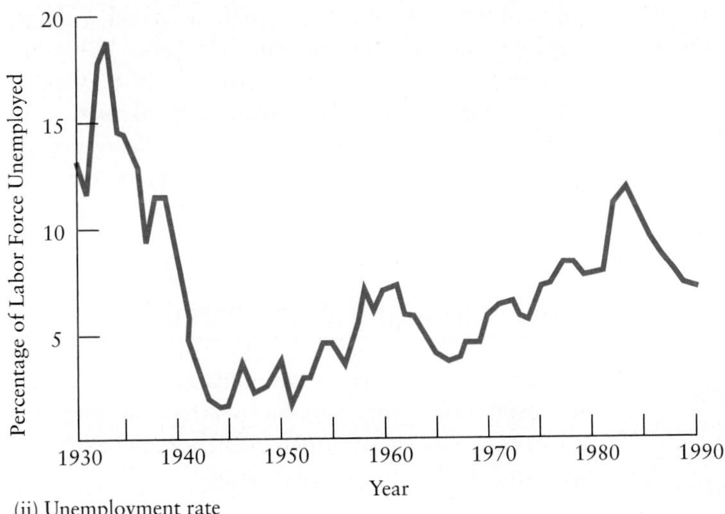

(ii) Unemployment rate

(i) The labor force and employment have grown since the 1930s with only a few interruptions. The size of the Canadian labor force has more than doubled since 1930, and so has the number of the employed. The fall in the labor force in the early 1940s was in the civilian labor force. The missing workers were in the military. Unemployment, the gap between the labor force and employment, has fluctuated. It reached a peak of 800,000 in 1933 and did not reach that level again until 1977. In 1983 it reached 1.5 million, although as we see in (ii), as a fraction of the labor force this is smaller than the 1933 figure.

(ii) The unemployment rate responds to the cyclical behavior of the economy. Booms are associated with low unemployment, slumps with high unemployment. The Great Depression of the 1930s produced record unemployment rates for an entire decade. During World War II, unemployment rates fell to very low levels. Since 1945, however, the unemployment rate has demonstrated a gradual upward trend. The recession of the early 1980s produced unemployment rates second only to those of the 1930s; these rates were extremely high by the standards of the post–World War II behavior of the Canadian economy. Over the period 1983–1986 the rate fell slowly but steadily, reaching 7.5 percent at the end of 1989. *Sources:* M. C. Urquhart, ed., *Historical Statistics of Canada*; Department of Finance, *Economic Review*; 1990 data are for June.

percent in 1933; in the post–World War II period the unemployment rate fell as low as 3.4 percent in 1956 and rose as high as 12.6 percent in 1982.

The high unemployment rate of the Great Depression in the early 1930s tends to dwarf the fluctuations in unemployment that have occurred since then. Nonetheless, the fluctuations in unemployment in recent decades have been neither minor nor unimportant.

Unemployment can rise either because employment falls or because the labor force rises. In recent decades the number of people entering the labor force has exceeded the number leaving it. The resulting rise in the labor force has meant that unemployment has sometimes grown even in periods when employment was also growing.

Why Unemployment Matters

The social and political significance of the unemployment rate is enormous. The government is blamed when it is high and takes credit when it is low. Few macroeconomic policies are planned without some consideration of how they will affect it. No other summary statistic, with the possible exception of the inflation rate, carries such weight as a source of both formal and informal policy concern as the percentage of the labor force unemployed.

Unemployment causes economic waste and human suffering. The economic waste is obvious. Human effort is the least durable of economic commodities. If a fully employed economy with a constant labor force has 12 million people who are willing to work in 1990, their services must either be used in 1990 or wasted. When the services of only 10.8 million are used because 10 percent of the labor force is unemployed, one year's potential output of 1.2 million workers is lost forever. In an economy in which there is not enough output to meet everyone's needs, many people feel that any waste of potential output is undesirable and that large wastes are tragic.

Severe hardship can be caused by prolonged periods of unemployment. A person's spirit can be broken by a long period of desiring but being unable to find work. Research has shown that crime, divorce, and general social unrest tend to be positively associated with unemployment.

In the not-so-distant past, only private charity or help from friends and relatives stood between the unemployed and starvation. Today, welfare and unemployment insurance have softened those effects, particularly when unemployment is for short periods, as is often the case. However, when an economic slump is deep and prolonged, as in the mid 1970s and again in the early 1980s, people begin to exhaust their unemployment insurance and must fall back on savings, welfare, or charity. In the early 1980s many people sank below the poverty level for the first time in their lives. They did so because they had used up their unemployment insurance but were unable to find jobs because of a persistently high unemployment level.

The Relationship Between Output and Employment

Output and employment (and therefore unemployment) are all closely related. If more is to be produced, either more workers must be used in production or existing workers must produce more. The first change means a rise in employment; the second means a rise in output per person employed, which is called a rise in *labor productivity*. Increases in productivity are a major source of economic growth. (Productivity was discussed in Chapter 11 and will be discussed again in Chapter 38.)

Changes in productivity and in the labor force dominate the long-term trends of output and employment, but productivity and the labor force generally change only slowly. As we study the main elements of macroeconomic theory over the next few chapters, we will treat both the labor force and productivity as constant. Under these assumptions, a rise in output means a rise in employment and a fall in unemployment. Output is positively associated with employment and negatively associated with unemployment. Taking productivity and the labor force as constant not only greatly simplifies our discussion but also is a reasonable approximation of reality when we are dealing with the *short-term* behavior of the economy. In later chapters we shall study changes in both productivity and the labor force.

Other Important Macro Variables

In addition to the macro variables that we have just discussed, three other variables warrant our attention at this stage. They are the interest rate, the exchange rate, and the balance of payments.

The Interest Rate

If a bank loans you money, it will usually ask you to agree to a schedule for repayment. Furthermore, it will charge you interest for the privilege of borrowing the money. If, for example, you are lent $1,000 today, repayable in one year's time, you may also be asked to pay $10 per month in interest. This makes $120 in interest over the year, which can be expressed as an interest rate of 12 percent per annum [(120/1,000) × 100 percent].

The **interest rate** is the price that is paid to borrow money for a stated period of time and is expressed as a percentage amount per dollar borrowed. For example, an interest rate of 12 percent per annum means that the borrower must pay 12 cents per year for every dollar that is borrowed.

Just as there are many prices of goods in the economy, so there are many interest rates. The bank will lend money to an industrial customer at a lower rate than it will lend money to you—there is a lower risk of not being repaid. The rate charged on a loan that is not to be repaid for a long time will usually differ from the rate on a loan that is to be repaid quickly.

When economists speak of "the" interest rate, they mean a rate that is typical of all the various interest rates in the economy. Dealing with one interest rate obscures much detail, but it does allow us to deal with overall changes in the level of interest rates. The prime rate of interest, the rate that banks charge to their regular business customers, may be thought of as "the" interest rate since, when the prime rate changes, most other rates change in the same direction.

The interest rate and inflation. How does inflation affect the rate of interest? Imagine that your friend lends you $100 and that it is repayable in one year. The amount that you pay her for making this loan, measured in money terms, is the **nominal interest rate**. If you pay her $108 in one year's time, $100 will be repayment of the amount of the loan (which is called the *principal*) and $8 will be payment of the interest. In this case, the nominal interest rate is 8 percent [(8/100) × 100 percent].

How much purchasing power has your friend gained or lost as a result of making this loan? The answer will depend on what happens to the price level during the year. The **real rate of interest** tells us the return on a loan, measured in terms of purchasing power. It is given by the nominal interest rate minus the inflation rate. This is because, as earlier examples have illustrated, a percentage payment equal to the inflation rate is needed just to compensate for the reduction in purchasing power of the amount loaned before any real return has been earned on the investment.

If the price level remains constant over the year, the real rate of interest that your friend earns would also be 8 percent, because she can buy 8 percent more goods and services with the $108 that you repay her than with the $100 that she lent you. However, if the price level rises by 8 percent, the real rate of interest would be zero, because the $108 that you repay her buys the same quantity of goods as the $100 that she originally gave up. If she is unlucky enough to lend money at 8 percent in a year in which prices rise by 10 percent, the real rate of interest that she earns is −2 percent.

If lenders and borrowers are concerned with real costs, measured in terms of purchasing power, the nominal interest rate will be set at the real rate to which they agree as a return on their money *plus* an amount to cover any expected rate of inflation. Consider a one-year loan that is meant to earn a real return to the lender of 5 percent. If the expected rate of inflation is zero, the nominal interest rate set for the loan will be 5 percent. If 10 percent inflation is expected, the nominal interest rate will be 15 percent.

To provide a given expected real rate of interest, the nominal interest rate must be set at the desired real rate of interest plus the expected annual rate of inflation.

Because they often overlook this point, people can be surprised at the high nominal interest rates that exist during periods of rapid inflation. For example, when the nominal interest rates rose drastically in 1980, many commentators expressed shock at the "unbearably" high rates. Most of them failed to notice that with inflation running at about 12 percent, an interest rate of 15 percent represented a real rate of only 3 percent. Had the Bank of Canada given in to the pressure to hold interest rates to the more "reasonable" level of 10 percent, it would have been imposing a *negative* real rate of interest. The purchasing power that lenders would get back, including interest, would be less than the purchasing power of the amount that was originally lent.

Concern about the burden of borrowing should be directed at the real, not the nominal, rate of interest.

For example, a nominal interest rate of 8 percent combined with a 2 percent rate of inflation is a much greater real burden on borrowers than a nominal rate

FIGURE 26-6 Real and Nominal Interest Rates, 1950–1990

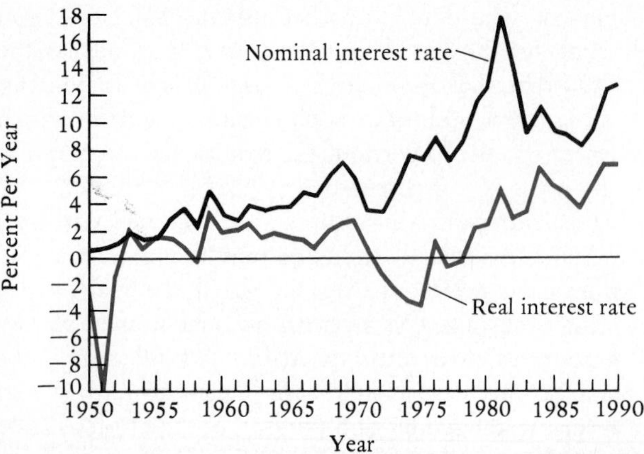

The inflationary trend in the postwar era has meant that the real interest rate has almost always been less than the nominal interest rate. The data for the nominal interest rate show the average rate of interest on three-month treasury bills in each year from 1950. The real interest is calculated as the nominal interest rate minus the actual rate of inflation over the same period. For the most part, the real interest rate has been below 3 percent throughout the period. Through much of the 1970s, the real interest rate was negative, indicating that the inflation rate exceeded the nominal interest rate. The 1980s saw real interest rates rise to heights that were unprecedented in the past. In the middle of the decade, as inflation moderated, both real and nominal interest rates fell, only to rise again.

of 16 percent combined with a 14 percent rate of inflation.

Figure 26-6 shows the nominal interest rate and the real rate of interest paid on short-term government borrowing since 1950. Interest rates were high and volatile during the early part of the 1980s; they fell somewhat in mid decade, only to rise again.

The Exchange Rate and the Balance of Payments

The exchange rate. If you are going on a holiday to Mexico, you will need Mexican pesos to pay for your purchases. Most banks, as well as any foreign exchange bureau, will make the necessary exchange of currencies for you. They will sell you pesos in return for your dollars. If you get 2,500 pesos for each dollar that you give up, the two currencies are trading at a rate of \$1 = 2,500 pesos or, what is the same thing, 1 peso = 0.0004 dollars.

The exchange rate refers to the rate at which different currencies are traded for each other.

In particular, the **exchange rate** between the Canadian dollar and any foreign currency is the quantity of Canadian dollars that is needed to buy one unit of that currency. For example, at the beginning of April 1990, it cost 1.18 Canadian dollars to buy one U.S. dollar; put the other way, one Canadian dollar was worth 0.84 U.S. dollar.

The term **foreign exchange** refers to foreign currencies or claims to foreign currencies, such as bank deposits, checks, and promissory notes, that are payable in foreign money. The **foreign exchange market** is the market where foreign currencies are traded—at prices expressed by the exchange rates.

The value of the Canadian dollar can be looked at in two ways. The *internal value of the dollar* refers to its power to purchase goods in Canadian domestic markets. We have already seen that the price level and the internal value of the dollar are negatively related: The higher the price level, the lower the purchasing power of a dollar. The *external value of the dollar* refers to its power to purchase foreign currencies. This external value is negatively related to the exchange rate, which, as you will recall, measures the dollar cost of a unit of foreign exchange. The lower the dollar's external value (that is, the less foreign currency it will buy), the higher the exchange rate (that is, the greater the number of Canadian dollars that must be used to purchase a unit of foreign exchange).

Figure 26-7 shows two indicators of the external value of the Canadian dollar since 1971. The first is the Canadian dollar price of one U.S. dollar; the second is an index of the weighted-average Canadian dollar price of the currencies of a group of 10 major industrial countries, called the G-10. Since the United States is such a major trading partner for Canada, the U.S. dollar gets a strong weight in the index, and the two series give a very similar picture.

For the first half of the 1970s, the external value of the Canadian dollar was relatively stable, fluctuating only moderately and not showing any trend. From 1976 through 1986, the external value of the

FIGURE 26-7 Canadian Dollar Exchange Rates, 1971–1990

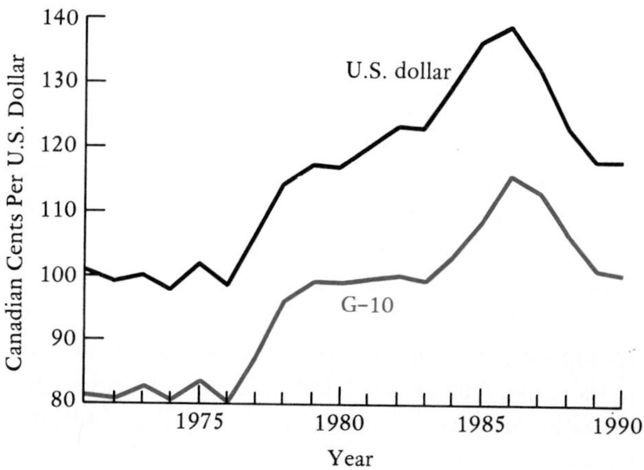

The Canadian dollar depreciated steadily from the mid 1970s through the mid 1980s; from 1986 through mid 1990 it appreciated. The black line shows the Canada-U.S. exchange rate, defined as the Canadian currency price, measured in cents, of one U.S. dollar. That price rose steadily from about $1.00 in 1976 to almost $1.40 in 1986; the rise in the price of U.S.dollars meant that the external value of the Canadian dollar was falling. From 1986 through mid 1990, the price of U.S. dollars fell continually, indicating a rising external value of the Canadian dollar.

The colored line shows the Canadian dollar exchange rate in terms of a weighted average of the currencies of 10 major industrial countries known as G-10. It is expressed as an index, with 1981 set equal to 100. This weighted average shows a similar pattern of a rising price of foreign exchange from 1976 through 1986 and a falling price from 1986 through mid 1990. *Sources: Bank of Canada Monthly Review,* various issues; 1990 data are for June.

Canadian dollar declined sharply, as both measures of the exchange rate rose over that period. (The period from 1980 to 1982 is interesting in that the external value of the Canadian dollar fell relative to the U.S. dollar but remained relatively stable relative to the G-10 average. During this period the U.S. dollar was very strong, and its external value rose relative to virtually all countries. The Canadian dollar actually strengthened relative to many of the G-10 countries, but its fall in terms of the U.S. dollar was enough to stabilize the average.)

From 1986 through mid 1990, the external value of the Canadian dollar strengthened, as both measures of the exchange rate fell; by mid 1990, both were back to approximately their 1980 levels. As the 1990s started, the strong external value of the Canadian dollar was a major point of controversy; Bank of Canada Governor John Crow argued that it was a necessary by-product of his commitment to fighting inflation (and thus stabilizing the internal value of the dollar), while many Canadian manufacturers said that it was destroying the competitiveness of Canadian industry by making foreign imports into Canada too cheap and making Canadian exports too expensive on world markets. We return to these debates in the chapters that follow.

The balance of payments. In order to know what is happening to the course of international trade and international capital movements, governments keep an account of the transactions among countries. These accounts are called the **balance-of-payments accounts**. They record all international payments that are made for the buying and selling of both goods and services, as well as financial assets such as stocks and bonds.

Figure 26-8 shows one part of the balance of payments that caused much controversy throughout the 1980s. This is the balance of payments on the *trade account,* or, as it is sometimes called, the *merchandise account.* This covers all trade in visible goods. (Services are recorded in another part of the account.) The balance is the difference between the value of Canadian exports and the value of Canadian imports. As can be seen from Figure 26-8, Canadian exports and imports both rose steadily in the 1970s and 1980s, and the balance of trade fluctuated slightly but remained at or near a roughly balanced position.

As we shall see in later chapters, the balance of trade is at the center of a number of economic controversies.

Cycles and Trends

Why are the price level, national income, and employment what they are today? What causes them to change? These are some of the questions that macroeconomics seeks to answer.

To study them, we make a number of assumptions that serve to simplify the analysis and that can be dropped later, once we have mastered the simpler

FIGURE 26-8 Canadian Imports, Exports, and Balance of Trade, 1970–1989

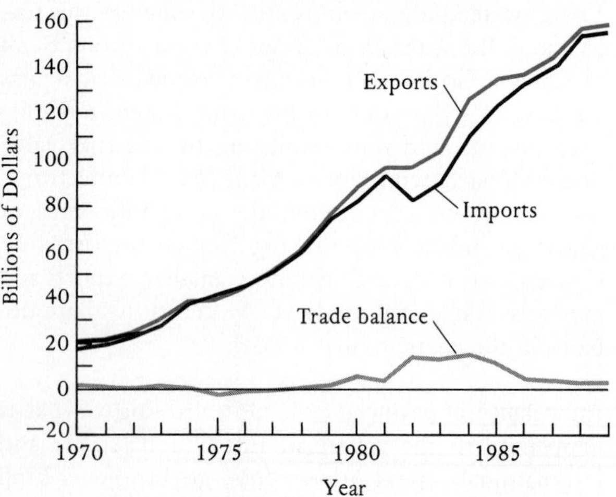

Though imports and exports are each quite large and have grown steadily, the balance of trade stays roughly in balance. The nominal value of imports and of exports rose steadily in the 1970s and 1980s, due both to price increases and to quantity increases. The sharp recession that Canada experienced in the early 1980s was accompanied by a sharp fall in imports, and the subsequent recovery was spurred in part by increased export sales (primarily to the United States). As a result, the balance of trade moved into a surplus in the 1980s, although it subsequently returned to its historical norm of being roughly in balance. *Sources: Bank of Canada Monthly Review,* various issues.

cases. Earlier in the chapter we encountered two such assumptions: Productivity and the labor force are assumed to be constant in the short run, implying that any increase in national income will be accompanied by an increase in employment and a decrease in unemployment. Hence the theory of national income that we will develop over the next few chapters will also explain both employment and unemployment.

As we have seen already in this chapter, national income and the price level exhibit long-term trends and short-term fluctuations around those trends. The analysis of the next few chapters is to be understood as establishing how the price level and national income will behave *relative to their trend.* A fluctuation that takes the price level or national income above its long-term trend will be indicated by an increase in its value, and a fluctuation that takes the price level or national income below its trend will be indicated by a decrease in its value.

Much of macroeconomics studies relatively short-term movements in the economy (that is, in terms of months or, at most, a few years). In order to concentrate on these movements, it is easiest to treat the longer-term trends of income, prices, and all other macro variables as zero. Thus in the next few chapters, when we talk about national income falling by 3 percent, we mean that it falls by 3 percent *relative to its growth trend.* If, for example, its long-term trend is to grow at 2 percent per year, a 3 percent fall (relative to that trend) actually would mean an observed fall of only 1 percent. Similarly, a force that causes the price level to fall by 4 percent below its trend will cause the price level to rise by 2 percent when its long-term trend is to rise at 6 percent per year. For the sake of simplicity, we call such a change a 4 percent fall in the price level, but it is important to remember that this means a 4 percent fall below its trend.

SUMMARY

1. Macroeconomics examines the behavior of such broad aggregates and averages as the price level, national income, potential national income, the output gap, employment, and unemployment.
2. Index numbers are summary measures the give the average percentage change in a set of related items between a base year and another given year.
3. The price level has displayed a continual upward trend since 1930. The inflation rate measures the rate of change in the price level. Although it fluctuates considerably, the inflation rate has been consistently positive.

4. The value of total production of goods and services is called national product. Since production of output generates income in the form of claims on that output, it is common also to talk of national income. One of the most commonly used measures of national income is gross domestic product (GDP). Nominal national income evaluates output in current prices. Real national income evaluates output in base period prices. Changes in real national income reflect changes in quantities of output produced.
5. Fluctuations of national income around its potential level are associated with the business cycle. Recoveries pass through peaks and turn into recessions, which in turn pass through troughs to become recoveries. Although these movements are systematic rather than random, they are by no means predictably regular.
6. Potential real national income measures the capacity of the economy to produce goods and services when factors of production are employed at their normal intensity of use. The output gap is the difference between potential and actual real national income.
7. The unemployment rate is the number of workers over 15 who are not employed and who are actively searching for a job, expressed as a percentage of the labor force. The labor force and employment both have grown steadily for the past half century. The unemployment rate fluctuates considerably from year to year. Unemployment imposes serious costs on the economy in the form of economic waste and human suffering.
8. Other important macroeconomic variables include nominal and real interest rates; exchange rates, which refer to the cost of a unit of foreign currency in terms of Canadian dollars; and the balance of payments, which is a record of all international transactions made by Canadian firms, households, and governments. The trade balance is a part of the balance of payments that refers to the difference between the value of exports and the value of imports of visible goods.
9. The dominant historical trends of the economy are growth of the price level, real output, and employment over the long term. This growth has never been entirely smooth; there have always been fluctuations in the price level, output, and unemployment around their trend growth rates. The study of these fluctuations is simplified by always stating and explaining the differences between the actual value of each variable and its trend value. Stated values, therefore, give deviations from the trend value; the actual, observed value is obtained by adding the trend value to the stated value. (If the trend value were zero, each stated value would be the same as that variable's actual value.)

TOPICS FOR REVIEW

Price level and rate of inflation
Real and nominal national income
Potential and actual national income and the output gap
Employment, unemployment, and labor force
Real and nominal interest rates
Exchange rate and balance of payments
Anticipated and unanticipated inflation

DISCUSSION QUESTIONS

1. Classify the issues raised in the following newspaper headlines as microeconomic, macroeconomic, or both.
   a. "Lettuce crop spoils as strike hits B.C. lettuce producers."
   b. "Analysts fear rekindling of inflation as economy recovers toward full employment."
   c. "Index of industrial production falls by 4 points."
   d. "Price of bus rides soars in Centerville as city council withdraws transport subsidy."
   e. "A fall in the unemployment rate signals the beginning of the end of the recession in the Edmonton area."
   f. "Silicon chip technology brings falling prices and growing sales of microcomputers."
   g. "Rising costs of imported raw materials cause most Canadian manufacturers to raise prices."
2. Most of the films on the list of 10-biggest-ever money makers have been made in the recent past. Does this mean that the best films are the most recent ones?
3. Between 1979 and 1986, employment in Canada grew by over 10 percent, from 10.4 million to 11.6 million. However, over that same period, unemployment grew from 836,000 to 1.2 million, and the unemployment rate rose from 7.4 percent to 9.6 percent. How do you reconcile these apparently conflicting statistics? Which do you think gives the most accurate description of developments in the economy?
4. During the economic recovery from 1983 through 1990, GDP at current prices grew at an average rate of 8.5 percent per year. To what extent does this imply an improvement in the economic circumstances of the average Canadian? What would we need to know in order to distinguish the effects on (a) a bank manager in Halifax, (b) an auto worker in Oshawa who was unemployed in 1982, (c) a pensioner living in retirement in Victoria, British Columbia, and (d) an oil field rigger living in Alberta?
5. Discuss the following statements about unemployment.
   a. "Unemployment is a personal tragedy and a national waste."
   b. "No one needs to be unemployed these days; just look at the help wanted ads in the newspapers and the signs in the stores."
   c. "Unemployment insurance is a boondoggle for the lazy and unnecessary for the industrious."
6. If you thought the inflation rate was going to be 10 percent next year, why would most people be unwilling to lend money at 5 percent interest? Say that 5 percent was all they could get and they had money they didn't want to spend for a year. Would they do better just to hold the money? What could they do that would be better than lending your money at 5 percent?
7. What might lie behind the allegation that "inflation is legalized government robbery" and the reply that "inflation only hurts the ignorant because no one with reasonable foresight needs to lose through inflation"?
8. In the good old days at the turn of the century you could buy a drink for $.05 and a full meal for $.25. Were they, then, good old days of high purchasing power for the average person?

Chapter 27

Measuring Macro-economic Variables

Our ultimate goal is to understand the type of macroeconomic events that were outlined in Chapter 26. Our first step is to look in some detail at the measurement and interpretation of one key set of variables—those relating to national output and national income.[1] We need to study national output and national income in order to develop the concepts used in macroeconomic theory and also to be able to interpret measures that play a prominent role in everyday discussion.

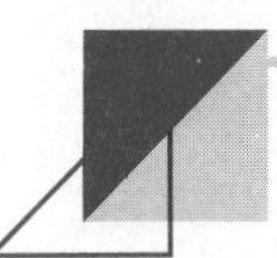

National Output Concepts

We are concerned in this chapter with measuring the nation's output and the income that is generated by its production. We start by asking two questions: What do we mean by output, and how do we distinguish real from nominal changes in output (and income)?

Value Added As Output

It may seem strange to ask what we mean by output. Surely the town bakery knows what it produces, and if General Motors does not know its own output, what does it know? If each firm knows the value of its total output, all the national income statisticians have to do is to add up each separate output value to get the nation's output—or is that all?

The reason that getting a total for the nation's output is not quite so simple as it seems is that one firm's output is another firm's input. The local baker uses flour that is the output of the flour milling company, and the flour milling company in turn uses wheat that is the farmer's output. What is true in bread production is true of most commodities.

Production occurs in stages: Some firms produce outputs that are used as inputs by other firms, and these other firms in turn produce outputs that are used as inputs by yet other firms.

If we merely added up the market values of all outputs of all firms, we would obtain a total that was greatly in excess of the value of the economy's actual output.

[1] We saw in Chapter 26 how to measure the price level by means of a price index. The measurement of labor force variables was also discussed briefly in that chapter; a more detailed discussion can be found in Chapter 37.

The local baker provides an example. If we added the total value of the sales of the wheat farmer, the miller, and the baker, we would be counting the value of the wheat three times, the value of the milled flour twice, and the value of the bread once.

The errors that would arise in estimating the nation's output by adding all sales of all firms is called **double counting**. *Multiple counting* would be a better term, since if we added up the values of all sales, the same output would be counted every time that it was sold from one firm to another.

The problem of double counting is solved by distinguishing between two types of output. **Intermediate goods** are outputs of some firms that are in turn inputs for other firms. **Final goods** are goods that are not, in the period of time under consideration, used as inputs by other firms. The term **final demand** refers to the purchase of final goods for consumption, for investment (including inventory accumulation), for use by governments, and for export. It does not include goods that are purchased by firms for use as inputs during the period under consideration.

If the sales of firms could be readily disaggregated into sales for final use and sales for further processing by other firms, measuring total output would still be straightforward. It would equal the value of all *final goods* produced by firms, excluding all intermediate goods. However, when Stelco sells steel to the Ford Motor Company, it does not care, and usually does not know, whether the steel is for final use (say, construction of a new warehouse) or for use as an intermediate good in the production of automobiles.[2] The problem of double counting must therefore be resolved in some other manner.

To avoid double counting, statisticians use the important concept of *value added*. Each firm's value added is the value of its output minus the value of the inputs that it purchases from other firms (and were in turn the outputs of those other firms). Thus a steel mill's value added is the value of its output minus the value of the ore that it buys from the mining company, the value of the electricity and fuel oil that it uses, and the values of all other inputs that it buys from other firms. A bakery's value added is the value of the baking products that it produces minus the value of the flour and other inputs that it buys from other firms.

The total value of a firm's output is the gross value of its output. The firm's value added is the net value of its output. It is this latter figure that is the firm's true contribution to the nation's total output. It is what its own efforts add to the value of what it takes in as inputs.

Value added is useful in avoiding the statistical problem of double counting; it is the correct measure of each firm's contribution to total output, the amount of market value that is produced by that firm.

The concept of value added is further illustrated in Box 27-1. In this simple example, as in all more complex cases, the value of total output of final goods is obtained by summing all the individual values added.

Gross Domestic Product

The sum of all values added in the economy is a measure of the economy's total output. This measure of total output is called **gross domestic product (GDP)**. It is a measure of all final output that is produced by all productive activity in the economy. Table 27-1 shows the composition of Canadian GDP by industry for 1989. The table also introduces a distinction between GDP valued at factor cost and GDP valued at market prices. The two differ because of indirect taxes—taxes on the production and sale of goods and services—and subsidies.

Suppose that a firm's value added as measured by the market value of its sales less the market value of its purchases of intermediate goods is \$10 and that \$1 of this represents excise taxes. Then only \$9 of the value added is attributable to the costs of factors used producing the output. Thus while the market value of its value added is \$10, in terms of factor costs its value added is only \$9. The other dollar represents the government's claim on the market value of the firm's value added.

Government subsidies on goods and services also cause the two measures of value added to differ. For example, consider a firm that produces a product with a market value of \$25,000, which, after subtracting \$15,000 worth of inputs purchased from other firms, has a value added of \$10,000. This is the firm's value added at market prices. But also assume

[2] Even if we use our earlier example of bread, a bakery cannot be sure that its sales are for final use, since the bread may be further "processed" by a restaurant prior to its final sale to a customer for eating.

BOX 27-1

Value Added Through Stages of Production

Because the output of one firm often becomes the input of other firms, the total value of goods sold by all firms greatly exceeds the value of the output of final products. This general principle is illustrated by a simple example in which Firm R starts from scratch and produces goods (raw materials) valued at $100; the firm's value added is $100. Firm I purchases raw materials valued at $100 and produces semimanufactured goods that it sells for $130. Its value added is $30 because the value of the goods is increased by $30 as a result of the firm's activities. Firm F purchases the semimanufactured goods for $130, works them into a finished state, and sells the final products for $180. Firm F's value added is $50. The value of the final goods, $180, is found either by counting only the sales of Firm F or by taking the sum of the values added by each firm. This value is much smaller than the $410 that we would obtain if we merely added up the market value of the commodities sold by each firm.

Transactions at three different stages of production

	Firm R	Firm I	Firm F	All firms
A = purchases from other firms	$ 0	$100	$130	$230 Total interfirm sales
B = purchases of factors of production (wages, rent, interest, profits)	100	30	50	180 Total value added
A + B = gross value of product	$100	$130	$180	$410 Total value of all sales

that the firm's wages and other production costs (excluding inputs for other firms) amounted to $14,000, with the extra $4,000 being covered by a government subsidy. The firm's value added measured at factor cost is therefore $14,000.

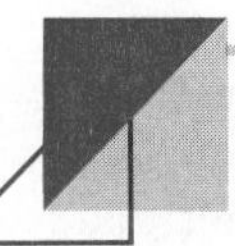

National Income Accounting

In Chapter 26 we used the generic terms *national income* to describe both the value of output produced and purchased and the value of income generated by that production. Earlier in this chapter we studied how output could be measured by summing values added; we called this aggregate measure GDP, and calculating GDP by summing values added is referred to as the *output approach*. Now we shall examine two other methods of calculating GDP and then relate GDP to other aggregate measures that are sometimes encountered.

It is useful to look again at Figure 3-1, on page 51, which shows the circular flow of expenditure and income. The bottom half of the circular flow focuses on expenditure to purchase the nation's output in product markets, and the top half focuses on factor markets where the receipts of firms are distributed to the factors used in producing the nation's output.

Corresponding to these two halves of the circular flow are two ways of measuring national income: the value of what is produced and the value of incomes generated by production. We can add up the total expenditure on each of the main components of final output; this is called the *expenditure approach*. We can also measure the incomes generated by the act of production; this is called the *income approach*.

The expenditure approach and the income approach are two different ways of looking at one magnitude: the market value of the nation's output.

The two approaches are conceptually identical and result in measures of GDP that differ in practice only because of errors of measurement. Each approach is of interest, however, because each gives a different and useful breakdown of national income. Also, hav-

TABLE 27-1 Real Gross Domestic Product, 1989

	Billions of 1981 dollars	Percent of GDP
Value added by sector		
Agriculture, fishing, and forestry	12.2	3.1
Mines, quarries, and oil wells	23.3	5.8
Manufacturing	77.3	19.3
Construction	30.1	7.5
Electric power, gas, and water utilities	11.5	2.9
Transportation, storage, and communication	31.7	7.9
Retail and wholesale trade	50.4	12.6
Financial, insurance, and real estate	58.2	14.5
Community, business, and personal services	40.8	10.2
Nonbusiness sector	64.2	16.1
GDP (at factor cost)	400.0	100.0
Plus: Indirect taxes less subsidies	65.1	
GDP (at market prices)	465.1	

Source: Statistics Canada, 11-003E; 15–001.

GDP, a measure of total output produced in Canada, can be decomposed into the contribution to that total by each of a number of sectors. GDP at factor cost equals the sum of values added of each sector. As can be seen, manufacturing is the largest sector, contributing over 19 percent. To convert *GDP at factor cost* to *GDP at market prices*, we have to add indirect taxes net of subsidies to the former.

ing two independent ways of measuring the same thing also provides a useful check on statistical procedures and unavoidable measurement errors.

National income accounting is the set of rules and techniques for measuring the total flow of output produced and the total flow of incomes generated by this production.

The conventions of double-entry bookkeeping require that all value produced must be accounted for by a claim someone has to that value.

Thus it is merely a matter of accounting convention that the two measures of GDP should be equal. (Measured values differ only to the extent that measurement errors arise. Any discrepancy arising from such errors is then reconciled so that one common total is given as *the* measure of GDP; that common total is also reconciled with the measure of GDP obtained using the output approach studied earlier in this chapter.)

The Expenditure Approach

The expenditure approach calculates GDP as the market value of final output by adding up the expenditures made to purchase final output. Total expenditure on final output is the sum of four broad categories of expenditure: consumption, investment, government, and net exports.

Consumption Expenditure

Consumption expenditure includes expenditure on all goods and services produced and sold to their final users during the year (with the exception of residential housing, which is counted as investment). It includes services such as haircuts, medical care, and legal advice; nondurable goods such as fresh meat, clothing, cut flowers, and fresh vegetables; and durable goods such as cars, television sets, and air conditioners. We denote actual, measured, consumption expenditure by the symbol C^a.

Investment Expenditure

Investment expenditure is expenditure on the production of goods not for present consumption, including inventories; capital goods such as factories, machines, and warehouses; and residential housing. Such goods are called **investment goods**.

Inventories. Almost all firms hold stocks of their inputs and their own outputs. These stocks are called

inventories. Inventories of inputs and unfinished materials allow firms to maintain a steady stream of production in spite of short-term fluctuations in the deliveries of inputs bought from other firms. Inventories of outputs allow firms to meet orders in spite of temporary fluctuations in the rate of output or sales.

Inventories require an investment of the firm's money, since the firm has paid for the goods but has not sold them yet. An accumulation of inventories counts as current investment because it represents goods produced but not used for current consumption. A drawing down, often called a *decumulation*, counts as disinvestment because it represents a reduction in the stock of finished goods that are available to be sold.

Additions to inventories are a part of the economy's final production of investment goods. These are valued in the national income accounts at market value, which includes the wages and other costs that the firm incurred in producing them and the profit that the firm will make when they are sold. Thus in the case of inventories of a firm's own output, the expenditure approach measures what will have to be spent to purchase them when they are sold rather than what has so far been spent to produce them.

Plant and equipment. All production uses capital goods—manufactured aids to production such as tools, machines, and factory buildings. The economy's total quantity of capital goods is called its **capital stock.** Creating new capital goods is an act of investment called *fixed business investment*, or simply **fixed investment**.

Residential housing. A house is a durable asset that yields its utility over a long period of time. For this reason, housing construction is counted as investment expenditure rather than as consumption expenditure. This is done by assuming that the investment is made by the firm that builds the house and that the sale to a user is a mere transfer of ownership that is not a part of national income.

Gross and net investment. The total investment that occurs in the economy is called **gross investment**. Gross investment is divided into two parts: replacement investment and net investment. **Replacement investment** is the amount of investment that just maintains the existing capital stock intact; it is called the **capital consumption allowance** or **depreciation**. Gross investment minus replacement investment is **net investment**. Positive net investment increases the economy's total stock of capital; replacement investment keeps the existing stock intact by replacing what has been used up.

All of gross investment is included in the calculation of national income. This is because all investment goods are part of the nation's total output, and their production creates income (and employment) whether the goods produced are a part of net investment or are merely replacement investment. Actual (that is, measured) total investment expenditure is denoted by the symbol I^a.

Government Expenditure on Goods and Services

When governments provide goods and services that households want, such as roads and air traffic control, it is obvious that they are adding to the total of valuable output in the same way as private firms that produce the trucks and airplanes that use the roads and air lanes. With other government activities, the case may not seem so clear. Should expenditures by the federal government to send a scientific probe into space or to pay a civil servant to refile papers from a now defunct department be regarded as contributions to national income? Some people believe that many (or even most) activities "up in Ottawa" or "down at City Hall" are wasteful, if not downright harmful. Others believe that it is governments, not private firms, that produce many of the important things of life, such as education and pollution control.

National income statisticians do not speculate about which government expenditures are or are not worthwhile. Instead, they include all government expenditures on goods and services as part of national income. (Government expenditure on investment goods is included as government expenditure rather than investment expenditure.) Just as the national product includes, without distinction, the output of both gin and Bibles, it also includes tanks and the upkeep of parks, along with the services of RCMP agents, senators, and even Revenue Canada investigators. Actual **government expenditure** on goods and services is denoted by the symbol G^a.

Government output is typically valued at cost rather than at the market value. In many cases there is really no choice. What, for example, is the market value of the services of a court of law? No one knows. We do know, however, what it costs the government to provide these services, so we value them at their cost of production.

Although valuing at cost is the only possible thing to do with many government activities, it does have one curious consequence. If, due to an increase in productivity, one civil servant now does what two used to do, and the displaced worker shifts to the private sector, the government's contribution to national income will register a decline. Conversely, if two workers now do what one worker used to do, the government's contribution will rise. Both changes could occur even though what the government actually does has not changed. This is an inevitable but curious consequence of measuring the value of the government's output by the cost of the factors, mainly labor, that are used to produce it.

It is important to recognize that only government expenditure on currently produced goods and services counts as part of GDP. A great deal of government expenditure does not count as part of GDP. For example, when Health and Welfare Canada sends a pension cheque to a retired person, the government is not purchasing any currently produced goods or services from the retiree. The payment itself adds neither to employment of factors nor to total output. The same is true of payments on account of unemployment insurance, family allowance, and welfare. All such payments are examples of **transfer payments**, which are government expenditures that are not made in return for currently produced goods and services. They are not a part of expenditure on the nation's total output, and they are not included in the measurement of GDP.

Thus when we refer to government expenditure as part of national income or use the symbol G^a, we include all government expenditure on currently produced goods and services, and we *exclude* all government transfer payments. (The term *government outlays* can be used to describe all government spending, including transfer payments.)

Net Exports

The fourth category of aggregate expenditure, and one that is increasingly important to the Canadian economy, arises from foreign trade. How do imports and exports influence the national income?

Imports. One country's national income is the total value of final commodities produced in that country. If your cousin spends $15,000 on a new car that was made in Japan, only a small part of that value will represent expenditure on Canadian production. Some of it represents payment for the services of the Canadian dealers and for transportation; the rest is the output of Japanese firms and expenditure on Japanese products. If you take your next vacation in Italy, much of your expenditure will be on goods and services produced by Italians and thus will contribute to Italian GDP.

Similarly, when a Canadian firm makes an investment expenditure on a Canadian-produced machine tool that was made partly with imported raw materials, only part of the expenditure is on Canadian production. The rest is expenditure on the production by the countries that are supplying the raw materials. The same is also true for government expenditure on such things as roads and dams; some of the expenditure is for imported materials, and only part of it is for domestically produced goods and services.

Consumption, investment, and government expenditures all have an import content. To arrive at total expenditure on Canadian products, we need to subtract from total Canadian expenditure any expenditure on imports, which is given the symbol M^a.

Exports. If Canadian firms sell goods to German households, the goods are a part of German consumption expenditure but also constitute expenditure on Canadian output. Indeed, all goods and services that are produced in Canada and sold to foreigners must be counted as part of Canadian production and income; they create incomes for the Canadians who produce them. To arrive at the total value of expenditure on Canadian domestic product, it is necessary to add in the value of Canadian exports. Actual exports are denoted by the symbol X^a.

It is customary to group actual imports and actual exports together as **net exports**. Net exports are defined as total exports minus total imports ($X^a - M^a$). When the value of exports exceeds the value of imports, net exports are positive. When, as in recent years, the value of imports exceeds the value of exports, net exports are negative.

Total Expenditures

Gross domestic product from the expenditure side is the sum of the four expenditure categories that we

TABLE 27-2 Components of GDP According to the Expenditure Approach, 1989

Expenditure category	Billions of dollars	Percentage of GDP
Consumption	350	58.2
Government	113	18.8
Investment	132	22.0
Net exports	4	1.0
Statistical discrepancy	2	—
	601	100

Source: Department of Finance, *Quarterly Economic Review,* 1990.

GDP measured from the expenditure side of the national accounts gives the size of the major components of aggregate expenditure. Consumption was by far the largest expenditure category, equal to almost 60 percent of GDP. Government and investment each accounted for about 20 percent. Whereas exports and imports are both quite large (each about 20 percent of GDP), net exports are quite small; in 1989 they represented a mere 1 percent of GDP.

have just discussed. These are shown in Table 27-2 for Canada in 1989.

GDP, calculated from the expenditure side, is the sum of consumption, investment, government, and net export expenditures.

The Income Approach

The production of the nation's output generates income. Labor must be employed, land must be rented, and capital must be used. The calculation of GDP from the income side involves adding up factor incomes and other claims on the value of output until all of it is accounted for. We have noted already that because all value produced must be owned by someone, the value of production must equal the value of income claims generated by that production.

Factor Payments

National income accountants distinguish four main factor incomes: wages, rent, interest, and profits.[3]

Wages. Wages and salaries (which national income accountants call *compensation to employees* but are usually just called *wages*) are the payment for the services of labor. Wages include take-home pay, taxes withheld, social insurance, pension fund contributions, and other fringe benefits. They represent the portion of the value of production attributable to labor.

Rent. Rent is the payment for the services of land and other factors that are rented. For the purposes of national income accounting, homeowners are viewed as renting accommodations from themselves. The amount of rent in the GDP thus includes payments for rented housing plus "imputed rent" for the use of owner-occupied housing. This allows national income measures to reflect the value of all housing services used, whether or not the housing is owned by its user.

Interest. Interest includes interest that is earned on bank deposits, interest that is earned on loans to firms, and miscellaneous other investment income.

Profits. Some profits are paid out as *dividends* to owners of firms; the rest are retained for use by firms. The former are called **distributed profits**, and the latter are called **undistributed profits** or **retained earnings**. Both distributed and undistributed profits are included in the calculation of GDP. For accounting purposes, total profits are reported in two separate categories—corporation profits and incomes of unincorporated businesses (mainly small businesses, farmers, partnerships, and professionals).

[3] The concepts of wages, rent, interest, and profits that are used in macroeconomics do not correspond exactly to the concepts with the same names that are used in microeconomics, but the details of the differences need not detain us.

Profits and interest together represent the payment for the use of capital—interest for borrowed capital and profits for capital contributed by the owners of firms.

Net domestic income at factor cost. The sum of the four components of factor incomes—wages, rent, interest, and profits—is called **net domestic income at factor cost**. It represents the share of total production that goes as income to the factors of production, labor, land, and capital; the rest is capital consumption and net business taxes.

Indirect Business Taxes Net of Subsidies

When using the income approach, we must distinguish between national income valued *at factor cost* and national income valued *at market prices*. The difference between the two is created by two effects—those of indirect business taxes and those of subsidies.

As we have seen, when summing values added to determine GDP, it is necessary to add in the part of the total market value of output that is the government's claim arising out of its taxes on goods and services. Recall also that it is necessary to subtract government subsidies on goods and services, since these allow the value of output, and hence incomes, to *exceed* the market value of output.

Net domestic product at market prices. Adding indirect business taxes to the four components of factor incomes and subtracting subsidies gives **net domestic product at market prices**. Taxes and subsidies are often combined into a single term, called *indirect taxes net of subsidies.*

Net domestic product at market prices equals the sum of wages, rent, interest, profits, and indirect taxes net of subsidies.

Depreciation

Another component on the income side arises from the distinction between net and gross investment. One claim on the value of final output is depreciation, or capital consumption allowance. This is the value of final output that embodies capital that has been used up in the process of its production. It is part of gross profits, but being the part needed to compensate for capital used up in the process of production, it is not part of net profits. Hence it is not income earned by any factor of production. Instead, it is value that must be reinvested just to maintain the existing stock of capital equipment.

Total Product

Adding depreciation to net domestic product at market prices gives **gross domestic product at market prices**.

From the income side, GDP is the sum of the factor incomes that are generated in the process of producing final output *plus* indirect taxes net of subsidies *plus* depreciation.

The various components of the income side of GDP in the Canadian economy in 1989 are shown in Table 27-3.

Income Produced and Income Received: An Important Distinction

GDP provides a measure of total output *produced in Canada* and of the total income generated as a result of that production. However, the total income received by Canadians can differ from GDP for two reasons. Some Canadian production creates factor earnings for foreigners who have previously invested in Canada or who sell services to producers in Canada; on this account, income received by Canadians will be less than Canadian GDP. Second, many Canadians earn income as a result of foreign investments and of factor services sold abroad; on this account, income received by Canadians will be greater than Canadian GDP.

As with total output produced, total income received by Canadians can be measured using either the income or the expenditure approach. The term **gross national product (GNP)** is used to describe total income received by Canadians as measured by the income approach. The term **gross national expenditure (GNE)** describes the same total measured using the expenditure approach. Hence GNE and GNP give conceptually identical measures of national income.[4]

Total output produced in the economy, measured by GDP, differs from total income re-

[4] In the United States, the term *GNP* is used to describe *both* measures, and the term *GNE* is not used in official statistics.

TABLE 27-3 Components of GDP According to the Income Approach, 1989

	Billions of dollars	Percentage of GDP
Compensation to employees	326	54.2
Corporate profits (before taxes)	62	10.3
Net interest	45	7.5
Rental income	37	6.2
Net domestic income at factor cost	470	78.2
Net indirect taxes	65	10.8
Net domestic income at market prices	535	89.0
Capital consumption allowance	68	11.3
Statistical discrepancy	−2	—
GDP at market prices	601	100.0

Source: Department of Finance, *Quarterly Economic Review,* 1990.

GDP measured from the income side of the accounts gives the size of the major components of the income that is generated by producing the nation's output. The largest category, equal to almost 55 percent of GDP, was compensation to employees, which includes wages and salaries plus employers' contributions to unemployment insurance, pensions, and similar schemes. The sum of compensation to employees, corporate profits, interest, and rental income equals net domestic income at factor cost. Adding net indirect taxes yields net domestic income at market prices. Adding the capital consumption allowance, which is the part of the earnings of businesses that is needed to replace capital used up during the year, and allowing for the statistical discrepancy yields GDP at market prices.

ceived by Canadians, measured by GNP and GNE, due to net foreign factor payments.

Reconciling GDP with GNP and GNE. Table 27-4 shows the reconciliation of GDP with GNP and hence with GNE. Recall that GNP and GNE both measure income received by Canadians, whereas GDP measures output produced in Canada. Since Canada has had a long history of importing capital from abroad, factor payments to foreigners exceed factor payments received from foreigners, and hence GDP exceeds GNP. (This does not mean that the net effects of Canada's foreign borrowing has been to reduce incomes of Canadians; most estimates show that foreign investment has contributed more to GDP than it has to the repatriation of factor payments and hence has increased GNP. We return to this important issue in Chapter 41.)

Other Income Concepts

Gross national income, however it is measured, is the most comprehensive income concept. The next most comprehensive measure is net domestic product. As we saw in building up the income approach, this is GDP minus the capital consumption allowance. Net domestic product is thus a measure of the

TABLE 27-4 Reconciling GDP with GNP

	Billions of dollars
GDP at market prices (from Table 27-3)	601
Plus: Investment income received from foreigners	11
Less: Investment income paid to foreigners	29
GNP (and GNE) at market prices	583

Source: Department of Finance, *Quarterly Economic Review,* 1990.

GNP, income owned or received by Canadians, is equal to GDP, income produced in Canada, plus factor income received from foreigners, less factor income paid to foreigners. Since Canada has traditionally experienced significant net foreign investment, investment income paid to foreigners is large, and hence net international factor payments for Canada are negative. As a result, GNP (and GNE, since GNE equals GNP) is less than GDP.

net output of the economy after deducting from gross output the amount needed to maintain intact the existing stock of capital. It is the maximum amount that could be consumed without actually running down the economy's capital stock.

Personal income is income that is earned by or paid to individuals before allowing for personal income taxes on that income. Some personal income goes for taxes, some goes for savings, and the rest goes for consumption. A number of adjustments to net domestic product are required to arrive at personal income. The most important are (1) subtracting *indirect business taxes net of subsidies*, which are the part of the market value of output that goes directly to governments (this, as we have seen, gives net domestic income at factor cost); (2) subtracting profits retained by corporations; (3) subtracting income taxes paid by business; and (4) adding transfer payments to households. The first three are parts of the value of output not paid to households; the fourth is paid to households and thus is income that households have available to spend or to save, even though the payments are not part of GNP.

Disposable personal income is the amount of current income that households have available for spending and saving; it is personal income minus personal income taxes.

Disposable personal income is GNP *minus* any part of it that is not actually paid to households *minus* personal income taxes paid by households *plus* transfer payments received by households.

The relationships among these various measures are shown in Table 27-5.

TABLE 27-5 Various National Income Measures, 1988

	Billions of dollars[a]
Gross domestic product at market prices	601
Less: Net foreign investment income	−18
Gross national product at market prices	583
Less: Capital consumption allowance	−68
Net domestic product at market prices	515
Less: Indirect taxes net of subsidies	−65
Net domestic income at factor cost	450
Less: Retained earnings and business taxes	−16
Plus: Government transfer payments to households	+71
Personal income	505
Less: personal income taxes	−112
Disposable personal income	393

[a] Figures may not match because of rounding.

Each of the six related national income measures focuses on a different aspect of the national output. Gross domestic product measures total output produced in Canada. Gross national product measures the market value of total income received by Canadians. Net domestic product measures the net value of national income after an allowance for maintaining the capital stock. Net domestic income at factor cost converts market price values to factor costs by adjusting for government indirect taxes net of subsidies. Personal income measures income earned or received by Canadians before personal income taxes. Disposable income measures Canadians' after-tax income; it is the amount they have available to spend or to save.

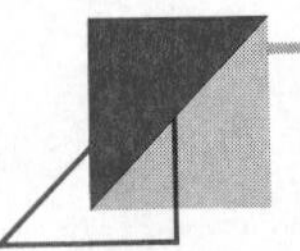

Interpreting National Income Measures

The information provided by national income data is useful, but unless it is carefully interpreted, it can be misleading. Furthermore, each of the specialized measures gives different information. Thus each may be the best statistic for studying a particular range of problems. Any statistical measure will be determined partly by some arbitrary decisions that might have been decided in another way. Some of these are discussed further in Box 27-2. The most important matters of interpretation will be dealt with now.

Real and Nominal Measures

In Chapter 26 we distinguished between real and nominal measures of national income and output. When we add up money values of outputs, expenditures, or incomes, we end up with what are called *nominal values*. Suppose that we found that a measure of nominal GDP had risen by 70 percent between 1980 and 1990. If we wanted to compare *real GDP* in 1990 to that in 1980, we would need to determine how much of that 70 percent nominal increase was due to increases in prices and how much was due to increases in quantities produced. Although there are

BOX 27-2

The Significance of Arbitrary Decisions

National income accounting uses many arbitrary decisions. Goods that are finished and held in inventories are valued at market value, thereby anticipating their sale, even though the actual sales price may not be known. In the case of a Ford in a dealer's showroom, this practice may be justified because the *value* of this Ford is perhaps virtually the same as that of an identical Ford that has just been sold to a customer. However, what is the correct market value of a half-finished house or an unfinished novel? Accountants arbitrarily treat goods in process at cost (rather than at market value) if the goods are being made by firms. They ignore completely the value of the novel in progress. Though these decisions are arbitrary, so would any others be. Clearly, practical people must arrive at some compromise between consistent definitions and measurable magnitudes.

The definition of final goods provides further examples. Business investment expenditures are treated as final products, as are all government purchases. Intermediate goods purchased by business for further processing are not treated as final products. Thus when a firm buys a machine or a truck, the purchase is treated as a final good; when it buys a ton of steel, the steel is treated as a raw material that will be used as an input into the firm's production process. If the steel sits in inventory, however, it is regarded as a business investment and thus *is* a final good.

Such arbitrary decisions surely affect the size of measured GDP. Does it matter? The surprising answer, for many purposes, is no. In any case, it is wrong to believe that just because a statistical measure falls short of perfection (as all statistical measures do), it is useless. Crude measures often give estimates to the right order of magnitude, and substantial improvements in sophistication may make only second-order improvements in these estimates.

In the third century B.C., for example, the Alexandrian astronomer Eratosthenes measured the angle of the sun at Alexandria at the moment that it was directly overhead 500 miles south at Aswan, and he used this angle to calculate the circumference of the earth to within 15 percent of the distance as measured today by the most advanced measuring devices. For the knowledge he wanted—the approximate size of the earth—his measurement was satisfactory. To launch a modern earth satellite, it would have been disastrously inadequate.

Absolute figures mean something in general terms, although they cannot be taken seriously to the last dollar. In 1989, GDP was measured as $601.5 billion. It is certain that the market value of all production in Canada in that year was neither $10 billion nor $10 trillion, but it might well have been $590 billion or $620 billion had different measures been defined with different arbitrary decisions built in.

International and intertemporal comparisons, though tricky, may be meaningful when they are based on measures all of which contain roughly the same arbitrary decisions. Canadian per capita GDP is a little less than three times Spanish per capita GDP and one-third higher than Japanese per capita GDP. Other measures might differ, but it is unlikely that any other would reveal that either Spanish or Japanese per capita GDP was higher than the Canadian. However, the statistics also show that per capita GDP was 2 percent higher in the United States than in Canada, a difference too small to have much meaning. Canadian output grew at 4.9 percent per year for the 30 years following World War II; it is unlikely that another measure of output would have indicated a 7 percent increase. Further, Japanese output grew at about 9 percent per year over the same period. It is inconceivable that another measure would alter the conclusion that Japanese national output rose faster than Canadian national output in those three decades.

BOX 27-3

Calculation of Nominal and Real National Income

To see what it involved in calculating nominal national income, real national income, and the implicit deflator, an example may be helpful. Consider a simple hypothetical economy that produces only two commodities, wheat and steel.

Table 1 gives the basic data for output and prices in the economy for two years.

TABLE 1 Data for a Hypothetical Economy

	Quantity produced		*Prices*	
	Wheat (bushels)	**Steel (tons)**	**Wheat (dollars per bushel)**	**Steel (dollars per ton)**
Year 1	100	20	10	50
Year 2	110	16	12	55

Table 2 shows nominal national income, calculated by adding the money values of wheat output and of steel output for each year. In year 1 the value of both wheat and steel production was $1,000, so nominal income was $2,000. In year 2 wheat output rose and steel output fell; the value of wheat output rose to $1,320 and that of steel fell to $880. Since the rise in value of wheat was bigger than the fall in value of steel, nominal income rose by $200.

TABLE 2 Calculation of Nominal National Income

Year 1 (100 × 10) + (20 × 50)	= $2,000
Year 2 (110 × 12) + (16 × 55)	= $2,200

Table 3 shows real national income, calculated by valuing output in each year by year 2 prices; that is, year 2 becomes the base year for weighting purposes. In year 2, wheat output rose but steel output fell. Using year 2 prices, the value of the fall in steel output between years 1 and 2 exceeded the value of the rise in wheat output, and real national income fell.

TABLE 3 Calculation of Real National Income Using Year 2 Prices

Year 1 (100 × 12) + (20 × 55)	= $2,300
Year 2 (110 × 12) + (16 × 55)	= $2,200

In Table 4 the ratio of nominal to real national income is calculated for each year and multiplied by 100. This ratio implicitly measures the change in prices over the period in question and is called the *implicit deflator.*

TABLE 4 Calculation of the Implicit Deflator

Year 1 (2,000 ÷ 2,300) × 100	= 86.96
Year 2 (2,200 ÷ 2,200) × 100	= 100.00

The implicit deflator shows that the price level increased by 15 percent between year 1 and year 2.

In Table 4 we used year 2 as the base year for comparison purposes, but we could have used year 1. The implicit deflator would then have been 100 in year 1 and 115 in year 2, and the increase in price level would still have been 15 percent.

many possible ways of doing this, the basic principle is always the same. It is to compute the value of output, expenditure, and income in each period by using a common set of *base period prices.* When this is done we speak of real output, expenditure, or income as being measured in *constant dollars.*

GDP valued at current prices is a nominal measure. GDP valued at base period prices is a real measure.

Any *change* in nominal GDP reflects the combined effects of changes in quantities and changes in prices.

TABLE 27-6 GDP in Current and Constant Dollars

Year	(1) GDP in billions of current dollars	(2) GDP in billions of 1981 dollars	(3) Implicit national income deflator (1981 = 100)
1935	4,301	34,685	12.4
1945	11,863	66,585	16.8
1955	29,250	109,104	26.8
1965	57,523	175,359	32.8
1975	171,540	283,187	60.5
1980	309,891	343,384	90.2
1985	479,446	393,817	121.7
1989	601,508	447,779	134.3

Sources: M. C. Urquhart, ed., *Historical Statistics of Canada*; Department of Finance, *Economic Review*.

Current dollar GDP tells us about the money value of output; constant dollar GDP tells us about changes in physical output. GDP in current dollars gives the total value of all final output in any year, valued in the selling prices of that year. GDP in constant dollars gives the total value of all final output in any year, valued at the prices prevailing in one particular year, in this case, 1981.

The ratio of *GDP in current dollars* to *GDP in constant dollars* times 100 is the implicit GDP deflator. (It is in effect a price index with current year quantity weights.)

However, when real income is measured over different periods by using a common set of base period prices, changes in real income reflect only changes in real output.

The Implicit Deflator

If nominal and real GDP changes by different amounts over some time period, this must be because prices have changed over that period. Comparing what has happened to nominal and real GDP over the same period implies the existence of a price index measuring the change in prices over that period. We say "implies" because no price index was used in calculating real and nominal GDP. However, an index can be inferred by comparing these two values. Such an index is called an *implicit price index* or an *implicit deflator.* It is defined as follows:

$$\textbf{Implicit deflator} = \frac{\textbf{GDP at current prices}}{\textbf{GDP at base period prices}} \times 100\%$$

Implicit deflators are the most comprehensive indexes of the price level because they cover all the goods and services that are produced by the entire economy. Although some other indexes use fixed weights, implicit deflators are variable-weight indexes. They use the current year's "bundle" of production to compare the current year's prices with those prevailing in the base period. Thus the 1990 deflator uses 1990 output weights, and the 1991 deflator uses 1991 output weights.

Box 27-3 illustrates the calculation of real and nominal national income and an implicit deflator for a simple hypothetical economy that produces only wheat and steel.

Any change in any nominal measure of national income can be split into a change due to prices and a change due to quantities. For example, in 1989, Canadian nominal GDP was 7.8 percent higher than in 1988. This increase was due to a 4.8 percent increase in prices and a 2.9 percent increase in real GDP.[5] Table 27-6 gives nominal and real income and the implicit deflator for selected years since 1935.

[5] The nominal change is not equal to the sum of the price and the quantity changes. Instead, the relationship is multiplicative. Prices and quantities are 1.048 and 1.029 times their original values, respectively. This makes nominal GDP equal to (1.048)(1.029) = 1.078 times its original value, which is an increase of 7.8 percent.

Total Values and Per Capita Values

The rise in real GDP during this century has had two main causes: an increase in the amounts of land, labor, and capital used in production and an increase in output per unit of input. In other words, more inputs have been used, and each input has become more productive. For some purposes, such as assessing a country's potential military strength or the total size of its market, we want to measure total output. For other purposes, such as studying changes in living standards, we require per capita measures, which are obtained by dividing a total measure such as GDP by the population.

There are many useful per capita measures. GDP divided by the total population gives a measure of how much GDP there is on average for each person in the country; this is called **per capita GDP**. GDP divided by the number of persons employed tells us the average output per employed worker. GDP divided by the total number of hours worked measures output per hour of labor input. A widely used measure of the purchasing power of the average person is disposable income per capita in constant dollars. This measure is shown in Figure 27-1.

The Significance of Omissions

Several types of economic activity are not included in GDP and are therefore also excluded from other

FIGURE 27-1 Disposable Income Per Capita in Canada, in Constant (1981) Dollars

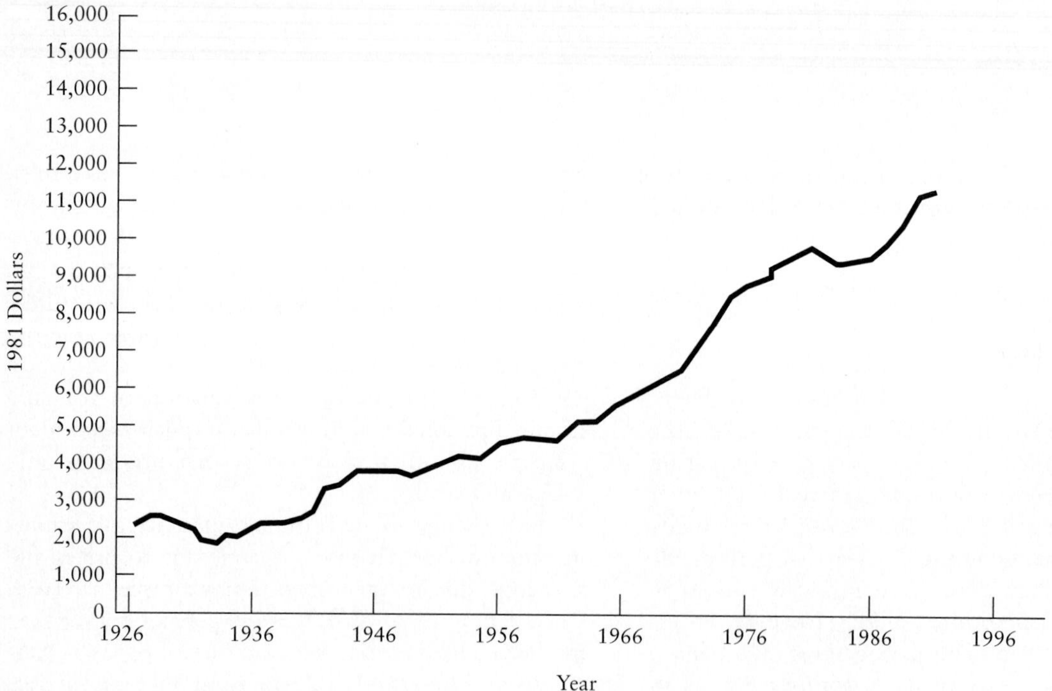

Disposable income per capita in constant dollars provides a measure of the real purchasing power available to the average Canadian household. Disposable income per capita fell during the early 1930s and late 1940s but has risen in every decade since. It underestimates the average living standard because it leaves out the contribution of government expenditures on such items as police, fire, justice, defense, and recreation. *Sources:* M. C. Urquhart, ed., *Historical Statistics of Canada*; *Bank of Canada Review.*

measures based on GDP. The importance of these omissions depends on the purpose for which the data are to be used.

Illegal activities. GDP does not measure illegal activities, even though many of them are ordinary business activities that produce goods and services sold on the market and generate factor incomes. The liquor industry during Prohibition in the United States (1919–1933) is an important example, because it accounted for a significant part of that nation's total economic activity. Today the same is true of illegal gambling, prostitution, and the drug trade. To gain an accurate measure of the *total* demand for factors of production in the economy, of *total* marketable output, or of incomes generated, we should include these activities, whether or not we as individuals approve of them. The omission of illegal activities is no trivial matter. The drug trade alone is a multibillion dollar business in North America.[6]

Unreported activities. An important omission from the measured GDP is the so-called underground economy. The transactions that occur in the underground economy are perfectly legal in themselves. The only illegal thing about them is that they are not reported for tax purposes. One example of this is the carpenter who repairs a leak in your roof and takes payment in cash or in kind in order to avoid tax. Because such transactions go unreported, they are omitted from GDP.

There are many reasons for the growth of the underground economy. Taxes, safety regulations, minimum wage laws, antidiscrimination regulations, and social insurance payments all may be avoided. The growth of the underground economy is also facilitated by the rising importance of services in the nation's total output. It is much easier for a carpenter to pass unnoticed by government authorities than it is for a manufacturing establishment.

Estimates of the value of income earned in the underground economy run from 2 to 15 percent of GDP. In some countries the figures are far higher. The Italian underground economy, for example, has been estimated at close to 25 percent of that country's total GDP!

[6] Some of these activities do get included in national accounting measures because people sometimes report their earnings from illicit activities as part of their earnings from legal activities. They do this to avoid the fate of Al Capone, a famous Chicago gangster in the 1920s, who, having avoided conviction on many counts, was finally caught for tax evasion.

Nonmarketed activities. If a homeowner hires a firm to do some landscaping, the value of the landscaping enters into GDP; if the homeowner does the landscaping herself, the value of the landscaping is omitted from GDP. Such omissions also include, for example, the services of homemakers, any do-it-yourself activity, and voluntary work such as canvassing for a political party, helping to run a volunteer day-care center, or leading a scout troop.

In most advanced industrial economies, the nonmarket sector is relatively small. The omissions become serious, however, when GDP or disposable income figures are used to compare living standards in very different economies. Generally, the nonmarket sector of the economy is larger in rural than in urban settings and in less developed than in more developed economies. Be a little cautious, then, in interpreting data from a country with a very different climate and culture. When you hear that the per capita GDP of Nigeria is about $900 per year, you should not imagine living in Winnipeg on that income.

Other omitted factors. Many factors that contribute to human welfare are not included in GDP. Leisure is one of these. Although a shorter work week may make people happier, it will reduce measured GDP.

GDP also does not allow for the capacity of different goods to provide different satisfactions. A million dollars that is spent on a bomber or a missile makes the same addition to GDP as a million dollars that is spent on a school or on candy bars; these are expenditures that may produce very different amounts of consumer satisfaction.

Do the Omissions Matter?

If we wish to measure the flow of goods and services through the market sector of the economy or to account for changes in the opportunities for employment for households that sell their labor services in the market, most of these omissions will not matter. If, however, we wish to measure the overall flow of goods and services available to satisfy people's wants, whatever the source of the goods and services, then the omissions are undesirable and potentially serious.

Is There a Best Measure?

To ask which is the best income measure is something like asking which is the best carpenter's tool. The answer is that it all depends on the job to be done. The decision concerning which measure to use will depend on the problem at hand, and solving some problems may require information provided by several different measures or information not provided by any conventional measures. If we wish to predict households' consumption behavior, disposable income may be the measure that we need to use. If we wish to account for changes in employment, constant dollar GDP may be the measure that we want. For an overall measure of economic welfare, we may need to supplement or modify conventional measures of national income, none of which measure the quality of life. To the extent that material output is purchased at the expense of overcrowded cities and highways, polluted environments, defaced countrysides, maimed accident victims, longer waits for public services, and a more complex life that entails a frenetic struggle to be happy, conventional measures of national income include only part of the things that contribute to human well-being.

Even if economists do come to use some new measures for some purposes, it is unlikely that GDP (and its relatives) will be discarded. Economists and policymakers who are interested in changes in market activity and in employment opportunities for factors of production will continue to use GDP and other relative measures because they are the ones that come closest to telling them what they need to know.[7]

[7] Concepts that come closer to measuring economic welfare have been developed. One was worked out by Professors William Nordhaus and James Tobin. It tries to measure consumption of things that provide utility to households rather than total production; it gives value to such nonmarketed activities as leisure and makes subtractions for such "disutilities" as pollution and congestion.

SUMMARY

1. Each firm's contribution to total output is equal to its value added. This is the gross value of its output minus the value of all intermediate goods and services—that is, the outputs of other firms—that it uses. Goods that count as part of the economy's output are called final goods; all others are called intermediate goods. The sum of all the values added produced in the economy is its total output, which is called gross domestic product (GDP).
2. GDP can also be calculated from either the expenditure or the income side. One gives the total value of expenditures required to purchase the nation's output, while the other gives the total value of incomes generated by the production of that output. By standard accounting conventions, these two aggregations define the same total.
3. From the expenditure side, GDP = $C^a + I^a + G^a + (X^a - M^a)$. C^a is consumption expenditures of households. I^a is investment in plant and equipment, residential construction, and inventory accumulation. Gross investment can be split into replacement investment (necessary to keep the stock of capital intact) and net investment (net additions to the stock of capital). G^a is government expenditures except transfer payments. $X^a - M^a$ is net exports, or exports minus imports; it will be negative if imports exceed exports.
4. GDP measured from the income side adds up all claims to the market value of production. Wages, rent, interest, profits, depreciation (capital consumption allowance), and indirect business taxes net of subsidies are the major categories.
5. Gross domestic product (GDP) measures production occurring in Canada, whereas gross national product (GNP) measures income accruing to Canadians. The difference is due to the balance between Canadian claims to incomes that are generated abroad and foreign claims to incomes that are generated in Canada.
6. Real measures of national income are calculated to reflect changes in

real quantities. Nominal measures of national income are calculated to reflect changes in both prices and quantities. Any change in nominal income can be split into a change in real income and a change due to prices. Appropriate comparisons of nominal and real measures yield implicit deflators.

7. Several related but different income measures are used in addition to GDP. Net domestic product measures total output after deducting the capital consumption allowance. Personal income is income actually earned by households before any allowance for personal taxes. Disposable personal income is the amount actually available to households to spend or to save, that is, income minus taxes.
8. GDP and related measures of national income must be interpreted with their limitations in mind. GDP excludes production resulting from activities that are illegal, that take place in the underground economy, or that do not pass through markets. Moreover, GDP does not measure everything that contributes to human welfare.
9. Notwithstanding its limitations, GDP remains a useful measure of the total economic activity that passes through the nation's markets and means of accounting for changes in the employment opportunities of households that sell their labor services on the market.

TOPICS FOR REVIEW

Value added
Gross domestic product (GDP) as the sum of all values added
Intermediate and final goods
GDP from the expenditure and income sides
National income measured at factor cost and at market prices
Gross national product (GNP)
Measures of real and nominal national income
Implicit deflator
Net domestic income, net domestic product, personal income, and disposable income
The significance of omissions from measured income

DISCUSSION QUESTIONS

1. If Canada and the United States were to join together as a single country, what would be the effect on their total GDP (assuming that output in each country is unaffected)? Would any of the components in their GDP change significantly?
2. In 1986 Statistics Canada switched from reporting national income in terms of GNP to reporting it in terms of GDP. How do these two measures differ? Do you think GDP is a better or worse measure of national income than GNP? Does your answer depend on the purpose the measure is being used for?
3. "Every time you rent a U-Haul, brick in a patio, grow a vegetable, fix your own car, photocopy an article, join a food co-op, develop your own film, sew a dress, stew fruit, or raise a child, you are commiting a productive act, even though these activities are not reflected in the gross domestic product." To what extent are each of these things "productive acts"? Are any of them included in GDP? If they are excluded, does the exclusion matter?
4. In measuring GDP from the expenditure side, which of the following expenditures are included? Why?
   a. Expenditures on automobiles by consumers and by firms

b. Expenditures on food and lodging by tourists and by business people on expense accounts
c. Expenditures on new machinery and equipment by firms
d. The purchase of one corporation by another corporation
e. Increases and decreases in business inventories

5. What would be the effect of the following events on the measured value of Canada's real GDP? Speculate on the effects of each event on the true well-being of Canadians.
a. Destruction of thousands of homes and stores by floodwater
b. Complete cessation of all imports from South Africa
c. An increase in the amount of acid rain that falls
d. An increase in the amount of spending on devices that reduce pollution at a major hydroelectricity plant

6. Consider the effect on measured GDP and on economic well-being of each of the following:
a. Reduction in the standard work week from 40 hours to 30 hours
b. Hiring of all welfare recipients as government employees
c. Increase in the salaries of priests and ministers as a result of increased contributions of churchgoers

7. In the United States a Social Security Administration study, using 1972 data, found the "average American housewife's value" to be U.S. $4,705 per year. Update the total to a current dollar figure. The study arrived at this total by adding up the hours that she spent cooking multiplied by a cook's wage, the hours spent with her children multiplied by a babysitter's wage, and so on. Should the time that a parent spends taking children to a concert be included? Are dollar amounts that are assigned to such activities a satisfactory proxy for market value of production? For what, if any, purposes would such values be excluded from or included in national income?

8. Use the table that appears on the endpaper at the back of this book to calculate the percentage increase over the most recent two decades of each of the following magnitudes. Can you account for the relative size of these changes?
a. GDP in current dollars
b. GDP in constant dollars
c. Disposable income in constant dollars
d. Disposable income per capita in constant dollars

9. A recent newspaper article reported that Switzerland was considered the "best" place in the world to live. In view of the fact that Switzerland does not have the highest per capita income in the world, how can it be ranked as the "best"?

Chapter 28

National Income and Aggregate Expenditure

In Chapters 26 and 27 we encountered a number of important macroeconomic variables. We described how they are measured and how they have behaved over the past half century or so. We now turn to a more detailed study of what *causes* these variables to behave as they do. In particular, we study the forces that determine national income (and hence employment and unemployment) and the price level.

The first things that we want to know are what determines the size of real national income and what makes it change. Because it is easier to do things one at a time, rather than all at once, this chapter deals with these questions on the assumption that the price level is constant. In Chapter 29 we shall see what happens when the price level varies.

Our ability to explain the behavior of national income depends on our understanding of what determines the amount that households and firms spend and why they change their spending. For this reason, we begin with an examination of the *expenditure decisions* of households and firms. As a first step, we distinguish between *desired* expenditure and *actual* expenditure.

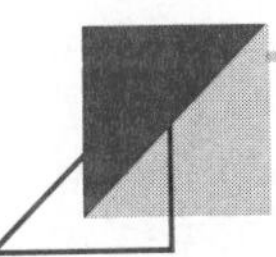

Desired Expenditure

In Chapter 27 we discussed how national income statisticians measure gross national expenditure by summing its components: consumption, C^a; investment, I^a; government, G^a; and net exports, $X^a - M^a$.

In this chapter we are concerned with a different concept. It is variously called *desired, planned,* or *intended* expenditure. Of course, all people would like to spend virtually unlimited amounts, if only they had the money. Desired expenditure does not refer, however, to what people would like to do under imaginary circumstances. It refers, instead, to what people want to spend out of the resources at their command. The *actual* values of the various categories of expenditure are indicated by C^a, I^a, G^a, and $X^a - M^a$. We use the same letters without the superscript *a* to indicate the *desired* expenditure in the same categories: C, I, G, and $X - M$.

Everyone with money to spend makes expenditure decisions. Fortunately, it is unnecessary for our purposes to look at each of the millions of such individual decisions. Instead, it is sufficient to consider four main groups of decision makers: domestic households, firms, governments, and foreign purchasers of domestically produced commodities. Their actual purchases account for the four main categories of expenditure that we studied in Chapter 27: consumption, investment, government, and exports. Their desired expenditures, made up of desired consumption, desired investment, desired government purchases, and desired exports, account for total desired expenditure. To allow for the fact that some of the commodities desired by each group will have an import content, we subtract import expenditure. The result is total desired expenditure on domestically produced goods and services, called **aggregate expenditure,** AE:

$$AE = C + I + G + (X - M)$$

Desired expenditure need not equal actual expenditure, either in total or in any individual category. For example, firms may not plan to invest in inventory accumulation this year but may do so unintentionally. If they produce goods to meet estimated sales but demand is unexpectedly low, the unsold goods that pile up on their shelves are undesired, and unintended, inventory accumulation. In this case actual investment expenditure, I^a, will exceed desired investment expenditure, I.

National income accounts measure *actual expenditures* in each of the four categories: consumption, investment, government, and net exports. The theory of national income deals with *desired expenditures* in each of these four categories.

To develop a theory of national income determination, we need to examine the determinants of each component of desired aggregate expenditure.

In this chapter we focus on desired consumption. It is the largest single component of aggregate expenditure, and as we will see, it provides the single most important link between desired aggregate expenditure and national income. We also look briefly at desired net exports, which provide a second link between desired aggregate expenditure and national income. For example, when residents of foreign countries decide to cut down on their purchases of Canadian goods because their prices are too high, this reduces the desired aggregate expenditure on Canadian output.

Although desired investment and government expenditures are treated only briefly here, they will be discussed in more detail in later chapters.

Before proceeding, we need to recall the important distinction between *autonomous* and *induced* expenditure, first introduced in Chapter 2. Components of aggregate expenditure that do *not* depend on national income are called *autonomous expenditures.* Autonomous expenditures can and do change, but such changes do not occur systematically in response to changes in national income. Components of aggregate expenditure that *do* change in response to changes in national income are called *induced expenditures.* As we will see, the induced response of aggregate expenditure to a change in national income plays a key role in the determination of equilibrium national income.

Desired Consumption Expenditure

Households can do one of two things with their disposable income: spend it on consumption or save it. **Saving** is all disposable income that is not consumed.

Since by definition there are only two possible uses of disposable income, spending or saving, when the household decides how much to put to one use, automatically it has decided how much to put to the other use.

What determines the division between the amount that households decide to spend on goods and services for consumption and the amount that they decide to save? The factors that influence this decision are summarized in the consumption function and the saving function.

The Consumption Function

The **consumption function** relates the total desired consumption expenditure of all households to the factors that determine it. It is, as we shall see, one of the central relationships in macroeconomics.

Although we are ultimately interested in the relationship between consumption and national income, the underlying behavior of households depends on the income that they actually have to spend—their disposable income. Therefore, we shall start with the relationship between consumption and disposable income, which we denote by Y_d, and then go on to relate consumption to national income.

Consumption and Disposable Income

It should not surprise us to hear that a household's expenditure is related to the amount of income that it has at its disposal. There is, however, more than one way in which this relationship could work. To see what is involved, consider two quite different households.

The first household is headed by the proverbial prodigal son. It spends everything it receives and puts nothing aside for a rainy day. When overtime results in a large paycheck, the household goes on a binge. When short hours are worked during periods of slack demand, the household's take-home pay is small and its members cut their expenditures correspondingly. This household's expenditure each week is thus directly linked to each week's take-home pay, that is, its current disposable income.

The second household is the opposite of the first. It thinks about the future as much as the present, and it makes plans that stretch over its lifetime. It puts money aside for retirement and for the occasional rainy day when disposable income may fall temporarily—it knows that it must expect alternating bouts of good and bad times. It also knows that it will need to spend extra money while the family is being raised and educated and that its income will probably be higher later in life when the children have left home and the husband and wife have finally reached the peaks of their personal careers. The household may borrow to meet higher expenses earlier in life, paying back out of the higher income that the household expects to attain later in life. A temporary, unexpected windfall of income may be saved. A temporary, unexpected shortfall may be cushioned by spending the savings that were put aside for just such a rainy day. In short, this household's current expenditure will be closely related to its expected *lifetime income,* so that fluctuations in its *current income* will have little effect on its current expenditure, unless such fluctuations also cause it to change its expectations of lifetime income, as would be the case, for example, if an unexpected promotion came along.

John Maynard Keynes, the English economist who developed the basic theory of macroeconomics—and, incidentally, gave his name to *Keynesian economics*—populated his theory with prodigal sons. For them, current consumption expenditure depended only on current income. A consumption function based on this assumption is called a *Keynesian consumption function.*

Later, two American economists, Franco Modigliani and Milton Friedman, both of whom were subsequently awarded the Nobel Prize in Economics, analyzed the behavior of prudent households. Their theories, which Modigliani called the *life-cycle theory* and which Friedman called the *permanent-income theory,* explain some observed consumer behavior that cannot be explained by the Keynesian consumption function. (For more details, see the appendix to this chapter.) However, the differences between the theories of Friedman and Modigliani, on the one hand, and Keynes, on the other hand, are not as great as might seem at first sight. To see why this is so, let us return to our two imaginary households and see why their actual behavior may not be quite so divergent as we so far described it.

Even the household that is headed by the prodigal son may be able to do some smoothing of expenditures in the face of income fluctuations. Most households have some money in the bank and some ability to borrow, even if it is just from friends and relatives. As a result, every income fluctuation will not be matched by an exactly equivalent expenditure fluctuation.

Although the second household wants to smooth its pattern of consumption completely, it may not have the borrowing capacity to do so. Its bank manager may not be willing to lend money for consumption when the security consists of nothing more than the expectation that the household's income will be much higher in later years, even if that expectation is quite reasonable. This may mean that the household's consumption expenditure fluctuates more with its current income than it would wish.

This discussion suggests that a household's consumption expenditure will fluctuate to some extent with its current disposable income and to some extent with its expectations of future disposable income. To develop our basic theory, we make the simplifying assumption that consumption expenditure is primarily determined by current disposable income. Once we understand the principles of the determination of national income, it will be an easy matter to allow for the fact that consumption expenditure is also influenced by expectations of future income.

Notice that whenever a change in current income is expected to be permanent, both current and expected future income change in the same way. This is true, for example, if households do not get an expected raise in pay this year and decide that this reflects a permanent but unforeseen downturn in business conditions. A second example is when what is expected to be a permanent tax reform leaves households with more take-home pay. In the first case their current disposable income and the income that they expect to receive in the future will both fall; in the second case they both rise. Relating expenditures to changes in current or to expected future income will then give the same answer—that expenditures will rise when income rises and fall when income falls.

The term *consumption function* describes the relationship between consumption and the variables that influence it; in the simplest theory, consumption is determined by current disposable income.

In Chapter 27 we examined the calculation of disposable personal income; for the purposes of this discussion, all we need to know is that disposable personal income tends to be a relatively constant percentage of national income.

Some consumption expenditure is *autonomous*, but most is *induced*; that is, most varies with disposable income and hence with national income. A schedule relating disposable income to desired consumption expenditure for a hypothetical economy appears in the first two columns of Table 28-1. In this example, autonomous consumption expenditure is \$100 billion, whereas induced consumption expenditure is 80 percent of disposable income. In what follows, we use this hypothetical example to illustrate the various properties of the consumption function.

Average and marginal propensities to consume. To discuss the consumption function concisely, economists use two technical expressions.

The **average propensity to consume (APC)** is total consumption expenditure divided by total disposable income. The third column of Table 28-1

TABLE 28-1 The Calculation of Average Propensity to Consume (APC) and Marginal Propensity to Consume (MPC) (*billions of dollars*)

Disposable income (Y_d)	Desired consumption (C)	$APC = C/Y_d$	ΔY_d (change in Y_d)	ΔC (change in C)	$MPC = \Delta C/\Delta Y_d$
0	100	—			
			100	80	0.80
100	180	1.800			
			300	240	0.80
400	420	1.050			
			100	80	0.80
500	500	1.000			
			500	400	0.80
1,000	900	0.900			
			1,000	800	0.80
2,000	1,700	0.850			
			1,000	800	0.80
3,000	2,500	0.833			
			1,000	800	0.80
4,000	3,300	0.825			

***APC* measures the proportion of disposable income that households desire to spend on consumption; *MPC* measures the proportion of any *increment* to disposable income that households desire to spend on consumption.** The data are hypothetical. We call the level of income at which desired consumption equals disposable income the break-even level; in this example it is \$500 billion. APC, calculated in the third column, exceeds unity—that is, consumption exceeds income—below the break-even level. Above the break-even level, APC is less than unity. It is negatively related to income at all levels of income.

The last three columns are set between the lines of the first three columns to indicate that they refer to changes in the levels of income and consumption. MPC, calculated in the last column, is constant at 0.80 at all levels of Y_d. This indicates that in this example, 80 cents of *every* additional dollar of disposable income is spent on consumption and 20 cents is used to increase savings.

shows the *APC*s calculated from the data in the table.

The **marginal propensity to consume (*MPC*)** relates the change in consumption to the *change* in disposable income that brought it about. *MPC* is the change in disposable income divided into the resulting consumption change: $MPC = \Delta C/\Delta Y_d$ (where the Greek letter Δ, delta, means "a change in"). The last column of Table 28-1 shows the *MPC*s calculated from the data in the table. [31]

The slope of the consumption function. Part (i) of Figure 28-1 shows a graph of the consumption function plotted from the first two columns of Table 28-1. The consumption function has a slope of $\Delta C/\Delta Y_d$, which is, by definition, the marginal propensity to consume. The positive slope of the consumption function shows that the *MPC* is positive; increases in income lead to increases in expenditure.

Using the concepts of the average and marginal propensities to consume, we can summarize the properties of the short-term consumption function as follows:

1. There is a break-even level of income at which *APC* equals unity. Below this level, *APC* is greater than unity; above it, *APC* is less than unity.
2. *MPC* is greater than zero but less than unity for all levels of income.

FIGURE 28-1 The Consumption and Saving Functions (*billions of dollars*)

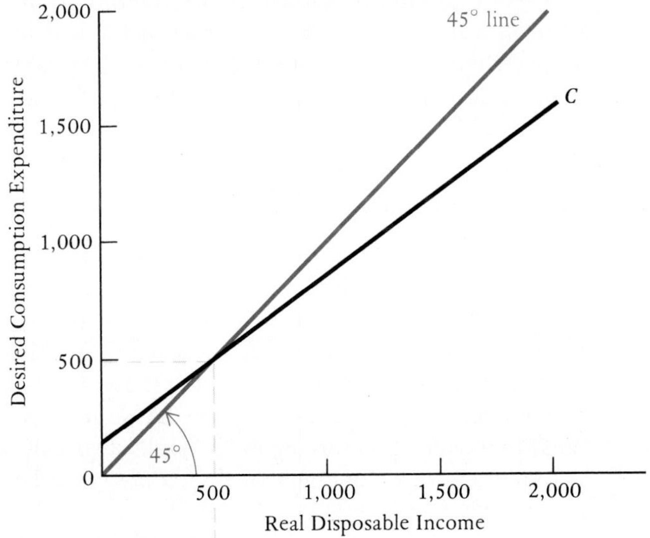

(i) Consumption function

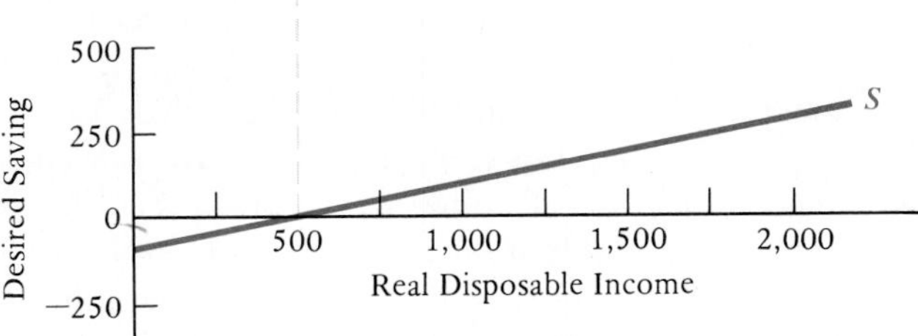

(ii) Saving function

Both consumption and saving rise as disposable income rises. Line *C* in (i) relates desired consumption expenditure to disposable income by using the hypothetical data from Table 28-1. Its slope, $\Delta C/\Delta Y_d$, is the marginal propensity to consume (*MPC*). The consumption line cuts the 45° line at the break-even level of disposable income, $500 billion in this case.

Saving is all disposable income that is not spent on consumption ($S = Y_d - C$). The relationship between desired saving and disposable income is derived in Table 28-2 and is shown in (ii) by line *S*. Its slope, $\Delta S/\Delta Y_d$, is the marginal propensity to save (*MPS*). The saving line cuts the horizontal axis at the break-even level of income. The vertical distance between *C* and the 45° line in (i) is by definition the height of *S* in (ii); that is, any given level of disposable income must be accounted for by the amount consumed plus the amount saved.

The 45° line. Figure 28-1(i) contains a line that is constructed by connecting all points where desired consumption (measured on the vertical axis) equals disposable income (measured on the horizontal axis). Since both axes are given in the same units, this line has a positive slope of unity, or (what is the same thing) it forms an angle of 45° with the axes. The line is therefore called the **45° line**.

The 45° line makes a handy reference line. In Figure 28-1(i) it helps to locate the break-even level of income at which consumption expenditure equals disposable income. The consumption function cuts the 45° line at the break-even level of income, in this instance \$500 billion. (The 45° line is steeper than the consumption function because the *MPC* is less than unity.)

The Saving Function

Households decide how much to consume and how much to save. As we have said, this is a single decision: how to divide disposable income between consumption and saving. It follows that once we know the dependence of consumption on disposable income, we also automatically know the dependence of saving on disposable income. (This is illustrated in Table 28-2.)

Two saving concepts are exactly parallel to the consumption concepts of *APC* and *MPC*. The **average propensity to save (*APS*)** is the proportion of disposable income that households want to save, derived by dividing total desired saving by total disposable income, $APS = S/Y_d$. The **marginal propensity to save (*MPS*)** relates the *change* in total desired saving to the *change* in disposable income that brought it about, $MPS = \Delta S/\Delta Y_d$.

There is a simple relationship between the saving and the consumption propensities. *APC* and *APS* must sum to unity, and so must *MPC* and *MPS*. Since income is either spent or saved, it follows that the fractions of incomes consumed and saved must account for all income ($APC + APS = 1$). It also follows that the fraction of any increment to income consumed and saved must account for all of that increment ($MPC + MPS = 1$). **[32]**

Calculations from Table 28-2 will allow you to confirm these relationships in the case of the example given. *MPC* is 0.80 and *MPS* is 0.20 at all levels of income, while, for example, at an income of \$2 trillion *APC* is 0.85 and *APS* is 0.15.

Part (ii) of Figure 28-1 shows the saving schedule given in Table 28-2. At the break-even level of income, where desired consumption equals disposable income, desired saving is zero. The slope of the saving line $\Delta S/\Delta Y_d$ is *MPS*.

TABLE 28-2 Consumption and Saving Schedules (*billions of dollars*)

Disposable income	Desired consumption	Desired saving
0	100	−100
100	180	− 80
400	420	− 20
500	500	0
1,000	900	+100
2,000	1,700	+300
3,000	2,500	+500
4,000	3,300	+700

Saving and consumption account for all household disposable income. The first two columns repeat the data from Table 28-1. The third column, desired saving, is disposable income minus desired consumption. Consumption and saving both increase steadily as disposable income rises. In this example, the break-even level of disposable income is \$500 billion.

Consumption and Wealth

We have seen that current disposable income is an important factor in the consumption-versus-saving decision. A second important factor is the real value of each household's wealth. A household's **wealth** is the sum of all the valuable assets that it owns minus its liabilities. This includes its car, its house and contents, the value of its money in the bank, its pension or retirement fund, and any stocks, bonds, or other investments that it holds.

Households save in order to add to their wealth. Many have target values for their wealth. They are willing to save now in order to be wealthier later—but only within limits. Other things being equal, an unexpected rise in their wealth will lead them to save less so that they can consume more now as well as be wealthier later. Conversely, an unexpected fall in their wealth will lead them to save more so that they can at least partly restore their targeted wealth positions. Obviously, it is the real value of wealth that matters. Should the money value of wealth and the price level change in the same proportion, leaving real wealth unchanged, the household's incentive to save will be unchanged.

A rise in wealth tends to cause a larger fraction of disposable income to be spent on consumption and a smaller fraction to be saved. This shifts the consumption function upward and the saving function downward, as shown in Figure 28-2. A fall in wealth increases the incentive to save in order to restore wealth. This shifts the consumption function downward and the saving function upward.

Individual households experience both expected and unexpected changes in wealth. For example, both planned saving and unplanned bequests will increase wealth. Similarly, both planned dissaving and unexpected declines in stock market values reduce wealth.

Many unexpected changes in wealth cancel out across households and so are unimportant for the macroeconomic consumption function. We will see, however, that inflation can be an important source of unexpected changes in wealth in most households.

Planned increases in wealth as a result of past accumulation of wealth can be important for the whole society and can lead to upward shifts in the macroeconomic consumption function as wealth accumulates. This effect operates only slowly, since wealth accumulates only slowly.

Because for the moment we are focusing on short-term issues, the consumption function used in this chapter does not include the effects of changes in wealth.

FIGURE 28-2 Wealth and the Consumption Function (*billions of dollars*)

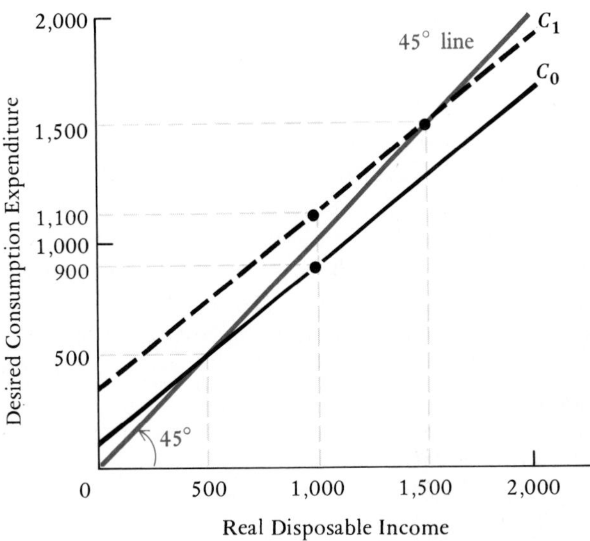

(i) The consumption function shifts upward with an increase in wealth

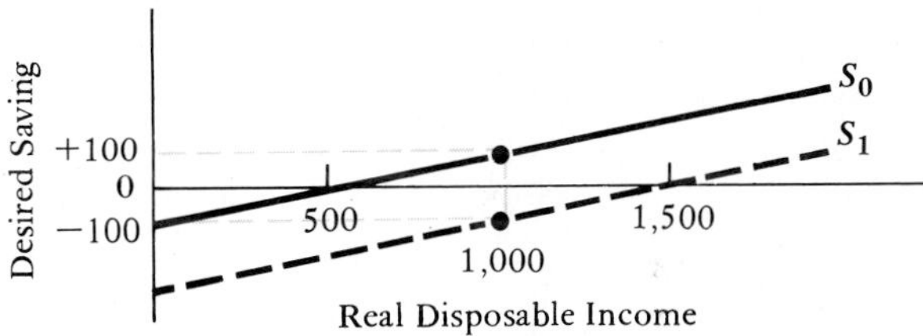

(ii) The saving function shifts downward with an increase in wealth

Changes in wealth shift consumption as a function of disposable income. In (i) line C_0 reproduces the consumption function from Figure 28-1(i). An increase in the level of wealth raises desired consumption at each level of disposable income, thus shifting the consumption line up to C_1. In the figure the consumption function shifts up by \$200, so with disposable income of \$1,000, for example, desired consumption *rises* from \$900 to \$1,100. As a result of the rise in wealth, the break-even level of income rises to \$1,500.

The saving function in (ii) shifts down by \$200, from S_0 to S_1. Thus, for example, at a disposable income of \$1,000, saving *falls* from plus \$100 to minus \$100.

Consumption and National Income

Desired consumption is related to *disposable* income. For a theory of the determination of national income, however, we need to know how consumption is related to national income.

The transition from a relationship between consumption and disposable income to one between consumption and national income is readily accomplished, since disposable income and national income are themselves related.

The relationship between disposable income and national income. Earlier we saw how to derive disposable income from national income. Since transfer payments (the major addition to national income) are smaller than total income taxes (the major subtraction from national income), the net effect is for disposable income to be substantially less than national income. (It was about 70 percent of GDP in 1990.)

Relating desired consumption to national income. If we know how consumption relates to disposable income and how disposable income relates to national income, we can derive the relationship between consumption and national income.

As an example, assume that disposable income is always 90 percent of national income. Then, whatever the relationship between C and Y, we can always substitute $0.9Y$ for Y_d. Thus if changes in consumption were always 80 percent of changes in Y_d, changes in consumption would always be 72 percent (80 percent of 90 percent) of Y. **[33]**

Table 28-3 shows that we can write desired consumption as a function of Y as well as of Y_d. We can then derive the marginal response of consumption to changes in Y by determining the proportion of any change in *national income* that goes to a change in desired consumption.

The marginal response of consumption to changes in *national income* ($\Delta C/\Delta Y$) is equal to the marginal propensity to consume out of *disposable income* ($\Delta C/\Delta Y_d$) multiplied by the fraction of national income that becomes disposable income ($\Delta Y_d/\Delta Y$).

We now have a function that shows how desired consumption expenditure varies as national income varies. The relationship is defined for real income and real expenditure (i.e., income and expenditure measured in constant dollars). For every given level of real income, measured in terms of purchasing power, households desire to spend some fraction of that purchasing power and to save the rest.

TABLE 28-3 Consumption As a Function of Disposable Income and National Income (*billions of dollars*)

(1) National income (Y)	(2) Disposable income ($Y_d = 0.9Y$)	(3) Desired consumption ($C = 100 + 0.8Y_d$)
100	90	172
1,000	900	820
2,000	1,800	1,540
3,000	2,700	2,260
4,000	3,600	2.980

If desired consumption depends on disposable income, which in turn depends on national income, desired consumption can be written as a function of either income concept. The data are hypothetical. They show deductions of 10 percent of any level of national income to arrive at disposable income. Deductions of 10 percent of Y imply that the remaining 90 percent of Y becomes disposable income. The numbers also show consumption as $100 billion plus 80 percent of disposable income.

By relating columns 2 and 3, one sees consumption as a function of disposable income. By relating columns 1 and 3, one sees the derived relationship between consumption and national income. In this example, the change in consumption in response to a change in disposable income (i.e., the *MPC*) is 0.8, and the change in consumption in response to a change in national income is 0.72.

Desired Net Exports

Canada is rich in natural resources and raw materials, which it exports to many other countries that are less favorably endowed. Also, Canada's manufacturing sector is both specialized and export-oriented. As we will see, fluctuations in exports play a key role in explaining fluctuations in the level of economic activity in the Canadian economy.

Similarly, imports play an important role in the Canadian economy; Canadian households typically consume a wide range of imported goods, and Canadian industry uses imported parts and components. A large segment of the Canadian economy is involved in foreign trade—primarily, but not exclusively, with the United States.

The Net Export Function

Exports depend on spending decisions made by foreign households that purchase Canadian goods and services. Exports, therefore, do not necessarily change as a result of changes in Canadian national income.

Imports, however, depend on the spending decisions of Canadian households. All categories of expenditure have an import content; domestic cars, for example, use large quantities of imported components in their manufacture. Thus imports rise when the other categories of expenditure rise. Because consumption rises with income, imports of foreign-produced consumption goods and materials that go into the production of domestically produced consumption goods also rise with income.

Desired net exports are negatively related to national income because of the positive relationship between desired expenditure on imports and national income.

This negative relationship between net exports and national income is called the *net export function*. Data for a hypothetical economy with constant exports and with imports that are 10 percent of national income are given in Table 28-4 and illustrated in Figure 28-3. In this example, exports form the autonomous component and imports form the induced component of the desired net export function.

Shifts in the Net Export Function

We have seen that the net export function relates net exports ($X - M$) to national income. It is drawn on the assumption that everything that affects net exports, except domestic national income, remains constant. The major factors that must be held constant are foreign national income, domestic and foreign prices, and the exchange rate. A change in any of these will affect the amount of net exports that will occur at each level of Canadian national income and hence will shift the net export function.

Notice that anything that affects Canadian exports will change the values in the export column in Table 28-4 and so will shift the net export function

FIGURE 28-3 The Net Export Function (*millions of dollars*)

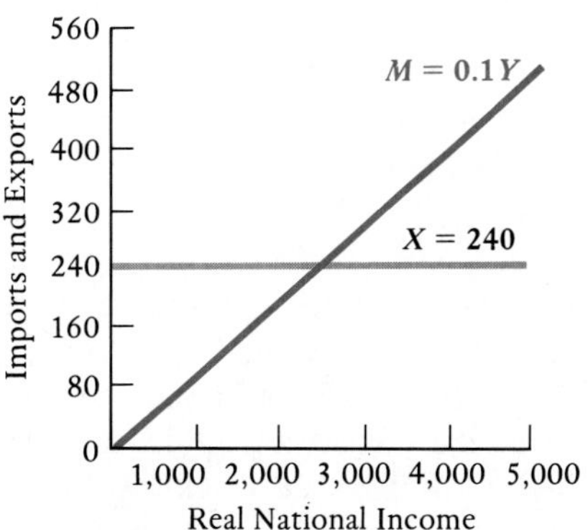

(i) Export and import functions

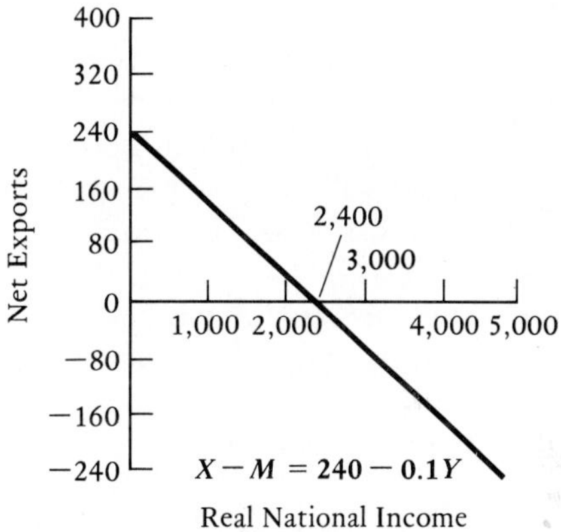

(ii) Net export function

Net exports, defined as the difference between exports and imports, are inversely related to the level of national income. In (i) exports are constant at $240 million, while imports rise with the national income. Therefore, net exports, shown in (ii), decline with national income. The figure is based on the hypothetical data in Table 28-4. With national income equal to $2,400 million, imports are equal to exports at $240 million, and net exports are zero. For levels of national income below $2,400 million, imports are less than exports, and hence net exports are positive. For levels of national income above $2,400 million, imports are greater than exports, and hence net exports are negative.

(Note that this is the only income-expenditure diagram with different scales on the two axes. If we had made both scales the same, the curve showing $X - M$ would have been virtually indistinguishable from the income axes.)

TABLE 28-4 A Net Export Schedule (*billions of dollars*)

National income (Y)	Exports (X)	Imports ($M = 0.10Y$)	Net exports
1,000	240	100	140
2,000	240	200	40
2,400	240	240	0
3,000	240	300	−60
4,000	240	400	−160
5,000	240	500	−260

Net exports fall as national income rises. The data are hypothetical. They assume that exports are constant and that imports are 10 percent of national income. Net exports are then positive at low levels of national income and negative at high levels of national income.

parallel to itself, upward if exports increase and downward if exports decrease. Also notice that anything that affects the proportion of income that Canadians wish to spend on imports will change the values in the import column in Table 28-4 and thus will change the slope of the net export function by making imports more or less responsive to changes in domestic income.

Foreign income. An increase in foreign income, other things being equal, will lead to an increase in the quantity of Canadian goods demanded by foreign countries, that is, to an increase in Canadian exports. The increase is in the constant X of the net export function, which shifts upward as a result. A fall in foreign income leads to a downward shift in the net export function.

Foreign prices. An increase in foreign prices will cause both foreign and domestic agents to substitute cheaper Canadian goods for the now more expensive foreign goods. This will cause changes in both exports and imports. Exports will rise, and the amount of imports associated with any given level of Canadian national income will fall. As a result, the net export function will shift upward. A fall in foreign prices has the reverse effect, with substitution away from Canadian goods in favor of foreign goods and a downward shift in the net export curve.

Domestic prices. An increase in domestic prices leads both foreign and domestic agents to substitute foreign goods for the now more expensive Canadian goods. The export part of net exports falls, and more imports will be associated with each level of domestic income. As a result, the net export function shifts downward. A fall in domestic prices leads to substitution in favor of Canadian goods and an upward shift in the net export function.

The exchange rate. A depreciation of the Canadian dollar means that foreigners must pay less of their money to buy one Canadian dollar, while Canadians must pay more dollars to buy a unit of any foreign currency. As a result, expenditure shifts away from foreign goods and toward Canadian goods. Canadians will import less at each level of Canadian national income, and foreigners will buy more of our export goods. The net export function thus shifts upward. An appreciation of the Canadian dollar has the opposite effect, causing substitution of foreign for Canadian goods, thus shifting the net export function downward.

Other Expenditure Categories

We have seen that desired consumption expenditure and desired net export expenditure each have an autonomous and an induced component. The induced components cause desired aggregate expenditure to depend on national income.

The relationship between desired aggregate expenditure and national income depends not only on desired consumption and net exports but also on the behavior of the other major expenditure categories, I and G. As we shall see in later chapters, changes in each of these play an important role in understanding changes in national income. For our present purposes of understanding how the equilibrium level of national income is determined, it is useful to keep things as simple as possible. Where we can, we treat these components as constant and include them in autonomous expenditure.

Desired investment expenditure. For the present it is convenient to study how the level of national income adjusts to a fixed level of planned real investment. So we assume that firms plan to make a constant amount of fixed business investment in plant and equipment each year and that they plan to hold their inventories constant. In Chapter 31 we shall drop these assumptions and study the important effects on national income that are caused by changes in the level of desired investment.

Desired government expenditure on goods and services. Governments intend to spend, and succeed in spending, many billions of dollars on currently produced goods and services. In this chapter we take desired and actual real government expenditure as a constant. We assume that the real value of government expenditure does not change as the circumstances of the economy change. This assumption allows us to see how national income adjusts to a constant level of real government expenditure. In Chapter 32 we shall drop this assumption and study how national income responds to changes in desired and actual government expenditure.

The Aggregate Expenditure Function

The aggregate expenditure function relates the level of desired real expenditure to the level of real national income. Total desired expenditure on the nation's output is the sum of desired consumption, investment, government, and net export expenditures, or

$$AE = C + I + G + (X - M)$$

Table 28-5 illustrates how such a function can be calculated, given the consumption function and the levels of desired investment, government, and net export expenditures at each level of income. In this specific case, autonomous expenditures are investment, government, exports, and the constant term in the consumption function. Induced expenditures are the induced part of consumption ($0.72Y$) and imports ($0.10Y$), and hence net imports ($X - M$). The resulting aggregate expenditure function is illustrated in Figure 28-4.

The Propensity to Spend Out of National Income

Earlier we defined propensities to consume and to save that together account for all household disposable income. We now define propensities to spend and not to spend that together account for all national income.

The fraction of any increment to national income that will be spent on domestic production is measured by the change in aggregate expenditure divided by the change in income, symbolized by $\Delta AE/\Delta Y$. It is called the economy's **marginal propensity to spend**. The value of the marginal propensity to spend, which is something greater than zero but less than one, may be indicated by the letter z. The amount $1 - \Delta AE/\Delta Y$ is the fraction of any increment in national income that is not spent. This is the **marginal propensity not to spend.**[1] This makes the value of the marginal propensity not to spend $1 - z$.

To illustrate this, suppose that the economy pro-

[1] More fully, these terms would be called the marginal propensity to spend *on national income* and the marginal propensity not to spend *on national income*. Expenditures on imports are included in the latter. The marginal propensity not to spend ($1 - z$) is often referred to as the *marginal propensity to withdraw*. Not spending a part of one's income amounts to a *withdrawal* from the circular flow of income, as described in Figure 3-1.

TABLE 28-5 The Aggregate Expenditure Function (*billions of dollars*)

National income (Y)	Desired consumption expenditure ($C = 100 + 0.72Y$)	Desired investment expenditure ($I = 250$)	Desired government expenditure ($G = 170$)	Desired net export expenditure ($X - M = 240 - 0.10Y$)	Desired aggregate expenditure ($AE = C + I + G + [X - M]$)
100	172	250	170	230	822
400	388	250	170	200	1,008
500	460	250	170	190	1,070
1,000	820	250	170	140	1,380
2,000	1,540	250	170	40	2,000
3,000	2,260	250	170	−60	2,620
4,000	2,980	250	170	−160	3,240
5,000	3,700	250	170	−260	3,860

The aggregate expenditure function is the sum of desired consumption, investment, government, and net export expenditures. The table is based on the hypothetical data given in Tables 28-3 and 28-4. The autonomous components of desired aggregate expenditure are desired investment, desired government, and desired export expenditures plus the constant term in desired consumption expenditure. The induced components are the second term in desired consumption expenditure ($0.72Y$) and desired imports ($-0.10Y$).

The marginal response of consumption to a change in national income is 0.72, calculated as the product of the marginal propensity to consume (0.8) times the fraction of national income that becomes disposable income (0.9). Because this exceeds the marginal propensity to import out of national income (0.1), desired aggregate expenditure is positively related to national income, as shown in the column at the far right. The marginal response of desired aggregate expenditure to a change in national income, $\Delta AE/\Delta Y$, is 0.62.

duces $1.00 of extra income and that the response to this is governed by the relationships in Tables 28-3 and 28-4. Since 10 cents is collected by the government as taxes, 90 cents is converted into disposable income, and 80 percent of this amount (72 cents) becomes consumption expenditure. However, import expenditure also rises by 10 cents, so expenditure on domestic goods, that is, aggregate expenditure, rises by 62 cents. Thus z, the marginal propensity to spend, is 0.62 (0.62/1.00). What is not spent on domestic output includes the 10 cents in taxes, the 18 cents of disposable income that is saved, and the 10 cents of import expenditure, for a total of 38 cents. Hence the marginal propensity not to spend, $1 - z$, is $1 - 0.62 = 0.38$.

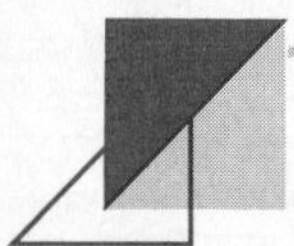

Determining Equilibrium National Income

We are now ready to see what determines the *equilibrium* level of national income. Recall from Chapter 4 that equilibrium is a state of balance between opposing forces. When something is in equilibrium, there is no tendency for it to change; forces are acting on it, but they balance out, so the net result is *no change*. Any conditions that are required for something to be in equilibrium are called its *equilibrium conditions*.

Table 28-6 illustrates the determination of equilibrium national income for our simple hypothetical economy. Suppose that firms are producing a final output of $1,000 billion, and thus national income is $1,000 billion. According to the table, aggregate desired expenditure is $1,380 billion at this level of income. If firms persist in producing a current output of only $1,000 billion in the face of an aggregate desired expenditure of $1,380 billion, one of two things must happen.[2]

One possibility is that households, firms, and governments will be unable to spend the extra $380 billion that they would like to spend, so lines or waiting lists of unsatisfied customers will appear. These will send a signal to firms that they can increase their sales if they increase their production. When the firms increase production, national income rises. Of course, the individual firms are interested only in their own sales and profits, but their individual actions have as their inevitable consequence an increase in GDP, that is the total of all firms' current production (the total of their values added).

[2] A third possibility, that prices would rise, has been excluded by assumptions in this chapter but will become important in later chapters.

FIGURE 28-4 An Aggregate Expenditure Curve *(billions of dollars)*

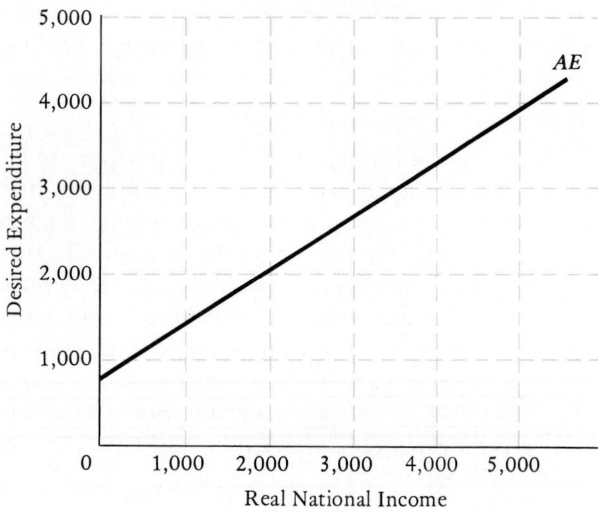

The aggregate expenditure curve relates total desired expenditure to national income. The *AE* curve in the figure plots the data from the first and the last columns of Table 28-5, which are repeated in Table 28-6. Its intercept (which in this case is $760 billion) shows autonomous expenditure. Its slope (which in this case is 0.62) shows the marginal propensity to spend.

The second possibility is that all spenders will spend everything that they wanted to spend. Then, however, expenditure will exceed current output, which can happen only when some expenditure plans are fulfilled by purchasing inventories of goods that were produced in the past. In this example, the fulfillment of plans to purchase $1,380 billion worth of commodities in the face of a current output of only $1,000 billion will reduce inventories by $380 billion. As long as inventories last, more goods can be sold than are currently being produced.

Eventually, inventories will run out, but before this happens, firms will increase their output as they

TABLE 28-6 The Determination of Equilibrium National Income (*billions of dollars*)

National income (Y)	Desired aggregate expenditure ($AE = C + I + G + [X - M]$)	
100	822	Pressure on
400	1,008	income to
500	1,070	rise
1,000	1,380	↓
		Equilibrium
2,000	2,000	income
		↑
3,000	2,620	Pressure on
4,000	3,240	income to
5,000	3,860	fall

National income is in equilibrium where aggregate desired expenditure equals national income. The data are copied from Table 28-5. When national income is below its equilibrium level, aggregate desired expenditure exceeds the value of current output. This creates an incentive for firms to increase output and hence for national income to rise. When national income is above its equilibrium level, aggregate desired expenditure is less than the value of current output. This creates an incentive for firms to reduce output and hence for national income to fall. Only at the equilibrium level of national income is aggregate desired expenditure exactly equal to the value of the current output.

see their inventories being depleted. Extra sales can then be made without a further depletion of inventories. Once again, the consequence of each individual firm's behavior, in search of its own individual profits, is an increase in national income. Thus the final response to an excess of aggregate desired expenditure over current output is a rise in national income.

At any level of national income at which aggregate desired expenditure exceeds total output, there will be pressure for national income to rise.

Next, consider the $4,000 billion level of national income in Table 28-6. At this level, desired expenditure on domestically produced goods is only $3,240 billion. If firms persist in producing $4,000 billion worth of goods, $760 billion worth must remain unsold. Therefore, inventories must rise. However, firms will not allow inventories of unsold goods to rise indefinitely; sooner or later they will reduce the level of output to the level of sales. When they do, national income will fall.

At any level of income for which aggregate desired expenditure falls short of total output, there will be a pressure for national income to fall.

Finally, look at the national income level of $2,000 billion in Table 28-6. At this level, and only at this level, aggregate desired expenditure is exactly equal to national income. Purchasers fulfill their spending plans without causing inventories to change. There is no incentive for firms to alter output. Since total output is the same as national income, national income will remain steady; it is in equilibrium.

The equilibrium level of national income occurs where aggregate desired expenditure equals total output.

This conclusion is quite general and does not depend on the numbers that are used in the specific example. **[34]**

Equilibrium Illustrated

Figure 28-5 shows the determination of the equilibrium level of national income. The line labeled AE graphs the aggregate expenditure function. Its slope is the marginal propensity to spend. The line labeled $AE = Y$ shows the equilibrium condition that desired aggregate expenditure, AE, equals national income, Y. Since the $AE = Y$ line plots points where the vertical distance equals the horizontal distance, it forms an angle of 45° with the axes. Any point on this line is a possible equilibrium.

Graphically, equilibrium occurs at the level of income at which the aggregate desired expenditure line intersects the 45° line. This is the level of income where desired expenditure is just equal to total national income and therefore is just sufficient to purchase total final output.

Now we have explained the equilibrium level of national income that rises at a *given price level*. Next we shall study the forces that cause equilibrium income to change. We shall see that shifts in desired consumption and investment expenditure can cause major swings in national income. We shall also see

FIGURE 28-5 Equilibrium National Income

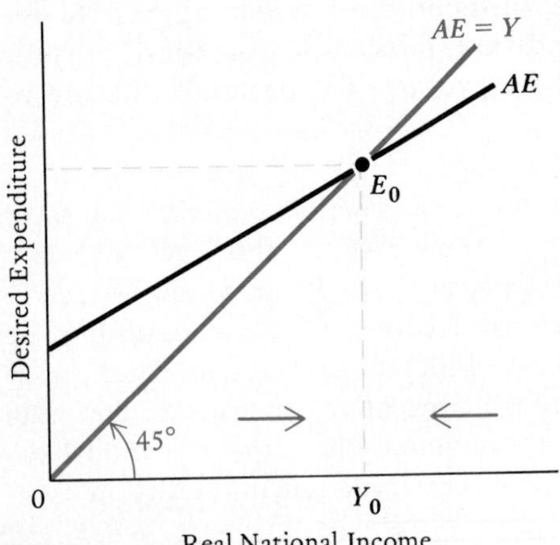

Equilibrium national income occurs at E_0, where the desired aggregate expenditure line intersects the 45° line. If real national income is below Y_0, desired aggregate expenditure will exceed national income, and production will rise. This is shown by the arrow to the left of Y_0. If national income is above Y_0, desired aggregate expenditure will be less than national income, and production will fall. This is shown by the arrow to the right of Y_0. Only when real national income is Y_0 will desired aggregate expenditure equal real national income.

that changes in government spending and taxation policies can do the same.

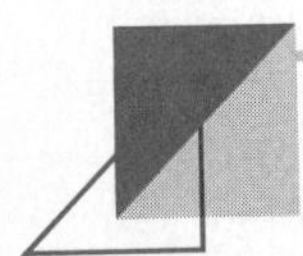

Changes in National Income

Since the *AE* function plays a central role in our explanation of the equilibrium level of national income, you should not be surprised to hear that the behavior of the *AE* function also plays a central role in explaining why national income changes. (We continue to assume that the price level is constant.) To understand this influence, we must recall an important distinction first encountered in Chapter 4.

Suppose that desired aggregate expenditure rises. This may be either a response to a change in national income or the result of an increased desire to spend at each level of national income. A change in national income causes a *movement along* the aggregate expenditure function. An increased desire to spend at each level of national income causes a shift in the aggregate expenditure function. Figure 28-6 illustrates this important distinction.

Shifts in the Aggregate Expenditure Function

For any specific aggregate expenditure function there is a unique level of equilibrium national income. If the aggregate expenditure function shifts, the equilibrium will be disturbed, and national income will change. Thus if we wish to find the causes of changes in national income, we must look for the causes of shifts in the *AE* function.

The aggregate expenditure function shifts when one of its components shifts, that is, when there is a shift in the consumption function, in desired investment expenditure, in desired government expenditure on goods and services, or in desired net exports. Such shifts were defined earlier as changes in *autonomous* aggregate expenditure.

Upward Shifts in Aggregate Expenditure Functions

What will happen if households permanently increase their levels of consumption spending at each level of disposable income, if the Ford Motor Company increases its rate of annual investment by $25 million in order to meet the threat from imported cars, if the government increases its defense spending, or if grain exports soar? (In considering these questions, remember that we are dealing with continuous flows measured as so much per period of time. An upward shift in the expenditure function means that the desired expenditure associated with each level of national income rises to and stays at a higher amount.)

Because any such increase shifts the entire aggregate expenditure function upward, the same analysis applies to all of the changes mentioned. Two types of shift in *AE* can occur. First, if the same addition to expenditure occurs at all levels of income, the *AE* curve shifts parallel to itself, as shown in Figure 28-7(i). Second, if there is a change in the propensity to spend out of national income, the slope of the *AE* curve changes, as shown in Figure 28-7(ii). (Recall that the slope of the *AE* curve is z, the marginal propensity to spend.)

FIGURE 28-6 Movements Along and Shifts of the *AE* Curve

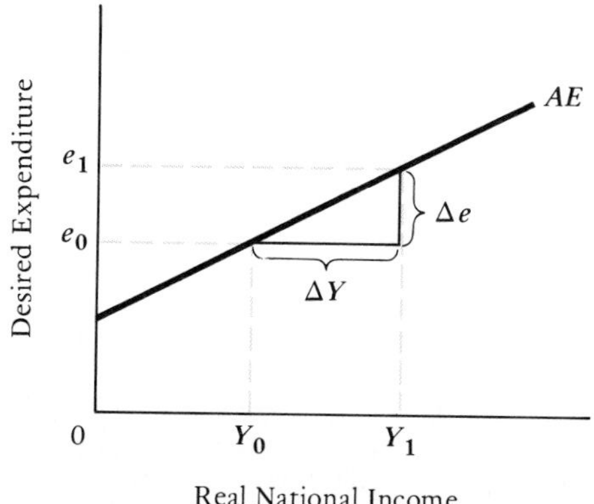

(i) A movement along the *AE* curve

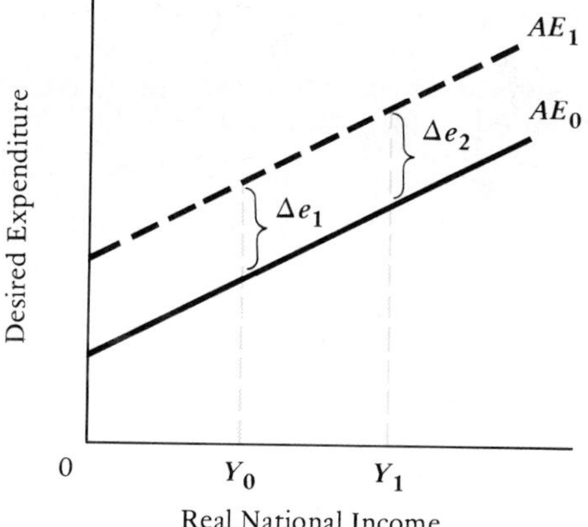

(ii) A shift of the *AE* curve

A movement along the aggregate expenditure curve occurs in response to a change in income; a shift of the *AE* curve indicates a different level of desired expenditure at each level of income. In (i) a change in income of ΔY, from Y_0 to Y_1, changes desired expenditure by Δe, from e_0 to e_1. In (ii) a shift in the expenditure curve from AE_0 to AE_1 raises the amount of expenditure associated with *each* level of income. At Y_0, for example, desired aggregate expenditure is increased by Δe_1; at Y_1 it is increased by Δe_2. (If the aggregate expenditure curve shifts parallel to itself, $\Delta e_1 = \Delta e_2$.)

Figure 28-7 shows that upward shifts in the aggregate expenditure function increase equilibrium national income. After the shift in the *AE* curve, income is no longer in equilibrium at its original level because at that level desired expenditure exceeds national income. Equilibrium national income now occurs at the higher level indicated by the intersection of the new *AE* curve with the 45° line, along which aggregate expenditures equal real national income.

Downward Shifts in Aggregate Expenditure Functions

What will happen to national income if consumption, investment, government spending, or exports decrease? All these changes shift the aggregate expenditure function downward. A constant reduction in expenditure at all levels of income shifts *AE* parallel to itself. A fall in the marginal propensity to spend out of national income reduces the slope of the *AE* function.

Changes in Tax Rates

If tax rates change, the relationship between disposable income and national income changes.[3] For the same level of national income there will be a different level of disposable income and thus a different level of consumption. This is illustrated in Table 28-7. Consequently, z, the marginal propensity to spend out of national income, will have changed.

Consider a decrease in tax rates. If the government decreases its rate of income tax so that it collects 5 cents less out of every dollar of national income, disposable income rises in relation to national income. Thus consumption also rises at every level of national income. This results in a (nonparallel) upward shift of the *AE* curve, that is, a change in the slope of the curve, as shown in Figure 28-7(ii). The result of this shift will be a rise in equilibrium national income, as is also shown in Figure 28-7(ii).

A rise in taxes has the opposite effect. A rise in tax rates results in less disposable income and hence less consumption expenditure at each level of national income. This results in a (nonparallel) downward shift of the *AE* curve and thus decreases the

[3] Effective tax rates can be changed either by changes in the percent of taxable income that is taken in taxes or by changes in the percent of national income that is taxable. For the sake of simplicity, in the text we have assumed that all national income is taxable.

FIGURE 28-7 Shifts in the *AE* Curve

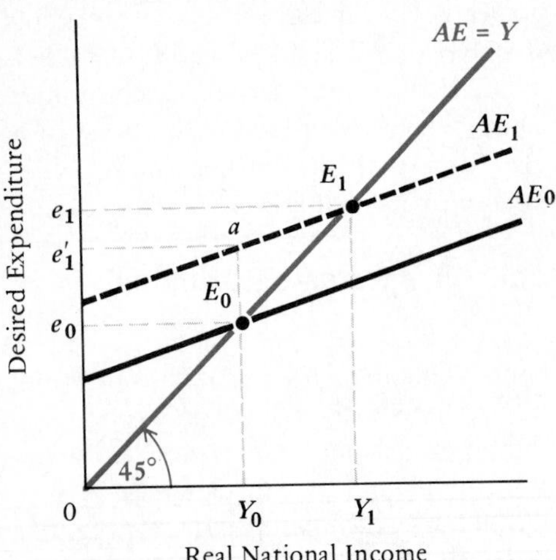

(i) A parallel shift in *AE*

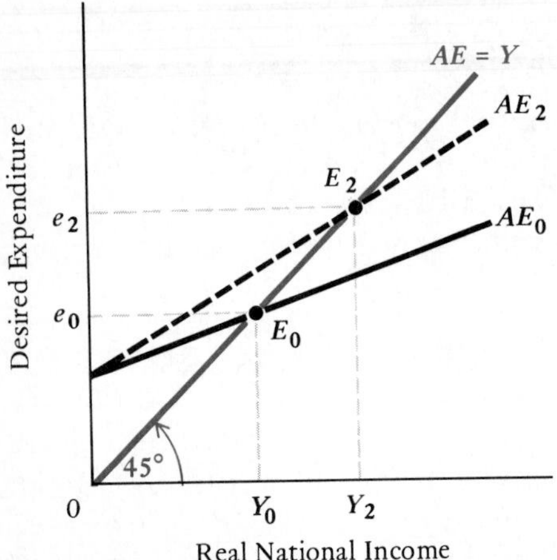

(ii) A change in the slope of *AE*

Upward shifts in the *AE* curve increase equilibrium income; downward shifts decrease equilibrium income. In both (i) and (ii) the aggregate expenditure curve is initially AE_0, with national income Y_0.

In (i) a parallel upward *shift* in the *AE* curve from AE_0 to AE_1 means that desired expenditure has increased by the same amount at each level of national income. For example, at Y_0 desired expenditure rises from e_0 to e_1' and therefore exceeds national income. Equilibrium is reached at E_1, where income is Y_1 and expenditure is e_1. The increase in desired expenditure from e_1' to e_1 represented by a *movement along* AE_1, is an induced response to the increase in income from Y_0 to Y_1.

In (ii) a nonparallel upward shift in the *AE* curve, say, from AE_0 to AE_2, means that the marginal propensity to spend at each level of national income has increased. This leads to an increase in equilibrium national income. Equilibrium is reached at E_2, where the new level of expenditure e_2 is equal to income Y_2. Again, the initial *shift* in the *AE* curve induces a *movement along* the new *AE* curve.

Downward shifts in the *AE* curve, from AE_1 to AE_0 or from AE_2 to AE_0, lead to a fall in equilibrium income to Y_0.

level of equilibrium national income. This, too, is illustrated in Figure 28-7(ii).

The results restated. Now we have derived two important general predictions of the elementary theory of national income.

1. **A rise in the amount of desired consumption, investment, government, or export expenditure that is associated with each level of national income will increase equilibrium national income.**

2. **A fall in the amount of desired consumption, investment, government, or export expenditure that is associated with each level of national income will lower equilibrium national income.**

A change in desired consumption in relation to national income can arise, as we have seen, either because the consumption function shifts or because the relationship between disposable income and national income is altered.

TABLE 28-7 Tax Changes Shift the Function Relating Consumption to National Income (*billions of dollars*)

	Disposable income equal to 80 percent of national income (tax rate = 0.2)		Disposable income equal to 90 percent of national income (tax rate = 0.1)	
(1) National income (Y)	(2) Disposable income ($Y_d = 0.8Y$)	(3) Consumption ($C = 100 + 0.8Y_d$)	(4) Disposable income ($Y_d = 0.9Y$)	(5) Consumption ($C = 100 + 0.8Y_d$)
100	80	164	90	172
500	400	420	450	460
1,000	800	740	900	820

The consumption function shifts if the relationship between disposable and national income changes. The table is based on the simplified hypothetical consumption function from Table 28-1 combined with the assumption that Y_d is a constant fraction of Y. Initially, $Y_d = 0.8Y$. This yields a schedule relating consumption to national income that is given in columns 1 and 3 and is described by the equation $C = 100 + 0.64Y$. Income tax rates are then decreased so that now 90 percent of national income becomes disposable income. Column 4 indicates the Y_d that corresponds at the decreased tax rate to each level of Y shown in column 1. With an unchanged consumption function, consumption at the new tax rate is given by column 5. Columns 1 and 5 give the new schedule relating consumption to national income, described by the equation $C = 100 + 0.72Y$.

The Multiplier

Now we can predict the *direction* of the changes in national income that occur in response to various shifts in the aggregate expenditure function. We would like also to be able to predict the *magnitude* of these changes.

Economists need to know the *size* of the effects of changes in expenditures in both the private and the public sectors. During a recession the government often takes measures to stimulate the economy. If these measures have a larger effect than estimated, demand may rise too much, and full employment may be reached with demand still rising. This outcome will have an inflationary impact on the economy. If the government greatly overestimates the effect of its measures, the recession will persist longer than is necessary. In this case there is a danger that the policy will be discredited as ineffective, even though the current diagnosis is that too little of the right thing was done.

Definition. A measure of the magnitude of changes in income is provided by the multiplier. We have just seen that a shift in the aggregate expenditure curve will cause a change in equilibrium national income. Such a shift will be caused by a change in any autonomous component of aggregate expenditure, for example, an increase or a decrease in investment or government spending. An increase in desired aggregate expenditure increases equilibrium national income by a multiple of the initial increase in autonomous expenditure. The **multiplier** is the ratio of the change in income to the change in autonomous expenditure, that is, the change in national income *divided by* the change in autonomous expenditure that brought it about.

Why the multiplier is greater than unity. What will happen to national income if, with unchanged tax rates, the government increases its spending on road construction by $1 billion per year?

Initially, the road construction program will create $1 billion worth of new national income and a corresponding amount of employment for households and firms on which the initial $1 billion is spent, but this is not the end of the story. The increase in national income of $1 billion will cause an increase in disposable income, which will cause an induced rise in consumption expenditure. Road crews and road contractors, who gain new income directly from the government's road construction program, will spend some of it on food, clothing, entertainment, cars, television sets, and other commodities. When output expands to meet this demand, employment will increase in all the affected industries. New incomes will then be created for workers and firms in these industries. When they in turn spend their newly earned incomes, output and employment will rise further. More income will be created, and more expenditure will be induced. Indeed, at this stage we might wonder whether the increases in income will ever come to an end. To deal with this concern, we need to consider the multiplier in somewhat more precise terms.

The simple multiplier. Consider an increase in autonomous expenditure of ΔA, which might be, say, \$1 billion per year. Remember that ΔA stands for *any* increase in autonomous expenditure; this could be an increase in investment, in government purchases, in exports, or in the autonomous component of consumption. The new autonomous expenditure shifts the aggregate expenditure function upward by that amount. National income is no longer in equilibrium at its original level, since desired aggregate expenditure now exceeds income. Equilibrium is restored by a *movement along* the new AE curve.

The **simple multiplier** measures the change in equilibrium national income that occurs in response to a change in autonomous expenditure *at a constant price level*. We refer to it as "simple" because we have simplified the situation by assuming that the price level is fixed. Figure 28-8 illustrates the simple multiplier and makes clear that it is greater than unity.[4] Box 28-1 provides a numerical example.

The Size of the Simple Multiplier

The size of the simple multiplier depends on the slope of the AE function, that is, on the marginal propensity to spend, z. This is illustrated in Figure 28-8.

A high marginal propensity to spend means a steep AE curve. The expenditure induced by any initial increase in income is large, with the result that the final rise in income is correspondingly large. By contrast, a low marginal propensity to spend means a relatively flat AE curve. The expenditure induced by the initial increase in income is small, and the final

[4] In our discussion in the text, we have assumed that the entire initial change in autonomous spending is all on domestically produced goods. If the initial increase involves some spending on imports, as it often does with investment spending, the ratio of the change in equilibrium income to the change in total autonomous spending can be less than one, although the ratio to the change in autonomous spending on domestic goods will still exceed unity.

FIGURE 28-8 The Simple Multiplier

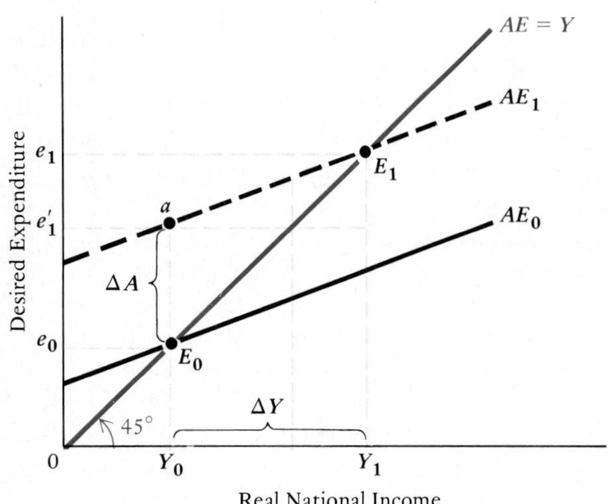

An increase in the autonomous component of desired aggregate expenditure increases equilibrium national income by a multiple of the initial increase. The initial equilibrium is at E_0, where AE_0 intersects the 45° line. At this point, desired expenditure, e_0, is equal to national income, Y_0. An increase in autonomous expenditure of ΔA then shifts the desired expenditure function upward to AE_1. If national income stays at Y_0, desired expenditure rises to e_1' (the coordinates of point a are Y_0 and e_1'). Since this level of desired expenditure is greater than national income, national income will rise.

Equilibrium occurs when income rises to Y_1. Here desired expenditure, e_1, equals income, Y_1. The extra expenditure of $e_1'e_1$ represents the induced increases in expenditure. It is the amount by which the final increase in income, ΔY, exceeds the initial increase in autonomous expenditure, ΔA. Since ΔY is greater than ΔA, the multiplier is greater than unity.

BOX 28-1

The Multiplier: A Numerical Example

Consider an economy that has a marginal propensity to spend out of national income of 0.80. Suppose that autonomous expenditure increases by $1 billion per year because the government spends an extra $1 billion per year on new roads. National income initially rises by $1 billion, but that is not the end of it. The factors of production involved in road building that received the first $1 billion spend $800 million. This second round of spending generates $800 million of new income. This new income in turn induces $640 million of third-round spending, and so it continues, with each successive round of new income generating 80 percent as much in new expenditure. Each additional round of expenditure creates new income and yet another round of expenditure.

The table carries the process through 10 rounds. Students with sufficient patience (and no faith in mathematics) may compute as many rounds in the process as they wish; they will find that the sum of the rounds of expenditures approaches a limit of $5 billion, which is five times the initial increase in expenditure. [35] The graph of the cumulative expenditure increases shows how quickly this limit is approached. The multiplier is 5, given the assumption about the marginal propensity to spend. Had the marginal propensity to spend been lower, say, 0.667, the process would have been similar, but it would have approached a limit of 3 instead of 5 times the initial increase in expenditure.

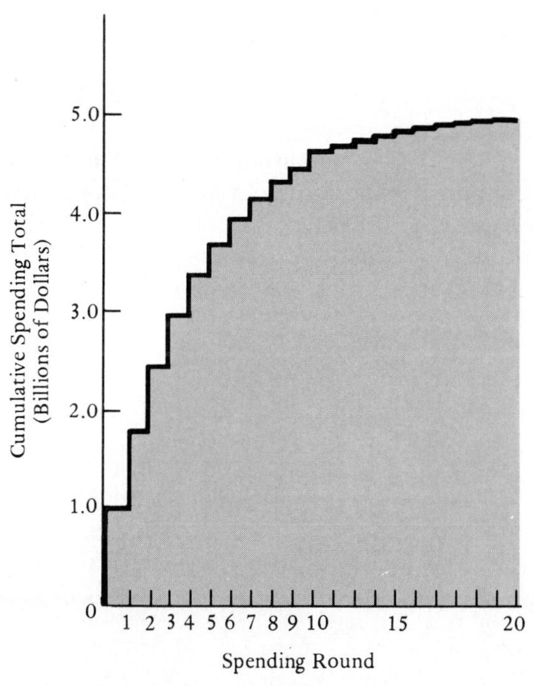

Round of spending	Increase in expenditure (millions of dollars)	Cumulative total (millions of dollars)
Initial increase	1,000.0	1,000.0
2	800.0	1,800.0
3	640.0	2,440.0
4	512.0	2,952.0
5	409.6	3,361.6
6	327.7	3,689.3
7	262.1	3,951.4
8	209.7	4,161.1
9	167.8	4,328.9
10	134.2	4,463.1
11 to 20 combined	479.3	4,942.4
All others	57.6	5,000.0

rise in income is not much larger than the initial rise in autonomous expenditure that brought it about.

The larger the marginal propensity to spend, the steeper the aggregate expenditure function and the larger the multiplier.

The precise value of the simple multiplier can be derived by using elementary algebra. (The derivation is given in Box 28-2.) The result is that the simple multiplier, which we call K, is

$$K = \frac{\Delta Y}{\Delta A} = \frac{1}{1 - z}$$

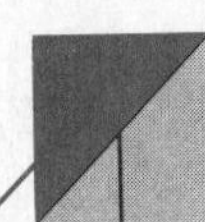

BOX 28-2

The Multiplier: An Algebraic Approach

High school algebra is all that is needed to derive the exact expression for the multiplier. Readers who feel at home with algebra may want to follow this derivation. Others can skip it and rely on the graphical and numerical arguments that have been given in the text.

First, we derive the equation for the AE curve. Aggregate expenditure is divided into autonomous expenditure, A, and induced expenditure,* N, so we write

$$AE = N + A \qquad [1]$$

Since N is expenditure on domestically produced output that varies with income, we can write

$$N = zY \qquad [2]$$

where z is the marginal propensity to spend out of national income. (It is a positive number between zero and unity.) Substituting Equation 2 in Equation 1 yields the equation of the AE curve:

$$AE = zY + A \qquad [3]$$

Now we write the equation of the 45° line,

$$AE = Y \qquad [4]$$

which states the equilibrium condition that desired aggregate expenditure must equal national income. Equations 3 and 4 are two equations with two unknowns, AE and Y. To solve them, we substitute Equation 3 in Equation 4 to obtain

$$Y = zY + A$$

Subtracting zY from both sides yields

$$Y - zY = A$$

Factoring out Y yields

$$Y(1 - z) = A$$

Dividing through by $1 - z$ yields

$$Y = \frac{A}{1 - z}$$

This tells us the equilibrium value of Y in terms of autonomous expenditures A and the propensity not to spend out of national income $(1 - z)$. The expression $Y = A/(1 - z)$ tells us that if A changes by ΔA, the change in Y, which we call ΔY, will be

$$\Delta Y = \frac{\Delta A}{1 - z}$$

Dividing through by ΔA gives the value of the multiplier, which we designate by K:

$$K = \frac{\Delta Y}{\Delta A} = \frac{1}{1 - z}$$

* In simple models N is mainly consumption expenditure, but in other models it may include other types of expenditure. All that matters is that there is one class of expenditure, N, that varies with income and another class, A, that does not.

where z is the marginal propensity to spend out of national income. (As we have seen, z is the slope of the aggregate expenditure function.)

As we saw earlier, the term $1 - z$ stands for the marginal propensity not to spend out of national income. For example, if 80 cents of every dollar of new national income is spent ($z = 0.80$), then 20 cents is the amount not spent. The value of the multiplier is then calculated as $K = 1/0.20 = 5$.

The simple multiplier can be written as the reciprocal of the marginal propensity not to spend.

From this we see that if $1 - z$ is small, the multiplier will be large (because extra income induces much extra spending). What if $1 - z$ is large? The largest possible value of $1 - z$ is unity, which arises when z equals zero, indicating that none of any ad-

FIGURE 28-9 The Size of the Simple Multiplier

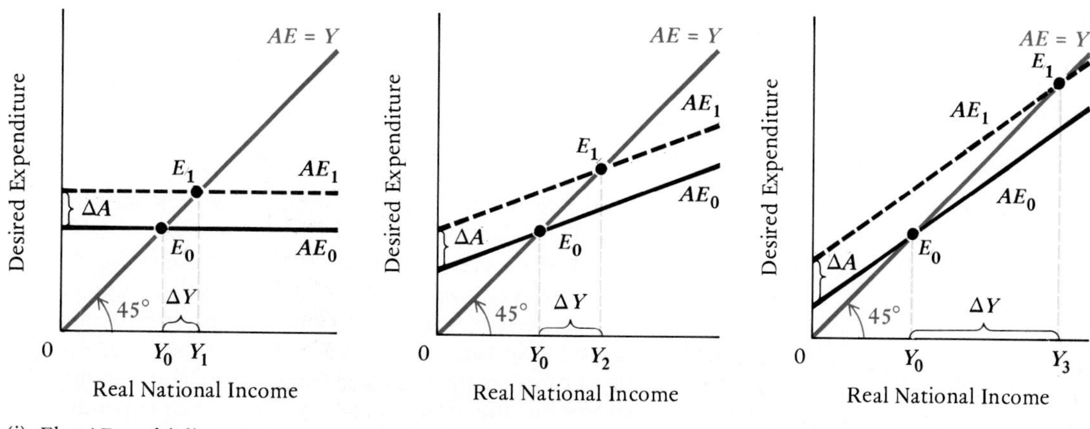

(i) Flat AE, multiplier unity (ii) Intermediate case (iii) Steep AE, multiplier large

The larger the marginal propensity to spend out of national income (z), the steeper the AE curve and the larger the multiplier. In each part of the figure the initial aggregate expenditure function is AE_0 and equilibrium is at E_0 with income Y_0. The AE curve then shifts upward to AE_1 as a result of an increase in autonomous expenditure of ΔA. The size of the shift, ΔA, is the same in each part. The new equilibrium is at E_1.

In (i) the AE function is horizontal, indicating a marginal propensity to spend of zero ($z = 0$). The change in income ΔY is only the increase in autonomous expenditure, since there is no induced expenditure by those who receive the initial increase in income. The simple multiplier is then unity, its minimum possible value.

In (ii) the AE curve is positively sloped but is still relatively flat (z is low). The increase in national income to Y_2 is only slightly greater than the increase in autonomous expenditure that brought it about. The simple multiplier is only slightly greater than one.

In (iii) the AE function is quite steep (z is high). Now the increase in income to Y_3 is much larger than the increase in autonomous expenditure that brought it about. The simple multiplier is quite large.

ditional national income is spent. In this case the multiplier itself has a value of unity; the increase in equilibrium national income is confined to the initial increase in autonomous expenditure. There are no induced additional effects on spending, so national income increases only by the original increase in autonomous expenditure. The relation between $1 - z$ and the size of the multiplier is illustrated in Figure 28-9.

To estimate the size of the multiplier in an actual economy, we need to estimate the value of the marginal propensity not to spend out of national income in that economy, that is, $1 - z$. Evidence suggests that the Canadian value is larger than the 0.2 that we used in our example.

The various elements of national income that are "not spent" include income taxes, savings, and import expenditures. For the Canadian economy in the late twentieth century, this leads to a realistic estimate of a little more than 0.5 for $1 - z$. Thus the simple multiplier is something less than 2, not 5, as in the example.

The simple multiplier is a useful starting point for understanding the effects of expenditure shifts on national income; however, as we shall see in subsequent chapters, many complications will arise.

SUMMARY

1. Desired aggregate expenditure consists of desired consumption, desired investment, desired government expenditures, and desired net exports. It is the amount that decision makers want to spend on purchasing the national product.
2. A change in disposable income leads to a change in consumption and saving. The responsiveness of these changes is measured by the marginal propensity to consume (*MPC*) and the marginal propensity to save (*MPS*), which are both positive and sum to 1.
3. A change in wealth tends to cause a change in the allocation of disposable income between consumption and saving. The change in consumption is positively related to the change in wealth, and the change in saving is negatively related to this change.
4. Since desired imports increase as national income increases, desired net exports decrease as national income increases, other things being equal. This gives rise to a negatively sloped net export function.
5. In the simple theory of this chapter, investment expenditures, government expenditures, export expenditures, and the constant term in the consumption function are all autonomous expenditures, whereas imports and the part of consumption that responds to income are induced expenditures.
6. At the equilibrium level of national income, purchasers wish to buy neither more nor less than what is being produced. At incomes above equilibrium, desired expenditure falls short of national income, and output will sooner or later be curtailed. At incomes below equilibrium, desired expenditure exceeds national income, and output will sooner or later be increased.
7. Equilibrium national income is represented graphically by the point at which the aggregate expenditure curve cuts the 45° line, that is, where total desired expenditure equals total output.
8. With a constant price level, equilibrium real national income is increased by a rise in the desired consumption, investment, government, or export expenditure that is associated with each level of the national income. Equilibrium national income is decreased by a fall in desired expenditures.
9. Equilibrium national income is negatively related to the amount of tax revenue that is associated with each level of national income.
10. The magnitude of the effect on national income of shifts in autonomous expenditure is given by the multiplier. It is defined as $K = \Delta Y/\Delta A$, where ΔA is the change in autonomous expenditure.
11. The simple multiplier is the multiplier when the price level is constant. It is equal to $1/(1 - z)$, where z is the marginal propensity to spend out of national income. Thus the larger z is, the larger the multiplier is. It is a basic prediction of national income theory that the simple multiplier is greater than unity.

TOPICS FOR REVIEW

Desired expenditure
Consumption function
Average and marginal propensities to consume and to save
Aggregate expenditure function
Marginal propensities to spend and not to spend
Equilibrium national income at a given price level
Shifts of and movements along expenditure curves
Effect on national income of changes in desired expenditures

Effect on national income of changes in tax rates
The simple multiplier
The size of the multiplier and the slope of the *AE* curve

DISCUSSION QUESTIONS

1. "The concept of an equilibrium level of national income is useless because the economy is never in equilibrium. If it ever got there, no economist would recognize it anyway." Discuss this quotation.
2. Interpret each of the following statements either in terms of the shape of a consumption function or the values of *MPC* and *APC*.
   a. "Tom Green has lost his job, and his family is existing on its past savings."
   b. "The Grimsby household is so rich that it used all the extra income it earned this year to invest in a wildcat oil-drilling venture."
   c. "The widow Hammerstein can barely make ends meet by clipping coupons on the bonds left to her by dear Henry, but she would never dip into her capital."
   d. "We always thought Harris was a miser, but when his wife left him, he took to wine, women, and song."
   e. "Inflation has made the Schultzes feel so poor that they are adding an extra $100 a week to their account at the savings bank."
   f. "The last stock market crash led young Ross to cancel two planned trips abroad, even though her job as a broker was never at risk."
3. Why might an individual's marginal propensity to consume be higher in the long run than in the short run? Why might it be lower? Is it possible for an individual's average propensity to consume to be greater than unity in the short run? In the long run? Can a country's average propensity to consume be greater than unity in the short run? In the long run?
4. What relationship holds along the 45° line between total expenditures and total income? In determining equilibrium graphically, are we restricted to choosing identical vertical and horizontal scales?
5. Explain carefully why national income changes when desired aggregate expenditure does not equal national income. Sketch scenarios that fit the cases of too much and too little desired expenditure.
6. Explain how a sudden unexpected fall in consumer expenditure would initially cause an increase in investment expenditure by firms.
7. What relationship is suggested by the following newspaper headline: "Auto sales soar as recovery booms"?
8. State the implied impact on the *AE* curve, and hence on equilibrium national income, relating to each of the following headlines.
   a. "Ottawa's planned spending up 10 percent."
   b. "Soviet Union agrees to buy more Canadian wheat."
   c. "Major Canadian companies expected to cut capital outlays."
   d. "Ottawa considers decreasing personal income tax rates."
   e. "Import car boom spells trouble for Canadian auto industry."
9. Find and discuss at least two current news stories that imply shifts in the *AE* curve.
10. Homer Hardcrust, chairman of the Economic Council of Cornwall, proposes that because of current heavy unemployment, the federal government should prepare an austerity program and cut government expenditures to set an example for private households. What do you think the effects of his policy would be?

Appendix to Chapter 28

The Permanent-Income and Life-Cycle Hypotheses of Household Consumption

In the Keynesian theory of the consumption function, current consumption expenditure is related to current income—either current disposable income or current national income. As we saw in Chapter 28, more recent theories relate consumption to some longer-term concept of income than the income that the household is currently earning.

The two most influential theories of this type are the **permanent-income theory (PIT)**, developed by Professor Friedman, and the **life-cycle theory (LCT)**, developed by Professors Modigliani, Ando, and Brumberg. Although there are differences between these, it is their similarities that are important. In particular, note that in both the PIT and the LCT, household behavior tends to smooth the time pattern of consumption relative to that of disposable income.

We use the term *permanent-income theories* to describe this general property, common to both specific versions. In discussing this "consumption-smoothing" issue, it is important to ask: What variables do these theories seek to explain? What assumptions do they make? What are the major implications of these assumptions?

Variables. Three variables need to be considered: consumption, saving, and income. Keynesian-type theories seek to explain the amounts that households spend on purchasing goods and services for consumption. This concept is called *consumption expenditure*. Permanent-income theories seek to explain the actual flows of consumption of the *services* that are provided by the commodities that households buy. This concept is called *actual consumption.*[1]

With services and nondurable goods, expenditure and actual consumption occur more or less at the same time, and the distinction between the two concepts is not important. Consumption of a haircut, for example, occurs at the time that it is purchased, and an orange or a package of corn flakes is consumed very soon after it is purchased. Thus if we knew when purchases of such goods and services were made, say, last year, we would also know last year's consumption of those goods and services.

This, however, is not the case with durable consumer goods. A house is purchased at one point in time, but it yields its services over a long period of time, possibly the purchaser's lifetime. The same is true of a personal computer and a watch and, over a shorter period of time, of a car and a dress. For such products, if we know last year's purchases, we do not necessarily know last year's consumption of the services that the products yielded.

Thus one important characteristic of durable goods is that *expenditure* to purchase them is not necessarily synchronized with *consumption* of the stream of services that the goods provide. If in 1992 Ms. Smith buys a car for $12,000, uses it for six years, and then discards it as worn out, her expenditure on automobiles is $12,000 in 1992 and zero for the next five years. Her consumption of the services of automobiles, however, is spread out at an average annual rate of $2,000 for six years. If everyone followed Ms. Smith's example and bought a new car in 1992 and replaced it in 1998, the automobile industry would undergo wild booms in 1992 and 1998 with five intervening years of slump, even though the actual consumption of automobiles would be spread more or less evenly over time. This example is extreme, but it illustrates the possibilities, where consumer durable goods are concerned, of quite different time paths of *consumption expenditure,* which is the subject of Keynesian theories of consumption, and *actual consumption,* which is the subject of permanent-income theories.

Now consider saving. The change in emphasis from consumption expenditure to actual consumption implies a change in the definition of saving.

[1] Because Keynes' followers did not always distinguish between the concepts of consumption expenditure and actual consumption, the word *consumption* often is used in both contexts. We follow this normal practice, but where there is any possible ambiguity, we will refer to *consumption expenditure* and *actual consumption.*

FIGURE 28A-1 Current Income and Permanent Income

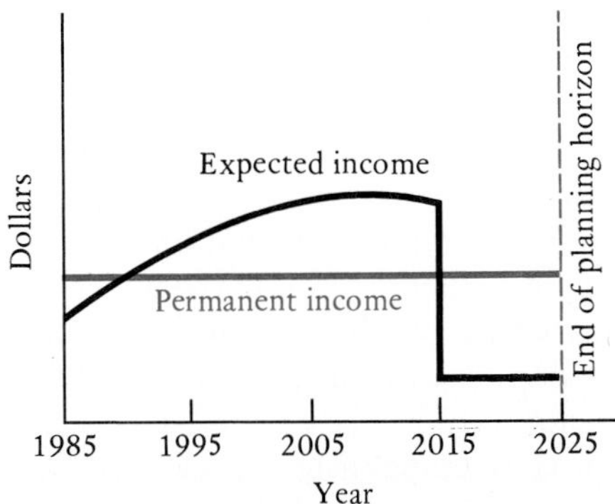

Expected current income may vary greatly over a lifetime; expected permanent income is defined to be the constant annual equivalent. The graph shows a hypothetical expected income stream from work for a household whose planning horizon was 40 years from 1985. Current income rises to a peak, then falls slowly for a while, and finally falls sharply on retirement. The corresponding permanent income is the amount that the household could consume at a steady rate over its lifetime by borrowing early against future earnings (as most newly married couples do), then repaying past debts, and finally saving for retirement when income is at its peak without either incurring debt or accumulating new wealth to be passed on to future generations.

Saving is no longer income minus consumption expenditure; it is now income minus the value of actual consumption. When Ms. Smith spent $12,000 on her car in 1992 but used only $2,000 worth of its services during that year, she was actually consuming $2,000 and saving $10,000. The purchase of a durable consumer good is thus counted as saving, and only the value of its services actually consumed is counted as consumption.

The third important variable is income. Instead of using current income, the theories use a concept of long-term income. The precise definition varies from one theory to another, but basically it is related to the household's expected income stream over a fairly long planning period. In the LCT it is the income that the household expects to earn over its lifetime, called its *lifetime income.*

Every household is assumed to have a view of its lifetime income. This is not as unreasonable as it might seem. Students who are training to become doctors have a very different view of expected lifetime income than those who are training to become schoolteachers. Both expected income streams—for a doctor and for a schoolteacher—will be different from that expected by an assembly line worker or a professional athlete. One possible lifetime income stream is shown in Figure 28A-1.

The household's expected lifetime income is then converted into a single figure for annual **permanent income**. In the life-cycle theory this permanent income is the maximum amount that the household could spend on consumption each year into the indefinite future without accumulating debts that are passed on to future generations.[2] If a household were to consume a constant amount that was equal to its permanent income each year, it would add to its debts in years when current income was less than permanent income and reduce its debt or increase its assets in years when its current income exceeded its permanent income. Over its lifetime, however, it would just break even, leaving neither accumulated assets nor debts to its heirs. If the interest rate were zero, permanent income would be just the sum of all expected incomes divided by the number of expected years of life. With a positive interest rate, permanent income will diverge from this amount because of the cost of borrowing and the extra income that can be earned by investing savings.

Assumption. The basic assumption of this type of theory, whether the PIT or the LCT, is that the household's actual consumption is related to its permanent rather than to its current income. Two households that have the same permanent income (and are similar in other relevant characteristics) will have similar consumption patterns, even though the current income of each may behave differently.

Implications. The major implication of these theories is that changes in a household's current income will affect its actual consumption only so far as they affect its permanent income. Consider two income

[2] In the PIT the household has an infinite time horizon, and the relevant permanent-income concept is the amount that the household could consume forever without increasing or decreasing its present stock of wealth.

changes that could occur in a household with a permanent income of $20,000 per year and an expected lifetime of 30 or more years. In the first case, suppose that the household receives an unexpected extra income of $2,000 *this year only*. The increase in the household's permanent income is small. If the rate of interest were zero, the household could consume an extra $66.66 per year for the rest of its expected life span; with a positive rate of interest, the extra annual consumption would be more because money not spent this year could be invested and would earn interest.[3] In the second case, suppose that the household gets a totally unforeseen increase of $2,000 per year *for the rest of its life*. In this event the household's permanent income has risen by $2,000 because the household can actually consume $2,000 more every year without accumulating new debts. Although in both cases current income rises by $2,000, the effect on permanent income is very different.

Keynesian theory assumes that *consumption expenditure* is related to current income and therefore predicts the same change in this year's consumption expenditure in each of the cases just discussed. Permanent-income theories relate *actual consumption* to permanent income and therefore predict different changes in actual consumption in each case. In the first case, there would be only a small increase in actual annual consumption; in the second case, there would be a large increase.

In the permanent-income theories, any change in current income that is thought to be temporary will have only a small effect on permanent income and hence on actual consumption.

Implications for the economy. According to the permanent-income theories, actual consumption is not affected much by temporary changes in income. Does this mean that aggregate expenditure, $C + I + G + (X - M)$, is not affected much? This is not necessarily true. Consider what happens when households get a temporary increase in income. If actual consumption is not greatly affected by this, households must be saving most of this increase. However, from the point of view of these theories, households save when they buy a durable good just as much as when they buy a financial asset, such as a stock or a bond. In both cases actual current consumption is not changed.

Thus spending a temporary increase in income on bonds or on new cars is consistent with the permanent-income theories, but it makes a great deal of difference to the short-run behavior of the economy which one of these choices is made. If households buy stocks and bonds, aggregate expenditure on currently produced final goods will not rise when income rises temporarily.[4] If households buy automobiles or other durable consumer goods, aggregate expenditure on currently produced final goods will rise when income rises temporarily. Thus the theories leave unsettled the question that is critical in determining the size of the multiplier: What is the reaction of household *expenditures* on currently produced goods and services, particularly durables, to short-term, temporary changes in income?

Assume, for example, that a recessionary gap emerges and that the government attempts to stimulate recovery by giving tax rebates and by cutting tax rates—both on an announced, temporary basis. This will raise households' current disposable incomes by the amount of the tax cuts, but it will raise their permanent incomes by only a small amount. According to the PIH, the flow of actual current consumption should not rise much. Yet it is quite consistent with the PIH that households should spend their tax savings on durable consumer goods, the consumption of which can be spread over many years.

In this case, even though actual consumption this year would not respond much to the tax cuts, expenditure would respond a great deal. Since current output and employment depend on expenditure rather than on actual consumption, the tax cut would be effective in stimulating the economy. However, it is also consistent with the PIH that households spend only a small part of their tax savings on consumption goods and seek to invest the rest in bonds and other financial assets. In this case the tax cuts may have only a small stimulating effect on the economy.

[3] If the rate of interest were 7 percent, the household could invest the $2,000, consume an extra $161 per year, and have nothing left at the end of 30 years.

[4] There may still be an indirect effect on aggregate expenditure; if the increased demand for financial assets causes interest rates to fall, some increase in interest-sensitive spending (see Chapter 31) may occur.

Chapter 29

National Income and the Price Level in the Short Run

The economy is constantly being buffeted by shocks. On the supply side, the prices of imported materials that are used by Canadian manufacturing firms change frequently and sometimes dramatically, as when oil prices soared in 1974–1975 and 1979–1980. On the demand side, a boom in less developed countries can increase the exports of Canadian-made goods that go to those countries, as happened during the 1970s. An income tax cut can lead to an increase in spending, as happened during the 1980s.

Virtually all such shocks affect both national income and the price level; that is, they have both real and nominal effects, at least initially. To understand these effects, we need to drop the assumption that the price level is constant and also to develop some further tools, called the *aggregate demand curves* and *aggregate supply curves*.

We make the transition to a variable price level in two steps. First, we study the consequences for national income of *exogenous* changes in the price level—changes that happen for reasons that are not explained by our model of the economy. Then we use our theory to determine both national income *and* the price level, and to explain why they change.

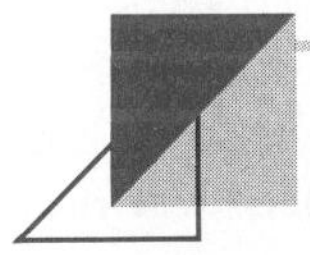

Exogenous Changes in the Price Level

What happens to equilibrium national income when the price changes for some exogenous reason, such as a rise in the price of imported raw materials? To find out, we need to understand how the change affects the desired aggregate expenditure curve.

Shifts in the *AE* Curve

There is one key result that we need to establish. A rise in the price level shifts the aggregate expenditure curve downward, and a fall in the price level shifts it upward. In other words, the price level and the desired aggregate expenditure are negatively related. The explanation lies in two effects: what the change in the price level does to desired consumption expenditure and what it does to net exports.

In most cases it is sufficient to look in detail at the implications of an increase in the price level, since a decrease merely reverses everything.

Changes in Consumption

Much of the private sector's total wealth is held in the form of assets with a fixed nominal money value. One obvious example is money itself—cash and bank deposits. Other examples are provided by many kinds of debt, including treasury bills and bonds. When a bill or a bond matures, the owner is repaid a stated sum of money. What that money can buy—its real value—depends on the price level. A rise in the price level lowers the real value of all assets that are denominated in money units and hence lowers the wealth of their owners.

How does a fall in the real value of the private sector's wealth affect the aggregate expenditure curve?[1] As we saw in Chapter 28 (see Figure 28-2 on page 595), there is a relationship between wealth and consumption. Because households have less wealth, they increase their saving so as to restore their wealth to the level that they desire for such purposes as retirement. An increase in saving of course implies a reduction in consumption.

A rise in the domestic price level lowers the real value of total wealth, which leads to a fall in desired consumption; this in turn implies a downward shift in the desired aggregate expenditure curve. A fall in the domestic price level leads to a rise in wealth and desired consumption and thus to an upward shift in the desired aggregate expenditure curve.

We have concentrated here on the direct effect of the change in wealth on desired consumption expenditure. There is also an indirect effect that operates through the interest rate. Although this effect is potentially very powerful, we cannot study it until we have studied the macroeconomic role of money and interest rates. Further discussion of this point must therefore be postponed until Chapter 34.[2]

Changes in Net Exports

When the domestic price level rises, Canadian goods become more expensive relative to foreign goods. As we saw in Chapter 28, this change in relative prices causes Canadians to reduce their purchases of domestic goods, which have now become relatively more expensive, and to increase their purchases of foreign goods, which have now become relatively less expensive. At the same time, consumers in other countries reduce their purchases of the now relatively expensive Canadian goods. We saw in Chapter 28 that these changes can be summarized as a downward shift in the net export function.

A rise in the domestic price level shifts the net export function downward, which means a downward shift in the desired aggregate expenditure curve. A fall in the domestic price level shifts the net export function and the desired aggregate expenditure curves upward.

In simple language, if Canadian goods become more expensive, less of them will be bought by foreigners, so total desired expenditure on Canadian output will fall; if Canadian goods become cheaper, more will be bought, and total desired expenditure on them will rise.

Changes in Equilibrium Income

Because it causes downward shifts in both the net export and the desired consumption curves, a rise in the price level causes a downward shift in the aggregate desired expenditure curve, as shown in Figure 29-1. The figure also allows us to reconfirm what

[1] It is worth noting that changes in the real value of a person's wealth do not necessarily change the total wealth of the private sector. In many cases the change in wealth of a creditor is exactly offset by the change in wealth of a debtor. For example, a rise in the price level lowers the real wealth of a bondholder but raises the real wealth of the bond issuer, who will have to part with less purchasing power when the bond is redeemed. However, many assets held by individuals are government debt, and hence any change in the price level causes a net change in the wealth of the private sector.

[2] Here is a brief summary of what is involved. When the price level rises, firms and households need to cover their increased money expenses between one payday and the next. This means that they wish to hold more money on average. The increased demand for money bids up the price that must be paid to borrow money (the interest rate). Firms that borrow money to build plants and to purchase equipment and households that borrow money to buy consumer goods and housing respond to rising interest rates by choosing to spend less on a host of items such as capital goods, housing, automobiles, and many other durable goods. This means that there is a decrease in the aggregate demand for the nation's output.

FIGURE 29-1 Aggregate Expenditure and the Price Level

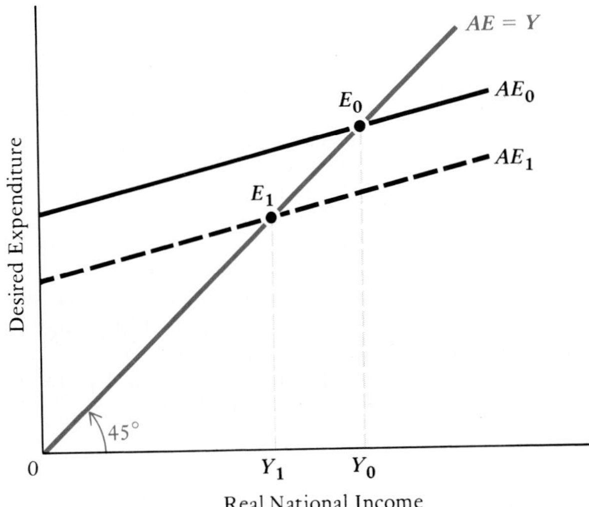

Changes in the price level cause the *AE* curve to shift and thus cause equilibrium national income to change. At the initial price level, the *AE* curve is given by the solid line AE_0, and hence equilibrium national income is Y_0. An increase in the price level reduces desired aggregate expenditure and thus causes the *AE* curve to shift downward to the dashed line, AE_1. As a result, equilibrium national income falls to Y_1.

Starting with the dashed line, AE_1, a fall in the price level increases desired aggregate expenditure, shifting the *AE* curve up to AE_0 and raising equilibrium national income to Y_1.

we already know from Chapter 28: When the *AE* curve shifts downward, the equilibrium level of national income falls.

Since a rise in the domestic price level causes the aggregate expenditure curve to shift downward, it reduces equilibrium national income.

Now suppose that there is a fall in the price level. Since this is the opposite of the case that we have just studied, we can summarize the two key effects briefly. First, Canadian goods become relatively cheaper internationally, so net exports rise. Second, the purchasing power of some existing assets that are denominated in money terms is increased, so households spend more. The resulting increase in desired expenditure on Canadian goods causes the *AE* curve to shift upward and hence raises equilibrium national income. This is also shown in Figure 29-1.

Since a fall in the domestic price level causes the aggregate expenditure curve to shift upward, it increases equilibrium national income.

The Aggregate Demand Curve

We now know from the behavior underlying the aggregate expenditure curve that the price level and real national income are negatively related; that is, a change in the price level changes equilibrium national income in the opposite direction. This negative relationship can be shown in an important new concept, called the *aggregate demand curve*.

Recall that the *AE* curve relates national income to desired expenditure for a given price level, plotting income on the horizontal axis. The **aggregate demand (*AD*) curve** relates equilibrium national income to the price level, again plotting income on the horizontal axis. Because the horizontal axes of both the *AE* and *AD* curves measure real national income, the two curves can be placed one above the other so that the level of national income on each can be compared directly. This is shown in Figure 29-2.

Now let us see how the *AD* curve is derived. Given a value of the price level, equilibrium national income is determined in part (i) of Figure 29-2 at the point where the *AE* curve crosses the 45° line. In part (ii) of Figure 29-2, the combination of the equilibrium level of national income and the corresponding value of the price level is plotted, giving one point on the *AD* curve.

When the price level changes, the *AE* curve shifts, for the reasons just seen. The new position of the *AE* curve gives rise to a new equilibrium level of national income that is associated with the new price level. This determines a second point on the *AD* curve, as shown in Figure 29-2(ii).

Any change in the price level leads to a new *AE* curve and hence to a new level of equilibrium

FIGURE 29-2 The *AD* Curve and the *AE* Curve

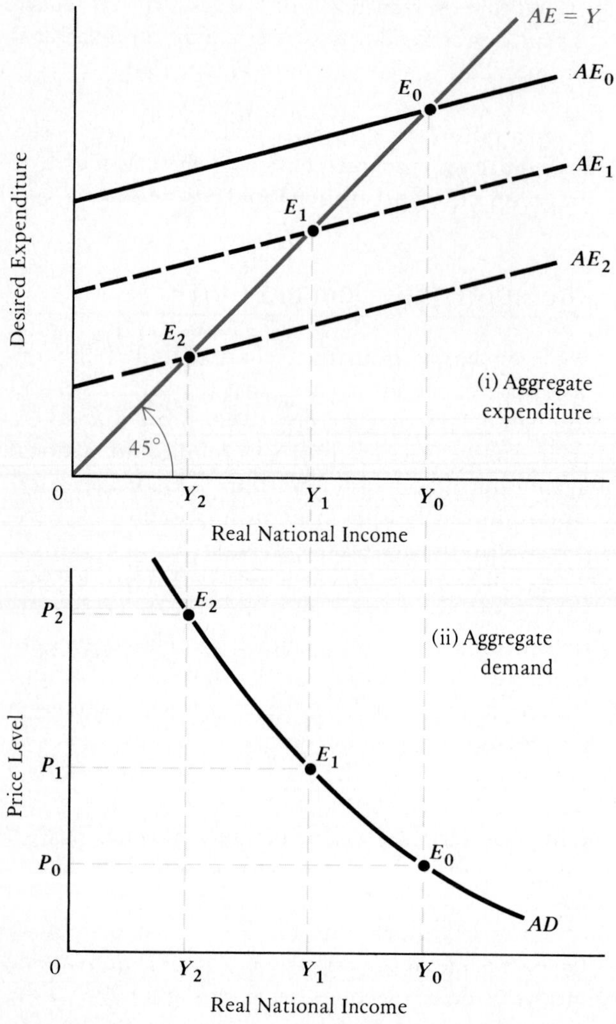

Equilibrium income is determined by the *AE* curve for each given price level; the level of income and its associated price level yield a point on the *AD* curve. When the price level is P_0, the *AE* curve is AE_0, and equilibrium income is Y_0 in (i). (This is the initial equilibrium from Figure 29-1.) Plotting Y_0 against P_0 yields the point E_0 on the *AD* curve in (ii).

An increase in the price level to P_1 causes AE_0 in (i) to shift downward to AE_1, reducing equilibrium income to Y_1. Plotting this lower level of income, Y_1, against the higher price level, P_1, yields a second point, E_1, on the *AD* curve in (ii). If the price level rises to P_2, the *AE* curve in (i) shifts downward to AE_2, reducing equilibrium income to Y_2. Plotting Y_2 against P_2 yields a third point, E_2, on the *AD* curve in (ii).

Thus a change in the price level causes a shift of the *AE* curve and a movement along the *AD* curve.

income. Each combination of equilibrium income and its associated price level becomes a particular point on the *AD* curve.

Note that since the *AD* curve relates equilibrium national income to the price level, changes in the price level that cause *shifts in* the *AE* curve cause *movements along* the *AD* curve. A movement along the *AD* curve thus traces out the response of equilibrium income to a change in the price level.

The Slope of the *AD* Curve

Figure 29-2 has already provided us with sufficient information to establish that the *AD* curve is negatively sloped.

1. **A *rise* in the price level causes the aggregate expenditure curve to shift downward and hence leads to a movement upward and to the left along the *AD* curve, reflecting a *fall* in the equilibrium level of national income.**

BOX 29-1

The Shape of the Aggregate Demand Curve

It is tempting to think that the properties of the aggregate demand curve arise from the same behavior that gives rise to the individual demand curves that we studied in Chapter 4. Unfortunately, life is not so simple. Let us see why we cannot take such an approach.

If we assume that a downward-sloping aggregate demand curve can be derived in the same manner as downward-sloping individual market demand curves, we would be committing the fallacy of composition. This is to assume that what is correct for the parts must be correct for the whole.

Consider a simple example of the fallacy. An art collector can add to her private collection of nineteenth century French paintings provided only that she has enough money. However, to assume that because any one person can do this, everyone could do so simultaneously is plainly wrong. The world's stock of nineteenth century French paintings is totally fixed. All of us cannot do what any one of us with enough money can do.

How does the fallacy of composition relate to demand curves? An individual demand curve describes a situation in which the price of one commodity changes while the prices of all other commodities and consumers' money incomes are constant. Such an individual demand curve is negatively sloped for two reasons. First, as the price of the commodity rises, each consumer's given money income will buy a smaller *total* amount of goods, so a smaller quantity of each commodity will be bought, other things being equal. Second, as the price of the commodity rises, consumers buy less of it and more of the now relatively cheaper substitutes.

The first reason has no application to the aggregate demand curve, which relates the total demand for all output to the price level. All prices and total output are changing as we move along the *AD* curve. Since the value of output determines income, consumers' money incomes will also be changing along this curve.

The second reason does have some limited application to the aggregate demand curve. A rise in the price level entails a rise in domestic commodity prices. There is no incentive to substitute among domestic commodities whose prices do not change relative to each other. However, it does give rise, as we saw earlier in this chapter, to some substitution between domestic and foreign goods. Domestic goods rise in price relative to imported goods, and the switch in expenditure will lower desired aggregate expenditure on domestic output and hence will lower equilibrium national income.

2. **A *fall* in the price level causes the aggregate expenditure curve to shift upward and hence leads to a movement downward and to the right along the *AD* curve, reflecting a rise in the equilibrium level of national income.**

Early in our study (Chapter 4) we saw that demand curves for individual goods such as carrots or automobiles are negatively sloped. However, the reasons for the negative slope of the *AD* curve are different from the reasons for the negative slope of individual demand curves that are used in microeconomics; this important point is discussed further in Box 29-1.

Points off the *AD* Curve

The *AD* curve depicts combinations of national income and the price level that give equilibrium between aggregate desired expenditure and actual output in the sense that aggregate desired expenditure equals actual output. These points are said to be *consistent* with expenditure decisions.

The national income given by any point on the aggregate demand curve is such that if that level of output is produced, aggregate desired expenditure, *at the given price level,* will exactly equal the output.

FIGURE 29-3 **The Relationship Between the *AE* and *AD* Curves**

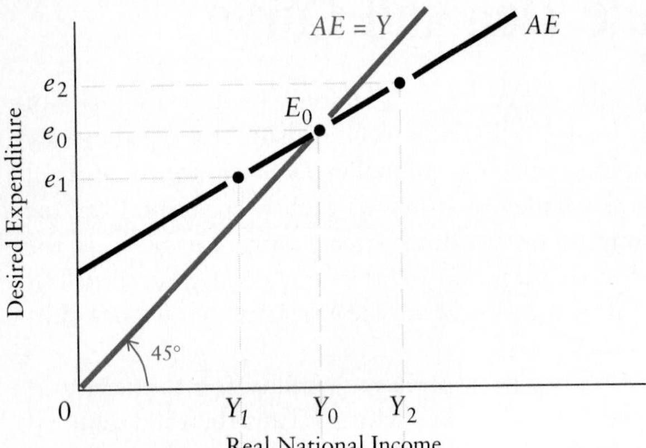

(i) Aggregate expenditure

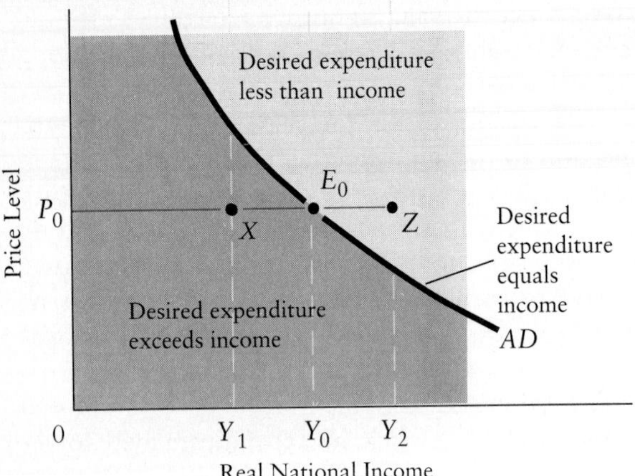

(ii) Aggregate demand

The *AD* curve plots the price level against the level of national income consistent with expenditure decisions at that price level. With the price level P_0, equilibrium national income is Y_0, shown by the intersection of *AE* and the 45° line at E_0 in (i) and by the point E_0 on the *AD* curve in (ii).

With the price level constant at P_0, consider a level of national income of Y_1, which is less than Y_0. As can be seen in (i), if national income were equal to Y_1, desired aggregate expenditure would be e_1, which is greater than Y_1. Hence Y_1 is not an equilibrium level of national income when the price level is P_0, and the combination (P_0, Y_1) is not on the *AD* curve in (ii), as shown by point *X*.

Now consider a level of national income of Y_2, which is greater than Y_0. As can be seen in (i), if national income were equal to Y_2, desired aggregate expenditure would be e_2, which is less than Y_2. Hence Y_2 is not an equilibrium level of national income when the price level is P_0, and the combination (P_0, Y_2) is not on the *AD* curve in (ii), as shown by point *Z*.

Repeating the same analysis for each given price level tells us that for all points to the left of the *AD* curve (dark-shaded area), desired expenditure exceeds income, whereas for all points to the right of the *AD* curve (light-shaded area), desired expenditure is less than income.

Points to the left of the *AD* curve show combinations of national income and the price level that cause aggregate desired expenditure to exceed output. There is thus pressure for income to rise because firms could sell more than current output. Points to the right of the *AD* curve show combinations of national income and the price level for which aggregate desired expenditure is less than current income. There is thus pressure for income to fall because firms will not be able to sell all of their current output. These relationships are illustrated in Figure 29-3.

Shifts in the *AD* Curve

Since the *AD* curve plots equilibrium national income as a function of the price level, anything that alters equilibrium national income *at a given price level* must shift the *AD* curve. In other words, any change other than a change in the price level that causes the *AE* curve to shift will also cause the *AD* curve to shift. (Recall that a change in the price level causes a *movement along* the *AD* curve.) Such a shift is called an **aggregate demand shock**. For example, in the 1980s changes in the tax laws led to an increase in

FIGURE 29-4 The Simple Multiplier and Shifts in the *AD* Curve

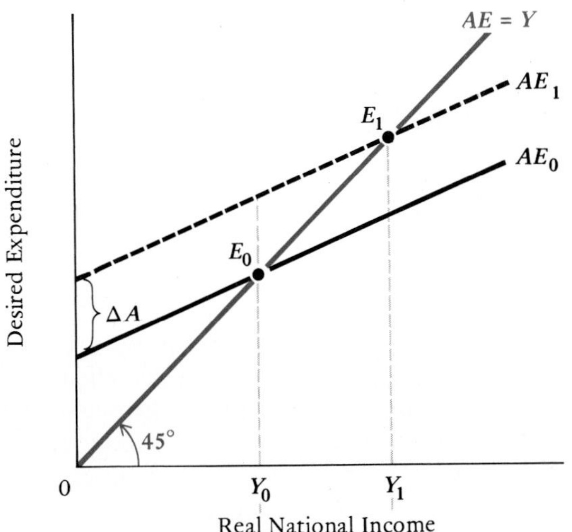

(i) Aggregate expenditure

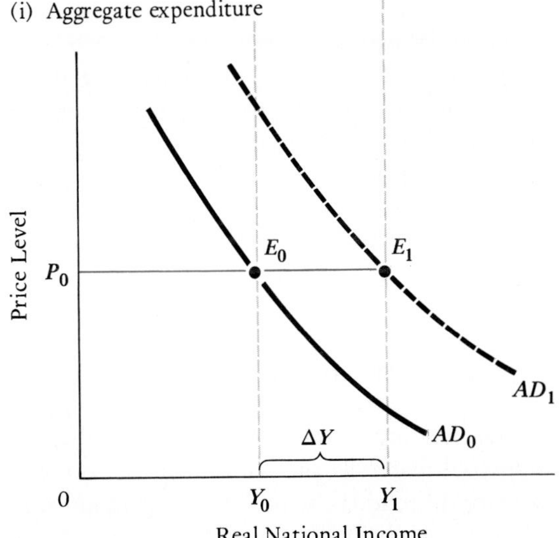

(ii) Aggregate demand

A change in autonomous expenditure changes equilibrium national income for any given price level, and the simple multiplier measures the resulting horizontal shift in the aggregate demand curve. The original desired expenditure curve is AE_0 in (i). Equilibrium is at E_0, with national income Y_0 at price level P_0. This yields point E_0 on the curve AD_0 in (ii).

The *AE* curve in (i) then shifts upward from AE_0 to AE_1, due to an increase in autonomous expenditure of ΔA. Equilibrium income now rises to Y_1, with the price level still constant at P_0. Thus the *AD* curve in (ii) shifts to the right to point E_1, indicating the higher equilibrium income Y_1 associated with the same price level P_0. The magnitude of the shift, ΔY, is given by the simple multiplier.

A fall in autonomous expenditure can be analyzed by shifting the *AE* curve from AE_1 to AE_0, which shifts the *AD* curve from AD_1 to AD_0 at price level P_0. The equilibrium value of national income falls from Y_1 to Y_0.

the amount of consumption expenditure that was associated with each level of national income. This was an expansionary demand shock that shifted the *AD* curve to the right.

Using our new concepts, the conclusions on page 604 now can be restated as follows:

A rise in the amount of desired consumption, investment, government, or net export expenditure that is associated with each level of national income shifts the *AD* curve to the right. A fall in any of these expenditures shifts the *AD* curve to the left.

The Simple Multiplier and the *AD* Curve

We saw in Chapter 28 that the simple multiplier measures the magnitude of the *change* in equilibrium national income in response to a change in autonomous expenditure when the price level is constant. It follows that this multiplier gives the magnitude of the *horizontal* shift in the *AD* curve in response to a change in autonomous expenditure. This is shown in Figure 29-4.

The simple multiplier measures the horizontal shift in the *AD* curve in response to a change in the autonomous expenditure.

If the price level remains constant and firms are willing to supply everything that is demanded at that price level, the simple multiplier will also show the change in equilibrium income that will occur in response to a change in autonomous expenditure.

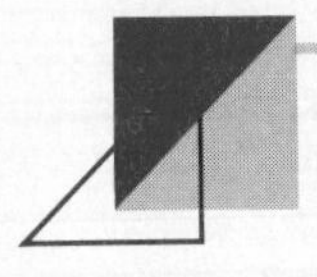

Equilibrium National Income and the Price Level

So far we have explained how the equilibrium level of national income is determined *when the price level is taken as given* and how that equilibrium changes as the price level is changed exogenously. By assuming that firms will produce all that is demanded at the going price level, we have effectively ignored the firms' supply decisions. We are now ready to take an important step: providing an *explanation* of the behavior of the price level. In order to do this, we need to take account of the supply decisions of firms.

The Aggregate Supply Curve

Aggregate supply refers to the total output of final goods and services that firms wish to produce, assuming that they can sell all that they wish to sell. Aggregate supply thus depends on the decisions of firms to use workers and all other inputs to produce goods and services to sell to households, governments, and other firms, as well as for export.

An *aggregate supply curve* relates aggregate supply to the price level. It is necessary to define two types of such curves. The **short-run aggregate supply (*SRAS*) curve** relates the price level to the quantity that firms would like to produce and to sell *on the assumption that the prices of all factors of production remain constant*. The *long-run aggregate supply (LRAS) curve*, which we will define more fully later, relates the price level to desired sales after a full adjustment has been made to that price level. For the moment we confine our attention to the *SRAS* curve.

The Slope of the Short-Run Aggregate Supply Curve

To study the slope of the *SRAS* curve, we need to see how costs are related to output and then how prices and outputs are related.

Costs and output. Suppose that firms wish to increase their outputs above current levels. What will this to do to their costs per unit of output—their **unit costs**? The short-run aggregate supply curve assumes that the prices of all factors of production that firms use, such as labor, remain constant. This does not, however, mean that unit costs will be constant. Less efficient standby plants may have to be used, and less efficient workers may have to be hired, and existing workers will have to be paid overtime rates for additional work. For these and other similar reasons,[3] unit costs will tend to rise as output rises, even when input prices are constant.

Unit costs and output are positively associated.

Prices and output. To consider the relationship between price and output, we need to distinguish two distinct types of markets: those in which firms are price takers and those in which firms are price setters. Some industries, including those that produce most basic industrial materials and some energy products, contain many individual firms (including many foreign firms with which Canadian firms must compete). In these cases each one is too small to influence the market price, which is set by the overall forces of demand and supply. Each firm must accept whatever price is set on the open market and adjust its output to that price. The firms are said to be *price takers* and *quantity adjusters*. When the market price changes, these firms will react by altering their production.

[3] Readers who have studied microeconomics will recognize the law of diminishing returns as a potent reason why costs rise in the short run as firms squeeze more output out of a fixed quantity of capital equipment.

FIGURE 29-5 A Short-Run Aggregate Supply Curve

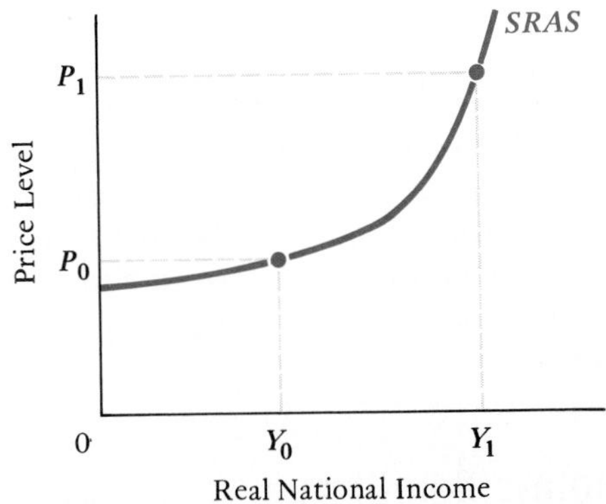

The *SRAS* curve is positively sloped. The positive slope of the *SRAS* curve shows that with the prices of labor and other inputs given, total desired output and the price level will be positively associated. Thus a rise in the price level from P_0 to P_1 will be associated with a rise in the quantity of total output supplied, from Y_0 to Y_1.

Because their unit costs rise with output, price-taking firms produce more when price rises and less when price falls.

Many other industries, including most of those that produce manufactured products, contain so few firms that each can influence market prices. Most such firms sell products that differ from one another but are similar enough to be thought of as the single commodity produced by one industry. For example, no two kinds of automobiles are the same, but all automobiles are sufficiently alike so that we have no trouble talking about the automobile industry and the commodity automobiles. In such cases each firm must quote a price at which it is prepared to sell each of its products; that is, the firm is a price setter. If the demand for the output of price-setting firms increases sufficiently to take their outputs into the range in which their unit costs rise (e.g., because overtime is worked and standby plants are brought into production), these firms will not increase their outputs unless they can pass at least some of these extra costs on through higher prices. When demand falls, they will reduce output, and competition among them will tend to cause a reduction in prices whenever their unit costs fall.

Price-setting firms will increase their prices when they expand output into the range in which unit costs are rising.

This is the basic behavior of firms in response to the changes in demand and prices when factor prices are constant, and it explains the slope of the *SRAS* curve, such as the one shown in Figure 29-5.

The actions of both price-taking and price-setting firms cause the price level and total output to be positively associated; the graphical expression of this relationship is the positively sloped, short-run aggregate supply curve.

Shifts in the *SRAS* Curve

Shifts in the *SRAS* curve, which are shown in Figure 29-6, are called **aggregate supply shocks**. Two sources of aggregate supply shocks are of particular importance: changes in the price of inputs and increases in productivity.

Changes in input prices. Factor prices are held constant along the *SRAS* curve, and when they change, the curve shifts. If factor prices rise, firms will find the profitability of their current production reduced. For any given level of output to be produced, an increase in the price level will be required. If prices do not rise, firms will react by decreasing production.[4] For the economy as a whole, this means that there will be less output at each price level than before the increase in factor prices. Thus if factor prices rise, the *SRAS* curve shifts upward. (Notice that when a positively sloped curve shifts upward, it also shifts to the left.)

Similarly, a fall in factor prices causes the *SRAS* curve to shift downward (and to the right). This increase in supply means that more will be produced and offered for sale at each price level.

[4] Readers who have studied microeconomics will recognize that such an upward shift in a firm's marginal cost curve leads to a decrease in the output that is profitable for the firm to produce. This was discussed in Chapter 12.

FIGURE 29-6 Shifts in the *SRAS* Curve

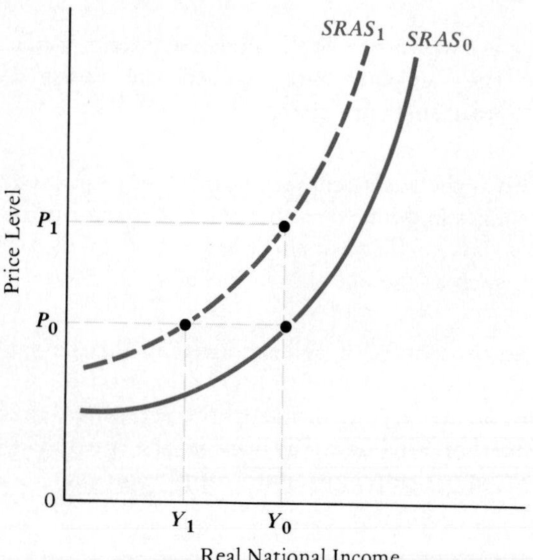

A shift to the left of the *SRAS* curve reflects a decrease in supply; a shift to the right reflects an increase in supply. Starting from (P_0, Y_0) on $SRAS_0$, suppose that there is an increase in input prices. At price level P_0, only Y_1 would be produced. Alternatively, to get output Y_0 would require a rise to price level P_1. The new supply curve is $SRAS_1$, above and to the left of $SRAS_0$. An increase in supply, caused, say, by a decrease in input prices, would shift the *SRAS* curve downward and to the right, from $SRAS_1$ to $SRAS_0$.

Increases in productivity. If labor productivity rises, meaning that each worker can produce more, the unit costs of production will fall as long as wage rates do not rise sufficiently to fully offset the productivity rise. Lower costs generally lead to lower prices. Competing firms cut prices in attempts to raise their market shares, and the net result of such competition is that the fall in production costs is accompanied by a fall in prices.

Since the same output is sold at a lower price, this causes a downward shift in the *SRAS* curve. This shift is an increase in supply, as illustrated in Figure 29-6.

A rightward shift in the *SRAS* curve, brought about, for example, by an increase in productivity with no increase in factor prices, means that firms will be willing to produce more national income with no increase in the price level. This result has been the object of many government policies that seek to encourage increases in productivity.

A change in either factor prices or productivity will shift the *SRAS* curve because any given output will be supplied at a different price level than previously. An increase in factor prices shifts the *SRAS* curve to the left; an increase in productivity or a decrease in factor prices shifts it to the right.

Macroeconomic Equilibrium

We have now reached our objective: We are ready to see how both real national income and the price level are simultaneously determined by the interaction of aggregate demand and aggregate supply.

The equilibrium values of national output and the price level occur at the intersection of the *AD* and *SRAS* curves, as shown by Y_0 and P_0, which intersect at point E_0 in Figure 29-7. We describe the combination of national income and price level that is on both the *AD* and the *SRAS* curves as a *macroeconomic equilibrium*.

To see why this pair of points is the only macroeconomic equilibrium, first consider what Figure 29-7 shows would happen if the price level were below P_0. At this lower price level, the desired output of firms, as given by the *SRAS* curve, is less than the level of output that is consistent with expenditure decisions, as given by the *AD* curve. If firms were to produce their desired level of output, desired expenditure would exceed the amount of goods supplied. Firms that found that they could sell more than their current outputs would increase their outputs, thus causing national income to change. Hence there can be no macroeconomic equilibrium when the price level is below P_0.

Similarly, Figure 29-7 shows that when the price level is above P_0, the behavior underlying the *SRAS* and *AD* curves is not consistent. In this case producers will wish to supply more than the level of income that is consistent with demand at that price level. If firms were to produce their desired levels of output, desired expenditure would not be large

FIGURE 29-7 Macroeconomic Equilibrium

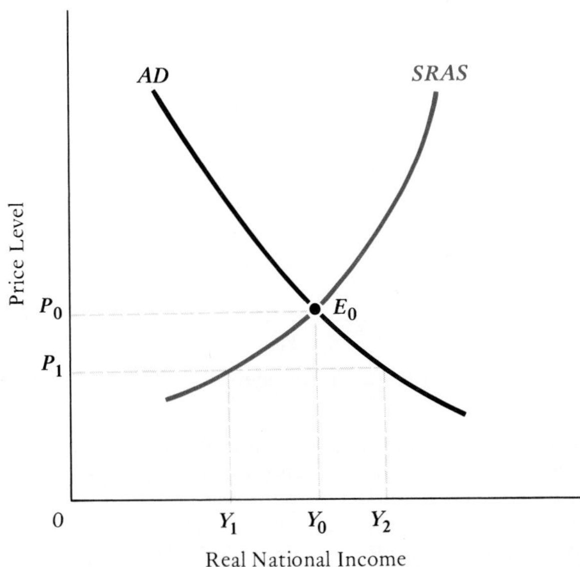

Macroeconomic equilibrium occurs at the intersection of the *AD* and *SRAS* curves and determines the equilibrium values for national income and the price level. Given the *AD* and *SRAS* curves in the figure, macroeconomic equilibrium occurs at E_0, with national income equal to Y_0 and the price level equal to P_0. At P_0 the desired output of firms, as given by the *SRAS* curve, is equal to the level of national income that is consistent with expenditure decisions, as given by the *AD* curve.

If the price level were equal to P_1, less than P_0, the desired output of firms, given by the *SRAS* curve, would be Y_1. However, at P_1 the level of output that is consistent with expenditure decisions, given by the *AD* curve, would be Y_2, greater than Y_1. Hence when the price level is P_1, or any other level less than P_0, the desired output of firms will be less than the level of national income that is consistent with expenditure decisions.

Similarly, for any price level above P_0, the desired output of firms, given by the *SRAS* curve, would exceed the level of output that is consistent with expenditure decisions, given by the *AD* curve.

The only price level where the supply decisions of firms are consistent with desired expenditure is at macroeconomic equilibrium. At P_0 firms wish to produce Y_0. When they do so, they generate a national income of Y_0; when income is Y_0, decision makers wish to spend exactly Y_0, thus purchasing the nation's output. Hence all decisions are consistent.

enough to purchase everything that would be produced.

Only at the combination of national income and price level, given by the intersection of the *SRAS* and *AD* curves, are spending behavior and supply behavior consistent.

When the price level is less than its equilibrium value, expenditure behavior is consistent with a level of national income that is greater than the desired output of firms. When the price level is greater than its equilibrium value, expenditure behavior is consistent with a level of national income that is less than the desired output of firms.

Macroeconomic equilibrium thus requires that two conditions be satisfied. The first is familiar to us from Chapter 28: At the prevailing price level, desired aggregate expenditure must be equal to national income, which means that purchasers are just willing to buy all that is produced. The second is introduced by consideration of aggregate supply: At the prevailing price level, firms must wish to produce the prevailing level of national income, no more and no less.

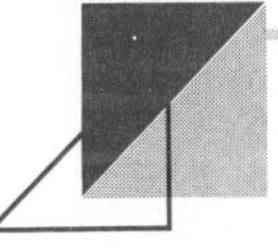

Changes in National Income and the Price Level

The aggregate demand and aggregate supply curves can now be used to show how various shocks to the economy change both national income and the price level.

A shift in the *AD* curve is called an *aggregate demand shock*. A *rightward* shift in the *AD* curve is an *increase* in aggregate demand; it means that at all price levels, expenditure decisions will now be consistent with a *higher* level of real national income. Similarly, a *leftward* shift in the *AD* curve is a *decrease* in aggregate demand; it means that at all price levels, expenditure decisions will now be consistent with a *lower* level of real national income.

A shift in the *SRAS* curve is called an *aggregate supply shock*. A *rightward* shift in the *SRAS* curve is an *increase* in aggregate supply; at any given price level, *more* real national income will be supplied. A *leftward* shift in the *SRAS* curve is a *decrease* in aggregate supply; at any given price level, *less* real national income will be supplied.[5]

What happens to real national income and to the price level when one of the aggregate curves shifts?

A shift in either the *AD* or the *SRAS* curve leads to changes in the equilibrium values of the price level and real national income.

Box 29-2 deals with the special case of a perfectly elastic *SRAS* curve. In that case only, the aggregate supply curve determines the price level by itself, and the aggregate demand curve determines real national income by itself.

FIGURE 29-8 Aggregate Demand Shocks

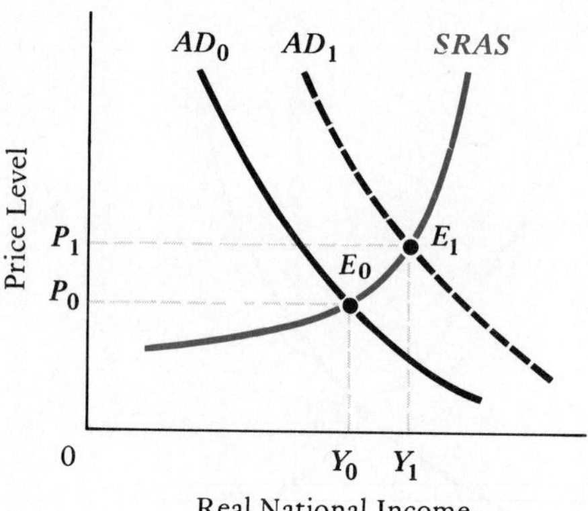

Shifts in aggregate demand cause the price level and real national income to move in the same direction. An increase in aggregate demand shifts the *AD* curve to the right, say, from AD_0 to AD_1. Macroeconomic equilibrium moves from E_0 to E_1. The price level rises from P_0 to P_1, and real national income rises from Y_0 to Y_1, reflecting a movement along the *SRAS* curve.

A decrease in aggregate demand shifts the *AD* curve to the left, say, from AD_1 to AD_0. Equilibrium moves from E_1 to E_0. Prices fall from P_1 to P_0, and real national income falls from Y_1 to Y_0, again reflecting a movement along the *SRAS* curve.

Aggregate Demand Shocks

Figure 29-8 shows the effects of an increase in aggregate demand. This increase could have occurred because of, say, increased investment or government spending; it means that more national output would be demanded at any given price level. For now we are not concerned with the source of the shock; we are interested in its implications for the price level and real national income.[6] As is shown in the figure, following an increase in aggregate demand, both the price level and real national income rise.

Figure 29-8 also shows that both the price level and real national income fall as the result of a decrease in demand.

Aggregate demand shocks cause the price level and real national income to change in the same direction; both rise with an increase in aggregate demand, and both fall with a decrease in aggregate demand.

An aggregate demand shock means that there is a shift in the *AD* curve (for example, from AD_0 to AD_1 in Figure 29-8). Adjustment to the new equilibrium following an aggregate demand shock involves a movement along the *SRAS* curve (for example, from point E_0 to point E_1).

The Multiplier When the Price Level Varies

We saw earlier in this chapter that the simple multiplier gives the extent of the horizontal shift in the *AD* curve in response to a change in autonomous expenditure. If the price level remains constant *and* if firms are willing to supply all that is demanded at the existing price level, the simple multiplier gives the increase in equilibrium national income.

Now that we can use aggregate demand and aggregate supply curves, we can answer a more interesting question: What happens in the more usual case

[5] The distinction between movements along and shifts of curves that we encountered in Chapter 4 and again in Chapter 28 is also relevant here. Recall that the phrase "a change in quantity demanded" refers to a *movement along* a demand curve, whereas "a change in demand" refers to a *shift of* the demand curve. A similar distinction applies to the supply curve.

Note that for either the *AD* or the *SRAS* curve, a shift to the right means an increase, and a shift to the left means a decrease. If we speak of upward and downward shifts, however, the meaning differs for the two curves. An upward shift of the *AD* curve reflects an increase in aggregate demand, but an upward shift in the *SRAS* curve reflects a *decrease* in aggregate supply.

[6] Later (starting in Chapter 32) we shall also study how government policy can influence these variables.

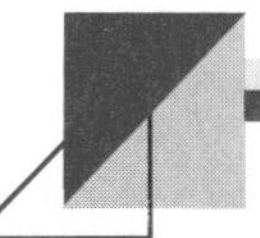

BOX 29-2

The Keynesian *SRAS* Curve

In this box we consider an extreme version of the *SRAS* curve that is horizontal over some range of national income. It is called the **Keynesian short-run aggregate supply curve**, after John Maynard Keynes, who in his famous book *The General Theory of Employment, Interest and Money* (1936) pioneered the study of the behavior of economies under conditions of high unemployment.

The behavior that gives rise to the Keynesian *SRAS* curve can be described as follows. When real national income is below potential national income, individual firms are operating at less than normal-capacity output. Firms respond to cyclical declines in demand by holding their prices constant at the level that would maximize profits if production were at normal capacity. They then respond to demand variations below that capacity by altering output. In other words, they will supply whatever they can sell at their existing prices as long as they are producing below their normal capacity. This means that the firms have horizontal supply curves and that their output is *demand-determined*.*

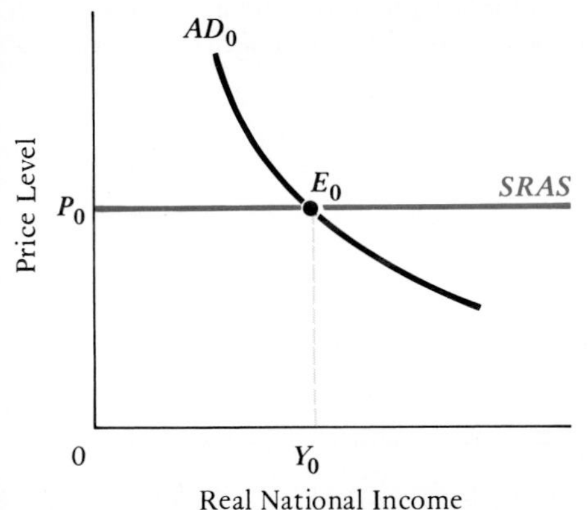

Under these circumstances, the economy has a horizontal aggregate supply curve, indicating that any output up to potential output will be supplied at the going price level. The amount that is actually produced is then determined by the position of the aggregate demand curve, as shown in the figure. Thus we say that real national income is demand-determined.

If demand rises enough so that firms are trying to squeeze more than normal output out of their plants, their costs will rise, and so will their prices. Thus the horizontal Keynesian *SRAS* curve is assumed to apply only to national incomes below potential income.

* The evidence is strong that firms, particularly in the manufacturing sector, do behave like this in the short run. One possible explanation for this is that changing prices frequently is too costly, so firms set the best possible (profit-maximizing) prices when output is at normal capacity and then do not change prices in the face of short-term fluctuations in demand. This is discussed further in Chapter 14.

in which the aggregate supply curve is positively sloped? In this case a rise in national income caused by an increase in aggregate demand will be associated with a rise in the price level. However, we have seen that a rise in the price level (by reducing net exports and by lowering the real value of household wealth) shifts the *AE* curve downward, which lowers equilibrium national income, other things being equal. The outcome of these conflicting forces is easily seen using aggregate demand and aggregate supply curves.

As can be seen in Figure 29-8, when the *SRAS* curve is positively sloped, the change in real national income that has been caused by a change in autonomous expenditure is no longer equal to the size of the horizontal shift in the *AD* curve. A shift to the right of the *AD* curve causes the price level to rise, which in turn causes the rise in national income to be less than the horizontal shift of the *AD* curve. Part of the expansionary impact of an increase in demand is dissipated by a rise in the price level, and only part is transmitted to a rise in real output. Of

FIGURE 29-9 The *AE* Curve and the Multiplier When the Price Level Varies

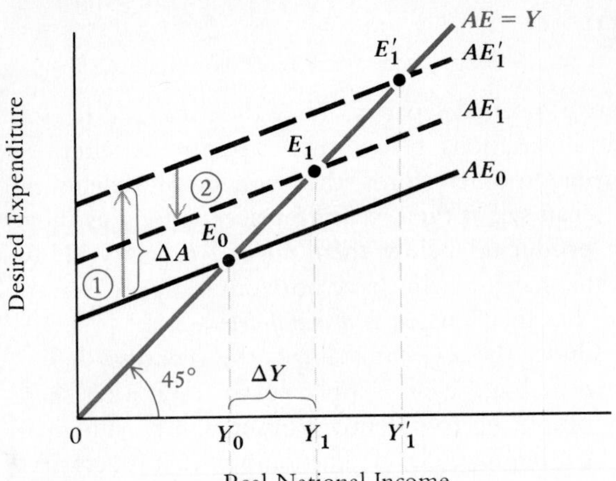

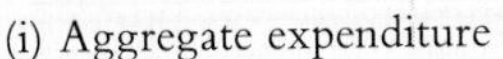
(i) Aggregate expenditure

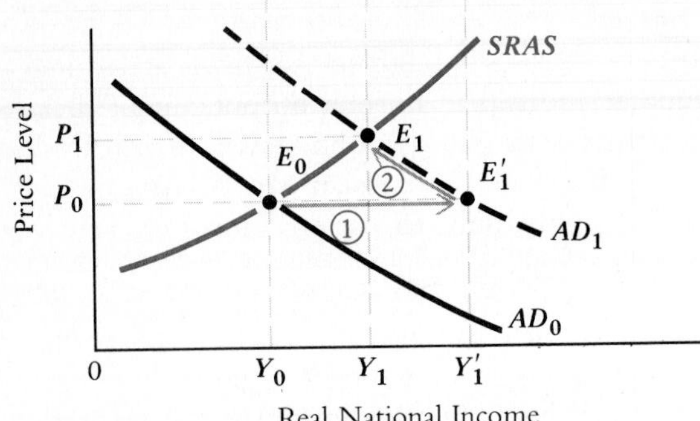

(ii) Aggregate demand

An increase in autonomous expenditures causes the *AE* curve to shift upward, but the rise in the price level causes it to shift part of the way down again. Hence the multiplier effect on income is smaller than when the price level is constant. Originally, equilibrium is at point E_0 in both (i) and (ii), with real national income at Y_0 and price level at P_0. Desired aggregate expenditure then shifts by ΔA to AE_1', as shown by arrow 1 in (i), taking the aggregate demand curve to AD_1. If the price level had remained constant at P_0, the new equilibrium would have been E_1' and real income would have risen to Y_1'. The amount Y_0Y_1' is the change called for by the simple multiplier, as shown by arrow 1 in (ii).

Instead, however, the shift in the *AD* curve raises the price level to P_1 because the *SRAS* curve is positively sloped. The rise in the price level shifts the aggregate expenditure curve down to AE_1, as shown by arrow 2 in (i). This is shown as a movement along the *AD* curve, as shown by arrow 2 in (ii). The new equilibrium is thus at E_1. The amount Y_0Y_1 is ΔY, the actual increase in real income, whereas the amount Y_1Y_1' is the shortfall relative to the simple multiplier due to the rise in the price level.

The multiplier, adjusted for the effect of the price increase, is the ratio of $\Delta Y/\Delta A$ in (i).

course, there still is an increase in output, so a multiplier still may be calculated, but its value is not the same as that of the simple multiplier.

When the *SRAS* curve is positively sloped, the multiplier is smaller than the simple multiplier.

Why is the multiplier smaller when the *SRAS* curve is positively sloped? The answer lies in the behavior that is summarized by the *AE* curve. To understand this, it is useful to think of the final change in national income as occurring in two stages, as shown in Figure 29-9.

First, with prices remaining constant, an increase in autonomous expenditure shifts the *AE* curve upward and therefore shifts the *AD* curve to the right. This is shown by a shift upward of the *AE* curve in part (i) of the figure and a shift to the right of the *AD* curve in part (ii). The horizontal shift in the *AD* curve is measured by the simple multiplier, but this cannot be the final equilibrium position because firms are unwilling to produce enough to satisfy the extra demand at the existing price level.

Second, we take account of the rise in the price level that occurs due to the positive slope of the *SRAS* curve. As we have seen, a rise in the price level, via its effect on net exports and on wealth, leads to a downward shift in the *AE* curve. This second shift of the *AE* curve partly counteracts the initial rise in national income and so reduces the size of the multiplier. The second stage shows up as a downward shift of the *AE* curve in part (i) of Figure 29-9 and a movement upward and to the left along the *AD* curve in part (ii).

The Importance of the Shape of the *SRAS* Curve

We now have seen that the shape of the *SRAS* curve has important implications for how the effects of an aggregate demand shock are divided between changes in real national output and changes in the price level. Figure 29-10 highlights this by considering *AD* shocks in the presence of an *SRAS* curve that exhibits three distinct ranges. Box 29-3 explores some possible reasons for such an increasing slope of the *SRAS* curve.

FIGURE 29-10 The Effects of Increases in Aggregate Demand

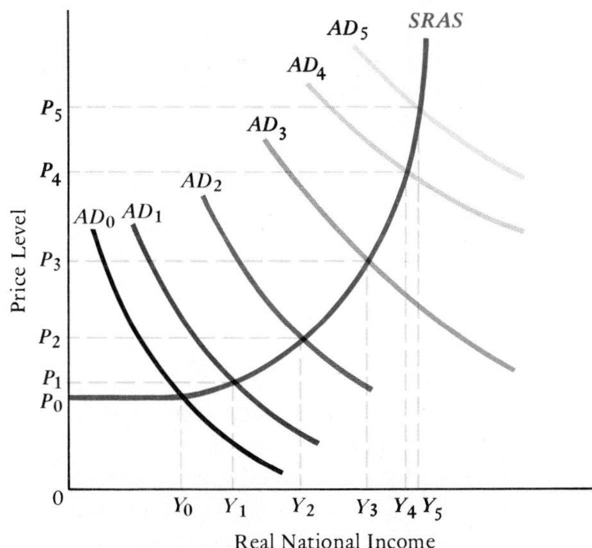

The effects of increases in aggregate demand are divided between increases in real income and increases in prices, depending on the shape of the *SRAS* curve. Because of the increasing slope of the *SRAS* curve, increases in aggregate demand up to AD_0 have virtually no impact on price. When aggregate demand increases from AD_0 to AD_1, there is a relatively small increase in price, from P_0 to P_1, and a relatively large increase in output, from Y_0 to Y_1. Successive further increases bring larger price increases and relatively smaller output increases. By the time aggregate demand is at AD_4, virtually all of the effect is on the price level.

Over the *flat* range, from 0 to Y_0, any change in aggregate demand leads to little change in prices and, as seen earlier, a response of output nearly equal to that predicted by the simple multiplier.

Over the *intermediate* range, along which the *SRAS* curve is positively sloped, from Y_1 to Y_4, a shift in the *AD* curve gives rise to appreciable changes in both real income and the price level. As we saw earlier in this chapter, the change in the price level means that real income will change by less in response to a change in autonomous expenditure than it would if the price level were constant.

Over the *steep* range, for output above Y_4, virtually nothing more can be produced, however large the demand is. This range deals with an economy near its capacity constraints. Any change in aggregate demand leads to a sharp change in the price level and to virtually no change in real national income. The multiplier in this case is nearly zero.

How do we reconcile what we have just discovered with the *AE* analysis of Chapter 28, where shifts in *AE always* change national income? The answer is that each *AE* curve is drawn on the assumption that there is a constant price level. A rise in *AE* shifts the *AD* curve to the right. However, a steep *AS* curve means that the price level rises significantly, and this shifts the *AE* curve downward, offsetting some of its initial rise. This interaction is seen most easily if we study the extreme case, shown in Figure 29-11, where the *SRAS* curve is vertical. An increase in autonomous expenditure shifts the *AE* curve upward, thus raising the amount demanded. However, a vertical *SRAS* curve means that output cannot be expanded to satisfy the increased demand. Instead, the extra demand merely forces prices up, and as prices rise, the *AE* curve shifts downward once again. The rise in prices continues until the *AE* curve is back to where it started. Thus the rise in prices offsets the expansionary effect of the original shift and as a result leaves both real aggregate expenditure and equilibrium real income unchanged.

The discussion of Figures 29-10 and 29-11 illustrates a general proposition:

The effect of any given shift in aggregate demand will be divided between a change in real output and a change in the price level, depending on the conditions of aggregate supply. The

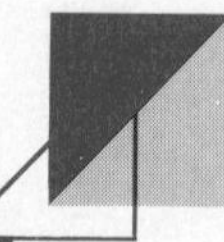

BOX 29-3

Another Look at the Shape of the *SRAS* Curve

The *SRAS* curve relates the price level to the quantity of output that producers are willing to sell. Notice two things about the shape of the *SRAS* curve that is shown in Figure 29-5. It has a positive slope, and the slope increases as output rises.

Positive Slope

The most obvious feature of the *SRAS* curve is its positive slope, indicating that a higher price level is associated with a higher volume of real output, other things being equal. Since the prices of all of the factors of production are being held constant along the *SRAS* curve, why is the curve not horizontal, indicating that firms would be willing to supply as much output as might be demanded with no increase in the price level?

You have already encountered an answer to this question. Even though *input prices* are constant, *unit costs of production* rise as output increases. Thus a higher price level for increasing output—rising short-run aggregate supply—is necessary to compensate firms for rising costs.

The preceding paragraph addresses the question "What has to happen to the price level if national output increases, with the price of factors of production remaining constant?" One may ask a different question: "What will happen to firms' willingness to supply output if product prices rise with no increase in factor prices?" If there is an increase in the prices of products that firms sell, while the prices of the factors of production that firms use to make their products remain constant, production becomes more profitable. Since firms are interested in making profits, when production becomes more profitable, they will usually produce more.* Thus when the price level of final output rises while factor prices are held constant, firms are motivated to increase their outputs. This is true for the individual firm and also for firms in the aggregate. This increase in the amount that will be produced leads to an upward slope of the *SRAS* curve.

Thus whether we look at how the price level will respond in the short run to increases in output or how the level of output will respond to an increase in the price level with input prices being held constant, we find that the *SRAS* curve has a positive slope.

Increasing slope. A somewhat less obvious but in many ways more important property of a typical *SRAS* curve is that its slope *increases* as output rises. It is rather flat to the left of potential output and rather steep to the right. Why? Below potential output, firms typically have unused capacity—some plant and equipment are idle. When firms face unused capacity, only a small increase in the price of their output may be needed to induce them to expand production—at least up to normal capacity.

Once output is pushed far beyond normal capacity, however, unit costs tend to rise quite rapidly. Many higher-cost expedients may have to be adopted. Standby capacity, overtime, and extra shifts may have to be used. Such expedients raise the cost of producing a unit of output. These higher-cost methods will not be used unless the selling price of the output has risen enough to cover them. The further output is expanded beyond normal capacity, the more rapidly unit costs rise and hence the larger is the rise in price that is needed to induce firms to increase output even further.

This increasing slope is sometimes called the *first important asymmetry* in the behavior of aggregate supply. (The second, which is a consequence of *sticky wages*, will be discussed in Chapter 30.)

* Readers who have studied microeconomics can understand this in terms of perfectly competitive firms being faced with higher prices and thus expanding output *along* their marginal cost curves until marginal cost is once again equal to price.

FIGURE 29-11 Demand Shocks When the *SRAS* Curve Is Vertical

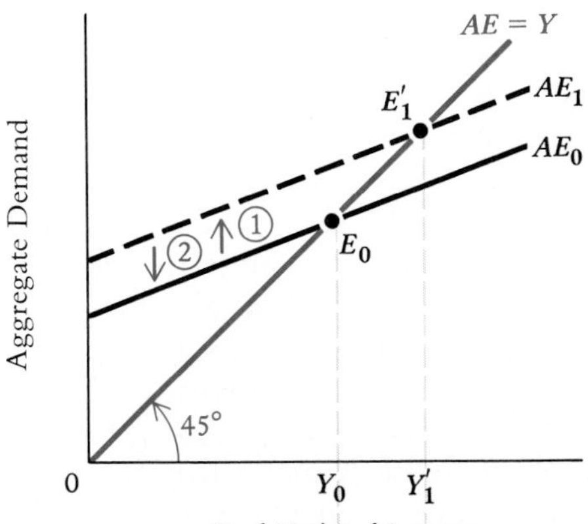

(i) Offsetting shifts in *AE*

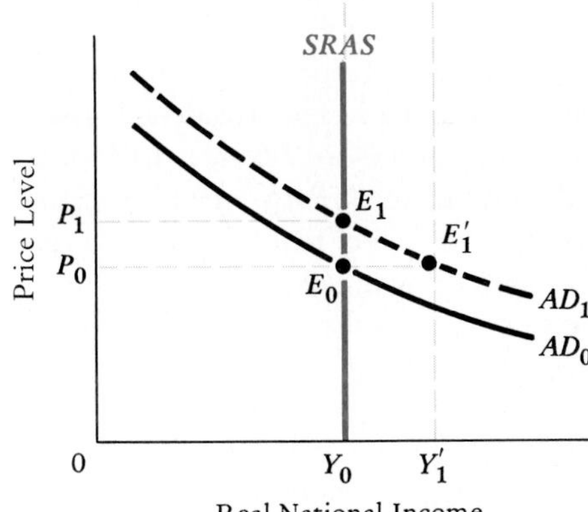

(ii) Shift in AD_0 and offsetting movement along AD_1

If the *SRAS* curve were vertical, the effect of an increase in autonomous expenditure would be solely a rise in the price level. An increase in autonomous expenditure shifts the *AE* curve upward from AE_0 to AE_1, as shown by arrow 1 in (i). Given the initial price level P_0, equilibrium would shift from E_0 to E_1', and real national income would rise from Y_0 to Y_1'. (Primes are used on these variables because these results cannot persist, since real national income cannot rise to Y_1'.) However, the price level does not remain constant. This is shown by the *SRAS* curve in (ii). Instead, the price level rises to P_1. This causes the *AE* curve to shift back down all the way to AE_0, as shown by arrow 2 in (i), and equilibrium income stays at Y_0. In (ii) the new equilibrium is at E_1 with income at Y_0, which is associated with the new price level, P_1.

FIGURE 29-12 Aggregate Supply Shocks

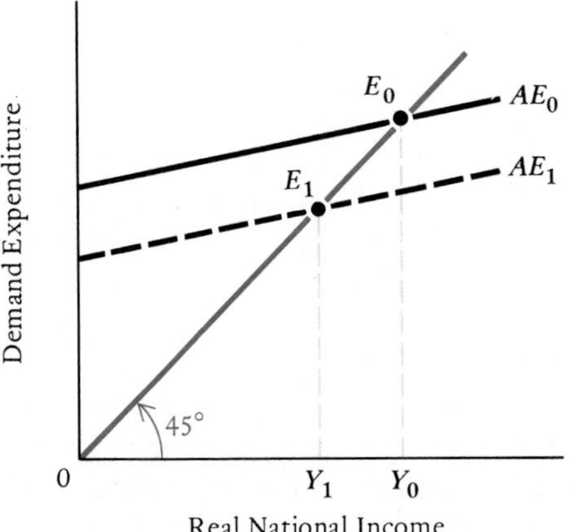

(i) Induced shift in *AE*

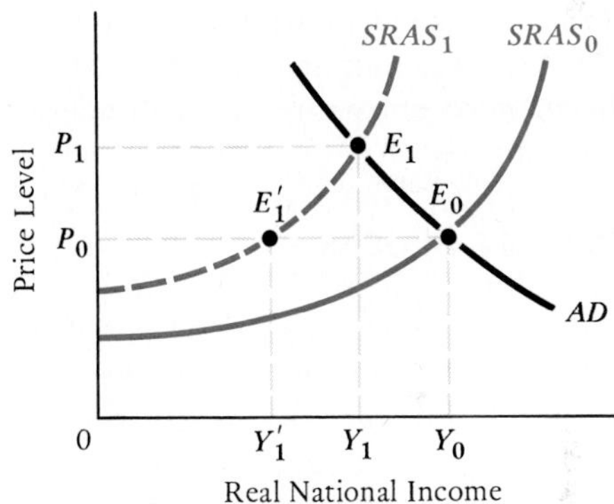

(ii) Shift in *SRAS* and movement along *AD*

Shifts in aggregate supply cause the price level and real national income to move in opposite directions. The original equilibrium is at E_0, with national income of Y_0 appearing in both parts of the figure. The price level is P_0 in (ii), and at that price level, the desired aggregate expenditure curve is AE_0 in (i).

An aggregate supply shock now shifts the *SRAS* curve in (ii) to $SRAS_1$. At the original price level P_0, firms are now only willing to supply Y_1'. The fall in supply, with no corresponding fall in demand, causes a shortage that leads to a rise in the price level along $SRAS_1$. The new equilibrium is reached at E_1, where the *AD* curve intersects $SRAS_1$. At the new, and higher, equilibrium price level of P_1, the *AE* curve has fallen to AE_1, as shown in (i), which is consistent with equilibrium national income of Y_1.

steeper the *SRAS* curve, the greater the price effect and the smaller the output effect.

For reasons discussed in Boxes 29-2 and 29-3, many economists think that the *SRAS* curve is shaped like that in Figure 29-8, that is, relatively flat for low levels of income and becoming steeper as the level of national income increases. This shape of the *SRAS* curve implies that at low levels of national income (well below potential), shifts in aggregate demand affect mainly output, and at high levels of national income (above potential), shifts in aggregate demand affect mainly prices.

Of course, as we have noted already, treating wages and other factor prices as constant is appropriate only when the time period under consideration is short. Hence the *SRAS* curve is used only to analyze short-run, or *impact*, effects. In Chapter 30 we shall see what happens in the *long run* when factor prices respond to changes in national income and the price level. First, however, our analysis of the short run needs to be rounded out with a study of aggregate supply shocks.

Aggregate Supply Shocks

A decrease in aggregate supply is reflected in a shift to the left in the *SRAS* curve and means that less national output will be supplied at any given price level. An increase in aggregate supply is reflected in a shift to the right in the *SRAS* curve and means that more national output will be produced at any given price level.

Figure 29-12 illustrates the effects on the price level and real national income of aggregate supply shocks. As can be seen from the figure, following the decrease in aggregate supply, the price level rises and real national income falls. This combination of events is called *stagflation*, a rather inelegant word that has been derived by combining *stagnation* (a term that is sometimes used to mean less than full employment) and *inflation*.

Figure 29-12 also shows that an increase in aggregate supply leads to an increase in real national income and a decrease in the price level.

Aggregate supply shocks cause the price level and real national income to change in opposite directions; with an increase in supply, the price level falls and income rises; with a decrease in supply, the price level rises and income falls.

An aggregate supply shock means that the *SRAS* curve shifts (for example, from $SRAS_0$ to $SRAS_1$ in Figure 29-12). Adjustment to the new equilibrium following the shock involves a movement along the *AD* curve (for example, from E_0 to E_1).

Oil prices have provided four major examples of aggregate supply shocks in recent decades. Massive increases in oil prices in 1974–1975 and 1979–1980 caused leftward shifts in the *SRAS* curve. National income fell and the price level rose, causing stagflation. In 1990 oil prices again rose sharply. During the mid 1980s oil prices fell substantially. This shifted the *SRAS* curve to the right, increasing existing pressures for national income to rise and decreasing existing pressures for the price level to fall.

We can see now how a rightward shift in the *SRAS* curve, which is brought about by an increase in productivity without a fully offsetting increase in factor prices, raises real national income and lowers the price level. As we shall see in Chapter 30, this happy combination of rising output and falling prices has proved to be difficult to achieve in practice.

SUMMARY

1. The *AE* curve shows desired aggregate expenditure for each level of income at a particular price level. Its intersection with the 45° line determines equilibrium national income for that price level, on the assumption that firms will produce everything that they can sell at the going price level. Equilibrium income then occurs where desired aggregate expenditure equals national income (output). A change in the price level is shown by a *shift* in the *AE* curve: upward when the price level falls and downward when the price level rises. This leads to a new equilibrium level of national income.
2. The *AD* curve plots the equilibrium level of national income that corresponds to each possible price level. A change in equilibrium national income following a change in the price level is shown by a *movement along* the *AD* curve.

3. A rise in the price level lowers exports and lowers consumers' spending (because it decreases consumers' wealth). Both of these changes lower equilibrium national income and cause the aggregate demand curve to have a negative slope. The *AD* curve shifts when any element of autonomous expenditure changes, and the simple multiplier measures the magnitude of the shift. This multiplier also measures the size of the change in real equilibrium national income when the price level remains constant *and* firms produce everything that is demanded at that price level.
4. The short-run aggregate supply (*SRAS*) curve, drawn for given factor prices, is positively sloped because unit costs rise with increasing output and because rising product prices make it profitable to increase output. An increase in productivity or a decrease in factor prices shifts the curve to the right. A decrease in productivity or an increase in factor prices has the opposite effect.
5. Macroeconomic equilibrium refers to equilibrium values of national income and the price level, as determined by the intersection of the *AD* and *SRAS* curves. Shifts in the *AD* and *SRAS* curves, called aggregate demand shocks and aggregate supply shocks, change the equilibrium values of national income and the price level.
6. When the *SRAS* curve is positively sloped, an aggregate demand shock causes the price level and national income to move in the same direction. The division of the effects between a change in national income and a change in the price level depends on the shape of the *SRAS* curve. When the *SRAS* curve is flat, shifts in the *AD* curve affect mainly real national income. When the *SRAS* curve is steep, shifts in the *AD* curve affect mainly the price level.
7. An aggregate supply shock moves equilibrium national income along the *AD* curve, causing the price level and national income to move in opposite directions. A leftward shift in the *SRAS* curve causes stagflation—rising prices and falling national income. A rightward shift causes an increase in real national income and a fall in the price level. The division of the effects between a change in national income and a change in the price level depends on the shape of the *AD* curve.

TOPICS FOR REVIEW

Effects of a change in the price level
Relationship between the *AE* and *AD* curves
Negative slope of the *AD* curve
Positive slope of the *SRAS* curve
Macroeconomic equilibrium
Aggregate demand shocks
The simple multiplier when the price level varies
Aggregate supply shocks
Stagflation

DISCUSSION QUESTIONS

1. Explain the following by shifts in the aggregate demand curve, the aggregate supply curve, or both. Pay attention to the initial position before any shift occurs.
   a. Output and unemployment rise, while prices hold steady.
   b. Prices soar, but employment and output hold steady.
   c. Inflation accelerates as the recession in business actively deepens.
2. A survey of private economic forecasters in mid 1989 showed that the consensus economic outlook for 1990 was cautiously optimistic—

most thought that real growth would remain roughly constant while unemployment would fall slightly; more worry was expressed that inflation might rise well above the 5 percent level. Explain what factors underlying the *AD* and *SRAS* curves would give rise to such a forecast. In retrospect, how accurate were these forecasts? What happened to the underlying determinants to cause actual events to differ from the forecasts?

3. In 1991 Canada introduced a new sales tax, the GST. Many economists argued that this would lead to a short burst of extra inflation and a fall in employment. Explain this in terms of shifts in the aggregate demand or aggregate supply curve, or both.
4. Indicate whether each of the following events was the cause or the consequence of a shift in aggregate demand or supply. If it was a cause, what do you predict will be the effect on the price level and on real national income?
   a. Unemployment decreases in 1989.
   b. OPEC raises oil prices in 1990.
   c. OPEC is forced to accept lower oil prices in 1985.
   d. In the late 1960s and early 1970s Canada experiences rapid inflation under conditions of approximately full employment.
   e. In France in 1981 income and employment continue to fall while the price level is quite stable.
   f. Defense spending is cut following an arms control agreement between the United States and the USSR.
   g. Canadian exports fall in response to a high value of the Canadian dollar and intense competition from foreign suppliers.
   h. Inflationary pressures build as economic expansion continues through 1989.
5. A number of economists argued that as a result of the major tax reform introduced in 1987 by the Canadian government, a number of "disincentives to work" were being removed, and hence there would be an improvement in productivity and an increase in labor force participation. If this proved true, what would you expect to be the effects on national income and the price level?
6. Following are the combinations of output and price level, given by indexes for GDP and the CPI, respectively, for some recent years. Treat each pair as if it is the intersection of an *AD* and *AS* curve. Plot these and indicate in each case the direction of shift of the *SRAS* or *AD* curve that could have caused the changes from one year to the next. Assume that only one curve shifts unless two shifts are needed to explain the data. Why might you be uncertain about some of the shifts?

	GDP (billions of 1981 dollars)	CPI (1981 = 100)
1980	343.4	89.8
1981	356.0	100.0
1982	344.5	107.2
1983	355.4	111.2
1984	377.9	117.4
1985	395.9	120.8
1986	408.1	126.8
1987	426.4	132.4
1988	447.8	135.9
1989	460.6	140.9

Chapter 30

National Income and the Price Level in the Long Run

Every labor leader knows that it is relatively easy to bargain for wage increases during a boom when the demand for labor is high. The same leaders also know that it is difficult to get wage increases during a recession when high unemployment signals a low demand for labor. Every businessperson knows that the cost of needed materials tends to rise rapidly during business expansions and to fall—often dramatically—during recessions. It is high time, therefore, to go beyond the assumption of fixed factor prices that we used to study the initial effects of aggregate demand and aggregate supply shocks in Chapter 29. To do this we need to see what happens in a longer-term setting when changes in national income *induce* changes in factor prices.

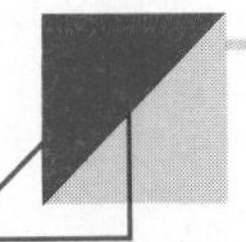

Induced Changes in Factor Prices

The first thing we need to do is to look again at two key concepts encountered in Chapter 26: potential income and the output gap.

Another Look at Potential Income and the Output Gap

Recall that potential income is the total output that can be produced when all productive resources—especially labor and capital equipment—are being used at their *normal rates of utilization*. When the nation's actual national income diverges from its potential income, the difference is called the output gap. (See Figure 26-4 on page 560.)

Although growth in potential income has powerful effects on all of us from one decade to another, its change from one year to another is small enough to be ignored when studying the year-to-year behavior of national income and the price level. So in this chapter we continue with the assumption that was made in Chapter 26 that potential income is constant. This means that variations in the output gap are determined solely by variations in actual national income around a given potential national income.

Figure 30-1 shows actual national income being determined by the intersection of the *AD* and *SRAS* curves. Potential income is constant, and it is shown by identical vertical lines in the two parts of the figure. In part (i) the *AD* and *SRAS* curves intersect to produce an equilibrium national income that falls short of potential income. The result is a positive output gap. In part (ii) the *AD* and *SRAS* curves intersect to produce an equilibrium national income that exceeds potential income, resulting in a negative output gap.

FIGURE 30-1 **Actual Income, Potential Income, and the Output Gap**

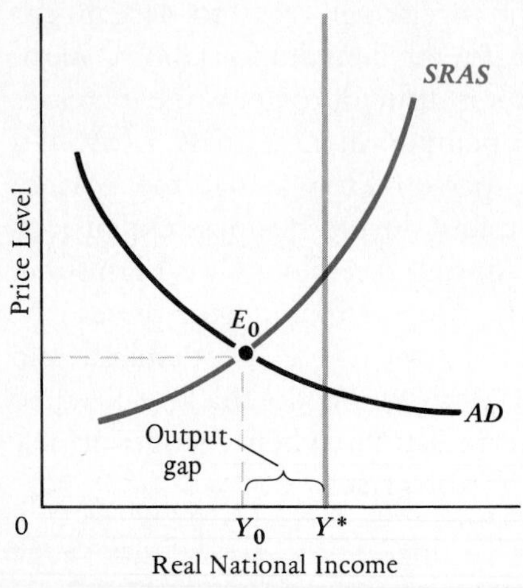

(i) A positive output gap

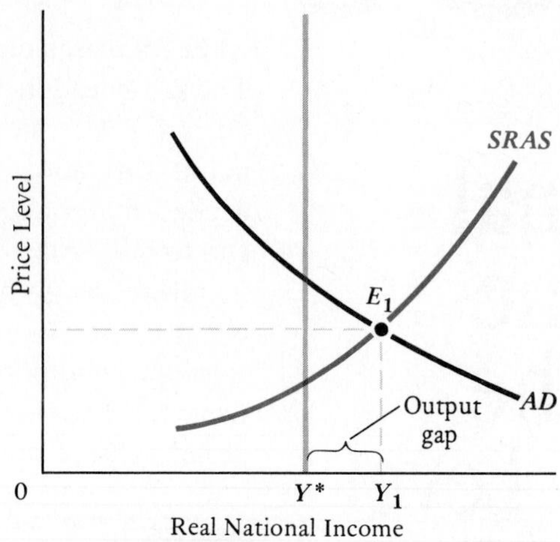

(ii) A negative output gap

The output gap is the difference between potential national income, Y^*, and actual national income, Y. Potential national income is shown by a vertical line because it refers to a given, constant national income. Actual national income is determined by the intersection of the aggregate demand (*AD*) and short-run aggregate supply (*SRAS*) curves.

In (i) the positions of the *AD* and *SRAS* curves result in a positive output gap. This is because equilibrium is at E_0, so actual national income is given by Y_0, which is less than potential income. The output gap is thus $Y^* - Y_0$.

In (ii) the positions of the *AD* and *SRAS* curves result in a negative output gap. Although potential income is unchanged at Y^*, equilibrium is now at E_1, so actual national income is given by Y_1, which is greater than potential income. The output gap is thus $Y^* - Y_1$.

Factor Prices and the Output Gap

The output gap provides a convenient measure of the pressure of demand on factor prices. When national income is high relative to potential income, demand for factors will also be high. When national income is low relative to potential income, demand for factors will be correspondingly low. This is true of all factors. The discussion that follows can be simplified, however, by focusing on one key factor, *labor*, and on its price, the *wage rate*. Earlier we referred to average costs per unit of output as *unit costs*; to focus on labor costs, we now use average wage costs per unit of output, which we refer to as *unit labor costs*.

When there is a negative output gap, the demand for labor services will be relatively high.

When there is a positive output gap, the demand for labor services will be relatively low.

Each of these situations will have implications for wages. Before turning to a detailed analysis of each, we first consider our benchmark for the behavior of wages.

Upward and downward wage pressures. Negative output gaps exert upward pressure on wages, and positive output gaps exert downward pressure on wages. To what do the upward and downward pressures relate? One answer is that upward pressure means that wages would rise, and downward pressure means that wages would fall. However, most wage bargaining starts from the assumption that, other things being equal, workers get the benefit of increases in their own productivity by receiving higher wages. Because of this, when national income is at its potential level, so that there are neither upward nor downward pressures on wages caused by output gaps, wages tend to be rising at the same rate as productivity is rising.[1] When wages and productivity change proportionately, labor cost per unit of output, which we have earlier called *unit labor costs*, remains unchanged. For example, if each worker produces 4 percent more and earns 4 percent more, unit labor costs will remain constant. This, then, is the benchmark:

When there is neither excess demand nor excess supply in the labor market, wages will tend to be rising as fast as labor productivity is rising; in this case unit labor costs will remain constant.

Note that with unit labor costs remaining constant, there is no presure coming from the labor market for the *SRAS* curve to shift and hence no pressure for the price level to rise or to fall.

In comparison with this benchmark, upward pressure on wages means that there is pressure for wages to rise faster than productivity is rising. When this occurs, unit labor costs will also be rising. For example, if money wages rise by 8 percent while productivity rises by only 4 percent, labor cost per unit of output will be rising by about 4 percent. In this case the *SRAS* curve will be shifting leftward, and hence there will be upward pressure coming from the labor market.

Downward pressure on wages means that there is pressure for wages to rise less fast than productivity. When this occurs, unit labor costs will be falling. For example, if productivity rises by 4 percent while money wages rise by only 2 percent, labor costs per unit of output will be falling by about 2 percent. In this case the *SRAS* curve will be shifting rightward, and hence there will be downward pressure coming from the labor market.

[1] Ongoing inflation would also influence the normal pattern of wage changes. Wage contracts often allow for changes in prices that are expected to occur during the life of the contract. For now we make the simplifying assumption that the price level is expected to be constant; hence changes in money wages also are expected to be changes in real wages. The distinction between changes in money wages and real wages and the important role played by expectations of price level changes will be discussed in Chapters 36 and 40.

A negative output gap. Sometimes the *AD* and *SRAS* curves intersect where actual output exceeds potential output, as illustrated in part (ii) of Figure 30-1. Firms are producing beyond their normal-capacity output, so there is an unusually large demand for all factor inputs, including labor. Labor shortages will emerge in some industries and among many groups of workers, particularly skilled workers. Firms will try to bid workers away from other firms in order to maintain the high levels of output and sales made possible by the boom conditions.

As a result of tight labor market conditions, workers will find that they have considerable bargaining power with their employers, and they will put upward pressure on wages.[2] Firms, recognizing that demand for their goods is strong, will be eager to maintain a high level of output. Thus to prevent their workers from either striking or quitting and moving to other employers, firms will be willing to accede to some of these upward pressures.

The boom associated with a negative output gap generates a set of conditions—high profits for firms and unusually large demand for labor—that exerts upward pressure on wages.

A positive output gap. Sometimes the *AD* and *SRAS* curves intersect where actual output is less than potential output, as illustrated in part (i) of Figure 30-1. In this situation firms will be producing below their normal-capacity output, so there is an unusually low demand for all factor intputs, including labor. The general conditions in the market for labor will be the opposite of those when actual output exceeds potential. There will now be labor surpluses in some industries and among some groups of workers. Firms will have below normal sales and will not only resist upward pressures on wages but will also tend to offer wage increases below productivity increases and may even seek reductions in wages.

The slump associated with a postive output gap generates a set of conditions—low profits for firms, unusually low demand for labor, and a desire on the part of firms to resist wage demands and even to push for wage concessions—that exerts downward pressure on wages.

[2] Additional upward pressures on wages may be created by the fact that the price level, P_1, will be higher than P^*, the price level that would have prevailed had output attained its potential level.

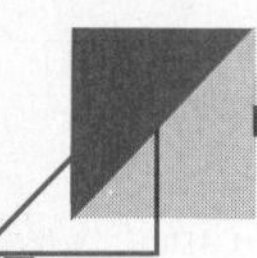

BOX 30-1

The Phillips Curve and the Shifting *SRAS* Curve

In the early 1950s Professor A. W. Phillips of the London School of Economics was doing path-breaking research on macroeconomic policy. He included in his early models an equation that related the rate of inflation to the difference between actual and potential income, $Y - Y^*$. Later he investigated the empirical underpinnings of this equation by studying the relationship between the rate of increase of wage costs and the level of unemployment. In 1958 he reported that a stable relationship had existed between these two variables for 100 years in the United Kingdom. This is the form of the relationship which came to be known as the Phillips curve.

The **Phillips curve** provided an explanation, rooted in empirical data, of the speed with which wage changes shifted the *SRAS* curve by changing unit labor costs. The empirical relationship that Phillips studied was between unemployment and wage rates. One reason he studied this was because he thought that unemployment provided a better measure of demand pressures in the labor market than output gaps did. More important, however, unemployment data were available as far back as the mid nineteenth century, while very little data on output gaps was available when he did his pioneering empirical work.

Nonetheless, his curve can be translated into one that relates wage changes to output gaps by noting that unemployment and the gaps are negatively related. A recessionary gap is associated with high unemployment, and an inflationary gap is associated with low unemployment. Thus the Phillips curve can also be drawn with national income on the horizontal axis, as in the figures shown here.

Both figures show the same information. Inflationary gaps (which correspond to low unemployment rates) are associated with *increases* in wages, whereas recessionary gaps (which correspond to high unemployment rates) are associated with slow *decreases* in wages.

The Phillips curve must be clearly distinguished from the *SRAS* curve. The *SRAS* curve has the *price level* on the vertical axis, whereas the Phillips curve has the *rate of wage inflation* on the vertical axis. Therefore, the Phillips curve tells us how fast the *SRAS* curve is shifting when actual income does not equal potential income. (Recall that it is wage changes relative to productivity growth that matters; for simplicity, in this box we assume zero productivity growth.)

Only when $Y = Y^*$ is the *SRAS* curve not shifting because of demand pressures. When income is at its potential level, aggregate demand for labor equals aggregate supply; the only unemployment would thus be frictional and structural. There would be neither upward nor downward pressure of demand on wages. Thus the Phillips curve cuts

Adjustment asymmetry. At this stage we encounter an important asymmetry in the economy's aggregate supply behavior. Boom conditions, along with severe labor shortages, do cause wages (and the price level) to rise rapidly. When there is a large excess demand for labor, wage (and price) increases often run well ahead of productivity increases. Money wages might be rising by 10 or 15 percent, while productivity might be rising at only 2 or 3 percent. This means that unit labor costs will be rising rapidly.

The experience of many economies suggests, however, that downward pressures on wages during slumps often do not operate as quickly as the upward pressures during booms. Even in quite severe recessions, when the price level is fairly stable, money wages may continue to rise, although their rate of increase tends to fall below that of productivity. For example, productivity might be rising at, say, 1.5 percent, while money wages are rising at 0.5 percent. In this case unit labor costs are falling but only at about 1 percent per year, so the leftward shift in the *SRAS* curve and the downward pressure on the price level are correspondingly slight.[3] Money wages ac-

[3] This is the second asymmetry in aggregate supply that we have encountered. The first refers to the changing slope of the *SRAS* curve, as discussed in Box 29-3.

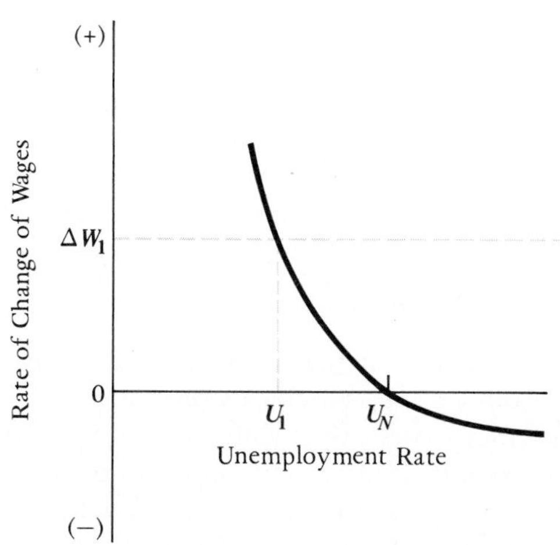

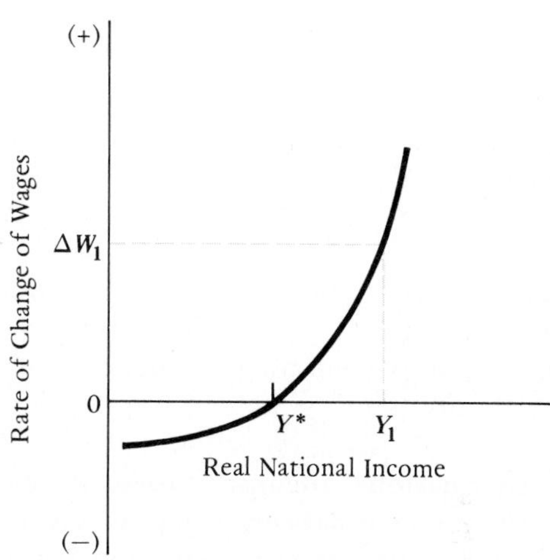

the axis at potential income Y^* and at the corresponding level of unemployment U_N. This is how Phillips drew his curve; later we shall see that things are not so simple.

The Phillips curve soon became famous. It provided a link between national income models and labor markets. This link allowed macroeconomists to drop the uncomfortable assumption, which they had often been forced to use in many of their earlier formal models, that money wages were rigidly fixed and neither rose nor fell as national income varied. The Phillips curve relationship between money wages and national income determines (in conjunction with productivity changes) the speed at which the *SRAS* curve shifts.

Consider, for example, the situation that is shown in part (ii) of Figure 30-1, where the level of income determined by the *AD* and *SRAS* curves is Y_1. Plotting Y_1 on the Phillips curve in part (ii) of the figure in this box tells us that wage costs will be rising at ΔW_1. Then the *SRAS* curve in Figure 30-1(ii) will be shifting upward by that amount. The same information can be seen in the figure in this box, where a national income of Y_1 in part (ii) corresponds to unemployment of U_1 in part (i).

tually may fall, reducing unit wage costs even more, but the reduction in unit labor costs in times of the deepest recession has never been as fast as the increases that have occurred during several of the strongest booms.

Both upward and downward adjustments to unit wage costs do occur, but there are differences in the speed at which they typically occur. Excess demand can cause unit labor costs to rise very rapidly; excess supply often causes unit labor costs to fall more slowly.

Box 30-1 discusses the wage-cost adjustment process, including its asymmetries, in terms of a famous relationship called the *Phillips curve.*

The inflationary and recessionary gaps. The asymmetry in the economy's speed of adjustment in response to positive and negative output gaps can be emphasized by some terminology.

Since a negative output gap will normally be accompanied by rising unit costs, the *SRAS* curve will be shifting upward. This will in turn push the price level up. Indeed, the most obvious event accompanying a negative output gap is likely to be significant inflation. Large, negative output gaps will bring rapid inflation. To emphasize this salient feature, negative output gaps are referred to as **inflationary gaps**.

A positive output gap, as we have seen, will be associated with unemployment of labor and other productive resources. Unit labor costs will fall only slowly, leading to a slow downward shift in the *SRAS* curve. Hence the price level will be falling only slowly, so that unemployment will be the positive output gap's most obvious result. Large, positive output gaps will bring high rates of unemployment. To emphasize this salient feature, positive output gaps are referred to as **recessionary gaps**.

From now on we will use these more vivid and descriptive terms:

When actual national income exceeds potential income, there is an inflationary gap; when actual national income is less than potential income, there is a recessionary gap.

The induced effects of output gaps on unit labor costs and consequent shifts in the *SRAS* curve play an important role in our analysis of the long-run consequences of aggregate demand shocks, to which we now turn.

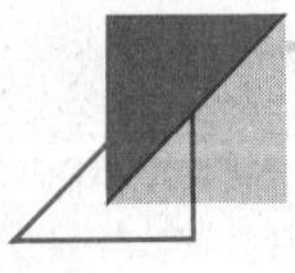

The Long-Run Consequences of Aggregate Demand Shocks

We can now extend our study to cover the longer-run consequences of aggregate demand shocks, which cause factor prices to change. We need to examine separately the effect of aggregate demand shocks on factor prices for expansionary and for contractionary shocks, since the behavior of unit costs is not symmetrical for the two cases. In what follows we make the simplifying assumption that labor productivity is constant, so all changes in wages are also changes in unit labor costs and hence cause the *SRAS* curve to shift. Do not forget, however, that the more general result is that the *SRAS* curve shifts upward whenever money wages rise faster than productivity and downward whenever they rise more slowly than productivity.

Expansionary Shocks

Suppose that the economy starts off with a stable price level at full employment, so that actual income equals potential. This is shown by the initial equilibrium in Figure 30-2(i).

Now suppose that this happy situation is disturbed by an increase in autonomous expenditure, perhaps caused by a sudden boom in investment spending. Part (i) of Figure 30-2 shows the effects of this aggregate demand shock in raising both the price level and national income. Now actual national income exceeds potential income, and there is an inflationary gap.

We have seen that an inflationary gap leads to increases in wages, which cause unit costs to rise. The *SRAS* curve then shifts leftward as firms seek to pass on their increases in input costs by increasing their output prices. For this reason the initial increases in the price level and in real national income shown in Figure 30-2(i) are *not* the final effects of the demand shock. As seen in part (ii) of the figure, the leftward shift of the *SRAS* curve causes a further rise in the price level, but this time the price rise is associated with a fall in output.

The cost increases (and the consequent leftward shifts of the *SRAS* curve) go on until the inflationary gap has been removed, that is, until income returns to Y^*, its potential level. Only then is there no abnormal demand for labor, and only then do wages and unit costs, and hence the *SRAS* curve, stabilize.

This important expansionary demand-shock sequence can be summarized as follows:

1. Starting from full employment, a rise in aggregate demand raises the price level and raises income above its potential level as the economy expands along a given *SRAS* curve.
2. The expansion of income beyond its normal capacity level puts heavy pressure on factor markets; factor prices begin to rise, shifting the *SRAS* curve to the left.
3. The shift of the *SRAS* curve causes national income to fall along the *AD* curve. This process continues *as long as* actual income exceeds potential income. Therefore, actual income eventually falls back to its potential level. The price level, however, is now higher than it was after the initial impact of the increased aggregate demand, but inflation will have come to a halt.

The ability to wring more output and income from the economy than its underlying potential out-

FIGURE 30-2 Demand-Shock Inflation

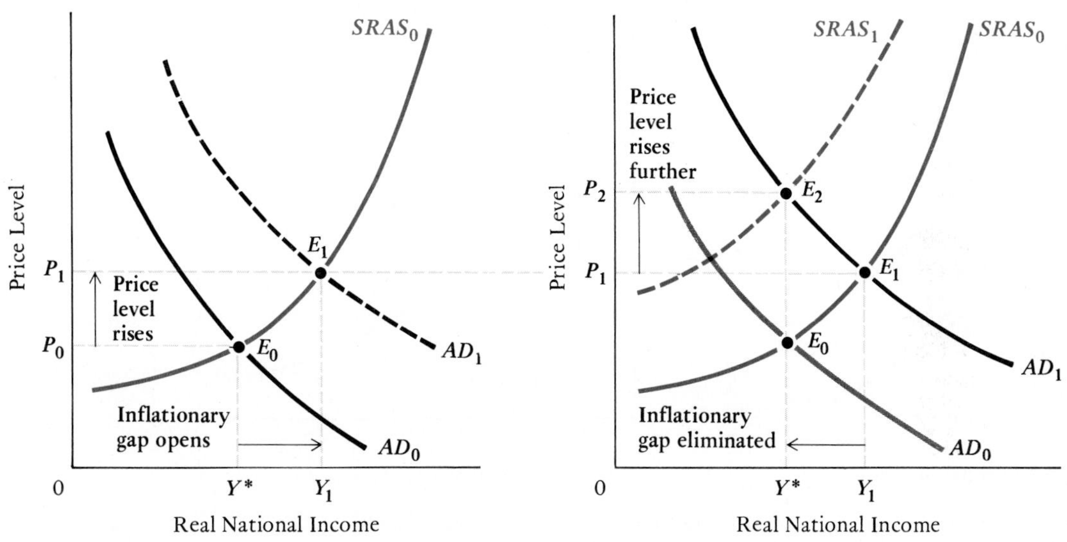

(i) Autonomous increase in aggregate demand (ii) Induced shift in aggregate supply

A rightward shift of the *AD* curve first raises prices and output along the *SRAS* curve. It then induces a shift of the *SRAS* curve that further raises prices but lowers output along the *AD* curve. In (i) the economy is in equilibrium at E_0, at its level of potential output, Y^*, and price level P_0. The *AD* curve then shifts to AD_1. This moves equilibrium to E_1, with income Y_1 and price level P_1, and opens up an inflationary gap of $Y^* - Y_1$.

In (ii) the inflationary gap results in an increase in wages and other input costs, shifting the *SRAS* curve leftward. As this happens, income falls, and the price level rises along AD_1. Eventually, when the *SRAS* curve has shifted to $SRAS_1$, income is back to Y^* and the inflationary gap has been eliminated. However, the price level has risen to P_2.

put (as in point 2) is only a short-term possibility. National income greater than Y^* sets up inflationary pressures that tend to push national income back to Y^*.

A self-adjustment mechanism brings any inflation caused by a one-time demand shock to an eventual halt by returning output to its potential level and thus removing the inflationary gap.

Contractionary Shocks

Let us return to that fortunate economy with full employment and stable prices. It appears again in part (i) of Figure 30-3, which is similar to Figure 30-2(i). Now assume that there is a *decline* in aggregate demand, perhaps due to a major reduction in investment expenditure.

The first effects of the decline are a fall in output and some downward adjustment of prices, as shown in part (i) of the figure. As output falls, unemployment rises. The difference between potential output and actual output is the recessionary gap that is shown in Figure 30-3(i).

Flexible wages. What would happen if severe unemployment did cause wage rates to fall rapidly? Falling wage rates would lower unit costs, causing a rightward shift of the *SRAS* curve. As shown in Figure 30-3(ii), the economy would move along its fixed *AD* curve with falling prices and rising output until full employment was restored at potential national income Y^*. We conclude that *if* wages were to fall whenever there was unemployment, the resulting fall in the *SRAS* curve would restore full employment.

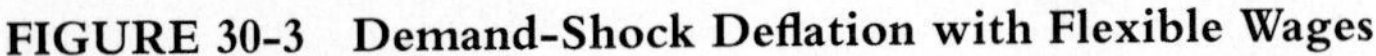

FIGURE 30-3 Demand-Shock Deflation with Flexible Wages

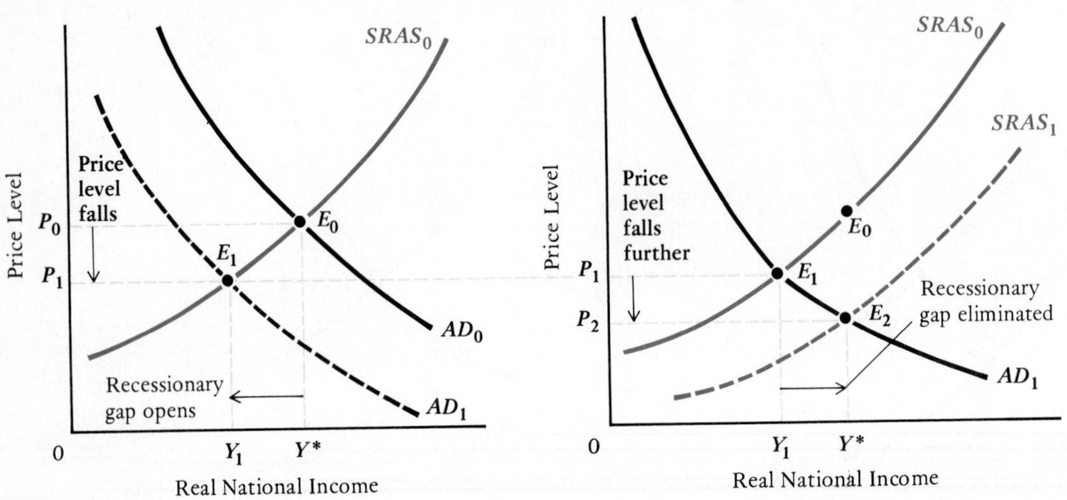

(i) Autonomous fall in aggregate demand (ii) Induced shift in aggregate supply

A leftward shift of the *AD* curve first lowers price and output along the *SRAS* curve and then induces a (slow) shift of the *SRAS* curve that further lowers prices but raises output along the *AD* curve. In (i) the economy is in equilibrium at E_0, at its level of potential output, Y^*, and price level P_0. The *AD* curve then shifts to AD_1, moving equilibrium to E_1, with income Y_1 and price level P_1, and opens up a recessionary gap of $Y^* - Y_1$.

Part (ii) shows the adjustment back to full employment that would occur from the supply side of the economy if wages were sufficiently flexible downward. The fall in wages would shift the *SRAS* curve to the right. Real national income would rise, and the price level would fall further along the *AD* curve. Eventually, the *SRAS* curve would reach $SRAS_1$, with equilibrium at E_2. The price level would stabilize at P_2 when income had returned to Y^*, eliminating the recessionary gap.

Flexible wages that fell when there was unemployment would provide an automatic adjustment mechanism that would push the economy back toward full employment whenever output fell below potential.[4]

Box 30-2 takes up the interesting case of how the adjustment mechanism might work if aggregate demand shocks were anticipated.

Sticky wages. Boom conditions, along with severe labor shortages, do cause wages to rise rapidly, shifting the *SRAS* curve upward. However, as we noted when we encountered the second asymmetry of aggregate supply behavior, the experience of many economies suggests that wages typically do not fall rapidly in response to recessionary gaps and their accompanying unemployment. It is sometimes said that wages are "sticky" in a downward direction. This does not mean that wages never fall; they do. Typically, however, they do not fall as fast in response to recessionary gaps as they rise in response to inflationary gaps. If wages are sluggish in their response to recessionary gaps, unit labor costs will fall only slowly. This in turn means that the rightward shifts in the *SRAS* curve occur slowly, and the adjustment mechanism that depends on these shifts will act sluggishly.

The weakness of the automatic adjustment mechanism does not mean that slumps must always be prolonged. What it means is that speedy recovery to

[4] Recall that what determines unit costs is how money wages behave relative to productivity. Since we are assuming productivity to be constant, we can talk about increases or decreases in wages. However, this must always be understood to mean increases or decreases relative to the change in productivity.

BOX 30-2

Anticipated Demand Shocks

Suppose that the increase in aggregate demand, which is illustrated in Figure 30-2, was widely anticipated well before it occurred. For example, as an election approached, it might become widely believed that the administration would stimulate the economy in order to improve its electoral chances.

Further suppose that most employers and employees believe that one of the effects of the demand stimulation will be inflation. Now workers might press for wage increases so that the purchasing power of their earnings would not be eroded by the coming price increases. Firms, knowing that demand for their products was likely to rise, enabling them to raise their selling prices, might be persuaded to grant wage increases now and pass these on to consumers in terms of higher prices.

A demand stimulus that was widely expected to occur and whose inflationary effects were widely understood could lead to upward pressure on wages, even without any inflationary gap opening up.

If this were to occur, the leftward shift in the *SRAS* curve that is depicted in part (ii) of Figure 30-2 could occur quickly, perhaps accompanying, or even preceding, the rightward shift in the *AD* curve in part (i). Given *perfect* anticipation of the effects of the demand stimulus and *full* adjustment to it in advance, the equilibrium would go straight from E_0 to E_2. The intermediate position, E_1, with its accompanying inflationary gap (with national income in excess of potential income), would be completely bypassed.

A similar story might be told for an anticipated fall in aggregate demand. The effects of an unanticipated fall are shown in the two parts of Figure 30-3. However, if the fall were widely anticipated and its effects were generally understood, firms might reduce their wage offers and workers might accept the decreases because they expect that prices will fall as well. In this case it is conceivable that the economy could bypass the recessionary stage and go straight to a lower price level at an unchanged level of real national income.

This possibility, that anticipated demand shocks might have no real effects on real national income and hence on unemployment, plays a key role in some important controversies concerning the effectiveness of government policies. We shall study these in detail in Chapter 40.

In the meantime, we may notice that the complete absence of real effects in the transitionary period, with the only change being in the price level, requires that everyone has full knowledge, both of the exact amount of the stimulus that the governent will induce and of the new equilibrium values of the relevant prices and wages. In other words, everyone knows what the new equilibrium will be and goes directly to it. If people do not have such perfect knowledge and foresight, there may be some groping toward the equilibrium and some real effects until the final equilibrium set of wages and prices is reached.

full employment must be generated mainly from the demand side. If the economy is to avoid a lengthy period of stagnation, the force leading to recovery must usually be an upward shift of the *AD* curve rather than a downward drift of the *SRAS* curve.

The *SRAS* curve shifts upward fairly rapidly when national income exceeds Y^*, but it shifts downward only slowly when national income is less than Y^*.

The asymmetry. This difference in speed of adjustment is a consequence of the important asymmetry in the behavior of aggregate supply that was noted earlier in this chapter. This asymmetry helps to explain two key facts about our economy. First, unemployment *can* persist for quite long periods without causing large decreases in unit costs and prices (which, when they do occur, help to remove the unemployment). Second, booms, along with labor shortages and production beyond normal capacity, do not persist for long periods without causing large increases in unit costs and prices.

The Long-Run Aggregate Supply (*LRAS*) Curve

The automatic adjustment mechanism leads us to an important concept: the **long-run aggregate supply (*LRAS*) curve**. This curve relates the price level to real national income *after wage rates and all other input costs have been fully adjusted to eliminate any unemployment or overall labor shortages.*[5]

Shape of the *LRAS* curve. Once all the adjustments that are required have occurred, the economy will have eliminated any excess demand or excess supply of labor. In other words, full employment will prevail, and output will be at its potential level, Y^*. It follows that the aggregate supply curve becomes a vertical line at Y^*, as shown in Figure 30-4.[6]

Notice that the vertical *LRAS* curve does not represent the same thing as the vertical portion of the *SRAS* curve (see Figure 29-10). Over the vertical range of the *SRAS* curve, the economy is at its utmost limit of productive capacity, when no more can be squeezed out, as might occur in an all-out war effort. The vertical shape of the *LRAS* curve is due to the workings of an adjustment mechanism that brings the economy back to its potential output, even though it may stray in the short run. It is called the *long-run* aggregate supply curve because it refers to adjustments that take a substantial amount of time.

Along the *LRAS* curve all the prices of *all outputs* and *all inputs* have been fully adjusted to eliminate any excess demands or supplies.[7] Proportionate changes in money wages and the price level (which, by definition, will leave real wages unaltered) will also leave equilibrium employment and output unchanged. The key concept is this: If the price of absolutely everything (including labor) doubles, nothing real changes. When the price of everything bought *and* sold doubles, neither workers nor firms gain any advantage and hence neither has any incentive to alter behavior. Output, therefore, is unchanged. The level of output will be what can be

FIGURE 30-4 The Long-Run Aggregate Supply (*LRAS*) Curve

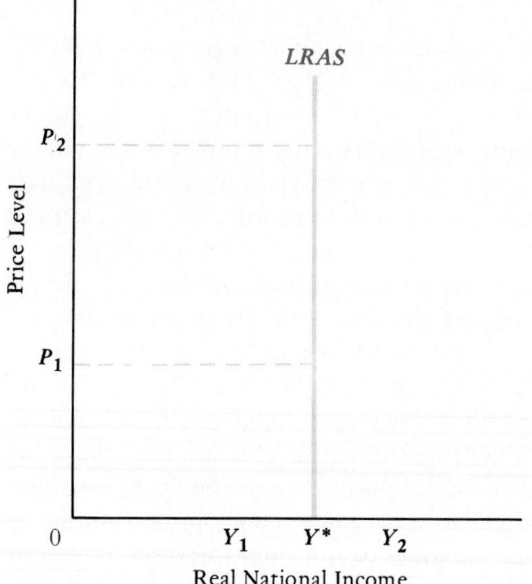

The long-run aggregate supply curve is a vertical line drawn at the level of national income that is equal to potential income, Y^*. It is a vertical line because the total amount of goods that the economy produces when all factors are efficiently used at their normal rate of utilization does not vary with the price level. If the price level were to rise from P_1 to P_2 *and* wages and all other factor prices were to rise by the same proportion, the desired output of firms would remain at Y^*.

If income were Y_1, which is less than Y^*, wages would be falling, and the *SRAS* curve would be shifting rightward; hence the economy would not be on its *LRAS* curve. If income were Y_2, which is greater than Y^*, wages would be rising, and the *SRAS* curve would be shifting leftward; hence the economy would not be on the *LRAS* curve.

[5] Students who have studied microeconomics will notice that this use of the term *long run* appears from its meaning in microeconomics. Note, however, the key similarity that the long run has more flexibility for adjustment than the short run.

[6] The *LRAS* curve is sometimes called the Classical aggregate supply curve because the Classical economists were concerned mainly with the behavior of the economy in long-run equilibrium.

[7] Stocks of assets that are denominated in money terms must also be adjusted so that there are no wealth effects on spending of changes in the price level.

produced in the economy when all factors of production, including labor, are used at "normal capacity."

The vertical *LRAS* curve shows that given full adjustment of input prices, potential income, Y^*, is compatible with *any* price level.

Long-Run Equilibrium

Figure 30-5 shows the equilibrium output and the price level as they are determined by the intersection of the *AD* curve and the vertical *LRAS* curve. Because the *LRAS* curve is vertical, shifts in aggregate demand change the price level but not the level of equilibrium output, as shown in part (i). In contrast, a shift in aggregate supply changes both output and the price level, as shown in part (ii). For example, a rightward shift of the *LRAS* curve increases national income and leads (eventually) to a fall in the price level.

With a vertical *LRAS* curve, output is determined solely by conditions of supply, and the role of aggregate demand is simply to determine the price level.

Of course, these are only long-term tendencies. To see the short-term impact of demand and supply shocks, we need to use the short-run aggregate supply curve. Because downward adjustments of wages, unit costs, and prices may take a long time, there may be long periods when the economy is well away from its long-run equilibrium.[8]

Supply-Side Economics

Both of Ronald Reagan's U.S. presidential campaigns featured a theory of economic policy that came to be known as *supply-side economics*. President Bush once called it "voodoo economics," but apparently he has since changed his mind. To some observers in Canada as well as in the United States, the policy promised a quick cure for both high inflation and low growth in real national income. To others it seemed an exercise in wishful thinking.

The theoretical tools that have been developed in this chapter can be used to explore both the theory

FIGURE 30-5 Long-Run Equilibrium and Aggregate Supply

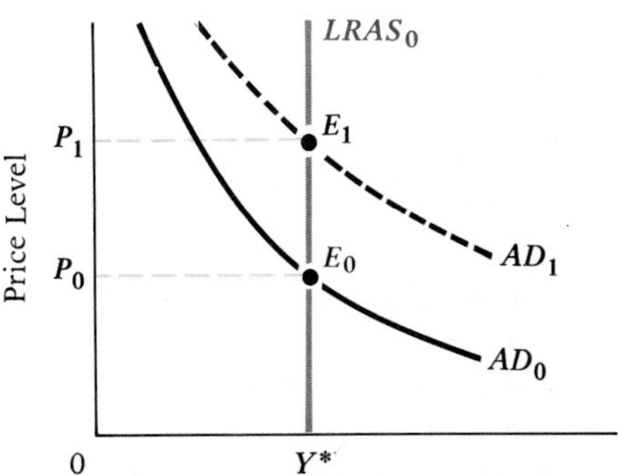

(i) A rise in aggregate demand

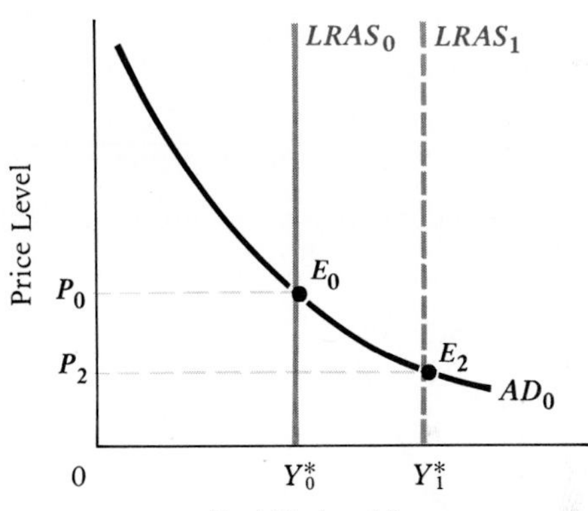

(ii) A rise in long-run aggregate supply

When the *LRAS* curve is vertical, aggregate supply determines the long-run equilibrium value of national income at Y^*. Given Y^*, aggregate demand determines the long-run equilibrium value of the price level. In both parts of the figure, the initial long-run equilibrium is at E_0, so the price level is P_0 and national income is Y_0^*.

In (i) a shift in the *AD* curve from AD_0 to AD_1, with the *LRAS* curve remaining unchanged, moves the long-run equilibrium from E_0 to E_1. This raises the price level from P_0 to P_1 but leaves national income unchanged at Y_0^* in the long run.

In (ii) a shift in the *LRAS* curve from $LRAS_0$ to $LRAS_1$, with the aggregate demand curve remaining constant at AD_0, moves the long-run equilibrium from E_0 to E_2. This raises national income from Y_0^* to Y_1^* but lowers the price level from P_0 to P_2.

[8] The rest of this chapter may be omitted without loss of continuity.

and the doubts about it. Although supply-side economics has many aspects, here we are concerned specifically with the effects of supply-side policies on the price level and on real national income, starting from a situation with a large inflationary gap. When Ronald Reagan became president in January 1981, the inflation rate was about 10 percent and unemployment was about 7 percent; any policy that would decrease them both would have been welcomed.

How It Was Supposed to Work

The theory of supply-side economics called for adopting measures that would shift the *LRAS* curve to the right far enough to reduce inflationary pressures. In the most favorable case there would be no offsetting demand-side effects. This case is illustrated in Figure 30-6.

A major part of supply-side economics was the provision of tax incentives that would increase potential national income by increasing the nation's supplies of labor and capital. Incentives were given to firms to increase their investment, thus, it was hoped, increasing national productive capacity. Personal taxes were cut across the board to give everyone an incentive to work more. It was argued that people who were already employed would be more inclined to work longer and harder when they were able to keep a larger percentage of their pretax earnings, and people outside the labor force would be drawn in as a result of the higher after-tax wages. Extra tax breaks were given to persons at high income levels to increase the incentives for work and risk taking on the part of the most productive people. Supporters of this policy argued that the resulting increases in productive capacity and in productivity

FIGURE 30-6 The Theory of Anti-inflationary Supply-Side Policies

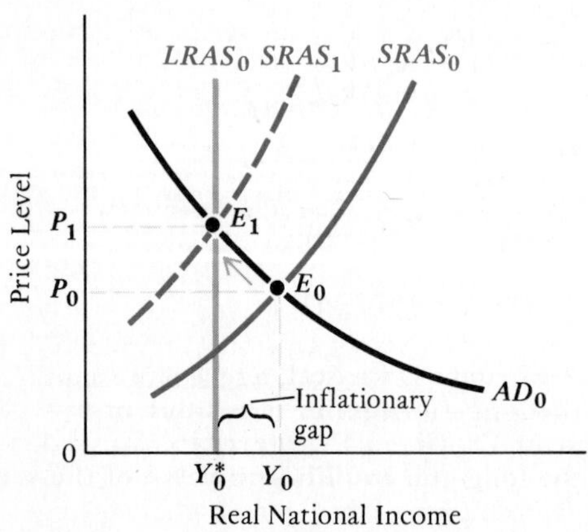

(i) An inflationary situation

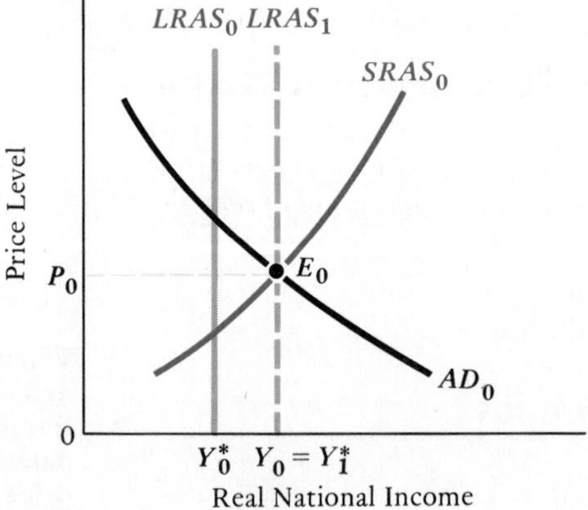

(ii) Supply-side success

Supply-side policies sought to eliminate an inflationary gap by shifting the *LRAS* curve to the right without changing aggregate demand. Part (i) shows an economy in short-run equilibrium at E_0 and AD_0 and $SRAS_0$, with income Y_0 and price level P_0. As a result of the inflationary gap, $Y_0^* - Y_0$, the *SRAS* curve will shift upward, taking the equilibrium along AD_0 (as shown by the arrow), with falling national income and rising price level. Other things being equal, inflation will come to a halt once the curve has reached $SRAS_1$ and equilibrium is established at E_1, with price level P_1 and national income at its potential level Y_0^*.

Part (ii) shows the same economy after supply-side measures shift the *LRAS* curve to $LRAS_1$. This makes Y_1^* the new level of potential income and removes the inflationary gap. The fall of income and rise in the price level shown in (i) are both prevented.

would shift the *LRAS* curve to the right, thus raising equilibrium national income and further reducing inflationary pressure.

Supply siders also argued that the cuts in tax rates and increases in tax exemptions would not increase the federal government's budget deficit. They believed that the increase in national income would create an increase in the tax base sufficient to generate larger tax *revenues* in spite of the lower tax *rates*. For example, if a 10 percent cut in tax rates were followed by a 10 percent increase in real national income, it would leave tax revenues approximately the same.[9]

Critics of the Theory

One major worry of critics of the theory was that demand-side effects would swamp any supply-side effects for at least the first several years. Whatever the long-term effects are on the supply side, economic theory is clear about the short-term effects of these measures on the demand side. Cuts in personal tax rates that are expected to be permanent leave households with an increase in their current and expected future disposable incomes. As a result, they spend more, causing a rightward shift in the aggregate demand curve. Also, we know that an increase in investment increases aggregate demand. In the short run the extra expenditure on capital goods creates new incomes for the factors of production that produce these goods and, through the multiplier process, new incomes for others as well.

Thus the short-run effect of supply-side measures would surely be to shift the aggregate *demand* curve to the right. In the least favorable situation, if all the demand-increasing effects and none of the favorable aggregate supply effects were to occur, the result would be an increase in the inflationary gap. This possibility is illustrated in Figure 30-7.

FIGURE 30-7 Demand Effects of Supply-Side Measures

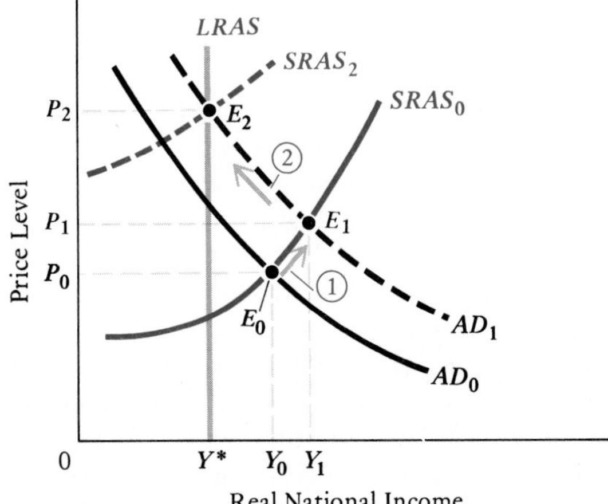

The effect of supply-side measures on aggregate demand is inflationary. The figure shows the economy in the same short-run initial equilibrium at E_0 as in Figure 30-6(i). However, it assumes that demand-side effects of the policy measures occur and are fully felt before any supply-side effects come into play. The *AD* curve shifts to the right to AD_1, and the economy moves to equilibrium at E_1, as shown by arrow 1. This gives a temporary increase in output to Y_1 at the cost of an immediate rise in the price level to P_1. However, the inflationary gap is also increased, to $Y^* - Y_1$. Now the *SRAS* curve starts to shift upward, taking the equilibrium along AD_1 in the direction shown by arrow 2, along with falling output and rising prices. If nothing else happens, inflation will finally come to an end at price level P_2 and output Y^*. As a result of the supply-side measures, the rise in the price level, from P_0 to P_2, is *greater* than it would have been without the measures, that is, from P_0 to P_1.

Supply siders with training in economics knew that the short-term effects via aggregate demand would occur. However, they believed that the supply-side shifts of long-run aggregate supply would be large enough and quick enough to dominate them. Critics not only doubted this view as to timing but also questioned whether the tax changes proposed would have the desired effects even in the long run. Economic theory makes no definite prediction about the effects of tax cuts on how much people will work. Cuts might make them work more because they earn more for each additional hour that they work, but cuts might make them work less because they can, if they wish, have both more disposable income and more leisure. For example, if in response to a tax cut that increased after-tax wages by 10 percent they worked 5 percent less, they would have approximately 5 percent more disposable income and

[9] Students who have read Chapter 24 and have encountered the Laffer curve (see pages 504–505) will see that believers in that phenomenon had an even more direct reason to believe that tax cuts would increase government revenues.

5 percent more leisure. (This is discussed in greater detail in Chapter 40.)

Evaluating the Theory

It is difficult to resolve all the factual matters at issue in the supply-side debate on the basis of the Reagan adminstration's experiences. First, the proposed measures were never fully implemented. Second, the inflationary conditions postulated in the theory were removed by both the course of events—no further cost-side pressures from rising oil and raw material prices—and monetary policy (these issues are discussed in Chapter 36). Nonetheless, some conclusions can be ventured.

First, it is clear that the aggregate demand effects of the policy were stronger than its supply-side effects in the short term. Consumer expenditures rose dramatically. The United States enjoyed a rapid recovery from the deep recession of the early 1980s, while many other industrial countries took much longer to recover.

Second, it is even clearer that the induced rise in national income was not sufficient to restore the government revenue that was lost when tax rates were cut. All through the 1980s the U.S. government's budget deficit was a cause of concern for economists, and at the end of the decade, the deficit remained substantially unchecked.

Finally, the anticipated supply-side effects are harder to locate. It is in the nature of these positive effects that they are diffused throughout the whole economy, which makes them difficult to identify and to measure. The incentives to business investment were accompanied by a rise in investment spending later in the decade, but it was too little and too late, and some of it would no doubt have occurred anyway. To what extent the reductions in tax rates provided effective incentives is more difficult to assess. The possibility that the supply-side reforms had major effects in improving the functioning of the economy cannot, however, be dismissed lightly. We will return to this issue in a later chapter.

SUMMARY

1. Potential income is treated as given and is represented by a vertical line at Y^*. The output gap is equal to the horizontal distance between Y^* and the actual level of income, as determined by the intersection of the *AD* and *SRAS* curves.
2. A negative output gap means that demand in the labor market is relatively high. As a result, wages rise faster than productivity, causing unit costs to rise. The *SRAS* curve shifts leftward, and the price level rises. Thus any excess of actual national income over potential national income is called an inflationary gap.
3. A positive output gap means that demand in the labor market is relatively low. Though there is some resulting tendency for wages to fall relative to productivity, asymmetrical behavior means that the strength of this force will be much weaker than that indicated in summary point 2. Unit costs will fall slowly, so the output gap will persist. Any shortfall of actual national income relative to potential is called a recessionary gap.
4. An expansionary demand shock creates an inflationary gap that causes wages to rise faster than productivity. Unit costs rise, shifting the *SRAS* curve to the left, resulting in a higher level of prices, with output eventually falling back to its potential level.
5. A contractionary demand shock will work in the opposite direction. If, however, factor prices are sticky, the automatic adjustment process may be slow, and a recessionary gap may not be quickly eliminated.
6. The long-run aggregate supply (*LRAS*) curve relates the price level and national income after all wages and other costs have been adjusted fully to long-run equilibrium. The *LRAS* curve is vertical at the level of potential income, Y^*.
7. Because the *LRAS* curve is vertical, output in the long run is determined by the position of the *LRAS* curve, and the only long-run role of the *AD* curve is to determine the price level.

8. Supply-side economics in an inflationary situation seeks to reduce an inflationary gap and increase output through tax cuts and other incentive measures that are designed to shift the *LRAS* curve to the right and thus increase potential output. In the short run such measures increase aggregate demand, thus adding to inflationary pressures. In the long run this may increase the rate at which the *LRAS* curve is shifting to the right due to economic growth.

TOPICS FOR REVIEW

The output gap and the labor market
Inflationary gap
Recessionary gap
Asymmetry of wage adjustment
Changes in aggregate demand shocks and induced wage changes
Wages, productivity, and unit costs
Long-run aggregate supply (*LRAS*) curve
Supply-side economics

DISCUSSION QUESTIONS

1. "Starting from a full-employment equilibrium, an increase in government spending can produce more output and employment at the cost of a once-and-for-all rise in the price level."

   "Increased spending can never lead to a permanent increase in output above its full employment level."

   Discuss these two statements in terms of short- and long-run *aggregate supply curves.*
2. Identify the effects of each of the following events on the *SRAS* and the *LRAS* curves.
   a. Increase in the price of imported raw materials that are used in key manufacturing industries
   b. Increase in the price of imported consumption goods such as coffee or bananas
   c. Increased restrictions on pollution emissions in an attempt to combat acid rain
   d. Projections of reduced federal government deficits over the next five years
   e. An improved economic outlook leading to an investment boom
   f. Increased labor force participation rate of key sectors of the population
3. Interpret each of the following news items in terms of *AD* and *SRAS* curves. (Assume that the statements are correct for the purposes of drawing your curves.)
   a. "Management representative calls union wage demands irresponsible in the face of current high unemployment rates."
   b. "Government spokesman says that although the recovery is expected to be vigorous, it will witness only modest reductions in the unemployment rate."
   c. "Wage increases have failed to keep up with inflation during the current boom."
   d. "Innovations in microelectronic technology will lead to an increase in both national output and unemployment."
   e. "The government's caving in to public-sector unions early in its term worsened inflation over the next few years."
4. Comment on the following newspaper headline: "More growth seen as cure for inflation."

5. Politicians are sometimes accused of adopting policies that bring "short-term gain at the cost of long-term pain," while statesmen offer "short-term pain to buy long-term gain." What policies that shift aggregate demand or aggregate supply curves might come under one or the other of these descriptions?
6. Over 20 percent of Canadian national income is generated through exports to the United States. Why do Canadians worry that "when the United States gets an (economic) cold, Canada gets (economic) pneumonia"?
7. If downward flexibility of money wages would allow the automatic adjustment mechanism to eliminate recessionary gaps quickly, why do workers usually resist wage cuts during times of economic slump?
8. Show the effects on the price level and output of income tax cuts that induce people to work more in an economy currently experiencing an inflationary gap.

Chapter 31

Business Cycles: The Ebb and Flow of Economic Activity

Changing, always changing—that is the dominant characteristic of national income as far back as we have records. As we saw in Chapter 26, GDP—like most economic time series—exhibits two types of change. The upward trend in GDP indicates long-term change, which we call economic growth, while shorter-term oscillations in GDP represent temporary changes, which we call the business cycle.

Economic growth and the business cycle both reflect changes in total real output and hence in employment and unemployment. Both are also the subject of much public debate and the object of government policies. Later in this book we shall study policy in some detail. It is important at this stage to distinguish carefully between the causes and implications of long-term growth and those of short-term fluctuations.

Cycles and Growth

Figure 31-1 illustrates the three alternative ways in which GDP can be increased. As shown in part (i) of the figure, an increase in aggregate demand will yield a one-time increase in real GNP. If that increase occurs when there is a recessionary gap, it pushes GDP toward potential income and thus bypasses the working of the automatic adjustment mechanism that eventually would have achieved the same outcome by depressing wages and other costs. (The operation of this automatic adjustment mechanism is discussed in detail in Chapter 30.) If the demand shock pushes GDP beyond potential income, the rise in GDP will be only temporary; the inflationary gap will cause wages and other costs to rise, shifting the *SRAS* curve to the left. This drives GDP back toward potential so that the only lasting effect is on the price level.

Increases in aggregate supply will also lead to an increase in GDP. Here it is useful to distinguish between two possible kinds of increases that might occur—those that leave the *LRAS* curve unchanged and those that shift it.

Part (ii) of Figure 31-1 shows the effects of a temporary increase in aggregate supply due, say, to a bumper agricultural crop. This will shift the *SRAS* curve to the right but will have no effect on the *LRAS* curve or, hence, on potential income. The shock will thus cause GDP to rise relative to potential, but the increase will be soon reversed—in this case possibly even before any significant impact on wages and other costs can be detected.

Part (iii) of Figure 31-1 shows the effects of permanent increases in aggregate supply that shift the *LRAS* curve. A once-

FIGURE 31-1 Three Sources of Increases in National Income

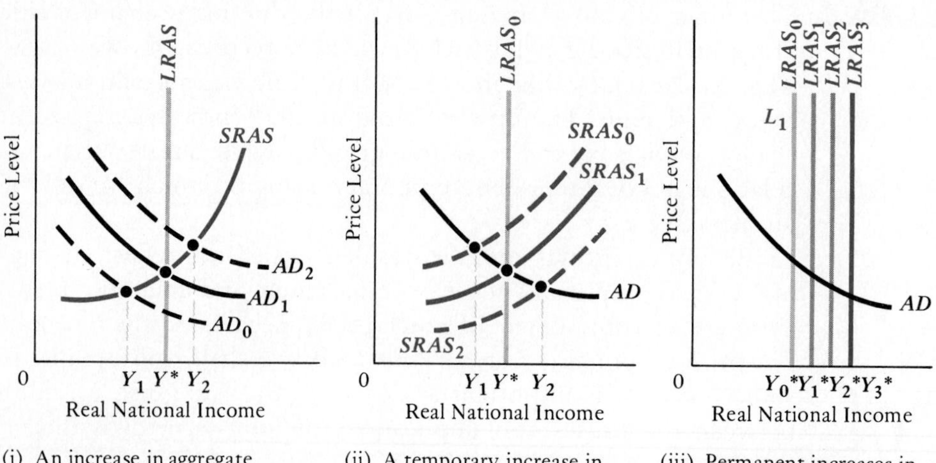

(i) An increase in aggregate demand

(ii) A temporary increase in aggregate supply

(iii) Permanent increases in aggregate supply

National income will increase in response to an increase in aggregate demand or an increase in aggregate supply. The increase will be permanent if the *LRAS* curve shifts, but if the *LRAS* curve does not shift, any divergences of GDP from potential will only be temporary; the output gap that is created will set in motion the wage adjustments that we studied in Chapter 30. The *LRAS* curve does not shift in (i) and (ii), but in (iii) it does.

In (i) the *AD* curve shifts to the right. If the initial level of income is Y_1, the shift from AD_0 to AD_1 eliminates the recessionary gap and raises national income to Y^*. If the initial level of income is Y^*, the shift from AD_1 to AD_2 raises national income to Y_2 and thereby opens up an inflationary gap.

In (ii) the *SRAS* curve shifts to the right. If the initial level of income is Y_1, the shift from $SRAS_0$ to $SRAS_1$ eliminates the recessionary gap and raises national income to Y^*. If the initial level of income is Y^*, the shift from $SRAS_1$ to $SRAS_2$ raises national income to Y_2 and thereby opens up an inflationary gap.

In the cases shown in (i) and (ii), any increase in GDP beyond potential is temporary, since, in the absence of any additional shocks, the inflationary gap will cause wages and other factor prices to rise; this will cause the *SRAS* curve to shift upward and hence national income to converge to Y^*.

In (iii) the *LRAS* curve shifts to the right so that potential income increases. Whether or not actual income increases immediately depends on what happens to the *AD* and *SRAS* curves. Since, in the absence of other shocks, actual income eventually converges to potential income, a rightward shift in the *LRAS* curve eventually leads to an increase in actual GDP. If the shift in the *LRAS* curve is recurrent, national income will grow continually.

and-for-all increase due, say, to a labor market policy that reduces the level of structural unemployment will lead to a one-time increase in potential GDP. A recurrent increase that is due, say, to population growth, capital accumulation, or ongoing improvements in productivity causes a continual rightward shift in the *LRAS* curve, giving rise to a continual increase in the level of potential GDP.

A gradual but continual rise in potential GDP, or what we have called *economic growth*, contributes significantly to improvements in the standard of living. Eliminating a severe recessionary gap will cause a once-and-for-all increase in national income of perhaps 4 percent, while eliminating structural unemployment will raise it by somewhat less. However, a growth rate of 3 percent per year raises national income by 10 percent in three years and *doubles* it in about 24 years. We shall study the factors influencing economic growth in detail in Chapter 38; in this chapter we focus on *cyclical fluctuations* in GDP.

Cyclical Fluctuations

Figure 31-1 allows us to distinguish the causes of trend growth in potential GDP from the causes of cyclical fluctuations.

Cyclical fluctuations in GDP are caused by shifts in the *AD* and *SRAS* curves that cause actual GDP to deviate temporarily from potential GDP.

These shifts are in turn caused by changes in a variety of factors, including interest rates, exchange rates, consumer and business confidence, and government policy. Although the resulting deviations of actual from potential GDP are described as "temporary," recall from Chapter 30 that the automatic adjustment mechanism may work so slowly that the deviations can persist for some time, perhaps several years.

The Concept of the Business Cycle

The business cycle was introduced in Chapter 26, where we saw that it refers to the continual ebb and flow of economic activity.[1] The pattern of a sequence of high values for some key series followed by a sequence of low values, followed again by another sequence of high values, is the source of the term *cyclical* that is used to describe such economic fluctuations. A stylized representation of the phases of the cycle was given in Figure 26-3, in which the continual oscillations in GDP were apparent.

The complexity of the business cycle cannot be fully captured by a single statistic, even one as important as GDP. Figure 31-2 shows three other economic series. Each of these, as well as a dozen others that might be studied, tells us something about the general variability of the economy. It is clear that some series vary more than others and that they do not all move exactly together.

The behavior suggested by Figures 26-3 and 31-2 is not one of occasional sharp shifts in the aggregate demand and aggregate supply curves. If it were, we would expect national income to show occasional sharp changes, followed by long periods of little or no change. Instead, the short-term situation is one of continual change at varying rates.

FIGURE 31-2 Three Indicators of Changes in Economic Activity, 1962–1989

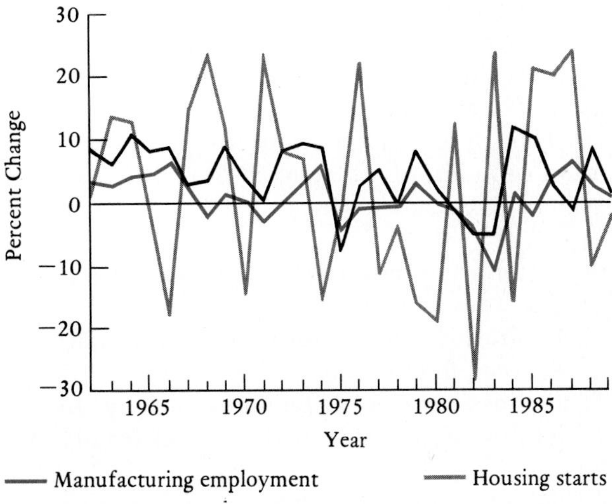

Fluctuations follow similar, but by no means identical, patterns for various series that can serve as indicators of aggregate economic activity. The cyclical pattern of fluctuations is easily seen in all three series, although the amplitudes are quite different. Housing starts tend to fluctuate more, and employment in manufacturing fluctuates somewhat less, than the series for industrial production. *Source:* Statistics Canada, 11-003E.

Evidently, there are forces at work causing economic activity to display continual short-term fluctuations around the economy's long-term growth trend.

Though all cycles are not alike in duration or intensity, each appears to exhibit movements that cumulate for a while and then eventually reverse themselves. This was true long before governments attempted to intervene in order to stabilize their economies, and it is true still.

Alvin Hansen, a distinguished American authority on business cycles, once reported that there were 17 cycles in the U.S. economy between 1795 and 1937, with an average duration of 8.35 years. A shorter "inventory cycle" of 40 months' duration

[1] We noted in Chapter 26 that when economists wish to analyze monthly or quarterly data, they often try to remove fluctuations that can be accounted for by a regular seasonal pattern. The business cycle refers to fluctuations that remain after the seasonal adjustment has been made.

was also found, as well as longer cycles associated with building booms (15 to 20 years). The Russian economist N. D. Kondratieff thought that he could identify long cycles, associated with the introduction of major innovations, of 40 to 50 years. Some economists have argued that in many Western democracies a political business cycle is associated with the pattern of elections.

Though the evidence is diverse, it is nevertheless possible to identify some basic characteristics of the pattern of business cycles:

1. **A common pattern of variation more or less pervades all economic series.**
2. **Economic series differ in their particular patterns of fluctuations.**
3. **Business cycles differ substantially in the length and the size of the swings involved.**

Explaining Business Cycles

An explanation of the business cycle must answer two questions: (1) What are the factors that cause GDP and other key macro variables to fluctuate? (2) What are the factors that cause those fluctuations to form a cyclical pattern? These two questions are taken up in the two main sections that follow.

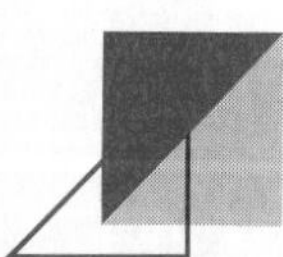

Why Do Income and Employment Fluctuate?

Although unresolved issues and hence points of controversy remain among economists who study business cycles, there is general agreement that over the course of Canadian economic history, the business cycle has been caused mainly by fluctuations in aggregate demand. Nevertheless, particular cycles can sometimes be explained in part by aggregate supply shocks. Indeed, the oil price shocks that occurred in the 1970s made citizens of advanced industrial countries acutely aware of supply-side causes.

Aggregate demand shocks are a major source of fluctuations in GDP; aggregate supply shocks are another source.

Figure 31-3 illustrates the two simple cases that we encountered earlier, in Chapter 29. In part (i) all fluctuations in GDP are the result of fluctuations in the *AD* curve, while both the *SRAS* and *LRAS* curves remain stationary. In part (ii) all fluctuations in GDP are the result of fluctuations in the *SRAS* curve, while both the *AD* curve and the *LRAS* curve remain stationary. These two cases form the basis for most of the discussion in this chapter. They use two key simplifications that should be noted.

First, neither of the two sources of fluctuation in Figure 31-3 affects the *LRAS* curve or, hence, the level of potential output. In this chapter we focus on short-term fluctuations, and so it is useful to ignore the underlying trend of potential output and its determinants. We shall return to a discussion of economic growth in Chapter 38.[2]

Second, Figure 31-3 ignores any *induced* shifts in the *SRAS* curve. Recall, however, that when the actual level of GDP differs from potential GDP, wages and other costs will tend to adjust, causing the *SRAS* curve to shift and thus inducing further changes in actual GDP. (See Figures 30-2 and 30-3 in Chapter 30.) To explain why GDP fluctuates, we focus on why the *AD* and *SRAS* curves shift exogenously; later, in order to explain why fluctuations tend to be cyclical, we focus on induced shifts in the *SRAS* curve.

Sources of Aggregate Demand Shocks

What are the sources of the continual disturbances to aggregate demand? The theory of income determination suggests four main candidates: shifts in each of the four main components of aggregate expenditure.

Changes in Consumption

Consumption is the largest single component of aggregate expenditure—about two-thirds of the total. When searching for the causes of income changes, we are not concerned with changes in consumption *in response* to changes in income but instead with *shifts* in the function relating consumption to income. Such shifts can have many causes.

[2] In that chapter we also encounter the possibility that the same forces that cause fluctuations also cause changes in potential output. This possibility—which essentially means that there are simultaneous shifts in the *SRAS* and *LRAS* curves, and hence simultaneous shifts in actual and potential GDP—is the subject of recent developments in the literature on *equilibrium business cycles* and *real business cycles*.

FIGURE 31-3 Demand-driven and Supply-driven Business Cycles

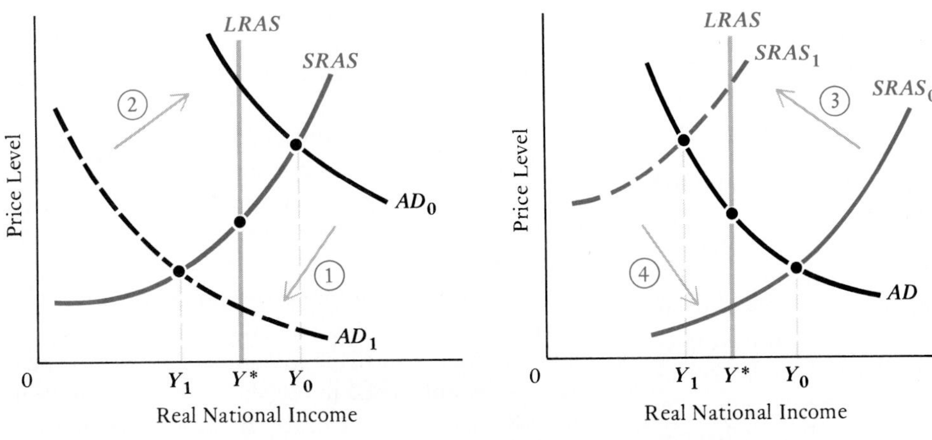

(i) *AD* fluctuations

(ii) *SRAS* fluctuations

Fluctuations in aggregate demand or aggregate supply can cause fluctuations in national income and employment. In (i) the *AD* curve oscillates regularly. Starting from a high level of demand, as depicted by AD_0 and an income level at a peak of Y_0, the *AD* curve then shifts leftward continually, as shown by arrow 1. As a result of this fall in demand, income falls—first reaching Y^* and then falling further to a trough at Y_1. The *AD* curve then starts to shift continually to the right, as shown by arrow 2. Income thus rises, first to Y^* and then reaching Y_0 again at the next peak.

In (ii) the *SRAS* curve oscillates regularly. Starting from a high level of supply, as depicted by $SRAS_0$ and an income level at a peak of Y_0, the *SRAS* curve then shifts leftward continually, as shown by arrow 3. As a result of this fall in supply, income falls—first reaching Y^* and then falling further to a trough at Y_1. The *SRAS* curve then starts to shift continually to the right, as shown by arrow 4. Income thus rises, first to Y^* and then reaching Y_0 again at the next peak.

Changes in tastes. Changes in how consumers divide their income between consumption and savings will lead to a change in desired aggregate expenditure. In the mid 1980s there was a significant increase in the demand for North American cars. If the income that was spent on automobiles had been saved previously, this would have represented a significant rightward shift in the *AD* curve. Jobs and incomes would first be gained in the automobile industry. The induced increase in spending by auto workers would then set up a multiplier effect as increases in output, income, and spending spread throughout the economy.

Changes in expectations and interest rates. Expectations of future inflation may lead to a burst of spending to buy now while goods are cheap. Conversely, a wave of uncertainty about the future may lead to a rise in saving and hence a cut in spending. High interest rates can be a powerful incentive to postpone buying durable goods. For example, in 1990 rates of over 15 percent helped to depress the markets for automobiles and other consumer durables.

In an inflationary world, it is important to distinguish between the real and the nominal rate of interest. (See Chapter 26 for a detailed discussion.) Recall that the real rate of interest is the difference between the nominal rate of interest and the expected rate of inflation. It is the real rate of interest that matters for most expenditure decisions.

Changes in taxes. As we saw in Chapter 29, tax changes can also shift the aggregate consumption function. Income tax cuts mean that more *total* income becomes *disposable* income, leading to an increase in consumer spending; income tax increases have the opposite effect.

Changes in transfer payments. As we also saw in Chapter 29, changes in transfer payments can influence aggregate expenditure through their effects on personal consumption. These effects can be substantial, since government transfer payments amount to roughly one-eighth of personal income.

Changes in Government Purchases

World War II brought a rapid expansion of economic activity. Government spending was a major contributing factor. Wars generally result in a large increase in governmental purchases as men and materials are shifted from civilian to military use. This shift is usually reversed in the postwar period. For example, federal government purchases of goods and services rose from $683 million in 1939 to $4.98 billion in 1944 and fell back to $1.54 billion by 1947. Changes in government purchases of goods and services from 1940 to 1946 were the dominant influence on GDP.

Aside from periods of major wars, government expenditures have not often been destabilizing. For peacetime periods before 1940, government expenditures were both small and relatively stable. Since 1955 they have been large and stable and growing rather steadily. Thus whatever their potential for being a major source of cyclical instability, they have not proved to be such except during wars.

As Figure 31-4 shows, the shocks caused by changing government expenditure have been much smaller on average than the shocks caused by either changing net exports or changing private investment expenditure.

Changes in Net Exports

A country such as Canada, in which foreign trade plays a large role, is subject to destabilizing influences from foreign demand. Since about one-half of all goods produced in Canada are exported, fluctuations in the national income of other countries can be transmitted to our economy through fluctuations in their demand for our exports. Changes in merchandise exports played an important role during the Great Depression. The fall in export demand triggered by the depression in the economies of our major trading partners led to a fall in our exports, thereby reinforcing the early stages of the recession in Canada. Similarly, during World War II exports boomed at the same time that the domestic economy was expanding.

Similar influences of exports on the domestic economy can be seen throughout the period. One notable episode was the boom in the economy during the early 1970s followed by the decline in the mid 1970s. Exports rose sharply from 1971 to 1973 and then fell sharply in the years 1973–1975. More recently, the severe recession in the United States in 1980–1982 and the sustained recovery from 1982 until 1989 caused Canadian exports first to fall and then to rise, contributing to a business cycle in Canada that followed a pattern roughly similar to that in the United States.

Factors other than foreign incomes also affect Canadian exports. One of the most important is the ability of Canadian firms to compete in international markets, as influenced in the short run by changes in the exchange rate and more directly by changes in domestic costs relative to foreign costs. Labor costs as reflected in wages are important, as are the costs of material inputs and energy.

Some further aspects of the relationship of net exports to cyclical movements in income are discussed in Box 31-1.

Shifts in consumption, government, and net export expenditures cause major fluctuations in national income and employment.

Changes in Investment

Changes in investment expenditure are a major source of economic fluctuations. For example, the Great Depression witnessed a dramatic fall in investment. Total investment in the Canadian economy fell from $1.2 billion in 1929 (almost double the amount that was needed to replace the capital goods that were being used up in the process of producing GDP) to just $145 million in 1933, less than one-sixth the amount that was needed just to keep the stock of capital intact. Similarly, at the trough of the recession of the early 1980s, investment expenditure was less than one-sixth its average level of the previous five years.

As Figure 31-4 shows, investment expenditure is very volatile. Quite large shocks, due to changes in investment expenditure, hit the economy frequently. The change in investment from one year to the next has been on average about three times the change in government purchases.

Changes in investment are also quite closely cor-

FIGURE 31-4 Changes in GDP and Selected Components, 1950–1989

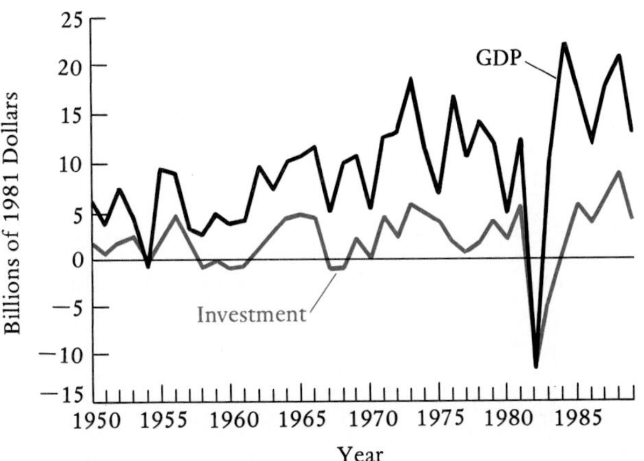

(i) Changes in GDP and investment

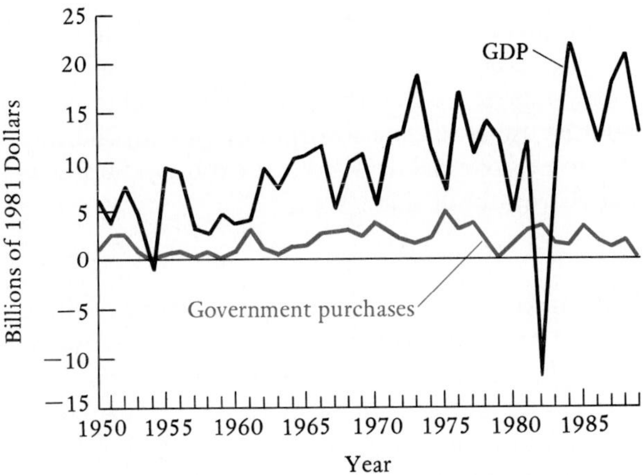

(ii) Changes in GDP and government purchases

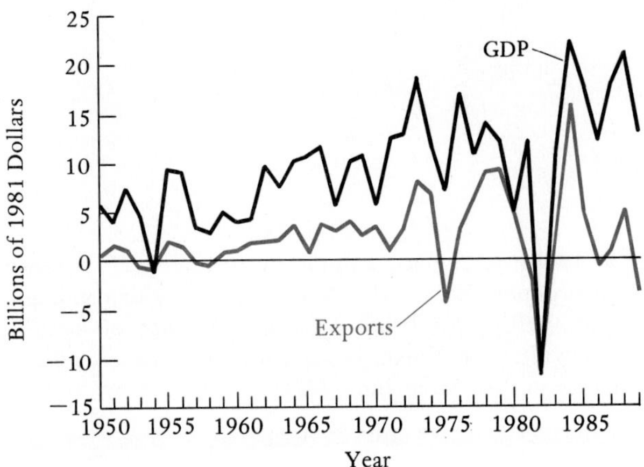

(iii) Changes in GDP and exports

Changes in GDP have been closely related to investment expenditures and exports. Part (i) shows that changes in GDP and changes in investment are closely correlated, tending to rise and fall together. For example, the recessions in the mid 1970s and the early 1980s were both accompanied by sharp drops in investment spending, and the recovery from each of these recessions was accompanied by sustained increases in investment spending.

Part (ii) shows that changes in government purchases are quite smooth over the period shown and consequently are not an important contributor to fluctuations in GDP.

Part (iii) shows that changes in exports are closely correlated with changes in GDP. For example, the recession in the early 1980s witnessed a dramatic fall in exports, and the subsequent recovery in GDP was accompanied by a sharp rise in exports. *Source:* Statistics Canada, 13-531, 13-201, 11-003E.

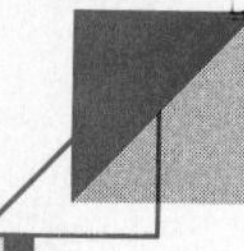

BOX 31-1

National Income and the Balance of Trade

Exports are an important source of demand for domestically produced goods. A key determinant of a country's exports is the level of activity in its major trading partners. When, for example, the United States experiences a slump, as it did in the early 1980s, there is a reduction in its demand for Canadian exports. In turn, via the multiplier process, the decrease in exports causes a contraction in Canadian income. Similarly, when the United States experiences a boom, as it did during 1984–1989, American demand for foreign goods increases. Again, the change in exports causes a multiplier effect, this time leading to an increase in Canadian national income.

The *export multiplier* causes the business cycles of major trading partners to be closely synchronized.

As we saw in Chapter 30, expenditure on imports will grow as domestic national income grows. Imports represent spending on other countries' outputs, and they therefore raise the economy's *marginal propensity not to spend,* denoted by $1 - z$. As we also saw in Chapter 30, this reduces the size of the multiplier. [36]

A smaller multiplier is undesirable because it reduces the effectiveness of domestic policies that attempt to change the level of domestic income. It is desirable because it reduces the impact that fluctuations in autonomous expenditure (such as investment and exports) have on national income.*

Net Exports and Domestic Absorption

The model of national income determination that we outlined in Chapter 28 provides an important perspective on the determination of net exports. Recall the basic condition for equilibrium national income:

$$Y = C + I + G + (X - M)$$

The sum of $C + I + G$ corresponds to total expenditure on all goods and services (domestic and foreign) for use within the economy; this total is often referred to as **domestic absorption (A)**. The equilibrium relationship can therefore be rewritten as

$$Y = A + (X - M)$$

The right-hand side of this equation is desired aggregate expenditure on domestic goods and services, represented as the sum of expenditure for internal use (domestic absorption) plus expenditure due to net external demand (net exports). Subtracting A from both sides, we get

$$Y - A = X - M$$

This makes it clear that net exports can be positive only if national income exceeds domestic absorption—that is, only if total demand for goods and services to be used in Canada is less than total output of goods and services in Canada. And if net exports are positive, it must be the case that national income exceeds the absorption of goods and services within Canada.†

* The consequence of the latter effect is that imports act as a *built-in stabilizer.* We will encounter built-in stabilizers again in Chapter 32 in our analysis of fiscal policy.

† Note that foreigners can influence the demand for Canadian goods and services in two ways: by demanding exports and by investing in Canada. An increase in exports will, other things being equal, lead to a smaller increase in national income. [37]

related with changes in national income, as shown in Figure 31-4. Rising investment tends to be associated with rapidly rising GDP, and falling investment tends to be associated with *slowly* rising or falling GDP. This is consistent with the view that investment shocks are a major cause of changes in national income.

Changes in investment expenditures play a key role in most theories of cyclical fluctuations.

Why Does Investment Change?

Changes in investment are a prime cause of fluctuations in the economy, but we need to know why investment fluctuates.

The Interest Rate and Investment

Empirical evidence shows that investment responds to many influencing factors. One of the most important of these factors is the rate of interest. Other things being equal, the higher the interest rate, the higher the cost of borrowing money for investment purposes and the less the amount of investment expenditure.[3]

Although each dollar of investment has the same consequences for aggregate demand, different types of investment respond to different sets of causes. Thus it is useful to discuss separately the determinants of the three major types of investment expenditure: inventories, residential housing construction, and business fixed investment. In so doing we can see why the interest rate is such an important influence on investment, and we can determine what other factors are important.

Inventories. Inventory changes represent only a small percentage of private investment in a typical year, but their average size is not an adequate measure of their importance. They are one of the more volatile elements of total investment and therefore have a major influence on shifts in total investment expenditure.

[3] In reality, there are many interest rates; however, it is usually possible to speak of movements in the general level of these interest rates, since they tend to rise and fall together. This trend is what we refer to in basic theory as "the interest rate." Later in this chapter we will study the complicated link between the interest rate and investment expenditure that operates through the stock market.

Studies show that the stock of inventories that are held tends to rise as production and sales rise. Because the size of inventories is related to the level of sales, the *change* in inventories (which is current investment) is related to the *change* in the level of sales.

A firm may decide, for example, to hold inventories of 10 percent of its sales. Thus if sales are $100,000, it will wish to hold inventories of $10,000. If sales increase to $110,000, it will want to hold inventories of $11,000. Over the period during which its stock of inventories is being increased, there will be a total of $1,000 new inventory investment.

The higher the level of production and sales, the larger the desired stock of inventories. Changes in the rate of production and sales cause temporary bouts of investment (or disinvestment) in inventories.

When a firm ties up funds in inventories, those same funds cannot be used elsewhere to earn income. As an alternative to holding inventories, the firm could lend the money out at the going rate of interest. Thus the higher the real rate of interest, the higher the opportunity cost of holding an inventory of a given size; the higher that opportunity cost, the smaller the inventories desired.

The higher the real rate of interest, the lower the desired stock of inventories. Changes in the rate of interest cause temporary bouts of investment (or disinvestment) in inventories.

Residential housing construction. Since 1970 spending on residential housing construction has varied between one-fifth and one-third of all gross private investment in Canada and between 3.5 percent and 6.5 percent of GDP. Because expenditures for housing construction are both large and variable, they exert a major impact on the economy.

Many influences on residential housing construction are noneconomic and depend on demographic or cultural considerations, such as new family formation. However, households must not only want to buy houses but also be able to do so. Periods of high employment and high average family earnings tend to lead to increases in housing construction.

Periods of high unemployment and falling earnings tend to lead to decreases in such construction.

Almost all houses are purchased with money that is borrowed by means of mortgages. Interest on the borrowed money typically accounts for over one-half of the purchaser's annual mortgage payments; the remainder is repayment of principal. It is for this reason that sharp variations in interest rates exert a substantial effect on the demand for housing.

This importance was borne out by experiences from 1979 to 1982 when mortgage rates rose from less than 11 percent to over 15 percent and housing starts fell from 197,000 units in 1979 to 126,000 in 1982. (Since inflation fell after 1980, the increased nominal interest rates also meant increased real rates.) The construction industry itself and its major suppliers, such as the cement and the lumber industries, felt the blow of a dramatic drop in demand. Conversely, during the mid 1980s interest rates fell sharply and there was a boom in the demand for new housing; that boom persisted until late 1988, when interest rates started to rise again.

Expenditures for residential construction tend to vary positively with changes in national income and negatively with interest rates.

Business fixed investment. Investment in plant and equipment is the largest component of domestic investment. Over one-half is financed by firms' retained profits (profits that are not paid out to their shareholders). This means that current profits are an important determinant of investment.

A second major determinant of investment is the rate of interest. As became abundantly clear during the early 1980s, very high interest rates greatly reduce the volume of investment as more and more firms find that their expected profits from investment do not cover the interest on borrowed investment funds. Other firms that had cash on hand found that purchasing interest-earning assets provided a better return than investment in plant and equipment; for them, the increase in real interest rates meant that the opportunity cost of investing had risen.

A third major determinant of investment is changes in national income. If there is a rise in aggregate demand that is expected to persist and that cannot be met by existing capacity, investment in new plant and equipment will be needed. Once the new plants have been built and put into operation, however, the rate of new investment will fall.

This further illustrates an important characteristic of investment that we have encountered already in the case of inventories:

If the desired stock of capital goods increases, there will be an investment boom while the new capital is being produced.

However, if nothing else changes, and even if business conditions continue to look rosy enough to justify the increased stock of capital, investment in new plant and equipment will cease once the larger capital stock is achieved. This aspect of investment leads to the *accelerator* theory of investment, which we look at more closely in the appendix to this chapter.

Sources of Aggregate Supply Shocks

In Chapter 29 we saw that the *SRAS* curve can shift for many reasons, including changes in input prices and productivity. (See especially Figure 29-6.) When the *SRAS* curve shifts, GDP and employment change.

As we noted also in Chapter 29, one episode in which an aggregate supply shock played an important role in the Canadian economy occurred in 1974, when the members of the Organization of Petroleum Exporting Countries (OPEC) acted to raise the price of oil fourfold. Since imported oil was a major input, used by many Canadian industries, the OPEC shock served to raise costs in those industries. As a result, the *SRAS* curve shifted up and to the left, leading to stagflation—an increase in prices and a fall in output and employment.

Changes in the Canadian dollar exchange rate can also cause aggregate supply shocks. During the 1980s movements in the exchange rate had direct effects on costs in industries that were using imported raw materials and goods in their production. Such changes in the exchange rate also can have indirect effects on aggregate supply, since their effects on imported consumer goods can feed through to wages.

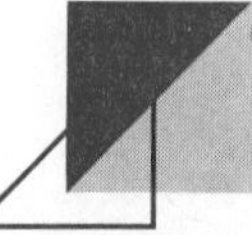

Why Do Fluctuations Exhibit Cyclical Patterns?

Explanations for the *cyclical* patterns of economic fluctuations fall into two categories. The various explanations are not necessarily competing ones, since several together often provide a better overall explanation than any one on its own. In the first category, the economy converts *random shifts* in the *AD* and *SRAS* curves into cyclical outcomes. In the second category, *cyclical shifts* in the *AD* curve cause cyclical fluctuations in the economy.

Random Shocks and Lags

One model of the business cycle suggests that random shifts in expenditure are transformed into systematic cycles of output and employment.

This theory begins with lags. For example, if a fall in the rate of interest makes an investment in a new project profitable, it may take six months to plan it, three months to write and sign contracts, six months before spending builds up to its top rate, and another 24 months to complete the project. These lags mean that changes in, say, the rate of interest will cause reactions in investment expenditure that are distributed over quite a long period of time.

Another source of lags comes from the response of production decisions to changes in demand. In many industries it takes weeks, months, or even longer to bring new or mothballed capacity into production and to hire and train new workers. As a result, changes in demand give rise to changes in output that are spread out over a substantial period of time. An increase in demand, for example, may lead to a gradual increase in output that builds up over several months. Then, as output does change, the automatic adjustment mechanism is set into action. As an inflationary gap opens up, wages and costs start to rise, and the *SRAS* curve shifts leftward.

Thus a once-and-for-all demand shock gives rise to a cyclical output response, with GDP first rising because of the rightward shift in the *AD* curve and then falling because of the leftward shift in the *SRAS*.

Each major component of aggregate expenditure has sometimes undergone shifts large enough to disturb the economy significantly. Adjustment lags can convert such shifts into cyclical oscillations in national income.

Cyclical Spending Behavior

Several factors can cause fluctuations in spending behavior themselves to follow a cyclical pattern. Some explanations focus on cyclical patterns in government behavior; we shall examine this possibility shortly.

The multiplier-accelerator model and related theories provide some basis for expecting investment and consumption to behave cyclically. The key is that a disturbance that causes an increase in income might also trigger further expenditure increases that respond to that increase. Business fixed investment, desired inventories, and spending on housing construction will all respond to the *change* in national income. Hence an initial change will set in motion further *cumulative* changes in spending and national income. Thus an initial positive shock to spending and income will tend to be followed by further increases, and an initial negative shock to spending will tend to be followed by further decreases. These interactions, which generate cyclical tendencies in private spending, are discussed further in the appendix to this chapter.

Policy-induced Cycles

Another theory of the business cycle is based on the allegation that government-induced demand shocks have sometimes caused cyclical fluctuations. Why should the government administer potentially disturbing demand shocks? Several reasons have been suggested.

A political business cycle. As early as 1944 the Polish-born Keynesian economist Michael Kalecki warned of a political business cycle. He argued that once governments had learned to manipulate the economy, they would engineer an election-geared business cycle. In preelection periods they would raise spending and cut taxes. The resulting expansionary demand shock would create high employment and good business conditions that would attract voters' support for the government, but the resulting inflationary gap would lead to a rising price level. So after the election was won, the government would depress demand to remove the inflationary gap and to provide some slack for expansion before the next election.

This theory invokes the image of a cynical government manipulating employment and national income solely because it wants to stay in power. Few people believe that governments deliberately do this all the time, but the temptation to do it some of the time, particulary before elections, may prove irresistible.

Alternating policy goals. A variant of the policy-induced cycle does not require a cynical government and an easily duped electorate. Instead, both sides need only to be rather shortsighted and to have rather narrow vision.

In this theory, when there is a recession and relatively stable prices, the public and the government identify unemployment as the number one economic problem. The government then engineers an expansionary policy shock through some combination of tax cuts and spending increases. This, plus such natural cumulative forces as the multiplier-accelerator, expands economic activity. Unemployment falls and income rises, but as income rises above potential national income, the price level begins to rise. It first rises along the stable *SRAS* curve and then rises further as boom conditions raise factor prices and shift the *SRAS* curve upward. (See Figure 30-2.)

At this point the unemployment problem is declared solved. Now inflation is seen as the nation's number one economic problem. A contractionary demand shock is engineered. The natural cumulative forces again take over, causing a recession. The inflation subsides, but unemployment rises, setting the stage once again for an expansionary shock to solve the unemployment problem.

Many economists have criticized government policy over the past few decades as sometimes causing fluctuations by alternately pushing expansion to cure unemployment and then pushing contraction to cure inflation. We shall see in Chapter 40 that this charge is particularly strong against monetary policy. But whatever the policy, the charge is that policymakers have sometimes been too shortsighted in alternating their concern between unemployment and inflation.

Misguided stabilization policy. In a variant of the preceding theory, the government tries to hold the economy at potential national income by countering fluctuations in private-sector expenditure with offsetting changes of its own through spending and taxes. The government can, in principle, dampen such cyclical fluctuations by its stabilization policies. But unless it is very sophisticated, bad timing may accentuate rather than dampen fluctuations. We shall return to this possibility in subsequent chapters.

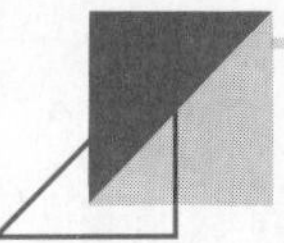

Securities Markets (Stock Markets)

Stock market values have sometimess displayed cumulative upward movements and at other times cumulative downward movements. The first are called *bull markets,* and the second are called *bear markets.* Most people also know that the Great Depression of the 1930s was preceded by the great stock market crash of 1929.

So an association between fluctuations in the stock market and in the economy is clear—but is there a causal connection? Do stock market booms contribute to business cycle booms, and do stock market slumps cause business cycle slumps? Before we can answer these questions, we need to learn a bit about such markets.

The Function of Securities Markets

When a household buys shares that have been newly issued by a company, it becomes one of the firm's owners. If, at some future date, the household wishes to cease being a shareholder in the firm, the firm will *not* repurchase the shares, except in the rare event that the firm is liquidated. If the household wishes to get its money back, it can only do so by persuading someone else to buy its shares in the company.

When a household buys a bond from a company, it becomes one of the firm's creditors. It cannot get its money back from the company before a specified date. For example, if you bought a 2010 bond in 1990, the bond would be redeemed by the company (i.e., the loan would be paid back) only in 2010. If you wished to get your money back sooner, all you could do would be to sell the bond to someone who was willing to become one of the company's creditors.

An organized market in which stocks and bonds are bought and sold is called a **securities market** or a **stock market**. The best known is probably the New York Stock Exchange. The biggest in Canada is the Toronto Stock Exchange (TSE). The trading of *existing* shares on the stock market indicates that ownership is being transferred; it does not indicate that companies are raising new money from the public, although firms also do raise funds by issuing new shares.

Securities markets are important because they allow people to put their savings into stocks and bonds that are not directly or quickly redeemable by their issuer.

For example, if I want to invest in a particular stock that I think will earn an attractive yield, I may do so, even though I know that I will want my money back after only a year. I can be confident that I will be able to sell the security a year from now. Nevertheless, although securities markets provide for the quick sale of stocks and bonds, they do not guarantee the price at which they can be sold. The price at any time is the one that equates the demand and supply for a particular security, and rapid fluctuations in stock prices are common.

Prices on the Stock Market

Figure 31-5 shows the wide swings in a well-known index of stock market prices, the Toronto Stock Exchange Industrial Composite Index. The most recent swing in the period covered in the figure began from a trough in September 1982 when the index was around 1,500. The index then rose, almost without interruption, until in early 1987 it reached a value of 3,740, a rise of 150 percent in just over four years. Then on Black Monday, October 19, 1987, it suffered a dramatic fall, losing 883 points. After continuing to fall for a number of weeks, the market then recovered steadily through mid 1989, climbing from below 2,900 to reach a new peak of 4,010 in July. On Black Friday, October 13, 1989, it again fell sharply but then recovered quickly, reaching 3,970 by the end of 1989.

This was only one in a series of "booms" and "busts" that have periodically interrupted the long-term trend for stock market prices to rise over the years. There had also been two large swings in the mid 1970s. Between 1979 and May 1981 the average stock price rose by 80 percent, yielding large gains for people who were wise or lucky enough to have bought at the beginning and sold at the end of this upswing. But then a downward movement occurred, with stock prices losing more than 30 percent of their value within a little over a year. Earlier, in 1973, stocks had lost 20 percent of their value and then recovered quite rapidly.

Commentators are often careless about making the key distinction between the *number of points* by which the index changes over some period and the *percentage* change in that index over the same period. For example, when the TSE Industrial Composite fell by just over 800 points from a value of 3,740 in two weeks in October 1987, newspaper reporters were quick to point out that this was one of the largest two-week falls ever, measured by the number of points. This was indeed a serious loss, and larger than many episodes, but the 25 percent that it represented is dwarfed by the loss everyone hopes will never be repeated: the more than 80 percent drop in stock values over the four-year period from 1929 to 1933!

Causes of Stock Market Swings

What causes such rapid gains and losses, and what do they have to do with business cycles?

When investors buy a company's stocks, they are buying rights to share in the stream of dividends to be paid out by that company. They are also buying an asset that they can sell in the future for a gain or a loss.

The value of that stock thus depends on two factors: first, what people expect the stream of future dividend payments to be and, second, what capital gains or losses people expect to realize when the stocks are sold. Both influences make dealing in stocks an inherently risky operation. Will the company in which people are investing pay high dividends in future years? Will the company's value rise so that these people can sell their shares for more than what they bought them for? The dividend policies of most established companies tend to be fairly stable, but stock prices are subject to wide swings.

The Influence of Present and Future Business Conditions

Many influences affect stock market prices; these include the state of the business cycle and the stance of government policies. Box 31-2 takes up the interesting possibility of self-reinforcing speculative booms.

Cyclical forces. If investors expect a firm's earnings to increase, the firm will become more valuable, and the price of its stock will rise. Such influences cause stock prices to move with the business cycle, being high when current profits are high and low when current profits are low. It also causes stock prices to vary with a host of factors that influence expectations

FIGURE 31-5 Fluctuations in an Index of Stock Prices, 1956–1990

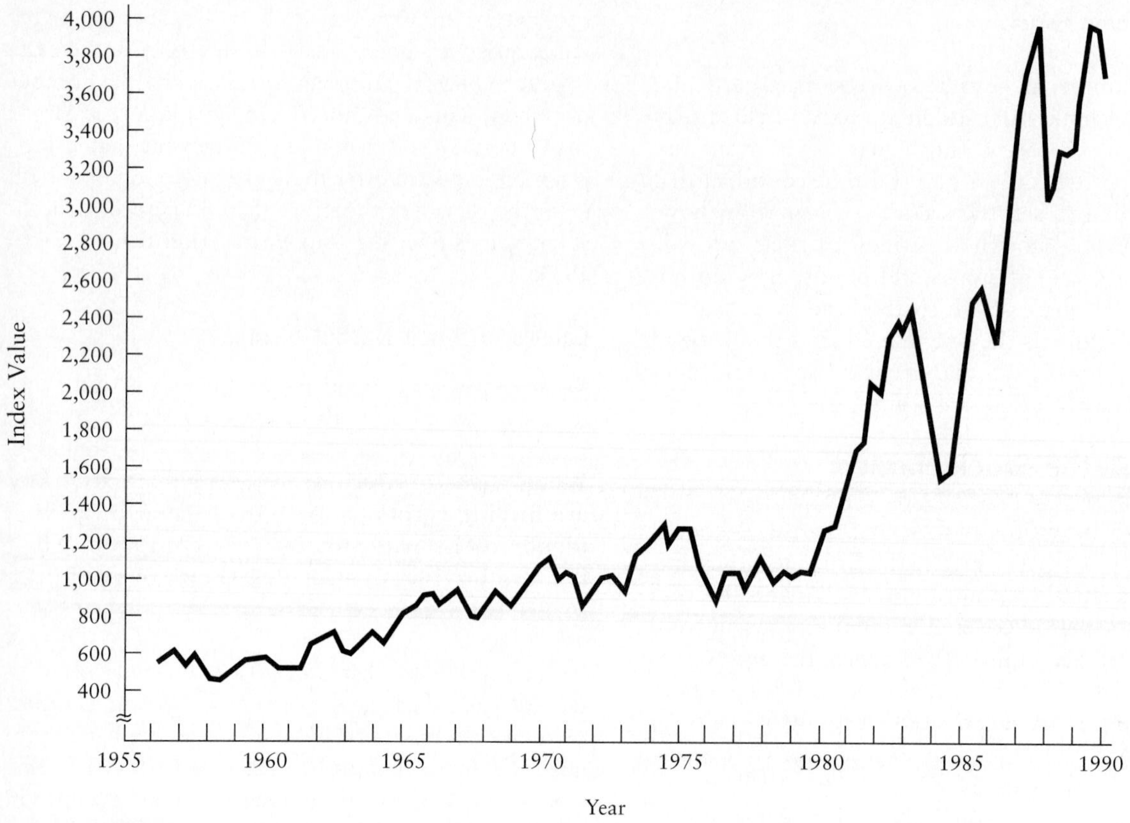

Stock market fluctuations are very sharp and irregular and have experienced a significant increase. The graph shows quarterly variations in the Toronto Stock Exchange Industrial Composite Index. The index showed an upward trend from 1958 to 1976. However, it did fluctuate sharply, and it is these fluctuations that make large speculative gains and losses possible. Two notable falls in the index occurred during economic downturns in 1970.

The market began to rise again in 1980, and after one major interruption in 1985, it reached just over 3,700 at the beginning of 1987 and then fell dramatically in late October to under 3,000. It climbed to a new peak of 4,010 in mid 1989 before suffering another October setback. Note that because the index is plotted on an arithmetic scale, equal percentage fluctuations look larger the higher the index is.

of future profits. A poor crop, destruction of trees by acid rain, an announcement of new defense spending, a change in the foreign exchange value of the dollar, or a change in the political complexion of the administration can all affect profit expectations and hence stock prices.

Policy factors. We shall see later in this book that major changes in monetary policy can cause major changes in interest rates. Such changes, or just the expectation of them, will have major effects on stock prices. Suppose that interest rates rise rapidly. Investors will see that they can now earn an increased amount by holding government bonds. As a result, they will wish to alter their investment portfolios to hold more bonds and fewer stocks. Everyone cannot do this, however, since only so many stocks and bonds are available to be held at any given time. As all investors try to sell their stocks, prices fall. The fall will stop only when the expected rate of return to investment in stocks, based on their lower purchase price, makes stocks as attractive as bonds. Then investors will no longer try to shift out of bonds *en masse*.

Stock Market Swings: Cause or Effect of Business Cycles?

Stock markets tend often to lead, and sometimes to follow, booms and slumps in business activity. In both cases the causes usually run from real business conditions, whether actual or anticipated, to stock market prices. This is the dominant theme, the stock market as a reflector.

Stock market fluctuations are more typically a consequence than a cause of the business cycle.

It is also possible for the stock market to be a causal factor in the business cycle. The value of the stock market influences the wealth of households, which ultimately own the stocks, either directly or through their pension funds. Thus stock prices can be expected to influence their consumption spending. (Recall the wealth effect from Chapter 28; see Figure 28-2.) Firms also use the stock market to issue new shares in order to finance investment spending; when stock market prices are low, they find this an unattractive way to raise new money and thus may choose to cancel, or at least postpone, investments. As a result, many people believed that the dramatic fall in stock values that were experienced in the October 1987 crash would cause households to curtail their consumption spending in response to their perceived fall in wealth. On this basis many forecasters predicted that the stock market fall of Black Monday would lead to a serious downturn in the economy. After the event, such gloom-and-doom forecasts turned out to be inaccurate; apparently, people did not perceive the fall in the stock market as an indication that their permanent incomes or wealth had fallen dramatically and hence did not reduce their consumption spending.

In many cases the stock market and the business cycle both reflect the common influence of other factors. For example, stock markets often react to changes in interest rates that may be caused by government policy; as we have seen, such interest-rate changes can also play a causal role in cyclical fluctuations in the economy. Typically, the stock market responds more quickly than the economy to such influences, and for this reason many observers look to it as a "leading indicator" of likely future economic developments.

The relationship between the stock market and the economy is further complicated by the existence of occasional speculative booms and busts. There are often real economic forces influencing expectations of stock prices, but, at least for a while, the prices may become dominated by speculative psychology. (This is discussed in Box 31-2.) Unfortunately, speculative behavior causes the stock market to react to many events that turn out to have little or no enduring implications for the economy. As one wag put it, the stock market has predicted seven out of the last two recessions!

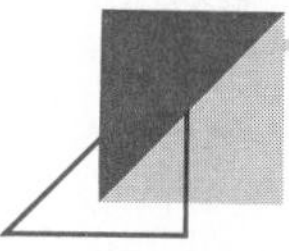

Causes of Business Cycles: A Consensus View?

Economists have debated long and bitterly about the "best" explanation of the recurrent cyclical behavior of the economy.

Today most economists agree that there is no single cause to which all business cycles can be attributed.

In an economy that has tendencies for both cumulative and self-reversing behavior, any large shock, from without or from within, can initiate a cyclical swing. Wars are important, and so are major technical innovations. A rapid increase in interest rates and a general tightening of credit can cause a sharp decrease in investment. Expectations can be changed by a political campaign or by a development in another part of the world. The list of possible impulses, autonomous or induced, is long.

It is probably true that the characteristic cyclical pattern involves many outside shocks that sometimes initiate, sometimes reinforce, and sometimes dampen the economy's cumulative tendencies.

Cycles differ also in terms of their structure. There are variations in timing, duration, and amplitude. In some cycles full employment of labor may

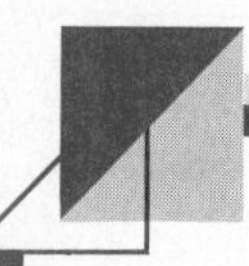

BOX 31-2

Speculative Booms

In addition to responding to a host of factors that influence the earnings of companies, stock prices often develop an upward or downward movement of their own, propelled by little more than speculation that feeds on itself.

In major stock market booms, people begin to expect rising stock prices and hurry to buy while stocks are cheap. This action bids up the prices of shares and creates the capital gains that justify the original expectations. This is an example of *self-realizing expectations.* Investors get rich on paper, in the sense that the market value of their holdings rises. Making money now looks easy to others, who also rush in to buy stocks, pushing up prices still further. Attention to current earnings all but ceases. If a stock can yield, say, a 50 percent capital gain in one year, it does not matter much if the current earnings represent only a small percentage yield on the purchase price of the stocks. Everyone is "making money," and their attempts to buy bid up prices still further. In such speculative booms, current earnings represent an ever-diminishing percentage yield on the current price of the stocks.

Investors may buy stocks on margin, that is, borrow money to buy them, using the stocks themselves as security for the loans. In doing this, many investors may be borrowing money at a rate of interest that is considerably in excess of the yield from current dividends. Suppose that $50,000 is borrowed at 10 percent (interest payments are $5,000 per year) to buy stocks yielding a current dividend return of only 4 percent (dividend receipts are $2,000 per year). Never mind, says the investor's logic, for the stocks can be sold in a year or so for a handsome capital gain that will more than repay the $3,000 of interest not covered by dividends. Some people have the luck or good judgment to sell out near the top of the market, and they actually make money. Others wait eagerly for ever-greater capital gains, and in the meantime they get richer and richer—on paper.

Eventually, something breaks the period of unrestrained optimism. Some investors may begin to worry about the very high prices of stocks in relation not only to current yields but also to possible future yields, even when generous allowances for growth are made. Or the prices of stocks may fall slightly when some people try to sell in order to realize their capital gains. As they offer their securities on the market, they cannot find purchasers without some fall in prices. Even a modest price fall may be sufficient to persuade others that it is time to sell. However, every share that is sold must be bought by someone. A wave of sellers may not find new buyers at existing prices, causing prices to fall. Panic selling may then occur.

A household that borrowed $50,000 to buy stock near the top of the market may find the paper value of its holdings sliding below $50,000. How will it repay its loan? The household may sell now before it loses too much, or its broker may "sell the customer out" to liquidate the loan. This causes prices to fall even further and provides another example of self-realizing expectations. If enough people think that prices are going to come down, their attempt to sell out at the present high prices will create the fall in prices, the expectations of which caused the selling.

be the bottleneck that determines the peak. In others high interest rates and shortages of investment funds may nip an expansion and turn it into a recession at the same time that the unemployment of labor is still an acute problem. In some cycles the recession phase is short; in others a full-scale period of stagnation sets in. In some cycles the peak develops into a severe bout of inflation; in others the pressure of excess demand is hardly felt, and a new recession sets in before the economy has recovered fully from the last

This is a very simple and stylized description of a speculative cycle, yet it describes the basic elements of market booms and busts that have recurred throughout stock market history. The biggest boom of all began in the mid 1920s and ended on Black Tuesday, October 29, 1929. The collapse was dramatic, with stocks losing about one-half of their value in about two months. Nor did it stop there. For three long years stock prices continued to decline, until the average value of stock sold on the New York Stock Exchange had fallen from its 1929 high of $89.10 per share to $17.35 per share by late 1933. It also happened, although less dramatically, in the booms and busts of the 1970s and 1980s.

Speculative behavior means that stock market prices do not always just reflect the fundamentals that underlie the expected profitability of companies; in this sense, the stock market is sometimes said to be overvalued or undervalued. However, the extent of the overvaluation or undervaluation is very hard to determine, and hence it is hard to predict when prices will "correct" and by how much. For example, consider the long upswing that more than doubled stock prices in just over three years between early 1984 and October 1987. At the time the economy enjoyed a very strong recovery, and the rising stock prices no doubt reflected the resulting favorable profit outlook of companies. However, many observers doubted that the full increase was justified by underlying business opportunities and hence felt that there may have been a speculative component to the rise in stock values. These people argued that the dramatic fall that occurred on Black Monday represented a "correction" that removed much of the speculative component from the prices. Of course, this is easy to say after the fact. If any of us had known in advance when and by how much prices would correct, we would have been able to make a huge profit.

Stock Markets: Marketplaces or Casinos?

Stock markets fulfill many important functions. It is doubtful that the great aggregations of capital that are needed to finance modern firms could be raised under a private-ownership system without them. There is no doubt, however, that they also provide an unfortunate attraction for many naive investors, whose get-rich-quick dreams are more often than not destroyed by the fall in prices that follows the occasional speculative booms that they help to create.

To some extent public policy has sought to curb the excesses of stock market speculation through supervision of security issues. This is an area of complex overlap between federal and provincial jurisdiction. Public policy seeks, among other things, to prevent both fraudulent or misleading information and trading by "insiders" (people in a company who have confidential information). Moreover, the regulators can limit the ability of speculators to trade on margin.

All in all, the stock market is both a real marketplace and a place to gamble. As in all gambling situations, players who are less well informed and less clever than the average player tend to be losers in the long term.

trough. Some cycles are long in duration; others are short.

In this chapter we have suggested reasons why an economy that is subjected to periodic external shocks will tend to generate a continually changing pattern of fluctuations, as cumulative and then self-reversing forces alternatively come into play. In the next chapter we shall study how governments seek to influence the cycle and remove some of its extremes through the use of fiscal policy.

SUMMARY

1. The economy experiences continual change. Long-term change represents what is referred to as economic growth; short-term fluctuations are referred to as the business cycle.
2. Most theories of the business cycle hold that short-term fluctuations in GDP are usually, though not always, the result of variations in aggregate demand. Overall, these fluctuations show a fairly clear pattern that is described as cyclical. Despite the overall pattern, the evidence is that the cycles are irregular in amplitude, in timing, and in duration, as well as in the way in which they affect particular industries and sectors of the economy.
3. Any explanation of the business cycle must explain both *why* income fluctuates and *how* those fluctuations get transformed into cycles.
4. Shifts in consumption, government purchases, and net export expenditures cause fluctuations in aggregate demand and hence in national income and employment.
5. Changes in investment expenditure are a major source of fluctuations in national income. The three principal components of private investment are changes in business inventories, residential housing construction, and business fixed investment. The interest rate is an important determinant of investment spending.
6. Changes in business inventories often account for an important fraction of the year-to-year changes in the level of investment. They respond both to changes in the level of production and sales and to the rate of interest.
7. Residential housing construction shows a cyclical pattern of its own. House building varies directly with the level of national income and inversely with the rate of interest.
8. Business fixed investment depends on a number of variables. These include innovation, expectations about the future, level of profits, rate of interest, and changes in national income.
9. There are several explanations for the cyclical pattern of economic fluctuations. They all involve either lags, which transform random shocks into cyclical responses, or theories of systematic behavior of spending patterns. The latter can apply both to private consumption and investment expenditure and to government purchases.
10. Securities (stock) markets allow firms to raise new capital from the sale of newly issued securities and allow the holders of existing securities to sell their securities to other investors. Prices on the stock market tend to reflect the public's expectations, both of firms' future earnings and of future changes in prices (for whatever reason). This necessarily gives a strong speculative dimension to security prices, and large speculative swings do occur. Such swings can be accentuated by the phenomenon of self-realizing expectations.

TOPICS FOR REVIEW

Economic growth and business cycles
Causes of fluctuations in GDP
Components of investment
Causes of cyclical fluctuations
Political business cycle
The stock market

DISCUSSION QUESTIONS

1. How and in what direction might each of the following shift the function relating consumption expenditure to disposable income?
   a. Introduction of free dental care
   b. A change in attitudes so that we become a nation of conspicuous conservers rather than conspicuous consumers, taking pride in how little we eat or spend for housing, clothing, and so on
   c. Increases in income taxes
   d. News that due to radical new medical advances, everyone can count on more years of retirement than ever before
   e. A spreading belief that all-out nuclear war is likely within the next 10 years
   f. Sharp increases in the down payments required on durable goods
2. Suppose that the government wished to reduce private investment in order to reduce an inflationary gap. What policies might it adopt? If it wished to do so in such a way as to have a major effect on residential housing and a minor effect on plant and equipment expenditures, which measures might it use?
3. What effect on total investment—and on which categories of investment—would you predict as a result of each of the following?
   a. Widespread endorsement of zero population growth by young couples
   b. A sharp increase in the frequency and duration of strikes in the transportation industries
   c. Forecasts of very low growth rates of real national income over the next five years
   d. Tax reform that introduces deductions for property taxes in computing taxable personal income
4. When interest rates rose sharply during the early 1980s, home construction fell dramatically, but sales of mobile homes increased. How do these changes relate to the notion that investment responds to the rate of interest?
5. Empirical studies show that as the volume of a firm's sales increases, the size of its inventories of raw materials tends to increase in proportion. It is common for business firms to speak of such inventories in terms of "a 20-day supply of coal" rather than "52,000 tons of coal" or "$280,000 worth of coal." Why should relative size be more important than absolute quantity or dollar value?
6. Which "cause" of business investment is being relied on in each of the following quotes?
   a. An aluminum industry spokesman, justifying a 50-cent-per-pound increase in aluminum prices: "We must have it to build the new capacity we need."
   b. Bethlehem Steel, in a newspaper ad: "We need lower taxes, not cheaper money or government deficits, to help lower barriers to capital formation."
   c. "The government used a credit crunch to bring on a recession and reduce inflation."
7. Since different series behave differently, does it make sense to talk about a business cycle? Predict the comparative behavior of the following pairs of series in relation to fluctuations in GDP.
   a. Purchases of food and purchases of consumer durables
   b. Tax receipts and bankruptcies
   c. Unemployment and birthrates
   d. Employment in Halifax and employment in Oshawa

   Check your predictions against the facts for the past decade.

Appendix to Chapter 31

The Accelerator Theory of Investment

According to the accelerator theory, usually called the **accelerator**, investment is related to the rate of change of national income. When income is increasing, it is necessary to invest in order to increase the capacity to produce consumption goods; when income is falling, it may not even be necessary to replace old capital as it wears out, let alone to invest in new capital.

The main insight that the accelerator theory provides is the emphasis on the role of net investment as a phenomenon of *disequilibrium*—the situation in which the actual stock of capital goods differs from what firms and households would like it to be. Anything that changes the desired size of the capital stock can generate investment. The accelerator focuses on one such source of change, changing national income. This gives the accelerator its particular importance in connection with *fluctuations* in national income. As we shall see, it can itself contribute to those fluctuations.

How the Accelerator Works

To see how the accelerator theory works, suppose that a particular capital stock is needed to produce each given level of an industry's output. The ratio of the value of capital to the annual value of output is called the **capital-output ratio**. Suppose that the industry is producing at capacity and that the demand for its product increases. If the industry is to produce the higher level of output, its capital stock must increase. This necessitates new investment.

Table 31A-1 provides a simple numerical example of the accelerator theory of investment. Working through the data step by step leads to three conclusions:

1. **Rising rather than high levels of sales are needed to call forth net investment.**
2. **For net investment to remain constant, sales must rise by a constant amount per year.**
3. **The amount of net investment will be a multiple of the increase in sales because the capital-output ratio is greater than one.**[1]

The data in Table 31A-1 are for a single industry, but if many industries behave in this way, one would expect aggregate net investment to bear a similar relationship to changes in national income. This is what the accelerator theory predicts. **[38]**

The accelerator theory says nothing directly about replacement investment, but it does have implications for such investment. When sales are constant (no net investment required), replacement investment will be required to maintain the capital stock at the desired level. When sales are increasing from a position of full capacity, both net investment and replacement investment will be required. When sales are falling, not only will net investment be zero, but also there will be a tendency to reduce replacement investment.

Limitations of the Accelerator

Taken literally, the accelerator posits a rigid response of investment to changes in sales (and thus, aggregatively, to changes in national income). In fact, the relationship is more subtle.

Changes in sales that are thought to be temporary will not necessarily lead to new investment. It is usually possible to increase the level of output for a given capital stock by working overtime or extra shifts. Although this solution would be more expensive per unit of output in the long run, it is usually preferable to making investments in new plants and equipment that would lie idle after a temporary spurt of demand had subsided. Thus expectations about what the required capital stock will be may lead to a much less rigid response of investment to income than the accelerator suggests.

Another limitation of the accelerator theory is that it takes a limited view of what constitutes investment. The fixed capital-output ratio emphasizes investment in what economists called **capital wid-**

[1] In the example in Table 31A-1, the capital-output ratio is 5:1. It is not unreasonable to spend $5 to purchase a machine that produces only $1 of output *per year*, provided that the machine will last enough years to repay the $5 plus a reasonable return on this investment.

TABLE 31A-1 An Illustration of the Accelerator Theory of Investment

(1) Year	(2) Annual sales	(3) Changes in sales	(4) Required stock of capital, assuming a capital-output ratio of 5:1	(5) Net investment: increase in required capital stock
1	$10	$0	$ 50	$ 0
2	10	0	50	0
3	11	1	55	5
4	13	2	65	10
5	16	3	80	15
6	19	3	95	15
7	22	3	110	15
8	24	2	120	10
9	25	1	125	5
10	25	0	125	0

With a fixed capital-output ratio, net investment occurs only when it is necessary to increase the stock of capital in order to change output. Assume that it takes $5 of capital to produce $1 of output per year. In years 1 and 2 there is no need for investment. In year 3 a rise in sales of $1 requires investment of $5 to provide the needed capital stock. In year 4 a further rise of $2 in sales requires an additional investment of $10 to provide the needed capital stock. As columns 3 and 5 show, the amount of net investment is proportional to the *change* in sales. When the increase in sales tapers off in years 7–9, investment declines. When sales no longer increase in year 10, net investment falls to zero because the capital stock of year 9 is adequate to provide output for year 10's sales.

ening, the investment in additional capacity that uses the same ratio of capital to labor as existing capacity. It does not explain **capital deepening**, which is the increase in the amount of capital per unit of labor that occurs, say, in response to a fall in the rate of interest. Neither does the theory say anything about investments that have been brought about as a result of new processes or new products. Furthermore, it does not allow for the fact that investment in any period is likely to be limited by the capacity of the capital-goods industry.

For these and other reasons, the accelerator does not by itself give anything like a complete explanation of variations in business fixed investment. It should not be surprising that a simple accelerator theory provides a relatively poor overall explanation of changes in investment. Yet accelerator-like influence do exist, and empirical evidence continues to suggest that they play a role in the cyclical variability of investment.

Chapter 32

An Introduction to Fiscal Policy

As we have seen, national income fluctuates continually, primarily due to shifts in aggregate demand and short-run aggregate supply. **Fiscal policy** involves the use of government spending and tax policies to pursue any of the government's many objectives. In this chapter we focus on the use of spending and tax policies, which we call *policy variables*, to influence the *AD* curve and, to a lesser degree, the *SRAS* curve. This is sometimes done in order to dampen fluctuations in the economy.

Any policy that attempts to stabilize national income at or near a desired level (usually potential national income) is called **stabilization policy**. This chapter deals first with the theory of fiscal policy as a tool of stabilization policy and then with the experience of using it.

Since government expenditure increases aggregate demand and taxation decreases it, the *direction* of the required changes in spending and taxation is generally easy to determine once we know the direction of the desired change in national income. However, the *timing*, *magnitude*, and *mixture* of the changes pose more difficult questions.

There is no doubt that the government can exert a major influence on national income. Prime examples are the massive military spending during major wars. During World War II the Canadian government's expenditures rose from 12.2 percent of national income in 1939 to 41.8 percent in 1944. At the same time, the unemployment rate fell from 11.4 percent to 1.4 percent. Economists agree that the increase in government spending helped bring about the fall in unemployment and the associated rise in GDP. Similar experiences occurred in the United States and most European countries before or immediately following the outbreak of the war in 1939.

When used appropriately, fiscal policy can be an important tool for stabilizing the economy. In the heyday of fiscal policy, from 1945 to late 1965, many economists were convinced that the economy could be adequately stabilized just by varying the size of the government's taxes and expenditures. That day is past. Today most economists are aware of the limitations of fiscal policy.

Fiscal Policy and the Budget

Changes in government expenditure and tax policies have financial implications for the government. As a result, fiscal policy is often referred to as the government's *budgetary policy* or simply as the *budget*.

• KEY IDEAS IN •
MACROECONOMICS

This section provides important diagrams and captions from the text as reminders of basic economic concepts at a glance. If you need to refresh your memory concerning a principle being shown here, look in the appropriate chapter for a full explanation.

CHAPTER 28 Shifts in the *AE* Curve

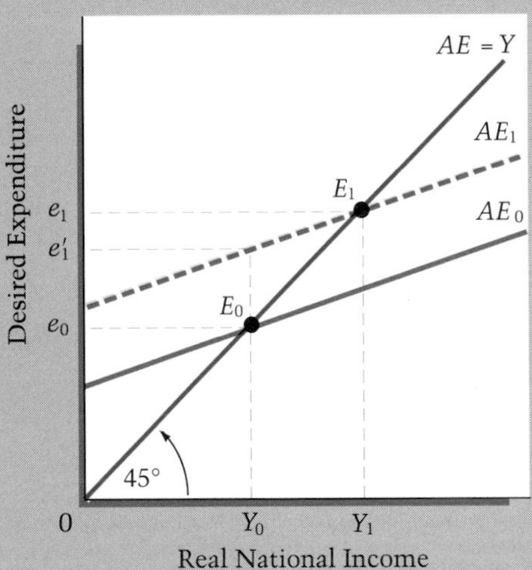

(i) A parallel shift in *AE*

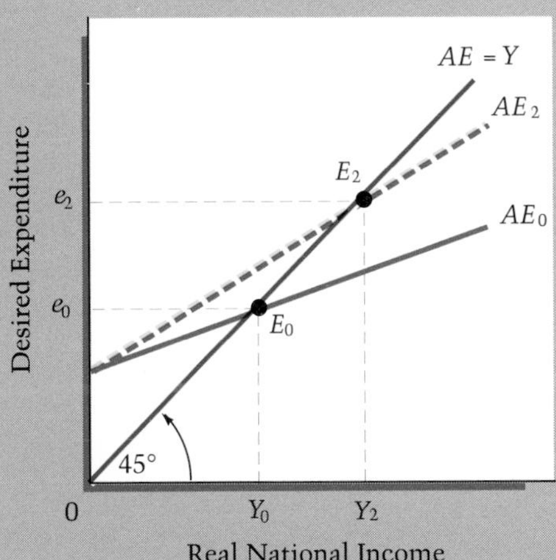

(ii) A change in the slope of *AE*

Upward shifts in the *AE* curve increase equilibrium income; downward shifts in the *AE* curve decrease equilibrium income.

CHAPTER 29 The *AD* Curve and the *AE* Curve

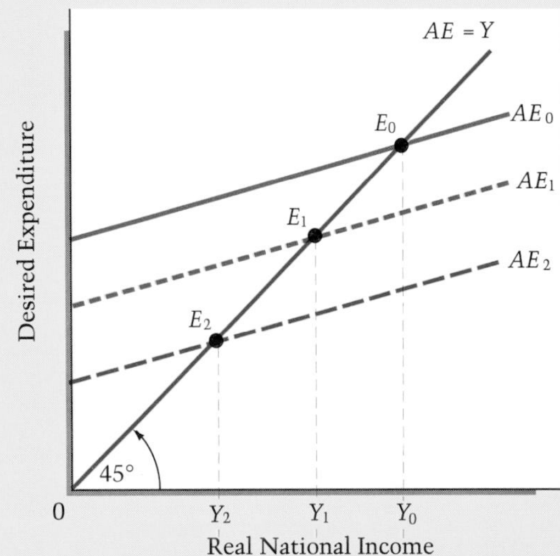

(i) Aggregate expenditure

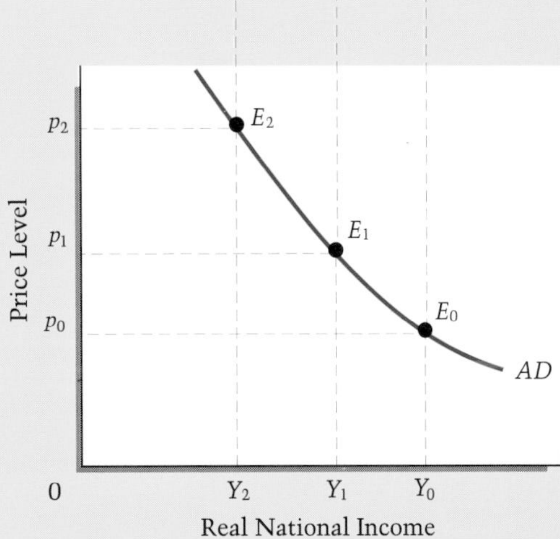

(ii) Aggregate demand

Equilibrium income is determined by the *AE* curve for each given price level; the level of income and its associated price level are then plotted to yield the *AD* curve.

CHAPTER 29 The Simple Multiplier and Shifts in the *AD* Curve

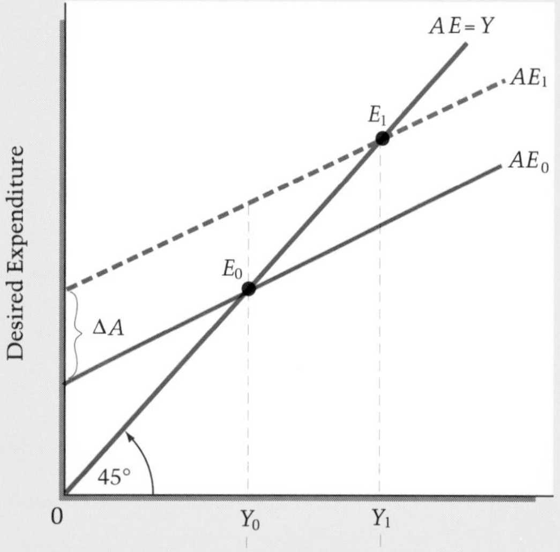

(i) Aggregate expenditure

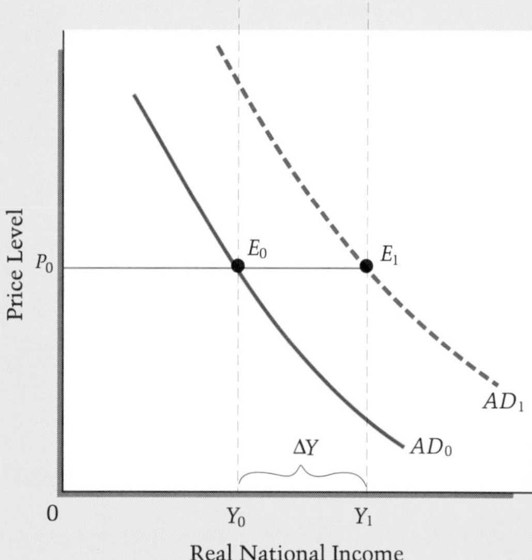

(ii) Aggregate demand

A change in autonomous expenditure changes equilibrium national income for any given price level. The simple multiplier measures the resulting horizontal shift in the aggregate demand curve.

CHAPTER 29 Macroeconomic Equilibrium

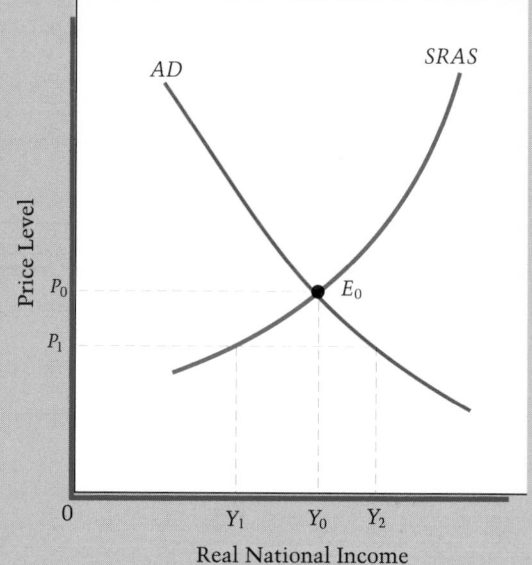

Macroeconomic equilibrium occurs at the intersection of the *AD* and *SRAS* curves and determines the equilibrium values for national income and the price level.

CHAPTER 29 The *AE* Curve and the Multiplier When the Price Level Varies

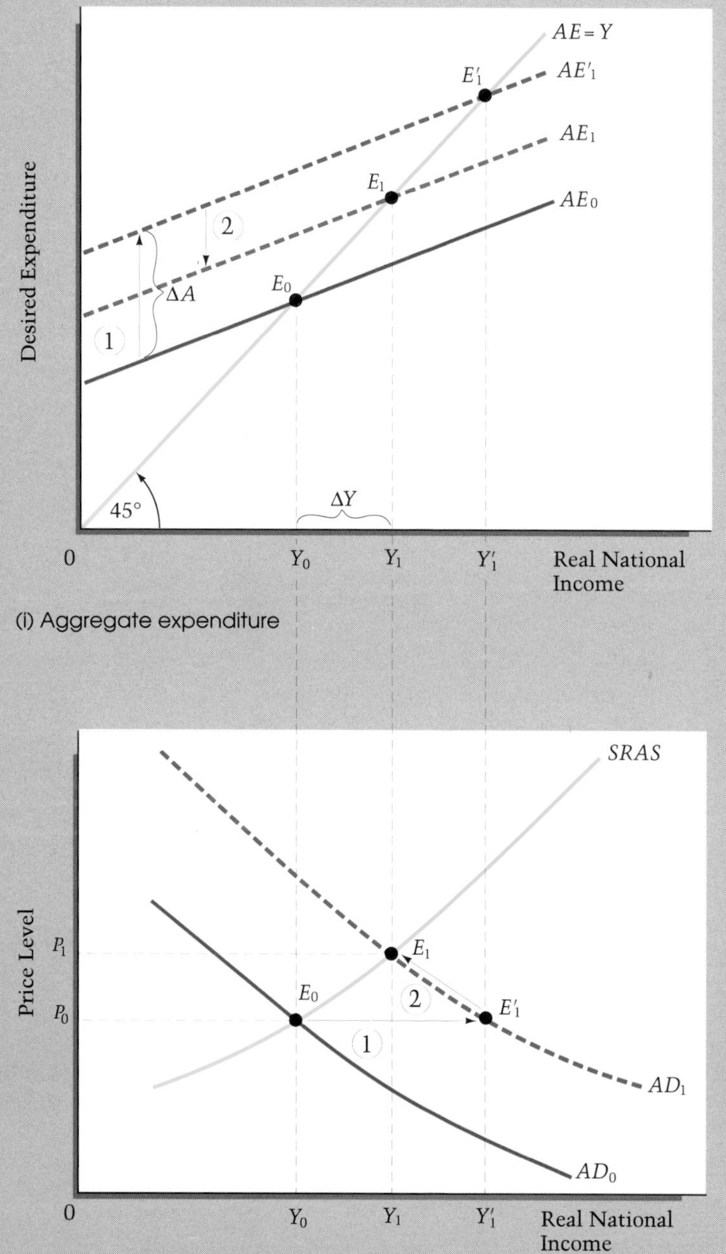

An increase in autonomous expenditures causes the *AE* curve to shift upward, but the rise in the price level causes it to shift part of the way down again. Hence, the multiplier effect on income is smaller than when the price level is constant.

CHAPTER 31 Three Sources of Increases in National Income

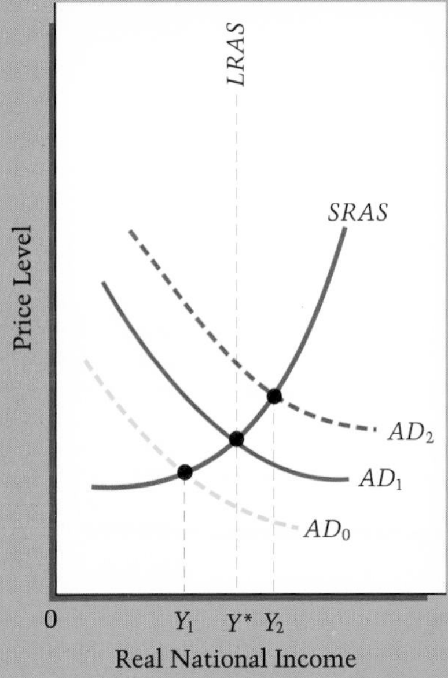

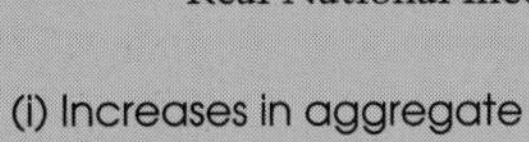
(i) Increases in aggregate demand

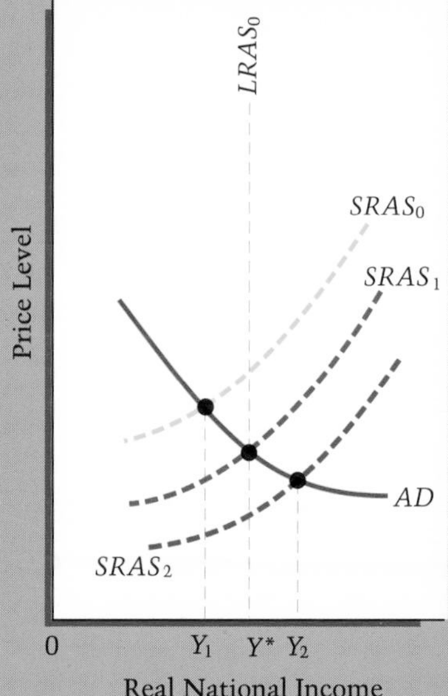

(ii) Temporary increases in short-run aggregate supply

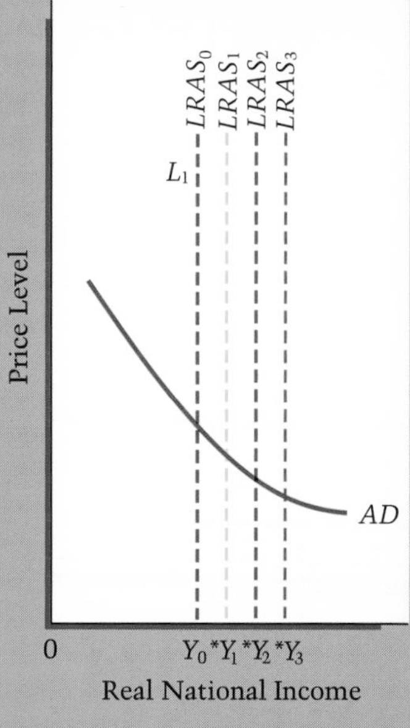

(iii) Permanent increases in long-run aggregate supply

National income will increase in response to an increase in aggregate demand or an increase in aggregate supply. The increase will be permanent if the *LRAS* curve shifts, but, if the *LRAS* curve does not shift, any divergences of actual GDP from potential GDP will only be temporary.

The Budget Balance

The **budget balance** is the difference between total government revenue and total government expenditure. In this definition *government expenditure* includes both transfer payments and purchases of currently produced goods and services.

The budget balance is the difference between government *budget receipts* (the money it takes in as revenue) and government *budget outlays* (the money it pays out).

If receipts are exactly equal to outlays, the government has a **balanced budget**. If receipts exceed outlays, there is a **budget surplus**; if receipts are less than outlays, there is a **budget deficit**. Changes in either government spending or tax policies influence the budget balance. If the government raises its outlays without raising taxes, the extra expenditure is said to be *deficit-financed*. If the extra outlays are accompanied by an increase in tax rates that yields an increase in receipts equal to the increase in outlays, we speak of a *balanced budget* change in spending.

When the government spends more than it raises, where does the money come from? If the government raises more than it spends, where does the money go? The difference between expenditure and current revenue shows up as changes in the government's debt, referred to as the **national debt**. A deficit requires that the government borrow money by selling financial instruments, usually referred to as *government bonds*.[1] A surplus allows the government to reduce its debt; it can use its excess tax revenue to redeem some of its outstanding bonds.

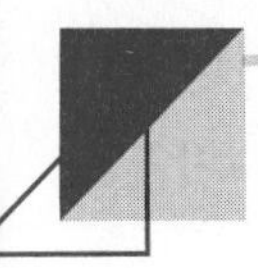

The Theory of Fiscal Policy

Since the stabilization objective of fiscal policy is to remove any existing output gaps, the appropriate fiscal policies appear quite straightforward. All that is needed is a once-and-for-all fiscal change that will shift the *AD* curve in the appropriate direction to remove the output gap.

The Basic Theory of Fiscal Stabilization

A reduction in tax rates or an increase in government expenditure shifts the *AD* curve to the right, causing an increase in GDP. An increase in tax rates or a cut in government expenditure shifts the *AD* curve to the left, causing a decrease in GDP. (For discussion, see Figures 29-8 and 29-9.)

A more detailed look at what is involved will provide a useful review. It will also help to show what complications might make the policy decisions more difficult.

A recessionary gap. The removal of a recessionary gap is illustrated in Figure 32-1. There are three possible ways in which the gap may be removed.

First, the recessionary gap may eventually drive wages and other factor prices down by enough to shift the *SRAS* curve to the right and thereby reinstate full employment and potential income (at a lower price level). The evidence is, however, that this process takes a substantial period of time.

Second, the natural cyclical forces of the economy could induce a demand-side recovery for the reasons spelled out in Chapter 30 (see page 640). This would cause the *AD* curve to shift rightward, moving the economy back toward full employment and potential income. The evidence is that such recoveries do occur. Often they happen quickly; sometimes, however, a recession can be both deep and prolonged.

Third, government expenditure can be increased or taxes can be cut in order to shift the *AD* curve to the right. The advantage of using fiscal policy is that it may substantially shorten what would otherwise be a long recession. One disadvantage is that it may stimulate the economy just before private-sector spending recovers due to natural causes. If it does, the economy may overshoot its potential output, and an inflationary gap may open up.

An inflationary gap. Figure 32-2 shows the three ways in which an inflationary gap can be removed.

First, wages and other factor prices may be pushed up by the excess demand. This will shift the *SRAS* curve to the left, eventually eliminating the gap, reducing income to its potential level, and raising the price level.

Second, a cyclical reduction in aggregate demand

[1] A wide variety of financial instruments is used. Some, called treasury bills, are short-term, promising to repay a stated amount at some specified date between 90 days and 1 year from the date of issue. A government *bond* represents a promise to pay a stated sum of money in the more distant future—as much as 25 years from the date of issue. We shall learn more about these in Chapter 34.

FIGURE 32-1 Removal of a Recessionary Gap

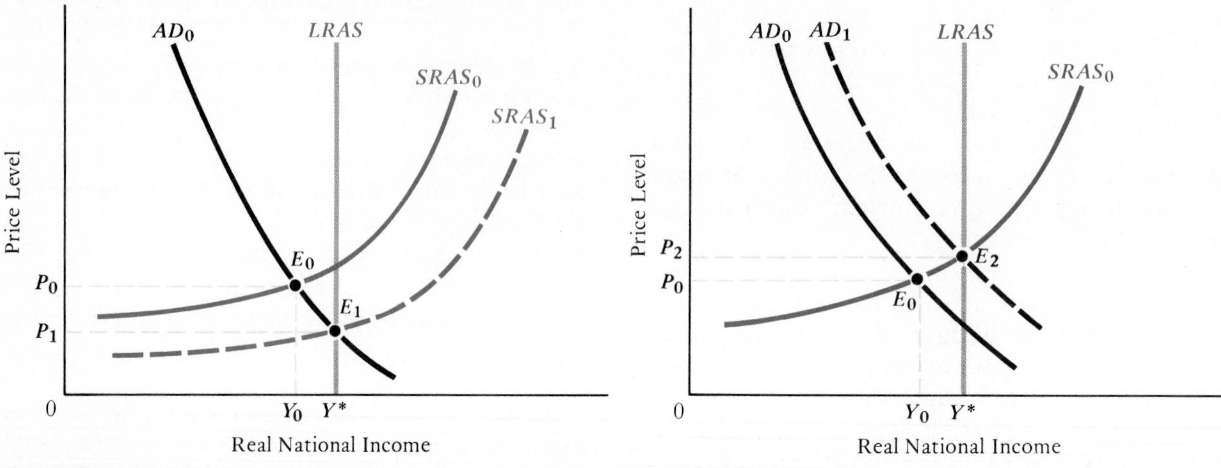

(i) A recessionary gap removed by a rightward shift in ***SRAS*** (ii) A recessionary gap removed by a rightward shift in ***AD***

A recessionary gap may be removed by a (slow) rightward shift of the *SRAS* curve, a natural revival of private-sector demand, or a fiscal policy–induced increase in aggregate demand. Initially, equilibrium is at E_0, with national income at Y_0 and the price level at P_0. The recessionary gap is Y_0Y^*.

As shown in (i), the gap might be removed by a shift of the *SRAS* curve to $SRAS_1$. This increase in aggregate supply could occur as a result of reductions in wage rates and other input prices. The shift of the *SRAS* curve causes a movement down and to the right along AD_0. This establishes a new equilibrium at E_1, achieving potential income, Y^*, and lowering the price level to P_1.

As shown in (ii), the gap might also be removed by a shift of the *AD* curve to AD_1. This increase in aggregate demand could occur either because of a natural revival of private-sector expenditure or because of a fiscal policy–induced increase in expenditure. The shift of the *AD* curve causes a movement up and to the right along $SRAS_0$. This shifts the equilibrium to E_2, taking income to Y^* and the price level to P_2.

may occur for the reasons outlined in Chapter 29. This might reduce income to its potential level without the rise in the price level that is associated with a shift of the *SRAS* curve. However, unless aggregate demand declines quickly, rising wages and other input prices will lead to a shift of the *SRAS* curve to the left and hence to rising prices.

Third, the government, by raising taxes or cutting spending, may reduce aggregate demand sufficiently to remove the inflationary gap. The advantage of this approach is that it avoids the inflationary increase in prices that accompanies the first method. One disadvantage is that if private-sector expenditures fall due to natural causes, national income may be pushed below potential, thus opening up a recessionary gap.

A key proposition. When the automatic adjustment mechanisms either fail to operate quickly enough or give rise to undesirable side effects such as rising prices, fiscal policy can play a potentially stabilizing role.

Government taxes and expenditure, by shifting the *AD* curve, can be used to remove persistent output gaps.

The Paradox of Thrift

Government tax revenues are related to the performance of the economy; they are high during booms and low during slumps. Thus if a government follows a balanced budget policy, its spending becomes

FIGURE 32-2 Removal of an Inflationary Gap

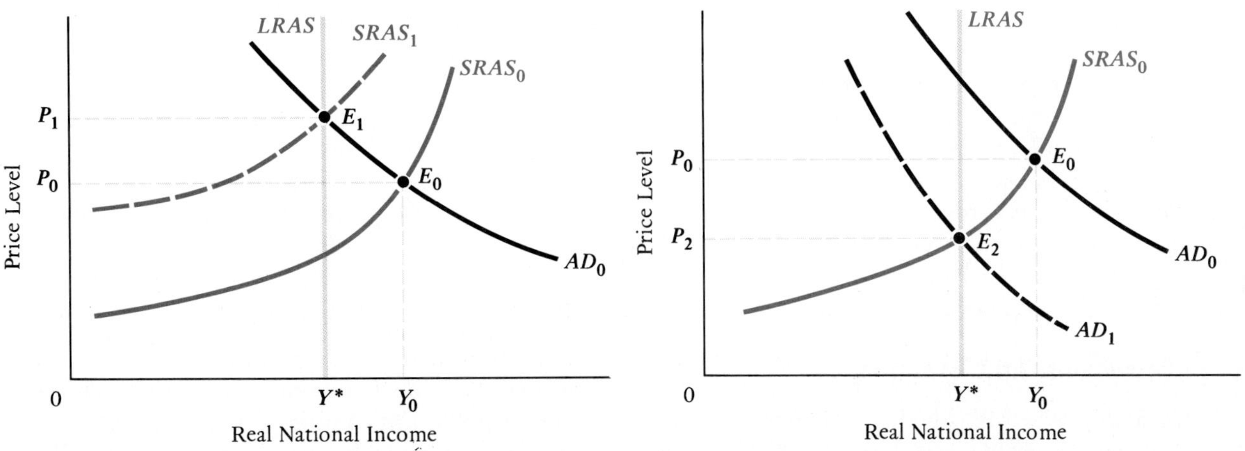

(i) An inflationary gap removed by a leftward shift in *SRAS*

(ii) An inflationary gap removed by a leftward shift in *AD*

An inflationary gap may be removed by a leftward shift of the *SRAS* curve, a natural reduction in private-sector demand, or a policy-induced reduction in aggregate demand. Initially, equilibrium is at E_0, with national income at Y_0 and the price level at P_0. The inflationary gap is Y^*Y_0.

As shown in (i), the gap might be removed by a shift of the *SRAS* curve to $SRAS_1$. This decrease in aggregate supply could occur as a result of increases in wage rates and other input prices. The shift of the *SRAS* curve causes a movement up and to the left along AD_0. This establishes a new equilibrium at E_1, reducing income to its potential level, Y^*, and raising the price level to P_1.

As shown in (ii), the gap might also be removed by a shift of the *AD* curve to AD_1. This decrease in aggregate demand could occur either because of a natural fall in private spending or because of contractionary fiscal policy. The shift of the *AD* curve causes a movement down and to the left along $SRAS_0$. This shifts the equilibrium to E_2, taking income to Y^* and the price level to P_2

procyclical. It will restrict its spending during a recession because its tax revenue is low, and it will increase its spending during a recovery when its tax revenue is rising. In other words, it rolls with the economy, raising and lowering its spending in step with everyone else.

Many people believe that a prudent government should always balance its budget. This view is based on an analogy with what seems to be prudent behavior for the individual household. It is a foolish household whose current expenditure exceeds its current revenue for a prolonged period so that it goes steadily further into debt. From this commonsense observation, some people argue that if balancing the budget is good for the individual, it must also be good for the nation. The *paradox of thrift*, however, suggests that the analogy between the government and the household may be misleading.

The theory of national income, developed in Chapters 26 through 30, predicts that if all spending units in the economy simultaneously try to increase the amount that they save, the combined increase in thrift will shift the *AD* curve to the left and hence *reduce* the equilibrium level of income.[2] The contrary case, a general decrease in thrift and increase in expenditure, shifts the *AD* curve to the right and hence increases national income. This prediction is known as the *paradox of thrift*.[3]

The policy implication of this prediction is that

[2] Indeed, income may fall enough that total savings falls, even though everyone's propensity to save has risen!

[3] The prediction is in fact not a paradox. It is a straightforward implication of the theory of the determination of income. The expectations that lead to the "paradox" are based on the fallacy of composition: the belief that what is true for the parts is necessarily true for the whole.

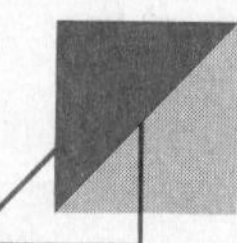

BOX 32-1

Fiscal Policy and the Great Depression

Failure to understand the implication of the paradox of thrift led many countries during the Great Depression to adopt policies that were disastrous. Failure to understand the role of built-in stabilizers has also led many observers to conclude, erroneously, that fiscal expansion had been tried in the Great Depression but had failed. Let us see how these two misperceptions are related.

The Paradox of Thrift in Action

In Canada, Prime Minister R. B. Bennett said in 1932, in the worst recession in recorded history, "We are now faced with the real crisis in the history of Canada. To maintain our credit we must practice the most rigid economy and not spend a single cent." His government that year brought down a budget based on the principle of trying to balance revenues and expenditures, and it included *increases* in tax rates.

U.S. President Franklin D. Roosevelt, in his first inaugural address (1933), urged: "Our great primary task is to put people to work. . . . [This task] can be helped by insistence that the federal, state, and local governments act forthwith on the demand that their costs be drastically reduced. . . . There must be a strict supervision of all banking and credits and investments."

Across the Atlantic, King George V told the British House of Commons in 1931, "The present condition of the national finances, in the opinion of His Majesty's Ministers, calls for the imposition of additional taxation and for the effecting of economies in public expenditure."

As the paradox of thrift predicts, these policies reduced aggregate demand and hence tended to worsen, not cure, the depression.

Interpreting the Deficit in the 1930s

Government deficits did increase in the 1930s, but they were not the result of a program of deficit-financed public expenditure. They were the result of the fall in tax yields brought about by the fall in national income as the economy sank into depression. Indeed, Professor E. Cary Brown of the Massachusetts Institute of Technology, after a careful study, concluded, "Fiscal policy seems to have been an unsuccessful recovery device in the 'thirties—not because it did not work, but because it was not tried."

The performance of the North American economies from 1930 to 1945 is quite well explained by modern national income theory. It is clear that the governments did not use fiscal measures effectively to stabilize their economies. War cured the depression because war demands made acceptable a level of government expenditure sufficient to remove the recessionary gap. Had the Canadian and American governments been able to do the same, they might have ended the waste of the Depression many years sooner.

substantial unemployment is correctly combated by encouraging governments, firms, and households to spend more, *not* to save more. In times of unemployment and depression, frugality will only make things worse. This prediction goes directly against the idea that we should tighten our belts when times are tough. The notion that it is not only possible but also acceptable to spend one's way out of a depression touches a sensitive point with people raised on the belief that success is based on hard work and frugality and not on prodigality; as a result, the idea often arouses great hostility.

Applications. As discussed in Box 32-1, the implications of the paradox of thrift were not generally understood during the Great Depression, and most governments followed procyclical spending policies in order to balance their budgets. However, by the middle of the 1930s, many economists had concluded that such government behavior did not make the most of its potential to stabilize the economy. Why, they asked, should not the government try to stabilize the economy by doing just the opposite of what everyone else was doing—by increasing its demand when private demand was falling and by lowering its demand when private demand was rising? If completely successful, this policy could hold aggregate demand constant even though its individual components were fluctuating.

When Milton Friedman said, "We are all Keynesians now," he was referring in part to the general acceptance of the view that the government's budget is much more than just the revenue and expenditure statement of a very large organization. Whether we like it or not, the sheer size of the government's budget inevitably makes it a powerful tool for influencing the economy.

Limitations. The paradox of thrift concentrates on shifts in aggregate demand that have been caused by changes in saving (and hence spending) behavior. Consequently, it applies only in the short run, when the *AD* curve plays an important role in the determination of national income.

In the long run, when the economy is on its *LRAS* curve and hence aggregate demand is not important for the determination of national income (see Figure 30-5), the paradox of thrift ceases to apply. The more people save, the larger the supply of funds available for investment. The more people invest, the greater the growth of potential income. Increased potential income causes the *LRAS* curve to shift to the right.

These longer-term effects are taken up in Chapter 38. For now, we concentrate on the short-run demand effects of saving and spending.

The paradox of thrift is based on the short-run effects of changes in saving and investment on aggregate demand.

Balanced Budget Changes

In Figures 32-1 and 32-2 we considered the effects of changes in either government expenditure or taxes. Another policy that is available to the government is to make a balanced budget change by introducing equal changes in spending and taxes. Say the government increases tax rates enough to raise an extra $1 billion that it then uses to purchase goods and services. Aggregate expenditure would remain unchanged if, and only if, the $1 billion that the government takes from the private sector would otherwise have been spent by the private sector. If that is the case, the government's policy would reduce private expenditure by $1 billion and raise its own spending by $1 billion. Aggregate demand, and hence national income and employment, would remain unchanged.

However, this is not the usual case. When an extra $1 billion in taxes is taken away from households, they usually reduce their spending on domestically produced goods by less than $1 billion. If the marginal propensity to consume out of disposable income is, say, 0.75, consumption expenditure will fall by only $750 million. If the government spends the entire $1 billion on domestically produced goods, aggregate expenditure will increase by $250 million. In this case the balanced budget increase in government expenditure has an expansionary effect, because it shifts the aggregate expenditure function upward and hence shifts the *AD* curve to the right.

A balanced budget increase in government expenditure will have an expansionary effect on national income, and a balanced budget decrease will have a contractionary effect.

The **balanced budget multiplier** measures these effects. It is the change in income divided by the balanced budget change in government expenditure that brought it about. Thus if the extra $1 billion of government spending, financed by the extra $1 billion of taxes, causes national income to rise by $500 million, the balanced budget multiplier is 0.5; if income rises by $1 billion, it is 1.0.

Now compare the sizes of the multipliers for a balanced budget and a deficit-financed increase in government spending. With a deficit-financed increase in expenditure, there is no increase in tax rates and hence no consequent decrease in consumption expenditure to offset the increase in government expenditure. With a balanced budget increase in expenditure, however, the increase in tax rates and a partially offsetting decrease in consumption does occur. Thus the balanced budget multiplier is much lower than the multiplier that relates the change in income to a deficit-financed increase in government expenditure with tax rates being held constant.

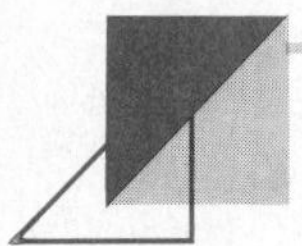

Judging the Stance of Fiscal Policy

The *stance* of fiscal policy refers to its expansionary or contractionary effects on the economy. An expansionary fiscal policy increases aggregate demand and thus tends to increase national income; a contractionary fiscal policy reduces aggregate demand and tends to lower national income. In Chapter 31, we looked separately at taxes, purchases of goods and services, and transfer payments as means of influencing aggregate demand. However, people want a summary measure—one number to express the government's effect on the economy.

The Inadequacy of the Deficit As a Measure of the Fiscal Stance

Not surprisingly, people tend to focus on the government's budget deficit in order to judge the stance of fiscal policy. An increase in the government deficit is often taken as an indication of an expansionary fiscal policy, and a decrease in the deficit is often taken as an indication of a contractionary fiscal policy. However, a number of problems make the deficit an unreliable guide to judging the fiscal stance.

The deficit is the difference between the government's outlays and receipts, its receipts consisting largely of tax revenues. However, tax revenues is the result of the interaction of tax rates, which the government sets, and the level of national income, which is influenced by many forces beyond the government's control.

The major tools of fiscal policy are government expenditure and tax *rates*. The government budget balance is the relationship between government expenditure and tax *revenues*.

Assume, for example, that government expenditure is constant at $200 billion and that at current tax rates the government takes 20 percent of national income in taxes. Suppose that national income is $1 trillion, so tax revenues are also $200 billion. Now assume that tax revenues sink to $150 billion, opening up a $50 billion budget deficit. This could be the result of a discretionary cut in tax rates so that now they yield only 15 percent of an unchanged national income. It could also be the result of a fall in national income itself to $750 billion, with tax rates being held constant. In the first case, a conscious change in the government's fiscal stance causes the fall in tax revenues. In the second case, a fall in national income that is not the result of fiscal policy causes tax revenue to fall; the increase in the deficit reflects the fall in tax revenues caused by the fall in national income.

This example illustrates why judging changes in the stance of fiscal policy from changes in the government's budget balance can be misleading. Doing so confuses changes in the deficit due to fluctuations in national income, which may not be the result of shifts in fiscal policy, with changes in the deficit that are the result of shifts in fiscal policy.

The Cyclically Adjusted Deficit

Changes in the stance of fiscal policy can be measured by estimating changes in the budget balance that would occur were national income constant at some base level. Measuring what the deficit would be at some constant level of national income ensures that measured changes in the budget balance are due to changes in policy. The base level most commonly used is potential national income. Because estimating the budget balance for a given level of national income eliminates the effect of cyclical fluctuations in expenditures and tax revenues, it is referred to as making the *cyclical adjustment*; the resulting measure is referred to as the *cyclically adjusted budget balance*, or **cyclically adjusted deficit (*CAD*)**.[4] It is an estimate of government expenditure minus government tax revenues, not as they actually are but as they would be if national income had been at its potential level. Table 32-1 shows the actual and cyclically adjusted deficit on an annual basis since 1970.

Because they reflect *exogenous* changes in the government's policy instruments and control for *endogenous* changes in actual spending and revenues, changes in the cyclically adjusted deficit are a useful indicator of changes in the stance of fiscal policy.

Box 32-2 discusses how using the *budget deficit function*, along with the cyclically adjusted deficit,

[4] This concept used to be called the *full-employment surplus*. The change from *full-employment* to *cyclically adjusted* came when the amount of unemployment that is associated with potential income rose rapidly during the 1970s, and hence referring to so much unemployment as *full employment* became embarrassing. The change from *deficit* to *surplus* occurred because during the 1960s people were trying to stress depressing effects of surpluses, while during the 1980s people wanted to stress the harmful effects of deficits.

BOX 32-2

The Budget Deficit Function

The distinction between changes in the budget balance due to changes in the fiscal stance and those due to cyclical changes in the economy is easily seen in what is called the government's *budget deficit function*.

The budget deficit function (curve B in the figure) expresses the difference between the government's expenditures and its tax revenues at each level of national income for given levels of government expenditure and tax rates. The curve in part (i) shows that deficits are associated with low levels of income and surpluses with high levels of income; this is because at a given tax *rate,* tax *revenue* rises with national income.

Changes in the government's budget balance induced by changes in national income are shown by *movements along* a given budget deficit function. Changes in the budget balance due to policy-induced changes in the level of government expenditure or tax rates are shown by *shifts in* the budget deficit function. Such shifts indicate a different budget at each level of national income.

In part (ii), a fall in national income from Y_0 to Y_1 causes the actual budget to go from a surplus of D_0 to a deficit of D_1. Government expenditure and tax rates are unchanged; that is, the fiscal policy stance is unchanged. The unchanged fiscal stance is correctly captured by the constant cyclically adjusted deficit, CAD, measured at the (constant) level of potential national income, Y^*.

Part (iii) illustrates a contractionary change in the stance of fiscal policy. A government expenditure cut or a tax rate increase shifts the budget deficit function from B_0 to B_1. Now there is a smaller budget deficit *at each level of national income.* This change is correctly captured by the fall in the cyclically adjusted deficit from CAD to CAD', both measured at the constant level of potential national income, Y^*.

To see the misleading effects of judging changes in the policy stance from changes in the measured deficit, suppose that national income had fallen from Y_0 to Y_1 at the same time that the budget deficit function shifted from B_0 to B_1. In that case the measured balance would have gone from surplus (D) to deficit (D') despite the fall in the cyclically adjusted deficit from CAD to CAD'. Thus the measured balance would have indicated an expansionary fiscal policy when the fiscal stance had in fact become contractionary.

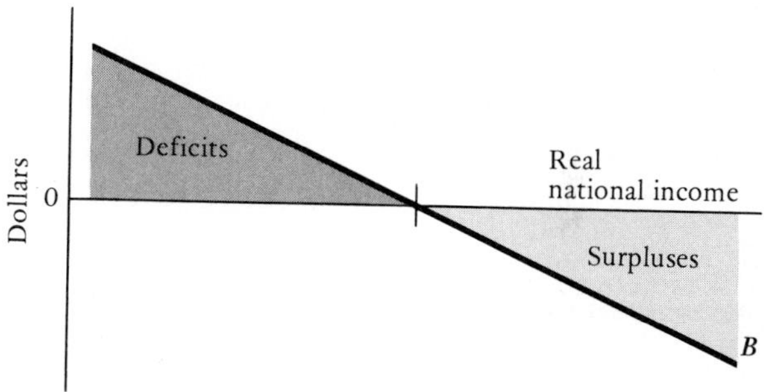

(i) The budget deficit function

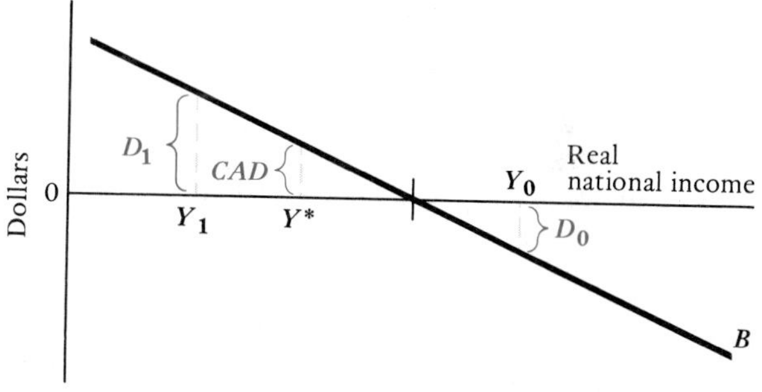

(ii) Changes in the measured deficit

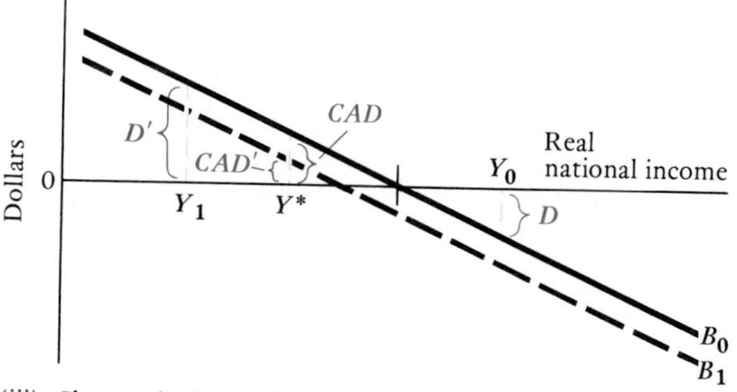

(iii) Changes in the cyclically adjusted deficit

TABLE 32-1 Actual and Cyclically Adjusted Federal Government Budget Balances, 1970–1989 (*billions of dollars, National Accounts basis*)

Year	Actual budget deficit*	Cyclical adjustment	Cyclically adjusted budget deficit*
1970	−0.2	−0.2	−0.4
1971	0.1	−0.2	−0.1
1972	0.5	−0.1	0.4
1973	−0.4	0.8	0.4
1974	−1.3	0.7	−0.6
1975	3.8	−0.6	3.2
1976	3.3	0.1	3.4
1977	7.3	0.1	7.4
1978	10.9	0.1	11.0
1979	9.4	0.6	10.0
1980	10.7	−0.4	10.3
1981	7.3	0.1	7.4
1982	20.3	−7.1	13.2
1983	25.0	−7.2	17.8
1984	30.0	−4.2	25.8
1985	31.4	−1.9	29.5
1986	24.0	−1.0	23.0
1987	22.9	0.7	23.6
1988	20.5	3.7	24.2
1989	23.9	3.6	27.5

Source: Department of Finance, *Economic Review*.
* A minus sign indicates a surplus.

Changes in the actual budget balance reflect both the fiscal actions of the government and the effects of the level of economic activity on government revenues and expenditures; the cyclical adjustment provides a correction for the latter influence, and the cyclically adjusted deficit thus gives a better measure of changes in fiscal policy. The cyclical adjustment corrects for the cyclical behavior of the economy. It shows the effect on the deficit arising from the existing output gap.

When there is a recessionary gap, meaning that actual output is below potential, the adjustment is negative, so the cyclically adjusted deficit is smaller than the actual deficit. This was the situation during the period 1982–1986, for example.

When there is an inflationary gap, meaning that actual output is above potential, the adjustment is positive, so the cyclically adjusted deficit is greater than the actual deficit. This was the situation during the period 1987–1989, for example.

Variations in the cyclically adjusted deficit give an indication of variations in the fiscal stance. For example, fiscal policy was contractionary in 1981, when the *CAD* fell from \$10.3 to \$7.4 billion, and expansionary in 1989, when the *CAD* rose from \$24.2 to \$27.5 billion.

makes it possible to avoid the errors that arise from using the current budget balance as an indicator of the stance of fiscal policy. (We encounter some related issues in Chapter 39 when we discuss some of the controversies surrounding the persistently large deficits that the federal government experienced in the 1980s.)

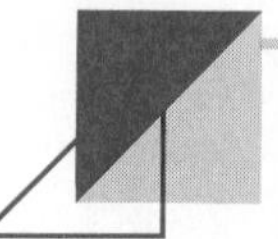

Implementing Fiscal Policy

The theory that we have just outlined makes the implementation of fiscal policy appear rather straightforward. However, there are complications that make the practice of fiscal policy a controversial issue.

As we saw in Chapter 31, private expenditure functions are constantly changing. Investment expenditure shifts with business conditions, and consumption functions sometimes shift upward as the public goes on a spending spree or downward as people become cautious and increase their saving. Further, any output gaps that do arise set in motion changes in wages and other factor costs that cause the *SRAS* curve to shift and that thus cause the gap itself to change. Also, shifts in the *LRAS* curve change potential GDP and thus make it hard to determine whether changes in actual GDP also imply that the output gap has changed. These and other considerations make stabilization policy much more difficult than it would be if it were possible simply to identify a stable inflationary or recessionary gap and then take steps to eliminate it once and for all.

Discretionary and Automatic Fiscal Policies

As a first step toward understanding some of the controversies involved in implementing fiscal policy, it is helpful to distinguish between *discretionary* and *automatic* fiscal policies.

We have seen that when persistent output gaps arise, it is possible for changes in tax rates and spending to offset the gaps. **Discretionary fiscal policy** refers to such changes in policy variables when they are made in a conscious effort to stabilize the econ-

TABLE 32-2 The Effect of Tax Rates on the Marginal Propensity to Spend Out of National Income

Marginal rate of tax	Change in national income (millions) ΔY	Change in tax revenue (millions) ΔT	Change in disposable income (millions) ΔY_d	Change in consumption (millions) ΔC	Marginal propensity to spend out of national income $\Delta C/\Delta Y$
0.2	$1,000	$200	$800	$640	0.64
0.4	1,000	400	600	480	0.48

The higher the marginal rate of tax, the lower the marginal propensity to spend out of national income. When national income changes by $1,000, disposable income changes by $800 when the tax rate is 20 percent and by $600 when the tax rate is 40 percent. Although the *MPC* out of disposable income is 0.8 in both examples, consumption changes by $640 in the first case and by only $480 in the second. Although households' *MPC* out of their disposable income is unchanged, an increase in tax rates lowers the marginal propensity to spend out of national income on which the size of the multiplier depends.

omy. **Automatic fiscal policy** does not require changes in the government policy variables; it occurs as the result of the operation of *built-in stabilizers.*

Automatic Fiscal Tools: Built-in Stabilizers

As we saw in Box 31-1, imports act as a *built-in stabilizer* because they reduce the marginal propensity to spend out of national income and hence reduce the value of the multiplier. In general, a **built-in stabilizer** is anything that automatically lessens the magnitude of the fluctuations in national income caused by changes in autonomous expenditures such as investment. The role of the government in the economy gives rise to a number of features that act as built-in stabilizers; note that they do so without the government's having to react consciously to each change in national income as it occurs.

Three principal government built-in stabilizers are taxes, government purchases of goods and services, and government transfer payments.

Taxes

Income taxes act as a built-in stabilizer because they reduce the marginal propensity to spend out of national income. To illustrate, consider two situations. In the first case, there are no income taxes, so every change in national income of $1 causes a $1 change in disposable income.[5] With a marginal propensity to consume out of disposable income (*MPC*) of, say, 0.8, consumption would change by 80 cents. In the second case, income taxes are a flat 40 percent of income. Now when national income changes by $1, disposable income changes by 60 cents, and taxes payable change by 40 cents. Hence consumption expenditure will change by 48 cents (0.8 times 60 cents) even though the *MPC* is still 0.8.

Table 32-2 illustrates the stabilizing effects of taxes by comparing the effects of two different marginal tax rates on the marginal propensity to spend out of national income in otherwise identical situations. The general proposition can be stated as follows:

Income taxes reduce the magnitude of fluctuations in disposable income that are associated with any given fluctuation in national income. Hence for a given marginal propensity to consume out of disposable income, they reduce the marginal propensity to spend out of national income.

Tax rates have increased greatly throughout the twentieth century. Although citizens complain about

[5] Undisturbed profits and other minor items would still hold disposable income below national income. We ignore these in the text because taxes (including subsidies and transfer payments) are the major source of the discrepancy between national income and disposable income.

the burden of high taxes—perhaps with good reason—few are aware that high taxes have helped to reduce swings in national income and employment.

Government Purchases

Government purchases of goods and services tend to be relatively stable in the face of cyclical variations in national income. Much of government spending is already committed by earlier legislation, so only a small proportion can be varied at the government's discretion from one year to the next, and even this small part is slow to change. In contrast, private consumption and investment expenditure tend to vary with national income.

Thus the higher the share of government spending in the economy, the lower the cyclical instability of total expenditure. The twentieth century rise in the importance of the government's role in the economy may be a mixed blessing. One benefit, however, has been to put a large built-in stabilizer into the economy.

Government Transfer Payments

Government transfer payments to individuals often rise during recessions and fall during booms. This stabilizes disposable income and personal consumption, reducing the size of the multiplier and thus acting as a built-in stabilizer.

Social insurance and welfare services. Welfare payments rise with the unemployment that accompanies falling national income. Many welfare schemes are financed by taxes based on payrolls or earnings, and these taxes yield less when income is low. Thus welfare schemes act to make net additions to disposable income in times of slumps. They also make net subtractions in times of boom, when payments are low and revenues high.

The Canada Pension Plan is financed by taxes (called *contributions*) paid jointly by employers and employees. Unemployment insurance is financed by a payroll tax on employers and employees. During recessions these tax collections decrease while payments to the unemployed rise.[6]

[6] The Unemployment Insurance Act requires the federal government to adjust the payroll tax (referred to as the *unemployment insurance premiums*) annually so as to finance some of the changes in benefits paid out. This greatly reduces the automatic stabilizing influence of the unemployment insurance scheme.

Agricultural support policies. When there is a slump in the economy, there is a general decline in the demand for all goods, including agricultural products. The free market prices of agricultural goods fall, and government agricultural supports come into play. This means that government transfers, which support agricultural disposable income, rise as national income falls. An added feature of these policies is that they focus the transfers on particular regions.

Transfer payments act as built-in stabilizers. They tend to stabilize disposable income, and hence consumption expenditure, in the face of fluctuations in national income.

Suppose that national income falls as a result of a fall in investment expenditure and that in the absence of transfer payments this would reduce disposable income by $6 billion. With an *MPC* out of disposable income of 0.8, this $6 billion reduction would cause an initial induced fall in consumption expenditure of $4.8 billion. Now assume instead that the fall in national income is accompanied by an increase in transfer payments of $4 billion. Instead of falling by $6 billion, disposable income now falls by only $2 billion. With the *MPC* out of disposable income still at 0.8, the initial induced fall in consumption expenditure is only $1.6 billion instead of $4.8 billion.

The Role of Built-in Stabilizers

Most built-in stabilizers are fairly new phenomena. Sixty years ago high marginal tax rates, high and stable government expenditures, farm stabilization policies, and large unemployment and other transfer payments were unknown in Canada. Each of these built-in stabilizers was the unforeseen by-product of policies originally adopted for other reasons. The progressive income tax arose out of a concern to raise government revenue while making the distribution of income less unequal. Social insurance and agricultural support programs were adopted more because of a concern with the welfare of the individuals and groups involved than with preserving the stability of the economy. Unforeseen or not, they work—even governments can be lucky.

No matter how lucky governments have been in finding built-in stabilizers, these stabilizers cannot reduce fluctuations to zero; they work by producing stabilizing reactions to changes in income. However, until income changes, these stabilizers are not even brought into play.

Discretionary Fiscal Policy

We have now seen that many short-term, minor fluctuations are dampened automatically by built-in stabilizers. We have seen also that large and persistent gaps nevertheless sometimes appear. We can now examine the role of discretionary changes in taxes and spending in offsetting these gaps. To do this effectively, the government must periodically make conscious decisions to alter fiscal policy. The Department of Finance must study current economic trends and predict the probable course of the economy. If the predicted course is unsatisfactory, the cabinet must be persuaded to adopt the appropriate fiscal stance.

In considering discretionary fiscal policy, we first ask whether the government can expect to be able to "fine tune" the economy so as to remove virtually all output gaps.

Fine Tuning

In the heyday of Keynesian fiscal policy, from 1945 to 1970, many economists advocated the use of fiscal policy to remove even minor fluctuations in national income around its potential level. Fiscal policy was to be altered frequently and by relatively small amounts to hold national income almost precisely at its potential level. This is referred to as **fine tuning** the economy.

A necessary condition for fiscal fine tuning is a relatively short **decision lag**, the period of time between perceiving a problem and deciding how to react to it. Many things contribute to the length of this decision lag. Experts must study the economy and agree among themselves on what fiscal changes are most desirable. They must persuade the government to initiate the action that they endorse.

The American form of government makes the decision lag rather long; in contrast, both the British system—used not only in Canada but in most of the rest of the English-speaking world—and the political systems in most European countries make the decision lag relatively short. Fine tuning has often been tried in these countries. Careful assessment of the results shows that their successes, if any, have fallen far short of what was hoped. One basic reason lies in the complexity of any economy. Although economists and policymakers can identify broad and persistent trends, they do not have detailed knowledge of what is going on at any moment, of all the forces that are operating to cause changes in the immediate future, and of all the short-term effects of small changes in the various government expenditure and tax rates.

Further difficulties for fine tuning also arise because of an **execution lag**, the time that it takes to put policies in place after the decision has been made, and because of lags between the introduction of a given policy measure and its effects being felt in the economy. Often by the time the effects of a given policy decision are felt, circumstances in the economy have changed, and the policy is no longer appropriate.

Fine tuning has often done as much to encourage fluctuations in the economy as to remove them.

As a result of these experiences, fine tuning is currently out of favor. If consciously fine tuning the economy, which involves constantly changing the government's policy variables, is undesirable, must we say that nothing can be done through discretionary fiscal policy to reduce or to eliminate output gaps?

There is a middle ground. Rather than either doing nothing or fine tuning, one might attempt *gross tuning*—altering fiscal policy less frequently by responding only to gaps that appear to be large and persistent.

Gross Tuning

If an output gap persists for a long enough period of time, its major causes can be studied and understood, and fiscal remedies can be planned and executed carefully. Such *gross tuning* can effectively shorten the period that it takes for the gaps to be eliminated. However, even gross tuning is not a simple matter.

The Need for Reversibility

Consider a *temporary* slump in private investment that opens up a large recessionary gap. Suppose that the government decides to adopt some combination of tax cuts and spending increases to push the economy back toward full employment. If private investment recovers to its preslump level and the government does not quickly reverse this policy, an inflationary gap will open up as the combination of rising investment expenditure and continuing fiscal stimulus takes national income into the inflationary range. The result is illustrated in Figure 32-3.

Alternatively, assume that starting from the same situation of approximately full employment, a temporary investment boom opens up an inflationary gap. Rather than let the inflation persist, the government reduces expenditure and raises taxes to remove the gap. If, when the investment boom is over and investment expenditure returns to its original level, the government does nothing, a recessionary gap will open up, and a slump may ensue. This, too, is analyzed in Figure 32-3.

Fiscal policies that are designed to remove persistent output gaps, resulting from abnormal levels of private expenditure, will destabilize the economy unless the policies can be reversed rapidly once private expenditure returns to its more normal level.

Even if the output gaps persist long enough for fiscal changes to be agreed on and to be made, subsequent rapid changes in private expenditure may require a quick reversal of the fiscal stance—a reversal that cannot always be made easily. As a result, many economists argue that caution dictates responding only to large output gaps that are expected to persist and even then attempting to close only part of a gap in anticipation of some stabilizing change in private expenditure.

"Temporary" Versus "Long-lasting" Changes

Consider the attempt to remove a persistent output gap through changes in tax rates. Such a gap, though persistent, is unlikely to be a permanent feature of the economy. The relevant tax changes should therefore be advocated only "for the duration," that is, for as long as the government thinks the gap would persist without the tax changes. A discretionary fiscal policy designed to remove such a gap might take the form, say, of a surcharge on income taxes for a two-year period. Similarly, a recession might be fought by temporary tax rebates.

FIGURE 32-3 Effects of Fiscal Policies That Are Not Reversed

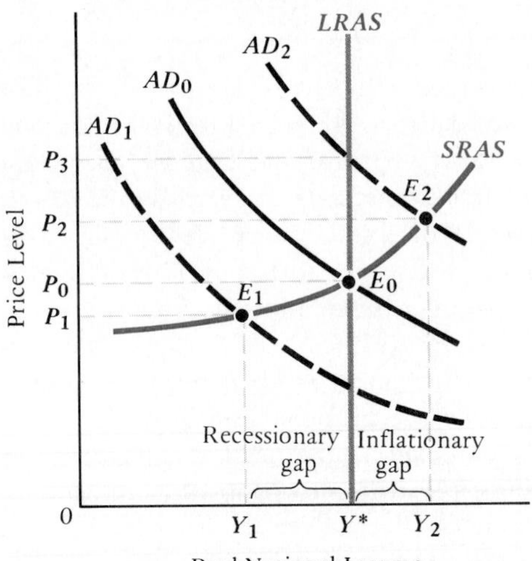

Fiscal policies that are initially appropriate may become inappropriate when private expenditure shifts. The normal level of the aggregate demand function is assumed to be AD_0, leaving income normally at Y^* and the price level at P_0. Suppose that a slump in private investment shifts aggregate demand to AD_1, lowering national income to Y_1 and causing a recessionary gap of Y^*Y_1.

The government now introduces fiscal expansion to restore aggregate demand to AD_0 and national income to Y^*. Suppose that private investment then recovers, raising aggregate demand to AD_2. If fiscal policy can be quickly reversed, aggregate demand can be returned to AD_0 and income stabilized at Y^*. If the policy is not quickly reversed, equilibrium will be at E_2, and an inflationary gap Y^*Y_2 will open up. This will cause wages to rise and thus shift the *SRAS* curve leftward and eventually restore Y^* at price level P_3.

Now suppose that starting from equilibrium E_0, a persistent investment boom takes AD_0 to AD_2. In order to stop the price level from rising in the face of the newly opened inflationary gap, the government introduces fiscal restraint, thereby shifting aggregate demand back to AD_0. Further assume, however, that the investment boom then comes to a halt, so that the aggregate demand curve shifts downward to AD_1. Unless the fiscal policy can be rapidly reversed, a recessionary gap will open up, and equilibrium income will fall to Y_1.

Such tax changes cause changes in household disposable income and hence in consumption expenditure. Consumption expenditure increases as tax rebates rise in times of recessionary gaps and decreases as tax surcharges rise in times of inflationary gaps. These effects of short-term tax changes rely on the dependence of household consumption on current disposable income.

Permanent-income theories. Some theories of the consumption function predict that a household's expected *permanent income* or *lifetime income,* rather than its *current* income, is the major determinant of consumption. (These theories were discussed in Chapter 28 and developed in detail in its appendix.)

According to such theories, households have expectations about their lifetime incomes and adjust their consumptions to those expectations. When temporary fluctuations in income occur, households maintain their long-term consumption plans and use their stocks of wealth as buffers to absorb income fluctuations. Thus when there is a purely temporary rise in income, households will save all the extra income; when there is a purely temporary fall in income, households will maintain their long-term consumption plans by using up part of their wealth that has been accumulated through past saving.

Such behavior has serious consequences for short-lived tax changes. A temporary tax rebate raises households' disposable income, but households, recognizing it as temporary, would not revise their expenditure very much and would instead save most of the extra disposable income. Thus the increase in aggregate expenditure would be smaller than hoped for. Similarly, a temporary rise in tax rates reduces disposable income, but this might lead to an almost offsetting drop in saving. Thus total expenditure is again little changed, and a temporary surcharge fails to have much effect on the inflationary gap.[7]

The more closely household consumption expenditure is related to lifetime income rather than to current income, the smaller will be the effects on current consumption of tax changes that are known to be of short duration.

Experience that lends support to this proposition occurred in the United States in 1968, when large military expenditures that were associated with the Vietnam War gave rise to an inflationary gap. In mid 1968, Congress approved a temporary tax surcharge that raised effective tax rates for a period of about 18 months and produced a substantial budget surplus. The object was to slow inflation by removing the inflationary gap. The restraining effect on inflation was disappointingly small because consumption expenditure was little affected.[8]

The advantage of having households perceive tax rate changes as long-lasting is in conflict with the need for the reversibility of cuts and surcharges if they are not to destabilize the economy at a later date.

This conflict reduces the usefulness of changes in tax rates as a stabilizing tool.

Some Preliminary Policy Conclusions

What can the government reasonably expect to achieve by using fiscal policy when private-expenditure functions are shifting continually, and when lags and an uncertain response of households and firms make the timing of the effects of fiscal policy uncertain?

We have seen that the attempt to use fine tuning to eliminate the continual but small and transitory fluctuations that dominate business cycle behavior is no longer favored by most economists. However, the economy does occasionally develop severe and persistent output gaps. For example, a recessionary gap developed between 1981 and 1983 when the United States and Canada, along with many other Western countries, experienced the deepest and longest lasting recession since the 1930s. Many economists who do not believe in the value of fine tuning nevertheless do feel that fiscal policy can aid in re-

[7] The permanent-income theory is not as devastating for fiscal policy as may initially appear. As the Appendix to Chapter 28 makes clear, it is necessary to distinguish between consumption of services from durables and expenditure on durables. When a household purchases a consumer durable, such as a computer or a car, the services of which it plans to consume for many years, it is in fact saving. Thus a transitory tax cut that leads to a transitory increase in disposable income may lead to increased saving that is also increased expenditure.

[8] Of course, many other factors that influence consumption also changed during this period, and there remains a controversy whether the failure of consumption to fall was the result of these other factors or whether it was due to the *ineffectiveness* of the tax cuts.

moving such persistent gaps. These economists argue that caution dictates responding only to large output gaps that are expected to persist and even then attempting to close only part of the gap in anticipation of some stabilizing change in private behavior.

Other economists believe that even with persistent gaps, the risks that fiscal policy will destabilize the economy are still too large. They would have the government abandon any attempt at stabilization policy, instead setting its budget solely in relation to such long-term considerations as the desirable size of the public sector and the need to obtain a satisfactory long-term balance between revenues and expenditures. Furthermore, many would argue that the failure to correct persistent, large deficits in the mid 1980s contributed to the emergence of an inflationary gap later in the decade. We shall return to this debate in Chapters 39 and 40.

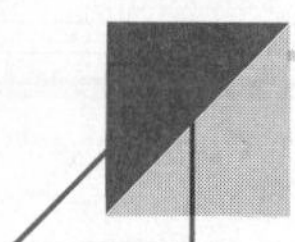

Fiscal Policy in Action

We have seen that the very size of the government budget guarantees that it will have a major impact on GDP. The conscious use of the budget to influence GDP that constitutes fiscal policy is, however, not inevitable.

Fiscal *impact* is unavoidable, but fiscal *policy* is a matter of choice.

The Fiscal Policy Record

An important legacy of World War II was a radically altered view of the role of government expenditures and taxes as instruments of government policy. The 1945 White Paper on Employment and Income established the principle that the federal government had a responsibility to maintain high and stable levels of employment and income. However, the implementation of this policy was greatly complicated by the unsettled state of federal-provincial relations. As early as 1940 a proposal to widen federal jurisdiction had been made by the Rowell-Sirois Commission, but—as discussed in Chapter 24—the division of powers has continued to be a contentious issue. Nevertheless, through a succession of temporary agreements, the federal government has retained sufficient power to operate a flexible fiscal policy. As a result, consideration of the desired degree of fiscal stimulus or restraint has become an important element in the federal budgets presented to Parliament.

Since World War II, the Canadian economy has experienced a series of cyclical swings that fiscal policy sometimes moderated and sometimes aggravated.

The 1960s and 1970s

In comparison with earlier and later periods, the quarter century following World War II was one of prosperity and steady growth. One prolonged but moderate slump occurred in 1958–1963. By 1965 the recessionary gap had been virtually eliminated, but policymakers apparently misjudged the situation and allowed the economy to develop an inflationary gap. Fiscal restraint was imposed in 1966–1968, but the effects came too late to prevent the buildup of inflationary forces. At the end of the 1960s, tight monetary policy reinforced the fiscal restraint, and unemployment started to rise in 1969.

The 1970s thus began with a substantial recessionary gap. Expansionary policies were put into place. However, as discussed in more detail in Chapter 36, sharp increases in the world price of oil and food caused a leftward shift in the long-run aggregate supply curve and created an inflationary gap. The shift in the *LRAS* curve and its implications were not fully understood at the time, and as a result the government's expansionary policy inadvertently served to widen the inflationary gap.

In late 1974 a series of shocks caused a downturn in the world economy. As Table 32-1 shows, the federal budget moved to a deficit position in 1975, and the actual and cyclically adjusted deficits grew steadily through the rest of the decade. This reflects discretionary fiscal policy actions as well as the influence of other factors, including more generous unemployment insurance provisions and a relatively high rate of inflation. The latter caused outlays to grow rapidly because many federal transfer payments such as old age pensions were indexed to inflation. Though tax revenues also rose due to inflation, the difference between them also grew.

Tax cuts were introduced in 1977 and 1978 when, despite steady but gradual growth, the economy was thought to be operating below capacity. In December 1979 the minority Progressive Conservative government introduced a budget that aimed to reduce the size of the deficit. Although the Conservative government fell on the issue of the budget, in early 1980 the newly elected Liberal government reintroduced two of the tax measures proposed in the defeated Conservative budget.

The 1960s and 1970s were thus years of fiscal activism. Discretionary tax and expenditure changes were constantly used in an attempt to stabilize the economy. Much of the reason active fiscal policy was so much in vogue was the dramatic success of tax cuts introduced in the United States in 1964. This episode, still cited by proponents of fiscal activism, is discussed in Box 32-3.

The overall evidence from the period, however, suggests that the record of fiscal activism was mixed: Sometimes fiscal policy moderated cyclical swings, and sometimes it accentuated them. As a result, fiscal activism fell from favor in most circles.[9]

The 1980s

In the early 1980s, fiscal policy was complicated by two major problems. First, as already noted (see Table 32-1), the federal budget deficit had become so large that worries were emerging about its implications. Second, the rate of inflation was unacceptably high despite an equally unacceptable high rate of unemployment. (Inflation was about 10 percent and unemployment was over 8 percent at the beginning of 1980; this *stagflationary* situation is discussed in more detail in Chapter 36.) For the first time since the federal government had accepted responsibility for stabilizing the economy, the direction—not simply the extent—of desired changes in the stance of fiscal policy was an issue. Reducing the recessionary gap called for an expansionary fiscal stance; reducing inflation and concern about the deficit called for a contractionary fiscal stance. Successive budgets in the early 1980s introduced offsetting changes in the overall fiscal stance, being pulled one way and the other by the two competing objectives.[10]

In late 1981 a major worldwide downturn set in, turning 1982 into the worst recession since the Great Depression. Still caught on the horns of the dilemma, in 1982 the government introduced only moderate expansion in the fiscal stance. In 1983 the budget tried to resolve the dilemma with short-term measures aimed at unemployment and longer-term measures aimed at the deficit. The budget introduced a moderate stimulus—about $6 billion phased in over two years—combined with a series of measures, including tax increases, to offset this stimulus later. This *tilt*—stimulus now, restraint later—was widely viewed as an appropriate way to stimulate the economy without increasing the future high-employment deficit.

In 1983 there was a strong recovery. Real output grew by over 6 percent, and inflation slowed dramatically. The February 1984 budget maintained a steady course, with very little change in the stance of fiscal policy. It also did very little to address the persistent budget deficit.

A Conservative government was elected in fall 1984, and it appeared committed to reversing the trend of rising government deficits. In November 1984 it published an agenda paper that laid out a number of "fundamental principles" to guide fiscal policy, including these three:

1. To achieve sizable year-over-year reductions in the deficit
2. To ensure that the majority of the reduction in the deficit was achieved through better management and expenditure restraint
3. To reduce the growth rate of the national debt to less than that of national income by the end of the decade

One remarkable feature of these three principles is that no specific reference is given to stabilization

[9] The fall from favor of fiscal policy activism was given a further push with the election of U.S. President Ronald Reagan, an avowed fiscal conservative, in 1980. Ironically, despite the Reagan administration's disavowal of fiscal *policy,* its actions had significant fiscal *effects*. Many economists believe that the dramatic increase in the deficit under Reagan played a major role in stimulating the economy and ending the recession. It also stimulated an extensive public debate about the consequences of persistent budget deficits, and Congress debated and passed legislation (the Gramm-Rudman-Hollings Bill) to try to reduce the deficit. This is taken up in more detail in Chapter 39.

[10] One important feature of the October 1980 budget was the introduction of the National Energy Program, designed to increase the federal government's share of the revenues from petroleum production mainly at the expense of the industry. Also, to help increase Canadian participation in the industry, a series of grants for exploration and development that would increase with the Canadian ownership of a firm were introduced. The NEP was dismantled by the Conservative government in 1984.

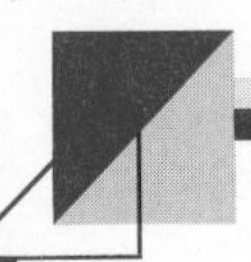

BOX 32-3

Fiscal Drag and the 1964 U.S. Tax Cuts: A Fiscal Policy Success

Fiscal drag, first diagnosed in the late 1950s, is the problem that is produced by economic growth acting on stable government expenditure and fixed tax rates. In such circumstances, growth leads to a falling cyclically adjusted budget deficit. (In terms of the figure in Box 32-2, the drag is due to a movement along the budget deficit function as potential income grows.)

Throughout the 1950s potential output rose 2 to 3 percent per year because of economic growth. Such growth increases aggregate supply, but since higher output means higher income earned, aggregate demand was also shifting outward. With both demand and supply increasing, it might seem that maintaining full employment would be no problem. There was a problem, however, and it lay with the tax system.

With tax rates being held constant, rising national income causes rising tax revenues. These revenues are money that does not become disposable income for households. If the government spends all its extra tax revenues, aggregate demand is not depressed. Since at the time, however, there was a relatively stable level of government expenditure, rising tax revenues exerted a drag on the growth of aggregate demand by taking income away from households that would have spent it and transferring it to governments that did not. There was thus a falling cyclically adjusted deficit.

This is illustrated in the figure, where we start with the curves AD_0, $LRAS_0$, and $SRAS_0$. These yield equilibrium at E_0 and potential income at Y_0^*. Economic growth now shifts the supply curves to $LRAS_1$ and $SRAS_1$. As a result of fiscal drag, however, the aggregate demand curve shifts only to AD_1 rather than to AD_2, which would have been required to sustain full employment. An output gap of $Y_1Y_2^*$ is thus created.

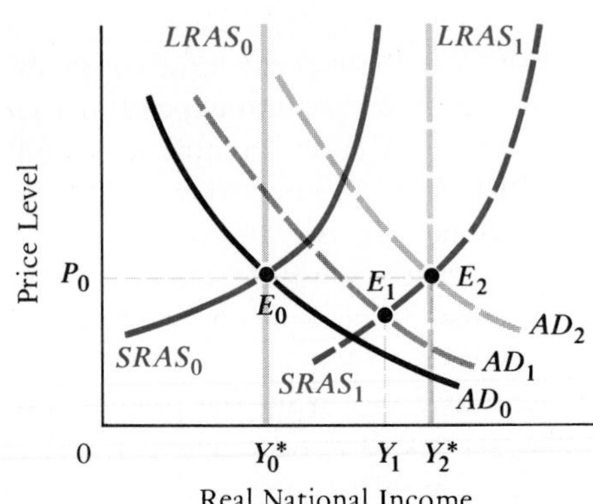

To prevent the exertion of an ever-stronger depressing effect on national income by a falling *CAD*, it is periodically necessary either to increase government spending or to reduce tax rates. This problem arose in the American economy during the 1950s. Economic growth was producing a declining *CAD*. As a result, each cyclical upswing was weaker than the one before it, and the average level of unemployment over the cycle was creeping upward. By the beginning of the 1960s, many economists were calling for a tax cut to remove the drag and to restore full employment. Their concern was not with cyclical stabilization of the economy but with solving a problem that is associated with long-term economic growth.

When the 1964 tax cut was enacted, the predicted effects occurred. The tax cuts increased disposable income, causing an increase in consumption expenditure that in turn caused an increase in national income and employment.

objectives of controlling unemployment and inflation. In part this reflects the fall from favor of fine tuning, and in part it reflects the concern that the large budget deficits and growing public debt greatly constrained the government's ability to use fiscal policy to achieve stabilization objectives. As it turned out, the rest of the decade witnessed sustained recovery and relatively stable inflation. As can be seen from Table 32-1, the cyclically adjusted deficit remained relatively stable through this period.

How did the government's fiscal actions stack up against its three fundamental principles?

Some success was achieved with regard to the first fiscal principle: As can be seen in Table 32-1, the deficit peaked in 1985 and fell in each of the next three years. Each of Finance Minister Wilson's budgets received some vote of confidence from financial market participants, although the vote was in most cases reserved rather than enthusiastic; the deficit cuts were in fact smaller than many market participants had hoped for. Despite the cuts that were introduced, the deficit remained an issue of concern, and this was reinforced in 1989 when the deficit rose. The February 1990 budget again had as its main focus the establishment of a credible downward trend in the government deficit.

There was also progress on the commitment to achieve deficit reduction largely through better management and expenditure restraint. Total program spending (all spending exclusive of interest payments on the national debt) declined not only as a share of GDP but also in absolute terms in fiscal 1985–1986, the first such decline in 25 years. Program spending continued to fall, and by fiscal 1989–1990 it had reached 16 percent of GDP, down from its 1984–1985 peak of 19.5 percent. Nevertheless, budgets throughout this period also involved substantial tax increases. Although the government's emphasis was on tax reform (as discussed in detail in Chapter 24), personal income taxes and the federal sales tax were increased. (The federal sales tax was scheduled to be replaced by the Goods and Services Tax on January 1, 1991; see Chapter 24 for a discussion.)

The last principle—reducing the rate of growth of debt to below that of GDP, which is the necessary condition for the debt-to-GDP ratio to fall—proved to be an elusive target. Though success appeared to be within reach several times, deficits turned out to be larger than projected, and hence there was slippage in the expected date at which the debt-to-GDP ratio would actually turn down. For example, in the summer of 1986 there was a dramatic fall in the world price of oil and a collapse in the international markets for Canadian agricultural exports. Automatic stabilizers in the form of increased payments under the terms of various agricultural support programs and reduced tax revenue from the energy sector were thus triggered. Furthermore, the government decided to provide farmers with an additional $1 billion in discretionary funds. Also, at the end of the decade, interest rates were much higher than had been expected, and as a result government debt service payments were much higher than had been projected. All of these events made the deficit larger than it would have otherwise been. The debt-to-GDP ratio rose steadily throughout the decade, and in its February 1990 budget the government was projecting that it would not start to fall until 1992 or 1993. By mid 1990 continued high interest rates had put even that prospect in doubt.

Thus while progress in controlling the federal deficit was certainly visible, the reductions were modest. After six years of sustained economic growth, and after six federal budgets that focused on deficit reduction, government deficits remained large by historical standards. Many commentators felt that these persistent federal government deficits posed a serious threat to future economic performance in Canada. In the mid 1980s a new phenomenon began to emerge as a source of concern—provincial government deficits. We return to these issues in Chapter 39, where we discuss the implications of persistent large government deficits and consequent growth of the national debt.

SUMMARY

1. Fiscal policy uses government expenditure and tax policies to influence the economy. Changes in either government spending or tax policies also influence the budget balance.
2. Stabilization policy involves the use of government fiscal (and other) policies to dampen fluctuations in the economy by trying to reduce or to eliminate output gaps that arise.

3. The government's budget balance is the difference between its receipts and its outlays. A budget deficit requires that the government borrow money by issuing bonds.
4. The so-called paradox of thrift is not a paradox at all. It applies to the short-run effects of saving and investment on aggregate demand. It predicts that severe recessions can be combated by encouraging an increase in spending.
5. Changes in the stance of fiscal policy may be reasonably judged by changes in the cyclically adjusted deficit. This is the balance between revenues and expenditures as they would be if full employment prevailed.
6. Short-term stabilization by fiscal policy operates largely through such automatic stabilizers as tax revenues that vary directly with national income, expenditures on goods and services that do not vary with national income, and transfer payments that vary negatively with national income.
7. Discretionary fiscal policy is also used sometimes to attack large and persistent gaps. Such policies must be reversible; otherwise, the economy may overshoot its target, once private investment recovers from a temporary slump or falls back from a temporary boom.
8. Tax changes also need to be perceived as relatively long-lived if they are to induce major changes in household spending patterns. Temporary changes may merely affect the current saving rate and not expenditure. The need to have tax changes perceived as long-lived, however, conflicts with the need to have fiscal policy easily reversible.
9. Fine tuning, the attempt to hold the aggregate expenditure function virtually constant by offsetting even small fluctuations in private expenditure, has been largely discredited. Many economists still believe, however, that large and persistent gaps can be offset by gross tuning, using fiscal policy.
10. Since the 1960s, the Canadian economy has undergone a series of cyclical swings that fiscal policy has sometimes aggravated and sometimes resisted. Concern about persistent budget deficits and mounting public debt dominates current fiscal policy debates.

TOPICS FOR REVIEW

Fiscal policy
Budget balance, balanced budget, budget surplus, and budget deficit
The paradox of thrift
The stance of fiscal policy
Actual budget balance and cyclically adjusted budget balance
Built-in stabilizers
Discretionary fiscal policy
Fine tuning and gross tuning

DISCUSSION QUESTIONS

1. In 1986, falling world energy prices and collapsing world agricultural markets caused a slowdown in the Canadian economy. The operation of automatic stabilizers in the face of these adverse shocks meant that the deficit would be larger than anticipated, and in addition the government announced an additional $1 billion discretionary expenditure program to assist farmers. Write a brief critique of the government's decision to let the deficit rise relative to its target path in these circumstances.

2. Which of the following would be built-in stabilizers?
   a. Food allowances for the needy
   b. Cost-of-living escalators in government contracts and pensions
   c. Income taxes
   d. Subsidized training allowances for unemployed workers after six months of unemployment
3. In his first inaugural address, U.S President Franklin D. Roosevelt expounded the doctrine of "sound finance"—that the government's budget should always be balanced. Under his "New Deal" policies, however, government spending rose faster than taxes, and deficits resulted. How would the effectiveness of the New Deal on employment have been changed if Roosevelt had been successful in keeping the budget balanced?
4. The 1945 White Paper on Employment and Income made no explicit mention of price stability as an objective of national income policy. Why do you suppose this was so? What is the relationship between fiscal policy and the price level?
5. Look at Table 32-1 and explain the rather different patterns that the actual and the cyclically adjusted deficits have followed since 1985. (*Hint:* What other economic time series would you need information about in order to be able to answer this question fully?)
6. As the recovery from the 1982 recession entered its eighth year in 1989, government deficits remained historically large, and concern over them was widespread. Another concern, however, was that in the event of a downturn, emphasis on the deficit might lead to procyclical fiscal policy. Explain how this might happen. Focus on what measure might allow it to be avoided. Should it be avoided?
7. "Fiscal policy has been a relatively weak instrument in Canada because of our heavy dependence on foreign trade and because of the wide regional disparities in employment opportunities." Discuss.
8. "Our current account deficit is closely related to important imbalances in domestic consumption, saving, and investment, and a correction of those imbalances is necessary to achieve a satisfactory adjustment on the external side." Why are these external imbalances related to the internal ones? What policies might the quote give support to?

PART 9

MONEY, BANKING, AND MONETARY POLICY

Chapter 33

The Nature of Money and Monetary Institutions

What is the significance of money to the economy, and how did it come to play its present role? Many people believe that money is one of the important things in life and that there is never enough of it. Yet economists argue that increasing the world's money supply would not make the average person better off. The reason for this is that although money allows those who hold it to buy someone else's output, the total amount of goods and services that are available for everyone to buy depends on the total output that is produced, not on the total amount of money that people possess. Increasing the world's money supply would not necessarily change the total quantity of goods produced and hence available for consumption, although it would likely cause the price level to rise.

The Real and Monetary Sectors of the Economy: The Classical Dichotomy

Early in the history of economics, eighteenth century economists developed theories in which the economy was conceived of as being divisible into a "real" part and a "monetary" part.

The real sector. According to these eighteenth century economists, the allocation of resources is determined in the real sector of the economy by demand and supply. Whether, for example, a lot of beef is produced relative to pork depends on the relative prices of beef and pork, not on the money price of either. If the price of beef is higher than the price of pork and both commodities cost about the same to produce, there is an incentive to produce beef rather than pork. At prices of $1 per pound for pork and $3 per pound for beef, the *relative* incentive is the same as it would be at $2 per pound for pork and $6 per pound for beef. As with beef and pork, so it is with all other commodities:

The allocation of resources among alternative uses depends on relative prices.

The monetary sector. According to the early economists, the price *level* is determined in the monetary sector of the economy. In the beef and pork example just given, an increase in the total money available might double all prices, thus raising the price of pork from $1 to $2 per pound and the price of beef from $3 to $6 per pound, but in equilibrium it would leave their *relative* prices unchanged. Hence it would have no effect on the real part of the economy, that is, on the amount of resources allocated to beef and to pork production (or to anything else).

An increase in the money supply leads to an increase in all money prices.

If the quantity of money were doubled, *other things being equal*, the prices of all commodities and money income would all double. Everyone earning an income would be made no better or worse off by the change.

Thus, in equilibrium, the real and the monetary parts of the economy were believed to have no effect on each other. The doctrine that the quantity of money influences the level of money prices but has no effect on the real part of the economy is called the **neutrality of money**. Because early economists believed that the most important questions—How much does the economy produce? What share of it does each group in the society get?—were answered in the real sector, they spoke of money as a "veil" behind which occurred the real events that affected material well-being.

The modern view. Modern economists still accept the insights of the early economists that relative prices are a major determinant of the allocation of resources and that the quantity of money has a lot to do with determining the absolute level of prices. They accept the neutrality of money in long-run equilibrium when all forces causing change have fully worked themselves out. We shall see in Chapter 34, however, that they do not accept the neutrality of money when the economy is undergoing change from day to day, that is, when the economy is not in a state of long-run equilibrium.

In this chapter we look first at the experience of price level changes—one aspect of the importance of money—and then at the nature of money itself and the operation of the modern institutions that comprise the monetary system of our economy.

Historical Experience

In Chapter 26 we discussed some important introductory material related to the price level itself and to inflations and deflations, that is, to changes in the price level. The material there should be reviewed at this stage. In this chapter we present some further details of the behavior of the price levels over very long periods of time. Figure 33-1 shows the course of producer (or wholesale) prices in Canada from 1867 through 1990. Considerable year-to-year fluctuations are apparent. Despite the large fluctuations that occurred during the nineteenth century, the price trend during that period was neither upward nor downward. In contrast, the twentieth century has seen large fluctuations *and* a distinct rising trend in the price level.

Although admittedly a long time, even two centuries may still not be enough to give us a clear perspective of very long term price fluctuations. The experience of the period since 1946 looks much more dramatic and unusual when it is compared only with the nineteenth century than when it is considered in longer perspective. For an indication of the longer-term course of price levels, we can look across the Atlantic. Figure 33-2 shows the course of the price level in southern England over seven centuries. It shows that there was an overall inflationary trend but that it was by no means evenly spread over the centuries.

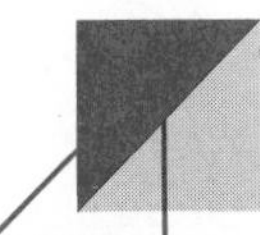

The Nature of Money

Inflation is a monetary phenomenon in the sense that a rise in the general level of prices is the same thing as a decrease in the purchasing power of money. But what exactly is money? More folklore and general nonsense are believed about money than about any other aspect of the economy. In this section we describe the functions of money and briefly outline its history. This will allow us to refute some of these misconceptions. In addition, continuing interest in the gold standard makes some discussion of early monetary systems relevant.

What Is Money?

In economics *money* has usually been defined as any generally accepted medium of exchange. A **medium of exchange** is anything that will be widely accepted in a society in exchange for goods and services. Money is more than this, however. **Money** has several functions:

Money acts as a medium of exchange, as a store of value, and as a unit of account.

Different kinds of money vary in the degree of efficiency with which they fulfill these functions. As we shall see, a variety of measures for the money supply

FIGURE 33-1 Index of Canadian Wholesale Prices, 1867–1990

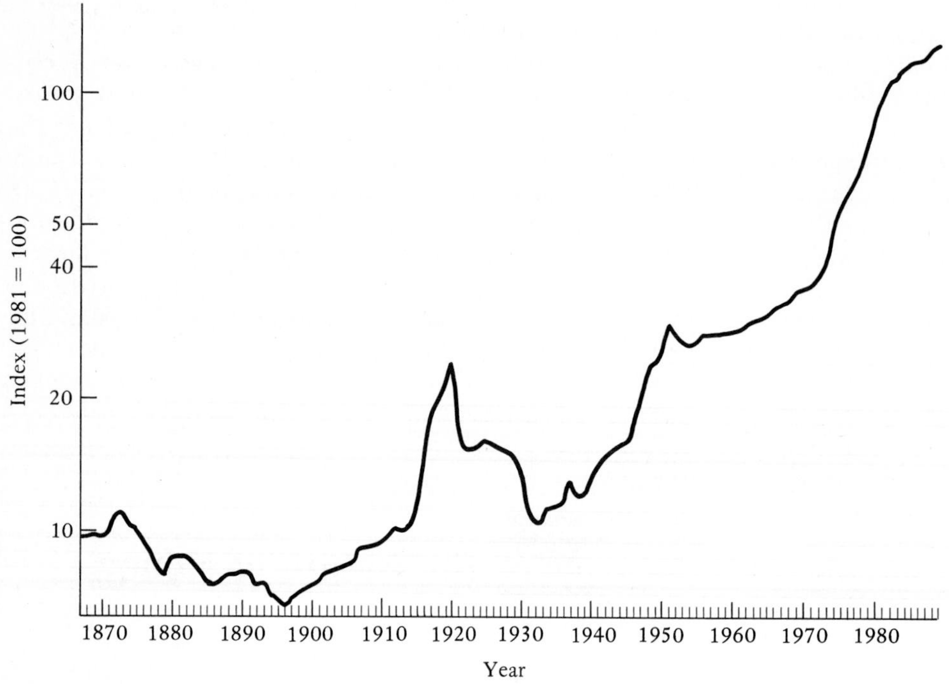

Persistent peacetime inflation is only a recent problem in Canada. Although the price level has fluctuated throughout Canadian history, no long-term trend was visible during the period from confederation to 1940. From the time of World War II to the present, the price level has shown a consistent upward trend. *Source:* Statistics Canada, Industrial Price Index, 62–0112.

are available, each using different definitions of what "money" is.

A Medium of Exchange

If there were no money, goods would have to be exchanged by barter (one good being swapped directly for another). We discussed this cumbersome system in Chapter 3. The major difficulty with barter is that each transaction requires a *double coincidence of wants*. For a barter exchange to occur between Helen and Tom, not only must Helen have what Tom wants, but Tom must have what Helen wants. If all exchange were restricted to barter, anyone who specialized in producing one commodity would have to spend a great deal of time searching for satisfactory transactions.

The use of money as a medium of exchange removes these problems. People can sell their output for money and subsequently use the money to buy what they wish from others.

The double coincidence of wants is unnecessary when a medium of exchange is used.

Without money, the economic system, which is based on specialization and the division of labor, could not function, and we would have to return to primitive forms of production and exchange. It is not without justification that money has been called one of the great inventions contributing to human freedom and well-being.

To serve as an efficient medium of exchange, money must have a number of characteristics. It

FIGURE 33-2 A Price Index of Consumables in Southern England, 1275–1959

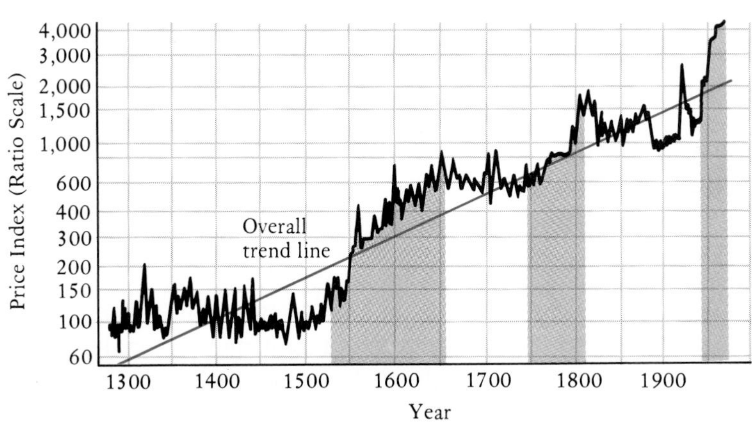

Over the past seven centuries, long periods of stable prices have alternated with long periods of rising prices. This remarkable price series shows an index of the prices of food, clothing, and fuel in southern England from 1275 through 1959. The trend line shows that the average change in prices over the whole period was 0.5 percent per year. The shaded areas indicate periods of unreversed inflation. The series also shows that even the perspective of a century can be misleading, because long periods of stable or gently falling prices tended to alternate with long periods of rising prices. *Source: Lloyds Bank Review,* No. 58, October 1960.

must be readily acceptable. It must have a high value relative to its weight (otherwise it would be a nuisance to carry around). It must be divisible, because money that comes only in large denominations is useless for transactions having only a small value. It must not be readily counterfeitable, because if money can be easily duplicated by individuals, it will lose its value.

A Store of Value

Money is a convenient way to store purchasing power; goods may be sold today, and money may be stored until it is needed. The money provides a claim on someone else's goods that can be exercised at a future date. The two sides of the transaction can be separated in time, with the obvious increase in freedom that this confers.

To be a satisfactory store of value, however, money must have a relatively stable value. When the price level is stable, the purchasing power of a given sum of money is also stable. When the price level is highly variable, this is not so, and the usefulness of money as a store of value is undermined. An extreme example is discussed in Box 33-1.

Although money can serve as a satisfactory store of accumulated purchasing power for a single individual, it cannot do so for the society as a whole. If a single individual accumulates a pile of dollars, he or she will, when the time comes to spend it, be able to command the current output of some other individual. All of society cannot do this. If all individuals were to save their money and then retire simultaneously to live on their savings, there would be no current production to purchase and consume. The society's ability to satisfy wants depends on goods and services being available; if some of this want-satisfying capacity is to be stored up for the whole society, goods that are currently produced must be left unconsumed and carried over to future periods.

A Unit of Account

Money may also be used purely for accounting purposes without having a physical existence of its own. For instance, a government store in a truly communist society might say that everyone had so many "dollars" to use each month. Goods could then be assigned prices and each consumer's purchases recorded, the consumer being allowed to buy until the allocated supply of dollars was exhausted. These dollars need have no existence other than as entries in the store's books, yet they would serve as a perfectly satisfactory unit of account.

Whether they could serve also as a medium of exchange between individuals depends on whether the store would agree to transfer dollar credits from one customer to another at the customer's request. Banks will transfer dollars credited to demand deposits in this way, and thus a bank deposit can serve

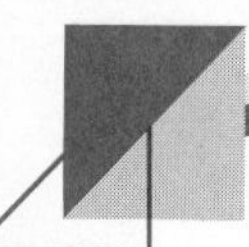

BOX 33-1

Hyperinflation

Can the price level ever rise so rapidly that money loses its usefulness either as a medium of exchange or as a store of value? The answer appears to be that very occasionally this has happened. Inflation rates of 50, 100, and even 200 percent or more per year have occurred year after year and have proved to be manageable as people adjust their contracts to real terms. Though there are strains and side effects, the evidence shows such situations to be possible without causing money to become useless.

Does this mean that there is no reason to fear that rapid inflation will turn into hyperinflation that will destroy the value of money completely? The historical record is not entirely reassuring. There have been a number of cases in which prices began to rise at an ever-accelerating rate until the nation's money ceased to be a satisfactory store of value even for the short period between receipt and expenditure and hence ceased also to be useful as a medium of exchange.

The index of wholesale prices in Germany during and after World War I is given in the table. The index shows that a good purchased with one 100-mark note in July 1923 would have required *ten million* 100-mark notes for its purchase only four months later! Although Germany had experienced substantial inflation during World War I, averaging more than 30 percent per year, the immediate postwar years of 1920 and 1921 gave no sign of an explosive inflation. Indeed, during 1920 prices were stable, but in 1922 and 1923 the price level exploded. On November 15, 1923, the mark was officially repudiated, its value wholly destroyed. How could this happen?

When inflation becomes so rapid that people lose confidence in the purchasing power of their currency, they rush to spend it. People who have goods become increasingly reluctant to accept the rapidly depreciating money in exchange. The rush to spend money accelerates the increase in prices until people finally become unwilling to accept money on any terms. What was once money ceases to be money.

The price system can then be restored only by repudiation of the old monetary unit and its replacement by a new unit. This destroys the value of monetary savings and of all contracts specified in terms of the old monetary unit.

There are about a dozen documented instances of hyperinflation in world history, among them the collapse of the continental during the American Revolution, the ruble during the Russian Revolution, the drachma during and after the German occupation of Greece in World War II, the pengö in Hungary during 1945 and 1946, and the Chinese national currency between 1946 and 1948. Every time, hyperinflation was accompanied by great increases in the money supply; new money was printed to give governments purchasing power that they could not or would not obtain by taxation. Further, each occurred in the midst of a major political upheaval in which grave doubts existed about the stability and the future of the government itself.

Is hyperinflation likely in the absence of civil war, revolution, or collapse of the government? Most economists think not. Further, it is clear that high inflation rates over a period of time do not mean the inevitable or even likely onset of hyperinflation, however serious the distributive and social effects of such rates may be.

Date		German wholesale price index (1913 = 1)
January	1913	1
January	1920	13
January	1921	14
January	1922	37
July	1922	101
January	1923	2,785
July	1923	74,800
August	1923	944,000
September	1923	23,900,000
October	1923	7,096,000,000
November	1923*	750,000,000,000

* The mark was repudiated on November 15, 1923.

as both a unit of account and a medium of exchange. Notice that the use of *dollars* in this context suggests a further sense in which money is a unit of account. People think about values in terms of the monetary unit with which they are familiar.

Another related function of money is sometimes distinguished. It can be used as a standard of deferred payments. Payments that are to be made in the future, on account of debts and so on, are reckoned in money. Money is used as a unit of account with the added dimension of time because the account will not be settled until later.

The Origins of Money

The origins of money are lost in antiquity; most primitive tribes that are known today make some use of it. The ability of money to free people from the cumbersome necessity of barter must have led to its early use as soon as some generally acceptable commodity appeared.

Metallic Money

All sorts of commodities have been used as money at one time or another, but gold and silver proved to have great advantages. They were precious because their supplies were relatively limited, and they were in constant demand by the rich for ornament and decoration. Also, they did not easily wear out. Thus they tended to have a high and stable price. They were easily recognized and generally known to be commodities that because of their stable price would be readily accepted. They were also divisible into extremely small units.

Precious metals thus came to circulate as money and to be used in many transactions. Before the invention of coins, it was necessary to carry the metals in bulk. When a purchase was made, the requisite quantity of the metal was carefully weighed on a scale. A sack of gold and a highly accurate set of scales were the common equipment of the merchant and the trader.

The invention of coinage eliminated the need to weigh the metal at each transaction. The ruler weighed the precious metal, added some base metal for strength and durability, and made a coin out of it to which the ruler's seal was affixed, guaranteeing the amount of precious metal that it contained. If a coin was certified to contain exactly 1/16 ounce of gold and a commodity was priced at 1/8 ounce of gold, two coins could be given over without weighing the gold. This was clearly a great convenience, as long as traders knew that they could accept the coin at its "face value." The face value was nothing more than a statement that a certain weight of metal was contained therein.

Abuses of metallic money. The ruler's subjects, however, could not let a good opportunity pass. Someone soon had the idea of clipping a thin slice off the edge of the coin. If he collected a coin that was stamped as containing 1/2 ounce of gold, he could clip a slice off the edge and pass the coin off as still containing 1/2 ounce of gold. ("Doesn't the stamp prove it?") If he got away with this, he would have made a profit equal to the market value of the clipped metal.

Whenever this practice became common, even the most myopic traders noticed that things were not what they seemed to be in the coinage world. It became necessary to weigh each coin before accepting it at its face value; out came the scales again, and much of the usefulness of coins was lost. To get around this problem, the idea arose of minting the coins with a rough edge. The absence of the rough edge would immediately be apparent and would indicate that the coin had been clipped. This practice, called *milling,* survives on some coins as an interesting anachronism to remind us that there were days when the market value of the metal in the coin (if it were melted down) was equal to the face value of the coin.

Debasement of metallic money. Not to be outdone by the cunning of their subjects, the rulers were quick to seize the chance of getting something for nothing. The power to mint placed rulers in a good position to work a profitable fraud. When faced with debts that could not be paid or repudiated, rulers merely used some suitable occasion—a marriage, an anniversary, an alliance—to remint the coinage. Subjects would be ordered to bring their gold coins into the mint to be melted down and coined afresh with a new stamp. The subjects could then go away with one new coin for every old coin that they had brought in. Between the melting down and the recoining, however, the rulers had only to toss some further inexpensive base metal in with the molten gold to earn a handsome profit. If the coinage were debased by adding, say, 1 pound of new base metal to every 4 pounds of old coins, five coins could be made for every four that were turned in. For every four coins brought in, the rulers could return four and have one left as profit with which to pay off debts.

Since gold and silver are softer and more malleable than most base metals, an experienced trader could usually tell if a coin had been seriously debased by testing its hardness. This is why, in films depicting ancient markets, you will often see a merchant biting a coin to see how easily it can be bent.

The result of debasement was inflation. The subjects had the same number of coins as before and hence could demand the same quantity of goods. When rulers paid their bills, however, the recipients of the extra coins could be expected to spend them. This caused a net increase in demand. The extra demand would bid up prices. Debasing the coinage thus led to a rise in prices.

It was the experience of such inflation that led early economists to propound the *quantity theory of money and prices*. They argued that there was a relationship between the average level of prices and the quantity of money in circulation, such that an increase in the quantity of money would lead to a proportionate increase in the price level. (This theory is discussed in more detail in Box 34-2.)

Gresham's law. The early experience of currency debasement led to the observation known as **Gresham's law**, after the Elizabethan financial expert, Sir Thomas Gresham. Gresham's hypothesis that "bad money drives out good" has stood the test of time.

When Queen Elizabeth I came to the throne of England in the middle of the sixteenth century, the coinage had been severely debased. Seeking to help trade, Elizabeth minted new coins, which contained their full face value in gold. However, as fast as she fed these new coins into circulation, they disappeared. Why? Gresham reasoned as follows to the young queen.

Suppose that you possessed one new and one old coin, each with the same face value, and had a bill to pay. What would you do? Clearly you would use the debased coin to pay the bill and keep the undebased one. (You part with less gold that way.) Suppose that you wanted to obtain a certain amount of gold bullion by melting down the gold coins (as was frequently done). Which coins would you use? Clearly, you would use new, undebased coins because you would part with less "face value" that way. The debased coins would thus remain in circulation, and the undebased coins would disappear. Whenever people got hold of an undebased coin, they would hold on to it; whenever they got a debased coin, they would pass it on. The example in Box 33-2 shows that Gresham's law is as applicable in the twentieth century as it was in the sixteenth century.

Paper Money

The next important step in the history of money was the evolution of paper currency. Artisans who worked with gold required secure safes, and the public began to deposit their gold with such goldsmiths for safekeeping. Goldsmiths would give their depositors receipts promising to hand over the gold on demand. When a depositor wished to make a large purchase, she could go to her goldsmith, reclaim some of her gold, and hand it over to the seller of the goods. If the seller had no immediate need for the gold, he would carry it back to the goldsmith for safekeeping.

If people knew the goldsmith to be reliable, there was no need to go through the cumbersome and risky business of physically transferring the gold. The buyer needed only to transfer the goldsmith's receipt to the seller, who would accept it, secure in the knowledge that the goldsmith would hand over the gold whenever it was needed. If the seller wished to buy a good from a third party, who also knew the goldsmith to be reliable, this transaction, too, could be effected by passing the goldsmith's receipt from the buyer to the seller. The convenience of using pieces of paper instead of gold is obvious.

Thus when it first came into being, paper money represented a promise to pay on demand a certain amount of gold, the promise being made first by goldsmiths and later by banks. Banks, too, became known for their vaults ("safes"), where the precious gold was stored and protected. As long as the institutions were known to be reliable, their pieces of paper would be "as good as gold." Such paper money was *backed* by precious metal and was *convertible on demand* into this metal. When a country's money is convertible into gold, the country is said to be on a *gold standard*.

In nineteenth century Canada, private banks operating initially under provincial charters commonly issued paper money nominally convertible into gold.

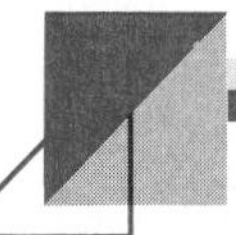

BOX 33-2

Where Has All the Coinage Gone?

Tourists who were traveling in Chile during the 1970s and in other countries with rapid inflation often wondered aloud why paper currency was used even for transactions as small as the purchase of a newspaper or a pack of matches. Metallic currency in such places was scarce and sometimes nonexistent. Similarly, the silver dollar, silver half dollar, silver quarter, and silver dime had disappeared from circulation in North America. The reason for these things is an example of Gresham's law.

Consider a country that has three different "tokens," each of which is legal tender in the amount of 25 cents. One is a silver quarter with 10 cents' worth of recoverable silver in it; a second is made of cheaper metals, with 5 cents' worth of recoverable metal in it; the third is a 25-cent bill, a colored piece of paper money that says plainly on its face "legal tender for all debts public and private."

If prices are stable and the government produces all three forms of money, there is no reason why they should not all circulate freely and interchangeably. Each is legal tender, and each is worth more as money than as anything else.

However, suppose that inflation starts and prices, including proportionally the prices of silver and other metals, begin to rise sharply. By the time prices have tripled, the silver quarters will have disappeared because the silver in each one is now worth 30 cents, and people will hoard them or melt them down rather than spend them to buy goods at an exchange value of only 25 cents. Although not everyone will do this, coins passing from hand to hand will eventually reach someone who withdraws them from circulation.

What about the coins made of cheaper metal? Since prices have tripled, they now contain metal worth 15 cents, still less than their face value. Will they too disappear? They will if there is further inflation of, say, 100 percent. This raises the market value of the metal in the coin above its face value. The coins will disappear as they are melted down. By that time, only the paper money will be in circulation. The "bad" paper money will have driven out the "good" metal money.

Thus inflation, and even the expectation of inflation, may make some money "good" and some money "bad" in Gresham's sense. If it does, the bad will displace the good.

Bank notes represented banks' promises to pay. They remained an important part of the money supply well into the twentieth century, and they were not completely supplanted by government-issued paper money until 1950.

Fractionally backed paper money. For most transactions, individuals were content to use paper currency. It was soon discovered that it was not necessary to keep an ounce of gold in the vaults for every claim to an ounce circulating as paper money. It was necessary to keep some gold on hand because paper would not do for some transactions. If someone wished to make a purchase from a distant place where her local bank was not known, she might have to convert her paper into gold and ship the gold. Further, she might not have perfect confidence in the bank's ability to honor its pledge to redeem the notes in gold at a future time. Her alternative was to exchange her notes for gold and to store the gold until she needed it.

For these and other reasons, some holders of notes demanded gold in return for their notes. However, some of the bank's customers would receive gold in various transactions and store it in the bank for safekeeping. They accepted promises to pay (i.e., bank notes) in return. At any one time, then, some of the bank's customers would be withdrawing gold, others would be depositing it, and most would be trading in the bank's paper notes without any need or desire to convert them into gold. Thus the bank was able to issue more money redeemable in gold than the amount of gold that it held in its vaults. This was good business, because the money could be invested profitably in interest-earning loans to households and firms.

This discovery was made by the early goldsmiths. From that time to the present, banks have had many more claims outstanding against them than they actually had in reserves available to pay those claims. We say that the currency issued in such a situation is *fractionally backed* by the reserves.

The major problem with a fractionally backed, convertible currency was maintaining its convertibility into the precious metal by which it was backed. The imprudent bank, which issued too much paper money, would find itself unable to redeem its currency in gold when the demand for gold was even slightly higher than usual. It would then have to suspend payments, and all holders of its notes would suddenly find that the notes were worthless. The prudent bank, which kept a reasonable relationship between its note issue and its gold reserve, would find that it could meet a normal range of demand for gold without any trouble.

If the public lost confidence and *en masse* demanded redemption of its currency, the banks would be unable to honor their pledges. The history of nineteenth and early twentieth century banking on both sides of the Atlantic is full of examples of banks that were ruined by "panics," or sudden runs on their gold reserves. When this happened, the banks' depositors and the holders of their notes would find themselves with worthless pieces of paper.

Fiat currencies. As time went on, note issue by private banks became less common, and central banks took control of the currency. Central banks, in turn, became governmental institutions. In time *only* central banks were permitted to issue notes. Originally, the central banks issued currency that was fully convertible into gold. In those days gold would be brought to the central bank, which would issue currency in the form of "gold certificates" that asserted that the gold was available on demand. The gold supply thus set some upper limit on the amount of currency.

However, central banks could issue more currency than they had in gold because in normal times only a small fraction of the currency was presented for payment at any one time. Thus even though the need to maintain convertibility under a gold standard put an upper limit on note issue, central banks had substantial discretionary control over the quantity of currency outstanding.

During the period between World Wars I and II, almost all of the countries of the world abandoned the gold standard; their currencies were no longer convertible into gold. Money that is not convertible by law into anything valuable depends on its acceptability for its value. Money that is declared by government order, or fiat, to be legal tender for settlement of all debts is called **fiat money**.

Today almost all currency is fiat money.

Today, few countries preserve the fiction that their currency is backed by gold, but no country allows its currency to be converted into gold on demand. Gold backing for Canadian currency was eliminated in 1940, although note issues continued to carry the traditional statement "will pay to the bearer on demand" until 1954. The holder of a $20 bill who took this seriously and demanded $20 could hand over the $20 bill and receive in return a different but identical $20 bill! Today's Bank of Canada notes simply say, "This note is legal tender." It is, in other words, fiat money pure and simple.

Legal tender is anything that by law must be accepted when offered either for the purchase of goods or services or to discharge a debt. If you are offered something that is legal tender in payment for a debt and you refuse to accept it, the debt is no longer legally collectible.

Not only is our modern currency fiat money, but so is our coinage. Modern coins, unlike their historical ancestors, contain a value of metal that is characteristically a minute fraction of the value of the coin. Modern coins, like modern paper money, are merely tokens.

Why Is Fiat Money Valuable?

Today paper money and coinage are valuable because they are generally accepted. Because everyone accepts them as valuable, they *are* valuable; the fact that they can no longer be converted into anything has no effect on their functioning as a medium of exchange.

In the early days of the gold standard, paper money was valuable because everyone believed that it was convertible into gold on demand. Experience during periods of crisis, when there was often a temporary suspension of convertibility into gold, and of panic, when there were bank failures, served to demonstrate that the mere *promise* of convertibility was not sufficient to make money valuable. Gradually, the realization grew that neither was convertibility necessary.

Fiat money is valuable because it is accepted in payment for the purchase of goods or services and for the discharge of debts.

Many people are disturbed to learn that present-day paper money is neither backed by nor convertible into anything more valuable—that it consists of nothing but pieces of paper whose value derives from common acceptance and from confidence that it will continue to be accepted in the future. Most people believe that their money should be more substantial than that; after all, what of the "bedrock solidity" of the Swiss franc? But money is, in fact, made of nothing more than pieces of paper. There is no point in pretending otherwise.

If paper money is acceptable, it is a medium of exchange; if its purchasing power remains stable, it is a satisfactory store of value; and if both of these things are true, it will also serve as a satisfactory unit of account.

Modern Money

By the twentieth century, private banks had lost the authority to issue bank notes. Yet they did not lose the power to create deposit money.

Deposit Money

Banks' customers frequently deposit coins and paper money with the banks for safekeeping, just as in former times they deposited gold. Such a deposit is recorded as an entry on the customer's account. A customer who wishes to pay a debt may come to the bank and claim the money in dollars and then pay the money to another person. This person may then redeposit the money in a bank.

Like the gold transfers, this is a tedious procedure, particularly for large payments. It is more convenient to have the bank transfer claims to this money on deposit. The common cheque is an instruction to the bank to make the transfer. As soon as such transfers became easy and inexpensive, and cheques became widely accepted in payment for commodities and debts, the deposits became **deposit money**, which is money held by the public in the form of deposits in banks that can be withdrawn on demand.

When Anne deposits $100 in a bank, the bank credits Anne's account with $100. This is the bank's promise to pay $100 cash on demand. If Anne pays Bruce $100 by writing a cheque that Bruce then deposits in the same bank, the bank merely reduces Anne's account by $100 and increases Bruce's by the same amount. Thus the bank still promises to pay on demand the $100 that originally was deposited, but it now promises to pay it to Bruce rather than to Anne. What makes all this so convenient is that Bruce can actually deposit Anne's cheque in any bank, and the banks will arrange the transfer of credits.

Cheques are in some ways the modern equivalent of old-time bank notes issued by commercial banks. The passing of a bank note from hand to hand transferred ownership of a claim against the bank. Similarly, a cheque on a deposit account is an order to the bank to pay the designated recipient, rather than oneself, money credited to the account. Cheques, unlike bank notes, do not circulate freely from hand to hand; thus cheques themselves are not currency. The balance in the demand deposit *is* money; the cheque transfers money from one person to another. Because cheques are easily drawn and deposited and because they are relatively safe from theft, they are widely used. In 1990 approximately 7 billion cheques were drawn in Canada. During the last two decades the number of cheques drawn increased by about 7 percent per year.

Thus when chartered banks lost the right to issue notes of their own, the form of bank money changed, but the substance did not. Today banks have money in their vaults (or on deposit with the central banks) just as they always did. Once it was gold; today it is the legal tender of the times—fiat money. It is true today, just as in the past, that most of the bank's customers are content to pay their bills by passing among themselves the bank's promises to pay money on demand. Only a small proportion of the transactions made by the bank's customers is made in cash.

Bank deposits are money. Today, just as in the past, banks can create money by issuing more promises to pay (deposits) than they have cash reserves available to pay out.

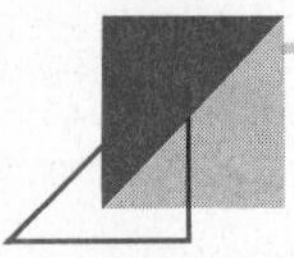

The Banking System

Many types of institutions make up a modern banking system such as exists in Canada today. The **central bank** is the government-owned and -operated institution that serves to control the banking system. Through it, the government's monetary policy is conducted. In Canada the central bank is the Bank of Canada, also referred to as the Bank.

Financial intermediaries are privately owned institutions that serve the general public. They are called intermediaries because they stand between savers, from whom they accept deposits, and investors, to whom they make loans. In this chapter we focus on an important class of financial intermediaries, the *commercial banks*; in Canada these are also referred to as the *chartered banks*.

Central Banks

All advanced free market economies have, in addition to commercial banks, a central bank. Many of the world's early central banks were private, profit-making institutions that provided services to ordinary banks. Their importance, however, led to their developing close ties with government. Central banks soon became instruments of the government, though not all of them were publicly owned. The Bank of England (the "Old Lady of Threadneedle Street"), one of the world's oldest and most famous central banks, began to operate as the central bank of England in the seventeenth century, but it was not "nationalized" until 1947.

The similarities in the functions performed and the tools used by the world's central banks are much more important than the differences in their organization. Although our attention is given to the operations of the Bank of Canada, its basic functions are similar to those of the Bank of England, the Bank of Greece, or the Federal Reserve System in the United States.

Organization of the Bank of Canada

The Bank of Canada is a publicly owned corporation; all profits accruing from its operations are remitted to the government of Canada. The responsibility for the bank's affairs rests with a board of directors composed of the governor, the senior deputy governor, the deputy minister of finance, and 12 directors. The governor is appointed by the directors, with the approval of the cabinet, for a seven-year term. In January 1987, John Crow was appointed governor, replacing Gerald Bouey, who retired after serving two seven-year terms.

The organization of the Bank of Canada is de-

TABLE 33-1 Assets and Liabilities of the Bank of Canada, December 1989 *(millions of dollars)*

Assets		Liabilities	
Government of Canada securities	23,590	Notes in circulation	22,093
Advances to banks	312	Government of Canada deposits	21
Foreign-currency assets	370	Deposits of chartered banks	1,787
Other assets	508	Foreign-currency liabilities	209
Total	24,780	Other liabilities and capital	670
		Total	24,780

Source: Bank of Canada Review, April 1990.

The balance sheet of the Bank of Canada shows that it serves as banker to the chartered banks and the government and as issuer of our currency; it also suggests the bank's role as regulator of money markets and the money supply. The principal liabilities of the Bank are the basis of the money supply. Bank of Canada notes are currency, and the deposits of the chartered banks give them the reserves they use to create deposit money. The bank's holdings of Government of Canada securities arise from its operations designed to regulate the money supply and financial markets.

signed to keep the operation of monetary policy free from day-to-day political influence. Thus the Bank is not responsible to Parliament for its day-to-day behavior in the way that the Department of Finance is for the operation of fiscal policy. Nonetheless, the governor of the Bank and the minister of finance consult regularly. Furthermore, in the case of fundamental disagreement over policy, the governor must resign or acquiesce to the cabinet's desired policy as enunciated by the minister.[1]

Basic Functions of the Bank of Canada

A central bank serves four main functions: as a banker for private banks, as a bank for the government, as the controller of the nation's supply of money, and as a supporter of financial markets. The first three functions are revealed by a study of Table 33-1, which shows the balance sheet of the Bank of Canada.

Banker to the chartered banks. The central bank accepts deposits from the chartered banks and will, on order, transfer them to the account of another bank. In this way the central bank provides the chartered banks with the equivalent of a chequing account and with a means of settling debts to other banks. The deposits of the chartered banks with the central bank appear in Table 33-1. Notice that the cash reserves of the chartered banks deposited with the central bank are *liabilities* of the central bank, because it promises to pay them on demand.

Historically, one of the earliest services provided by central banks was that of "lender of last resort" to the banking system. Central banks would lend money to private banks that had sound investments (such as government securities and safe loans to individuals) but were in urgent need of cash. If such banks could not obtain ready cash, they might be forced into insolvency because they could not meet the demands of their depositors, in spite of their being basically sound. Today's central banks continue to be the lenders of last resort.

U.S. banks borrow extensively from the Federal Reserve System in order to maintain their reserves, but the corresponding institutional arrangement that Canadian banks use is somewhat more complicated. Some Bank of Canada holdings of government securities, shown in Table 33-1, are held under **purchase and resale agreements (PRA)**. Rather than rely on loans from the Bank of Canada, the chartered banks meet their immediate cash requirements by varying the amount of **day-to-day loans** they make available to a group of investment dealers who carry inventories of Government of Canada securities. When necessary, these dealers can obtain financing from the Bank of Canada under PRA; that is, they can sell securities to the Bank of Canada and agree to buy them back at a later date. Thus when the chartered banks reduce their day-to-day loans, they induce an increase in PRA. The result is the same as if the banks had borrowed from the Bank of Canada directly.

Banker to the government. Governments, too, need to hold their funds in an account into which they can make deposits and on which they can write cheques. The government of Canada keeps its chequing deposits at the Bank of Canada, replenishing them from much larger accounts kept at the chartered banks. When the government requires more money, it too needs to borrow, and it does so by printing bonds. Most are sold directly to the public, but occasionally the government raises funds by selling securities (mostly short-term) to the central bank, which "buys" them by crediting the government's account with a deposit for the amount of the purchase. In December 1989 the Bank of Canada held over $23 billion in Government of Canada securities.

Controller and regulator of the money supply. One of the most important functions of a central bank is to control the money supply. From Table 33-1 it is clear that the overwhelming proportion of a central bank's liabilities (its promises to pay) are either notes (money) or the reserves of the chartered banks, which underlie the deposits (money) of households and firms.

The central bank can change the levels of its assets and liabilities in many ways, and as its liabilities rise and fall, so does the money supply. Consider a single example. Suppose that the central bank buys $100 million worth of newly printed bonds from the government of Canada. The bank's assets (government bonds) rise by $100 million, and so do its liabilities

[1] In 1962 when James Coyne was governor, such a fundamental disagreement arose and Coyne was eventually forced to resign. This incident established the precedent that the final responsibility for monetary policy lies with the government, not the governor.

(Government of Canada deposits). The government has an extra $100 million of purchasing power to spend. As easy as printing money, you say. Indeed, it is the same thing.

Regulator and supporter of money markets. Central banks usually assume a major responsibility to support the country's financial system and to prevent serious disruption by wide-scale panic and resulting bank failures. Various institutions are in the business of borrowing on a short-term basis and lending on a long-term basis. To some extent the chartered banks do this when they take in demand (or savings) deposits and lend money for various terms. But trust and mortgage loan companies are the major institutions for this kind of transaction. They receive deposits from the public and lend the money on long-term mortgages.

Large, unanticipated increases in interest rates tend to squeeze these institutions. The average rate they earn on their investments rises only slowly as old contracts mature and new ones are made, but they must either pay higher rates to hold on to their deposits or accept wide-scale withdrawals that could easily bring about insolvency. To prevent such financial disasters, central banks often buy and sell government bonds either to slow the rate of change in interest rates or to narrow the range over which the rates are allowed to fluctuate.

Conflicts among functions. The several functions of the central bank are not always compatible. For example, in pursuit of an anti-inflationary policy, the Bank may cause interest rates to rise. The resulting squeeze makes life uncomfortable for banks and other financial institutions and makes borrowing expensive for the government. If the Bank chooses to ease those problems, say, by lending money to chartered banks, it is relaxing its anti-inflationary policy.

The Bank must strive to balance conflicting objectives. We discuss a number of aspects of this conflict in Chapter 35. However, at this stage we note that many critics think that the Bank does not always succeed in finding the right balance between its conflicting objectives.

The Canadian System

There are two main types of modern commercial banking systems. One has a small number of banks, each with a large number of branch offices; the other consists of many independent banks, many of which are quite small. Canada and Britain have the first type, with only a few large banks accounting for the overwhelming bulk of the business. The American system is of the second type. The functioning of the banking system is, however, essentially the same in both systems.

A wide variety of banking systems exist, but they all function in essentially the same manner.

The Canadian banking system is controlled by the provisions of the Bank Act, first passed in 1935 and revised several times since. Under the Bank Act, charters can be granted to financial institutions to operate as banks, and until 1980 there were only a few chartered banks, most of which were very large and each of which operated under identical regulatory provisions.

The 1980 revisions to the Bank Act allowed for foreign banks to commence operations in Canada, although it severely limited the scale and scope of their activity. Subsequent revisions have altered some of these restrictions and made it easier to obtain new banking charters, but the revisions have maintained the distinction between these newer institutions and banks operating under what are essentially the pre-1980 provisions of the Bank Act. The original provisions, in slightly modified form, are now known as Schedule A of the Bank Act; the foreign banks and the new, smaller domestic banks operate under Schedules B and C. The term **chartered banks** is usually reserved for the Schedule A banks.

The chartered banks have common attributes: They hold deposits for their customers; they permit certain deposits to be transferred by cheque from an individual account to other accounts held in any bank branch in the country; they make loans to households and firms; and they invest in government securities.

Banks are not the only financial institutions in the country. Many other privately owned, profit-seeking institutions, such as trust companies and credit unions, accept savings deposits and grant loans for specific purposes. Finance companies make loans to households for practically any purpose—sometimes at very high effective interest rates. The post office and the telegraph system will transfer money, and credit card companies will extend credit so that purchases can be made on a buy-now, pay-later basis.

The banks (including Schedule B and C banks) are subject only to federal regulations and are required to hold reserves with the Bank of Canada against their deposit liabilities. Other institutions do not face reserve requirements, but most are subject to various federal and provincial regulations concerning ownership and control and the types of financial activities they are allowed to engage in. Thus there are differences among all types of financial institutions, not just between banks and others.

The chartered banks have historically been such a stable and dominant group that the terms *chartered banks* and *banking system* have been considered virtually synonymous. However, recent events may serve to break this identification. First, there have been dramatic changes in the makeup of the chartered banks—in 1985 two relatively new, regionally based chartered banks failed, and since then banks have merged in two instances and two Canadian banks were taken over by foreign banks. Second, the federal government and several provincial governments have recently proposed extensive changes in regulations, including the abolition of reserve requirements for the chartered banks, that would further blur the distinction between the chartered banks and other financial institutions. Third, there have been sweeping changes *internationally* in the structure and functining of financial markets; some of these developments are discussed further in Box 33-3.

Interbank Activities

Chartered banks have a number of interbank cooperative relationships. For example, banks often share loans. Even the biggest bank cannot meet all the credit needs of a giant corporation, and often a group of banks will offer a "pool loan," agreeing on common terms and dividing the loan up into manageable segments.

Another form of interbank cooperation is the bank credit card. Visa and MasterCard are the two most widely used credit cards, and each is operated by a group of banks.

Probably the most important form of interbank cooperation is cheque clearing and collection. Bank deposits are an effective medium of exchange only because banks accept each other's cheques. If a depositor in the Bank of Montreal writes a cheque to someone who deposits it in the Toronto Dominion Bank, the Bank of Montreal now owes money to the Toronto Dominion Bank. This creates a need for the banks to present cheques to each other for payment.

There are millions of such transactions in the course of a day, and they result in an enormous sorting and bookkeeping job. Multibank systems make use of a **clearing house** where interbank debts are settled. At the end of the day, all the cheques drawn by the Bank of Montreal's customers and deposited in the Toronto Dominion Bank are totaled and set against the total of all the cheques drawn by the Toronto Dominion's customers and deposited in the Bank of Montreal. It is necessary only to settle the difference between the two sums. The actual cheques are passed through the clearing house back to the bank on which they were drawn. Both banks are then able to adjust the individual accounts by a set of book entries. A flow of cash between banks is necessary only when there is a net transfer of cash from the customers of one bank to those of another. This flow of cash is accompanied by a transfer of deposits held by the chartered banks with the Bank of Canada.

Profit Seeking

Banks are private firms that start with invested capital and seek to "earn money" in the same sense as firms making neckties or bicycles. A chartered bank provides a variety of services to its customers: a safe place to store money, the convenience of demand deposits that can be transferred by personal cheque, a safe and convenient place to earn a modest but guaranteed return on savings, and often financial advice and estate management services. The bank earns some revenue by charging for these services, but such fees are a small part of the bank's total earnings. The largest part (typically about five-sixths) of a bank's earnings is derived from the bank's ability to invest profitably the funds placed with it.

Principal Assets and Liabilities

Table 33-2 is the combined balance sheet of the chartered banks in Canada. The bulk of a bank's liabilities are deposits owed to its depositors. The principal assets of a bank are the *securities* it buys (including government bonds), which pay interest or dividends, and the *loans* it makes to individuals and to businesses. A bank loan is a liability to the borrower

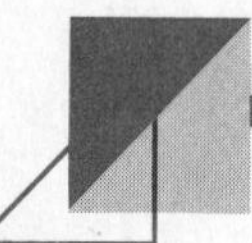

BOX 33-3

The Globalization of Financial Markets

Technological innovations in communication and the desire to avoid onerous government regulations have recently led to a globalization of the financial service industry. Computers, satellite communication systems, reliable telephones with direct worldwide dialing, electronic mail, and fax machines—all coming into widespread use only within the past decade—have put people in instantaneous contact anywhere in the world.

As a result of these new technologies, borrowers and lenders can learn about market conditions and then move their funds instantly anywhere in search of the most favorable loan rates. Large firms need transaction balances only while banks in their area are open. Once banks close for the day in each center, the firms know that they will not need these balances until tomorrow's reopening; thus the funds can be moved to another market, where they are used until it closes. They are then moved to yet another market. Funds are thus free to move from London to Toronto to Tokyo and back to London on a daily rotation. This is a degree of global sophistication that was inconceivable before the advent of the computer, when international communication was much slower and costlier than it now is. To facilitate the movement in and out of various national currencies, increasing amounts of bank deposits are denominated in foreign rather than domestic currencies.

One of the first developments in this movement towad globalization was the growth of the foreign currency markets in Europe in the 1960s. At first the main currency involved was the U.S. dollar, and hence *Eurodollar* markets were the first to develop. Today the *Eurobond* market is an international market where bonds of various types, denominated in various national currencies, are issued and sold to customers located throughout the world. The customers are mainly public corporations, international organizations, and multinational enterprises. The *Eurocurrency* market is a market for short-term bank deposits and bank loans denominated in various currencies. In both markets, the U.S. dollar accounts for the largest single volume of transactions, but many other currencies are also used.

The original attraction of the Eurodollar market was the freedom from the restrictions placed by the Federal Reserve on American commercial banks. By operating in offshore markets, the banks could avoid reserve requirements and interest-rate ceilings imposed on various types of deposits. This allowed the banks to operate on lower reserve margins and to cut unit costs by dealing in large volume at the wholesale level. They could then offer rates that were higher for lenders and lower for borrowers than those prevailing in the United States.

The progressive worldwide lifting of interest-rate ceilings and other capital market restrictions—including exchange controls, which were lifted after most countries abandoned fixed exchange rates in the 1970s—led to a further globalization of the fi-

(who must pay it back) but an asset to the bank. The bank expects not only to have the loan repaid but also to receive interest that more than compensates for the paperwork involved and the risk of nonpayment.

Banks attract deposits by paying interest to depositors and by providing them, for a fee that does not cover the banks' full cost, with services such as clearing cheques and providing regular monthly statements. Banks earn profits by lending and investing money deposited with them for more than they pay their depositors in terms of interest and other services provided.

Competition for Deposits

Competition for deposits is active among banks and between banks and other financial institutions. Financial deregulation, which removed restrictions on the activities of various financial institutions, has contributed to this competition.

Interest paid on deposits, special high-interest

nancial markets. Although this removed some of the original reasons for their growth, the Euromarkets prospered. First, they allowed banks to avoid the remaining domestic restrictions, such as minimum reserve requirements. Second, the advantage of having an international market dealing in many different national currencies was sufficient to sustain the markets.

The increasing sophistication of information transfer also led to a breakdown of the high degree of specialization that had characterized financial markets in earlier decades. When information was difficult to obtain and analyze, an efficient division of labor called for a host of specialist institutions, each with expertise in a narrow range of transactions. As a result of the new developments in communication technology, economies of large scale came to dominate the efficiencies of a detailed division of labor. The integration of various financial operations within one firm then became increasingly common. For example, banks have moved into the markets where securities are traded, while many security-trading fims have begun to offer a range of banking services. As the scale of such integrated firms increases, they find it easier to extend their operations geographically as well as functionally.

It has often been difficult for government regulations to keep up with these rapid changes. Governments that relaxed their regulations first in face of the evolving realities often allowed their financial institutions to gain important advantages in international competition. The U.K. government has been quick to react to these developments, and as a result London has retained its strong position in the international financial world. In contrast, the U.S. government has been slow to adapt. For example, it still limits interstate banking and prevents U.S. banks from extending their operations beyond the ones traditionally reserved for banks. As a result, the U.S. banks have lost out heavily to European and Japanese banks.

The Canadian government has also been slow to react, although the barriers between the traditional "four pillars" of the Canadian financial sector (banking, trust, insurance, and securities) have been crumbling. Some provinces—particularly Quebec—have moved more quickly than others. It seems a safe bet that in 1990s the agenda for deregulation of the financial sector will remain full, often driven by international developments such as those noted here.

The kinds of government intervention into domestic capital markets and government control over international capital flows that characterized the 1950s and 1960s are no longer possible. International markets are just too sophisticated. Globalization is here to stay, and by removing domestic restrictions and exchange controls, governments in advanced countries are only bowing to the inevitable.

deposits (such as CICs), advertising, personal solicitation of accounts, giveaway programs for new deposits to existing accounts, and improved services are all forms of competition for funds. Among the special services are payroll and pension accounting for industrial customers. The *lockbox* is another kind of service: Banks establish locked post office boxes to which retail customers of large companies send their payments. The bank opens the remittances, deposits them to the company's account, and forwards notices of payment to the company. All these services are costly to the bank, but they serve as inducements to customers to maintain deposits with the financial institution.

Reserves

The Need for Reserves

All bankers would as a matter of convenience and prudence keep sufficient cash on hand to be able to meet depositors' day-to-day requirements for cash.

TABLE 33-2 Consolidated Balance Sheet of Canadian Chartered Banks, December 31, 1989 (*billions of dollars*)

Assets		Liabilities	
Reserves (including deposits with Bank of Canada)	10	Demand deposits	25
Loans (determined in Canadian dollars)	270	Savings deposits	184
Government of Canada securities	21	Time deposits	64
Foreign-currency assets	172	Foreign-currency liabilities	180
Other assets	78	Other liabilities	70
Total	551	Capital account	28
		Total	551

Source: Bank of Canada Review, April 1990.

Reserves are only a small fraction of deposit liabilities. If all the bank's customers who held demand deposits tried to withdraw them in cash, the banks could not meet this demand without liquidating $15 billion of other assets. This would be impossible without assistance from the Bank of Canada.

But just as the goldsmiths of old discovered that only a fraction of the gold they held was ever withdrawn at any given time, and just as banks of old discovered that only a small fraction of convertible bank notes was actually converted, so too have modern banks discovered that only a small fraction of their deposits will be withdrawn in cash at any one time.

The reserves needed to ensure that depositors can withdraw their deposits on demand will be quite small in normal times.

In abnormal times, however, nothing short of 100 percent might do the job if the commercial banking system had to stand alone. Should a few bank failures cause a general loss of confidence in banks' ability to redeem their deposits, the results would be devastating. Until relatively recent times, such an event—or even the rumor of it—could lead to a run on banks as depositors rushed to withdraw their money. Faced with such a panic, banks would have to close until they had borrowed funds or liquidated enough assets to meet the demand or until the demand subsided. However, banks could not instantly turn their loans into cash since the borrowers had the money tied up in such things as real estate or business enterprises. Neither could the banks obtain cash by selling their securities to the public since payments would be made by cheques, which would not provide cash with which to pay off depositors.

The difficulty of providing sufficient liquidity to meet abnormal situations can be alleviated by the central bank.

Because it controls the supply of bank reserves, the central bank can provide all the reserves that are needed to meet any abnormal situation. It can do this in two ways. First, it can lend reserves directly to the chartered banks, using as collateral bank assets that are sound but not easy to liquidate quickly. Second, it can enter the open market and buy all the securities that the commercial banks need to sell. Once the public finds that deposits can be turned into cash, the panic will usually subside, and any further drain of cash out of banks will cease.

The possibility of panic withdrawals is also greatly diminished by the provision of government deposit insurance, which guarantees that depositors will get their money back even if a bank fails completely. Most depositors will not withdraw their money as long as they are *certain* they can get it when they need it.

Although deposit insurance confers a number of benefits on the operation of the financial system, it has also been subject to considerable criticism in recent years. This is taken up in Box 33-4.

Actual and Required Reserves

Look again at Table 33-2 and observe that the banking system's cash reserves are just a fraction of its deposits. If the holders of even 40 percent of its demand deposits had demanded cash sometime in January 1990, the commercial banking system would have been unable to meet the demand without outside help.

The Canadian banking system is a *fractional reserve system*, with banks holding reserves of much less than 100 percent of their deposits.

A bank's **reserve ratio** is the fraction of its deposit liabilities that it holds as reserves, either as cash or as deposits with the central bank. The chartered banks also hold liquid assets, such as interest-bearing Government of Canada bonds and treasury bills. These assets generally earn a lower yield than loans, but they act as *secondary reserves* that can be converted into cash quickly should cash holdings be run down.

In the past, legal requirements imposed by the Bank Act have required the chartered banks to hold reserves. These requirements were thought necessary not only to ensure the stability of the banking system but also, as we shall discuss later in this chapter, to enhance the Bank of Canada's ability to control the money supply. The reserves that the Bank Act requires the banks to hold are called **required reserves**. As of mid 1990, banks were required to hold reserves of 10 percent against demand deposits and 2 percent against notice deposits; on average, this works out to a total reserve requirement of 4 percent of total deposit liabilities.

The size of the reserves held by the banking system reflects not only the legal requirements imposed by the Bank Act but also the judgment of bankers. We call the fraction of deposits that a bank wishes to hold as reserves its **target reserve ratio**. The corresponding level of reserves is called its **target reserves**, and any reserves it holds in excess of these target reserves are called its **excess reserves**.[2]

Many analysts have argued that the legal requirement that chartered banks hold some of their assets as reserves, which do not pay interest, places them at a disadvantage relative to their competitors, including Canadian nonbank financial institutions and some foreign commercial banks, that are not subject to such requirements. For example, trust companies in Canada do not face reserve requirements yet compete directly with the chartered banks in attracting deposits and making loans. Globalization of financial markets has brought domestic financial institutions into direct competition with foreign ones, and continuing deregulation of financial markets has enhanced the competition between banks and nonbank financial institutions. These developments have strengthened the argument for a "level playing field" in the sense of making the regulations on competing institutions more similar. Recently the Bank of Canada has announced its intention to eliminate reserve requirements for the banks.

Although reserve requirements are to be eliminated, the chartered banks will continue to hold reserves, as do other financial institutions not currently subject to reserve requirements.

The banks will hold reserves not only because it is prudent financial management to keep liquid assets on hand to meet the needs of its customers but also because they must maintain deposits with the Bank of Canada in order to facilitate clearing transactions with other financial institutions. These deposits are referred to as *clearing balances*; the *clearing house* role of the Bank of Canada was discussed earlier in this chapter. Clearing balances are used to settle the net transfers that occur as a result of imbalances in the transactions between banks.

The Bank of Canada expects that under its proposed new system, its ability to influence the chartered banks' clearing balances will enable it to control the money supply. The system is designed to ensure that the banks will hold reserves that are stable in relation to their deposits since the Bank of Canada will impose financial penalties on any chartered bank that does not maintain sufficient balances to meet its clearing needs. The prediction that such a system will function effectively is borne out by the experience of other countries such as the United Kingdom where required reserves were eliminated many years ago.

We return to this issue of the ability of the Bank of Canada to control the money supply after we have examined how the money supply is determined. Our analysis of the money supply process is based on the following behavior of the chartered banks:

Chartered banks will wish to maintain some target level of reserves equal to its target ratio of reserves to deposits. This target ratio may be partly or wholly a legally imposed requirement

[2] In previous editions we defined *any* reserves held over and above required reserves as excess reserves. Our current usage is slightly different since the *target* level of reserves could exceed the required level. In a system with *zero* required reserves, this will necessarily be the case. Thus *excess reserves* is now taken to mean more reserves than the banks wish to hold, taking into account required reserves and other reasons for wanting to hold reserves.

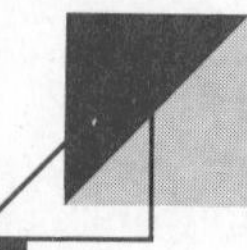

BOX 33-4

Deposit Insurance and the Financial System

Deposit insurance assures depositors that their funds are secure whatever the fate of their deposit institution. This is a great boon for depositors, but experience has shown that it is a double-edged sword.

On the one hand, deposit insurance provides security to depositors. This is a good thing in itself. It also helps to stabilize the economy in times of financial distress by preventing large losses of wealth when financial institutions fail.

On the other hand, deposit insurance creates an incentive for financial intermediaries to pursue riskier investments than they would if depositors had to worry about losing their deposits should the institution fail. Because of deposit insurance, depositors have no reason to select deposit institutions according to the riskiness of their investments. They are free instead to select the institution that pays the highest interest without worrying about the associated risk.

Deposit insurance is thus an example of an important class of government institutions that create situations whereby *heads, the private investor wins, and tails, the taxpayer loses.* In the financial sector, such institutions take in depositors' insured funds; if the owners place them in risky ventures that pay off, the owners get the profits; if the owners place the funds in ventures that fail, the taxpayers must meet the bill by repaying those who provided the capital (the depositors).

The Experience of U.S. S&Ls

The conflict between the two roles played by deposit insurance is illustrated by the crisis of the savings and loan associations (S&Ls) in the United States. These institutions take in deposits from the public and invest the funds in mortgages.

In 1988, rising interest rates meant that the interest costs paid by the S&Ls on deposits rose quite sharply. However, since most of their assets were long-term, their interest return on assets did not rise in step. These problems were intensified by reductions in real estate values in many parts of the country. S&Ls holding mortgages concentrated in these areas suffered poor collection rates and high default rates. The problems were also intensified by increased competition from foreign institutions as a result of the globalization of financial markets, and from other domestic financial institutions as a result of deregulation of financial markets. This experience led to a period of sustained losses for many S&Ls in the late 1980s. As a result, owners had little, if any, capital of their own left in their companies; liabilities were as large as assets, and owner equity had been reduced to virtually zero.

The reaction to this difficult economic situation was influenced by the regulatory situation. Government deposit insurance gave the owners strong incentives to make very risky investments—investments that carried risks that their depositors would

or partly or wholly a self-determined target dictated by prudent financial management.

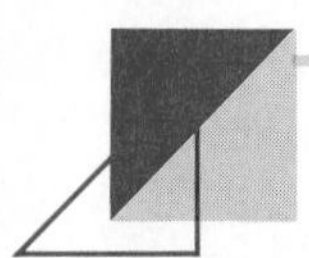

Money Creation by the Banking System

The fractional reserve system provides the leverage that permits commercial banks and other financial institutions to create money. The process is important and needs to be examined in some detail.

Some Simplifying Assumptions

To focus on the essential aspects of how banks create money, assume that banks can invest in only one kind of asset, loans, and that there is only one kind of deposit, a demand deposit.

Two other assumptions are provisional. When we have developed the basic ideas concerning the bank's creation of money, these assumptions will be relaxed.

never have agreed to accept. But this calculation was never relevant because the insurance provided a buffer between the providers of the funds and the users of the funds. If the high-risk investment worked out, the owners would reap large profits. If it failed, the owners lost little of their own capital, since the institutions already had almost zero net worth, and the depositors, who did have capital in the institutions, were repaid by deposit insurance.

While some of the S&L losses were due to normal operations in the face of adverse circumstances, some were due to risky decisions made by owners who did not bear the losses themselves. (This is an example of *moral hazard*, a concept first encountered in Chapter 8.)

The Canadian Experience

Though the Canadian financial system has never suffered the dramatic problems faced by the U.S. S&Ls, Canadian financial institutions have occasionally failed, including two western banks in the mid 1980s. When those institutions went under, depositors were repaid by the Canadian Federal Deposit Insurance Corporation (FDIC). Although the legal ceiling on deposit insurance was $60,000, deposits in excess of that amount were also repaid, using taxpayer money. This created the precedent that ceilings on deposit insurance were not be taken seriously. Any amount would be likely to be repaid. Hence no investor need worry about the financial probity of the investments made by the institutions in which his or her money was deposited.

What Can Be Done?

Several reforms are possible. They fall into two types: those that would keep deposit insurance and provide the necessary accompanying regulations and those that would take deregulation to its logical conclusion of ending deposit insurance.

The implications of deposit insurance for the investment behavior of financial intermediaries suggests that if deposit insurance is to be maintained, other regulations concerning capital requirements and investment standards need to be applied. In addition, the deposit insurance system might be reformed in order to relate the cost of insurance for a particular institution to the risks implied by that institution's asset position.

Many economists believe that if deregulation of financial institutions is regarded as desirable, it should be accompanied by a reform of deposit insurance so that the people who use the funds will be more accountable to those who provide them.

1. *Fixed reserve ratio.* It is assumed that all banks maintain the same, constant reserve ratio, which does not change. In our numerical illustration we shall assume that this *target reserve ratio* is 20 percent (i.e., 0.20); that is, at least $1 of reserves are held for every $5 of deposits.[3] Thus we assume that all banks want to invest any reserves that they have in excess of their target reserves; this implies that they always believe that there are profitable investments—loans, in our example—to be made when they have excess reserves.
2. *No cash drain from the banking system.* It is assumed that the public holds a fixed amount of currency in circulation. Thus changes in the money supply will take the form of changes in deposit money.

[3] This assumption of a constant *target reserve ratio* could reflect either a system with a constant and binding *required* reserve ratio or a system with zero required reserves combined with chartered banks maintaining a constant desired reserve ratio. In either case, we speak of the banks as holding zero excess reserves.

The Creation of Deposit Money

A hypothetical bank's balance sheet is shown in Table 33-3. The hypothetical Canadian Immigrants

TABLE 33-3 Initial Balance Sheet of the Canadian Immigrants Bank of Commerce (*thousands of dollars*)

Assets		Liabilities	
Cash and other reserves	200	Deposits	1,000
Loans	900	Capital	100
Total	1,100	Total	1,100

The CIBC has a reserve of 20 percent of its deposit liabilities. The chartered bank earns money by finding profitable investments for much of the money deposited with it. In this balance sheet, loans are its earning assets.

Bank of Commerce (CIBC) has assets of $200 of reserves (all figures are in thousands of dollars), held partly as cash on hand and partly as deposits with the central bank, and $900 of loans outstanding to its customers. Its liabilities are $100 to those who initially contributed capital to start the bank, and $1,000 to current depositors. The bank's ratio of reserves to deposits is 200/1,000 = 0.20, exactly equal to its minimum requirement.

A Single New Deposit

An immigrant arrives in the country and opens an account by depositing $100 with the CIBC. This is a wholly new deposit for the bank, and it results in a revised balance sheet (Table 33-4). As a result of the immigrant's new deposit, both cash assets and deposit liabilities have risen by $100. More important, the CIBC's ratio of reserves to deposits has increased from 0.20 to 0.27 (300/1,100). The bank

TABLE 33-4 Balance Sheet of CIBC After an Immigrant Deposits $100 (*thousands of dollars*)

Assets		Liabilities	
Cash and other reserves	300	Deposits	1,100
Loans	900	Capital	100
Total	1,200	Total	1,200

The immigrant's deposit raises deposit liabilities and cash assets by the same amount. Since both cash and deposits rise by $100, the cash reserve ratio, formerly 0.20, increases to 0.27. The bank has more cash than it needs to provide a 20 percent reserve against its deposit liabilities.

TABLE 33-5 CIBC Balance Sheet After a New Loan and Cash Drain of $80 (*thousands of dollars*)

Assets		Liabilities	
Cash and other reserves	220	Deposits	1,100
Loans	980	Capital	100
Total	1,200	Total	1,200

The bank lends its surplus cash and suffers a cash drain. The bank keeps $20 as a reserve against the immigrant's new deposit of $100. It lends $80 to a customer who writes a cheque to someone who deals with another bank. When the cheque is cleared, the CIBC suffers an $80 cash drain. Comparing Tables 33-3 and 33-5 shows that the bank has increased its deposit liabilities by the $100 deposited by the new immigrant and increased its assets by $20 of cash reserves and $80 of new loans. It has also restored its reserve ratio of 0.20.

now has $80 in excess reserves; with $1,100 in deposits, its required reserves are only $220.

The CIBC will now lend the $80 excess reserves that it is holding. Table 33-5 shows the position after this has been done and after the proceeds of the loan have been withdrawn to be deposited to the account of a customer of another bank. The CIBC once again has a 20 percent reserve ratio.

So far, of the $100 initial deposit in the CIBC, $20 is held by the CIBC as reserves against the deposit and $80 has been lent out in the system. However, other banks have received new deposits of $80 stemming from the loans made by the CIBC; persons receiving payment from those who borrowed the $80 from the CIBC will have deposited those payments in their own banks. Note that while the banking system suffers no cash drain (i.e., all the money lent out is returned to the banking system as deposits), the CIBC does suffer a cash drain (i.e., most of the money lent out is not redeposited at the CIBC).

The banks that receive deposits from the proceeds of the CIBC's loan are sometimes called *next-generation banks* or, more specifically according to the situation, *second-generation, third-generation,* and so on. In this case the second-generation banks receive new deposits of $80, and when the cheques clear, they have new reserves of $80. Because they require only $16 in additional reserves to support the new deposits, they have $64 of excess reserves. They now increase their loans by $64. After this money is spent by the borrowers and has been deposited in other, third-

TABLE 33-6 Changes in the Balance Sheets of Second-Generation Banks (*thousands of dollars*)

Assets		Liabilities	
Cash and other reserves	+ 16	Deposits	+ 80
Loans	+ 64		
Total	+ 80	Total	+ 80

Second-generation banks receive cash deposits and expand loans. The second-generation banks gain new deposits of $80 as a result of the loan granted by the CIBC, which is used to make payments to customers of the second-generation banks. These banks keep 20 percent of the cash they acquire as their reserve against the new deposit, and they can make new loans using the other 80 percent. When the customers who borrowed the money make payments to the customers of third-generation banks, a cash drain occurs.

generation banks, the balance sheets of the second-generation banks will have changed, as in Table 33-6.

The third-generation banks now find themselves with $64 of new deposits. Against these they need hold only $12.80 in cash, so they have excess reserves of $51.20 that they can immediately lend out. Thus begins a long sequence of new deposits, new loans, new deposits, and new loans. The stages are shown in Table 33-7. The series in the table should look familiar, for it is the same convergent process we met when dealing with the multiplier in Chapter 28.

If v is the reserve ratio, the ultimate effect on the deposits of the banking system of a new deposit will be $1/v$ times the new deposit.[4] [39] The banking system has created new deposits and thus new money, although each banker can honestly say, "All I did was invest my excess reserves. I can do no more than manage wisely the money I receive." At the end of the process depicted in Table 33-7, the change in the combined balance sheets of all the banks in the system is shown in Table 33-8.

[4] The "multiple expansion of deposits" that has just been worked through applies in reverse to a withdrawal of funds. Deposits of the banking system will fall by $1/v$ times any amount withdrawn from the bank and not redeposited at another.

TABLE 33-7 Sequence of Loans and Deposits After a Single Initial Deposit (*thousands of dollars*)

Bank	New deposits	New loans	Addition to reserves
CIBC	100.00	80.00	20.00
Second-generation bank	80.00	64.00	16.00
Third-generation bank	64.00	51.20	12.80
Fourth-generation bank	51.20	40.96	10.24
Fifth-generation bank	40.96	32.77	8.19
Sixth-generation bank	32.77	26.22	6.55
Seventh-generation bank	26.22	20.98	5.24
Eighth-generation bank	20.98	16.78	4.20
Ninth-generation bank	16.78	13.42	3.36
Tenth-generation bank	13.42	10.74	2.68
Total first 10 generations	446.33	357.07	89.26
All remaining generations	53.67	42.93	10.74
Total for banking systems	500.00	400.00	100.00

The banking system as a whole can create deposit money whenever it receives new reserves. The table shows the process of the creation of deposit money on the assumptions that all the loans made by one set of banks end up as deposits in another set of banks (the next-generation banks), that the target reserve ratio (v) is 0.20, and that there are no excess reserves. Although each bank suffers a cash drain whenever it grants a new loan, the system as a whole does not, and the system ends up doing in a series of steps what a monopoly bank would do all at once; that is, it increases deposit money by $1/v$, which in this example is five times the amount of any increase in reserves that it obtains.

TABLE 33-8 The Combined Balance Sheets of All the Banks in the System Following the Multiple Expansion of Deposits (*thousands of dollars*)

Assets		Liabilities	
Cash and other reserves	+ 100	Deposits	+ 500
Loans	+ 400		
Total	+ 500	Total	+ 500

The reserve ratio is returned to 0.20. The entire initial deposit of $100 ends up as reserves of the banking system. Therefore, deposits rise by (1/0.2) times the initial deposit, that is, by $500.

Many Deposits

A more realistic picture of deposit creation is one in which new deposits accrue simultaneously to all banks, perhaps because of changes in the monetary policy of the government. (We shall study monetary policy in detail in Chapter 35.)

Say, for example, that the community contains 10 banks of equal size and that each receives new deposits of $100 in cash. Now each bank is in the position shown in Table 33-4, and each can begin to expand deposits based on the $100 of excess reserves. (Each bank does this by granting loans to customers.)

Because each bank does one-tenth of the total banking business, an average of 90 percent of any newly created deposit will find its way into other banks as the customer pays other people in the community by cheque. This will represent a cash drain from the lending bank to the other banks. However, roughly 10 percent of each new deposit created by each of the other nine banks should find its way into this bank. All banks receive new cash and all begin creating deposits simultaneously.

The expansion can go on with each bank watching its own ratio of cash reserves to deposits, expanding deposits as long as the ratio exceeds 1/5 and ceasing when it reaches that figure. The process will come to a halt when each bank has created $400 in additional deposits, so that for each initial $100 cash deposit, there is now $500 in deposits backed by $100 in cash.

The general rule, if there is no cash drain, is that a banking system with a reserve ratio of v can change its deposits by $1/v$ times any change in reserves.

Variable Reserve Ratios and Cash Drains

The two simplifying assumptions made earlier can now be relaxed.

Variable reserve ratio. If banks do not choose to invest excess reserves, the multiple expansion discussed will not occur. Turn back to Table 33-4. If the CIBC had been content to hold 27 percent reserves, it might well have done nothing more. Other things being equal, banks will choose to invest excess reserves because of the profit motive. But there may be times when they believe that the risk is too great. It is one thing to be offered a good rate of interest on a loan, but if the borrower defaults on the payment of interest and principal, the bank will be the loser. Similarly, if the bank expects interest rates to rise in the future, it may hold off making loans now so that it will have reserves available to make more profitable loans after the interest rate has risen.

Deposit creation does not happen automatically; it depends on decisions of bankers. If banks do not choose to use excess reserves to expand their loans, there will be no expansion of deposits.

The money supply is thus at least partly determined by the chartered banks in response to such forces as changes in the level of economic activity or in interest rates. However, the upper limit of deposits is determined by the banks' willingness to hold reserves and by the reserves available to them, both of which are under the influence of the Bank of Canada.

Cash drain. We now extend our analysis to make it a little more realistic. Suppose that firms and households were to keep a fixed *fraction* of their money holding in cash (say, 5 percent of their deposits) instead of a fixed *amount* of dollars. In that case an extra $100 in money supply will not all stay in the banking system; some will remain on deposit, and the rest will be added to cash in the hands of the public. In such a situation, any multiple expansion of bank deposits will be accompanied by a cash drain to the public that will reduce the maximum expansion below what it was when the public was content to hold all its new money as bank deposits.

The story of deposit creation when all banks receive new deposits and there is a cash drain to the

TABLE 33-9 The Combined Balance Sheets of All the Banks in the System Following the Multiple Expansion of Deposits with a Cash Drain *(thousands of dollars)*

Assets		Liabilities	
Cash and other reserves	+ 80	Deposits	+ 400
Loans	+ 320		
Total	+ 400	Total	+ 400

The reserve ratio is 0.20 and cash drain is 0.05. Only $80 of the initial deposit of $100 ends up as reserves of the banking system. Therefore, deposits rise by (1/0.2) times the $80, that is, by $400.

public goes like this. Each bank starts creating deposits and suffers no significant cash drain to other banks. But because approximately 5 percent of newly created deposits are withdrawn to be held as cash, each bank suffers a cash drain to the public. The expansion continues, each bank watching its own ratio of cash reserves to deposits, expanding deposits as long as the ratio exceeds $\frac{1}{5}$ and ceasing when it reaches that figure. Because the expansion is accompanied by a cash drain, it will come to a halt with a smaller deposit expansion than in the case of no cash drain.[5]

Table 33-9 shows the consolidated balance sheets of the banking system after the deposit expansion arising from an initial injection of $100 when there is a cash drain. As shown, since there is a cash drain of $20, reserves rise by only $80 and deposits rise by only $400.

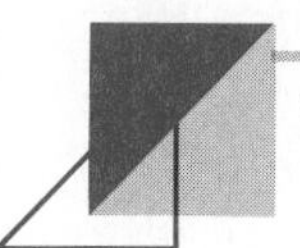

The Money Supply

The total stock of money in the economy at any moment is called the **money supply** or the **supply of money**. Economists use several alternative definitions for the money supply, most of which are regularly reported in the *Bank of Canada Review*. Typically, the definitions involve the sum of currency in circulation plus some types of deposit liabilities of financial institutions; definitions vary in terms of what deposits are included. Different definitions become more or less useful as the importance of different types of deposits changes.

Kinds of Deposits

Most of the deposits held by the average person are either demand deposits or savings deposits.

Demand Deposits

A **demand deposit** means that the customer can withdraw the money on demand (i.e., without giving any notice of intention to withdraw). Demand deposits are transferable by cheque. A cheque instructs the bank to pay without delay a stated sum of money to the person to whom the cheque is made payable.

Savings Deposits

Prior to recent changes in the Bank Act, a **savings deposit** was an interest-bearing deposit legally withdrawable only after a certain notice period. (Hence another term for savings deposit used to be *time deposit.*) In practice, although it was impossible to pay a bill by writing a cheque on a savings deposit, such deposits were always quickly convertible into a medium of exchange. A depositor wishing to use a savings deposit to pay a bill had to withdraw money from a savings account and then either pay the bill in cash or deposit the funds in a demand account and write a cheque on the demand account.

The Disappearing Distinction

For decades interest rates on savings deposits amounted to only a few percent, and people were content to keep most of their money in savings deposits and their reserves of cash for ordinary transactions in demand deposits. Then interest rates available on savings deposits and other safe liquid investments grew, and it became more and more expensive (in terms of lost interest) to keep cash in demand deposits, even for a week or two. Starting in the early 1970s, a number of changes in banking practices occurred that made it easier to convert interest-bearing deposits into demand deposits transferable by cheque.

Chequable savings accounts are now common, and most banks offer a service whereby fixed sums

[5] It can be shown algebraically that the percentage of cash drain must be added to the reserve ratio to determine the maximum possible expansion of deposits. [40]

are automatically transferred from a customer's savings account to his or her demand account when funds in the demand account become insufficient to meet newly presented cheques. The effective distinction is no longer between demand and savings accounts but rather among a multitude of types of accounts, each offering different combinations of interest payments, services provided, and service charges levied. The deposit that is genuinely tied up for a period of time now takes the form of a *term deposit,* which is purchased with a statement of a particular withdrawal date, a minimum of 30 days into the future, and which pays a much reduced interest rate in the event of early withdrawal.

Demand deposits offer other services to compensate for the lack of interest earnings. These include free traveler's cheques, detailed monthly statements, and return of canceled cheques.

Nonchequable deposits and some other liquid assets are so easily (sometimes automatically) converted into a medium of exchange that the distinction between what is and is not legally a medium of exchange is of diminishing significance.

TABLE 33-10 Canadian Money Supply, January 1990 (*billions of dollars*)

Currency	18.4
+ Demand deposits	21.0
= M1	39.4
+ Personal savings deposits and nonpersonal notice deposits	203.7
= M2	243.1
+ Nonpersonal fixed-term deposits and foreign-currency deposits	46.8
= M3	289.9

Source: Bank of Canada Review, June 1990.

The money supply can be defined in a variety of ways: M1, M2, and M3 figures are all published regularly by the Bank of Canada. M1 is the narrowly defined money supply that includes items that serve directly as media of exchange. M2 includes additional categories of bank deposits that serve the store-of-value function and can be readily converted into demand deposits or currency. M3 adds in bank term deposits that cannot be converted easily because the funds must remain on deposit for a fixed term and foreign-currency deposits whose value in terms of Canadian dollars varies with the exchange rate. (A series called M2+ adds to M2 related deposits with trust companies, credit unions, and Quebec savings institutions called *caisses populaires.*)

Definitions of the Money Supply

Different definitions of the money supply include different types of deposits. The narrowly defined money supply, called **M1**, includes currency and deposits that are themselves usable as media of exchange. Broader definitions, such as **M2** and **M3**, include savings accounts and term deposits. These are liquid assets that serve the temporary-store-of-value function and are in practice quickly convertible into a medium of exchange at a known price ($1 on deposit in a savings account is always convertible into a $1 demand deposit or $1 in cash).

Table 33-10 shows the principal elements in these definitions of the money supply. The details of the differences are not important at this stage; what matters is that broadly defined, money comprises a spectrum of closely related financial assets that their holders regard as highly substitutable for each other.

Near Money and Money Substitutes

Over the past two centuries what has been accepted by the public as money has expanded from gold and silver coins to include first bank notes and then bank deposits subject to transfer by cheque. Until recently, most economists would have agreed that money stopped at that point. No such agreement exists today, and an important debate centers on the definition of money appropriate to present circumstances.

If we concentrate only on the medium-of-exchange function of money, there is little doubt about what is money in Canada today. Money consists of notes, coins, and deposits subject to transfer by cheque or chequelike instruments. No other asset constitutes a generally accepted medium of exchange.

The problem of deciding what is money arises because some media of exchange—currency, which carries no interest yield, and demand deposits, whose interest yield tends to be quite low—may provide relatively poor ways to meet the store-of-value function (see Table 33-11). Assets that earn a higher-interest return will do a better job of meeting this function of money than currency or demand deposits. At the same time, however, these other assets are less capable of filling the medium-of-exchange function.

TABLE 33-11 The Dollar As a Store of Value Since 1962

$1 put aside in	Had the purchasing power five years later of	Its average annual loss of value over the five-year period was
1962	$0.86	2.8%
1967	0.79	4.2
1972	0.47	10.7
1977	0.37	12.6
1982	0.76	4.3
1985	0.80	4.2

The dollar has become an increasingly less satisfactory store of value since the 1960s. The second column shows the purchasing power, measured by the Consumer Price Index, of $1 five years after it was saved (assuming that it earned no interest). In order for it to have maintained its real purchasing power, it would have had to earn the annual after-tax percentage return shown in the last column. The increase in the required return explains the growing use of near money and money substitutes that (unlike currency and demand deposits) earn interest.

Near Money

Assets that fulfill adequately the store-of-value function and are readily converted into a medium of exchange but are not themselves a medium of exchange are sometimes called **near money**. Deposits at a trust company are a characteristic form of near money. When you have such a deposit, you know exactly how much purchasing power you hold (at current prices), and, given modern banking practices, you can turn your deposit into a medium of exchange—cash or a chequing deposit—at a moment's notice. Furthermore, your deposit will earn some interest during the period that you hold it.

Why then does not everybody keep their money in such deposits instead of in demand deposits or currency? The answer is that the inconvenience of continually shifting money back and forth may outweigh the interest that can be earned. One week's interest on $100 (at 10 percent per year) is only about 20 cents, not enough to cover carfare to the bank or the cost of mailing a letter. For money that will be needed soon, it would hardly pay to shift it to a time deposit.

In general, whether it pays to convert cash or demand deposits into interest-earning savings deposits for a given period will depend on the inconvenience and other transactions costs of shifting funds and on the amount of interest that can be earned.

There is a wide spectrum of assets in the economy that pay interest and also serve as reasonably satisfactory temporary stores of value. The difference between these assets and savings deposits is that their capital values are not quite as certain as those of savings deposits. If I elect to store my purchasing power in the form of a treasury bill that matures in 30 days, its price on the market may change between the time I buy it and the time I want to sell it, say, 10 days later. If the price changes, the purchasing power available to me changes. But because of the short horizon to maturity, the price will not change very much. (After all, the government will pay the face value in a few weeks.) Such a security is thus a reasonably satisfactory short-run store of purchasing power. Indeed, any readily salable capital asset whose value does not fluctuate significantly with the rate of interest will satisfactorily fulfill this short-term store-of-value function.

Money Substitutes

Things that serve as temporary media of exchange but are not a store of value are sometimes called **money substitutes**. Credit cards are a prime example. With a credit card, many transactions can be made without either cash or a cheque. The evidence of credit, the credit slip you sign and hand over to the store, is not money because it cannot be used to make other transactions. The credit card serves the short-run function of a medium of exchange by allowing you to make purchases even though you have no cash or bank deposit currently in your possession. But this is only temporary; money remains the final medium of exchange for these transactions when the credit account is settled.

Conclusion

Since the eighteenth century, economists have known that the amount of money in circulation is an important economic variable. As theories became more carefully specified in the nineteenth and early twentieth centuries, they included a variable called the "money supply." But for theories to be useful, we must be able to identify real-world counterparts of these theoretical magnitudes.

What is an acceptable enough medium of exchange to count as money has changed and will continue to change over time. New monetary assets are continually being developed to serve some, if not all, the functions of money, and they are more or less readily convertible into money. There is no single, timeless definition of what is money and what is only near money or a money substitute. Indeed, as we have seen, our monetary authorities use several definitions of money, and these definitions change from year to year.

SUMMARY

1. Early economic theorists regarded the economy as divided into a real part and a money part. The real sector is concerned with production, allocation of resources, and distribution of income—determined by relative prices. The level of prices at which all transactions take place is determined by the monetary sector, that is, by the demand for and supply of money. With the demand for money constant, an increase in the money supply would cause all equilibrium money prices to increase, but relative prices, and hence everything in the real sector, would be left unaffected.
2. Traditionally in economics, money has referred to any generally accepted medium of exchange. A number of functions of money may be distinguished. The major ones are serving as a medium of exchange, a store of value, and a unit of account.
3. Money arose because of the inconvenience of barter, and it developed in stages from precious metal, to metal coinage, to paper money convertible to precious metal, to token coinage and paper money fractionally backed by precious metals, to fiat money, and to deposit money. Societies have shown great sophistication in developing monetary instruments to meet their needs.
4. The banking system in Canada consists of two main elements: chartered banks and the central bank, the Bank of Canada. Each has an important effect on the money supply.
5. The Bank of Canada, a publicly owned corporation, is Canada's central bank. It serves as the banker to the chartered banks and to the federal government, regulator of financial markets, and controller of the money supply.
6. Chartered banks are profit-seeking institutions that allow their customers to transfer demand deposits from one bank to another by means of cheques. They create and destroy money as a by-product of their commercial operations—by making or liquidating loans and various other investments.
7. Because most customers are content to pay their accounts by cheque rather than by cash, banks need only small reserves to back their deposit liabilities. Consequently, banks are able to create deposit money. When the banking system receives a new cash deposit, it can create new deposits to some multiple of this amount. The amount of new deposits created depends on the legal minimum reserves the Bank of Canada enforces on the banks, the amount of cash drain to the public, and whether the banks choose to hold excess reserves.
8. The money supply—the stock of money in the country at a specific moment—can be defined in various ways. M1 is currency plus demand deposits plus chequable substitutes, the narrowest definition now in use. (M1 was about $40 billion in 1990.) M3, the widest commonly used definition, adds in all time and savings deposits. (M3 was about $290 billion in 1990.)
9. Near money includes interest-earning assets that are convertible into money on a dollar-for-dollar basis but are not currently included in

the definition of money. Money substitutes such as credit cards temporarily serve as a medium of exchange but are not money.

TOPICS FOR REVIEW

Real and monetary sectors of the economy
Functions of money
Gresham's law
Fully backed, fractionally backed, and fiat money
The banking system and the central bank
Creation and destruction of deposit money
Target reserve ratio, required reserves, and excess reserves
Demand and savings deposits
The money supply
Near money and money substitutes

DISCUSSION QUESTIONS

1. "The love of money is the root of all evil" (I Timothy 6:10). If a nation were to become a theocracy in which money was illegal, would you expect the level of national income to be affected? How about the productivity of labor?
2. Consider each of the following with respect to its potential use as a medium of exchange, a store of value, and a unit of account. Which would you think might be regarded as money?
   a. A $100 Bank of Canada note
   b. An American Express credit card
   c. A painting by Picasso
   d. A treasury bill payable in three months
   e. A savings account with a trust company in London, Ontario
   f. One share of General Motors stock
   g. A lifetime pass to the Art Gallery of Ontario
3. When the Austrian government minted a new 1,000-shilling gold coin—worth $78 face value—the 1-inch-diameter coin came into great demand among jewelers and coin collectors. By law, the number of such coins to be minted each year is limited. Lines of people eager to get the coins formed outside the government mint and local banks. "There is exceptional interest in the new coin," said a Viennese banker. "It's a numismatic hit and a financial success." It has disappeared from circulation, however. Explain why.
4. When the rate of exchange was near par, so that $1 Canadian was within 3 cents of $1 U.S., American and Canadian coins circulated side by side, exchanging at their face values. Use Gresham's law to predict which coinage disappeared from circulation in Canada when the Canadian dollar fell to 75 U.S. cents. Why did a 3-cent differential not produce this result?
5. Some years ago a strike closed all banks in Ireland for several months. What do you think happened during the period?
6. During hyperinflation in several foreign countries after World War II, American cigarettes were sometimes used in place of money. What made them suitable?
7. Assume that on January 1, 1990, a family had $25,000 that they wished to hold for use one year later. Use library sources to calculate which of the following would have been the best store of value over that period. Will the best store of value over that period necessarily be the best over the next 24 months?
   a. The dollar

b. Stocks whose prices moved with the Toronto Stock Exchange Industrial 300 average
c. A Labatts 11¾ percent 2005 bond
d. Gold
e. Silver

8. If all depositors tried to turn their deposits into cash at once, they would find that there are not sufficient reserves in the system to allow all of them to do this at the same time. Why then do we not still have panicky runs on the banks? Would a 100 percent reserve requirement be safer? What effect would such a reserve requirement have on the banking system's ability to create money? Would it preclude any possibility of a panic?

9. What would be the effect on the money supply of each of the following?
a. Declining public confidence in the banks
b. A desire on the part of banks to increase their levels of reserves
c. Monopolizing of the banking system into a single superbank
d. Increased use of credit cards
e. Transfer of deposits from banks to new nonbank institutions

Chapter 34

The Role of Money in Macroeconomics

At one time or another, most of us have known the surprise of opening our wallet and discovering that we had either more or less money than we thought. There can be pleasure in deciding how to spend an unexpected windfall in the first case, just as there can be pain in deciding what expenditure to eliminate in the second.

What determines how much money people hold in their wallets and in the bank? What happens when people discover that they are holding more, or less, money than they wish to? These turn out to be key questions for our study of the influence of money on output and prices.

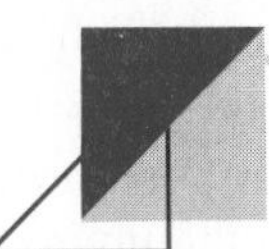

Financial Assets

At any one moment, households have a stock of wealth that they hold in many forms. Some of it is money in the bank or in the wallet; some is in short-term securities, such as treasury bills; some is in long-term bonds; and some is in real capital, which may be held directly (in the form of family businesses) or indirectly (in the form of shares of stock that indicate ownership of a corporation's assets).

Kinds of Assets

These ways of holding wealth may be grouped into three main categories: (1) assets that serve as a medium of exchange, that is, paper money, coins, and bank deposits on which cheques may be drawn; (2) financial assets, such as bonds earning a fixed rate of interest, that will yield a fixed money value at some future date (called the *maturity date*) and can usually be sold before maturity for a price that fluctuates on the open market; and (3) claims (i.e., stocks or shares) on capital, such as factories and machines.

To simplify our discussion, we will regroup wealth into just two categories, which we will call money and bonds. By *money* we mean M1, as defined in Chapter 33, and by *bonds* we mean all other forms of wealth. Money therefore includes currency, demand deposits, and chequable savings deposits. Bonds include all other interest-earning financial assets *plus* claims on real capital.[1]

[1] This simplification can take us quite a long way. However, for some problems it is necessary to treat debt and equity as distinct assets, in which case three categories—money, debt (bonds), and equity stocks—are used.

The Rate of Interest and the Price of Bonds

A bond is a promise by the issuer to pay a stated sum of money as interest each year and to repay the face value of the bond at some future maturity date, often many years distant. The time until the maturity date is called the **term to maturity**, or the **term**, of the bond. Some bonds, called *perpetuities,* pay interest forever and never repay the principal.

The **present value (*PV*)** of a bond, or of any asset, refers to the value now of the future payment or payments to which the asset represents a claim. The present value is thus the amount that someone would be willing to pay now to secure the right to the future stream of payments conferred by ownership of the asset. This amount depends critically on the rate of interest, most easily seen in the case of a perpetuity. Assume that such a bond will pay $100 per year to its holder forever. The *present value* of the bond depends on how much $100 per year is worth, and this in turn depends on the rate of interest.

A bond that will produce a stream of income of $100 per year forever is worth $1,000 at 10 percent interest because $1,000 invested at 10 percent per year will yield $100 interest per year forever. However, the same bond is worth $2,000 when the interest rate is 5 percent per year, because it takes $2,000 invested at that rate to yield $100 interest per year. The lower the rate of interest obtainable on the market, the more valuable a bond paying a fixed amount of interest.

Similar relations apply to bonds that are not perpetuities, though the calculation of present value must allow for the lump-sum repayment of principal at maturity. (Further details on the calculation of present value are given in Box 34-1.)

The present value of any asset that yields a stream of money over time is negatively related to the interest rate.

This proposition has two important implications: (1) If the rate of interest falls, the value of an asset producing a given income stream will rise; and (2) a rise in the market price of an asset producing a given income is equivalent to a decrease in the rate of interest earned by the asset. Thus a promise to pay $100.00 one year from now is worth $92.59 when the interest rate is 8 percent and only $89.29 when the interest rate is 12 percent: $92.59 at 8 percent interest ($92.59 × 1.08) and $89.29 at 12 percent interest ($89.29 × 1.12) are both worth $100.00 in one year's time.

The present value of bonds that are not perpetuities becomes increasingly dominated by the fixed redemption value as the maturity date approaches. For example, a rise in the interest rate from 8 to 12 percent will lower the value of $100 payable in one year's time by 3.6 percent, but it will lower the value of $100 payable in 10 years' time by 37.9 percent.[2]

The sooner the maturity date of a bond, the less the bond's value will change with a change in the rate of interest.

Consider an extreme case. The present value of a bond that is redeemable for $1,000 in one week's time will be very close to $1,000 no matter what the interest rate is. Thus its value will not change much, even if the rate of interest leaps from 5 percent to 10 percent during that week. Note that the interest-earning assets included in our definition of money are so short-term that their values remain unchanged when the interest rate changes.

The discussion should make clear that the present value of an asset determines its market price. If the market price of any asset is greater than the present value of the income stream that it produces, no one will want to buy it, and the market price will fall. If the market value is below its present value, there will be a rush to buy it, and the market price will rise. These facts lead to the following conclusion:

In a free market, the equilibrium price of any asset will be the present value of the income stream that it produces.

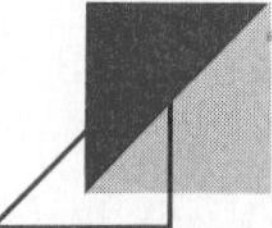

Supply of Money and Demand for Money

The Supply of Money

The money supply is a stock. (It is so many billions of dollars, *not* a flow of so much per unit of time.) In January 1990, M1 was approximately $39 billion.

[2] The example assumes annual compounding. The first case is calculated from the numbers of the previous example: (92.58 − 89.29)/92.58. The 10-year case uses the formula

$$\text{Present value} = \frac{\text{principal}}{(1 + r)^n}$$

which gives $46.30 at 8 percent and $28.75 at 12 percent. The percentage fall in value is thus (46.30 − 28.75)/46.30 = 0.379.

We saw in Chapter 33 that deposit money is created by the commercial banking system, but only within limits set by their reserves. Since, as we shall see in Chapter 35, the reserves of the commercial banking system are under the control of the Bank of Canada, ultimate control of the money supply is also in the hands of the Bank. In this chapter we simply assume that the money supply can be precisely controlled by the Bank.

The Demand for Money

The amount of wealth that everyone in the economy wishes to hold in the form of money balances is called the **demand for money**. Because households are choosing how to divide their given stock of wealth between money and bonds, it follows that if we know the demand for money, we also know the demand for bonds. With a *given level of wealth,* a rise in the demand for money necessarily implies a fall in the demand for bonds; if people wish to hold \$1 billion more money, they must wish to hold \$1 billion less of bonds. It also follows that if households are in equilibrium with respect to their money holdings, they are in equilibrium with respect to their bond holdings.

When we say that on January 1, 1990, the quanity of money demanded was \$39 billion, we mean that on that date the public wished to hold money balances that totaled \$39 billion, but why do firms and households wish to hold money balances at all? There is a cost to holding any money balance. The money could have been used to purchase interest-earning bonds.[3]

The opportunity cost of holding any money balance is the extra interest that could have been earned if the money had been used instead to purchase bonds.

In terms of the distinction between the real and nominal rates of interest that were noted in Chapter 26, the nominal rate of interest is the opportunity cost of holding money. However, since in this chapter we assume that there is no ongoing inflation, the nominal and real rates of interest are the same; both are measured by the market rate of interest.

Clearly, money will be held only when it provides services that are valued at least as highly as the opportunity cost of holding it. Three important services that are provided by money balances give rise to the transactions, precautionary, and speculative motives for holding money. We examine each of these motives in detail.

The Transactions Motive

Most transactions require money. Money passes from households to firms to pay for the goods and services produced by firms; money passes from firms to households to pay for the factor services supplied by households to firms. Money balances that are held to finance such flows are called **transactions balances**.

In an imaginary world in which the receipts and disbursements of households and firms are perfectly synchronized, it would be unnecessary to hold transactions balances. If every time a household spent \$10 it received \$10 as part payment of its income, no transactions balances would be needed. In the real world, however, receipts and disbursements are not perfectly synchronized.

Consider the balances that are held because of wage payments. Suppose, for purposes of illustration, that firms pay wages every Friday and that households spend all their wages on the purchase of goods and services, with the expenditure spread out evenly over the week. Thus on Friday morning firms must hold balances equal to the weekly wage bill; on Friday afternoon households will hold these balances.

Over the week, households' balances will be drawn down as a result of purchasing goods and services. Over the same period, the balances held by firms will build up as a result of selling goods and services until, on the following Friday morning, firms will again have amassed balances equal to the wage bill that must be met on that day.

The transactions motive arises because of the nonsynchronization of payments and receipts.

What determines the size of the transactions balances to be held? It is clear that in our example total transactions balances vary with the value of the wage

[3] As we saw in Chapter 33 (see especially Table 33-10), M1 includes some interest-bearing chequable deposits. This complicates but does not fundamentally alter the analysis of the demand for money. In particular, it means that the opportunity cost of holding those interest-bearing components of M1 is not the *level* of interest rates paid on bonds but the *difference* between that rate and the rate paid on M1 assets. For the sake of simplicity, we treat the interest rate on all M1 assets as being zero so that we can identify the *level* of the interest rate on bonds as the opportunity cost of money.

BOX 34-1

Calculating Present Value

An asset held now will generate returns in the future. What the stream of future income provided by an asset is worth now is called the asset's *present value*. In general, present value (PV) refers to the value *now* of one or more payments to be received in the future.

This box provides some background details concerning the calculation of present value that will prove helpful for understanding the material in the text. If you have studied microeconomics first, the material will be familiar from Chapter 18, and this box provides a useful review.

Present Value of a Single Future Payment

One period hence. To learn how to find the present value, we start with the simplest possible case. How much would someone be prepared to pay *now* to purchase a bond that will produce a single payment of \$100 in one year's time? One way to answer this question is to discover how much the person would have to lend out in order to have \$100 a year from now. Suppose for the moment that the interest rate is 5 percent, which means that \$1.00 invested today will be worth \$1.05 in one year's time.

If we use PV to stand for this unknown amount, we can write $PV(1.05) = \$100$ (which means PV *multiplied by 1.05*). Thus $PV = \$100/1.05 = \$95.24$. This tells us that the present value of \$100 receivable in one year's time is \$95.24 when the interest rate is 5 percent. Anyone who lends out \$95.24 for one year at 5 percent interest will get back \$95.24 plus \$4.76 in interest, which makes \$100. When we calculate this present value, the interest rate is used to *discount* (i.e., reduce to its present value) the \$100 to be received one year hence. The maximum price that anyone would be willing to pay for this bond is \$95.24, assuming that the relevant interest rate is 5 percent.

To see why, let us start by assuming that some sellers offer to sell the bond at some other price, say, \$98. If, instead of paying this amount for the bond, a potential buyer lends its \$98 out at 5 percent interest, it would have at the end of one year more than the \$100 that the bond will produce. (At 5 percent interest, \$98 yields \$4.90 in interest, which when added to the principal makes \$102.90.) Clearly, no well-informed individual would pay \$98—or by the same reasoning any sum in excess of \$95.24—for the bond. The person could do better by using the funds in other ways.

Now say that the bond is offered for sale at \$90. A potential buyer could borrow \$90 to buy the bond and would pay \$4.50 in interest on the loan. At the end of the year, the bond yields \$100. When this is used to repay the \$90 loan and the \$4.50 in interest, \$5.50 is left as profit. Clearly, it would be worthwhile for someone to buy the bond at the price of \$90 or, by the same argument, at any price less than \$95.24.

The actual present value that we have calculated depended on our assuming that the interest rate is 5 percent. What if the interest rate had been 7 percent? At that interest rate, the present value of the \$100 receivable in one year's time would be $\$100/1.07 = \$93.46$.

These examples are easy to generalize. In both cases we have found the present value by dividing the sum that is receivable in the future by 1 plus the rate of interest.* In general, the present value

* Notice that in this type of formula the interest rate is expressed as a decimal fraction where, for example, 7 percent is expressed as 0.07, so $1 + i$ equals 1.07.

bill. If the wage bill doubles for any reason, the transactions balances held by firms and households on this account will also double. As it is with wages, so it is with all other transactions: The size of the balances held is positively related to the value of the transactions.

Next we ask how the total value of transactions is related to national income. Because of the double

of R dollars one year hence at an interest rate of i per year is

$$PV = \frac{R}{1 + i} \qquad [1]$$

Several periods hence. Now we know how to calculate the present value of a single sum that is receivable one year hence. The next step is to ask what would happen if the sum were receivable at a later date. What, for example, is the present value of \$100 to be received *two* years hence if the interest rate is 5 percent? This is \$100/(1.05)(1.05) = \$90.70. We can check this by seeing what would happen if \$90.70 were lent out for two years. In the first year the loan would earn an interest of (0.05)(\$90.70) = \$4.54, and hence after one year the lender would receive \$95.24. In the second year the interest would be earned on this entire amount; interest earned in the second year would thus equal (0.05)(\$95.24) = \$4.76. Hence in two years the lender would have \$100. (The payments of interest in the second year on the interest income earned in the first year is known as *compound interest.*)

In general, the present value of R dollars after t years at i percent is

$$PV = \frac{R}{(1 + i)^t} \qquad [2]$$

All that this formula does is to discount the sum, R, by the interest rate, i, repeatedly, once for each of the t periods that must pass until the sum becomes available. If we look at the formula, we see that the higher i or t is, the higher the whole term $(1 + i)^t$. This term, however, appears in the denominator, so that PV is *negatively* related to both i and t.

The formula $PV = R/(1 + i)^t$ shows that the present value of a given sum payable in the future will be smaller the more distant the payment date and the higher the rate of interest.

Present Value of a Continuous Stream of Payments

Finally, consider the present value that a buyer would place on a bond that produces a stream of payments of \$100 a year forever. To find the present value of \$100 payable every year in the future, we ask how much money would have to be invested now at an interest rate of 10 percent per year to obtain \$100 every year in the future. This present value is simply 0.1 (PV) = \$100, where PV is the sum required. In other words, PV = \$100/0.1 = \$1,000. This tells us that \$1,000 invested at 10 percent interest forever would yield a constant stream of income of \$100 per year; put the other way around, when the interest rate is 10 percent, the present value of \$100 per year forever is \$1,000.

To generalize for any interest rate, we merely write i for the interest rate and R for the revenue to be received each year. Now we wish to find the amount PV that, invested at i, will yield R per year forever. This is $i(PV) = R$, or

$$PV = \frac{R}{i} \qquad [3]$$

Here, as before, PV is related to the rate of interest: The higher the interest rate, the less the (present) value of any stream of future receipts and hence the lower the price that anyone would be prepared to pay to purchase the bond.

counting problem, which we first discussed in Chapter 27, the value of all transactions exceeds the value of the economy's final output. When the miller buys wheat from the farmer and when the baker buys flour from the miller, both are transactions against which money balances must be held, although only the value added at each stage is part of national income.

We now make an added assumption that there is a stable, positive relationship between transactions and national income. A rise in national income also leads to a rise in the total value of all transactions and hence to an associated rise in the demand for transactions balances. This allows us to relate transactions balances to national income. [41]

The larger the value of national income, the larger the value of transactions balances that will be held.

The Precautionary Motive

Many goods and services are sold on credit. The seller can never be certain when payment will be made, and the buyer can never be certain of the day of delivery and thus when payment will fall due. As a precaution against cash crises, when receipts are abnormally low or disbursements are abnormally high, firms and households carry money balances. These are called **precautionary balances**; they provide a cushion against uncertainty about the timing of cash flows. The larger such balances are, the greater is the protection against running out of money because of temporary fluctuations in cash flows.

How serious the risk of a cash crisis is depends on the penalties for being caught without sufficient money balances. A firm is unlikely to be pushed into insolvency, but it may incur considerable costs if it is forced to borrow money at high interest rates in order to meet a temporary cash crisis.

The precautionary motive arises because households and firms are uncertain about the degree to which payments and receipts will be synchronized.

The protection provided by a given quantity of precautionary balances depends on the volume of payments and receipts. A $100 precautionary balance provides a large cushion for a household whose volume of payments per month is $800 and a small cushion for a firm whose monthly volume is $25,000. Fluctuations of the sort that create the need for precautionary balances tend to vary directly with the size of the firm's cash flow. To provide the same degree of protection as the value of transactions rises, more money is necessary.[4]

The precautionary motive, like the transactions motive, causes the demand for money to vary positively with the money value of national income.

The Speculative Motive

Firms and households hold some money in order to provide a hedge against the uncertainty inherent in fluctuating prices of other financial assets. Money balances held for this purpose are called **speculative balances**. This motive was first analyzed by Keynes, and the classic modern analysis was made by Professor James Tobin, the 1981 Nobel Laureate in Economics.

When a household or a firm holds money balances, it forgoes the extra interest income that it could earn if it held bonds instead. However, market interest rates fluctuate, and so do the market prices of existing bonds (since their present values depend on the interest rate). Because their prices fluctuate, bonds are a risky asset. Many households and firms do not like risk; they are said to be *risk-averse*.

In choosing between holding money or holding bonds, wealth holders must balance the extra interest income that they could earn by holding bonds against the risk that bonds carry. At one extreme, if a household or a firm holds all its wealth in the form of bonds, it earns extra interest on its entire wealth, but it also exposes its entire wealth to the risk of changes in the price of bonds. At the other extreme, if the household or firm holds all its wealth in the form of money, it earns less interest income, but it does not face the risk of unexpected changes in the price of bonds. Wealth holders usually do not take either extreme position. They hold part of their wealth as money and part of it as bonds; that is, they *diversify* their holdings.

Influence of wealth. Suppose that Ms. B. Smart elects to diversify her wealth by holding 5 percent of her wealth in money and the other 95 percent in bonds.

[4] Institutional arrangements affect precautionary demands. In the past, for example, a traveler would have carried a substantial precautionary balance in cash, but today a credit card covers most unforeseen expenses that may arise while traveling.

If her wealth is $50,000, her demand for money will be $2,500. If her wealth increases to $60,000, her demand for money will rise to $3,000. Thus

The speculative motive means that the demand for money varies positively with wealth.

Although an individual's wealth may rise or fall rapidly, the total wealth of a society changes only slowly. For the analysis of short-term fluctuations in national income, the effects of changes in wealth are fairly small, and we shall ignore them for the present. Over the long term, however, variations in wealth can have a major effect on the demand for money.

Influence of interest rates. Wealth that is held in cash earns no interest; hence the reduction in risk involved in holding more money carries a cost in terms of forgone interest earnings. The speculative motive leads households and firms to add to their money holdings until the reduction in risk obtained by the last dollar added is just balanced (in each wealth holder's view) by the cost in terms of the interest forgone on that dollar.

When the rate of interest falls, the opportunity cost of holding money falls. This leads to more money being held both for the precautionary motive (to reduce risks caused by uncertainty about the flows of payments and receipts) and for the speculative motive (to reduce risks associated with fluctuations in the market price of bonds). When the rate of interest rises, the cost of holding money rises. This leads to less money being held for speculative and precautionary motives.

The precautionary and speculative motives both cause the demand for money to be negatively related to the rate of interest.

Real and Nominal Money Balances

In referring to the demand for money, it is important to distinguish real from nominal values. Real values are measured in purchasing power units; nominal values are measured in money units.

First, consider the demand for money in real terms. This means the number of units of purchasing power that the public wishes to hold in the form of money balances. In an imaginary one-product wheat economy, this would be measured by the number of bushels of wheat that could be purchased with the money balances held. In a more complex economy, it could be measured in terms of the number of "baskets of goods" represented by a price index such as the CPI that could be purchased with the money balances held. When we speak of the demand for money in real terms, we speak of the amount demanded in constant dollars:

The real demand for money is the nominal quantity demanded divided by an index of the price level.

For example, in the decade from 1980 to 1990, the nominal quantity of M1 balances held in Canada increased by 66.7 percent, from $23.7 billion to $39.5 billion. Over the same period, however, the price level, as measured by the CPI, rose by about 77 percent. This tells us that the real quantity of M1 actually fell slightly, from $23.7 billion to $22.3 billion, measured in constant 1980 dollars.

From real demand to nominal demand. Our discussion has identified the determinants of the demand for real money balances as real national income, real wealth, and the interest rate. Notice that the real demand for money depends, among other things, on real national income; it is not influenced by the price level.

Now suppose that with the interest rate, real wealth, and real national income being held constant, the price level doubles. Since the demand for real money balances will be unchanged, the demand for nominal balances must double. If the public previously demanded $30 billion in nominal money balances, it will now demand $60 billion. This keeps the real demand unchanged at $60/2 = $30 billion. The money balances of $60 billion at the new, higher price level represents exactly the same purchasing power as $30 billion at the old price level.

Other things being equal, the nominal demand for money balances varies in proportion to the price level; when the price level doubles, desired nominal money balances also double.

This is a central proposition of the quantity theory of money, which is discussed further in Box 34-2.

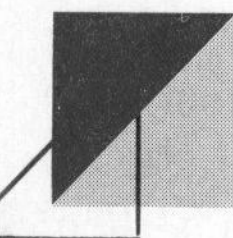

BOX 34-2

The Quantity Theory of Money

The quantity theory of money can be set out in terms of four equations. Equation 1 states that the demand for money balances depends on the value of transactions as measured by nominal income, which is real income multiplied by the price level:

$$M^D = kPY \qquad [1]$$

Equation 2 states that the supply of money, M, is set by the central bank:

$$M^S = M \qquad [2]$$

Equation 3 states the equilibrium condition that the demand for money must equal the supply:

$$M^D = M^S \qquad [3]$$

Substitution produces a relationship among P, M, and Y:

$$M = kPY \qquad [4]$$

The original classical quantity theory assumes that k is a constant given by the transactions demand for money and that Y is constant because full employment is maintained. Thus increases or decreases in the money supply lead to proportional increases or decreases in prices.

Often the quantity theory is presented by using the concept of the **velocity of circulation (V)**, defined as national income divided by the quantity of money:

$$V = \frac{PY}{M} \qquad [5]$$

Rearranging this gives us the *equation of exchange*:

$$MV = PY \qquad [6]$$

Velocity may be interpreted as showing the average amount of "work" done by a unit of money. If annual national income is $400 billion and the stock of money is $100 billion, on average, each dollar's worth of money is used four times to create the values added that comprise the national income.

There is a simple relationship between k and V. One is the reciprocal of the other, as may be seen immediately by comparing Equations 4 and 6. Thus it makes no difference whether we choose to work with k or V. Further, if k is assumed to be constant, this implies that V must also be treated as being constant.

An example may help to illustrate the interpretation of each. Assume that the stock of money that people wish to hold is equal to one-fifth of the value of total transactions. Thus k is 0.2 and V, the reciprocal of k, is 5. This indicates that if the money supply is to be one-fifth of the value of annual transactions, each dollar must be "used" on average five times.

Modern versions of the quantity theory do not assume that k is exogenously fixed. However, they do argue that k will not change in response to a change in the quantity of money.

Total Demand for Money: Recap

Figure 34-1 summarizes the influences of national income, the rate of interest, and the price level, the three variables that account for most of the short-term variations in the nominal quantity of money demanded. The function relating money demanded to the rate of interest is often called the **liquidity preference (LP) function**.

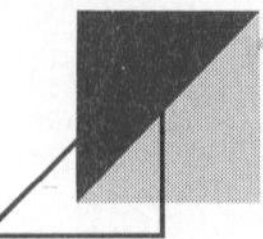

Monetary Forces and National Income

We are now in a position to examine the relationship between monetary forces, on the one hand, and the equilibrium values of national income and the price level, on the other. The first step in explaining this

FIGURE 34-1 The Demand for Money As a Function of Interest Rates, Income, and the Price Level

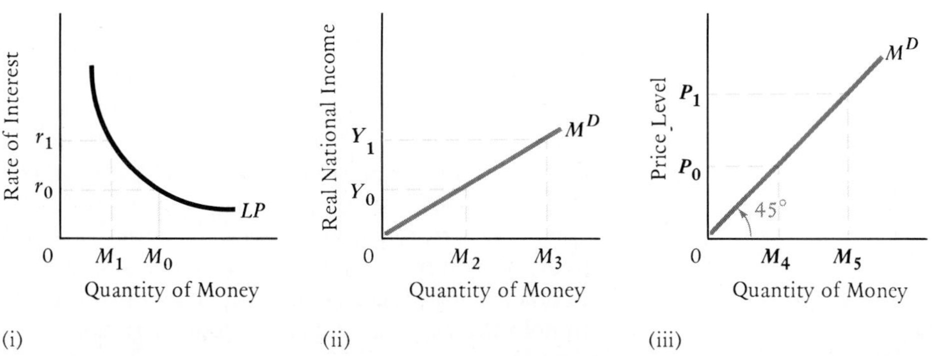

The quantity of money demanded varies negatively with the rate of interest and positively with both national income and the price level. In (i) the demand for money is shown varying negatively with the interest rate along the liquidity preference function. When the interest rate rises from r_0 to r_1, households and firms reduce the quantity of money demanded from M_0 to M_1.

In (ii) the demand for money varies positively with national income. When national income rises from Y_0 to Y_1, households and firms increase the quantity of money demanded from M_2 to M_3.

In (iii) the demand for money varies in proportion to the price level. When the price level doubles from P_0 to P_1, households and firms double the quantity of money demanded from M_4 to M_5.

relationship is a new one: the link between monetary equilibrium and aggregate demand. The second is familiar from earlier chapters: the effects of shifts in aggregate demand on equilibrium values of national income and the price level.

Monetary Equilibrium and Aggregate Demand

Monetary equilibrium occurs when the demand for money equals the supply of money. In Chapter 4 we saw that in a competitive market for some commodity such as carrots, the price will adjust so as to ensure equilibrium. The rate of interest does the same job with respect to money demand and money supply.

The Liquidity Preference Theory of Interest

Figure 34-2 shows how the interest rate will change in order to equate the demand for money with its supply. When a single household or firm finds that it has less money than it wishes to hold, it can sell some bonds and add the proceeds to its money holdings. This transaction simply redistributes given supplies of bonds and money among individuals; it does not change the total supply of either money or bonds.

Now assume that all of the firms and households in the economy have an excess demand for money balances. They all try to sell bonds to add to their money balances, but what one person can do, all persons cannot do. At any moment the economy's total supply of money and bonds is fixed; there is just so much money and there are just so many bonds in existence. If everyone tries to sell bonds, there will be no one to buy them, and the price of bonds will fall.

We saw that a fall in the price of bonds means a rise in the rate of interest. As the interest rate rises, people economize on money balances, because the opportunity cost of holding such balances is rising. This is what we saw in Figure 34-1(i), where the quantity of money demanded falls along the liquidity preference curve in response to a rise in the rate of interest. Eventually, the interest rate will rise enough that people will no longer be trying to add to their

FIGURE 34-2 The Liquidity Preference Theory of Interest

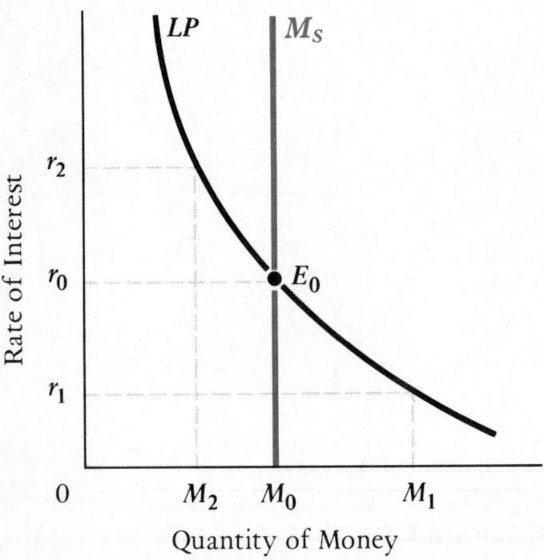

The interest rate rises when there is an excess demand for money and falls when there is an excess supply of money. The fixed quantity of money, M_0, is shown by the completely inelastic supply curve M_S. The demand for money is *LP*; its negative slope indicates that a fall in the rate of interest causes the quantity of money demanded to increase. Equilibrium is at E_0, with a rate of interest of r_0.

If the interest rate is r_1, there will be an excess demand for money of M_0M_1. Bonds will be offered for sale in an attempt to increase money holdings. This will force the rate of interest up to r_0 (the price of bonds falls), at which point the quantity of money demanded is equal to the fixed available quantity of M_0. If the interest rate is r_2, there will be an excess supply of money M_2M_0. Bonds will be demanded in return for excess money balances. This will force the rate of interest down to r_0 (the price of bonds rises), at which point the quantity of money demanded has risen to equal the fixed supply of M_0.

money balances by selling bonds. At that point there is no longer an excess supply of bonds, and the interest rate will stop rising. The demand for money again equals the supply.

Assume next that firms and households hold larger money balances than they would like. A single household or firm would purchase bonds with its excess balances, achieving monetary equilibrium by reducing its money holdings and by increasing its bond holdings. However, just as in the previous example, what one household or firm can do, all cannot do. At any moment the total quantity of bonds is fixed, so everyone cannot simultaneously add to personal bond holdings. When all households enter the bond market and try to purchase bonds with unwanted money balances, they bid up the price of existing bonds, and the interest rate falls. Hence households and firms become willing to hold larger quantities of money; that is, the quantity of money demanded increases along the liquidity preference curve in response to a fall in the rate of interest. The rise in the price of bonds continues until firms and households stop trying to convert bonds into money. In other words, it continues until everyone is content to hold the existing supply of money and bonds.

Monetary equilibrium occurs when the rate of interest is such that the existing supply of money is willingly held, that is, when the demand for money equals its supply.

The determination of the interest rate, depicted in Figure 34-2, is often described as the *liquidity preference theory* of interest and sometimes as the *portfolio balance theory.*

As we shall see, a shift in either the demand for money or the supply of money will lead to a change in the interest rate. However, as we saw in Chapter 31, desired aggregate expenditure is sensitive to changes in the interest rate. Here, then, is a link between monetary factors and real expenditure flows.

The Transmission Mechanism

The mechanism by which changes in the demand for and the supply of money affect aggregate demand is called the **transmission mechanism**. The transmission mechanism operates in three stages: The first is the link between monetary equilibrium and the interest rate, the second is the link between the interest rate and investment expenditure, and the third is the link between investment expenditure and aggregate demand.

From monetary disturbances to changes in the interest rate. The interest rate will change if the supply of money changes or if there is a shift in the demand for money. For example, as shown in Figure 34-3(i), an increase in the supply of money, with an unchanged liquidity preference function, will give rise to an excess supply of money at the original interest

FIGURE 34-3 Monetary Disturbances and Interest Rate Changes

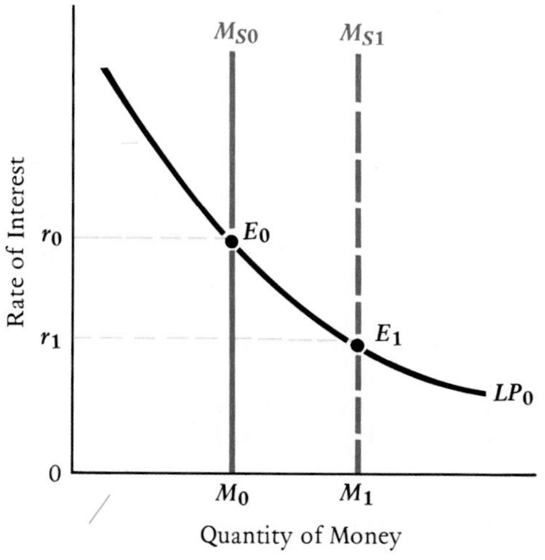

(i) A change in the supply of money

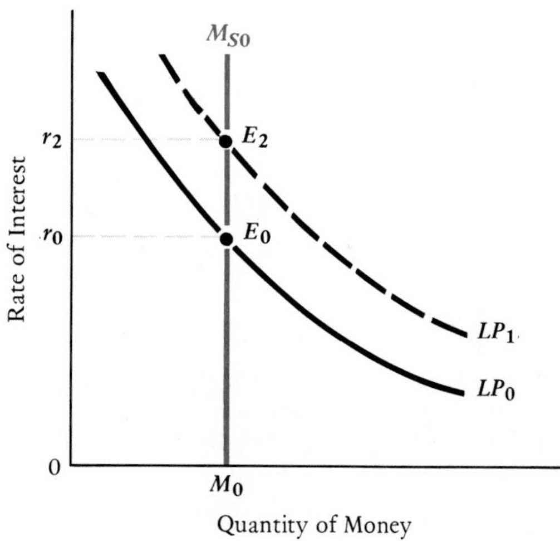

(ii) A change in the demand for money

Shifts in the supply of money or in the demand for money cause the equilibrium interest rate to change. In both parts of the figure, the money supply is shown by the vertical curve M_{S0}, and the demand for money is shown by the negatively shaped curve LP_0. The initial equilibrium is at E_0, with corresponding interest rate r_0.

In (i) an increase in the money supply causes the money supply curve to shift to the right from M_{S0} to M_{S1}. The new equilibrium is at E_1, where the interest rate is r_1, less than r_0. Starting at E_1 with M_{S1} and r_1, it can be seen that a decrease in the money supply to M_{S0} leads to an increase in the interest rate from r_1 to r_0.

In (ii) an increase in the demand for money causes the LP curve to shift to the right from LP_0 to LP_1. The new equilibrium occurs at E_2, and the new equilibrium interest rate is r_2, greater than r_0. Starting at E_2, we see that a decrease in the demand for money from LP_1 to LP_0 leads to a decrease in the interest rate from r_2 to r_0.

rate. As we have seen, an excess supply of money will cause the interest rate to fall. As also shown in part (i) of Figure 34-3, a decrease in the supply of money will cause the interest rate to rise.

As shown in Figure 34-3(ii), an increase in the demand for money, with an unchanged supply of money, will give rise to an excess demand for money at the original interest rate and will cause the interest rate to rise. As also shown in part (ii) of Figure 34-3, a decrease in the demand for money will cause the interest rate to fall.

Monetary disturbances, which can arise due to changes in either the demand for or the supply of money, cause changes in the interest rate.

From changes in the interest rate to shifts in aggregate expenditure. The second link in the transmission mechanism relates interest rates to expenditure. We saw in Chapter 31 that investment, which includes expenditure on inventory accumulation, residential construction, and business fixed investment, responds to changes in the rate of interest. Other things being equal, a decrease in the rate of interest makes borrowing cheaper and generates new investment expenditure.[5] This negative relationship between in-

[5] In Chapter 31 we saw that purchases of durable consumer goods also respond to changes in interest rates. In this chapter we concentrate on investment expenditure, which may be taken to stand for *all* interest-sensitive expenditure.

FIGURE 34-4 The Effects of Changes in the Money Supply on Investment Expenditure

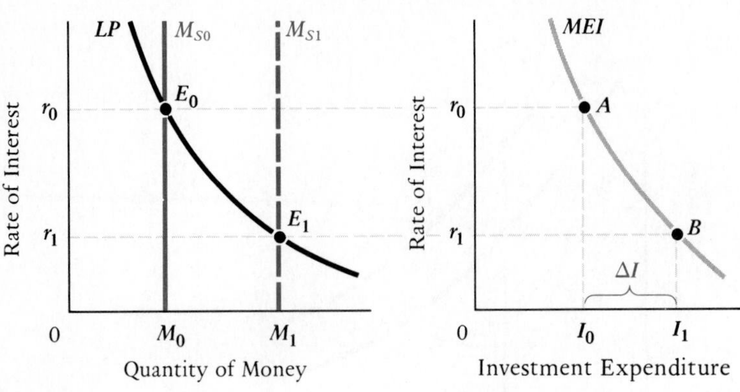

(i) Money demand and supply

(ii) The marginal efficiency of investment

Increases in the money supply reduce the rate of interest and increase desired investment expenditure. Equilibrium is at E_0, with a quantity of money of M_0 (shown by the inelastic money supply curve M_{S0}), an interest rate of r_0, and an investment expenditure of I_0 (point *A*). The Bank of Canada then increases the money supply to M_1 (shown by the money supply curve M_{S1}). This lowers the rate of interest to r_1 and increases investment expenditure by ΔI to I_1 (point *B*). A reduction in the money supply from M_1 to M_0 raises interest rates from r_1 to r_0 and lowers investment expenditure by ΔI, from I_1 to I_0.

vestment and the rate of interest is called the **marginal efficiency of investment (*MEI*) function**.

The first two links in the transmission mechanism are shown in Figure 34-4. We concentrate for the moment on changes in the money supply, although, as we have seen already, the process can also be set in motion by changes in the demand for money. In part (i) we see that a change in the money supply causes the rate of interest to change in the opposite direction. In part (ii) we see that a change in the interest rate causes the level of investment expenditure to change in the opposite direction. Therefore, changes in the money supply cause investment expenditure to change in the same direction.

An increase in the money supply leads to a fall in the interest rate and an increase in investment expenditure. A decrease in the money supply leads to a rise in the interest rate and a decrease in investment expenditure.

From shifts in aggregate expenditure to shifts in aggregate demand. Now we are back on familiar ground. In Chapter 29 we saw that a shift in the aggregate expenditure curve can lead to a shift in the *AD* curve. This is shown again in Figure 34-5.

A change in the money supply, by causing a change in desired investment expenditure and hence a shift in the *AE* curve, causes the *AD* curve to shift. An increase in the money supply causes an increase in investment expenditure and therefore an increase in aggregate demand. A decrease in the money supply causes a decrease in investment expenditure and therefore a decrease in aggregate demand.

The transmission mechanism connects monetary forces and real expenditure flows. It works from a change in the demand for or the supply of money to a change in bond prices and interest rates, to changes in investment expenditure, and to a shift in the aggregate demand curve.

This is illustrated in Figure 34-6 for the case of an expansionary monetary shock, that is, a shift in money demand or money supply that tends to increase aggregate demand. Details on how the openness of the economy affects the transmission mechanism are presented in Box 34-3.

Aggregate Demand, the Price Level, and National Income

We have just seen that a change in the money supply shifts the aggregate demand curve. If we want to know what it does to real national income and to the price level, we need to know the slope of the aggre-

FIGURE 34-5 The Effects of Changes in the Money Supply on Aggregate Demand

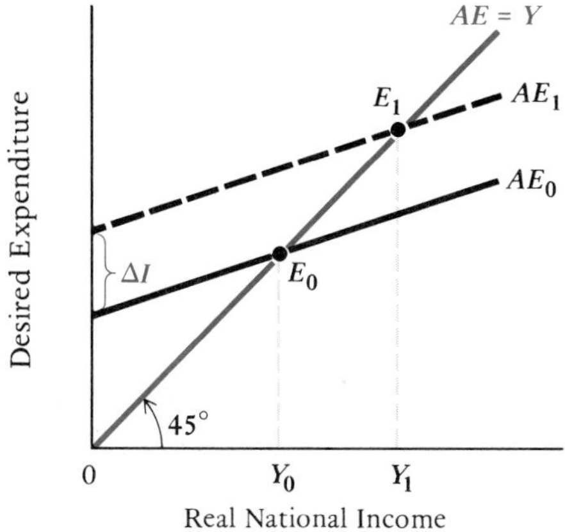

(i) Shift in aggregate expenditure

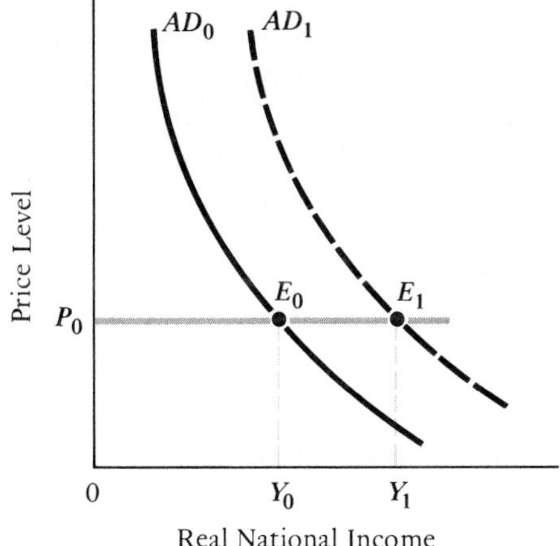

(ii) Shift in aggregate demand

Changes in the money supply cause shifts in the aggregate expenditure and aggregate demand functions. In Figure 34-4 an increase in the money supply increased desired investment expenditure by ΔI. In (i) the aggregate expenditure function shifts up by ΔI (which is the same as ΔI in Figure 34-4), from AE_0 to AE_1. At the fixed price level P_0, equilibrium income rises from Y_0 to Y_1, as shown by the horizontal shift in the aggregate demand curve from AD_0 to AD_1 in (ii)

When the supply of money falls (from M_{S1} to M_{S0} in Figure 34-4), investment falls by ΔI, thereby shifting aggregate expenditure from AE_1 to AE_0. At the fixed price level P_0, this reduces equilibrium income from Y_1 to Y_0.

FIGURE 34-6 Transmission Mechanism for an Expansionary Monetary Shock

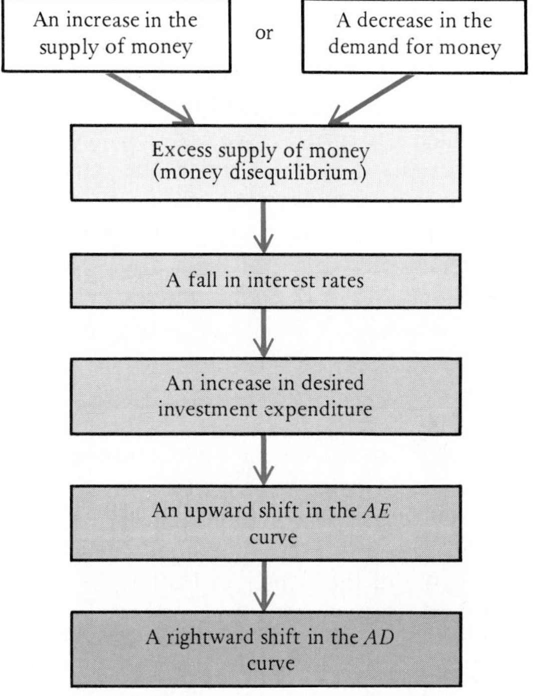

An increase in the supply of money or a decrease in the demand for money leads to an increase in aggregate demand. The excess supply of money following an expansionary monetary disturbance leads to a fall in the interest rate and an increase in investment. This causes an upward shift in the *AE* curve and thus a rightward shift in the *AD* curve. The effects of a contractionary monetary shock can be traced through the flowchart simply by reversing the effects at each stage. A decrease in the supply of money (or an increase in the demand for money) creates an *excess demand* for money; this leads in turn to a *rise* in interest rates, a *decrease* in desired investment expenditure, a *downward* shift in the *AE* curve, and a *leftward* shift in the *AD* curve.

gate supply curve. This step, which is familiar from earlier chapters, is recalled in Figure 34-7.[6]

[6] Since the demand for money in general will depend on the level of national income, as shown in Figure 34-1(ii), our analysis at this stage is incomplete. The induced change in equilibrium national income will lead to a shift in the liquidity preference function in Figure 34-2. For the sake of simplicity, we have assumed in the text that the demand for money function does not shift in response to a change in national income.

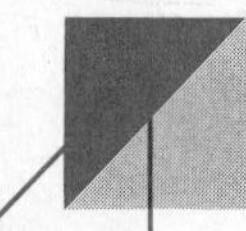

BOX 34-3

The Transmission Mechanism in an Open Economy

The text focuses on the interest rate as the channel through which the effects of monetary policy are transmitted to the economy. However, in an open economy such as Canada's, two additional complications must be allowed for. First, the effects of monetary contraction or expansion are weakened because the domestic interest rate is closely linked to interest rates in the rest of the world. This restricts the scope for domestic interest rates to change in response to monetary policy. Second, there is an added channel through which the effects of monetary policy are transmitted to real aggregate demand. This is through changes in the external value of the Canadian dollar on the foreign exchange market.

The Link Between Interest Rates and the External Value of the Canadian Dollar

If Canadian interest rates rise relative to those in other countries, the demand for Canadian dollar assets will also rise. Canadians will be less inclined to invest in assets of other countries, and foreigners will have a strong demand to invest in high-yielding Canadian assets. In order to invest in these assets, foreigners need to buy Canadian dollars, and their demand for these dollars on the foreign exchange rate will appreciate the Canadian dollar.

Low Canadian interest rates have the opposite effect. Canadians will want to invest in foreign assets, and foreigners will be less anxious to invest in Canadian assets. Foreigners will demand fewer Canadian dollars, and Canadians will be selling more Canadian dollars in order to obtain foreign currencies to invest in higher-yielding foreign assets. This will cause a depreciation of the Canadian dollar on the foreign exchange market.

Other things being equal, the higher Canadian interest rates are, the higher will be the external value of the Canadian dollar, and the lower Canadian interest rates are, the lower will be the external value of the Canadian dollar.

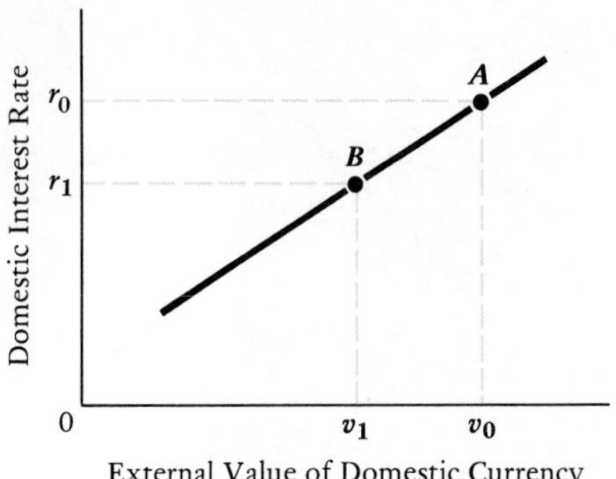

This *positive* relationship between the interest rate and the external value of the Canadian dollar is shown in the figure. It is this relationship that is often featured in newspaper and television discussions about movements in the exchange rate. For example, an appreciation of the Canadian dollar, say from U.S.$0.80 to U.S.$0.85, will often be the result of a rise in Canadian interest rates relative to those in the United States.

The Impact of Changes in the Money Supply

Suppose that in order to stimulate the economy, the Bank of Canada increases the money supply. The initial effects will be exactly the same as in the closed economy analyzed in the text. The chartered banks will find that they have excess reserves and will want to make more loans and expand their deposits; households and firms will want to add to their holdings of interest-earning assets. Their combined actions will cause Canadian interest rates to fall.

It is at this point that open economy forces come into play. As Canadian interest rates fall, foreigners and Canadians will start to sell Canadian assets in order to purchase foreign assets that now earn interest rates higher than those prevailing in Canada.

Since people are selling Canadian dollar assets, the fall in Canadian interest rates is mitigated. In this way Canadian interest rates are constrained by those abroad; the availability of interest-earning assets in foreign currencies that investors think are substitutes for Canadian securities implies that Canadian interest rates do not move as much in response to changes in the money supply as they would in a closed economy.

People who have sold their Canadian dollar assets will now wish to sell Canadian dollars in order to buy foreign exchange, which they will use to purchase foreign assets. This causes a depreciation of the Canadian dollar on the foreign exchange market.*

These effects of an increase in the money supply can be shown in terms of the figure as a movement from point A with the interest rate of r_0 and the value of the Canadian dollar of v_0 to point B with a lower interest rate r_1 and a lower value of the dollar of v_1.

An increase in the money supply will lead to a fall in domestic interest rates and a depreciation of the Canadian dollar.

A decrease in the money supply will have the opposite effects, resulting in an increase in interest rates and an appreciation in the Canadian dollar.

The Transmission Mechanism

How are impacts on the interest rate and the external value of the Canadian dollar transmitted into changes in the level of economic activity? The reduced response of interest rates to monetary policy implies less effect, for a given change in the money supply, on interest-sensitive expenditures. However, the induced changes in the value of the Canadian dollar add a new channel by which monetary policy is transmitted to the economy. As we saw in Chapter 28, a depreciation of the Canadian dollar, other things being equal, makes Canadian-produced goods more competitive on world markets and thus increases exports and decreases imports.

Because an increase in the money supply leads to a depreciation of the Canadian dollar, it stimulates net exports and thereby raises aggregate demand.

Similarly, a decrease in the money supply will lower aggregate demand because it leads to an appreciation of the Canadian dollar and hence to a fall in net exports.

In the late 1980s, for example, a tight Canadian monetary policy drove Canadian interest rates considerably above those in the United States and caused the value of the Canadian dollar to appreciate from around U.S. \$0.82 to about U.S. \$0.88. This caused a reduction in some Canadian exports and a shrinking in the incomes earned by others that were sold for prices set in U.S. dollars.

The operation of this channel of the transmission mechanism can be seen in terms of the definition of aggregate demand from Chapter 28:

$$AD = C + I + G + (X - M)$$

In a closed economy, monetary policy operates through changes in the interest rate influencing investment expenditure (I) as well as any interest-sensitive consumption expenditures (C); in the open economy, that channel is weakened, but the effects on aggregate demand are reinforced through the effects of changes in the exchange rate on net exports ($X - M$).

Though the channels are different, the ability of monetary policy to affect national income remains. In the rest of this chapter, we maintain the simple closed economy analysis for simplicity; we return to the open economy issues in Chapter 41.

* Equilibrium will occur when the Canadian dollar has depreciated so much that people expect it to appreciate later (i.e., the exchange rate "overshoots" its long-run value), and that expected appreciation compensates investors for the lower nominal interest rate on Canadian bonds. This theory is discussed in more detail later in Chapter 41.

FIGURE 34-7 The Effects of Changes in the Money Supply

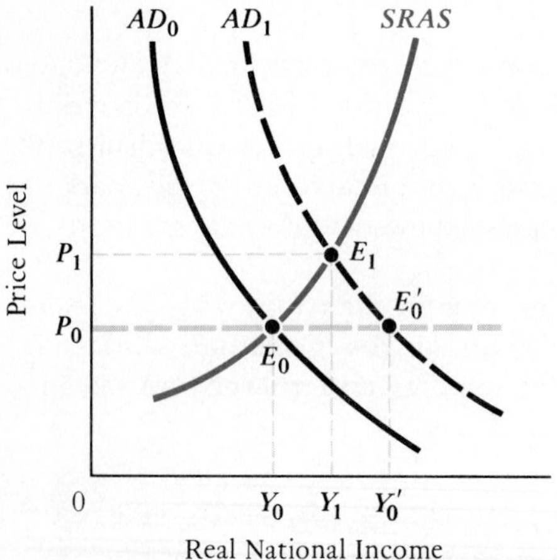

A change in the money supply leads to a change in national income that is smaller than the horizontal shift in the *AD* curve. An increase in the money supply causes the *AD* curve to shift to the right, from AD_0 to AD_1. With the price level being held constant, national income would rise from Y_0 to Y_0'. With the positively sloped *SRAS* curve, income rises to only Y_1, while the price level rises as well—to P_1.

The key result is that the increase in equilibrium real income is less than the horizontal shift in the *AD* curve. This is because part of this shift is dissipated by a rise in the price level: Because the *AD* curve is negatively sloped, the rise in the price level means that the rise in real output is smaller than the horizontal shift of the *AD* curve.[7]

The slope of the *AD* curve. We can now use the transmission mechanism to explain the negative slope of the *AD* curve, that is, to explain why equilibrium national income is negatively related to the price level. In Chapter 29, when we explained the negative slope of the *AD* curve, we mentioned three reasons: the wealth (or real balance) effect, the substitution of domestic for foreign goods, and the indirect effect operating through interest rates. Until now we have focused on the wealth effect because it was simple and direct. Now that we have developed a theory of money and interest rates, we are able to understand the indirect effect that works through the transmission mechanism.

The essential feature of this indirect effect is that a rise in the price level raises the money value of transactions. This leads to an increased demand for money, which brings the transmission mechanism into play. People try to sell bonds to add to their money balances, but, collectively, all they succeed in doing is forcing up the interest rate. The rise in the interest rate reduces investment expenditure and so reduces equilibrium national income.

This effect is important because, empirically, the interest rate is the most important link between monetary factors and real expenditure flows. The third reason for the negative slope of the *AD* curve is discussed in more detail in the appendix to this chapter.

The Monetary Adjustment Mechanism

Suppose that an economy, in equilibrium with real national income equal to its potential level, were disturbed by an increase in the money supply. Since real national income would increase, there would be an inflationary gap, as shown in Figure 34-8(i). Let us now examine the mechanism by which such an inflationary gap is eliminated. This involves an important but subtle implication of the theory.

A sufficiently large rise in the price level will eliminate any inflationary gap, provided that the nominal money supply remains constant.

Operation of the monetary adjustment mechanism. Because it causes excess demand in factor markets, the inflationary gap will cause factor prices to rise. This will shift the *SRAS* curve upward and will take the price level with it. This raises the money value of transactions, and the resulting increase in the demand for money raises interest rates. Hence at any level of real income, desired real expenditure falls. The fall in real expenditure as the price level rises is shown by a movement upward to the left *along* the *AD* curve. This reduces the inflationary gap. When the price level has risen enough, the inflationary gap disappears, and the price level stops rising.

[7] If you draw the graph, you will see that if the *AD* curve were vertical, the rise in the price level would not diminish the effect on real output; real output would rise by an amount equal to the horizontal shift of the *AD* curve.

FIGURE 34-8 The Monetary Adjustment Mechanism

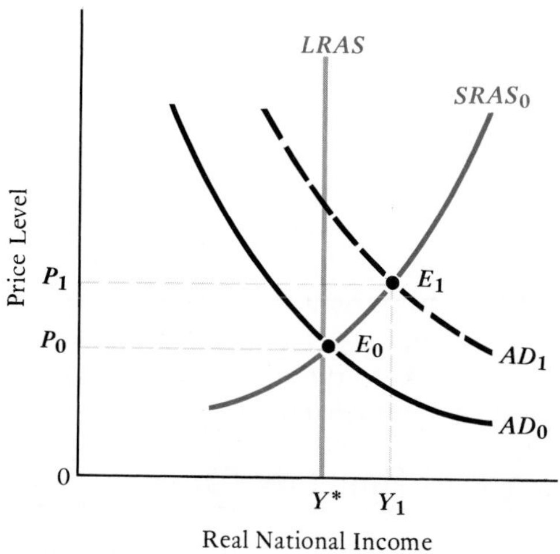

(i) Inflationary gap created

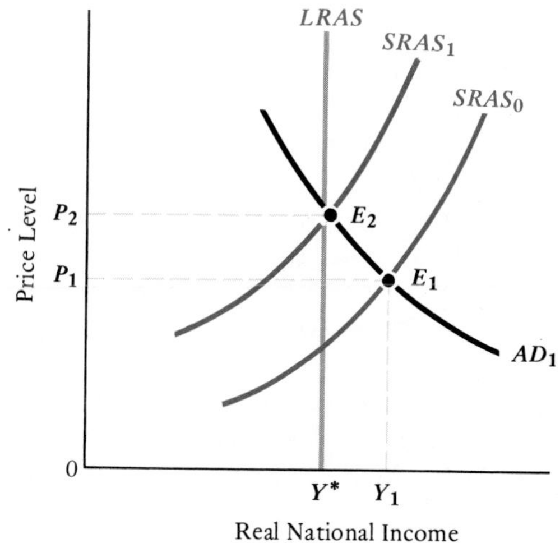

(ii) Inflationary gap eliminated

A rise in the price level will eliminate an inflationary gap. The economy is initially in long-run equilibrium at E_0, with price level P_0 and real income Y^*. In (i) some disturbance shifts the *AD* curve to the right, leading to equilibrium E_1, with a higher price level P_1 and an inflationary gap of Y^*Y_1.

E_1 is also shown in (ii). The inflationary gap causes wages to rise, shifting the *SRAS* curve to the left so that the price level starts to rise. The monetary adjustment mechanism (working through a rising interest rate and falling investment) lowers aggregate expenditure so that the economy moves upward along the *AD* curve. Eventually, the inflationary gap is eliminated and equilibrium is reached at E_2, with income at Y^* and price level P_2.

This mechanism, illustrated in Figure 34-8(ii), may be called the *monetary adjustment mechanism*. It works through the transmission mechanism.

The monetary adjustment mechanism will eliminate any inflationary gap, provided that the nominal money supply is held constant.

Thus inflationary gaps tend to be self-correcting as long as the money supply does not increase. They will cause the price level to increase, but the increase sets in motion a chain of events in the markets for financial assets that will eventually remove the inflationary gap.

The self-correcting mechanism is the reason that price levels and the money supply have been linked for so long in economics. Many things can cause the price level to rise for some time. Yet whatever the reason for the rise, unless the money supply is expanded, the increase in the price level sets up forces that will remove the initial inflationary gap and so bring demand inflation to a halt.

Frustration of the monetary adjustment mechanism. The self-correcting mechanism for removing an inflationary gap can be frustrated indefinitely if the money supply is increased at the same rate that prices are rising. Say that the price level is rising by 10 percent per year under the pressure of a large inflationary gap. Demand for nominal money balances will also be rising by about 10 percent per year. Now suppose that the Bank increases the money supply by 10 percent per year. No excess demand for money will develop, since the extra money needed to meet the rising demand will be forthcoming. The real interest rate will not rise, and the inflationary gap

FIGURE 34-9 Frustration of the Monetary Adjustment

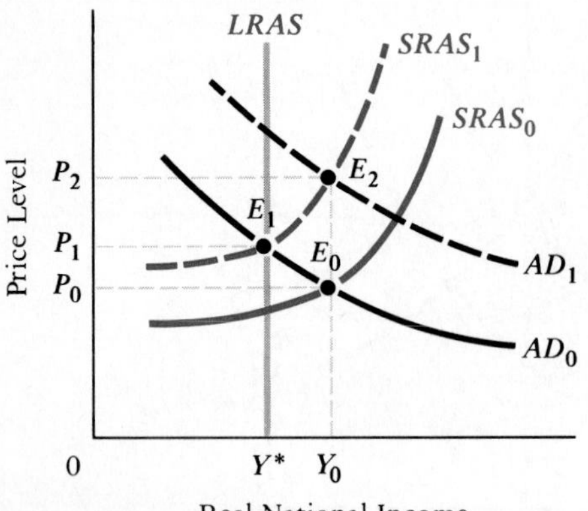

An inflationary gap can persist indefinitely if the money supply increases as fast as the price level. Suppose that the economy is at E_0, with income Y_0 and price level P_0. Since potential income is Y^*, there is an inflationary gap of Y^*Y_0. The price level now rises, which tends to shift the economy upward along any given *AD* curve, thereby tending to reduce the excess aggregate demand. However, the Bank of Canada increases the money supply, so that the *AD* curve shifts outward, thereby tending to increase excess aggregate demand. If the two forces just balance each other, by the time the price level has risen, to P_2, the curve will have shifted to AD_1, leaving the inflationary gap unchanged, with equilibrium at E_2.

will not be reduced. This process is analyzed in Figure 34-9.

If the money supply increases at the same rate as the price level rises, the real money supply and hence the real interest rate will remain constant, and the monetary adjustment mechanism will be frustrated.

Inflation is said to be *validated* when the money supply is increased as fast as the price level so that the monetary adjustment mechanism is frustrated. Validated inflation can go on indefinitely, although, as we shall see in Chapter 36, not at a constant rate.

A recessionary gap. In principle, the monetary adjustment mechanism will also operate to eliminate a recessionary gap. If the recessionary gap leads to a fall in factor prices, the *SRAS* curve would shift to the right, causing the price level to fall and national income to rise. However, as we saw in Chapter 30, many economists argue that wages and other factor costs are slow to fall in the face of a recessionary gap. (This was referred to as the second asymmetry of aggregate supply; see the discussion surrounding Figure 30-3.) In this circumstance the monetary adjustment mechanism will not be effective in causing national income to return quickly to its potential level. Thus many economists argue that aggregate demand should be stimulated in the face of a recessionary gap, either through fiscal policy, which we studied in Chapter 32, or through monetary policy, which we shall study in Chapter 35.

The Strength of Monetary Forces

How much will a given change in the money supply cause national income to increase? As can be seen in Figure 34-7, this will depend on both aggregate demand and aggregate supply.

The Role of Aggregate Demand

The size of the shift in the *AD* curve in response to an increase in the money supply depends on the size of the increase in investment expenditure that is stimulated. This in turn depends on the strength of the two key linkages that make up what is called the *transmission mechanism*.

The first consideration is how much interest rates fall in response to the increase in the money supply. The more interest-sensitive the demand for money, the less interest rates will have to fall to induce firms and households willingly to hold the increase in the money supply.

The second consideration is how much investment expenditure increases in response to the fall in interest rates. The more interest-sensitive investment expenditure is, the more it will increase in response to any given fall in the interest rate.

It follows that the size of the shift in aggregate demand in response to a change in the money supply depends on the shapes of the demand for money and marginal efficiency of investment curves. The influence of the shapes of the two curves is shown in Figure 34-10 and may be summarized as follows:

1. **The steeper (less interest-sensitive) the *LP* function, the greater the effect a change in the money supply will have on interest rates.**

FIGURE 34-10 Two Views on the Strength of Monetary Changes

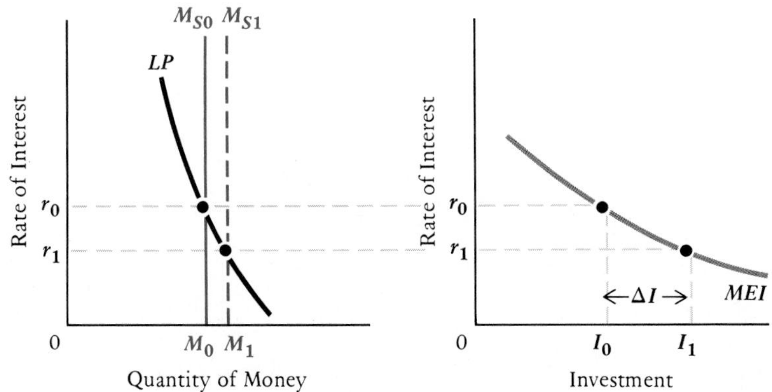

(i) Changes in the money supply effective

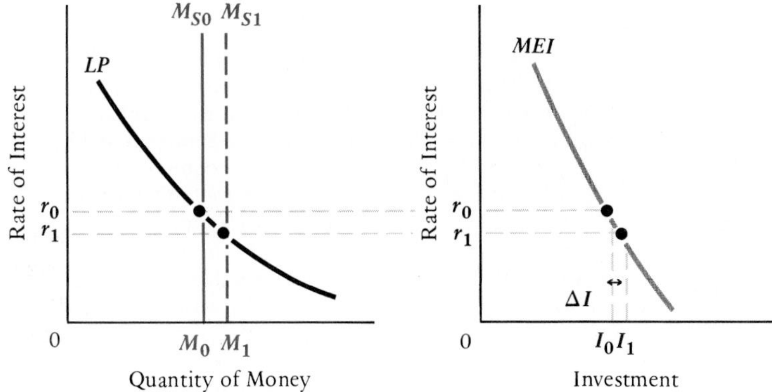

(ii) Changes in the money supply ineffective

The strength of the effect of a change in the money supply on investment and hence on aggregate demand depends on the interest elasticity of both the demand for money and desired investment expenditure. Initially, the money supply is M_{S0}, and the economy is in equilibrium, with an interest rate of r_0 and investment expenditure of I_0.

In both parts of the figure, the central bank expands the money supply from M_{S0} to M_{S1}. The rate of interest thus falls from r_0 to r_1, as shown in each of the left panels. This causes an increase in investment expenditure of ΔI, from I_0 to I_1, as shown in each of the right panels.

In (i) the demand for money is highly interest-inelastic, so the increase in the money supply leads to a large fall in the interest rate. Further, desired investment expenditure is highly interest-elastic, so the large fall in interest rates also leads to a large increase in investment expenditure. In this case the change in the money supply will be effective in stimulating aggregate demand.

In (ii) the demand for money is interest-elastic, so the increase in the money supply leads only to a small fall in the interest rate. Further, desired investment expenditure is highly interest-inelastic, so the small fall in interest rates also leads to only a small increase in investment expenditure. In this case the change in the money supply will not be effective in stimulating aggregate demand.

2. **The flatter (more interest-sensitive) the *MEI* function, the greater the effect a change in the interest rate will have on investment expenditure and hence on aggregate demand.**

The combination that produces the largest effect on aggregate demand for a given change in the money supply is a steep *LP* function and a flat *MEI* function. This combination is illustrated in Figure 34-10(i). It accords with the view, which we shall see later is often associated with so-called monetarists, that monetary policy is relatively effective as a means of influencing the economy. The combination that produces the smallest effect is a flat *LP* function and a steep *MEI* function. This combination is illustrated in Figure 34-10(ii). It accords with the view, which we shall see later is associated with some so-called Keynesians, that monetary policy is relatively ineffective.

The monetarist and Keynesian views just identified are closely related to their differing interpretations of one of the most dramatic episodes in the history of the Canadian economy, the Great Depression.

The Role of Aggregate Supply

As we saw in Chapter 30, the response of real national income and the price level to any given shift in the *AD* curve depends on the behavior of aggregate supply. Two aspects of this behavior are relevant.

The slope of the *SRAS* curve. As shown in Figure 29-10, the steeper the *SRAS* curve is, the larger will be the change in the price level and the smaller will be the change in real national income following a shift in the *AD* curve. Many economists think that when the level of real national income is near (or above) its capacity level, the *SRAS* curve is very steep. Thus

When the economy is operating near its capacity level of output, increases in aggregate demand (including those caused by increases in the money supply) will not lead to large increases in real national income but will have a substantial effect on the price level.

Shifts in the *SRAS* curve. As we saw in Figure 34-8, shifts in the *SRAS* curve can offset the expansionary effects of an increase in aggregate demand. In Figure 34-8 such shifts were induced by changes in factor prices that arose in response to an inflationary gap. However, many economists think that such offsetting shifts in the *SRAS* curve can also occur if the *AD* shock was caused by an increase in the money supply that was *anticipated*. (In Box 30-2 we also examined the possibility that expectations effects can cause the *SRAS* curve to shift for any anticipated shift in the *AD* curve.)

Figure 34-11 illustrates the case of an increase in the money supply that is perfectly foreseen by workers and employers alike. As in Figure 34-8, the monetary disturbance shifts the *AD* curve rightward. Workers, knowing that the prices of goods that they buy are going to rise, would demand increases in wages to compensate. Employers, knowing that the price of their output is going to rise, would be willing to grant the wage increases. Thus the *SRAS* curve immediately shifts leftward; this *expectations effect* means that the monetary adjustment mechanism operates very quickly, thus reducing the effect of a monetary disturbance on real national income.

How far does the *SRAS* curve shift in anticipation of a future shock? In the extreme case where there was no disagreement about the extent or the implications of the initial monetary disturbance, wages would rise so as to offset the price increase completely. Real wages would thus remain unchanged. If real wages were unchanged, real output would also be unchanged, so the *SRAS* curve must shift enough to offset completely the expansionary effects on real national income, as shown in the figure. Thus:

It is possible that in the case of a perfectly foreseen monetary disturbance, all the effects fall on money wages and prices and none fall on real wages or real national output.

Of course, most monetary disturbances are, at best, imperfectly foreseen, and typically there is considerable uncertainty about the exact nature and implications of any particular disturbance. Hence the

FIGURE 34-11 Expectations and the Effects of Monetary Changes

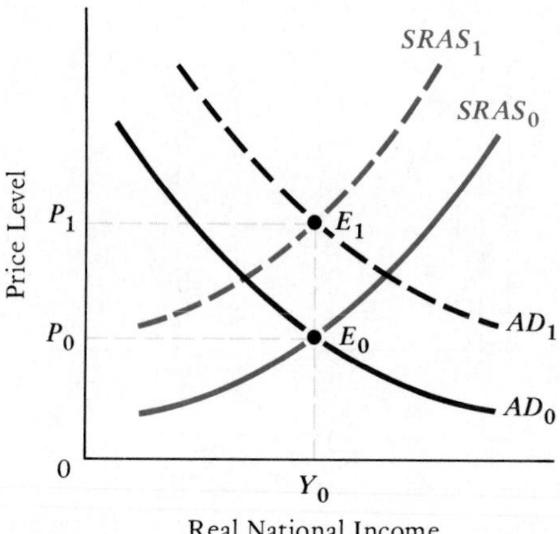

An increase in the money supply that is widely foreseen and understood might cause wages to rise, thus eliminating any effect on real national income. The economy is initially in equilibrium at E_0, with price level P_0 and real national income at Y_0. An increase in the money supply causes the *AD* curve to shift rightward from AD_0 to AD_1. Because the increase was perfectly foreseen and because workers and employers agreed that its effects would be inflationary, wages rise so that the *SRAS* curve shifts leftward. The shift will be such that the new equilibrium is at E_1, where real wages and real national income are unchanged. Hence wages rise until the *SRAS* curve reaches $SRAS_1$ and the new price level is P_1. Real national output remains unchanged at Y_0.

result that the effects on real national income are completely offset is extreme, and any monetary disturbance can be expected to have at least some temporary effect. However, the expectations effects complicate the analysis of the effects of monetary disturbances and create problems for economists who are trying to predict the effects of current monetary events or to advise governments on the use of monetary policy. We will encounter this issue repeatedly in the next few chapters as we study monetary policy and other macroeconomic problems and controversies.

SUMMARY

1. For the sake of simplicity, we divide all forms in which wealth is held into money, which is a medium of exchange, and bonds, which earn a higher interest return than money and can be turned into money by selling them at a price that is determined on the open market.
2. The price of bonds varies negatively with the rate of interest. A rise in the interest rate lowers the prices of all bonds. The longer its term to maturity, the greater the change in the price of a bond for a given change in the interest rate.
3. The value of money balances that the public wishes to hold is called the *demand for money*. It is a stock (not a flow), measured as so many billions of dollars.
4. Money balances are held, despite the opportunity cost of bond interest forgone, because of the transactions, precautionary, and speculative motives. They have the effect of making the demand for money vary positively with real national income, the price level, and wealth and negatively with the rate of interest. The nominal demand for money varies proportionally with the price level.
5. When there is an excess demand for money balances, people try to sell bonds. This pushes the price of bonds down and the interest rate up. When there is an excess supply of money balances, people try to buy bonds. This pushes the price of bonds up and the rate of interest down. Monetary equilibrium is established when people are willing to hold the fixed stocks of money and bonds at the current rate of interest. The liquidity preference (*LP*) function is the relationship between money demand and the interest rate.
6. A change in the interest rate causes desired investment to change along the marginal efficiency of investment (*MEI*) function. This shifts the aggregate desired expenditure function and causes equilibrium national income to change. This means that the aggregate demand curve shifts.
7. Points 5 and 6 together describe the transmission mechanism that links money to national income. A decrease in the supply of money tends to reduce aggregate demand. An increase in the supply of money tends to increase aggregate demand.
8. The negatively sloped aggregate demand curve indicates that the higher the price level, the lower the equilibrium national income. The explanation lies with the monetary adjustment mechanism: Other things being equal, the higher the price level, the higher the demand for money and the rate of interest, the lower the aggregate expenditure function, and thus the lower the equilibrium income.
9. The monetary adjustment mechanism that causes the aggregate demand curve to have a negative slope means that a sufficiently large rise in the price level will eliminate any inflationary gap. However, this mechanism can be frustrated if the Bank of Canada validates

the price rise by increasing the money supply as fast as the price level is rising.

10. The steeper the *LP* curve and the flatter the investment curve, the greater the effect of a given change in the money supply on aggregate demand. The steeper the *SRAS* curve or the faster wages adjust, the smaller the transitory effect of a given shift in the *AD* curve on national income. If the change in the money supply was widely foreseen and understood, the *SRAS* curve might shift very quickly so as to reduce any effects on national income.

TOPICS FOR REVIEW

Interest rates and bond prices
Transactions, precautionary, and speculative motives for holding money
Liquidity preference (*LP*) function
Monetary equilibrium
Transmission mechanism
Marginal efficiency of investment (*MEI*) function
Monetary adjustment mechanism
Expectations and the strength of monetary forces

DISCUSSION QUESTIONS

1. "Central banker says using monetary policy to lower interest rates now would only cause inflation to rise and lead to higher interest rates in the future." Explain how this might be so.
2. "Bond prices pressed downward by news of M1's sharp rise, economy's rebound." Does this *Wall Street Journal* headline necessarily contradict our theory about the direct link between money supply and bond prices?
3. Historically, construction of new houses has been one of the most interest-sensitive categories of spending. In 1989 the financial press carried a number of stories suggesting that due to financial deregulation and innovations in housing finance, this interest sensitivity had apparently decreased. If this were true, what would be the implications for monetary policy?
4. Describing a possible future "cashless society," a public report recently said, "In the cashless society of the future, a customer could insert a plastic card into a machine at a store and the amount of the purchase would be deducted from his 'bank account' in the computer automatically and transferred to the store's account. No cash or checks would ever change hands." What would such an institutional change do to the various motives for holding money balances? What functions would remain for commercial banks and for the central bank if money, as we now know it, disappeared in this fashion? What benefits and disadvantages can you see in such a scheme?
5. What motives do you think explain the following holdings?
   a. Currency and coins in the cash register of the local supermarket at the start of each working day
   b. The payroll account of the Ford Motor Company in the local bank
   c. Term deposits that mature after one's retirement
   d. Government bonds held by private individuals

6. What would be the effects on the company if Parliament were to vote a once-and-for-all universal social dividend of $5,000 paid to every Canadian over the age of 15, to be financed by the creation of new money?
7. In 1989 economists Christina and David Romer produced a study of post–World War II policies of the U.S. Federal Reserve Board. They examined six episodes in which the Fed tightened monetary policy to reduce inflation and found that each time, following the tightening of monetary policy, the unemployment rate rose sharply and industrial production fell. Further, they estimated that these effects persist, so that unemployment is at its peak $2\frac{1}{2}$ years after the policy is initiated, and "there is only a limited tendency for economic activity to return to its previous path subsequently." Interpret these results in terms of the theoretical framework developed in this chapter.
8. Suppose that you alone know that the Bank of Canada is going to engage in policies that will decrease the money supply sharply, starting next month. How might you make speculative profits by purchases or sales of bonds now?
9. What would happen if, starting from a situation of a 10 percent rate of inflation and of monetary expansion, the Bank cut the rate of monetary expansion to 5 percent?
10. Trace the full sequence of events by which the monetary adjustment mechanism would work if, in the face of a constant money supply, workers and firms insisted on actions that raised prices continually at a rate of 10 percent per year. "Sooner or later in this situation, something would have to give." What possible things could "give"? What would be the consequence of each "giving"?

Appendix to Chapter 34

More About the Slope of the Aggregate Demand Curve

The *AD* curve relates the price level to the equilibrium level of real national income. Its negative slope means that the higher the price level, the lower the equilibrium national income. The main reason for this negative slope is found in the transmission mechanism.

Let us look at this process in detail. Although the argument contains nothing new, it does require that you follow carefully through several steps.

We start with an initial equilibrium position, corresponding to a given price level P_0, shown by the 0 subscripts in the two figures. Figure 34A-1, which reproduces the relationships depicted in Figure 34-4, shows the determination of the interest rate by the conditions of monetary equilibrium in part (i); that in turn determines the level of desired investment spending by the marginal efficiency of investment schedule in part (ii). Figure 34A-2, which reproduces

FIGURE 34A-1 Changes in the Price Level: Interest Rates and Investment

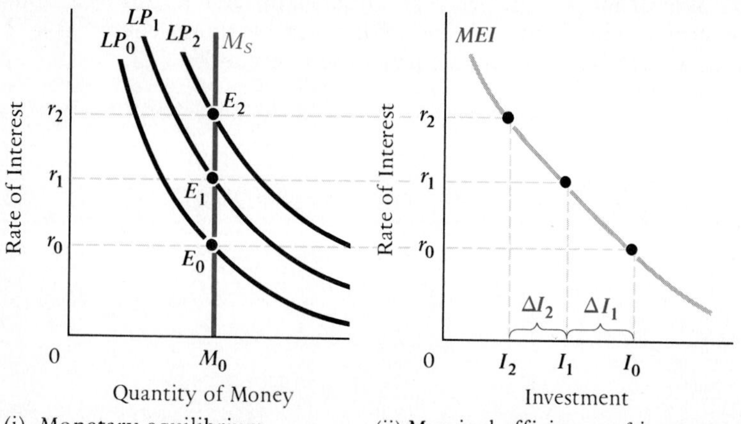

Changes in the price level influence the demand for money and hence cause the level of interest rates and desired investment spending to change; other things being equal, the higher the price level, the lower the level of desired investment spending. Monetary equilibrium is shown in (i). The money supply is fixed at M_0. The *LP* curve shows how the demand for money varies with the interest rate, with the price level given. Initially money demand is given by LP_0, equilibrium is at E_0, and the interest rate is r_0. Given that interest rate, desired investment spending is I_0, as shown in (ii) by the marginal efficiency of investment (*MEI*) schedule.

An increase in the price causes an increase in the demand for money, and hence the *LP* curve shifts upward to LP_1. Equilibrium is at E_1, the interest rate rises to r_1, and desired investment spending falls by ΔI_1 to I_1.

A further increase in the price level causes a further increase in the demand for money, to LP_2. Equilibrium is at E_2, the interest rate rises to r_2, and desired investment spending falls by ΔI_2 to I_2.

FIGURE 34A-2 Changes in the Price Level: Aggregate Expenditure and National Income

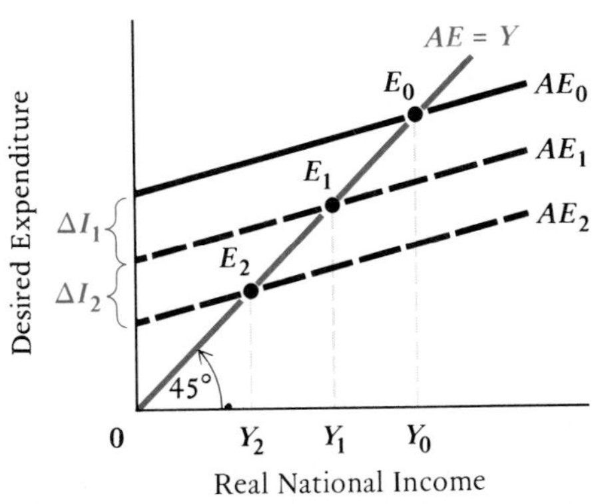

(i) Equilibrium national income

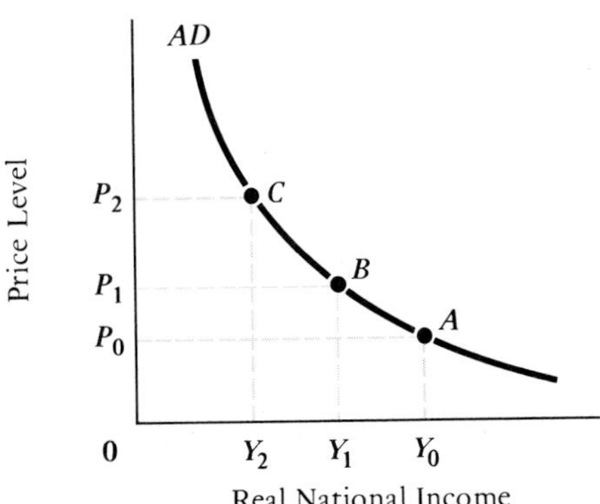

(ii) The aggregate demand curve

Changes in the price level lead to changes in desired aggregate expenditure and hence in the equilibrium level of national income; other things being equal, the higher the price level, the lower the equilibrium level of national income. Equilibrium national income is determined in (i). At a given initial price level—hence an initial level of desired investment spending of I_0 from Figure 34A-1—desired aggregate expenditure is shown by AE_0. Equilibrium is at E_0, and the equilibrium level of national income is Y_0. In (ii) the level of equilibrium national income Y_0 is plotted against the price level P_0 to give point A on the AD curve.

An increase in the price level causes a decrease of ΔI_1 in the level of desired investment spending, as determined in Figure 34A-1 and shown in (i) here. Thus desired aggregate expenditure falls and the AE curve shifts down to AE_1. Equilibrium is at E_1, and the equilibrium level of national income falls to Y_1. In (ii) the higher price level P_1 is plotted against the lower equilibrium level of income Y_1 as point B on the AD curve.

A further increase in the price level causes a further decrease of ΔI_2 in the level of desired investment spending, as determined in Figure 34A-1 and shown in (i) here. Thus desired aggregate expenditure falls, and the AE curve shifts downward to AE_2. Equilibrium is at E_2, and the equilibrium level of national income falls to Y_2. In (ii) the higher price level P_2 is plotted against the lower equilibrium level of income Y_2 as point C on the AD curve.

the relationships depicted in Figure 34-5, shows the *AE* curve, drawn for that level of investment spending, and the determination of equilibrium national income in part (i); that level of national income is then plotted against the price level to give point *A* on the *AD* curve in part (ii).

A rise in the price level raises the money value of transactions and increases the quantity of money demanded at each possible value of the interest rate. As a result, the liquidity preference function shifts upward, raising the interest rate and reducing the level of desired investment expenditure, as shown in Figure 34A-1. The reduction in investment spending in turn causes the *AE* curve to shift downward, leading to a reduction in the equilibrium level of national income, as shown in part (i) of Figure 34A-2. The combination of the higher price level and the lower equilibrium level of national income can be plotted as another point, say, point *B*, on the *AD* curve in part (ii).

Changes in the price level lead to changes in the interest rate and hence in desired aggregate expenditure and the equilibrium level of national income; other things being equal, the higher the price level, the lower the equilibrium level of national income.

The negative relationship between the price level and equilibrium real income shown by the *AD* curve occurs because, other things being equal, a rise in the price level raises the *demand for money*. Notice the qualification "other things being equal." It is important for this process that the nominal money *supply* remain constant. The monetary adjustment mechanism operates because the demand for money increases when the price level rises while the money supply remains constant. The attempt to add to money balances by selling bonds is what drives the interest rate up and reduces desired expenditure, thereby reducing equilibrium national income. (This argument is conducted in terms of the nominal supply of and demand for money. Arguing in terms of the real demand and supply of money leads to identical results.) **[42]**

Chapter 35

Monetary Policy

The Bank of Canada conducts monetary policy in order to influence such key macroeconomic variables as real national income, employment and unemployment, inflation, interest rates, and the exchange rate. The primary way in which it exerts influence on these variables is through control of the money supply.

Later in this chapter we study in detail how the Bank of Canada chooses to conduct monetary policy and what is involved in choosing among alternative possible operating procedures and deciding how much emphasis to place on each of its policy targets. We begin by examining how the Bank controls the money supply.

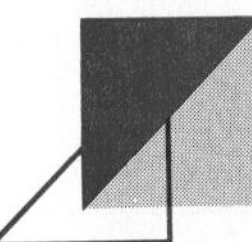

Control of the Money Supply

Deposit money is the most important part of the money supply. Demand deposits at the chartered banks account for over 50 percent of M1, the narrowest definition of money. Chequable deposits in those institutions account for over 25 percent of M2, the next broadest measure. As we have seen, the ability of commercial banks to create deposit money depends on their reserves.

The ability of the central bank to affect the money supply is critically related to its ability to affect the reserves of the banking system.

Constant target reserve ratio. In the following sections we shall discuss two ways in which the central bank affects the reserves of the banking system and hence the money supply. In Chapter 33 we identified the *target reserve ratio* of the chartered banks as the ratio of reserves they wished to hold relative to their deposit liabilities.[1] At this stage of our discussion of open-market operations, we suppose that the target reserve ratio is constant.

Open-Market Operations

One important tool that the Bank of Canada uses for influencing the supply of money is the purchase or sale of government securities on the open market. These actions are known as **open-market operations**. Just as there are stock markets, there are active and well-organized markets for government securities. You

[1] Recall that the target reserve ratio includes the influence of any reserve requirements as well as the banks' desire to hold reserves to meet their customers' needs and to facilitate clearing transactions with other banks.

or I, General Motors, the Toronto Dominion Bank, or the Bank of Canada can enter this market and buy or sell negotiable government securities at whatever price supply and demand establishes.

At the start of 1990 the Bank of Canada held more than $20 billion in government securities. In a typical year the Bank of Canada may accumulate $1 billion or even $2 billion worth of additional government securities by purchasing them; during the year its total purchases and sales on the open market amount to many times this amount. What is the effect of these purchases and sales?

Purchases on the open market. When the Bank of Canada buys a bond from a household or a firm, it pays for the bond with a cheque drawn on the central bank and payable to the seller. The seller deposits this cheque in a chartered bank, which then presents the cheque to the Bank of Canada for payment. The Bank of Canada then makes a book entry, increasing the deposit of the chartered bank at the central bank.

Table 35-1 shows the changes in the balance sheets of the several parties involved in a Bank of Canada purchase of $100,000 in government securities from a household. At the end of these transactions, the central bank has acquired a new asset in the form of a security and a new liability in the form of a deposit by the chartered bank. The seller has reduced its security holdings and increased its deposits. The chartered bank has increased its deposit liabilities and its reserves by the amount of the transaction. Typically, when the central bank buys securities on the open market, the entire banking system gains new reserves.

Given a constant target reserve ratio, after the transactions shown in Table 35-1 are completed, the chartered banks have excess reserves, that is, reserves over and above those needed to maintain their target reserve ratio. Thus they are in a position to expand their loans and deposits. Indeed, after the household deposits the proceeds of its sale of the security in its chartered bank account, its bank is placed in the same position as the bank in Table 33-4 that received the new deposit from the immigrant.

When the central bank buys securities on the open market, the reserves of the chartered banks are increased. These banks can then expand deposits, thereby increasing the money supply.

TABLE 35-1 Balance Sheet Changes Caused by an Open-Market Purchase from a Household (*thousands of dollars*)

Assets		Liabilities	
Private households			
Bonds	−$100	No change	
Deposits	+ 100		
Chartered banks			
Reserves (deposits with central bank)	+$100	Demand deposits	+$100
Central bank			
Bonds	+$100	Deposits of chartered banks	+$100

The money supply is increased when the Bank of Canada makes an open-market purchase from the nonbank private sector. When the Bank of Canada buys a $100,000 bond from a household, the household gains money and gives up a bond. The chartered banks gain a new deposit of $100,000 and thus new reserves of $100,000. Chartered banks can now engage in a multiple expansion of deposit money of the sort analyzed in Chapter 33.

Sales on the open market. When the Bank of Canada sells a security to a household or firm, it receives in return the buyer's cheque drawn against a deposit in a chartered bank. The central bank presents the cheque to the private bank for payment. Payment is made by a book entry that reduces the private bank's deposit at the central bank.

The changes in this case are the opposite of those shown in Table 35-1. The central bank has reduced its assets by the value of the security it sold and reduced its deposit liabilities to the chartered banks. The household or firm has increased its holdings of securities and reduced its deposit with a chartered bank. The chartered bank has reduced its deposit liability to the household or firm and reduced its reserves (on deposit with the central bank) by the same amount. In each case the asset change is balanced by a liability change.

Given a constant target reserve ratio, the chartered bank finds that by suffering an equal reduction in its reserves and its deposit liabilities, its actual ratio of reserves to deposits falls below its target ratio.[2] Banks whose actual reserve ratios are pushed below their target ratios will take steps to restore their reserve ratios. The necessary reduction in deposits can be accomplished by not granting new loans when old ones are repaid or by selling (liquidating) existing investments. (If the central bank requires that the banks maintain some minimum reserve ratio and their actual ratio falls below this, they *must* take immediate steps. In the short term they may borrow from the Bank of Canada to increase their reserve holdings.)

When the central bank sells securities on the open market, the reserves of the chartered banks are decreased. These banks can in turn contract deposits, thereby decreasing the money supply.

Although the process just described reflects the mechanics of an open-market sale, it does not accurately portray some of the subtleties involved in how the Bank of Canada pursues a tight monetary policy. These are discussed further in Box 35-1.

Shifting Government Deposits

As the government's fiscal agent, the Bank of Canada manages a large amount of government funds. It maintains government accounts on its own books, into which funds are deposited and from which funds are withdrawn. In addition, it manages some government accounts with the chartered banks.

The major tool the Bank of Canada uses in its day-to-day operations involves shifting government deposits between itself and the chartered banks.

When the Bank of Canada transfers government deposits, it influences the reserves of the banking system relative to its target level of reserves, thereby inducing an expansion or contraction of the money supply.

For example, suppose that the Bank of Canada were to transfer $100 million from the government's account with it to the government's account with a chartered bank. The transactions involved are illustrated in Table 35-2. From the government's view, nothing substantial has changed, since its deposits with one financial institution will have fallen but its deposits with another have risen by the same amount. However, the chartered bank in question will find that its deposit liabilities and reserves will each have risen by $100 million, and hence its ratio of reserves to deposits will have risen. If we again suppose that the bank's target reserve ratio is unchanged, the bank will have excess reserves. As with the situation following a Bank of Canada purchase of government securities on the open market, the bank will be in the position shown by Table 33-4. It will wish to loan out some of its excess reserves, thus setting in motion an expansion of deposits.

When the central bank transfers government deposits to the chartered banks, the reserves of the chartered banks are increased. These banks can then expand deposits, thereby increasing the money supply.

A transfer of government deposits from the chartered banks to the Bank of Canada has the opposite effect. The reserves and deposit liabilities of the banking system fall by the same amount, thus driving the actual reserve ratio below the target reserve ratio. Banks will now have insufficient reserves and will begin to call in existing loans and stop making new ones, setting in motion a process of deposit contraction.

When the central bank transfers government deposits from the chartered banks, the reserves of the chartered banks are decreased. These banks will then contract deposits, thereby decreasing the money supply.

Implications for the Money Supply

Notice in Table 33-1 that the Bank of Canada's holdings of government securities and its deposit liabilities to the government are both large. Either through open-market operations or switching those govern-

[2] Consider a bank with $10 million in deposits backed by $1 million cash in fulfillment of a 10 percent target reserve ratio. As a result of the Bank of Canada's open-market sales of $100,000 in bonds, the bank loses $100,000 of deposits *and* reserves. Reserves are now $900,000 while deposits are $9.9 million, and the reserve ratio has fallen to 9.09 percent.

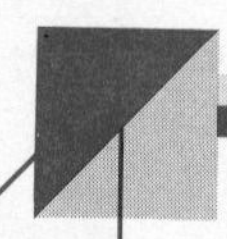

BOX 35-1

Further Aspects of Contractionary Monetary Policy

Two further issues that arise with a contractionary monetary policy are taken up in this box.

Can the Bank Always Find Buyers for Securities?

One way in which the Bank of Canada pursues a contractionary monetary policy is to sell government securities on the open market, thus reducing the reserves available to the banking system. What if the public does not wish to buy the securities the Bank of Canada wishes to sell? Can it force the public to do so?

The answer is that there is always a price at which the public will buy. The Bank of Canada in its open-market operations must be prepared to have the price of the securities fall if it insists on selling a large volume of them. As we have seen, a fall in the price of securities is the same thing as a rise in interest rates, so if the Bank of Canada wishes to decrease the money supply by selling bonds, it will usually also drive up interest rates.

Do Reserves and the Money Supply Actually Fall?

In every year since 1950, real growth and inflation have combined to ensure that nominal national income has risen. The result has been a growing transactions demand for money. In every year in that period, the nominal money supply has also grown, reflecting the Bank of Canada's decision to supply additional reserves to the banking system to meet the growing demand for money.

Does this mean that the Bank of Canada has never followed a contractionary monetary policy? The answer is no. In an economy in which real income growth and inflation result in continually growing nominal national income, the stance of monetary policy depends on the rate at which the money supply is allowed to grow *relative to* the rate of growth of the demand for money. A contractionary monetary policy occurs when the growth in the money supply is pushed below the rate of growth in the demand for money.

For example, if nominal national income and the demand for money are growing at 10 percent per year, the Bank of Canada would be following a contractionary monetary policy if it reduced the rate of growth of the money supply from 10 percent to 7 percent. This would create excess demand for money, causing interest rates to rise. In turn, the higher interest rates would feed through the transmission mechanism to cause reduced spending and a slowing in real growth or inflation (or both).

In an economy in which nominal national income is continually growing, a contractionary monetary policy occurs when the rate of growth of the money supply is reduced below the rate of growth of money demand; it does not require a fall in the absolute size of the money supply.

This point is analogous to our discussion in Chapter 26 (pages 567–568) where we noted that reductions in national income or in the price level are to be interpreted as reductions *relative to the trend* rather than as absolute declines.

ment deposits, the Bank can change the reserves of the chartered banks sharply.

Open-market operations and control of government deposits give the central bank a potent weapon for affecting the size of chartered bank reserves and thus for affecting the money supply.

Changing target reserve ratio. Changes in the money supply in response to Bank of Canada actions to change the chartered banks' reserves are not automatic but depend on the response of the chartered banks to the changes in their reserve positions. In the preceding discussion, we assumed that the banks maintained a constant target reserve ratio and hence that changes in their actual reserve ratio would set in

TABLE 35-2 Balance Sheet Changes Caused by a Transfer of Government Deposits from the Bank of Canada to a Chartered Bank (*millions of dollars*)

Chartered bank

Assets		Liabilities	
Reserves	+ 100	Government deposits	+ 100

Bank of Canada

Assets		Liabilities	
		Government deposits	− 100
		Chartered bank deposits	+ 100

A transfer of government deposits from the Bank of Canada to a chartered bank leads to an increase in the money supply. When the Bank of Canada transfers $100 of government deposits to a chartered bank, the chartered bank's account with the Bank of Canada is credited with a deposit of $100. Thus the decrease in the Bank of Canada's deposit liabilities to the government is exactly balanced by the increase in its deposit liabilities to the chartered bank. The chartered bank's increase in its deposit liabilities to the government is balanced by the increase in its reserves on deposit with the Bank of Canada. Since its deposits and its reserves have risen by the same amount, it is in the same excess reserve situation as the bank whose balance sheet is shown in Table 33-4, and the potential is created for multiple expansion of deposit money as analyzed in Chapter 33.

motion expansion or contraction of deposits. However, the target reserve ratio, and hence the reserves that the banks wish to hold, will vary with economic conditions. For example, banks may wish to hold larger reserves in times of business recession (when there is a low demand for loans and low interest rates) than they do in periods of boom (when the demand for loans is great and interest rates are high).

Changes in the chartered banks' target reserves can lead to a change in the money supply without any actions on the part of the central bank. And if the central bank increases the reserves of the banking system at the same time as the chartered banks decide to hold more, the increase in reserves will not lead to an increase in the money supply.

The significance of the potential for the banks' target reserve ratio to change is that it weakens the link between the creation of reserves by the Bank of Canada and money creation. But it does not destroy the link, since, other things being equal, an increase in reserves will lead to some undesired excess reserves and hence to some deposit creation, and a decrease in reserves will lead to a shortage of reserves and hence to some deposit contraction.

Increasing the reserves of the banking system makes it *possible* for the chartered banks to expand the money supply, and an increase in reserves by the central bank will generally lead to some deposit creation and hence to an increase in the money supply.

Other Tools for Influencing the Money Supply

In addition to open-market operations and transferring government deposits, two other tools—moral suasion and changes in the bank rate—are available to the Bank of Canada.[3]

Moral Suasion

The term *moral suasion* is generally used to describe attempts by the central bank to enlist the cooperation of private financial institutions in the pursuit of some objective of monetary policy. In a country such as Canada, where there are only a few banks, the central bank can easily communicate its view to the chartered banks. In some cases moral suasion involves general discussions aimed at improving understanding of the current financial situation and the objectives of policy. In other cases specific requests have been issued to the banks. For example, on a number of occasions in recent years, the Bank of Canada has attempted to restrain the growth of term deposits by requesting the observance of ceilings either on the interest rates offered or on the volume of deposits.

[3] Changing the reserve requirements that the banking system must maintain is also a potential method of inducing changes in the money supply. However, this is a ponderous method for changing excess reserves; open-market operations or switches in government deposits can be applied much more flexibly to achieve the same effects on the money supply. Although reserve requirements have been changed in Canada a number of times (and under current proposals are to be eliminated), these changes have been motivated for other reasons than short-term control of the money supply. This option will disappear completely when the Bank of Canada adopts its zero-required reserve policy. Changes in reserve requirements have on occasion been used in the United States for purposes of controlling the money supply.

Under the proposed new system in which reserve requirements are abolished, the Bank of Canada will monitor closely the reserves (and especially those reserves of the banking system held in the form of clearing balances with the Bank of Canada). It is possible that this system will lead the Bank to increase its reliance on moral suasion: It could, for example, use its position to put pressure on the banks to increase their clearing balances when the Bank of Canada judges those balances to be inadequate. However, the new system will also likely involve penalties in the form of interest charges on banks whose clearing balances are inadequate to meet their clearing obligations in a given period. If those interest charges are high enough to impose real penalties on banks whose reserves fall short, they will exert a strong influence on the banks' desire to hold reserves; that is, they will influence the banks' target reserve ratio. If, in turn, those interest charges can be varied according to how the Bank of Canada perceives the need for expansion or contraction of the money supply, this may reduce the emphasis on moral suasion in the new system.

Changes in the Bank Rate

Under the pre-1990 system whereby the chartered banks were required to hold some required reserves, they were able to borrow reserves from the Bank of Canada if their reserve holdings fell short of their required reserves. The rate of interest at which the Bank of Canada makes loans to the chartered banks is called the **bank rate**. In principle, a higher bank rate would have induced the banks to hold more reserves in view of the higher cost of borrowing they would have incurred if they suffered a loss of cash and were forced to seek a loan from the Bank to meet their reserve requirements.

Although this mechanism operates in the United States, it has not been of much importance in Canada because the chartered banks rarely borrowed from the Bank of Canada. Typically, their week-to-week need for reserves was accommodated by the Bank through switching government deposits, as discussed earlier. However, in pursuit of its policy objectives, the Bank also focused on controlling the growth of reserves over time. If this meant slowing the growth of reserves and the money supply, it also meant rising interest rates; the bank rate was widely viewed as a signal of the Bank's intentions.

Prior to March 1980 the bank rate was simply set by the Bank of Canada. Changes in the rate had an "announcement effect"—such changes were widely interpreted as a signal of changes in the stance of monetary policy, which would cause market interest rates quickly to move in the same direction. Since March 1980 the bank rate itself has become a "market rate." It is now set at a premium of one-quarter of a percentage point over the average rate determined in the weekly Thursday auction of three-month treasury bills.

Most observers believed that a market-determined bank rate would lessen the role played by the bank rate by eliminating the announcement effect; however, the financial press now gives even more attention to changes in the bank rate, and it is not at all clear that it is less important as a signal about monetary policy. The Bank of Canada is a major participant in the market for treasury bills, and its purchases or sales clearly influence the bank rate by influencing the treasury bill rate. But its purchases and sales also influence the money supply. Hence the bank rate now signals actual rather than intended monetary policy.

Effects of Changes in the Money Supply: A Review

We have now seen how the Bank of Canada can alter the money supply. Before turning to a more detailed discussion of the Bank's operating procedure and the policy choices it faces, we review the analysis in Chapter 34 of the effects of changes in the money supply.

Suppose that initially the economy is in equilibrium at less than potential income. The Bank then buys bonds on the open market, increasing the reserves of the banking system and putting downward pressure on interest rates (which is the same as upward pressure on the price of bonds). This leads to an increase in the money supply and a fall in interest rates. As a result, there is an increase in desired investment expenditure, which in turn shifts the aggregate demand curve rightward, thus raising equilibrium national income. This process is shown in Figures 34-4 and 34-5.

When the Bank sells bonds, this reduces the reserves of the banking system and puts upward pressure on interest rates. The money supply falls, and interest rates rise. The increased interest rate causes a reduction in investment expenditure. This in turn shifts the aggregate demand curve leftward and lowers equilibrium income.

Monetary policy works through the transmission mechanism to shift the aggregate demand curve and so to change equilibrium national income. An increase in the money supply is expansionary; a decrease is contractionary.

As a result, changes in the money supply will cause real national income and the price level to change in the same direction, as shown in Figure 34-8.

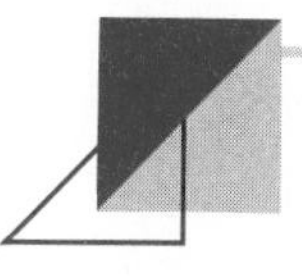

Instruments and Objectives of Monetary Policy

The Bank of Canada conducts monetary policy in order to influence real national income and the price level. These ultimate objectives of the Bank's policy are called **policy variables**. The variables that it controls *directly* in order to achieve these objectives are called its **policy instruments**. Variables that are neither policy variables nor policy instruments but nevertheless can play a key role in the execution of monetary policy are called **intermediate targets**; their importance lies in their close relationship to policy variables.

Policy Variables

The Bank of Canada's twin policy variables are real national income and the price level. In practice, the two are often lumped into a single variable, nominal national income.

Nominal national income as a policy variable. Changes in nominal national income reflect changes both in real national income and in the price level. In principle, the central bank is concerned about how a given change in nominal national income is divided between these two components.

We saw in Chapter 34 that monetary policy operates by influencing aggregate demand, and the short-run effects of a monetary policy that shifts the *AD* curve will be divided between the price level and real output in a manner determined by the slope of the *SRAS* curve. This link between the monetary actions of the central bank and the determination of the price level and real national income is summarized in Figure 35-1.

Thus even though the central bank cares about the separate reactions of the price level and of real output, there is little it can do in the short run to control such goals independently. For any price level response that is achieved, the real output consequence must be accepted. Alternatively, for any real output response that is achieved, the price level consequence must be accepted.

Monetary policy is not capable of pursuing two objectives of pushing the price level (*P*) and national income (*Y*) toward independently determined targets.

For this reason, central banks often focus on nominal national income (*PY*) as the target for monetary policy in the short run.

The price level as the policy variable in the long run. We have seen that in the long run, when the level of wages is fully adjusted to the price level, the *LRAS* curve is vertical and hence the major impact of monetary policy will be on the price level.

Though monetary policy influences both real output and the price level in the short run, its main effects in the long run are on the price level.

Policy Instruments

Having selected its policy variables and formulated targets for their behavior, the Bank of Canada must decide how to achieve these targets. How can the policy variables be made to perform in the way that the Bank of Canada wishes?

Since the Bank of Canada can control neither income nor the price level directly, it must employ its policy instruments, which it does control directly, to influence aggregate demand in the desired manner.

The primary instruments used by the Bank of Canada to conduct monetary policy are open-market operations and switching government deposits at the chartered banks.

Open-market operations and transfers change the size of the Bank of Canada's monetary liabilities,

FIGURE 35-1 Monetary Policy and Macroeconomic Equilibrium

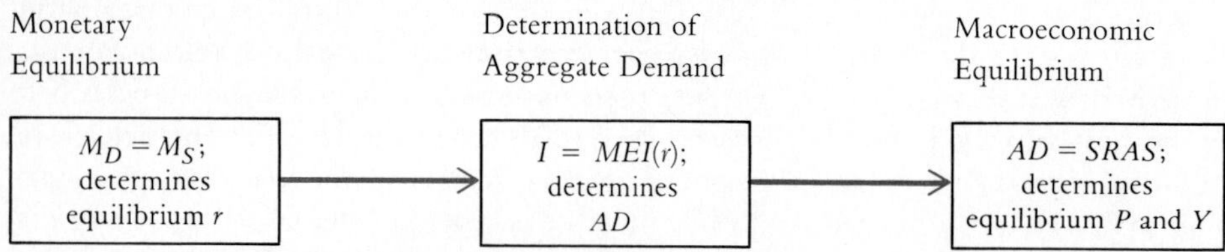

Monetary policy influences aggregate demand through the transmission mechanism, and macroeconomic equilibrium determines the price level P and the level of real output Y. Monetary equilibrium requires that the interest rate be such that the money supply equal the quantity of money demanded; for a given money supply this gives rise to the liquidity preference theory of interest, as illustrated in Figure 34-2.

Monetary equilibrium is linked to the determination of aggregate demand via the transmission mechanism, as illustrated in Figure 34-6: Changes in the money market give rise to changes in interest rates and hence, via the transmission mechanism, to changes in desired aggregate expenditure.

Aggregate demand and short-run aggregate supply together determine the equilibrium values for the price level P and real national income Y. Changes in aggregate demand thus give rise to changes in P and Y; the exact combination of changes in P and Y depends on the slope of the $SRAS$ curve, as shown in Figure 29-10.

which are the sum of currency in circulation plus reserves of the chartered banks (see Tables 33-1 and 33-2). Chartered bank reserves are held on deposit with the Bank of Canada, and they are the Bank's liability because they can be redeemed on demand. The Bank's monetary liabilities, as we saw in Chapter 33, form the *base* on which chartered banks can expand and create deposits. For this reason, its liabilities are often referred to as the **monetary base**.

The central bank cannot expect to be able to use its ability to influence the reserves of the banking system to control both the interest rate and the monetary base independently.

This is because of the liquidity preference function, which relates the quantity of money to the rate of interest. The Bank of Canada must therefore choose between two alternative procedures in determining the reserves of the banking system.

For example, it may set the *price* (and hence the interest rate) at which it sells or buys bonds on the open market. In this case the quantity of bonds sold or purchased is determined by market demand. If the Bank of Canada wishes to change its policy, it must change the price at which it is willing to buy and sell bonds. This approach is called **interest rate control**, and under it the interest rate is properly viewed as a policy instrument.

Alternatively, the Bank of Canada may choose to set the *quantity* of open-market sales or purchases. It does this in order to set the reserves of the chartered banks. In this case it is the price of bonds, and hence the interest rate, that is determined by market demand. If the Bank of Canada wishes to change its policy, it changes the amount of its open-market purchases or sales. (Of course, this means that the interest rate at which these transactions are made may also change.) In this case, where the Bank of Canada chooses to set the quantity of its open-market operations, it is directly deciding how much the monetary base will change. For this reason, it is said to be using **base control**, and the monetary base is properly viewed as the policy instrument.

The operation of these two alternative policy instruments is illustrated in Figure 35-2.

Intermediate Targets

Major changes in the direction or method of monetary policy are usually made only infrequently. Decisions regarding the implementation of policy must,

FIGURE 35-2 Alternative Policy Instruments

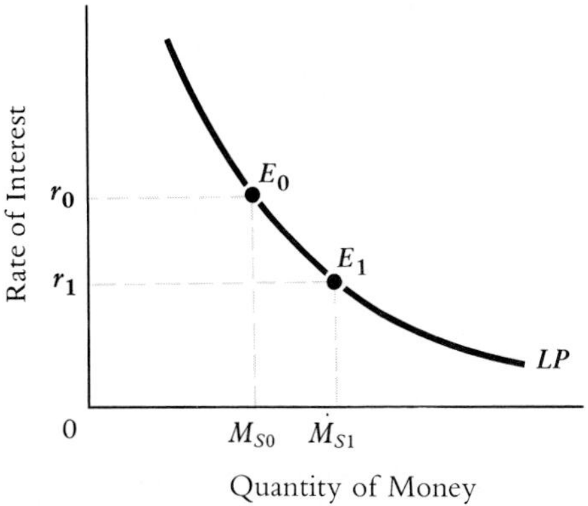

The central bank can use either the interest rate or the monetary base as its policy instrument. The demand for money is given by the negatively sloped, black liquidity preference function, *LP*, which is reproduced from Figure 34-2.

Suppose that the central bank chooses to set the interest rate at r_0. The money supply will then adjust to M_{S0}, the level consistent with money demand. If the money supply were larger, say, M_{S1}, then at r_0 there would be an excess supply of money. Households and firms would attempt to reduce their money holding by buying bonds. In order to maintain the interest rate at r_0, the central bank would meet this demand for bonds. Thus the monetary base and the money supply would fall; this would continue until the money supply fell to its equilibrium level. If the money supply were too small, a similar process would cause it to rise to its equilibrium level. For example, suppose that the economy is in equilibrium at E_0 and that the central bank then chooses to maintain the interest rate at the lower level r_1. Then the money supply, M_{S0}, would be too small; firms and households would sell bonds in order to increase their money holdings. The central bank would buy the bonds, thus increasing the monetary base and the money supply. This would continue until the money supply reached M_{S1}.

If, instead, the central bank were to choose to control the monetary base and hence the money supply, the interest rate would then adjust to ensure monetary equilibrium. For example, if the central bank were to set the monetary base so that the money supply was M_{S0}, the interest rate would adjust to r_0. If, instead, the central bank were to set the monetary base so that the money supply was M_{S1}, the interest rate would adjust to r_1. This is just the liquidity preference theory of interest rates that we encountered in Figure 34-2.

however, be made almost daily. Given the values that the Bank of Canada wishes its policy variables to take on, and given the current state of the economy, are purchases or sales on the open market called for? How big a purchase? How big a sale? At what interest rate? Such questions must be answered continually in the Bank's day-to-day operations.

Daily information about the policy variables, however, is rarely available. Inflation and unemployment rates are available only on a monthly basis and with a considerable lag. National income figures are available even less frequently; they appear on a quarterly basis. Thus the policymakers do not know exactly what is happening to the policy variables when they make decisions regarding their policy instruments.

How, then, does the Bank of Canada make decisions? Central banks have typically used *intermediate targets* to guide them when implementing monetary policy in the very short run. To serve as an intermediate target, a variable must satisfy two criteria. First, information about it must be available on a frequent basis, daily if possible. Second, its movements must be closely correlated with those of the policy variable so that changes in it can reasonably be expected to indicate that the policy variable is also changing.

The two most commonly used intermediate targets have been the money supply and the interest rate. Since the two are not independent of each other, it is important that the central bank not choose a target for one that is inconsistent with the other. By the same token, since the two are closely related, it might appear not to matter much which one is used.

For example, if the Bank of Canada wishes to remove an inflationary gap by forcing interest rates up, it will sell securities and thus drive their prices down. These open-market sales will also contract bank reserves and lead to a fall in the money supply. It is largely immaterial whether the Bank of Canada seeks to force interest rates up or to contract the money supply; doing one accomplishes the other. Similarly, driving interest rates down by open-market purchases of government securities will tend to expand the money supply as the public gains money in return for the securities it sells to the Bank of Canada.

In spite of what we have just said, there are differences between a monetary regime where interest rates are taken as an intermediate target and a regime that uses the money supply as target. As we shall see, these differences have led to changes in the Bank of Canada's use of intermediate target variables.

Choice of intermediate targets. Over the years there has been controversy over the intermediate target that the Bank should rely on most. In the earlier part of the postwar period, many central banks relied mainly on interest rates.

Many economists, and particularly monetarists, have long been critical of the practice of using the interest rate as an intermediate target. These economists pointed out that since interest rates tended to vary directly with the business cycle, rising on the upswing and falling on the downswing, it was difficult for the central bank to determine the impact of its monetary policy by observing the interest rate alone. They cited historical examples where central banks tried to restrain a boom and were lulled into thinking that their policy was pushing toward restraint by the observation that the interest rate was rising sharply. In retrospect it was concluded, however, that the expansion occurring at the time was an unusually strong one and that it was the resulting unusually high demand for money that was pushing up interest rates. In other words, the high interest rates were due to a strong demand for money rather than a restrictive supply.

As a result of such criticisms, many central banks, including the Bank of Canada, turned to rely almost exclusively on the narrow monetary aggregate M1. When M1 turned out to be a less than completely reliable guide, broader monetary aggregates were used.

Today, however, after more than a decade's experience with such monetary aggregates, similar criticisms can be levied at exclusive concentration on them. The reason is that changes in the money supply are reliable indicators of the direction of monetary policy *only* if the demand for money is relatively stable. Recent experience suggests that the demand for money can change quite substantially and that a central bank can discover what is happening to this demand only after much time-consuming research. Critics of the use of monetary aggregates as intermediate targets can point to historical circumstances in which a central bank incorrectly thought it was exerting a restraining force on the economy through a restrictive monetary policy because monetary aggregates were growing slowly. In retrospect, however, it turned out that monetary policy had been expansionary. There was an excess supply rather than an excess demand for money, the reason being that the demand for money had fallen more than had been appreciated at the time. Today some central banks still try to target on a money supply figure while others, including the Bank of Canada, use no single target but try to assess their monetary stance by looking at interest rates, various money supply measures, and other targets.

A cental bank's *operating regime* refers to its selected combination of intermediate targets and the policy instruments used to achieve those targets. Whichever operating regime is adopted, attempts to use monetary policy to fine-tune the economy remain fraught with dangers. The problems come mainly from the lags between a change in the policy instruments and the reaction of the policy variables that the Bank wishes to control. The way in which long lags can make stabilization policy destabilizing has already been discussed in Chapter 32 in the context of fiscal policy, and it is discussed further in Box 35-2 in the context of monetary policy.

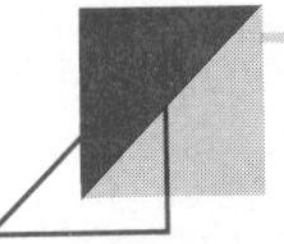

Monetary Policy in Action

Throughout the 1950s and 1960s, the Bank of Canada used interest rates as its main intermediate target. Although it was frequently difficult to judge the stance of monetary policy by observing interest rates, in some instances the stance was clear. For example, there is little doubt that monetary policy was contractionary in 1968 and 1969 when the Bank tried to insulate Canada from rising U.S. inflation.[4] There is also little doubt that monetary policy was quite expansionary in the early 1970s. In 1974 inflation was close to the double-digit level *before* the first OPEC shock that sent oil prices, and then the general price level, soaring.

By the mid 1970s there was wide consensus that using interest rates as the main intermediate tar-

[4] The attempt was frustrated by the Bank's commitment to a fixed rate of exchange between the Canadian dollar and the U.S. dollar. As we shall see in Chapter 42, monetary policy cannot simultaneously control the money supply and the exchange rate.

get was inappropriate, and central banks around the world began to focus instead on monetary aggregates.

Monetary Gradualism: 1975–1980

In 1975 the Bank of Canada announced its policy of "monetary gradualism." This involved gradually reducing the rate of growth of the money supply (narrowly defined as M1) in an effort to reduce the inflation rate slowly. A target range for money supply growth was publicly announced and periodically revised downward.

The Bank was quite successful at keeping actual money growth inside the target range, although there was considerable movement within that range. But after some reduction during the early periods of gradualism, the inflation rate accelerated, and by the end of the decade it was not far below the rate prevailing when the policy was introduced in 1975.

The restraint sought through gradual reduction in the rate of growth of the money supply was offset by shifts in the demand for money.

Some of the shifts were caused by the very inflation that the policy was attempting to curb. Inflation raises the cost of holding non-interest-bearing M1 balances, since one consequence of rapid inflation is a high nominal rate of interest. This provides an incentive to economize on M1 balances and invest the funds in interest-earning assets.

A series of spectacular institutional changes showed just how adaptive financial systems can be to changes in the needs of its users and in the information and technology available to them (many of these changes were noted in Chapter 33). Firms learned how to reduce their M1 balances by careful cash management and were often able to lend their operating balance on an overnight basis, thus earning interest on funds that would otherwise have been idle. Banks introduced automatic transfer systems where money could be held in interest-earning accounts and transferred to chequing accounts only when needed. As a result of such changes, the demand for M1 balances often fell faster than the supply was being restricted. Thus M1 control did not always create the desired conditions of tight money.

Shifts in the demand for money meant that monetary aggregates were an unreliable indicator on which to base monetary policy.

In 1982 the Bank of Canada formally abandoned monetary targeting, although it remained committed to trying to control the economy through aggregate demand. It stated, however, that no observed relationship between M1 or any other monetary magnitude on the one hand and national income on the other hand was stable enough to make complete reliance on monetary aggregates useful.

Monetary Stringency: 1981–1983

The early 1980s saw an extremely restrictive monetary policy, with interest rates rising to unprecedented levels; the rate on 90-day government treasury bills reached almost 20 percent, as shown in Figure 35-3. Inflation fell to low levels, but at the cost of a very severe recession. The Bank of Canada was following the lead of the U.S. Fed, and hence the period is best studied by observing the forces operating in the United States.

The U.S. Experience

In 1980 the Fed embarked on a policy of monetary restraint aimed at fighting inflation. The rise in interest rates, as shown in Figure 35-3, helped choke off the recovery that had just started. The subsequent rise in rates in early 1982 fed the downturn and helped make it the most serious recession since the 1930s.

These high interest rates, and the recession they wrought, were more severe than might have been expected from the relatively moderate slowdown in the rate of growth of the money supply.

An unanticipated surge in the U.S. demand for money led to a much tighter monetary policy than the Fed had intended.

This unplanned tight monetary policy did not occur because money supply targets were missed but because money demand rose. (This was the opposite of the shift in the demand for money that disrupted Canadian monetary gradualism in the 1970s.) By June 1982, M1 was back in its target range. The serious weakness in the economy and the "room for monetary ease" created by the return of M1 to its

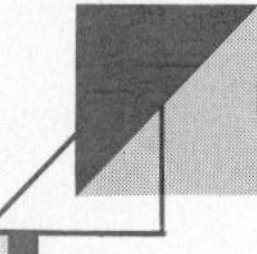

BOX 35-2

How Monetary Policy Can Be Destabilizing

The full effects of monetary policy occur only after quite long time lags. *Execution lags*, lags that occur after the decision is made to implement the policy, can have important implications for the conduct of monetary policy.

Sources of Execution Lags

1. Open-market operations affect the reserves of the chartered banks. The full increase in the money supply occurs only when the banks have extended enough new loans and made enough investments to expand the money supply by the full amount permitted by existing reserve ratios.
2. The division of all assets into just two categories, money and bonds, is useful for showing the underlying forces at work in determining the demand for money. In fact, however, there is a whole series of assets—currency and demand deposits, term deposits, treasury bills, short-term bonds, long-term bonds, and equities. When households find themselves with larger money balances than they require, a chain of substitution occurs as households try to hold less money and more interest-earning assets. The resulting fall in interest rates in turn affects interest-sensitive expenditures. These adjustments can take considerable time to work out.
3. It takes time for new investment plans to be drawn up, approved, and put into effect.
4. The increased investment expenditures set off the multiplier process that increases national income. This, too, takes some time to work out.

Furthermore, although the end result is fairly predictable, the speed with which the entire expansionary or contractionary process works itself out can vary from time to time in ways that are hard to predict. Similar considerations apply to contractionary monetary policies that seek to shift the aggregate expenditure function downward.

Monetary policy is capable of exerting expansionary and contractionary forces on the economy, but it operates with a time lag that is long and unpredictably variable.

Implications of Execution Lags

To see the significance of execution lags for the conduct of monetary policy, assume that the execution lag is 18 months. If on December 1 the Bank of Canada decides that the economy needs a stimulus, it can be increasing the money supply within days, and by the end of the year a significant increase may be registered.

But because the full effects of this policy take time to work out, the policy may prove to be destabilizing. By the fall of the next year, a substantial inflationary gap may have developed due to cyclical forces unrelated to the Bank's monetary policy. However, the full effects of the monetary expansion initiated nine months earlier are just being felt, so an expansionary monetary stimulus is adding to the existing inflationary gap.

If the Bank now applies the monetary brakes by contracting the money supply, the full effects of this move will not be felt for another 18 months. By that time a contraction may have already set in

target range led to a loosening of monetary policy in the second half of 1982.

The Canadian Reaction

The very tight monetary policy in the United States led to similar monetary restraint in Canada. Two reasons are probably important.

One is that if Canadian interest rates were held below those in the United States, one would have expected a sharp fall in the external value of the Canadian dollar (see Box 34-3). This would have made inflation worse in Canada, as there would have been upward pressure on the Canadian prices of many internationally traded goods. (This matter is discussed further in Chapter 43.) Given that the Bank of Canada was concerned with reducing, not raising, the Canadian inflation rate, it chose to allow interest

because of the natural cyclical forces of the economy. If so, the delayed effects of the monetary policy may turn a minor downturn into a major recession.

The long execution lag of monetary policy makes monetary fine tuning difficult and possibly destabilizing.

If the execution lag were known with certainty, it could be built into the Bank of Canada's calculations. But the fact that the lag is highly variable makes this nearly impossible. Of course, when a persistent gap has existed and is predicted to continue for a long time, monetary policy may still be stabilizing.

A Monetary Rule?

The poor record of monetary policy as a short-run stabilizer has lent force to the monetarists' persistent criticisms of monetary fine tuning. Monetarists argue that (1) monetary policy is a potent force of expansionary and contractionary pressures, (2) monetary policy works with lags that are both long and variable, and (3) the Bank of Canada is in fact given to sudden and sharp reversals of its policy stance. Consequently, monetary policy has a destabilizing effect on the economy.

Monetarists argue from this position that the stability of the economy would be much improved if the Bank stopped trying to stabilize it. What, then, should the Bank of Canada do? Since growth of population and of productivity lead to a rising level of output, the Bank ought to expand the money supply year in and year out at a constant rate equal to the rate of growth of real income. When the growth rate shows signs of long-term change, the Bank can adjust its rate of monetary expansion. It should not, however, alter this rate with a view to stabilizing the economy against short-term fluctuations. Many other economists think that fine tuning monetary policy can *in principle* reduce cyclical fluctuations below what they would have been under constant-rate rule, particularly when output gaps are persistent. However, the experience of the 1970s convinced many economists that:

Whatever may be true of the *best conceivable* monetary policy, the Bank of Canada's *actual* policy made cyclical fluctuations larger than they would have been under a constant rate.

Subsequent experience has shown, however, that the demand for money can sometimes shift quite substantially. A stable money supply rule in the face of demand instability guarantees monetary shocks rather than monetary stability. This undermines confidence in the appropriateness of a monetary rule. The daunting challenge for central banks in this situation is to offset such shifts in the demand for money without overreacting so as to destabilize the economy.

rates to rise with those in the United States (see Figure 35-3).

The second reason is that the Bank of Canada, discouraged by the failure of gradualism to control inflation, welcomed the opportunity to follow the United States in a more severe bout of monetary restraint. By the early 1980s many commentators had begun to wonder if the problem of inflation was intractable. If it could be solved, the failure of gradualism suggested that a severe jolt of very restrictive policy might be necessary.

The severe monetary restraint caused interest rates to soar, and a severe recession occurred. By the end of that year the unemployment rate reached 12.8 percent, its highest level since the Great Depression of the 1930s. The monetary restraint also reduced inflation from its peak of 12.7 percent in the third quarter of 1981 to 4.6 percent at the end of 1983.

FIGURE 35-3 **Short-Term Interest Rates, Canada and the United States, 1979–1990**

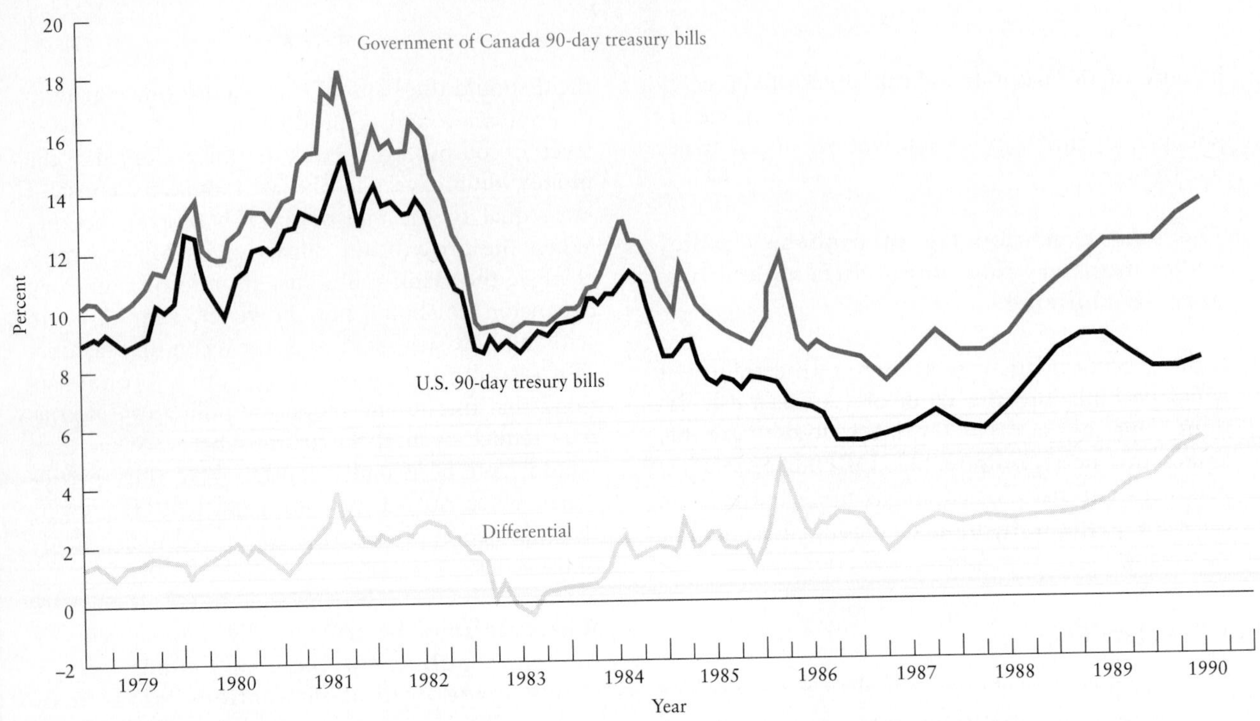

Until very recently, short-term interest rates have moved together in Canada and the United States, both rising and falling together. During 1979 and 1980, interest rates displayed an upward trend, reflecting increases in inflation. Tight monetary policy then led to sharp increases in interest rates in 1981. Subsequent declines in inflation then led to declines in nominal interest rates.

The interest differential shows that Canadian interest rates were typically a little higher than American interest rates. The differential was especially large in 1981 and 1982 when sharp increases in U.S. rates were more than matched by increases in Canadian rates, and in late 1985 and early 1986 when sharp decreases in U.S. rates were not matched by decreases in Canadian rates. In 1989 U.S. rates declined somewhat, while in late 1989 and early 1990, Canadian rates rose sharply; the differential reached an unprecedented 5.6 percent. *Source: Bank of Canada Review,* various issues.

The fall in inflation brought with it a fall in nominal interest rates; for example, the 90-day commercial bond rate fell from a peak of just over 17 percent in mid 1982 to 9.3 percent by the end of 1983. (Real interest rates did not fall as much, if indeed they fell at all, as inflation also fell.)

Low Inflation and Economic Recovery: 1983–1987

In early 1983 a sustained recovery began, and by mid 1987 national income had moved back toward potential. Much of the growth was centered in the export-oriented manufacturing industries in Ontario and Quebec. Although painfully slow for Canadians who remained unemployed, the first four years of the recovery saw a record 890,000 jobs created and cumulative output growth of 15.7 percent.

The main challenge for monetary policy in this period was to create sufficient liquidity to accommodate the recovery without triggering a

return to the high inflation rates that prevailed at the start of the decade.

The reentry problem. This task was not as simple as it may appear. Economic recovery at low inflation led to what has become known as the *reentry problem* for monetary policy. The combination of falling nominal interest rates and rising national income led to a sharp increase in the demand for real money balances. Since an increase in real balances can be achieved by either slow growth in the price level or a rapid increase in the nominal money supply, the Bank of Canada basically had two alternatives.

It could continue its restrictive monetary policy, restricting the rate of growth of the nominal money supply. This would restrain aggregate demand and thus guard against the risk of a resurgence of inflation, but at the cost of slowing the pace of the recovery. Under this policy, real balances would begin to increase only when the rate of price increase fell below the rate of monetary growth. For that to occur, national income would have to be kept below potential for a prolonged period.

Alternatively, the Bank could allow a short but rapid burst of growth in the nominal money supply, thus generating the desired increase in real money balances. Once the new level of real balances was achieved, money growth could again be cut back to a rate consistent with low inflation, allowing for the underlying rate of growth in real income. But the trick with this policy was to avoid triggering expectations of renewed inflation—essentially, the Bank had to generate a one-shot increase in the level of the money supply without creating the impression that it was raising the long-term rate of growth of the money supply.

Most economists agreed that the second policy was preferable *in principle*. But there was wide disagreement over the size and duration of the required monetary expansion and hence whether the Bank's actual policy was appropriate. In late 1983 and early 1984, when growth in monetary aggregates first started to surge, many voiced the fear that the Bank was being overly expansionary and was risking a return to higher inflation. As the reentry problem came to be more widely understood and as inflation pressures failed to reemerge, these criticisms subsided, and the consensus appeared to be that the Bank had done a commendable job of handling the reentry problem.

Continued Recovery and Rising Inflation: 1987–1990

Whatever the judgment of monetary policy in the 1983–1986 period, by mid 1987 many observers began to worry that Canadian policymakers were too complacent in accepting the 4 percent range that Canadian inflation settled into.[5] Further, there was concern that inflationary pressures were starting to build; as shown in Table 35-3, monetary aggregates were growing quickly, real output growth was strong, the unemployment rate was falling, and inflation was rising.

In 1987 many economists argued that if monetary policy were not tightened, Canada would experience gradually increasing inflation until once again a severe monetary restriction would be necessary.

The Bank of Canada apparently agreed with these views.

In January 1988, Governor John Crow announced that "price stability" was the Bank's long-term objective for monetary policy.

Specifically, he said that "monetary policy should be conducted so as to achieve a pace of monetary expansion that promotes stability in the value of money. This means pursuing a policy aimed at achieving and maintaining stable prices."[6] This explicit adoption of a zero inflation target set off a heated debate about the appropriate stance for monetary policy.

The debate was fueled by Crow's decision to give a high profile to his policy by repeatedly articulating and defending it in speeches and public appearances. It was also fueled by developments in the economy that occurred in the two years following Crow's initial announcement. Some of these are summarized in Table 35-3.

[5] In 1974, when inflation rose to the "unprecedented peak" of 4 percent, it was considered a national emergency that led to the introduction of wage and price controls in the United States and their serious consideration in Canada! See Chapter 36 for further discussion.

[6] John W. Crow, "The Work of Canadian Monetary Policy," speech given at the University of Alberta, January 18, 1988; reprinted in *Bank of Canada Review,* February 1988. A detailed analysis of this policy is presented in Richard G. Lipsey (ed.), *Zero Inflation* (Toronto: C. D. Howe Institute, 1990).

TABLE 35-3 Macroeconomics Indicators, 1986–1990

Year	Interest rate	Exchange rate (Canadian dollars per U.S. dollar)	Monetary growth M1	Monetary growth M2	Real output growth	Unemployment rate	Inflation rate
1986	8.99%	1.37	5.0%	8.7%	3.1%	9.5%	4.0%
1987	8.19	1.39	12.9	10.1	4.5	8.8	4.3
1988	9.42	1.33	6.1	7.6	5.0	7.8	4.4
1989	12.02	1.23	4.6	13.1	2.9	7.5	5.3
1990[a]	12.68	1.18	−1.1	3.1	2.0	7.6	5.4

Source: Bank of Canada Review.

[a] 1990 figures are for the first quarter.

The various indicators gave mixed signals about the economic situation and about the stance of monetary policy. Short-term interest rates rose sharply in 1988 and especially in 1989, indicating a tight monetary policy. This view was reinforced by the increase in the external value of the dollar, as reflected in the decrease in the price in terms of Canadian dollars of one U.S. dollar.

Monetary growth rates gave mixed signals. Although the growth of M1 slowed steadily throughout the period, growth in M2 rose sharply in 1989.

However, real output growth remained quite strong, and the unemployment rate fell steadily until early 1990. Furthermore, inflation rose steadily through most of the period.

Was the zero inflation target appropriate? For opponents of the Bank's policy, the sharp rise in interest rates and in the external value of the Canadian dollar provided evidence that the effects of a tight money policy were so severe that the costs clearly outweighed any potential benefits from reducing inflation. The combination of high interest rates and a strong dollar did cause many hardships, especially in traded goods industries; there were large numbers of layoffs, plant closings, and bankruptcies to provide further evidence in support of this view.

Defenders of the Bank's policies not only supported the goal of price stability but also pointed to the persistent strength in the economy as shown by real output growth and the stability of the unemployment rate to suggest that the actual costs of the policy were much less than might have been expected, given the levels of interest rates and exchange rates that had occurred. In Chapter 36 we return to a more detailed discussion of the benefits and costs of reducing inflation.

Was monetary policy effective? Some commentators argued that monetary policy was no longer effective. This view followed from observing the strength of the economy and the persistence of inflation in 1988 and 1989 despite the tight monetary policy that the Bank claimed to be following and that high interest rates and the strong dollar indicated was being followed. Proponents of this view felt that since monetary policy was ineffective in reducing inflation, it was not worth imposing the costs associated with high interest rates on the economy.

Was monetary policy tight? A number of commentators noted that monetary growth (especially M2) was quite high in 1989 and hence, they argued, despite the Bank of Canada's public rhetoric, monetary policy had not been very tight at all. According to this view, the Canadian economy had been experiencing a significant demand boom (partly fueled by large investment spending due to the signing of the Free Trade Agreement in 1988). Thus the Bank of Canada, though intending a tight enough monetary policy to reduce inflation, had in fact simply been "leaning against the wind" and had not even fully offset the inflationary pressures inherent in such a demand boom. Proponents of this view noted that the inflation rate rose rather than fell in 1989, giving further weight to the notion that the Bank of Canada's monetary policy had not been tight, at least in the sense of doggedly pursuing its goal of price stability.

These competing views give ample testimony to the problems involved for both policymakers and their critics in trying to assess the current stance of monetary policy.

It is difficult to sort out the extent to which developments in the economy are due to changes in the demand for money and to changes in monetary policy.

The competing views illustrate why most central banks have abandoned attempts to guide their policy decisions by exclusive focus on any single variable in the table but rather look at all indicators as they gather information in order to make their policy choices.

The particular developments shown in Table 35-3 were further complicated by the fact that this was a period during which macroeconomic forecasting seemed particularly inaccurate. Starting in 1988 and continuing through 1990, many forecasters, inside and outside of government, were on record as predicting a sharp downturn in the economy, accompanied by lower inflation and interest rates and a weaker Canadian dollar. In fact, the economy continued to outperform the forecasts, with output and employment growth continually outstripping predicted levels; the higher demand meant that interest rates and inflation remained higher than expected, and the Canadian dollar remained stronger. (A discussion of this experience and of the problems it created for monetary policy can be found in the 1989 annual report of the Bank of Canada.)

In mid 1990 many economists were still forecasting a sharp slowdown in the economy. One fear was that in the face of the failure of so many similar forecasts to come true in the previous two years, monetary policy would be slow to adjust to any downturn that did occur. If that happened, monetary policy would quickly become excessively tight and would cause the slowdown to turn into a severe recession. Whether that would at least serve the purpose of ratcheting down the inflation rate is a question we return to in Chapter 36.

Some Tentative Conclusions

It is now widely accepted that the economy is too complicated for a single magnitude to provide all the information that the Bank needs in developing an effective monetary policy.

For example, with regard to monetary aggregates, the extensive substitutability among M1, M2, and M3 means that all three magnitudes must be surveyed for the information that they can provide. Furthermore, institutional developments mean that the degree of substitutability is subject to continual change and so no one magnitude can be taken as a proxy for all three.

It is also widely accepted that interest rates convey information that might not be available from monetary aggregates alone. For example, the important lesson to be drawn from the 1970s is that even if all the monetary aggregates are increasing only slowly, real interest rates that are low or negative probably indicate major reductions in the demand for money. In that situation the low real interest rates suggest that monetary policy is more expansionary than the behavior of any monetary aggregate would reveal.

New goals of monetary policy in addition to the traditional ones of income and price level have emerged. The two new goals of greatest importance are the health of the financial system and the behavior of exchange rates.

Stabilizing the Financial System

The enormous debt that third-world countries, particularly oil exporters, piled up in the 1970s became unsustainable in the 1980s. Much of this debt was owed to banks in the developed countries, the United States and Canada being important creditors. As oil revenues fell, the oil-exporting countries found it impossible to pay the interest on their debt without further loans, let alone trying to repay any of the principal. Central banks became acutely aware that a sudden default of these debtor countries could cause a financial crisis in the banking system. It also became aware that every time the interest rate rose 1 percent, the burden on these debtor countries was measured in billions of dollars of extra payments.

There was no hope that these countries could ever generate the revenues necessary to repay the principal of these loans. What the banking community of the developed world could at most try to do was to delay the final day of reckoning by rescheduling some of the loans and lending some of the money needed to repay the remaining interest until the major banks could adjust their portfolios sufficiently to write off enormous loans without going into insolvency.

The Role of the Exchange Rate

The exchange rate has always been important in Canada. Its behavior influences the health of domestic industries that either export or compete with imports and therefore has an important influence on domestic economic performance.

Other Policy Issues

The Bank of Canada seems to have come more and more to take nominal national income as its target variable. In the past the Bank has often concentrated on real national income as its goal of stabilization policy (by removing recessionary or inflationary gaps) and the price level as its traditional goal of preserving the purchasing power of the nation's currency. Recently, however, the understanding has spread that the Bank can, at best, influence the *AD* curve; how this influence divides itself between income and the price level depends on the shape of the *SRAS* curve, which is beyond the Bank's control. The Bank is still concerned with the long-term trend in the price level as its most important goal, but in the shorter term it seems to accept that it can influence nominal national income and adjust its policies to the behavior of that variable, which is a composite of changes in real income and the price level.

As the enormous federal budget deficit is reduced, there may be a need for the Bank to adopt a compensating monetary policy. The reduction in the deficit means some combination of tax increases and expenditure decreases on the part of the government. As we saw in Chapter 32, both of these changes reduce aggregate demand and tend to contract economic activity. To offset these forces, the Bank could engage in a once-and-for-all monetary expansion. As we saw in Chapter 34, this increases aggregate demand. There is no reason in theory why a change in the mix of macroeconomic policy to a more restrictive fiscal policy and a more expansionary monetary policy cannot leave the level of aggregate demand unchanged. This would mean that the policy changes did not significantly affect either national income or the price level. This shift in policy mix requires that the Bank be willing to play a more sophisticated role than merely following blind rules for the growth of monetary aggregates. This is a role that some would say is fraught with dangers of trying to do things that are beneficial in theory but that, given the imperfections of practical policy, may turn out to be harmful in practice—harmful in the specific way of increasing inflationary pressures. Whether or not this is a serious worry should become apparent by the end of the 1990s.

SUMMARY

1. The major tool the Bank of Canada uses to control the supply of money is control of reserves of the banking system. Increases in the reserves of the banking system lead to an increase in the money supply; decreases in reserves lead to a contraction in the money supply.
2. The Bank of Canada can affect the reserves of the banking system through open-market operations or by switching government deposits between itself and the chartered banks. Purchases of bonds on the open market or switching government deposits to the chartered banks increases the reserves of the banking system. Sales on the open market or withdrawing government deposits from the chartered banks reduces bank reserves.
3. Other instruments of monetary policy include changing the bank rate (the rate of interest at which the Bank of Canada will lend to chartered banks) and applying moral suasion.
4. The ultimate objectives of monetary policy are called policy variables. In principle these include real national income and the rate of change of the price level. However, in practice nominal income is

often taken to be the policy variable in the short term, since the Bank of Canada cannot expect to be able to influence the composition of changes in nominal income between real growth and inflation.

5. Where the Bank of Canada cannot influence its policy variables directly, it must work through policy instruments that it can control and that will in turn influence its policy variables. Intermediate targets are used to guide decisions about policy instruments. The money supply and the interest rate may both be either intermediate targets or policy instruments.
6. National income can be influenced by open-market operations. Since it cannot control both independently, the Bank must choose between the interest rate and the money supply as the intermediate target of such operations. To reduce national income, the Bank sells bonds on the open market, thereby reducing bank reserves, driving up the rate of interest, and shifting the *AD* curve to the left. To increase national income, the Bank buys bonds on the open market, thereby increasing reserves, driving down the rate of interest, and shifting the *AD* curve to the right.
7. Until 1975 the Bank of Canada used interest rates as its main intermediate target. In that year the Bank converted to monetarism in that it based its monetary policy on targets for the rate of increase of the money supply (defined as M1). In the period of monetary gradualism from 1975 to 1980, the stance of monetary policy was meant to be restrictive by gradually reducing the rate of increase of the money supply. However, due to innovations in banking practices, the demand for M1 often fell faster than the supply, making monetary policy expansive rather than restrictive.
8. In the period of stringency (1981–1983), the U.S. Federal Reserve Bank, followed by the Bank of Canada, adopted a policy of severe monetary restraint. Interest rates soared to unprecedented heights, and the aggregate demand curves of both countries were driven sharply to the left. This led to a severe recession and a sharp fall in inflation.
9. During the long recovery from the recession that broke the inflation, the Bank largely accommodated the increase in the demand for real balances that resulted from the fall in the inflation rate and the rise in national income. At the end of the 1980s the Bank was explicitly advocating a policy of "zero inflation," but strong demand growth kept income and prices rising despite very high interest rates and a strong Canadian dollar.
10. It is generally agreed that rapid changes in the money supply and interest rates can have large effects on the economy. There is disagreement, however, on how much monetary policy can and should be used as a device for stabilizing national income at its potential level or coping with temporary bouts of rising prices.

TOPICS FOR REVIEW

Open-market operations
Shifting government deposits
The bank rate
Policy variables, policy instruments, and intermediate targets
Variability of monetary policy and monetary rules
Appropriateness of monetary targets when money demand is shifting

DISCUSSION QUESTIONS

1. One common criticism of Bank of Canada policy in the 1980s was that it was too contractionary in 1983–1985, too expansionary in 1987–1988, and too contractionary again in 1990. Use the data in Table 35-3 and other data that you might think relevant to evaluate this view. To what extent is this "cheap criticism" that draws too readily on "perfect hindsight"?
2. During the recovery of the Canadian economy from 1983 to 1985, two different views were often expressed. Some analysts said that adherence to a long-run constant growth rate rule for monetary aggregates was particularly important lest inflationary expectations be rekindled by an overly fast rate of monetary expansion. Others said that encouraging the recovery required a temporary burst of monetary expansion. Discuss these two views.
3. The U.S. Federal Reserve Board runs a facility in Culpeper, Virginia, that costs $1.8 million per year to maintain and to guard against robbery, according to Senator William Proxmire of Wisconsin. Inside this "Culpeper switch," a dugout in the side of a mountain, the government has hidden $4 billion in new currency for the purpose, it says, of "providing a hedge against any nuclear attack that would wipe out the nation's money supply." Comment on the sense of this policy.
4. Describe the chief weapons of monetary policy available to the Bank of Canada, and indicate whether—and if so, how—they might be used for the following purposes:
   a. To create a mild tightening of bank credit
   b. To signal that the Bank of Canada favors a sharp curtailment of bank lending
   c. To permit an expansion of bank credit with existing reserves
   d. To supply banks and the public with a temporary increase of currency for Christmas shopping
5. It is often said that an expansionary monetary policy is like "pushing on a string." What is meant by this statement? How does this contrast with a contractionary monetary policy?
6. In what situations might the following pairs of objectives come into conflict?
   a. Lowering the cost of government finance and using monetary policy to change aggregate demand
   b. Ending a deep recession and maintaining a currently achieved target for monetary growth
   c. Maintaining stable interest rates and controlling inflation
   d. Stimulating the economy and supporting the value of the dollar on foreign exchange markets
7. In 1988 the Bank of Canada announced that it was committed to achieving "price stability," but it did not commit itself to a particular target growth rate for any monetary aggregate that would be consistent with achieving its price stability target. Why do you think it failed to make such a commitment? Write a brief report either defending or criticizing the Bank's strategy.

PART 10

ISSUES AND CONTROVERSIES IN MACROECONOMICS

Chapter 36

Inflation

If you look back at Figure 26-1 on page 553, you will see that for 20 years following World War II, inflation remained low. The only exceptions were the "bubbles" immediately following World War II and the Korean War. During the second half of the 1960s, the inflation rate slowly inched upward and reached the double-digit range in the mid 1970s. By then inflation had been declared public enemy number one. Even more worrisome, it fell only slightly during the late 1970s in the face of a concerted anti-inflationary policy, which included statutory control of wages and prices and an apparently restrictive monetary policy. It rose again to the double-digit level in 1980, then remained quite stubbornly high during the recession of 1981–1982. At last, in 1983 inflation fell dramatically to around 4 percent, where it remained through 1987. Although this was an improvement over the double-digit inflation rates experienced earlier, 4 percent was historically a high inflation rate to be experienced at the end of a serious recession. Then during the latter half of 1988, the rate crept up to over 5 percent, where it stayed through 1989 and the early part of 1990. The Bank of Canada's attempt to push inflation down—first back to the 4 percent level, where it had been stabilized for years, and then over the longer term to zero—caused renewed controversy about the methods, the costs, and the benefits of controlling inflation.

What are the causes of inflation? Can inflation be prevented from skyrocketing into the double-digit range again? Why is it so difficult to reduce inflation that has persisted for several years? Can inflation ever be eliminated altogether?

Inflationary Shocks

We start by noting a key distinction:

It is important to distinguish between the forces that can cause a once-and-for-all increase in the price level and the forces that can cause a continuing (or sustained) increase.

The distinction between *once-and-for-all* and *continuing* rises in the price level is important. In this book we use the term *inflation,* as it is commonly used, to mean *any* rise in the price level. We then make the distinction by referring to *temporary* or *once-and-for-all* inflation on the one hand and to *continuing* or *sustained* inflation on the other.[1]

Any event that tends to drive the price level upward is called an *inflationary shock*. To examine the causes and consequences of such shocks, we begin with an economy in long-run equilibrium: The price level is stable, and national income is at its potential level. We then study the economy as it is buffeted by different types of inflationary shocks.

Supply Shocks

Suppose that there is a decrease in short-run aggregate supply; that is, that the *SRAS* curve shifts upward and to the left. Anything that causes a rise in the price level that is associated with each level of total output will cause such a shift. Examples are a rise in the costs of imported raw materials or a rise in domestic wage costs per unit of output, both of which will be passed on in terms of increased prices, and a rise in provincial sales taxes or the federal goods and services tax (GST), both of which directly raise the prices of most products.

When any of these events occur, the equilibrium price level rises while the equilibrium output falls. The rise in the price level shows up as a temporary burst of inflation. (See Figure 36-1.)

What happens next depends on whether the shock to the *SRAS* curve is an isolated event or one of a series of recurring shocks. We choose import price increases as an example of an isolated supply shock because such shocks have occurred during the past two decades. We choose continued wage-cost push inflation as an example of a repeated supply shock because, as we shall see later in this chapter and again in Chapter 40, this possibility has often worried economists.

What happens also depends on how the Bank of Canada reacts. If it responds by increasing the money supply, we say that the supply shock has been *accommodated*. If it holds the money supply constant, the shock is not accommodated. (Recall that our terminology distinguishes between the Bank's response to a supply shock, which we describe as accommodating the shock, and its response to a demand shock, which we describe as *validating* the shock.)

[1] Recall that the positively sloped *SRAS* curve either shifts upward and to the left or downward and to the right, while the negatively sloped *AD* curve either shifts downward and to the left or upward and to the right.

FIGURE 36-1 Monetary Accommodation of a Single Supply Shock

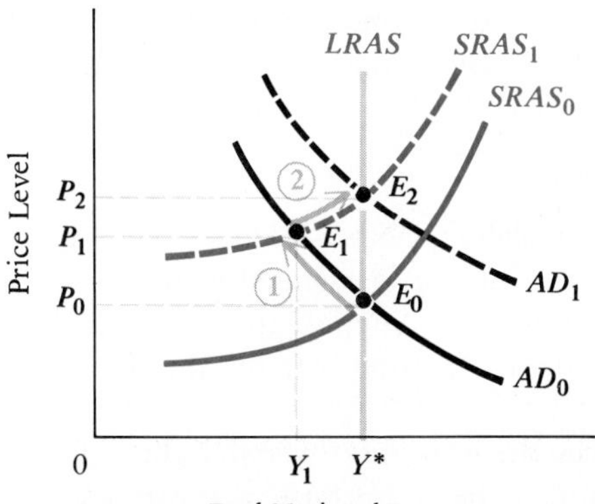

Monetary accommodation of a single supply shock causes costs, the price level, and the money supply all to move in the same direction. A supply shock causes the *SRAS* curve to shift leftward from $SRAS_0$ to $SRAS_1$ as shown by arrow 1. Equilibrium is established at E_1.

If there is no monetary accommodation, the unemployment would put downward pressure on wages and other costs, causing the *SRAS* curve to shift slowly back to the right to $SRAS_0$. Prices would fall and output would rise until the original equilibrium was restored.

If there is monetary accommodation, the *AD* curve shifts from AD_0 to AD_1, as shown by arrow 2. This reestablishes full-employment equilibrium at E_2 but with a higher price level, P_2.

Isolated Supply Shocks

Suppose that the leftward shift in the *SRAS* curve is an isolated event; say that it is caused by a once-and-for-all increase in the cost of imported raw materials. How does monetary policy affect the economy's response to such an isolated supply shock?

No monetary accommodation. The upward shift in the *SRAS* curve causes the price level to rise and pushes income below its full-employment level, opening up a recessionary gap. Pressure now mounts for wages and other factor costs to fall. When they do, the *SRAS* curve shifts downward, causing a return of income to full employment and a fall in the price level. In this case the period of inflation accompanying the original supply shock is eventually followed by a period of deflation, that is, a fall in the average level of all prices. Deflation continues until the original long-run equilibrium is reestablished. This is discussed in the second paragraph of the caption to Figure 36-1. Given that wages and prices fall slowly, the recovery to full employment takes a long time.

Monetary accommodation. Now let us see what happens if the money supply is changed in response to the isolated supply shock. Suppose that the monetary authorities decide to accommodate the supply shock because relying on cost deflation to restore full employment forces the economy to suffer through an extended slump. The monetary accommodation shifts the aggregate demand curve to the right and causes both the price level and output to *rise*. When the recessionary gap is eliminated, the price level, rather than falling back to its original value, rises further. The effects are illustrated in Figure 36-1.

Monetary accommodation of a supply shock causes the initial rise in the price level to be followed by a further rise, resulting in a higher price level than if the recessionary gap were relied on to reduce costs and prices.

Repeated Supply Shocks

Now assume that powerful unions are able to raise wages in the absence of excess demand for labor and even in the face of significant excess supply. Large manufacturing firms pass these higher wages on in the form of higher prices. This type of repeated supply shock causes what is called **wage-cost push inflation**: an increase in the price level due to increases in money wages that are not associated with excess demand for labor.

No monetary accommodation. Suppose that the Bank does not accommodate these supply shocks. The initial effect of the leftward shift in the *SRAS* curve is to open up a recessionary gap, as shown in Figure 36-1. If unions continue to negotiate increases in wages, subjecting the economy to further supply shocks, prices continue to rise and output continues to fall. Eventually, the trade-off between higher wages and unemployment will become obvious to everyone, and unions will cease forcing up wages in order to maintain jobs for workers who are still employed.

Once the wage-cost push ceases, there are two possible scenarios. First, the unions may succeed in holding on to their high wages but not push for further increases. The economy then comes to rest with a stable price level and a large recessionary gap. Second, the persistent unemployment may eventually erode the power of the unions, so that wages begin to fall. In this case the supply shock is reversed, and the *SRAS* curve shifts downward until full employment is eventually restored.

A nonaccommodated wage-cost push is self-limiting because the rising unemployment that it causes tends to restrain further wage increases.

Monetary accommodation. Now suppose that the Bank accommodates the shock with an increase in the money supply, thus shifting the aggregate demand curve to the right, as shown in Figure 36-1. In the new full-employment equilibrium, both money wages and prices have risen. The rise in wages has been offset by a rise in prices. Workers are no better off than they were originally, although those who remained in jobs were temporarily better off in the transition after wages had risen (taking equilibrium to E_1 in Figure 36-1) but before the price level had risen (taking equilibrium to E_2).

The stage is now set for the unions to try again. If they succeed in negotiating further increases in money wages, they hit the economy with another supply shock. If the Bank again accommodates the shock, full employment is maintained but at the cost of a further round of inflation. If this process goes on repeatedly, it can give rise to a continual wage-cost push inflation. The wage-cost push tends to cause stagflation, with rising prices and falling output. Monetary accommodation tends to reinforce the rise in prices but to offset the fall in output. This case is illustrated in Figure 36-2.

Two things are required for wage-cost push inflation to continue. First, powerful groups, such as industrial unions or government employees, must press for and employers must grant increases in money wages, even in the absence of excess demand for labor and goods. Second, the central bank must accommodate the resulting inflation by increasing the money supply and so prevent the unemployment that would otherwise occur. The process set up by

FIGURE 36-2 Monetary Accommodation of a Repeated Supply Shock

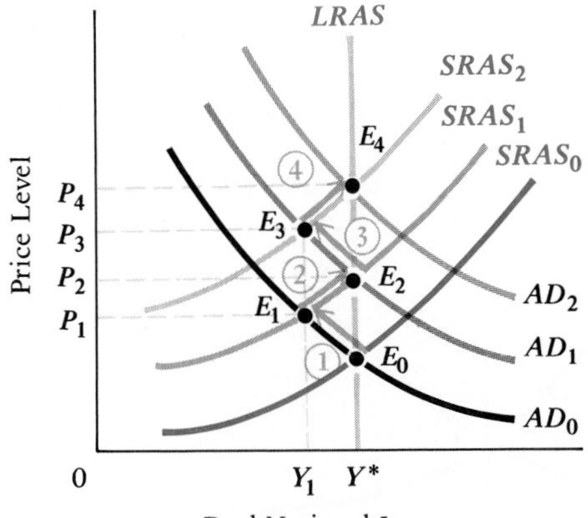

Monetary accommodation of a repeated supply shock causes continuous inflation in the absence of excess demand. The initial equilibrium is at E_0. A supply shock then takes equilibrium to E_1, just as in Figure 36-1. This is the stagflation phase of rising prices and falling output; it is indicated by arrow 1.

The Bank of Canada then accommodates the supply shock by increasing the money supply, taking the *AD* curve to AD_1 and equilibrium to E_2. This is the expansionary phase of rising prices and output (arrow 2).

A second supply shock, followed by monetary accommodation, takes equilibrium to E_3 (arrow 3) and then to E_4 (arrow 4). As long as the supply shocks and monetary accommodation continue, inflation continues.

this sequence of wage-cost push and monetary accommodation is often called a *wage-price spiral.*

Is monetary accommodation desirable? Once started, a wage-price spiral can be halted only if the Bank stops accommodating the supply shocks that are causing the inflation. The longer the Bank waits to do so, the more entrenched will be the expectations that it will continue its policy of accommodating the shocks. These entrenched expectations may cause wages to continue to rise after accommodation has ceased. Because employers expect prices to rise, they go on granting wage increases. If expectations are firmly enough entrenched, the wage push can continue for quite some time, in spite of the downward pressure caused by the rising unemployment associated with the growing recessionary gap.

Because of this possibility, some economists argue that the process should not be allowed to begin. One way to ensure this is to refuse to accommodate any supply shock whatsoever.

To some people, caution dictates that no supply shocks should be accommodated lest a wage-price spiral be set up. Others are willing to risk accommodating isolated shocks in order to avoid the severe, though transitory, recessions that otherwise accompany them.

This key issue is discussed further in Chapter 40.

Demand Shocks

Now suppose that an initial equilibrium is disturbed by a rightward shift in the aggregate demand curve. This causes the price level and output to rise, as shown in Figures 36-3 and 36-4. The shift in the *AD* curve could have been caused by either an increase in autonomous expenditure or an increase in the money supply.[2] As with a supply shock, it is important to distinguish between the case in which the Bank reacts and the case in which it does not. As we have seen, when the Bank reacts to the demand shock by increasing the money supply, it is said to be validating the shock.

No monetary validation. The case of no monetary validation is shown in Figure 36-3. Because the initial *AD* shock takes output above the full-employment level, an inflationary gap opens up. The pressure of excess demand soon causes wages and other costs to rise, shifting the *SRAS* curve upward and to the left. As long as the Bank holds the money supply constant, the rise in the price level brings the monetary adjustment mechanism (discussed in detail in Chapter 34) into play: The economy moves upward and to the left along the fixed *AD* curve, and the rise in the price level acts to reduce the inflationary gap. Eventually, the gap is eliminated as equilibrium is established at a higher but stable price level and with income at its potential level. In this case the initial period of inflation is followed by further inflation that lasts only until the new equilibrium is reached.

[2] As we saw in Chapter 34, an increase in the money supply works through the transmission mechanism—excess supply of money, higher price of bonds, the lower interest rates, increased investment expenditure—to shift the *AD* curve to the right.

FIGURE 36-3 An Unvalidated Demand-Shock Inflation

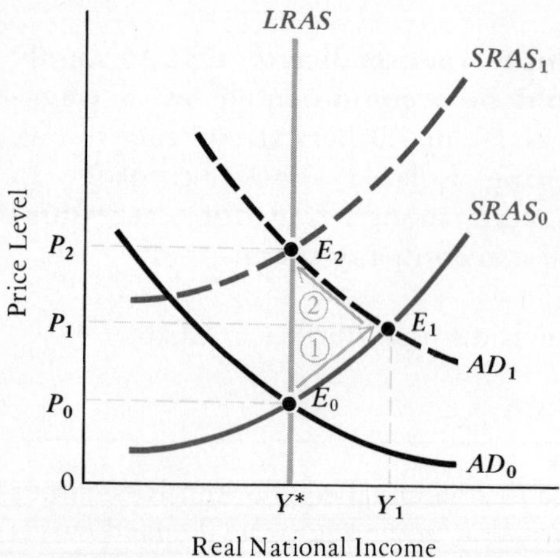

An unvalidated demand shock raises the equilibrium price level but leaves equilibrium income unchanged. The initial equilibrium is at E_0, with potential income Y^* and the price level P_0. A demand shock shifts the *AD* curve from AD_0 to AD_1, shifting equilibrium from E_0 to E_1, as shown by arrow 1. At E_1 income is Y_1 and the price level is P_1. The inflationary gap of Y^*Y_1 causes wages to rise, shifting the *SRAS* curve to the left. Equilibrium moves along AD_1 to E_2, as shown by arrow 2. At E_2 income has returned to Y^*, removing the inflationary gap, while the price level has risen to P_2.

FIGURE 36-4 A Validated Demand-Shock Inflation

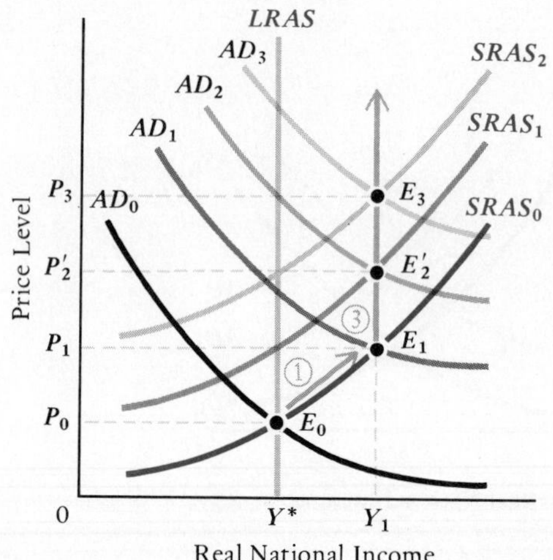

Monetary validation will cause the *AD* curve to shift rightward, offsetting the leftward shift in the *SRAS* curve and so leaving an inflationary gap in spite of the ever-rising price level. As in Figure 36-3, an initial demand shock shifts equilibrium from E_0 to E_1, taking income to Y_1 and the price level to P_1. The resulting inflationary gap then causes the *SRAS* curve to shift to the left. This time, however, the money supply is increased, shifting the *AD* curve to the right. By the time the aggregate supply curve has reached $SRAS_1$, the aggregate demand curve has reached AD_2. Now instead of being at E_2 as in Figure 36-3, equilibrium is at E'_2. Income remains constant at Y_1, leaving the inflationary gap constant at Y^*Y_1, while the price level rises to P'_2.

The persistent inflationary gap continues to push the *SRAS* curve to the left, while the continued monetary validation continues to push the *AD* curve to the right. By the time the aggregate supply reaches $SRAS_2$, the aggregate demand has reached AD_3. The price level has risen still further to P_3, but because of the frustration of the monetary adjustment mechanism, the inflationary gap remains unchanged at Y^*Y_1. As long as this monetary validation continues, the economy moves along the vertical path of arrow 3.

Monetary validation. Next, suppose that after the demand shock has created an inflationary gap, the Bank frustrates the monetary adjustment mechanism by increasing the money supply when output starts to fall. This is the case that is illustrated in Figure 36-4.[3] Two forces are now brought into play. Spurred by the inflationary gap, the wage increases cause the *SRAS* curve to shift to the left. Fueled by the expansionary monetary policy, the *AD* curve shifts to the right. As a result of both of these shifts, the price level rises, but output need not fall. Indeed, if the shift in the *AD* curve exactly offsets the shift in the *SRAS* curve, the inflationary gap will remain constant.

Validation of a demand shock turns what would have been transitory inflation into sustained inflation fueled by monetary expansion.

[3] Although we distinguish between a single supply shock and a continuing one, we do not make a similar distinction with a demand shock. This is because the accommodation of a single supply shock restores full-employment equilibrium, whereas the validation of a demand shock perpetuates the disequilibrium.

Because of the validation process, all subsequent shifts in the *AD* curve that perpetuate the inflation are caused by monetary forces.

Inflation As a Monetary Phenomenon

There has been heated debate among economists about the extent to which inflation is a monetary phenomenon. Does it have purely monetary causes—changes in the demand or the supply of money? Does it have purely monetary consequences—only the price level is affected? One slogan that states an extreme position on this issue was made popular many years ago by Milton Friedman: "Inflation is *everywhere* and *always* a monetary phenomenon."

To consider these issues, let us summarize what we have learned already. First, look at causes.

1. On the demand side, anything that shifts the *AD* curve to the right will cause the price level to rise. This includes such expenditure changes as an autonomous increase in investment or government expenditure and such monetary changes as an increase in the money supply or a decrease in money demand. On the supply side, anything that increases costs of production will shift the *SRAS* curve to the left and cause the price level to rise.
2. Such increases in the price level can continue for some time without any increases in the money supply.
3. The price level increases must eventually come to a halt, unless monetary expansion occurs.

Points 1 and 2 provide the sense in which, looking at causes, a temporary burst of inflation need not be a monetary phenomenon. It need not have monetary causes, and it need not be accompanied by monetary expansion. Point 3 provides the sense in which, looking at causes, sustained inflation must be a monetary phenomenon. If a rise in prices is to continue, it must be accompanied by continuing increases in the money supply (or decreases in money demand). This is true regardless of the cause that set the rise in motion.[4]

Second, let us summarize the consequences of inflation on the assumption that actual national income is initially at its potential level ($Y = Y^*$).

1. In the short run, demand-shock inflation tends to be accompanied by an increase in national income.
2. In the short run, supply-shock inflation tends to be accompanied by a decrease in national income.
3. When all costs and prices are adjusted fully (so that the relevant supply-side curve is the *LRAS* curve), shifts in either the *AD* or *SRAS* curve leave national income unchanged and affect only the price level.

Points 1 and 2 provide the sense in which, looking at consequences, inflation is not, in the short run, a purely monetary phenomenon. Point 3 provides the sense in which, looking at consequences, inflation is a purely monetary phenomenon from the point of view of long-run equilibrium.

We have now reached three important conclusions:

1. Without monetary accommodation, supply shocks cause temporary bursts of inflation, accompanied by recessionary gaps. The gaps are removed if and when wages fall, restoring equilibrium at potential income and at the initial price level.
2. Without monetary validation, demand shocks cause temporary bursts of inflation, accompanied by inflationary gaps. The gaps are removed as rising costs push the *SRAS* curve to the left, returning national income to its potential but at a higher price level.
3. With an appropriate response from the central bank, inflation initiated by either supply or demand shocks can continue indefinitely; an ever-increasing money supply is necessary for ever-continuing inflation.

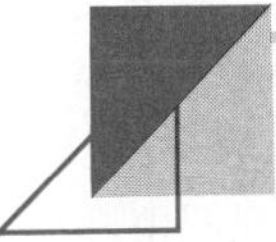

Sustained Inflation

Why do we have sustained inflation of either the rapid sort, as in the 1970s, or the more gradual sort, as in the 1980s? What are the costs and benefits of reducing or eliminating such inflation?

Before we can deal with these questions, we must

[4] The statement that inflation is everywhere and always a monetary phenomenon depends on a restricted and specific definition of the term *inflation*. To justify the statement, a temporary burst of inflation with nonmonetary causes must be called *a rise in the price level*, and the term *inflation* must be reserved for increases in the price level that are sustained long enough so that they must be accompanied by monetary expansion.

look in greater detail at what is involved in sustained inflation. We have already stressed the role of monetary validation in allowing the *AD* curve to shift up continually. We now focus on the forces that cause the *SRAS* curve to shift upward.

Upward Shifts in the *SRAS* Curve

A rise in the cost of producing each unit of output, which is called *unit cost,* will cause the *SRAS* curve to shift upward. What is it, then, that causes unit costs to rise?

Influence of wage rates and productivity. We have already seen that increases in wage rates do not necessarily cause unit costs to rise because these costs depend on the relationship between the price of labor and labor productivity (output per unit of labor input). For example, if wage rates and productivity both rise by 3 percent, each unit of labor costs 3 percent more but also produces 3 percent more, and labor costs per unit of output remain unchanged.

In this chapter, it is simplest to assume that productivity does not change, so that unit costs are positively related to money wage rates. To apply the analysis to cases in which productivity is changing, the statements "wages rise" and "wages fall" need to be understood to mean rise or fall *relative to the change in productivity.*

Why Wages Change

Let us now ask what we know about the behavior of money wages and hence of the *SRAS* curve. Up to now it has been enough to say that an inflationary gap implies excess demand for labor, low unemployment, upward pressure on wages, and, hence, an upward-shifting *SRAS* curve.

We now need to look in more detail at three forces that can cause wage costs to change and thus shift the *SRAS* curve upward. These are demand for labor, expectations, and random forces. Much of what we say in the case of demand forces is a recapitulation, but the points are important enough to bear repeating.

Demand Forces

The excess demand for labor that is associated with an inflationary gap puts upward pressure on wages relative to productivity. Wages rise more rapidly than productivity is rising.

The excess supply of labor associated with a recessionary gap puts downward pressure on wages relative to productivity. Wages rise more slowly than productivity is rising. The absence of either an inflationary or a recessionary gap means that demand forces do not exert any pressure on wages either to rise or to fall.

The NAIRU.[5] We saw in Chapter 26 that when current national income is at its potential level ($Y = Y^*$), unemployment is not zero. Instead, there may be a substantial amount of frictional and structural unemployment caused by the movement of people between jobs. Recall that the amount of unemployment that exists when national income is at its potential level is called the *NAIRU* (U_N). It follows from this definition that when current national income exceeds full-employment income ($Y > Y^*$), current unemployment will be less than the NAIRU ($U < U_N$). When current national income is less than full-employment income ($Y < Y^*$), current unemployment will exceed the NAIRU ($U > U_N$).

We can now restate the three results about the pressure that is put on wage rates, and through them on the *SRAS* curve, by inflationary and recessionary gaps.

When unemployment is below the NAIRU, demand forces exert upward pressure on money wages and hence on unit costs. When unemployment is above the NAIRU, demand forces exert downward pressure on money wages and on unit costs. When unemployment is at the NAIRU, demand forces exert neither upward nor downward pressure on money wages and unit costs.

The influence of demand forces on wages can be shown by the *Phillips curve,* discussed in Box 30-1.

Expectational Forces

A second force that can influence wages is *expectations.* Suppose, for example, that both employers and

[5] Recall that these initials stand for *nonaccelerating inflationary rate of unemployment.* The reason for using this mouthful to describe the amount of unemployment associated with Y^* will become clear later in the chapter.

employees expect a 4 percent inflation next year. Unions will start negotiations from a base of a 4 percent increase in money wages, which would hold their real wages constant. Firms also may be inclined to begin bargaining by conceding at least a 4 percent increase in money wages, since they expect that the prices at which they sell their products will rise by 4 percent. *Starting from that base,* unions will attempt to obtain some desired increase in their real wages. At this point such factors as profits and bargaining power become important.

The general expectation of an *x* percent inflation creates pressures for wages to rise by *x* percent and hence for unit costs and the *SRAS* curve to shift by *x* percent.

Random Forces

Wage changes are also affected by forces that are associated with neither excess demand nor expected inflation. These forces can be positive, pushing wages higher than they otherwise would go, or negative, pushing wages lower than they otherwise would go. We assume that there are many such forces and that they are independent of one another. This means that they will exert an overall random influence on wages, sometimes speeding wage increases up a bit and sometimes slowing them down a bit but having a net effect that is more or less cancelled out over several years. Over the long term, they may be regarded as random events and hence are referred to as *random shocks*.

One such force occurs when an exceptionally strong union or exceptionally weak management comes to the bargaining table and produces a wage increase that is a percentage point or two *above* what would have occurred under more typical bargaining conditions. Another example is when a new government policy that is favorable to management causes this year's negotiated wage rates to be a percentage point or two *below* what they would have been.

Random shocks may be important causes of temporary bursts of inflation, but they are not causes of sustained inflation. Although they may have a large positive or negative effect in any one year, over a longer period of time positive shocks in some years will tend to be offset by negative shocks in other years so that in total they contribute little to the long-term trend of the price level.

Overall Effect

The overall change in wage costs is a result of the three basic forces that we have just studied. We may express this as follows:

$$\text{Percentage increase in money wages} = \text{demand effect} + \text{expectational effect} + \text{random-shock effect}$$

It is important to realize that what happens to wage costs is the net effect of all three of these forces. Consider two examples.

For the first example, assume that both labor and management expect 3 percent inflation next year and are willing on this account to allow wages to increase by 3 percent. This would leave the relationship between wages and other prices unaltered. Now assume that there is a significant inflationary gap with an associated labor shortage. The demand pressure causes wages to rise by 2 percentage points more than they otherwise would have risen. Further assume that there is a shock, in the form of a temporary concern on the part of labor unions with foreign competition, which moderates wage claims by 1 percentage point this year. The final outcome is that wages rise by 4 percent, which is the net effect of +3 from expectations, +2 from demand forces, and −1 from the random shock.

For the second example, assume again that expected inflation is 3 percent but that this time there is a recessionary gap. The associated heavy unemployment exerts downward pressure on wage bargains, and hence the demand effect now works to moderate wage increases, say, to the extent of 2 percentage points. Finally, assume that some unusual cost-plus government contracts reduce employer resistance to wage raises to the extent that they contribute upward pressure on wage bargains of 1 percentage point. Wages rise by +2 percent, which is the net effect of +3 from expectations, −2 from demand forces, and +1 from shock effects.

The overall effect of the three forces acting on wage costs—demand, expectations, and random shocks—determines what happens to the *SRAS* curve.

Inflationary gaps, expectations of inflation, and positive random shocks put pressure on wage rates to rise relative to productivity and hence on the *SRAS* curve to shift upward. Recessionary gaps, expectations of deflation, and negative random shocks put pressure on wage rates to fall and hence on the *SRAS* curve to shift downward. What happens to the *SRAS* curve in any one year is the overall effect of all of these forces.

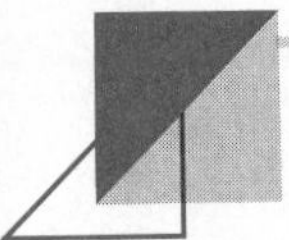

Inflationary Situations

We can now study some of the ways in which inflation that is generated from the demand side of the economy can become a problem for policymakers. The inflationary phases that we study here are found over and over again in actual practice. They were encountered in Chapter 35 when we discussed the experience of monetary policy, and we encounter them later in this chapter when we study recent inflationary experience.

The Outbreak of Inflation

Start by considering an economy that is currently experiencing a recessionary gap. That gap has persisted for long enough to remove any expectational inflation. Since there is no upward demand pressure on prices, the price level is relatively stable.

Now suppose that a recovery begins. Aggregate demand rises, pushing national income toward its potential level. The rise in income causes an increase in the amount of money that is demanded for transactions purposes. If the Bank holds the money supply constant, the increasing demand for money will bid up interest rates (as people try to sell bonds to add to their money balances). Instead, however, assume that the Bank decides to provide the additional money needed to finance the extra transactions. The Bank will enter the open market, buying bonds so as to increase the money supply at the same rate as the demand for money is rising (due to the rise in income). Now there will be no upward pressure on interest rates, because the demand for and the supply of money will expand together.

If the recovery takes national income beyond its potential level, an inflationary gap will open up, and the rise in money wages and unit costs will begin to shift the *SRAS* curve upward, taking the price level upward with it. The transactions demand for money will continue to rise with nominal income, and if the Bank goes on expanding the money supply at the same rate as money demand is rising, it will find itself accommodating the demand-shock inflation in the manner that was shown in Figure 36-4.

Nominal interest rates will begin to rise because an inflationary premium must be added to the real rate if the real rate is to remain constant. For example, if the short-term real rate remains constant at 4 percent, a rise in the inflation rate from 2 percent to 5 percent will raise short-term nominal rates from 6 percent to 9 percent. What happens to long-term rates will depend on expectations about the *future* path of inflation. If the higher inflation rate is expected to rule over the duration of longer-term bonds, their rates will fully follow the short-term rates. If, however, the rise in inflation is thought to be temporary, longer-term rates will rise only enough to cover the average inflation rate over the life of the bond.

In these circumstances, the public is likely to complain about the crushing burden of higher interest rates, and commentators are likely to accuse the Bank of Canada of applying a tight monetary policy because market interest rates are rising. Both of these accusations may be wide of the mark. First, the high nominal interest rates may not provide the heavy real burden that is being alleged. After all, the burden of interest rates depends primarily on real, not nominal, rates. If prices and wages are rising at 5 percent per year, a 9 percent nominal interest rate implies no higher burden on private and corporate borrowers than does a 6 percent nominal rate when prices and wages are rising at 2 percent per year. Second, the tightness of monetary policy depends on the real interest rate. Those who borrow to spend money—particularly large corporate borrowers—usually look at real, not nominal, rates.

It follows that the monetary transmission mechanism works by altering real interest rates. For example, a *fall* in the real rate, caused by nominal rates rising only from 5 to 7 percent when inflation goes from 2 to 6 percent, is expansionary, not contractionary.

Once the rise in the inflation rate attracts general attention, the Bank will be urged to take steps to bring it down. The Bank can do this by reducing its purchases of bonds on the open market, thus lowering the rate of monetary expansion. As a result, nominal interest rates will rise sufficiently to make real rates rise as well. For simplicity, we assume that the Bank raises interest rates sufficiently to reduce the rate of monetary expansion to zero. This will stop the aggregate demand curve from shifting rightward and bring the monetary adjustment mechanism into play as shown in Figure 34-6 on page 735.

Recall how the adjustment mechanism works. As long as prices keep rising, firms and households will need more money balances to finance the increasing nominal value of their transactions. The rising demand for money, in conjunction with a more slowly expanding money supply, causes a money shortage. People who are trying to sell bonds in order to obtain additional money balances to finance the rising values of their transactions will be unable to obtain funds by selling bonds. As long as the Bank is not purchasing bonds, the attempt on the part of the public to sell bonds merely drives bond prices down and hence drives the interest rate up. This reduces investment expenditure, causing equilibrium national income to fall toward potential income.

This is shown in Figure 36-3. As the *SRAS* curve goes on shifting upward, equilibrium moves to the left along a fixed *AD* curve, lowering national income and thus reducing the inflationary gap. (This is the path of arrow 2, which shows what happens when a demand shock is not validated by an increase in the money supply.)

Interest Rates and Inflation

At this point a controversy often breaks out—as it did in 1989–1990—over the effect of the increase in the interest rate on inflation. One group will point out that the rise in the interest rate increases business costs and that passing the extra costs on in higher prices adds to inflation. They will condemn the Bank of Canada's tight monetary policy as being inflationary. Others will argue that the rising interest rate signifies the slowdown in the rate of monetary expansion that has occurred in order to curb inflation.

The first group is correct in pointing out that the rise in interest rates can cause a one-time increase in the price level. The rise in interest costs shifts the *SRAS* curve upward, just as does a rise in wage costs. This, however, has only a one-time effect on the price level. This group is wrong, therefore, in asserting that the Bank's policy of driving up interest rates is contributing to a long-term increase in the rate of inflation.

The second group is correct in saying that the rise in the interest rate is a necessary part of an anti-inflationary policy. If the Bank were to try to hold interest rates down, it would enter the open market and buy bonds to keep their prices up. Buying bonds, however, increases the money supply. This rise in the money supply shifts the *AD* curve to the right and counteracts the effects of the leftward shift in the *SRAS* curve, thus frustrating the monetary adjustment mechanism.

If the Bank is to succeed in slowing the rate of monetary expansion, it must allow the interest rate to rise temporarily as people try to sell bonds to replenish their insufficient holdings of money.

The rise in the interest rate is what puts the monetary adjustment mechanism into play. It reduces aggregate desired expenditure and takes equilibrium national income upward along a fixed *AD* curve as the price level rises. This will reduce the inflationary gap and eliminate it altogether when income falls back to its potential level. (See also Figure 36-3.)

Accelerating Inflation

If the Bank of Canada accedes to the call to hold interest rates down, it will find itself increasing the money supply as fast as the demand for money is rising. The result is fully validated inflation with a constant inflationary gap, such as is shown in Figure 36-4.

What now happens to the rate of inflation is predicted by the **acceleration hypothesis**, which says that when the central bank engages in whatever rate of monetary expansion is needed to hold the inflationary gap constant, the actual inflation rate will accelerate. The Bank may start by validating a 3 percent inflation, but soon 3 percent will become 4 percent, and if the Bank insists on validating 4 percent, the rate will become 5 percent, and so on without limit, until the Bank finally stops trying to maintain a constant inflationary gap.

The reasoning behind this acceleration hypothesis consists of several steps. The first concerns the development of inflationary expectations.

Expectational effects. When the inflation shown in Figure 36-4 has persisted for some time, people will

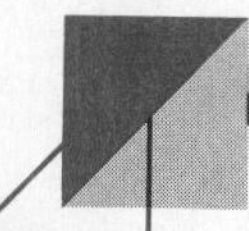

BOX 36-1

The Phillips Curve and Accelerating Inflation

Professor Phillips was interested in studying the short-run behavior of an economy subjected to cyclical fluctuations (see Box 30-1). Others, however, treated the curve as establishing a long-term trade-off between inflation and unemployment.

Let the government stabilize income at Y_1 (and thus unemployment at U_1), as shown in the figures. To do this it must validate the ensuing wage inflation of ΔW_1 per year. It now appears to have been able to choose a particular combination of inflation and unemployment, with lower levels of unemployment being attained at the cost of higher rates of inflation.

In the 1960s, Phillips curves were fitted to the data for many countries, and governments made decisions about where they wished to be on the trade-off between inflation and unemployment. Then in the late 1960s, in country after country, the rate of wage and price inflation associated with any given level of unemployment began to rise. Instead of being stable, the Phillips curves were shifting upward. The explanation lay primarily in a shifting relationship between the pressure of demand and wage increases due to expectations, as discussed in the text.

It was gradually understood that the original Phillips curve concerned only the influence of demand and left out inflationary expectations. This proved to be an important and unfortunate omission. An increase in expected inflation shows up as an upward shift in the original Phillips curve that was drawn in Box 30-1.

The importance of expectations can be shown by drawing what is called an **expectations-augmented Phillips curve**, as shown here. The heights of the Phillips curves above the axis at Y^* and at U_N show the expected inflation rate. This is the amount that wages will rise when there is neither excess demand nor excess supply pressure in labor markets. The actual wage increase is shown by the augmented curve, with the increase in wages exceeding expected inflation when $Y > Y^*$ ($U < U_N$) and falling short of expected inflation when $Y < Y^*$ ($U > U_N$).

The demand component shown by the simple Phillips curve tells us by how much wage changes will deviate from the expected inflation rate.

Now we can see what was wrong with the idea of a stable inflation-unemployment trade-off. Targeting on income Y_1 or unemployment U_1 in the figures is fine as long as no inflation is *expected*, but once some particular rate of inflation comes to be expected, people will demand that much just to

expect that monetary validation, and hence inflation, will continue. As these inflationary expectations emerge, additional upward pressure will be put on wages as the inflationary effect comes into play. Now that the demand effect on wages has been augmented by an expectational effect, the *SRAS* curve will begin to shift upward more rapidly.

More rapid monetary validation required. If the Bank still wishes to hold the level of output constant, it must increase the rate at which the money supply is growing. This is because to hold Y constant, the *AD* curve must be shifted more rapidly to compensate for the more rapid shifts in the *SRAS* curve.

An increasing rate of inflation. As a result of the increasingly rapid upward shifts in both the *AD* and *SRAS* curves, the rate of inflation must now be increasing. The rise in the actual inflation rate will in turn cause an increase in the expected inflation rate. This will then cause the actual inflation rate to increase, which will in turn increase the expected in-

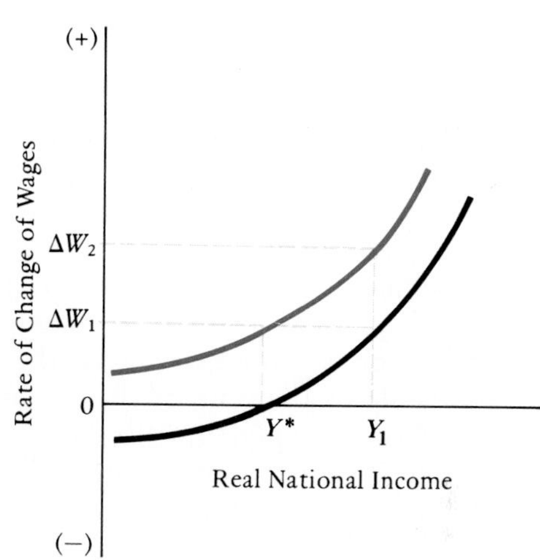

hold their own. The Phillips curve will shift upward to the position shown in the figures. Now there is inflation ΔW_2 because of the combined effects of expectations and excess demand.

However, this higher rate is above the expected rate. Once this higher rate comes to be expected, the Phillips curve will shift upward once again.

The expectations-augmented Phillips curve shows that the actual rate of inflation exceeds the expected rate whenever there is an inflationary gap.

Sooner or later this will cause inflationary expectations to be shifted upward. The inflation rate associated with any given level of Y or U rises over time. This is the phenomenon of accelerating inflation that is further discussed in this chapter.

The shifts in the Phillips curve are such that most economists agree that in the long run, when inflationary expectations have adjusted to actual inflation, there is no trade-off between inflation and unemployment. That is, they believe that the long-run Phillips curve is a vertical line at the NAIRU.

flation rate, and so on. The net result is a *continually increasing rate of inflation.*[6]

According to the acceleration hypothesis, as long as an inflationary gap persists, expectations of inflation will be rising, and this will lead to increases in the actual rate of inflation.

[6] Now we see the reason for the name *NAIRU*. At any lower level of unemployment, national income is above Y^*, and the inflation rate tends to accelerate. So the NAIRU is the lowest level of unemployment consistent with a nonaccelerating rate of inflation.

The tendency for inflation to accelerate is discussed further in Box 36-1.

Constant Inflation

Must sustained inflation always accelerate, or is it possible for inflation to go on at a constant rate indefinitely?

The answer is that not all sustained inflation must accelerate. When the demand effect is absent and all inflation is thus expectational, inflation can persist indefinitely at a constant rate. Let us see why this is so.

When national income is at its potential level, there is neither an inflationary nor a recessionary gap. In this case there is no demand effect operating on wage bargains. Leaving random shocks aside, the only force operating on wages is expectations. Say, for example, that both workers and employers expect 4 percent inflation and that employers are prepared to raise wages by 4 percent per year to keep wages in line with everything else. Wages will rise by 4 percent per year, and the *SRAS* curve will shift upward by that amount each year. If the Bank of Canada validates the resulting inflation by increasing the money supply by 4 percent each year, the *AD* curve will also be shifting upward by that amount.

This case is illustrated in Figure 36-5. Here wage costs are rising due to expectations of inflation, and these expectations are being fulfilled.

Steady inflation at potential income results when the rate of monetary growth, the rate of wage increase, and the expected rate of inflation are all consistent with the actual inflation rate.

The key point about pure expectational inflation at a constant rate is that there is no demand effect operating on wage bargains. Wages rise at the expected rate of inflation, and this is just enough to preserve the existing relationship between wages and all other prices. The labor shortages that accompany an inflationary gap are absent, as are the labor surpluses that accompany a recessionary gap.

If all forces worked precisely as described in the simple theoretical model, steady inflation would occur only when income was exactly at its potential level. In practice, however, stable inflation rates also seem to be compatible with modest recessionary gaps.

In such circumstances there is a tendency for wages to fall (relative to productivity), forcing the *SRAS* curve downward. However, the negative demand effect of a recessionary gap is rather weak. Thus when the gap is relatively small, the demand effect may be swamped by the expectational and random-shock effects, so that an approximately stable inflation rate is the net result. Ths is what seems to have occurred in the mid 1980s, when a fairly stable inflation rate persisted for several years in spite of a modest recessionary gap.

FIGURE 36-5 Steady Inflation at the NAIRU

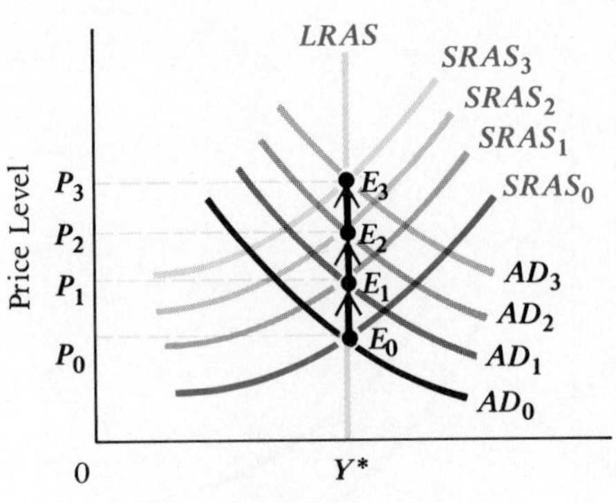

When income equals Y^* (and hence unemployment equals U_N), there is no demand effect on wages, and steady inflation can proceed at a rate that is consistent with inflationary expectations. With no demand effect, the *SRAS* curve shifts upward at the expected rate of inflation. If the Bank of Canada raises the money supply at the same rate, the upward shift in the *AD* curve will match that of the *SRAS* curve. Output will stay at Y^*, unemployment will be at the NAIRU, and inflation will be steady. The steady inflation is shown by the rising price level as equilibrium moves along the arrows from E_0 to E_1 to E_2 to E_3 in the figure.

Breaking Entrenched Inflation

Because inflation cannot be reduced instantaneously, there are costs associated with reducing the inflation rate over time. The longer a given rate has persisted, the more firmly will expectations that the rate will persist be built into people's behavior, and the more costly will it be to reduce the rate. The major costs are those inflicted by a temporary rise in interest rates above their long-term equilibrium levels and a temporary fall in national income below its equilibrium levels.

The Debate

Reducing the rate of inflation requires creating a monetary shortage by reducing the rate of growth of the money supply below the rate of growth of money demand. This forces up interest rates. The main objective is to work through the monetary adjustment mechanism to lower real aggregate demand. The incidental effect, however, is to hurt all borrowers, including homeowners who have mortgages and new firms that are expanding on the basis of borrowed money. The decline in real aggregate demand reduces real national income and, as we shall see in detail shortly, tends to create a recessionary gap that can be large and quite persistent. This hurts owners of firms, who lose profits and their investment if bankruptcies rise, and employees, who lose jobs as a result of declining output.

So reducing inflation has costs and always raises this question: Are the transitory costs of reducing inflation justified by the benefits of establishing the lower rate?

This question has been debated since 1988 when Bank of Canada governor John Crow announced his policy of slowly pushing the inflation rate down to zero. At the time the inflation rate had been stabilized at around 4 percent for several years. This was long enough for people to become accustomed to 4 percent inflation and to build it into their expectations. The Bank's first announcement was made in January 1988, and as it became increasingly apparent that "zero inflation" was the Bank's medium-term objective, controversy increased.

Critics said that the costs of breaking the inflation that was entrenched at about 4 percent would be too high. Supporters said that 4 percent was an unacceptably high rate and that something much closer to zero was the appropriate long-term goal of monetary policy. The controversy continued for several years. Since a policy of reducing the inflation rate requires (during the period when inflation is being reduced) higher real interest rates than does a policy of accepting the current inflation rate, controversy over the Bank's zero inflation policy will no doubt go on until either something close to zero is achieved or the Bank stops trying. (The controversy, however, has a cyclical component, dying down when interest rates are falling due to cyclically declining demand and breaking out anew when rates are rising due to cyclically rising demand.)

This was not the first time that such a controversy had aroused great passions in Canada. In the early 1980s the inflation rate had risen to about 12 percent, a rate that halves the purchasing power of money every six years! In response, the Bank adopted a tough anti-inflationary stance, and interest rates were driven up to unprecedented heights, the short-term rate rising to over 20 percent in 1982–1983. At that time critics said that the harm done by anti-inflationary policy was not worth the gain, while supporters said that inflation at the rate of 12 percent, which threatened to rise even further, was intolerable and hence that large, short-run costs were a necessary price to pay for getting the rate back to a reasonable level.

The Analysis

What is at issue in these debates? To answer this question in its simplest form, we study a policy of reducing the entrenched rate very quickly. A policy of doing the same thing more gradually means that interest rates are not driven up so high and that monetary expansion is not reduced so fast. This reduces the harm at any moment of time but spreads it out over a longer period of time.

Reducing entrenched inflation quickly incurs high costs for a short period of time; reducing it slowly incurs lower costs but for a longer period of time.

Whether the total costs incurred are greater by suffering a lot of pain for a short time or by suffering less pain for a longer period of time is an unsettled question.

Our analysis of the breaking of an entrenched inflation begins with a situation of a continuing, fully validated inflation, with actual income above its potential level ($Y > Y^*$). Inflation has been going on for some time, and people expect it to continue. Firmly held expectations of a continuation of the current inflation rate are what leads to the concept of *entrenched inflation*.

Now suppose that the Bank of Canada decides to reduce the inflation rate by reducing its rate of monetary validation. The events that follow generally fall into three phases.

Phase 1: Removing the inflationary gap. The first phase, shown in Figure 36-6(i), consists of slowing the rate of monetary expansion below the current rate of inflation. This slows the rate at which the *AD* curve is shifting upward. To illustrate, we take an extreme case: the "cold turkey approach," in which the rate of monetary expansion is cut to zero so that the upward shift in the *AD* curve is halted abruptly.

FIGURE 36-6 Eliminating Entrenched Inflation

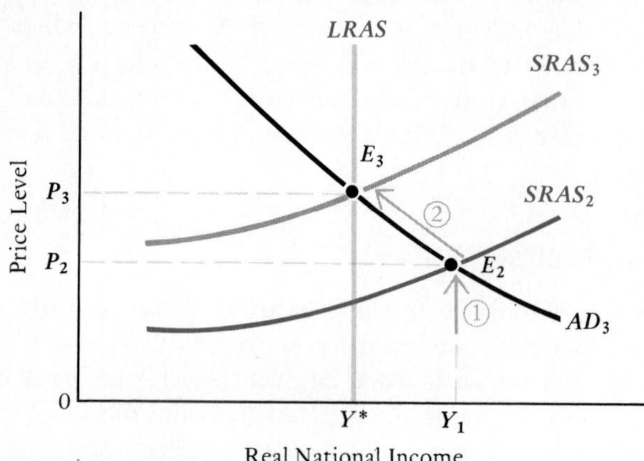

(i) Phase 1: Removing the inflationary gap

(i) Phase 1: The elimination of entrenched inflation begins with a demand contraction to remove the inflationary gap. Fully validated inflation of the type shown in Figure 36-4 is taking the economy along the path shown by arrow 1 here. When the curves reach $SRAS_2$ and AD_3, the Bank of Canada stops expanding the money supply, thus stabilizing aggregate demand at AD_3. Wages continue to rise, taking the *SRAS* curve leftward. The economy moves along arrow 2, with income falling and the price level rising. When aggregate supply reaches $SRAS_3$, the inflationary gap is removed, and equilibrium is established at income Y^* and price level P_3.

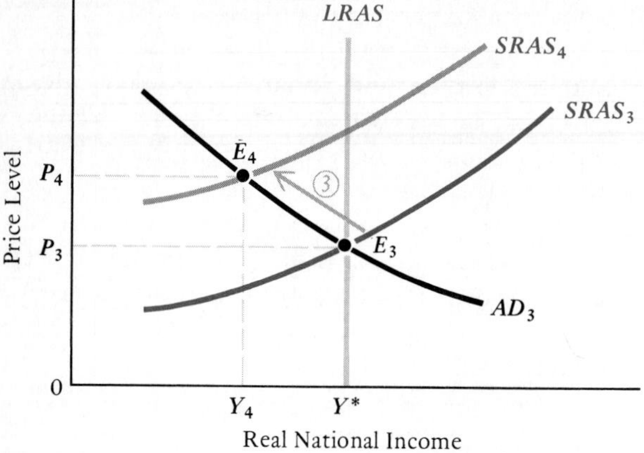

(ii) Phase 2: Stagflation

(ii) Phase 2: Expectations and wage momentum lead to stagflation, with falling output and continuing inflation. The economy moves along the path shown by arrow 3. The driving force is now the *SRAS* curve, which continues to shift because inflationary expectations cause wages to continue to rise. The recessionary gap grows as income falls. Inflation continues, but at a diminishing rate. If wages stop rising when income has reached Y_4 and the price level has reached P_4, the stagflation phase is over, with equilibrium at E_4.

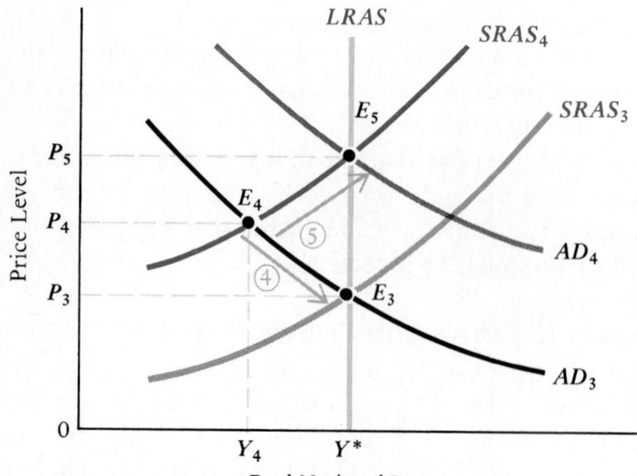

(iii) Phase 3: Recovery

(iii) Phase 3: After expectations are reversed, recovery takes income to Y^*, and the price level is stabilized. There are two possible scenarios for recovery. In the first the recessionary gap causes wages to fall (slowly), taking the *SRAS* curve back to $SRAS_3$ (slowly), as shown by arrow 4. The economy retraces the path originally followed in (ii) back to E_3. In the second scenario, the Bank increases the money supply sufficiently to shift the *AD* curve to AD_4. The economy then moves along the path shown by arrow 5. This restores potential income at the cost of further temporary inflation that takes the price level to P_5. Full employment and a stable price level are now achieved.

This implies a large and rapid increase in both nominal and real interest rates.

Under the combined influence of an inflationary gap and expectations of continued inflation, wages continue to rise, and the *SRAS* curve thus continues to shift upward. Eventually, the gap is removed. If the only influence on wages were demand, that would be the end of the story. At Y^* there is no upward demand pressure on wages. Wages would stop rising, the *SRAS* curve would be stabilized, and the economy would remain at full employment with a stable price level.

Phase 2: Stagflation. Governments around the world many times have wished that things were really so simple. However, wages depend not only on excess demand but also on inflationary expectations. Once inflationary expectations have been established, it is not always easy to get people to revise them downward, even in the face of changed monetary policies. Thus the *SRAS* curve continues to shift upward, causing the price level to continue to rise and income to fall further.

Expectations may cause inflation to persist after its original causes have been removed. What was initially demand inflation due to an inflationary gap becomes expectational inflation.

This is phase 2, shown in Figure 36-6(ii).

The emerging recessionary gap has two effects. First, there is rising unemployment. Thus the demand influence on wages becomes negative. Second, as the recession deepens and monetary restraint continues, people revise their expectations of inflation downward. When they have no further expectations of inflation, there are no further increases in wage costs, and the *SRAS* curve stops shifting. The stagflationary phase is over. Inflation has come to a halt, but a large recessionary gap now exists. At this point nominal interest rates will fall because they no longer need to include an inflationary premium. Furthermore, the Bank can allow real interest rates to fall, since it no longer wishes to exert contractionary pressure through the monetary adjustment mechanism.

The duration of phase 2 depends on two key factors. The first is the speed with which wages respond to the rising unemployment. The second is the speed with which inflationary expectations fall to reflect the Bank's new anti-inflationary monetary policy. The sooner both of these things happen, the sooner the *SRAS* curve will stop shifting upward.

Phase 3: Recovery. The final phase is the return to full employment. When the economy comes to rest at the end of the stagflation, the situation is exactly the same as when the economy is hit by an isolated supply shock (see Figure 36-1). The move back to full employment can be accomplished in either of two ways. First, the recessionary gap can be relied on to reduce wages, thus shifting the *SRAS* curve downward. Second, the money supply can be increased to shift the *AD* curve to a level that is consistent with full employment. These two possibilities are illustrated in Figure 36-6(iii).

Some economists worry about waiting for wages and prices to fall because they fear that the process will take a very long time. Others worry about a temporary burst of monetary expansion because they fear that expectations of inflation may be rekindled when the Bank increases the money supply. If inflationary expectations are revived, the Bank will then have an unenviable choice. Either it must let another severe recession develop to break these new inflationary expectations, or it must accommodate the inflation in order to reduce unemployment. In the latter case it is back where it started, with validated inflation on its hands.[7]

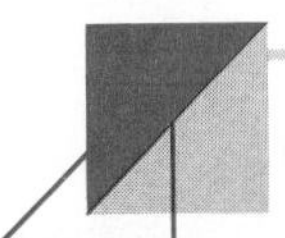

Anti-inflation Policy in Canada

The early 1970s witnessed quite expansionary fiscal and monetary policies. The money supply was expanded rapidly, and an inflationary gap opened up as national income exceeded potential income. As a result, inflation began to rise. Expansion continued until early 1974, and inflation rose throughout that period. Then a recession set in. As a recessionary gap began to open up, the normal expectation was that inflation would moderate. Just then, however, the first OPEC shock hit. The prices of oil and the myriad petroleum-related products soared. This supply shock sent inflation into the double-digit range. The result was stagflation.

[7] This is the so-called reentry problem that was discussed in detail in Chapter 35.

Wage and Price Controls and Monetary Gradualism: 1975–1980

Canadian policymakers interpreted the stagflation as accelerating wage-push inflation in a time of world recession. Having failed in an attempt to secure agreement of labor in a voluntary incomes policy, the Canadian cabinet decided in the autumn of 1975 to impose wage and price controls. The Anti-Inflation Board (AIB) was set up and given power to control wages and prices for three years. At roughly the same time, the Bank of Canada adopted a policy of "monetary gradualism" by announcing its intention to reduce gradually the rate at which the money supply was growing.

Whether by accident or by design, the two policies made a coherent package. The monetary policy was meant to reduce the speed with which the *AD* curve was shifting upward. Wage-price controls were meant to reduce the speed with which the *SRAS* curve was shifting upward. If the upward rush of the two curves could be slowed at the same rate, the inflation rate could be reduced without having to endure the stagflation phase (phase 2 in Figure 36-6), which occurs when the rise of the *AD* curve is checked faster than that of the *SRAS* curve.

At first all seemed to go well. The inflation rate fell in successive years starting in 1975. Then in 1979 and in 1980 the rate rose, back to where it had been at the peak of the 1975 crisis. Five years of gradualism seemed to have accomplished almost nothing.

One reason was a substantial supply-side shock due to a large increase in the world price of oil due to a second round of OPEC output restrictions. A second reason was that sharp reductions in the demand for M1 balances over that period meant that money was becoming more plentiful *relative to demand*. Thus instead of operating its intended contractionary monetary policy, the Bank was presiding over an expansionary policy.

As we have noted earlier, the propositions that a loose monetary policy stimulates the economy and leads to inflation and that a tight monetary policy does the opposite remained valid. The key conclusions illustrated by the failure of monetary gradualism in the 1970s are that demand-side measures can be offset by unfavorable supply-side shocks and that it is not always possible to identify a tight or loose policy solely by the rate of growth of the money supply.

The failure of gradualism did not upset any basic economic theory. What it did upset was the proposition that aggregate demand could be precisely controlled by merely controlling the supply of money.

Indeed, if central banks had paid more attention to the interest rate—which had been discredited as an intermediate target—they might have realized that monetary policy was not restrictive. Several times during this period the real interest rate (the money rate corrected for the rate for inflation) was negative.

Stabilizing Inflation: 1981–1988

Inflation rose during the 1970s. By the turn of the decade it was firmly entrenched, and a major controversy arose over how to reduce it. Most people agreed on the goal of returning to a much lower inflation rate, but there was disagreement as to the means of achieving the goal.

Monetarists advocated breaking the inflation with monetary restraint in the manner analyzed earlier in this chapter. Since they felt that there would be a short phase 2, they were willing to rely exclusively on monetary policy to bring about the transition from a high to a low inflationary environment.

Keynesians agreed that a low rate of monetary growth was a necessary condition for returning to a low rate of inflation. However, because they felt that phase 2 would be long—some talked in terms of 5 to 10 years—they were reluctant to use monetary policy alone during the transition. As a result, many Keynesians advocated using **incomes policies**, a term that covers any direct government intervention used to affect wage and price setting. They hoped that such intervention would shorten phase 2 by helping to break inflationary expectations. This and other possible uses of incomes policies are discussed in Box 36-2.

The Reduction of Inflation: 1981–1984

In 1981 the Bank of Canada chose to follow the United States in adopting a highly restrictive monetary policy. In the budget of June 1982, the Canadian government felt that fiscal restraint was not appropriate in the face of the recession, but it tried to contribute to the disinflation process by introducing a package of controls on civil service compensation—the so-called *6&5 Program*.

There is still debate over the effects of the program. Some feel it stiffened the resistance of private-sector firms to continued inflationary wage increases. Be that as it may, serious recession, falling sales, and falling profits eventually had to have an effect in moderating wage increases. When it came, the fall in inflation was dramatic: from a peak of 13 percent in mid 1981 to around 5 percent by early 1984.

By 1984 the restrictive policies had succeeded in reducing inflation to a level not seen since the early 1960s, but it had also produced a major recession with all its attendant costs, including unemployment, lost output, business bankruptcies, and foreclosed mortgages.

The results came out somewhere between the extremes that had been predicted. Keynesians were right in predicting that the anti-inflationary policies would induce a severe recession. But the inflation rate came down much faster than Keynesians had predicted. Jobs rather than wages quickly became the focus of many contract settlements. Not only were new wage agreements moderated in response to the excess supply of labor, but also some existing contracts were reopened and lower wages agreed on.

As so often happens with great debates, neither the extreme pessimists nor the extreme optimists were right. The truth lay somewhere in between. Whatever the reasons, during the early 1980s inflation fell faster than many Keynesians had expected, and the slump was deeper and more prolonged than many monetarists had expected.

A Stable Inflation Rate: 1985–1988

For several years following 1984, the Canadian inflation rate stabilized at a figure around 4 percent, and it was a time of low inflation in the world as a whole. There was no reason for the inflation rate to rise since there was no inflationary gap in the Canadian economy. The inflation seemed purely expectational: People expected a 4 percent inflation rate, and the Bank accommodated that rate through monetary expansion.

But since there clearly was a recessionary gap, why did inflation not fall further? The answer here seems to be that the weak demand forces that work toward deceleration when there is excess supply were swamped by the forces of expectational inflation and random shocks.

Accelerating Inflation

In 1988 the Canadian economy was approaching its potential national income. Although there were considerable regional disparities in unemployment rates, the industrial sectors of Ontario and Quebec and some of the resource sectors of the western provinces were at, and sometimes even beyond, full employment. (See Figure 37-1, which suggests that the overall economy was developing an inflationary gap.) The inflation rate began to creep upward, going over 5 percent in 1989.

Fearing an erosion of its hard-won gains in reducing inflation earlier in the decade, the Bank of Canada reacted by adopting a restrictionist monetary policy. Interest rates were driven up, and as discussed on page 736, the Canadian dollar rose, putting tradable goods producers under heavy competitive pressure. The country's economic expansion proved remarkably resilient. The inflationary gap, and the 5 percent inflation rate, persisted for over a year in spite of very high interest rates and a strong Canadian dollar.

The Bank came under very strong criticism. Many commentators felt that the Bank should not continue its contractionary monetary policy. They feared that the effects of high interest rates and a strong dollar would be too harmful to make the effort worthwhile. These people would accept higher current inflation rates—creeping beyond 5 percent, and possibly higher if monetary policy were relaxed—as a price of avoiding the costs of reducing the inflation rate to 4 percent.

One problem with this advice was that reducing entrenched inflation is costly, and if the costs are always to be avoided, each rise in the inflation rate will become permanent as it is accommodated by more rapid monetary expansion. In this case there would seem little to prevent the inflation rate from ratcheting upward once again into the two-digit range and beyond. Sooner or later the rate would become so high that everyone would agree that it

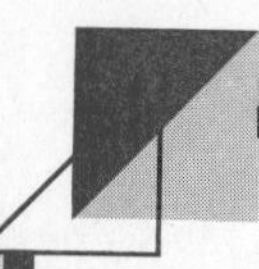

BOX 36-2

Incomes Policies

In the past, Keynesian economists have often recommended the use of **incomes policies** as an anti-inflationary device. There is a wide range of such policy measures. Voluntary guidelines for wage and price increases can be set, as they were in the United States under the Kennedy administration in the 1960s. The government may consult labor and business leaders with a view to moderating their wage demands and price hikes, as has often been done in European countries. More drastically, compulsory controls may be imposed on wage, price, and profit increases. A proposal commonly made in the 1970s and early 1980s was for a **tax-related incomes policy (TIP)**, which would operate through the tax system to provide penalties for "excessive" wage and price hikes and rewards for moderate ones.

Incomes policies might be used for three quite distinct purposes: (1) to suppress demand inflation, (2) to break expectational inflation, and (3) to control permanent wage-cost push inflation. We discuss the first two purposes in this box and the third in Chapter 40.

Demand Inflation

One reason that incomes policies have a bad reputation throughout the world is that they have often been used, as they were in the United States during Richard Nixon's presidency, in a futile attempt to stop demand inflation. To see why such an attempt is futile, consider the situation shown at E_1 in Figure 36-3. If nothing else is done, the inflationary gap will cause the price level to rise to P_2. Wage and price controls could be used to hold the price level at P_1, but once the controls are removed, the excess demand will cause prices to rise.

The conclusion that using incomes policy in an attempt to control demand inflation will be ineffective (while the cost in terms of social stress and economic disruption can be enormous) is borne out not only by the U.S. experience of the early 1970s but by the experience of Britain and a number of other European countries as well.

Expectational Inflation

When entrenched inflation exists, incomes policies may help to break expectations. If successful, incomes policies will greatly reduce the stagflation phase. This could happen if, once phase 1 is over and the inflationary gap has been eliminated, incomes policies were used to stop wages and prices from rising because of the expectational effect. The *SRAS* curve would not continue to shift upward and thereby open up a recessionary gap. Once ex-

must be brought down, as happened in 1981. The higher the inflation rate, the deeper the ensuing recession when entrenched inflation is finally attacked by a restrictive monetary policy.

Nonetheless, many Canadian economists were critical of the Bank and felt that it should have operated a looser monetary policy in spite of the tendency of inflation to accelerate. Others argued that to postpone the pain of the anti-inflationary measures would imply that much tougher measures would be required a year or two in the future.

Despite the pressure to ease up, the Bank continued its tight monetary policy, and by the middle of 1990 the inflation rate began to fall appreciably. By autumn it had returned to the 4 percent plateau from which it had accelerated two years earlier.[8] The Bank however, persisted in its tight policy on the grounds that it had to be sure that the inflationary pressures were really removed from the economy. This prompted even stronger pressure on it to ease up on its tight policy and to accept, at least temporarily, a 4 percent rate until the economy had a chance to

[8] This was the inflation rate as measured as a percentage increase over the same month a year ago. On a month-to-month basis, the inflation rate had been running significantly below 4 percent for several months.

pectations have adjusted to the new anti-inflationary monetary policy and to the existing stable price level, the controls could be removed. The economy would then be at a position of stable prices and full employment.

The sequence of events seems almost too good to be true. The stagflation phase is eliminated, and the economy goes directly from phase 1, with an inflationary gap, to the final situation of an equilibrium at Y^*. If such a policy had been tried as many advocated during the early 1980s, *and if it had worked*, the recession of the early 1980s, with all of its consequent unemployment and lost output, would have been avoided.

Controls were used when the AIB formed part of a package to counter the explosive double-digit inflation of the 1974–1975 period. Detailed studies by several Canadian economists have shown that the AIB probably reduced the rate of inflation by about 2 percentage points. It did this by helping to break generally held expectations that the inflation would not respond rapidly to monetary restraint.

What Can We Conclude?

Opponents of incomes policies believe that the costs of using incomes policies will exceed the alleged benefits. First, they argue that the benefits, in terms of shortening the stagflation phase, would be small because the policies would not be wholly successful in restraining wage and price increases. Second, they argue that the costs, in terms of direct administrative burdens and indirect frustration of the workings of the price system, would be large.

Although most experience internationally is with incomes policies used in a futile attempt to control demand inflation, the evidence about the costs of using such policies may be relevant, even where the objective is not futile. The evidence suggests that when prices are set by government administrators rather than market forces, the allocation of resources becomes increasingly arbitrary, with serious consequences for the efficient working of the economic system.

recover from the battering it had received from the high interest rates and strong Canadian dollar resulting from the successful fight to eliminate the accelerating inflation.

One of the new critics was Queen's University professor Thomas Courchene, who had reported on several studies monitoring the Bank's monetary policy since the 1960s. Courchene called the Bank's policy wrong-headed for a number of reasons. First, since major companies can bypass high Canadian interest rates, the bulk of the harm falls on smaller borrowers such as farmers and mortgage holders; second, except for its effect through a high value of the dollar, the Bank's high interest rate policy has little effect until the economy "snaps" (i.e., enters a severe recession); third, the high interest rates are increasing the burden of debt service for the federal government and crowding out spending on social services and other important categories.

Whatever the verdict of history on this particular episode, two questions remain unanswered. First, what monetary policy would the critics have had the Bank follow during 1989 and 1990, and what would have been its consequences? Second, since many of the comments suggest that monetary policy will not work in the future as it did until the mid 1980s, what is the new theory of the behavior of the economy, and what are its consequences for the Bank's control of inflation in the future?

Supporters of the Bank argued that monetary restraint was always painful and so would always arouse criticism. Furthermore, they predicted that the Bank's anti-inflation policy would be seen to work more or less as it always has in the past (making allowance for the offsetting effects of rising aggregate demand because of the investment boom), and that the policy would soon be eased as the inflation rate came down below 4 percent by the end of 1990. They also added that the predictions that the economy is behaving in some totally new way will go into oblivion just as did similar predictions made during the 1970s when conventional macroeconomics seemed unable to explain stagflation (which, as readers of this chapter know, it now can do).

By late 1990, the economy was clearly into a recession. At that time many who supported the Bank's longer-term policy called for a little fine tuning. They felt that the Bank could mitigate the recession by easing up on its tight monetary policy, returning to it once the next recovery had begun. How the Bank responded to this advice will be known by the time this passage is read.

Zero Inflation?

When he became governor of the Bank of Canada, John Crow lost no time in announcing the policy of zero inflation mentioned earlier in the chapter. This was a new type of gradualism. It was intended to reduce the rate of monetary expansion slowly until the inflation rate had been reduced to approximately zero over a period of years. For technical reasons to do with bias in index numbers, the CPI would probably show an inflation rate of between ½ and 1 percent even if the price level was in fact constant.[9] This was the Bank's objective: zero actual inflation and less than 1 percent measured inflation.

This policy sparked off a bout of controversy. The controversy was somewhat confused by the fact that the zero inflation policy got mixed up with the policy of trying to contain and reverse the acceleration of inflation from 4 to nearly 6 percent that occurred in the years 1988–1990.

Critics of the zero inflation policy felt that the costs of reducing the inflation rate below 4 percent would be excessive. They would prefer to have the economy adjust to that rate than to undergo the costs of reducing the rate to 2 percent, let alone to zero. Supporters pointed out that 4 percent inflation cut the purchasing power of money in half in about 18 years and that 4 percent was a high inflation rate by the standards as far back as records go. (See the series going back to the thirteenth century in England in Figure 33-2.)

Governor Crow argued that the only credible, stable rate is zero. If the Bank chooses, for example, 2 percent as a long-term goal, it might ease up to 3 or 4 percent later. In contrast to all other numbers, zero is harder to revise as a goal; people will believe a goal of zero where they will not believe a goal of, say, 2 percent. This was the governor's argument. But if one chooses any number x as the long-term goal, one might revise it subsequently to $x + 2$ or $x - 2$. To say that zero is harder to revise than any other number is to turn zero into a magic number with special "sticky" properties that no other number has. If it means anything, the governor's position must be about psychology: People will believe you are serious about your zero target more than a nonzero target. This may be true, although no body of evidence presently exists to support such a view.

The Bank's policy of zero inflation rekindled a debate that had recurred at various times in the past: *Is full employment compatible with a stable price level?* If the Bank persists with its zero inflation policy, this debate will become an important one in Canada in the 1990s.

As long as the *SRAS* curve shifts only because of demand, expectational, and random-shock effects, as we assumed earlier in this chapter, the answer is yes, full employment *is* compatible with stable prices. What worries some observers, however, is the possibility of a cost push that pushes wages up faster than productivity once the fear of unemployment is reduced by the continued achievement of potential income. As far back as the 1940s many Keynesians were worried that once the government was committed to maintaining full employment, much of the discipline of the market would be removed from wage bargains. The scramble of every group trying to get ahead of every other group would lead to wage-cost push inflation. The commitment to full employment would then lead to accommodating increases in the money supply.

[9] These technical reasons are many and varied. For example, price indexes have difficulty coping with quality increases. When prices rise, this may be partly to cover a rise in quality and only partly to cover a pure price increase per unit of real service delivered.

There is evidence that something like this has happened periodically over the past 40 years in Britain and in many of the countries of continental Europe. Most economists are more skeptical that it has been a serious force in North America. Nonetheless, some observers still worry that full employment and a low, stable inflation rate may in the end prove incompatible. They argue for some permanent form of incomes policy. (See Box 36-2.)

Some economists argue that the best way to ensure that the two objectives can be obtained most of the time is for governments to make clear that a stable price level, rather than full employment, is their overriding commitment and that whenever the two come into short-run conflict, price stability will be given priority over full employment. They argue that once this message has been accepted by the public, there will be two benefits. First, wage-cost push inflation may not occur, even at full employment. Second, incipient inflation of the supply- or demand-shock variety will be easy to quell with only minor recessions because inflationary expectations and inertia will never have a chance to become strongly entrenched. In this environment, major policy-induced recessions would not be required to control an outbreak of inflation. Paradoxically, by abandoning its full-employment commitment, the government might make the maintenance of something close to full employment much more likely—at least, that is how the argument goes.

Other economists argue that a commitment to stable prices will condemn the economy to operate on average well below its level of potential income. They believe that at or even near potential income, wage-push inflation becomes strong. As inflation begins to develop, the Bank will quickly adopt a contractionary monetary policy that will cut off expansions before they are fully developed.

Conclusion

Throughout the history of economics, inflation has been recognized as a harmful phenomenon. This view was given renewed strength as a result of the worldwide experiences of high inflation rates since the 1960s. The resolve is there, at least in advanced industrial countries, to prevent another outbreak of rapid inflation and, should one occur for reasons of unavoidable supply-side shocks, to prevent it from continuing long enough to become firmly entrenched in people's expectations. The resolve is, however, much weaker among the general public, as revealed by the strong criticisms of the Bank's attempts at the turn of the decade to push inflation back to its 1980s plateau of 4 percent. It remains to be seen who will dominate policy in the 1990s: those who would resist, even at major cost, any tendency for the inflation rate to rise and would try to lower it or those who are unwilling to accept the costs of strong anti-inflation policies. Either way, the outcome of the debate will affect us all.

SUMMARY

1. Inflationary supply shocks lead to a rise in the price level and a fall in national income. Inflationary demand shocks lead to a rise in the price level and in national income.
2. Without monetary expansion, inflation cannot continue indefinitely. Continuous monetary expansion can create continuous demand-shock inflation or accommodate continuous supply-shock inflation.
3. Sustained price inflation will also be accompanied by a closely related growth in wages and other factor costs, so that the *SRAS* curve is shifting upward. Factors that influence shifts in the *SRAS* curve can be divided into three main categories: demand, expectations, and random shocks.
4. The influence of demand can be expressed in terms of the inflationary and recessionary gaps, which relate national income to potential income, or in terms of the difference between the actual and the NAIRU.
5. Expectations of inflation tend to cause wage settlements that preserve the expected real wage and hence lead to nominal wage increases.
6. If the central bank accommodates the increasing demand for money

as the economy recovers from a serious recession, it can easily find itself validating demand-shock inflation once the economy develops an inflationary gap. If the Bank of Canada wishes to stop the inflation, it will have to reduce its rate of monetary expansion. This will raise interest rates and reduce aggregate desired expenditure, eventually eliminating the inflationary gap. Although the rise in interest rates does cause a once-and-for-all upward shift in the *SRAS* curve, the rise is a necessary part of an anti-inflationary policy that slows the rate of growth of the money supply.

7. It is impossible to have sustained, steady inflation when income exceeds its potential level. As expectations constantly catch up to the existing inflation rate, this rate, which is the sum of the expectations and demand effects, must accelerate.
8. It is possible to have sustained inflation at potential national income (and hence at the natural rate of unemployment). There is no demand pressure on prices, but expectations can cause wages and hence prices to grow at the same rate as the money supply.
9. Stopping entrenched inflation through a restrictive monetary policy will lead to temporary high interest rates and a recession. The length and depth of the recession will depend on the strength of the downward pressure on wages and on the speed with which inflationary expectations adjust.
10. Canadian policy was to reduce inflation from its two-digit levels in the early 1980s and from its 4 percent plateau in the late 1980s. Critics have argued that the immediate costs exceed the long-term benefits.
11. Some economists believe that zero inflation is an achievable goal of the policy of price stability; others believe that a gradual upward drift of the price level on the order of 1 to 2 percent per year must be accepted.
12. Some observers doubt that sustained full employment is compatible with stable prices. They advocate permanent incomes policies to control wage inflation and to make the two objectives compatible. Many economists are skeptical that such policies are needed in Canada and see no compelling evidence that full employment and stable prices cannot coexist in a flexible market economy.

TOPICS FOR REVIEW

Temporary and sustained inflation
Monetary accommodation of supply shocks
Monetary validation of demand shocks
Expectational inflation
The NAIRU
Accelerating inflation
Entrenched inflation
Zero inflation and price stability
Incomes policies

DISCUSSION QUESTIONS

1. On what source or sources of inflation do the following statements focus attention?
   a. "The one basic cause of inflation is the government's spending more than it takes in. The cure is a balanced budget."
   b. "Wage bargains currently being negotiated in autos and several other basic industries will soon cause inflation to accelerate."

c. "Canadians have become so accustomed to 4 percent inflation that it would be difficult for the Bank of Canada to induce the transition to 1 or 2 percent inflation."
d. "As the Canadian business expansion continued, inflationary pressures seemed to be building up across the country."

2. When OPEC radically increased the price of oil in 1974, the world was hit with a severe supply shock. The Bank of Canada decided to accommodate this with a rapid burst of monetary expansion, while the U.S. Federal Reserve Board decided on a policy of nonaccommodation. What do you think happened to the inflation rate and the national incomes of the two countries over the following two years?

3. When the entrenched inflation of the early 1980s was broken, the economies of many industrial countries came to rest with a relatively low inflation rate and high unemployment. People who feared the outbreak of inflation opposed even a temporary increase in the rate of monetary expansion. Use aggregate demand and aggregate supply analysis to show why some people felt that a *temporary* burst of monetary expansion might bring increases in employment without increases in inflation.

4. What theory or theories of inflation are suggested by each of the following quotations?
a. Canadian newspaper headline in 1986: "February producer prices steady—fall in energy costs largest in 6 years."
b. Newspaper editorial in Manchester, England: "If American unions were as strong as those in Britain, American inflationary experience would have been as disastrous as Britain's."
c. Study issued in 1980 by the Worldwatch Institute: "The nation's spiraling inflation reflects a global depletion of physical resources and therefore cannot be cured by traditional fiscal and monetary tools."
d. Article in the London *Economist*: "Oil price collapse will reduce today's inflation rate."
e. A Canadian newspaper article in October 1990: "The combination of the Kuwaiti crisis and an emerging recession is a sure recipe for worldwide stagflation."

5. In an article on the harmful effects of inflation written early in the 1980s, a reporter wrote, "With the rise in mortgage interest rates to 11 percent, heaven only knows the price of what was once idealized as 'the $100,000 house.' " At the time the inflation rate was 8 percent. Did the 11 percent interest rate represent a heavy burden of inflation on the new homeowner? What do you think the mortgage interest rate would have been if the inflation rate had been zero? Which situation would have meant a heavier real burden on the purchaser of a new house?

6. Discuss the apparent conflict between the following views. Can you suggest how they might be reconciled using aggregate demand and aggregate supply analysis?
a. "A rise in interest rates is deflationary, since breaking entrenched inflation with a tight monetary policy usually requires that interest rates rise steeply."
b. "A rise in interest rates is inflationary, since interest is a major business cost and, as with other costs, a rise in interest will be passed on by firms in terms of higher prices."

Chapter 37

Employment and Unemployment

Figure 26-5 on page 563 shows the course of employment and unemployment in Canada. Canadian unemployment, which is the subject of most of this chapter, follows a cyclical path, rising during periods of recession and falling in periods of business expansion. Unemployment does not, however, show any significant long-term trend to rise over time.

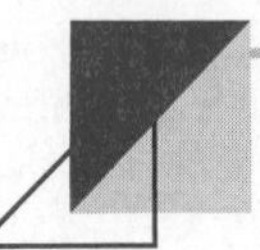

Employment in Canada

Looked at over the long term, the most striking feature of the economy revealed by Figure 26-5 is the course of employment rather than that of unemployment. The economy shows a strong capacity to generate a net increase in new jobs fast enough to prevent unemployment from growing steadily over time.

Changes in Total Employment

On the demand side, every year both economic growth and the natural cycle of growth and decay followed by many individual firms destroy many existing jobs. Economic growth causes some sectors of the economy to decline while other sectors expand. Jobs are lost in the contracting sectors (as well as in those where sales, and hence output, do not expand as fast as the productivity of the industry's existing factors is growing). Also, many firms go out of business for a number of reasons associated with the firm itself.

On the supply side, in virtually every year since the end of the Second World War in 1945, the labor force has expanded. The causes have included entry into the labor force of young persons born in Canada 15 to 25 years previously; increased labor force participation by various groups, especially women; and immigration of working-age persons. Nevertheless,

In most years, enough new jobs have been created both to replace the old jobs that are destroyed and to provide jobs for the increased numbers in the labor force. The result has been a net increase in employment in almost all years.

In most recessions, unemployment does not increase because total employment falls. Instead, unemployment increases because the net creation of new jobs, though positive, falls below the net increase in the size of the labor force. Only in the deepest recessions does the actual number of jobs decrease.

Some observers feared that the Canada-U.S. Free Trade Agreement (FTA) would cause massive unemployment by destroying hundreds of thousands of jobs soon after it began to take effect in January 1989. Instead, the number of people employed continued to rise through the rest of the decade. At the beginning of the recession in mid 1990, total employment in Canada was 179,000 higher than it had been in January 1989.

Kinds of Employment

Table 37-1, compiled by the Economic Council of Canada, shows that between 1967 and 1988 Canadian employment rose in all major sectors of the economy with the sole exception of primary goods–producing industries (forestry, mining, fishing, etc.), where it fell only marginally.

Although the total number of jobs held by Canadians has risen decade by decade, the table shows that the relative importance of the types of job has changed dramatically. The most striking change is in the relative shift of employment from manufacturing to services. The goods sector, which provided just over 40 percent of all jobs in 1967, provided less than 30 percent in 1988, while services rose from just under 60 percent in 1967 to just over 70 percent in 1988.

Types of Service Production

Many of the service industries, particularly those classified by the Economic Council as dynamic services, provide inputs to the goods-producing industries. Thus the value of their outputs is incorporated in the market value of the goods they help to produce.

TABLE 37-1 Employment Shares and Employment Growth, by Industry, 1967–1988

	INDUSTRY EMPLOYMENT		
	As a share of total employment		Annual growth rate, 1967–1988
	1967	1988	
Service sector	59.4%	70.9%	3.4%
Dynamic services	19.7	23.0	3.2
Transportation, communications, and utilities	9.0	7.4	1.5
Wholesale trade	4.5	4.6	2.7
Finance, insurance, and real estate	4.3	5.9	4.1
Business services	1.9	5.1	7.3
Traditional services	21.7	25.7	3.3
Retail trade	12.1	13.1	2.8
Personal services	9.6	12.6	3.8
Nonmarket services	18.0	22.2	3.5
Health and social services	6.2	8.9	4.3
Education	5.8	6.6	3.2
Public administration	6.0	6.7	3.0
Goods sector	40.6	29.1	0.9
Primary industries	10.3	6.0	−0.1
Manufacturing	23.9	17.2	0.9
Construction	6.5	5.9	2.1
Both sectors	100.0	100.0	2.5

Source: Economic Council of Canada, *Good Jobs, Bad Jobs* (Ottawa: Ministry of Supply and Services, 1990), p. 5.

The proportion of Canadians employed in the service sectors has been rising while the proportion in the goods sectors has been falling. The only service sector shown that has not increased its share of total employment is transportation, communications, and utilities. All three goods sectors shown have accounted for declining shares of total employment.

Other service industries, particularly those classified by the council as traditional, are sold directly to consumers. They are consumption commodities, such as personal services and entertainment.

Finally, the nonmarket service industries provide services that do not cover their costs of production by selling their outputs to consumers on free markets. Instead, their production costs are paid for by governments, largely out of tax revenues, and the services are then provided to their users free of charge (or sometimes for a small fee that does not cover the full cost of production). These industries are key contributors to our standard of living, as in the case of health care, and to the international competitiveness of the goods-producing sector, as in the case of education. They depend, however, on the other sectors of the economy to generate sufficient income to be able to bear the taxes needed to pay for their costs of production.

The Relation of Various Sectors

Surveying the employment provided by both the goods and the service sectors of the economy, the Economic Council of Canada had this to say:

> Sectoral interdependencies mean that a healthy goods sector is a key ingredient of total employment and output growth. By and large, goods industries operate in markets where international competition is a fact of daily life. Their competitiveness is fundamental to the demand for services. . . .
>
> Services themselves are important sources of employment and output in their own right. Moreover, both commercial and nonmarket services are major contributors to overall competitiveness, since they form a large part of the inputs to goods production and since they play a key role in creating an environment that promotes competitiveness [through such activities as education and health].
>
> To say that the Canadian economy is either goods-based or service-based would be inaccurate; it is, in fact, an economy in which both sectors are essential to one another in a complex and linked whole. As the two become more closely linked and as each increasingly takes on features of the other, the traditional distinction between them is becoming less relevant. In many respects, goods and services are converging.[1]

[1] Economic Council of Canada, *Good Jobs, Bad Jobs: Employment in the Service Economy* (Ottawa: Ministry of Supply and Services, 1990), p. 10.

Good Jobs and Bad Jobs

In its survey of service-sector jobs, the Economic Council divided them into "good jobs" and "bad jobs." Good jobs require substantial skills, pay good wages, and provide reasonable job security. Bad jobs are mainly unskilled, pay lower wages, are often part-time, and have little job security.

The council provides evidence that the emergence of these two types of jobs may be leading to a division in employees between the "haves" in good services jobs, largely located in what the council calls the dynamic service sector and the nonmarket service sector, and the "have-nots" in bad jobs, largely in what the council calls the traditional services sector but also partly in the nonmarket service sector.

The possible growth of two distinct income and employment classes is worrying. It is too early, however, to assess the seriousness of this labor market development. There are several reasons why not all "bad jobs" are actually bad from the employees' point of view.

First, many Canadians are unskilled, because of below average mental or physical endowment and/or inadequate education. Since, for these persons, it is often a case of a "bad job" or no job at all, they are fortunate that such jobs are available. It should not be forgotten that a mere 20 years ago pessimists who were surveying the changes in goods production—including the replacement of mass-production techniques by automated methods that replaced unskilled workers with robots—were predicting massive unemployment among the unskilled. The growth of "bad jobs" in the service sector more than compensated for the loss of unskilled jobs in the manufacturing sector.

Second, although almost half of those who work in part-time jobs say that they would prefer full-time jobs if such jobs were available, the other half *want* part-time employment. This group is made up of many types, including second (or third) income earners in a family, students working part-time to support their education, and people looking for jobs in other sectors in which they feel they are qualified but who need support in the meantime. For these people, the provision of part-time employment is an advantage, not a shortcoming, of the demand side of the labor market. This suggests an important point. Since there are so many more multi-income-earning families today than a decade or two ago, real income comparisons are often more revealing when they compare family incomes rather than incomes of individual employees.

Third, many of the part-time workers are people gaining their first job experience while continuing in education or before deciding to enter the work force full-time. For them, the profusion of part-time jobs in places such as the fast food industry provides important experience. They acquire basic but essential human capital in the knowledge and attitudes needed to be successful members of the modern labor force. The importance of this can be seen when people who do not get this experience early in life find it increasingly difficult to get a job as their age advances.

Nonetheless, when all these qualifications have been made, there is also little doubt that some of the workers who are today in "bad," dead-end jobs would prefer to be in good, career-oriented jobs. Some of these already have the skills to be in such jobs, and others could acquire them. Whether the problem of potentially good workers in "bad jobs" is a serious problem in terms of numbers, whether it is more serious than it was 30 years ago, and what, if anything, can be done about it will no doubt be a matter of considerable research and policy debate in the 1990s.

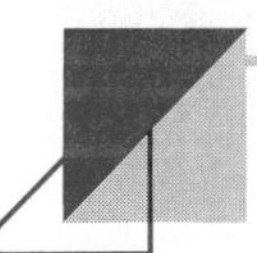

Unemployment in Canada

In the early 1980s worldwide unemployment rose to high levels. It remained high in many advanced industrial countries and only began to come down, and then very slowly, during the latter half of the decade. Canada's experience reflected these international developments rather closely. From a high of 12.8 percent in late 1982, Canada's unemployment rate fell to 7.7 percent in mid 1990, a point very close to the NAIRU.

As we shall see later in this chapter, those overall figures hide large variations in rates for specific groups. For example, in 1989 the unemployment rate was 6.9 percent for males over 25 years of age and 13.9 percent for males between the ages of 15 and 24.

Many social policies designed to alleviate the short-term economic consequences of unemployment have been instituted since the 1930s, and their success may be counted as a real triumph of economic policy. Being unemployed, even for some substantial period of time, is no longer the economic disaster that it once was. But the longer-term effects of high unemployment rates in terms of the disillusioned who have given up trying to make it within the system and who contribute to social unrest should be a matter of serious concern to the haves as well as the have-nots.

The case for concern about high unemployment when it occurs has been put eloquently by American economist Alan Blinder:

> A high-pressure economy provides opportunities, facilitates structural change, encourages inventiveness and innovation, [and] opens doors for society's underdogs. . . . All these promote the social cohesion and economic progress that make democratic mixed capitalism such a wonderful system when it works well. A low-pressure economy slams the doors shut, breeds a bunker mentality that resists change, stifles productivity growth, and fosters both inequality and mean-spirited public policy. All this makes reducing high unemployment a political, economic, and moral challenge of the highest order.[2]

Kinds of Unemployment

For purposes of study, the unemployed are classified in various ways. They can be grouped by personal characteristics, such as age, sex, degree of skill or education, and ethnic group. They can also be classified by geographical location, by occupation, by the duration of unemployment, or by the reasons for their unemployment.

In this chapter we are concerned mainly with the reasons for unemployment. Although it is not always possible to say why a particular unemployed person does not have a job, it is often possible to gain some idea of the total number of people unemployed for each major cause.

In Chapter 26 we distinguished three types of unemployment: *cyclical* unemployment, which is unemployment due to a recessionary gap, and *frictional* and *structural* unemployment, both of which may exist when national income is at its potential level and hence there is neither a recessionary gap nor an inflationary gap.

In this chapter we discuss each type of unemployment in more detail, and we also discuss *real-*

[2] Alan S. Blinder, "The Challenge of High Unemployment," *American Economic Review,* 78:2 (1988), p. 1.

wage unemployment, which may prevent an economy from reaching potential income.

Frictional Unemployment

Frictional unemployment refers to the normal turnover of labor. An important source of frictional unemployment is young people who enter the labor force and look for jobs. Another source is people who leave their jobs. Some may quit because they are dissatisfied with the working conditions; others may be fired. Whatever the reason, they must search for new jobs, which takes time. Persons who are unemployed while searching for jobs are said to be frictionally unemployed.

The normal turnover of labor would cause frictional unemployment to persist, even if the economy were at potential income and the structure of jobs in terms of skills, industries, occupations, and location were unchanging.

When Keynes examined the causes of unemployment, he made a basic distinction between voluntary and involuntary unemployment. In his view, *voluntary unemployment* occurs when there is a job available but the unemployed person is not willing to accept it at the going wage rate. *Involuntary unemployment* occurs when a person is willing to accept a job at the going wage rate but cannot find one. In Box 37-1, in which we discuss *search unemployment* in more detail, we see that the distinction between voluntary and involuntary unemployment is not always as clear as Keynes suggested.

Structural Unemployment

Structural adjustments of the economy can cause unemployment. When the pattern of demand for goods changes, the demand for labor changes. Until labor adjusts fully, *structural unemployment* develops. This has been defined as unemployment caused by a mismatch between the structure of the labor force—in terms of skills, occupations, industries, or geographical location—and the structure of the demand for labor. In Canada today, structural unemployment exists, for example, in the fish-processing towns of the Atlantic provinces and in the textile industry.

Natural causes. Economic growth can cause structural unemployment. As the economy grows, the mix of required inputs changes, as do the proportions in which final goods are demanded. These changes require considerable economic adjustment. Structural unemployment occurs when such adjustments are slow enough that severe pockets of unemployment develop in areas, industries, and occupations in which the demand for factors of production is falling faster than the supply.

Changes that accompany economic growth shift the structure of the demand for labor. Demand rises in such expanding areas as Ontario and British Columbia and falls (at least relatively) in other regions. Demand rises for workers with certain skills, such as computer programming and electronics engineering, and falls for workers with other skills, such as stenography and assembly line work. To meet changing demands, the structure of the labor force must change. Some existing workers can retrain and some new entrants can acquire fresh skills, but the transition is often difficult, especially for experienced workers whose skills become economically obsolete.

Increases in international competition can have effects similar to those of economic growth. As the geographical distribution of world production changes, so does the composition of production and labor demand in any one country. Labor adapts to such shifts by changing jobs, skills, and locations, but until the transition is complete, structural unemployment exists.

Structural unemployment will increase if there is either an increase in the speed at which the structure of the demand for labor is changing or a decrease in the speed at which labor is adapting to these changes.

Policy causes. Government policies can influence the speed with which labor markets adapt to changes. Some European countries such as the United Kingdom have used policies that discourage movement among regions, industries, and occupations. These policies tend to raise structural unemployment. Others, such as Sweden, have done the reverse and have encouraged workers to adapt to change. Partly for this reason, Sweden's unemployment rates were well below the European norm during the 1980s.

Policies that discourage firms from replacing human labor with machines may protect employment over the short term. If, however, such policies lead to the decline of an industry because it cannot com-

BOX 37-1

Search Unemployment

Some frictional unemployment is involuntary: The job seeker has not yet found an acceptable job in an appropriate occupational and skill category. Often, however, it is voluntary. The unemployed person is aware of available jobs but is searching for better options. Voluntary frictional unemployment is often called **search unemployment**.

The existence of search unemployment shows that the distinction between voluntary and involuntary unemployment is not as clear as it might seem at first. How, for example, should we classify an unemployed woman who refuses to accept a job at a lower skill level than the one for which she feels she is qualified? What if she turns down a job for which she is trained because she hopes to get a higher wage offer for a similar job from another employer?

In one sense people in search unemployment are voluntarily unemployed, because they could find some job; in another sense they are involuntarily unemployed, because they have not yet succeeded in finding the job for which they feel that they are suited at a rate of pay that they believe is attainable.

Workers do not have perfect knowledge of all available jobs and rates of pay, and they may be able to gain information only by searching the market. Faced with this uncertainty, it may be sensible for them to refuse a first job offer, for the offer may prove to be a poor one in light of further market information. Too much search—for example, holding off while being supported by others in the hope of finding a job better than a job for which one is really suited—is an economic waste. Thus search unemployment is a gray area: Some of it is useful, and some of it is wasteful.

It is socially desirable for there to be sufficient search unemployment to give unemployed people time to find an available job that makes the best use of their skills.

How long it will pay for people to remain in search unemployment depends on the economic costs of being unemployed. By lowering the costs of being unemployed, unemployment insurance tends to increase the amount of search unemployment. This may or may not increase economic efficiency, depending on whether or not it induces people to search beyond the point at which they acquire new and valuable information about the labor market.

pete effectively with innovative foreign competitors, serious structural unemployment can result in the long run.

Minimum wage laws can cause structural unemployment by pricing low-skilled labor out of the market. In Canada they are set by the provinces—sometimes too low to have much effect on labor markets, sometimes high enough to raise significantly the wages of unskilled persons who retain employment. As we saw in Chapter 19, effective minimum wage laws have two effects: They reduce employment of the unskilled, and they raise the wages of the unskilled who retain their jobs.

The potential effect of minimum wages on employment can be illustrated by an example. Consider an elderly person who may be prepared to supplement his social insurance pension by working for $150 per week as a caretaker of an apartment building. Suppose that the owner believes that this person is capable of doing what is needed, but the minimum wage is $170 per week. If there were no minimum wage, the elderly person would get the job. Because of the minimum wage, however, the owner has to pay more than she needs to and therefore hires someone else who can provide more services than are needed. She reasons that since she has to pay more, she might as well get something extra for it.

The same considerations apply to an inexperienced worker, just out of school, who would accept $150 per week for a first job. A potential employer is willing to pay this wage, but say the minimum wage is $170 per week. Once again the employer hires someone else who is overqualified for the job. A further unfortunate effect is that such young workers do not get on-the-job training and experience, which would enable them to hold down a stable, higher-paying job a year or two later.

Minimum wage policies are not the only types of policies that affect the structure of relative wages, although they are by far the most important policies that are likely to have such effects in Canada. Generally, policies that substitute imposed wage structures for market-determined ones tend to transfer employment from those whose relative wages are raised to those whose relative wages are lowered. The effect on overall employment is uncertain. However, when policies that affect the structure of wages lead to an increase in the average wage paid, they can contribute to what we will call *real-wage unemployment,* which we discuss later in this chapter.

The relationship between frictional and structural unemployment. As with many distinctions, the one between structural and frictional unemployment becomes blurred at the margin. In a sense structural unemployment is really long-term frictional unemployment. Consider a change that requires labor to move from one sector to another. If the reallocation occurs quickly, we call the unemployment *frictional*; if the reallocation occurs slowly, we call the unemployment *structural*.

The major characteristic of both frictional and structural unemployment is that there is a job available, an unfilled vacancy, for each unemployed person.

In the case of pure frictional unemployment, the job vacancy and the searcher are matched. The only problem is that the searcher has not yet located the vacancy. In the case of structural unemployment, the job vacancy and the searcher are mismatched in one or more relevant characteristics, such as occupation, industry, location, or skill requirements.

The sum of frictional and structural unemployment is what is called the *NAIRU*. Later in this chapter we consider policies that might change the NAIRU by changing the level of both frictional and structural unemployment.

Cyclical Unemployment

The term *cyclical unemployment* refers to unemployment that occurs because total demand is insufficient to purchase all the output that could be produced by a fully employed labor force. It is the unemployment that exists because there is a recessionary gap. As a result, there are fewer available jobs than there are unemployed persons. Cyclical unemployment can be measured as the number of persons currently employed minus the number of persons who would be employed at potential income. (It is thus the unemployment counterpart of the recessionary gap.) When cyclical unemployment is zero, there is some job available for every person unemployed. In this situation unemployment persists for either structural or frictional reasons. This is the level of unemployment that occurs at the NAIRU.

National income theory seeks to explain the causes of and cures for unemployment in excess of frictional and structural unemployment. *Full employment* does not mean zero unemployment; it means that all unemployment is frictional or structural.

Real-Wage Unemployment

Unemployment that occurs because real wages are too high is called **real-wage unemployment** or sometimes **classical unemployment**. This latter term is used because many economists, whom Keynes dubbed the Classical economists, believed that unemployment in the 1930s was caused by excessively high real wages. The remedy that they suggested for unemployment was to reduce wages. Keynes argued that the unemployment was due to too little aggregate demand, and his remedy was to raise demand, not to cut wages. Keynesians won that debate, and the majority of economists now agree that the unemployment of the 1930s was caused primarily by deficient aggregate demand rather than excessive real wages.

Because the debates of the 1930s aroused strong emotions, some modern Keynesians have refused to believe that *any* unemployment could be caused by too high real wages. There was concern, however, that much of the unemployment in Western Europe and elsewhere during the 1980s could be traced to

• KEY IDEAS IN •

MACROECONOMICS

This section provides important diagrams and captions from the text as reminders of basic economic concepts at a glance. If you need to refresh your memory concerning a principle being shown here, look in the appropriate chapter for a full explanation.

CHAPTER 32 The Budget Deficit Function

The actual deficit is negatively related to real national income, but the cyclically adjusted deficit only changes when the stance of fiscal policy changes.

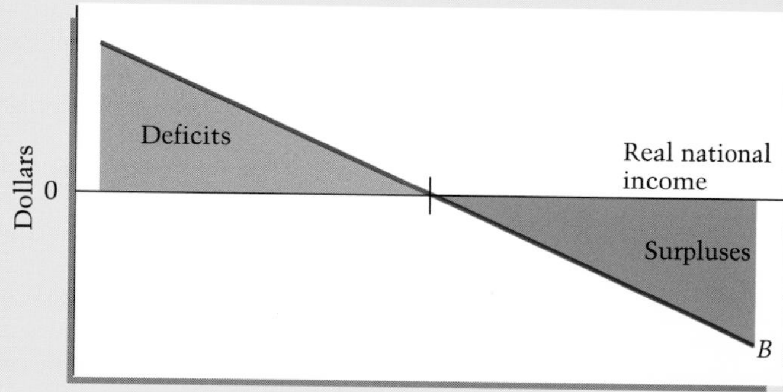

(i) The budget deficit function

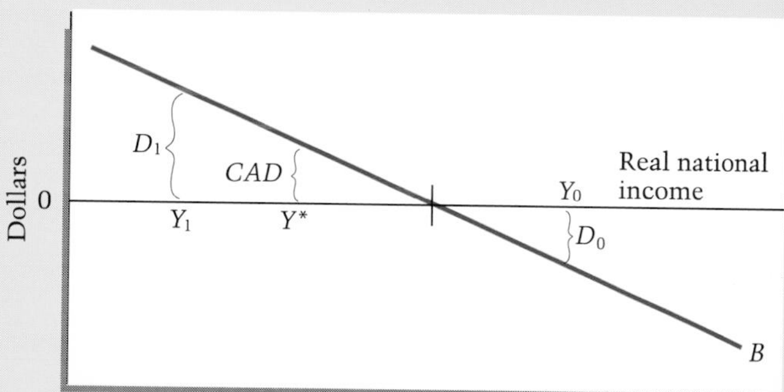

(ii) Changes in the measured deficit

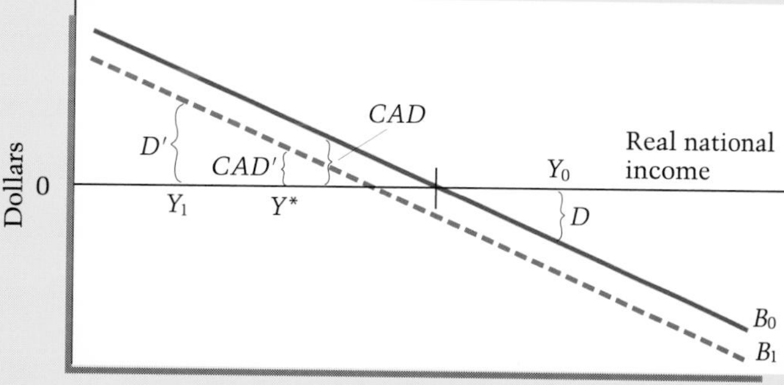

(iii) Changes in the cyclically adjusted deficit

CHAPTER 34 The Transmission Mechanism for an Expansionary Monetary Shock

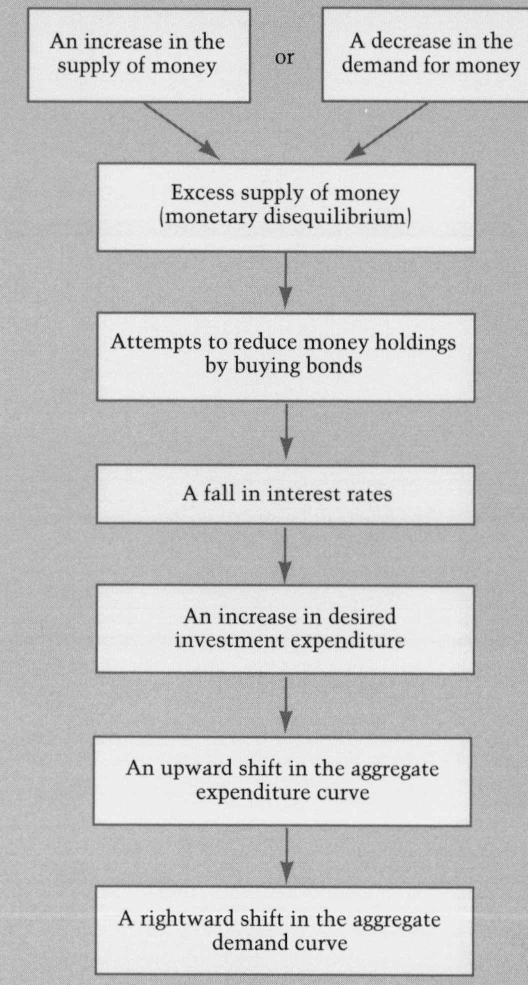

An increase in the supply of money or a decrease in the demand for money leads to an increase in aggregate demand. The excess supply of money following an expansionary monetary disturbance leads to a fall in the interest rate and an increase in investment. This causes an upward shift in the *AE* curve and thus a rightward shift in the *AD* curve.

CHAPTER 36 Monetary Accommodation of a Single Supply Shock

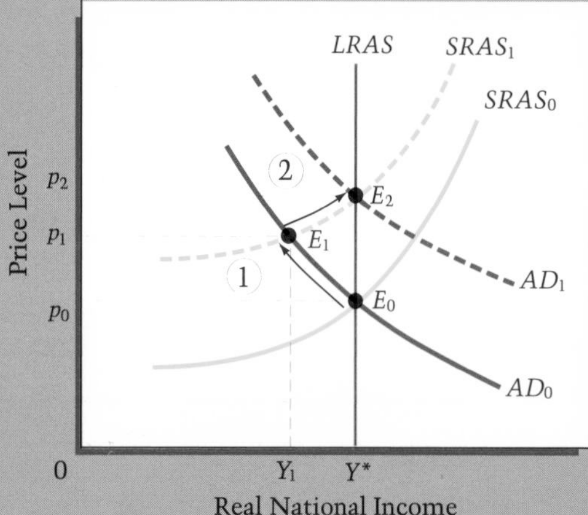

Monetary accomodation of a single supply shock causes costs, the price level, and money supply all to move in the same direction.

CHAPTER 36 An Unvalidated Demand-Shock Inflation

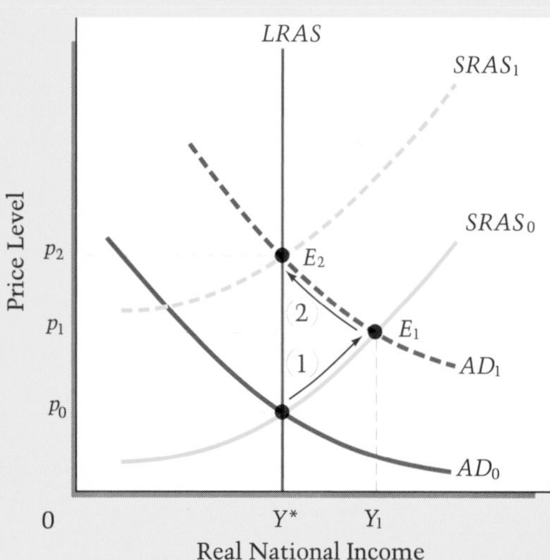

An unvalidated demand shock raises the equilibrium price level but leaves equilibrium income unchanged

CHAPTER 36 Eliminating an Entrenched Inflation

(i) Phase 1: The elimination of an entrenched inflation begins with a demand contraction to remove the inflationary gap. A fully validated Inflation is taking the economy along the path that is shown by arrow 1. When the Bank of Canada stops expanding the money supply, the economy moves along arrow 2.

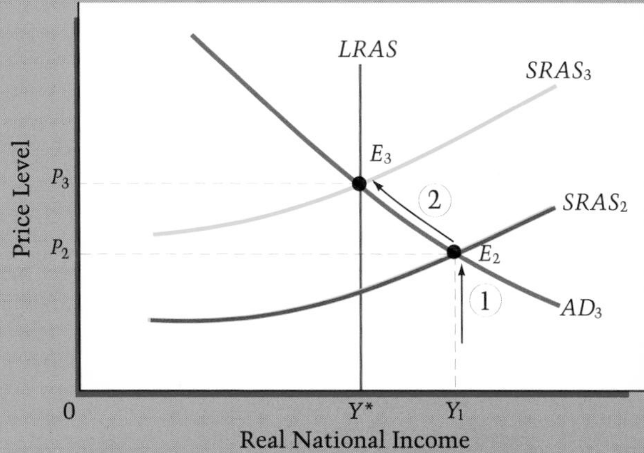

(i) Phase 1: Removing the inflationary gap

(ii) Phase 2: Expectations and wage momentum lead to a stagflation, with falling output and continuing inflation. The economy moves along the path that is shown by arrow 3.

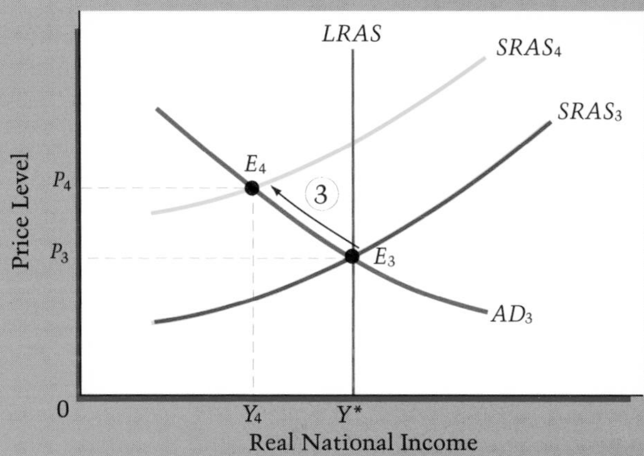

(ii) Phase 2: Stagflation

(iii) Phase 3: After expectations are revised, recovery takes income to Y^* and the price level is stabilized. There are two possible scenarios for recovery: either the recessionary gap can be relied on to cause wages to fall (slowly), taking the *SRAS* curve back to $SRAS_3$, arrow 4, or the Bank can increase the money supply sufficiently to shift the *AD* curve to AD_4, arrow 5.

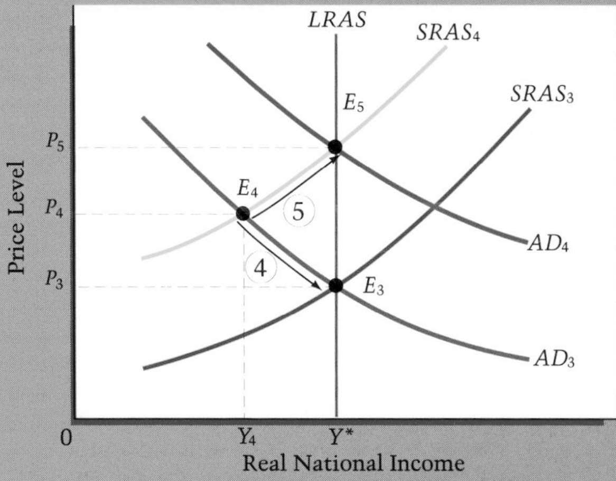

(iii) Phase 3: Recovery

CHAPTER 41 Effects of an Increase in the Domestic Currency Price of an Exported Good (Wheat)

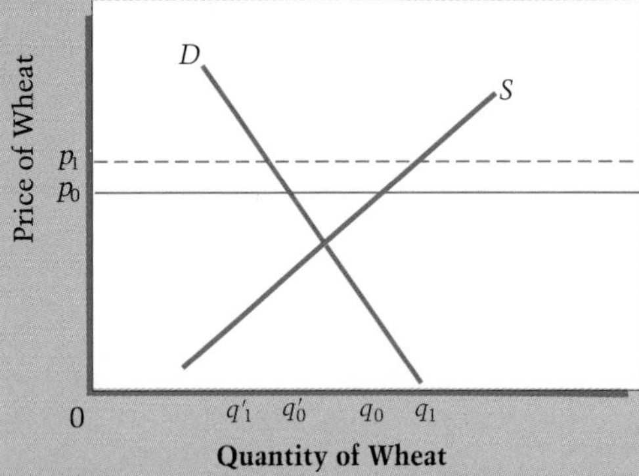

An increase in the domestic currency price of export goods leads to an increase in the volume of exports.

CHAPTER 42 A Stabilized Exchange Rate

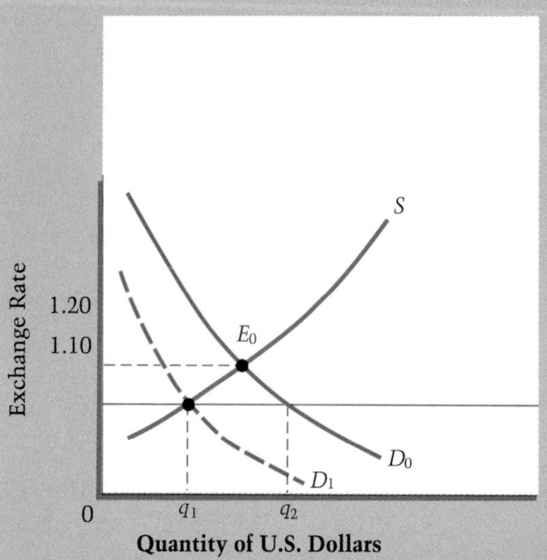

When an exchange rate is fixed at other than the equilibrium rate, either excess demand or excess supply will persist.

real wages that were so high that it did not pay private employers to provide employment for all who sought it at the going wage. How might this have come about?

So far in this book we have used the term *real wages* to mean the purchasing power of money wages. This is measured by deflating the money wage by the Consumer Price Index. In this discussion we are concerned with the real cost to the employer of hiring a worker. We call this the **real product wage**. The nominal cost to the employer includes the pretax wage, any extra benefits such as pension plan contributions, and any government payroll taxes such as employers' contributions to the social insurance funds. The hourly real product wage is the nominal cost of hiring labor for one hour, divided by the value of the output produced by labor during the same time period. Thus, for example, if it costs $10 per hour to employ labor that produces output valued at $15, the real product wage is 0.667, which says that labor costs absorb two-thirds of the value of output.

Too high a real product wage can affect employment through forces operating both in the short run and in the long run. Consider the short run first. At any moment in time, many industries will have an array of plants, ranging from those that embody the oldest technologies in use and can do little more than cover their variable costs to those that embody the latest technology and can make a handsome return over variable costs. A rise in the real product wage of 10 percent will mean that some plants can no longer cover their variable costs and so will close down. If, for example, a particular plant had wages of 70 cents and other variable costs of 25 cents for every dollar of sales, production would be worthwhile, since 5 cents of every dollar of sales would be available as a return on already invested capital. Now suppose that the product wage rose so that 77 cents for every dollar of sales was paid to labor. In this case the plant would be shut down, since the product price of $1.00 would not even cover the variable costs of $1.02. The plant's employees would then lose their jobs. This analysis can be extended to the economy as a whole.

An economywide rise in real product wages, other things being equal, means that some plants and firms will no longer be able to cover their variable costs and will shut down. When they do, the unemployment rate will rise.

Now consider a period of time that is long enough so that the demand for labor can fully respond to an increase in the real product wage. When the real product wage rises, firms will replace old plant and equipment with new capital that requires higher capital-labor ratios. Over time, firms will adopt technologies that replace expensive labor with less expensive capital, and this will increase the amount of real-wage unemployment. Thus when the real wage is too high across the whole economy, a structural mismatch will develop between the labor force and the capital stock. This mismatch will show up as unemployment; when the capital stock is working at full capacity, there is still unemployed labor. The unemployment will continue until one of two things happens. Unemployment may force down the real wage until it pays firms to employ all of the existing labor. Alternatively, new technologies may be invented that make profitable use of the unemployed labor, in spite of its high real product wage.

There is a strong danger that real-wage unemployment will develop when sustained inflation is being broken. If wages go on rising after price inflation is checked, the real product wage goes on rising and can become too high to permit full employment. If wages are slow to adjust to the unemployment that develops, real-wage unemployment can persist for some time. It will persist until the real product wage falls to a level at which it is profitable to employ the entire labor force.

Box 37-2 outlines an important technique for distinguishing between frictional and structural unemployment on the one hand and cyclical and real-wage unemployment on the other hand.

Why Does "Involuntary" Unemployment Persist?[3]

The existence of cyclical and real-wage unemployment poses a serious problem for both the economy and economic theory. Why do real wages fail to fall rapidly enough and far enough to eliminate all unemployment that is not frictional or structural? Indeed, the case could be made that structural unem-

[3] This section can be omitted without any loss of continuity.

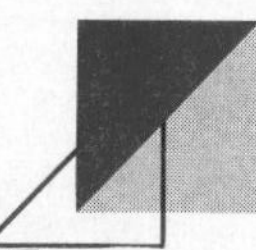

BOX 37-2

Distinguishing Types of Unemployment

One useful measure of the NAIRU is the percentage of the labor force unemployed when the number of unfilled job vacancies is equal to the number of persons seeking jobs. When these two are equal, there is a job opening for every person seeking a job. Any unemployment that remains must be either frictional or structural.

This measure is illustrated in the figure, which plots the number of unfilled vacancies (v) against the number of unemployed (u). The 45° line is the locus of points where $u = v$. On that line there is some job available to match every unemployed person, so there is no cyclical unemployment. The *uv* curve shows the actual relationship between unemployment and vacancies that is suggested by empirical evidence. In an economy with the relation uv_1, zero cyclical unemployment occurs at the point x, with frictional plus structural unemployment given by the amount a measured on either axis.

When a boom occurs, employers seek to hire more workers, so more vacancies open up. Since there are more jobs available, the unemployed spend less time searching before finding an acceptable job. Thus the number of unemployed falls. A boom therefore takes the economy to some point such as y, where there are more vacancies than unemployed. A slump takes the economy to some point such as z, where there are fewer vacancies than unemployed.

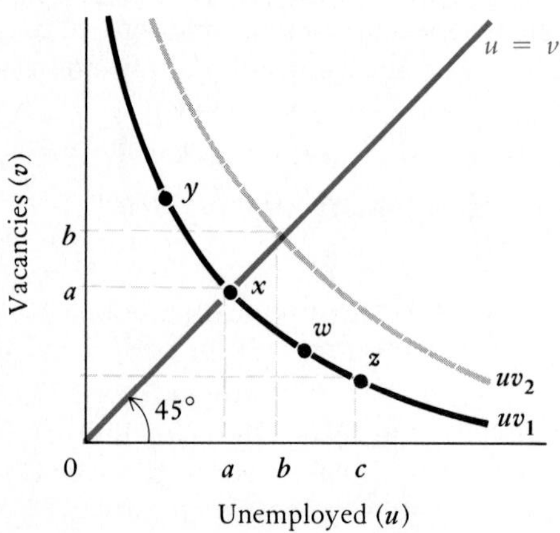

A change in structural plus frictional unemployment shifts the *uv* curve. For example, if people lose their jobs in Alberta while more jobs are created in Toronto, there may be a rise in the number of unemployed (in Alberta) and a rise in the number of unfilled job vacancies (in Toronto). Hence both u and v increase. In the graph, a shift to uv_2 indicates a rise in frictional plus structural unemployment from a to b.

In most countries where reliable vacancy data are available, the *uv* relation shifted outward in the 1970s, indicating a rise in the NAIRU.

Cyclical Unemployment

We can measure cyclical unemployment as total unemployment minus estimated frictional plus structural unemployment. Graphically, it is actual unemployment minus unemployment where the *uv* relation cuts the 45° line. If the economy is at point z, this measure is ac in the figure.*

Real-Wage Unemployment

Unemployment due to excessive increases in the real wage will show up in the figure approximately as a movement along the existing *uv* curve, say from point x to w, rather than as a shift of that curve. There will be a large rise in unemployment and a small fall in vacancies (which would otherwise have resulted from the normal turnover of labor in the now-closed plants). A general rise in the real product wage can lead to a general rise in unemployment that looks like cyclical unemployment because there is a rise in unemployment with no corresponding rise in unfilled vacancies.

* Notice that the measure is not current unemployment minus current vacancies but current unemployment minus the vacancies that would exist were there no output gap.

ployment would be greatly reduced if real wages were sufficiently flexible. Except in times of high cyclical unemployment, such as the Great Depression of the 1930s, someone who is unemployed because of a drop in demand for, say, skilled machinists could presumably find some sort of work, although the person might have to take a large cut in pay and status.

New theories, designed to explain involuntary unemployment, start by examining the forces that determine how quickly wages in actual labor markets will respond to changes in economic conditions. If wages do not respond quickly, supply and demand will *not* be equated for extended periods of time.

These theories start with the observation that labor markets are not auction markets in which prices always respond to excess demand or excess supply. When unemployed workers are looking for jobs, they do not knock on employers' doors and offer to work at lower wages than are being paid to current workers; instead, they answer want ads and hope to get the jobs offered, but often they are disappointed. Nor do employers, seeing an excess of applicants for the few jobs that are available, go to their current workers and reduce their wages until there is no one who is looking for a job; instead, they pick and choose until they fill their needs and then hang out a sign saying "No help wanted."

Long-term relationships. One set of modern theories, associated with the work of Arthur Okun and Robert Hall, among others, explains the familiar observations made in the preceding paragraph as results of the advantages to both workers and employers of relatively long-term, stable employment relationships.[4] Workers want job security in the face of fluctuating demand. Employers want workers who understand the firm's organization, production, and marketing plans. Under these circumstances both parties care about things in addition to the wage rate, and wages become somewhat insensitive to fluctuating current economic conditions. Wages are, in effect, regular payments to workers over an extended employment relationship rather than a device for fine tuning the supply and demand for labor. Given this situation, the tendency is for employers to "smooth out" the income of employees by paying a steady money wage and letting profits and employment fluctuate to absorb the effects of temporary increases and decreases in demand for the firm's product.

Many labor market institutions work to achieve these results. For example, many long-term contracts provide for a schedule of money wages over a period of several years. Another example is fringe benefits, providing pensions, health care, and other benefits, which tend to bind workers to particular employers. As yet another example, pay that rises with years of service to the employer binds the employee to the company, while seniority rules for layoffs bind the employer to the long-term worker.

These things tend to be the adhesive that leads to long-term employment, despite the known fact that the output attributable to workers rises rapidly as they gain experience, reaches a peak, and then falls off as their age advances. Under gradually rising wages, experienced workers tend to get less than the value of the output that they produce[5] at earlier ages and more as they near retirement. But over the long pull they are paid, on average, the value of their output to the firm, just as microeconomic theory (see Chapter 19) predicts that they will be. Between wages that rise with age and dismissal in recessions in ascending order of seniority, employers and employees are held to each other, allowing payment of a more or less steady wage in the face of fluctuating economic circumstances.

In such labor markets the wage rate does not fluctuate to clear the market. Wages are written over what has been called the "economic climate" rather than the "economic weather." Because wages are thus insulated from short-term fluctuations in demand, any market clearing that occurs does so through fluctuations in the volume of employment rather than in wages. Of course, wages must respond to permanent shifts in market conditions, for example, the permanent and unexpected decline in the demand for the output of a particular industry.

Efficiency wages. The idea of the *efficiency wage* forms the core of a second strand of thinking about why wages do not readily fall in response to excess supply

[4] See Robert E. Hall, "Employment Fluctuations and Wage Rigidity," *Brookings Papers on Economic Activity,* 1 (1980), pp. 91–123, for a review of much of this literature.

[5] The relevant microeconomic concept is the marginal revenue product of labor.

in labor markets. For any of a number of reasons, employers may find that they get more output per dollar of wages paid (i.e., a more *efficient* work force) when they pay labor somewhat more than the minimum amount that would induce workers to work for them.

Suppose that it is costly for employers to monitor workers' performance on the job so that some workers will be able to shirk some of their duties with a fairly low probability of being caught.[6] Given the institutions of the labor market, it is generally impossible for employers to fine employees for shirking on the job. The employees could just leave their jobs rather than pay the fines. Further, if the workers can easily find new jobs that are just as good as their old ones, firing is not much of a threat. However, if there is a group of potential employees who are currently unemployed and who would like to work at the going wage, the threat of firing workers in order to discipline them is much enhanced. Under these conditions employees who are fired will be made worse off by being fired precisely because it is difficult to find work at the going wage.

Efficiency wage theory says that firms may find it advantageous to pay high enough wages so that working is a clearly superior alternative to being laid off. This will improve the quality of workers' output without firms' having to spend large resources monitoring workers' performance.

Firms will pay efficiency wages as long as there is some reason that paying more than the market-clearing wage will increase the value of workers' output by more than it increases wages paid. Put this way, the idea is quite plausible. It is well established that workers who believe that they are well treated work harder than those who believe that they are treated badly.[7] This fact alone provides a potential justification for the efficiency wage idea, depending again on whether the increased output that arises from treating workers well covers the increased cost of doing so.

[6] This is an example of the principal-agent problem in microeconomics, discussed in Chapter 16.

[7] See George A. Akerlof, "Labor Contracts As Partial Gift Exchange," *Quarterly Journal of Economics,* 92 (1982), pp. 543–569.

A variant of efficiency wage theory is especially promising as an explanation of why firms do not cut wages during recessions. If workers feel unfairly treated when their wages are reduced, wage reductions (at least in response to moderate recessions) may cost firms more (in lost output from unhappy employees) than they save in reduced wages.[8] If so, real wages may not fall rapidly enough to eliminate cyclical and real-wage unemployment.

The basic message of new theories of unemployment is that competitive labor markets cannot be relied on to eliminate unemployment by equating current demand for labor with current supply.

New-Classical Views

Economists do not all agree on the importance of these new microeconomic explanations of why cyclical and real-wage unemployment can persist for long periods of time. Indeed, not all economists agree that such unemployment *can* persist. According to a number of economists, who have come to be known as *new-Classical* theorists (see Chapter 40), involuntary unemployment can arise only as a temporary result of unanticipated changes in economic circumstances. The new-Classical theorists argue that errors of this kind are quickly corrected in the labor market. Most economists have difficulty reconciling this view with the levels of unemployment that prevailed throughout most of the industrialized world in the 1930s and in the early 1980s or that persisted in much of Western Europe throughout the 1980s. However, to doubt the new-Classical interpretation as a complete explanation of unemployment is not the same thing as to embrace the new Keynesian theories that we have discussed here. Until business cycle fluctuations in unemployment are eliminated, it seems safe to say that economists will continue to search for and argue about their causes and cures.

[8] See Daniel Kahneman, Jack Knetsch, and Richard Thaler, "Fairness As a Constraint on Profit Seeking," *American Economic Review,* 76 (1986), pp. 728–741, for an interesting discussion, by a psychologist and two economists, of ways in which notions of fairness can complicate and illuminate economic analysis.

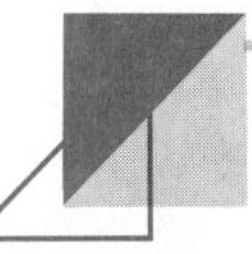

The Experience of Unemployment

Measured and Nonmeasured Unemployment

In Chapter 26, we discussed how unemployment is measured in Canada through a monthly sample survey. We also noted that some people who would be willing to accept jobs at the going wage rate are not recorded as unemployed, while some of those who are so recorded would not in fact accept a job. (See Box 26-2 on page 562.) It is not clear whether the net effect of these under- and overrecordings is to make the overall figure too high or too low.

The Overall Unemployment Rate

Figure 26-5 shows the behavior of the unemployment rate since the end of World War II. Until 1970 the rate fluctuated cyclically but showed no clear rising or falling trend. From 1970, however, the cyclical fluctuations appear to be superimposed on a rising trend. The *low* figure of 5.3 percent unemployment for the post-1970 period was above the *average* of 4.7 percent for the previous two decades, and the high figure of 12.8 percent was the highest since the Great Depression of the 1930s. The average rate of unemployment was 6.6 percent during the 1970s and 9.3 percent during the 1980s.

Figure 37-1 presents one estimate of the NAIRU. It takes into account the effects of variables measuring demographic, policy, institutional, and sectoral changes. This estimate shows the NAIRU rising steadily in the 1970s to a peak in 1978. After 1978 it declines to 1982, then rises to 1985, and then begins to fall again. We shall discuss some of the reasons for these movements in the NAIRU shortly.

The excess of actual unemployment over the NAIRU is due to a combination of deficient-demand and above-equilibrium real wages and is called cyclical unemployment. The estimate in Figure 37-1 thus indicates that by 1988 the prolonged upswing had eliminated cyclical unemployment.

The rise in the actual unemployment rate over the 1970s was accompanied by a rise in the NAIRU; since then the NAIRU has probably fallen somewhat.

FIGURE 37-1 Actual Unemployment and the NAIRU, 1971–1988

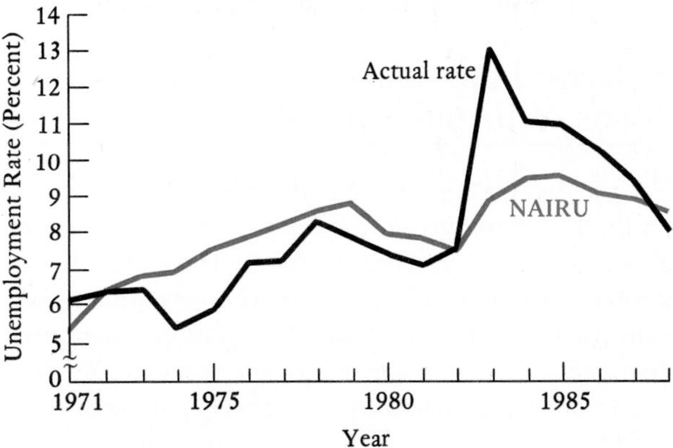

The NAIRU changes slowly, mainly due to structural changes in the labor market; the actual rate of unemployment fluctuates, mainly due to changes in aggregate demand. This estimate of the NAIRU shows it rising from 6 percent in 1971 to 9.5 percent in 1985, then falling to about 8 percent in 1988. The actual rate was below the NAIRU from 1973 to 1981, indicating tight labor market conditions for a decade. The recession in 1983 saw the actual rate soar above the NAIRU; the long, slow recovery over the next years saw the gap gradually narrow. In 1988 the actual rate fell below the NAIRU, indicating the return of tight labor market conditions. Although estimates for the NAIRU were not available for 1989 and 1990, the behavior of the actual rate suggests that the tight labor market conditions continued until about the middle of 1990. *Source:* David T. Coe, "Structural Determinants of the Natural Rate of Unemployment in Canada," *IMF Staff Papers,* March 1990.

Expressed as percentage points, the difference between 1.5 percent and 3.5 percent cyclical unemployment may not seem very big, but a reduction of two percentage points in the unemployment rate means that over a quarter of a million more people have jobs.

It is important to know how much cyclical unemployment exists. Raising aggregate demand when national income is already at its potential level, and hence when there is no cyclical unemployment, would open up an inflationary gap. This would accelerate inflation while achieving only a transitory fall in unemployment. We return to this later.

Relative Importance of the Various Kinds of Unemployment

At the beginning of 1990 there were just over 1 million unemployed in Canada, about 7.7 percent of the labor force. According to the most widely accepted estimates, nearly all of this unemployment was frictional and structural. The cyclical unemployment that existed at the end of the recession in 1982 was slowly eliminated by the subsequent recovery.

Figure 37-2 gives some idea of the current duration of the spells of unemployment.[9] Data are given for 1982, a year of severe recession, and for 1989, when the economy was at its potential income. The differences between the two sets of figures are due mainly to the reduction in cyclical unemployment over the period.

In 1989 nearly two-thirds of the unemployed had been out of work for 13 weeks or less. Long-term unemployment accounted for only 13 percent of the unemployed in that year. These figures represent an enormous improvement over the recession year 1982, when only 18 percent of the unemployed had been without jobs for 4 weeks or less and 52 percent for more than 13 weeks. But the 1989 figures were not yet back to the more favorable ones for 1979, when national income was also at its potential level. In that year just less than one-third of the unemployed had been out of work for more than 13 weeks.

Three facts stand out about the unemployed. First, a group of marginal workers who move in and out of jobs, sometimes several times a year, account for a significant fraction of the unemployment totals. Second, most spells of unemployment are of short duration. Third, the bulk of total unemployment is accounted for by the long-term unemployed. Observers are often surprised that both the second and third points can be true. Their consonance can be demonstrated, however, by a simple example. Consider four people, each unemployed for a week, and a fifth who is unemployed for nine months. For this group of five people, 80 percent of the individual spells of unemployment are short-term, but the long-term spell counts for 90 percent of the total weeks of unemployment.

FIGURE 37-2 Duration of Unemployment

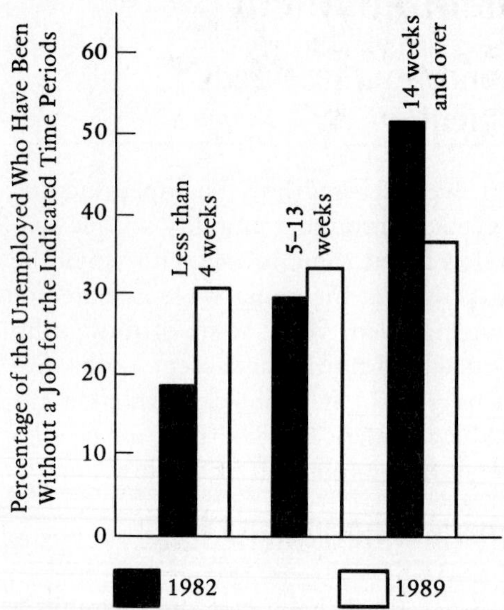

In recession years, the average duration of unemployment rises. In 1982, a year of severe recession and high overall unemployment, over half of the unemployed were without jobs for more than 13 weeks, while less than one-fifth were without jobs for less than 4 weeks. In 1989, a year of relative prosperity, only 36.5 percent of the unemployed were without jobs for more than 13 weeks, while over a quarter were without jobs for less than 4 weeks. *Source:* Statistics Canada.

Potentially soul-destroying spells of prolonged periods without a job are confined to a relatively small part of the labor force, but a part that rises significantly in recessions.

Figures 37-3 and 37-4 document some of the inequalities in unemployment rates. Males and females,

[9] The figures are based on the Labor Force Survey, which asks currently unemployed individuals how long they have been out of work. Notice that this gives us the duration of *currently uncompleted* bouts of unemployment. It gives different and shorter figures than the duration of *completed bouts* of unemployment, which is obtained by asking people who have just found a job how long they were out of work.

FIGURE 37-3 **Variations in Experience of Unemployment, 1982 and 1989**

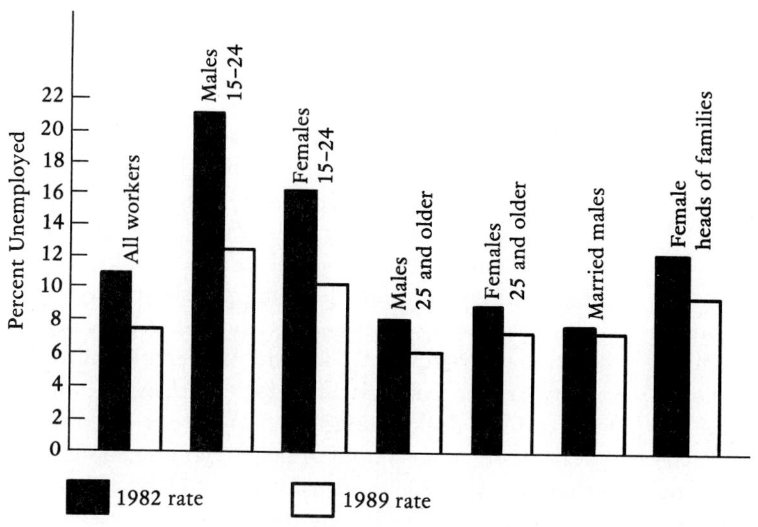

Unemployment is very unevenly divided among sex and skill groups. The overall unemployment rates of 11.0 and 7.5 percent in 1982 and 1989, respectively, concealed large variations in the unemployment rates of different groups. The recession of 1982 led to higher unemployment rates for most groups, but the difference between the 1982 rate and the 1989 rate varied considerably from group to group, with the largest decline being experienced by males between 15 and 24. The unemployment rate for this group fell from 21.2 percent in 1982 to the still high rate of 12.4 percent in 1989. *Source: Canadian Statistical Review.*

the young and the experienced have very different unemployment experiences, as Figure 37-3 shows. Equally dramatic are the differences between sectors, as shown in Figure 37-4.

Why Does the NAIRU Change?

We have noted that structural unemployment can increase because the pace of change accelerates or the

FIGURE 37-4 **Unemployment Rates by Sector, 1982 and 1989**

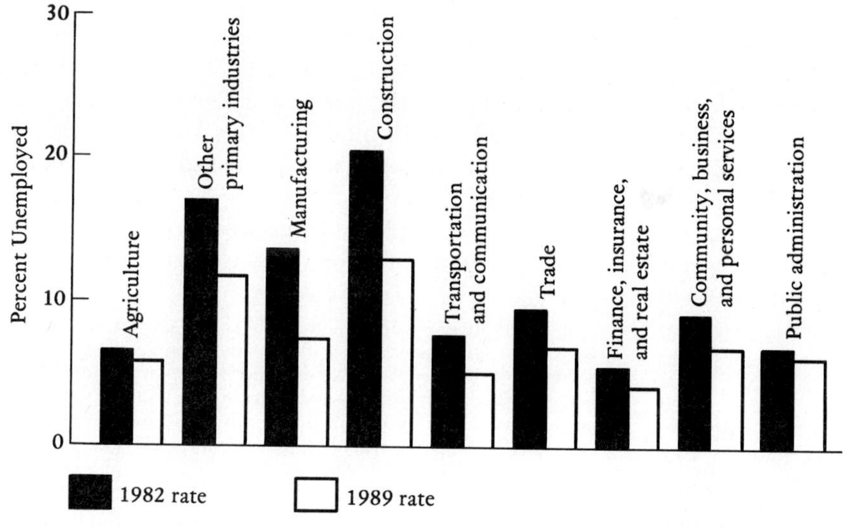

Unemployment rates vary greatly across sectors in both recessions and booms. Unemployment was highest in construction and lowest in finance, insurance, and real estate in both the recession year 1982 and the relatively prosperous year 1989. The ranking of unemployment rates by sector was unchanged between the two years, but there were considerable changes in the differences between sectors. *Source:* Statistics Canada.

pace of adjustment to change slows down. An increase in the rate of growth, for example, usually speeds up the rate at which the structure of the demand for labor is changing. The adaptation of labor to the changing structure of demand may be slowed by such diverse factors as a decline in education and new regulations that make it harder for workers in a given occupation to take new jobs in other provinces. Any of these changes will cause the natural rate of unemployment to rise. Changes in the opposite direction will cause the natural rate to fall.

Demographic changes. Because people usually try several jobs before settling into one for a longer period of time, young or inexperienced workers have higher unemployment rates than experienced workers. The proportion of inexperienced workers in the labor force rose significantly as the baby boom generation of the 1950s entered the labor force along with an unprecedented number of women who elected to work outside the home. It is estimated that these demographic changes added nearly a percentage point to the natural rate of unemployment. Since birthrates were low in the 1960s and a further increase in the percentage of females entering the labor force is unlikely, some demographically induced fall in this type of unemployment has been occurring recently and will continue over the next decade.

Although the NAIRU, and youth unemployment in particular, should fall as the baby boom generation passes on to middle age, many observers worry that although the brighter, the more energetic, and the luckier of that generation will do well, many others will not. Learning through on-the-job experience is a critical part of developing marketable labor skills. Many unemployed young people have been denied that experience early in their working careers. They may be condemned to remain at best marginal workers who take temporary jobs at low pay and with little future job security.

Other significant changes include the large increase in female participation rates and the related increase in the number of households with more than one income earner. In 1960 only 30 percent of females 20 years and older were in the labor force; in 1972 the figure was 38 percent; by 1990 it had jumped to 51 percent. When both husband and wife work, it is possible for one to support both while the other looks for "a really good job" rather than accepting the first job offer that comes along.

Wage and price rigidity. Recent research suggests that the speed with which wages and prices adjust to changing market conditions may have slowed over the years. Anything that slows the speed of adjustment to the economy's ever-changing conditions will create a larger pool of structural unemployment.

Social programs. Minimum wage laws are of real help to those who keep their jobs when their wages are forced up. They hurt those who lose their jobs as a result of the higher wage rates. They may also have a longer-term harmful effect. Employers are discouraged from hiring young people at low wages while providing on-the-job training. During a period of training, employees acquire marketable skills that allow them subsequently to command a higher wage. By discouraging such practices, minimum wage laws create a pool of people without skills who alternate between low-paid jobs and bouts of unemployment, thus raising the number of people who are in structural or frictional unemployment at any one time.

As discussed in Box 37-1, enriched unemployment insurance benefits will make it easier for the unemployed to maintain living standards while searching for a new job. As a result, they can afford to turn down job offers in anticipation of potential better offers. This serves to increase the amount of search unemployment and probably played a role in the increase in the natural rate in the 1970s that persisted into the 1980s.[10]

Hysteresis. Recent models of unemployment show that the level of the NAIRU can be influenced by the actual rate of unemployment.[11] Such models get their name from the Greek word *hysteresis,* meaning "lagged effect." In models of this kind, the normal intensity of use of labor is affected by the actual intensity of use.

A number of plausible mechanisms might lead to some hysteresis in labor markets. One mechanism,

[10] It is important in discussions such as this one to distinguish between positive statements and normative judgments. Accepting the positive statement that UI raises frictional unemployment does *not* imply accepting the judgment that UI is undesirable. Most economists support UI while accepting that it does cause some unemployment. Some would like to reform the UI rules, but few advocate abandoning the whole system.

[11] See, for example, Olivier Blanchard and Lawrence Summers, "Hysteresis and the European Unemployment Problem," *NBER Macroeconomics Annual* (1986), pp. 15–78.

emphasized by commentators on Western Europe, which has a heavily unionized labor force, is based on the notion that in times of high unemployment people who are currently employed (insiders) use their bargaining power to ensure that their own status is maintained and prevent new entrants to the labor force (outsiders) from competing effectively. In an *insider-outsider* model of this type, a period of prolonged, high unemployment—whatever its initial cause (e.g., cyclical fluctuations)—will tend to become "locked in" to the normal functioning of the labor market. If outsiders are denied access to the labor market, their unemployment will fail to exert downward pressure on wages, and the NAIRU will tend to rise.

Another mechanism that can lead to hysteresis in labor markets arises from the importance of experience and on-the-job training. Suppose, for example, that a period of recession causes a significant group of new entrants to the labor force to have unusual difficulty in obtaining their first jobs. As a result, the unlucky group will be slow to acquire the important skills that workers generally learn in their first jobs. When demand increases again, this group of workers will be at a disadvantage relative to workers with normal histories of experience, and the unlucky group will tend to have unemployment rates that will be higher than average. Thus the NAIRU will be higher than it would have been had there been no recession.

The empirical importance of hysteresis in Canada has not been settled. In some countries in Western Europe, there is evidence that hysteresis may be quite important.

Increasing structural change. The amount of resource reallocation across industries and areas appears to have increased in the 1970s and again in the 1980s. In part this is the result of the increasing integration of the Canadian economy with the rest of the world and the globalization of world markets. Most observers feel that overall this integration has been beneficial. One less fortunate consequence, however, is that Canada is increasingly affected by changes in demand and supply conditions anywhere in the world—changes that require adjustments throughout the world's trading sectors.

Structural changes have created a continuing need for rapid adjustments over the past few decades: increases in the demand for food due to the failure of agricultural industries in Eastern Europe; increases in the supply of agricultural products due to the green revolution in less developed countries; enormous OPEC-induced increases in the price of oil in the 1970s and early 1980s, followed by almost equally precipitous declines in the mid 1980s; the rise of Japanese industrial might, including its challenge to the North American auto industry; the communications revolution leading to the decentralization of industry, with components produced in various countries and assembled in others; robotization, which increased industrial productivity and reduced the demand for assembly line workers; the growth of knowledge-intensive industries that require highly educated work forces and are relatively footloose geographically; the globalization of competition, with fewer and fewer firms serving home markets that are sheltered by natural or artificial barriers; the decline of employment in manufacturing; and the enormous growth in service industries.

The pace of technological change since the start of the 1970s has contributed greatly to an increase in the level of structural unemployment.

Recent experience. Canadian unemployment has tended to exceed U.S. unemployment for at least a decade. Earlier, both the average levels and the cyclical patterns of unemployment were quite similar in the two countries.

The persistently higher Canadian unemployment rates suggests a rise in the Canadian NAIRU early in the 1980s. Various investigators have shown that the obvious explanations of differences in aggregate demand, relative wages, unionization, and labor market regulations at most explain only part of the differences.

It has been argued by three Queen's University economists—Rose Milbourne, Douglas Purvis, and David Scoones—that much of the change is the result of the unemployment insurance system. Since 1977, Canadian unemployment benefits have been more generous, the higher the level of unemployment. Although this aspect of UI may be desired on grounds of social justice, it has the effect of encouraging people to prolong their job searches and remain in the labor force during recessions, thus increasing measured unemployment. If these extra unemployed would otherwise have withdrawn from the labor force, there is no real loss in counting them as unemployed. If they would otherwise have been working, the generous UI payments have a cost in terms of forgone employment and output.

Future outlook. Certain factors may work to reduce NAIRU in the future. First, the proportion of youths and females newly entering the labor force will diminish as the baby boom generation ages and the female participation rate stabilizes. Second, educational systems in some or all provinces may be revamped to give students better job-related training. Third, governments may become more aware of the importance of structural changes in the economy and of the need for policies to encourage rather than inhibit adaptability and flexibility in the economy.

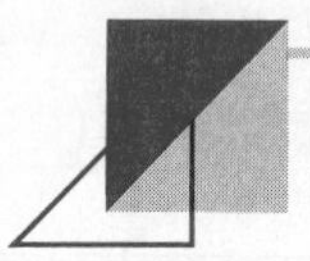

Reducing Unemployment

The economic cost of unemployment is measured by the output that could have been produced had unemployed workers been employed. Yet reducing unemployment is also costly. For example, retraining and reallocation schemes designed to reduce structural unemployment use scarce resources.

It would be neither possible nor desirable to reduce unemployment to zero. The causes of unemployment could never be removed completely, and reducing the amount of unemployment stemming from those causes is costly.

Unemployment insurance is one method of helping people cope with unemployment. Certainly, it has reduced significantly the human costs of the bouts of unemployment that are inevitable in a changing society. Nothing, however, is without cost. Though unemployment insurance alleviates the suffering caused by some kinds of unemployment, it can itself contribute to unemployment in that it encourages search unemployment, as we have observed.

Supporters of unemployment insurance emphasize its benefits. Critics emphasize its costs. As with any policy, a rational assessment of the value of unemployment insurance requires a balancing of its undoubted benefits against its undoubted costs. Most Canadians seem convinced that when this calculation is made, the benefits greatly exceed the costs, although many also recognize the scope for reform of certain aspects of the program, as discussed in Chapter 25.

Cyclical Unemployment

We do not need to say much more about this type of unemployment since its control is the subject of stabilization policy, which we have studied in several earlier chapters. A major recession that occurs due to natural causes can be countered by monetary and fiscal policy to reduce cyclical unemployment.

The mid 1970s and late 1980s and the early 1990s saw the emergence of *policy-induced* cyclical unemployment. This occurred when the government's anti-inflation policy led to drastic contractionary policies that opened up large recessionary gaps. As we saw in Chapter 36, a temporary bout of cyclical unemployment was the price of reducing inflation.

Real-Wage Unemployment

Whenever real-wage unemployment becomes a major problem, its cure is not an easy matter. What is required is a fall in the real product wage. This requires that money wages rise less slowly than money prices. In labor markets that are sluggish in their responses to excess supply, this can take a long time. If wages rise 2 percent more slowly than prices, it will take five years for the real product wage to fall from 80 cents in the sales dollar to 70 cents.

Frictional Unemployment

The turnover that causes frictional unemployment is an inevitable part of the functioning of the economy. Insofar as it is caused by ignorance, increasing the knowledge of workers about market opportunities may help. But such measures have a cost, and that cost has to be balanced against the benefits.

Some frictional unemployment is an inevitable part of the learning process. New entrants have to try jobs to see if they are suitable, and this leads to a high turnover rate among the young and hence high frictional unemployment.

Structural Unemployment

The reallocation of labor among occupations, industries, skill categories, and regions that gives rise to structural unemployment is an inevitable part of growth. There are two basic approaches to reducing structural unemployment: First, try to arrest the changes that accompany growth, and second, accept the changes and try to speed up the adjustments. Throughout history, labor and management have advocated, and governments have tried, both approaches. Box 37-3 gives a cautionary tale concerning the choice between the two.

Resisting change. Since the beginning of the Industrial Revolution, workers have often resisted the introduction of new techniques to replace the older techniques at which they were skilled. This is understandable. New techniques often destroy the value of the knowledge and experience of workers skilled in the displaced techniques. Older workers may not even get a chance to start over with the new technique. Employers may prefer to hire younger persons who will learn the new skills faster than older workers who are set in their ways of thinking. From society's point of view, new techniques are beneficial because they are a major source of economic growth. From the point of view of the workers they displace, new techniques can be an unmitigated disaster.

Here are two characteristic ways in which economic change has been resisted. First, a declining industry may be supported with public funds. If the market would support an output of X, but subsidies are used to support an output of $2X$, jobs are provided for, say, half the industry's labor force who would otherwise become unemployed and have to find jobs elsewhere. Second, change may be accepted but agreement reached to continue to employ workers who would otherwise be made redundant by the new technology. Both these policies are attractive to the people who would otherwise become unemployed. It may be a long time before they can find other jobs, and when they do, their skills may not turn out to be highly valued in their new occupations.

Over the long term, however, such policies run into increasing difficulties. Agreements to hire unneeded workers raise costs and can hasten the decline of an industry threatened by competitive products. An industry that is declining due to economic change becomes an increasingly large burden on the public purse as economic forces become less and less favorable to its success. Sooner or later, public support is withdrawn, and an often precipitous decline then ensues.

In assessing these remedies for structural unemployment, it is important to realize that although they are not viable in the long run for the entire economy, they may be the best alternatives for the affected workers during their lifetimes.

There is often a genuine conflict between workers threatened by structural unemployment, whose interests lie in preserving their jobs, and the general public, whose interest is served by economic growth, which raises living standards.

Aiding adjustments to change. Another policy to deal with structural change is to accept the decline of industries and the destruction of specific jobs that go with it and try to reduce the cost of adjustment for those affected. Retraining and relocation grants make movement easier and reduce structural unemployment without inhibiting economic change and growth.

A number of policies have been introduced in Canada. These have focused on two sources of adjustment problems. One is imperfections in capital markets that make it difficult for workers to borrow funds in order to retrain or relocate. The other is the lack of good information about current and future job prospects.

A major aspect of labor market policies is education. Between 1960 and 1990, university enrollment rose from 107,000 to 514,000, and community college enrollment increased from 50,000 to 315,000. Over the same period, the number of persons undertaking technical training increased from fewer than 5,000 to over 350,000, partly under the stimulus of the Adult Occupational Training Act of 1967.

Policies to improve the flow of information include the creation of job banks and information centers and initial steps toward a nationwide computerized information system called Jobscan. Job creation programs such as the Local Employment Assistance Programme, Canada Community Services Projects, New Technology Employment Programme, and Summer Canada are also major labor market policies aimed at structural unemployment.

A number of programs that aid adjustment in a variety of ways exist under the National Training Act and the Labour Adjustment Benefits Act. The Canadian Mobility Programme, which finances relocation and travel assistance, spends about $8 million annually and each year helps about 5,000 work-

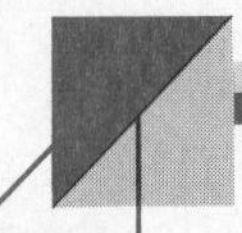

BOX 37-3

Industrial Change: An Economist's Cautionary Tale

The audience hushed as the royal commissioners filed into the room. The chief forecasting wizard—behind his back some called him the economic soothsayer—began his report. "I have identified beyond resonable doubt the underlying trends now operating," he declared to an expectant audience. "The nation's leading industry, industry X, is in a state of decline. From its current position of employing 50 percent of our work force it will, within the duration of one human lifetime, employ only 5 percent."

"Forty-five percent of the nation's jobs destroyed within one lifetime!" proclaimed the newspaper headlines.

"Where can new jobs possibly come from at so rapid a pace?" asked a labor leader.

"We must protect industry X; we just cannot let all these jobs go down the tubes," argued an employer.

"Perhaps we should identify and promote new 'sunrise industries,' " said a mandarin. Indeed, it was widely believed that a new high-tech product, product Y, would be the wave of a future new transportation revolution, and a call went out for subsidies and tax expenditures to back its development.

"Is there any hope that the private sector might provide the new jobs?" someone asked.

"Possibly," said a junior economist, more out of desperation than hope, "the new product Z that is being produced by a few people in backyard sheds might grow to be a significant employer."

He was immediately pounced on by a chorus of more realistic thinkers. "Product Z! It's noisy, it's smelly, and it's a plaything for the rich. Surely *it* will never provide significant employment."

All of the economic facts in the above tale are true; only the royal commission and the policy initiatives are fictitious.

The country was Canada.

The time was 1900.

Industry X, the employer of 50 percent of the work force, was agriculture.

Product Y, the sunrise industry, was zeppelins.

Product Z, the scorned plaything of the rich, was automobiles.

The decline of some traditional industries is a cause for concern. Some are suffering a temporary decline, and some are declining permanently. In either event, the hardships on those losing their jobs are severe. The tale does, however, have a serious message. Here are a few of the lessons that can be gleaned from a look at the Canadian economy of 1900:

1. The economy is constantly changing. Indeed, the motto of any market economy could be "nothing is permanent." New products appear continually, while others disappear.

At the early stage of a new product, total demand is low, costs of production are high, and many small firms are each trying to get ahead of their competitors by finding the twist that appeals to consumers or the technique that slashes costs.

ers relocate permanently and another 20,000 temporarily. Women's employment counseling centers serve 5,000 women entering or reentering the work force each year. Other services meet the special needs of such groups as the physically disabled, criminal offenders, and youths.

In 1985 the Conservative government introduced the Canadian Job Strategy. This strategy involved federal expenditures of about $1.4 billion annually toward six programs, the biggest of which were Job Development, Job Entry, and Skill Shortages. These programs were meant to be directed to groups such as women, aboriginal peoples, and disabled persons, who were perceived as being "disadvantaged" in labor markets. The funds are allocated on a regional basis. The $1.4 billion does not, however, all repre-

Sometimes new products never get beyond that phase—they prove to be passing fads. Others, however, do become items of mass consumption.

Successful firms in growing industries buy up, merge with, or otherwise eliminate their less successful rivals. Simultaneously, their costs fall, owing to scale economies. Competition drives prices down along with costs.

Eventually, at the mature stage, a few giant firms often control the industry. They become large, conspicuous, and important parts of the nation's economy. Sooner or later, new products arise to erode the position of the established giants. Demand falls off, and unemployment occurs as the few firms run into financial difficulties.

A large, sick, declining industry may appear to many as a national failure and a disgrace. At any moment, however, firms can be found in all phases—from small firms in new industries to giant firms in declining industries. Large declining industries are as much a natural part of a healthy changing economy as large stable industries and small growing ones.

2. The policy of shoring up the declining industries of the 1980s could be just as destructive of our living standards as the policy of protecting the agricultural sector from decline in 1900 would have been. (Policies that ease the human cost of the adjustment are, however, to be recommended.)

3. To tell where the new employment will come from requires the kind of crystal ball our young economist would have needed in 1900 to stick by his wild guess of identifying the new plaything of the rich as the massive automobile industry 30 years later.

Economists are continually asked, "Where will the new employment come from?" The answer "we don't know" is *wrongly* taken to mean "it won't come." In the past, the new jobs have come, and we see no new identifiable forces to prevent their coming in the future. For example, in the course of the current recovery, many people gaining employment are starting in *new* jobs—jobs with firms and in locations that did not exist or would not have been predicted even five years ago.

4. Picking winners and backing them by government policy is a sure way to waste public funds and inhibit the development of the real winners. People risking their own money and diversifying risks over many ventures are a surer route to employment creation than governments risking taxpayers' money and mesmerized by a few current fads and fashion.

5. The industrial policy we do need is one that encourages private initiatives and risk taking. Small businesses are often, if not always, the route to the creation of new employment. Risk taking and the growth of small firms should not be discouraged by such things as complicated regulatory rules and tax laws.

sent new expenditures, as a number of existing labor market adjustment programs—including the Industry and Labour Adjustment Program and the Canadian Industrial Renewal Program—were discontinued.

Some of the changes appeared to be mere window dressing, but some real changes were effected. The government defended the changes on the grounds that the old programs provided only "short-term responses to labor market fluctuations," whereas the new programs concentrated on directing help to individuals who needed it most. Critics of the changes argued that short-term assistance was all that was needed to promote adjustment and that the changes in some cases replaced proadjustment policies with disguised welfare payments, often distributed in a manner more geared to the political interests of the government than to the adjustment needs of the economy.

As global economic competition becomes more and more severe and as new knowledge-driven methods of production spread, the ability to adjust to economic change will become increasingly important.[12] Countries that succeed in the global marketplace, while also managing to maintain humane social welfare systems, will be those that best learn how to *cooperate* with change. This will mean avoiding economic policies that inhibit change while adopting social policies that reduce the human cost of adjusting to change. This is an enormous challenge for future Canadian economic and social policies.

[12] This was one of the main themes emphasized by the Macdonald Commission on Canada's Economic Prospects, whose report was published in 1985.

SUMMARY

1. Unemployment may be voluntary or involuntary. Involuntary unemployment is a serious social concern, both because it causes economic waste due to lost output and because it is a source of human suffering.
2. Looking at causes, it is useful to distinguish among several kinds of unemployment: (a) frictional unemployment, which is caused by the length of time that it takes to find a first job and to move from job to job as a result of normal labor turnover; (b) structural unemployment, which is caused by the need to reallocate resources among occupations, regions, and industries as the structure of demands and supplies changes; (c) cyclical unemployment, which is caused by too low a level of aggregate demand; and (d) real-wage unemployment, which is caused by too high a real product wage. Together, the amounts of frictional unemployment and structural unemployment make up what is now called the NAIRU.
3. There is a great deal of disagreement among economists regarding the causes of persistent cyclical and real-wage unemployment. Recent theories have focused on the long-term nature of employer-worker relationships and on the possibility that it is efficient for employers to pay wages that are above the level that would clear the labor market.
4. Measured unemployment figures may overestimate or underestimate the actual number of unemployed, for they may include some people who are voluntarily unemployed and omit discouraged workers who have left the labor force.
5. The natural rate of unemployment has risen in recent years. This is due in part at least to demographic changes in the work force, increasing wage and price rigidity in the economy, increasingly generous unemployment compensation and other social insurance programs, and increasing structural change in the economy.
6. Unemployment insurance helps to alleviate the human suffering that is associated with inevitable unemployment. It also increases unemployment by encouraging voluntary unemployment.
7. Unemployment can be reduced by raising aggregate demand, by making it easier to move between jobs, by slowing down the rate of change in the economy, and by raising the cost of staying unemployed. However, in a growing, changing economy populated by real people who wish to change jobs for many reasons, it is neither possible nor desirable to reduce unemployment to zero.

TOPICS FOR REVIEW

Voluntary and involuntary unemployment
Cyclical unemployment
Frictional unemployment
Structural unemployment
Real-wage unemployment
Efficiency wages
Hysteresis
Effects of demographic and structural changes on unemployment

DISCUSSION QUESTIONS

1. Interpret the following statements from newspapers in terms of types of unemployment:
   a. "Recession hits local factory; 2,000 laid off."
   b. "A job? I've given up trying," says a mother of three.
   c. "We closed down because we could not meet the competition from Taiwan," says a local manager.
   d. "When they raised the minimum wage, I just could not afford to keep all of these retired policemen on my payroll as security guards," says the owner of a local shopping center.
   e. "Slack sales put local foundry on short time."
   f. "Of course, I could take a job as a dishwasher, but I'm trying to find something that makes use of my high school training," says a local teenager in our survey of the unemployed.
   g. "Retraining main challenge in increased use of robots."
   h. "Modernization and tariff cuts may reduce textile employment."
   i. "Uneven upturn: Signs of recovery in Ontario, but B.C. and the Atlantic provinces still in recession."
2. Discuss the following recommendations made by the Economic Council of Canada in 1990.
   a. "We recommend that reform of the federal government's labor market strategy move in the direction of supporting skill development and employability as the primary objective."
   b. "We recommend that the federal government increase the UI funds available for retraining and relax the eligibility restrictions for training under the UI program."
   c. "We recommend that the federal government allocate increased funds to the Industrial Adjustment Service to be used as 'seed money' for the development of sector-specific human-resource plans in industries that have chosen to initiate such plans."
   d. "We support the adoption of legislation on all jurisdictions that will provide for the inclusion of part-time employees with an ongoing employer attachment, on a prorated basis, in all employee-benefit programs normally available to full-time employees."
   e. "Governments should be alert to the possibility that labor market trends may necessitate further rethinking of the overall approach to retirement income security in the 1990s."
3. Discuss the following views:
   a. "Canadian workers should resist automation, which is destroying their jobs," says a labor leader.
   b. "Given the fierce foreign competition, it's a case of automate or die," says an industrialist.
4. Use the latest *Bank of Canada Review* to compare the percentage of total unemployment that is long-term, in the last year available, with

the figures for earlier years given in the text of this chapter. Can you think of any reasons why the figures have changed?

5. What theories can you suggest to explain why unemployment rates stay persistently above average for youths and below average for males over 25?

6. It is often argued that the true unemployment figure for Canada is much higher than the officially reported figure. What are possible sources of "hidden unemployment"? On the other side, are there reasons for expecting some exaggeration of the number of people who are reported as unemployed? Would the relative strength of these opposing forces change over the course of the business cycle? What would you expect if a short recession turned into a long and deep depression?

7. At a time when the Canadian unemployment rate stood at close to 10 percent, the press reported, "Skilled labor shortage plagues many firms—newspaper ads often draw few qualified workers; wages and overtime are up." What type of unemployment does this suggest is important?

8. What differences in approach toward the problem of unemployment are suggested by the following facts?

a. In the 1960s and 1970s, Britain spent billions of dollars on subsidizing firms that would otherwise have gone out of business, in order to protect the jobs of the employees.

b. Sweden has been a pioneer in spending large sums to retrain and to relocate displaced workers.

Chapter 38

Economic Growth

A dramatically inefficient allocation of resources, such as follows from removing most market price signals for resource allocation, can greatly reduce living standards. This lesson was learned by the countries of Eastern Europe in the decades that followed the Second World War. Removing these extreme inefficiencies, by introducing market-determined prices and allowing individuals to respond to them, can greatly increase living standards once full adjustments are made. However, in economies that already allow the price system to work sufficiently to produce an allocation of resources that is not wildly inefficient,[1] economic growth becomes the single most powerful engine for raising living standards over the decades. This economic growth is the story, in the words of economic historian Nathan Rosenberg, of how the Western countries grew rich:

> Over a year, or even over a decade, the economic gains [of the late eighteenth and the nineteenth centuries], after allowing for the growth of population, were so little noticeable that it was widely believed that the gains were experienced only by the rich, and not by the poor. Only as the West's compounded growth continued through the twentieth century did its breadth become clear. It became obvious that Western working classes were increasingly well off and that the Western middle classes were prospering and growing as a proportion of the whole population. Not that poverty disappeared. The West's achievement was not the abolition of poverty but the reduction of its incidence from 90 percent of the population to 30 percent, 20 percent, or less, depending on the country and one's definition of poverty.[2]

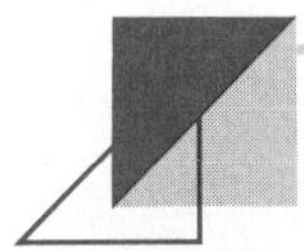

Sources of Increasing Real National Income

Several sources of increases in real national income must be distinguished. Later we shall concentrate on those that cause long-term economic growth.

[1] It is important to be careful about this point. In economies in which prices are not free to adjust to clear markets, the allocation of resources *can be* wildly inefficient. In economies in which prices more or less clear markets and people are more or less free to respond to these price signals, the allocation of resources is much less inefficient. *Perfect* efficiency in resources allocation—what economists call an optimal allocation of resources—requires a set of conditions that cannot be fulfilled by any modern real-world economy.

[2] N. Rosenberg and L. E. Birdzell, Jr., *How the West Grew Rich* (New York: Basic Books, 1986), p. 6.

Shifts in Aggregate Demand and Aggregate Supply

Popular debate is bedeviled by confusion about the various causes of changes in national income. For example, some commentators argue that governments can spend their way into a rising national income, while others argue that although expansionary government policies may stimulate the economy in the short run, they often have adverse effects on growth in the economy in the long run.

Figure 38-1, which reproduces Figure 31-1, illustrates some of the most important possible causes of rising national income. If there is a recessionary gap, raising aggregate demand will yield a once-and-for-all increase in national income. However, once potential income is achieved, further increases in aggregate demand yield only transitory increases in real income but lasting increases in the price level.

Measures that reduce structural unemployment can also increase the employed labor force and thus increase potential income. The resulting increase in income might not be very large, but social gain would result from the reduction in unemployment, especially in the long-term unemployment that occurs when people are trapped in declining areas, industries, or occupations.

Over the long haul, however, the main cause of rising national income is **economic growth**—the increase in potential income due to changes in factor

FIGURE 38-1 Ways of Increasing National Income

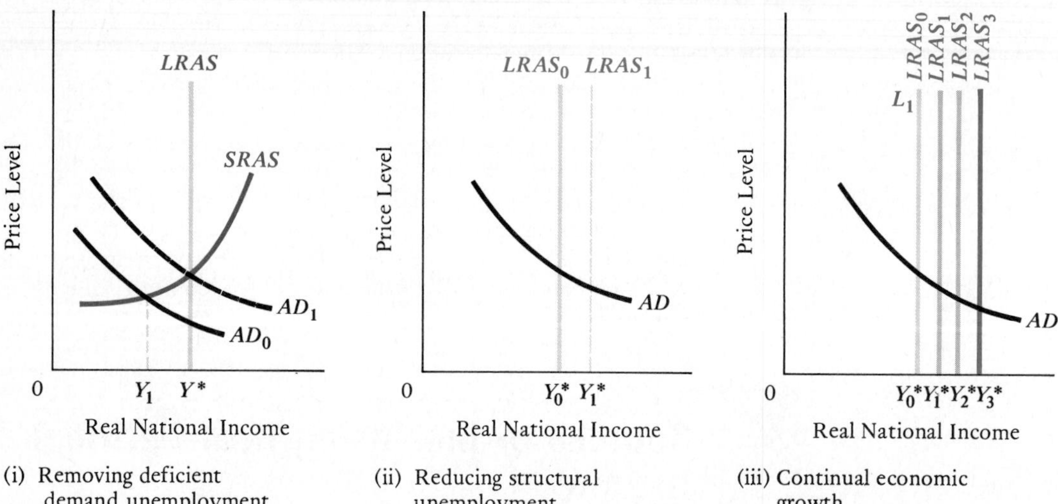

(i) Removing deficient demand unemployment

(ii) Reducing structural unemployment

(iii) Continual economic growth

A once-and-for-all increase in national income can be obtained by raising aggregate demand to remove a recessionary gap or by shifting the *LRAS* curve by cutting structural unemployment. Continued increases in national income are possible by shifting the *LRAS* curve through continued economic growth. In (i), with the aggregate demand curve at AD_0, there is a recessionary gap of Y_1Y^*. An increase in aggregate demand from AD_0 to AD_1 achieves a once-and-for-all increase in national income from Y_1 to Y^*.

In (ii) potential output rises from Y_0^* to Y_1^* due to measures that reduce structural unemployment. The *LRAS* curve shifts from $LRAS_0$ to $LRAS_1$ because people who were formerly unemployed due to having the wrong skills or being in the wrong place are now available for employment.

In (iii) increases in factor supplies and productivity lead to increases in potential income. This *continually* shifts the long-run aggregate supply curve outward. In successive periods it moves from $LRAS_0$ to $LRAS_3$, taking potential income from Y_0^* to Y_1^* to Y_2^*, and so on, as long as growth continues.

supplies (labor and capital) and in the productivity of factors (output per unit of factor input). The removal of a serious recessionary gap or the elimination of all structural unemployment might raise national income by, say, 6 percent. However, a modest growth rate of 3 percent per year raises national income by 10 percent in 3 years and *doubles* it in about 24 years.

Over any long period of time, economic growth, rather than variations in aggregate demand or in structural unemployment, exerts the major effect on real national income.

Saving and Investment

Both saving and investment affect real national income. To understand their influence, it is critical to distinguish between their short-run and long-run effects.

Short-Run and Long-Run Effects of Investment

The theory of income determination that we studied in Part 8 is a short-run theory. It takes potential income as constant and concentrates on the effects of all types of expenditure—including investment—on aggregate demand. The theory thus concentrates on variations of actual national income around a given potential income. This short-term viewpoint is the focus of Figure 38-1(i).

In the long run, by adding to the nation's capital stock, investment raises potential income. This effect is shown by the continuing shift of the *LRAS* curve in Figure 38-1(iii).

The theory of economic growth is a long-run theory. It ignores short-run fluctuations of actual national income around potential income and concentrates on the effects of investment in raising potential income.

The contrast between the short- and long-run aspects of investment is worth emphasizing. In the short run, any activity that puts income into people's hands will raise aggregate demand. Thus the short-run effect on national income is the same whether a firm invests in digging holes and refilling them or in building a new factory. The long-run growth of potential income, however, is affected only by the part of investment that adds to a nation's productive capacity, that is, by the factory but not by the refilled holes.

Similar observations are true of public-sector expenditure. Any expenditure will add to aggregate demand and raise national income if there are unemployed resources, but only some expenditures increase full-employment income. While public investment expenditure on such things as roads and health may do so, expenditure that shores up a declining industry in order to create employment may have an adverse effect on growth. Such expenditure may prevent the reallocation of resources in response to shifts both in the pattern of world demand and in the country's comparative advantage. Thus in the long run the country's capacity to produce commodities that are demanded on open markets may be diminished.

Short-Run and Long-Run Effects of Saving

The short-run effects of an increase in saving are to reduce aggregate demand. If, for example, households elect to save more, this means that they spend less. The resulting downward shift in the consumption function lowers aggregate demand and thus lowers equilibrium national income.

In the longer term, however, higher savings are necessary for higher investment. Firms usually reinvest their own savings, and the savings of households pass to firms, either directly through the purchase of stocks and bonds or indirectly through financial intermediaries. In the long run, the higher the level of savings, the higher the level of investment—and the higher the level of investment, the higher the level of real income due to the accumulation of more and better capital equipment.

In the long run, there is no paradox of thrift; societies with high savings rates have high investment rates and, other things being equal, high levels of real income.

The Cumulative Nature of Growth

Growth is a much more powerful method of raising living standards than the removal of either recessionary gaps or structural unemployment, *because it can go on indefinitely*. For example, a growth rate of 2 percent per year may seem insignificant, but if it continues for a century, it will lead to a more than sevenfold increase in real national income!

BOX 38-1

Case Studies of Rapid Growth: Japan and Korea

The real national income of Japan was 5.4 times as large in 1973 as it was in 1953. During that period, Japan's economic growth rate was more than double the average rate in the 10 major North American and European countries. Starting a little later and from a lower level, Korea also has experienced rapid growth in the past quarter century, and it increasingly rivals Japan in world markets for many manufactured goods. From 1960 through 1985, growth in Korea was even faster than in Japan; real per capita GNP in Korea rose from 12 percent of the U.S. level to 31 percent, while in Japan it rose from 33 to 77 percent.

In one study of Japan's growth success, Edward Denison and William Chung found that no single factor was responsible for Japan's high postwar growth rate. More recently, Rudiger Dornbusch and Yung Chul Park found similar results for Korea; they found that both economies benefited from several major sources of growth: an increase in the quantity and the quality of labor, an increase in the quantity of capital, improved technology in production, and economies of scale. For example, Japan gained more in each of these respects than any of the 10 other countries that were studied by Denison and Chung.*

* E. F. Denison and W. K. Chung, *How Japan's Economy Grew So Fast: The Sources of Postwar Expansion* (Washington, D.C.: Brookings Institution, 1976); R. Dornbusch and Y. C. Park, "Korean Growth Policy," *Brookings Papers on Economic Activity* (1987).

In addition, in both countries employment and output in manufacturing rose much faster than GNP as a whole, with resources being transferred from agriculture to manufacturing. Since productivity is generally higher in manufacturing than in agriculture, a shift of this kind raises average productivity and thereby contributes to growth even without an increase in output per person in either sector. This is a source of overall productivity gain that the United States and Canada enjoyed—and exhausted—in the first half of the twentieth century.

Both expansions have been characterized by an exceptional rise in exports and by high investment spending as a share of GNP. Both countries have pursued activist policies of import restrictions, subsidies, and credit allocation aimed at encouraging manufacturing and export industries in particular. The allocation of investment was, to a degree, centrally directed through subsidies and credit allocation; although some mistakes were made in the process, for the most part investment was concentrated in sectors that developed into highly competitive export industries.

Dornbusch and Park argue that Korea's success had depended on the interaction of that investment strategy with its educated work force and wage moderation. Koreans work an average of 54 hours per week, and the educational level of the work force has risen steadily since 1960. Although unit labor costs in Korean manufacturing rose sharply during the 1970s relative to those in Japan and in

The cumulative effect of small annual growth rates is large.

To appreciate the cumulative effect of what seem to be very small differences in growth rates, examine Table 38-1. Notice that if one country grows faster than another, the gap in their respective standards will widen progressively. If, for example, countries A and B start from the same level of income and if country A grows at 3 percent per year while country B grows at 2 percent per year, A's income per capita will be twice B's in 72 years. You may not think that it matters much whether the economy grows at 2 percent or 3 percent per year, but your children and grandchildren will! (A helpful approximation device is the *rule of 72*. Divide 72 by the annual growth rate, and the result is approximately the number of years that it will take for income to double.) **[43]**

Canada, Korea continued to expand the range and total volume of its manufacturing exports. Investment and a large pool of skilled workers allowed the Korean manufacturing sector to expand and to employ advanced technology that had been developed abroad. Although relative unit labor costs were rising on average, labor costs continued to be low in the manufacturing sectors in which Korean workers were employed with the newest technology and ample capital. This, together with a policy that maintained an undervalued exchange rate, led to improved competitiveness over a growing range of manufactured goods.

The remarkable growth records of Korea and Japan were possible partly because of their low initial *levels* of productivity. It is easier to improve from a low base than from a high one. Productivity is still much lower in Japan and Korea than in Canada, even after eliminating the effects of differences between the countries in working hours, composition and allocation of the labor force, amounts of capital and land, size of markets, and cyclical positions of the two economies. There is thus an obvious potential for still further growth in those countries relative to Canada.

Toward the end of the 1980s Korea experienced a wage explosion that took money wages up by as much as 30 percent per year. This rise in money costs, combined with an appreciation of the Korean currency, put its export industries at a severe competitive disadvantage. It was not immediately clear how quickly the economy could overcome these setbacks.

A question is, then, "Can Japan's and Korea's growth rates be sustained?" While the probability of a decline in the growth rate as the various ways of securing fast growth by "catching up" are successively exhausted, the potential remains for fairly high rates of long-term growth throughout the rest of this century. (Denison and Chung's prediction of continued Japanese growth of between 5 and 8 pecent per year proved accurate for the decade following the period covered by their study.) If these rates do continue, by the year 2000, Japan will be enjoying the highest standard of living of any industrialized country in the world, and Korea will not be far behind.

The experiences of two high-growth economies, Japan and Korea, are discussed in Box 38-1.

Economic Growth, Efficiency, and Redistribution

Observing that economic growth is the most important force for raising living standards over the long term in no way implies that policies designed to increase economic efficiency or to redistribute income are unimportant.

If at any moment in time national income could be increased by removing certain inefficiencies, such gains would be valuable. After all, any increase in national income is welcome in a world where many wants go unsatisfied. Furthermore, inefficiencies may themselves serve to reduce the growth rate. For example, the policy of rent control, which can be

TABLE 38-1 The Cumulative Effect of Growth

	Rate of growth per year				
Year	1%	2%	3%	5%	7%
0	100	100	100	100	100
10	111	122	135	165	201
30	135	182	246	448	817
50	165	272	448	1,218	3,312
70	201	406	817	3,312	13,429
100	272	739	2,009	14,841	109,660

Small differences in growth rates make enormous differences in levels of potential national income over a few decades. Assume that potential national income is 100 in year 0. At a rate of growth of 3 percent per year, it will be 135 in 10 years, 448 after 50 years, and over 2,000 in a century. The compounding of sustained rates of growth is a powerful force!

criticized for violating efficiency conditions in the housing market, can also be criticized for reducing the geographical mobility of labor that is a necessary part of the growth process.

Next consider redistribution. Economic growth has made the poor vastly better off than they would have been if they had lived 100 years ago. Yet that is little consolation when they see that they cannot afford the basic medical treatment for themselves or schooling for their children that is currently available to higher-income citizens. After all, people compare themselves with others in their own society, not with their counterparts at other times or in other places. Because we care about relative differences among individuals, we continue to have policies to redistribute income and to make such basic services as health and education available to everyone, at least to some minimum acceptable degree.

Nonetheless, over the long term,

The income-raising potential of economic growth vastly exceeds that of removing inefficiencies or redistributing the existing national income.

Interrelations among the policies. Economists once assumed that the policies of redistributing income, increasing efficiency, and ensuring growth could each be treated separately. For example, policies that cause extreme inefficiencies or a distribution of income unrelated to the market value of work can adversely affect the growth rate. It follows that policies designed to reduce inefficiencies or redistribute income need to be examined carefully for any effects that they may have on growth. A policy that reduces growth *may* be a bad bargain, even if it increases the immediate efficiency of the economy or creates a more equitable distribution of income. Consider a hypothetical redistributive policy that raises the incomes of lower-income people by 5 percent but lowers the rate of economic growth from 2 to 1 percent. In 10 years those who gained from the policy would be no better off than if they had not received the redistribution of income while the growth rate had remained at 2 percent (and, of course, everyone who did not gain from the redistribution would be worse off from the beginning). After 20 years' time, those who had gained from the redistribution would have 5 percent more of a national income that was 12 percent smaller than it would have been if the growth rate had remained at 2 percent.

Conversely, a policy that creates a more equitable distribution of income at only a small cost in terms of a lower growth rate may be judged a good, or at least an acceptable, trade-off. Deciding among such competing policy goals requires value judgments that take us beyond economics. Economists play an important part, however, in establishing these interrelationships. Misguided policies are likely to be followed if policymakers think that measures adopted to get closer to any one of these goals will have no effect on the others.

Of course, not all redistribution policies have unfavorable effects on the growth rate. Some may have no effect, and others—by raising health and educational standards of ordinary workers—may raise the growth rate. Some related policy issues are discussed in Box 38-2.

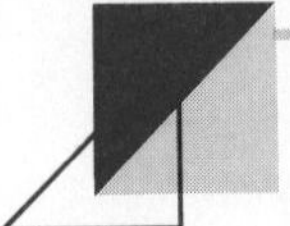

Theories of Economic Growth

So far we have learned (1) that long-term growth is associated with shifts in the aggregate supply curve, (2) that these shifts are positively related to savings and investment, and (3) that such growth is a powerful determinant of changes in long-term living standards.[3]

In the rest of this chapter we study long-term growth, its causes and its consequences.

Neo-Classical Growth Theories

The distinguishing feature of the so-called neo-Classical view of growth is the existence of diminishing returns to investment: Each unit of investment is presumed to add less to production than each subsequent unit. In the neo-Classical view of growth, innovation is a key factor. To understand its importance, we first study a world without it.

Growth Without Innovation

Suppose that there is a known and fixed stock of projects that might be undertaken. Suppose also that nothing ever happens to increase either the supply of such projects or knowledge about them. Whenever the moment is right, some of the investment opportunities are used, thereby increasing the stock of capital goods and depleting the reservoir of unused investment opportunities. Of course, the most productive opportunities will be used first.

Such a view of investment opportunities can be represented by a fixed marginal efficiency of capital (*MEC*) schedule of the kind presented in Chapter 18. Such a schedule is graphed in Figure 38-2. It relates the stock of capital to the productivity of an additional unit of capital. The productivity of a unit of capital is calculated by dividing the annual value of the additional output resulting from an extra unit of capital by the value of that unit of capital. Thus, for example, a marginal efficiency of capital of 0.2 means that a dollar of new capital adds 20 cents per year to the stream of output.

The downward slope of the *MEC* schedule indicates that with knowledge being held constant, increases in the stock of capital bring smaller and smaller increases in output per unit of capital; that is, the rate of return on successive units of capital declines. This shape is a consequence of the law of diminishing returns, which was first discussed in Chapter 10.

[3] The whole section on the very long run in Chapter 11 could be read now and treated as part of this chapter.

FIGURE 38-2 The Marginal Efficiency of Capital Schedule

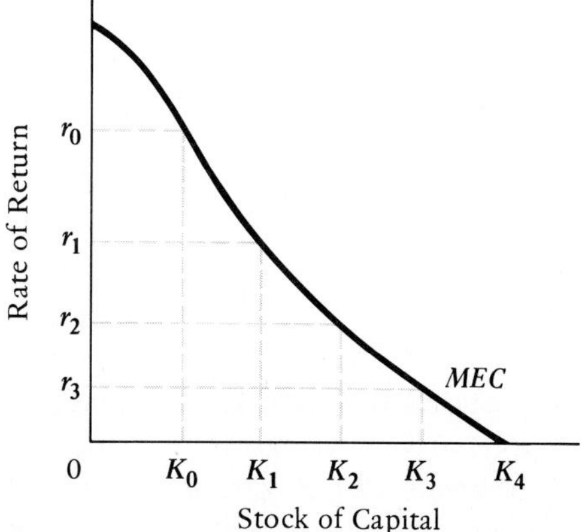

A negatively sloped *MEC* schedule shows that successive increases to the capital stock bring smaller and smaller increases in output and thus a declining rate of return. A fixed *MEC* schedule can represent the theory of growth in an economy with some unused investment opportunities but no learning. Increases in investment that increase the capital stock from K_0 to K_1 to . . . K_4 lower the rate of return from r_0 to r_1 to . . . zero. Because the productivity of successive units of capital decreases, the capital-output ratio rises.

If, with land, labor, and knowledge being held constant, more and more capital is used, the net amount added by successive increments will diminish and may eventually reach zero. As capital is accumulated in a state of constant knowledge, the society will move down its *MEC* schedule. In such a "nonlearning" world, in which new investment opportunities do not appear, growth occurs only so long as there are unutilized opportunities to use capital effectively in order to increase output.

So far we have discussed the *marginal* efficiency of capital. The *average* efficiency of capital refers to the average amount produced in the whole economy per unit of capital employed. It is common in discussions of the theory of growth to talk in terms of the *capital-output ratio*, which is the reciprocal of output per unit of capital. In a world without learning, the capital-output ratio increases.

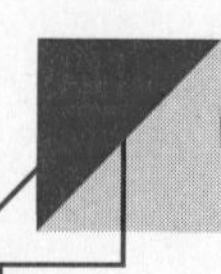

BOX 38-2

Policy Options Concerning Economic Growth

As in most areas of economic policy, sharp differences arise between strategists who wish to let market forces determine the economy's growth and those who favor government intervention.

Some economists, often referred to as *supply siders*, feel that in a stable environment free from government interference, growth will take care of itself. Large firms will spend a lot of money on research and development. Where they fail, or where they suppress inventions to protect monopoly positions, the genius of backyard inventors will come up with new ideas and will develop new companies to challenge the positions of the established giants. Left to itself, the economy will prosper as it has in the past, provided only that an inquiring scientific spirit and the profit motive are not suppressed.

Other economists, whom we may call *interventionists*, are less certain about the ability of market forces to produce growth. They recognize the importance of invention and innovation, but they fear the dead hand of monopoly and cautious business practices that choose security over risk taking. Therefore, the state needs at the very least to give a nudge here or there to help the growth process along.

Interventionists thus tend to support general policies that make the macroeconomic climate favorable to growth. They typically promote subsidization or favorable tax treatment for research and development or for the purchasing of plant and equipment. Measures to lower interest rates temporarily or permanently are also often urged as favorable to investment and growth. Conservatives argue that such government intervention only reduces market efficiency.

The Broader Supply-Side Agenda

Given the large web of government rules, regulations, and perverse tax incentives that has grown over many years, the supply-side agenda for promoting growth includes *opposition* to a number of existing policies thought to inhibit growth. In an assessment of the supply-side proposal to eliminate each of these policies, problems arise in evaluating the existence and importance of the alleged harmful effects of each policy and, since the government needs revenue, in finding alternative revenue sources that will have less harmful effects than the ones being criticized.

Reduce support for declining industries. Supporting declining industries causes resources that could be employed more productively elsewhere to leave the industry more slowly. Most economists agree that such policies are costly, harmful to growth, and self-defeating in the end.

Picking winners. Some interventionists support what is called *picking* and *backing* winners in one

In a world without learning, growth in the capital stock will lead to a continually declining marginal efficiency of capital and a rising capital output ratio. Eventually the MEC may reach zero, bringing the growth of output to a complete halt.

Growth with Innovation

The steady depletion of growth opportunities with constant knowledge results from the assumption that new investment opportunities are never discovered or created. In fact, investment opportunities are continually created as well as used up with the passage of time. As a result the *MEC* schedule shifts outward over time, so that the effects of increasing the capital stock are offset by the shifting *MEC* curve, as illustrated in Figure 38-3.

Researchers develop basic ideas for new ways of producing existing products or wholly new products Firms spend money to develop these ideas into usable

way or another. Advocates of this view, such as Professor Lester Thurow of the Massachusetts Institute of Technology, want governments to pick the industries (usually new ones) that have potential for future success and then to back them with subsidies, government contracts, research funds, and all the other encouragements at the government's command.

Supply siders argue that picking winners requires foresight and that there is no reason to expect that the government will have better foresight than private investors. Indeed, since political considerations inevitably get in the way, the government may be less successful than the market in picking winners. If so, channeling funds through the government rather than through the private sector may hurt rather than help growth rates. However, some supporters respond that since governments in other countries pursue such policies, even if our own policies are imperfect, we harm our competitive position relative to state-supported foreign producers if we fail to respond with policies of our own.

High rates of income tax. Supply siders allege that high taxes discourage work. Yet the effect of high taxes may actually be one of making people work either harder or less hard. Theory is silent on which is more likely, and no hard evidence has yet shown that lowering current tax rates makes people work harder. Many elements of the tax reform that was introduced in 1987, which saw tax bases broadened and tax rates reduced, were well received by supply siders. Tax changes that encouraged saving were also widely viewed as being progrowth.

Taxing consumption, not savings. Savings are a cause of investment and growth. Currently, income is taxed when it is earned and saved, and the return is taxed again when it accrues to the investor. Supply-side reformers would tax consumption only. Savings would be untaxed; taxes would be collected only when the income produced by savings was consumed. Aside from increasing equity by removing the double taxation of savings, this policy would encourage economic growth by encouraging domestic saving and investment.

Policy Agreement

One important potential area of agreement can be identified. As we will see later in this chapter (see especially Box 38-3), a number of economists have recently stressed the importance of "knowledge," broadly defined, as a key difference between high-growth, high-income countries and low-growth, low-income ones. If this view prevails, many supply-side economists might in principle come to support government intervention that encourages "learning" and technological advance.

form. Together such research and development (R&D) provides a fund of new investment opportunities. When learning occurs, what matters is how rapidly the *MEC* schedule shifts relative to the amount of capital investment being undertaken.

Gradual reduction in investment opportunities: The Classical view. If, as in Figure 38-3(i), investment opportunities are created, but at a slower rate than they are used up, there will be a tendency toward a falling rate of return and an increasing ratio of capital to output. The predictions in this case are the same as those given for the world without learning.

This figure illustrates the theory of growth that was held by most early economists. They saw the economic problem as one of fixed land, a rising population, and a gradual exhaustion of investment opportunities. These conditions, they believed, would ultimately force the economy into a static situation, with no growth, high capital-output ratios, and the

FIGURE 38-3 **Shifting Investment Opportunities: Three Cases**

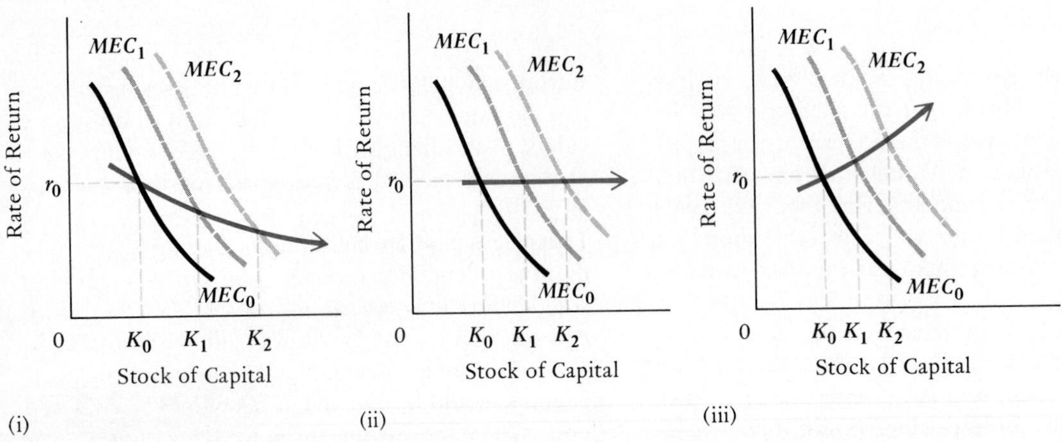

When both knowledge and the capital stock grow, the actual marginal efficiency of capital depends on their relative rates of growth. In each case the economy at period 0 has the MEC_0 curve, a capital stock of K_0, and a rate of return of r_0. In period 1 the curve shifts to MEC_1 and there is investment to increase the stock of capital to K_1. In period 2 the curve shifts to MEC_2 and new investment increases the capital stock to K_2. It is the relative size of the shift of the *MEC* curve and the additions of the capital stock that are important.

In (i) investment occurs more rapidly than increases in investment opportunities, and the rate of return falls along the colored arrow. In (iii) investment occurs less rapidly than increases in investment opportunities, and the rate of return rises along the colored arrow. Part (ii) is the borderline case where investment and investment opportunities increase at the same rate, which means that the rate of return is constant along the colored line.

marginal return on additional units of capital forced downward toward zero.

Constant or rising investment opportunities: The contemporary view. The pessimism of the Classical economists came from their failure to anticipate the possibility of really rapid innovation—of technological progress that could push investment opportunities outward as they were used up or even more rapidly, as shown in parts (ii) and (iii) of Figure 38-3.

In a world with rapid innovation:

1. **Successive increases in capital accumulation may prove highly productive, and the capital-output ratio may be constant or decreasing.**
2. **Despite large amounts of capital accumulation, the marginal efficiency of new capital may remain constant or even increase as new investment opportunities are created.**

The historical record suggests that outward shifts in investment opportunities over time lead to the reality of sustained growth. Evidently, modern economies have been successful in generating new investment opportunities at least as rapidly as old ones were used up.

Increasing Returns Theories

The neo-Classical theories assume that investment is always subject to diminishing returns. Some modern theories have emphasized the possibility of *increasing returns to investment.*

A number of sources of increasing returns can be noted. (1) Early investment in a country, province, or town may result in new skills and attitudes in the work force that are then available to all subsequent investors and lower their costs below those encountered by early investors. (2) Each new investor may find the environment more and more favorable to its investment because the infrastructure has been created by those who came before. (3) The first investment in a new product may encounter countless problems of production and of product acceptance among customers that, once overcome, cause no problems to subsequent investors. All of these cases, and many more that could be mentioned, are examples of a single phenomenon:

Many investments require fixed costs, the advantages of which are then available to other investors; this can make the investment costs for "followers" substantially less than the investment costs for "pioneers."[4]

More generally, many of the sources of increasing returns are variations on the following single general theme: Doing something really new is difficult, both technically and in terms of customer acceptance, while making further variations on an accepted and developed new idea become progressively easier—both because the costly knowledge developed by earlier pioneers often becomes freely available to followers and because customer resistance is slowly eroded. This leads to the following net result:

For many reasons, successive increments of investment in a whole country, in one industry, and in one firm may often yield a range of increasing returns as costs that are incurred in earlier investment expenditure provide publicly available knowledge and as customer attitudes become more receptive to new products.[5]

[4] The general phenomenon discussed here has been the object of intense study since the early 1970s. Increasing returns to scale result from fixed costs of developing any activity, be it one product or a whole financial sector in one town; the results of development exenditures are then available to all subsequent investors in that activity.

[5] Slow acceptance of new products by customers is not necessarily irrational. When a sophisticated new product comes on the market, no one is sure if it will be a success, and the first customers to buy it take the risk that the product may subsequently be regarded as a failure. They also incur the costs of learning how to use it effectively. Many potential users take the not unreasonable attitude of letting others try a new product and follow only after the product's success has been demonstrated.

Further Causes of Growth

So far we have looked at capital accumulation as a cause of growth in worlds with and without innovation. Contemporary studies suggest that other causes of growth are also important.

Quantity of Capital Per Worker

Human beings always have been tool users. It is still true that more and more tools tend to lead to more and more output. As long as a society has unexploited investment opportunities, productive capacity can be increased by increasing the stock of capital. The effect on output per worker of "mere" capital accumulation is so noticeable that it was once regarded as virtually the sole source of growth.

However, if capital accumulation were the only source of growth, it would lead to movement down the *MEC* schedule and to a rising capital-output ratio and a falling rate of return on capital. The evidence does not support these predictions. The facts suggest that investment opportunities have expanded at least as rapidly as investments in capital goods, roughly along the pattern of Figure 38-3(ii). While capital accumulation has taken place and has accounted for much observed growth, it cannot have been the only source of growth.

Quality of Capital: Innovation

New knowledge and inventions can contribute markedly to the growth of potential national income, even without capital accumulation. To see this, assume that the proportion of the society's resources that is devoted to the production of capital goods is just sufficient to replace capital as it wears out. Thus if the old capital were merely replaced in the same form, the capital stock would be constant, and there would be no increase in the capacity to produce. However, if there were a growth of knowledge, so that as old equipment wore out it was replaced by different, more productive equipment, national income would be growing.

Increases in productive capacity that are intrinsic to the form of capital goods in use are called **embodied technical change**. The historical importance of embodied technical change is clear: The assembly line and automation transformed much of manufacturing, the airplane revolutionized transportation, and electronic devices now dominate the information technology industries. These innovations plus less well known but no less profound ones—for example, improvements in the strength of metals, the productivity of seeds, and the techniques for recovering basic raw materials from the ground—create new investment opportunities.

Less obvious but nonetheless important changes occur through **disembodied technical change**, that is, changes in the organization of production that are not embodied in the form of the capital goods or raw materials used. One example is improved techniques of managerial control.

Most innovations involve both embodied and disembodied changes. Whatever the form of innovation, the nature of the goods and services consumed and the way in which they are made change continually as innovations occur. Major innovations of the past century have resulted from the development of such key products as the telephone, the automobile, the airplane, plastics, the assembly line, the coaxial cable, xerography, the computer, the transistor, and the silicon chip. It would be hard for us to imagine life without them.

Modern economists debate how to incorporate innovation into their theories. The neo-Classical view is that innovation shifts the *MEC* curve and that investment moves the economy downward along that curve. Some modern theories, of the type discussed under the heading of "Increasing Returns Theories," imply that this neo-Classical view may be misleading. In these newer theories, an initial investment in any new line of endeavor yields less to its owners than it costs, whereas subsequent investment in similar lines yields more than it costs.

If this latter view is confirmed by careful empirical studies, it will have profound implications for our views on how growing economies behave and on how government policies can affect growth.

The Quality of Labor

The "quality" of labor—or what is often called *human capital*—has several aspects. One involves improvements in the health and longevity of the population. Of course, these are desired as ends in themselves, but they have consequences for both the size and the productivity of the labor force. There is no doubt that they have increased productivity per worker-hour by cutting down on illness, accidents, and absenteeism. At the same time, the extension of the normal life span, with no comparable increase in the working life span, has created a larger group of retired persons that exercises a claim on total output. Whether health improvements alone have increased output per capita in Canada is not clear.

A second aspect of the quality of human capital concerns technical training, from learning to operate a machine to learning how to be a scientist. Training is clearly required to invent, operate, manage, and repair complex machines. More subtly, there are often believed to be general social advantages to an educated population. It has been shown that productivity improves with literacy and that in general, the longer a person has been educated, the more adaptable, and thus, in the long run, the more productive that person is to new and changing challenges. However, education may also increase feelings of alienation in a society that is thought to be arbitrary or unjust. Box 38-3 explores some related issues that arise from recent research on *endogenous* growth.

The Quantity of Labor

The size of a country's population and the extent of its participation in the labor force affect the quantity of a factor of production. For any given state of knowledge and supplies of other factors of production, the size of the population can affect the level of output per capita. Every child born has both a mouth and a pair of hands; over a lifetime each person will be both a consumer and a producer. Thus, on average, it is meaningful to speak of overpopulated or underpopulated economies, depending on whether the contribution to production of additional people would raise or lower the level of per capita income.

Because population size is related to income per capita, we can define a theoretical concept, *optimal population*, that maximizes income per capita.

Many countries have or have had conscious population policies. Canada has consistently sought immigrants, as did Australia until recently. Greece in the 1950s and 1960s tried to stem emigration to Western Europe. All are examples of countries that believed that they had an insufficient population, though the motives were not in every case purely economic. In contrast, many less developed countries in South America, Africa, and Asia desire to limit population growth.

Structural Change

Changes in the economy's structure can cause large fluctuations in its growth rate. For example, an expansion in such a low-productivity sector as personal services and a decline in such a high-productivity sector as manufacturing will temporarily lower the measured aggregate growth rate.

When one type of energy (say, solar) supplants another type (say, oil), much existing capital stock specifically geared to the original energy source may become too costly to operate and will be scrapped. New capital, geared to the new energy source, will be built. During the transition, investment expenditure is high, thus stimulating aggregate demand, but there is little, if any expansion in the economy's output capacity because the old capital goods have been scrapped. Gross investment is high, but net investment is low, since the capital expenditure *transforms* the capital stock but does not *increase* it. Similarly, new pollution control laws will affect investment expenditure but will not lead to growth in capacity. (The reduction in pollution may nonetheless be socially desirable.)

A rise in the international price of *imported* energy will also lower productivity. Although the same volume of goods can be produced with a given input of labor, a smaller portion of the output's value now accrues as income to domestic workers and firms because more must be used to pay for the energy imports. The higher-priced imported energy input means that domestic *value added* falls and with it GDP per worker. This shows up in the statistics as a decline in productivity and a temporary fall in growth rates.

These are some of the many factors that were operative in the 1970s and early 1980s. They worked to depress growth rates for some considerable period of time, but they are not permanent factors. When the structural adjustments are complete, their depressing effects will pass. Further, many of the effects were reversed when oil prices fell in early 1986, giving a boost to the productivity of many domestic factors of production.

Institutional Considerations

Almost all aspects of a country's institutions can foster or deter the efficient use of a society's natural and human resources. Social and religious habits, legal institutions, and traditional patterns of national and international trade are all important. So, too, is the political climate.

Historians of economic growth, such as Nathan Rosenberg, attribute much of the growth of the Western economies in the postmedieval world to the development of *new institutions* such as the joint-stock company and limited liability. Many students of modern growth suggest that institutions are as important today as they were in the past. They suggest that the societies that are most successful in developing the new institutions that are needed in today's knowledge-intensive world of globalized competition will be the ones in the forefront of new economic growth.

Among the major contributors to rapid economic growth are a capital stock that is steadily growing and improving in quality, a healthy and well-educated labor force, and a rate of population growth that is small enough to permit per capita growth in capital and, most important, the capacity to develop and market new innovations in products and production processes.

These factors are likely to be more effective in some institutional settings than in others.

Though much remains to be learned about economic growth, an important tentative conclusion of recent studies is that improvements in the quality of capital—human as well as physical—have played a larger role than increases in the quantity of capital in the economic growth of Canada and the United States since 1900. Whether quality, rather than quantity, of capital is also the more important source of growth for countries with different cultural patterns, more acute population problems, or more limited natural resources is a matter of continuing research.

Growth and Competitiveness in Advanced Industrial Economies

Recent shifts in apparent competitive advantage among industrial nations have aroused an active debate about the sources of continued growth in advanced industrial countries. In particular, many industries in the United States and some in Canada worry about losing their competitive edge to firms

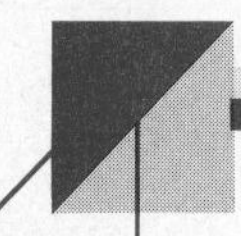

BOX 38-3

Endogenous Growth Models

During the 1950s, economists began to develop mathematical models to aid their understanding of economic growth. The simplest version of the resulting "neo-Classical" growth model treated the economy's output as if it were a single good, produced from homogeneous capital and labor through an "aggregate production function." The stock of capital grew as a result of saving and investment, and the labor force grew with increases in the population. Because the marginal efficiency of capital was assumed to fall as the stock of capital per head rose (see Figure 38-2), balanced growth—called a "steady state"—was reached when the increases in output due to investment just balanced the growth in the labor force. Thus the capital stock and total output both grew at the same rate as the labor force, and *output per head was constant.* Thus as far as per capita real income growth is concerned (the growth on which personal welfare depends), neo-Classical growth models are models of *nongrowth.*

Though this simple neo-Classical growth model has proved valuable for helping to understand the behavior of growing economies, it has a number of unsatisfactory characteristics.

First, the evidence suggests that the accumulation of capital and growth in the labor force accounts for only a small part of the growth in total and per capita output that most advanced industrialized economies enjoyed in the post–World War II period. The residual, representing the excess of actual over "explained" growth, was dubbed the "measure of our ignorance," and it was substantial. This problem was resolved by assuming that the economy experienced *exogenous* technical progress: As time passed, productivity increased and hence growth in total output exceeded growth in inputs, and output per head rose. (The key difference between this model and that of the first paragraph is that in the first model there is no "learning.")

Second, and related, is the criticism that the model does not really explain the rate of growth of the economy: Since the population and technical growth rates are both *exogenous,* so is the rate of growth. Hence no predictions of the rate of growth or the variables that affect it are possible. For example, changes in the rate of saving in this model do not change the equilibrium rate of growth but only change per capita GDP in the steady state.

Third, since most technology can flow quite freely across borders, and since technical change plays a key role in explaining growth, the model predicts that the growth rate of per capita GDP in various countries will converge to a worldwide constant. This prediction is at odds with the evidence of wide and persistent differences between individual countries' growth rates.

In reaction to these weaknesses, economists such s Gene Grossman, Elhanan Helpman, and Paul Romer have recently developed models of *endogenous* growth. These models stress the role of learning and investment in knowledge in influencing technical change and hence the rate of growth of the economy.

Knowledge is treated as a capital good: An individual firm's production is a function of the firm's own level of knowledge and of the stock of knowl-

in Japan and Western Europe. An entire new field of study has grown up concerning competitiveness in advanced industrial countries and the relation between competitiveness and economic growth.

The modern industrial world is dominated by a number of key characteristics. (1) Transnational corporations control much of production and can locate their production of individual components of any one commodity wherever costs are lowest.[6] (2) This leads to globalized competition among transnational firms whereby firms in one country compete with firms in many other countries. (3) In contrast, much innovative activity is done by individual entrepre-

[6] See Box 9-1 on page 178 for further discussion of the importance of transnationals.

edge in the economy. The stock of knowledge creates an *externality* in production: Firms that did not create it nonetheless benefit from it. The externality means that accumulation does not force the economy to move downward along a negatively sloped *MEC* curve, as in Figure 38-2, but rather along a horizontal or rising path, such as shown by the arrow in parts (ii) and (iii) of Figure 38-3. For example, the accumulation of human capital by one worker, or one group of workers, might increase not only that worker's or group's own productivity but also that of others in the economy who now work in a better-trained work force. Further, those others may find that the returns to further investment in their own human capital have increased. Thus an increase in the stock of knowledge may set up a series of actions that *permanently* increase the level and rate of growth of output.

The external effects of knowledge mean that an initial investment in human capital can make further investments more productive; thus increased savings in the form of investment in human capital can permanently increase the economy's rate of growth.

The possibility for the level and rate of growth of output to be *permanently* affected by shocks is often referred to as *hysteresis* in the growth process.

Another possibility, captured by these models, is *learning by doing* in production, whereby productivity in an industry increases with the cumulative volume of production in that industry. (This is discussed in detail in Chapter 21.) Learning by doing means that countries with initial high levels of skill can specialize in producing products that permit faster accumulation of human capital and thus have permanently higher rates of growth than those specializing in lower-growth industries.

These models also point to ways in which economies can increase their rates of growth. Government investment in infrastructure, such as roads, airports, and other communication and transportation networks, as well as schools and training centers, can affect growth.* In particular, the models stress that the accumulation of human capital should be fostered through both specific worker training and general education. Also, an immigration policy that discriminates in favor of highly trained, skilled workers could raise the general level of productivity and enhance growth.

The importance of government investment in infrastructure highlights the fact that not all government spending is the same. For example, a government that spends less and therefore creates fewer jobs in the short run but provides the economic underpinnings for private-sector investment may eventually produce higher standards of living through increased growth. Furthermore, too much government expenditure can reduce growth opportunities, just as too little can.

* The development of cities and their tremendous capacity for the generation of wealth is often cited as an example of the external effects of human capital.

neurs, who raise their capital in angel markets and, as they grow, look to more traditional capital markets for funds.[7] (4) As new firms with new ideas succeed, they look to becoming globally competitive; at this point, it is often more profitable to sell the firm, with its ideas, to an established transnational rather than to incur the enormous cost of developing a global marketing organization to sell the firm's product. (5) Much modern production—both in transnational and in small, innovating firms—is knowledge-intensive; it will go where the human

[7] Angels are individuals who have money and who wish to finance risky new entrepreneurial activities. Venture capital brokers introduce angels to entrepreneurs with the object of financing new firms to exploit a new idea. There are well-developed angel markets in most countries, including Canada.

capital is and where that capital is supplied cheapest; traditional natural resource motivations for industrial location are becoming less and less important in many lines of production. (6) In today's rapidly changing, globally competitive world, each firm's competitive advantage increasingly depends on its ability to innovate at a rate sufficiently rapid to stay on the cutting edge of product and production process development.

For these and many more reasons, governments of many advanced nations, including Canada, are asking themselves what is needed to sustain competitive advantage in a rapidly evolving world and thereby sustain economic growth. Some consensus views have emerged: (1) Market incentives must be stressed—subsidization and other traditional supports end up supporting industries that cannot compete over the long term. (2) Many government policies inhibit competitiveness and need to be revised. (3) Climate-type encouragement to innovative activity is valuable—examples are changes in the tax system to tax consumption rather than savings; keeping capital gains taxes to moderate levels; and reducing double taxation of firm income so that when corporations pay taxes, these are fully deductible by the individuals who own corporate equities. (4) To the extent that future production will be knowledge-intensive, comparative advantage in advanced, high-value-added, high-wage-producing industries may be determined by educational systems; on this count Canada, with its high rate of functional illiteracy and innumeracy, must worry about becoming a lower-value-added, lower-wage-generating country similar to today's less developed economies.

Broad incentives, such as encouraging both R&D and overall savings, as well as altering education to produce more people trained to provide comparative advantage in knowledge-intensive industries, seem productive.

Debate continues over more specific policies. Should governments pick specific industrial winners and back them? The evidence is that they should not, for two reasons. First, there is no evidence that civil servants risking taxpayers' money will do better than private investors risking their own money. Second, when given the chance to exercise discretion, governments often make decisions directed to winning the next election rather than maximizing economic advantage.

If governments are not to back winning firms, should they not back winning activities? They could, for example, give tax advantages to R&D. The case for encouraging more R&D than the market would provide lies with what microeconomists call externalities. In our earlier discussion of increasing returns in the growth process, we saw that the results of early R&D are often freely available to firms that enter the market at a later date. This means that the initial firms create valuable knowledge with their R&D that they cannot fully appropriate in their own profits. To the extent that the value of their R&D is not translated into their own private incomes, they will invest in less R&D than is socially desirable. There is then a case for encouragement of R&D activity by the state. The case is not to back particular R&D ventures, which requires the state to act as an entrepreneur, but to reduce the cost of all R&D so that the private cost to the firm reflects only the benefits it is able to appropriate for itself and not the benefits it is freely providing to others.

A more vexing problem involves foreign government interventions into the processes of growth, competition, and innovation that have been rejected by the domestic government—such as direct subsidies to specific innovating firms. If some governments are engaging in a host of such interventionist industrial policies, can other governments afford to leave all such activity to market forces? It is all very well to say that the market is the best arbitrator of success or failure, but if other governments are playing an intervention game, won't firms in countries with noninterventionist governments be outcompeted by subsidized firms in the interventionist countries? Does this not provide a reason for the Canadian government to copy the behavior of interventionist governments just to put its entrepreneurial players on a level playing field with those in the interventionist countries? Possibly it does. Yet if direct detailed government intervention is counterproductive, the argument that what one country does, others must do in self-defense will lead to a high world level of unproductive intervention.[8]

[8] This is similar to the problem that arises with tariffs. Everyone agrees that a high level of world tariffs is harmful to all the world's trading nations. Yet one country can sometimes gain a selfish advantage by levying tariffs. If one country does so, others are likely to follow in self-defense. The net result can be rounds of tariffs that end up lowering all countries' living standards.

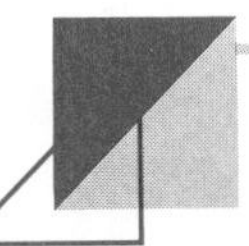

Benefits and Costs of Growth

The remainder of this chapter outlines some more general considerations concerning economic growth. We start by looking at the benefits and then the costs of growth. Boxes 38-4 and 38-5 outline the popular arguments on both sides of the growth debate.

Benefits of Growth

Growth in Living Standards

A country whose per capita output grows at 3 percent per year doubles its living standards about every 24 years.

A primary reason for wanting growth is to raise general living standards.

The extreme importance of economic growth in raising income can be illustrated by comparing the real income of a father with the real income of the son who follows in his father's footsteps. If the son neither rises nor falls in the relative income scale compared with his father, his share of the country's national income will be the same as his father's. If the son is 30 years younger than his father, he can expect to have a real income that is nearly twice as large as the one that his father enjoyed when his father was the same age. These figures assume that the father and the son live in a country such as Canada where the growth rate has been 2 or 3 percent per year. If they live in Japan, where growth has been going on at a rate of about 8 percent per year, the son's income will be about 10 times as large as his father's.

For those who share in it, growth is a powerful weapon against poverty. A family that is earning $15,000 today can expect an income of $22,000 within 10 years (in constant dollars) if it shares in a mere 4 percent growth rate. The transformation of the life-style of blue-collar workers in North America (as well as in Europe and Japan) in a generation provides a notable example of the escape from poverty that growth makes possible.

Growth and Income Redistribution

Not everyone benefits equally from growth. Many of the poorest are not even in the labor force and thus are least likely to share in the higher wages that, along with profits, are the primary means by which the gains from growth are distributed. For this reason, even in a growing economy, redistribution policies will be needed if poverty is to be averted.

Economic growth makes many kinds of redistribution easier to achieve. For example, a rapid growth rate makes it more feasible politically to alleviate poverty. If existing income is to be redistributed, someone's standard of living will actually have to be lowered. However, when there is economic growth and when the increment in income is redistributed (through government intervention), it is possible to reduce income inequalities without actually having to lower anyone's income. It is much easier for a rapidly growing economy to be generous toward its less fortunate citizens—or neighbors—than it is for a static economy.

Growth and Life-Style

A family often finds that a big increase in its income can lead to a major change in the pattern of its consumption—that extra money buys important amenities of life. In the same way, the members of society as a whole may change their consumption patterns as their average income rises. Not only do markets in a country that is growing rapidly make it profitable to produce more cars, but also the government is led to produce more highways and to provide more recreational areas for its newly affluent and mobile citizens. At yet a later stage, a concern about litter, pollution, and ugliness may become important, and their correction may then begin to account for a significant fraction of GDP. Such "amenities" usually become matters of social concern only when growth has assured the provision of the basic requirements for food, clothing, and housing of a substantial majority of the population.

National Defense and Prestige

When one country is competing with another for power or prestige, rates of growth are important. If our national income is growing at 2 percent while

BOX 38-4

An Open Letter to the Ordinary Citizen from a Supporter of the "Growth Is Good" School

Dear Ordinary Citizen:

You live in the world's first civilization that is devoted principally to satisfying *your* needs rather than those of a privileged minority. Past civilizations have always been based on leisure and high consumption for a tiny upper class, a reasonable living standard for a small middle class, and hard work with little more than subsistence consumption for the great mass of people.

The continuing Industrial Revolution is based on mass-produced goods for you, the ordinary citizen. It ushered in a period of sustained economic growth that has dramatically raised consumption standards of ordinary citizens. Reflect on a few examples: travel, live and recorded music, art, good food, inexpensive books, universal literacy, and a genuine chance to be educated. Most important, there is leisure to provide time and energy to enjoy these and thousands of other products of the modern industrial economy.

Would any ordinary family seriously prefer to go back to the world of 150 or 500 years ago in its same relative social and economic position? Surely the answer is no. However, for those with incomes in the top 1 or 2 percent of the income distribution, economic growth has destroyed much of their privileged consumption position. They must now vie with the masses when they visit the world's beauty spots and be annoyed, while lounging on the terrace of a palatial mansion, by the sound of charter flights carrying ordinary people to inexpensive holidays in far places. Many of the rich complain bitterly about the loss of exclusive rights to luxury consumption, and it is not surprising that they find their intellectual apologists.

Whether they know it or not, the antigrowth economists are not the social revolutionaries that they think they are. They say that growth has produced pollution and wasteful consumption of all kinds of frivolous products that add nothing to human happiness. However, the democratic solution to pollution is not to go back to where so few people consume luxuries that pollution is trivial but rather to learn to control the pollution that mass consumption tends to create.

It is only through further growth that the average citizen can enjoy consumption standards (of travel, culture, medical and health care, etc.) now available only to people in the top 25 percent of the income distribution—which includes the intellectuals who earn large royalties from the books that they write in which they denounce growth. If you think that extra income confers little real benefit, just ask those in the top 25 percent to trade incomes with average citizens.

Ordinary citizens, do not be deceived by disguised elitist doctrines. Remember that the very rich and the elite have much to gain by stopping growth and even more by rolling it back, but you have everything to gain by letting it go forward.

Onward! *A. N. Optimist*

another country's national income is growing at 5 percent, the other country will only have to wait for our relative strength to dwindle. Moreover, the faster its productivity is growing, the easier a country will find it to bear the expenses of an arms race or a program of foreign aid.

More subtly, growth has become part of the currency of international prestige. Countries that are engaged in persuading other countries of the might or right of their economic and political systems point to their rapid rates of growth as evidence of their achievements.

BOX 38-5

An Open Letter to the Ordinary Citizen from a Supporter of the "Growth Is Bad" School

Dear Ordinary Citizen:

You live in a world that is being despoiled by a mindless search for ever-higher levels of material consumption at the cost of all other values. Once upon a time, men and women knew how to enjoy creative work and to derive satisfaction from simple activities. Today the ordinary worker is a mindless cog in an assembly line that turns out ever more goods that the advertisers must work overtime to persuade the worker to consume.

Statisticians count the increasing flow of material output as a triumph of modern civilization. You arise from your electric-blanketed bed, clean your teeth with an electric toothbrush, open a can of the sad remnants of a once-proud orange with an electric can opener, and eat your bread baked from superrefined and chemically refortified flour; you climb into your car to sit in vast traffic jams on exhaust-polluted highways.

Television commercials tell you that by consuming more you are happier, but happiness lies not in increasing consumption but in increasing the ratio of *satisfaction of wants* to *total wants*. Since the more you consume, the more the advertisers persuade you that you want to consume, you are almost certainly less happy than the average citizen in a small town in 1900, whom we can visualize sitting on the family porch, sipping lemonade, and enjoying the antics of the children as they jump rope with pieces of old clothesline.

Today the landscape is dotted with endless factories, producing the plastic trivia of the modern industrial society. They drown you in a cloud of noise, air, and water pollution. The countryside is despoiled by strip mines, petroleum refineries, acid rain, and dangerous nuclear power stations, producing energy that is devoured insatiably by modern factories and motor vehicles. Worse, our precious heritage of natural resources is being fast used up.

Now is the time to stop this madness. We must stabilize production, reduce pollution, conserve our natural resources, and seek justice through a more equitable distribution of existing total income.

A long time ago, Malthus taught us that if we do not limit population voluntarily, nature will do it for us in a cruel and savage manner. Today the same is true of output: If we do not halt its growth voluntarily, the halt will be imposed on us by a disastrous increase in pollution and a rapid exhaustion of natural resources.

Citizens, awake! Shake off the worship of growth, learn to enjoy the bounty that is yours already, and reject the endless, self-defeating search for increased happiness through ever-increasing consumption.

Upward! *I. Realvalues*

Costs of Growth

The benefits of growth suggest that it is a great blessing. It is surely true that, other things being equal, most people would regard a fast rate of growth as preferable to a slow one, but other things are seldom equal.

Social and Personal Costs of Growth

Industrialization can cause deterioration of the environment. Unspoiled landscapes give way to highways, factories, and billboards; air and water become polluted; and unique and priceless relics of earlier ages—from flora and fauna to ancient art and ruins—

often disappear. Urbanization tends to move people away from the simpler life of farms and small towns into the crowded, slum-ridden, and often darkly evil life of the urban ghetto. Those remaining behind in the rural areas find that rural life, too, has changed. Larger-scale farming, the decline of population, and the migration of children from the farm to the city all have their costs. The stepped-up tempo of life brings joy to some but tragedy to others. Accidents, ulcers, crime rates, suicides, divorces, and murders all tend to be higher in periods of rapid change and in more developed societies.

An economy that is growing is also changing. Innovation renders some machines obsolete and also leaves some people partly obsolete. No matter how well trained workers are at age 25, in another 25 years most will find that their skills are at least partly obsolete. A rapid growth rate requires rapid adjustments, which can cause much upset and misery to the affected individuals.

It is often argued that costs of this kind are a small price to pay for the great benefits that growth can bring. Even if this is true in the aggregate (which is a matter of debate), these personal cost are very unevenly borne. Indeed, many of those for whom growth is most costly (in terms of jobs) share least in the fruits of growth. Yet it is also a mistake to see only the costs of growth—to yearn for the good old days while enjoying higher living standards that growth alone has made possible.

The Opportunity Cost of Growth

In a world of scarcity, almost nothing is free. Growth requires heavy investments of resources in capital goods, as well as in activities such as education. Often these investments yield no immediate return in terms of goods and services for consumption; thus they imply that sacrifices have been made by the current generation of consumers.

Growth, which promises more goods tomorrow, is achieved by consuming fewer goods today. For the economy as a whole, this sacrifice of current consumption is the primary cost of growth.

An example will suggest the magnitude of this cost. Suppose that the fictitious economy of Kanata has full employment and is experiencing growth at the rate of 2 percent per year. Its citizens consume 85 percent of the GDP and invest 15 percent. The people of Kanata know that if they are willing to decrease immediately their consumption to 77 percent, they will produce more capital and thus shift at once to a 3 percent growth rate. The new rate can be maintained as long as they keep saving and investing 23 percent of the national income. Should they do it?

Table 38-2 illustrates the choice in terms of time paths of consumption. How expensive is the "invest now, consume later" strategy? Using the assumed figures, it takes 10 years for the actual amount of consumption to catch up to what it would have been had no reallocation been made. In the intervening 10 years, a good deal of consumption is lost, and the cumulative losses in consumption must be made up before society can really be said to have broken even.

TABLE 38-2 The Opportunity Cost of Growth

Year	(1) Level of consumption at a 2% growth rate	(2) Level of consumption at a 3% growth rate	(3) Cumulative gain (loss) in consumption
0	85.0	77.0	(8.0)
1	86.7	79.3	(15.4)
2	88.5	81.8	(22.1)
3	90.3	84.2	(28.2)
4	92.1	86.8	(33.5)
5	93.9	89.5	(37.9)
6	95.8	92.9	(40.8)
7	97.8	95.0	(43.6)
8	99.7	97.9	(45.4)
9	101.8	100.9	(46.3)
10	103.8	103.9	(46.2)
15	114.7	120.8	(28.6)
20	126.8	140.3	19.6
30	154.9	189.4	251.0
40	189.2	255.6	745.9

Transferring resources from consumption to investment goods lowers current income but raises future income. The example assumes that income in year 0 is 100 and that consumption of 85 percent of national income is possible with a 2 percent growth rate. It is further assumed that to achieve a 3 percent growth rate, consumption must fall to 77 percent of income. A shift from (1) to (2) decreases consumption for 10 years but increases it thereafter. The cumulative effect on consumption is shown in (3); the gains eventually become large.

It takes an additional 9 years before total consumption over the whole period is as large as it would have been if the economy had remained on the 2 percent path. **[44]**

A policy of sacrificing present living standards for a gain that will not begin to be reaped for a generation is hardly likely to appeal to any but the altruistic or the very young. The question of how much of its living standards one generation is prepared to sacrifice for its heirs (who are in any case likely to be richer) is troublesome. As one critic put it: Why should we sacrifice for them? What have they ever done for us?

Many governments, particularly those that are seeking a larger role in world affairs, have chosen to force the diversion of resources from consumption to investment. The Germans under Hitler, the Russians under Stalin, and the Chinese under Mao Tse-tung adopted four-year and five-year plans that did just this. Many less developed countries are using such plans today. Such shifts in resources are particularly important when actual growth rates are small (say, less than 1 percent), for without some current sacrifice, there is little or no prospect of real growth in the lifetimes of today's citizens. The very lowest growth rates are frequently encountered in the very poorest countries. This creates a cruel dilemma—the vicious circle of poverty.

Are There Limits to Growth?

Many opponents of growth argue that sustained world growth is undesirable; some argue that it is impossible. Of course, all terrestrial things have an ultimate limit. Astronomers predict that the solar system itself will die as the sun burns out in another 6 billion or so years. To be of practical concern, a limit must be within some reasonable planning horizon.

Resource Exhaustion

The years since World War II have seen a rapid acceleration in the consumption of the world's resources, particularly fossil fuels and basic minerals. World population has increased from under 2.5 billion to over 5 billion in that period, and this alone has increased the demand for all the world's resources. However, the single fact of population growth greatly understates the pressure on resources.

Calculations by Professor Nathan Keyfitz of Harvard University and others focus on the resources used by those who can claim a life-style of the level enjoyed by 90 percent of North American families. This so-called middle class, which today includes about one-sixth of the world's population, consumes 15 to 30 times as much oil per capita and, overall, at least 5 times as much of the earth's scarce resources per capita as the "poor" five-sixths of the population.

The world's poor are not, however, content to remain poor forever. Whether they live in the USSR, Argentina, Indonesia, or Kenya, they have let their governments understand that they expect policies to be created that will generate enough growth to give *them* the higher consumption levels that all of *us* take for granted. This upward aspiration is being fulfilled to some degree in many countries. The growth of the middle class has been nearly 4 percent per year—twice the rate of population growth—over the postwar period. The number of persons realizing middle-class living standards is estimated to have increased from 200 million to 1 billion between 1950 and 1990 and is predicted almost to double again by the turn of the twenty-first century.

This growth is a major factor in the recently recognized or projected shortages of natural resources. Yet the 4 percent growth rate of the middle class, which is too fast for present resources, is too slow for the aspirations of the billions who live in underdeveloped countries and who see the fruits of development all around them. Thus the pressure on world resources of energy, minerals, and food is likely to accelerate, even if population growth is reduced.

Another way to look at the problem of increasing pressure on natural resources is to note that present technology and resources could not possibly support the present population of the world at the standard of living of today's average North American family. For example, the demand for oil would increase 5 to 10 times. Since these calculations (most unrealistically) assume no population growth anywhere in the world and no growth in living standards for the richest one-sixth of the world's population, it is evident that resources are insufficient.

Most economists, however, agree that conjuring up absolute limits to growth, based on the assumptions of constant technology and fixed resources, is not warranted. Technology changes continually, as do stocks of resources. For example, no one would

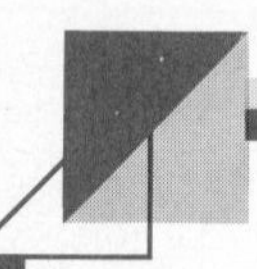

BOX 38-6

The Brundtland Commission and "Sustainable Development"

The 1980s witnessed a major increase in public awareness of the environmental problems that all nations of the world face. Problems such as global warming, ozone depletion, soil erosion, and acid rain have risen to the top of the political agenda around the world. As barges laden with toxic waste are shunted around the world in search of a country that is willing to accept their cargo, policymakers have come to recognize that even problems that once were considered to be purely local in nature, such as garbage disposal, have become international in scope.

In 1983 the United Nations created the World Commission on Environment and Development (called the Brundtland Commision after its chairman, Gro Harlem Brundtland) to examine global environmental and development problems and to design solutions to them. In its report, *Our Common Future*, published by Oxford University Press in 1987, the Brundtland Commission outlined a broad agenda for integrating economic development and environmental policy. The commission stressed the view that economic growth and environmental protection are interdependent: Growth cannot long continue at the present rate of environmental degradation. Its report introduced the concept of *sustainable development*, defined as "development that meets the needs of the present without compromising the ability of future generations to meet their own needs." (Note that the concept underlying this definition can be thought of as a "broadening" of the concept of "permanent income," which was introduced in Chapter 28.)

The idea that economic growth is limited by "nature" is not new. In the early 1970s the Club of Rome focused on the limits to growth arising from the supply of natural resources: It extrapolated from the shortages in oil, caused by the formation of OPEC and the attendant price increases, that industrialized countries faced an absolute limit to growth. This prediction was confounded by experience, as higher prices for fuel have led to increases in both supply and the efficiency with which it has been used. The bounds to growth envisioned by the Brundtland Commission are not absolute but rather a function of the "present state of technology" and the capacity of the "biosphere to absorb the effects of human activity." The environment imposes limits to growth because it is the fundamental capital upon which economic development is based. As technology and economic organization improve, the stream of wealth that flows from this stock of "environmental capital" can continue to increase. The concept of sustainable development stresses the role of the environment as capital, which, if exhausted, cannot be replaced.

Regardless of whether they are government agencies, small firms, or transnational corporations, the Brundtland Commission's message applies: All institutions that affect the environmental base of the economy must respect the needs of future generations. Governments need to expand their role in the collection and the dissemination of information and, where possible, should produce an annual account of the nation's environment and resource base "to complement the traditional annual fiscal budget and economic development plans." Recall from Chapter 27 that the national income accounts measure *net* national income by subtracting depreciation of capital from *gross* national product. The Brundtland Commission's recommendations involve expanding this concept to subtract some measure of the deterioration of the environment in calculating the level and rate of growth of net national income and derivative measures such as disposable income per capita. The idea is that the environment is part of our capital, and when we degrade it, we reduce our ability to generate real income in the future, just as when a machine used for producing consumer goods depreciates.

Some of the Brundtland Commission's recommendations require more government involvement in economies in order to produce and enforce environmental regulations. While the Brundtland Commission recognizes the value of economic incentives in generating the cost reductions that flow from more efficient use of resources, it also feels that there are limits to the ability of competitive industry to reduce waste voluntarily: "Regulations imposing uniform performance standards are essential to ensure that industry makes the investments necessary to reduce pollution and waste and to enable them to compete on an even footing." (In microeconomic terms, this is seen as an intervention, justified by market failure, and a distinction between private and social costs, as discussed in Chapter 23.)

In other cases, what is required is *less* government intervention, and the report calls on governments to examine whether existing policies and subsidies contribute to resource-efficient practices. For example, agricultural policy that protects farmers in industrialized countries is criticized for being "studded with contradictions that encourage the degradation of the agricultural resource base and, in the long run, do more harm than good to the agricultural industry." The solution lies in "reducing incentives that force overproduction and noncompetitive production in the developed market economies and enhancing those that encourage food production in developing countries."

More specific recommendations are made for reforming international organizations, in which an "extensive institutional capacity exists that could be redirected towards sustainable development"; thus most of the proposed changes "will not require additional financial resources but can be achieved through a reorientation of existing mandates, programmes, and budgets and a redeployment of existing staff." The efficacy of existing institutions is reduced by their "fragmented" nature and a "weakness of coordination." Key to these reforms is the requirement that sustainable development be made central to the mandate of all international bodies such as UN agencies and the IMF and World Bank. The United Nations Environment Program (established in 1972) should be strengthened to become a clearing house for information and to become the "principal advocate" for cooperation on environmental issues. The funding of nongovernmental organizations (NGOs) should be increased, and these groups should be more fully integrated into intergovernmental organizations, as NGOs can "often provide an efficient and effective alternative to public agencies."

Our Common Future is a hopeful document, but its hope is tempered with the realization that unless major conservation initiatives are acted on quickly, the current serious rate of environmental degradation will soon start to harm the health and welfare of all of us.

have thought 30 years ago that the world could produce enough food to feed its present population of over 5 billion people, let alone the 10 billion at which the population is projected to stabilize sometime in the twenty-first century. Yet this now seems feasible. Famines do occur, but they are often the result of government policy during a civil war, as in Ethiopia and the Sudan, or of climatic changes plus poor land conservation policies, as in the Sahel region of central Africa. There will never be full protection from the vagaries of nature or from willful or ignorant mismanagement. Over the world as a whole, however, too much rather than too little food production is today's problem.

In 1990 the developed world was struggling not with a food shortage but with a food glut. Farm support policies in the European Community turned the countries of Europe into food exporters rather than food importers, as they had been in past centuries. These subsidies greatly hurt agricultural producers in countries that would export agricultural produce under free market prices. A mere 3 percent of U.S., Canadian, and European labor applied to limited farmland with modern technology was producing more food than the world markets could absorb. The problem in 1990 was how to reduce subsidized production, not how to produce more.

It is possible that 30 years from now, the energy problem could be as much a thing of the past as the food shortage problem is today. Technology could by then have produced a cheap, nonpolluting energy source (possibly based on solar energy or atomic fusion).

The future is always uncertain, and it is instructive to recall how many things that we accept as commonplace today would have seemed miraculous a mere 25 years ago.

Yet there is surely cause for concern. Although many barriers can be overcome by technological advances, this is not done in an instant, and certainly not automatically. There is a critical problem of timing: How soon can we discover and put into practice the knowledge required to solve the problems that are made ever more imminent by the growth in the population, the affluence of the rich nations, and the aspirations of the billions who now live in poverty?

There is no guarantee that a whole generation may not be caught in transition, with social and political consequences that promise to be enormous, even if they are not cataclysmic.

One positive outgrowth of concern over environmental issues is the recent attention given to the concept of "sustainable development," discussed further in Box 38-6.

Renewable Resources

Furthermore, the demands placed on renewable resources threaten to destroy their natural recuperative cycle. Throughout history, for example, fishermen were a small part of the predatory process. Now the demands of 5 billion people have made fish a scarce resource, threatening to destroy the fish-generating capacity in many oceans. In the Mediterranean, many species of fish that were once the staple food of ordinary people are now consumed mainly by well-off tourists.

Pollution

A further problem is how to cope with pollution. The earth's natural processes had little trouble coping with the pollution generated by its 1 billion inhabitants in 1800. Air, water, and earth are polluted by all sorts of natural activities, and through billions of years the environment has coped with these. But the more than 5 billion people who now exist on the earth put demands on resources for pollution removal that threaten to become unsustainable. Smoke, sewage, chemical waste, hydrocarbon emissions, and a host of other pollutants threaten to overwhelm the earth's natural regenerative processes.

Conscious management of pollution and of renewable resources was unnecessary when the world's population was 1 billion, but they have become a pressing matter of survival now that more than 5 billion people are seeking to live in the same space and off the same resources.

SUMMARY

1. Real national income can be increased on a once-for-all basis, from the demand side by removing recessionary gaps and from the supply side by reducing structural unemployment. Sustained increases, however, are due mainly to economic growth, which continuously pushes the *LRAS* curve outward.
2. Investment has short-term effects on national income through aggregate demand and long-term effects through growth in potential national income. Such growth is frequently measured by using rates of change of potential real national income per person or per hour of labor employed.
3. Savings reduce aggregate demand and therefore reduce national income in the short run, but in the long run savings finance the investment that leads to growth in potential income.
4. The cumulative effects of even small differences in growth rates become large over periods of a decade or more.
5. Understanding growth involves understanding both the use of existing investment opportunities and the process of creating new investment opportunities. The source of economic growth was once thought to be almost entirely capital accumulation and the use of a backlog of unexploited investment opportunities. Today most economists recognize that many investment opportunities can be created, and much attention is given to the sources of outward shifts in the *MEC* schedule through technical change.
6. Neo-Classical growth models look to innovation to shift the *MEC* schedule outward but assume that, other things being equal, additions to capital stock are always subject to diminishing returns. Increasing returns models stress that innovations in new products and new processes may encounter a large range of increasing returns as successive units of investment in the new activities each yield higher returns than each previous unit.
7. Causes of growth, other than increases in the quantity and quality of capital, are increases in the quantity and quality of labor, structural changes, and innovations in institutions.
8. The most important benefit of growth lies in its contribution to the long-run struggle to raise living standards and to escape poverty. It also makes more manageable the policies that would redistribute income among people. Growth also plays an important role in some countries' national defense and struggle for international prestige.
9. Growth, while often beneficial, is never costless. The opportunity cost of growth is the diversion of resources from current consumption to capital formation. For individuals who are left behind in a rapidly changing world, the costs are higher and more personal. The optimal rate of growth involves balancing benefits and costs. Most people do not wish to forgo the benefits that growth can bring, but neither do they wish to maximize growth at any cost.
10. Recently, the advanced industrial countries have become increasingly concerned with maintaining their international competitiveness in order to continue their economic growth. Globalized competition and the increasing pace of technological change, particularly of the knowledge-driven variety, have made countries acutely aware of how easy it is to lose one's position at or near the forefront of the innovating nations whose growth in productivity keeps them competitive and helps to preserve their growth performance.
11. The critical importance of increasing knowledge and new technol-

ogy in sustaining growth is highlighted by the great drain on existing natural resources, resulting from the explosive growth of population and output of recent decades. Without continuing new knowledge, the present needs and aspirations of the world's population cannot come anywhere close to being met.

12. Of particular concern is the pressure that the rising population and rising real incomes places on resources. Although resources will not be exhausted in general, particular resources, such as petroleum, will be. They will have to be replaced by new resources that new technologies permit to do the same job as the exhausted resources. Furthermore, resources that renewed themselves without help from humans when the world's population was 1 billion can easily be exhausted unless they are consciously controlled now that the world's population has exceeded 5 billion. This enormous increase in population has similar effects on pollution: The earth's environment could cope naturally with much of human pollution 200 years ago, but the present population is so large that control of pollution has outstripped nature's coping mechanisms.

TOPICS FOR REVIEW

Short-run and long-run effects of investment and saving
Cumulative nature of growth
Factors affecting growth
Effects of capital accumulation with and without new knowledge
Growth with increasing returns
Embodied and disembodied technical change
Benefits and costs of growth
Resource depletion and pollution

DISCUSSION QUESTIONS

1. We usually study and measure economic growth in macroeconomic terms, but in a market economy, who makes the decisions that lead to growth? What kinds of decisions and what kinds of actions cause growth to occur? How might a detailed study of individual markets be relevant to understanding economic growth?
2. Discuss the following quote from a newspaper article that appeared in the summer of 1989:

   "Economics and the environment are not strange bedfellows. Environment-oriented tourism is one creative way to resolve the conflict between our desire for a higher standard of living and the realization that nature cannot absorb everything we throw at it. The growing demand for eco-tourism has placed a premium on the remaining rain forests, undisturbed flora and fauna, and endangered species of the world."
3. Almost all international migration tends to be from lower- to higher-income countries. What does this suggest about ordinary people's preferences for economic growth?
4. Critics of the no-growth solution to environmental problems feel technological improvements will simultaneously produce growth and the solution to many environmental problems. These critics point out that the automobile replaced the horse just in time to stop cities from being swamped with horse manure, which was unsightly, smelly, and disease carrying. The pollution brought by the automobile was small per unit of transportation services compared to what the horse produced. They also point out that death from

food poisoning was common at the beginning of the century and that when food additives were introduced—additives to which we now seek a superior alternative—food-poisoning deaths were reduced to a tenth of their former magnitude. In the light of such facts, consider two views. First, technology has been the source of our rising living standards and will be the source of the solutions to the environmental questions that now face us. Second, technology is a curse, and the best way to save the world is to suspend technological change, holding living standards where they now are.

5. Many people worry that Canadian living standards will fall progressively behind those of the more dynamic countries. Does it matter? If the reason is a lack of innovative activity in Canada, is there anything that the government could do about it?

6. Throughout the 1980s and early 1990s, many Canadian observers saw a conflict between the "corporate agenda" and the "people's agenda" for economic policy, the former stressing the conditions for business profitability, and the latter the conditions for ordinary people's welfare. Others said that "all Canadians are in the same boat": If business becomes uncompetitive internationally, both owners and workers will suffer, while if business competes successfully in international markets, everyone—employers and employees—will be the gainers. what do you think?

7. Dr. David Suzuki recently has argued that, despite the fact that "in the twentieth century the list of scientific and technological achievements has been absolutely dazzling, the costs of such progress are so large that negative economic growth may be right for the future." Policies to achieve this include "rigorous reduction of waste, a questioning and distrustful attitude towards technological progress, and braking demands on the globe's resources." Identify some of the benefits and costs of economic growth, and evaluate Dr. Suzuki's position.

8. *Family Weekly* recently listed among "inventions that have changed our lives" microwave ovens, digital clocks, bank credit cards, freeze-dried coffee, tape cassettes, climate-controlled shopping malls, automatic toll collectors, soft contact lenses, tubeless tires, and electronic word processors. Which of these would you hate to do without? Which, if any, will have a major impact on life in the twenty-first century? If there are any that you believe will not, does this mean that they are frivolous and unimportant?

9. "The case for economic growth is that it gives man greater control over his environment, and consequently increases his freedom." Explain why you agree or disagree with this statement by Nobel Laureate W. Arthur Lewis.

10. Suppose that solar energy becomes the dominant form of energy in the twenty-first century. What changes will this make in the growth rates of Africa and northern Europe?

11. Discuss the following newspaper headlines in terms of the sources, costs, and benefits of growth.

a. "Stress addiction: 'Life in the fast lane' may have its benefits"
b. "Education: An expert urges multiple reforms"
c. "Industrial radiation risk higher than thought"
d. "Developments in the field of management design are looking ahead."
e. "Environmentalists move to stop dam construction."
f. "Emigration of firms to the U.S. worries Ontario voters."

Chapter 39

Government Budget Deficits

The federal government's budget deficit soared from \$8 billion in 1979 to over \$31 billion in 1985, and it remained at historically record levels at the end of the 1980s. No single measure associated with the government has ever been the focus of so much attention and controversy in the media, on the campaign trail, and in coffee shops and bars across the nation. Extreme views about the deficit and its potential effects are not hard to come by. One extreme is that the deficit is a "time bomb ticking away" that "if unchecked, threatens the jobs and prosperity of all Canadians." At the other extreme is the view that the deficit itself is not a problem at all and that the only threat it poses to Canadians arises from the possible effects of severe policy actions that might be taken on the misguided advice of deficit alarmists.

The average Canadian has some idea of the size of the federal budget deficit (or at least the idea that it is too big). Many Canadians have been concerned about the size of the deficit for almost a decade now. Yet it persists at record levels. Why is our budget deficit so large? Why do Canadians worry so much about it? Is it really such a big problem?

Facts About the Deficit

The recent emergence of record federal budget deficits is clear from Figure 39-1. Part (i) shows total federal spending (on goods and services and transfers) and total federal revenues since 1967 as a share of GDP. Part (ii) shows the deficit, again measured as a share of GDP—this is the shaded area between the two lines in part (i).

Over the period 1975–1980, expenditures were a relatively constant fraction of GDP, while tax revenues fell sharply. This is the basis for the Department of Finance's view that discretionary tax cuts introduced in the 1970s were initially responsible for rapid growth in the deficit. Other analysts, however, argue that it was the failure to constrain expenditures in the face of the tax cuts that is responsible and that there was also a switch toward delivering some transfers through tax concessions rather than direct expenditure.

The increase in the deficit that occurred from 1981 to 1983 reflects the combined effects of the severe recession in 1982, some mild discretionary fiscal expansion, and increased interest payments on the government's debt. This last was due to both the sharp rise in interest rates that occurred and the cumulative effect of the persistent deficits on the size of the government debt.

FIGURE 39-1 Federal Revenues, Expenditures, and Budget Balances, 1967–1989 (*percentage of GDP, National Accounts Basis*)

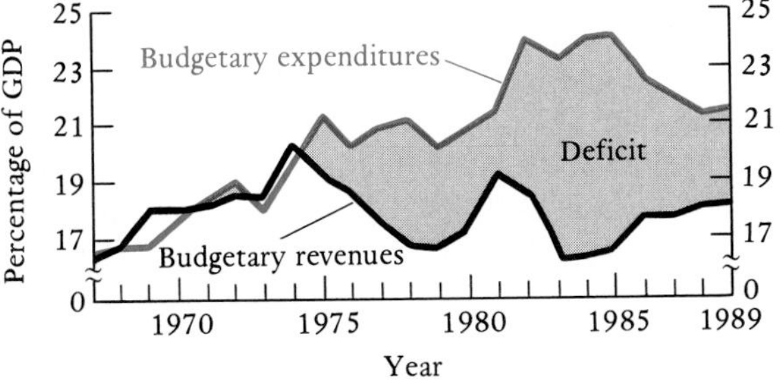

(i) Revenues and expenditures

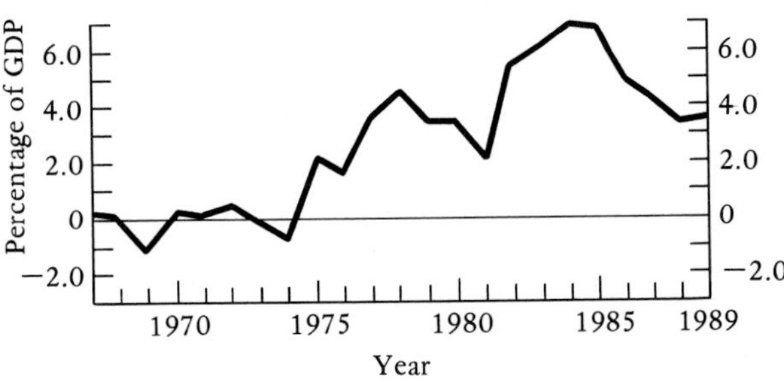

(ii) The budgetary deficit

The deficit has grown sharply in recent years, reflecting rapid increases in expenditures relative to revenues. The graphs in (i) show expenditures and revenues of the federal government, both as a percentage of national income. The difference is the federal deficit, shown in (ii).

From 1967 through 1973, expenditures grew steadily while revenue fluctuated around a rising trend; as a result, the budget balance fluctuated between deficit and surplus positions but showed no clear trend. Persistent deficits emerged in the next five years as expenditures remained roughly constant while revenues fell.

In the 1980s the deficit increased dramatically. In the early part of the decade, the growth in the deficit reflected the effects of the recession; cyclical adjustment grew sharply in this period. Revenues fell sharply and have recovered only slowly since. Expenditures rose rapidly, in part reflecting the operation of automatic stabilizers. More recently, government restraint curtailed growth in program spending, but this was more than offset by the rapid growth in interest payments on the national debt, so that, as shown, total expenditure continued to rise. Since 1988 the deficit has fallen as a percentage of GDP. (*Source*: Department of Finance, *Budget Papers*, February 1990.)

The government budget had been in deficit prior to 1982, although as a percentage of GDP the deficit had not been unusually large by historical standards. After 1982, however, the deficit increased dramatically as a share of GDP. As can be seen from Table 32-1 (see page 680), the cyclically adjusted deficit grew even more than the annual deficit over the period 1982–1985 and has fallen only marginally since then.

So far we have focused on the federal government budget balance. We could also consider the total deficit of all levels of government, equal to the federal deficit plus the deficits of the provincial and municipal governments. For most of the past two decades, provincial and municipal governments have experienced only relatively small budget imbalances, and hence most of the concern about budget deficits in Canada has been focused on the federal government. In fact, throughout the 1970s and early 1980s, the total government deficit was smaller than the federal government deficit, reflecting the combined surpluses of the other two levels of government. But since 1986, the total government deficit has been larger than the federal deficit.

In the late 1980s, reductions in the deficit of the federal government have been largely offset by increases in the deficits of provincial and municipal governments.

In 1986 all 10 provincial governments were running deficits. Although deficits had been the order of the day in certain provinces, they had traditionally been offset by surpluses in other provinces. In 1986 a deficit emerged in Alberta, which had typically been a surplus province due to large oil revenues. It began running a deficit in response to depressed economic conditions brought about by adverse shocks to the agricultural and energy sectors. Most worrisome, perhaps, was the deficit in Ontario, a province that had been experiencing a sustained economic boom since 1983. By the end of the decade, only British Columbia was running a small surplus; all other provinces were still incurring deficits.

Deficits and the National Debt

The national debt is the total debt owed by the governments of Canada; it represents the *cumulative* effect of past deficits. When a government runs a deficit in any one year, it must borrow and therefore add to the total debt that it owed at the start of the year. When it runs a surplus, it pays off some of its past borrowing and therefore reduces its total debt.

A deficit increases the national debt; a surplus reduces it.

As we shall see, much of the concern about government budget deficits arises from their cumulative effect on the national debt and therefore on the government's interest obligations.

Facts About the Debt

The national debt in January 1990 was over $320 billion, which represents more than $12,000 for every man, woman, and child in the country. About 15 percent of the debt was held by the government itself and by the Bank of Canada; interest payments on this part of the debt are only bookkeeping transactions.[1] The other 85 percent is held privately by Canadians and foreigners.

The national debt represents money that the federal government has borrowed by selling bonds to Canadian and foreign households, firms, pension funds, and financial institutions.

In this sense, the national debt is owed by all of us to some of us and to foreigners.

The debt in relation to GDP. The figures for debt per person, which are often quoted in an attempt to shock, require interpretation. For a government, as for a household, the significance of debt depends on what it represents and on whether the income is available to pay the interest. No one would be shocked, for example, to find that a Canadian family of four earning $70,000 a year had a mortgage of $60,000 on a $120,000 home.

As with the deficit, in evaluating the national debt and the government's interest payments on it, it is useful to consider them *relative* to the size of the economy. Worries about the debt arise primarily when the debt grows faster than the economy; it is really the *debt-to-GDP ratio* that matters. A national debt of $300 billion clearly has different implications when GDP is $50 billion than when it is $500 billion.

Figure 39-2 shows historical data for the debt and interest payments on it as a proportion of GDP. Part (i) shows that national debt as a proportion of GDP started to fall at the end of World War II and continued to fall until 1975. The debt rose relative to GDP after 1977, and by 1989 it had reached almost 54 percent of GDP. That figure is still much less than it was at the postwar peak, when it exceeded 100 percent. Nevertheless, the trend is worrisome, and most projections suggest that the debt-to-GDP ratio will continue to rise.

Interest payments. Consider next the interest payments on the debt, often called the *debt service payments,* shown in Figure 39-2(ii). The current ratio of 4.6 percent is very high by historical standards.

In fiscal year 1989–1990 debt service payments exceeded the total federal deficit, indicating that the government's *primary budget balance* (which excludes debt service payments) was in surplus.

The primary budget balance is discussed further in Box 39-1.

Another perspective on debt service payments is their share of government revenues and expenditures. In 1989–1990 the debt service payments of $33 billion represented 25 percent of total federal government spending and over 30 percent of total revenues. Both are very high by historical standards; for example, they are more than double the corresponding fractions in 1970.

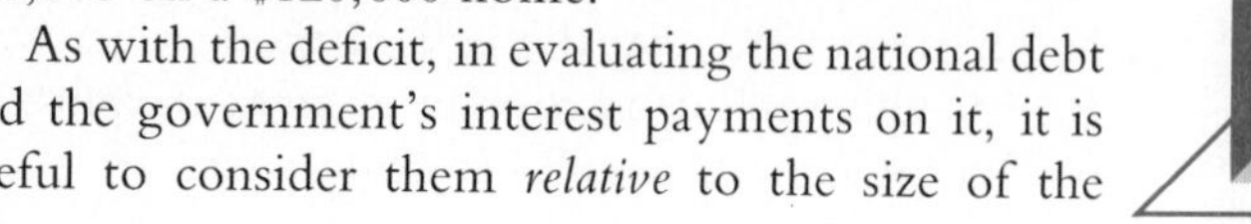

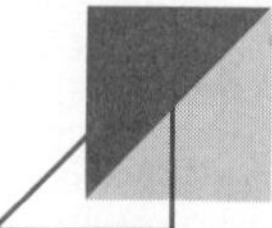

Why Worry About Deficits?

Some economists have argued that deficits and public debt have no important effects on the economy. The logic underlying this belief is called the *Ricardian neutrality proposition.* It is discussed in the appendix to this chapter, where we show that the conditions

[1] The Bank of Canada buys government bonds in the course of operating monetary policy (see Chapter 35). Government departments sometimes acquire government bonds with funds that they do not need for relatively short periods of time.

FIGURE 39-2 Relative Significance of the National Debt, 1938–1989

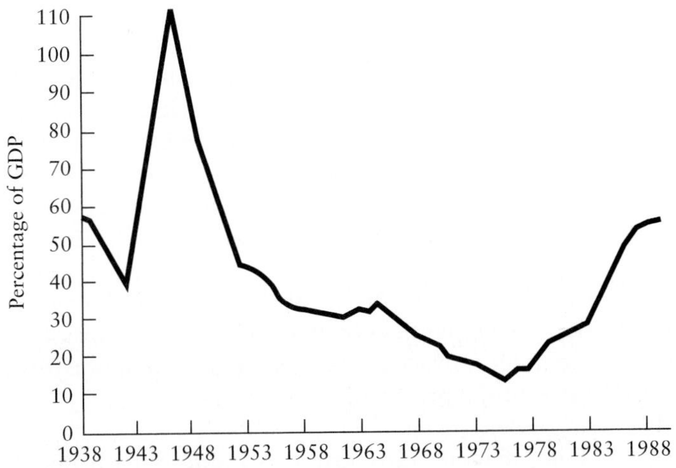

(i) Net government debt

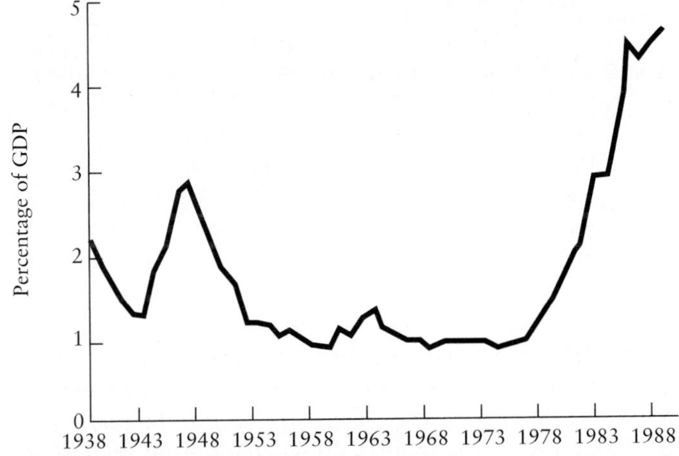

(ii) Net interest on government debt

After falling for 30 years, the national debt and interest payments on it have both started to rise as a share of national income. Net federal government debt is plotted in (i), net interest payments made by the federal government in (ii), both expressed as a percentage of GDP.

The national debt, after rising sharply through World War II, was a declining fraction of GDP until 1975. Since 1975 there has been a continuing rise, increasing quite sharply in the past few years. In 1989 the ratio reached 53.4 percent.

Interest payments on the national debt have followed a similar pattern; since interest rates rose in the late 1970s and early 1980s, the upturn in interest payments was sharper and occurred sooner than with the debt. Interest payments on the debt reached 2.9 percent of national income in 1948 and remained under 3 percent for the next 33 years. In 1983 they rose to 3.3 percent, and since 1986 they have fluctuated around 4.5 percent. (*Source*: *Public Accounts*, Department of Finance.)

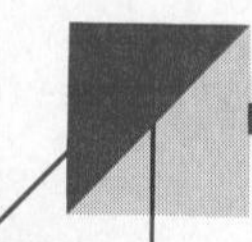

BOX 39-1

Another Perspective on the Deficit

For some purposes it can be useful to examine the deficit by looking at the interest payments on the national debt separately from other government expenditures, called *program expenditures*. The difference between the government's program expenditures and its revenues is called its *primary deficit*. The total deficit is equal to the primary deficit plus the government's debt service payments.

Columns 1–5 of the accompanying table show the evolution of the federal government deficit over the period 1984–1990 in terms of this breakdown and reveal a number of interesting facts. Column 1 shows that the government has succeeded to a considerable extent in controlling the growth of its program expenditures; they have fallen from 19.5 percent of GDP in 1984–1985 to 16.5 percent in 1989–1990. Comparing columns 1 and 2 shows that program expenditures have grown much more slowly than revenues, and since 1987–1988 revenues have exceeded program expenditures. Thus since 1987 the primary balance has been in surplus (as shown by the negative entries in column 3). This in turn means that since that time, debt service payments, which grew steadily throughout the period as shown in column 4, exceeded the total government deficit (as shown by comparing columns 4 and 5).

These observations have led a number of commentators to suggest that the overall deficit is not the serious problem that government critics have alleged; their view is that basic government programs are being financed out of current tax revenues, and the deficit is merely a reflection of the large national debt.

This less alarming view of the deficit is reinforced when one takes into account the impact of inflation on the measurement of the debt service payments. As we have seen in Chapter 26, nominal interest rates can be divided into a real interest component and an inflation premium. The *inflation adjustment* involves making the same distinction when assessing the government's debt service payments.

Debt service payments made by the government also have a real and an inflation premium component. The real component constitutes a transfer from the government to holders of the government debt as payment for use of the principal; the inflation premium does not. This is because the inflation premium is exactly offset by a reduction in the real value of the principal.

The inflation adjustment is made by subtracting the inflation premium component of government debt service payments from the measured deficit.

The inflation adjustment is shown in column 6 in the table. For example, in 1988–1989 the government debt was approximately $320 billion, the inflation rate was about 5.3 percent, and the government had a total deficit of $28.7 billion. On an inflation-adjusted basis, the deficit was only $11.7 billion. This is the increase in the real value—or purchasing power—of the debt: The debt rose by $28.7 billion in *nominal* terms due to the measured deficit, but its *real* value depreciated by over $17 billion due to the effects of the 5.3 percent inflation on the purchasing power of the $321 billion stock of debt. As column 7 shows, the inflation-adjusted deficit is much smaller than the total deficit; in 1989–1990 it amounted to only one-third of the total deficit.

Whether making the inflation adjustment is appropriate for assessing the impact of the deficit depends on the response of household consumption spending to inflation-induced changes in their real wealth. Economists who argue for the adjustment hold that the net effect on aggregate demand of this

Fiscal year	Program expenditures (1)	Revenue (2)	Primary deficit (3)	Debt service payments (4)	Total federal deficit (5)	Inflation adjustment (6)	Inflation-adjusted deficit (7)
1984–1985	86.8	70.9	15.9	22.5	38.3	8.4	30.0
1985–1986	85.8	76.8	9.0	25.4	34.4	9.3	25.1
1986–1987	89.7	85.8	3.9	26.7	30.6	11.4	19.2
1987–1988	96.5	97.5	−0.9	29.0	28.1	12.9	15.2
1988–1989	99.5	104.0	−4.4	33.2	28.7	17.0	11.7
1989–1990[a]	103.5	112.4	−8.9	39.4	30.5	20.2	10.3

Source: The Federal Budget, February 20, 1990. All figures are in billions of dollars.
[a] Estimate.

component of the deficit will be approximately zero—the government's outlay will be offset by an increase in private saving as wealth holders attempt to recoup the inflation-induced fall in their real wealth. Economists who argue against making the adjustment hold that private-sector saving will not rise by enough to offset the inflation component completely.* Although the magnitude of the short-run response of household spending is a source of some controversy, most economists hold that household spending will adjust completely in the long run and hence that if one's concern is with the long-run effects of persistent deficits, the adjustment should be made.

* The balanced budget multiplier (see Chapter 32) indicates another reason for adjusting the measured deficit in order to assess its impact on the economy. The balanced budget multiplier suggests that a dollar of spending will increase aggregate demand by more than a dollar of tax revenue will decrease it. Therefore, to obtain a proper measurement of the effect of fiscal actions on aggregate demand, a more sophisticated measure, called the *weighted cyclically adjusted deficit,* which takes account of these differential effects, is often used.

Professor Pierre Fortin of the University of Quebec in Montreal has led a small but vocal group of economists who argue on the basis of this line of reasoning that the deficit is not so large as to be considered a major problem.† Other economists argue that the long-run concerns are best captured by the evolution of the debt-to-GDP ratio. Since both real growth in the economy and inflation cause the denominator, nominal GDP, to increase, the debt-to-GDP ratio automatically allows for their effects. If the ratio increases, the deficit was large enough to cause the nominal stock of debt to increase faster than nominal GDP. If the ratio falls, the deficit was so small that the nominal stock of debt grew slower than nominal GDP. On this basis many economists view the rapid run-up in the debt-to-GDP ratio that occurred in the 1980s (see Figure 39-2) as evidence that the deficit is large enough to constitute a serious problem. We return to this issue in Box 39-3.

† Pierre Fortin, "Federal Debt Trends in Perspective," in M. Prachowny (ed.), *John Deutsch Institute Policy Forum on the 1990 Federal Budget* (Kingston, Ont.: Queens University Press), 1990.

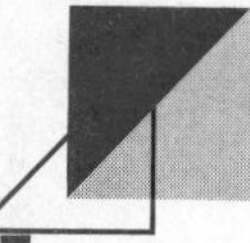

BOX 39-2

Does the National Debt Matter? The Owe-It-to-Ourselves View

A few economists have argued that since the national debt simply involves a debt of some Canadians payable to other Canadians, it imposes no net burden on the country. Of course, these economists recognize that the debt is a burden to taxpayers in general who must ultimately provide the funds for the government to make interest payments on the debt. But, the "owe it to ourselves" argument holds, that burden is exactly offset by the interest payments that are made to Canadians who own government bonds.

The owe-it-to-ourselves view thus argues that the major effect of the national debt is that interest payments on it merely redistribute income from the general taxpayer toward bondholders. Since government bonds are widely held, being a major component of most public and private pension funds, the argument holds that even this redistribution of income is not a serious matter.

This contention raises several issues.

Crowding Out

First, suppose that the basic facts alleged in the owe-it-to-ourselves view are true—that is, that virtually all Canadian government debt is in fact held by Canadians. Even in this case, it does not follow that there is no net burden to the Canadian economy arising from the government debt.

Economic theory and evidence suggest that government bonds are held instead of claims on income streams produced by real capital. That is, if the debt did not exist, people would still wish to hold assets to provide for future consumption; in the absence of the government debt, they would have invested in corporations engaged in producing goods and services. Thus the bonds, which on net contribute nothing to the economy but merely redistribute income from one group to another, crowd out investment in real capital that would have created wealth and income for Canadians.

International Capital Mobility

The basic contention that the debt is merely owed to ourselves is not completely true. Though the vast majority of Canadian government bonds are held by Canadian citizens, government bonds are also sold on international markets, so some are held by foreigners. Accordingly, the interest payments on these bonds, which must be financed by Canadian taxpayers, accrue to foreign nationals.

required for deficits and the debt to be irrelevant are very stringent.[2] A less formal argument that the national debt is of no concern to the nation as a whole since it is something that we as citizens owe to ourselves is discussed in Box 39-2.

For most economists, the relevant question is not whether deficits have effects but the form and magnitude of those effects.

One way in which deficits influence the economy is through their short-run stabilizing or destabilizing effects.

This stabilization role was emphasized in Chapter 32, where we saw (see Box 32-2) that complications arise when measuring the deficit in order to judge

[2] Briefly, the argument is that the government's decision of whether to finance current expenditure by levying current taxes or by issuing debt is irrelevant for the economy, since all that the latter decision does is postpone the taxes. Issuing bonds raises the current government deficit and raises current household disposable income, but according to this theory, neither has any implications for the performance of the economy. Forward-looking consumers will know that they have to pay higher taxes later and hence will not increase their current consumption expenditures. Thus the theory holds that there will be no stimulus to the economy from the deficit.

The fact that some Canadian government debt is held abroad is enough to refute the owe-it-to-ourselves view. But in fact the situation is even more complicated—and more damaging to this view.

Suppose that a Canadian corporation wishes to float a new debt issue in order to finance expansion of its existing capacity. Although it might expect to sell a large fraction of the new bonds on the Canadian market, the fact that the Canadian government is flooding that market with debt in order to finance its budget deficit means that the Canadian corporation will have to sell at least some of its debt abroad. (Ontario Hydro and Quebec Hydro are examples of organizations that have found themselves in this position in recent years.)

Again there will be a burden to the national debt, not in the form of a reduced capital stock in Canada but in the form of reduced income and wealth for Canadians. Foreign nationals will now own claims to the income from the new Canadian investment projects, and some of the income from these Canadian projects will accrue to those foreign nationals who acquired these financial claims.

In this case the burden to the national debt arises *indirectly* because of the need that it creates for Canadian firms to finance their investment by selling bonds and equities abroad. Once this indirect effect is recognized, simply looking at the share of foreign ownership of the national debt does not give a good indication of how much is owed to ourselves and how much is actually owed to foreign nationals.

What Limits the Acceptable Size of the Deficit?

The arguments given in the text provide a case for balancing the need for short-run fiscal stabilization with longer-run concerns for fiscal prudence. But the owe-it-to-ourselves view is not helpful in this regard.

If the owe-it-to-ourselves view were correct, why would we not want a $200 billion deficit, or even a $500 billion one, rather than the controversial $30-plus billion one of the 1980s and early 1990s? Surely the politicians would like that, as it would allow them to avoid many of the hard decisions involved in restraining expenditures and raising taxes. Of course, no one would seriously advocate such a deficit. But if the owe-it-to-ourselves view were correct, there would be no reason for objecting to such a deficit.

the stance of fiscal policy for stabilization purposes. The strength of the economic recovery meant that the GDP gap shrank during that period and hence that the *cyclically adjusted deficit* rose relative to the actual deficit.

The persistence of a large *CAD*, along with a large actual deficit and a rising debt-to-GDP ratio, reinforces the concerns that many economists have about the deficit.

A second way in which deficits can influence the economy is through their potential to affect income and welfare adversely in the long run. People worry about the long-run effects of persistent deficits for many reasons. We will look at several.

Will a Deficit Cause Inflation?

Neither economic theory nor the available evidence suggests that deficits by themselves are sufficient to cause inflation. The worry that persistent deficits may cause inflation arises out of the fear that a persistent deficit will eventually cause the Bank of Canada to increase the money supply, which, as we saw in Chapter 36, is a necessary condition for a sustained inflation to occur. To date, however, this has not been a problem, as the deficit has been financed by government borrowing in private-sector capital markets; only if it were financed by selling bonds to the Bank would the growth rate in the money supply be increased. (When this happens, the Bank *creates* the money to finance the deficit by giving the government new deposits in return for its new bonds.) If this increase in the money supply is too rapid, then—as we saw in Chapter 34—it will cause inflation.

Deficits financed by the continual creation of new money cause continual inflation; deficits financed by private-sector borrowing do not.

Will the Deficit Crowd Out Private Investment?

People fear that deficit spending may lead to a more or less equivalent reduction in private-sector investment spending. Government borrowing to finance its deficit can absorb a significant proportion of private savings. In 1990, for example, the federal deficit was nearly two-thirds of total private-sector savings by households and firms. The fear is that heavy government borrowing drives up the interest rate, and the higher interest rate reduces private investment expenditure. This "crowding out" process is illustrated in Figure 39-3.

If government borrowing to finance the deficit drives up the interest rate, some private investment expenditure will be crowded out.

This effect can be seen by referring to the definition of aggregate expenditure as the sum of consumption, investment, and government expenditure plus net exports:

$$AE = C + I + G + (X - M) \quad [1]$$

The argument is that, other things being equal, the rise in interest rates caused by a government deficit will lead to a fall in investment spending, I, and thus to a fall in desired aggregate expenditure, AE.

This effect is more likely when the economy is close to full employment. When there is a large recessionary gap, the rise in income will increase the volume of savings (as households move along their savings functions, as shown in Figure 28-1 on page 593). In this case the new savings generated by the rise in income help to finance the deficit so that less crowding out of existing private-sector borrowing need occur.

Will the Deficit Crowd Out Net Exports?

In a relatively small trading country such as Canada, a budget deficit tends to crowd out exports rather than private investments. This phenomenon is analyzed more fully in Chapter 43. In the meantime, however, we can see how it works in broad outline.

The government borrowing to finance a large budget deficit tends to push up interest rates. But as soon as Canadian rates rise significantly above those in the rest of the world, funds flow into Canada, attracted by the higher rates to be earned here; this was discussed in Box 35-1 on page 752.

In an open economy such as Canada's, instead of driving up interest rates sufficiently to crowd out private investment, the government budget deficit tends to attract foreign capital.

The rush to buy Canadian dollars in order to invest in Canada drives up the value of the Canadian dollar on the foreign exchange market. This reduces Canadian exports and encourages Canadian imports.

A persistent government budget deficit appreciates the Canadian dollar on foreign exchange markets and causes net exports to fall.

This type of crowding out can also be seen in terms of Equation 1, where now it is $X - M$ that falls.

Will the Debt Harm Future Generations?

To the extent that government borrowing to finance current expenditures crowds out private investment, there will be a smaller stock of capital to pass on to future generations. Less capital means less output; this is the long-term burden of the debt.

Despite large deficits, investment was sustained at high levels throughout the 1980s. Does this mean that we do not need to worry about a burden arising from the large deficits? Unfortunately, the answer is no. Because private investment has been maintained, foreign lenders have supplied much of the funds.[3] Thus while future generations of Canadians may well inherit a capital stock that is not significantly reduced as a result of the deficit, they will inherit an increased

[3] As we shall see in Chapter 41, the capital inflows from abroad are matched by a deficit on the current account, and the association of the current account deficit with the government budget deficit has become known as the *twin-deficits problem.*

FIGURE 39-3 **Crowding Out of Private Investment by Government Borrowing**

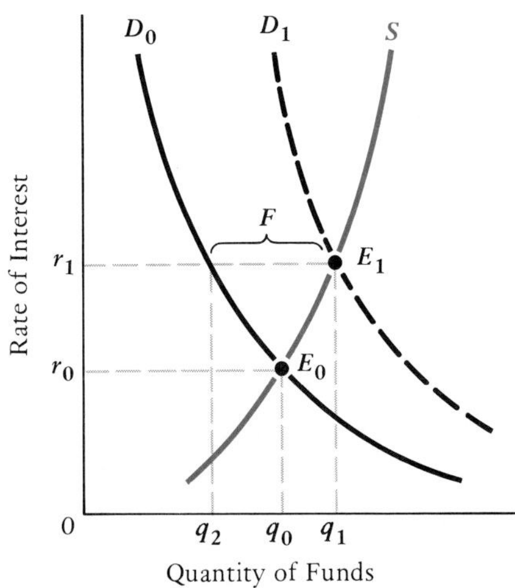

(i) Effects of government borrowing with constant national income

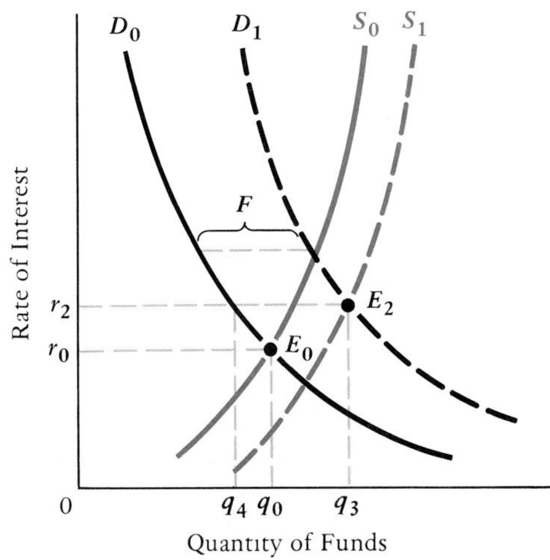

(ii) Effects of government borrowing with increased national income

Government borrowing may crowd out private-sector borrowing and investing. In (i), the supply of funds available to be lent, S, is fairly insensitive to the interest rate. Initially, the demand to borrow funds is D_0, giving an equilibrium interest rate of r_0 and a quantity of funds borrowed for all purposes of q_0.

Government spending now increases by F, all of which is borrowed. This shifts the demand for funds to the right, from D_0 to D_1, taking equilibrium to E_1. The interest rate rises to r_1, and the quantity of funds borrowed rises to q_1. However, q_2q_1 of these go to the government, so the private sector borrows only q_2, which is q_2q_0 less than it was able to borrow, and hence invest, before the deficit forced the government into the market.

If, however, the extra government expenditure increases national income, it will raise saving. The savings function will then shift to the right, say, from S_0 to S_1 in (ii). Crowding out will then be lessened. At equilibrium E_2 the interest rate rises to r_2, and private borrowing is only q_4q_0 less than before the government entered the market.

stock of foreign liabilities. Either way, their wealth will have been reduced relative to what it would have been without the deficits.

Payments of interest and dividends on liabilities owed abroad will lower GNP (income owned by Canadians) in relation to GDP (output produced in Canada), since some income generated by the output will accrue to foreigners. These payments will also lower GNP relative to what it would have been without the deficits.

Borrowing from abroad entails a transfer of purchasing power to domestic residents when the borrowing occurs and a transfer back to foreigners when interest payments and repayments of principal occur.

Does the Size of the Debt Hamper Economic Policy?

In 1989 over 30 percent of all tax revenues went to pay interest on the national debt! The magnitude of this obligation puts a severe strain on all government policies. Four ways in which it does this deserve mention.

First, to meet growing interest payments, expenditure on many existing programs must be cut, and many desirable new programs cannot be adopted.

During the first six years of the Conservative government's tenure, program expenditure fell as a fraction of GDP, but most of the saving went to pay the rising interest bill on the national debt rather than to cutting the deficit.

Second, fiscal stabilization policy is made difficult. According to the theory of stabilization policy, the government should run a surplus or a small deficit in boom times and a large deficit during slumps. (Built-in stabilizers will do much of the job automatically *if* the government's fiscal position is satisfactory on average over the cycle.) The persistent deficits over the past few years have meant that to some extent the government has been stimulating the economy during a boom. Even more worrisome is the possibility that in order to eliminate the deficit and control the growth of the national debt, it may have to go on trying to cut its deficit even if a severe slump emerges.

Third, the fiscal deficit greatly complicates the Bank of Canada's anti-inflationary policy.

Because the government's deficits were stimulating the economy, the Bank had to drive interest rates up sufficiently to counteract that stimulus and then even further to get the desired contractionary pressures.

Because of this, since the mid 1980s many economists have been publicly urging the government to alter the balance between fiscal and monetary policies. A major reduction in the budget deficit would be contractionary, and this would allow a less restrictive monetary policy with its accompanying lower interest rates. If desired, the two effects could be adjusted so as approximately to offset each other so that aggregate demand would be unaffected.

Fourth, every time the Bank pushes up interest rates, it adds to the government's budget deficit by increasing the interest bill on existing debt. With a national debt of over $320 billion, much of which was short-term, it was estimated in 1990 that every 1 percent increase in the interest rate added just over $3 billion to the federal government's budget deficit.

In view of these costs of persistent deficits and growing national debt, many economists and others have argued that the government's fiscal policies are imprudent and have called for a commitment to control the deficit.

Proposals to Control the Deficit

As we have seen, government deficits contribute to aggregate demand and hence can play a useful role in dampening cyclical fluctuations in the economy. As we have also seen, government deficits contribute to increases in the national debt and hence in the long term might lead to a reduction in living standards of the average Canadian. This conflict between the short-term stabilization role of deficits and the long-term adverse effects of a large public debt has been a subject of constant debate among economists and others.

Views range from those who dismiss the long-run costs of the national debt and hence are not concerned about the deficit to those who wish to eschew the short-term stabilization role for the deficit entirely and impose a virtual straitjacket on the government, requiring it always to balance its budget. We now look at some of the specific proposals that have been put forward; some of the general options are illustrated in Figure 39-4.

An annually balanced budget? Much current rhetoric of fiscal restraint calls for a balanced budget. In the United States, the Gramm-Rudman-Hollings bill, passed in late 1985, mandates expenditure cuts in order to eliminate the federal deficit by 1993. It failed to do so, and much of the deficit reduction that it did achieve came from "window dressing." This term refers to such dodges as shifting expenditures to accounts that are not covered in the budget and once-and-for-all shifts of tax revenue to get them into an earlier year.

The discussion earlier in this chapter suggests that an annually balanced budget would be extremely difficult, perhaps impossible, to achieve. With fixed tax rates, tax revenues fluctuate as national income fluctuates. Much government expenditure is fixed by past commitments, and most of the rest is hard to change quickly.

But suppose that an annually balanced budget, or something approaching it, were feasible. What would its effects be? Would they be desirable?

We saw earlier that a large government sector whose expenditures on goods and services are not very sensitive to the cyclical variations in national income is a major built-in stabilizer. To insist that annual government expenditure be tied to annual tax receipts would be to abandon the present built-in

FIGURE 39-4 Balanced and Unbalanced Budgets

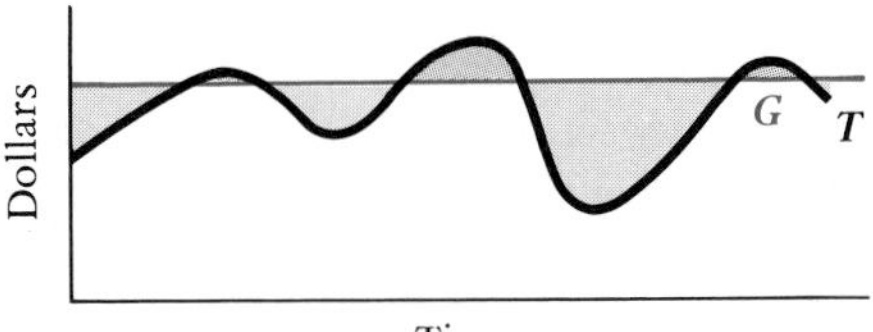

(i) A cyclically unbalanced budget

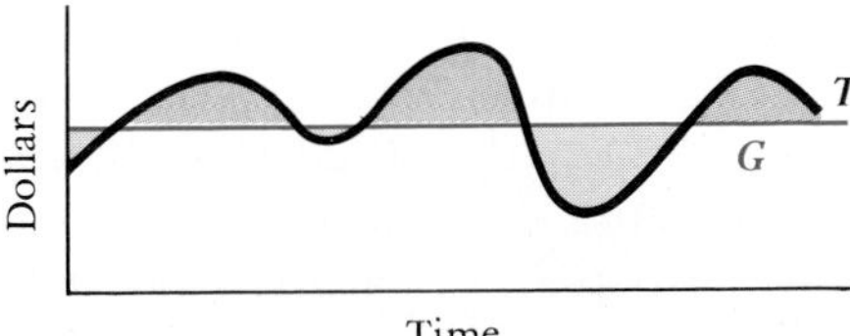

(ii) A cyclically balanced budget

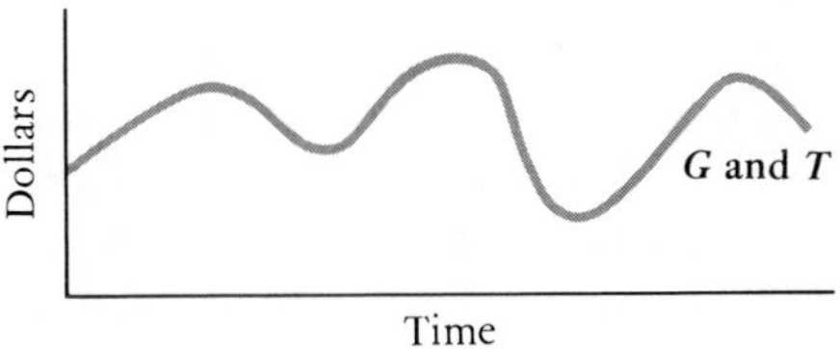

(iii) A constantly balanced budget

An annually (constantly) balanced budget is a destabilizer; a cyclically balanced budget is a stabilizer. The flow of tax receipts, *T*, is shown varying over the business cycle, while in (i) and (ii) government expenditure, *G*, is shown at a constant rate.

In (i) deficits (dark areas) are common and surpluses (light areas) are rare because the average level of expenditure exceeds the average level of taxes. Such a policy will tend to stabilize the economy against cyclical fluctuations, but the average fiscal stance of the government is expansionary. This has been the characteristic Canadian budgetary position over the past several decades.

In (ii) government expenditure has been reduced until it is approximately equal to the average level of tax receipts. The budget is now balanced cyclically. The policy still tends to stabilize the economy against cyclical fluctuations because of deficits in slumps and surpluses in booms. However, the average fiscal stance is neither strongly expansionary nor strongly contractionary.

In (iii) a balanced budget has been imposed. Deficits have been prevented, but government expenditure now varies over the business cycle, which tends to destabilize the economy by accentuating the cyclical swings in aggregate expenditure.

stability provided by the government. Government expenditure would then become a major *destabilizing* force. Tax revenues necessarily rise in booms and fall in slumps; an annually balanced budget would force government expenditure to do the same. Changes in national income would then cause induced changes not only in household consumption expenditure but also in government expenditure. This would greatly increase the economy's marginal propensity to spend and hence increase the value of the multiplier. In the terminology of Chapter 32, this would serve as a *built-in destabilizer*!

An annually balanced budget would accentuate the swings in national income that accompany changes in such autonomous expenditure flows as investment and exports.

A cyclically balanced budget. An alternative policy, one that would prevent continual deficits (and could also inhibit the growth in the size of the government sector), would be to balance the budget over the business cycle. This would be more feasible than the annually balanced budget, and it would not make government expenditure a destabilizing force.

Although more attractive in principle than the annually balanced budget, a cyclically balanced budget carries problems of its own. Government might well spend in excess of revenue in one year, leaving the next government the obligation to spend less than current revenue in following years. Could such an obligation to balance over a period of several years be made binding? What one government commits itself to in one year does not necessarily restrict what it (or its successor) does the next year.

Perhaps even more of a problem is that there is always room for some disagreement about the current state of the business cycle. A requirement to balance the budget over the business cycle can only be implemented on the basis of some forecast of future economic conditions. Forecasting of the level of economic activity is imperfect, to say the least, and there will be genuine disagreement among economists about what stage of the business cycle the economy is in and where the economy is headed. Compounding the difficulty that rises from such uncertainty is the fact that politicians will have a stake in the economic forecast. Those who favor increased government spending will tend to argue that *this* year is an unusually bad one, and the deficits of this year

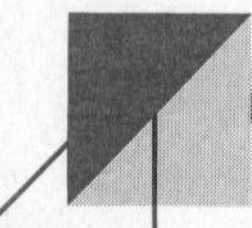

BOX 39-3

Debt, Deficits, and Sustainability

One way of checking whether concern about persistent government budget deficits is justified is to ask whether the current fiscal plan is *sustainable*. A sustainable fiscal plan is one that will not lead to continued growth in the debt-to-GDP ratio.

An unsustainable fiscal plan leads to a debt, and hence to interest payments, which are an ever-increasing fraction of GDP. If the current fiscal plan is unsustainable, the government will eventually have to introduce some fiscal correction; otherwise its deficit would eventually absorb all of the tax revenues in interest payments on the debt.

To examine this issue more fully, we need to introduce a fundamental equation that describes the evolution of the debt-to-GDP ratio over time. To do this, we let B stand for the size of the government debt, Y for national income as measured by GDP, and b for the ratio of the two; that is, $b = B/Y$, the debt-to-GDP ratio. Next let b' stand for the change in the debt-to-GDP ratio over time. A positive value for b' means that the ratio is increasing, and a negative value for b' means that the ratio is decreasing.

Using basic calculus, b' can be expressed as the sum of the two terms on the right side of Equation 1. **[45]**

$$b' = (g - t) + (i - n)b \qquad [1]$$

The first term is the primary deficit (which was introduced in Box 39-1), measured as a percentage of GDP; it is expressed as the difference between government program expenditure g and government tax revenue t, each measured as a fraction of GDP. The second term is the debt-to-GDP ratio b multiplied by the difference between the interest rate i and the rate of growth of GDP, n.

To see the role of these two terms, we consider each in isolation. First, suppose that the primary deficit is zero (i.e., that $g = t$); Equation 1 shows that in this case the change in the debt-to-GDP ratio is equal to the term $(i - n)b$. This tells us that there are two competing pressures on b'. Interest payments (ib) have to be financed by issuing new debt, so there is upward pressure of this amount on b. This tends to make b' positive. However, since we are concerned with the ratio of debt to GDP, growth in GDP serves to reduce the ratio; this term ($-nb$) puts downward pressure on the ratio and hence tends to make b' negative. Thus whether the ratio rises or falls (that is, whether b' is positive or negative) depends on whether the interest rate i is greater than or less than the growth rate n.

Now suppose that the interest rate i is just equal to the growth rate n. This makes the second term in Equation 1 zero, so the change in the ratio is equal to $g - t$. Now we see that a primary deficit (program spending, g, greater than tax revenue, t) will cause the debt-to-GDP ratio to rise over time (b' positive) since financing the primary deficit requires that more debt be issued. A primary surplus (g less than t) means that the government can gradually retire debt and thus the debt-to-GDP ratio will fall over time (b' negative).

We can now examine the conditions that must be satisfied if the "deficit" is to be sustainable. There are two cases, depending on the relation between the interest rate, i, and the growth rate, n.

First, consider the case where the interest rate i is less than the growth rate n. In this case, even if there is a primary deficit (g greater than t) that makes b' positive, the ratio will eventually stabilize since b' will eventually turn down. Initially, the primary deficit, the $g - t$ term, will cause the debt-to-GDP ratio b to grow. However, this growth in

b increases the weight given to the second term in Equation 1, which is negative. As this second term grows in absolute size, the rate at which the debt grows, given by b', falls. Eventually, b' will reach zero, and hence the ratio b will be constant.*

Second, consider the case where the interest rate, i, is greater than the growth rate, n. In this case the second term in Equation 1 is positive. For b' to be zero in this case requires a primary surplus so that that the negative value of $g - t$ offsets the positive value of $(i - n)b$.

A further difficulty arises in this second case because it involves an inherent instability. Any increase in b, say, due to a temporary primary budget deficit, will tend to make b' positive and thus cause further increases in b. This is because the initial rise in b increases the weight given to the second term in Equation 1 (where the interest payment effect, ib, outweighs the growth effect, nb). In order to limit this self-reinforcing and potentially explosive effect, the government would have to undertake discretionary fiscal actions to create a primary surplus so that the negative effects of the first term again offset the positive effects of the second term.

In its budgets and other public documents throughout the late 1980s and early 1990s, the Canadian government repeatedly focused on the implications of current and projected fiscal measures for the evolution of the debt-to-GDP ratio. The April 1989 budget, for example, stated explicitly, "The focus of the government's fiscal strategy is to stabilize and then reduce the size of the federal debt relative to GDP." In terms of Equation 1, this means lowering b' first to zero and then to below zero.

The government also noted that this objective had been difficult to achieve since the interest rate had exceeded the economy's growth rate in every year since 1981 (i.e., the second term in Equation 1 was positive). Early in the decade there had also been a significant primary deficit (i.e., the first term in Equation 1 was also positive), and as a result the debt-to-GDP ratio grew rapidly. A key part of the government's fiscal strategy was to reduce the primary deficit, and it fell from a peak of 5 percent in 1984 to a position of balance by 1988 and in 1989 turned to a surplus. However, in 1989–1990 the debt-to-GDP ratio continued to grow since the positive effect of the interest-growth differential (the second term) outweighed the negative effect of the primary surplus (the first term). Had the 1989–1990 primary surplus been attained earlier in the decade when the debt was a smaller fraction of GDP, the debt ratio would have started to fall.

The government's strategy to halt the growth in the debt ratio relied on three developments. First, the primary surplus had to be increased further. Second, as the strategy started to work and the growth in the debt ratio slowed, it was hoped that interest rates would fall. Third, the government projected increased economic growth as a result of some of its policies such as free trade with the United States, deregulation and privatization, and the replacement of the manufacturer's sales tax with the GST. (The hoped-for rise in n would serve to reduce the magnitude of the second term in Equation 1.)

* The value at which b will be stabilized is found by setting $b' = 0$ in Equation 1, and then solving for b. This particular value, which we label b^*, is given by $b^* = -(g - t)/(i - n)$. If i and n can be taken as given, the government can choose the "steady state" debt ratio b^* by choosing the appropriate value of $g - t$.

can be made up by the surpluses in (better) years to come. On the other side, some will always tend to find this year to be unusually good, a time to run surpluses against the hard times to follow.

Though a budget balanced over the course of the business cycle is in principle an acceptable way of reconciling short-term stabilization and long-term prudence, the business cycle may not be well enough defined to make the proposal operational.

Allowing for growth. A further problem is that the goal of budget *balance,* whether applied annually or over the cycle, is in fact stricter than is required to avoid a rising debt-to-GDP ratio. Growth in GDP (due either to growth in real output or to inflation) means that some growth in the debt, and hence a (small) deficit, is consistent with a stable debt-to-GDP ratio.

For economists who think of a stable debt-to-GDP ratio as the appropriate indicator of fiscal prudence, *budget balance* means a deficit such that the debt grows at the same rate as nominal GDP.

In the past few years the government has emphasized the need to stabilize the debt-to-GDP ratio and has included projections of the debt-to-GDP ratio in the documents accompanying its budget papers. These projections have in turn often been the focus of post-budget debates, with commentators often expressing the view that the government is too optimistic in its beliefs about growth or interest rates, and thus its projections about the debt-to-GDP ratio are also too optimistic.

The Medium-Term Fiscal Plan

Debt reduction. When the Progressive Conservatives formed the government in 1984, they made reduction of the large and growing budget deficit a major policy commitment. In their first two years, they eliminated the built-in tendencies for the deficit to rise rapidly. The fiscal plan then called for reducing the absolute value of the deficit over the next few years. This proved difficult, partly because of political pressures to spend rather than to economize and partly because of economic events beyond the government's control. World interest rates remained higher than expected, and the buildup of inflationary pressures in Canada induced the Bank to push Canadian rates significantly above world rates in the course of its anti-inflation policy. The extremely high Canadian interest rates increased the cost of servicing the growing stock of national debt. Other domestic problems caused major expenditures. For example, the agricultural crisis among grain farmers, caused by sagging international markets and poor harvests at home, raised support grants to farmers by about $2 billion.

Reducing the debt-to-GDP ratio. The main objective of the government's fiscal plan was first to stabilize the debt-to-GDP ratio at a level below 60 percent and then to have the ratio slowly fall to a lower level. Although the budget deficits were not reduced as much as had been hoped, they were stabilized at just less than $30 billion per year. The continued growth of the GDP stabilized the debt-to-GDP ratio, which meant that the debt was growing no faster than national income. However, a ratio of nearly 60 percent was generally believed to be too large. It meant, among other things, that government revenues were heavily committed to paying interest on the national debt and that there was little room for new fiscal initiatives. The deficit was also highly sensitive to swings in the interest rate.

Many critics called for much larger reductions in the budget deficit. However, as long as the rate of growth of the debt could be held below the rate of growth of GDP, the crucial debt-to-GDP ratio would fall. This would reduce the burden of the debt as measured by the proportion of national income needed to be raised in taxes just to service that debt.

Evaluation. In a study written for the Macdonald Commission in the mid 1980s, Professors Neil Bruce and Douglas Purvis of Queen's University addressed the issue of fiscal prudence by evaluating the government's medium-term fiscal plan.

Bruce and Purvis defined the *imprudent deficit* as the part of projected deficits that contributes to growth in the debt-to-GDP ratio above some target level. Thus they allow for trend growth in the economy and for projected inflation. Their calculation showed the imprudent deficit to be significant. They concluded that there was cause for concern about the long-term implications of projected deficits and that some concerted but systematic phasing in of budget cuts was in order. Further, they argued that even though the actual cuts could be implemented gradually, the process had to be shared quickly so that the programs for reestablishing fiscal prudence would be flexible enough that the short-term objectives of fiscal stabilization need not be abandoned.

Summary. The need for fiscal prudence is accepted by virtually everyone. How to evaluate it and enforce it, however, is still subject to controversy. Indeed, there is serious doubt that the idea of a balanced budget over any time period is operational.

Many economists believe that a superior alternative to insisting on a precise balance is to pay attention to the balance without making a fetish of never adding to the national debt.

Some further aspects of the concern about growth in the debt-to-GDP ratio are discussed in Box 39-3.

The Political Economy of the Debt

Almost all economists accept that if the debt got so large that it could not be serviced without either putting a crushing burden on taxpayers or forcing the government to create new money to service it, there would be serious problems. But many think we are still a long way from that point. To them the overriding principle is that the debt should be changed according to the needs of stabilization policy.

An alternative view is what has come to be called *fiscal conservatism*. The main premise of fiscal conservatives is that governments are not passive agents who do what is necessary to create full employment and maximize social welfare. Instead, governments are composed of individuals—elected officials, legislators, and civil servants—who, like everyone else, seek mainly to maximize their own well-being. Their welfare is best served by a big role for government and by a satisfied electorate. Thus they tend to favor spending and to resist tax increases. This creates a persistent tendency toward deficits that is quite independent of any consideration of a sound fiscal policy.

The debate reflects deeply held views about the role of government, the nature and motivation of public officials, and the desirability of stabilization. Keynesians are more likely to emphasize the potential benefits from active fiscal policy and to regard substantial government intervention as essential to an effective and humane society. Fiscal conservatives are likely to see public intervention, however well motivated, as probably inept and ultimately destabilizing.

The deficits of the past decade have also received enough public attention so that the majority of both Keynesians and fiscal conservatives consistently argue that the deficit must be reduced. In spite of the fact that deficit reduction is politically uncontroversial in principle, it has proved very difficult to effect in practice. This is not entirely surprising. As we have seen, most of the harm that will arise from deficits will only appear over the very long term, in the form of potentially reduced living standards in the future. To do something about deficits, politicians must raise taxes and cut spending today, imposing real costs on today's voters, when the uncertain benefits of those actions will only be reaped in the relatively distant future.

SUMMARY

1. The recent record of persistent, large government budget deficits has attracted enormous attention and generated heated debate over the policy options. In order to put the growth of the deficit in perspective, it is useful to measure it relative to GDP. After roughly balancing, on average, for the 1960s and early 1970s, the government budget deficit rose from less than 1 percent of GDP at the start of the decade to over 6 percent in 1984 and remained high through the remainder of the 1980s.
2. Deficits influence the economy through their short-run stabilizing or destabilizing role and through their potential to affect income and welfare adversely in the long run. The latter effects arise from the buildup of the debt-to-GDP ratio.
3. Canadian national debt and debt service payments have risen and fallen as a percentage of national income, but recently they have

shown an upward trend. Recent increases in these ratios reflect the cumulative effects of persistently large deficits dating back to the mid 1970s. Persistent deficits are a cause for concern for several reasons, including inflation, crowding out of investment and net exports, and reducing national income in the long run.

4. An annually balanced budget would be unfeasible; even if it were possible, it would destabilize the economy. A cyclically balanced budget would act as a stabilizer and would also curb the growth of the government sector.
5. In a growing economy, the concept of budget balance allows for a small but positive deficit such that the stock of debt grows at the same rate as nominal GDP.
6. Keynesians tend to take a relatively sanguine view of the effect of active fiscal policy on the national debt. As long as the national debt does not grow rapidly as a proportion of national income, they view its short-term fluctuations as a stabilizing device and its long-term upward trend as a reasonable price to pay for economic stability.
7. Fiscal conservatives mistrust government and view insistence on a balanced budget as the only effective means of curtailing reckless government spending that wastes scarce resources and feeds the fires of inflation.

TOPICS FOR REVIEW

Short-run and long-run effects of deficits
The relationship between deficits and the national debt
Debt service payments
Debt-to-GDP ratio
Cyclically balanced budget
Keynesian and fiscal conservative views of debt

DISCUSSION QUESTIONS

1. In 1990 the Canadian economy appeared to be sliding into a recession, while the deficit and, in particular, debt service payments continued at record levels. The first development led many people to call for fiscal stimulus, while the second developments led to calls for fiscal restraint. Write a brief analysis of the bases for these competing views; then review the record to see what was actually done and why.
2. Consider the typical annual expenditures and revenues of the organizations listed here. Comment on the appropriate debt policy for each, taking into account their respective goals, life span, and resources.
   a. Family household
   b. Two private corporations, one growing rapidly and the other a mature firm
   c. A village of 5,000 inhabitants
   d. The Canadian government
   e. The United Nations
3. Evaluate each of the following proposals to "control the deficit" in order to avoid the long-run burden of the debt.
   a. Maintaining a zero cyclically adjusted deficit
   b. Keeping the debt-to-GDP ratio constant
   c. Limiting government borrowing in each year to some fixed percentage of national income in that year

4. In the August 27, 1990, issue of the *Globe and Mail,* former federal deputy minister of finance Grant Reuber argued that in preparing its 1991 budget, the finance minister must regain the "steady path of deficit reduction" and that to do so "probably at least $2 billion would have to be found through lower spending." Evaluate his views in the context of the state of the economy and of the government budget at that particular juncture. Why does he emphasize expenditure cuts?
5. Judith Maxwell, chairman of the Economic Council of Canada, has warned that "when interest rates are higher than the economic growth rate, the ratio of debt to GDP acquires dangerous upward momentum." Discuss why this is so. Does the current Canadian situation reflect this combination?
6. What problems for budgetary control are posed by the fact that economic forecasting is imperfect? How might these problems be minimized?
7. How does the decision of whether to raise taxes or issue bonds in order to finance the unusually high government expenditures incurred during a war influence "who pays" for the war?
8. John Crow, governor of the Bank of Canada, has expressed concern about the persistent government deficit and the growing level of debt in the economy. Why should this concern him?
9. In 1989, U.S. Congressional Budget Office director Robert Reischaner said: "We have a long way to go before the [government budget] deficit is brought down to a level where Americans should feel comfortable." Arguing that the borrowing caused by the deficit erodes living standards for future generations, "How well do you want your children and grandchildren to live?" he asked. Write a critique either supporting or challenging Reischaner's views.

Appendix to Chapter 39

Does the Deficit Matter? The Ricardian Neutrality Proposition

Analysts who focus on the deficit as a summary description of the government's influence on the economy presuppose that tax-financed government expenditure contributes less to aggregate demand than bond-financed government expenditure, since the latter leads to a larger deficit. Note that deficit financing of government expenditure can be viewed as a deferral of taxes, increasing current disposable income and reducing future disposable income. This rearrangement of the timing of taxes may leave expected permanent income basically unchanged compared with the case in which taxes are levied at the same time as the government expenditure occurs. Whereas the Keynesian consumption function predicts that consumption would increase with the increase in current disposable income, the permanent-income hypothesis (PIH), discussed in the Appendix to Chapter 28, predicts that households' consumption is related to their lifetime or permanent income, not their current disposable income. If the PIH is an accurate description of behavior, deficit finance will have little effect on consumption behavior.

Thus it is possible to identify a set of conditions that would mean that government expenditure has the same effect on the economy whether it is financed by raising current taxes or by issuing government bonds. This imaginary world, first considered by David Ricardo in 1817 and recently revived by Professor Robert Barro, is populated by farsighted individuals whose consumption decisions depend on their "permanent" income only. Thus changes in the time pattern of income receipts that leave their permanent income unchanged would have no effect on private-sector expenditure decisions.

In this world, government bonds would not be net wealth, because the financial value of a bond would be matched exactly by a corresponding liability for future tax payments needed to service the debt. Specifically, households would be indifferent between paying $1 of current taxes and paying a stream of future taxes that has a present value of $1 when discounted at the market interest rate. In this case the government deficit would not matter; bond rather than tax finance would represent merely a rearrangement in the timing of income receipts that the private sector could (and would) offset in capital markets. Issuing bonds now and raising taxes later would be viewed as equivalent to raising taxes now.

The theory underlying this analysis requires that households have an infinite planning horizon, as in the PIH that was discussed in the Appendix to Chapter 28. Otherwise taxes accruing after the household's lifetime would not offset interest payments received during the household's lifetime, and government bonds would be viewed as net wealth by the household. Hence deficits would increase households' perceived net wealth, households would increase their consumption, and deficit-financed government expenditure would be more expansionary than tax-financed expenditure.

Barro's contribution was to show that debt neutrality could arise even in the context of the life-cycle theory if the household's concern for its heirs caused its planning horizon to extend beyond its own lifetime. Suppose that the typical household, when it is making its own lifetime consumption plans, also plans for a positive bequest that it intends to leave to its heirs. Now consider the effects of a government decision to sell bonds rather than to increase taxes in order to finance previously announced government expenditure; this, of course, increases the government budget deficit. (Thus we are focusing on the effects of the method of financing the expenditure, not on the effects of the expenditure itself.) If the household wishes, it could simply spend the disposable income that it did not have to pay as current taxes to finance the government expenditure, thus leaving the next generation with a liability to pay the taxes that will have to be levied when the government redeems the bonds. If the recipients behave in this manner, the fiscal authority's decision to rely on deficit financing will have stimulated the economy by inducing an increase in spending.

However, this behavior would reduce the net value of the bequest that the typical household would be leaving to its heirs, since the heirs now face an increased tax liability. This violates the notion that the members of a typical household make a rational plan that includes targets for its own consumption and for the bequest that it wishes to leave to its heirs, since the government action does not change the options open to current households. The current household could have achieved this redistribution away from future generations toward itself without the government action simply by increasing its own consumption and reducing the value of the estate that it leaves to its heirs.

If the current household wishes to preserve its initial plan, all that it needs to do is maintain its spending plans and increase saving by the full amount of its disposable income that it did not have to pay to finance its share of the government budget deficit. The resulting increase in the value of the next generation's inheritance will exactly offset the increase in tax liabilities that it faces. Thus a government deficit that issues bonds now and "promises" taxes in the future would have no effect even if the taxes were expected only after the current generation was dead.

Note that the level of government expenditure is still important in this model—only the method of financing is irrelevant. However, there are a number of reasons to believe that future taxes that have a present value of $1 are not equivalent to present taxes of $1 and thus that this debt-neutral Ricardian model does not provide an accurate description of the working of a modern economy. (Ricardo himself rejected it.) Let us cite just three reasons.

The private sector borrows on terms different from those of the government sector. This is perhaps the most important reason why deficit financing is not neutral in practice. In many circumstances households and to some extent firms face constraints that prevent them from borrowing all that they would like at the prevailing market interest rate. Alternatively, they may be able to borrow but at a much higher interest rate than that of the government. Consequently, when the government substitutes future taxes for present taxes by running a deficit, these "constrained" private-sector agents will feel wealthier and will consequently spend more.

Myopic perception. If some households imperfectly perceive the future tax liabilities implied by the government deficit, they will not offset government dissaving with private saving.

Finite lifetimes. Another reason why households might view future taxes as not equivalent to current taxes is that future taxes may extend beyond the expected lifetime of the household. Thus the household may anticipate escaping taxes by dying! As Barro points out, this would make no difference if households "care about their heirs"; in this case living households would simply alter any bequests that they had planned to leave to their heirs by an amount equal to the expected increase in future taxes borne by their heirs. However, if households that are currently alive do not care or are unable to alter their bequests (perhaps because such bequests cannot be reduced below their current zero level), living households will, in fact, react to a change in the deficit in a manner that does not completely offset it.

Conclusions

The basic feature of the economy that makes government deficits and the public debt matter is that to a significant extent, current private-sector expenditure is tied to current private-sector income. The government deficit influences the current income of the private sector, since for a given level of government expenditure, a larger deficit means lower current taxes and hence larger current private disposable income. In the first instance, this debt finance simply causes an intertemporal rearrangement of private-sector income. However, for the reasons noted, the private sector is not indifferent to this rearrangement of its income receipts. In particular, current private-sector expenditure rises in response to the increase in current income. This influence of government deficits on private spending not only creates the potential for a stabilization role for deficits over the business cycle but also creates the mechanism by which persistent deficits become costly and undesirable in the longer run.

Chapter 40

Macroeconomic Controversies

How well do markets work? Can government improve market performance? In various guises these two questions are the basis of most disagreements over economic policy. We shall see that different answers to these questions imply big differences in macroeconomic policy prescriptions.

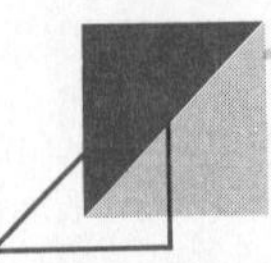

Interventionists and Noninterventionists

Broadly speaking, we can identify a noninterventionist view and an interventionist view with respect to each of the economic policy goals that we have encountered throughout this book. The noninterventionist view says that the unaided market economy functions well and needs little help from government in achieving the policy goal in question. The interventionist view says that government policy can substantially improve the economy's performance with respect to that question. For the purposes of our study, we can identify two extreme positions. The people we call *noninterventionists* are noninterventionist on all issues, whereas those we call *interventionists* support government intervention at all times. Only a few people may actually be noninterventionist or interventionist in this sense, since most would favor intervention on some issues and nonintervention on others. Many, however, would still identify themselves as either noninterventionist or interventionist because they were more often on one side than on the other.

Noninterventionist Views

Noninterventionists believe that the free market economy performs quite well on balance. Although shocks do hit the system, they lead rather quickly, and often painlessly, to the adjustments dictated by the market system. For example, relative prices in booming sectors rise, drawing in resources from declining sectors or regions. As a result, resources (and particularly labor) usually remain fully employed, so there is no need for full-employment policies.

Noninterventionists hold that macroeconomic performance will be most satisfactory if it is determined primarily by the workings of the free market.

Of course, few believe that the market system functions perfectly. However, whereas interventionists call for discretionary policies to improve economic performance, the noninterventionist view is that the market system works well enough to preclude any significant constructive role for policy. Indeed, many noninterventionists believe that policies are often so crude and their effects so uncertain with regard to both strength and timing that their use may impair rather than improve the economy's performance.

In a modern economy, some government presence is inevitable. Thus a stance of *no* intervention is impossible; rather, noninterventionists advocate minimal direct intervention in the market system. This involves the government's bearing responsibility for providing a *stable environment* in which the private sector can function. This has given rise to a debate that is popularly known as *rules versus discretion*, which is discussed further in Box 40-1.

Providing a Stable Environment

Creating a stable environment, as the noninterventionists advocate, may be easier said than done. One major problem is that macro variables are interrelated. The stability of one may imply the instability of another. In such cases, a choice must often be made. How much instability of one aggregate can we tolerate to secure stability in another related aggregate? We now consider the prescriptions for establishing stable fiscal and monetary policies.

Fiscal rules. Suppose that the government decides to adopt the goal of stability in the budget balance as part of the stable environment. This "stability" would require great *instability* in tax and expenditure policy. Tax revenues depend on the interaction between tax rates and the level of national income. With given tax rates, tax revenues change with the ebb and flow of the business cycle. A stable budget balance would require that the government raise tax rates and cut expenditures in slumps and lower tax rates and raise expenditures in booms.

Not only does this squander the budget's potential to act as a stabilizer (see the discussion in Chapter 32), but also continual changes in tax rates and expenditure levels cause great instability of the fiscal environment. A stable fiscal environment requires stability in government expenditures and tax rates so that the private sector can make plans for the future in a climate of known patterns of tax liabilities and government demand.

Any target budget balance must be some average over a period long enough to cover a typical cycle. Stability from year to year should be found in tax rates and expenditure programs, *not* in the size of the budget balance.

This in turn requires that the budget deficit vary cyclically, showing its largest deficits in slumps and its largest surpluses in booms.

Monetary rules. Advocates of a stable monetary environment are actually advocating stable inflation. (Whether a *zero* rate is feasible or not is discussed on page 790.) The central bank is urged to set a target rate of increase in the money supply and to hold it. To establish the target, the cental bank estimates the rate at which the demand for money would be growing if actual income equaled potential income and the price level were stable. This then becomes the target rate of growth of the money supply. The key proposition is that the money supply should be changing gradually along a stable path that is independent of short-term variations in the demand for money caused by cyclical changes in the economy. This is referred to as the ***k* percent rule.**

Will the *k* percent rule really provide monetary stability? The answer is not necessarily. Assuring a stable rate of monetary growth does not assure a stable monetary environment. Monetary shortages and surpluses depend on the relationship between the supply of and the demand for money. Problems for the *k* percent rule arise when the demand for money shifts. For example, payment of interest on checking deposits increases the demand for M1. In this event, if the central bank adheres to a *k* percent rule, there will be an excess demand for money, and interest rates will rise. Thus contractionary pressure will be put on the economy.

One disadvantage of a monetary rule is that it may set up speculative behavior. For example, if there is too much money when weekly money supply figures are announced, speculators know that in the future the price of bonds will most likely fall because the central bank will sell more bonds to reduce the surplus. Speculators are thus induced to sell bonds now, hoping to rebuy them at bargain prices later when the central bank acts.

Monetary rules can introduce instability into interest-rate behavior.

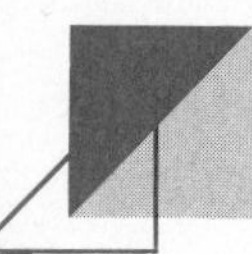

BOX 40-1

Rules Versus Discretion

Policymakers can indulge in *gross tuning* of the economy, which means that they try to influence its trends of inflation, economic growth, and other aspects. They can also engage in *fine tuning*, which means trying to remove recessionary and inflationary gaps that emerge due to short-term fluctuations mainly in aggregate demand. Our discussion is of fine tuning.

Three of the main issues involved in the rules versus discretion debate are problems that are created by lags, the type of stabilization needed, and the adequacy of information.

Lags

Economists who are hostile to discretionary policy emphasize the long and variable lags of both fiscal and monetary policy. Monetary policy can be put into effect quickly, but it takes 6 to 18 months for the full effects of a change in interest rates to be felt in terms of altered private-sector expenditures. It often takes a long time to put fiscal policy into effect, since federal budgets are usually several months in the making. Once the changes are made, however, their effects spread quickly throughout the economy.

Noninterventionists feel that these lags destroy the presumption that discretionary full-employment policy will usually be stabilizing. Interventionists feel that although the lags are serious, discretionary policies can be effective in reducing persistent recessionary gaps. Few interventionists, however, now call for fine tuning.

A Stable Climate for Planning

Supporters of rules emphasize the need for a stable climate so that firms and households can plan for the future. They argue that continual changes in tax rates and the money supply, which are designed to stabilize the economy, are destabilizing because they create a climate of uncertainty that makes long-term planning difficult.

Supporters of discretionary policy argue that they want discretion exercised only when the occasional serious recession develops and that large fluctuations in income and employment can be as upsetting to long-term planning as the occasional changes in tax rates and expenditures that are required by stabilization policy.

Do We Know Enough?

Discretionary stabilization policy requires that we forecast what the state of the economy will be in the absence of that policy. Generally, actual information is available only when there is a lag. Policymakers know approximately what the GDP was last quarter and what unemployment was last month. (The first preliminary figures for many economic variables can be subject to substantial errors. Often these estimates are revised several times over subsequent months and even years.) On the basis of these data, projections of future behavior of the economy must be made and policy must be set.

Supporters of discretionary policy accept that errors in projections may be large in relation to the recessionary gaps that are created by minor recessions, but they believe that the errors are small in relation to major recessions. They argue that in major recessions policymakers will not be in doubt about the existence of a large recessionary gap or the need for some significant stimulus, even though the exact amount of the gap or the stimulus cannot be determined precisely.

A second disadvantage of a monetary rule is that to preserve its credibility, the central bank may fail to take discretionary action that would otherwise be appropriate. For example, after an entrenched inflation is broken, the economy may come to rest with substantial unemployment and a stable price level. There is then a case for a once-and-for-all discretionary expansion in the money supply to get the economy back to full employment. The *k* percent rule precludes this, condemning the economy to a slump. (This possibility is discussed in detail on pages 763–764.)

Despite these problems, noninterventionists believe that the *k* percent rule is superior to any known alternative. Some would agree that in principle the central bank could improve the economy's performance by occasional bouts of discretionary monetary policy to offset such things as major shifts in the demand for money. However, they also believe that once given any discretion, the central bank would abuse it in an attempt to fine tune the economy. The resulting instability would, they believe, be much more than any instability resulting from the application of a *k* percent rule in an environment subject to some change.

Interventionist Views

Interventionists believe that the functioning of the market economy is often far from satisfactory. Sometimes markets show weak self-regulatory forces, and the economy settles into prolonged periods of heavy unemployment. At other times markets tend to "overcorrect," causing the economy to lurch between the extremes of large recessionary and inflationary gaps.

Interventionists believe that the outcomes that arise from the workings of the market system can be improved by judicious government intervention.

Even though interventionist policies may be imperfect, they may be good enough to improve the functioning of the economy with respect to all three main goals of macro policy.[1]

Interventionist Prescriptions

Interventionists call for discretionary fiscal and monetary policies to offset significant inflationary and recessionary gaps and thus to stabilize national income at its capacity level. Some interventionists, particularly a group called *post-Keynesians*, believe that control of the money supply may not be enough to achieve full employment and stable prices simultaneously. This is because they accept the wage-cost push theory of inflation, which was briefly discussed in Chapter 36.

Some interventionists call for incomes policies to restrain the wage-cost push and so make full employment compatible with stable prices. They believe that such policies should become permanent features of the economic landscape. Many economists accept that wage and price controls might work as *temporary* measures to break inflationary inertia (see Chapter 36) but that they would introduce inefficiencies and rigidities as permanent features.

More permanent incomes policies might be of two types. The first type, commonly used in Europe in past decades but now out of favor, is often called a *social contract*. Labor, management, and the government consult annually and agree on target wage changes. These are calculated to be noninflationary, given the government's projections for the future and its planned economic policies. Such a scheme is most easily initiated in a centralized economy such as Germany's, where a few giant firms and unions exert enormous power, or in a country such as Great Britain, where the party in power during much of the period in which social contracts were used had strong official links with the labor unions.

The other main type of incomes policy is the *tax-related incomes policy (TIP)* that was first discussed in Chapter 36. TIPs provide tax incentives for management and labor to conform to government-established wage and price guidelines. For example, increases in wages and prices in excess of the guidelines would be taxed heavily.

TIPs rely on tax incentives to secure voluntary conformity with wage and price guidelines, whereas wage and price controls try to impose conformity by law.

Advocates of TIPs argue that their great advantage is that decisions on wages and prices are left in the hands of labor and management while they influence behavior by altering the incentive system. Critics, however, argue that they would prove to be an administrative nightmare. Although they have been strongly backed by some economists in the past,

[1] Note that both opposing views are optimistic in this respect. Noninterventionists say that the economy functions well without government assistance; interventionists say that it functions poorly but government intervention can improve its performance. A pessimistic view would be that the economy does exhibit the unstable behavior described in the text but that government intervention would only make it worse.

TIPs have never been tried and currently have few vocal advocates.

The Working of the Automatic Adjustment Mechanism

For almost 40 years following World War II, disagreements among macroeconomists were dominated by the ongoing debate between two groups—the monetarists and the Keynesians. Monetarists are often identified with noninterventionist views, and Keynesians are often identified with interventionists. Both groups accepted the key features of the macroeconomic model of the economy, which we have outlined elsewhere in this book. The relevant features are these:

1. In the long run, national income is equal to its capacity level, as determined by the position of the vertical *LRAS* curve. The level of income at this *full-employment* position is not influenced by fluctuations in aggregate demand.
2. In the short run, national income is determined by the intersection of the *SRAS* and *AD* curves. This level can deviate from the capacity level, giving rise to either an *inflationary gap* or a *recessionary gap*. In the short run, national income can be influenced by aggregate demand, which can in turn be influenced by monetary and fiscal policies.
3. Deviations of national income from its capacity level give rise to changes in wages and prices that if allowed to operate would eventually restore full employment. (This was referred to as the *automatic adjustment mechanism*.)

Given that both groups apparently accepted these "core" propositions, how is it that they could disagree about the behavior of the economy and about the appropriate role of policy? The basic course of their disagreements lay in their different views about the strength of the automatic adjustment mechanism. Their different views relate to their different answers to the question, "What behavior in the individual markets for goods and factors of production is implied by the macroeconomic model?" This issue concerns what are called the *micro foundations*, or *micro underpinnings,* of macro models.

Monetarist Views

Most monetarists view markets as competitive. They realize, of course, that perfect competition does not exist everywhere in the economy, but they believe that the forces of competition are strong enough that analysis based on the theory of perfect competition will be close to the real behavior of the economy.

One important characteristic of competitive markets is that prices and wages are flexible; they adjust to establish equilibrium at all times. When a competitive market is in equilibrium (see Chapter 4), the market is said to have *cleared.* Competitive markets clear only at the equilibrium price. At any other price, there are either unsatisfied purchasers (excess demand) or unsatisfied sellers (excess supply).

When a competitive market has cleared, every purchaser has been able to buy all that he or she wishes to buy at the going price and every seller has been able to sell all that he or she wishes to sell at that price. When each and every market is in equilibrium, there is full employment of all resources. The prices that clear markets are called **market-clearing prices**.

According to monetarists, strong market forces ensure that departures from full-employment equilibrium are quickly rectified; that is, monetarists believe that the automatic adjustment mechanism works quite efficiently.

Monetarists recognize the existence of cyclical fluctuations in output and unemployment and the role of aggregate demand in influencing them, but they argue that for the purposes of interpreting the behavior of the economy and for formulating policy recommendations, it is best to treat the economy *as if* there were continuous full employment.

Further, according to Friedman and his followers, long and variable lags in the operation of monetary policy make interventionist monetary policy counterproductive. In their view, monetary policy that seeks to stabilize the economy against cyclical fluctuations has actually served to destabilize it in the past. Given this and the belief that the economy's automatic adjustment mechanism works quickly, the best course for monetary policy is to follow the *k* percent rule: Set the rate of increase of the money supply at some given value and hold it there. This will ensure a relatively small and stable rate of inflation while leaving output gaps to be removed by the economy's wage and price adjustment mechanisms.

Keynesian Views

Keynesian micro foundations emphasize the noncompetitive nature of the economy. Most firms are seen as setting their own prices rather than as accepting those set in competitive markets. Their per unit output costs tend to be fairly constant, and they set prices by adding a relatively inflexible markup to their costs.[2] They then sell what they can at the going price. Cyclical fluctuations in aggregate demand cause cyclical fluctuations in the demand for each firm's products, which in turn cause individual firms to make cyclical variations in output and in employment rather than in price. A similar argument holds for labor markets in the Keynesian model. Wages respond to the price level and productivity but are relatively insensitive to short-term cyclical fluctuations in demand. (This is discussed in detail in Chapter 37, and we return to these issues later in this chapter when we encounter the new Keynesian economics.)

In the monetarist model, the main short-run impact of fluctuations in aggregate demand is on prices; in the Keynesian model, their main impact is on output and employment.

Thus Keynesians tend to believe that the economy lacks strong natural corrective forces that will always cause it easily and quickly to move back to full employment. In particular, though they believe that the price level rises quite quickly to eliminate inflationary gaps, they believe that the price level does not fall quickly to eliminate recessionary gaps. Keynesians thus stress the asymmetries, noted in Chapter 30 (see page 638). As a result,

Keynesians believe that recessionary gaps can persist for significant periods of time unless they are eliminated by active stabilization policy.

These supply-side issues that arise from differences concerning the operation of the automatic adjustment mechanism anticipate some of the current macroeconomic controversies that we take up next.

[2] Complete cyclical inflexibility of markups is not necessary. What matters is that firms do not adjust prices continually and are thus willing to sell further units at the same price. This much price inflexibility need not imply an absence of profit maximization. Instead, it may follow from profit maximization when it is costly to alter prices. This is discussed further in Chapter 14.

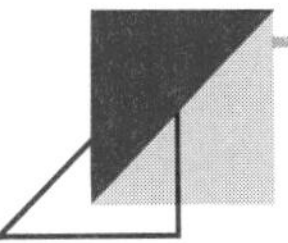

Current Controversies

A spate of recent research, stimulated by concern about the ability of the common core model to provide further insights into the operation of the economy and economic policy, has resulted in a number of schools of thought that espouse models that represent sharp departures from the common core model, which is the one studied so far in this book. We shall consider three of the most important. Debate about the merits of the models still rages today. The issues are important; because they are at the frontier of modern research, they are also difficult. The analysis depends on material that is treated in detail in more advanced courses. At this stage, therefore, we can discuss the issues only in broad outline.

New Classical Economics

The *new classical economists* follow Professors Robert Lucas and Thomas Sargent in holding that temporary departures from full employment occur mainly because people make mistakes. This viewpoint can be best understood in terms of the proposition, derived from microeconomics, that individual supply and demand behavior depends only on the structure of relative prices.[3]

To follow their argument, let us start by assuming that each of the economy's markets is in equilibrium; there is full employment, prices are stable, and the actual and expected rates of inflation are zero. Now suppose that the government increases the money supply by 5 percent. People find themselves with unwanted money balances, which they seek to spend.[4] For the sake of simplicity, assume that this leads to an increase in desired expenditure on all

[3] The new classical economists espouse many of the same policy views, which we have just discussed, as the monetarists; both are essentially *noninterventionist* in their approach to economic policy. Sometimes the new classical economists are referred to as *new classical monetarists*, and the original monetarists are sometimes referred to as *traditional monetarists*.

[4] Most monetarists (new classical and traditional) accept the theory of the transmission mechanism (discussed in Chapter 34), according to which the excess money balances are used to buy financial assets, thus driving down interest rates and stimulating expenditure *indirectly*. However, most monetarists tend to stress the relative importance of the *direct* expenditure effects created by excess money balances.

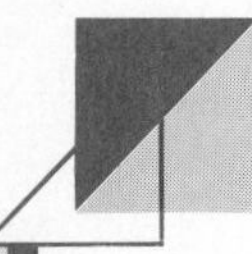

BOX 40-2

Nonlinear Dynamics and Chaos

Like economists, scientists in other fields, including physics, biology, and ecology, abstract from many complications and focus on the problem at hand using models that present a simplified picture of the real world. Scientists have found that the analysis and simulation of such models can contribute greatly to the understanding of real-world events.

Recently, there have been some startling discoveries about the behavior of models that involve *nonlinearities* in their structures. In a *linear* system, cause and effect are *proportionately* related; for example, if production is linear, doubling all inputs will double the output. In a nonlinear system, the relationship between cause and effect is more complicated; for example, doubling all inputs may more than double the output.

In clasical linear dynamics, a stable system either settles down at a constant rate of change or in a regular cycle; such a system's behavior can be disturbed by random shocks, but their effects normally die out fairly quickly. For example, in a model of economic growth that is built on linear dynamic systems, real income may follow the growth path of potential income, or it may also exhibit regular cyclical fluctuations around that growth path.

Nonlinear dynamic systems do not always behave in these simple ways. For example, a nonlinear model of economic growth may exhibit steady growth for a while, then quite suddenly move to regular cycles and then quite suddenly again produce irregular fluctuations that never repeat themselves. Although there is no random behavior in the system's equations, the behavior may look random in that it exhibits an irregular pattern of fluctuations that never repeats itself. This seemingly random behavior is caused by the system's deterministic but nonlinear laws.

Nonlinear systems that behave as we have just described are called *chaotic*. A chaotic system is one that has the capacity to magnify small differences in its initial conditions into two paths that diverge from each other to a point where they eventually do not resemble each other at all. Such systems are often characterized by phase transitions and positive feedback loops.

A phase transition occurs, for example, when water is cooled steadily. At first the speed of the random movement of its molecules falls continuously. Then, at freezing temperature, there is an abrupt change. The molecules stop moving about and become fixed in a definite pattern. A similar *phase transition* occurs when the water is heated and goes abruptly from a liquid to a gaseous state.

commodities; the demand for each commodity shifts to the right, and all prices, being competitively determined, rise. Individual decision makers see their selling prices go up and mistakenly interpret this increase as a rise in their own relative price. This is because they expect the overall rate of inflation to be zero. Firms will produce more, and workers will work more; both groups think that they are getting an increased *relative price* for what they sell. Thus total output and employment rise.

When both groups eventually realize that their own relative prices are in fact unchanged, output and employment fall back to their initial levels. The extra output and employment occur only while people are being fooled. When they realize that *all* prices have risen by 5 percent, they revert to their initial behavior. The only difference is that now the price level has risen by 5 percent, leaving relative prices unchanged.

According to the new classical theory, deviations from full employment occur only because people make mistakes that cause markets to clear at more or less than full-employment output. People do not encounter constraints in their attempts to sell as many commodities or as

The nonlinear model of economic growth that we have described went through two phase changes: first, when it began to exhibit regular cycles around its growth trend and, second, when it began to fluctuate in an irregular manner.

Positive-feedback loops occur when a given divergence from any state of the system is magnified rather than dampened. A normal competitive market such as we studied in Chapter 4 is a negative-feedback system. If price diverges from equilibrium, market forces push price back toward the equilibrium. However, if we reverse the labels of the *D* and *S* curves, we have a positive-feedback system. Now a slight increase in price above the equilibrium value will create excess demand, and this will cause price to rise even further.

Another example of positive feedback can occur when two different technologies that do the same job are competing with each other in the early stages of their development. The positive-feedback mechanism is that most R&D expenditure tends to be allocated toward the technology that is currently the more successful. A slight advantage of one technology over another will tend to cause more and more of the R&D effort to be directed to that technology, magnifying its lead over the other. The losing technology may be superior to the winning one in some fundamental way, but if a small, even random advantage develops for the inferior technology, it may gain a decisive lead over the superior one. This is because of the positive R&D feedback loop, which has the potential to magnify small, possibly random divergences into large, irreversible divergences. With a positive-feedback loop, the *first*, rather than the *best*, technology to enter the field has the best chance of winning.

Just as engineers still use Newtonian mechanics to build bridges, so economists will continue to use classical equilibrium theory to analyze the behavior of markets that are dominated by negative-feedback systems. Many believe, however, that the behavior of some individual markets, particularly financial markets, may be described by nonlinear, even chaotic systems. Many also believe that large systems, such as those describing economic growth that involve invention, knowledge diffusion, innovation, and possible increasing returns to investment, may be characterized by nonlinear dynamic equations, positive-feedback loops, occasional chaotic behavior, and decision making that is, at best, bounded in its rationality.

much labor as they wish; the contraction or expansion in output is voluntary.

New classical economists focus on the role of changes in relative prices when they are signaling appropriate information in a world where tastes and technology are constantly changing. They hold that fluctuations in the money supply will lead to increased fluctuations in all prices. This makes it hard for households and firms to distinguish between changes in relative prices, to which they do wish to respond, and changes in the price level, to which they do not wish to respond. Such confusion, created by fluctuations in the money supply, thus leads to mistakes in supply and demand decisions.

The Lucas aggregate supply curve. The behavior just described gives rise to the **Lucas aggregate supply curve**.

The Lucas aggregate supply curve posits that national output will vary positively with the ratio of the actual to the expected price level.

This is often also referred to as the *surprises-only supply curve*, since it implies that only changes in the price level that are unexpected (surprises) will give rise to fluctuations in aggregate supply.

To see this, consider what happens if there is again an increase in the money supply, but this time suppose that it has been widely expected by firms and households. Again, prices will rise. Most firms will now take this to mean only that the *observed* change in the price of their own output has roughly matched the *expected* change in the average of all other prices. Hence they will not interpret it as a rise in the relative price of their own output and will maintain their production at its normal level. National income will not rise above potential income, despite the rise in the general price level.

According to the new classical theory, expected changes in the price level do not lead to fluctuations in national income.

New classical policy views. New classical economists support the *k* percent rule, just as the traditional monetarists do. They believe that firms and households make better decisions when monetary and fiscal policies are stable than when they are highly variable. They believe that active interventionist policies, designed to stabilize the economy, make it harder for people to interpret the signals that are generated by the price system and so lead them to make more errors in forming their expectations. This then increases rather than reduces the fluctuations of output around its full-employment level and increases rather than reduces the fluctuations of unemployment around the NAIRU.

According to the new classical theory, active use of monetary policy in an attempt to stabilize the economy will lead to confusion about relative and absolute prices. This will cause people to make mistakes in their output and purchasing decisions and will therefore increase aggregate output fluctuations.

This conclusion depends on the particular view adopted by the new classical economists about how people form predictions or expectations—a subject that has recently become an important part of macroeconomic debates.

The Theory of Rational Expectations

The new classical model is augmented by the theory of *rational expectations.* People look to the government's current macroeconomic policy to form their expectations of future inflation. They understand how the economy works, and they form their expectations rationally by predicting the outcome of the policies being pursued. People learn fairly quickly from their mistakes; though random errors occur, systematic and persistent errors do not. In an obvious sense, expectations formed in this way are *forward-looking*.

According to the theory of rational expectations, people do not make persistent, systematic errors in predicting the overall inflation rate; they may, however, make unsystematic errors.

This discussion highlights a controversial methodological aspect of new classical economics. The economy is assumed to be simple enough that individual households and firms can understand it fully and can use current information to make rational forecasts. This paradigm of deterministic, fully rational, equilibrium systems is derived from the analogous view of the physical world that was propounded by Isaac Newton. However, the Newtonian paradigm has recently come under attack in many of the natural sciences; this is taken up in Box 40-2.

Policy invariance. Rational expectations, combined with the Lucas aggregate supply curve, give rise to the *new classical policy invariance proposition*, or policy neutrality proposition, with this result:

Systematic attempts to use monetary policy to stabilize the economy will lead to systematic changes in the price level but will not influence the behavior of output.

This happens because *systematic* monetary policy will lead only to systematic aggregate demand shocks and thus will not be a source of confusion to households and firms. Only unsystematic monetary policy will have real effects. Hence, according to the new classical economists, monetary policy can do harm—by creating confusion about the source of price changes—but cannot do good, except by random chance. Thus even in the face of major recessions, laissez faire is the best conceivable stabilization policy.

Let us review how this follows from combining the monetarist micro foundations with the theory of rational expectations.

1. According to the new classical theory's micro foundations, deviations from full employment occur only because of errors in predicting the price level (which cause workers and firms to mistake changes in the price level for changes in relative prices).
2. According to the theory of rational expectations, only random errors in predicting the price level occur.
3. It follows from the first two points that there is no room for active government policy to stabilize the economy. The causes of fluctuations are random.[5] It is in the nature of random fluctuations that they cannot be foreseen and offset. Thus there is no room for stabilization policy to reduce the fluctuations in the economy by offsetting the disturbances that emanate from the private sector.

For new classical economists who espouse this model, the contrast with the Keynesians is extreme. Box 40-3 takes up some other aspects of the important differences between the two groups that play a role in the ongoing controversies.

Real Business Cycle Models

Recently, a number of economists have pursued a research strategy that gives rise to what they have termed *real business cycle theory*. As Professor Alan Stockman of the University of Rochester states, "The purpose of real business cycle (RBC) models is to explain aggregate fluctuations in business cycles without reference to monetary policy."[6]

The Research Strategy

RBC research has evolved from an attempt to explain cyclical fluctuations in the context of models in which equilibrium prevails at all times. In this sense the models can be seen as a further extension of the new classical approach. (The early prototypes in this literature were referred to as *equilibrium business cycle models*.) The desire to model *equilibrium* outcomes reflects the researchers' dissatisfaction with the lack of a clear understanding of *how* monetary policy affects real outcomes in the traditional macro model. The focus on *real* disturbances reflects their skepticism about the evidence, showing the strength of those alleged effects from both the traditional macro model and from the new classical models.

Essentially, the view of the business cycle that arises in these models is that fluctuations in national income are caused by fluctuations in the vertical *LRAS* curve; this is illustrated in Figure 40-1. The contrast with the theory of fluctuations, which was shown in Figure 31-3 on page 655, is apparent.

The explanation of cyclical fluctuations that arises in RBC models is based on the role of supply shocks originating from sources such as oil price changes and technical progress.

Key Propositions and Criticisms

The RBC approach is controversial. Although its proponents claim a number of major accomplishments, its critics have pointed to a number of serious shortcomings.

The major claims made for the approach include the following:

1. It has been able to explain the recent behavior of the American economy quite well, while disavowing any role for *AD* fluctuations in the business cycle. The approach, therefore, obviously provides for no role for stabilization policy operating through monetary and fiscal policies that act to influence aggregate demand.
2. It suggests that an integrated approach to understanding cycles and growth may be appropriate, since both reflect forces that affect the *LRAS* curve. The distinction it makes is that some shocks are temporary (and thus have cyclical effects) and some are permanent (and therefore affect the economy's growth).
3. It provides valuable insights into how shocks, regardless of their origin, spread over time to the different sectors of the economy. By abstracting from monetary issues and from the automatic adjustment mechanism, more details concerning technology and household choice concerning intertemporal trade-offs in consumption and labor-leisure choice can be dealt with.
4. It has focused on explaining a number of stylized facts that other modern approaches have ignored. These include the comparison of seasonal and cyclical fluctuations, the fact that consumption varies less than output, and the procyclical movements of hours worked and of the average productivity of labor.

However, critics of the approach focus on some implausible results of the model, express concern over

[5] However, long lags may cause macro variables to display *cyclical* fluctuations, as was discussed in Chapter 31.

[6] Alan C. Stockman, "Real Business Cycle Theory: A Guide, an Evaluation, and New Directions," *Federal Reserve Bank of Cleveland Monthly Review*, 1988.

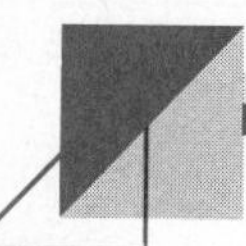

BOX 40-3

Unemployment in Alternative Models

One of the most important differences between the Keynesian models, on the one hand, and the monetarist and new classical models, on the other hand, relates to the distinction between voluntary and involuntary unemployment.

In the latter models, all unemployment and below capacity output are voluntary. Workers decide to be unemployed, and firms decide to produce less than capacity output as a result of the errors that they make in predicting the general price level (and therefore the relative price of what they sell). So if they had been surveyed, the millions of unemployed around the world during the early 1980s would have said that they could have had a job at the going wage but had refused to accept it because, given their expectations about inflation, the expected real wage was too low.

In the Keynesian model, prices and wages do not fluctuate to clear markets. Unemployment and production below capacity are involuntary, in the sense that unemployed workers would like jobs at the going wage rate but cannot find them, and firms would like to sell more at going prices but customers are not forthcoming.* So if they had been surveyed, the millions of unemployed around the world during the early 1980s would have said that they would have accepted a job at the going wage rate but that none was available.

This distinction between voluntary and involuntary unemployment leads to a striking difference in the policy recommendations of the two schools. The new classicists and the traditional monetarists argue that monetary policy should not be used actively to stabilize the economy. This is for two reasons: (1) Fluctuations in the money supply are a major source of fluctuations in output and inflation, and (2) there is no long-term trade-off between inflation and national income.†

One aspect of the new classical and monetarist models that is particularly controversial is the belief in downward flexibility of prices, which leads to the prediction that as long as national income is below its full-employment level, the price level will *fall* at an ever-accelerating rate. Keynesians say that the observed downward inflexibility of the price level refutes this view. They reject the prediction that the main cause of recessionary gaps is *voluntary* reductions in employment and output, due to errors in reading the signals that are provided by the price system. Most Keynesians do not believe that output deviates from its potential level *only* because workers and firms make mistakes, and thus they believe that stabilization policy should be used to eliminate recessionary gaps.

Major current research and debate center around issues such as what determines the degree of wage and price flexibility in the economy, the conditions under which people can be expected to form accurate expectations and act on them, and the potential for destabilizing the economy by pursuing an active stabilization policy. Views on how the economy behaves at both the micro and macro levels will be influenced by the progress of the debate, and so will views on the place of fiscal and monetary policy as possible ways to eliminate inflationary or recessionary gaps. We encounter a number of the most important issues in this chapter.

* Some economists argue that this unemployment is voluntary, because the workers had earlier voluntarily agreed to contracts at the going wage.

† Most economists accept the view that monetary forces are important in influencing inflation and unemployment, but many do not agree that monetary forces are the *most* important force. Most economists also agree that inflation will tend to accelerate if income is held permanently above its full-employment level.

FIGURE 40-1 Real Business Cycles

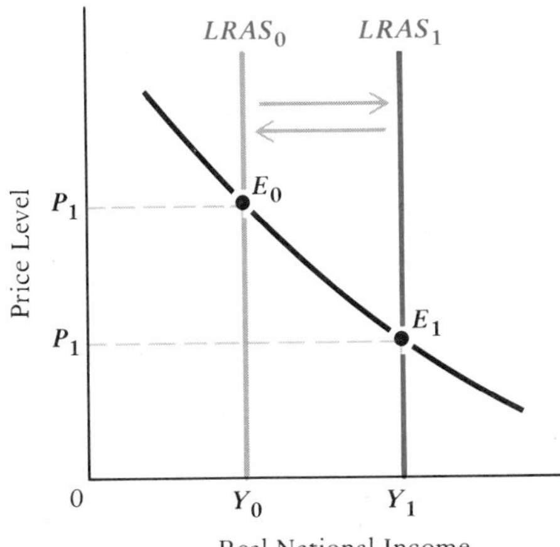

Real business cycle theory views fluctuations in national output as being caused by fluctuations in the long-run aggregate supply curve. Shocks to technology and changes in availability of key products, such as oil, cause the *LRAS* curve to shift back and forth between $LRAS_0$ and $LRAS_1$. Because the *LRAS* curve is vertical, these shifts give rise to identical fluctuations in national income; that is, national income fluctuates between Y_0 and Y_1. If the aggregate demand curve were stable, as shown by *AD*, the price level would fluctuate between P_0 and P_1. However, whatever the behavior of the *AD* curve, the behavior of national income would be unchanged.

assumptions about underlying behavioral parameters, and, most important, are skeptical about a model in which monetary issues are completely ignored. For example, they point out that RBC models are unable to provide any insights into the issue of the correlation between money and output that was at the heart of the monetarist-Keynesian debate in earlier decades and that they are unable to provide insights into empirical regularities involving nominal variables, such as the fact that prices apparently vary less than quantities or that nominal prices are procyclical.

Policy Implications

As we have noted, the structure of RBC models rules out any role for using policy to manage the economy via aggregate demand. However, the models do provide some basis for believing that the use of such demand management policies can be harmful and thus give rise to a noninterventionist policy prescription.

The basis for this view is that cycles in the economy will, according to the RBC model, represent efficient responses to the real shocks that are hitting the economy. If policymakers mistakenly interpret cyclical fluctuations as aggregate-demand-inspired deviations from full employment and therefore try to stabilize the output fluctuations, all they will succeed in doing is to distort the decisions made by households and firms. In turn, this will cause the responses to the real shocks to be inefficient.

While only a minority of economists espouse these models as complete or even reasonable descriptions of the business cycle, and thus only a minority take seriously the strict implications for policy, most accept the general message that real disturbances can play an important role in business cycles and that this militates against the active use of stabilization policy.

New Keynesian Macroeconomics

The first two modern research programs that we have discussed involve extensions of the market-clearing theories. The third one, which we turn to now, involves a number of separate approaches to providing micro foundations for the sticky-price Keynesian model.

Traditional Keynesian macroeconomic theories argue that prices or wages, or both, are sticky in the short run; because the oligopolists selling differentiated products, who make up most of the manufacturing sector and much of the service sector, must fix their own prices, and because it is costly to change these prices, it is the quantity of output that initially adjusts to changes in aggregate demand. However, the price stickiness is not explicitly derived as optimal behavior by consumers and firms. Thus the models are said to lack microeconomic foundations. Furthermore, the equilibrium theories just described allow no role for government intervention.

New Keynesian macroeconomics is the name that has been given to the attempts by some economists to develop theories of macroeconomic fluctuations that both have microeconomic foundations and allow a role for government stabilization policy. In contrast to equilibrium theories, which assume prices to be flexible so that all markets clear, new Keynesian theories seek explanations for rigidities that prevent markets from clearing at their optimal level. The effect of these rigidities may either be transient—simply slowing adjustment of output toward the unique optimal level—or permanent, if the model has more than one equilibrium and shocks can cause the economy to move from one such equilibrium to another with possibly different levels of output and employment.

Explaining Slow Adjustment

Explaining how prices and wages could be slow to adjust to changes in purely nominal demand within a model of maximizing agents is difficult, as it requires an explicit model of price setting. (Equilibrium models that are based on perfectly competitive markets do not address the problem of *how* prices are set.)

For prices to be set, agents must have some degree of market power, and so new Keynesian models assume that markets for output are imperfectly competitive.[7] However, imperfect competition alone is insufficient to generate a role for government stabilization policy. If, for instance, the money supply is increased, profit-maximizing price setters who knew precisely what was happening might respond to the increase in demand by increasing prices; if so, the price level would simply rise, and there need be no output effects. Thus new Keynesian models require additional features that make some price rigidity optimal. Among the possible explanations explored are menu costs, implicit contracts, and efficiency wages.

Menu costs. When a firm incurs costs by changing its prices, it may be said to face *menu costs*. The term is an allusion to the fixed cost that a restaurant faces when it reprints its menu because it has adjusted its prices. For a firm to operate at the profit-maximizing level of output, its marginal cost will equal its marginal revenue, and hence a small change in output will create only a small effect on profits, particularly if its cost curves for its products are flat. Therefore, if the firm faces menu costs and responds to a change in demand by changing its price and its output, the cost of the change in price may well outweigh any gain in profit from its changed sales.

For example, frequent price changes for a company that sells a wide variety of items could involve considerable costs in terms of keeping track of customer accounts and printing new catalogs; optimal behavior for the company may be to change prices at regular intervals, say, four times per year, rather than to adjust them constantly. Since most firms in the economy would set prices at fixed intervals, changes in nominal demand would be matched by changes in real output, and government stabilization policy would have real effects.

For an imperfectly competitive, profit-maximizing firm selling a wide range of differentiated products, sufficiently high menu costs will mean that small changes in demand will be accommodated by changes in output rather than price.

However, in order for changes in output to be large, the amount of labor employed must vary considerably without large changes in the wage rate. Many of the other features of new Keynesian models that we discuss next attempt to examine the conditions needed for there to be an elastic labor supply.

Implicit contracts. Many of the models that are proposed by new Keynesian economists are characterized by a degree of attachment between agents that surpasses the atomistic behavior assumed by models of pure competition. This accords well with everyday experience; however, while many of these attachments are formalized in contracts, others are not, and so models of *implicit contracts* have been developed to explain why agents may form lasting relationships, even in the absence of formal ties.

According to implicit-contract theory, short-term wage inflexibility can stem from rational behavior on the part of firms and workers. If wage rates adjust to clear labor markets, wages will vary over the cycle. *All* workers will then bear the uncertainty that is associated with the cyclical movements in wages. However, if wages are set in response to long-term considerations but do not vary cyclically so as to clear labor markets, cyclical fluctuations in demand will cause employment to fluctuate.

[7] The role of imperfect competition in providing micro foundations for Keynesian macroeconomics is discussed briefly in Chapter 14.

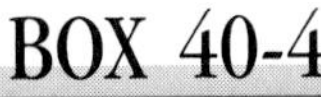

The Progress of Economics

In this chapter we have discussed a number of current controversies about the behavior of the economy and the evidence that relates to these controversies. General acceptance of the view that the validity of economic theories should be tested by confronting their predictions with the mass of all available evidence is fairly new in economics.

Since 1936, when Keynes' *General Theory of Employment, Interest, and Money* was published, great progress has been made in economics in relating theory to evidence. This progress has been reflected in the superior ability of governments to achieve their policy objectives. The financial aspects of World War II were handled far better than those of World War I. When U.S. President Franklin Roosevelt tried to reduce unemployment in the 1930s, his efforts were greatly hampered by the failure even of economists to realize the critical importance of budget deficits in raising aggregate demand and in injecting newly created money into the economy. When the Vietnam War forced the American government to adopt expansive fiscal and monetary policies, economists had no trouble in predicting the outcome. More involvement abroad was obtained at the cost of heavy inflationary pressure at home.

The general predictions of theories are tested in such important policy areas as managing wartime economies, curing major depressions, and coping with inflation, even if all of their specific predictions are not. In some sense, then, economic theories have always been subjected to empirical tests. When they were wildly at variance with the facts, the ensuing disaster could not help being noticed, and the theories were discarded or amended in the light of what was learned.

The advances of economics in the past half century reflect economists' changed attitudes toward empirical observations. Today economists are much less likely to dismiss theories just because they do not like them and to refuse to abandon theories just because they do like them. Economists are more likely to try to base their theories as much as possible on empirical observation and to accept empirical relevance as the ultimate arbiter of the value of theories. As human beings, we may be anguished at the upsetting of a pet theory; as scientists, we should try to train ourselves to take pleasure in it because of the new knowledge gained thereby. It has been said that one of the great tragedies of science is the continual slaying of beautiful theories by ugly facts. It must always be remembered that when theory and fact come into conflict, theory, not fact, must give way.

Implicit contracts that give rise to wage rigidity and employment variability can be a form of insurance provided by firms, which are in a better position to bear risk, to workers, who wish to avoid risk.

This insurance can increase workers' welfare *and* allow firms to reduce the wage level and thus increase profits.

Seniority can also play a role in this model. Since most layoffs and rehiring are based on seniority, employment fluctuations are all borne by the 10 or 20 percent of workers who have the least seniority. The majority of workers then will have little uncertainty in the face of cyclical fluctuations in demand, since all the uncertainty will have been placed on the minority, who have the least seniority. Thus contracts that fix wages over the cycle and allow employment to vary may be preferred by the majority of workers over contracts that allow wages to vary in order to clear the labor market continually and thus prevent unemployment.

Note that implicit contracts in the labor market cannot "explain" involuntary unemployment. First, all workers agree to the arrangement before demand shocks occur, and thus all those who become unemployed do so voluntarily, in the sense that they agreed to a contract that exposed them to the risk of unemployment. If unemployment were a major concern of workers, the insurance could be against variations in employment rather than wages. Also, the predictions of these models rely heavily on the assumed attachment between firms and workers. If alternative employment were available to workers during layoffs, of course, no unemployment would result; furthermore, in times of high demand, workers who are being paid a wage equal to their average productivity across the cycle could be bid away from the firm by competitors who are willing to pay them their marginal product.

Note also that the rigidity that arises in these models relates to real, not nominal, wages. Thus changes in nominal aggregate demand may not affect employment in these models. This property will change, however, if costs of changing wages, similar to the menu costs that we just discussed, make it optimal to fix nominal wages in the short run. In practice, wages are adjusted infrequently and often at quite regular time intervals, rather than as a function of the state of demand.[8] For example, most major Canadian unions sign three-year contracts whose only flexibility within that period will be given by a cost-of-living clause.

It also has been suggested that implicit contracts exist between firms and their customers. Thus a product's price may be only one concern to its consumers; for example, in the case of intermediate goods, purchasers may "insure" against unpredictable price fluctuations and allow delivery time to absorb demand shocks.

Efficiency wages. Efficiency wage models, which we discussed in Chapter 37, also offer an explanation of why wages may be used for purposes other than clearing the labor market. Imperfectly competitive firms paying wages above market clearing may not, in the presence of costs of changing prices and wages, adjust wages as a result of changes in nominal demand. Therefore, government stabilization policy can be effective.

Multiple Equilibria

Another class of new Keynesian models involves multiple equilibria. In these models imperfections do not necessarily retard the adjustment to equilibrium; however, the models have more than one equilibrium, and the equilibrium reached may not be optimal. Included in this class are models that are based on union behavior in the labor market and on the existence of an externality in the goods market.

Unions and the insider-outsider hypothesis. Most models of union behavior assume that unions negotiate on behalf of their membership and recognize that in many cases not all of these workers may be employed. Potential workers who are not union members may enter the unions' calculations only peripherally or not at all. This idea is formalized as the *insider-outsider hypothesis,* in which union members (insiders) negotiate in a self-interested manner, ignoring the interests of the unemployed (outsiders).

Consider a simple but extreme case in which union membership is equated with the previous period's employment. In this case sufficient union power may result in inflexible real wages and thus in equilibrium unemployment levels higher than those that policymakers consider optimal. Furthermore, the unemployment is truly involuntary, as the unemployed wish to work at the union wage but cannot.

Nominal rigidities that are created by insider-outsider behavior can provide a rationale for government stabilization policy.

It is interesting to note that in this situation stabilization policy can have long-lasting effects by moving the economy to a new equilibrium; once-and-for-all changes in labor demand may alter union membership and therefore alter *insider* behavior.[9]

[8] The absence of agreements that are explicitly based on detailed descriptions of the "state of the world" is sometimes attributed to "bounded rationality," which refers to the limited ability of agents to understand the precise state of the world, as well as the practical difficulty of writing contracts contingent on it. The first of these, as well as the related notion of asymmetric information, in which firms and workers have different information about the state of the world, can be invoked to motivate nominal wage rigidity in implicit contracts.

[9] Such permanent changes in equilibrium unemployment rates, which, as we saw earlier, are sometimes called *hysteresis,* can also be caused by a decline in the employability of unemployed workers due to a deterioration of their work skills or by the cyclical dependence of unemployment insurance parameters, which adjusts the generosity of benefits countercyclically. In both of these cases, temporary changes in aggregate demand may permanently alter the equilibrium rate of unemployment.

Taken together, these microeconomic foundations, which underpin new Keynesian macroeconomics, are far from a unified theory. However, given that these models are still in the early stages of development, this should be expected. Only time will tell which of the ideas that we have just discussed will come to dominate the research agenda of new Keynesians. Some related issues are taken up in Box 40-4.

SUMMARY

1. Views about the role that policy plays in improving macroeconomic performance range between two extremes. The noninterventionist view is that there is only a minimum role for policy; macroeconomic performance will be most satisfactory when the market system is allowed to function as freely as possible. The interventionist view is that active use of policy will improve macroeconomic performance.
2. Noninterventionists see the role of policy as providing a stable environment for individual decision makers. This involves maintaining a consistent set of "fiscal rules of the game," in terms of expenditure and tax rates and in terms of providing steady but gradual growth in the money supply.
3. Interventionists have specific prescriptions for each policy variable. They advocate active use of discretionary monetary and fiscal policy to stabilize output and employment. Despite imperfections that are caused by lags and incomplete knowledge, they believe such policies to be helpful. Similar policies can be combined with incomes policies to stabilize the fluctuations in the price level that arise from various sources and are subject to an upward bias. They also support policies to promote growth through subsidization, tax favors, and more specific intervention.
4. It is common to identify monetarists with noninterventionists and Keynesians with interventionists. Monetarists believe that because the economy is inherently stable, the goal of dampening the business cycle is best achieved by avoiding fluctuations in policy, especially monetary policy. Hence they advocate a *k* percent rule. Keynesians believe that the economy is inherently unstable in that expenditure functions shift regularly and the economy's self-corrective mechanisms are weak. Hence they believe in an active role for both monetary and fiscal policy as a way to stabilize the business cycle.
5. Monetarists believe that inflation is everywhere and always a monetary phenomenon, and so they advocate the same noninterventionist policies to avoid price instability as they advocate to minimize policy-induced cycles in output. They also argue that to control inflation, the long-term growth rate of the money supply must not be too high. Keynesians accept the view that monetary expansion is necessary for inflation to persist in the long term, but they take seriously the role of other factors in causing short-term but substantial inflation. Hence they believe in an active role for policy as a way to offset these factors in the short term.
6. Monetarists view markets as competitive and hence believe that departures from full-employment equilibrium are quickly rectified. As a result, they believe that fluctuations in aggregate demand lead primarily to fluctuations in the price level rather than in the level of output. They believe that the best course for monetary policy is to follow a *k* percent rule. For traditional monetarists, this is because they believe that long and variable lags in the effect of monetary

policy mean that an interventionist monetary policy would destabilize output.

7. Keynesians emphasize the oligopolistic nature of the economy. As a result, they believe that fluctuations in aggregate demand lead primarily to fluctuations in output rather than in the price level. In this view, an interventionist stabilization policy can be effective in stabilizing fluctuations in output.
8. New classical economists believe that departures from full-employment output occur only when people make mistakes in predicting the price level. When this belief is combined with the theory of rational expectations, it leads to the policy invariance proposition. New classical monetarists support the *k* percent rule because they believe that an interventionist monetary policy will not be effective in stabilizing output.
9. Real business cycle models posit that fluctuations in national income can be explained as the result of real shocks, which cause the vertical *LRAS* curve to fluctuate; they eschew any role for *AD* fluctuations, including those caused by monetary and fiscal policies.
10. New Keynesian macroeconomics encompasses a wide variety of models that try to explain why wages and prices may be sticky and hence why aggregate demand fluctuations have an important impact on national income. These include the role of menu costs, implicit contracts, efficiency wages, and unions.

TOPICS FOR REVIEW

Noninterventionists and interventionists
Traditional Keynesians and monetarists
Micro foundations
The *k* percent rule
New classical economics
Lucas aggregate supply curve
Theory of rational expectations
Policy invariance proposition
Real business cycle models
New Keynesian economics

DISCUSSION QUESTIONS

1. To what extent is today's unemployment a serious social problem? If people could vote in order to choose between 10 percent unemployment combined with zero inflation and 2 percent unemployment combined with 10 percent inflation, which alternative do you think they would choose? Which groups might prefer the first alternative, and which groups might prefer the second?
2. Some economists urge the government to fight inflation and combat unemployment by encouraging private-sector saving and investment. How might expanded saving and investment help to reduce inflation and to combat unemployment?
3. Nobel Laureate Paul Samuelson quoted a "conservative economist friend" as saying in mid 1980, "If you're contriving a teensy-weensy recession for us, please don't bother. It won't do the job. What's needed is a believable declaration that Washington will countenance *whatever* degree of unemployment is needed to bring us back on the path to price stability, and a demonstrated willingness to *stick* to that resolution no matter how politically unpopular the short-run joblessness, production cutbacks, and dips in profit might be." Discuss

the "conservative friend's" view of inflation. Does experience since 1980 suggest that the friend's advice was followed? If so, what was the consequence?

4. An ad that appeared in the *New York Times* in the early 1980s had this to say about inflation: "First [our politicians] blamed wage increases and price hikes for inflation. Then when 'voluntry guidelines' were established, the blame shifted to OPEC oil prices. Both explanations were wrong. Government policy is responsible for inflation—paying for deficit spending by 'creating money out of thin air.' " What theories of inflation are rejected and accepted by the writers of this ad?

5. In the mid 1980s, a fervent national debate developed concerning the need to protect North American industries from foreign competition. How do the pro and con views of protectionism relate to the noninterventionist and interventionist policies for promoting long-term growth?

6. In late 1989 a newspaper headline read: "Loss of consumer confidence sparks downturn in economy." What basic macroeconomic model did the writer likely have in mind?

7. A number of key microeconomic policy issues are listed below. Present both the noninterventionist case for "letting the market work" and the interventionist case in favor of a particular policy prescription. (Although the issues listed are "microeconomic" issues, their impact on the macroeconomic issues—in particular, economic growth—can be important.)

a. Rent controls (Chapter 6)
b. Minimum wage laws (Chapter 19)
c. Paying for social benefits (Chapter 25)
d. Financing health care (Chapter 25)
e. Increasing tariffs and other restrictions on imports (Chapter 21)

PART 11

INTERNATIONAL MACROECONOMICS

Chapter 41

Exchange Rates and the Balance of Payments

The value of the Canadian dollar on foreign exchange markets matters to many people. It affects the decisions of a Japanese firm wanting to sell cars in Canada, a Canadian person wanting to buy a German government bond, a French exporter selling kitchen appliances to Canada, a Canadian firm hoping to sell commuter airplanes to American feeder airlines, and exporters of Canadian wood and mineral products in markets where prices are quoted in U.S. dollars. It also matters to Canadian tourists cashing their Canadian dollar traveler's cheques in Miami, London, Athens, or Bangkok. It even matters to Canadians who have neither bought nor sold foreign currency or even heard of the exchange rate. This is because the exchange rate helps to determine the cost of imported goods as well as the amount of employment offered by firms that sell on foreign markets or compete with imports for sales in the Canadian market.

In this chapter we are concerned with what it means to speak of the "external value of the dollar" and what causes that external value to change. The discussion will bring together material on three topics studied elsewhere in this book: the theory of supply and demand (Chapter 4), the nature of money (Chapter 33), and international trade (Chapter 20).

We shall examine the simple case of a *small open economy (SOE),* an economy that can exert no influence on the world prices of traded goods. The quantities it exports and imports are small in relation to the total volume of world trade in these commodities, so its exporters and importers must buy and sell at prices that are established in world markets. For many commodities, such as wheat, forest products, and minerals, this is the correct assumption. For Canada as a whole this is a useful simplification.

A small open economy faces international terms of trade that are fixed in world markets and hence beyond its control.

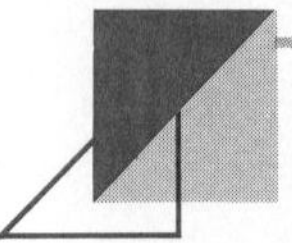

The Nature of Foreign Exchange Transactions

We have seen that money, which consists of any accepted medium of exchange, is vital in any economy that relies on specialization and exchange. Yet money as we know it is a *national* matter, closely controlled by national governments. If you live in Sweden, you will earn kronor and spend kronor; if you run a business in Austria, you borrow schillings and meet your payroll with schillings. The currency of a country is acceptable within the borders of that country, but it will not usually be accepted by households and firms in another country. The Stockholm bus company will accept kronor for a fare but not Austrian schillings. The Austrian worker will not take Swedish kronor for wages but will accept schillings.

The situation is similar in Canada except that our proximity to the United States leads many Canadian sellers to accept U.S. dollars over the counter. Because U.S. dollars are so well known and so common, Canadian merchants are willing to accept them and then do what the customer would otherwise have had to do: take the U.S. money to the bank and exchange it for Canadian money. For international transactions, however, this is the rare exception rather than the rule.

When Canadian producers sell their products, they require payment in Canadian dollars. They must meet their wage bills, pay for their raw materials, and reinvest or distribute their profits. There is no problem when they sell to Canadian purchasers. However, when they sell their goods to Japanese importers, either the Japanese must exchange their yen to acquire dollars to pay for the goods, or the Canadian producers must accept yen. They will accept yen only if they know that they can exchange the yen for the dollars that they require. The same holds true for producers in all countries: They must eventually receive payment for the goods that they sell in terms of the currency of their own country.

Trade between nations would be greatly hampered if it were not possible to exchange the currency of one nation for that of another.

The exchange rate. International payments that require the exchange of one national currency for another can be made in a bewildering variety of ways, but in essence they involve the exchange of currencies between people who have one currency and require another. Suppose that a Canadian firm wishes to acquire £3,000 for some purpose. The firm can go to a seller of foreign currency and buy a check that will be accepted in the United Kingdom as £3,000. How many *Canadian dollars* the firm must pay to obtain this check will depend on the price of sterling in terms of dollars.

The exchange of one currency for another is done on the foreign exchange market. The term *foreign exchange* refers to the actual foreign currency or various claims on it, such as bank deposits or promises to pay, that are traded for each other. The *exchange rate* is the price at which purchases and sales of foreign currency or claims on it take place; it is the amount of home currency that must be paid in order to obtain one unit of the foreign currency. For example, if one must give up $1.20 Canadian to get one U.S. dollar, the exchange rate between the U.S. and Canadian dollars[1] is 1.2.

A rise in the price of foreign exchange (i.e., a rise in the exchange rate) is a **depreciation** of the home currency. *Because foreign currencies have become more expensive, the relative value of the home currency has fallen.* For example, if the exchange rate between Canadian and U.S. dollars rises from 1.2 to 1.4, the Canadian dollar has depreciated in value because it now takes more Canadian dollars to buy one U.S. dollar. A fall in the price of foreign exchange (i.e., a fall in the exchange rate) is an **appreciation** of the home currency. *Because foreign currencies have become cheaper, the relative value of home currency has risen.* For example, when the exchange rate between Canadian and U.S. dollars falls from 1.2 to 1.1, the Canadian dollar has appreciated in value because it now takes fewer Canadian dollars to buy one U.S. dollar.

The relation between the exchange rate and the value of the domestic currency on the foreign exchange market, called the *external value of the currency,* can be confusing and should be committed to memory:

The exchange rate is the amount of domestic currency needed to buy a unit of foreign currency. It is negatively related to the external value of the domestic currency. A rise in the exchange rate is a depreciation of the domestic currency, and a fall in the exchange rate is an appreciation of the domestic currency.

The mechanism of foreign exchange transactions. Let us see how foreign exchange transactions are carried

[1] This expresses the relative values of the two currencies in terms of the Canadian dollar price of one U.S. dollar. Alternatively, one could consider the U.S. dollar price of a Canadian dollar, which in this example is 0.833. The first, 1.2, is the exchange rate from the Canadian point of view; the second, 0.833, is the external value of the Canadian dollar, that is, how much foreign currency can be bought with one Canadian dollar. From the U.S. point of view, 0.833 is the exchange rate while 1.2 is the external value of the U.S. dollar. Both measures are commonly used in the press.

TABLE 41-1 Changes in the Balance Sheets of Two Banks As a Result of International Payments

U.K. bank			Canadian bank		
Assets	Liabilities		Assets	Liabilities	
No change	(1) Deposits of car exporter	+£15,000	No change	(1) Deposits of car importer	−$25,000
	(2) Deposits of refrigerator importer	−£15,000		(2) Deposits of refrigerator exporter	+$25,000
	Net change	0		Net change	0

International transactions involve a transfer of deposit liabilities among banks. The table records two separate international transactions at an exchange rate of £1.00 = $1.66 Canadian: (1) a Canadian purchase of a British car for £15,000 (= $25,000) and (2) a British purchase of Canadian refrigerators for $25,000 (= £15,000). The Canadian's import of a car reduces deposit liabilities to Canadian residents and increases deposit liabilities to British residents. The Britisher's import of refrigerators does the opposite. When several transactions are equal in value, there is only a transfer of deposit liabilities among individuals within a country. The Canadian refrigerator manufacturer received (in effect) the dollars the Canadian car purchaser gave up to get a British-made car.

out. Suppose that a Canadian firm wishes to purchase a British sports car to sell in Canada. The British firm that made the car requires payment in pounds sterling. If the car is priced at £15,000, the Canadian firm will go to its bank, purchase a cheque for £15,000, and send the cheque to the British seller. Let us suppose this requires that the firm pay $25,000.[2] The British firm deposits the cheque in its bank. (The exchange rate in this transaction is 1.667, because it costs $1.667 to buy one British pound sterling; the external value of the Canadian dollar measured in sterling is 0.60 because that is the amount of sterling one Canadian dollar will buy.)

Now assume that in the same period a British wholesale firm purchases 25 Canadian commercial refrigerators to sell in Britain. If the refrigerators are priced at $1,000 each, the Canadian seller will have to be paid $25,000. To make this payment, the British importing firm goes to its bank, writes a cheque on its account for £15,000, and receives a cheque drawn on a Canadian bank for $25,000. The cheque is sent to Canada and deposited in a Canadian bank.

The effects of the two transactions are shown in Table 41-1. The transactions balance, and there is no net change in international liabilities. No money need pass between British and Canadian banks; each bank merely increases the deposit of one domestic customer and decreases the deposit of another. Indeed, as long as the flow of payments between the two countries is equal (Canadians pay as much to British residents as British residents pay to Canadians), all payments can be managed as in the example, and there will be no need for a net payment from British banks to Canadian banks.

All these calculations involve comparing magnitudes measured in different currencies. These comparisons are done using exchange rates. We now turn to an analysis of how such exchange rates are determined.

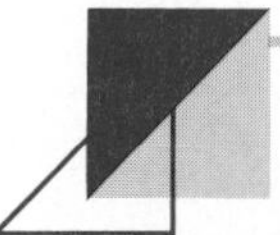

Determination of Exchange Rates

As a first step we must look at the link between exchange rates and the prices of a country's imports and exports.

Exchange Rates and the Domestic Prices of Traded Goods

A small open economy faces prices of internationally traded goods that are fixed in foreign currency. The exchange rate translates these into domestic prices. If, for example, the price of wheat is U.S.$3.00 a bushel on international wheat markets, the Canadian dollar price that is earned by Canadian wheat ex-

[2] Banks charge a small commission for making currency exchanges, but for simplicity, we shall ignore this and assume that parties can exchange moneys back and forth at the going exchange rate.

porters depends on the exchange rate. When the rate is C$1.20 to the U.S. dollar, the Canadian domestic price of wheat is C$3.60. This is because the U.S.$3.00 earned from the foreign sale of a bushel of wheat is converted into C$3.60 when it is sold on the foreign exchange market at a rate of C$1.20 for every U.S. dollar sold.

In Figures 4A-1 and 4A-2 (pages 76 and 77) we showed how imports and exports were determined in a small open economy facing given world prices for traded goods. We drew the domestic demand and supply curves plotted against domestic prices. We then used the world price, *stated in units of domestic currency,* to determine the quantity of imports and exports of a product. To do this we needed an exchange rate to convert world prices into local currency, although we did not say so at the time. (Recall that we express the exchange rate, e, as the number of units of domestic currency needed to buy one unit of foreign currency.)

The domestic price of traded goods, p_d, is thus the *world* price of traded goods expressed in foreign currency, p_f, multiplied by the exchange rate:

$$p_d = ep_f$$

To repeat the example given earlier, when the international price of wheat is U.S.$3.00 per bushel and the exchange rate is C$1.20 to the U.S. dollar, the Canadian dollar price of wheat is U.S.$3.00 per bushel times C$1.20 per U.S. dollar, which is C$3.60 per bushel.

It is now a simple matter to see the effect of a change in the exchange rate on the domestic prices of traded goods. Say that the value of the Canadian dollar appreciates so that it takes only C$1.10 to buy one U.S. dollar. The domestic price of a bushel of wheat that costs U.S.$3.00 is now only C$3.30, since C$3.30 is all the Canadian dollars that can be bought with U.S.$3.00. (The formula $p_d = ep_f$ gives the right answer, since C$1.10 per U.S. dollar times U.S.$3.00 per bushel equals C$3.30 per bushel.) As a second example, say that the external value of the Canadian dollar depreciates so that it now takes C$1.40 to buy one U.S. dollar. Now the Canadian dollar price of wheat rises to $4.20 since that is the number of Canadian dollars that U.S.$3.00 will buy on the foreign exchange market.

An appreciation of the external value of the domestic currency lowers the domestic prices of internationally traded goods; a depreciation raises them.

To study the effects of changes in the exchange rate further, we return to the example given in the Appendix to Chapter 4, a country that is exporting wheat and importing cloth.

First consider depreciation of the country's currency. A 10 percent depreciation, for example, would mean that the domestic currency prices of the two goods must rise by 10 percent. Look first at the export good, wheat. Since the sale of a unit of wheat abroad still yields the same amount of foreign exchange, it now yields 10 percent more in terms of domestic currency. Domestic purchasers too will have to pay 10 percent more, for if the domestic price did not rise, producers would sell only in the export market. Similarly, the purchase of cloth still requires the same amount of foreign currency, but 10 percent more of the domestic currency must be paid to obtain the required amount of foreign currency. Thus the domestic currency price of imported cloth also rises by 10 percent.

The effects of these price changes are illustrated in Figures 41-1 and 41-2. In the market for wheat, the increase in the domestic price causes the quantity supplied domestically to rise and the quantity demanded domestically to fall. As a result, the quantity of wheat exported, which is equal to the excess of the quantity supplied domestically over the quantity demanded domestically, *rises* (see Figure 41-1). In the market for cloth, the increase in the domestic price also causes the quantity supplied domestically to increase and the quantity demanded domestically to fall. Since domestic demand exceeded domestic supply in the initial situation, this response *reduces* the excess demand. As a result, the quantity of cloth imported *decreases* (see Figure 41-2).

For a small country, a depreciation of the domestic currency causes the domestic prices of traded goods to rise, thereby increasing the quantity supplied and decreasing the quantity demanded domestically. Therefore, the volume of exports rises while the volume of imports falls.

As a result of these changes, net exports, $X - M$, rise. Since net exports are a component of aggregate demand, the depreciation increases the country's

FIGURE 41-1 Effects of an Increase in the Domestic Currency Price of an Exported Good (Wheat)

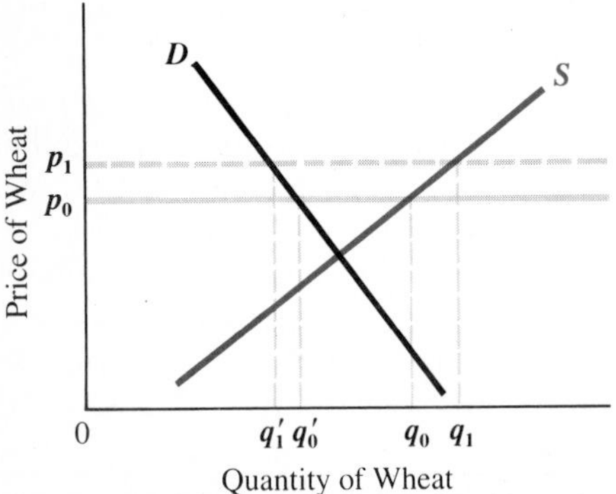

An increase in the domestic currency price of export goods leads to an increase in the volume of exports. Exports of wheat are determined by the domestic excess supply of the tradable good at the domestic price. (The domestic price is the world price adjusted by the exchange rate.) D and S are the domestic demand and supply schedules. If the world price expressed in domestic currency is p_0, quantity q_0 will be produced, of which q_0' will be consumed domestically and $q_0'q_0$ will be exported. A depreciation of the domestic currency or an increase in the world price causes the domestic currency price to rise to p_1. As a result, domestic consumption falls to q_1', quantity supplied rises to q_1, and exports rise to $q_1'q_1$.

FIGURE 41-2 Effects of an Increase in the Domestic Currency Price of an Imported Good (Cloth)

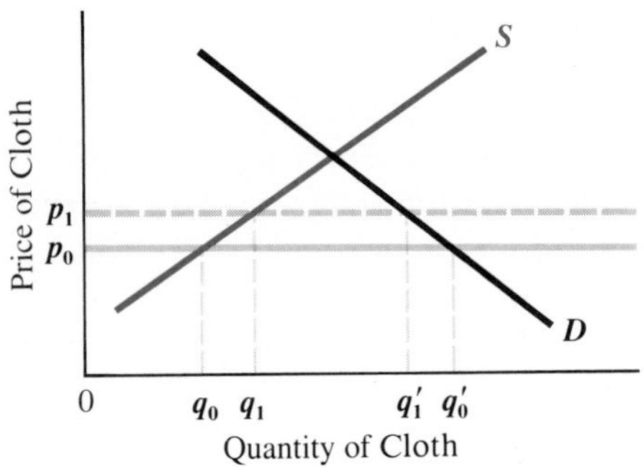

An increase in the domestic currency price of import goods leads to a decrease in the volume of imports. Imports of cloth are determined by the domestic excess demand for cloth at the domestic price. (The domestic price is the world price adjusted by the exchange rate.) D and S are the domestic demand and supply schedules. If the world price expressed in domestic currency is p_0, quantity q_0' will be consumed, of which q_0 will be produced domestically and $q_0'q_0$ will be imported. A depreciation of the domestic currency or an increase in the world price causes the domestic currency price to rise to p_1. As a result, quantity supplied rises to q_1, domestic consumption falls to q_1', and imports fall to $q_1'q_1$.

aggregate demand. This in turn tends to increase equilibrium national income.

Next consider an *appreciation* of the domestic currency. This will *lower* the domestic prices of traded goods. For both cloth and wheat, this leads to a reduction in the quantity supplied domestically and an increase in the quantity demanded domestically. The quantity of cloth that is imported now rises while the quantity of wheat that is exported falls. This is also shown in Figures 41-1 and 41-2.

For a small country, an appreciation of the domestic currency causes the domestic prices of traded goods to fall, thereby decreasing the quantity supplied and increasing the quantity demanded domestically. Therefore, the volume of exports falls while the volume of imports rises.

As a result of these changes, net exports fall. This causes a decrease in aggregate demand and hence a fall in equilibrium national income.

The Exchange Rate Between Two Currencies

For simplicity, we shall consider an example involving trade between Canada and the United States and the determination of the exchange rate between their two currencies, the Canadian dollar and the U.S. dollar. The two-country example simplifies things, but the principles apply to all foreign transactions. Thus in our example U.S. dollars stand for foreign exchange in general, and the price of U.S. dollars stands for foreign exchange rates in general.

We can relate our example to the demand and supply analysis of Chapter 4. To do so we need only recognize that *in the market for U.S. dollars,* the holders of Canadian dollars who want U.S. dollars are *demanders* of U.S. dollars, and the holders of U.S. dollars who want Canadian dollars are *suppliers* of U.S. dollars. We could also look at the same transaction in terms of the market for Canadian dollars: The holders of Canadian dollars who want U.S. dollars are suppliers of Canadian dollars, and the holders of U.S. dollars who want Canadian dollars are demanders of Canadian dollars. Both views are different ways of looking at the same transactions.

Because one currency is traded for another on the foreign exchange market, an offer to buy Canadian dollars implies a willingness to sell foreign exchange, and an offer to sell Canadian dollars implies a desire to buy foreign exchange.

Consider a simple example. When the U.S. dollar exchange rate is 1.2 (i.e., U.S.$1.00 costs C$1.20), a U.S. importer who offers to buy C$6.00 with U.S. dollars must be offering to sell U.S.$5.00. Similarly, a Canadian importer who offers to sell C$6.00 for U.S. dollars must be offering to buy U.S.$5.00. As this example illustrates, a theory of the exchange rate between Canadian and U.S. dollars can deal with *either* the demand for and the supply of Canadian dollars *or* the demand for and the supply of U.S. dollars; both sets of demands and supplies need not be considered. We shall concentrate on the demand, supply, and price of U.S. dollars.

Figure 41-3 plots the *quantity of U.S. dollars* on the horizontal axis and the exchange rate, the *price of one U.S. dollar* measured in Canadian dollars, on the vertical axis. Moving down the vertical scale to *lower exchange rates,* the foreign currency (U.S. dollars) becomes *cheaper*; it is depreciating on the foreign exchange market while the domestic currency (the Canadian dollar) is *appreciating*. Moving up the scale to higher exchange rates, the foreign currency (U.S. dollars) becomes *more expensive*; it is appreciating while the Canadian dollar is depreciating.

FIGURE 41-3 The Market for Foreign Exchange

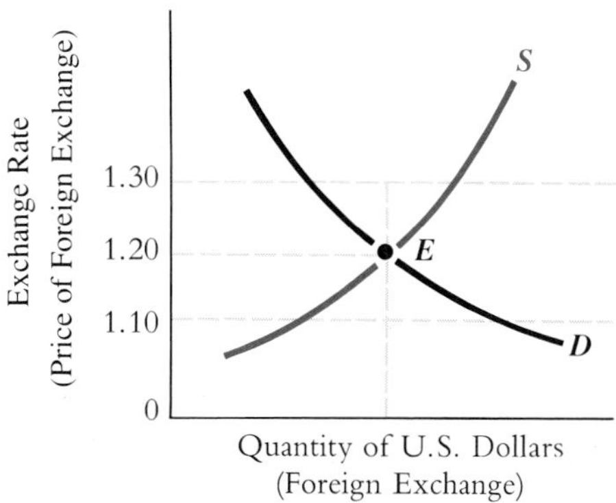

The equilibrium exchange rate is the price that equates the demand and supply of foreign exchange. In this example the U.S. dollar stands for all foreign exchange and the exchange rate is the number of Canadian dollars required to buy one U.S. dollar. The *S* curve is the supply of U.S. dollars to the foreign exchange market to be used to make purchases in Canada. The *D* curve is the demand for U.S. dollars on the foreign exchange market to be used to make purchases in the United States. The quantity of U.S. dollars demanded is equal to the quantity supplied at an exchange rate of 1.20. When the exchange rate is low, say, 1.10, there is an excess demand for U.S. dollars, which bids the price up. When the exchange rate is high, say, 1.30, there is an excess supply of U.S. dollars, which bids the price down.

Supply of U.S. Dollars

U.S. dollars are supplied on the foreign exchange market to finance purchases by foreigners from Canadian residents. In addition to the purchase of Canadian exports, such as wheat, there are purchases of assets previously owned or newly issued by Canadian firms and governments. Such purchases give rise to *capital flows.* These play an important role in exchange markets, and we study them in detail later in this chapter; for the present, we continue to focus on imports and exports of goods and services.

Our representative Canadian export is wheat. We saw in Figure 41-1 that a rise in the Canadian exchange rate (a depreciation of the Canadian dollar) led to an increase in the *quantity* of wheat exports. Since in our simplified model the *U.S. dollar price* of wheat is set on the international wheat market and is unaffected by any changes in the exchange rate, the total U.S. dollar value of Canadian wheat exports must rise. Foreign purchasers must be spending more U.S. dollars to buy Canadian wheat, and these U.S.

dollars go to purchase the Canadian dollars needed to pay Canadian sellers for this wheat. It follows that a rise in the exchange rate will increase the supply of U.S. dollars offered on the foreign exchange market.

By the same argument, a fall in the exchange rate (an appreciation in the Canadian dollar) leads to a decrease in the quantity of wheat exports. Since these are sold at an unchanged U.S. dollar price, the U.S. dollar value of Canadian sales of wheat must fall. Thus a fall in the exchange rate will decrease the supply of U.S. dollars offered on the foreign exchange market.

The foregoing analysis tells us the sign of the slope of the supply curve of U.S. dollars on the foreign exchange market, since it shows that the exchange rate and the quantity of U.S. dollars offered to buy Canadian exports are positively related.

The supply curve of U.S. dollars on the foreign exchange market is positively sloped when plotted against the Canadian dollar price of U.S. dollars—that is, against the exchange rate.

The common sense of this result is that since Canadian exports of wheat are sold at a given U.S. dollar price, anything that increases the quantity of their sales must increase the total value of U.S. dollars spent on them. This spending takes the form of offering U.S. dollars on the foreign exchange market to buy the Canadian dollars needed to pay Canadian exporters.

Demand for U.S. Dollars

In our two-country example, the demand for U.S. dollars on the foreign exchange market is merely the opposite side of the supply of Canadian dollars. Who wants to sell Canadian dollars for foreign exchange? In our example, Canadians seeking to purchase the representative U.S. export, cloth, will require foreign exchange to make their purchases. Hence they will wish to supply Canadian dollars in exchange for U.S. dollars.[3]

When the exchange rate rises (the Canadian dollar depreciates in value), the Canadian price of U.S. cloth rises. As we saw in Figure 41-2, Canadians will import less of the now more expensive U.S. cloth. Since the U.S. dollar price of cloth is unchanged, buying less cloth means needing fewer U.S. dollars to pay for it. Thus the Canadian demand for U.S. dollars falls.

Now consider the opposite case in which the exchange rate falls. American cloth exports to Canada become cheaper, and more will be sold. Since the U.S. dollar price of cloth is unchanged, buying more means spending more U.S. dollars. Thus there is an increase in the amount of U.S. dollars demanded on the foreign exchange market.

Together these two reactions tell us the sign of the slope of the demand curve for U.S. dollars.

The demand curve for U.S. dollars on the foreign exchange market is negatively sloped when plotted against the Canadian dollar price of U.S. dollars—that is, against the exchange rate.

Equilibrium Exchange Rates in a Competitive Market

The exchange rate between Canadian and U.S. dollars is set in a competitive market by the forces of demand and supply. (Even when the Bank of Canada intervenes to influence the exchange rate, it does so by adding its own demand or supply to what is coming from the private sector.)

Assume that the current exchange rate is so low (say, 1.05 in Figure 41-3) that the quantity of U.S. dollars demanded exceeds the quantity supplied. U.S. dollars will be in scarce supply. Some people who require U.S. dollars to make payments to the United States will be unable to obtain them, and the price of U.S. dollars—the exchange rate—will be bid up.

As the exchange rate rises, the domestic market price of Canadian imports rises; hence the quantity of imports falls, as does the quantity of U.S. dollars demanded on the foreign exchange market to pay for these imports. This is a movement along the demand curve, *D*, in Figure 41-3. However, the depreciation of the dollar also leads to a rise in the dollar price of Canadian exports and a resulting increase in the quantity sold abroad. Thus the amount of U.S. dollars offered to buy more Canadian exports at an unchanged U.S. dollar price must rise. This is a movement along the supply curve, *S*, in Figure 41-3. Thus a rise in the exchange rate reduces

[3] A demand for U.S. dollars may also result from capital flows if Canadians seek to buy U.S. assets. Like the supply of U.S. dollars to purchase Canadian assets, we neglect this until later in the chapter.

the quantity of U.S. dollars demanded and increases the quantity of U.S. dollars supplied. Where the two curves intersect, quantity demanded equals quantity supplied, and the foreign exchange market is in equilibrium.

What happens if the price of foreign exchange is too high? The quantity of U.S. dollars demanded will be less than the quantity of U.S. dollars supplied. With U.S. dollars in excess supply, some people who wish to convert U.S. dollars into Canadian dollars will be unable to do so. The price of U.S. dollars will fall, fewer U.S. dollars will be supplied, more will be demanded, and equilibrium will be reestablished.

In the foreign exchange market, as in other competitive markets, the forces of demand and supply establish an equilibrium exchange rate at which quantity demanded equals quantity supplied.

Changes in Exchange Rates

What causes exchange rates to vary? The simplest answer to this question is changes in demand or supply in the foreign exchange market. Anything that shifts the demand curve for U.S. dollars to the right or the supply curve for U.S. dollars to the left leads to a rise in the exchange rate. Anything that shifts the demand curve for U.S. dollars to the left or the supply curve for U.S. dollars to the right leads to a fall in the exchange rate. This is nothing more than a restatement of the laws of demand and supply, applied now to the market for foreign exchange.

The trick in applying demand and supply theory to the foreign exchange market is knowing what causes the demand and supply curves to shift. There are many causes, some of them transitory and some persistent, and we shall study several of the most important.

Foreign Inflation

What happens when the rest of the world experiences inflation while our domestic economy does not? Domestic costs and the prices of domestic (nontraded) goods remain unchanged. However, world prices of all traded goods rise. As a result, at the initial exchange rate, the domestic prices of all traded goods rise.

We saw in Figures 41-1 and 41-2 that the rise in the prices of exported and imported goods leads domestic firms to increase the quantities of their exports while decreasing the quantities of their imports. These changes cause shifts in the demand and supply curves in the foreign exchange market. More Canadian exports sold at a higher world price mean more foreign exchange offered in return for Canadian dollars. The supply curve of foreign exchange shifts right, as shown in Figure 41-4. Fewer imports purchased at higher foreign prices means less spent on imports—at least as long as the percentage fall in the quantity demanded exceeds the percentage rise in the price.[4] The demand curve for foreign exchange thus shifts leftward, as shown in Figure 41-4.

Now, at the original exchange rate, there is an excess supply of foreign exchange, and the market exchange rate falls to a new equilibrium level.

Other things being equal, foreign inflation will lead to an appreciation of the Canadian dollar (a fall in the exchange rate).

Domestic Inflation

Suppose now that foreign prices are constant but there is domestic inflation. This means increases in domestic wages, in other domestic costs of production, and in the prices of domestic goods and services (things such as haircuts and restaurant meals that are not traded internationally). As a result of the rise in costs, the domestic supply curves for traded goods (both imports and exports) will shift upward. As a result of the rise in prices of nontraded goods, the domestic demand curves for traded goods will shift upward. This is because at any given exchange rate, traded goods are now cheaper relative to nontraded goods, so more will be demanded and less will be supplied. As a result of these various changes, the quantity of imports will rise and the quantity of exports will fall. This situation is shown in Figure 41-5.

[4] This is true as long as the elasticity of demand for imports is greater than unity—the fall in the volume of imports will then swamp the rise in price, and hence fewer dollars will be spent on them. This elasticity condition is related to a famous long-standing issue in international economics. In what follows, we adopt the standard case of the condition's being met. In a more general form, it is called the *Marshall-Lerner condition* after two famous economists who first studied the problem.

FIGURE 41-4 Foreign Inflation and the Exchange Rate

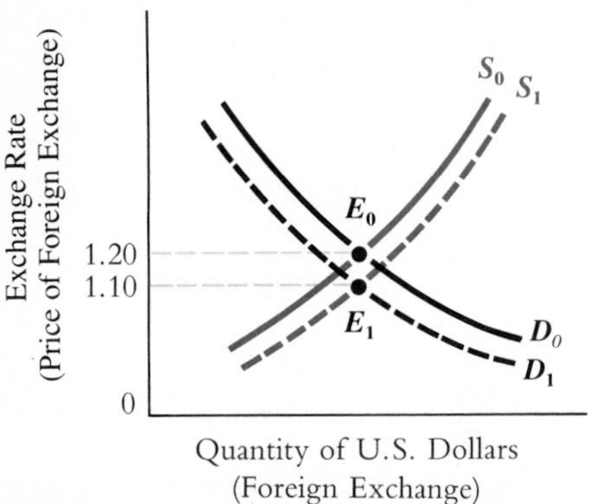

Foreign inflation will increase the supply of foreign exchange and decrease the demand, thus causing a fall in the exchange rate. The initial demand and supply curves are shown by the solid curves (labeled D_0 and S_0), and the initial equilibrium is at E_0. Now suppose that foreign inflation occurs. This raises the foreign price of all tradable goods. At any given exchange rate, this will cause an increase in the Canadian dollar price of traded goods, and as we saw in Figures 41-1 and 41-2, the quantity of Canadian exports will increase and the quantity of Canadian imports will decrease as a result. The increase in Canadian exports gives rise to an increase in the supply of U.S. dollars, as shown by the shift in the supply curve from S_0 to S_1. The decrease in Canadian imports gives rise to a decrease in the demand for foreign exchange, as shown by the shift in the demand curve from D_0 to D_1. As a result, the exchange rate falls from 1.20 to 1.10.

At any given exchange rate, these changes in the quantities of imports and exports will cause the supply and demand of foreign exchange to change. The decrease in exports will cause the quantity of U.S. dollars supplied to the foreign exchange market to decrease. The increase in imports will cause the quantity of U.S. dollars demanded in the foreign exchange market to increase. As a result, the equilibrium exchange rate rises; that is, the Canadian dollar depreciates.

Other things being equal, a localized Canadian inflation will lead to depreciation of the Canadian dollar (a rise in the exchange rate).

Inflation in All Countries

Now consider a case in which the domestic country experiences exactly the same rate of inflation as the rest of the world. Now the demand and supply curves for traded goods in Figure 41-5 shift upward as before, but so does the world price of imports and exports. (The rise in the world price is not shown in the figure.) The two shifts offset each other: The upward shifts in the demand and supply curves reduce exports and increase imports, while the upward shift in world prices increases exports and reduces imports. With equal rates of inflation in Canada and the rest of the world, the prices of nontraded Canadian goods remain unchanged *relative to* internationally traded goods at the original exchange rate. There is no reason to expect any change in any country's demand for imports or its supply of exports at the original exchange rate. Hence there is no change in the demand for and supply of foreign exchange.

The effects of equal rates of inflation in all trading countries offset each other, leaving unchanged the incentive to import and to export and the equilibrium exchange rate.

Unequal Inflation

The results we have just seen show that the *relative rates of inflation* between any two trading countries is an important determinant of the exchange rate between their two currencies. Differences in the inflation rates will cause changes in imports and exports and hence changes in quantities demanded and supplied on the foreign exchange market. Thus the exchange rate between the two currencies will change. An important general conclusion follows from a simple extension of the cases just studied:

If the price level of one country is rising relative to that of another country, its currency will be depreciating relative to that of the second country (that is, its exchange rate will be rising).

Capital Movements

Capital flows influence exchange rates. For example, an increased Canadian desire to invest in assets in the United States will cause holders of Canadian dollars to demand the U.S. dollars needed to buy U.S. assets. This shifts the demand curve for U.S. dollars

FIGURE 41-5 Domestic Inflation and International Trade

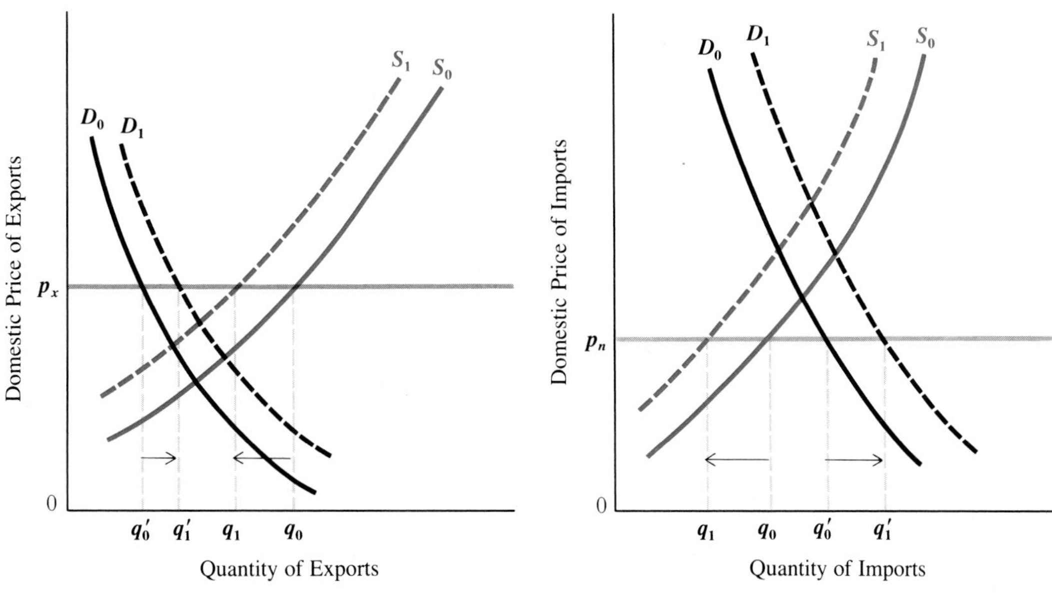

(i) The fall in exports

(ii) The rise in imports

Domestic inflation unmatched in the rest of the world increases the domestic demand for traded goods and reduces the domestic supply; as a result, the quantity of exports falls and the quantity of imports rises. The initial supply and demand curves are shown by the solid lines D_0 and S_0 in both parts of the figure. In each market the initial quantity supplied is given by q_0 and the initial quantity demanded by q_0'. Initial exports are given in (i) by $q_0'q_0$ and initial imports in (ii) by q_0q_0'.

Domestic inflation causes the demand curves for each traded good to shift rightward from D_0 to D_1 and the supply curve for each to shift leftward from S_0 to S_1. As a result, quantity demanded rises from q_0' to q_1' and quantity supplied falls from q_0 to q_1.

In the market for exports, where domestic supply initially exceeded demand, the inflation thus causes exports to fall, from $q_0'q_0$ to $q_1'q_1$. (In turn, this means that the supply of U.S. dollars in the foreign exchange market falls, as shown by a shift from S_1 to S_0 in Figure 41-4.)

In the market for imports, where domestic demand initially exceeded supply, the inflation thus causes Canadian imports to rise, from q_0q_0' to q_1q_1'. (In turn, this means that the demand for U.S. dollars on the foreign exchange market rises, as shown by a shift from D_1 to D_0 in Figure 41-4.)

to the right, causing the exchange rate to rise (i.e., causing the value of the Canadian dollar to depreciate). The reverse would happen if Americans wished to invest in Canada: The increased supply of U.S. dollars would reduce the exchange rate (the Canadian dollar would appreciate).

A movement of investment funds has the effect of appreciating the currency of the capital-importing country and depreciating the currency of the capital-exporting country.

This statement is true for all capital movements, short-term or long-term. Since the motives that lead to large capital movements are usually different in the short and long terms, each must be considered separately.

Short-term capital movements. A major incentive for short-term capital flows is international differences in interest rates. If one major country's short-term rate of interest rises above the rates in most other countries, there will tend to be a large inflow of short-term capital into that country to take advantage of the differential. The extra demand for the country's currency will tend to appreciate its value on the foreign exchange market. Conversely, if the short-term interest rate falls, there will be a movement of short-term funds out of the country. The increased supply of that country's currency on the foreign exchange market (in order to buy the foreign currency needed to move funds to other countries) will depreciate that country's currency.

A second motive for short-term capital movements is speculation about a country's exchange rate. If foreigners expect the Canadian dollar to appreciate, they will rush to buy assets that pay off in Canadian dollars. The supply of U.S. dollars to the foreign exchange market pushes the exchange rate down, causing the expected appreciation of the value of the Canadian dollar to occur. Conversely, if foreigners expect the Canadian dollar to depreciate, they will be reluctant to hold Canadian securities. They will seek to sell Canadian dollars, demanding U.S. dollars in exchange. This pushes the exchange rate up and causes the depreciation of the Canadian dollar that was expected. This is another example of the phenomenon of *self-realizing expectations* that we have encountered at several earlier points in this book.

Long-term capital movements. Long-term capital movements are largely influenced by long-term expectations about various countries' profit opportunities and exchange rates. A U.S. firm would be more willing to invest in Canada than in the United States if it expects the Canadian investment to earn more *U.S. dollars* than the U.S. investment. This could happen if the Canadian investment earned greater profits (translated into U.S. dollars) than the U.S. investment at the current exchange rate. It could also happen if the profits were the same, translated at the current exchange rate, but the U.S. firm expected future appreciation of the Canadian dollar relative to the U.S. dollar.

Structural Changes

Structural change is an omnibus term for changes in costs of production, the invention of new products, or anything else that affects the pattern of comparative advantage. For example, when the quality of one country's products do not improve as rapidly as those of a second country, consumer demand (at fixed prices) shifts slowly away from the first country's products toward those of the second country. This causes a slow depreciation of the first country's currency because its demand curve is shifting slowly leftward.

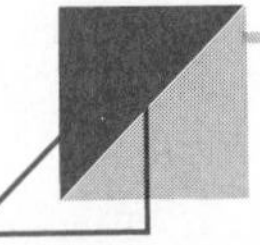

The Balance of Payments

Balance-of-Payments Accounts

To know what is happening to the course of international trade, governments keep track of the transactions among countries. The record of such transactions is kept in the *balance-of-payments accounts*. Each transaction, such as a shipment of exports or the arrival of imported goods, is classified according to the payments or receipts that would typically arise from it. Table 41-2 shows the major items in the Canadian balance-of-payments accounts for 1989.

Current Account

The **current account** records payments arising from trade in goods and services and from income in the form of interest, profits, and dividends arising from capital owned in one country and invested in another. The current account is divided into two main sections.

The first is variously called the **visible account** and the **merchandise account**. It records payments and receipts arising from the imports and exports of tangible goods such as computers, cars, wheat, and shoes. Canadian imports require the use of foreign exchange and hence are entered as debit items on the visible account. Canadian exports earn foreign exchange and hence are recorded as credit items.

The second section of the current account is called **traded service account**. It records payments arising out of trade in services and payments for the use of capital. Trade in such services as insurance, shipping, and tourism is entered in this account. The balance on the first two sections is called the *balance of trade* and refers to trade in both goods and services. The third section is called *capital servicing* and includes such items as payments of interest, dividends, and profits made for capital used in one country but owned by residents of another country. The sum of the second and third sections is called the balance on **invisible account.**

Items that use foreign exchange, such as pur-

TABLE 41-2 Canadian Balance of International Payments, 1989 (*billions of dollars*)

Current account	
Merchandise exports	+ 142.1
Merchandise imports	− 134.5
Balance of merchandise trade	+ 7.6
Exports of services	+ 20.8
Imports of services	− 28.0
Balance of trade	+ 0.4
Net investment income	− 22.2
Transfers	+ 5.1
Balance on current account	− 16.9
Capital account	
Long-term capital flows	+ 24.4
Short-term capital flows	− 6.1
Balance on capital account	+ 18.3
Current plus capital account	+ 2.4
Statistical discrepancy[a]	− 3.1
Use of official reserves (increase −, decrease +)	− 0.7
Overall balance of payments	(Always zero)

Source: Bank of Canada Review, September 1990.

[a] In balance-of-payments accounts, the "statistical discrepancy" item results from the inability to measure some industrial items accurately. For example, many capital transactions are not recorded.

The overall balance of payments always balances, but the individual components do not have to. In 1989 Canada shows a positive (surplus) merchandise trade balance (exports exceed imports) and a negative (deficit) balance on current account. There is a positive (surplus) balance on capital account because capital exports exceeded capital imports. The capital *plus* current account balance is what is commonly referred to as the *balance of payments.* It is exactly matched by the balance in the official account, that is, the use of official reserves.

chases by Canadian residents of foreign insurance and shipping services, travel abroad by Canadians, and payments to foreign residents of interest earned in Canada, are entered as debit items. Items that earn foreign exchange, such as purchases of Canadian insurance and shipping services by foreigners, travel by foreigners in Canada, and payments to Canadian residents of interest earned abroad, are entered as credit items.

Given Canada's long history of being a net international borrower, the payment of interest and dividends on foreign loans and investments is a substantial item in the Canadian balance-of-payments accounts. When an American corporation owns a subsidiary in Canada, it receives dividend payments in Canadian dollars. If the American owners wish to spend these dividends at home, they will need to exchange Canadian for American dollars. Interest and dividends paid to foreigners thus use up foreign exchange and are entered as debit items on the balance of payments.

Usually the debt-servicing entry is sufficiently large to cause the current account to be in overall deficit, even when the trade account shows a substantial surplus.

Capital Account

The second main division in the balance of payments is the **capital account**, which records transactions related to international movements of financial capital. The export of funds from Canada, called a *capital export*, uses foreign exchange and so is entered as a debit item in the Canadian payments accounts. The import of funds into Canada, called a *capital import*, earns foreign exchange and so is entered as a credit item in the payments statistics.

It may seem odd that the export of capital is a debit item on the capital account when the export of a good is a credit item on the current account. To see that there is no contradiction in the treatment of goods and capital, consider the export of Canadian funds for investment in a U.S. bond. The capital transaction involves the purchase, and hence the *import*, of a U.S. bond, and this has the same effect on the balance of payments as the purchase, and hence the import, of a U.S.-made good. Both items involve payments to foreigners, and both use foreign exchange. Both are thus debit items in Canadian balance-of-payments accounts.

The capital account distinguishes between movements of short-term and long-term capital. Short-term capital is money held in the form of highly liquid assets, such as bank accounts and short-term treasury bills. If a nonresident merchant buys dollars and places them in a deposit account in Toronto, this represents an inflow of short-term capital into Canada, and it will be recorded as a credit item on short-term capital account. Long-term capital represents funds coming into Canada (a credit item) or leaving Canada (a debit item) to be invested in less liquid assets such as long-term bonds or physical capital such as a new car assembly plant.

The two major subdivisions of the long-term part of the capital accounts are direct investment and portfolio investment. **Direct investment** relates to changes in nonresident ownership of domestic firms and resident ownership of foreign firms. Thus one form of direct investment in Canada is capital investment in a branch plant or subsidiary corporation in Canada in which the investor has voting control. Another form is a takeover in which a controlling interest in a firm previously controlled by residents is acquired by foreigners. **Portfolio investment**, by contrast, is investment in bonds or a minority holding of shares that does not involve legal control.

Use of Official Reserves

The final section in the balance-of-payments accounts represents transactions in the *official reserves* held by a country's central bank. These transactions reflect the financing of the balance on the remainder of the accounts. The central banks of most countries hold reserves of funds that they can use to buy and sell in the foreign exchange market. Some of these reserves are held in gold, some in foreign exchange, some as claims on various major foreign currencies, and some in an international currency called special drawing rights (which we study in Chapter 42).

The Bank of Canada, operating on behalf of the government, can intervene in the market for foreign exchange to influence the Canadian dollar's exchange rate. For example, to prevent the exchange rate from falling, the Bank must buy foreign exchange, which it then adds to its reserves. When the Bank wishes to stop the Canadian exchange rate from rising in value, it enters the market and sells foreign exchange. This will deplete its holdings of foreign exchange reserves.

The Meaning of Payments Balances and Imbalances

We have seen that the payments accounts show the total of receipts of foreign exchange (credit items) and payments of foreign exchange (debit items) in each category of payment. It is also common to calculate the *balance* on separate items or groups of items. The concept of the balance of payments is used in a number of ways. These can be confusing, so we must approach this issue in steps.

The Balance of Payments Must Balance Overall

Notice two things about the payments accounts. First, they record *actual payments*, not *desired payments*. Second, they attempt to record *all payments*, whatever the reason for which they were made.

It is quite possible that at the existing exchange rate between dollars and yen, holders of yen want to purchase more dollars than holders of dollars want to sell in exchange for yen. In this situation, the quantity of dollars demanded exceeds the quantity supplied. However, holders of yen cannot actually buy more dollars than holders of dollars actually sell; every yen that is bought must have been sold by someone, and every dollar that is sold must have been bought by someone.

It follows that if we add up all the receipts arising from (1) payments received by Canadian residents on account of Canadian exports of goods and services, (2) capital imports, and (3) purchase of foreign exchange or gold by the Bank of Canada, these must be exactly equal to all payments made by holders of dollars arising from (1) Canadian imports of goods and services, (2) exports of capital, and (3) sale of foreign exchange or gold by the Bank.

This relation is so important that it pays us to write it out in symbols. We let C, K, and F stand for current account, capital account, and use of official reserves, respectively, and use P for payments (debit items) and R for receipts (credit items). Now we can write

$$C_R + K_R + F_R = C_P + K_P + F_P \qquad [1]$$

All this tells us is that if we add up across all transactions, payments must equal receipts in total.

Although the relation given in the equation is necessarily true, it often worries students who feel that it need not be true. To help clarify the issue, some apparent exceptions are considered in Box 41-1.

Payments on Specific Parts of the Accounts Need Not Balance

Although the overall total of payments must equal the overall total of receipts, the same zero balance does not have to hold on subsections of the overall accounts. We now look at the balances on parts of the accounts, first in relation to particular countries and then in relation to particular subsectors of the account.

Country balances. When all foreign countries are taken together, each country's overall payments must balance, but one country can have bilateral surpluses or deficits with other individual foreign countries or groups of countries. In general, the **multilateral**

balance of payments refers to the balance between one country's payments to and receipts from the rest of the world. When all items are considered, every country must have a zero multilateral payments balance with the rest of the world, although it can have bilateral surpluses or deficits with individual countries. This important principle is illustrated in the second part of Box 41-1.

Subsection balances. The balance on visible, or merchandise, account refers to the difference between the value of Canadian exports of goods and the value of imports of goods. A surplus occurs when exports of goods exceed imports of goods; a deficit occurs when imports exceed exports. The balance on invisibles refers to the difference between the value of receipts on invisibles and the value of payments for invisibles. The **current account balance** is the sum of the balances on the visible and invisible accounts. It gives the balance between payments and receipts on all income-related items.

As a carryover from a long-discredited eighteenth century economic doctrine called mercantilism, a credit balance on current account (receipts exceeding payments) is called a **favorable balance of payments**, and a debit balance (payments exceeding receipts) is called an **unfavorable balance of payments**.

Mercantilists, both ancient and modern, hold that the gains from trade arise from having a favorable balance of trade. This misses the whole point of the principle of comparative advantage discussed in Chapter 20. That principle shows that countries can gain from a *balanced increase* in trade between themselves because of the opportunity it provides for each country to specialize according to its comparative advantage. The modern resurgence of mercantilist views is discussed in Box 41-2.

The balance on capital account gives the difference between receipts of foreign exchange and payments of foreign exchange arising out of capital movements. A surplus ("favorable") balance on capital account means that a country is a *net importer of capital*; a deficit ("unfavorable") balance means that the country is a *net exporter of capital*.

Notice that a deficit on capital account, which is referred to as an unfavorable balance, merely indicates that a country is investing abroad. Investing abroad and accumulating assets that will earn income in the future may be desirable. So once again we observe that there is nothing necessarily unfavorable about having an "unfavorable" balance on any of the payments accounts.

A credit balance on official settlements account means that the Bank of Canada has bought more gold and foreign exchange than it has sold. This adds to its reserves of foreign exchange. A deficit balance means that the Bank has sold more gold and foreign exchange than it has bought. This reduces its foreign exchange reserves.

The Relations of Various Balances

Two important points require notice. First, since overall payments must balance, the terms *balance-of-payments deficit* and *balance-of-payments surplus* refer to the balance on *some part* of the payments accounts. Second, because of the necessity for the balance of payments to balance overall, a deficit on any one part of the accounts implies an offsetting surplus on the rest of the accounts.

Two important applications of this second point will be considered. The first concerns the balances on current and capital accounts, and the second concerns the use of official reserves and the balances on the remainder of the overall accounts.

The current and capital account balances. To help clarify the relation between current and capital balances, suppose that the Bank of Canada does not engage in any foreign exchange transactions. This means that the use of official reserves is zero because both F_R and F_P in Equation 1 are zero.

Now any deficit or surplus on current account must be matched by an equal and opposite surplus or deficit on capital account. For example, if a country has a credit balance on current account, the foreign exchange earned must appear as a debit item in the capital account. The foreign exchange may be used to buy foreign assets or merely stashed away in foreign bank accounts. In either case there is an outflow of capital from Canada. It is recorded as a debit item because it uses foreign exchange.

We can see this clearly if we return to Equation 1 and set F_R and F_P equal to zero to indicate no transactions by the Bank of Canada. This gives

$$C_R + K_R = C_P + K_P \qquad [2]$$

Now subtract C_P and K_R from both sides of the equation to get

$$C_R - C_P = K_P - K_R \qquad [3]$$

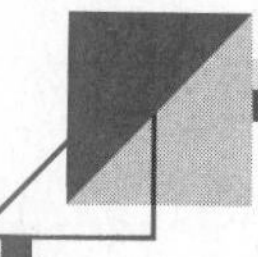

BOX 41-1

Why Total Payments Always Balance: An Illustration

Trade Between Two Countries

Suppose that the sole international transaction made this year by a small country called Myopia was an export to Canada of Myopian coconuts worth \$1,000. Further suppose that the Myopian central bank issues a local currency, the stigma, but does not operate in the foreign exchange market, so there is no official financing. Finally, suppose that Myopia's self-sufficient inhabitants want no imports. Surely, then, you might think Myopia has an overall favorable balance of \$1,000, which is a current account receipt, C_R, with no balancing item on the payments side.

To see why this is wrong, we must ask what the exporter of coconuts did with the dollars he received for his coconuts. If he deposited them in a Toronto bank, this transaction represents a capital export from Myopia. Myopians have accumulated claims on foreign exchange, which they hold in the form of a deposit with a foreign bank. Thus there are two entries in the Myopian accounts—one a credit item for the export of coconuts (C_R) = \$1,000) and the other a debit item for the export of capital (K_P = \$1,000). The fact that the same person made both transactions is irrelevant. Although the current account shows a credit balance, the capital account exactly balances this with a debit item. Hence looking at the *balance of payments as a whole*, the two sides of the account are equal. The balance of payments has balanced—as always it must.

Consider now a slightly more realistic case. If the coconut exporter wants to turn his \$1,000 into Myopian stigmas so that he can pay his coconut pickers in local currency, he must find someone who wishes to buy his dollars in return for Myopian currency. But we have assumed that no one in Myopia wants to import, so no one wants to sell Myopian currency for current account reasons. Assume, however, that a wealthy Myopian landowner would like to invest \$1,000 in Toronto by buying shares in a Canadian firm. To do so he needs \$1,000. The coconut exporter can sell his \$1,000 to the landowner in return for stigmas. Now he can pay his local bills. The landowner sells his stigmas to the exporter in return for dollars. Now he can buy the Canadian shares.

This expresses in equation form what we have just stated in words: A surplus on current account must be balanced by a deficit on capital account (i.e., an outflow of capital), and a deficit on current account must be matched by a surplus on capital account (i.e., an inflow of capital).

One important implication relates to capital transfers. A country that is importing capital has a surplus on capital account and so it *must* have a deficit on current account. This is the position that the United States was in during all of the 1980s and that Canada was in during the latter part of the decade. Because of the borrowing requirements of a large government budget deficit, there was a capital inflow into that country. This inflow made a current account deficit inevitable. As long as the capital inflow persisted, no policy measure could remove the current account deficit. It has also been the position throughout much of Canada's history when the country has been a net importer of capital. This issue is considered in more detail in Chapter 43.[5]

[5] Commentators sometimes assume that the capital inflow must be to buy new government debt directly. The shortfall between the government's borrowing requirements plus private requirements for funds on the one hand and Canadian savings on the other had to be covered by foreign capital. In practice, much of the foreign capital was invested in the Canadian private sector, leaving the Canadian public to buy Canadian government debt. Thus the government debt helped to increase foreign ownership of Canadian private-sector debt and equity.

Once again the Myopian balance of payments will show two entries, equal in size but opposite in sign. The credit item for the export of coconuts (the sale of coconuts that earned foreign exchange) and the debit item for the export of capital (the purchase of the Canadian shares that used foreign exchange) balance each other out.

Trade Involving Many Countries

In the example, Myopia had what is called a bilateral payments balance with Canada. The *bilateral balance of payments* between any two countries is the balance between the payments and receipts flowing between them. If there were only two countries in the world, their overall payments would have to be in bilateral balance; that is, one country's payments to the other would be equal to its receipts from the other. This is not true when there are more than two countries.

Suppose that one year later Myopia again sells $1,000 worth of coconuts to Canada but that the landowner does not wish to invest further in Canada. Now suppose, however, that the Myopian people wish to buy 200,000 yen's worth of parasols from Japan. (Assume also that on the foreign exchange market, $1.00 Canadian trades for 200 yen.) Finally, assume that a Japanese importer wishes to buy $1,000 worth of skateboards from a Canadian company.

What in effect happens is that the Myopian coconut exporter sells his $1,000 to the Japanese skateboard importer for 200,000 yen, which the coconut dealer then sells to the Myopian parasol importer in return for Myopian stigmas. (In the real world the exchanges are usually made through financial institutions, but this is what happens in effect.) Now the Myopian payment statistics will show a $1,000 bilateal payment surplus with Canada—receipts of $1,000 from Canada on account of coconut exports and no payments to Canada—and a bilateral deficit with Japan of 200,000 yen (equal to $1,000)—$1,000 of payments to Japan on account of parasol imports and no receipts from Japan. But when both countries are considered, Myopia's *multilateral payments* are in balance.

Use of official reserves. When people speak of a country as having an overall balance-of-payments deficit or surplus, they are usually referring to the *balance of all accounts excluding the use of official reserves.* A balance-of-payments surplus means that the central bank is adding foreign exchange reserves to its holdings; a balance-of-payments deficit means that the central bank is reducing its reserves.

If the central bank does not operate in the foreign exchange market, there can be no overall balance-of-payments deficit or surplus on current plus capital account. Suppose that holders of Canadian dollars are trying to buy more foreign exchange than holders of foreign currencies wish to sell in return for dollars. There will be an excess supply of dollars and an excess demand for foreign exchange. The dollar will depreciate on the foreign exchange market until demand equals supply. At this point both desired and actual international payments are in balance.

If exchange rates are completely free to vary, balance-of-payments deficits and surpluses will be eliminated through exchange rate adjustments.

Today, though no country need have a balance-of-payments problem, many do have them. As long as governments intervene in foreign exchange markets, there will be balance-of-payments deficits and

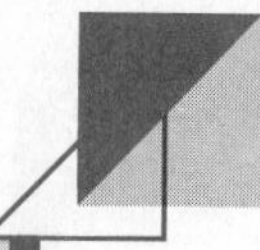

BOX 41-2

The Volume of Trade, the Balance of Trade, and the New Mercantilism

Media commentators, political figures, and much of the general public often judge the national balance of payments as they would the accounts of a single firm. Just as a firm is supposed to show a profit, the nation is supposed to secure a balance-of-payments surplus, with the benefits derived from international trade measured by the size of that surplus.

This view is related to the exploitation doctrine of international trade. Since one country's surplus is another country's deficit, one country's gain, judged by its surplus, must be another country's loss, judged by its deficit.

People who hold such views today are echoing an ancient economic doctrine called *mercantilism*. The mercantilists were a group of economists who preceded Adam Smith. They judged the success of trade by the size of the trade balance. In many cases this doctrine made sense in terms of their objective, which was to use international trade as a means of building up the political and military power of the state rather than raising the living standards of its citizens. A balance-of-payments surplus allowed the nation (then and now) to acquire foreign exchange reserves. (In those days the reserves took the form of gold. Today they are a mixture of gold and claims on the currencies of other countries.) These reserves could then be used to pay armies, composed partly of foreign mercenaries; to purchase weapons from abroad; and to finance colonial adventures.

People who advocate this view in modern times are called *neomercantilists*. Insofar as their object is to increase the power of the state, they are choosing means that could achieve their ends. Insofar as they are drawing an analogy between what is a sensible objective for a business interested in its own material welfare and what is a sensible objective for a government interested in the material welfare of its citizens, their views are erroneous, for the analogy is false.

If we take the view that the object of economic activity is to promote the welfare and living standards of ordinary citizens rather than the power of governments, the mercantilist focus on the balance of trade makes no sense. The law of comparative advantage shows that average living standards are maximized by having individuals, regions, and countries specialize in the things they can produce comparatively best and trading to obtain the things they can produce comparatively worst. The more specialization, the more trade.

In this view the gains from trade are to be judged by the volume of trade. A situation in which there is a *large volume of trade* but each country has a *zero balance of trade* can thus be regarded as quite satisfactory. Furthermore, a change in commercial policy that results in a balanced increase in trade between two countries will bring gain, because it allows for specialization according to comparative advantage even though it causes no change in either country's trade balance.

To the business interested in private profit and to the government interested in the power of the state, it is the balance of trade that matters. To the person interested in the welfare of ordinary citizens, it is the volume of trade that matters.

It follows that when we are evaluating any new initiative such as the Canada–U.S. Free Trade Agreement, we need to look at its effects on the volume, not the balance, of trade. A large and equal increase in both exports and imports following the agreement would indicate substantial mutual gains for trade in both countries. A negligible increase in imports and exports would suggest that the agreement was failing to produce the anticipated benefits.

surpluses. Surpluses will occur whenever the currency is held below its equilibrium level. Persistent deficits will cause persistent losses of reserves; they are evidence that the government is trying to resist longer-term trends for changes in the exchange rate.

SUMMARY

1. International trade is greatly facilitated because it is possible to exchange the currency of one country for that of another. The exchange rate between two currencies is the amount of the home currency that must be paid to purchase one unit of a foreign currency. Where more than two currencies are involved, there is an exchange rate between each pair of currencies.
2. The determination of exchange rates in the free market is simply an application of the laws of supply and demand studied in Chapter 4; the item being bought and sold is foreign exchange.
3. The supply of foreign exchange arises from Canadian exports of goods and services and from long-term and short-term capital flows into Canada. The demand for foreign exchange arises from Canadian imports of goods and services and from capital flows out of Canada.
4. A depreciation of the dollar (a rise in the exchange rate) raises the domestic price of traded goods. This increases the quantity of such goods supplied domestically and reduces the quantity demanded. As a result, the volume of exports rises and with it the supply of foreign exchange. But the volume of imports falls and with it the demand for foreign exchange. Thus the supply curve for foreign exchange is upward-sloping and the demand curve for foreign exchange is downward-sloping when the quantities demanded and supplied are plotted against the price of foreign exchange measured in terms of Canadian dollars—that is, against the exchange rate.
5. A currency will tend to depreciate if there is a shift to the right of the demand curve for foreign exchange or a shift to the left of the supply curve. Shifts in the opposite directions will tend to appreciate the currency. Shifts are caused by such things as changes in the prices of imports and exports, the rates of inflation in different countries, capital movements, structural changes, expectations about future trends in earnings and exchange rates, and the level of confidence in the currency as a source of reserves.
6. Actual transactions among the firms, households, and governments of various countries are kept track of and reported in the balance-of-payments accounts. In these accounts, any transaction that uses foreign exchange is recorded as a debit item and any transaction that produces foreign exchange is recorded as a credit item. If all transactions are recorded, the sum of all credit items necessarily equals the sum of all debit items since the foreign exchange that is bought must also have been sold.
7. Major categories in the balance-of-payments account are the balance of trade (exports minus imports), current account, capital account, and official financing. The so-called balance of payments is the balance of the current plus capital accounts; that is, it excludes the transactions on official account. Ignoring official settlements, a balance on current account must be matched by a balance on capital account of equal magnitude but opposite sign.
8. There is nothing inherently good or bad about deficits or surpluses. Persistent deficits or surpluses cannot be sustained because the former will eventually exhaust a country's foreign exchange reserves and the latter will do the same to a trading partner's reserves.

TOPICS FOR REVIEW

Foreign exchange and exchange rates
Appreciation and depreciation
Sources of the demand for and supply of foreign exchange
Effects on exchange rates of capital flows, inflation, interest rates, and expectations about exchange rates
Balance of trade and balance of payments
Current and capital accounts
Official financing items
Mercantilist views on the balance and volume of trade

DISCUSSION QUESTIONS

1. What is the probable effect of each of the following on the exchange rate between the Canadian and U.S. dollars?
   a. The quantity of Canadian oil exports is greatly increased.
   b. Canada's inflation rate rises well above the U.S. inflation rate.
   c. Falling unit labor costs in Canada increase the competitiveness of Canadian exports in world markets.
   d. The federal government greatly increases its foreign borrowing in order to finance its deficit in the face of falling domestic savings.
   e. A major boom occurs with rising employment.
   f. The Bank of Canada drives up interest rates sharply in pursuit of its anti-inflation policy.
   g. Canadian consumers increase their purchases of Japanese cars in preference to North American models.
2. In the mid 1980s the United States became a major importer of capital, partly to finance the large internal budget deficit and partly because the American boom and the European slump made the United States a highly attractive place in which to invest foreign funds. Predict the effects of this large capital inflow on the U.S. dollar exchange rate and on the balance of payments on current account. Would these developments have anything to do with the upsurge of protectionist sentiment in the U.S. Congress during the latter part of the 1980s?
3. In the mid 1980s money wages rose substantially faster in Canada than in the United States. Many Canadians expressed the fear that the rapidly rising wages would price them out of U.S. markets. Would this fear be well founded if the Canada-U.S. exchange rate were fixed? Is it well founded when, as was the case, the external value of the Canadian dollar was free to vary on the open market?
4. Indicate whether each of the following transactions increases the demand for Canadian dollars on the foreign exchange market, the supply of Canadian dollars, or neither.
   a. IBM moves $10 million from bank accounts in Canada to banks in Paris to expand operations in France.
   b. The Canadian government extends a grant of $3 million to the government of Peru, which Peru uses to buy farm machinery from a Winnipeg firm.
   c. Canadian investors, responding to higher profits of American rather than Canadian corporations, buy stocks through the New York Stock Exchange.
   d. Several less-developed countries stop interest payments on their large debts to Canadian and American banks.
   e. Lower interest rates in Montreal than in New York encourage British firms to borrow in the Montreal money market, converting the proceeds into sterling for use at home.

5. What must be the balance of payments on current account when Canada is a major importer of foreign capital? Does it matter if this capital is used to build productive facilities, as it largely was in the late 1970s, or to finance an excess of government spending for current purposes over government tax revenue, as it largely was in the late 1980s?
6. "The necessity of the government to stabilize the balance of payments through the use of official reserves is a relic of the past. It was a by-product of the adherence to a policy of fixed exchange rates." Do you agree?
7. "If a country solves its balance-of-payments problems, it will have solved its foreign trade problems." Discuss.
8. Outline the reasoning behind the following 1983 newspaper headline: "U.S. dollar tumbles as British interest rates weaken."

Chapter 42

Alternative Exchange Rate Systems

Over the centuries, many different international monetary systems have been used. No system is without problems, and periods of crisis have alternated with periods of stability.

The twentieth century began with a system of fixed exchange rates under the gold standard. That system had served the world well over several centuries but broke down under heavy pressures placed on it in the early part of the twentieth century. The Great Depression of the 1930s was a period of experimentation, with both market-determined and fixed exchange rates. Some of the policy problems of that period are discussed in Box 42-1.

This period of experimentation ended with World War II, when all major governments again fixed exchange rates. In 1944 a system of government-stabilized exchange rates was formalized by international agreement at a conference in Bretton Woods, New Hampshire. The Bretton Woods system lasted for over a quarter of a century, but its shortcomings, and the periods of crisis that it induced, finally prevailed over its advantages and the periods of stability that it afforded. After several attempts to patch it up in the 1970s, the system finally broke down and was abandoned as countries turned one by one to market-determined, flexible exchange rates.

The International Monetary Fund (IMF, also called simply the Fund) was created as part of the Bretton Woods system. Under its original charter, the Fund had several tasks. It tried to ensure that countries kept their exchange rates fixed in the short run. It was supposed to ensure that any exchange rate changes were really needed to remove persistent payments disequilibria and that a single devaluation did not set off a self-cancelling round of devaluations. In doing this, it was to avoid the rounds of self-defeating exchange rate devaluations that helped to destabilize world trade in the 1930s (discussed in Box 42-1). It also made loans—out of funds subscribed by member nations—to governments to support their exchange rates in the face of temporary payments deficits. The Bretton Woods system was abandoned in 1973, but the Fund survives, although its tasks have changed.

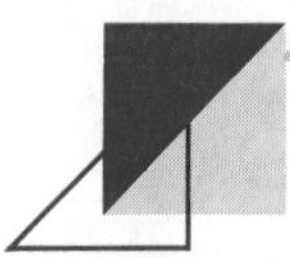

Exchange Rate Systems

Two extreme exchange rate systems can be distinguished. The first is a system of **fixed exchange rates** in which rates are fixed at given par values that central banks cannot alter simply by

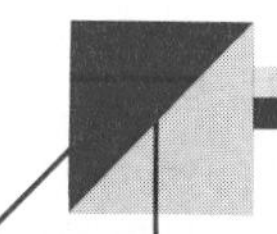

BOX 42-1

Beggar-My-Neighbor Policies, Past and Present

During the Great Depression of the 1930s, concern over massive unemployment came to dominate economic policies in almost every country. All measures, including exchange rate manipulations, seemed fair game for dealing with unemployment. Many of the policies adopted at this time were acts of desperation that would have made long-term sense only if other countries had not also been in crisis. Governments, hoping to gain short-term advantages before their policies provoked the inevitable reaction from others, tended not to consider the long-term effects of the policies that they adopted on trade or on their trading partners.

The use of devaluations to ease domestic unemployment rested on a simple and superficially plausible line of analysis: If a country has unemployed workers at home, why not substitute home production for imports and thus give jobs to one's citizens instead of to foreigners? One way to do this is to urge Canadians to buy Canadian rather than foreign goods (while Americans are being urged to buy U.S. goods, the English to buy English goods, and so on). Another, probably more effective way is to lower the prices of domestic goods relative to those of imports. The devaluation of one's currency does this by making foreign goods much more expensive. Of course, if this policy works, other countries will find *their* exports falling and unemployment rising as a consequence. Because such policies attempt to solve one country's problems by inflicting them on others, they are called **beggar-my-neighbor policies**, described as attempts to "export one's unemployment."

In a situation of inadequate world demand, a beggar-my-neighbor policy on the part of one country can work only in the unlikely event that other countries do not react by changing their policies to protect themselves. A situation in which all countries devalue their currencies in an attempt to gain a competitive advantage over one another is called a situation of **competitive devaluations**.

This is what happened during the 1930s. One country would devalue its currency in an attempt to reduce its imports and stimulate exports, but because other countries were suffering from the same problems of unemployment, retaliation was swift, and devaluation followed devaluation. The simultaneous attempt of all countries to cut imports without suffering a comparable cut in exports is bound to be self-defeating.

These policies, along with other restrictive trade policies, such as import duties, export subsidies, quotas, and prohibitions, led to a declining volume of world trade and brought no relief from the worldwide depression.

To avoid a recurrence of the beggar-my-neighbor policies of the 1930s, trading nations designed some important institutions. The International Monetary Fund (IMF) was supposed to reduce the chances of competitive devaluations, and the General Agreement on Tariffs and Trade (GATT) was supposed to reduce the chances of competitive increases in tariffs and other trade restrictions. These institutions worked well for over 30 years.

Although we no longer have fixed exchange rates, most countries have resisted the temptation to use devaluation of the currency to try to gain a competitive advantage for their exports. Beggar-my-neighbor policies are currently confined mainly to tariffs and other trade restrictions.

deciding to support a different rate in foreign exchange markets. The gold standard is the prime example. Under this system, each country's currency had a fixed value set by the amount of gold into which it could be converted, called the currency's *gold content*. The exchange rate between two currencies was then set by their relative gold content. For example, the British pound sterling was convertible throughout most of the nineteenth century into 4.86 times as much gold as was the U.S. dollar. Thus the exchange rate was £1.00 sterling = U.S.$4.86. As long as the gold content of each national currency was fixed, exchange rates were fixed.

The second system is one of freely fluctuating exchange rates. In this system rates are determined by market demand and supply, in the absence of government intervention. Some countries have come close to operating such a system, first in the 1930s and then since 1971.

Between these two "pure" systems lies a variety of possible intermediate cases. The two that we will encounter are known as the *adjustable peg* and the *managed float*. The managed float, the principal system in use today, is a mixture of the adjustable peg and the freely fluctuating systems. In order to understand the managed float, therefore, we must first study how these other two systems work. A further reason for studying the adjustable peg is that there is considerable interest in some quarters in returning to that type of system. Recently, several Canadian economists have suggested an adjustable peg for the Canadian dollar.

An Adjustable Peg System

When the gold standard was abandoned in the early 1930s, currencies were no longer convertible into gold. If a country wished to have a fixed exchange rate, it did this by pegging the rate between its currency and the currency of some important trading country. But an exchange rate that was fixed by government policy could easily be changed by government policy. Thus the fixed-rate systems that succeeded the gold standard were **adjustable peg systems**, which means that the rate was pegged from day to day but subject to periodic adjustment. When an exchange rate is changed under an adjustable peg system, the domestic currency is said to be **devalued** when its external value is lowered (the exchange rate is raised) and **revalued** when its external value is raised (the exchange rate is lowered). The act of devaluing a currency is called **devaluation**; the act of revaluing it is called **revaluation**.

The Bretton Woods system was a cooperative attempt to stabilize exchange rates by international agreement. According to the Bretton Woods agreement, each participating country undertook to fix its exchange rate. This was done through central bank intervention in the foreign exchange market to prevent the external value of its currency from going outside a narrow band on either side of its stated par value.

One immediate difficulty in this system is that one country must take a passive role with respect to its exchange rate. This is because there is one less exchange rate to be determined than there are countries. In a two-country world, containing only Japan and the United States, for example, if the Bank of Japan fixes the exchange rate at 150 yen to the dollar, the U.S. Federal Reserve cannot fix a different rate, making the dollar worth, say, 200 yen. Under the Bretton Woods system, all foreign countries fixed their exchange rate against the U.S. dollar. The Fed adopted the passive role; it was the only central bank in the world that did not have to intervene to support a particular value of its currency.

Having picked a fixed exchange rate for its currency against the U.S. dollar, each foreign central bank then had to manage matters so that the chosen rate could actually be maintained. Each central bank had to be prepared to offset imbalances in demand and supply through its own sales or purchases of foreign exchange. In the face of short-term market fluctuations, each central bank tried to maintain its fixed exchange rate by entering the market and buying and selling as required.

To do this the central bank has to hold reserves of acceptable foreign exchange. When there is an abnormally low demand for its country's currency in the foreign exchange market, the bank keeps the currency from depreciating by selling foreign exchange and buying up domestic currency. This depletes its reserves of foreign exchange. When there is an abnormally high demand for its country's currency in the foreign exchange market, the bank prevents the currency from appreciating by selling domestic currency for foreign exchange. This action increases its stocks of foreign exchange.

As long as the central bank is trying to maintain an exchange rate that equates demand and supply for its currency *on average*, the policy can be successful. Sometimes the bank will be buying, and other times it will be selling, but its reserves will fluctuate around a constant average level.

If, however, there is a permanent shift in demand for or supply of a nation's currency in the foreign exchange market, the long-term equilibrium rate will move away from the **pegged rate**, that is, its par value. It will then be difficult to maintain the pegged rate. For example, if major inflation occurs in Canada while prices are stable in the United States, the equilibrium value of the Canadian dollar will fall. In a free market, the Canadian dollar would depreciate and the U.S. dollar would appreciate. However, a fixed exchange rate is not a free market rate. If the Bank of Canada persisted in trying to maintain the original exchange rate, it would have to meet the excess demand for U.S. dollars by selling from its reserves. Such a policy can persist only as long as the Bank has reserves that it is willing to spend to maintain an artificially high price of Canadian dollars. However, the Bank cannot do this indefinitely. Sooner or later the reserves that it has, and those that it can borrow, will be exhausted.

The management of a fixed rate is illustrated in Figure 42-1. The example used is the maintenance by the Bank of Canada of a fixed exchange rate between the Canadian dollar and the U.S. dollar.

When the fixed rate is not near the free market equilibrium rate, controls of various sorts may be introduced in an attempt to shift the demand curve for foreign exchange so that it intersects the supply curve at a rate close to the fixed rate. This is usually done by restricting imports of goods and services or by restricting the export of capital. If the Bank cannot shift demand and supply in order to keep the equilibrium rate approximately as high as the fixed rate, it will have no alternative but to devalue its currency.

FIGURE 42-1 A Stabilized Exchange Rate

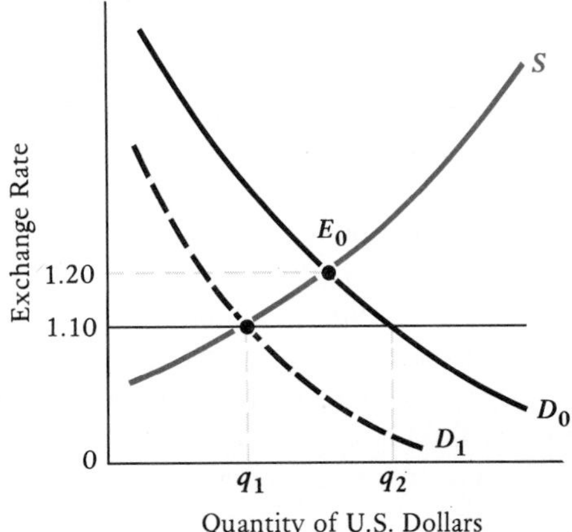

When an exchange rate is fixed at other than the equilibrium rate, either excess demand or excess supply will persist. Suppose that the demand and supply curve of U.S. dollars in the absence of government controls are D_0 and S; equilibrium is at E_0, with a price of \$1.20 Canadian per U.S. dollar. Now the Canadian authorities peg the price of the U.S. dollar at \$1.10 Canadian. They have overvalued the Canadian dollar in relation to the U.S. dollar. As a result, there is an excess demand for U.S. dollars of q_1q_2. One way to maintain the fixed rate is to shift either the demand curve or the supply curve (or both) so that the two intersect at the fixed rate. For example, the demand curve might be shifted to D_1 by reducing imports. A second way to maintain the fixed rate if the curves are not shifted is for the Bank of Canada to sell U.S. dollars in the amount of q_1q_2 per period out of its reserves.

Problems with Adjustable Peg Systems

Three problems typically arise with an adjustable peg system of exchange rates: (1) providing sufficient reserves, (2) adjusting to long-term trends, and (3) dealing with speculative crises.

Providing sufficient reserves. Reserves are needed to accommodate short-term balance-of-payments fluctuations arising from the current and capital accounts. On current account, trade is subject to many short-term variations—some systematic and some random. This means that even if the value of imports does equal the value of exports on average over several years, there may be considerable imbalances over shorter periods.

With a market-determined exchange rate, fluctuations in current and capital account payments would cause the exchange rate to fluctuate. To prevent such fluctuations when rates are fixed, the monetary authorities buy and sell foreign exchange as required. These operations require that the authorities hold reserves of foreign exchange. If they run out of reserves, they cannot maintain the pegged rate.

The Bretton Woods system had difficulty in providing sufficient reserves. This was because the ultimate reserve was gold, and there was not enough of it. As a result, the world's central banks held much of their reserves in U.S. dollars and British pounds sterling. Currencies that are widely held for this purpose are called **reserve currencies**.

This system worked well enough as long as these reserve currencies had a stable value. However, in the mid 1960s fear of an impending devaluation of the pound sterling arose, and in the early 1970s a similar fear arose regarding the U.S. dollar. In both cases the fears were well founded: The pound sterling was devalued in late 1967, and the dollar was devalued in 1971 and again in 1973.

The devaluation of a reserve currency reduces the value of the reserves of that currency held by the world's central banks. Fear that a devaluation will occur reduces the acceptability of a currency as a means of holding reserves.

The problem of providing reserves, though serious, need not be insurmountable in any future system of fixed rates. After all, a balanced portfolio, composed of some holdings of a number of currencies, could be held as reserves. This would reduce the risks from holding reserves, since whenever one currency fell in value against a second currency, the second currency would rise in value against the first.

Adjusting to long-term trends. With fixed exchange rates, long-term disequilibria can be expected to develop because of lasting shifts in the demands for and supplies of foreign exchange. There are three important reasons for these shifts. First, different trading countries have different rates of inflation. Chapter 41 explained how these varying rates produce changes in the equilibrium rates of exchange; if the rate is fixed, the differences in inflation rates would produce excess supply or excess demand in each country's foreign exchange market. Second, changes in the demands for and supplies of imports and exports are associated with long-term economic growth. Because the economies of different countries grow at different rates, their demands for imports and their supplies of exports can be expected to shift at different rates. Third, structural changes, such as major innovations or a change in the price of oil, cause major changes in imports and exports.

The associated shifts in demand and supply in the foreign exchange market imply that there is no reason to believe that the exchange rate consistent with equilibrium in the market for foreign exchange will remain unchanged.

The exchange rate consistent with balance-of-payments equilibrium will change over time; over a decade the change can be substantial.

Governments may react to long-term disequilibria in at least three ways.

First, the exchange rate can be changed whenever it is clear that a balance-of-payments deficit or surplus is the result of a long-term shift in demands and supplies in the foreign exchange market and not the result of some transient factor.

Second, domestic price levels can be allowed to change in an attempt to make the present fixed exchange rate become the equilibrium rate. To restore equilibrium, countries with overvalued currencies need deflation and countries with undervalued currencies need inflation. However, changes in domestic price levels have all sorts of domestic repercussions. Deflation is difficult and costly to accomplish (e.g., reductions in aggregate demand, intended to lower the price level, are likely to raise unemployment), and often an explicit goal of government policy is to avoid inflation. Often governments will be more willing to change exchange rates than to try to change their price levels.

Third, restrictions can be imposed on trade and foreign payments. Imports and foreign spending by tourists and governments can be restricted, and the export of capital can be slowed or even stopped. Surplus countries are often quick to criticize such restrictions on international trade and payments. However, as long as exchange rates are fixed and price levels prove difficult to manipulate, deficit countries have little option but to restrict the quantity of foreign exchange that their residents are permitted to obtain.

Since restrictions on trade and foreign payments are undesirable in a world economy that is characterized by large-scale international trade and foreign investment and since deflation of the price level is difficult and costly to bring about, most countries want to preserve the possibility of making occasional changes in their exchange rates, even if fixed rates are the main rule of the day.

Several major rounds of exchange rate adjustments took place under the Bretton Woods system.

Handling speculative crises. When enough people begin to doubt the government's ability to maintain the current exchange rate, a speculative crisis develops. The most important reason for such a crisis is that over time, equilibrium exchange rates get further and further away from any given set of fixed rates. When the disequilibrium becomes obvious to everyone, traders and speculators come to believe that a realignment of rates is due. There is a rush to buy currencies that are expected to be revalued and a rush to sell currencies that are expected to be devalued. Even if the authorities take drastic steps, there may be doubt that these measures will work before the exchange reserves are exhausted. Speculative flows of funds can reach large proportions, and it may be impossible to avoid changing the exchange rate under such pressure.

Under an adjustable peg system, opportunities often arise for speculators to make large profits; this occurs when everyone knows the direction in which an exchange rate will be changed, if it is to be changed at all.

As the equilibrium value of a country's currency changes, possibly under the impact of high inflation, it becomes obvious that the central bank is having more and more difficulty holding the pegged rate. So when a crisis arises, speculators sell the country's currency. If it is devalued, they can buy it back at a lower price and earn a profit. If it is not devalued, they can buy it back at the price at which they sold it and lose only the commission costs on the deal. This asymmetry, with speculators having a chance to make large profits by risking only a small loss, eventually destroyed the Bretton Woods system.

Flexible Exchange Rates

Under a system of flexible exchange rates, demand and supply determine the rates without any government intervention. (This was illustrated in Figure 42-1 on page 907.) Such rates are called **free, flexible,** or **floating exchange rates**. Since the foreign exchange market always clears, the government can turn its attention to domestic problems of inflation and unemployment, leaving the balance of payments to take care of itself—at least so went the theory before flexible rates were introduced.

For reasons that we analyze later in this chapter, this optimistic picture did not materialize when the world went over to flexible exchange rates. Free market fluctuations in rates were far greater and hence potentially more upsetting to the performance of national economies and to the flow of international trade than many economists had anticipated. As a result, central banks have felt the need to intervene quite frequently and extensively to stabilize exchange rates.

Managed Floats

The system of **dirty**, or **managed**, **floats** has two characteristics that make it a mixture of the systems of adjustable pegs and flexible rates that we have just studied. First, it is like a fully flexible system because the exchange rate is often left to fluctuate according to normal market forces. Second, it is like an adjustable peg because the central bank often intervenes in the market to keep exchange rates near some target value that it has set. However, unlike the adjustable peg system, these targets are usually not publicly known and can be changed from time to time without public announcement. Central banks are thus free to adjust their exchange rate targets as circumstances change. Sometimes they leave the rate completely free to fluctuate, and at other times they interfere actively to alter the exchange rate from its free market value.

Some countries have opted for what is called a *currency block* by pegging their exchange rates against each other and then indulging in a joint float against the outside world. The best-known currency block is the **European monetary system (EMS)**. Under this arrangement most of the countries of the EC maintain fixed rates among their own currencies but allow them to float as a block against the dollar. As Europe moves toward increased economic integration in 1992, momentum is also building for the creation of a common currency area, with one European currency issued by a European central bank.

What Determines the Exchange Rate in a Floating System?

The average value of exchange rates over the long term depends on their **purchasing power parity (PPP) exchange rate** values. The PPP exchange rate equals the purchasing power of any two currencies when one is translated into the other currency at that rate. For example, suppose that the average price of a representative bundle of goods is U.S.$10.00 in the United States and C$12.00 in Canada to buy the same bundle of goods. In this case, the Canadian PPP rate for the U.S. dollar is 1.2. Converting the U.S. average price of the representative bundle to Canadian dollars yields U.S.$10.00 × C$12. The PPP rate has the important property that it adjusts for the relative change in the two countries' price levels. If, for example, a Canadian inflation drives the Canadian average price of the representative bundle of goods up to \$14, the Canadian PPP rate rises to 1.4 (or the PPP value of the Canadian dollar depreciates to US\$0.714, which is the same thing).

The PPP exchange rate is the rate that keeps the relative price of the two nations' goods (measured in the same currency) constant; to do this the PPP rate changes by the amount needed to compensate exactly for differences in national inflation rates.

As long as the actual exchange rate remains equal to the PPP rate, the competitive positions of producers in the two countries will be unchanged. Firms that are located in countries with high inflation rates will still be able to sell their outputs on international markets, since the exchange rate adjusts to offset the effect of the higher domestic prices.

Figure 42-2 shows that the exchange rate between U.S. dollars and three major currencies has followed the PPP rate over the long run. Notice also, however, the large fluctuations around the PPP rate.

Because the Canadian and the U.S. currencies both have the same name, many people assume that the correct long-term relation is that one Canadian dollar should equal one U.S. dollar. This is not so. There is no more reason why one Canadian dollar should equal one U.S. dollar than one Mexican peso or one British pound should equal one U.S. dollar. The exchange rate around which the currency should fluctuate is the PPP rate, which at the beginning of the 1990s made one Canadian dollar worth about 80 to 82 U.S. cents, which was several cents less than the current market rate.

During the Bretton Woods period of fixed exchange rates, the advocates of floating rates argued that speculators would stabilize the actual rates within a narrow band around the PPP rates. The argument was that since everyone knew that the normal value was the PPP rate, speculators who were seeking a profit when the rate deviated from its PPP level would quickly force the rate back to that level. To illustrate, suppose that the PPP rate is C\$1.00 = US\$1.20 and that the actual rate falls to C\$1.10. Speculators who hold Canadian dollars would rush to buy U.S. dollars at C\$1.10, expecting to sell them at C\$1.20 when the rate returned to its PPP level. This very action would raise the demand for the U.S. dollar and help push its value back toward C\$1.20.

Such speculative behavior would stabilize the exchange rate near its PPP value if speculators could be sure that the deviations would be small and short-lived. However, in practice, the swings around the

FIGURE 42-2 The Dollar and Purchasing Power Parity, 1973–1988

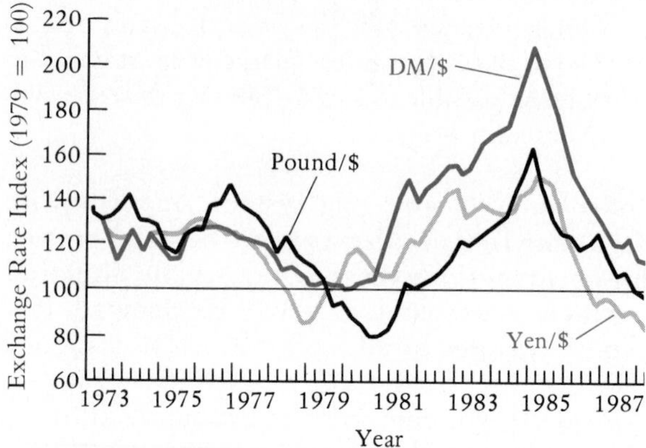

Deviations from PPP can be substantial in the short run, but over the long run exchange rates tend to converge to their PPP values. The figure shows the bilateral real value of the U.S. dollar in terms of three major currencies—the Japanese yen, the West German deutsche mark (DM), and the U.K. pound sterling. The series are calculated by multiplying the nominal exchange rate by the relative price levels of the two countries, and an index number is then calculated by setting the value for 1979 equal to 100. (In 1979 the U.S. current account was roughly in balance, and many economists argue that PPP can be assumed roughly to hold then.)

If PPP were always to hold, the series would be constant. However, as can be seen, in the early 1980s the real value of the U.S. dollar rose sharply in terms of all three currencies. This reflected a sharp rise in the foreign exchange value of the dollar that was not offset by relatively high foreign inflation. As a result, there was a real appreciation of the U.S. dollar, and U.S. goods became very expensive relative to those produced in the other countries. In 1985 the real value of the dollar started to fall, and by mid 1988 it had returned to its 1979 value in terms of the pound sterling *adjusted for changes in the relative price levels.* Further, at the end of 1988, the U.S. dollar was actually lower in real terms relative to the yen than it had been in 1979, and it had almost fallen to its 1979 real value in terms of the deutsche mark.

PPP rate have been wide and have lasted for long periods. Thus if the U.S. dollar fell to C$1.10, speculators would know that it could go as low as, say, C$1.00 and stay there for quite a while before returning to C$1.20. In that case it might be worth speculating on a price of C$1.05 next week rather than a price of C$1.20 in some indefinite future.

The wide swings in exchange rates that have occurred show that speculative buying and selling cannot be relied on to hold exchange rates close to their PPP values.

Why have these wide fluctuations occurred? One of the most important reasons is associated with international differences in interest rates.

Exchange Rate Overshooting

Suppose that Canadian interest rates rise above those prevailing in other major financial centers, as they did towards the end of the 1980s. A rush to lend money at the profitable rates found in Canada will lead to an appreciation of the Canadian dollar.

This process will stop only when the rise in value of the Canadian dollar in foreign exchange markets is large enough that investors will expect the dollar subsequently to fall in value. This expected future depreciation then just offsets the interest premium from lending funds in Canadian dollars.

To illustrate, assume that interest rates are 4 percentage points higher in Toronto than in New York, due to a restrictive monetary policy in Canada. Investors believe that the PPP rate is C$1.20 = U.S.$1.00, but as they rush to buy Canadian dollars to take advantage of the higher Canadian interest rates, they drive the exchange rate down to, say, C$1.10 = U.S.$1.00. (Recall that since it now takes fewer Canadian dollars to buy one U.S. dollar, the Canadian currency has appreciated in value.) However, investors do not believe that this rate will be sustained and instead expect the Canadian dollar to lose value. If foreign investors expect it to depreciate at 4 percent per year, they will be indifferent between lending money in New York and doing so in Toronto. The extra 4 percent per year of interest that they earn in Toronto is exactly offset by the 4 percent that they expect to lose when they turn their money back into their own currency.

Any policy that raises domestic interest rates above world levels will cause the domestic currency to appreciate enough to create an expected future depreciation that will be sufficient to offset the interest differential.

A central bank that is seeking to meet a monetary target may have to put up with large fluctuations in the exchange rate. If, in the example, the high Canadian interest rates were the result of a restrictive monetary policy, the overshooting of the Canadian dollar beyond its PPP rate may put export- and import-competing industries under temporary but severe pressure from foreign competition. Something very much like this happened in 1988 and 1989. In an attempt to restrain a rising inflation rate, the Bank of Canada drove rates up to about 4 percentage points above the U.S. rate, and the Canadian dollar rose well above its PPP rate. This put Canadian export industries at a competitive disadvantage in the U.S. market.

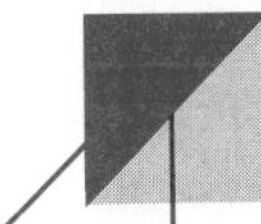

Current Problems

The Lack of an Alternative to the U.S. Dollar As a Reserve Currency

Governments that operate dirty floats need reserves, just like governments that operate adjustable pegs. The search for an adequate supply of reserves has continued unabated since the demise of the Bretton Woods system.

One major form in which reserves are held is U.S. dollars; another form—one that is growing in size—is the **special drawing rights (SDRs)** held with the IMF. First introduced in 1969, SDRs were designed to provide a supplement to existing reserve assets. The Special Drawing Account of the IMF was set up and kept separate from all other operations of the Fund. Each member country was assigned an SDR quota that was guaranteed in terms of a fixed gold value. Each country could use its quota to acquire an equivalent amount of convertible currencies from other participants. SDRs could be used without prior consultation with the Fund, but only to cope with balance-of-payments difficulties. SDR allocations grew from about $10 billion in 1970 to well over $50 billion in 1988.

Why does the world not turn to an international paper reserve system based on SDRs or some similar creation? Such a solution has much support from academic economists, who see an appropriate international institution managing the supply of international currency to accommodate growth and to avoid inflation.

Critics of such a system—among them most of the world's central bankers—distrust the concept of an international paper currency, pointing out that few countries have managed their own money supplies effectively. However difficult the task of the U.S. Federal Reserve may be, the task of a World Reserve Bank would be even more difficult. Further, private acceptance and use of the SDR has been virtually nonexistent, indicating the enormous difficulties inherent in creating a new currency.

Some who are skeptical of an international paper monetary standard have urged a return to the gold standard. This approach has critical disadvantages. In fact, the IMF and the U.S. government have at various times taken the lead in an attempt to "demonetarize" gold completely.

For the moment at least, the world cannot agree on an international monetary reserve. Until it does, there will be crises whenever there is a desire to shift from one to another of the multiple sources of reserves: dollars, gold, SDRs, marks, francs, and yen. The speculative opportunities inherent in such a system remain large, as evidenced by the recent behavior of the price of gold, shown in Figure 42-3.

FIGURE 42-3 Price of Gold, 1971–1990

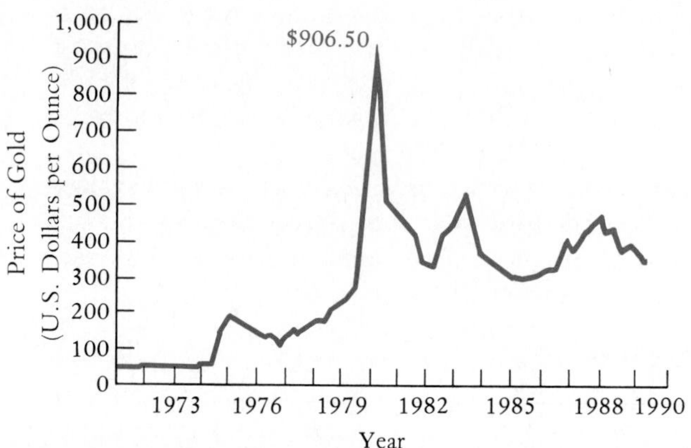

Gold soared in value and proved to be highly volatile after convertibility of the dollar was suspended in 1973. The two devaluations of the U.S. dollar in terms of gold that occurred under the adjustable peg system are barely visible. The effects of speculation on the price of gold is seen in subsequent experience. The price of gold more than quadrupled from 1977 to 1979, reaching a peak of over $900 per ounce. It subsequently fell to around $300 by 1982. Since that time it has fluctuated around the $400 level, sometimes rising above it and sometimes falling below it, but with no long-term trend visible during the 1980s.

The Management of Exchange Rates

The 1970s witnessed the replacement of a system of managed fixed exchange rates with a system of managed flexible exchange rates. The problems of the latter may have been revealed by the events of the decade, but they cannot be said to have been solved.

Policy Problems

Managing floating rates poses several potential problems for the international monetary system.

Inconsistent exchange rate policies. Different governments may try to fix their exchange rates at levels that are inconsistent with each other. For example, if the Bank of Canada's target is that the U.S. dollar should be worth $1.20 Canadian while the Fed's target is that the Canadian dollar should be worth 90 U.S. cents, both policies cannot succeed. If both banks persist in trying to meet such inconsistent targets, they can destabilize exchange markets.

Competitive devaluations. Countries may get involved in bouts of competitive devaluations that are similar to those that destabilized exchange markets during the 1920s and 1930s and were discussed in Box 42-1. For example, if one country devalues its currency in order to get a competitive advantage for its exports and other countries respond by devaluing their currencies, the rounds of successive devaluations will destabilize the exchange market without giving any country's exports a permanent advantage.

Destabilizing speculation. Speculative behavior can destabilize exchange markets. Before the system of floating exchange rates was adopted, many economists felt that rates would stay fairly close to their equilibrium values. Economists expected that speculators would then stabilize rates even further by buying currencies that seemed temporarily low in price and by selling those that seemed temporarily high in price. In that event, however, very large and persistent deviations of exchange rates from the long-run equilibrium values occurred. This left speculators less clear on which way a particular rate was likely to go in the near future. When a particular currency started to fall in value, speculators might conclude that a large and persistent fall was just beginning. In this case their rush to sell the currency before its expected further fall would bring the fall about.

Overshooting. The overshooting problem analyzed on page 911 can cause serious disruptions to flows of international trade. When a country's currency is pushed far above its PPP rate, its export- and import-competing industries are placed under severe competitive pressure. Firms that can compete at the PPP rate may be driven out of business, forcing major adjustments in labor and capital that then have to be reversed when the overshooting comes to an end.

Policy Responses

The Group of Seven. To help manage exchange rates and especially to prevent exchange rate overshooting, in 1982 a group of five major trading nations agreed to meet annually and to set policies of coordinated intervention into exchange markets. Later in the decade, the original group of Germany, France, the United Kingdom, the United States, and Japan was expanded to include Canada and Italy and became known as the Group of Seven, or G7. It is important to realize that the group does not have the power to fix exchange rates at whatever levels it desires. The G7 countries know that they cannot resist strong, fundamental market pressures. For example, if the yen is undervalued and market traders know this, sooner or later the yen's value will be driven up. What the G7 can do is iron out shorter-term fluctuations in exchange rates and resist overshooting that can take a major currency far away from its PPP value for long periods of time.

The IMF. The IMF has published guidelines designed to assist in orderly exchange rate management. It emphasizes that exchange rate policy is a matter for international consultation and surveillance by the IMF and that intervention practices by individual central banks should be based on three principles:

1. Exchange authorities should prevent sudden and disproportionate short-term movements in exchange rates and ensure an orderly adjustment to longer-term pressures.
2. In consultation with the IMF, countries should establish a target zone for the medium-term values of their exchange rates and keep the actual rate within that target zone.
3. Countries should recognize that exchange rate management involves joint responsibilities and is not just the responsibility of the individual country in question.

Recent experience has underlined one of the most important unsolved problems of managed floating rates: coping with the massive volume of short-term funds that can be switched rapidly among financial centers.

Capital flows often prevent the quick return of exchange rates to their PPP values. Various attempts have been made to limit such capital flows. Italy has adopted a two-tier foreign exchange market, with one price for foreign exchange to finance current account transactions and another price (and another set of controls) for foreign exchange to finance capital movements. Germany has used direct controls on overseas borrowing. There has also been a considerable extension of arrangements under which central banks in surplus countries lend the funds that they are accumulating back to central banks in deficit countries. Such arrangements enhance the ability of banks to maintain stable exchange rates in the face of short-term speculative flights of capital.

The major problem in managing speculative flows is to identify them accurately. Experience suggests that exchange rate management can smooth out temporary fluctuations but cannot resist underlying trends in equilibrium rates, caused by relative inflation rates, structural changes, and persistent nonspeculative capital flows. In day-to-day management, it is not always easy to distinguish among them.

Nevertheless, the excessive variability and persistent misalignment of exchange rates that continued

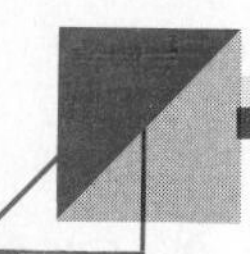

BOX 42-2

Proposals for International Monetary Reform

The high degree of variability and persistent misalignment of exchange rates that plagued the flexible exchange rate system for the first 20 years of its operation led during the mid 1980s to a number of proposals for reform.

Fixed Exchange Rates

Some observers advocated a return to fixed exchange rates. In fact, some even wanted the new system to be based on gold or some other group of commodities. This proposal was apparently motivated by the belief that *ruling out* exchange rate changes would allow some of the problems that we have noted in this text to be avoided.

This proposal has not received wide support among economists, since most believe that the flaws that led to the demise of the Bretton Woods system were indeed fatal and that a system of fixed exchange rates would have performed worse, not better, than flexible exchange rates did in the face of the shocks that have disturbed the world economy since Bretton Woods was abandoned. Proponents of fixed exchange rates counter that many of those shocks were in fact the result of bad policies that were made possible only by the freedom for independent domestic policy that exists under flexible exchange rates. They argue that the discipline imposed by fixed exchange rates would have improved the performance of policy over the period.

Target Exchange Rate Zones

Another proposal was for establishing *target zones* for exchange rates. Some advocates proposed "hard" zones, that is, narrowly defined zones with automatic intervention required whenever exchange rates moved outside the defined limits. This amounts to a fixed exchange rate system, and not surprisingly, debate on this type of proposal paralleled that on fixed exchange rates.

Alternatively, some advocates proposed "soft" zones, defined more loosely and departures from which simply served as a signal to authorities that some policy reaction might be appropriate. Although these "soft" zones were more acceptable to some observers, many expressed a good deal of skepticism about what such weak arrangements might accomplish.

"Sand in the Gears"

The enormous variability of exchange rates led to proposals to "throw sand in the gears of international financial markets" in order to limit the international mobility of capital. These proposals were motivated by the view that exchange rate variability is the result of large pools of liquid capital that move from currency to currency in anticipation of capital gains that are due to exchange rate changes. Such movements, of course, could themselves give rise to dramatic exchange rate changes—sometimes self-fulfilling and sometimes self-defeating but always disruptive to international trade and investment. The "sand in the gears" would involve levying taxes on "unproductive" capital movements in an attempt to discourage them and therefore to stabilize exchange rates. (These proposals were also sometimes called *dual exchange rates,* since the tax means that, effectively, a different exchange rate is used for taxed transactions than for untaxed ones.)

Many economists, however, oppose such schemes. They express worries about the problems of identifying "unproductive" capital movements and the potential distortions that would arise if the taxes were misapplied. They also argue that black markets would evolve that would allow many capital movements to avoid the taxes, thereby rendering them largely ineffective but still burdening the economy with the administrative costs of trying to enforce them. They also question whether the scheme would achieve its goal, even if it could be implemented, citing markets such as real estate, rare art, and fine wine in which transactions costs are high but prices are still volatile.

to plague the flexible exchange rate system led to a number of proposals for reform. These are discussed further in Box 42-2.

Conclusion

One of the most impressive aspects of the international payments history of the past 30 years has been the steady rise of effective international cooperation. When the gold standard collapsed and the Great Depression struck, "every nation for itself" was the rule of the day. Rising tariffs, competitive exchange rate devaluations, and all forms of beggar-my-neighbor policies abounded.

After World War II, countries cooperated in bringing the Bretton Woods system and the IMF into being. The system itself was far from perfect, and it finally broke down as a result of its own internal contradictions. Nevertheless, the international cooperation that was necessary to set up the system survived. The joint cooperative actions of central banks allowed them to weather temporary crises during the 1970s and 1980s that would have forced them to devalue their currencies during the 1950s.

Thus the collapse of the Bretton Woods system did not plunge the world into the same chaos that followed the breakdown of the gold standard. The world was also better able to cope with the terrible strains that were caused by the sharp rise in oil prices during the 1970s. Of course, enormous oil-related problems remain, and they are matters for continuing international dialogue. Further, it is not yet clear how well the world economy will weather the upsurge of American protectionism that began in the mid 1980s. Prior to this upsurge, the United States provided essential leadership as it worked for lower restrictions on international trade. It is a serious question, then, whether other nations will now follow the American lead to *increased* protectionism and thus join in a mutually destructive round of competitive tariff increases and other restrictions.

Whatever the problems of the future will be, the world has a better chance of solving them—or even of just learning to live with them—when countries cooperate through the IMF and other international organizations than when each country seeks its own solution without concern for the interests of other countries.

SUMMARY

1. A fully fixed exchange rate is determined by some force other than central bank intervention into exchange markets, such as the relative gold content of currencies as under the gold standard. A fully flexible exchange rate is set by free markets in which the central bank does not intervene. Under an adjustable peg, the rate is stabilized within a narrow band on either side of a publicly announced par value by central bank intervention into the foreign exchange market, but the pegged rate is subject to periodic change. Under a dirty or managed float, the rate is free to fluctuate on the free market, but the central bank intervenes from time to time in pursuit of exchange rate targets that it does not need to state publicly.
2. In practice, any "fixed-rate system" in today's world is an adjustable peg system because what the authorities set they can easily change.
3. Any adjustable peg system must encounter three major problems: (a) providing sufficient international reserves, (b) adjusting to long-term trends in receipts and payments, and (c) handling periodic speculative crises.
4. Under a system of flexible, or floating, exchange rates, the exchange rate is market-determined by supply and demand for the currency.
5. Since their adoption in the mid 1970s, flexible exchange rates have fluctuated substantially. As a result, central banks often have intervened to stabilize the fluctuations, thus moving to a system of managed or dirty floats.

6. Fluctuations in exchange rates can be understood as fluctuations around a trend value that is determined by the purchasing power parity (PPP) exchange rate. The PPP rate adjusts in response to differences in national inflation rates. Departures from the PPP rate can be large and sustained for long periods of time, thus subjecting a country's tradable goods sector to large and sustained shocks.
7. The main current problem of exchange rate management is better handling of the system of dirty floats. Problems include the setting of inconsistent exchange rates, competitive devaluations, destabilizing speculative behavior, and exchange rate overshooting. Two organizations, the Group of Seven major trading nations, which includes Canada, and the IMF, have tried to respond to these problems by encouraging international cooperation and coordination of macroeconomic policies.

TOPICS FOR REVIEW

Fixed and flexible exchange rates
Managed floats
Adjustable peg system
Bretton Woods system
International Monetary Fund (IMF)
Exchange rate overshooting
Reform of the international monetary system

DISCUSSION QUESTIONS

1. From mid 1985 through the end of 1986, the U.S. dollar fell sharply in terms of the Japanese yen and the major European currencies. However, the U.S. current account deficit did not fall. Can you think of any reasons why? What happened to the Canadian dollar over this period? What were the implications for Canada?
2. The Canadian dollar is no longer convertible into gold because of a change in government policy. Does this lack of convertibility make the dollar any less useful as a medium of international exchange?
3. Several Canadian economists have recently advocated that the Bank of Canada adopt a fixed exchange rate between the Canadian dollar and the U.S. dollar. What implications would this have for Canadian monetary policy and for the Canadian rates of interest and inflation? What would be the consequences of a large increase in the U.S. desire to invest in Canada under such a system? What exchange rate should be set in the first place? Might Canadian exporters prefer this system to the present one in which exchange rates vary quite widely according to variations in the demand and supply for foreign exchange?
4. "Under a flexible exchange rate system, no country need suffer unemployment, for if its prices are low enough, there will be more than enough demand to keep its factories and farms fully occupied." The evidence suggests that flexible exchange rates have not generally eliminated unemployment. Can you explain why? Can changing exchange rates ever cure unemployment?
5. The OPEC oil price increases during the 1970s caused grave problems in international payments and increased the need for IMF loans. Why did market adjustment of exchange rates not solve the problem?
6. In December a major Canadian political party advocated fighting a developing recession by driving down the Canadian interest rate from 14 to 10 percent and the external value of the Canadian dollar from US$0.86 to US$0.80. Predict some of the effects of these policies.

7. At the beginning of 1991, Canada, the United States, and Mexico were considering negotiating a joint free trade agreement. If such an agreement is achieved, what would be some of the advantages and disadvantages of adopting one or the other of the following payments systems: freely fluctuating exchange rates, managed floats, adjustable pegs, a common currency (which could be called the North American dollar)?
8. Might a person who regards inflation as the number one economic danger favor a return to the pre-1914 gold standard? Would you predict noninflationary results if, in order to restore the gold standard, the price of gold had to be set at U.S.$1,600 per ounce, either all at once or gradually?

Chapter 43

Macroeconomic Policy in an Open Economy

When we shift our attention to an *open economy*, new complications arise for the study of macroeconomic policy. New complications arise. These include the behavior of the terms of trade and their influence on net exports and national income, the nature and extent of foreign borrowing, and changes in foreign interest or inflation rates. The response of the economy to various policies is altered. For example, we shall see in this chapter that since Canadian interest rates are closely tied to those prevailing in foreign markets, the mechanism by which macroeconomic policies influence the economy can differ sharply from the closed economy mechanisms studied earlier in this book.

Consideration of the openness of the economy also introduces some new policy objectives that may be in conflict with policy objectives arising solely from domestic considerations. We introduce the study of macroeconomic policy in an open economy by considering these possibly conflicting objectives, taking a simple example in which there is one internal (domestic) and one external (international) policy objective. These objectives are stated simply in terms of a *target value* for the variable in question.

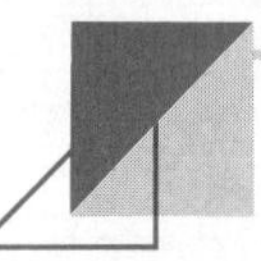

Internal and External Balance

In this chapter we take the typical domestic policy objective to be to achieve a target level of real national income—the target being potential income. Restricting attention to one domestic policy target is for simplicity only. It is in any case more general than might first appear. For example, if one objective is to reduce the domestic rate of inflation, we know from our analysis in Chapter 36 that this can be accomplished by achieving a target level of real national income below potential income. When real national income is at its target level, we say that the economy has achieved **internal balance**.

For the moment, we focus on the trade account as a typical external policy objective. When the trade account is equal to its target level, we say that the economy has achieved **external balance**. We take the target value of the trade balance to be zero, but it could just as well be some other specific amount.[1]

[1] For example, a nation with a large undeveloped natural resource base may have a low current national income yet anticipate a high future national income when the resource base is developed. High current investment to develop the resource base and high current consumption in anticipation of that high future income will together lead to high imports and a trade account deficit. Hence the target for the trade account in such a circumstance may well be a deficit.

To begin, we treat the exchange rate as fixed. Later in the chapter we study the complications that arise when the capital account and a flexible exchange rate are considered.

The conditions for internal and external balance are illustrated in Figure 43-1.

Conflicting Objectives

When policies that are used to move the economy closer to one objective simultaneously move the economy further from another objective, the two objectives are said to be *in conflict*.

Policies that raise national income will influence the trade account. They will do this by causing a movement along the negatively sloped net export function (which we studied in Chapter 28 and which is graphed again in Figure 43-2). Whether there is a conflict between the objectives of internal and external balance depends on how the current values of the trade account and real national income compare to their target values.

Since the target level of real national income is potential income, Y^*, and the target for the trade account is a zero balance, we can identify the initial situation relative to the targets in terms of the signs of the output gap and the trade account balance.[2] There are four possible cases:

1. A trade account *deficit* combined with an *inflationary gap* poses no conflict because the contraction of aggregate demand needed to eliminate the inflationary gap leads to a reduction in imports and hence reduces the trade deficit.
2. A trade account *deficit* combined with a *recessionary gap* does pose a conflict because the expansion of aggregate demand needed to eliminate the recessionary gap leads to an increase in imports and hence a worsening of the trade deficit.
3. A trade account *surplus* combined with a *recessionary gap* poses no conflict because the expansion of aggregate demand to eliminate the recessionary gap increases imports and hence reduces the trade surplus.
4. A trade account *surplus* combined with an *inflationary gap* does pose a conflict because the contraction of aggregate demand to eliminate the inflationary gap leads to a reduction in imports and hence an increase in the trade surplus.

The four cases are depicted in Figure 43-2.

In case 2 in our list, the trade account deficit calls for a decrease in national income, but the recessionary gap calls for an increase. In case 4 the trade account surplus calls for an increase in national income, but the inflationary gap calls for a decrease.

A conflict arises between the objectives of internal and external balance when the two require the level of national income to change in opposite directions.

Basically, the conflicts arise from *movements along* the net export function, and we shall see that their resolution requires *shifts in* the net export function.

Case 2 has attracted the most attention, perhaps because a trade deficit is generally viewed as a more serious problem than a trade surplus, and in the past unemployment was considered a more serious problem than inflation. Case 2 is often referred to as a

FIGURE 43-1 Internal and External Balance

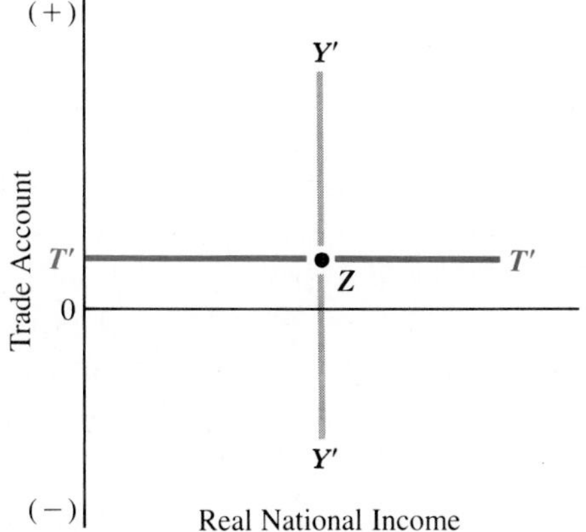

Internal and external balance are simultaneously attained at point Z. Internal balance is defined in terms of a target level of real national income and is depicted by the vertical line $Y'Y'$. External balance is here defined in terms of a target level of the trade account and is depicted by the horizontal line $T'T'$. Only at the intersection, point Z, are both internal and external balance attained.

[2] We emphasize that this assumption is made only to simplify the discussion and that the actual targets may often differ from these. The same principles apply regardless of the actual values of the targets.

FIGURE 43-2 Conflicts Between Internal and External Balance

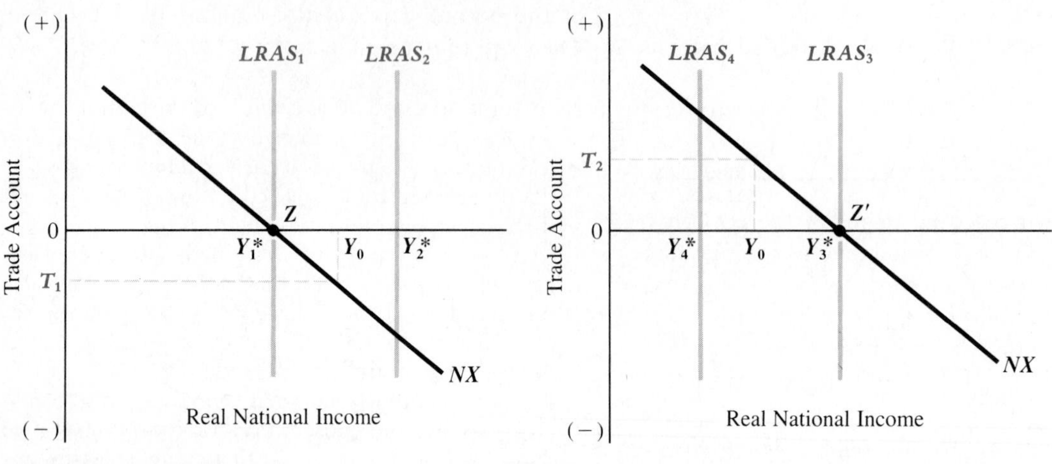

(i) A trade account deficit

(ii) A trade account surplus

Of the four different possible combinations of signs of the output gap and the trade account, only two pose conflicts. In both parts of the figure, the net export function, which relates the trade account to real national income, is shown by the black line labeled *NX*. The actual level of income is given by Y_0, so in (i) there is a trade account deficit of T_1, while in (ii) there is a trade account surplus of T_2.

In (i), if potential output is given by Y_1^* so there is an inflationary gap (case 1), there is no conflict, since adjustment of actual real national income to achieve one target will also achieve the other target, at point *Z*. However, if potential output is given by Y_2^* so there is a recessionary gap (case 2), there is a conflict, since movement of actual real national income to achieve either target will cause a movement away from the other target.

In (ii), if potential income is given by Y_3^* so there is a recessionary gap (case 3), there is no conflict, since adjustment of actual real national income to achieve one target will also achieve the other target, at point *Z*′. However, if potential output is given by Y_4^* so there is an inflationary gap (case 4), there is a conflict, since a change in actual real national income to achieve either target will cause a movement away from the other target.

situation in which there is a "balance-of-payments constraint" on domestic stabilization policy.

Expenditure-changing and Expenditure-switching Policies

As a first step in studying how the conflicts between internal and external balance can be resolved, we repeat the basic equilibrium condition that national income equal aggregate desired expenditure.

$$Y = C + I + G + (X - M) \qquad [1]$$

The total $C + I + G$ is often referred to as *domestic absorption*, or simply *absorption*. This concept, which was discussed in Box 31-1 on page 658, refers to total expenditure on goods for use in the domestic economy. Denoting absorption by the letter *A*, we can rewrite the national income equilibrium condition as

$$Y = A + (X - M) \qquad [2]$$

This condition states that equilibrium national income is equal to aggregate desired expenditure, which is in turn equal to domestic absorption plus net exports.

Equation 2 is useful in distinguishing between two types of policies that can be used to maintain internal and external balance. Policies that do not change the *level* of aggregate desired expenditure but change its *composition* between domestic absorption and net exports are called **expenditure-switching policies**. Policies that change aggregate desired expenditure are called **expenditure-changing policies**.

Expenditure-changing policies involve *moving along* a given net export function, so changes in the trade balance and national income must be *negatively related*; a rise in national income worsens the trade balance, whereas a fall in national income improves the balance. If the initial situation calls for income and the trade balance to move in the same direction, the use of expenditure-changing policies necessarily involves a conflict.

Expenditure-switching policies involve *shifting* the net export function. We shall see that this can lead to *positively related* changes in the trade balance and national income. Examples of expenditure-switching policies are changes in the exchange rate, restrictions on international trade such as tariffs or quotas, and domestic inflation or deflation relative to foreign conditions.[3] If the initial situation calls for national income and the trade balance to move in opposite directions, the use of expenditure-switching policies necessarily involves a conflict.

The conflicts between the two objectives of internal and external balance arise from the use of only one policy, *either* expenditure changing *or* expenditure switching.

With both expenditure-changing and expenditure-switching policies available, we can now see how to deal with each of the four cases that we described earlier. We first consider the two cases where the trade account is in deficit and then go on to the two cases where it is in surplus.

A Trade Account Deficit

Equation 2 shows that when there is a trade account deficit (so that $X - M$ is negative), national income is less than domestic absorption. Now consider policies to eliminate the trade account deficit.

Case 1—A deficit combined with an inflationary gap: No conflict. If the economy already has an inflationary gap, increasing national income will take it further away from its target level. The trade account deficit indicates that domestic absorption is above the current level of national income and hence, by virtue of the inflationary gap, above the level of potential income. To eliminate the deficit, absorption must be lowered. In other words, if net exports are to rise, resources must be released through a reduction in domestic usage. This calls for *expenditure-reducing* policies such as reductions in the money supply, cuts in government expenditure, and increases in taxes. No conflict for expenditure-changing policies arises in this case because the expenditure reduction cuts the inflationary gap and improves the trade account by inducing a movement along the net export function.

Case 2—A deficit combined with a recessionary gap: Conflict. When national income is below its capacity level, income can be increased to get closer to the potential income target. However, an expansion in national income with a fixed net export function would worsen the trade account, so expenditure-increasing policies are not appropriate. A reduction in national income to reduce the deficit would take national income further away from its target value, so expenditure-reducing policies are not appropriate. What is needed is a *switch* in expenditure away from foreign goods (thus reducing the trade deficit) and toward domestic goods (thus reducing the recessionary gap).

Policies to induce a *switch* of some expenditure from foreign goods to domestic goods—thereby *shifting* the net export function rightward and raising national income—will alleviate the conflict posed by a recessionary gap combined with a trade deficit.

Such policies include devaluation of the currency and measures to restrict imports. This is illustrated in Figure 43-3.[4]

[3] When restrictions on international trade, such as tariffs or quotas, are used in this manner, they are referred to as *commercial policy*. Commercial policy may in some circumstances be useful for macroeconomic purposes, but it is never indispensable; other expenditure-switching policies will have the same macroeconomic effects.

[4] From the discussion in Chapter 41, it would appear that there should be two shifts in the *NX* function. The first is due to the switch in expenditure; the second, which will be in the opposite direction to the first, is due to the induced change in the price of domestic goods as national income changes. The analysis in Figure 43-3, and in this chapter, incorporates this second effect in the response of *NX* national income by using the *SRAS* curve to capture the price effect. **[46]**

FIGURE 43-3 A Trade Deficit and a Recessionary Gap

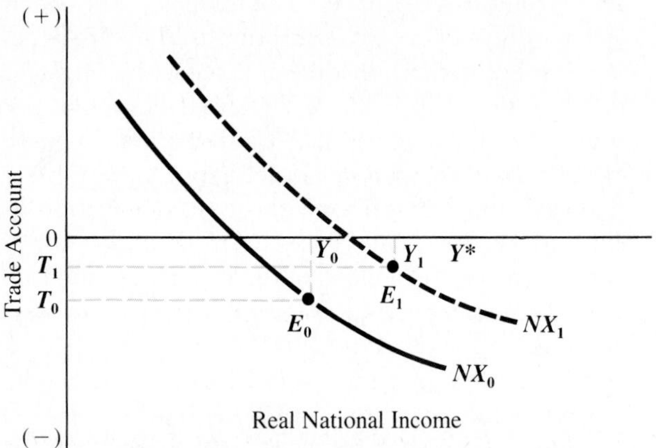

(i) Net export function

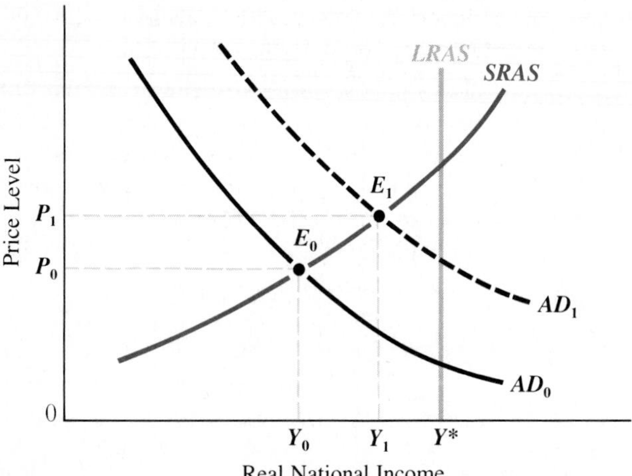

(ii) Determination of national income

A policy to switch expenditure away from foreign goods and toward domestic goods can be used to resolve the conflict posed by a trade deficit combined with a recessionary gap. Initially, the net export function is given by NX_0 in (i), and aggregate demand is given by AD_0 in (ii). Equilibrium is at E_0 with real national income equal to Y_0. There is a recessionary gap of Y_0Y^* and a trade deficit of T_0.

An expenditure-switching policy raises net exports at each level of income, so the net export function shifts right to NX_1 in (i). The policy also raises aggregate demand, so the *AD* curve shifts right to AD_1 in (ii). The new equilibrium is at E_1, with real national income of Y_1 and a trade deficit of T_1. Hence both the recessionary gap and the trade deficit are reduced.

A Trade Account Surplus

Cases 3 and 4 in our list both involve a trade account surplus. An expansion of national income will therefore cause a move toward external balance by raising imports. Hence in case 3, where there is a recessionary gap, no conflict arises, and expenditure-raising policies will lead to movement toward both targets. In case 4, where there is an inflationary gap, a conflict does arise; external balance calls for expenditure increases, but internal balance calls for expenditure reduction. What is needed is a *switch in expenditure* away from domestic goods (thus reducing the inflationary gap) and toward foreign goods (thus reducing the trade account surplus).

Policies to induce a switch of expenditure from domestic goods to foreign goods—thereby *shifting* the net export function leftward and lowering national income—will alleviate the con-

flict posed by an inflationary gap combined with a trade surplus.

This is illustrated in Figure 43-4.

A General Statement

We have now seen the difference in the effects of the two types of expenditure policies in an open economy.

To achieve internal and external balance, a combination of expenditure-changing and expenditure-switching policies is generally required.

In conflict situations, expenditure-switching policies will result in a movement *toward* both targets. Expenditure switching alone cannot, however, achieve both internal and external balance *exactly*. Hence both types of policies are generally required. Expenditure-switching policies are necessary to shift

FIGURE 43-4 A Trade Surplus and an Inflationary Gap

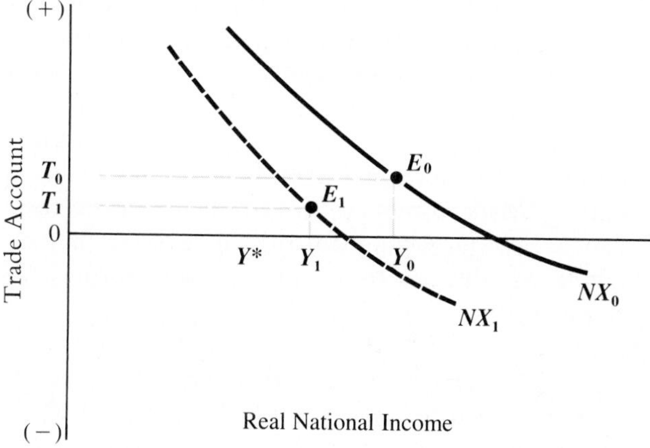

(i) Net export function

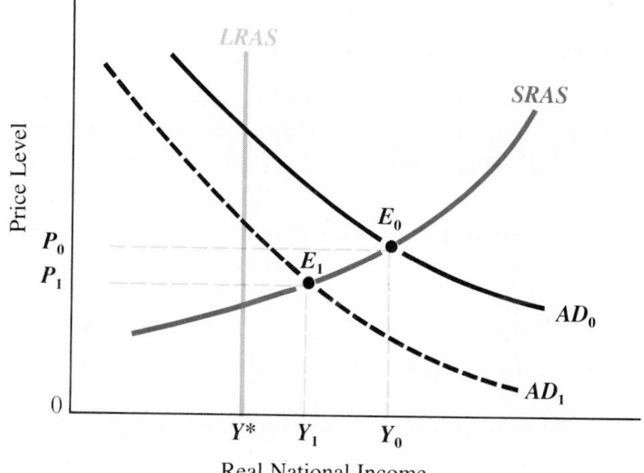

(ii) Determination of national income

A policy to switch expenditure away from domestic goods and toward foreign goods can be used to solve the conflict posed by a trade surplus combined with an inflationary gap. Initially, the net export function is given by NX_0 in (i), and aggregate demand is given by AD_0 in (ii). Equilibrium is at E_0 with real national income equal to Y_0. This is an inflationary gap of Y^*Y_0 and a trade surplus of T_0.

An expenditure-switching policy lowers net exports at each level of income, so the net export function shifts left to NX_1 in (ii). The policy also lowers aggregate demand, so the aggregate demand curve shifts left to AD_1 in (ii). The equilibrium moves from E_0 to E_1, real national income falls to Y_1, and the trade surplus falls to T_1. Hence both the inflationary gap and the trade surplus are reduced.

the net export function in order to make the two objectives consistent. In terms of Figures 43-3(i) and 43-4(i), this means that expenditure-switching policies can be used to ensure that the net export curve cuts the horizontal axis at Y^*. There is no assurance, however, that the effects of such policies on the aggregate demand curve will cause national income to equal Y^*. Expenditure-changing policies can then be used to attain both internal and external balance simultaneously by changing national income and moving along the now-shifted net export functions.

Some long-run aspects of such policies are taken up in Box 43-1.

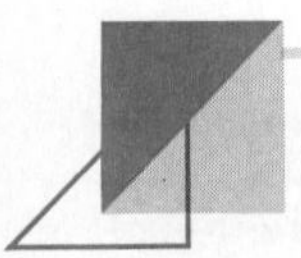

Macroeconomic Policy and the Capital Account

The capital account of the balance of payments records international movements of investment funds. When foreign investors buy securities issued by Canadian corporations or governments or invest in Canadian industry, this capital inflow is recorded as a receipt in the balance of payments because it involves foreign currency being offered for Canadian dollars in the foreign exchange market. Conversely, the acquisition of foreign assets by Canadians represents a capital outflow and is recorded as a payment because foreign currency is used up by such transactions.

The primary means by which capital flows can be influenced by the government is through domestic interest rates. If short-term interest rates are raised in Canada, this will induce an inflow of short-run capital to take advantage of the higher Canadian rates. A lowering of Canadian interest rates will have the opposite effect as capital moves elsewhere to take advantage of the now relatively higher foreign rates.

Long-term capital flows are typically less sensitive to interest-rate differentials, but they are nevertheless likely to show some response. In particular, Canadian corporations and governments attempt to minimize the cost of long-term borrowing by selling bonds in foreign markets when foreign interest rates are lower than Canadian rates.

In discussing the trade account in the first part of this chapter, we did not distinguish between the effects of monetary and fiscal policy. However, capital flows respond to interest rates, and monetary and fiscal policies that have the same influence on national income have opposite effects on interest rates. As we saw in Chapter 34, expansionary monetary policy operating in a closed economy exerts its influence on income by *reducing* interest rates. Fiscal policy influences aggregate demand directly, and fiscal-policy-induced increases in national income create an excess demand for money, which in a closed economy causes interest rates to *rise*. In discussing capital flows in an open economy, it is therefore necessary to distinguish between monetary and fiscal policies.

Fiscal Policy and the Capital Account

The effects of fiscal policy on the capital acount of an open economy are related to the interest-rate changes that it would bring about in a closed economy. Expansionary fiscal policy, for example, is usually accompanied by increased federal government borrowing in domestic capital markets. In a closed economy this forces interest rates up; in an open economy it forces other domestic borrowers to import their capital requirements from foreign financial centers. Many provincial governments finance their deficits by borrowing abroad themselves, thereby giving rise directly to a capital account surplus. In summary:

An expansionary fiscal policy will put upward pressure on interest rates and lead to an inflow of foreign capital, thereby moving the capital account toward a surplus. A contractionary fiscal policy will have the opposite effects.

Monetary Policy and the Capital Account

Since monetary policy influences interest rates in a closed economy, it will influence the capital account in an open economy.

An expansionary monetary policy will put downward pressure on interest rates and lead to an outflow of capital, thereby moving the capital account toward a deficit. A contractionary monetary policy will have the opposite effects.

An Alternative Target for External Balance

So far in this chapter we have used *external balance* to mean achieving some target for the balance of trade. Consideration of international capital flows

BOX 43-1

Expenditure-switching Policies in the Long Run

Use of expenditure-switching policies, such as allowing the country's currency to depreciate on the foreign exchange market, has often been very controversial. Supporters point to the increase in output and the reduction in the trade account deficit shown in Figure 43-3. Opponents focus on the inflationary impact indicated by the rise in the price level also shown in Figure 43-3. The controversy often hinges on disagreement about the relative size of these two effects. Some of the controversy can be defused by distinguishing between the long-run and short-run effects of such policies.

In the text we focused on the short-run effects of expenditure-switching policies, treating the *SRAS* curve as fixed and studying the shifts in the *NX* and *AD* curves. One alternative to using such policies is to do nothing, letting the monetary adjustment mechanism studied in Chapter 34 operate to eliminate the recessionary gap. (There are also automatic mechanisms that will establish external balance in the long run.) Justification for letting the currency depreciate, for example, in the face of a recessionary gap and a trade deficit is that these automatic adjustment mechanisms are very slow to operate. Hence support for depreciation and other expenditure-switching policies stems from their ability to influence output and the trade account *in the short run*.

Note, however, that such policies do not alter potential output—they do not shift the *LRAS* curve, and hence they have no effect on output in the long run. But by circumventing the monetary adjustment mechanism and stimulating aggregate demand, expenditure-switching policies ensure that when potential income is attained in the long run, the price level will be higher than it would have been in their absence. Opponents of such policies focus on this price-level effect, since that is the only long-run effect the policies have. Typically, these opponents believe the automatic adjustment mechanisms are strong enough so that the long-run effect can be achieved fairly quickly without intervention or that depreciation of the currency on the foreign exchange market sets up expectations of price rises that quickly feed into wages and hence create very little real response of output and employment even in the short run.

The key policy implication of this debate is that depreciation and other expenditure-switching policies should be directed toward the external target, but they should be combined with expenditure-changing policies that focus on the internal target. In particular, depreciation should be accompanied by expenditure-reducing policies to offset any inflationary gap caused by the depreciation in the short run and hence to avoid the price-level increase that would otherwise ensue in the long run.

suggests an expansion of this target to incorporate the capital account and interest payments on the foreign debt as well.

We now specify external balance in terms of a target level of the overall balance of payments. For simplicity, we take external balance to mean a zero overall balance of payments so that any current account imbalance is exactly offset by the opposite capital account imbalance.

Before turning to a discussion of how monetary and fiscal policy might be combined to achieve internal and external balance in this circumstance, it is useful to examine the relationship between the money supply and the overall balance of payments.

The Balance of Payments and the Money Supply

Suppose that Canada is experiencing a balance-of-payments deficit and that the Bank of Canada intervenes in the foreign exchange market to maintain the value of the Canadian dollar. The Bank will be selling foreign currency in exchange for Canadian dollars and thereby running down its stock of official reserves. Payment for the foreign currency acquired by private participants in the market will normally be made in the form of Canadian dollar cheques drawn on one of the chartered banks. These cheques will be cleared by reducing the deposits of the chartered bank at the Bank of Canada. These transactions are summarized in Table 43-1.

If there are no offsetting transactions, a balance-of-payments deficit will lead to a decrease in both commercial bank reserves and commercial bank deposits equal to the amount of foreign exchange sold by the central bank. A surplus will lead to an increase in commercial bank reserves and deposits.

Thus a balance-of-payments deficit will lead to a contraction of the money supply. The central bank has the option of preventing this from happening by undertaking other offsetting transactions. For example, the decrease in bank reserves can be offset by an open-market purchase of bonds, which will have the effect of increasing bank reserves. This procedure of engaging in offsetting open-market operations to insulate the domestic money supply from the effects of balance-of-payments deficits or surpluses in known as **sterilization**.

TABLE 43-1 Balance Sheet Changes Caused by a Sale of Foreign Currency by the Central Bank

Assets		Liabilities	
Nonbank private sector			
Foreign currency (equivalent value in Canadian dollars)	+100		
Deposits	−100		
Chartered banks			
Reserves (deposits with central bank)	−100	Demand deposits	−100
Central bank			
Foreign currency	−100	Deposits of chartered banks	−100

The money supply is reduced when the central bank sells foreign currency to maintain a fixed exchange rate when there is a balance-of-payments deficit. A deficit of $100 leads to an excess demand for foreign currency of $100, which is met by a reduction of official reserves by this amount. When the central bank receives payment in the form of a cheque drawn on a chartered bank, bank reserves fall by $100. There will then be a multiple contraction of deposit money through the process analyzed in Chapter 33.

Fixed Exchange Rates

Monetary Policy

To see the limitations of monetary policy under a fixed exchange rate, consider the following sequence of events. Suppose that interest rates in Canada are at levels similar to those in the rest of the world. Now the Bank of Canada, faced with a large recessionary gap, seeks to stimulate demand through an expansionary monetary policy. The Bank buys bonds in the open market, thereby increasing the money supply and reducing interest rates.

Lower interest rates stimulate an outflow of capital from Canada and thus a deficit on the capital account. To the extent that national income rises, movement along the net export function causes a deterioration in the trade account. Thus the overall balance of payments moves into deficit. To maintain the fixed exchange rate, the Bank will have to intervene in the foreign exchange market and sell foreign currency. This will have the effect of *reducing* the money supply and thus offsetting the increase brought about by the initial open-market operation.

If no other transactions are initiated by the Bank of Canada, national income and the money supply will fall and domestic interest rates will rise until all return to their initial levels. Thus the deficit will be self-correcting, and the Bank's expansionary policy will be nullified.

Suppose now that the Bank of Canada attempts to sterilize the impact on the money supply of the balance-of-payments deficit. The difficulty with this strategy is that it can be continued only as long as the Bank has sufficient reserves of foreign exchange. If capital flows are highly sensitive to interest rates, as a great deal of evidence suggests is the case, these reserves will be run down at a rapid rate, and the Bank will be forced to abandon its expansionary policy.

Under a fixed exchange rate, there is little scope for the use of monetary policy for domestic stabilization purposes because of the sensitivity of international capital flows to interest rates. The central bank will be forced to maintain domestic interest rates close to the levels existing in the rest of the world, and it will not be able to bring about substantial changes in the domestic money supply.

Fiscal Policy

Consider now the effectiveness of fiscal policy under fixed exchange rates. Suppose again that Canadian interest rates are in line with those of the rest of the world and that an expansionary fiscal policy is introduced, aimed at reducing a large recessionary gap. The fiscal expansion raises the level of domestic interest rates and national income.

Higher interest rates stimulate a flow of capital into Canada, thereby leading to a surplus on the capital account. If the capital flows are large, as they are likely to be in Canada because of the close integration of Canadian and American capital markets, the surplus on capital account will exceed the current account deficit arising from increased national income. Hence there will be an overall balance-of-payments surplus.

To maintain the fixed exchange rate, the Bank of Canada will have to intervene in the foreign exchange market and buy foreign currency. This will have the effect of increasing the money supply, thus reinforcing the initial fiscal stimulus.

Under a fixed exchange rate, interest-sensitive international capital flows stabilize the domestic interest rate and enhance the effectiveness of fiscal policy.

Combining Monetary Policy and Fiscal Policy

Consider an attempt to increase national income with an expansionary monetary policy that reduces interest rates and thereby stimulates investment and other interest-sensitive expenditures. The decline in domestic interest rates makes it more attractive to invest short-term capital abroad than at home. The outflow of short-term capital to be invested at more attractive rates in foreign financial centers worsens the balance of payments on the short-term capital account. Of course, if the expansionary policy succeeds in raising income, there will be additional strain on the balance of payments on current account as a consequence of the increased expenditure on imports caused by the rise in income.

Flexible Exchange Rates

A major advantage of a flexible exchange rate is that it lessens any conflict between domestic stabilization objectives and the balance of payments because deficits or surpluses tend to be reduced through movements in the exchange rate. In addition, a flexible rate may cushion the domestic economy against cyclical variations in economic activity in other countries. For example, if the U.S. economy goes into a recession, the decline in U.S. income will lead to a reduction in demand for Canadian exports. The fall in exports will reduce national income in Canada. If the value of the Canadian dollar is allowed to respond to market forces, it will also depreciate. This fall in the external value of our currency will stimulate demand for our exports and encourage the substitution of domestically produced goods for imports. Thus the depreciation will provide a stimulus to demand in Canada that will at least partly offset the depressing effect of the U.S. recession.

Fiscal Policy

Suppose that the government seeks to remove a recessionary gap by expansionary fiscal policy. An increase in government expenditures or a reduction in taxes (or both) will increase national income and reduce the size of the gap. This will also tend to cause a movement *along* the net export function, leading to a deterioration of the trade account. However, this is not the whole story, for there will also be repercussions on the capital account and the exchange rate.

Capital flows and the crowding-out effect. In a closed economy, fiscal policy causes domestic interest rates to rise. This causes interest-sensitive private expenditures to fall, thus partly offsetting the initial expansionary effect of the fiscal stimulus. As we saw in Chapter 39, this *crowding-out effect* plays an important role in the analysis of fiscal policy in a closed economy. In an open economy, the crowding-out effect will operate differently, due to international capital flows.

Higher domestic interest rates will induce a capital inflow and cause the domestic currency to appreciate. If capital flows are highly interest-elastic, the external value of the currency is likely to rise substantially. This will depress demand by discouraging exports and encouraging the substitution of imports for domestically produced goods. The initial fiscal stimulus will be offset by the expenditure-switching effects of currency appreciation.

Under flexible exchange rates, strong crowding out of net exports greatly reduces the effectiveness of fiscal policy.

It is possible, however, to eliminate the crowding-out effect by supporting the fiscal policy with an accommodating monetary policy. Suppose that the central bank responds to the increase in the demand for money induced by the fiscal expansion by increasing the supply of money so as to maintain domestic interest rates at their initial level. There will then be no capital inflow and no tendency for the currency to appreciate. Equilibrium national income will increase.

The effectiveness of fiscal policy under flexible exchange rates can be enhanced by an accommodating monetary policy.

Monetary Policy

We have seen that there is little scope under fixed exchange rates for the use of monetary policy for domestic stabilization purposes. Under flexible exchange rates the situation is reversed, and monetary policy becomes a very powerful tool.

Suppose that the Bank of Canada seeks to stimulate demand through an expansionary monetary policy. The Bank buys bonds in the open market, thereby increasing both bank reserves and the money supply and thereby reducing interest rates. Lower interest rates will cause an outflow of capital from Canada and thus a deficit on the capital account.

Under a fixed rate we saw that the Bank may be forced to reverse its policy in order to stem the loss of foreign reserves. Under a flexible rate, however, the Canadian dollar can be allowed to depreciate. This will stimulate exports and discourage imports so that the deficit on the capital account will be offset by a surplus on the current account.

Domestic employment will be stimulated not only by the fall in interest rates but also by the increased demand for domestically produced goods brought about by a depreciation of the currency. The monetary stimulus will be *reinforced* by the expenditure-switching effects of currency depreciation.

Under flexible exchange rates, monetary policy is a powerful tool for stabilizing domestic income and employment. If capital flows are highly interest-elastic, the main channel by which an increase in the money supply stimulates demand for domestically produced goods is a depreciation of the currency.

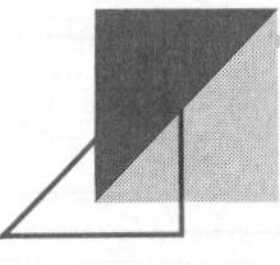

Canadian Stabilization Policy and External Balance

The foregoing analysis suggests that the existence of either a fixed or a flexible exchange rate can influence the operation of stabilization policy. It is instructive to examine recent Canadian experience from this perspective.

1950–1961: Introduction of Flexible Exchange Rates

Canada operated a flexible exchange rate regime from 1950 to 1961 while most of the rest of the world was on fixed rates. Large capital inflows occurred between 1955 and 1961 in response to attractive Canadian investment opportunities. The price of the U.S. dollar remained below $1 Canadian and at times fell to around 95 cents Canadian.

A serious recession that began in 1957, combined with a balance-of-payments surplus, presented policy-makers with the "no conflict" case 3 of Figure 43-2. The period 1959–1961 was characterized, however, by a very restrictive monetary policy.

An expansionary policy would have caused the Canadian dollar to depreciate and stimulated the economy. Unfortunately, the advantages of a flexible exchange rate were not used to deal with the serious unemployment problem, and the hoped-for expansion of the money supply and depreciation of the Canadian dollar did not occur until 1961.

1962–1970: Fixed Exchange Rate

The exchange rate was pegged at $1.08 Canadian to the U.S. dollar throughout the period 1962–1970—that is, the Canadian dollar was worth 92.5 cents U.S. This period witnessed the buildup of boom conditions in the United States. As is to be expected under a fixed exchange rate, the resulting rise in inflation in the United States spilled over into Canada. In the late 1960s the Canadian government decided that control of inflation was its primary policy objective. Contractionary monetary policy was introduced, and the restriction in aggregate demand had the desired domestic result: By 1970 inflation had fallen, but unemployment had risen.

The attempt to inflate at a slower rate than the United States was incompatible with fixed exchange rates; in the face of a high balance-of-payments surplus, either the economy had to be allowed to expand faster or the exchange rate had to be freed. The latter course was chosen.

1970–1975: Return to the Float

Once it was freed, the Canadian dollar rose rapidly in value almost to par with the U.S. dollar. The stage was now set for Canada to continue to pursue a lower rate of inflation than that in the United States. If Canada were to achieve this goal, the value of the Canadian dollar would have to *rise* at a rate approximately equal to the excess of the U.S. inflation rate over the Canadian inflation rate.[5]

However, the Bank of Canada, after adopting a flexible exchange rate in order to be able to pursue its anti-inflation policy, simultaneously adopted a more expansionary posture. In particular, it adopted a managed, or dirty, float.

There are two ways to manage a dirty float so that the exchange rate keeps to a target rate. One is to intervene directly in the foreign exchange market to stabilize the exchange rate. A balance-of-payments surplus such as Canada was experiencing at the time would mean that the Bank of Canada would have to buy foreign exchange to keep the Canadian dollar from appreciating. Of course, the purchase of foreign exchange by the Bank of Canada would have meant that the Canadian money supply would be rising.

The second method of managing a dirty float is to set domestic monetary conditions (rates of interest and rates of monetary expansion) so that the foreign exchange market clears at the desired rate without substantial government intervention in the foreign exchange market. Essentially, this means adopting the monetary policy that would be consistent with fixed rates (and hence might better be termed a "dirty fix").

The Bank of Canada chose the second method, and this led to a more rapid expansion of the money supply than would have been consistent with the goal of reducing inflation. Indeed, it led, predictably, to a rate of inflation roughly equal to that in the United States and higher than the target rate that had led to the monetary contraction of the late 1960s and the adoption of a flexible exchange rate in 1970. Indirectly, by maintaining policies consistent with a stable exchange rate, inflation was imported from the United States.

Canada appears to have missed an opportunity to avoid at least some of the inflation that plagued the world economy in the 1970s. The full benefits of a flexible rate were not realized because the Bank of Canada resisted the appreciation of the Canadian dollar and permitted high rates of growth in the money supply. The experience of this period illustrates dramatically the futility of trying to protect Canada's export industries by holding the value of the Canadian dollar below its equilibrium level. This could be done only by increasing the rate of growth of the money supply, which had the effect of raising the domestic rate of inflation.

1975–1980: Monetary Targeting

In 1975 the Bank of Canada's new policy of gradualism (discussed in Chapter 35) attempted to exploit the monetary independence created by flexible exchange rates. The Bank started announcing target rates of growth for the money supply. Though on the surface this policy appeared to meet some of the earlier objections to the use of monetary policy under flexible exchange rates, most economists believed nevertheless that the policy was still one of a dirty float.

In 1978 and 1979 a large number of wage con-

[5] The discussion of the PPP exchange rate in Chapter 42 could usefully be reviewed at this stage.

tracts were coming up for renewal, following the unwinding of wage and price controls. At the same time, the Canadian dollar was under substantial downward pressure. The Bank of Canada, worried that an inflationary surge coming from a depreciation would trigger an unacceptable increase in wages, intervened to support the dollar. (Recall that a depreciation of the currency raises the domestic prices of all internationally traded goods.) However, many economists were skeptical of the importance of the direct influence of the exchange rate on wages; they believed that the harmful disruptions to financial markets caused by the uncertainty arising from the Bank's departure from its pre-announced monetary stance were likely to be larger than any possible gains on the wage front. Shortly after, the Bank abandoned its policy of announcing explicit growth rate targets for the money supply.

1980–1983: Imported Monetary Restraint

In the early 1980s a problem for Canadian monetary and exchange rate management arose from the high average level and volatile behavior of interest rates in the United States. A rise in foreign interest rates leads, other things being equal, to large outflows of short-term capital and a depreciation of the domestic currency. Hence a rise in foreign interest rates such as occurred in the United States in 1980 and again in 1981 must be matched by a rise in Canadian rates, a depreciation of the Canadian dollar, or some combination of the two.

In 1980, Canadian interest rates rose, but by less than those in the United States. The resulting interest differential attracted capital to the United States, and as a result the Canadian dollar fell somewhat. When the next round of U.S. interest rate increases occurred in 1981, Canadian interest rates rose along with U.S. rates, and the dollar remained relatively stable. Again the Bank of Canada was criticized for pursuing a dirty float.

Although nominal interest rates in the United States fell in 1983, real interest rates remained high. The Bank of Canada walked a middle ground between high Canadian real interest rates and depreciation of the Canadian dollar. Though the value of the Canadian dollar fell slowly but steadily from 1982 on, it is widely agreed that the Bank of Canada acted to "protect the exchange rate" and that monetary policy in Canada was tighter than it would have been in the absence of the very tight U.S. monetary policy. This had benefits in the form of a substantial fall in inflation in the 1982–1984 period. It also had costs in terms of the severity of the 1982 recession and the persistent high unemployment of the 1983–1984 recovery.

1984–1987: Recovery and Stable Inflation

During the period 1984–1987 the Bank of Canada was able to reap the benefits of the monetary tightness that it had pursued in the first years of the decade. The economy experienced a sustained recovery, inflation remained stable in the 4 percent range, and interest rates fell dramatically. As a result, the central focus of monetary policy was the reentry problem discussed in Chapter 35—it had to accommodate the growth in the demand for money while not rekindling inflation. The exchange rate did not play a central role in the overall design or execution of monetary policy in this period, although exchange rate fluctuations were large.

The period was dominated by the dramatic fall in the value of the U.S. dollar in terms of the Japanese yen and the major European currencies. In late 1985 and early 1986 the Canadian dollar fell in terms of the U.S. dollar; during a brief period in January 1986, speculative pressures—apparently motivated by concern over Canada's large government budget deficit—drove the Canadian dollar below 70 cents U.S. The Canadian dollar thus experienced an even more dramatic depreciation in terms of the offshore currencies. The Bank of Canada took strong measures to counter the speculative attacks and kept to its medium-term goal of stabilizing the inflation rate. In late 1986 and early 1987 the market acknowledged its belief in the efficacy of these policies, and the Canadian dollar strengthened considerably in terms of the U.S. dollar, rising to around 74 cents U.S. This mitigated the depreciation experienced in terms of the overseas currencies, and the Canadian dollar stayed almost constant in terms of a trade-weighted average of all currencies.

1987–1990: Anti-inflation and an Appreciating Dollar

In 1987 the new Bank governor, John Crow, announced the policy, already discussed in Chapters 35 and 36, of gradually reducing the rate of inflation from its plateau of around 4 percent slowly to zero. Unfortunately, at the same time, the economy was developing an inflationary gap as a result of the longest sustained expansion since World War II. The inflation rate crept up into the 5 to 6 percent range.

Containing the rising inflation and reducing the rate toward zero both called for a tight monetary policy, and that was adopted. Interest rates were driven to historic highs over U.S. rates. At several times during the period, Canadian rates were an unprecedented 4 percentage points above corresponding U.S. rates. Attracted by the high interest rates, short-term investment funds flooded into Canada, driving the Canadian dollar to a value on the foreign exchange market well above its PPP rate. Exporters were hurt by their difficulties in selling profitably in the United States and by the high cost of funds at home. The Bank aruged that, although unfortunate, these were inevitable consequences of the need to fight inflation. Critics argued that the cure was worse than the disease and called for the Bank to accept the higher inflation rate as the cost of letting the dollar and interest rates fall significantly. At the turn of the decade, the debate was still going on.

SUMMARY

1. Policymakers in an open economy face policy targets or objectives relating to the foreign sector as well as to the domestic sector. Attaining these targets is often called achieving external and internal balance, respectively. When policies to move the economy toward one target cause it to move away from the other, the targets are said to be in conflict.
2. Expenditure-changing policy used to control the level of national income will also influence the trade balance by altering imports. There will be a conflict of objectives if there is a trade account deficit and a recessionary gap or if there is a trade account surplus and an inflationary gap. Expenditure-switching policies that shift the net export function can be used to deal with conflict situations.
3. In general, both expenditure-switching and expenditure-changing policies are needed to attain internal and external balance.
4. The capital account is influenced by both fiscal and monetary policy because both influence domestic interest rates.
5. Under a fixed exchange rate, there is little scope for the use of monetary policy for domestic stabilization purposes. Because of the sensitivity of international capital flows to interest rates, the central bank will be forced to maintain domestic interest rates close to the levels in the rest of the world, and it will not be able to bring about substantial changes in the domestic money supply.
6. Under a fixed exchange rate, capital flows will act to reinforce the effectiveness of fiscal policy.
7. Under a flexible exchange rate, fiscal policy actions will be offset by a crowding-out effect unless they are accompanied by an accommodating monetary policy that prevents changes in interest rates and the exchange rate.
8. Under a flexible exchange rate, monetary policy is a powerful tool. When capital flows are highly interest-elastic, the main channel by which an increase in the money supply increases demand for domestically produced goods is a depreciation of the exchange rate.
9. During the period 1950–1961, Canada was on a flexible exchange rate. The Bank of Canada failed to use monetary policy effectively to deal with a serious unemployment problem. In the late 1960s Canada was on a fixed exchange rate that prevented the authorities from avoiding the rising inflation rates experienced by other countries.
10. The floating of the Canadian dollar in 1970 did not remove the inflationary pressure coming from abroad because the Bank of Can-

ada permitted excessively high rates of growth of the money supply during the period 1971–1975.

11. From 1975 to 1980 the Bank of Canada followed a policy of controlling the rate of growth of the money supply. Nevertheless, there were episodes in which a dirty float was maintained.
12. From 1980 to 1983 the Bank of Canada tried to defend the value of the Canadian dollar. High U.S. interest rates led Canada both to import the tight U.S. monetary policy and to experience some depreciation of the Canadian dollar. From 1984 to 1987 the Bank accommodated the gradual recovery from the recession.
13. From 1987 to 1990 the Bank adopted a tough anti-inflationary stance. The objects were to stop the inflation rate from accelerating from its 4 percent plateau and eventually to force the rate down toward zero. The consequences were high Canadian interest rates, which attracted foreign capital, causing an appreciation of the Canadian dollar. This put the tradable goods sector under heavy competitive pressure and led to calls for an easing of monetary policy on the grounds that the cure was worse than the disease.

TOPICS FOR REVIEW

Internal and external balance
Conflicts between objectives
Expenditure-changing and expenditure-switching policies
Monetary and fiscal policy under fixed exchange rates
Sterilization
Monetary and fiscal policy under flexible exchange rates
Dirty float

DISCUSSION QUESTIONS

1. Explain how a country can influence the external value of its currency by (a) direct intervention in the foreign exchange market, (b) fiscal policy, (c) monetary policy.
2. One message of this chapter is that despite a formal commitment to flexible exchange rates, central banks often try to stabilize the exchange rate and to mimic policies adopted by their major trading partners. Why might a central bank oppose both a depreciation and an appreciation of its currency? How has Canadian monetary policy performed in this respect in the past few years?
3. In a speech in December 1980, Bank of Canada Governor Gerald Bouey stated that "the rapid run-up of U.S. short-term interest rates is bound to have a major impact on Canada through increases in interest rates here or through a fall in the foreign exchange value of the Canadian dollar, or some combination of the two." Why must one of these responses occur? What policies can the Bank of Canada follow in order to influence which of the possible responses occurs? Which is preferable?
4. In 1989 and 1990 the Bank of Canada was trying to remove an inflationary gap while Canadian exporters were complaining that the high external value of the Canadian dollar was preventing them from reaping the advantages of the new Canada–U.S. Free Trade Agreement. What classic policy conflict was the Bank encountering? What change in the policy mix was called for to remove the conflict? Why do you think that change did not occur? What alternatives did the Bank have, given that it could control only the monetary policy lever?

5. In his annual report for 1977, Bank of Canada Governor Gerald Bouey said: "If we in Canada continue our progress towards better control of our prices and costs, we shall unquestionably benefit from higher levels of employment and output than would otherwise be possible. Better price performance will improve the competitive position of Canadian suppliers in foreign markets and in relation to foreign goods in Canadian markets." Why should Canada be concerned with its competitive position under a flexible exchange rate? In what other ways might a lowering of the rate of inflation lead to increased employment?

6. Which of the following pairs of policy goals can be reached simultaneously using an appropriate macroeconomic policy, and which involve conflicting objectives? Indicate the policies you would advocate in each case.

a. Lower rate of inflation and a reduced trade deficit
b. Elimination of an inflationary gap and a trade deficit
c. Lower rate of unemployment and a reduced trade deficit
d. Lower rate of unemployment and a reduced overall balance-of-payments deficit

7. Explain why the use of monetary policy for domestic stabilization is limited under a fixed exchange rate.

8. A country that maintains a fixed exchange rate will have to allow its inflation rate to adjust to the level occurring in the rest of the world. Is this inconsistent with the various theories of inflation outlined in Chapter 36?

MATHEMATICAL NOTES

1. Since one cannot divide by zero, the ratio $\Delta Y/\Delta X$ cannot be evaluated when $\Delta X = 0$. However, the limit of the ratio as ΔX *approaches* zero can be evaluated, and it is infinity.

$$\lim_{\Delta X \to 0} \frac{\Delta Y}{\Delta X} = \infty$$

2. Many variables affect the quantity demanded. Using functional notation, the argument of the next several pages of the text can be anticipated. Let Q^D represent the quantity of a commodity demanded and

$$T, \overline{Y}, N, Y^*, p, p_j$$

represent, respectively, tastes, average household income, population, income distribution, the commodity's own price, and the price of the jth other commodity.

The demand function is

$$Q^D = D(T, \overline{Y}, N, Y^*, p, p_j), \; j = 1, \ldots, n$$

The demand schedule or curve is given by

$$Q^D = q(p) \Big|_{T, \overline{Y}, N, Y^*, p_j}$$

where the notation means that the variables to the right of the vertical line are held constant.

This function is correctly described as the demand function with respect to price, all other variables being held constant. This function, often written concisely as $q = q(p)$, shifts in response to changes in other variables. Consider average income. If, as is usually hypothesized, $\partial Q^D/\partial \overline{Y} > 0$, then increases in average income shift $q = q(p)$ rightward and decreases in average income shift $q = q(p)$ leftward. Changes in other variables likewise shift this function in the direction implied by the relationship of that variable to the quantity demanded.

3. Quantity demanded is a simple, straightforward but frequently misunderstood concept in everyday use, but it has a clear mathematical meaning. It refers to the dependent variable in the demand function from note 2:

$$Q^D = D(T, \overline{Y}, N, Y^*, p, p_j)$$

It takes on a specific value whenever a specific value is assigned to each of the independent variables. The value of Q^D changes whenever the value of any independent variable is changed. Q^D could change, for example, from 10,000 tons per month to 20,000 tons per month as a result of a *ceteris paribus* change in any one price, in average income, in the distribution of income, in tastes, or in population. Also it could change as a result of the net effect of changes in all of the independent variables occurring at once. Thus a change in the price of a commodity is a sufficient reason for a change in Q^D but not a necessary reason.

Some textbooks reserve the term *change in quantity demanded* for a movement along a demand curve, that is, a change in Q^D as a result of a change in p. They then use other words for a change in Q^D caused by a change in the other variables in the demand function. This usage gives the single variable Q^D more than one name, and this is potentially confusing.

Our usage, which corresponds to that in more advanced treatments, avoids this confusion. We call Q^D *quantity demanded* and refer to *any* change in Q^D as a *change in quantity demanded.* In this usage it is correct to say that a movement along a demand curve is a change in quantity demanded, but it is incorrect to say that a change in quantity demanded can occur only because of a movement along a demand curve (since Q^D can change for other reasons, for example, a *ceteris paribus* change in average household income).

4. Continuing the development of note 2, let Q^S represent the quantity of a commodity supplied and

$$G,X,p,w_i$$

represent, respectively, producers' goals, technology, the products' own price, and the price of the ith input.

The supply function is

$$Q^S = S(G,X,p,w_i),\ i = 1, 2, \ldots, m$$

The supply schedule or curve is given by

$$Q^S = s(p) \Big|_{G,X,w_i}$$

This is the supply function with respect to price, all other variables being held constant. This function, often written concisely as $q = s(p)$, shifts in response to changes in other variables.

5. Continuing the development of notes 2 through 4, equilibrium occurs where $Q^D = Q^S$. *For specified values of all other variables,* this requires that

$$q(p) = s(p) \qquad [1]$$

Equation 1 defines an equilibrium value of p; hence, although p is an *independent* variable in each of the supply and demand functions, it is an *endogenous* variable in the economic model that imposes the equilibrium condition expressed in Equation 1. Price is endogenous because it is assumed to adjust to bring about equality between quantity demanded and quantity supplied. Equilibrium quantity, also an endogenous variable, is determined by substituting the equilibrium price into either $q(p)$ or $s(p)$.

Graphically, Equation 1 is satisfied only at the point where demand and supply curves intersect. Thus supply and demand curves are said to determine the equilibrium values of the endogenous variables, price and quantity. A shift in any of the independent variables held constant in the q and s functions will shift the demand or supply curves and lead to different equilibrium values for price and quantity.

6. The definition in the text uses uses finite changes and is called *arc elasticity*. The parallel definition using derivatives is

$$\eta = \frac{dq}{dp} \times \frac{p}{q}$$

and is called *point elasticity*. Further discussion appears in the Appendix to Chapter 5.

7. The propositions in the text are proved as follows. Letting TR stand for total revenue, we can write

$$TR = pq$$

$$\frac{dTR}{dp} = q + p\frac{dq}{dp} \qquad [1]$$

From the equation in note 6, however,

$$q\eta = p\frac{dq}{dp} \qquad [2]$$

which we can substitute in Equation 1 to obtain

$$\frac{dTR}{dp} = q + q\eta = q(1 + \eta) \qquad [3]$$

Because η is a negative number, the sign of Equation 3 is negative if the absolute value of η exceeds unity (elastic demand) and positive if it is less than unity (inelastic demand).

8. The axis reversal arose in the following way. Marshall theorized in terms of "demand price" and "supply price," these being the prices that would lead to a given quantity being demanded or supplied. Thus

$$p^d = D(q) \qquad [1]$$

$$p^s = S(q) \qquad [2]$$

and the condition of equilibrium is

$$D(q) = S(q)$$

When graphing the behavioral relationships expressed in Equations 1 and 2, Marshall naturally put the independent variable, q, on the horizontal axis.

Leon Walras, whose formulation of the working of a competitive market has become the accepted one, focused on quantity demanded and quantity supplied *at a given price.* Thus

$$q^d = q(p)$$

$$q^s = s(p)$$

and the condition of equilibrium is

$$q(p) = s(p)$$

Walras did not use graphical representation. Had he done so, he would surely have placed p (his independent variable) on the horizontal axis.

Marshall, among his other influences on later generations of economists, was the great popularizer of graphical analysis in economics. Today we use his graphs, even for Walras' analysis. The axis reversal is thus one of those historical accidents that seem odd to people who did not live through the "perfectly natural" sequence of steps that produced it.

9. The relationship of the slope of the budget line to relative prices can be seen as follows. In the two-commodity example, a change in expenditure (ΔE) is given by the equation

$$\Delta E = p_C \Delta C + p_F \Delta F \qquad [1]$$

Along a budget line, expenditure is constant, that is, $\Delta E = 0$. Thus along such a line,

$$p_C \Delta C + p_F \Delta F = 0 \qquad [2]$$

whence

$$-\frac{\Delta C}{\Delta F} = \frac{p_F}{p_C} \qquad [3]$$

The ratio $-\Delta C/\Delta F$ is the slope of the budget line. It is negative because, with a fixed budget, to consume more F, one must consume less C. In other words, Equation 3 says that the negative of the slope of the budget line is the ratio of the absolute prices (i.e., the relative price). Although prices do not show directly in Figure 7-3, they are implicit in the budget line: Its slope depends solely on the relative price, whereas its position, given a fixed money income, depends on the absolute prices of the two goods.

10. Because the slope of the indifference curve is negative, it is the absolute value of the slope that declines as one moves downward to the right along the curve. The algebraic value, of course, increases. The phrase *diminishing marginal rate of substitution* thus refers to the absolute, not the algebraic, value of the slope.

11. The distinction made between an incremental change and a marginal change is the distinction for the function $Y = Y(X)$ between $\Delta Y/\Delta X$ and the derivative dY/dX. The latter is the limit of the former as ΔX approaches zero. Precisely this sort of difference underlies the distinction between arc and point elasticity, and we shall meet it repeatedly—in this chapter in reference to marginal and incremental *utility* and in later chapters with respect to such concepts as marginal and incremental *product, cost,* and *revenue.* Where Y is a function of more than one variable—for example, $Y = f(X,Z)$—the marginal relationship between Y and X is the partial derivative $\partial Y/\partial X$ rather than the total derivative.

12. The hypothesis of diminishing marginal utility requires that we can measure utility of consumption by a function $U = U(X_1, X_2, \ldots, X_n)$ where $X_1, \ldots, X_n$ are quantities of the n goods consumed by a household. It really embodies two utility hypotheses. First, $\partial U/\partial X_i > 0$, which says that for some levels of consumption the consumer can get more utility by increasing consumption of the commodity. Second, $\partial^2 U/\partial X_i^2 < 0$, which says that the marginal utility of additional consumption is declining.

13. *Marginal product,* as defined in the text, is really *incremental product.* More advanced treatments distinguish between this notion and *marginal* product as the limit of the ratio as ΔL approaches zero. Marginal product thus measures the rate at which total product is changing as one factor is varied and is the partial derivative of the total product with respect to the variable factor. In symbols,

$$MP = \frac{\partial TP}{\partial L}$$

14. We have referred specifically both to diminishing *marginal* product and to diminishing *average* product. In most cases, eventually diminishing marginal product implies eventually diminishing

average product. This is, however, not necessary, as the accompanying figure shows.

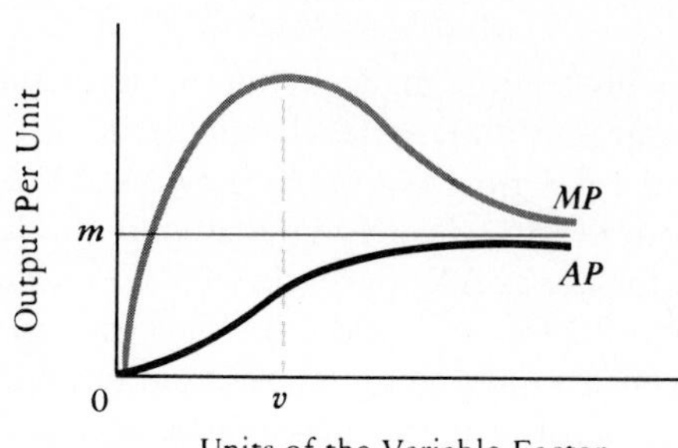

In this case marginal product diminishes after v units of the variable factor are employed. Because marginal product falls toward, but never quite reaches, a value of m, average product rises continually toward, but never quite reaches, the same value.

15. Let q be the quantity of output and L the quantity of the variable factor. In the short run,

$$TP = q = f(L) \qquad [1]$$

We now define

$$AP = \frac{q}{L} = \frac{f(L)}{L} \qquad [2]$$

$$MP = \frac{dq}{dL} \qquad [3]$$

We are concerned about the relationship between these two. Whether average product is rising, at a maximum, or falling is determined by its derivative with respect to L:

$$\frac{d\frac{q}{L}}{dL} = \frac{L\frac{dq}{dL} - q}{L_2} \qquad [4]$$

This may be rewritten

$$\frac{1}{L}\left(\frac{dq}{dL} - \frac{q}{L}\right) = \frac{1}{L}(MP - AP) \qquad [5]$$

Clearly, when MP is greater than AP, the expression in Equation 5 is positive and thus AP is rising. When MP is less than AP, AP is falling. When they are equal, AP is at a stationary value.

16. The text defines *incremental cost*. Strictly, marginal cost is the rate of change of total cost, with respect to output, q. Thus $MC = dTC/dq$. From the definitions, $TC = TFC + TVC$. Fixed costs are not a function of output. Thus we may write $TC = K + f(q)$, where $f(q)$ is total variable costs and K is a constant. From this we see that $MC = df(q)/dq$. MC is thus independent of the size of the fixed costs.

17. This point is easily seen if a little algebra is used:

$$AVC = \frac{TVC}{q}$$

but

$$TVC = L \times w$$

and

$$q = AP \times L$$

where L is the quantity of the variable factor used and w is its cost per unit. Therefore,

$$AVC = \frac{L \times w}{AP \times L} = \frac{w}{AP}$$

Since w is a constant, it follows that AVC and AP vary inversely with each other, and when AP is at its maximum value, AVC must be at its minimum value.

18. A little elementary calculus will prove the point:

$$MC = \frac{dTC}{dq} = \frac{dTVC}{dq}$$

$$= \frac{d\,(L \times w)}{dq}$$

If w does not vary with output,

$$MC = \frac{dL}{dq} \times w$$

However, referring to note 15, Equation 3, we see that

$$\frac{dL}{dq} = \frac{1}{MP}$$

Thus

$$MC = \frac{w}{MP}$$

Since w is fixed, MC varies negatively with MP. When MP is a maximum, MC is a minimum.

19. As we saw in note 16, $MC = dTVC/dq$. If we take the integral of MC from zero to q_0, we get

$$\int_0^{q_0} MC\, dq = TVC\, q_0 + K$$

The first term is the area under the marginal cost curve, while the constant of integration, K, is fixed cost.

20. Strictly speaking, the marginal rate of substitution refers to the slope of the tangent to the isoquant at a particular point, whereas the calculations in Table 11A-1 refer to the average rate of substitution between two distinct points on the isoquant. Assume a production function

$$Q = Q(K, L) \qquad [1]$$

Isoquants are given by the function

$$K = I(L, \overline{Q}) \qquad [2]$$

derived from Equation 1 by expressing K as an explicit function of L and Q. A single isoquant relates to a particular value ($\overline{Q}$) at which Q is held constant. Define Q_K and Q_L as an alternative, more compact notation for $\partial Q/\partial K$ and $\partial Q/\partial L$, the marginal products of capital and labor. Also, let Q_{KK} and Q_{LL} stand for $\partial^2 Q/\partial L^2$ and $\partial^2 Q/\partial K^2$, respectively. To obtain the slope of the isoquant, totally differentiate Equation 1 to obtain

$$dQ = Q_K dK + Q_L dL$$

Then, since we are moving along a single isoquant, set $dQ = 0$ to obtain

$$\frac{dK}{dL} = -\frac{Q_L}{Q_K} = MRS$$

Diminishing marginal productivity implies Q_{LL}, $Q_{KK} < 0$, and, hence, as we move down the isoquant of Figure 11A-1, Q_K is rising and Q_L is falling, so the absolute value of MRS is diminishing. This is called the *hypothesis of a diminishing marginal rate of substitution.*

21. Formally, the firm's problem is to maximize $Q = Q(K, L)$ subject to the budget constraint

$$p_K K + p_L L = C$$

To do this, form the Lagrangean

$$Q(K, L) - \lambda(p_K K + p_L L - C)$$

The first-order conditions for finding the saddle point on this function are

$$Q_K - \lambda p_K = 0;\ Q_K = \lambda p_K \qquad [1]$$

$$Q_L - \lambda p_L = 0;\ Q_L = \lambda p_L \qquad [2]$$

$$-p_K K - p_L L + C = 0 \qquad [3]$$

Dividing Equation 1 by Equation 2 yields

$$\frac{Q_K}{Q_L} = \frac{p_K}{p_L}$$

That is, the ratio of the marginal products, which is (-1) times the MRS, is equal to the ratio of the prices, which is (-1) times the slope of the isocost line.

22. Marginal revenue is mathematically the derivative of total revenue with respect to output, dTR/dq. Incremental revenue is $\Delta TR/\Delta q$. However, the term *marginal revenue* is used loosely to refer to both concepts.

23. For notes 23 through 25, it is helpful first to define some terms. Let

$$\pi_n = TR_n - TC_n$$

where π_n is the profit when n units are sold.

If the firm is maximizing its profits by producing n units, it is necessary that the profits at output q_n be at least as large as the profits at output zero. If the firm is maximizing its profits at output n, then

$$\pi_n \geq \pi_0 \qquad [1]$$

The condition says that profits from producing must be greater than profits from not producing. Condition 1 can be rewritten as

$$TR_n - TVC_n - TFC_n \geq TR_0 - TVC_0 - TFC_0 \qquad [2]$$

However, note that by definition

$$TR_0 = 0 \quad [3]$$

$$TVC_0 = 0 \quad [4]$$

$$TFC_n = TFC_0 = K \quad [5]$$

where K is a constant. By substituting Equations 3,4, and 5 into Condition 2, we get

$$TR_n - TVC_n \geq 0$$

from which we obtain

$$TR_n \geq TVC_n$$

This proves Rule 1.

On a per unit basis, it becomes

$$\frac{TR_n}{q_n} \geq \frac{TVC_n}{q_n} \quad [6]$$

where q_n is the number of units produced.

Since $TR_n = q_n p_n$, where p_n is the price when n units are sold, Equation 6 may be rewritten as

$$p_n \geq AVC_n$$

24. Using elementary calculus, we may prove Rule 2.

$$\pi_n = TR_n - TC_n$$

each of which is a function of output q. To maximize π, it is necessary that

$$\frac{d\pi}{dq} = 0 \quad [1]$$

and that

$$\frac{d^2\pi}{dq^2} < 0 \quad [2]$$

From the definitions,

$$\frac{d\pi}{dq} = \frac{dTR}{dq} - \frac{dTC}{dq} = MR - MC \quad [3]$$

From Equations 1 and 3, a necessary condition of maximum π is $MR - MC = 0$, or $MR = MC$, as is required by Rule 2.

25. To prove that for a negatively sloped demand curve, marginal revenue is less than price, let $p = p(q)$. Then

$$TR = pq = p(q) \times q$$

$$MR = \frac{dTR}{dq} = q\frac{dp}{dq} + p$$

For a negatively sloped demand curve, dp/dq is negative by definition, and thus MR is less than price for positive values of q.

26. A monopolist, selling in two or more markets, will set its marginal cost equal to marginal revenue in each market. Thus the condition $MC = MR_1 = MR_2$ is a profit-maximizing condition for a monopolist that is selling in two markets. In general, equal marginal revenues will mean unequal prices, for the ratio of price to marginal revenue is a function of elasticity of demand: The higher the elasticity, the lower the ratio. Thus equal marginal revenues imply a higher price in the market with the less elastic demand curve.

27. The marginal revenue produced by the factor involves two elements: first, the additional output that an extra unit of the factor makes possible and, second, the change in price of the product that the extra output causes. Let Q be output, R revenue, and L the number of units of labor hired. The contribution to revenue of additional labor is $\partial R/\partial L$. This in turn depends on the contribution of the extra labor to output $\partial Q/\partial L$ (the marginal product of the factor) and $\partial R/\partial Q$ (the firm's marginal revenue from the extra output). Thus

$$\frac{\partial R}{\partial L} = \frac{\partial Q}{\partial L} \cdot \frac{\partial R}{\partial Q}$$

We define the left side as marginal revenue product, MRP. Thus

$$MRP = MP \cdot MR$$

28. The condition that for profit maximization MRP must be downward-sloping at the point where $w = MRP$ is just an application of the proposition (proved in notes 23 and 24) that for profit maximization MC must cut MR from below. Consider the output added by the last unit of the variable factor. Its marginal cost is w, and its marginal revenue is MRP. Thus w must cut

MRP from below. Since w is a horizontal line, *MRP* must be falling.

If we put the matter in standard mathematical terms,

$$w = MRP \qquad [1]$$

is a first-order condition of *either* maximizing or minimizing. The second-order condition for maximization is

$$\frac{dw}{dq} > \frac{dMRP}{dq} \qquad [2]$$

Since

$$\frac{dw}{dq} = 0 \qquad [3]$$

the slope of *MRP* must be negative to satisfy Equation 2; that is, it must be declining.

29. The proposition that the marginal labor cost is above the average labor cost when the average is rising is essentially the same proposition proved in note 15. Nevertheless, let us do it again, using elementary calculus.

The quantity of labor depends on the wage rate: $L = f(w)$. Total labor cost is wL. Marginal cost of labor is $d(wL)/dL = w + L(dw/dL)$. Rewrite this as $MC = AC + L(dw/dL)$. As long as the supply curve slopes upward, $dw/dL > 0$, and therefore $MC > AC$.

30. Let t be the tax rate applied to the profits, π, of the firm. After-tax profits are $(1 - t)\pi$, where π is a function of output, q. To maximize profits after tax requires that

$$\frac{d(1 - t)\pi}{dq} = 0 \qquad \text{or}$$

$$(1 - t)\frac{d\pi}{dq} = 0$$

Dividing both sides of the last equation by $(1 - t)$ we see that $d\pi/dq = 0$ depends on the level of q and is independent of the tax rate.

31. In the text we define *MPC* as an incremental ratio. For mathematical treatments it is sometimes convenient to define all marginal concepts as derivatives: $MPC = dC/dY_d$, $MPS = dS/dY_d$, and so on.

32. The basic relationship is

$$Y_d = C + S$$

Dividing through by Y_d yields

$$\frac{Y_d}{Y_d} = \frac{C}{Y_d} + \frac{S}{Y_d}$$

or

$$1 = APC + APS$$

Next, take the first difference of the basic relationship to yield

$$\Delta Y_d = \Delta C + \Delta S$$

Dividing through by ΔY_d gives

$$\frac{\Delta Y_d}{\Delta Y_d} = \frac{\Delta C}{\Delta Y_d} + \frac{\Delta S}{\Delta Y_d}$$

or

$$1 = MPC + MPS$$

33. This involves using functions of functions. We have $C = C(Y_d)$ and $Y_d = f(Y)$. So, by substitution, $C = C[f(Y)]$. In the linear expressions that are used in the text, $C = a + bY_d$, where b is the marginal propensity to consume. $Y_d = hY$, so $C = a + bhY$, where bh is thus the marginal response of C to a change in Y.

34. The elementary theory of national income can be described by the following set of equations (or model):

$Y = E$	(equilibrium condition)	[1]
$E = C + I + G + (X - M)$	(definition of *AE*)	[2]
$C = a + bY_d$	(consumption function)	[3]
$M = mY$	(import function)	[4]
$Y_d = hY$	(disposable income)	[5]

where a, b, m, and h are parameters determined by behavior; I, G, and X are exogenous variables (i.e., are treated as constants); and Y, E (aggregate expenditure), C, M, and Y_d are all endogenous variables (i.e., are determined by this system of equations). Substituting Equations 3, 4, and 5 and collecting terms in Y, we can obtain the aggregate expenditure function by relating desired expenditure to income:

$$E = (a + I + G + X) + (bh - m)Y$$

where the first term (in parentheses) is autonomous expenditure and the second term is induced expenditure. Using Equation 1, we can derive the equilibrium level of income by solving

$$Y = (a + I + G + X) + (bh - m)Y$$

to obtain

$$Y = \frac{1}{1 - bh + m}(a + I + G + X) \qquad [6]$$

The z defined in the text is $(bh - m)$ in this model. The example in Table 28-5 has these values: $a = 100$, $I = 250$, $G = 170$, $X = 240$, $b = 0.80$, $h = 0.90$, and $m = 0.10$. Substituting into Equation 6 yields

$$Y = \frac{1}{1 - 0.72 + 0.10}(100 + 250 + 170 + 240)$$

$$= \frac{1}{0.38}(760) = 2{,}000$$

35. The total expenditure over all rounds is the sum of an infinite series. If we let A stand for the initiating expenditure and z for the marginal propensity to spend, the change in expenditure is ΔA in the first round, $z\Delta A$ in the second, $z(z\Delta A) = z^2\Delta A$ in the third, and so on. This can be written

$$\Delta A(1 + z + z^2 + \cdots + z^n)$$

If z is less than 1, the series in parentheses converges to $1/(1 - z)$ as n approaches infinity. The change in total expenditure is thus $\Delta A/(1 - z)$. In the example in Box 28-1, $z = 0.80$; therefore, the change in total expenditure is five times ΔA.

36. As we saw in Box 28-2, the simple multiplier, K, is equal to the reciprocal of the marginal propensity not to spend, $1 - z$, also called the marginal propensity to withdraw, w:

$$K = \frac{1}{w}$$

In an open economy the marginal propensity to withdraw is equal to the sum of the marginal propensity to save, $1 - b$, plus the marginal propensity to import, m. Hence the multiplier in an open economy

$$K_o = \frac{1}{(1 - b) + m}$$

is less than that in a closed economy

$$K_c = \frac{1}{1 - b}$$

if the two economies had a common marginal propensity to consume, b. Note that the denominator of K_o can be written as $1 - (b - m)$ where $b - m$ is the marginal propensity to consume *home goods.*

37. Using the multiplier derived in math note 36, we see that an autonomous increase in exports leads to an increase in national income given by

$$\Delta Y = \frac{1}{(1 - b) + m}\Delta X$$

The resulting increase in imports is given by the marginal propensity to import times the change in national income:

$$\Delta M = m\Delta Y$$

Combining, we can calculate the change in the trade balance, $\Delta T = \Delta X - \Delta M$, as

$$\Delta T = \frac{1 - b}{(1 - b) + m}\Delta X = (1 - b)\,\Delta Y$$

which is positive since b is less than 1.

38. The accelerator may be stated as a general macroeconomic theory. Define I_n as the volume of net investment this year and ΔY as the increase in national income from last year to this year. The accelerator theory is the relationship between I_n and ΔY.

Assume that the capital-output ratio is a constant: $K/Y = \propto$, so $K = \propto Y$. If Y changes, K must be changed accordingly:

$$\Delta K = \propto\Delta Y$$

However, the change in the capital stock (ΔK) is net investment, so

$$\Delta K = I_n = \propto \Delta Y$$

39. This is easily proved. In equilibrium the banking system wants sufficient deposits (D) to establish the target ratio (v) of deposits to reserves (R). This gives $R/D = v$. Any change in D of ΔD has to be accompanied by a change in R of ΔR of sufficient size to restore v. Thus $\Delta R/\Delta D = v$, so that $\Delta D = \Delta R/v$, and $\Delta D/\Delta R = 1/v$.

This can be shown also in terms of the deposits created by the sequence in Table 33-6. Let v be the reserve ratio. Let $e = 1 - v$ be the excess reserves per dollar of new deposits. If X dollars are initially deposited in the system, the successive rounds of new deposits will be X, eX, e^2X, e^3X . . . The series

$$X + eX + e^2X + e^3X \ldots = X[1 + e + e^2 + e^3 + \cdots]$$

has a limit

$$X\frac{1}{1-e} = X\left[\frac{1}{1-(1-v)}\right] = \frac{X}{v}$$

This is the total new deposits created by an injection of \$$X$ of new reserves into the banking system. For example, when $v = 0.20$, an injection of \$100 into the system will lead to an increase of \$500.

40. Suppose that the public wishes to hold a fraction, c, of deposits in cash, C. Now suppose that X dollars are injected into the system. Ultimately, this money will be held either as reserves by the banking system or as cash by the public. Thus we have

$$\Delta C + \Delta R = X$$

From the banking system's reserve behavior, we have $\Delta R = v\Delta D$, and from the public's cash behavior, we have $\Delta C = c\Delta D$. Substituting into the above equation, we get the result that

$$\Delta D = \frac{X}{v + c}$$

From this we can also relate the change in reserves and the change in cash holdings to the initial injection:

$$\Delta R = \frac{v}{v + c}X$$

$$\Delta C = \frac{c}{v + c}X$$

For example, when $v = 0.20$ and $c = 0.05$, an injection of \$100 will lead to an increase in reserves of \$80, an increase in cash in the hands of the public of \$20, and an increase in deposits of \$400.

41. The argument is simply as follows, where prime marks stand for first derivatives:

$$M^D = F_1(T),\ F_1' > 0$$

$$T = F_2(Y),\ F_2' > 0$$

Therefore,

$$M^D = F_1(F_2(Y)) = H(Y),\ H' > 0$$

where H is the function of the function combining F_1 and F_2.

42. Let $L(Y, r)$ give the real demand for money measured in purchasing power units. Let M be the supply of money measured in nominal units and P an index of the price level, so that M/P is the real supply of money. Now the equilibrium condition requiring equality between the demand for money and the supply of money can be expressed in real terms as

$$L(Y, r) = \frac{M}{P} \quad [1]$$

or by multiplying through by P in nominal terms as

$$PL(Y, r) = M \quad [2]$$

In Equation 1 a rise in P disturbs equilibrium by lowering M/P, and in Equation 2 it disturbs equilibrium by raising $PL\,(Y, r)$.

43. The rule of 72 is an approximation, derived from the mathematics of compound interest. Any measure X_t will have the value $X_t = X_0e^{rt}$ after t years at a continuous growth rate of r percent per year. Because $X_1/X_0 = 2$ requires $r \times t = 0.69$, a "rule of 69" would be correct for continuous growth. The rule of 72 was developed in

the context of compound interest, and if interest is compounded only once a year, the product of $r \times t$ for X to double is approximately 0.72.

44. The time taken to break even is a function of the *difference* in growth rates, not their level. Thus had 4 percent and 5 percent or 5 percent and 6 percent been used in the example, it still would have taken the same number of years. To see this quickly, recognize that we are interested in the ratio of two growth paths:

$$\frac{e^{r_1 t}}{e^{r_2 t}} = e^{(r_1 - r_2)t}$$

45. With $b = B/Y$, it follows from elementary calculus that

$$b' = \frac{B'}{Y} - \frac{bY}{Y} \quad [1]$$

Since Y'/Y is the rate of growth of nominal income, n, we can write

$$b' = \frac{B'}{Y} - bn \quad [2]$$

But B', the change in the stock of government bonds, is just equal to the government budget deficit. This in turn is equal to the sum of the primary deficit $(G - T)$ plus the government's debt service payments, iB. Expressing each of these terms as a percentage of national income, the B'/Y term in Equation 2 can be written as

$$\frac{B'}{Y} = (g - t) + ib \quad [3]$$

Substituting into the equation for b', we then have

$$b' = (g - t) + (i - n)b$$

which is Equation 1 in Box 39-3.

46. Net exports equals exports minus imports.

$$NX = X - M \quad [1]$$

Exports depend on foreign income, Y^f, and on the terms of trade.

$$X = X_0 + m^f Y^f - b^f\left(\frac{P}{eP^f}\right) \quad [2]$$

where X_0 is autonomous exports, m^f is the foreign marginal propensity to import, b^f is the response of exports to a change in relative prices, P is the domestic price level, e is the exchange rate, and P^f is foreign prices. Imports depend on domestic income and the terms of trade.

$$M = M_0 + mY + b\left(\frac{P}{eP^f}\right) \quad [3]$$

Combining Equations 1, 2, and 3, we can write

$$NX = (X_0 - M_0) + m^f Y^f - mY - c\left(\frac{P}{eP^f}\right) \quad [4]$$

where $c = b + b^f$. In Chapter 26 we considered this relationship in isolation, and hence the slope of the NX curve when it was drawn against national income was taken to be $dNX/dY = -m$, where the other variables in Equation 4 were held constant. Now we have to take into account the fact that P changes as Y changes.

Writing the $SRAS$ curve as

$$P = g(Y),\ g' > 0 \quad [5]$$

and substituting Equation 5 into Equation 4, we eliminate P to yield

$$NX = (X_0 - M_0) + mY^f - mY - c\left(\frac{g(Y)}{eP^f}\right) \quad [6]$$

The slope of the NX curve is now given by

$$\frac{dNX}{dY} = -(m + u') < 0 \quad [7]$$

where $u = cg'/ep^f > 0$. Hence as Y rises, NX falls, both because of the marginal propensity to import and because of substitution away from domestic goods as P rises.

GLOSSARY

absolute advantage When a given amount of resources can produce more of some commodity in one country than in another.

absolute price The amount of money that must be spent to acquire one unit of a commodity. Also called the *money price*.

acceleration hypothesis The hypothesis that when national income is held above potential, the persistent inflationary gap will cause inflation to accelerate, and when national income is held below potential, the persistent recessionary gap will cause inflation to decelerate.

accelerator The theory that relates the level of investment to the rate of change of national income.

adjustable peg system A system in which exchange rates are fixed in the short term but are occasionally changed in response to persistent payments imbalances.

administered price A price set by the conscious decision of the seller rather than by impersonal market forces.

ad valorem tariff An import duty that is a percentage of the price of the imported product.

ad valorem tax See *excise tax*.

adverse selection Self-selection, within a single risk category, of persons of above average risk.

AE See *aggregate expenditure*.

agents Decision makers including households, firms, and government bodies.

Aggregate demand Total desired purchases by all the buyers of an economy's output.

aggregate demand (*AD*) curve A curve showing the combinations of real national income and the price level that makes aggregate desired expenditure equal to national income; the curve thus relates the total amount of output that will be demanded to the price level of that output.

aggregate demand shock A shift in the aggregate demand curve.

aggregate expenditure (*AE*) Total expenditure on final output of the economy. $AE = C + I + G + (X - M)$, representing the four major components of aggregate desired expenditure.

aggregate expenditure (*AE*) function The function that relates aggregate desired expenditure to national income.

aggregate supply Total desired sales of all the producers of an economy's output.

aggregate supply (*AS*) curve See *short-run aggregate supply curve* and *long-run aggregate supply curve*.

aggregate supply shock A shift in the aggregate supply curve.

allocation of resources See *resource allocation*.

allocative efficiency A situation in which no reorganization of production or consumption could make everyone better off (or, as it is sometimes stated, make at least one person better off while making no one worse off).

appreciation (of currency) A rise in the free market value of domestic currency in terms of foreign currencies; that is, a fall in the exchange rate.

a priori Literally, "at a prior time" or "in advance," hence prior to actual experience.

arc elasticity A measure of the average responsiveness of quantity to price over an interval of the demand curve. For analytical purposes it is usually defined by the formula

$$\eta = \frac{\Delta q/q}{\Delta p/p}$$

An alternative formula often used where computations are involved is

$$\eta = \frac{(q_2 - q_1)/(q_2 + q_1)}{(p_2 - p_1)/(p_2 + p_1)}$$

where p_1 and q_1 are the original price and quantity and p_2 and q_2 are the new price and quantity.

With negatively sloped demand curves, elasticity is a negative number. Sometimes the expressions given here are therefore multiplied by -1 to make measured elasticity positive.

autarky A situation in which there is no international trade.

automatic fiscal policy Fiscal policy that does not require changes in government policy variables but has its effects via the operation of *built-in stabilizers*.

autonomous expenditure See *exogenous expenditure*.

autonomous variable See *exogenous variable*.

average cost (*AC*) See *average total cost*.

average fixed cost (*AFC*) Total fixed cost divided by the number of units of output.

average product (*AP*) Total product divided by the number of units of the variable factor used in its production.

average propensity to consume (*APC*) The proportion of income devoted to consumption; total consumption expenditure divided by total disposable income ($APC = C/Y_d$).

average propensity to save (*APS*) The proportion of disposable income devoted to saving; total saving divided by total disposable income ($APS = S/Y_d$).

average revenue (*AR*) Total revenue divided by quantity sold; this is the market price when all units are sold at one price.
average tax rate The ratio of total taxes paid to total income earned.
average total cost (*ATC*) Total cost of producing a given output divided by the number of units of output; it can also be calculated as the sum of average fixed costs and average variable costs. Also called *cost per unit, unit cost, average cost.*
average variable cost (*AVC*) Total variable costs divided by the number of units of output. Also called *direct unit cost, avoidable unit cost.*
avoidable cost See *total variable cost.*
avoidable unit cost See *average variable cost.*

balanced budget A situation in which current revenue is exactly equal to current expenditures.
balanced budget multiplier The change in income divided by the tax-financed change in government expenditure that brought it about.
balance-of-payments accounts A summary record of a country's transactions that involve payments or receipts of foreign exchange.
balance of trade The difference between the value of exports and the value of imports of visible items (goods).
bank notes Paper money issued by commercial banks.
bank rate The rate of interest at which the Bank of Canada makes loans to the chartered banks, often interpreted as a signal about the stance of monetary policy.
barter A system in which goods and services are traded directly for other goods and services.
beggar-my-neighbor policies Policies designed to increase a country's prosperity (especially by reducing its unemployment) at the expense of reducing prosperity in other countries (especially by increasing their unemployment).
benefit-cost analysis A technique for evaluating government policies. The sum of the opportunity cost to all parties is compared with the value of the benefits to all parties.
black market A situation in which goods are sold illegally at prices that violate a government price ceiling.
bond An evidence of debt carrying a specified amount and schedule of interest payments and (usually) a date for redemption of its face value.
bread-and-butter unionism A union movement whose major objectives are higher wages and better conditions of employment rather than political or social reform.
budget balance The difference between total government revenue and total government expenditure.
budget deficit Any shortfall of current revenue below current expenditure.
budget line Graphical representation of all combinations of commodities or factors that a household or firm may obtain if it spends a specified amount of money at fixed prices of the commodities or factors. Also called the *isocost line.*
budget surplus Any excess of current revenue over current expenditure.
built-in stabilizer Anything that automatically lessens the magnitude of the fluctuations in national income caused by changes in autonomous expenditures, such as investment.
business cycle The wavelike pattern of fluctuations of national income around its trend value, after seasonal fluctuations have been removed.
buyout When a group of investors buys up a controlling interest in a firm.

C Consumption expenditure.
capacity The level of output that corresponds to the firm's minimum short-run average total cost.
capital A factor of production consisting of all manufactured aids to further production. (See also *physical capital.*)
capital account That part of the balance-of-payments accounts that records payments and receipts arising from the import and export of long-term and short-term financial capital.
capital consumption allowance An estimate of the amount by which the capital stock is depleted through its contribution to current production. Also called *depreciation.*
capital deepening Adding capital to the production process in such a way as to increase the ratio of capital to labor and other factors of production.
capital-labor ratio A measure of the amount of capital per worker in an economy.
capital-output ratio The amount of capital divided by the amount of labor; it shows the amount of capital available on average to each unit of labor.
capital stock The aggregate quantity of capital goods.
capital widening Adding capital to the production process in such a way as to leave factor proportions unchanged.
cartel An organization of producers who agree to act as a single seller in order to maximize joint profits.
ceiling price See *price ceiling.*
central bank A bank that acts as banker to the commercial banking system and often to the government as well. In the modern world, usually a government-owned and -operated institution that controls the banking system and is the sole money-issuing authority.
centrally planned economy See *command economy.*
ceteris paribus Literally, "other things being equal"; usually used in economics to indicate that all variables except the ones specified are assumed not to change.
change in demand An increase or decrease in the quantity demanded at each possible price of the commodity, represented by a shift in the entire demand curve.
change in quantity demanded An increase or decrease in the specific quantity bought at a specified price, represented by a movement along a demand curve.
change in quantity supplied An increase or decrease in the specific quantity supplied at a specified price, represented by a movement along a supply curve.

change in supply An increase or decrease in the quantity supplied at each possible price of the commodity, represented by a shift in the entire supply curve.
chartered bank A privately owned, profit-seeking institution that provides a variety of financial services, such as accepting deposits from customers, which it agrees to transfer when ordered by a cheque, and making loans and other investments.
classical unemployment See *real-wage unemployment.*
clearing house An institution where interbank indebtedness, arising from transfer of cheques between banks, is computed, offset against each other, and net amounts owing are calculated.
closed economy An economy that does not engage in international trade.
collective bargaining The process by which unions and employers arrive at and enforce agreements.
collective consumption goods Goods or services that, if they provide benefits to anyone, can, at little or no additional cost, provide benefits to a large group of people, possibly everyone in the contry. Also called *public goods.*
collusion An agreement among sellers to act jointly in their common interest, for example, by agreeing to raise prices. Collusion may be overt or covert, explicit or tacit.
combine laws Laws that prevent firms either from combining into one unit or acting cooperatively so as to behave monopolistically.
command economy An economy in which the decisions of the government (as distinct from households and firms) exert the major influence over the allocation of resources. Also called a *centrally planned economy.*
commercial policy A government's policy involving restrictions placed on international trade.
commodities Marketable items produced to satisfy wants. Commodities may be either *goods,* which are tangible, or *services,* which are intangible.
common market An agreement among two or more countries to establish a single market among themselves by abolishing all tariffs on trade among themselves, by charging a common tariff on imports from nonmember countries, and by permitting a free flow of labor and capital among themselves.
common-property resource A natural resource that is owned by no one and may be used by anyone.
comparative advantage The ability of one nation, region, or individual to produce a commodity at a lesser opportunity cost of other products forgone than another nation, region, or individual.
comparative statics Short for *comparative static equilibrium analysis,* the derivation of predictions by analyzing the effect of a change in some exogenous variable on the equilibrium position.
competition policy Policies designed to prohibit the acquisition and exercise of monopoly power by business firms.
competitive devaluations A round of devaluations of exchange rates by a number of countries, each trying to gain a competitive advantage over the other and each failing to the extent that other countries also devalue their currencies.
complement Two commodities are complements when they tend to be used jointly. The degree of complementarity is measured by the size of the negative cross-elasticity between the two goods.
concentration ratio The fraction of total market sales (or some other measure of market occupancy) controlled by a specified number of the industry's largest firms, four-firm and eight-firm concentration ratios being most frequently used.
conglomerate merger See *merger.*
constant-cost industry An industry in which costs of the most efficient size firm remain constant as the entire industry expands or contracts in the long run.
constant dollar GDP See *real GDP.*
constant dollar national income See *real national income.*
constant returns A situation in which output increases in proportion to inputs as the scale of production is increased. A firm in this situation, and facing fixed factor prices, is a *constant-cost firm.*
Consumer Price Index (CPI) A measure of the average prices of commodities commonly bought by households; compiled monthly by *Statistics Canada.*
consumers' durables See *durable good.*
consumers' surplus The difference between the total value that consumers place on all units consumed of a commodity and the payment that they must make to purchase that amount of the commodity.
consumption The act of using commodities, either goods or services, to satisfy wants.
consumption expenditure Household expenditure on all goods and services except housing.
consumption function The relationship between total desired consumption expenditure and all the variables that determine it; in the simplest cases, the relationship between consumption expenditure and disposable income and consumption expenditure and national income.
contestable market A market is perfectly contestable if there are no sunk costs of entry or exit, so that *potential* entry may hold profits of existing firms to zero.
cooperative equilibrium The equilibrium reached when all the firms in an industry cooperate so as to maximize their joint profits.
corporation A form of business organization in which the firm has a legal existence separate from that of the owners, and ownership and financial responsibility are divided, limited, and shared among any number of individual and institutional shareholders.
cost To a producing firm, the value of inputs used to produce output.
cost minimization An implication of profit maximization that the firm will choose the method that produces specific output at the lowest attainable cost.
cost per unit See *average total cost.*
CPI See *Consumer Price Index.*
cross-elasticity of demand (η_{xy}) A measure of the responsiveness of the quantity of a commodity demanded

to changes in price of a related commodity, defined by the formula

$$\eta_{xy} = \frac{\text{percentage change in quantity demand of one good } X}{\text{percentage change in price of another good } Y}$$

cross-sectional data Several measurements or observations made at the same point in time.

crowding-out effect The offsetting reduction in private expenditure caused by the rise in interest rates that follows an expansionary fiscal policy.

crown corporation Business concerns owned by government; also known as *public enterprises.*

current account A part of the balance-of-payments accounts that records payments and receipts arising from trade in goods and services and from interest and dividends that are earned by capital owned in one country and invested in another.

current account balance The balance of payments on current account; the sum of the balances on the visible and the invisible accounts.

current dollar GDP See *nominal GDP.*

current dollar national income See *nominal national income.*

cyclically adjusted deficit (*CAD*) An estimate of the government budget deficit (expenditure minus tax revenue), not as it actually is but as it would be if national income were at its potential level.

cyclical unemployment Unemployment in excess of frictional and structural unemployment; it is due to a shortfall of actual national income below potential national income. Sometimes called *deficient-demand unemployment.*

day-to-day loan A loan made by a chartered bank to an investment dealer. Such loans make up part of the *secondary reserves* of the chartered banks.

debt Generally, amounts owed to one's creditors. From a firm's point of view, the portion of its money capital that is borrowed rather than subscribed by shareholders.

decision lag The period of time between perceiving some problem and reaching a decision on what to do about it.

decreasing returns A situation in which output increases less than proportionately to inputs as the scale of a firm's production increases. A firm in this situation, with fixed factor prices, is an *increasing-cost* firm.

deficient-demand unemployment See *cyclical unemployment.*

demand The entire relationship between the quantity of a commodity that buyers wish to purchase per period of time and the price of that commodity.

demand curve The graphical representation of the relationship between the quantity of a commodity that buyers wish to purchase per period of time and the price of that commodity, other things being equal.

demand deposit A bank deposit that is withdrawable on demand (without notice of intention to withdraw) and transferable by means of a cheque.

demand elasticity See *elasticity of demand.*

demand for money The total amount of money balances that the public wishes to hold for all purposes.

demand inflation Inflation arising from excess aggregate demand, that is, when national income exceeds potential income.

demand schedule A table showing for selected values the relationship between the quantity of a commodity that buyers wish to purchase per period of time and the price of that commodity, other things being equal.

demogrants Social benefits paid to anyone meeting only minimal requirements such as age or residence; in particular, *not* income-tested.

deposit money Money held by the public in the form of demand deposits with commercial banks.

depreciation (of capital) The loss in value of an asset due to physical wear and tear and to obsolescence. See also *capital consumption allowance.*

depreciation (of currency) A fall in the free market value of domestic currency in terms of foreign currency; that is, a rise in the exchange rate.

depression A persistent period of very low economic activity with very high unemployment and high excess capacity.

derived demand The demand for a factor of production that results from the demand for the products that it is used to make.

devalued A reduction of the external value of a country's currency under an adjustable peg system.

devaluation The act of devaluing a country's currency under an adjustable peg system.

differentiated product A group of commodities that are similar enough to be called the *same* product but dissimilar enough so that all of them do not have to be sold at the same price.

diminishing marginal rate of substitution The hypothesis that the marginal rate of substitution changes systematically as the amounts of two commodities being consumed vary.

direct burden Amount of money for a tax that is collected from taxpayers.

direct cost See *total variable cost.*

direct investment In balance-of-payments accounting, foreign investment in the form of a takeover or capital investment in a branch plant or subsidiary corporation in which the investor has voting control.

direct unit cost See *average variable cost.*

dirty float See *managed float.*

discounted present value See *present value.*

discount rate The rate of interest used to discount a stream of future payments to arrive at their present value.

discretionary fiscal policy Fiscal policy that is a conscious response (not according to any predetermined rule) to each particular state of the economy as its arises.

disembodied technical change Technical change that raises output without the necessity of building new capital to embody the new knowledge.

disequilibrium The absence of equilibrium. A market is in disequilibrium when there is either excess demand or excess supply.

disequilibrium price A price at which quantity demanded does not equal quantity supplied.

disposable personal income (Y_d) GDP minus any part of it not actually paid to households minus personal income taxes paid by households plus transfer payments to households; personal income minus personal income taxes.

distributed profits Profits paid out to owners of a firm. For incorporated firms, the distributed profits are called *dividends*.

dividends Profits paid out to the shareholders of a corporation.

division of labor The breaking up of a production process into a series of repetitive tasks, each done by a different worker.

domestic absorption (A) Total demand for goods for use by domestic residents; equal to $C + I + G$.

double counting In national income accounting, adding up the total outputs of all the sectors in the economy so that the value of intermediate goods is counted in the sector that produces them and every time they are purchased as an input by another sector.

dumping In international trade, the practice of selling a commodity at a lower price in the export market than in the domestic market for reasons that are not related to differences in costs of servicing the two markets.

duopoly An industry that contains only two firms.

durable good A good that yields its services over an extended period of time. Often divided into the subcategories *producers' durables* (e.g., machines, equipment) and *consumers' durables* (e.g., cars, appliances).

economic efficiency The least costly method of producing any output.

economic growth Increases in real, or constant dollar, potential GDP.

economic profits or **losses** The difference between the revenues received from the sale of output and the opportunity cost of the inputs used to make the output. Negative economic profits are economic losses. Also called *pure profits* or *pure losses* or simply *profits* or *losses*.

economic rent The surplus of total earnings over what must be paid to prevent a factor from transferring to another use.

economies of scale Reduction of costs per unit of output resulting from an increase in output; a negatively sloped *LRAC* curve over a range of output.

economies of scope Economies achieved by a firm that is large enough to engage efficiently in multiproduct production and associated large-scale distribution, advertising, and purchasing.

economy A set of interrelated production and consumption activities.

effective marginal tax rate The combined or *stacked* rate including the explicit marginal tax rate on income and the complicit marginal tax-back rate on social benefits.

effective rate of tariff The tax charged on any imported commodity expressed as a percentage of the value added by the exporting industry.

elastic demand The situation in which, for a given percentage change in price, there is a greater percentage change in quantity demanded; elasticity greater than unity.

elasticity of demand (η) A measure of the responsiveness of quantity of a commodity demanded to a change in market price, defined by the formula

$$\eta = \frac{\text{percentage change in quantity demanded}}{\text{percentage change in price}}$$

With negatively sloped demand curves, elasticity is a negative number. Sometimes the expression given here is multiplied by -1 to make measured elasticity positive. Also called *demand elasticity, price elasticity,* and *own price elasticity of demand.*

elasticity of supply (η_s) A measure of the responsiveness of the quantity of a commodity supplied to a change in the market price, defined by the formula

$$\eta_s = \frac{\text{percentage change in quantity supplied}}{\text{percentage change in price}}$$

embodied technical change Technical change that is intrinsic to the particular capital goods in use and hence that can be used only when new capital, embodying the new techniques, is built.

employment The number of adult workers (15 years of age and older) who hold jobs.

endogenous expenditure See *induced expenditure*.

endogenous variable A variable that is explained within a theory.

ends The goals that we seek to attain.

entry barrier Any natural or artificial impediment to entry into an industry, such as patents, economies of scale, and established brand preferences.

envelope Any curve that encloses, by being tangent to, a series of other curves. In particular, the *envelope cost curve* is the *LRAC* curve, which encloses the *SRATC* curves by being tangent to each without cutting any of them.

equalization payments Transfers of tax revenues from the federal government to the low-income provinces to compensate them for their lower potential per capita tax yields.

equilibrium condition A condition that must be fulfilled if some market or sector of the economy, or the whole economy, is to be in equilibrium.

equilibrium differential A difference in factor prices that would persist in equilibrium, without any tendency for it to be removed.

equilibrium price The price at which quantity demanded equals quantity supplied.

equity capital Funds provided by the owners of a firm the return on which depends on the firm's profits.

European Monetary System (EMS) An agreement among the countries of the European Community (except the United Kingdom) to fix exchange rates among their own currencies and then let their joint rate float against the U.S. dollar.

excess burden The value to taxpayers of the changes in behavior that are induced by taxes; the amount that taxpayers would be willing to pay, over and above the direct burden of taxes, to abolish the taxes.

excess capacity The amount by which actual output falls short of capacity output (which is the output that corresponds to the minimum short-run average total cost).

excess demand A situation in which, at the given price, quantity demanded exceeds quantity supplied. Also called a *shortage*.

excess reserves Reserves held by a commercial bank in excess of its *target reserves*.

excess supply A situation in which, at the given price, quantity supplied exceeds quantity demanded. Also called a *surplus*.

exchange rate The price of a unit of foreign currency expressed in terms of units of domestic currency.

excise tax A tax on the sale of a particular commodity; may be a *specific tax* (fixed tax per unit of commodity) or an *ad valorem tax* (fixed percentage of the value of the commodity).

execution lag The time that it takes to put policies in place after the decision has been made.

exhaustible resource See *nonrenewable resource*.

exogenous expenditure In macroeconomics, elements of expenditure that do not vary systematically with other variables, such as national income and the interest rate, but are determined by forces outside of the theory. Also called *autonomous expenditure*.

exogenous variable A variable that influences endogenous variables but is itself determined by factors outside the theory.

expectational inflation Inflation that occurs because decision makers raise prices (so as to keep their relative prices constant) in the expectation that the price level is going to rise.

expectations-augmented Phillips curve The relationship between unemployment and the rate of increase of money wages or between national income and the rate of increase of money prices that arises when the demand and expectations components of inflation are combined.

expenditure-changing policies Policies that change the level of aggregate desired expenditure.

expenditure-switching policies Policies that maintain the level of aggregate desired expenditure but change the relative proportions of its components, domestic absorption, and net exports.

external balance The balance-of-payments (or some subset) is at its target level.

external economies of scale Scale economies that cause the firm's costs to fall as *industry output* rises but are external to the firm and so cannot be obtained by the firm's increasing its own output.

externalities Effects, either good or bad, on parties not directly involved in the production or use of a commodity. Also called *third-party effects*.

factor markets Markets in which the services of factors of production are sold.

factor services The services of factors of production that are used to produce outputs.

factors of production Resources used to produce goods and services to satisfy wants; frequently divided into the basic categories of land, labor, and capital.

fair game A game of chance for which the expected value of the outcome is zero.

fair trade laws Laws providing import duties intended to eliminate unfair competition from foreign goods caused by foreign-government subsidies or predatory pricing by foreign producers. Also called *trade remedy laws*.

falling-cost industry An industry in which the lowest costs attainable by a firm fall as the scale of the industry expands.

favorable balance of payments A credit balance on some part of the international payments accounts (receipts exceed payments); often refers to a favorable balance on current plus capital account (that is, everything except the official settlements account).

fiat money Paper money or coinage that is neither backed by nor convertible into anything else but is decreed by the government to be legal tender and is generally accepted in exchange for goods and services and for the discharge of debts.

final demand Demand for the economy's output of final goods.

final goods Goods that are not used as inputs by other firms but are produced to be sold for consumption, investment, government, or exports during the period under consideration.

financial capital Money that a firm raises to carry on its business, including both equity capital and debt. Also called *money capital*.

fine tuning The attempt to maintain national income at or near its full-employment level by means of frequent changes in fiscal or monetary policy.

firm The unit that employs factors of production and produces goods and services to be sold to households, other firms, or the government.

fiscal drag The tendency for tax revenues to rise faster than government expenditure as full-employment income rises due to economic growth, thus causing a falling, cyclically adjusted budget deficit.

fiscal policy The use of the government's tax and spending policies in an effort to influence the behavior of such macro variables as the GDP and total employment.

fixed cost Any component of *total fixed cost*.

fixed exchange rate An exchange rate that is maintained within a small range around its publicly stated par value by the intervention of a country's central bank in foreign market operations. Also called a *pegged rate*.

fixed factor An input that cannot be increased beyond a given amount in the short run.

fixed investment Investment in plant and equipment.

flexible exchange rate An exchange rate that is left free to be determined by the forces of demand and supply on the free market, with no intervention by the monetary authorities. Also called a *free* or a *floating exchange rate*.

floating exchange rate See *flexible exchange rate.*

foreign exchange Actual foreign currencies or various claims on them, such as bank balances or promises to pay, that are traded for each other on the foreign exchange market.

foreign exchange market The market where different national currencies or claims to these currencies are traded.

foreign investment Investment in one country by firms owned in a foreign country or individuals resident in a foreign country.

45° line In macroeconomics, the line that graphs the equilibrium condition that aggregate desired expenditure should equal national income ($AE = Y$).

fractional reserve system A banking system in which commercial banks are required to keep only a fraction of their deposits in cash or on deposit with the central bank.

free exchange rate See *flexible exchange rate.*

free good A commodity for which the quantity supplied exceeds the quantity demanded at a price of zero; therefore, a good that does not command a positive price in a market economy.

free market economy An economy in which the decisions of individual households and firms (as distinct from the government) exert the major influence over the allocation of resources. Also called a *market economy.*

free trade The absence of any form of government intervention in international trade, which implies that imports and exports must not be subject to special taxes or restictions levied merely because of their status as imports or exports.

free trade association An agreement among two or more countries to abolish tariffs on all or most of the trade among themselves, while each remains free to set its own tariffs against other countries.

frictional unemployment Unemployment caused by the time that is taken for labor to move from one job to another.

fringe benefits Compensation other than wages for the benefit of labor, such as company contributions to pension and welfare funds, sick leave, and paid holidays.

full employment Employment that is sufficient to produce the economy's potential output; at full employment, all remaining unemployment is frictional and structural. Also called *high employment.*

function Loosely, an expression of a relationship between two or more variables. Precisely, Y is a function of the variables $X_1, \ldots, X_n$ if, for every set of values of the variables $X_1, \ldots, X_n$, there is associated a unique value of the variable Y.

functional distribution of income The distribution of total national income among the major factors of production.

G Government expenditure.

gains from trade The increased output due to the specialization according to comparative advantage that is made possible by trade.

GDP deflator See *implicit GDP deflator.*

GDP gap See *output gap.*

Giffen good An inferior good for which the negative income effect outweighs the substitution effect, so that the demand curve is positively sloped.

goods Tangible commodities, such as cars or shoes.

goods markets See *product markets.*

government All public officials, agencies, and other organizations belonging to or under the control of state, local, or federal governments.

government expenditure All government expenditure on currently produced goods and services, excluding government transfer payments.

Gresham's law The theory that "bad," or debased, money drives "good," or undebased, money out of circulation because people keep the good money for other purposes and use the bad money for transactions.

gross domestic product (GDP) National income as measured by the output approach; equal to the sum of all values added in the economy or, what is the same thing, the values of all final goods produced in the economy.

gross domestic product at market prices Net domestic product at market prices (wages, rent, interest, profit, plus indirect taxes net of subsidies) plus depreciation.

gross investment The total value of all investment goods produced in the economy during a stated period of time.

gross national expenditure (GNE) National income as measured by the expenditure approach; equal to the sum of expenditures on consumption, investment, government production, and net exports.

gross national product (GNP) National income as measured by the income approach; equal to the sum of all factor incomes earned plus depreciation plus (to get the valuation at market prices) indirect taxes minus subsidies.

high employment See *full employment.*

high-employment national income (Y^*) See *potential income.*

homogeneous product A product every unit of which is identical to every other unit in the eyes of purchasers.

horizontal merger See *merger.*

household All of the people who live under one roof and who make joint financial decisions or are subject to others' financial decisions.

human capital The capitalized value of productive investments in persons; usually refers to value derived from expenditures on education, training, and health improvements.

I Investment expenditure.

implicit GDP deflator An index number derived by dividing GDP, measured in current dollars, by GDP, measured in constant dollars, and multiplying by 100. In effect, a price index, with current-year quantity weights, measuring the average change in price of all the items in the GDP.

import quota A limit set by the government on the quantity of a foreign commodity that may be shipped into that country in a given time period.

import substitution industry (ISI) Domestic production for sale in the home market of goods that were previously imported; usually involves some form of protection or subsidy.

imputed costs The costs of using factors of production already owned by the firm, measured by the earnings that they could have received in their best alternative use.

income-consumption curve (1) A curve showing the relationship for a commodity between quantity demanded and income, *ceteris paribus*. (2) A curve drawn on an indifference curve diagram and connecting the points of tangency between a set of indifference curves and a set of parallel budget lines, showing how the consumption bundle changes as income changes, with relative prices being held constant.

income effect The effect on quantity demanded of a change in real income with relative prices held constant.

income elasticity of demand A measure of the responsiveness of quantity demanded to a change in income, defined by the formula

$$\eta_Y = \frac{\text{percentage change in quantity demanded}}{\text{percentage change in income}}$$

income-related benefits See *income-tested benefits*.

incomes policy Any direct intervention by the government to influence wage and price formation.

income statement A financial report showing the revenues and costs that arise from the firm's use of inputs to produce outputs over a specified period of time.

income-tested benefits Social benefits paid to recipients who qualify because their income falls below some critical level; in particular, more targeted than demogrants.

increasing returns A situation in which output increases more than proportionately to inputs as the scale of a firm's production increases. A firm in this situation, with fixed factor prices, is a *decreasing-cost* firm.

incremental cost See *marginal cost*.

incremental product See *marginal product*.

incremental revenue See *marginal revenue*.

indexation Automatic change in any money payment in proportion to the change in the price level.

index number An average that measures changes over time of such variables as the price level and industrial production; conventionally expressed as a percentage relative to a base period, which is assigned the value 100.

indifference curve A curve showing all combinations of two commodities that give the household an equal amount of satisifaction and between which the household is thus indifferent.

indifference map A set of indifference curves based on a given set of household preferences.

induced expenditure In macroeconomics, elements of expenditure that are explained by variables within the theory. In the aggregate desired expenditure function, it is any component of expenditure that is related to national income. Also called *endogenous expenditure*.

industry A group of firms that produce a well-defined product or group of related products.

inelastic demand The situation in which, for a given percentage change in price, there is a smaller percentage change in quantity demanded; elasticity less than unity.

infant industry argument for tariffs The argument that new domestic industries with potential for economies of scale, or learning by doing, need to be protected from competition from established, low-cost foreign producers so that they can grow large enough to achieve costs as low as those of foreign producers.

inferior good A good for which income elasticity is negative.

inflation A rise in the average level of all prices. Sometimes restricted to prolonged or sustained rises.

inflationary gap A negative output gap, that is, a situation in which actual national income exceeds potential income.

infrastructure The basic installations and facilities (especially transportation and communication systems) on which the commerce of a community depends.

injections Income earned by domestic firms that does not arise out of the spending of domestic households and income earned by domestic households that does not arise out of the spending of domestic firms.

innovation The introduction of an invention into methods of production.

inputs Intermediate products and factor services that are used in the process of production.

interest The payment for the use of borrowed money.

interest rate The price paid per dollar borrowed per period of time, expressed either as a proportion (e.g., 0.06) or as a percentage (e.g., 6 percent). Also called the *nominal interest rate* to distinguish it from the *real rate of interest*.

intermediate goods See *intermediate products*.

intermediate products All outputs that are used as inputs by other producers in a later stage of production.

intermediate targets Variables that the government cannot control directly and does not seek to control ultimately yet have an important influence on policy variables.

internal balance When real national income is at its target level.

internal economies of scale Scale economies that result from the firm's own actions and hence are available to it by raising its own output.

internalization A process that results in a producer's taking account of a previously external effect.

invention The discovery of something new, such as a new production technique or a new product.

inventories Stocks of raw materials, goods in process, and finished goods held by firms to mitigate the effect of short-term fluctuations in production or sales.

investment expenditure Expenditure on the production of goods not for present consumption.

investment goods Goods that are produced not for present consumption, namely, capital goods, inventories, and residential housing.

invisible account That part of the balance-of-payments account that records payments and receipts arising out of trade in services and payments for the use of capital. Also called a *service account.*

invisibles All items of foreign trade that are intangible; services as opposed to goods.

involuntary unemployment Unemployment due to the inability of qualified persons who are seeking work to find jobs at the going wage rate.

isocost line See *budget line.*

isoquant A curve showing all technologically efficient factor combinations for producing a specified amount of output.

isoquant map A series of isoquants from the same production function, each isoquant related to a specific level of output.

Keynesians Economists who hold the view, derived from the work of John Maynard Keynes, that active use of monetary and fiscal policy can be effective in stabilizing the economy. Often the term encompasses economists who advocate active policy intervention in general.

Keynesian short-run aggregate supply curve A horizontal aggregate supply curve indicating that when national income is below potential, changes in national income can occur with little or no accompanying changes in prices.

***k* percent rule** The proposition that the money supply should be increased at a constant percentage rate year in and year out, irrespective of cyclical changes in national income.

labor A factor of production consisting of all physical and mental efforts provided by people.

labor force The total number of persons employed plus the number of persons who are unemployed.

labor union See *union.*

Laffer curve A graph relating the revenue yield of a tax system to the marginal or average tax rate imposed.

laissez faire Literally, "let do"; a policy advocating the minimization of government intervention in a market economy.

land A factor of production consisting of all gifts of nature, including raw materials and land as understood in ordinary speech.

law of demand The assertion that market price and quantity demanded in the market vary inversely; that is, their demand curves are negatively sloped.

law of diminishing returns The hypothesis that if increasing quantities of a variable factor are applied to a given quantity of fixed factors, the marginal product and average product of the variable factor will eventually decrease. Also called the *law of variable proportions.*

law of variable proportions See *law of diminishing returns.*

learning curve A curve showing how a firm's costs of producing a *given* rate of output fall as the total amount produced increases over time due to accumulated learning of how to make the product efficiently using given equipment. Found in many industries when new products and/or new production processes are introduced.

legal tender Anything that by law must be accepted for the purchase of goods and services or in discharge of a debt.

less developed countries (LDCs) The lower-income countries of the world, most of which are in Asia, Africa, and South and Central America. Also called *underdeveloped countries, developing countries,* the *South.*

leveraged buyout (LBO) The practice of borrowing the money that is necessary to acquire controlling stock in a firm.

life-cycle theory A hypothesis that relates a household's actual consumption to its expected lifetime income rather than (as in early Keynesian theory) to its current income.

lifetime income See *permanent income.*

limited liability Limitation of the financial responsibility of an owner (shareholder) of a corporation to the amount of money that the shareholder has actually invested in the firm by purchasing its shares.

limited partnership A form of business organization in which the firm has two classes of owners: general partners, who take part in managing the firm and who are personally liable for all of the firm's actions and debts, and limited partners, who take no part in the management of the firm and who risk only the money that they have invested.

liquidity preference (*LP*) function The function that relates the demand for money to the rate of interest.

logarithmic scale A scale in which equal proportional changes are shown as equal distances (for example, 1 inch may always represent doubling of a variable, whether from 3 to 6 or 50 to 100). Also called *log scale* and a *ratio scale.*

logrolling The political practice in which two or more voters agree to support each other's programs in exchange for support for his or her own.

long run A period of time in which all inputs may be varied but the basic technology of production cannot be changed.

long-run aggregate supply (*LRAS*) curve A curve showing the relationship between the price level of final output and the total quantity of output supplied when all markets have fully adjusted to the existing price level; a vertical line at $Y = Y^*$.

long-run average cost (*LRAC*) curve The curve relating the least-cost method of producing any output to the level of output when all inputs can be varied.

long-run industry supply (*LRS*) curve A curve showing the relationship between the market price and the quantity supplied by a competitive industry when it is in equilibrium.

long-run Phillips curve (*LRPC*) A curve showing the relationship between national income and the price level when all goods and factor markets are in long-run equilibrium.

Lorenz curve A graph showing the extent of departure from equality of income distribution.

losses See *economic profits or losses*.

Lucas aggregate supply curve A curve expressing the hypothesis that national output varies positively with the ratio of the actual to the expected price level.

M Imports; a country's total expenditure on imports.

M1 Currency plus demand deposits plus other chequable deposits.

M2 M1 plus money market mutual balances, money market deposit accounts, savings accounts, and small denomination time deposits.

M3 M2 plus large-denomination time deposits (CDs), term repurchase agreements, and money market mutual funds held by institutions.

macroeconomics The study of the determination of economic aggregates, such as total output, total employment, the price level, and the rate of economic growth.

managed float Intervention in the foreign exchange market by a country's central bank to respond to particular circumstances in pursuit of an unofficial exchange rate target but not to maintain an announced par value. Also called a *dirty float*.

marginal cost (*MC*) The increase in total cost resulting from raising the rate of production by one unit. Mathematically, the rate of change of cost with respect to output. Also called *incremental cost*.

marginal cost pricing Setting price equal to marginal cost so that buyers are just willing to pay for the last unit bought the amount that it costs to make that unit.

marginal efficiency of capital (*MEC*) The marginal rate of return on a nation's capital stock. The rate of return on one additional dollar of net investment, that is, an addition of one dollar's worth of new capital to capital stock.

marginal efficiency of investment (*MEI*) function The function that relates the quantity of investment to the rate of interest.

marginal physical product (*MPP*) See *marginal product*.

marginal product (*MP*) The change in quantity of total output that results from using one unit more of a variable factor. Mathematically, the rate of change of output with respect to the quantity of the variable factor. Also called *incremental product, marginal physical product*.

marginal productivity theory of distribution The theory that factors are paid the value of their marginal products so that the total earnings of each type of factor of production equals the value of the marginal product of that factor multiplied by the number of units of that factor that are employed.

marginal propensity not to spend The fraction of any increment to national income that is not spent on domestic production (unity minus the marginal propensity to spend; that is, $1 - \Delta AE/\Delta Y$).

marginal propensity to consume (*MPC*) The change in consumption divided by the change in disposable income that brought it about; mathematically, the rate of change of consumption with respect to disposable income ($MPC = \Delta C/\Delta Y_d$).

marginal propensity to save (*MPS*) The change in total desired saving related to the change in disposable income that brought it about ($\Delta S/\Delta Y_d$).

marginal propensity to spend The fraction of any increment to national income that is spent on domestic production; it is measured by the change in aggregate expenditure divided by the change in income ($\Delta AE/\Delta Y$).

marginal rate of substitution (*MRS*) (1) In consumption, the slope of an indifference curve, showing how much more of one commodity must be provided to compensate for the giving up of one unit of another commodity if the level of satisfaction is to be held constant. (2) In production, the slope of an isoquant, showing how much more of one factor of production must be used to compensate for the use of one less unit of another factor of production if production is to be held constant.

marginal revenue (*MR*) The change in a firm's total revenue resulting from a change in its rate of sales by one unit. Mathematically, the rate of change of revenue with respect to output. Also called *incremental revenue*.

marginal revenue product (*MRP*) The addition of revenue attributable to the last unit of a variable factor ($MRP = MP \times MR$). Mathematically, the rate of change of revenue with respect to quantity of the variable factor.

marginal tax rate The amount of tax that a taxpayer would pay on an additional dollar of income; that is, the fraction of an additional dollar of income that is paid in taxes.

marginal utility The additional satisfaction obtained by a consumer from consuming one unit more of a good; mathematically, the rate of change of utility with respect to consumption.

market An area over which buyers and sellers negotiate the exchange of a well-defined commodity or group of related commodities.

market-clearing price Price at which quantity demanded equals quantity supplied, so that there are neither unsatisfied buyers nor unsatisfied sellers, that is, the equilibrium price.

market economy See *free market economy*.

market failure Failure of the unregulated market system to achieve optimal allocative efficiency or social goals because of externalities, market impediments, or market imperfections.

market for corporate control The buying and selling of control over firms using such methods as mergers, leveraged buyouts, and hostile and friendly takeovers.

market rate of interest The actual interest rate in effect at a given moment.

market sector That portion of an economy in which

commodities are bought and sold and in which producers must cover their costs from sales revenue.

market structure All features of a market that affect the behavior and performance of firms in that market, such as the number and size of sellers, the extent of knowledge about each other's actions, the degree of freedom of entry, and the degree of product differentiation.

means The methods of achieving our goals.

medium of exchange Anything that is generally acceptable in return for goods and services sold.

merchandise account See *trade account.*

merger When two firms join together to become a single firm. In a *horizontal* merger both firms are in the same line of business; in a *vertical* merger one firm is a supplier of the other; if the two are in unrelated industries, it is a *conglomerate* merger.

merit goods Goods such as housing and medical care that are deemed to be especially important.

microeconomic policy Activities of governments designed to alter resource allocation and/or income distribution.

microeconomics The study of the allocation of resources and the distribution of income as they are affected by the workings of the price system and by government policies.

minimum efficient scale (*MES*) The smallest output at which long-run average cost reaches its minimum because all available economies of scale in production and/or distribution have been realized. Also called *minimum optimal scale.*

minimum wages Legally specified minimum rate of pay for labor in covered occupations.

mixed economy An economy in which some decisions about the allocation of resources are made by firms and households and some by the government.

monetarists Economists who stress monetary causes of cyclical fluctuations and inflation and believe that an active stabilization policy is not normally required. Often the term encompasses conservative economists who oppose active policy intervention in general.

monetary base The sum of currency in circulation plus reserves of the commercial banks, equal to the monetary liabilities of the central bank.

monetary equilibrium A situation in which the demand for money equals the supply of money.

monetary policy An attempt to influence the economy by operating on such monetary variables as the quantity of money and the rate of interest.

money Anything that acts as a medium of exchange, a store of value, and a unit of account.

money capital See *financial capital.*

money income Income measured in monetary units per period of time.

money national income See *nominal national income.*

money price See *absolute price.*

money rate of interest See *interest rate.*

money substitute Something that serves as a temporary medium of exchange but is not a store of value.

money supply The total quantity of money in an economy at a point in time. Also called the *supply of money.*

monopolist A firm that is the only seller in some market.

monopolistic competition (1) A market structure of an industry in which there are many firms and freedom of entry and exit but in which each firm has a product somewhat differentiated from the others, giving it some control over its price. (2) More recently, any industry in which more than one firm sells differentiated products.

monopoly A market containing a single firm.

monopsony A market situation in which there is a single buyer.

moral hazard A situation in which an individual or a firm takes advantage of special knowledge while engaging in socially uneconomic behavior.

multilateral balance of payments The balance of payments between one country and the rest of the world taken as a whole.

multiplier The ratio of the change in national income to the change in autonomous expenditure that brought it about.

NAIRU (*Nonaccelerating inflationary rate of unemployment*) The rate of unemployment associated with potential national income and at which steady, nonaccelerating or nondecelerating inflation can be sustained indefinitely. Also called the *natural rate of unemployment.*

Nash equilibrium In the case of firms, an equilibrium that results when each firm in an industry is currently doing the best that it can, given the current behavior of the other firms in the industry.

national debt The current volume of outstanding federal government debt.

national income In general, the value of total output and the value of the income that is generated by the production of that output.

national income accounting The set of rules and techniques for measuring the flow of output produced in the economy and the income generated by that production.

natural monopoly An industry characterized by economies of scale sufficiently large that only one firm can cover its costs while producing at its minimum efficient scale.

natural rate of unemployment See *NAIRU.*

natural scale A scale in which equal absolute amounts are represented by equal distances.

near money Liquid assets that are easily convertible into money without risk of significant loss of value and can be used as short-term stores of purchasing power but are not themselves media of exchange.

negative income tax (NIT) A tax system in which households with incomes below taxable levels receive payments from the government that are based on a percentage of the amount by which their income is below the minimum taxable level.

net domestic income at factor cost The sum of the four components of factor incomes (wages, rent, interest, and profits).

net domestic product at market prices The sum of wages, rent, interest, profits, and indirect taxes minus subsidies.

net exports Total exports minus total imports; represented by the expression $(X - M)$ as a component of aggregate expenditure, where X is total exports and M is total imports.

net investment Gross investment minus replacement investment.

neutrality of money The doctrine that the money supply affects only the absolute level of prices and has no effect on relative prices and hence no effect on the allocation of resources or the distribution of income.

newly industrialized countries (NICs) Formerly underdeveloped countries that have become major industrial exporters since World War II.

nominal GDP Gross domestic product valued in prices prevailing at the time of measurement; year-to-year changes in current-dollar GDP reflect changes both in quantities produced and in market prices. Also called *current dollar national income.*

nominal interest rate See *interest rate.*

nominal national income Total national income measured in dollars; the money value of national income. Also called *money national income, current dollar national income.*

nominal rate of tariff The tax charged on any imported commodity.

noncooperative equilibrium Any equilibrium reached when firms calculate their own best policies without cooperation—tacit or explicit—with other firms.

nonmarket sector The portion of an economy in which commodities are given away and producers must cover their costs from some source other than sales revenue.

nonrenewable resource Any productive resource available as a fixed stock that cannot be replaced once it is used. Also called *exhaustible resource.*

nontariff barriers Restrictions, other than tariffs, designed to reduce the flow of imported goods.

nontradables Commodities that do not enter into international trade.

normal-capacity output The level of output that a firm hopes to maintain on average over the business cycle; typically, somewhat less than full-capacity output.

normal good A good for which income elasticity is positive.

normal profits The opportunity cost of capital and risk taking just necessary to keep the owners in the industry. They are usually included in what economists, but not businesspersons, call *total costs.*

normative statement A statement or theory about what ought to be true in an ethical sense, as opposed to what is, was, or will be true.

oligopoly An industry that contains two or more firms, at least one of which produces a significant portion of the industry's total output.

open economy An economy that engages in significant amounts of international trade.

open-market operations The purchase and sale by the central bank of securities (usually short-term government securities) on the open market.

opportunity cost The cost of using resources for a certain purpose, measured by the benefit given up by not using them in their best alternative use.

organization theory A set of hypotheses that predicts that the substance of the decisions of a firm is affected by its size and form of organization.

output gap Potential national income minus actual national income. Also called the *GDP gap.*

outputs The goods and services that result from the process of production.

overhead cost See *total fixed cost.*

Pareto-efficiency See *Pareto-optimality.*

Pareto-optimality A situation in which it is impossible by reallocation of production or consumption activities to make all consumers better off without simultaneously making others worse off (or, as it is sometimes put, to make at least one person better off while making no one worse off). Also called *Pareto-efficiency.*

partnership A form of business organizaton in which the firm has two or more joint owners, each of whom takes part in the management of the firm and is personally responsible for all of the firm's actions and debts.

paternalism Intervention in the free choices of individuals by others (including governments) to protect them against their own ignorance or folly.

pegged exchange rate See *fixed exchange rate.*

per capita GDP GDP divided by total population.

perfect competition A market structure in which all firms in an industry are price takers and in which there is freedom of entry into and exit from the industry.

perfectly contestable market See *contestable market.*

permanent income The maximum amount that a household can consume per year into the indefinite future without reducing its wealth. (A number of similar, but not identical, definitions are in common use.) Also called *lifetime income.*

permanent-income theory A hypothesis that relates actual consumption to permanent income rather than (as in the original Keynesian theory) to current income.

personal income Income earned by or paid to individuals before allowance for personal income taxes on that income.

Phillips curve Originally, a relationship between the percentage of the labor force unemployed and the rate of change of money wages. Now often drawn as a relationship between the percentage of the labor force employed and the rate of price inflation or between actual national income and the rate of price inflation.

physical capital See *real capital.*

point elasticity A measure of the responsiveness of quantity to price at a particular point on the demand curve. The formula for point elasticity of demand is

$$\eta = \frac{\Delta q}{\Delta p} \times \frac{p}{q}$$

where $\Delta q/\Delta p$ is the slope of the *tangent* to the demand curve at the point p,q. With negatively sloped demand curves, elasticity is a negative number. Sometimes the expression given here is multiplied by -1 to make elasticity positive.

point of diminishing average productivity The level of output at which average product reaches a maximum.

point of diminishing marginal productivity The level of output at which marginal product reaches a maximum.

policy instruments The variables that the government can control directly to achieve its policy objectives.

policy variables The variables that the government seeks to control, such as real national income and the price level.

political business cycle Cyclical swings in the economy generated by fiscal and monetary policy for the purpose of winning elections.

portfolio investment In balance-of-payments accounting, foreign investment in bonds or a minority holding of shares that does not involve legal control. See also *direct investment.*

positive statement A statement or theory about what is, was, or will be true as opposed to what ought to be true.

potential income (Y^*) The real gross domestic product that the economy could produce if its productive resources were fully employed at their normal levels of use. Also called *potential national income, national income, high-employment national income.*

precautionary balances Money balances held for protection against the uncertainty of the timing of cash flows.

present value (PV) The value now of one or more payments to be received in the future; often referred to as the *discounted present value* or the *capitalized value* of future payments.

price ceiling A government-imposed maximum permissible price at which a commodity may be sold. Also called a *ceiling price.*

price-consumption line A line connecting the points of tangency between a set of indifference curves and a set of budget lines where one absolute price is fixed and the other varies, money income being held constant.

price control policy Any government policy that regulates the price at which a commodity can be bought and sold; often used to refer to the imposition of maximum prices on one or more commodities.

price discrimination The sale by one firm of different units of a commodity at two or more different prices for reasons not associated with differences in cost.

price elasticity of demand See *elasticity of demand.*

price floor A government-imposed minimum permissible price at which a commodity may be sold.

price index A number that shows the average of some group of prices, expressed as a percentage of the average ruling in some base period. Price indexes can be used to measure the price level at a given time relative to a base period.

price level The average level of all prices in the economy, usually expressed as an index number. See *price index.*

price taker A firm that can alter its rate of production and sales without significantly affecting the market price of its product.

price theory The theory of how prices are determined; competitive price theory concerns the determination of prices in competitive markets by the interaction of demand and supply.

principal-agent problem The problem of inducing agents to act in their principals' best interests, which arises because contracts that ensure this result are difficult to write and costly to monitor.

principle of substitution Methods of production will change if relative prices of inputs change, with relatively more of the cheaper input and relatively less of the more expensive input being used.

private cost The value of the best alternative use of resources available to the private decision maker.

private sector The portion of an economy in which the organizations that produce goods and services are owned and operated by private units, such as households and firms.

producers' surplus The difference between the total amount that producers receive for all units sold of a commodity and the total variable cost of producing the commodity.

product differentiation The existence of similar but not identical types of a single generic product sold by an industry, such as breakfast foods or automobiles.

production The act of making commodities—either goods or services.

production function A functional relation showing the maximum output that can be produced by each and every combination of inputs.

production possibility boundary A curve that shows which alternative combinations of commodities can just be attained if all available resources are used; it is thus the boundary between attainable and unattainable output combinations. Also called the *production possibility curve.*

productive efficiency Production of any output at the lowest attainable cost for that level of output.

productivity Output produced per unit of some input; frequently used to refer to *labor productivity,* measured by total output divided by the amount of labor used.

product markets Markets in which outputs of goods and services are sold. Also called *goods markets.*

profit (1) In ordinary usage, the difference between the value of outputs and the value of inputs. (2) In microeconomics, the difference between revenues received from the sale of goods and the value of inputs, which includes the opportunity cost of capital, so that profits are *economic profits.* (3) In macroeconomics, profits exclude interest on borrowed capital but do not exclude the return on owner's capital.

progressive tax A tax that takes a larger percentage of income the higher the level of income.

proportional tax A tax that takes a constant percentage of income at all levels of income and is thus neither progressive nor regressive.

protectionism Any government policy that interferes with free trade in order to give some protection to domestic industries against foreign competition.

public goods See *collective consumption goods.*

public sector The portion of an economy in which production is owned and operated by the government or bodies appointed by it, such as nationalized industries.

purchase and resale agreement (PRA) An arrangement by which the Bank of Canada makes short-term advances as a lender of last resort to investment dealers. Government securities are sold to the Bank with an agreement to repurchase them.

purchasing power of money The amount of goods and services that can be purchased with a unit of money. The purchasing power of money varies inversely with the price level. Also called the *real value of money.*

purchasing power parity (PPP) exchange rate The exchange rate between two currencies that equates their domestic purchasing powers, and so adjusts for relative inflation rates.

pure profits or **losses** See *economic profits or losses.*

pure rate of interest The rate of interest that would prevail in equilibrium in a riskless economy where all lending and borrowing is for investment in productive capital.

pure return on capital The amount that capital can earn in a riskless investment; hence the transfer earnings of capital in a riskless investment.

quantity demanded The amount of a commodity that households wish to purchase in some time period. An increase (decrease) in quantity demanded refers to a movement down (up) the demand curve in response to a fall (rise) in price.

quantity exchanged The identical amount of a commodity that households actually purchase and producers actually sell in some time period.

quantity supplied The amount of a commodity that producers wish to sell in some time period. An increase (decrease) in quantity supplied refers to a movement up (down) the supply curve in response to a rise (fall) in price.

random sample A sample chosen from a group or population in such a way that every member of the group has an equal chance of being selected.

rate of inflation The percentage rate of increase in some price index from one period to another.

rational expectations The theory that people understand how the economy works and learn quickly from their mistakes so even though random errors may be made, systematic and persistent errors are not made.

ratio scale See *logarithmic scale.*

real capital The physical assets that a firm uses to conduct its business, composed of plant, equipment, and inventories. Also called *physical capital.*

real GDP Also called *constant dollar GDP.* Gross national product valued in prices prevailing in some base year; year-to-year changes in constant-dollar GDP reflect changes only in quantities produced.

real income Income expressed in terms of the purchasing power of money income, that is, the quantity of goods and services that can be purchased with the money income; it can be calculated as money income deflated by a price index.

real national income (*Y*) National income measured in constant dollars so that it changes only when quantities change.

real product wage The proportion of each sales dollar accounted for by labor costs (including the pretax nominal wage rate, benefits, and payroll taxes).

real rate of interest The money rate of interest corrected for the change in the purchasing power of money by subtracting the inflation rate.

real-wage unemployment Unemployment caused by too high a real product wage. Also called *classical unemployment.*

real value of money See *purchasing power of money.*

recession A sustained downturn in the level of economic activity.

recessionary gap A positive output gap; that is, a situation in which actual national income is less than potential income. Also called a *deflationary gap.*

regressive tax A tax that takes a lower percentage of income the higher the level of income.

relative price The ratio of the money price of one commodity to the money price of another commodity; that is, a ratio of two absolute prices.

renewable resources Productive resources that can be replaced as they are used up, as with physical capital; distinguished from nonrenewable resources, which are available in a fixed stock that can be depleted but not replaced.

rental price of capital The price paid to rent the services of a unit of capital for a period of time.

replacement investment The amount of investment that is needed to maintain the existing capital stock intact.

required reserves The reserves that a bank must, by law, keep either in currency or in deposits with the central bank.

reserve currencies Currencies (such as the U.S. dollar) that are commonly held by foreign central banks as international reserves.

reserve ratio The fraction of its deposits that a commercial bank holds as reserves in the form of cash or deposits with a central bank.

resource allocation The allocation of an economy's scarce resources of land, labor, and capital among alternative uses.

retained earnings See *undistributed profits.*

return to capital The total amount available for payments to owners of capital; the sum of pure returns to capital, risk premiums, and economic profits.

revalued An increase in the external value of a country's currency under an adjustable peg system.

revaluation The act of revaluing a country's currency under an adjustable peg system.

revenue sharing The return of some of the revenue collected by the federal government to a provincial or local government for unresticted expenditure.

rising-cost industry An industry in which the minimum cost attainable by a firm rises as the scale of the industry expands.

risk-averse individuals Individuals who do not like risk and will engage in a risky activity only if the expected return is high enough to compensate them for the risk they will have to bear.

risk lovers Individuals who like risk and will engage in some risky activities that do not have a positive expected return in order to get some of the pleasure that the risk entails.

risk-neutral individuals Individuals who are indifferent about the amount of risk a given activity involves but will engage in the activity as long as the expected return is positive.

satisficing A hypothesized objective of firms to achieve levels of performance deemed satisfactory rather than to *maximize* some objective.

saving All disposable income that is not spent on consumption.

savings deposit An interest-bearing deposit legally withdrawable only after a certain notice period. (Savings deposits were common prior to recent revisions in the Bank Act.) Also called a *time deposit.*

scatter diagram A graph of statistical observations of paired values of two variables, one measured on the horizontal axis and the other on the vertical axis. Each point on the coordinate grid represents the values of the two variables for a particular unit of observation.

search unemployment Unemployment caused by people continuing to search for a good job rather than accepting the first job that they come across after they become unemployed.

secondary reserves Interest-earning liquid assets held by banks. For purposes of the minimum ratio to deposits imposed by the Bank of Canada, secondary reserves are defined as holdings of *treasury bills, day-to-day loans,* and *excess cash reserves.*

sectors Parts of an economy.

securities market See *stock market.*

sellers' preferences Allocation of commodities in excess demand by decisions of those who sell them.

service account See *invisible account.*

services Intangible commodities, such as haircuts or medical care.

shareholders See *stockholders.*

shortage See *excess demand.*

short run A period of time in which the quantity of some inputs cannot be increased beyond the fixed amount that is available.

short-run aggregate supply (*SRAS*) curve A curve showing the relationship between the price level of final output and the quantity of output supplied on the assumption that all factor prices are held constant.

short-run equilibrium Generally, equilibrium subject to fixed factors or other things that cannot change over the time period being considered. For a competitive firm, the output at which market price equals marginal cost; for a competitive industry, the price and output at which industry demand equals short-run industry supply and all firms are in short-run equilibrium. Either profits or losses are possible.

short-run Phillips curve (*SRPC*) A curve showing the relationship between unemployment and the rate of wage inflation or between national income and the rate of price inflation, drawn for a given state of expectations about the future rate of inflation.

short-run supply curve A curve showing the relationship between quantity supplied and market price, with one or more fixed factors; it is the horizontal sum of marginal cost curves (above the level of average variable costs) of all firms in a perfectly competitive industry.

simple multiplier The ratio of the change in equilibrium national income to the change in autonomous expenditure that brought it about, calculated for a constant price level.

single proprietorship A form of business organization in which the firm has one owner who makes all the decisions and is personally responsible for all of the firm's actions and debts.

size distribution of income The distribution of income among households, without regard to source of income or social class of households.

slope The ratio of the vertical change to the horizontal change between two points on a curve.

small open economy An economy that is unable to influence the prices of its exports or its imports by altering the quantities that it sells or buys; a price taker in international markets.

social benefit The contribution that an activity makes to the society's welfare.

social cost The value of the best alternative use of resources available to society as valued by society. Also called *social opportunity cost.*

social regulations The regulation of economic behavior to advance social goals when competition and economic regulation will fail to achieve those goals.

special drawing rights (SDRs) Financial liabilities of the IMF held in a special fund generated by contributions of member countries. Members can use SDRs to maintain supplies of convertible currencies when these are needed to support their exchange rates.

specialization of labor An organization of production in which individual workers specialize in the production of particular goods or services (and satisfy their wants by trading) rather than produce everything they consume (and satisfy their wants by being self-sufficient).

specific tariff An import duty of a specific amount per unit of the product.

specific tax See *excise tax.*

speculative balances Money balances held as a hedge against the uncertainty of the prices of other financial assets.

stabilization policy Any policy designed to reduce the economy's cyclical fluctuations and thereby to stabilize national income at or near a desired level.

stagflation The coexistence of high rates of unemployment and high and sometimes rising rates of inflation.

sterilization Operations undertaken by the central bank to offset the effects on the money supply of balance-of-payments surpluses or deficits which require central bank purchases or sales of foreign exchange.

stockholders The owners of a corporation who have supplied money to the firm by purchasing its shares. Also called *shareholders.*

stock market An organized market where stocks and bonds are bought and sold. Also called a *securities market.*

structural unemployment Unemployment due to a mismatch between characteristics required by available jobs and characteristics possessed by the unemployed labor.

substitute Two commodities are substitutes for each other when both satisfy similar needs or desires. The degree of substitutability is measured by the magnitude of the positive cross-elasticity between the two.

substitution effect A change in the quantity of a good demanded that results from a change in its relative price, eliminating the effect on real income of the change in price.

supply The entire relationship between the quantity of some commodity that producers wish to sell per period of time and the price of that commodity, other things being equal.

supply curve The graphical representation of the relationship between the quantity of some commodity that producers wish to make and sell per period of time and the price of that commodity, other things being equal.

supply of effort The total number of hours of work that the population is willing to supply. Also called *total supply of labor.*

supply of money See *money supply.*

supply schedule A table showing for selected values the relationship between the quantity of some commodity that producers wish to make and sell per period of time and the price of that commodity, other things being equal

surplus See *excess supply.*

takeover When one firm buys another firm.

takeover bid See *tender offer.*

target reserve ratio The fraction of deposit liabilities that a bank *wishes* to hold as reserves; the ratio of *target reserves* to deposit liabilities.

target reserves The level of reserves that a bank *wishes* to hold, taking into account its deposit liabilities, any legally required reserves, and its own concerns about its ability to facilitate transactions with its customers and other financial institutions.

tariff A tax applied on imports.

tax base The aggregate amount of taxable income.

tax expenditures Tax concessions, such as exemptions and deductions from taxable income and tax credits, designed to induce market responses considered to be desirable. They are called expenditures because they have the same effect as having no concessions and then spending money on subsidies and other transfers to the groups getting the concessions.

tax incidence The location of the burden of a tax; that is, the identity of the ultimate bearer of the tax.

tax-related incomes policy (TIP) Tax incentives for labor and management to encourage them to conform to wage and price guidelines.

tax-rental arrangements An agreement by which the federal government makes a per capita payment to the provinces for the right to collect income taxes.

technical change See *technological change.*

technological change Any change in the available techniques of production. Also called *technical change.*

tender offer An offer valid for a limited period of time to buy some or all of the outstanding common stock of a corporation from its stockholders at a specified price per share in an attempt to gain control of the corporation. Also called a *takeover bid.*

term See *term to maturity.*

terms of trade The ratio of the average price of a country's exports to the average price of its imports, both averages usually being measured by index numbers; the quantity of imported goods that can be obtained per unit of goods exported.

term to maturity The period of time from the present to the redemption date of a bond. Also called simply the *term.*

third-party effects See *externalities.*

time deposit See *savings deposit.*

total cost (*TC*) The total cost to the firm of producing any given level of output; it can be divided into total fixed costs and total variable costs.

total fixed cost (*TFC*) All costs of production that do not vary with level of output. Also called *overhead cost* or *unavoidable cost.*

total product (*TP*) Total amount produced by a firm during some time period.

total revenue (*TR*) Total receipts from the sale of a product; price times quantity.

total supply of labor See *supply of effort.*

total utility The total satisfaction resulting from the consumption of a given commodity or group of commodities by a consumer in a period of time.

total variable cost (*TVC*) Total costs of production that vary directly with level of output. Also called *direct cost* or *avoidable cost.*

tradable emissions permits Government-granted rights to emit specific amounts of specified pollutants that private firms may buy and sell among themselves.

tradables Commodities that can enter into international trade.

trade account A section of the balance-of-payments accounts that records payments and receipts arising from the import and export of tangible goods. Also called *visible account, merchandise account.*

traded services account That part of the balance-of-payments accounts that covers trade in services (such as insurance and advertising).

trade remedy laws See *fair trade laws.*

traditional economic system An economy in which the allocation of resources is primarily determined by tradition, custom, and habit.

transactions balances Money balances held to finance payments because payments and receipts are not perfectly synchronized.

transactions costs Costs incurred in effecting market transactions (such as negotiation costs, billing costs, and bad debts).

transfer payment A payment to a private person or institution that does not arise out of current productive activity; typically made by governments, as in welfare payments, but also made by businesses and private individuals in the form of charitable contributions.

transmission mechanism The channels by which a change in the demand or supply of money leads to a shift of the aggregate demand curve.

transnational corporation (TNC) A firm with locations in more than one country, often many countries. Also sometimes called a *multinational enterprise (MNE).*

treasury bill The characteristic form of short-term government debt. A promise to pay a certain sum of money at a specfied time in the future (usually 90 days to one year from date of issue). Although treasury bills carry no fixed interest payments, holders earn an interest return because they purchase them at a lower price than their redemption value. Also called *treasury note.*

unavoidable cost See *total fixed cost.*

underdeveloped countries See *less developed countries.*

undistributed profits Earnings of a firm that are not distributed to shareholders as dividends but are retained by the firm. Also called *retained earnings.*

unemployment (*U*) The number of persons 15 years of age and older who are not employed and are actively searching for a job.

unemployment rate Unemployment expressed as a percentage of the labor force.

unfavorable balance of payments A debit balance on some part of the international payments accounts (payments exceed receipts); often refers to the balance on current plus capital account (that is, everything except the official settlements account).

union An association of workers authorized to represent them in bargaining with employers. Also called *trade union, labor union.*

unit cost See *average variable cost.*

utility The satisfaction that a consumer receives from consuming a commodity.

value added The value of a firm's output minus the value of the inputs that it purchases from other firms.

value of money See *purchasing power of money.*

variable A magnitude (such as the price of a commodity) that can take on a specific value that will vary with time and place.

variable cost Any component of *total variable cost.*

variable factor An input that can be varied by any desired amount in the short run.

velocity of circulation (*V*) National income divided by quantity of money.

vertical merger See *merger.*

very long run A period of time that is long enough for the technological possibilities available to a firm to change.

visible account See *trade account.*

visibles All items of foreign trade that are tangible; goods as opposed to services.

voluntary export restriction (VER) An agreement by an exporting country to limit the amount of a good exported to another country.

wage and price controls Direct government intervention into wage and price formation with legal power to enforce the government's decisions on wages and prices.

wage-cost push inflation An increase in the price level caused by increases in labor costs that are not themselves associated with excess aggregate demand for labor.

wealth The sum of all the valuable assets owned minus liabilities.

withdrawals Income earned by households and not passed on to firms in return for goods and services purchased, and income earned by firms and not passed on to households in return for factor services purchased.

X Exports; the value of all domestic production sold abroad.

X-inefficiency The use of resources at a lower level of productivity than is possible, even if they are allocated efficiently, so that the economy is at a point inside its production possibility boundary.

X* − *M See *net exports.*

INDEX

Canadian Labor Force, Employment, and Unemployment, 1930-1990

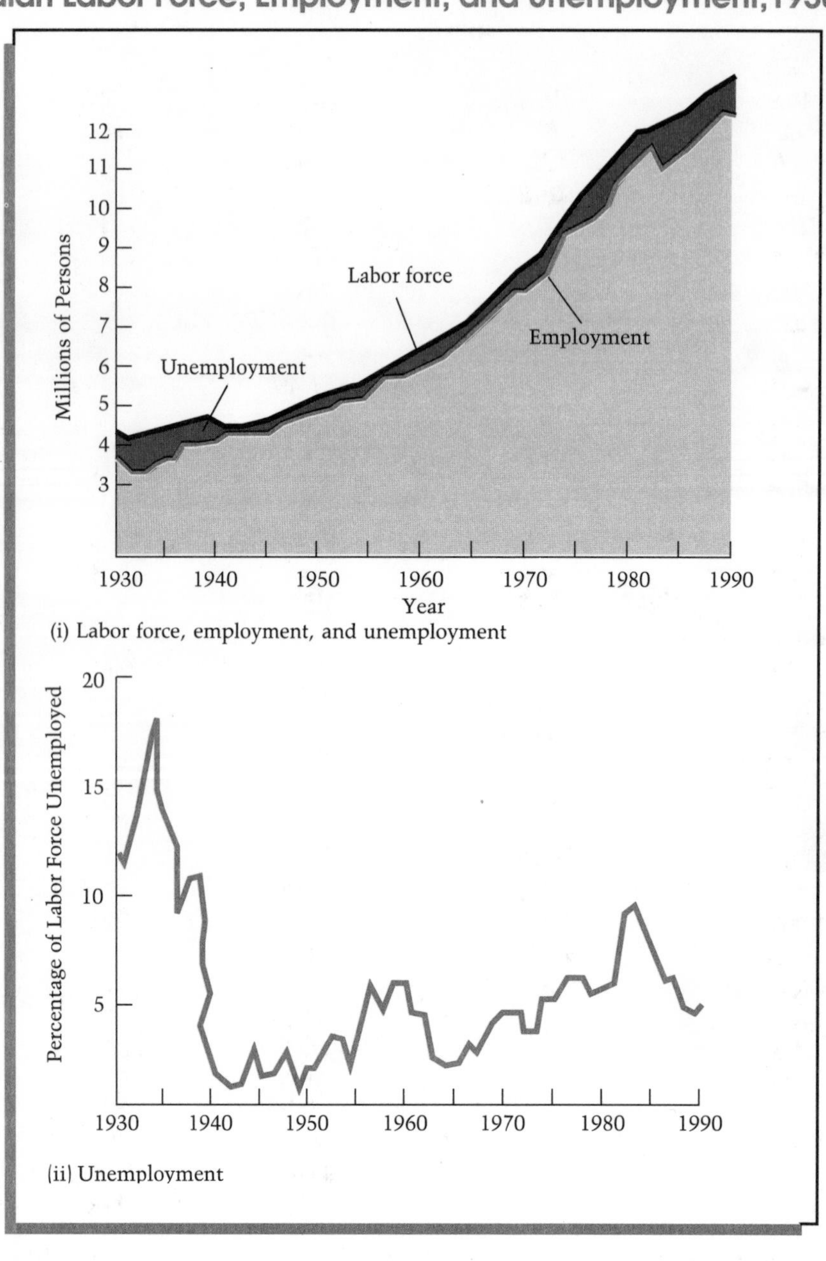

(i) Labor force, employment, and unemployment

(ii) Unemployment